Beyond Open Skies

KLUWER LAW INTERNATIONAL

Beyond Open Skies

A New Regime for International Aviation

Brian F. Havel

Wolters Kluwer

Law & Business

AUSTIN   BOSTON   CHICAGO   NEW YORK   THE NETHERLANDS

Published by:
Kluwer Law International
PO Box 316
2400 AH Alphen aan den Rijn
The Netherlands
Website: www.kluwerlaw.com

Sold and distributed in North, Central and South America by:
Aspen Publishers, Inc.
7201 McKinney Circle
Frederick, MD 21704
United States of America
Email: customer.care@aspenpubl.com

Sold and distributed in all other countries by:
Turpin Distribution Services Ltd.
Stratton Business Park
Pegasus Drive, Biggleswade
Bedfordshire SG18 8TQ
United Kingdom
Email: kluwerlaw@turpin-distribution.com

Printed on acid-free paper.

ISBN 978-90-411-2389-3

Printed in Great Britain.

Aviation Law and Policy Series

Volume 4

Series Editor

Pablo Mendes de Leon

International Institute of Air and Space Law, Leiden University

The global liberalization regime of the past two decades has fundamentally affected the operation of international air transport services.

This process calls for reflection and analysis across a wide range of legal and policy areas, including but not limited to public international air law and policy, with special reference to safety, security and environmental concerns, liability, competition law regimes, company law, and the complex relationship between European Community law and public international law.

The *Aviation Law and Policy Series* critically examines developments around liberalization of air services internationally resulting in the establishment of Open Aviation Areas; institutional questions such as the external powers of the European Community and the relationship between international organizations such as ICAO and EUROCONTROL; the coming into force of unlimited liability regimes and related case law; the granting of antitrust immunity to international airline alliances; and cooperation between competition authorities. Attention will also be paid to topical safety and security issues, and the growing impact of aviation in relation to the environment, dictating the design of emission trade systems. Last but not least, commercially oriented subjects such as aircraft financing and leasing will be addressed, both from the perspective of national and international legal regimes, taking into account practical cases and case law.

The objective of the *series* is to make a contribution to legal thinking on the multifaceted aspects of this important field of law. The publications are designed to document and anticipate the evolution of aviation law and policy in the twenty-first century.

The titles published in this series are listed in the back of this volume.

About the Author

Brian F. Havel is Professor of Law, Associate Dean, Director of the International Aviation Law Institute, and Director of the International and Comparative Law Program at DePaul University College of Law in Chicago. He is also Visiting Scholar at University College Dublin and held the 2007-08 Fulbright Visiting Chair in Comparative Law and Legal Pluralism at McGill University's Institute of Air and Space Law in Montreal. Before joining the DePaul faculty in 1994, he practiced transnational corporate and antitrust litigation at Paul, Weiss, Rifkind, Wharton & Garrison in New York City. His publications have had an interdisciplinary focus and include *In Search of Open Skies: Law and Policy for a New Era in International Aviation* (Kluwer, 1997), as well as a number of law review studies including *The Constitution in an Era of Supranational Adjudication* (North Carolina Law Review, 2000) and *In Search of a Theory of Public Memory: The State, the Individual, and Marcel Proust* (Indiana Law Journal, 2005). *Maestro of Crystal*, his biography of his father, Miroslav Havel, late chief designer of Waterford Crystal, was first published in Europe in 2005.

Foreword

By Jeffrey N. Shane
Under Secretary of Transportation for Policy,
U.S. Department of Transportation (2003-08)

In 1609, the Dutch jurist Hugo Grotius wrote, in *Mare Liberum* (*Free Seas*), that the oceans were international territory and thus open to seafaring by anyone. More than three centuries later, in 1944, most of the world's aviation powers came together in Chicago and established for aviation precisely the opposite principle. The United States had proposed a multilateral agreement guaranteeing commercial landing rights everywhere to the world's airlines without restriction. It didn't sell. What we got instead was the Chicago Convention, which specifically left the establishment of commercial traffic rights to be negotiated by governments on a market-by-market basis.

It was a fateful decision. By failing to establish an open global marketplace for international airline operations, the Chicago conference by implication created a closed market. Aviation, now as vital to global commerce as shipping, henceforth would be shackled by a host of government-imposed restrictions that would be treated as objectionable trade barriers in any other sector of economic activity. Airlines would not be allowed to fly between any two countries without first obtaining explicit permission from both. That permission would be granted, route by route, carrier by carrier, pursuant to carefully calibrated, highly mercantilist bilateral accords that would compromise the growth of aviation and limit its potential benefits for years to come.

The past three decades – dating from airline deregulation in the United States – have witnessed a gradual evolution toward a far more sensible approach to the regulation of international air services. The United States and the Netherlands pioneered a new 'open skies' approach to international aviation in a groundbreaking

1992 agreement – the first of 95 that the United States enjoys as of this writing. Increasingly, governments everywhere are backing away from their earlier micro-management of international aviation, allowing carriers to tap market opportunities where they can be found far more easily and responsively. All of this is a good thing.

But it is not enough. Vestigial legal constraints on the structure and operation of international air transport continue to impede the prospects for a more robust and competitive global airline industry. Even in a world characterized by open skies agreements, the diplomatic and regulatory framework for international aviation remains bafflingly anachronistic.

Laws against 'cabotage' – the carriage of domestic traffic by a foreign airline – are the most obvious evidence of the extent to which government-sponsored protectionism is still a major factor in the air transport sector. The longstanding requirement in bilateral aviation agreements that all commercial flights begin and end in the carrier's home territory is similarly inconsistent with contemporary thinking about trade in services. Why shouldn't Air France be allowed to set up a major hub in, say, Montreal? Or United in Milan?

A more serious impediment to the rethinking and restructuring that international aviation so badly needs is found in the ownership and citizenship requirements of most countries. Investment capital in most major industries is allowed to flow freely across national borders, enabling companies with global aspirations to establish a market presence wherever in the world commercial opportunities can be found. It is a well-established policy, and one that applies even to industries long thought essential to national and economic security, such as aerospace manufacturing, information technology, steel, and pharmaceuticals.

It is no small paradox that the one industry in which capital is *not* allowed to flow freely across national borders is the one that has facilitated the globalization of all the others. That is because most countries have strict rules governing the citizenship of the owners and sometimes even the senior managers of their airlines.

But it's worse than that. Most bilateral air services agreements require that, for an airline to conduct services between the territories of the two contracting States, it must be owned and controlled by citizens of one State or the other. What that means, quite simply, is that if a government has the good sense to allow foreign investors to make a sizeable capital contribution to an airline based in its territory, the airline is likely to be in violation of the bilateral agreements that define its access to foreign destinations. Access to those foreign markets could then be legally prohibited.

So we have a kind of 'double-whammy.' Most countries have laws prohibiting foreign ownership and control of their national airlines, and bilateral aviation agreements effectively prohibit the contracting countries from ever changing those laws, lest their airlines lose their ability to serve international destinations.

These archaic requirements aren't merely about the flow of capital. They are more importantly about the very structure of global aviation. By forbidding airlines to invest in each other across borders, both national laws and bilateral agreements effectively prohibit airlines from ever transforming themselves into the innovative and efficient global service providers they might otherwise be. In stark contrast to the astonishing pace of progress in so many industries that have been allowed to exploit the vast opportunities afforded by a globalized marketplace and the benefits that we all enjoy as a result, our airlines continue to limp along as local companies, locally owned, locally controlled, and effectively banned from full access to the global capital market.

Yes, we have made significant progress over the past three decades in liberalizing aviation. But we have a long way to go.

There is nothing very new or radical in that proposition. Drop in on any of the many international aviation conferences held each year around the world and you will discover that just about everybody agrees that greater liberalization – perhaps we should simply call it 'normalization' – would be a good thing for airlines, their customers, and indeed economies everywhere. Even high-ranking government officials themselves routinely call for fundamental change. Like the puzzled party-goers in Luis Buñuel's 1962 classic, *The Exterminating Angel*, who discover that they don't know how to leave the party even though they want to, governments are stuck in a regulatory paradigm they profess not to like but can't get out of.

Nobody has chronicled this public policy anomaly more effectively or with greater erudition than Brian Havel. A European who has taught for years in the United States, he brings a special transatlantic perspective to his work. His first book on the subject, *In Search of Open Skies*, published more than a decade ago, explored critically the approaches to aviation liberalization emerging in the United States and the European Union. The present volume tells the fascinating story of two likeminded leaders in the quest for a truly open aviation marketplace who, working together toward what appears to be a common vision in the most significant aviation negotiations we have witnessed since 1944, have been unable to achieve the ultimate breakthrough. Professor Havel proposes a breakthrough of his own in the book's final chapter, but I won't ruin the story by describing it here.

It is a book to be savored on two levels. First and most simply, it is just a very interesting and important story – one whose ending we still don't know. Professor Havel has cut through the fog of diplomacy to find the genuine drama in this long and important effort to conform international aviation to the principles we normally apply to trade in services, and he has made it a great read.

Second, his copious documentation is a treasure-trove of hard-to-find but vital scholarship and source material. Professor Havel's detailed footnotes are the analog equivalent of hyperlinks; they unlock a cornucopia of relevant material – never before collected so conveniently in one place – furnishing a rich and satisfying context that will enable readers to understand better the forces at work on both sides during these historic negotiations. The book will quickly take its place, I predict, as the most comprehensive and valuable reference that exists on the complex diplomacy that will define the future of international aviation.

Washington, D.C., November 2008

Preface

On March 30, 2008, the historic air transport agreement between the United States and the European Community went into provisional effect. In itself, it is a remarkable achievement, the culmination of a policy of international air transport liberalization pursued by the United States over the past 25 years under the optimistic sobriquet 'open skies.' Yet, despite its undoubted significance, the agreement is in reality more of a staging-post on the journey to a truly open transatlantic aviation marketplace. Attention has turned now to the agreement's provision for a second stage of negotiations. This book not only charts how the agreement emerged and how it fits into the contemporary regulatory context of the U.S. and EU air transport industries, but advocates a transformative agenda for the second stage that would end a regulatory order that has resisted opening airline ownership and control to foreign citizens. Abolition of the citizenship 'purity' test lies at the core of this book's proposal to move 'beyond open skies.'

Reading the runes at the beginning of the administration of President Barack Obama, one senses that the reform proposals presented here will gain only a little traction in the years ahead. Responding in 2007 to a questionnaire framed by the U.S. Air Line Pilots Association, candidate Obama declared that he would oppose any effort to allow non-U.S. investors to hold more than a minority stake in U.S. air carriers. Without American leadership on this pivotal issue, the old dogmas of airline nationality will not be renounced and the industry which has played such a central role in globalization will – as Jeffrey Shane reminds us in his Foreword – remain itself unglobalized.

Domestically, the landscape of regulatory policy may be transformed in any event by the financial crisis and the prospect of a lengthy downturn in the business cycle. Governments worldwide, including the U.S. Government, seem less ideologically discomfited by the prospect of State intervention or State assistance, and the airlines may well be tempted to retreat once again to their post-9/11 reliance on public aid and to accept some further measure of government reregulation.

This book, the successor to my 1997 work, *In Search of Open Skies: Law and Policy for a New Era in International Aviation*, again invites the reader to consider a very different perspective: that the global air transport regulatory system, a hodge-podge of inter-State bilateral treaties based on archaic domestic and international rules of nationality and citizenship, is so inadequate to the commercial demands of the modern industry that the imperatives for its reform transcend domestic debates about incremental public intervention in the business of providing air transport. By analyzing the law and policy of U.S. and EC airline deregulation, and integrating that analysis into the framework for the coming negotiations, this book argues for an intensification, rather than some kind of fashionable 'correction,' of the competitive forces that liberalization has stimulated at both the transatlantic and global levels. The arguments presented here seek to build upon the efforts of government officials, industry stakeholders, and academic commentators who have encouraged a progressive liberalization of air transport within the existing flawed system.

Perhaps, then, the runes will turn out to have been inaccurate. Perhaps the global airline industry's pressing need to overthrow a chauvinistic regime that emerged over 60 years ago from a conference held in Chicago – Mr. Obama's home city – will allow the negotiators to crown their work with an agreement that smashes all regulatory barriers to a global airline system. For this endlessly frustrating and endlessly fascinating industry, the world's most visible service industry, the journey 'beyond open skies' now begins.

Citations in this book follow the format recommended by the *Bluebook Uniform System of Citation* (18th Edition). To the extent that the exigencies of publishing allow, I have endeavored to state the law as of January 2009. (Updates to issues discussed in this book will be posted on the web-log of the International Aviation Law Institute of DePaul University College of Law, <http://lawprofessors.typepad.com/aviation>.)

Acknowledgements

I am most grateful to Jeffrey N. Shane, former Under Secretary for Policy at the U.S. Department of Transportation and now a partner at the Washington, D.C. law firm of Hogan & Hartson LLP, for contributing the Foreword to this book. A skilled writer and communicator, Jeff has tirelessly advocated airline regulatory reform for more than two decades. His intellectual comprehension of how governments should best steward the global air transport industry has been justly celebrated. It was my special pleasure to watch Jeff's masterful service as President of the 36th Triennial Assembly of the International Civil Aviation Organization in September 2007 – the first American to serve in that position since 1959. At the French delegation's reception during the Assembly, he graciously accepted my invitation to write the Foreword.

As well as Jeff, a number of the governmental *dramatis personae* in the U.S./EC air transport saga have given me their time and insights. I am particularly grateful to John Byerly, Deputy Assistant Secretary for Transportation Affairs at the U.S. Department of State; Daniel Calleja, Air Transport Director for the European Commission; Luisa Ragher, Head of the Transport, Energy, Environment, and Nuclear Matters Section of the European Commission Delegation to the United States; and Andy Steinberg, formerly Assistant Secretary for Aviation & International Affairs at the U.S. Department of Transportation.

I wish also to express my appreciation to my colleagues at my home institution, DePaul University College of Law, and to its Dean, Glen Weissenberger, for their interest, reassurance, and advice over the past three years. Dean Weissenberger generously supported this venture through grants from the Faculty Development Fund. I also wish to recognize the influence and leadership of my academic mentor, DePaul Emeritus Professor M. Cherif Bassiouni, whose global standing in public international law has been a constant inspiration.

This book evolved directly from my work as Director of the International Aviation Law Institute, established at DePaul in 2004. I pay tribute to the support

I have received from my fellow Director, Professor Michael S. Jacobs, as well as the Institute's Executive Director Stephen B. Rudolph, formerly with CCH Wolters Kluwer, where he was Editor of two prestigious publications, the *Aviation Law Reporter* and *Issues in Aviation Law and Policy*. It is gratifying that the Institute, under Steve's direction, has succeeded Wolters Kluwer as publisher of *Issues in Aviation Law and Policy*. My very personal thanks go to two energetic and gifted DePaul graduates, Gabriel S. Sanchez and Andrew C. Eastmond, who have served as FedEx/United Airlines Resident Research Fellows at the Institute. In that regard, I also wish to record my gratitude to Rush O'Keefe, General Counsel at FedEx, and Michael G. Whitaker, Senior Vice President for International and Regulatory Affairs and Alliances at United Airlines, who have each made an outstanding contribution to the evolution of the Institute and who continue to support its progress.

I am indebted to my student research assistants Louis Shansky, Shane Nix, and Elliott Riebman, and wish them every success in their careers. My peerless proofreader, Alice Rudolph (Steve's wife), has cast her usual meticulous eye over the text. And my deep appreciation goes also to the staff of the DePaul Rinn Law Library, most especially to my friend Dan Ursini.

Many others have helped me in this process. The aviation industry, in my experience and at the level at which I most frequently encounter it, comprises two types of people: those who are aviation law professors and those who could be aviation law professors if they were to leave the industry. In the former category, I have encountered a number of brilliant people who have helped me in my endeavors. I mention in particular Professor Pablo M.J. Mendes de Leon, Director of the International Institute of Air and Space Law at Leiden University, who has been a mentor and friend for nearly a decade; Professor Dr. Paul Stephen Dempsey, holder of the Tomlinson Chair in Global Governance and Director of the Institute of Air and Space Law at McGill University, who supported my application to spend a year at the Institute as Fulbright Visiting Chair in Comparative Law and Legal Pluralism and thereby enabled me to complete work on this book in the congenial setting of the Faculty of Law campus; Respicio A. Espirito Santo, Professor at the Federal University of Rio de Janeiro and President of the Brazilian Institute of Strategic Studies and Public Policies in Air Transport, whose passion for the study of air transport has been a tremendous source of encouragement and energy; and Professor Martin Staniland, Professor and Division Director for International Affairs in the Graduate School of Public and International Affairs at the University of Pittsburgh, who gave me my first public platform as an academic in the field of air transport law and policy when he invited me to his institution's Future of EU-U.S. Aviation Relations Conference at Pittsburgh in 2000. As to potential aviation law professors who are still in the industry, I make special mention of my dear friend Conor McAuliffe, a brilliant scholar who currently serves as Managing Director, European Affairs, for United Airlines.

My editor at Kluwer Law International, Ewa Szkatula, has been unstinting in her supervision of the publishing process and rigorous in setting the deadlines which make a project like this more than just an academic vagary. I am grateful for her patience, and glad that I just managed to avoid completely exhausting it.

Professor Graeme B. Dinwoodie, now at Oxford University, has brought all of his great academic expertise to bear on making sure that I finished this project while remaining in good humor.

Finally, for their love and support, I thank my family in Ireland and in the United States. To my mother, Betty, and to my father, Miroslav, I repeat the dedication I made on the opening page of *In Search of Open Skies*. My father, the 'Maestro of Crystal' as I proudly described him in a biography published in Ireland in 2005, passed away just weeks before I finished the manuscript for the present book. I dedicate it now to his memory.

Chicago, January 2009

Table of Contents

Chapter 4
Model Jurisdiction I: The United States   235
Airline Deregulation Within and Beyond a Unitary Airspace

List of Abbreviations

ABA	American Bar Association
ACA	Air Carrier Association of America
ACI-NA	Airports Council International-North America
ACMI	Aircraft, Crew, Maintenance and Insurance (lease)
ADA	Airline Deregulation Act of 1978 (U.S.)
AEA	Association of European Airlines
AIR-21	Wendell H. Ford Aviation Investment and Reform Act for the 21st Century (U.S.)
ALJ	Administrative law judge
ALPA	Air Line Pilots Association (U.S.)
AOC	Air operator certificate
APD	Air Passenger Duty
APEC	Asia-Pacific Economic Cooperation
ATA	Air Transport Association of America
ATM	Air Traffic Management
ATPCO	Airline Tariff Publishing Company
ATUC	Air Transport Users Council (EU)
BIT	Bilateral Investment Treaty (U.S.)
BSCA	Brussels South Charleroi Airport (Belgium)
CAA	Civil Aviation Authority (U.K.)
CAB	Civil Aeronautics Board (U.S.)
CAFTA	Central American Free Trade Agreement
CARICOM	Caribbean Community
CCH	Commerce Clearing House (Wolters Kluwer)
CFI	Court of First Instance (EU)
CFIUS	Committee on Foreign Investment in the United States
CLMV	Cambodia, Laos, Myanmar, and Vietnam

COREPER	Comité des Représentants Permanents (Committee of Permanent Representatives (EU)
CRAF	Civil Reserve Air Fleet (U.S.)
CRS	Computer Reservations System
DOD	Department of Defense (U.S.)
DOJ	Department of Justice (U.S.)
DOT	Department of Transportation (U.S.)
DPFI	Domestic Passenger Fare Investigation
EAS	Essential Air Service Program (U.S.)
EASA	European Aviation Safety Agency
EC	European Community
ECA	European Cockpit Association
ECAA	European Common Aviation Area
ECAC	European Civil Aviation Conference
ECJ	European Court of Justice
EEA	European Economic Area
EEC	European Economic Community
EFTA	European Free Trade Association
EIU	Economist Intelligence Unit
ELFAA	European Low Fares Airline Association
ET	Electronic ticketing
ETF	European Transport Workers Federation
ETS	Emissions Trading Scheme
EU	European Union
EUROCONTROL	European Organisation for the Safety of Air Navigation
FAA	Federal Arbitration Act (U.S.)
FAA	Federal Aviation Act of 1958 (U.S.)
FAA	Federal Aviation Administration (U.S.)
FDI	Foreign direct investment
FINSA	Foreign Investment and National Security Act of 2007 (U.S.)
FTC	Federal Trade Commission (U.S.)
GAO	Government Accountability Office (formerly General Accounting Office) (U.S.)
GATS	General Agreement on Trade in Services
GATT	General Agreement on Tariffs and Trade
GDS	Global Distribution System
HHI	Herfindahl-Hirschman Index
HST	High Speed Train (EU)
IAEAA	International Antitrust Enforcement Assistance Act of 1994 (U.S.)
IASA	International Aviation Safety Assessments Program
IASTA	International Air Services Transit Agreement
IATA	International Air Transport Association
IATCA	International Air Transportation Competition Act of 1979 (U.S.)

IATFCPA	International Air Transportation Fair Competitive Practices Act of 1974 (U.S.)
ICAO	International Civil Aviation Organization
ICSID	International Centre for Settlement of Investment Disputes
ITA	International Trade Administration (U.S.)
ITO	International Trade Organization
LCC	Low-Cost Carrier
MALIAT	Multilateral Agreement on the Liberalization of International Air Transportation
MFN	Most Favored Nation
MIDT	Market Information Data Tapes
MOC	Memorandum of Consultations
MOU	Memorandum of Understanding
NAFTA	North American Free Trade Agreement
NEB	National Enforcement Body (EU)
NERA	National Economic Research Associates
NPRM	Notice of Proposed Rulemaking (U.S.)
NT	National Treatment
OAA	Open Aviation Area
OECD	Organisation for Economic Cooperation and Development
OFT	Office of Fair Trading (U.K.)
OMB	Office of Management and Budget (U.S.)
PFC	Passenger Facility Charge (U.S.)
PICAO	Provisional International Civil Aviation Organization
PSO	Public service obligation (EU)
StB	Simplifying the Business Program (IATA)
SCASDP	Small Community Air Service Development Program (U.S.)
SES	Single European Sky
TABD	TransAtlantic Business Dialogue
TACO	Travel agency commission override
TCAA	Transatlantic Common Aviation Area
TRB	Transportation Research Board (U.S.)
TTE	Transport, Telecommunication and Energy Council (EC)
UNCLOS	UN Convention on the Law of the Sea
VAT	Value Added Tax
VISA	Voluntary Intermodal Sealift Agreement
WTO	World Trade Organization

Chapter 1

Introduction: Preparing for a New Era in International Aviation

I   REPLACING A FLAWED REGULATORY SYSTEM

Despite the 'perfect economic storm' that struck the global air transport industry after September 11, 2001[1] – compounded more recently by the pernicious effects of escalating kerosene prices[2] – despair about the future of the industry is not only uncalled-for but blinkered. With ambitious global brands like the Virgin Group agitating for long-denied access to the huge U.S. domestic aviation market (directly or by acquiring one of a number of ailing U.S. carriers),[3] while European airlines

---

1. AIR TRANSPORT ASSOCIATION, AIRLINES IN CRISIS: THE PERFECT ECONOMIC STORM 1 (2003) (submission to the Bush Administration).
2. According to the International Air Transport Association, the airline industry's global trade body, the airlines' fuel bill is expected to grow to $176 billion in 2008 – a $40 billion increase from 2007. Fuel has jumped from 14% of the airlines' operating expenses in 2003 to an estimated 34% for 2008. The end result for 2008 may be losses as high as $6.1 billion for the industry. *See* Press Release, International Air Transport Association, Fact Sheet – Fuel (Jul. 2008).
3. *See* Richard Branson, *Fair Competition: A True Revolution in Flight*, U.S. NEWS & WORLD REP., Dec. 2, 2002 (calling for opening up the U.S. domestic aviation market to foreign competition by removing restrictive rules that have 'stopped me' [*sic*] from setting up a U.S.-based airline, Virgin America, and predicting a 'breakthrough' in the international air transport regulatory system following recent rulings by the European Court of Justice, discussed *infra* Chapter 2, Part III(A)); *see also* Kerry Capell & Wendy Zellner, *Richard Branson's Next Big Adventure*, BUS. WEEK, Mar. 8, 2004, at 44. Branson's U.S. subsidiary commenced operations in 2007, but only after a regulatory donnybrook, driven by the 'restrictive rules' he had earlier decried, that forced Branson's Virgin Group to relinquish much of its planned control interests in his putative U.S. offspring. Effectively, Virgin Atlantic stands in a franchise relationship (through a flexible trademark license agreement) with its U.K. 'mother' organization, the Virgin Group – a state of affairs that may have prompted the inclusion of franchise opportunities in the U.S. domestic market for foreign airlines as part of the 2007 U.S./EC Air Transport Agreement. *See infra*

circle each other warily in anticipation of further consolidations and a new hierarchy of air service providers, the industry on both sides of the Atlantic will inevitably generate new paradigms of competitive market behavior. In that context fresh thinking is already needed on an appropriate legal and policy architecture to govern the industry in the decades ahead.[4] This book, therefore, continues the pursuit of the topic considered by *In Search of Open Skies*,[5] its predecessor: the contours of a legal regime that should govern international scheduled air passenger (and relatedly, air cargo) transport for the decades ahead.

Launched by a restrictive global convention in Chicago in 1944,[6] the existing regulatory regime has largely stood firm against the neoliberal free trade winds of the postwar era,[7] straitjacketing the world's airline industry within a system of bilateral, point-to-point air treaties that explicitly reserves to governments the power to parcel out (and to deny) access to national airspace by foreign airlines, to exclude foreign airlines from domestic air service ('cabotage'), and to prohibit foreign citizens (and their airlines) from owning and controlling national air carriers (the 'nationality' rule).[8] The present work seeks to expose the anticompetitive

---

Chapter 2, Part V(B); *see also* U.S. Dept. of Transp. [U.S. DOT], *Application of Virgin America Inc., For a Certificate of Public Convenience and Necessity Under 49 U.S.C. § 41102 To Engage in Interstate Scheduled Air Transportation of Persons, Property, and Mail*, Dkt. No. OST-2005-23307, Final Order (May 18, 2007), setting highly restrictive conditions, including compelled removal of Branson-designated Chief Executive Officer and freedom for the U.S. carrier to operate services without a Virgin brand identity if it chooses in order to approve Virgin America Inc. under the U.S. airline citizenship laws. These kinds of intrusive adjustments were not needed, however, for U.K.-owned Virgin Blue – Australia's second-largest carrier – when it began providing intra-Australian domestic air services following revocation of Australia's ownership and control rules for all-domestic airlines. *See* Yu-Chun Chang & George Williams, *Changing the Rules – Amending the Nationality Clauses in Air Services Agreements*, 7 J. AIR TRANSP. MGMT. 207, 209 (2001). (Majority ownership of Virgin Blue has lately come into Australian hands, with shareholders in Toll Holdings, an Australian logistics group, now having a 63% stake in the company. *Toll Taken*, FIN. TIMES (Asia Edition), Jul. 15, 2008, at 12.) For a fuller treatment of the Virgin America citizenship proceeding, *see infra* Chapter 3, Part V(B).

4. Or, to borrow a suspect bureaucratic coinage of the U.S. Department of Transportation (DOT), this book comprises an extended 'Visioning Session' on the future of air transportation. U.S. DOT, AVIATION IN THE 21ST CENTURY: BEYOND OPEN SKIES MINISTERIAL I (1999).

5. *See* BRIAN F. HAVEL, IN SEARCH OF OPEN SKIES: LAW AND POLICY FOR A NEW ERA IN INTERNATIONAL AVIATION (1997).

6. *See* Convention on International Civil Aviation, *opened for signature* Dec. 7, 1944, 61 Stat. 1180, 15 U.N.T.S. 295 (entered into force Apr. 4, 1947) [hereinafter Chicago Convention]. For more detailed analysis of the Chicago Convention, *see infra* Chapter 3.

7. Jürgen Basedow, *Verkehrsrecht und Verkehrspolitik als Europäische Aufgabe ('Transport Law & Policy as a European Task')* in EUROPÄISCHE VERKEHRSPOLITIK ('European Transport Policy') 8 (Gerd Aberle ed., 1987). Basedow chose the multilateral World Trade Organization/General Agreement on Tariffs and Trade (WTO/GATT) international trade regime and the regional European Union to portray the postwar success of a free trade philosophy.

8. The most advanced aircraft known to the participants at the conference that drafted the Chicago Convention were the Douglas DC-6 and the Lockheed Constellation. This study will argue that the Convention (unlike, for example, the United States Constitution), lacks the textual vitality to serve the era of the Boeing 787 and the Airbus A380. For a crisp historical review of the development of commercial jet air transportation, *see* ALEXANDER T. WELLS & JOHN WENSVEEN,

bias of this bilateral system contextually, through a systematic comparative analysis[9] of the legal and policy dimensions of airline deregulation by federal fiat in the United States and by supranational collaboration in the European Union (EU).[10] The book draws upon a variety of sources, including the transcripts and materials

AIR TRANSPORTATION: A MANAGEMENT PERSPECTIVE 29-67 (6th ed. 2007); *see also* Hasso Spode, '*Let Us Fly You Where the Sun Is:*' *Air Travel and Tourism in Historical Perspective, in* VITRA DESIGN MUSEUM, AIRWORLD 13 (2004) (tracing how technological advances spurred the development of postwar air travel and tourism).

9. For a recitation of the key principles of the discipline of comparative law, *see* JAMES MAXEINER, POLICY AND METHODS IN GERMAN AND AMERICAN ANTITRUST LAW 3-5 (1986).

10. Although in a strict legal and constitutional sense the European Union (EU) is the overarching constitutional fusion of three separate 'Communities,' the engine of the Member States' *economic* integration is the European Community (EC, formerly the European Economic Community). Constant alternation of the terms 'EC' and 'EU' seems to inspire confusion and annoyance rather than clarity. However, because the legislative work of air transport deregulation has been formally the province of the European Community, and because airlines under EC jurisdiction are legislatively designated as 'Community air carriers,' the narrow entity is preferred as more technically appropriate in the present work. (For example, the European parties to the 2007 U.S./EC Air Transport Agreement, which is a significant presence in this study, are *stricto sensu* the European *Community* and its 27 Member States.) Thus, the EC will be referred to throughout the book as a *source of law or policy*, while the EU is referenced as a political and geographical unit. *Cf.* Paul B. Stephan, *Global Governance, Antitrust, and the Limits of International Cooperation*, 38 CORNELL INT'L L.J. 173, 189 n.47 (2005). The nomenclatural thicket was finally to be brushed aside with the adoption of a modified treaty-based version of the failed 'European Constitution' in 2008. The rejection of the Treaty of Lisbon by the Irish electorate in Jun. 2008 has dampened the prospect that it would enter into force in 2009. *See* Europa, Treaty of Lisbon: Taking Europe into the 21st Century, <http://europa.eu/lisbon_treaty/index_en.htm> (official website of the treaty with full text and frequently updated news about its status); Press Release, Europa, Statement by [European Commission] President [José Manuel] Barroso Following the Irish Referendum on the Treaty of Lisbon, IP/08/941 (Jun. 13, 2008) (expressing the European Commission's disappointment at Ireland's rejection of the treaty). The 'European Union,' as such, was formed by the Treaty on European Union (the Maastricht Treaty), in effect since Nov. 1, 1993. Article A of Maastricht establishes the Union as 'founded on' the European Economic Community (retitled the 'European Community' by Article G(A)), the European Coal and Steel Community (ECSC) and the European Atomic Energy Community (Euratom), as well as a process of formal intergovernmental cooperation in the fields of foreign and security policy (Title V of Maastricht) and justice and home affairs (Title VI). The 'European Community' (EC) is the creation of the Treaty of Rome, in effect since Jan. 1, 1958 (as amended by the Maastricht Treaty). (The original text of the Rome Treaty appears at 298 U.N.T.S. 11. The original ECSC and Euratom Treaties appear at 261 U.N.T.S. 140 and 298 U.N.T.S. 167, respectively.) The European Community is the specific constitutional component of the European Union within which the Union's air transport policy has been (and continues to be) legislated. Thus, while reference to the 'EU airline industry' or to 'EU international aviation policy' is perfectly appropriate, as a legal matter it is more accurate to speak of the 'EC regulations on air transport' or 'the Community's power to negotiate international air transport relations.' To add an additional splash of confusion, the unified supranational institutions, within this dualistic framework, are the Council of the European Union (sometimes referred to as the 'Council of Ministers'), the Commission of the European Communities (referred to here as the 'European Commission'), the European Parliament, and the European Court of Justice. *See* JAMES D. DINNAGE & JOHN F. MURPHY, THE CONSTITUTIONAL LAW OF THE EUROPEAN UNION 3-4 (2d ed. 2008) (discussing the challenge of EU nomenclature).

of the Airline Commission appointed by President Bill Clinton in 1993,[11] as well as on very recent developments in U.S. and European Community (EC) international aviation law and policy, to propose a genuine multilateral system that will restore the economic opportunity that was only partially grasped at Chicago over 60 years ago.[12]

It is a recurrent theme of this book, moreover, that air transport should evolve beyond its historical preoccupation with abstract legal categories and toward a focus on tangible commercial opportunities. Thus, as we will see, the Chicago 'system' is managed by government delegations which trade specialized rights of airspace access, known (with no little irony) as the 'freedoms of the air,' and which were elaborated in two subsidiary conventions also concluded at Chicago in the mid-1940s.[13] The so-called freedoms of the air are, in reality, a protectionist artifice to imprint government control on every conceivable means of access to national airspace (directly, from the negotiating country, or indirectly, through third countries). In the reasoning adopted here, however, there ought to be no commercial difference between a U.S. passenger airline like Southwest Airlines serving the Chicago/San Francisco route and a U.S. all-cargo operator like FedEx moving local cargo traffic between Singapore and New Zealand. Nevertheless, international aviation law (and therefore the commercial reality of international air transport) assigns entirely different conceptual legal categories to these

---

11. By statute, the records and materials of the Airline Commission have been deposited with the National Archives and are available subject to certain copyright and security restrictions. Because of the historical value of the Airline Commission's archives, as well as the continuing force of its findings and recommendations, this book retains many of the references to Commission documents and personalities that characterized IN SEARCH OF OPEN SKIES. *Note:* All references to the Airline Commission's records and materials are in the form *Airline Commission Documents, Dkt. No.* (followed, where appropriate, by the six-digit file number assigned by the Airline Commission). Testimony given before the Commission will be cited as *Airline Commission Proceedings* with an appropriate reference to the testimony itself in the Commission's archives.

12. The present system, and therefore the industry it regulates, has probably earned the epithet 'dysfunctional' bestowed on it by Glenn Tilton, Chairman and Chief Executive Officer of United Airlines, in an address to the European Aviation Club in 2004. This observation was picked up and quoted by Daniel Calleja, Director, EC Air Transport Directorate, in a speech to the International Aviation Club. *See* Daniel Calleja, Speech to the International Aviation Club, Washington, D.C. (Nov. 16, 2004). Leo van Wijk, who held the equivalent post to Tilton at KLM, has remarked that if Hollywood operated under the same rules as the airline industry, the world would still be watching silent movies. Maintaining the Hollywood theme, Director Calleja referred to the aviation industry as a 'Jurassic Park.' *Id.*

13. In addition to the Chicago Convention, the Chicago Conference also adopted two other documents establishing the first five freedoms: International Air Services Transit Agreement, *opened for signature* Dec. 7, 1944, 59 Stat. 1693, 84 U.N.T.S. 389 (entered into force Jan. 30, 1945) (122 State parties as of 2006) [hereinafter Two Freedoms Agreement] and the International Air Transport Agreement, *opened for signature* Dec. 7, 1944, 59 Stat. 1701, 171 U.N.T.S. 387 (entered into force Jan. 30, 1945) (11 State parties as of 2006) [hereinafter Five Freedoms Agreement]. The freedoms of the air are formulated in an ascending order of liberality of market access. *See infra* Chapter 3, Part III.

services: the Chicago/San Francisco route is in legal form a 'cabotage' (or 'ninth freedom') service between points in the same State that can only be served by an airline owned and controlled by nationals of that State,[14] while FedEx's Singapore/New Zealand operation is in legal form a 'seventh freedom' service which States concede primarily for all-cargo operations, by an airline owned and controlled by nationals of one State and which runs a service between two third States.[15]

In succeeding *In Search of Open Skies*, this book once again takes up the challenge of imagining a set of core principles for an 'authentically' liberalized international aviation law and policy regime.[16] It does so with its gaze fixed on the historic 2007 U.S./EC Air Transport Agreement, which encoded a number of regulatory innovations including an historic loosening of the nationality rule.[17] Until the restrictive precepts of the Chicago Convention are rolled back, in the United States *and* among America's aviation trading partners, no authentic globalization of the international aviation system will be possible.

II   THE 'CHICAGO SYSTEM' AND A PROPOSAL
                  FOR ITS REFORM

At the very outset of this study, it is appropriate to offer a brief outline of some salient features of the international airline regulatory system that is in effect today, and to preview the recommendations for reform that will be advanced in Chapter 6. All of the subject matter introduced in this outline is considered in greater detail in later Chapters. (While many of the recommendations are based on the book's comparative analysis of the U.S. and EC approaches to deregulation of the airline industry, this may be an opportune moment to emphasize that the purpose of this study is not primarily to evaluate the *economic* performance of airline deregulation, the real or apparent economic benefits and detriments experienced by

---

14. *See infra* Chapter 3, Part IV.
15. *See infra* Chapter 3, Part V.
16. For a comment on the use of the term 'authentic' to modify liberalization, *see infra* Chapter 6, Part IV. Some U.S. aviation industry leaders, such as Glenn F. Tilton, have publicly espoused these themes of systemic change. *See, e.g.*, International Aviation Law Institute, DePaul University College of Law & Chicago Council on Global Affairs, *Sustainable Aviation Policies for America and the World: A Leadership Summit*, Synopsis of the Proceedings (Oct. 19, 2006) (containing a summary of Tilton's remarks to the DePaul University International Aviation Law Institute/Chicago Council on Global Affairs Second Annual Aviation Leadership Summit). In concluding an address on the state of global airline regulation, Tilton stated that '[w]e have an opportunity to take a fresh look at our aviation policies, and at regulatory biases too long left unexamined.'
17. A complete text of the agreement, along with its Annexes and the Memorandum of Consultations, can be found in the Official Journal of the European Union, 2007 O.J. (L 134) 4 (May 25, 2007) [hereinafter U.S./EC Air Transport Agreement], and reproduced *infra* Appendix III. This will be the version of the text used throughout this study. For further discussion of the Agreement, *see infra* Chapter 2.

consumers and providers of aviation services; this sometimes mercurial art has been well-practiced in the literature.)[18]

A   AN OVERVIEW OF THE GLOBAL AIR TRANSPORT INDUSTRY: PASSENGER/CARGO SERVICES

We begin with a selection of context-setting observations on the structure of the international airline industry. Two broad sectors of activity are usually identified, comprising passenger and cargo traffic respectively.[19] (The specialized express delivery sub-sector of air cargo transport – populated by handful of global names

---

18. *See, e.g.*, Government Accountability Office, GAO-06-630, *Airline Deregulation: Reregulating the Airline Industry Would Likely Reverse Consumer Benefits and Not Save Airline Pensions* (Jun. 2006) (concluding, for example, that the median airfare has declined almost 40% since 1980 as measured in 2005 dollars, and that markets have generally become more competitive under deregulation, with the average number of competitors increasing from 2.2 per market in 1980 to 3.5 in 2005). Earlier reports evidenced the same trends. The most recent study issued by the DOT reports that air fares have risen by 4.4% between the first quarter of 2007 and the first quarter of 2008 compared to a 4% inflation rate. *See* Press Release, U.S. DOT, Average First-Quarter Domestic Air Fares Rose 4.4% from 2007, BTS 36-0 (Jul. 23, 2008). Yet, from the first quarter of 1995 to the first quarter of 2008, fares rose a mere 11.7% compared to a cumulative 41% inflation rate. *See id.* An independent analysis offered at *The Boston Globe*'s travel web-log found, on the basis of the DOT statistics and adjusting for inflation, an overall 20% drop in air fares since 1995. *See* Posting of Paul Makishima, Globe Assistant Sunday Editor, to Globe-trotting: Travel News, Tips, Deals & Dispatches, <http://www.boston.com/travel/blog/> (Jul. 25, 2008, 7:30 EST). This trend has become the subject of some industry ire, most notably from former American Airlines CEO Robert Crandall. Crandall has proposed reregulating the setting of fares in order to better cover costs and maintain profitability. *See* Robert L. Crandall, Remarks to the Wings Club, New York, N.Y. (Jun. 10, 2008). Such a proposal could threaten many low-cost carrier operations, yielding higher fares and fewer choices for consumers. On the subject of fare reregulation generally, *see infra* Chapter 4, Part IV(C).

19. Transportation of air cargo occurs also through so-called 'combination' carriers which offer both passenger and cargo services. United Airlines, in addition to its passenger services, also operates United Cargo which, in 2005, carried just over 2 billion cargo-ton miles worldwide of freight and mail. *See* United Airlines, Fact Sheet, United's Worldwide Operations (Jan. 22, 2006), <http://www.unitedcargo.com/imggallery/FactSheet1stQtr06.pdf>. The DOT adopted the concept of sectoral divisions in its 1995 policy statement which contemplates future specialized sectoral agreements for liberalization of air cargo and charter services. *See* U.S. International Air Transport Policy Statement, 60 Fed. Reg. 21,841, 21,844 (May 3, 1995) [hereinafter 1995 Policy Statement]; *see also Airline Commission Proceedings*, testimony of Jeffrey N. Shane, former DOT Assistant Secretary for Policy, On Multilateral Approaches to Air Cargo Dereg-ulation (Jun. 24, 1993), at 47-48. Liberalization of air cargo traffic rights has tended to outpace that of air passenger traffic rights, in large part because cargo is a much less politically sensitive sector. Thus, even a traditionally closed economy like India introduced a largely unilateral 'open skies' policy for air cargo as early as 1990, at the very outset of its new governmental program of 'economic disengagement,' in order to counter the suppressive economic effects of chronic shortages in international air cargo capacity. *See* ICAO Secretariat, *Case Studies on Liberalization, presented at* Worldwide Air Transport Conference: Challenges and Opportu-nities of Liberalization, Montreal, Mar. 24-29, 2003, Case 2, ATConf/5-WP/5 (Feb. 17, 2003).

like DHL, FedEx, TNT, and UPS[20] – has experienced torrid rates of growth with revenues exceeding $64 billion in 2003, and provides jobs to 2.65 million people, a total likely to grow to 4.5 million by 2013.[21]) Within the category of passenger traffic, there has been a further sectoral distinction, increasingly blurred as deregulation advances, between 'scheduled' and 'nonscheduled' (or 'charter') services. Scheduled air traffic is assigned specific routes and times of arrival and departure, usually by license and international bilateral air treaty. Passenger traffic in 2007 accounted for 79% of the operating revenues of the world's scheduled (*i.e.*, non-charter) airlines.[22]

According to a definition proposed by the International Civil Aviation Organization (ICAO)[23] in 1952, a scheduled international air service (*inter alia*) operates to serve traffic between the same two or more points, either according to a published timetable or with flights so regular or frequent that they constitute a recognizable systematic series.[24] In contrast, in nonscheduled or charter air traffic, services are structured to meet a particular source of demand (sun or ski holidays predominate in Europe), and are frequently offered in conjunction with other services such as resort accommodation.[25] Charter traffic is not as intensively licensed,[26] but is nonetheless typically included in the scope of bilateral air treaty negotiations.

---

20. Traditional cargo movements have become separated from rapid-delivery services that use integrated multimodal transport systems. In fact, the four dominant companies are sometimes called 'express integrators.' These logistical networks transcend the archaic chains of forwarders, air carriers, agents, and surface transport providers that used to dominate the cargo field. Integrated multimodal transport, is based on a services 'product' – express delivery – rather than a specific mode of transport. In other words, if the express integrators could use Olympic sprinters to deliver iPods faster than they can do with airplanes, they would do so. In essentialist terms, therefore, the mode of transport is irrelevant. What is relevant is an integrated process to ensure on-time delivery. *See generally* OXFORD ECONOMIC FORECASTING, THE IMPACT OF THE EXPRESS DELIVERY INDUSTRY ON THE GLOBAL ECONOMY (2005).
21. In Europe, the express delivery industry has grown six times faster since 1998 than the European economy as a whole, with revenues rising by almost 80% in real terms. *See* OXFORD ECONOMIC FORECASTING, THE ECONOMIC IMPACT OF EXPRESS CARRIERS IN EUROPE 3 & 7 (2005). Worldwide, the industry since 1998 has grown at twice the rate of the global economy, soaring from 137.1 billion revenue ton kilometers (RTK) to a projected 470 billion RTKs in 2019. This tripling of services, as forecast by Boeing, represents an annual growth rate of 6.4%. *See* Press Release, Boeing, Boeing 20-Year Forecast Sees Strength in Air Cargo (Sept. 18, 2002).
22. Perry Flint, *A World Turned Upside Down*, AIR TRANSP. WORLD, July 2008, at 30, tbl.
23. ICAO is a public international organization for multilateral *technical* aviation cooperation among States that was established at the Chicago Conference in 1944. *See infra* Chapter 3, Part IX.
24. *See* ICAO, *Analysis of the Rights Conferred by Article 5 of the Convention*, ICAO Doc. 7278-C/ 841 (May 10, 1952), *compiled in Policy and Guidance Material on the Economic Regulation of International Transport*, ICAO Doc. 9587 (2d ed. 1999). *See also* I.H. PHILEPINA DIEDERIKS-VERSCHOOR, AN INTRODUCTION TO AIR LAW 19-21 (8th rev. ed. 2006). The definition retains its vitality, and appears in new EC legislation which synthesizes prior airline liberalization reform instruments into a single consolidated regulation. *See infra* Chapter 5, Part II.
25. *See generally* Andreas Papatheodorou, *Civil Aviation Regimes and Leisure Tourism in Europe*, 8 J. AIR TRANSP. MGMT. 381 (2002).
26. But charter traffic is nonetheless subject to a U.S. Department of Transportation licensing regime. *See* 14 C.F.R. § 380 (2003).

As liberalization has coursed through the U.S. and EU air transport industries, the nature of the economic bargain offered by charter operators (rigid, often unsocial, scheduling in return for more cost-based pricing) is increasingly trumped by an array of advance-purchase options from scheduled airlines, particularly the new paradigm low-cost, low-fare carrier.[27] Indeed, in the United States the downward trend of prices has reduced the size of the domestic charter industry to a small fraction of scheduled traffic.[28] In Europe, too, the recent emergence of a liberalized scheduled system is cutting into the historically high market share of charter operators, sending charter traffic spiraling downward from 2.4 million passenger journeys in 2000 to less than 900,000 by 2006.[29] The gradual confluence of the scheduled and non-scheduled sectors, reflected in their assimilation under the EC's airline deregulation project, explains this book's concentration on the former.[30]

B   A SYNOPTIC VIEW OF THE 'CHICAGO SYSTEM'

While the global air transport industry has been described (with some hyperbole) as 'probably the most complicated field of endeavo[u]r ever attempted by

---

27. *See* RIGAS DOGANIS, THE AIRLINE BUSINESS IN THE 21ST CENTURY 126-62 (2001) (analyzing the 'low-cost revolution'); *see also* Ryan Griffin, *State Aid, the Growth of Low-Cost Carriers in the European Union, and the Impact of the 2005 Guidelines on Financing Airports and Start-up Aid to Airlines Departing from Regional Airports*, 71 J. AIR L. & COM. 341, 344-46 (discussing the low-cost business model in the EU).

28. The passenger charter market in the United States is so small that a three-way merger between some of the largest passenger charter carriers (ATA, World Airways, and North American Airlines) was concluded in Apr. 2007. The transaction value of the deal, with ATA as the acquiror, was a relatively modest $31 million. *See* AIRLINE BUS., *Briefing: ATA Buys World and North American*, Apr. 23, 2007.

29. *See* George Williams, *The Future of Charter Operations, in* AVIATION AND TOURISM: IMPLICATIONS FOR LEISURE TRAVEL 85 (Anne Graham et al. ed., 2008). For background on how the European charter sector has handled the rise of low-cost competitors such as Ryanair and easyJet, *see* generally Cathy Buyck, *Flying Through Unchartered Skies: European Leisure Carriers Remain a Powerful Cluster, But the Industry is Changing Rapidly and Faces Some New Challenges*, AIR TRANSP. WORLD, Nov. 1, 2002, at 30 (noting concentration of 70% of charter production in the United Kingdom and Germany, a Europe-wide pattern of vertical and horizontal – transborder – integration of carriers, continued strength of charters in serving specific tourist-only destinations, and some evidence that charters have launched low-fare brands of their own). For two recent surveys of the European charter industry, *see* cb [*sic*], *New Horizons*, AIRLINE BUS., Sept. 2005 & Andrea Crisp, *Adapt or Die*, AIRLINE BUS., Aug. 2006 (noting continued resilience of the charter sector some four years later, marked by higher customer care and amenities to displace the old 'cattle truck' mentality of the charter experience, as well as a shift to medium- and long-haul destinations like Turkey, Egypt, the Middle East, Bali, and the United States, as low-cost competition has risen in big short-haul markets such as Nice. Meanwhile, charter carriers' embrace of the low-fare sector, either through alliances or their own brands, has remained a consistent trend as seat-only sales and Internet-driven customer demands for flexibility displace the traditional packaged tour). The fightback of the European charter industry has turned some of these operators into what Crisp calls 'multi-force' businesses that 'tr[y] to encompass all elements of the air transport market: package holidays, *ad hoc* charters, scheduled low-fare services, and two-class long haul flights.' *Id.*

30. Areas of continuing distinction, however, will be noted.

man,'[31] the legal regime which governs it is reducible to a very simple axiom: 'all commercial international air passenger transport services are forbidden except to the extent that they are permitted.'[32] Under what I call in this book the 'Chicago System,' government barter, not the entrepreneurial acumen of airline managements, has been the principal instrument of new transnational market development in this most technologically precocious industry.

Despite the ambition of the United States and other participants at Chicago, trading of the freedoms of the air has been conducted in a resolutely bilateral fashion, with each side committed to a kind of 'aeropolitics'[33] of restriction and artful compromise, classic zero-sum diplomacy, in defense of the market shares of one or more domestic carriers. Moreover, two of the key protectionist planks in the Chicago system, mentioned briefly in Part I, have been manifestly *non-negotiable*. Cabotage, originally a creature of the medieval law of maritime transport, prohibits foreign citizens from supplying domestic transport services (specifically, point-to-point flights within national territory);[34] while the nationality rule ensures that

---

31. M.J. Lester, 8 EUR. L. REV. 212 (1983) (reviewing C. CODRAI, EUROPEAN AIR FARES AND TRANS-PORT SERVICES (1982)). 'It is a field that employs more science and techniques, more supporting services and more personal attention than any other commercial enterprise. It produces inter-connecting air transport services throughout the world on a scale that makes Mr. Bradshaw's railway timetable look like a pamphlet on the London Underground system. It has been largely achieved in the . . . years since the Second World War not by politicians, not by regulators but by airline men negotiating through the medium of their trade association, IATA [the International Air Transport Association], the essential compromises in the technical, financial, legal and operational fields needed to make the system work.' Mr. Lester, as might be gathered from this hymn to the prevailing order, was not an advocate of what he disparaged as 'the Nirvana of cut-throat competition.' *Id.* IATA has itself taken increasing note of the complexity of the business it was formed to assist. The IATA 'Simplifying the Business' program (under the IATA-favored acronym StB) is leveraging Internet-based technologies to support electronic ticketing (ET), bar-coded boarding passes (BCBP), e-freight, and other enhancements to airline efficiency. The StB also supports an interlining partner search program with the appealing title of 'ET Matchmaker.' ET penetration has now reached over 80% of IATA's member airlines. *See* IATA, *Simplifying the Business Programme* (May 2007) and IATA's related website portal, <www.iata.org/stbsupportportal>.

32. Colin Thaine, *The Way Ahead from Memo 2: The Need for More Competition A Better Deal for Europe*, 10 AIR L. 90, 91 (1985).

33. On the possible origin of this phrase, *see infra* Chapter 6, note 260.

34. The principle of 'cabotage,' excluding foreign carriers from domestic transport services, has a long history in international commerce. For a comprehensive study of the origins and development of air transport cabotage, *see* PABLO M. J. MENDES DE LEON, CABOTAGE IN AIR TRANSPORT REGULATION (1992). As indicators of the non-negotiability of cabotage, *see* Andrew Zwaniecki, America.gov: Economics and Trade, U.S.-EU Aviation Talks Bring Prospect of Better Markets (May 27, 2008), <http://www.america.gov/st/econ-english/2008/May/20080523103412saik-ceinawz0.3800165.html> (containing Deputy Assistant Secretary in the Department of State John Byerly's remarks that there are no near-term prospects for the United States to change its cabotage laws); Transport Canada, Blue Sky: Canada's New International Air Policy 3 (2006), <http://www.tc.gc.ca/pol/en/ace/consultations/blueSky.pdf> (affirming that Canada's new approach to air transport policy does not include cabotage); THE BRATTLE GROUP, THE ECONOMIC IMPACT OF AN EU-US OPEN AVIATION AREA 28 (2002) (assuming the removal of cabotage restrictions to be a legal impossibility). Signs of movement away from this absolutism include the

airlines which provide a State's 'cabotage' services, or that are designated by the State to provide international services to other countries, remain owned *and* controlled by its own nationals (and, concomitantly, that any other State's airlines remain similarly owned and controlled by *its* nationals).[35] As we will see, the Chicago system is only partly the product of the solemn proceedings in 1944; the bilateral treaty network, and the unbending reliance on cabotage and nationality rules, evolved through subsequent State practice.[36]

The virtually universal approach among members of ICAO (the 190 parties to the Chicago Convention)[37] is that air services treaty negotiations are conducted separately from general trade diplomacy.[38] When government negotiators meet, they are often accompanied by nominees of their domestic airlines. (Only very recently, in fact, have U.S. airlines participated *directly*, rather than solely through trade associations, at U.S. negotiations.)[39] Based on the U.S. Department of

---

Australian Government's relaxation of cabotage while maintaining a relatively illiberal external policy. *See supra* note 3; *see also* Brian F. Havel, Moderator's Briefing Paper for the 2007 ABA Forum on Air & Space Law, Beyond Open Skies: Liberalization after the U.S.-EC Agreement (Oct. 4, 2007) (on file with author); *see also* Paul Waldie & Heather Scoffield, *Ottawa Urged to Unshackle Business*, GLOBE & MAIL, Jun. 27, 2008, at B1 (stating the opinion of Canada's Competition Bureau Commissioner Sheridan Scott that Canada should unilaterally open its airline industry to cabotage).

35.   For a recent critique of the nationality rule, *see* Brian F. Havel, *A New Approach to Foreign Ownership of National Airlines*, [2001-2004 Transfer Binder] ISSUES AVIATION L. & POL'Y ¶ 25,201, at 13,201 (2003). The source of the nationality restriction is a common provision of the International Air Services Transit Agreement and the International Air Transport Agreement. *See infra* Chapter 3, Part V. The restriction provides that 'each Contracting State reserves the right to withhold or revoke a certificate or permit to an air transport enterprise of another State in any case where it is not satisfied that substantial ownership and effective control are vested in nationals of a Contracting State.' The nationality restriction, incidentally, is only partly the product of these international agreements. The bilateral treaty network, and the unbending reliance on nationality (and cabotage) rules, evolved through subsequent State practice.

36.   *See infra* Chapter 3, Part III. Incidentally, as a matter of international treaty classification, a bilateral air transport agreement can be considered a *traité-contrat*, accomplishing a series of reciprocal commercial exchanges or concessions. In contrast, the 2007 product of the U.S./EC negotiations considered in this book, like the original Chicago Convention itself, has the attributes of a rarer species, the *traité-loi*, which establishes broad patterns of 'regular behavior' among States. MARK W. JANIS, INTERNATIONAL LAW 13-14 (5th ed. 2008).

37.   *See* ICAO, ICAO Documents, Doc 7300 Status, <http://www.icao.int/icaonet/dcs/7300.html>. (indicating that 190 States are currently contracting parties to the Chicago Convention).

38.   Thus, U.S. 'payments' for more liberal aviation regimes must be made in the context of the aviation agreement itself. As we will see, often the unit of payment is expanded route rights for the foreign carrier. Daniel P. Kaplan, *Foreign Investment in Domestic Airlines, in Airline Commission Documents*, Dkt. No. 001018 (Jul. 2, 1993), at 13. While the unique treatment of aviation is undoubtedly an historical anomaly, which occurred precisely because the Chicago Convention created a unique rule framework for international air transport competition, U.S. airlines have occasionally lobbied U.S. negotiators to use general trade imbalances, such as those with Japan, to leverage concessions in the air transport sector. Author's Interview with Mary Street, U.S. DOT Office of International Aviation (Dec. 4, 1995).

39.   But, for most of the negotiations leading to the Mar. 2007 U.S./EC Air Transport Agreement, the airlines on both sides were once again represented only through their trade associations.

Transportation's (DOT's) Model Open Skies Agreement,[40] and on a representative sampling of bilateral agreements,[41] there are six topics that predominate in typical bilateral air services negotiations: (i) route selection: the configuration of 'freedoms' that each party will concede, ranging from simple bilateral air traffic rights to more complex routing strategies that involve transit to or from third countries; also, the airports that will be the origin, destination or (for third-country traffic) the intermediate points for those routes; (ii) airline identity: designation of one or more airlines, typically including the national or 'flag' carrier, to serve the agreed routes; (iii) capacity: limitations on the number and frequency of flights, as well as type of aircraft ('gauge'), permitted on each approved route; (iv) pricing regimes: the degree of government approval required for airline tariff proposals; (v) provisions for charter and/or cargo transportation; and (vi) a number of ancillary topics, which in recent years have principally included fair operation of and access to computer reservations systems, authorization of 'code-sharing' arrangements,[42] and an assortment of issues concerning equitable treatment of non-national airlines in the supply and operation of airport slots, gates, and apron/terminal services.[43]

Route selection, airline designation, capacity, and pricing are the negotiating topics that chiefly define the marketplace created by each Chicago system bilateral.

See U.S./EC Air Transport Agreement, *supra* note 17, Attachment A, Delegation Lists (listing U.S. and EC 'Industry Observers' including *inter alia*, on the European side, the Association of European Airlines and the International Air Carrier Association, and on the U.S. side, the Air Transport Association and the National Air Carrier Association). As a general rule, any interested party (airlines, airports, trade associations, unions, etc.) may have one representative in the room during the plenary sessions of bilateral negotiations. There can, however, be more than one representative per entity in delegation meetings, though none in government-only sessions. In the U.S./EC negotiations, an exception was made only to allow representatives from trade associations to be present because of the large numbers involved. In fact, the very first session of the most recent round of U.S./EC talks had so many airline and industry representatives wishing to participate that many had to be seated in a separate room using a closed-circuit television feed. The compromise of inviting only trade association representatives soon followed. *Source*: Author's e-mail interview with Conor D. McAuliffe, Managing Director, Government and Environmental Affairs, United Airlines, Jul. 25, 2008. In any event, it would be naive to give the impression that all negotiations take place in bright sunshine. The chairs of each delegation often meet together in pre-policy or post-policy sessions, so that the real negotiations occur outside nongovernmental presence. These talks are often preceded, too, by exchanges of diplomatic cables.

40. *See* U.S. Dept. of State, Air Transport Agreement Between the Government of the United States of America and the Government of [country] (Jan. 1, 2008), <http://www.state.gov/documents/organization/19622.pdf> [hereinafter Model Open Skies Agreement]. The Model Agreement is reprinted as Appendix II to this book. Note that the Model Agreement is in constant evolution; the latest version can always be found at the homepage of the U.S. Department of State. *See* U.S. Dept. of State, Open Skies Agreements, <http://www.state.gov/e/eeb/tra/c661.htm>. On the content of the U.S. 'open skies' policy, *see infra* Part II(C).

41. The complete texts of all of the current U.S. bilateral air services agreements can be found in the third volume of Av. L. Rep. (CCH), beginning at ¶ 26,100.

42. Code-sharing is an arrangement between two or more airlines where all participating airlines market the same flight even though only one of them will serve as the operating carrier. This practice is a cornerstone of the current network of airline alliances. *See infra* Chapter 3, Part VIII.

43. The menu of 'ancillary' topics was considerably expanded in the 2007 U.S./EC Air Transport Agreement to include forms of mutual collaboration and notification (through a 'Joint

These core topics have always had an inherent conceptual elasticity. Governments that favor heavy protection of national airlines can adopt a 'closed' system, choosing to restrict foreign airlines to specific cities, or even specific airports, to narrow – or even to deny – opportunities for third-country traffic rights, and to swaddle a national (or 'flag') carrier in route systems that are true duopolies, served by one home carrier and one foreign carrier, with capacity subject to a rigid 50/50 split and the price structure constrained by government approval (at both ends) of all proposed tariffs. These protections could be buttressed further by formulas requiring cross-payments from one carrier to another should the capacity shares wobble too much in favor of one or other designated airline (a practice known as 'revenue pooling').[44]

While bilateralism is by no means a spent force (indeed, bilateral agreements remain the predominant approach used by States to expand international air transport services),[45] both the U.S. and EC air transport paradigms have undergone significant conceptual shifts in the past fifteen years. With some specific bilateral exceptions (notably the U.K./Netherlands air pact of 1984),[46] the EU's air transport industry prior to 1987 was a prototypical closed system of dueling air sovereignties. Today, within EU borders, supranational legislation has toppled the entire bilateral treaty network, gradually converting EU airspace, through a sequence of multilateral liberalization 'packages,' into a juridical confederation that (since the disappearance of intra-Member State cabotage in 1997) mirrors the unitary airspace of the U.S. federal system. Subject to the EC competition regime and to a very few regulatory safeguard mechanisms,[47] EU airlines have open access to all intra-Union international and domestic markets, without capacity or pricing restraints, without national ownership restrictions, and without the intruding presence of government aerodiplomacy.

C   Open Skies: Seeking Flexibility within the Chicago System

Meanwhile, U.S. officials, their deregulatory impulses stymied outside U.S. borders by the persistence of bilateralism, in the early 1990s invented a quasi-deregulatory doctrine called 'open skies.' This liberalizing concept was designed

---

Committee') on matters such as competition law investigations, public subsidies, wet-leasing policies, official government transportation practices, and other matters. *See infra* Chapter 2, Part V (summarizing the content of the 2007 agreement).

44.   European airlines prior to liberalization developed a special fondness for this practice. *See infra* Chapter 5, Part I.

45.   After the failure of the Five Freedoms Agreement discussed *supra* note 13, the bilateral treaty developed as the principal diplomatic and political vehicle for the exchange of traffic rights. As objects of purely bilateral exchange, however, the freedoms of the air were conceded only on the basis of defensive reciprocity. *See infra* Chapter 3, Part III(B).

46.   *See* HAVEL, *supra* note 5, Chapter 4, note 297.

47.   For example, EU Member States may impose what are known as 'public service obligations' on certain routes which are central to the economic development of the region they serve. *See infra* Chapter 5, Part II(C).

to temper the mercantilism (and hence the *raison d'être*) of the original restrictive bilateral model by giving the airlines of each contracting party unlimited access to operate services to and from any point in each other's territory, creating a virtually untrammeled pricing regime, and eliminating prescribed curbs on airline capacity (*i.e.*, frequency of flights).

Open skies was designed to stretch the negotiating framework of the Chicago system to its point of maximum tolerance. The United States launched various liberalizing initiatives of this kind, but the term *open skies* did not receive official imprimatur, or conceptual clarity, until a renewed initiative by the Bush Administration in early 1992, primarily directed toward European States, by then-Transportation Secretary Andrew Card.[48] Since then, the changes to international air transport prompted by open skies have been, in the words of former DOT Under Secretary for Policy Jeffrey Shane, 'an endless source of wonder.'[49] The open skies bill of fare, as refined by the U.S. DOT following extensive public comments, offers a highly liberalized interpretation of each of the key Chicago system negotiating points.[50] On route selection, the United States pursues an unrestricted 'gateway' policy, allowing foreign airlines to serve all cities (and airports) in U.S. territory, in return for reciprocal unlimited access in the other State. Routing flexibility is also featured, so that foreign carriers, again on condition of reciprocity, can (without capacity restrictions) board passengers at intermediate (third country) points for onward transit to the United States, or board passengers in the United States for onward transit to third countries (the so-called fifth freedom right).[51] 'Coterminalization rights' are also freely exchanged, so that a foreign carrier can link New York and Los Angeles, for example, as part of a continuing service (but without pick-up rights in New York).[52] As to airline identity, each side receives unlimited designation opportunities on each route.[53] Capacity (flight frequency) is also unrestricted on every route.[54]

On pricing structure, all airlines are free independently to set their own fares on each route they serve (subject only to U.S. and foreign law as to tariff 'filing'[55]).

---

48. Mr. Card subsequently returned to political prominence as the Chief of Staff to President George W. Bush.

49. Jeffrey N. Shane, Under Secretary for Policy, U.S. Department of Transportation, *Air Transport Liberalization: The U.S. Experience*, Speech at the ICAO Global Symposium on Air Transport Liberalization 6 (Sept. 18, 2006), <http://www.icao.int/icao/en/atb/ecp/dubai2006/Documentation/Shane.pdf> [hereinafter Shane, *Air Transport Liberalization*].

50. *See* In the Matter of Defining 'Open Skies,' final order issued by Jeffrey N. Shane, [former] Assistant Secretary for Policy and International Affairs, [March 2001] Av. L. Rep. (CCH) ¶ 26,960, at 23,901 (Aug. 5, 1992) (establishing DOT definition of 'open skies') [hereinafter DOT, *Open Skies*].

51. *Id.* ¶ 26,960, at 23,902.

52. *Id.*

53. *See id.*

54. *See id.*

55. Tariff filing has, for the most part, become obsolete under newer open skies bilaterals such as the 2007 U.S./EC Air Transport Agreement. *See* U.S./EC Air Transport Agreement, *supra* note 17, art. 13(1).

This flexibility results from typical adoption in open skies agreements of 'double disapproval' pricing, which requires *both* governments to reject a filed tariff. For routes involving third countries (such as fifth freedom traffic), the United States permits (once again, on a reciprocal basis) whatever price mechanism operates on the routes agreed between the United States and those third countries.[56]

Beyond these core elements of the package, the United States also offers liberal charter arrangements,[57] a liberal cargo regime that may include seventh freedom rights,[58] and a variety of liberalized provisions, very generally framed, concerning hard currency conversion of earnings, open code-sharing (including fifth freedom routes),[59] airport self-handling,[60] nondiscriminatory operation of and

---

56. DOT, *Open Skies, supra* note 50, ¶ 26,960, at 23,901. The European Community's final liberalization package precluded non-EU air carriers from price leadership on intra-Union routes. EU States negotiating their separate open skies bilaterals with the United States, therefore, faced legal difficulties in offering price leadership privileges on intra-Union fifth freedom routes (the United Kingdom, for example, could not assure Delta Air Lines equal treatment with British Airways to price-lead on the London/Frankfurt route). In a mood of compromise, the DOT announced that it would not 'insist' on price leadership in intra-Union markets. *Id.* The Department recognized, however, that open skies pricing at the very least required price-*matching* rights as 'essential for establishing a competitive presence in third-country markets.' *Id.* Although this prohibition on price leadership by U.S. airlines on intra-Union routes is maintained under the 2007 U.S./EC Air Transport Agreement, *see* U.S./EC Air Transport Agreement, *supra* note 17, art. 13(2), arguably a more liberal approach has been legislated by the 2008 regulatory consolidation of EC airline deregulation laws. *See infra* Chapter 5, Part II. For analysis of the European Community's provisions on tariff-setting, *see id.*
57. '[T]he least restrictive charter regulations of the two governments would apply, regardless of the origin of the flight.' DOT, *Open Skies, supra* note 50, ¶ 26,960, at 23,901. In response to criticism that charter arrangements were supererogatory in the U.S. open skies framework (given the small charter segment of the U.S. market), the DOT stated that it viewed charter operations 'as an important part of the air transport environment.' *Id.* The liberalizing provisions of the 2007 U.S./EC Air Transport Agreement include charter flights as well. *See* U.S./EC Air Transport Agreement, *supra* note 17, art. 3(4).
58. *See* DOT, *Open Skies, supra* note 50, ¶ 26,960, at 23,901. As noted previously, the less politically-charged air cargo industry has enjoyed somewhat more liberal regulatory favor than air passenger travel. The latest U.S. open skies template, for example, now offers all-cargo seventh freedom provisions (*i.e.*, the right to carry cargo traffic between two country points, neither of which is in the home State of the carrier). One of the earliest agreements to have an all-cargo seventh freedom provision is the 1997 U.S./El Salvador bilateral air services treaty. *See* Air Transport Agreement Between the Government of the United States of America and the Government of the Republic of El Salvador annex I [May 2005] Av. L. Rep. (CCH) ¶ 26,297a, at 22,209 (May 8, 1997) (offering each party's designated airlines the entitlement to offer all-cargo services for points between the other party's territory and 'any point or points'). The 2007 U.S./EC Air Transport Agreement, however, limits U.S. reciprocal seventh freedom all-cargo rights to the Czech Republic, France, Germany, Luxembourg, Malta, Poland and the Slovak Republic – countries which had swapped these rights with the United States before the Agreement.
59. *See infra* Chapter 3, Part VIII.
60. In effect, the right of an airline to perform its own 'ground-handling' in the territory of the other trading partner. *See* DOT, *Open Skies, supra* note 50, ¶ 26,960, at 23,903. 'The ability to self-handle is a crucial element in an airline's presentation of its product to the public, and the ability to self-handle guards against monopolistic and discriminatory practices at airports.' *Id.*

access to computer reservations systems, and a catch-all category of fair competitive opportunities, including access to airport slot and gate facilities.[61]

Finally, although antitrust immunity for intercarrier cooperation is not an element *per se* of the model open skies relationship, this vestigial DOT authority to allow airlines to cooperate *inter alia* on route planning, scheduling, 'frequent flier' programs, marketing, and pricing acquired prominence as a pivotal factor in persuading Germany to become the first 'big' EU Member State to subscribe to a liberalized air transport treaty.[62] The use of the bait of immunity (a process which could risk turning competitors into immunized price-fixers) has become a template for U.S. international aviation policy that is difficult for American negotiators to decline.[63] After 1992, open skies bilaterals *inter alia* with Austria, Belgium, France, Germany, the Netherlands, and Switzerland were each accompanied by antitrust immunity for alliances linking the national carriers of these countries with U.S. airline partners.[64] The 2007 U.S./EC Air Transport Agreement, in its Memorandum of Consultations, specifically confirms DOT policy that antitrust immunity will only be extended to agreements involving foreign carriers whose home States have concluded open skies agreements with the United States.[65] As we will

---

61. *See id.*
62. The history of the U.S./Germany aviation relationship suggests that it would probably have matured into open skies even without immunity. But the DOT award certainly helped to accelerate Germany's timetable. *See* HAVEL, *supra* note 5, Chapter 3, notes 273-74.
63. According to its participants, the last proposed American Airlines/British Airways integration was contingent on a U.S./U.K. open skies treaty and on U.S. antitrust immunity for the alliance. By Aug. 1996, however, the U.S./U.K. negotiations for a new treaty had stalemated on the prickly issue of unlimited fifth freedom rights for U.S. airlines. *See* Michael Skapinker, *US Assails British Tactics in 'Open Skies' Negotiations*, FIN. TIMES, Aug. 30, 1996, at 3. The two airlines reapplied for antitrust immunity before the DOT in 2001 after the DOT refused to process their original application following a breakdown in the U.S./U.K. negotiations. General Accounting Office, *Proposed Alliance Between American Airlines and British Airways Raises Competition Concerns and Public Interest Issues*, GAO-02-293R, at 1 (Dec. 21, 2001). Antitrust immunity and approval were eventually granted in 2002 subject to the condition that the parties divest 224 takeoff and landing slots to competitors seeking access to London Heathrow Airport – a condition neither could accept. *See* U.S. DOT, *U.S.-U.K. Alliance Case*, Dkt. No. OST-2001-11029-69, Order to Show Cause (Jan. 25, 2002); *see also* Laurence Zuckerman, *British Airways and American Cancel Alliance*, N.Y. TIMES, Jan. 26, 2002, at C1.
64. *See infra* Chapter 3, Part VIII.
65. *See* U.S./EC Air Transport Agreement, *supra* note 17, Memorandum of Consultations, para. 48. Thus, following the announcement of the U.S./EC agreement, U.S. carriers Delta Air Lines and Northwest Airlines, along with EU carriers Air France-KLM, Alitalia, and CSA Czech Airlines, applied for transatlantic antitrust immunity to deepen their relations as part of the SkyTeam Alliance. This complex collaboration would streamline and integrate two discrete alliance networks comprising Northwest's partnership with KLM and Delta's with Air France, Alitalia, and Czech Airlines. *See* U.S. DOT, *Joint Application of Alitalia-Linee Aeree Italiane-S.p.A., Czech Airlines, Delta Air Lines, Inc., KLM Royal Dutch Airlines, Northwest Airlines, Inc., & Société Air France for Approval of and Antitrust Immunity for Alliance Agreements*, Dkt. No. OST-2007-28644, Final Order (May 22, 2008); *see also* Paulo Prada, *Rules Eased for Airline Alliance*, WALL ST. J., Apr. 10, 2008, at B4. In a public statement, the DOT highlighted the U.S./EC agreement and its provision 'that transatlantic markets remain open' as part of its basis for granting the immunity. *See* Press Release, U.S. DOT, DOT Approves Expanded Transatlantic Alliance, DOT 73-08 (May 22, 2008).

see, the dual mechanisms of immunity and code-sharing provided the conceptual underpinning for the complex transatlantic alliances that have evolved over the past decade.[66]

Despite all of this upward ratcheting of rights and privileges, however, as previously noted the U.S. open skies experiment has remained a creature (albeit a 'late-model' creature) of the Chicago system in its homage to both the cabotage and nationality principles. To that extent, the United States has decided not to 'normalize' international aviation. Indeed, until its doomed 2005 initiative to moderate its application of the nationality rule,[67] the U.S. DOT had explicitly rejected any tampering with either principle, indicating statutory restrictions (which certainly exist to enforce both the cabotage and nationality rules), but also unspecified 'elements of policy' that would be addressed 'on a case-by-case basis.'[68] While the DOT could not unilaterally raze these twin structural pillars of bilateralism, the Department retains (and has used) some policy discretion, which will be addressed in Chapter 4, to modify their pure-form application.[69] Even the 'new-generation' bilaterals signed since 1995 sacralize the traditional treaty language that disqualifies foreign airlines from domestic point-to-point service[70] and from ownership

---

66. *See infra* Chapter 3, Part VIII.
67. Chapter 2 of this study will discuss a gallant effort by the U.S. Department of Transportation, intended to motivate EU Member State approval of the 2007 U.S./EC Air Transport Agreement, to introduce a more expansive interpretive approach to the control test component of the nationality rule. *See infra* Chapter 3, Part V(B). The new interpretation, shadows of which flicker in the final text of that historic Agreement, *see supra* note 3 (discussing Virgin America's 'franchise' relationship with the U.K.-based Virgin Group), would have cracked the nationality pillar but would not have caused it to crumble. Although this DOT effort failed (in part because of labor-inspired Congressional opposition), it signaled that U.S. aviation officials continue to show fidelity to the liberalizing instincts of the open skies era. One of those officials, former DOT Under Secretary for Policy Jeffrey N. Shane, comprehensively stated the implications of the agency's interpretive 'rulemaking' in Congressional testimony delivered at the peak of the controversy. *See* U.S. DOT, Office of Public Affairs, Statement of Jeffrey N. Shane, Under Secretary for Policy, Department of Transportation, Before the Aviation Subcommittee of the House Transportation and Infrastructure Committee (Feb. 8, 2006), <http://www.dot.gov/affairs/jeffshane020806.htm> (criticizing the unpredictable and subjective tests applied for U.S. citizen 'control' of U.S. airlines and suggesting that only a narrower set of objective ownership criteria, focused on shareholding, safety, and security rather than freedom of commercial decision-making, would not disturb the capital flows of a global economy and would allow the citizenship oversight process to 'add value').
68. DOT, *Open Skies*, *supra* note 50, ¶ 26,960, at 23,903.
69. For example, despite the DOT's relatively benign view of code-sharing arrangements ('an important element of the aviation landscape,' *id.* ¶ 26,960, at 23,903.), by allowing foreign air carriers to camouflage themselves on U.S. domestic routes using U.S. airline codes the DOT may be sanctioning a serious invasion of the pure cabotage principle. As to nationality, the DOT, as we will see, does have some flexibility in its treatment of the statutory indicia of ownership and control. *See infra* Chapter 3, Part V(B) (discussing the DOT's attempt to modify the indicia for the control test component of the nationality rule).
70. *See*, for example, Article 2 of the Model Open Skies Agreement, captioned *Grant of Rights*, which provides that '[n]othing in this Article shall be deemed to confer on the airline or airlines of one [p]arty the rights to take on board, in the territory of the other [p]arty, passengers, their baggage, cargo, or mail carried for compensation and destined for another point in the territory

and control of U.S. airlines.[71] As we will see, the 2007 U.S./EC Air Transport Agreement does not challenge this orthodoxy.[72]

III   A SUMMARY OF CORE PRINCIPLES FOR A
                     SECOND STAGE PLURILATERAL TREATY

In surveying the rigidity of the Chicago system, it is plain to see why this book turns for a remedial model to the comparative experiences of U.S. and EC airline deregulation. Although the wings of U.S. deregulation were clipped at America's external borders, successive U.S. administrations have attempted to export a simulacrum of the deregulated domestic system through various prescriptions for 'open skies.' The EU, surprising many of its own airlines, actually replaced the Chicago system in a multi-State environment, but the external aviation relations of the Member States, despite recent changes in the legal and policy environment, will remain bilaterally administered in some measure for the foreseeable future. While European commentators were once fond of protesting that the U.S. experience had little to teach the Community's air transport program,[73] it is nonetheless apparent that the coupling of these two jurisdictions in a unified airspace now presents an exceptional opportunity to transcend the Chicago system and to

---

of that other [p]arty.' Model Open Skies Agreement, *supra* note 40, art. 2(4). For analysis of similar exclusionary language in concluded bilaterals, *see infra* Chapter 3, Part IV.

71. *See* Article 4 of the Model Open Skies Agreement, captioned *Revocation of Authorization*, which provides for revocation or suspension of operating rights of a foreign airline where 'substantial ownership and effective control of that airline are not vested in the other [p]arty, the [p]arty's nationals, or both.' Model Open Skies Agreement, *supra* note 40, art. 4(1)(b). The treaty text provides that either party '*may* revoke [or] suspend' (emphasis added) if the ownership/control provisions are violated. *Id.* There is an element of subjective impression in the measurement of 'control' that inevitably transcends mathematical percentages of equity (or debt) ownership. *See* discussion of U.S. and other countries' ownership/control tests, *infra* Chapter 3, Part V. (Notice that, generally speaking, the applicable test will be that of the foreign airline's own domestic laws.)

72. *See* U.S./EC Air Transport Agreement, *supra* note 17, art. 3(6) & art. 5.

73. In earlier years, the European Commission took pains to distinguish its liberalization policies from the U.S. model. *See* The Community and the Aviation Sector: Commission Position, Commission Press Release, *ref:* IP(93)511, *in Airline Commission Documents*, Dkt. No. 001142, Annex (Jun. 24, 1993). The EC legislation included certain safeguard clauses to allow limited State intervention should specific dislocations occur. *See infra* Chapter 5, Part II. These mechanisms were included in an apparent effort to preclude the 'upheaval' that allegedly followed deregulation in the United States. *Id.* The Commission styled this combination of deregulation and safeguard clauses a 'middle-of-the-road' approach to liberalization. *See* European Commission, *The Way Forward for Civil Aviation in Europe*, paras. 20-25, COM (94) 218 final (Jan. 6, 1994). Despite the rapid evolution of the European aviation marketplace over the last 15 years, the Commission has not abandoned this approach even though it has abridged certain intervention powers in order to minimize market distortion. *See, e.g.*, European Commission, *Proposal for a Regulation of the European Parliament and of the Council on Common Rules for the Operation of Air Transport Services in the Community (Recast)*, Explanatory Memorandum, COM (2006) 396 final (Jul. 18, 2006) (explaining the need to clarify existing competition safeguard rules in the EC while refraining from wholesale elimination of such rules).

inspire a genuine 'globalization' of the world's air transport industry.[74] Toward that end, this book lays out a radical proposal for a plurilateral air transport treaty – pursued within the second stage negotiations already begun by the terms of the 2007 U.S./EC Air Transport Agreement – that joins the airspaces of the United States and the EU in a transcontinental zone of free and fair competition. As a plurilateral instrument, the new treaty will be open to all other aviation powers which subscribe to its 'highest common denominator' pitch of liberalization. Here, in summary form, are the seven guiding principles that would form the core of this next-generation treaty:[75]

Principle 1: Abrogating Managed Trade

All airlines, irrespective of national affiliation or quantum of public owner-ship, will compete under uniform, objective rules of nondiscrimination and equality of competitive opportunity, with freedom to access markets, establish prices and determine frequency of services. Accordingly, the plurilateral con-tracting parties will accept that it is no longer feasible, in a market environ-ment, for each country to have its own airline, and optimization of 'national' shares will no longer be retained as an objective of the international airline system. In effect, there will be only one 'freedom' of the air in the new dispensation, expressed in the maxim *suum cuique*: in other words, to each airline will belong the trade that it is able to attract and build, rather than the trade which its sponsor State is able to secure based on the mutating bargains of aeropolitical diplomacy.

Principle 2: Abrogating Chicago's Artifice of Freedoms

The plurilateral treaty will release all origin/destination points in and between all of its contracting parties, including all cabotage routes in the United States and European Union, into a grand network pool. Any airline carrier licensed within the territory of the plurilateral will have the commercial right to enter any of these origin/destination markets without *a priori* restrictions as to capacity or frequency of services. To the extent that the right might be cir-cumscribed in any way, it will be because of an infrastructural constraint that triggers nondiscriminatory safeguard measures notified to all contracting parties and possibly subject to appellate review by a new supranational author-ity (see below). There will be no requirement that services be connected to a 'home' origin or destination city, and there will be no advance determinations that only a certain number of airlines will be permitted to serve any given origin/destination combination.

Principle 3: Adopting A New Doctrine of 'Regulatory' Nationality

The plurilateral will dismantle the nationality rule – the citizenship purity test, as it is sometimes described in this book – by recasting the traditional

---

74. *See* discussion on 'globalization' of air transport in the DOT's 1995 Policy Statement, *supra* note 19, at 21,841-42 ('Changing Environment').

75. Detailed discussion of each of these principles begins *infra* Chapter 6, Part III(E).

airline/State identity as a 'right of establishment.' Under this approach, while an airline's nationality will still be legally significant, its 'regulatory' and 'commercial' nationality will be de-linked. An airline will still have a regulatory nationality, a State in which it is incorporated, where it has its principal place of business, where it pays taxes, employs local management and employees, obeys local environmental and labor and other laws, and is subject to local safety, security, and fiscal supervision. Even multinational airlines, therefore, will have to 'localize' themselves to operate to, from, and within the contracting States of the plurilateral. Otherwise, however, the commercial nationality of an airline – the national identity of its shareholders – will be a matter of regulatory indifference: if the plurilateral is 'open,' the shareholders can be from any State or States; if closed, they will have the nationality of one or more contracting parties to the plurilateral. The broad right of 'establishment' will enable airlines (and entrepreneurially-inclined citizens) to establish start-up or subsidiary operations in other territories of the plurilateral and to decide merger and acquisition strategy without restrictions of any kind on cross-border investment. Registration and licensing procedures will be administered nationally according to common criteria, while the Joint Committee established under the first-stage U.S./EC Agreement may be charged with the task of developing a central aircraft register.

Principle 4: Abrogating Pricing Controls

The plurilateral will not include any pricing protocols or government tariff approval procedures. Airlines will be free to set their prices in accordance with the competitive conditions of the marketplace, and to engage in price leadership (or price matching). The plurilateral will shun *a priori* surveillance of pricing predation. Thus, the only form of pricing control in the post-Chicago system will be through the *ex post* operation of the competition laws.

Principle 5: Adopting A 'Deep Integration' Program of Regulatory Convergence

To ensure a level commercial playing-field among all carriers, the plurilateral will seek 'deep integration' to elide remaining regulatory differences between the contracting parties. In particular, a balanced program will encompass regulatory convergence in three broad spheres of commercial interest. First, with respect to antitrust and competition regimes, the plurilateral will leverage the shared U.S./EC competition enforcement culture to propose a sectoralized common body of competition law applied within each jurisdiction and subject to supranational appellate jurisdiction (see below). Second, the plurilateral will reject *a priori* all publicly-funded operating aid for failing carriers, but otherwise public grants of aid will be filtered through objective criteria modeled on prior practices of the European Commission and of the World Trade Organization under its subsidies agreement. Again, supranational appellate review will be available with respect to public aid violations. Finally, the plurilateral will encourage an abstentionist regulatory 'mindset' that prefers market solutions to problems such as infrastructural congestion and potential bias in distribution systems and resists 'overexuberant' intervention in areas (such as airline passenger rights) where regulation adds costs but does not necessarily deliver optimal outcomes. Also, while recognizing disparities in labor laws not only between the United States and the European Community but also within the EU Member States, the plurilateral will set forth broad principles of labor policy that will assure labor unions on both continents that a market-based plurilateral settlement, built upon the 'right of establishment,' is capable of protecting and advancing their interests. Finally, regulatory convergence will continue in a second stage plurilateral by expanding the remit of the Joint Committee established under Article 18 of the 2007 U.S./EC Air Transport Agreement.

Principle 6: Adopting Mandatory Supranational Appellate Jurisdiction

The plurilateral will create a standing authority, the Air Transport Commission, to determine finally and on the basis of a developed body of global air transport law, the conflicting claims of public and private stakeholders in the international aviation industry in potentially any of their relationships governed by law. The Commission's appellate jurisdiction, will extend, in the first instance, to competition law and to all of the substantive regulatory issues (public aid, airport congestion controls, slot trading, and other sources of conflict) that will be addressed in the second-stage plurilateral. Decisions of the Commission will have the force of domestic law within each contracting party's jurisdiction, and no further domestic appeals or challenges will be permitted. To facilitate this regime, private corporations and citizens will have standing in all proceedings before the Commission.

Principle 7: Adopting the EC 'Community Designation Clause' For Third Countries Outside the Plurilateral

The European Court of Justice decided in a series of rulings in 2002 that tolerating Member State nationality-based designations of air carriers to serve external (third country) routes outside the European Union is discriminatory. The European Community, acting under this legal compulsion, is renegotiating all Member State bilateral air services agreements with non-Member States to insert a 'Community designation clause' that opens all Member State external routes to access by all EC-licensed air carriers. The contracting parties to the plurilateral will undertake a similar initiative in aeropolitical diplomacy, and adopt a similar joint designation clause, as a buffering mechanism to allow participating States to maintain their aviation relationships with third countries outside the plurilateral system. The Joint Committee will represent the contracting parties in this effort.

Amplifying these core principles of abrogation and adoption into a coherent proposal for change will be part of my task in the final Chapter of this study. Chapter 2, meanwhile, will offer a critical synthesis of the past decade and a half of unprecedented ferment in transatlantic air transport diplomacy. This was a period marked by aeropolitical timidity and boldness, as well as by bad timing and occasional fair winds, that culminated in the signing in 2007 of an historic – if necessarily template-driven – air transport liberalization agreement between the United States and the European Community.

Chapter 2

Prelude to Change: A Synthesis of Transatlantic Aviation Relations 1993-2008

I   INTRODUCTION: AN EPISTEMIC COMMUNITY RISES

Discussion of the fate of the so-called 'Chicago system' is indeed timely.[1] For nearly 15 years, the U.S. and EU aviation establishments have been seeking to frame new policies to supersede the archaic bilateral structures that have persisted for well over half a century. The EU has rebuilt its aviation regulatory system from the inside, but the effect (as noted in Chapter 1) has been to forge a union of sovereign airspaces that now mirrors the federally integrated airspace of the United States. Indeed, the EU developed – within its own jurisdiction – precisely the multilateral, multi-sovereign regulatory model that the United States might

---

1. As will be evident from this Chapter, the pace of recent events in international aviation has been swift. In a retrospective address made at the onset of the events chronicled here, Professor Andreas Lowenfeld, author of the seminal AVIATION LAW: CASES AND MATERIALS (1981), commented that he was regularly asked why he had not published a third edition of his book. He responded that his 'instinct' was that 'the legal regime governing civil aviation is in a prolonged period of transition, more suitable to weekly newsletters than to an effort at description and analysis with some perspective.' Andreas F. Lowenfeld, Competition in International Aviation: The Next Round, Address Before the International Conference on Air Transport and Space Application in the New World (Jun. 1993) (transcript on file with author). While I hope that this book might (in building on its predecessor) in some way confound Lowenfeld's pessimism about the wisdom of writing *au courant* books on aviation law, there is indeed ample evidence of an industry in dynamic transition in the pages of two excellent industry journals, AVIATION DAILY and AVIATION WEEK & SPACE TECHNOLOGY, both products of McGraw-Hill's Aviation Week Group. Another periodical publication that maintains superb coverage of aviation law and policy issues is the London-based monthly AIRLINE BUSINESS, published by Reed Business Information. AIRLINE BUSINESS, in fact, is sometimes called 'the airline industry's *Economist.*'

ultimately embrace for the global aviation system. The Americans, meanwhile, endeavored to export a replica (or, more correctly, a simulacrum) of their deregulated domestic market using an 'open skies' template for U.S. bilateral agreements. As a result of these concurrent initiatives, a powerful transatlantic consensus for reform of the bilateral system has emerged.

The past decade and a half, in fact, unlike any comparable period which preceded it, has produced a complex, extended, and multi-institutional transatlantic public policy discourse on the future contours of a common air transport regime for the United States and the EU. Although an historic U.S./EC (European Community) 'open skies' agreement was signed in April 2007, it would be fair to call that agreement a significant, but by no means culminating, moment in this evolving rapprochement. To understand what still lies in the future, it is necessary to synthesize all of the major initiatives of the past 15 years and to appreciate the complexity of the policy challenges that spurred efforts to liberate global air transport from the static regime of intergovernmental barter (described in Chapter 1) that has regulated its existence for seven decades. The beacons of progress in deepening the search for open skies have been the legal and policy initiatives of various State and non-State actors, notably including the U.S. and EU aviation administrations, the European Court of Justice,[2] the public and private international air transport organizations, the nongovernmental U.S. and EU airline representative organizations, and the endeavors of analysts and academics. As these actors interacted with and reinforced one another, 'webs of influence'[3] have evolved to deliver new principles for a transnational air transport regime and which will lead ultimately to the specific regulatory (and deregulatory) mechanisms of that regime.[4] In short, a transatlantic 'epistemic community' in aviation law and policy has been rising.[5]

In the succeeding Sections of this Chapter, we will begin the task of lending retrospective analytical coherence to these legal and policy initiatives of the past 15 years. In the robust *Realpolitik* atmosphere of transatlantic aeropolitical affairs, it is fair to say that they did not unfold with chronological or conceptual precision. But two principal phases of the prelude to a post-bilateral system can be identified for the purpose of exposition. The first phase begins with the convening of a U.S. presidential commission on the airline industry in 1993 and concludes, following a

---

2. 'Equivalent to a supreme court in the EC context,' according to the somewhat defensive language of a recent European Commission publication. European Commission, *EC External Aviation Policy: Why Does the EC Want to Modify Air Service Agreements Between Its Member States and Partner Countries?*, para. 2, Information Note. Nonetheless, in the evolution of a coherent EC air transport policy, the Commission has had reason to fear a scofflaw attitude by the Member States. *See infra* Part III.

3. 'Webs of influence' is a useful epistemological expression that undergirds a recent important study of the evolution of regulatory schemes for international business. *See* JOHN BRAITHWAITE & PETER DRAHOS, GLOBAL BUSINESS REGULATION 13 (2000).

4. *Id.* at 9.

5. The substitution of the adjective 'transatlantic' modifies the original phrase, 'global epistemic community,' used in Gunter Teubner, *'Global Bukowina': Legal Pluralism in the World Society*, *in* GLOBAL LAW WITHOUT A STATE (Gunter Teubner ed., 1997).

momentous ruling of the European Court of Justice, with the award of a formal mandate to the European Commission in 2003 to negotiate a comprehensive air services agreement with the United States on behalf of all of the EU Member States. If we take the 2003 mandate (which followed an earlier, more circum-scribed mandate granted in 1996) as the critical inflection point after a decade of change, the second phase then encompasses two periods of U.S./EC negotiations (starting in late 2003) and ends with the provisional entry into force of a new transatlantic air services agreement in March 2008.

II   RETHINKING BILATERALISM: THE OPEN SKIES
            DECADE 1993-2003

A   BEYOND BILATERALISM: THE BALILES AIRLINE COMMISSION

While bilateralism today is by no means a spent force (indeed, as already noted, bilateral agreements remain the prevailing approach used by States in expanding international air transport services),[6] U.S. international aviation policy since the early 1990s progressively tempered the mercantilism (and hence the *raison d'être*) of the original restrictive bilateral models through the policy of 'open skies' bilat-eral agreements discussed in Chapter 1.[7] While these new-generation bilaterals

---

6. The Montreal-based Secretariat of the International Civil Aviation Organization (ICAO) iden-tified over 900 bilateral air service agreements (including amendments or memoranda of understanding) that were concluded between 1995 and 2005. *See* International Civil Aviation Organization [ICAO], *Regulatory and Industry Overview*, para. 1.1, Information Paper (Aug. 15, 2006) [hereinafter ICAO, *Regulatory*]. According to ICAO, 'over 70[%] of these agreements and amendments contained some form of liberalized arrangements' such as unrestricted traffic rights, multiple airline designation, absence of flight capacity limitations, flexible pricing regimes, broader inward investment criteria, and other features. *Id.* Counting all informal exchanges, amendments, additions, and writings, the global number of extant bilateral air services agree-ments may be as high as 10,000. *See* Cornelia Woll, *The Activism of the European Commission in the Case of International Aviation* 6 (AICGS/DAAD, Working Paper Series, 2003).

7. In 1995, the Clinton Administration launched a revamped version of earlier efforts to 'export' U.S. airline deregulation, building on several precedents including President Jimmy Carter's relatively modest liberalized agreements beginning in 1977 as well as President George H. W. Bush's gateway-specific 'Cities Program' in 1990, and a more ambitious all-gateway 'Open Skies' policy in 1992. *See* Jeffrey N. Shane, Under Secretary for Policy, U.S. DOT, *Air Transport Liberalization: The U.S. Experience*, Speech at the ICAO Global Symposium on Air Transport Liberalization, at 6 (Sept. 18, 2006), <www.icao.int/icao/en/atb/ecp/dubai2006/Documentation/ Shane.pdf> [hereinafter Shane, *Air Transport Liberalization*] (summarizing emergence of the U.S. open skies regime, and charting how the skeptical reaction of incumbent U.S. airlines to international liberalization eased as their performance in international markets proved 'extraor-dinary'); *see also infra* Chapter 4, Part III. Former U.S. Secretary of Transportation Federico Peña chose the 50th anniversary commemoration ceremony of the signing of the Chicago Con-vention – a muted affair, held in the same Chicago hotel where the 1944 meeting gathered – to unveil a new, Clintonian U.S. international aviation policy. Secretary Peña's salute to the Chicago treaty, as revealed in his prepared remarks, was in pointed contrast to the views expressed to the Airline Commission in 1993 by senior U.S. aviation official Patrick Murphy. Commenting

will be analyzed in additional detail in Chapter 4,[8] for the present it is enough to note once again the critical systemic limitations of this U.S. policy – limitations that will become the ultimate coin of exchange in any multilateral dispensation. Although U.S. open skies policy relied on a globalist and cosmopolitan rhetoric,[9] the most current iteration of the policy, the U.S. DOT's 1995 *International Air*

on the U.S. failure to prise open aviation markets at the Chicago Conference, Murphy wryly observed that the Convention was then approaching its 50th anniversary, 'and some people actually want to celebrate that. They are actually going to have ceremonies to celebrate that.' *Airline Commission Proceedings*, testimony of Patrick V. Murphy, Deputy Assistant Secretary for Aviation and International Affairs, U.S. Department of Transportation (May 24, 1993), at 213. Peña's thematic focus on 'globalization' mirrored the dialectical approach of the Airline Commission. Pledging 'the power of the United States government' to the goal of superseding the Chicago bilateral system, he committed himself to a strategy of negotiating new 'open skies' bilaterals that would 'provide for moving toward full liberalization' while including unspecified 'adjustment provisions' for foreign carriers facing increased U.S. competition. Specifically, he offered 'attractive service opportunities to U.S. cities' as the incentive to encourage these new-generation bilaterals. Federico Peña, Secretary of Transportation, Remarks at the 50th Anniversary Commemoration, The Convention on International Civil Aviation (Nov. 1, 1994), *in* U.S. DOT, *Transportation Trends* (Nov. 1994); *see also* Press Release, U.S. DOT, News, DOT 156-64 (Nov. 1, 1994) Nine small European States, including seven EC members, and Canada, were invited to be the first participants in this new move 'toward free trade in aviation services.' *See* U.S. International Air Transport Policy Statement, 60 Fed. Reg. 21,841, 21,844 (May 3, 1995) [hereinafter 1995 Policy Statement].

8.　*See infra* Chapter 4, Part III. By the time formal negotiations began between the United States and European Community in 2003 for what would become the 2007 U.S./EC Air Transport Agreement, 2007 O.J. (L 134) 4 [hereinafter 2007 U.S./EC Air Transport Agreement], the United States had already entered into bilateral agreements with 11 of the then-15 (now 27) EU Member States. (Greece, Ireland, Spain, and the United Kingdom had remained impervious to the U.S. diplomatic *démarches*.) The agreement came into effect on Mar. 30, 2008, and is currently the subject of negotiations to further expand the scope of air liberalization between the two aviation powers. *See* John R. Byerly, Deputy Assistant Secretary for Transportation Affairs, U.S. Department of State, Remarks on the EU Open Skies Agreement (Sept. 29, 2007).

9.　The cosmopolitan *mentalité* had an unflattering half-life in the 20th century as part of the lexicon of the Stalinist Soviet Union, used to describe primarily the Jews, who had no homeland over nearly two millennia and were described as *bezrodniy kosmopolit*: rootless cosmopolitans. *See* GLEB STRUVE, SOVIET RUSSIAN LITERATURE: 1917-50 338-46 (1951). While disparaging Soviet dogma has become customary, the earliest glimmerings of cosmopolitanism in the life and thought of Diogenes of Sinope – an early Cynic philosopher – lent itself to being associated with individuals whose interests and loyalties are solipsistic and rapacious rather, as the contemporary ethos would have it, a 'citizen of the world.' *See* LUIS E. NAVIA, CLASSICAL CYNICISM: A CRITICAL STUDY 81-118 (1996); *but see* PHILO OF ALEXANDRIA, PHILO VOL. I: ON THE ALLEGORICAL INTERPRETATION OF GENESIS 2 AND 3 (F.H. Colson & G.H. Whitaker trans., 1929) (deploying the term *kosmopolites* to describe humanity as under one order of right); ERIC VOEGELIN, THE COLLECTED WORKS OF ERIC VOEGELIN VOLUME 17: ORDER AND HISTORY VOLUME IV: THE ECUMENIC AGE 77 (Michael Franz ed., 2000) (arguing against the grain that *kosmopolites* is a Philonic neologism and thus incorrectly attributed to Diogenes). The less pejorative sense of a cosmopolitan *mentalité* resurfaced and in some sense stabilized through the course of the twentieth century when intellectual trends in foreign relations conceived of humanity as a single moral community perceived as better, safer, and more enlightened than traditional tribalist understandings. Cosmopolitanism was tied closely to the emergence of international collaborative institutions like the United Nations, the International Monetary Fund, the European Economic

Transportation Policy Statement,[10] shrank from any reference, explicit or implicit, to elimination of the central legal pillars of the prevailing Chicago system of protective bilaterals – the principle of cabotage (the prohibition on awarding domestic traffic rights to foreign carriers[11]) and the nationality rule, the skein of restrictions on inward foreign investment in and control of national carriers.[12]

In 1993, as the U.S. air transport industry was returning weak results in the midst of a cyclical economic downturn,[13] the 15 voting members of President Bill Clinton's National Commission to Ensure a Strong Competitive Airline Industry (the Airline Commission) endorsed a multilateral 'open skies' replacement for the

---

Community and, in the context of international aviation, the International Civil Aviation Organization. *See generally* Eleftheriadis Pavlos, *The European Constitution and Cosmopolitan Ideals,* 12 K.C.L.J. 17 (2001); Richard Janda, *Toward Cosmopolitan Law,* 50 McGILL L.J. 967 (2005); Frederick Pollock, *Cosmopolitan Custom and International Law,* 29 HARV. L. REV. 565 (1916); William Smith & Robert Fine, *Kantian Cosmopolitanism Today: John Rawls and Jürgen Habermas on Immanuel Kant's* Foedus Pacificum, 15 K.C.L.J. 5 (2004).

10. *See supra* note 7. This was the first formal statement of U.S. international aviation policy since 1978 (when the Carter Administration published its *United States Policy for the Conduct of International Air Transportation Negotiations*). *See infra* Chapter 4, Part III(A).

11. 'Cabotage,' which in its peremptory meaning excludes foreign common carriers from the supply of domestic transport services, has a long history in international commerce. Its centrality to the Chicago aviation system is considered *infra* Chapter 3, Part IV. For a comprehensive study of the origins and development of air transport cabotage, *see* PABLO M. J. MENDES DE LEON, CABOTAGE IN AIR TRANSPORT REGULATION (1992).

12. *See* Richard Branson, *Fair Competition: A True Revolution in Flight,* U.S. NEWS & WORLD REP. , Dec. 2, 2002 (provocatively calling U.S. open skies agreements 'the last gasps of the old, archaic bilateral system'). Abolition of the nationality rule, and its restrictions on inward foreign investment, would be the most commercially (and juridically) attractive option for reform. If the nationality rule were abolished in the United States, for example, an EU airline could either buy an existing U.S. carrier (gaining access to the carrier's domestic route system) or 'establish' a subsidiary to serve U.S. domestic routes (as the Virgin Group originally hoped to do). *See infra* Chapter 3, Part V(B). Cabotage services, in contrast, assume that the EU carrier simply operates *qua* foreign carrier, but extends its network to serve U.S. domestic routes. Lifting the cabotage exclusion would be hard for a government to do (in addition to labor union objections), because under international treaty law (the Chicago Convention) foreign airlines which serve cabotage routes are still regulated by their home countries. *See* Brian F. Havel, *A New Approach to Foreign Ownership of National Airlines,* [2001-2004 Transfer Binder] ISSUES AVIATION L. & POL'Y ¶ 25,201, at 13,203 (2003). Moreover, the persistence of a visceral nationalism, even among advanced powers, can never be discounted. After the ignominious fall of Swissair in 2001, the Swiss Government might have wished to join an investor group and to purchase a foreign carrier, for example the German flagship Lufthansa, instead of funding the major burden of restarting a new airline, dubbed 'Swiss.' Scenarios of that kind are unworkable as long as the nationality rule persists.

13. Following the U.S. economic recession in the early 1980s, the airlines began rapidly to expand capacity, resulting in price wars and hard financial losses once the economy turned downward again in the early 1990s. According to the International Air Transport Association (IATA), net losses between 1990 and 1993 among its member airlines amounted to $15 billion. *See* RIGAS DOGANIS, THE AIRLINE BUSINESS 4 (2d ed. 2006). After 1994, many airlines returned to profitability until the 9/11 attacks began a series of staggering losses which eventually reached nearly $26 billion. *See id.*

patchwork of bilateral agreements developed under the Chicago Convention.[14] A decade later, its Chairman, former Virginia Governor Gerald L. Baliles, would write of his 'alarming sense of *dejà vu*' as another cyclical downturn took hold[15] and point once again to his Commission's recommendations to permit more substantial cross-border investment and to transcend bilateral air services agreements (in short, to migrate to a multilateral strategy).[16] A new Commission would not have to be

---

14. The President empanelled the Airline Commission pursuant to Section 204 of the Airport and Airway Safety, Capacity, Noise Improvement and Intermodal Transportation Act of 1992, 49 U.S.C. app. § 1371 note (as amended by Pub. L. No. 103-13 (Apr. 7, 1993)). The Commission's mandate, in broad brush, was to uncover the structural causes of the parlous financial condition of the U.S. airline industry in 1992. Under the rubric of international aviation policy, Section 204(d)(4)(B) required the Commissioners to examine 'the desirability of multilateral rather than bilateral negotiations.' The frenetic timetable imposed on the Commission – 90 days from appointment to final report – was surprising, given its broad mandate, and probably contributed to the slightness of its impact on most of the issues it surveyed. Calls for a new presidential commission to be formed have thus far gone unheeded, partly because so much of the 1993 Commission's work remains undone, and partly because much of the initiative in multilateral aviation has since slipped from the United States to the European Union. Indicative of this torch-passing was the establishment in 2006 of the High Level Group to advise the European Commission on the future of aviation regulation in the EC. The group's work, which ended in Jun. 2007, resulted in ten recommendations on topics including airport safety, the environment, and regulatory convergence. *See* HIGH LEVEL GROUP FOR THE FUTURE EUROPEAN REGULATORY FRAMEWORK, EUROPEAN AVIATION: A FRAMEWORK FOR DRIVING PERFORMANCE IMPROVEMENT (2007).
15. Gerald L. Baliles & Greg Principato, *Ever Get the Feeling We're Flying in Circles?*, WASH. POST, Mar. 2, 2003, at B5; *see also* Gerald L. Baliles, *Departures: Open Up Foreign Investment – Finally*, 357 AV. DAILY, Sept. 9, 2004, at 1 [hereinafter Baliles, *Departures*] (revisiting the recommendation of the Airline Commission to raise the ceiling on inward investment in U.S. airlines); Mark Murray, *In a Tailspin*, 41 NAT'L J., Oct. 12, 2002 (noting how the economic crisis of the first half of the new decade reprised the 'bleak' message of the 1993 Commission).
16. Other Commission recommendations recapitulated by the Governor in his 2003 retrospective included providing a stable predictable stream of revenue to the federal air traffic control system, expansion of airport infrastructure, and a 're-examination' of government-mandated fees and charges (the latter now even more pressing because of new security rules). *See* Baliles, *Departures*, *supra* note 15. In Brussels, at virtually the same time that the President's 1993 Commission nominees were deliberating in Washington D.C., the European Commission convened a panel of 'wise men,' literally called the *Comité des Sages*, to perform a similar diagnosis of the ailments of the European Union's commercial airline industry. While the *Comité* merely noted the absence of any 'blueprint for global air transport' (without attempting to invent one), its findings on the shortcomings of the bilateral system tracked many of those of its U.S. counterpart. *See* COMITÉ DES SAGES, EXPANDING HORIZONS: CIVIL AVIATION IN EUROPE, AN ACTION PROGRAMME FOR THE FUTURE (1994) [hereinafter Report of the *Comité des Sages*]. The Chairman of the *Comité*, striking a more rhapsodic note than any of the U.S. Commissioners, alluded in his opening message to 'the dream of Icarus.' *Id.* at 5. In the aftermath of the wise men's report, EC international aviation policy showed signs of unfolding in the direction of multilateral negotiation and exchange of air traffic rights (with the United States and other significant foreign markets). A recent proposal to appoint a new *Comité des Sages*, focused especially on transnational investment issues, has gained only limited traction. *See* Tony Barber, *EU Reins in Sarkozy 'Wise Men' Scheme*, FIN. TIMES, Dec. 6, 2007, at 9; *cf.* HIGH LEVEL GROUP FOR THE FUTURE EUROPEAN REGULATORY FRAMEWORK, *supra* note 14 (refraining from any treatment of the topic of transnational investment in EU aviation).

appointed, Baliles argued, '[because] the solutions needed today are the ones recommended ten years ago – and then largely ignored.'[17] Notwithstanding Baliles' gloomy perception of how events unfolded, however, the Airline Commission's treatment of international issues – and in particular its unexpected but deliberate embrace of the goal of multilateralism – did in fact resonate over the past decade with U.S. and EU governmental and industry planners.[18]

B   A BRIDGE TO MULTILATERALISM: THE STRATEGIC IMPLICATIONS OF U.S. OPEN SKIES

As noted in the preceding Section, the post-1995 U.S. bilateral strategy did not seek to ratchet back the restrictive policy on foreign ownership of U.S. air carriers. In the succeeding ten years, all U.S. open skies bilaterals – including the 2007 U.S./ EC Air Transport Agreement, which properly speaking takes the form of a 'bilateral' between the United States and the 27 Member States of the EC[19] – retained the conventional language on foreign ownership.[20] Clearly, the strategy pursued by

---

17. Baliles, *supra* note 15.
18. An early positive chord was struck by the European Commission's aborted attempt to start negotiations with the United States on a cargo-only agreement. The EU Member States, however, stymied any further progress. *See* John R. Byerly, Deputy Assistant Secretary for Transportation Affairs, U.S. Department of State, *U.S.-EU Aviation Relations – Charting the Course for Success*, Remarks at the International Aviation Club, Washington, D.C., at 5 (Jul. 13, 2004), <www.iacwashington.org/Byerly071304.pdf> [hereinafter Byerly, *Charting the Course*]; *see also EC, U.S. Open High-Level Meetings on Multilateral Air Freight Regime*, AV. DAILY, Feb. 17, 1994, at 1 (noting the conceptual inspiration for a multilateral cargo agreement that was provided both by the Airline Commission and the *Comité des Sages*). A segregated U.S./EC cargo agreement was always bound to be problematical, however, given the very high volume of transatlantic freight carried by so-called 'combination' (passenger/cargo) carriers and consequent likelihood of entanglement in the complex network of bilateral agreements covering passenger traffic. *See* Bruce Barnard, *EC-US Talks Face New Obstacle*, J. COMM., Mar. 28, 1994, at 7.
19. *See infra* Part V.
20. This open skies policy, revitalizing earlier similar but less ambitious policies, *see supra* note 7, adopted a minnow-to-shark strategy, beginning with a cluster of nine smaller European states, including six of the then Member States of the European Community. The nine states were (alphabetically) Austria, Belgium, Denmark, Finland, Iceland, Luxembourg, Norway, Sweden, and Switzerland. (Under this so-called 'encirclement' strategy, the sharks, including France, Germany, and the United Kingdom, would come later.) Iceland and Norway, while not EC members, do participate in a novel extension of the Community's commercial jurisdiction called the European Economic Area (EEA), which includes acceptance of the European Community's common air transport policy. In addition, the European Commission envisages a European Common Aviation Area (ECAA) operational by 2010 that is based on the Community's aviation *acquis* and that includes Iceland and Norway and those States of southeast Europe that have not yet become members of the Union (Albania, Bosnia and Herzegovina, Croatia, the former Yugoslav Republic of Macedonia, Serbia, Montenegro, and the former United Nations Mission in Kosovo), and eventually other States in the European Union's eastern and southern 'neighborhood.' Press Release, Europa, EC & South East Europe: First Steps Towards an Extended Single Aviation Market, IP/06/764 (Jun. 9, 2006) (emphasizing that

successive U.S. Secretaries of Transportation hewed precisely to the Airline Commission's recommended path of incremental change, using a model liberal aviation agreement that the United States, in effect, would 'export' on a

the core of the ECAA project is regulatory harmonization, including uniform economic, safety, security, air traffic management, competition, environmental, and consumer protection rules). *See infra* Chapter 5, Part III(D); *see also* European Commission, *Communication from the Commission on the Consequences of the Court Judgments of 5 November 2002 for European Air Transport Policy*, paras. 21-22, COM (2002) 649 final (Nov. 19, 2002) [hereinafter European Commission, *Consequences*]. The Commission has identified Ukraine as the next candidate for extension of its 'European Neighborhood Policy' to the east, along with strengthening its aviation relations with Russia and other countries in the Black and Caspian Sea region. *See* Press Release, Europa, EU and Ukraine Open Aviation Negotiations on Common Aviation Area, IP/07/1866 (Dec. 6, 2007). *See also* European Commission, *Communication from the Commission to the European Parliament and the Council: A Framework for Developing Relations with the Russian Federation in the Field of Air Transport*, COM (2005) 77 final (Mar. 14, 2005); Press Release, European Commission, Third Meeting of the Traceca (EU – Black Sea/ Caspian Basin) Working Group on Civil Aviation (Jul. 15, 2008). Regulatory convergence is also key to the Community's Euro-Mediterranean Aviation Agreement with Morocco, initialed in Dec. 2005. *See* Press Release, Europa, EU-Morocco Aviation Agreement: Morocco Joins Europe in the Aviation Field, IP/06/1770 (Dec. 12, 2006). (The new treaties are discussed *infra* Chapter 5, Part III(D); the EEA's embrace of air transport is considered *id.*) Swiss voters, ever solicitous of their country's neutral history, have repeatedly rejected EC/EEA adherence: 'The world outlook of the Swiss consists in the very fact that they do not look out upon the world.' Claudio Caratsch, *The Permanent Neutrality of Switzerland, in* NEUTRALITY AND NON-ALIGNMENT IN EUROPE 13 (Birnbaum/Neuhold eds., 1982). To supersede the EEA concept, Switzerland and the European Community signed a sweeping free trade package, including provisions on air transport, that Swiss voters approved by referendum in May 2000. As explained by a Swiss government website, the new package 'lays down the terms on which Swiss airline companies will have access to Europe's deregulated civil aviation market, on a reciprocal basis. The granting of commercial flying rights over a gradual period, together with a ban on discrimination, will give Swiss companies virtually the same opportunities as their European rivals, as well as the right to acquire a majority shareholding in airlines within the [European Community].' Civil Aviation Fact Sheet, Switzerland – European Union (Oct. 2005), <www. Europa.admin.ch/themen/00500/00506/00523/index.html?lang=en>. The agreement entered into force on Jun. 1, 2002 and supersedes all existing bilateral agreements among the Member States and Switzerland concerning any matter covered in the agreement. *See* Agreement Between the European Community and the Swiss Confederation on Air Transport, 2002 O.J. (L 114) 73. Among other things, Article 4 provides (reciprocally) that Swiss-owned airlines will have freedom of establishment (*i.e.*, to create subsidiaries or to invest in local carriers) in all EU Member States, while Article 15, concerned with traffic rights, envisages the eventual abolition of cabotage restrictions as between Switzerland and the EU Member States. Under Article 11, the agreement grants supervision and control over competition issues affecting Switzerland's aviation relations with the Community to the EC institutions (and recognizes the Community *acquis* in this sphere), but under Article 14 responsibility for policing illegal public subsidies is not so assigned other than allowing a consultative role for the 'Joint Committee' created by Article 21 of the agreement. Similarly, the Joint Committee may decide, upon request by one of the contracting parties, whether any Swiss environmental restrictions on landing rights are in conformity with the nondiscrimination and other provisions of the agreement (Article 18). (In Apr. 2001, despite the momentum generated by the new package, the Swiss people, again using the device of popular referendum, overwhelmingly rejected the opening of talks leading to membership in the European Union, although the matter is likely to recur in national policy debates.) *See The Swiss Say No*, ECONOMIST (U.S. Edition), Mar. 10, 2001.

country-by-country basis[21] and use as a lure to entice larger geographical neighbors (fearful of loss of traffic, for example, over the EU's porous borders) into

21. Oddly, the United States made more 'open skies' progress with EU Member States than with its neighbor and North American Free Trade Agreement (NAFTA) partner, Canada. An 'open transborder' agreement in 1995 left important restrictions in place with respect to access to Canada's international market. *See* Transport Canada, *Straight Ahead – A Vision for Transportation in Canada*, Policy Statement (Feb. 25, 2003) (noting that the 1995 agreement did not allow for unlimited rights to carry beyond traffic to third States from the other country's territory ('fifth freedom' rights, *see infra* Chapter 3, Part III(A)), prohibited all-cargo courier carriers from coterminalizing (*i.e.*, linking) points in the other country, and prevented price leadership by the other country's airlines in fifth freedom and 'sixth freedom' markets (the latter 'freedom' being the ability to carry traffic between two other States via the carriers' home country (*see infra* Chapter 3, Part III(A)), so that American Airlines, for example, could not undercut Air Canada prices in the Toronto/Mexico City market and conversely Air Canada was limited in the same fashion in the New York/Zurich market. *See* Robert Milton, CEO and President, Air Canada, Briefing to the Air Transport Association Board of Governors, Washington, D.C. (Dec. 13, 2001) [hereinafter Milton, Briefing]. In Mar. 2007, however, a new U.S./Canada open skies agreement removed these restrictions. *See* Press Release, U.S. Department of State, U.S. Signs Open Skies Aviation Agreement with Canada, 2007/182 (Mar. 12, 2007) (noting that, for cargo, the new agreement extended so-called 'seventh freedom' or 'stand-alone' rights, *i.e.*, allowing airlines to perform international cargo operations with no route connection to their home country). The U.S./Canada open skies breakthrough occurred in tandem with publication of Transport Canada's own 'open skies' blueprint, denominated 'Blue Sky.' *See* Transport Canada, *Blue Sky: Canada's New International Air Policy* (Dec. 2006) (stating as a 'primary objective' the negotiation of 'reciprocal "open skies"-type agreements') [hereinafter Canada, *Blue Sky*]. While Canada was obviously not part of the original 'cluster' strategy that the United States attempted in Europe, the use of a similar model bilateral, and the later open skies bilateral, indicated U.S. expectations that Canada would participate in any future multilateral concordat with the European Community. Although Canada did not commit resources to a North American aviation liberalization regime and did not join the U.S./EC discussions in progress since 1997, it did adopt an observer status at those discussions. *See* Joan M. Feldman, *Transatlantic Two-step*, AIR TRANSP. WORLD, Apr. 2003, at 43. Moreover, it was reported in mid-2007 that Canada, pursuing its Blue Sky agenda, had opened preliminary discussions toward its own open skies agreement with the now 27-member Union. *See* Madhu Unnikrishnan, *Canada Eyes EC Open Skies As Part of Blue Sky Program*, AV. DAILY, Jun. 5, 2007, at 4 (mentioning prior agreements with the United States, Serbia, Croatia, Ireland, Portugal, and Kuwait). These discussions resulted in a comprehensive agreement reached in 2008. *See* Press Release, Europa, Breakthrough in EU-Canada Negotiations, IP/08/1914 (Dec. 9, 2008). Through all of these new initiatives, however, Canada has remained, like the United States, firmly opposed to cabotage rights (the right for a foreign airline to carry domestic traffic between points in Canada) and resistant also to changing to changing its airline ownership rules (which match the U.S. cap of 25% stock ownership by foreign citizens). *See* Canada, *Blue Sky*, *supra*, at 3 (stating that 'in no circumstances' will cabotage be allowed); *but see* Don Carty, Chairman and CEO, American Airlines, Remarks to the Vancouver Board of Trade (Jun. 27, 2002) (while conceding that U.S. carriers would earlier have 'balk[ed]' at abolition of limits on cross-border ownership and introduction of reciprocal cabotage rights, identified a 'rapidly emerging consensus among U.S. airlines' for full liberalization of U.S./Canada commercial aviation, including a NAFTA-style open aviation agreement and Canadian participation in a future U.S./EC common aviation region); Press Release, *supra* (noting that the new EC/Canada agreement envisages a phased (although highly contingent) removal of investment and cabotage restrictions between the two sides). The Canadian attitude to post-open skies liberalization (the *Beyond Open Skies* of this book's title) has been ambivalent. Despite the *Blue Sky* embargo on cabotage

similar liberalized relationships.[22] This 'encirclement' strategy proved highly successful in the EU, picking off such high-profile targets as France and Germany.[23] But whatever the specific tactical successes of the policy, it is nevertheless important to recognize the strategic implication that the post-1995 open skies initiative was the *first* time that a U.S. administration officially articulated a strategy for (or even contemplated) the eventual demise of the existing system of bilateral treaties.[24]

(the document does not explicitly discuss foreign ownership issues), consolidation of the Canadian industry after Air Canada absorbed Canadian Airlines in 2000 prompted the Competition Bureau of Canada in 2005 to support 'reciprocal cabotage' and removal of all foreign ownership restrictions. *See* Sheridan Scott, Commissioner of Competition, Competition Bureau Canada, *Air Liberalization and the Canadian Airports System*, Speaking Notes for Remarks to the House of Commons Standing Committee on Transport (May 4, 2005) (finding 'no compelling economic reason' for Chicago system restrictions, while conceding that aviation policy concerns might limit the scope of liberalization to increasing the limit on foreign ownership of Canadian airlines to 49% and also required reciprocity in the eventual introduction of cabotage rights and the right of majority investment in domestic airlines – the 'right of establishment'). Scott also proposed that the U.S./Canada air transport market, the world's largest international air transport market (with 19.8 million passengers in 2005), should be transformed into a single aviation market mirroring that of the EU. *Id.*

22. *See* Statement of Neil Kinnock, former EC Transport Commissioner, *Commission Approves Draft Mandate to Negotiate 'Open Skies' Accord with the United States* (Apr. 26, 1995), *ref:* IP/95/414 (on file with Library of the EU Delegation, Washington, D.C.) (referring to 'the U.S. effort – which they frankly admit – to divide Europe in setting the ground rules for relations in the field of civil aviation and to impose pressure on the other Member States that are no[t] considering the "open skies" proposal'). The Commission's suspicions were borne out in the text of the 1995 Policy Statement, *supra* note 7, at 10: '[T]here may be strategic value in adopting liberal agreements with smaller countries where doing so puts competitive pressure on neighboring countries to follow suit.' As the proceedings of the Airline Commission foreshadowed, the U.S. policy of moving with alacrity to sign liberal agreements with smaller EU Member States preempted the possibility that the larger, more protectionist-minded EU States would be able to dominate (or ultimately to defeat) a future common EC external negotiating strategy. (Moreover, the smaller countries also represented useful points of access for U.S. carriers to those larger aviation markets.) *See Airline Commission Proceedings*, testimony of Richard B. Hirst, Senior Vice President and General Counsel, Northwest Airlines, Inc. (Jun. 3, 1993), at 212-16.

23. '... [T]he Encirclement Strategy worked.' Rex S. Toh, *Toward an International Open Skies Regime*, 3 J. AIR TRANSP. WORLD WIDE 61, 66 (1998) (crediting Michael E. Levine, then Director of the Bureau of Pricing and Domestic Aviation of the now-defunct Civil Aeronautics Board, with originally proposing pressure on larger aviation markets through open skies deals with their smaller neighbors, diverting traffic from those markets to other European or Asian gateways served by cheaper scheduled services and inexpensive charters under liberal pricing rules). France and Germany were induced to sign more liberal bilaterals (the latter feared inroads by KLM into U.S./Germany traffic). Japan, watching liberal agreements with South Korea, Singapore, and Thailand, eventually conceded multiple carrier designations. The United Kingdom allowed some liberalizing of Bermuda II, but mostly stood pat. This general view of encirclement is shared even by persistent liberalization critic Duane E. Woerth, former Chief Executive Officer of the Air Line Pilots Association. *See* Duane E. Woerth, Speech to the International Aviation Club, Jun. 28, 2001 ('[W]e predicted that the policy of encirclement would fail. We were wrong. With the notable exception of the United Kingdom, it has succeeded.').

24. *See* U.S. Department of State, History of the Department of State During the Clinton Presidency (1993-2001), 05. International Economic Policy, <www.state.gov/r/pa/ho/pubs/8521.htm>

Thus, the substantive limitations of the U.S. open skies policy were not as important as the existence of the policy itself, and its role as a conceptual bridge to multilateralism. In the late 1990s and early 2000s, the catalytic effects of the new U.S. thinking were becoming apparent on both sides of the Atlantic. By 1997, with the elimination of intra-Community cabotage restrictions, the EC had completed its own ambitious internal market deregulation. The 'single aviation market' now looked very much like the U.S. post-deregulation domestic model, even if the new market opportunities had yet to be fully subscribed.[25] But, although the United States secured open skies agreements with Germany in 1996, Italy in 1998, and France in 2001,[26] the momentum for new agreements – and for using open skies pacts with smaller countries to coax larger ones into liberalizing (the 'encirclement' policy[27]) – eventually stalled. The United Kingdom, in particular, would remain aloof until the signing of the U.S./EC Air Transport Agreement in 2007.[28]

(stating that the U.S. open skies policy 'set the table' internationally for the dismantling of the old bilateral system).

25. The Commission's ambitions with respect to EU aviation transcend economic integration and mirror some other significant features of the U.S. integrated federal airspace. Thus, with respect to aviation safety and navigation, the Commission has championed the creation of a European Aviation Safety Agency (EASA) with pretensions to becoming the EU analog of the U.S. Federal Aviation Administration in safety matters, as well as the air navigation initiative dubbed the 'Single European Sky' (SES). *See* Council Regulation 1592/2002, 2002 O.J. (L 240) 1; Council Regulation 549/2004, 2004 O.J. (L 96) 1; Council Regulation 550/2004, 2004 O.J. (L 96) 10; Council Regulation 551/2004, 2004 O.J. (L 96) 20; *see also* EUROCONTROL, EUROCONTROL and the Single European Sky (Jan. 24, 2006), <www.eurocontrol.int/ses/public/standard_page/sk_involvement.html> (discussing the role of the European Organisation for the Safety of Air Navigation (EUROCONTROL) in the development and oversight of the SES). The creation of the EASA was meant to remove market distortions brought about by inconsistent safety, security, and environmental regulations throughout the EU. *See* Daniel Calleja, Director of Air Transport, European Commission, Speech to the International Aviation Club, Washington, D.C. (Nov. 16, 2004). Similarly, the SES initiative is intended to promote regulatory convergence and operational efficiency in the area of air traffic management throughout the EU. *See* Niels Van Antwerpen, Cross-Border Provision of Air Navigation Services with Specific Reference to Europe: Safeguarding Transparent Lines of Responsibility and Liability (2008). For the elements of the Community's external aviation policy as imagined by the Commission, *see infra* Chapter 5, Part II(E); European Commission, *Communication from the Commission: A Community Aviation Policy Towards Its Neighbors*, COM (2004) 74 final (Feb. 9, 2004).

26. Portugal joined the open skies fold in 1999. The holdouts, in addition to the United Kingdom mentioned in the main text, were Ireland, Greece, and Spain, all of which are now parties to the 2007 U.S./EC Air Services Agreement. *See* U.S. Department of State, Office of Transportation Affairs, Open Skies Partners (Jun. 12, 2008), <http://2001-2009.state.gov/e/eeb/rls/othr/2008/22281.htm> (listing 92 open skies agreements by date of conclusion rather than date of signature or implementation; the years given for agreements mentioned in this footnote and in the main text follow that convention).

27. *See* Dawna L. Rhoades, Evolution of International Aviation 39-40 (2003) (noting that the policy operated on the assumption that the agreements would lower fares between the parties, thus resulting in passengers altering their travel plans to take advantage of cheaper tickets available through smaller countries' airports – a reasonable strategy given Europe's more compressed travel distances).

28. *See infra* Part IV. The United States policy had failed, moreover, to secure open skies agreements with Japan and China (as well as with major aviation powers such as Brazil, India,

C   THE EC RESPONDS TO OPEN SKIES: AN INCOMPLETE
                     FIRST 'MANDATE'

The U.S. open skies policy had the unintended (but ultimately condign) effect of sparking the European Commission's intense drive to secure a 'mandate' to negotiate the Community's external air transport relations on behalf of all Member States collectively,[29] deploying the real international treaty-making authority the 'European Community'[30] has garnered through a combination of explicit Treaty powers and predominantly favorable judicial rulings (most recently from the European Court of Justice in November 2002).[31] The Commission's initial motivation for seeking a mandate was that variations in bilateral agreements with non-Member States must inevitably distort the functioning of the Community's internal single market in aviation.

---

and Russia). The U.S.-Japan air services agreement, last modified in 1998 (but using a 1952 template), falls short of open skies. *See infra* Chapter 4, Part III(D). Recent talks have not dislodged some of the more restrictive elements of the agreement, such as double-approval pricing (where fares cannot be set unless each State approves). *See infra* Chapter 3, Part III(B); *see also* Madhu Unnikrishnan, *U.S., Japan Negotiators Go Home Empty-Handed*, AV. DAILY, Apr. 9, 2007, at 2. The U.S.-China 'aviation liberalization' agreement, announced in May 2007, is also not a member of the open skies directory (but comes close in the context of air cargo). *See* Press Release, U.S. Department of State, U.S. and China Initial Aviation Liberalization Agreement, 2007/414 (May 23, 2007) (indicating that formal open skies negotiations will commence in 2010). (The China agreement, in particular, holds the eventual promise of access to a huge domestic market and China must be considered a likely candidate for admission to the plurilateral arrangement canvassed in this study.) To the credit of U.S. policymakers, the 'encirclement strategy' as applied in Asia – always tentative because of Asia's scattered geography – is spurring calls within the Japanese aviation establishment for open skies, but airport capacity limitations remain a serious obstacle to liberalization. *See* Editorial, *Expanded Tokyo Service Must Precede 'Open Skies'*, DAILY YOMIURI (Tokyo), May 13, 2007, at 4 (noting how Japan's international airports are threatened by construction of large new airports in Asia, including Singapore and Shanghai, each of which has ambitions to become an air gateway to Asia). With respect to Latin America, the large variations in the economic conditions of those States (and the persistence of iconic flag carriers in many countries) has militated against a successful encirclement strategy.

29. The EU signed accession treaties that brought its total membership to 25 States on Jan. 1, 2004. The new admitted States were the Czech Republic, Estonia, Cyprus, Latvia, Lithuania, Hungary, Malta, Poland, Slovenia, and Slovakia. On Jan. 1, 2007, Bulgaria and Romania became the 26th and 27th Member States, respectively.

30. *See supra* text accompanying Chapter 1, note 10 (discussing the contexts that require – the admittedly annoying – alternation between the terms 'European Community' and 'European Union').

31. The Commission staked out the Community's supranational competence in intra-Union aviation through a series of liberalization 'packages' enacted between 1987 and 1992, considered *infra* Chapter 5, Part II. After the European Court of Justice ruling on nationality clauses in 2002, the Commission is gradually being mandated to negotiate air services agreements with certain third countries (including, most notably, the United States) on behalf of all of the Member States. *See infra* Chapter 5, Part III(D).

For international purposes (the Commission argued), the merger of the Community's separate national airspace sovereignties meant that all point-to-point international routes within the EU became, in legal effect, cabotage (*i.e.*, domestic) points comparable to the network of cabotage points inside the huge U.S. market, from which European carriers were historically excluded under the Chicago system.[32] By combining rights separately negotiated under different bilaterals, U.S. negotiators had won rights for American carriers to enplane passengers at destination cities in Europe for onward transit to other points in Europe. These so-called 'fifth freedom' rights[33] would permit United Airlines, for example, to pick up new passengers at London as an extension of its New York/London transatlantic service and to carry them onward to other EU destination cities such as Frankfurt or Rome.[34] The bilateral system places a premium on forceful diplomacy by making the *exercise* of these additional rights dependent on separate negotiations with the governments of both the granting State (in this example, the United Kingdom) and the receiving State (in this example, Germany or Italy).[35] A British Airways flight from London to New York, in contrast, is excluded by cabotage

---

32. *See U.S. International Aviation Issues in a Global Perspective*, U.S. Department of Transportation Issues Paper, *in Airline Commission Documents*, Dkt. No. 001207 (May 1993).

33. The various 'freedoms' of the air, the building blocks of market access under the Chicago system, are considered in more detail, *infra* Chapter 3, Part III.

34. The European Commission's view was that fifth freedom rights, while of relatively little value on the American side of the Atlantic (where there are few viable onward destinations for EU carriers to exploit), become much more important in the European Union, with many international markets in close proximity. By exploiting these 'third State' connections among EU Member States, U.S. carriers thereby gained a network purchase on what the Commission has called 'Europe's domestic market.' European Commission, *Consequences*, *supra* note 20, para. 14.

35. Although fifth freedom connections have been put in place by U.S. carriers throughout EU territory, enabling them to build route networks connecting multiple points in different Member States, in fact U.S. carriers have chosen to operate to internal EU points using code-share arrangements with their major EU alliance partners. Thus, although Delta accumulated fifth freedom rights under the U.S./Germany bilateral and other bilaterals with European countries, and at one time operated a successful European hub operation at Frankfurt, it shifted strategies to cooperate with Air France (through an immunized alliance). *See U.S. DOT, Joint Application of Delta Air Lines, Inc., Société Air France, Alitalia-Linee Aeree Italiane-S.p.A., and Czech Airlines, under 49 U.S.C. §§ 41308 and 41309 for Approval of and Antitrust Immunity for Alliance Agreements*, Dkt. No. OST-2001-10429-36, Final Order (Jan. 18, 2002) (granting approval of a four-way alliance which would coordinate service over the partners' respective route networks 'as if they were a single entity'); *see also* John R. Byerly, Deputy Assistant Secretary for Transportation Affairs, U.S. Department of State, *Turbulent Times: Regulation, Security, and Profitability in the Airline Industry*, Address to the Chatham House Conference, London (Mar. 5, 2007) (graphically describing the value to U.S. passenger carriers of intra-Union traffic rights as no more than 'decimal dust') [hereinafter Byerly, *Turbulent Times*]. As the Commission itself has conceded, however, the main users of intra-Union fifth freedom rights are U.S. cargo companies providing intra-Union parcel services. *See* European Commission, *Consequences*, *supra* note 20, para. 14. U.S. passenger carriers typically make onward intra-European connections using code-shares with EU airline partners.

from boarding new passengers in New York for continuing service to Los Angeles.[36] (EU carriers do exercise so-called 'coterminal' rights in the United States, which merely allow a British Airways continuing service to Los Angeles from New York, but only for passengers who boarded originally in London.) It must be added that U.S. negotiators have never agreed that the Commission's analogizing of fifth freedom rights to cabotage makes sense as a matter of international law.[37]

Thus, as both the European Commission and European Parliament observed, the unitary legal structure of the U.S. aviation market, bolted tight by the federal cabotage and national ownership rules, would prevent the development of authentic network rights by EU carriers operating to and from gateway points in the United States.[38] The Commission, in particular, took the view that intra-Union cabotage privileges should be a 'Community asset' that could be explicitly traded for similar rights of access to the huge domestic U.S. market (which still represents 30% of all global air traffic).[39] Accordingly, access to the New York/Los Angeles air transport market, for example, would be treated in collective EC aviation talks with the United States – if such talks emerged – as the juridical replica of the Union's

---

36. As will be seen, the practice of 'code-sharing,' where an EU carrier feeds its transatlantic services into the domestic network of a U.S. carrier, has arguably caused some dilution of the pure cabotage exclusion. *See infra* Chapter 3, Part VIII(C).

37. *See* Byerly, *Turbulent Times*, *supra* note 35 (noting that, under international law, the right to operate within the territory of another sovereign State – cabotage – is 'considered quite different from the authority to operate between separate sovereign countries'). For more detailed consideration of cabotage, *see infra* Chapter 3, Part IV.

38. Again, a qualification to this statement should be entered with respect to code-sharing. *See infra* Chapter 3, Part VIII(C); *see also, e.g., Air Transport: Do Europeans Need Cabotage Rights in the U.S.?*, EUROPEAN REPORT, No. 2032, Apr. 12, 1995, at 6 [hereinafter EUROPEAN REPORT No. 2032] (discussing the Resolution of the European Parliament adopted in plenary session on Apr. 7, 1995, which noted that 'bilateral [a]greements between the United States and certain Member States could give American companies access to intra-European routes without giving European operators the right of cabotage between American cities').

39. *See infra* Chapter 3, note 143 and accompanying text. *But see* Allan I. Mendelsohn, *Myths of International Aviation*, 68 J. AIR L. & COM. 519 (2003) (disputing European Commission's view that EU inter-State air routes – which, from the U.S. perspective, are fifth freedom routes – are a mirror image of the U.S. domestic cabotage market); *see also* Byerly, *Turbulent Times*, *supra* note 35 (agreeing that fifth freedom and cabotage rights are conceptually dissimilar in international law). Ironically, in 2005, the intra-Union market accounted for only 55% of the total market for EU airlines, EUROSTAT, PANORAMA OF TRANSPORT: EDITION 2007 121 (2007) (providing data on the EU-25 prior to the accession of Bulgaria and Romania), revealing a much higher dependency on true 'international' air transport than U.S. carriers, which generate over 90% of their revenue from their giant domestic market, Air Transport Association of America [ATA], Annual Traffic and Ops: U.S. Airlines (Jun. 7, 2008), <www.airlines.org/economics/traffic/Annual+US+Traffic.htm> (determined by passengers enplaned). Further mining of the statistical data reveals some interesting alternative perspectives, however. In terms of revenue passenger miles, for example, the value of U.S. international traffic rises to almost 30%. *See* ATA, *supra*. On the EU side, the extra-EU share is much higher for certain countries (*e.g.*, France (47%), the Netherlands (44%), and Germany (40%)). *See* EUROSTAT, *supra*, at 212.

London/Frankfurt market, from which U.S. carriers now would potentially be excluded.[40]

In 1995, then-EU Transport Commissioner Neil Kinnock launched a forensic assault attacking separately-concluded Member State bilateral air services agreements with the United States.[41] Kinnock used the enforcement proceedings of the Treaty of Rome against six apostate States (Austria, Belgium, Denmark, Luxembourg, Finland, and Sweden) that had subscribed to the revamped open skies policy announced by U.S. Secretary of Transportation Federico Peña in 1995.[42] In response, the Council of Ministers (as the EU's political body was then called) approved what might be called a 'split' mandate for the Commission to open multilateral aviation talks[43] with the United States.[44] The negotiations were

---

40. *See* International Air Transport Association [IATA], *Passenger and Freight Forecasts 2007 to 2011*, IATA Economic Briefing (Oct. 2007).

41. The Commission had been confident of its legal position in that jurisdictional tussle, placing reliance on the 1994 opinion of the European Court of Justice on the division of competence between EU institutions and Member States concerning negotiation and signature of certain instruments of the new World Trade Organization regime, including the General Agreement on Trade in Services. *See* WTO Case, Opinion 1/94, [1994] E.C.R. I-5267. The opinion, by no means a straightforward analysis of these complex issues, is discussed in some detail *infra* Chapter 5, Part II(E). The Commission's strategy was presented in its response to the Report of the *Comité des Sages*, entitled *The Way Forward for Civil Aviation in Europe*, COM (94) 218 final, Jun. 1, 1994 [hereinafter European Commission, *The Way Forward*]. Both the Kinnock proceedings and the subsequent 1998 challenges were founded on Article 226 of the Treaty Establishing the European Community (EC Treaty), which provides a mechanism for the Commission to bring an action before the European Court of Justice against a Member State that, in the Commission's consideration, 'has failed to fulfill an obligation under the [EC] Treaty.' As a procedural prerequisite, the Article obliges the Commission first to deliver a 'reasoned opinion' on the matter (under Article 249 of the Treaty, 'opinions' are not considered legally binding acts of the Community). *See infra* Chapter 5, Part II(B).

42. *See infra* Chapter 5, Part III.

43. As noted, in technical terms U.S./EC talks are 'bilateral,' although the European Commission would be representing all of the sovereign Member States of the European Union. For the reasons discussed *infra* Chapter 5, Part III(D), the Council at the time focused only on possible agreements with the United States.

44. The Council evidently feared (and calculated) that emerging transatlantic collaborations of would-be competitors might allow a select group of U.S. and EU carriers, cannibalizing each other's airline codes, to oligopolize international competition across the Atlantic. And, within the Union's single aviation market itself, similar strategies could enable U.S. carriers to enhance their existing fifth freedom penetration. *See generally* Press Release, European Commission, Airline Agreements (Jul. 3, 1996) (copy on file with the Library of the EU Delegation, Washington, D.C.) [hereinafter Press Release, Airline Agreements]. Indeed, in the wake of the announcement of a proposed American Airlines/British Airways alliance the European Commission opened an investigation into the competition implications of six transatlantic alliances. *See infra* Chapter 3, Part VIII(B). The Commission was concerned that the U.S. partners in these alliances would use intra-Union traffic rights (internal rights which EU carriers do not enjoy in the United States, except through code-sharing) to feed their expanding intercontinental routes. *See* Press Release, Airline Agreements, *supra*. The common aviation policy, directed solely to liberalization of air transport within Community airspace, at that time assigned no executive authority to the Commission to meet or deflect these external challenges to the integrity of the new single market. *But see infra* Chapter 5, Part II.

to be conducted in two discrete but mutually dependent cycles.[45] In the first cycle, which began in fall 1996, the Commission was authorized to negotiate so-called 'soft' regulatory issues such as competition policy and inward investment opportunities.[46] Only if 'significant results' were obtained in this first cycle would the Council approve a 'specific mandate for a second negotiating stage' that would feature the more economically significant – and hence divisive – 'hard' issues of traffic rights (including direct market access, without artificial devices like

---

45. Despite the resistance of the U.K. Government to *any* grant of supranational negotiating competence to the Commission, the EU's transport ministers approved a compromise in Jun. 1996 that attracted the support of other entrenched large-State bilateralists such as France and Spain. The United Kingdom was the only dissenting vote. *See European Union Approves Commission Mandate To Negotiate A Common Aviation Area With The United States*, EUROPEAN UNION NEWS, No. 35/96, Jun. 17, 1996. The positive French vote, in contrast, was unexpected, but was reportedly linked to pending Commission approval of a final tranche of public capital aid for Air France. *See Transport Ministers Near Agreement On Multilateral Talks With U.S.*, 6 AVIATION EUROPE, Jun. 6, 1996, at 1. It should be noted that the actual *content* of the approved mandate was never made public. Any assessment of its substance had to be drawn from the opaque diplomatic language of EU press statements, and from secondary news sources. Moreover, despite the phased nature of negotiations suggested by the first cycle/second cycle timetable, EU officials in Washington, D.C. indicated to me (in background interviews on the new mandate) that Commission negotiators anticipated no *a priori* restriction of the issues that could be canvassed, albeit not necessarily resolved, in the first cycle.
46. In particular, the mandate would examine the benefits that might flow from a harmonization of U.S. and EC regulations dealing with airline ownership, computer reservations systems, slot allocation, code-sharing, competition, groundhandling services, safety, and security. The issue of public capital assistance to EU national airlines would also be considered. There was no indication, however, that the mandate contemplated a complete liberalization of ownership restrictions, only an elevation of the permitted quantum of foreign ownership of U.S. airlines to the prevailing EC standard of 49% (or, more accurately, 49.9%). *See Commission's Multilateralism Mandate Comes in Phases, May Be Too Late*, 6 AVIATION EUR., Jun. 20, 1996, at 1 [hereinafter *Multilateralism Mandate*]. Contrary to a discernible trend in academic and official commentaries, the rule against foreign ownership and control of domestic airlines should not be regarded as a 'soft' right. *See, e.g.*, Wolfgang Hubner & Pierre Suavé, *Liberalisation Scenarios for International Air Transport*, 35 J. WORLD TRADE L. 973, 979 (2001) (suggesting, erroneously, that 'ownership and control' is a component of air transport that is 'not quite so jealously guarded' as hard traffic rights); *but see* United Nations Conference on Trade and Development, *Report of the Expert Meeting on Air Transport Services: Clarifying Issues to Define the Elements of the Positive Agenda of Developing Countries as Regards Both the GATS and Specific Sector Negotiations of Interest to Them*, para. 38, TD/B/COM.1/EM.9/3 (Aug. 23, 1999) (explicitly linking ownership and control with route and traffic rights as 'hard rights'). This view is supported by the exclusion of so-called 'hard' rights from the General Agreement on Trade in Services (GATS) 1995 Annex on Air Transport Services – rights of heightened economic significance dealing with route access and the exercise of traffic rights. *See generally* ICAO Economic Commission, *Report by the Council on Trade in Services*, A33-WP/7 (Jan. 28, 2000) (describing the GATS Annex on Air Transport Services). Given the fact that the ownership and control rule is used explicitly to assign route access and traffic rights on the basis of nationality, it is wholly consistent with the GATS classification to regard the rule as a 'hard' right.

code-sharing, to internal U.S. city-pair markets).[47] It was in response to this initiative, in fact, that the Commission suspended its pending legal action against the original open skies insurgents.[48]

Despite the pitfalls of the original mandate proposal,[49] the immediate success for the Commission was not so much the piecemeal donation of authority that this mandate imposed, but rather that the Council had dropped its resistance to the *principle* that traffic rights could be collectively negotiated.[50] Indeed, glossing

---

47. *See* Press Release, European Council, Council Formally Adopts the Common Position on Decision No. 1400/97/EC, PRES/96/172 (Jun. 18, 1996) [hereinafter Press Release, Common Position]. The second cycle (or 'stage') was never reached. *See* Feldman, *supra* note 21, at 43.

48. *See Multilateralism Mandate, supra* note 46. It is worth noting here that the split mandate ordained explicitly that existing – and even future – bilateral arrangements between EU Member States and the United States would continue to be tolerated. 'The present bilateral systems of relations between Member States and the United States will be maintained and kept working until an agreement on a Common Aviation Area is in place. In the meantime, Member States will be able *to open or pursue* negotiations and conclude bilateral agreements with the United States.' Press Release, Common Position, *supra* note 47 (emphasis added). In other words, the Commission's task – even in the more plenary second cycle, apparently – would have been to secure some undefined 'added value' that lay beyond the grasp of bilateral negotiators. Press Release, Europa, European Union Approves Draft Mandate to Negotiate a Common Aviation Area with the United States, IP/96/520 (Jun. 18, 1996). Thus, even after the so-called 'Common Aviation Area' had been put in place, and new bilateral negotiations were presumably halted, an existing bilateral agreement that varied from the joint negotiated position would prevail if its provisions were more 'favorable.' Press Release, Common Position, *supra* note 47. It may be assumed – although the Council does not say so – that the balance of 'favorableness' should be toward the EU party. (The 2003 mandates make no such assumptions.)

49. There was a glaring potential for acrimony in allowing existing external bilateral agreements to be maintained, at least under the prevailing Chicago system, that would eventually be addressed in 2007 through insisting on a single common agreement that includes recognition of 'seventh freedom' rights for all EU carriers from all EU airports to the United States. *See also infra* Chapter 6, Part III(E) (discussing management of air transport relations with third countries outside the proposed plurilateral). If the Council intended to grant competence to the Commission to award *all* extra-Union traffic rights, and to distribute these rights without discrimination to all EU carriers, this attribution of competence *would* necessarily be in conflict with each existing U.S./Member State bilateral treaty, which restricted traffic rights to carriers that were nationals of the parties to the treaty – and which must be, in that specific sense, more 'favorable' to each Member State than any collective imposition of rights. Arguably, for example, the European Commission might successfully negotiate 'cabotage' access to the United States for all EU airlines, while retaining the existing bilateral system of traffic rights exchanged by each Member State with the United States (which were awarded exclusively to each party's national airlines). Although certainly an example of 'added value,' that outcome would have offered U.S. airlines much more flexibility to access the EU market than EU carriers would have in providing services to the United States. EU carriers would still have been restricted to direct services from their homelands, a competition-depleting arrangement that would appeal only to weaker EU carriers. While the complex issue of assigning traffic rights is more fully treated later, *see supra* Chapter 5, Part III, it is apparent that the split mandate was a messy reconciliation of essentially bilateral interests.

50. What actually transpired after the original mandate was a series of informal consultations between U.S. and EU aviation officials that lasted several years. *See* INTERNATIONAL AIR CARRIER ASSOCIATION, TOWARDS REGULATORY CONVERGENCE: AN IACA VIEW (Jun. 2001) (noting U.S./EC aviation discussions held on Oct. 30/31, 1996, Apr. 3, 1997, and May 31, 2001). Despite

over the conditionality of the mandate, the Council's press announcement spoke rhetorically and positively of the eventual achievement of a 'Common Aviation Area where air carriers of both sides could freely provide their services in the European Union and in the [United States],' an agreement that would be 'without any precedent in the aeronautical sector.'[51]

D   WEBS OF INFLUENCE: INTERNATIONAL ORGANIZATIONS AND ACADEMIC COMMENTATORS

In tracing a gradual evolution toward the 2007 transatlantic agreement, it is important here to pause the 'macro-story' of U.S./EC public policymaking in order to give consideration to other actors, private and public, institutional and individual, involved in shaping the recent *Zeitgeist* of transatlantic aviation relations. Three of these 'webs of influence' (to use the useful coinage adopted earlier)[52] will be examined in the following Sections – international nongovernmental organizations, international governmental organizations, and academic commentators.

1   Webs of Influence I: International Nongovernmental Organizations

The most transformative development in U.S./EC air transport diplomacy since the 1993 Baliles Commission was the entry of EU public and private actors into what had been a U.S.-dominated laboratory of reform. In part because of the economic travails of the U.S. industry in the first decade of the new century,[53] the era of a unilateral Americanist policy has clearly been over for some time.

---

authorization from the EU Transport Council to negotiate multilaterally with the United States, the EU Member States restricted the scope of discussions to issues such as computer reservations systems, code-sharing, and ownership restrictions. In order to negotiate more substantial issues such as traffic rights, a further mandate would have been required. In the end, no formal agreements were ever concluded. *See* Sophie Meunier, *What Single Voice? European Institutions and EU-U.S. Trade Negotiations*, 51 INT'L ORG. 103, 130-31 (2000); *see generally* European Commission, *Consequences, supra* note 20.

51. Press Release, Common Position, *supra* note 47. Although informal talks were held, in negotiator John Byerly's view 'little progress was possible where one side lacked the ability to address the very core of an air services agreement: routes and rates.' Byerly, *Charting the Course, supra* note 18, at 4.

52. *See supra* note 3.

53. *See* Glenn Tilton, Chairman and Chief Executive Officer, United Airlines, *Moving the World: Global Aviation and the Global Economy*, Remarks to the Chicago Council on Foreign Relations (Apr. 21, 2005) (lamenting that, 'for the first time in the history of aviation, U.S. carriers are no longer the largest, strongest companies leading the way'). As a telling example of the parlous condition of his industry, Tilton noted that United Airlines was the launch customer in 1995 for the Boeing 777, whereas U.S. passenger airlines have placed only a handful of orders for the new Boeing 787 Dreamliner and none for the behemoth Airbus 380, the benchmark commercial aircraft of the new century's first decade. *See id.*

In Parts III and IV, we will examine, on the public side, how the 2007 U.S./EC Air Transport Agreement capped a sequence of convulsive events – including new mandates for the European Commission – set in motion by the so-called 'open skies' rulings of the European Court of Justice, the EU's highest court, in November 2002. But an early sign that Europe's cynicism toward ambitious changes in global aviation[54] had crested came in September 1999, when the private nongovernmental Association of European Airlines (AEA) published a 17-page 'Policy Statement,' bearing the tendentious caption *Towards a Transatlantic Common Aviation Area,*[55] which called for a 'unified system' – including strong regulatory convergence[56] – that would take advantage of likeminded regulatory instincts to give airlines operating in a new U.S./EC aviation union 'full commercial opportunities on an equal basis' under the dominion of a 'common body of aviation rules.'[57]

The so-called Transatlantic Common Aviation Area (TCAA) was aimed squarely at displacing the Chicago bilateral system, a trade-depleting miasma of agreements[58] that varied in content from one bilateral to another depending on the trade interests and negotiating power of the parties and a system, moreover, that could not accommodate complex international trade flows.[59] In aerodiplomatic terms, the TCAA proposal created a bridgehead for continuing U.S./EC contacts,[60]

---

54. *See* Calleja, *supra* note 25, at 18 (noting a reversal of roles as Europe pushed for comprehensive liberalization of the transatlantic aviation system).
55. *See* Association of European Airlines [AEA], *Towards a Transatlantic Common Aviation Area*, AEA Policy Statement (Sept. 1999).
56. *Id.* at 1. As will be seen, the proposals for comprehensive regulatory integration soured its reception in the United States. The proposal's drafter, however, envisaged regulatory convergence as a logical follow-up to 'the modest commonality in open skies agreements on ground-handling and computer reservations systems.' Kees Veenstra, Deputy Secretary General, Association of European Airlines, Speaking Notes to the University of Pittsburgh's The Future of EU-U.S. Aviation Relations Conference (Apr. 7, 2000) [hereinafter Veenstra, Remarks] (speaking notes on file with author). But Veenstra conceded that, particularly with respect to his proposal for supranational airline competition rulemaking and enforcement, existing global institutions like the World Trade Organization were characterized by a very limited interference in State sovereignty compared with what Venstra self-mockingly called 'the potential monstrosity of the guardians of the TCAA.' *Id.*
57. *Id.* The notion that the United States and EC were indeed 'likeminded' parties on transatlantic air transport liberalization was the conceit of the TCAA's author, Kees Veenstra. *See* Veenstra, Remarks, *supra* note 56. Moreover, to accomplish 'major reform,' Veenstra argued, there had to be likemindedness and also 'critical mass.' *Id.* Thus, while big global institutions like the World Trade Organization and the International Civil Aviation Organization had critical mass, unlike the U.S./EC aviation establishments they did not enjoy 'likemindedness.' *Id.*
58. There were estimated to be 1500 bilateral agreements concluded just by the EU Member States. *See* Woll, *supra* note 6, at 10.
59. *See* Veenstra, Remarks, *supra* note 56.
60. The TCAA proposal was ostensibly the brainchild of the AEA, an industry trade group, rather than of the European Commission itself. But the Commission undoubtedly provided policy inputs into the TCAA drafting process, while cloaking itself in the 'legitimacy' of an industry-inspired initiative. Woll, *supra* note 6, at 10.

albeit one punctuated at first by low-intensity skepticism about each side's motives and readiness to make concessions. Development of the TCAA proposal reflected at least an exploratory commitment by the European private sector to extraterritorial expansion of the single aviation market.

The AEA members perceived that the bilateral system, encrusted with discriminatory and restrictive regulation, had evolved into an inefficient exercise in 'zero-sum market division' incapable of producing the network growth demanded by a global trade environment.[61] Air services treaties needed to be recast to cede control over pricing and market access – the chief indicia of a deregulated system – to airline managements. This shift in attitude by leading European airlines, which could see their future international growth potential stifled by the peculiar legal restrictions of the bilateral system, illustrated a well-recognized consequentialist paradigm where policy is shaped by economics, and in turn law is shaped by policy.[62]

The economic backdrop to the emergence of the TCAA is instructive – and ironic. In 1993, the U.S. Airline Commission had described a retrenchment in the positions of foreign governments whose nationally controlled airlines were facing strong competition from U.S. fleets.[63] But, as EU flag carriers shed costs and strengthened their performances, while embracing privatization,[64] U.S. carriers gradually lost a transatlantic market share dominance that had seemed virtually structural.[65] European attitudes shifted accordingly. For EU airlines, services to

---

61. As will be seen, *infra* Chapter 3, Part VIII, airlines' network-building capabilities are hostage to the interconnectivity of bilateral agreements with different countries.

62. As TCAA author Kees Veenstra emphasized, it was 'incomprehensible' to the European airlines that transatlantic alliances, which themselves reflected a major restructuring of the global system, had not provoked 'a fundamental reappraisal' of the ownership and control rules. *See* Veenstra, *Remarks, supra* note 56. Thus, the burden of proof in a modern economic system should be on those who sought to maintain artificial barriers. *See id.*

63. As examples, France had 'denounced' (unilaterally terminated) its bilateral treaty with the United States, citing capture by U.S. airlines of 70% of traffic on the New York/Paris route. Chancellor Helmut Kohl of Germany had written a letter to President Clinton threatening denunciation of the U.S./Germany aviation pact as a 'post-war relic,' and noting the 60% share of bilateral traffic held by U.S. carriers. *Change, Challenge and Competition, The National Commission to Ensure a Strong Competitive Airline Industry: A Report to President and Congress*, Aug. 1993, at 20-21 [hereinafter *Airline Commission Report*]. U.S. aviation bilaterals typically provide for denunciation by written notification, to take effect one year following the date of receipt of notification.

64. This embrace had its structural limits. Between 1991 and 1997, the European Commission gave the green light to numerous injections of State aid into EU airlines for the express purpose of turning them into profitable enterprises. *See* RIGAS DOGANIS, FLYING OFF COURSE: THE ECONOMICS OF INTERNATIONAL AIRLINES 67-68 (3d ed. 2002).

65. Thus, by the full year ending 2003, U.S. airlines' share of the U.S./France and U.S./Germany markets had fallen back to 43% and 37%, respectively. *See* U.S. Department of Transportation, Office of the Assistant Secretary for Aviation and International Affairs, *U.S. International Air Passenger and Freight Statistics* (Mar. 2005), Table 4 (Top 25 Foreign Country Gateways). Most EU national flag carriers are now the strongest transatlantic operators to and from their home markets. However, U.S. carriers operate a higher number of frequencies over a higher number of transatlantic routes, reflecting the way that they have each developed several hubs

destinations outside the EU in 2006 generated about 70% of revenues, and the transatlantic market alone accounted for approximately 25%.[66] Accordingly, the implications of global liberalization would have consequences much more profound than the internal liberalization measures adopted by the Community between 1988 and 1992.[67]

Beyond the European setting, the International Air Transport Association (IATA), the oldest worldwide private league of airlines, also championed reform of the nationality rule. In particular, the organization promoted carrier designation criteria in bilateral agreements that would allow a separation of commercial control of the airline (the traditional narrow focus on the citizenship profiles of the investors) from its regulatory control.[68] While ownership of a carrier (its commercial control) could be multinational, in order to avoid risks of 'flags of convenience'[69] the regulatory control or licensure of the carrier would remain with the designating State.[70] Concomitantly, IATA called for liberalization also of national limitations on airline ownership.[71]

2 Webs of Influence II: International Governmental Organizations

In the decade ending in 2003, international governmental organizations also gradually joined the policy fray. In March 2003, IATA's fellow Montreal-based institution, the intergovernmental International Civil Aviation Organization (ICAO),

---

across the United States that they feed with traffic from a range of international destinations. *See* Press Release, Europa, European Commission Requests the Denunciation of the Bilateral Open Sky Agreements, IP/02/171 (Nov. 20, 2002) [hereinafter Press Release, Denunciation].

66. *See* AEA, OPERATING ECONOMY OF AEA AIRLINES 2007 7 (2007).

67. *See* European Cockpit Association [ECA], A Contribution by the European Cockpit Association to the Communication from the Commission on the Consequences of the European Court of Justice Judgments of 5 Nov. 2002 for the European Air Transport Policy, COM (2002) 649 (Dec. 19, 2002), <www.eurocockpit.be/content/view/127/274/> [hereinafter ECA, Contribution].

68. *See, e.g.*, IATA, *Airline Views on Liberalizing Ownership and Control*, Paper Presented to the ICAO Worldwide Air Transport Conference, ATConf/5-WP26 (Dec. 16, 2002) [hereinafter IATA, *Liberalizing*]; *see also* IATA, *Airline Views on Liberalising Ownership and Control* para. 4.1(a) (Int'l Air Transp. Ass'n Working Policy Paper, 2003).

69. *See infra* notes 81 & 89 (explaining this concept).

70. Incidents of regulatory control include air operator and airworthiness certificates and crew licenses, as well as the establishment of tax liability. Out of concern for safety regulation, IATA has also recommended an additional clause giving the receiving State the power to suspend or vary the operating authorization of another State's designated carriers based on ramp inspections or the denial of ramp inspections. *See* IATA, *Liberalizing, supra* note 68, para. 4.1(b).

71. As considered *infra* Chapter 3, Part V, dismantling of the traditional nationality rule will require that changes in bilateral designation criteria must be accompanied by abolition of national laws imposing the same or similar 'purity' tests. For the United States to designate a foreign-owned and controlled airline under the U.S./Japan bilateral agreement, for example, that non-U.S. quantum of investment would have to comply with U.S. domestic laws on airline ownership *as well as* with the designation clauses of the U.S./Japan bilateral agreement.

convened its fifth Worldwide Air Transport Conference to consider liberalization developments in air transport (domestically and internationally).[72] At its prior conference in 1994, the mood of ICAO's member States was largely inimical to abolition of the bilateral system,[73] but in 2003 the stringency of the competitive environment seemed to move delegates toward appreciation of the new paradigms suggested by multilateral options and toward embrace of a mantra of 'liberalization' in air services negotiations and with respect to the ownership and control laws.[74] Thereafter, a global symposium on liberalization in Dubai in September 2006 was followed by the 36th ICAO Assembly in September 2007, both of which recognized a rising preference for bilateral 'open skies' agreements derived from the U.S. paradigm.[75] A 2006 Working Paper of the Assembly offered a *tour d'horizon* of liberalization initiatives, including 11 regional liberalization projects[76] and

---

72. *See* ICAO Secretariat, *Liberalizing Air Carrier Ownership and Control*, Paper Presented to the ICAO Worldwide Air Transport Conference, ATConf/5-WP/7 (Oct. 21, 2002); *see also* ICAO Secretariat, *Background and Overview of Conference Task*, Paper Presented to ICAO Worldwide Air Transport Conference, ATConf/5-WP/4 (Feb. 11, 2003). Whether ICAO has any formal assigned role in evaluating economic (as opposed to safety and navigational) regulatory options is a matter of some controversy. *See generally* Ruwantissa I.R. Abeyratne, *The Economic Relevance of the Chicago Convention – A Retrospective Study*, 19-2 ANNALS AIR & SPACE L. 3 (1994); Richard Janda, *Passing the Torch: Why ICAO Should Leave Economic Regulation of International Air Transport to the WTO*, 20-1 ANNALS AIR & SPACE L. 409 (1995). At most, it could be said that ICAO's role is not so much legislative as it is advisory and recommendatory. *See* Taieb Cherif, *Mission Statement: Wings of Change in International Air Transport*, U.N. CHRON., 2004, <www.un.org/Pubs/chronicle/2003/issue4/0403p15.asp>.
73. *See* Press Release, ICAO, ICAO Conference Plots Future Course for International Air Transport Regulation, PIO 18/94 (Dec. 8, 1994).
74. *See* IATA, *Advancing the Liberalisation of Ownership and Control*, Paper Presented to the ICAO Assembly's 35th Session, para. 1.1, A35-WP/64 (Jul. 8, 2004) (noting that ICAO governments agreed for the first time at the Fifth Worldwide Air Transport Conference on a global framework of objectives, principles, and policies to liberalize international air transport) [hereinafter IATA, *Advancing the Liberalisation*]. All of the working papers for the 35th Session of the ICAO Assembly may be found (in up to six languages) at ICAO, 35th Session of the Assembly, Working Papers by WP Number, <www.icao.int/cgi/goto_m.pl?cgi/a35.pl?wp>.
75. Both IATA and ICAO have collaborated in seeking to build a 'practical nucleus' of States which, as a matter of law or policy or both, have or would consider relaxing the traditional nationality rule on airline ownership and control (which needs to be done at both domestic and bilateral levels). *See* International Air Transport Association, *Airline Views on Liberalizing Ownership and Control*, Paper Presented to the ICAO Worldwide Air Transport Conference, ATConf/5-WP26 (Dec. 16, 2002). An ICAO questionnaire circulated to its Member States in Sept. 2003 suggested more flexibility on both of these questions than might have been expected. Over two-thirds of the respondent States indicated a willingness to accept criteria other than traditional ownership and control, some on a case-by-case basis (the latter being a typical mannerism of U.S. bilateral practice). *See* IATA, *Advancing the Liberalisation, supra* note 74, para. 2.1.
76. Exhibiting more or less effectiveness, the principal regional groups, in addition to the pioneering European Community's Common Aviation Area and the Andean Pact, include the CARICOM Air Service Agreement of 1996 (14 Caribbean States), the Fortaleza Agreement of 1997 (six South American States), the Banjul Accord of 1997 (six West African States), the CLMV Agreement of 1998 (Cambodia, Lao PDR, Myanmar, Vietnam), an agreement in 1998 among 16 Arab Civil Aviation Commission Member States, an agreement in 1999 between six States of the Economic and Monetary Community of Central Africa, the U.S.-anchored Multilateral

continued efforts to expand the limited reach of the Air Transport Annex to the General Agreement on Trade in Services.[77]

The adoption of a conscious liberalization agenda marked a departure from ICAO's traditional State-centered thinking, which tended to view superannuated utilitarian treaties such as the International Air Services Transit Agreement (IASTA) (which provides for multilateral exchange of rights of overflight and non-traffic stopover)[78] as the zenith of multilateralism, and even as recently as 2003 the ICAO Secretariat promoted the IASTA as the 'cornerstone' of multilateralism in air transport.[79]

Meanwhile, the Paris-based Organization for Economic Cooperation and Development (OECD) also promoted a liberalization agenda, most notably with respect to cargo issues.[80] The principal intellectual contribution of the OECD's comprehensive 2002 report on liberalizing air cargo was an attempt to reframe an airline's 'home' jurisdiction in the regulatory terms favored by IATA. In particular, the report recommended a 'principal place of business' link between airline and State that would be defined by a number of variables including the jurisdiction where the primary corporate headquarters is located, where regular air transport is provided, where there is a substantial investment in physical facilities, where the airline pays income tax and registers its aircraft, and where it employs a significant number of nationals in managerial, technical, and operational positions.[81]

Agreement on the Liberalization of International Air Transportation (MALIAT) of 2001, *see infra* note 114, which includes nine States in Asia and North and South America. *See* ICAO, *Regulatory, supra* note 6, para. 2.2. Additionally, further efforts to establish a common aviation area in South America based on a multilateral open skies approach through a revised and modernized Fortaleza Agreement have also begun to take shape. *See* Respicio A. Espirito Santo Jr., *Building a Common Aviation Area in South America*, AERLINES MAGAZINE, Apr. 13, 2005, <www.aerlines.nl/issue_29/29_Santo_Building_a_Common_Aviation_Area.pdf>. However, the journey towards multilateral air liberalization on the African continent – specifically through the Yammoussoukro Decision – has been fraught with difficulties. *See* Charles E. Schlumberger, *Africa's Long Path to Liberalization: Status Quo of the Implementation of the Yammoussoukro Decision*, 33 ANNALS AIR & SPACE L. 194 (2008).

77. *See* ICAO Council, *Development and Economic Regulation of International Air Transport*, Paper Presented to the ICAO Assembly's 36th Session, A-36-WP/16 (Jun. 26, 2007). The World Trade Organization, custodian of the General Agreement on Trade in Services (GATS), has played only a peripheral role in the process of economic liberalization of air transport. The GATS Air Transport Annex, under its newest review schedule that began in 2005, may be extended to cover other auxiliary air transport services in addition to its current modest trifecta of aircraft repair and maintenance, selling and marketing of air transport, and computer reservations systems. *See infra* Chapter 6, Part III(C).

78. *See infra* Chapter 3, Part II.

79. *See* ICAO Secretariat, *Liberalization Developments Related to Market Access*, Paper Presented to the ICAO Worldwide Air Transport Conference, para. 2.1, ATConf/5-WP/21 (Mar. 3, 2003).

80. Three OECD working groups held on air cargo between 1999 and 2002 culminated in a comprehensive report published in 2002. *See* Directorate for Sci., Tech., and Indus., OECD, *Liberalisation of Air Cargo Transport*, DSTI/DOT (2002) 1/REV1 (May 2, 2002).

81. *See id.* para. 58. From the perspective of organized labor, insisting that bilateral designation must be based upon these indicia of attachment to a particular State reduces the risk that an airline will seek to relocate to States with lower social (including labor) costs – the so-called

3   **Webs of Influence III: Academic Commentators**

Academic commentators also sought to influence the emerging debate on both sides of the Atlantic. In April 2000, at the behest of Professor Martin Staniland of the Graduate School of Public and International Affairs at the University of Pittsburgh, the University's European Union Center hosted a policy conference on 'The Future of EU-U.S. Aviation Relations.'[82] This conference served as a kind of public debut, to an informed audience of U.S. policymakers, for the AEA's blueprint for a TCAA.[83] The document's author, Kees Veenstra, Deputy Secretary-General of the AEA, pitched to an uncomfortable U.S. audience his ideas that not only could traditional airline ownership and control and cabotage embargoes be scrapped, but that a common regulatory superstructure could be imagined for the American and European air transport industries.[84] In Professor Staniland's estimation, the AEA's advocacy of new supranational regulatory institutions for the aviation industry was 'anathema' to the U.S. participants at Pittsburgh.[85] To the U.S. mind, it seemed counterproductive, if not contrarian, to accompany a call for deregulation of international air transport with an entirely new proposal for regulation.[86]

On May 1, 2002, in anticipation of the open skies rulings of the European Court of Justice and of a fresh set of negotiating mandates for the European

---

'flag of convenience' problem. *See id.*; *see also infra* note 89. However, it should be noted that in the context of U.S./EC aviation relations, the likelihood of U.S. carriers 're-flagging' in a Member State of the European Union is slim, among other reasons, because of the absence of a significant disparity in air transport pay scales between the United States and Europe. *See* BRATTLE GROUP, THE ECONOMIC IMPACT OF AN EC-U.S. OPEN AVIATION AREA 13 (2002). EU carriers can already hire workers from lower-wage Member States without re-flagging. *See id.*

82.   Professor Staniland's interest in this topic has not dimmed. For a dynamic account of the development of the European airline industry from its earliest days through the era following the Chicago Convention and on to the most recent period of market integration and air transport liberalization, *see* MARTIN STANILAND, A EUROPE OF THE AIR?: THE AIRLINE INDUSTRY AND EUROPEAN INTEGRATION (2008).

83.   *See supra* note 55.

84.   *See generally* Martin Staniland, *The Future of EU-U.S. Aviation Relations: Issues and Implications*, Commentary for the Transatlantic Aviation Forum, <www.ucis.pitt.edu/euce/events/policyconf/FutureAviationRelations-00.pdf> (sketching how the AEA's policy statement proposed a plurilateral agreement for a common aviation area and therefore implicated a 'fundamental reappraisal of the traditional regulatory framework' of the international air transport system) [hereinafter Staniland, *Future*]; *see also* Martin Staniland, *Conference Report, University of Pittsburgh Conference on 'The Future of EC-U.S. Aviation Relations,'* 6 J. AIR TRANSP. MANAGEMENT 245-247 (2000).

85.   Staniland, *Future*, *supra* note 84, at 10. In the view of one U.S. observer, the TCAA proposal 'landed with a thud'. Woll, *supra* note 6, at 9. According to Woll, U.S. policymakers and airlines described the TCAA, without apparent intent to flatter, as 'a very "European" proposal.' *Id.* A few sentences later the U.S. bias becomes manifest: '[T]he TCAA proposal had "regulation" written everywhere. We counted the number of times the word appeared on the first couple of pages and came to fifteen!' *Id.*

86.   *See id.* at 9 (noting that the TCAA was in terms an invitation to the United States to join the EC's evolving common aviation area).

Commission, the present author and Dr. Dorothy Robyn (former economic advisor to President Clinton and partner in the Washington. D.C.-based economic consultancy, The Brattle Group), convened a working group in Washington, D.C., of U.S. and EU airline alliance executives, government officials, and pilot union leaders to discuss strategies for a future transatlantic agreement.[87] The Havel/Robyn 'Moderators' Understanding' concluded that, while the AEA policy statement 'launched a bold idea and fostered a valuable discussion of next steps,' as currently written it lacked support on the U.S. side in part because of a perception that 'it would add bureaucratic structures even as it eliminated economic restrictions.'[88]

While union leaders were troubled about issues of 'labor substitution' in a liberalized environment,[89] the group as a whole was nonetheless broadly sympathetic to the proposition that U.S. open skies agreements are 'a significant, but only partial step towards international aviation liberalization.'[90] With that in mind, the group examined a 'beyond open skies' agenda that would eschew cabotage rights in favor of an economic 'right of establishment' for non-national investors,[91]

---

87. The group, accorded the sobriquet 'the Havel Huddle' by the former general counsel of British Airways, Andrew Carr, focused on a series of issues that remained paramount in subsequent U.S./EC negotiations leading to the 2007 U.S./EC Air Transport Agreement and that still forms the agenda for the second stage of those negotiations after Mar. 2008. *See infra* Part III.

88. Brian F. Havel & Dorothy Robyn, *Understanding of the Moderators*, Paper Presented to the Working Meeting of Aviation Experts on U.S./EU Aviation Liberalization, Washington, D.C. (May 1, 2002) (copy on file with author).

89. The issue of labor substitution will be revisited in Chapter 6 in presenting the challenges of a 'beyond open skies' agenda. *See infra* Chapter 6, Part III(E). It remains a huge political obstacle to the liberalization of U.S. airline ownership and control laws. The primary concern of labor unions is that, in a regime where foreign carriers could acquire U.S. airlines or create their own U.S. airlines or subsidiaries, those carriers might replace U.S. mobile flight crews on international services with workers from countries with lower wages or more lax labor standards. At the extreme, labor fears that an airline might fly a foreign 'flag of convenience' to take advantage of low wages and taxes in another country. *See* Havel & Robyn, *supra* note 88, at 2. The potential for domestic substitution (*i.e.*, on intra-U.S. services) would be lessened by adoption of the so-called right or obligation of 'establishment.' *See* Chapter 3, Part V.

90. Havel & Robyn, *supra* note 88, at 1. Historically, open skies agreements approached the most liberal accord that U.S. executive branch agencies could support without eliminating statutory restrictions such as those on foreign ownership and control and cabotage. *See id.* at 1-2.

91. The economic notion of a 'right of establishment' is considered in greater detail, *infra* Chapter 3, Part V. It should be distinguished at the outset from the more limited 'right of establishment' in Articles 52-58 of the EC Treaty, the operative nucleus of the open skies rulings of the European Court of Justice in 2002. The Treaty speaks of a simple right of non-nationals to conduct a business or pursue a professional career without suffering local discrimination, and in that sense is indeed a legal right conferred by Community law. The broader notion of a right (or, more accurately 'obligation') of establishment, in the context of non-national aviation investment, would allow foreign investors to take majority ownership and control of domestic carriers, or to set up new airlines or subsidiaries of foreign airlines in a domestic market, but also *obligate* the foreign-owned entity to operate as a domestic-regulated carrier employing local labor and abiding by local labor, tax, immigration, registration, safety, security, and other laws. A right or obligation of establishment could be created merely by modifying the definition of 'citizen' in the relevant national laws while requiring that local air carriers under foreign ownership and control will be regulated as local corporations. As the Working Group discussed,

would require participation in the U.S. Civil Reserve Air Fleet program by U.S. airlines under foreign ownership and control,[92] would seek greater convergence in the application (as opposed to the substance) of competition laws as well as continued formal agency cooperation,[93] would ease restrictions

---

it is incorrect to assume that the elimination of restrictions on foreign ownership and control simultaneously would serve to authorize cabotage. *See* Havel & Robyn, *supra* note 88, at 2 n.2. Cabotage restrictions would continue to apply to all foreign carriers (which, under the Chicago Convention, are regulated for cabotage purposes by their home States, but foreign-owned domestically-regulated carriers would be able to serve cabotage routes. U.S. labor unions, it may be fair to say, do recognize that their fears about labor substitution would be much less likely to be realized in a purely domestic context under a right of establishment. As noted, however, their principal concern lies with substitution on international air routes, and there the issue is more contentious.

92. As will be discussed in further detail, *infra* Chapter 3, Part V(B), the U.S. Department of Defense has opposed elimination of restrictions on foreign ownership and control of U.S. airlines out of fear that liberalization of these rules would jeopardize the Department's Civil Reserve Air Fleet (CRAF) program. Under this program, U.S. carriers commit to supply airlift capacity in the case of a military emergency. The Department has expressed its concern that, if a U.S. carrier were bought by foreign investors, it could no longer be relied on to honor its CRAF commitments. The 2002 U.S./EU Aviation Working Group considered how a right or obligation of establishment could address the Department's concerns by giving the U.S. Government legal control over the U.S.-based but foreign-owned airline. License revocation would be one available penalty. *See* Havel & Robyn, *supra* note 88, at 3. As co-moderator Dorothy Robyn noted for the group, in the maritime equivalent of CRAF (the Voluntary Intermodal Sealift Agreement, VISA), the Department of Defense already allows participation by foreign-owned commercial ships that qualify as 'U.S. citizens' under maritime law. *Id.*

93. The AEA's policy statement on a Transatlantic Common Aviation Area, *see supra* note 55, foundered on the rock of U.S. dislike of regulatory convergence. U.S. Government officials repeated and emphasized this dislike at the Nov. 2007 Working Group in Dublin, Ireland. *See infra* text accompanying note 95. U.S. resistance cuts through a wide swathe of regulatory issues including safety, security, and the environment, but was most vigorously manifested with respect to the AEA's call for supranational competition rules and enforcement. The 2002 Working Group found the AEA's proposal on competition cooperation to be both 'legally problematic and politically unrealistic.' Havel & Robyn, *supra* note 88, at 4. In its place, the Group advocated convergence in the application of competition laws based on existing formal cooperation arrangements, *see infra* Chapter 6, Part III(E), a process that reflects a willingness to share nonconfidential information and similar approaches to key concepts such as market definition and market power. *See* Havel & Robyn, *supra* note 88, at 4. The cooperative spirit, which is about as far as U.S. regulators wished to commit themselves, could also include the competition responsibilities of the U.S. Department of Transportation. Although the Department is a regulatory agency confined by rules of procedure such as those with respect to *ex parte* communications, its representatives nevertheless indicated their interest in a 'deeper and more structured relationship' with their European Commission counterparts. *Id.* Interestingly, some (but not all) U.S. and EU airlines at the Working Group believed that the application of competition law to their industry lacks transparency and predictability. The suggestion was made, therefore, that U.S. and EC agencies should develop 'common guidelines' for aviation transactions, analogous to the merger guidelines of the U.S. Department of Justice and Federal Trade Commission. These guidelines would clarify the concept of market definition (agencies have applied both route- and network-based definitions) and promote remedies that rely on market incentives rather than administrative oversight. Guidelines might also serve to reduce political pressure on the agencies. Havel & Robyn, *supra* note 88, at 4. In this respect, the 2007

on domestic wet leasing,[94] and would proscribe all forms of government subsidy or State aid.[95]

In 2007, in the aftermath of the signing of the U.S./EC Air Transport Agreement, this author convened two further U.S./EC Working Groups. The first (again held in Washington, D.C.) took place on May 1, 2007, under the auspices of the International Aviation Law Institute at DePaul University College of Law. The second, in Dublin, Ireland, on November 8, 2007, was a collaboration between the DePaul-based Institute and the International Air and Space Law Institute of Leiden University and its Director, Professor Pablo Mendes de Leon. This second Working Group was timed to coincide with Dublin's hosting of the 19th Annual Conference of the European Air Law Association, the first time the Conference had been held in the Irish capital.

The participants in the 2007 Working Groups were by no means unanimous in welcoming the U.S./EC Agreement, not necessarily because it failed to enhance competition – to the contrary, it amplified competition in already contested markets – but because some saw the 2007 agreement as an historical missed opportunity. These participants had a sense that, notwithstanding the known political difficulties of

---

U.S./EC Agreement mirrors the circumscription of U.S. negotiators evinced at the May 2002 Working Group.

94. Wet leasing, the temporary provision of aircraft and crews by one carrier to another, is a normal operational arrangement in many countries and permits lease-out and lease-in of aircraft and crew to and from foreign airlines. *See* Kees Veenstra, Speaking Notes for the Future of EU-U.S. Aviation Relations Conference, Pittsburgh, Pa. (Apr. 7, 2000) [hereinafter Veenstra, Speaking Notes] (copy on file with author). Wet leasing from foreign carriers, however, has been more tightly restricted in the United States, particularly with respect to the domestic market, than in the EU. *See* Havel & Robyn, *supra* note 88, at 5. U.S. all-cargo carriers like Atlas, Evergreen, Southern, and Polar Air have significant wet-leasing operations on a global scale, but non-U.S. carriers do not enjoy wet-lease access to the U.S. market. *See* Veenstra, Speaking Notes, *supra*, at 5. The 2007 U.S./EC Air Transport Agreement relaxes the U.S. position with respect to international services, but inward wet leasing for domestic services remains impermissible in most circumstances. Wet leasing is particularly important to air cargo carriers because of their need to respond to seasonal peaks. U.S labor representatives told the 2002 Working Group that wet leasing creates opportunities for labor substitution, and some U.S. aviation safety officials posit that it could weaken national safety regulations. *See* Havel & Robyn, *supra* note 88, at 5.

95. The 2002 Working Group came together in the aftermath of the 9/11 tragedy and the U.S. Government's 'stabilization' assistance to the U.S. air transport industry. EU representatives drew unflattering comparisons between the European Community's tough State aids policy and the perceived largesse of the U.S. Government in compensating its stricken carriers. *See infra* Chapter 5, Part III(F) (discussing the European Commission's robust stand on State aid). The U.S. response was to point to a series of 'one-time, last-time' capital infusions by EU Member State governments into national carriers during the 1990s, which in some instances spilled over into the first decade of the new century. Borrowing the lexicon of Community State aids, U.S. members of the Working Group characterized post-9/11 aid also as 'unique and one-time,' leaving both sides *pro futuro* 'firmly committed to a policy of not providing subsidies to the airline industry.' Havel & Robyn, *supra* note 88, at 5. On the general subject of State subsidies in the EU, *see infra* Chapter 5, Part III(F).

tampering with the U.S. cabotage and investment laws, the trajectory of U.S./EC negotiations since 2003 had shown a progressive raising of reciprocal concessions and might have led, if additional effort could have been marshaled in convincing U.S. opponents, to a major breakthrough on the pivotal issue of liberalizing the U.S. airline ownership and control laws. In particular, some participants argued that it was a mistake for the United States to seek to decouple the DOT's proposed reform of the control criteria from progress in the U.S./EC negotiations;[96] to have made the Department's rulemaking initiative a *sine qua non* of reaching an agreement, as the EC negotiators sought to do on their side, might have been politically potent in overcoming domestic U.S. resistance. These views, which are consistent with the missiological zeal of the European Commission itself,[97] reflected disappointment that an unstoppable global momentum could have begun in 2007 rather than the second-best option of a return to the core unresolved issues of liberalization during a prolonged and uncertain 'second stage.' They may reflect also a darker view, sometimes expressed in Europe, that the first-stage agreement gave the United States everything it wanted (including open skies over Heathrow), but offered the EU only promises of future favor.[98]

But the Working Groups were not solely an echo chamber for voicing regrets. Working Groups have their moments of poetry, too. The November 2007 session closed with a ringing admonition from senior Dutch political leader Laurens Jan Brinkhorst, Chairman of the International Advisory Board of the Leiden institute, to sweep away parochial commercial considerations in the name of a larger trans-atlantic culture of collaboration. Responding to that summons, on the practical level of optimizing the second stage negotiations, the participants in both Working Groups considered legal and policy options that might enhance the palatability to key U.S. stakeholders of liberalizing or abolishing restrictions on inward investment. Of special importance, the participants agreed, was to build support in Congress for these changes. Industry representatives, for example, noted that most members of Congress are uninformed on airline investment issues, surrendering the initiative by default to outspoken opponents of reform such as House Transportation Committee Chairman James Oberstar.[99]

As an example of innovative thinking, the Group considered the potential applicability of the U.S. Foreign Investment and National Security Act of 2007 ('FINSA').[100] FINSA substantially modifies the 1988 'Exon-Florio' amendment granting the President of the United States broad powers to block or suspend

---

96. For more on ownership and control rules, *see infra* Chapter III, Part V.
97. *See infra* Chapter 6, Part IV for a further comment on the Commission's evangelical engage-ment in the reform of air transport.
98. The issue of whether the 2007 agreement maintained a fair balance between U.S. and EC negotiating objectives will be further considered *infra* Chapter 6, Part IV.
99. *See infra* text accompanying note 267 (discussing Oberstar's efforts to amend the ownership and control statute to make unlawful precisely the kinds of liberalizing changes that the DOT proposed to allow on a discretionary basis in its 2005/06 rulemaking).
100. Pub. L. No. 110-49, 121 Stat. 246 [hereinafter FINSA].

investments in and/or acquisitions of U.S. companies and assets by foreign entities if the transaction presents a 'credible' threat to national security.[101] That any foreign investment in U.S. airlines carries the potential to be blocked by the President under FINSA should not be in doubt.[102] As one commentator has already pointed out, the U.S. airline industry, with its perceived place as a 'symbolic national asset' and 'the potential security implications of dangerous or intentionally destructive airplane flights,' falls well within the scope of the President's statutory powers.[103] As under Exon-Florio, the duty to investigate proposed foreign investments is delegated to a cross-departmental consortium of U.S. federal agencies dubbed the Committee on Foreign Investment in the United States (CFIUS).[104]

The amended FINSA would undoubtedly assuage fears that foreign investment in U.S. airlines would put U.S. national security at risk.[105] But the statute does not address the issue of *economic* security, although amending language to that effect has been proposed nearly half-a-dozen times over the past two decades.[106] This omission is understandable, as prominent Exon-Florio lawyers Alan Larson and David Marchick have written, because the term itself is 'extraordinarily vague' and thus difficult to implement, and also because 'an economic security' test would regress into a protectionist vehicle for domestic industries to block foreign competition.[107] In the view of the Working Groups, those who

---

101. 50 U.S.C.A. § 2170(d)(4)(A)-(B) (West 2008).
102. Following FINSA's modifications, 'national security' must now be 'construed so as to include those issues relating to "homeland security," including its application to "critical infrastructure."' FINSA § 2. 'Critical infrastructure' is defined by FINSA as 'systems and assets, whether physical or virtual, so vital to the United States that the incapacity or destruction of such systems or assets would have a debilitating impact on national security.' *Id.* As noted in the main text, air transport clearly falls within these definitional parameters.
103. *See* Joseph Mamounas, *Controlling Foreign Ownership of U.S. Strategic Assets: The Challenge of Maintaining National Security in a Globalized and Oil Dependent World*, 13 LAW & BUS. REV. AM. 381, 395-96 (2007).
104. *See* Exec. Order No. 11,858, 40 Fed. Reg. 20,263 (May 7, 1975). FINSA's most critical adjustments are made to CFIUS's composition, *see* FINSA § 3 (expanding the composition of CFIUS and requiring its chairperson – the Secretary of the Treasury – to consult with the heads of other Federal agencies as the chairperson deems appropriate), mandate, *see id.* § 2 (specifying which transactions, including mergers, acquisitions or takeovers by or with foreign persons which could result in 'foreign control' fall under the statute, while expanding the factors CFIUS may examine during its investigation), and oversight, *see id.* § 7-8 (expanding the amount of Congressional oversight over CFIUS). Congressional oversight of CFIUS's activities became a hot button issue following approval of the controversial Dubai Ports World deal. *See* Editorial, *The Don't Invest in America Act*, WALL ST. J., Jul. 19, 2006; *see also infra* note 203 (discussing the Dubai Ports World transaction).
105. In instances where a national security concern presented itself, CFIUS has power to impose and enforce mitigating agreements with the parties involved in the transaction. *See* FINSA, *supra* note 100, § 5.
106. *See* Alan P. Larson & David M. Marchick, *Foreign Investment and National Security: Getting the Balance Right*, at 28, Council on Foreign Relations, CSR No. 18 (July 2006).
107. *See id.* Even without the economic security language, some commentators have drawn attention to the fact that the expanded composition of CFIUS and increased Congressional oversight

believe foreign investment in U.S. airlines will disrupt economic security –
displacing certain sectors of the U.S. air transport labor force – will take small
comfort from FINSA's strengthened national security focus.[108]

E   GLIMMERINGS OF MULTILATERALISM: SOME TENTATIVE
                     U.S. INITIATIVES

A common thread in the discourses considered in the previous Part was an
increasing awareness that any new paradigm should transcend the Chicago Convention's most pervasive commercial legacy, the restrictions on foreign ownership that
are keyed into all bilateral air services agreements.[109] This issue had been flagged,
albeit indirectly and incompletely, by the Airline Commission in 1993. The Commissioners endorsed a multilateral focus,[110] but felt unable to visualize precisely
how it should be achieved. Thus, while their most general recommendation – that the
long-range goal of an open multilateral system should shape immediate U.S.
international aviation policy – plainly influenced the language of the subsequent
1995 DOT policy statement,[111] their only *specific* nostrum was to endorse raising the
ceiling on foreign investment in U.S. air carriers closer to the new EC standard of
just below 50%,[112] in the context of bilateral agreements 'which are reciprocal

---

already 'create[s] new and additional opportunities and avenues for competitors of the parties
[involved] and/or opponents of a proposed transaction to have an impact on the CFIUS process
in order to block or heavily condition a transaction, or dissuade a potential buyer.' *See* Edward
L. Rubinoff & Henry Terhune, *New CFIUS Reform Act Presents Challenges to Foreign
Investment in the United States*, METRO. CORP. COUNSEL, Sept. 2007, at 29.

108. Another example of promoting private investment while protecting national security can be
found in the U.S. Bilateral Investment Treaty (BIT) Program. Every BIT allows for reciprocal
'right of establishment' and most-favored-nation treatment. *See* U.S. Department of State,
Treaty Between the Government of the United States of America and the Government of
[Country] Concerning the Encouragement and Reciprocal Protection of Investment, arts.
3-4, 2004 Model BIT (2004), <www.state.gov/documents/organization/38710.pdf>. The
BITs also include provisions for the maintenance of peace and security. *See id.* art. 18.

109. As noted, the Chicago Convention itself does not proscribe foreign ownership of domestic air
carriers. Those restrictions spread through the contagion of bilateralism. The foreign ownership rules, therefore, are more properly the legacy of the Chicago *system*, rather than of the
Convention itself, and are so treated in this book.

110. The Commission's report uses the term 'multi-national' [*sic*], a word that resonates with the
notion of global commercial enterprises, beginning with the huge American business corporations that dominated at mid-century. *See* ROBERT B. REICH, THE WORK OF NATIONS 65-66 (1992).
The choice of word is intriguing; the Commission spoke positively in its deliberations, and in
its final report, of the notion of ownership of airline carriers by nationals of one or more
countries. That airline companies, too, will become 'multinationals' will be the inevitable
consequence of true multilateralism. *Airline Commission Report, supra* note 63, at 21-23.

111. *See id.*

112. *Id.* (recommending a ceiling of 49%). Even the (second) Bush Administration, often portrayed
as jingoistic and reactionary in these matters, kept faith with earlier liberalizing initiatives by
asking Congress in 2003 to follow Europe's lead by raising the foreign voting stock ownership

and enhance the prospects of securing the ultimate goal of procompetitive, multinational agreements.'[113] A higher order of procompetitive bilaterals, therefore, would be the spur to a future multilateral settlement.

Some of these ideas were absorbed into the official thinking of U.S. aviation administrators. Although displaced as the lone pioneer in global aviation policy initiatives, the United States was not inactive during this first phase of the prelude to a post-bilateral order. In the waning days of the Clinton Administration, the United States sponsored a new Multilateral Agreement on the Liberalization of Air Transportation which was announced at Bandar Seri Begawan, Brunei, on November 15, 2000, and signed at Washington, D.C., on May 1, 2001.[114] This agreement, which entered into force on December 21, 2001, was an attempt to relaunch the open skies initiative multilaterally. The pact includes the United States and Asia-Pacific Economic Cooperation (APEC) partners Brunei, Chile, New Zealand, and Singapore.[115] Despite the exultant tone of U.S. Transportation Secretary Rodney E. Slater's accompanying press statement, the new agreement essentially stitched together the content of the individual bilateral open skies agreements and applied it multilaterally. Thus, misleadingly, the statement described the new agreement as a 'mirror' of the 'enormously successful U.S. Open-Skies [*sic*] bilateral agreements,' and expressed the hope that the new

---

cap to 49% from 25%. *See* Press Release, Air Transport Association, Statement on Foreign Ownership of U.S. Carriers (Jun. 13, 2003) [hereinafter Press Release, Foreign Ownership]. On the EC standard (conventionally understood to be 49.9%), *see infra* Chapter 3, Part V.

113. Press Release, Foreign Ownership, *supra* note 112. This proposal (like the Bush Administration proposal mentioned *supra* note 112) would require amendment of the Federal Aviation Act, which currently imposes a 25% cap on foreign ownership of the voting stock of U.S. airlines. Because only airlines that are owned and controlled by American citizens can legally offer domestic point-to-point service in the United States or be designated under U.S. bilateral agreements to provide international service from the United States, the practical effect of the ownership rule is to remove any incentive for a U.S. airline to sell itself to a foreign carrier and thereby forfeit its economic heritage. It appears that nothing in the federal aviation statutes would actually *prevent* such a sale; it is the citizenship consequences which constrain it. *See* F. Allen Bliss, *Rethinking Restrictions on Cabotage: Moving to Free Trade in Passenger Aviation*, 17 SUFFOLK TRANSNAT'L L. REV. 382, 399-401 (1994). On the citizenship tests generally, *see* discussion *infra* Chapter 3, Part V.

114. Multilateral Agreement on the Liberalization of International Air Transportation [May 2004] 3 Av. L. Rep. (CCH) ¶ 26,018, at 21,121 (Nov. 15, 2000) [hereinafter MALIAT]. For the complete text of the Agreement, and of a Protocol also signed at Washington on May 1, 2001 (among Brunei Darussalam, New Zealand, and Singapore), *see* MALIAT Homepage, <www.maliat.govt.nz/>.

115. *See* Press Release, U.S. DOT, United States, Asia-Pacific Aviation Partners Enter Multilateral Open Skies Agreement, DOT 222-00 (Nov. 15, 2000) [hereinafter Press Release, Asia-Pacific]. Though Australia signed but did not join the agreement, it has recently entered into a bilateral open skies agreement with the United States. *See* Press Release, U.S. Department of State, U.S. Reaches Open Skies Accord with Australia, 2008/115 (Feb. 15, 2008). For the text of the agreement, *see* Air Transport Agreement Between the Government of the United States and the Government of Australia [Feb. 2008] 3 Av. L. Rep. (CCH) ¶ 26,207g, at 21,850 (Feb. 14, 2008).

agreement '[would increase] the odds that the U.S. Open-Skies [*sic*] approach will become the international standard.'[116] Nevertheless, although the cabotage restriction remained, the agreement did modify the traditional ownership and control test in favor of a more plastic standard of 'effective control' by citizens of the designating party accompanied by incorporation and principal place of business in the State of the designating party.[117]

In December 1999, Secretary Slater, the last Clinton Administration Transportation Secretary, convened a multilateral meeting of transport ministers and directors-general of civil aviation from 93 countries in Chicago. The meeting had no anchoring in any existing assembly or organization. Secretary Slater labeled it a 'Ministerial;' as such, it was primarily a vanity invitation by the transportation supremo of the world's most formidable aviation power. The meeting, portentously captioned 'Aviation in the 21st Century: Beyond Open Skies,' nonetheless had the tonic effect of reinforcing a U.S. transition (in rhetorical terms, at least) to a multilateralist philosophy. In a press release, the United States pledged 'to initiate a policy dialogue on further liberalization, including possible plurilateral mechanisms for achieving a more open global aviation system.'[118] The discussions would be regional, focused on Europe (through the European Commission), Latin America, and Asia-Pacific (through APEC).[119] The press statement, interestingly, was only faintly echoed in the text of the conference final statement adopted on December 7, 1999. In a classically anodyne recitation of industry desiderata, the participants committed themselves merely to 'consider the possible advantages and disadvantages of new approaches for dealing with' challenges to aviation in the 21st century.[120] A separate 'Declaration on Next Steps,' adopted by open skies signatory countries, was hardly less vague, speaking of 'exploring the potential for aviation liberalization beyond Open Skies … including consideration of regional, multilateral and plurilateral systems.'[121]

---

116. Press Release, Asia-Pacific, *supra* note 115.
117. *See* MALIAT, *supra* note 114, art. 3.
118. Press Release, U.S. DOT, Slater: U.S. Prepared to Initiate Discussions Taking Aviation Agreements Beyond Open Skies, DOT 212-99 (Dec. 19, 1999) [hereinafter Press Release, Slater]. On the legal nature of plurilateral agreements, *see infra* note 121.
119. *See* Press Release, Slater, *supra* note 118.
120. U.S. DOT, Aviation in the 21st Century: Beyond Open Skies Ministerial 61 (1999) [hereinafter U.S. DOT, Aviation]. Otherwise, the statement recapitulated the history of bilateralism, and called for higher safety and security, an enhanced worldwide liability system, the promotion of efforts to improve provisions of airline operations in bilateral aviation agreements, assistance to developing countries, and attention to environmental issues. *See id.* Nonetheless, speakers did endorse aspects of multilateralism. The Dutch Minister of Transport and Public Works, for example, 'endorsed' the TCAA as 'a stepping-stone toward a multilateral aviation system.' *Id.* at 8.
121. *See* U.S. DOT, Aviation, *supra* note 120, at 66, app. V. Plurilateral agreements offer non-parties the opportunity to accede after the agreement has come into effect among its founding parties, but typically the latecomers must accept the terms of the agreement in their entirety.

In sum, there was a danger that the U.S. bridge to multilateralism would be a bridge to nowhere, merely incremental tinkering with existing open skies agreements but no bold *démarches* beyond the existing system. To force systemic change, in fact, a dynamic tribunal on the other side of the Atlantic, the European Court of Justice, would now play the critical role in delegitimizing the nationalist Chicago bilateral system.

III   FIXING A NEW HORIZON FOR OPEN SKIES: U.S./EC AVIATION RELATIONS AFTER 2003

The European Commission, as previously discussed, did battle with the EU Member States to uphold what the Commission took to be a principle of right: that the U.S. domestic aviation market juristically and commercially mirrors the EU's network of transnational but *intra-Union* air routes. By this reckoning, U.S. airlines should not be at liberty to serve intra-Union points (as fifth freedom extensions of transatlantic services) while Europe's airlines remained excluded from U.S. cabotage routes. Eventually, the Commission reached an existential appreciation that U.S. airlines already enjoyed commercially adequate access to the internal EU market through alliance-building with their larger EU confrères (and had been conspicuously pulling out of intra-EU fifth freedom routes operated as extensions of their transatlantic services).[122]

The Commission, therefore, articulated a reformulated position focused on the 'external' effects of open skies agreements. In this understanding, the bilateral

---

    See RESTATEMENT (THIRD) OF FOREIGN RELATIONS LAW OF THE UNITED STATES § 312 (1987). While the 2007 U.S./EC Air Transport Agreement is not *expressis verbis* a plurilateral, there is no doubt that its precedential force is well-understood by the U.S. and EC aviation administrations and that future iterations of this model may as a result be made explicitly plurilateral. In fact, this step would likely make sense initially for agreements that have a regional rather than transcontinental focus. The U.S. DOT, for example, revealed in mid-2007 that a huge trilateral open skies air transport agreement among the United States, Canada, and Mexico is in the contemplation of policymakers. This post-NAFTA initiative would offer seventh freedom rights, for example, that would allow Aeromexico to offer flights between Los Angeles and Toronto and Air Canada to compete with U.S. carriers on U.S./Europe routes as the agreement is looped into the liberalized U.S./EC traffic arrangements completed in 2007. For the official announcement of the initiative, *see* Press Release, U.S. DOT, U.S., Canada, Mexico Aim to Liberalize Air Transport in 10 Years (May 2, 2007) (noting unprecedented gathering of U.S., Canadian, and Mexican transportation ministers to discuss a 'vision' for North American transportation and to sign a Ministerial Declaration pledging a commitment to a trilateral open skies agreement); *see also* Andrzej Zwaniecki, *Plans for Open North American Aviation Market Inch Forward*, USINFO, Jun. 8, 2007.

122.   The plain fact is that U.S. carriers no longer use intra-Union traffic rights, having switched to code-shared connections with alliance partners. *See supra* note 43; *see also* Byerly, *Turbulent Times, supra* note 35. Thus, the U.S. carriers' commercial perception of the nonequivalency of intra-Union and intra-U.S. traffic rights now tracks the U.S. jurisprudential perception of this non-equivalency.

New York/Frankfurt market (for example) was reserved to German-owned carriers, and a potential rival like British Airways would be unable to exploit U.S./Germany traffic rights. This inbuilt rigidity, precisely the *raison d'être* of bilateral agreements, conflicted with the core tenets of national nondiscrimination animating the EU's single market enterprise. In the absence of coordinated 'Community' action, however, Member States have historically bargained individually with the United States and other foreign air powers.[123] Securing a common negotiating mandate would enable the European Commission to attack this discriminatory artifice, while also encouraging a consolidation of European airlines no longer bound to their domestic hubs.[124] As to the intra-United States cabotage argument, EU carriers were reportedly not directly interested in this privilege (fearing the costs of competition with U.S. carriers on the choicest routes),[125] but the liberalization of inward investment opportunities would certainly be a desirable alternative means of market access, and could also be secured as part of the Commission's future negotiating mandate.[126]

---

123. In setting out its transportation policy for the first decade of the 21st century, the European Commission called explicit attention to the disadvantageous position of EU carriers *vis-à-vis* their U.S. counterparts due to the nationality restrictions placed on the exercise of traffic rights under the open skies bilaterals. *See* European Commission, *White Paper on European Transport Policy for 2010: Time to Decide*, at 99, COM (2001) 370 final (Sept. 12, 2001). The Commission also noted that, as individual States, EU Member States had fared less well than the United States in negotiating access rights to third countries. As an example, the Commission pointed to the fact that EU carriers as a whole had a mere 160 slots at Tokyo's Narita airport while U.S. carriers held a staggering 640. *See id.* Such disparities, in the Commission's view, could only be rectified by the 'develop[ment] [of] an external dimension for [EU] air transport commensurate with the importance of the internal *acquis.*' *Id.*

124. In this process the Commission would also face the risk that third countries would not accord traffic rights to an airline operating from an EU Member State which was owned and controlled by nationals of other EU States. This structural resistance of the bilateral system would eventually have to be overcome by the sheer aeropolitical power of the European Union. *See infra* Chapter 6, Part III.

125. *See* EUROPEAN REPORT No. 2032, *supra* note 38, at 6. For further commentary, *see* remarks of Hermann de Croo, Chairman of the *Comité des Sages*, 142 Av. WK. & SPACE TECH. 29 (1995).

126. On the commercial and legal attraction of abolishing the nationality restriction rather than cabotage, *see infra* Part IV. It is worth indicating here that Article 21(2) of the 2007 U.S./EC Air Transport Agreement, *see supra* note 8, propounds a second stage agenda that implicitly contemplates cabotage ('further liberalization of traffic rights') and relaxation of inward investment restrictions ('additional foreign investment opportunities') as issues of 'priority interest.' As will be seen, *see infra* Chapter 4, Part III & Chapter 6, Part III, the U.S. position as articulated by its chief negotiator, U.S. Deputy Assistant Secretary of State for Transportation John Byerly, strongly resists any concession on cabotage in the second stage. Liberalization of foreign investment, on the other hand, is destined to be the crux of the next round of talks. *See U.S. Will Consider Relaxing Foreign Control Rules But Not Cabotage*, ATW DAILY NEWS, May 23, 2007, <http://www.atwonline.com/news/story.html?storyID=8981> [hereinafter ATW, *Not Cabotage*] (reporting Byerly's rhetorical query to the Baltimore/Washington International Airport Air Service Symposium: 'If British Petroleum is pumping gas into cars in the United States, why can't we have transnational airlines?').

And, more than all of that, the Commission argued that it could obtain a better value-added deal if it negotiated for the Community and its Member States as a whole.[127] Almost inevitably, given political realities on both sides of the Atlantic, such an outcome would be achieved by piecemeal stages rather than a negotiating donnybrook (or 'Armageddon,' as one U.S. official put it, though not for attribution).[128] And, within the EU itself, the Commission's quest for a negotiating mandate would unleash a high-stakes public policy competition among the EU legislative institutions, the Member States, and the aviation industry.

A   THE FORCE OF EC NONDISCRIMINATION LAW: THE EUROPEAN COURT DESTABILIZES THE NATIONALITY RULE

In 1998, the European Commission revived former Transport Commissioner Neil Kinnock's forensic strategy,[129] starting proceedings in the European Court of Justice for a declaration that seven Member States had concluded full open skies bilaterals with Washington that violated cardinal nondiscrimination and freedom of movement principles of the EC's commercial order.[130] The cases produced a jurisprudentially contentious but politically astute final opinion in November 2002,[131] spurring the European Commission to press the Council of the European Union (formerly the Council of Ministers) to appoint the Commission, the EU executive body, as sole negotiator for all Community external aviation relations.

    The Court, in fact, rejected the Commission's primary argument seeking *exclusive* Community competence to negotiate bilateral air services agreements with third countries.[132] Technically, therefore, the Court left Member States at

---

127. Byerly, *Charting the Course, supra* note 18, at 4.
128. Richard Carlson, Briefing Paper for the Air Transport Association 6 (Nov. 26, 2002) (copy on file with author).
129. *See supra* Part II(C).
130. *See* Cases C-467/98, C-468/98, C-469/98, C-471/98, C-472/98, C-475/98, and C-476/98, Comm'n v. Denmark, Sweden, Finland, Belgium, Luxembourg, Austria, and Germany, 2002 E.C.R. I-09519 *et seq.* An eighth defendant, the United Kingdom, was named although the U.S./U.K. relationship had never produced an open skies arrangement. *See* Case C-466/98, Comm'n *v.* U.K., 2002 E.C.R. I-09427. The U.S./U.K. agreement, popularly called 'Bermuda II,' *see infra* note 215, contained restrictive nationality provisions similar to those in the open skies agreements, but was much more circumscribed in its grant of traffic rights. *See* European Commission, *Consequences, supra* note 20, paras. 27-28.
131. Virgin Group chief Richard Branson's comment following publication of the ruling was typically pithy (and unsettling to authors of aviation law books): 'Never mind the detailed legal arguments, this decision is a major political statement.' Branson, *supra* note 12, at 2.
132. In summary, the Commission had argued that EC aviation law has developed so substantially that the Commission should, in accordance with existing Court jurisprudence (most notably the so-called 'AETR' principle), be granted exclusive competence over external aviation relations. The AETR principle, named after an eponymous European Court of Justice proceeding, provides that 'whenever the European Community ha[s] included in its internal legislative acts provisions relating to the treatment of nationals of non-member countries, it acquires an exclusive external competence in the spheres covered by those acts.' European

liberty to continue to negotiate third-country bilaterals provided they respected the specific areas identified by the Court where the Commission does have exclusive competence arising from prior EC legislation (*i.e.*, with respect to computer reservations systems, aspects of intra-Union fares, and take-off and landing slots),[133] and also honored the Court's ruling striking down the nationality clauses in bilateral agreements that require each Member State to designate only its own national airlines to serve air routes negotiated with third countries outside the EU.[134]

The propulsive element of the 2002 European Court of Justice ruling was its conclusion that the bilateral nationality restrictions in the challenged open skies agreements prevented full exercise (by 'Community air carriers'[135]) of the freedom (or 'right') of establishment embedded in the Rome Treaty.[136] The concept of the

---

Commission, *Consequences, supra* note 20, at 7. *See infra* Chapter 5, Part II(E). The Court, however, found that the trio of EC air transport liberalization 'packages' did not completely govern the situation of air carriers from non-Member States which operate within the European Union.

133. An illuminating speech by U.S. DOT Under Secretary for Policy, Jeffrey N. Shane questioned the bilateral pertinence of these areas of competence. *See* Jeffrey N. Shane, Under Secretary for Policy, U.S. Department of Transportation, *Open Skies Agreements and the European Court of Justice*, Remarks to the American Bar Association's Forum on Air and Space Law, Hollywood, Florida (Nov. 8, 2002) [hereinafter Shane, *Open Skies Agreements*]. On slots, Shane noted that the European Court of Justice found that 'not one of the bilateral agreements [challenged by the Commission] contained any such provision.' *Id.* On intra-Union prices, he observed that the European Community no longer regulates prices for intra-Union air services, and that, in any case, most U.S./EC Member State open skies agreements 'already recognize that [Community] law does not entitle U.S. airlines to be price leaders on [intra-Union] routes.' *Id.* With respect to computer reservations systems, Shane emphasized that no U.S. airline any longer owns a system in its own right and therefore the historic need to combat EU exclusivity and bias has been eliminated. Moreover, while U.S. and EC rules continue to show differences, they both exist to promote 'fair competition,' and he saw little purpose to maintaining computer reservations systems provisions in open skies agreements. *Id.* The Commission, reviewing the directory of EC legislation, has subsequently added several further dimensions to its realm of claimed 'exclusive' competence, including safety, commercial opportunities (groundhandling and consumer protection), customs duties (for aircraft supplies and aviation fuel), and environmental (including noise reduction) rules. *See* European Commission, *Consequences, supra* note 20, para. 31. In the Commission's view, other areas covered by EC legislation 'shape the trading environment' even though not directly addressed in international agreements – these areas include denied boarding compensation, air carrier liability, package travel, and data protection. *Id.* para. 32; *see also* European Commission, Press Release, Denunciation, *supra* note 65.

134. For a more detailed consideration of the issue of 'nationality' clauses in bilateral agreements, *see infra* Chapter 3, Part V; *see also* Shane, *Open Skies Agreements, supra* note 133 (comparing notion of EC 'competence' to U.S. doctrine of preemption of state governments by federal supremacy); *see generally* René Fennes, *The European Court of Justice Decision on Bilateral Agreements: The Future of Relations*, AIR & SPACE LAW., Winter 2003, at 17.

135. 'Community air carrier' is a defined term of EC legislation. *See infra* Chapter 5, Part II(C).

136. Article 43 of the EC Treaty provides as a principle of nondiscrimination that the freedom of 'establishment' includes the right to set up and manage undertakings under the conditions laid down for its own nationals by the legislation of the Member State in which establishment is effected.

'Community air carrier' appeared in a 1992 Community regulation which provides that airlines licensed in any Member State (under common EC criteria)[137] have the right to operate without discrimination as though licensed in any other Member State, and can be owned and controlled by any Member State or by the nationals of any Member State.[138] Moreover, since 1997 all 'Community air carriers' in principle enjoy unrestricted market access to all intra-Union air routes, including domestic ('cabotage')[139] routes within Member States. In the reasoning of the European Court of Justice, the nationality clause in a bilateral agreement between one of the defendant Member States and a third country (*in situ*, the United States) meant that Community air carriers from other Member States would always be excluded from the benefit of that agreement, while that benefit was assured exclusively to air carriers of the Member State which negotiated the agreement. Accordingly, EU airlines would suffer trade discrimination in being prevented by the negotiating Member State from benefiting from the treatment (access to third-country routes from airports in that State) accorded to the Member State's own national air carriers.[140]

Interestingly, the Court's finding invalidated not only the nationality provisos of the challenged open skies bilaterals, but similar provisions in *all* Member State bilaterals with third countries.[141] Thus, the most aggressive jurisprudential aspect of the Court's decision – as will be more fully canvassed in Chapter 5 – is how a relatively innocuous antidiscrimination provision, which previously had been applied in mundane matters of mutual recognition of qualifications and diploma equivalency,[142] could become the open sesame for bestowing third-country air traffic rights from each Member State upon all EC-licensed air carriers.[143]

---

137. *See infra* Chapter 5, Part III(E).
138. *See* Council Regulation 2407/92, 1992 O.J. (L 240) 1. For a more detailed treatment of the terms of this legislation, *see infra* Chapter 5, Part II(C). Note in particular that not only *can* the incidents of ownership and control be in the hands of any Member State or nationals of any Member State, these incidents *must* be in such hands under EC law as well as international bilateral treaty law.
139. On the origins and significance of cabotage in air transport law, *see infra* Chapter 3, Part IV.
140. The ECJ opinion on open skies will be analyzed in greater detail, *infra* Chapter 5, Part III(D).
141. *See* European Commission, *Communication from the Commission on Relations Between the Community and Third Countries in the Field of Air Transport*, paras. 36-41, COM (2003) 94 final (Feb. 26, 2003) [hereinafter European Commission, *Relations*]; *see also* Fennes, *supra* note 134, at 16.
142. *See generally* PAUL B. STEPHAN ET AL., THE LAW AND ECONOMICS OF THE EUROPEAN UNION 629 *et seq.* (2003) (considering representative cases).
143. As noted earlier in the main text, since the adoption of the third package of airline liberalization reforms in 1992, the requirements for the licensing of air carriers have been harmonized throughout the EC. Accordingly, an operating license issued in any EU Member State under the harmonized criteria must be recognized in all of the other Member States, creating the concept of a 'Community air carrier.' *See infra* Chapter 5, Part II(C). René Fennes has posited the following hypothetical, which arises from the simple premise of the Court's ruling on the nationality clauses:

    Olympic Airways could go to the French Government and apply for a permit to operate Paris to Lima just like a French carrier could. Should there be enough room in the applicable

Further, invocation of the right of establishment presupposes a preexisting 'subsidiary, branch, or agency' in the State from which those third-country traffic rights will be exercised.[144] If a Community carrier licensed in one Member State has only a ticketing office – or even just a telephone answering service – in another Member State, would the carrier be entitled (once again on grounds of nondiscrimination) to claim designation under the second State's bilaterals to serve third-country routes or, even more intrusively, the right to participate in the preparation and conduct of negotiations with respect to that State's air services agreements with third countries?[145] Assertion of these rights based solely on the right of establishment (which appears to generate national treatment rights from a mere modicum of business presence) would set up a normative conflict with the significantly more onerous requirements of the EC rules on operator and aircraft operator licenses.[146]

The European Commission quickly acknowledged the need for more legal coherence as it approached the task of reconciling all of the bilateral air services agreements of all the Member States with the prescriptions of Community antidiscrimination law.[147] A later regulatory clarification spoke of establishment as

---

bilateral to accommodate Olympic, then France would have to allow the operation. Should there not be enough or no sufficient room, then the authorities in France would have to ensure that Olympic would be eligible for such operation, similar [to] French carriers, once it became possible, or to the extent the operational room allowed, under non-discriminatory, consistent and transparent administrative rules. The only ones that would be able to stop the operation would be the Peruvians! But France would be under obligation to amend the bilateral agreement concerned to allow for all carriers established in France under Community rules.

Fennes, *supra* note 134, at 18. For a fuller treatment of the issue of allocating third-country rights under Member State bilateral air service agreements, *see infra* Chapter 5, Part III.

144. *See* EC Treaty art. 43.
145. *See* European Commission, *Relations, supra* note 141, para. 16.
146. *See infra* Chapter 5, Part III. Thus, as René Fennes also emphasizes, the applicable EC legislation restricts the grant of a license to airlines which have their 'principal place of business' and 'registered office' in the licensing Member State. Fennes, *supra* note 134, at 18. Accordingly, it may be necessary to set up a full-fledged subsidiary in the second Member State, rather than merely a branch or agency. *See generally* Michael F. Goldman, *Saving Open Skies Agreements In Light of The European Court's Recent Ground-Breaking Decision*, ACI-NA CENTERLINES, Spring 2003, at 20 (noting that some EC law experts believe that to exploit the right of establishment principle, an Irish carrier such as Aer Lingus would have to set up a subsidiary in France, obtain a French air operator's certificate, and operate French-registered aircraft; in other words, France would not be obliged to designate Aer Lingus under the U.S./France bilateral, but would be obliged to designate Aer Lingus (France), a French airline company owned by Aer Lingus.
147. *See* European Commission, *Relations, supra* note 141, para. 20. The Commission took the view that the Court's opinion had instantly invalidated *all* existing bilateral agreements (not just the open skies agreements in issue) to the extent they enforce a nationality-based exclusion on access to third-country routes. *See id.* But the Commission also accepted that the complexity of the situation, as well as the existence of incumbent access rights, should not be jeopardized by a legal imbroglio within the Community. Accordingly, the Commission pledged to 'limit . . . the changes needed to the balance of rights that has been achieved under the existing framework of bilateral agreements,' while maintaining that 'changes

'the effective and real exercise of air transport activity through stable arrange-ments,' while the legal form of such an establishment (branch, subsidiary, legal personality, and so forth) continued to be nondeterminative.[148] But this definition cannot, surely, be dispositive. On the contrary, it proposes a conceptual antinomy that separates an 'effective and real exercise of air transport activity' (*i.e.*, by which a carrier 'establishes' a presence in a Member State) from a 'principal place of business' which a carrier would maintain in a Member State *other than* the State of establishment. Clearly, the intention of the concept of 'establishment' is to allow a Community carrier, with a principal place of business in the United Kingdom, for example, to fly from the territory of Germany within the limits of the bilateral air services agreement between Germany and, let us say, Brazil.[149] How much busi-ness should the British carrier be doing in Germany to demand this exercise of rights in a Member State that is not its principal place of business or one of its principal places of business? The legislation appears to assume, casuistically, that something *less than* a principal place of business attachment should suffice, but nevertheless falls short of the definitional rigor that could distinguish 'establish-ment' through a ticket office from mere presence through a telephone answering service.[150]

B   Managing the Fallout: The Commission Secures
           A Second (Double) Mandate

Despite the Court's implicit finding that the crown jewels of bilateral deal-making – the award of route rights – remained legally within Member State

---

must be made to the current regime in order to bring existing relations with third countries into line with the Court's rulings of 5 November 200[2].' *Id.* para. 24. And the Commission went further, promising to 'add value' to the existing situation and not just to fill the legal vacuum forced by the Court's opinion. *Id.* In this regard, as a tactical matter, the Commission has correctly intuited that only a unified approach – in other words, deployment of the aeropolitical power of the EU – could coax third countries into compliance with the nondiscrimination standards imposed by the Court of Justice. *See id.* paras. 36-41.

148.   Council Regulation 847/2004, recital 10, 2004 O.J. (L 157) 7.
149.   *See* European Commission, *Relations, supra* note 141, para. 16.
150.   It is difficult to imagine that EC law would permit an air carrier licensed in one Member State which seeks access to another Member State's extra-Union routes to receive that access on the basis of merely having a business office (much less an answering service) in the second State. In light of the bilateral nature of the relationship (with a third country), it would seem appro-priate to require that the airline would also obtain an operating license and aircraft operator certificate from the granting State, so that the mere place of doing business would be coupled with a condition of regulatory oversight. *See* Fennes, *supra* note 134, at 18 (noting that 'it would be difficult to refuse carriers that have an [operating license] and [aircraft operator certificate] from another Member State and thus are perfectly safe to operate on intra-[Union] routes and allowed to do so under EC law').

competence,[151] the Commission managed the fallout from the Court's attack on nationality clauses to its own strategic advantage. Initially, the Commission caused disgruntlement (not just in the United States) when it imperiously summoned all Member States to denounce their existing bilateral agreements with the United States.[152] Although the Commission properly took its cue in this respect both from

---

151. A finding that prompted Jeffrey N. Shane, Under Secretary for Policy, U.S. Department of Transportation, to comment that the European Court had not rejected the 'central features' of the open skies agreements. Shane, *Open Skies Agreements, supra* note 133 (stating that '[t]raffic rights, in a real sense, are the *whole point* of an air services agreement' (emphasis in original)); *see also* Goldman, *supra* note 146, at 20-21.

152. *See* Press Release, Denunciation, *supra* note 65; *see also* European Commission, *Consequences, supra* note 20, para. 27. Procedurally, the Commission used the form of a blunt letter to EU Member States bearing the signature of the Commission's late Director General for Energy and Transport, François Lamoureux. The letter noted 'a series of diplomatic démarches by the United States' promoting bilateral adjustment of the problematic nationality clauses. 'I am writing to caution your government against entertaining any such approach from the United States,' M. Lamoureux declared. He insisted that, in the Commission's view, 'the only acceptable response to the [ruling of the Court of Justice] is for Member States to give notice of denunciation of the existing agreements with the United States and to proceed with the adoption of a mandate for a Community negotiation with the United States forthwith.' Forecasting legal action against Member States which did not comply with this 'only acceptable response,' M. Lamoureux closed by remarking that 'bilateral discussions on the basis of a foreign government's partial interpretation of our internal European legal system would be unlikely to result in a satisfactory final outcome for European countries.' A copy of the letter circulated widely at the time. It was described by one U.S. industry leader (somewhat hyperbolically) as 'not merely blunt . . . [but also] nasty.' (Lamoureux was subsequently described by his former EU superior, Pascal Lamy (now Director-General of the World Trade Organization), as someone whose passion for European integration sometimes impaired his sensitivity to political realities, leading to counterproductive outcomes. *See Obituary – Francois Lamoureux,* 12 EUROPEAN VOICE, Aug. 31, 2006. Interestingly, the so-called démarches did exist, coordinated through the U.S. carriers' trade association, the Air Transport Association. The proposed changes would have included deleting the computer reservations system annex from each bilateral, removing intra-Union prices from coverage by the pricing article, and ending the designation article to allow the other party to designate airlines established in its territory (through incorporation and principal place of business) but owned and controlled by any EU nationals. For a foreshadowing of this strategy, *see* Shane, *Open Skies Agreements, supra* note 133. (The Shane speech was posted on the website of the U.S. State Department and sent to all U.S. embassies, and was described by U.S. Deputy Assistant Secretary of State John Byerly, the State Department's chief EC negotiator, as 'personal and authoritative;' Carlson, *supra* note 128.) According to U.S. Government sources, the EU Member States (and incoming acceding States) were also puzzled by the Commission's denunciation strategy, and considered the existing bilateral agreements to remain in force. *See* Carlson, *supra* note 128. This attitude was particularly noticeable among countries with carriers in immunized alliances with U.S. carriers (*i.e.*, alliances which had the benefit of U.S. antitrust immunity). *See infra* Chapter 4, Part III(C). U.S. officials conveyed (through diplomatic cables) that continued antitrust immunity was based on the existence of an open skies agreement, not on comity and reciprocity. *See* Jeffrey N. Shane, Under Secretary for Policy, U.S. Department of Transportation, Remarks to the International Aviation Club, Washington, D.C., at 5 (Sept. 12, 2006), <www.iacwashington.org/speeches/JNS_IAC_Speech_Final_09-12-2006.pdf> (commenting that 'without legally secure open-skies agreements with their guarantee of open market entry, it is very difficult to see how we could continue to justify immunity

its Treaty-enshrined role as guardian of the EU treaties as well as from the earlier opinion of the Advocate-General,[153] it clearly appreciated that, as a matter of international law, the agreements continued to bind the United States despite the post-ruling 'domestic' irregularity within the Community.[154]

The Commission's call for denunciation was intended, it seems, to discourage Member States (and their bilateral partners) from treating the opinion as merely an abstract inconvenience that could be checked by the need to preserve international air commerce.[155] When sovereign States are the object of supranational legal rulings, there is inevitably the potential for delayed compliance.[156] The Commission needed

---

from antitrust enforcement for airlines that are potential competitors') [hereinafter Shane, IAC Remarks]. For further analysis of how the issue of antitrust immunity affected negotiations for the 2007 U.S./EC air services agreement, *see infra* Chapter 4, Part III(C).

153. *See* Calleja, *supra* note 25, at 7. With respect to the nationality clauses, the Advocate-General appeared to believe that the Member State defendants had a responsibility to renounce their U.S. bilaterals. *See* Cases C-466-69, 71-72, & 75-76, Opinion of Advocate General Tizzano, paras. 143-44 (Jan. 31, 2002); *see also* Joan M. Feldman, *Transatlantic Two-step*, AIR TRANSP. WORLD, Apr. 2002, at 43.

154. *See* European Commission, *Consequences, supra* note 20, para. 34 (noting that the Court 'could not have invalidated the agreements under international law'). The principle of *pacta sunt servanda* guides both Community and Member State law. *See* Fennes, *supra* note 134, at 17. *See also* AEA, POLICY STATEMENT ON EXTERNAL RELATIONS (2003) (recognizing importance 'for political reasons that the [European Union] as a whole and the Member States individually are seen to remain credible and reliable international partners') [hereinafter AEA, POLICY STATEMENT]. Indeed, the initial U.S. reaction to the European Court's ruling, expressed by Under Secretary for Policy Jeffrey N. Shane, was that the nationality clause problem was 'all about Europe, not about the [United States].' Shane, *Open Skies Agreements, supra* note 133. Choosing to ignore the equally restrictive effects of domestic legislation that precludes foreign ownership and control of national airlines, Shane also noted the essentially permissive nature of the bilateral nationality clauses, and that the United States has on occasion waived its rights under such provisions. *See* Shane, *Open Skies Agreements, supra* note 133 (recalling U.S. accommodation of multinational ownership for aviation partners from Scandinavia, Africa, and the Caribbean); *see also* Havel, *supra* note 12, at 13,208-09 (discussing examples of U.S. waiver policy with respect to nationality clauses in bilateral agreements).

155. EU aviation industry leaders were unsettled by the Commission's apparent *lèse majesté*. The leading industry trade lobbyist, the AEA, warned that 'strong statements made by the European Union institutions in this internal discussion may carry an unintended and possibly negative message to our foreign partners and the public.' AEA, POLICY STATEMENT, *supra* note 154. The AEA was particularly concerned to preserve the stability of 'the body of rights agreed between Member States and third countries.' *Id.*

156. This has already been the historical experience with the post-1995 World Trade Organization panel and Appellate Body rulings. *See, e.g.,* WTO Appellate Body Report, *United States – Section 211 of Omnibus Appropriations Act of 1998*, WT/DS176/AB/R (Jan. 2, 2002) (finding United States in violation of TRIPS); Modification of the Agreement, *United States – Section 211 of Omnibus Appropriations Act of 1998*, WT/DS176/14 (Dec. 24, 2003) (reporting agreement by United States and EC to extend the time for implementation of the rulings of the Dispute Settlement Body to Dec. 31, 2004); Modification of the Agreement, *United States – Section 211 of Omnibus Appropriations Act of 1998*, WT/DS176/15 (Dec. 21, 2004) (reporting agreement by United States and EC to again extend the period for implementation, this time to Jun. 30, 2005); Status Report by the United States, *United States – Section 211 of Omnibus*

a dramatic gesture to impress upon Member States, despite the 'tension and acrimony' engendered by the litigation,[157] the juristic inescapability of the ruling by the
Community's highest court that their bilaterals now violated EC law.[158] Moreover,
the ruling necessarily implied that the main reason for bilateral deals – to protect
national carriers on international routes – would no longer be legally viable.[159]

Appropriations Act of 1998, WP/DS176/11/Add.68 (Jul. 21, 2008) (reporting by United States
for the 68th time in five years on its failure to implement the Appellate Body's ruling); *but see*
Bruce Wilson, *Compliance by WTO Members with Adverse WTO Dispute Settlement Rulings:
The Record to Date*, 10 J. Econ. L. 397 (2007) (recording a 'quite good' compliance record by
WTO members with adverse rulings, but with significant exceptions and delays, and noting in
particular that legislative action presents more difficulties for compliance than simple administrative action).

157. Byerly, *Charting the Course, supra* note 18, at 5. In later assessing the reasons for the collapse
of the first post-ruling U.S./EC negotiations (in 2003/2004) Byerly contrasted what he called a
'broad consensus' in the United States among government and private sector stakeholders
(including a decade of open skies negotiations) with the resentment of Member States forced
into unhappy collaboration with the European Commission. *Id.*

158. The Commission's instruction to activate the typical one-year denunciation period was applied
to all of the then 15 Member States. *See* Press Release, Denunciation, *supra* note 65. The
Commission's strong position, in fairness, was legally correct as a matter of internal Community law. Article 10 (ex-Article 5) of the EC Treaty is crystalline in its requirement that
Member States 'shall take all appropriate measures, whether general or particular, to ensure
fulfillment of the obligations arising out of the Treaty or resulting from action taken by
institutions of the Community.' The Court did hold that, in the case of an infringement stemming from an international agreement, Member States cannot contract new international
commitments and cannot maintain in force any infringing commitments. *See id.*; *but see*
Dow Jones Business News, *France's Air Pact With China Tests New EC Aviation Laws*
(Feb. 27, 2003) (noting that, despite the new dispensation, in Jan. 2003 France signed a
new bilateral 'trade accord' granting exclusive routes for Air France into Canton, China);
see also Dow Jones Business News, *European Airlines Want Common Line on International
Air Pacts* (Mar. 11, 2003) (reporting U.K. reluctance to sign an agreement with China that was
not open to all EU Member States). Indeed, since the commencement of the action, France,
Italy, and Portugal had all entered new 'open skies' agreements with the United States. In
2004, the Commission brought new proceedings against these Member States in addition to the
Netherlands. *See* Press Release, Denunciation, *supra* note 65; Press Release, Delegation of the
European Commission to the U.S., EU Commission Takes Action to Enforce 'Open Skies'
Court Rulings, No. 116/04 (Jul. 20, 2004). As an aside, it is interesting that even in 2007, on the
brink of the signing of the U.S./EC Air Transport Agreement, *see supra* note 8, a major
European business leader could still state publicly that compliance with ECJ rulings could
not justify what he considered to be a 'bad deal.' Martin Broughton, Chairman, British Airways, Speech to the Chatham House Conference (Mar. 5, 2007) (stating that '[t]he German
Presidency and the rest of the Council [of the European Union] must not be satisfied with a bad
deal just to satisfy the Commission's legal obligations'). Aside from Mr. Broughton's mis-
conception of the universality of the Court's declaration of 'legal obligations,' the sentiment he
expresses appears to show that, among some EU elites, the jurisprudential 'stickiness' of the
Court's supranational rulings remains a work in progress.

159. 'The ownership and control clause is there precisely because of the nature of these agreements:
they are bilateral.' Fennes, *supra* note 134, at 17. Naturally, this realization helped persuade
Member States that common negotiations were the only way to preserve their negotiating
power with third countries.

The denunciation gambit, offensive as it appeared to many,[160] did achieve its minacious purpose. Spurred by an activist Transport Commissioner (former Spanish cabinet minister, the late Loyola de Palacio), in February 2003 the Commission presented a fresh set of 'mandate' proposals to the Council of the European Union (the Council of Ministers).[161] The proposals, written primarily by European Commission aviation official Ludolf van Hasselt, sought to capitalize on the momentum of the landmark Court of Justice judgment in November 2002.[162]

Ultimately, despite some political reservations,[163] the Council of Ministers erected the framework for an EC external aviation policy when it adopted two decisions in May 2003, in effect granting the Commission a dual or double negotiation mandate.[164] The first, and most radical, of the two mandates moved negotiation of all Member State bilaterals with the United States from the sovereign remit of each Member State to the executive and collective responsibility of the

---

160. And not just to the European side, as already observed *supra* note 152. After the EU Council of Transport Ministers' rejection of the U.S./EC draft agreement in 2004, *see infra* text accompanying note 177, the European Commission seemed to focus again, to U.S. dismay, on denunciation as a strategic option to propel change. *See* Byerly, *Charting the Course*, *supra* note 18, at 16 (noting that '[i]nternal [EU] squabbling over denunciation can only distract us from a focus on substantive negotiations ... and might even prevent the resumption of our negotiations').

161. *See supra* main text for an analysis of the Commission's strategies and tactics in obtaining the new mandates. The AEA anticipated the Court judgment and the new mandate request by commissioning an economic analysis of an EC agreement with the United States that might supersede the existing regime of bilaterals. *See* BRATTLE GROUP, *supra* note 81; *see also* BOOZ ALLEN HAMILTON, THE ECONOMIC IMPACTS OF AN OPEN AVIATION AREA BETWEEN THE EUROPEAN UNION AND THE UNITED STATES: FINAL REPORT (2007) (updating the 2002 Brattle Group report with further examination of the implications of the agreement for social and labor policy, along with covering implications for the cargo industry in greater detail). Creating an economic forecast of this kind, while it has some clear polemic merit, cannot reveal the dynamic network consequences of the plurilateral solution proposed in Chapter 6 *infra*. Incidentally, the Brattle Group's report did tend to confirm the fears expressed by EC officials that bilateral open skies agreements have drained traffic from larger aviation markets. *See supra* note 81. In its initial years, for example, the KLM/Northwest transatlantic alliance, *see infra* Chapter 3, Part VIII, caused an 80% increase in the number of German passengers traveling via Amsterdam (instead of using German airports) to New York between 1992 and 1995, even though the total number of German passengers from Germany to the United States remained stable. *See* Caroline Southey, *Brussels Concern Over Air Deals*, FIN. TIMES, Dec. 7, 1995.

162. The proposals had been heralded by a Commission Communication dated Nov. 19, 2002, which comprised a stocktaking of the European Community's external aviation relations after the Court's judgment. *See* European Commission, *Consequences*, *supra* note 20.

163. And a high level of mutual suspicion between the European Commission and the Member States. *See infra* note 182 (discussing comments of U.S. lead negotiator John Byerly).

164. The decisions were adopted based on submissions to the Council by the European Commission. *See* European Commission, *Relations*, *supra* note 141, paras 29, 35, & 75 (urging Council to take decisions to authorize Community negotiations on the creation of an Open Aviation Area, *see infra* note 166, with the United States, and on the designation of Community carriers on international routes to and from third countries and on matters within Community exclusive competence).

European Commission.[165] The Commission projected the potential outcome of this mandate as an 'Open Aviation Area' (OAA), intending to dissociate its new mandate from the much-derided TCAA.[166] Under the mandate, EC delegations pursued two consecutive sets of negotiations with their U.S. counterparts between October 2003 and March 2007; after rejection of a draft agreement by the Council of the European Union in June 2004, a revived set of negotiations culminated in an eventual U.S./EC air transport agreement signed in April 2007.[167] The Council's award of this comprehensive mandate truly represented a much broader grant of authority than what was necessitated by the European Court of Justice ruling.[168] In effect, the new mandate, through conclusion of a single agreement, would displace all of the existing directory of bilateral air services agreements between the 27 EU Member States and the United States.

The second mandate, known as the 'horizontal' mandate (and thereby to be distinguished from the 'vertical' mandate for comprehensive negotiations with the United States), authorized the Commission to conduct simultaneous bilateral treaty revisions with non-Member States (other than the United States) to bring all of these States' bilateral treaties with Member States into compliance – by inserting a small catalogue of standardized clauses – with the open skies rulings of the European Court of Justice. In Chapter 5, we will examine the horizontal mandate in more detail, as well as the Commission's quest for additional vertical mandates with other major air powers and its incremental extension of the single aviation

---

165. *See* Press Release, Europa, New Era for Air Transport: Loyola de Palacio Welcomes the Mandate Given to the European Commission for Negotiating an Open Aviation Area with the U.S., IP/03/806 (Jun. 5, 2003).

166. Woll, *supra* note 6, at 13. As noted below, however, *see infra* Part V, the substantive reach of the Open Aviation Area (OAA) reflected the agenda set by the TCAA. In that respect, of course, it did not correspond with U.S. expectations. But the phrase has entered the Commission's commonplace vocabulary, replacing TCAA more for terminological than conceptual reasons. As has been pointed out, 'on the one hand [TCAA] refers too much to an enlargement of the European Common Aviation Area, and on the other, by naming it "Transatlantic", it cannot extend itself in the future to include other areas beyond the Western Hemisphere and Europe.' H.S. Rutger Jan toe Laer, *The ECJ Decision: 'Blessing in Disguise'?*, 31 AIR & SPACE L. 19, 24 (2006).

167. The former EC Transport Commissioner, Loyola de Palacio, described the U.S./EC negotiations in 2003 as the Commission's 'uppermost priority' in international aviation relations. European Commission, Press Release, Open Skies: Commission Sets Out its International Aviation Policy, Brussels, Feb. 26, 2003, IP/03/281; *see also* AEA, POLICY STATEMENT, *supra* note 154 (describing a U.S./EC concordat as 'the priority issue that by far outweighs all others,' and proposing that harmonized U.S./EC policies should include 'security, information exchange and privacy protection, insurance and financial assistance,' as well as 'investment, open market access and [a] level playing field, and – with particular emphasis – convergence of competition policy').

168. Nevertheless, the mandate evidently did not include authority to negotiate fifth and seventh freedom rights outside the U.S./EU market. In that sense, it was described as '[n]ot fully complete' by one of the leading U.S. negotiators. *See* Byerly, *Charting the Course, supra* note 18, at 6.

market to the EU's eastern and southern geographic neighborhood – an unprecedented project to create a 'European Common Aviation Area' by 2010.[169]

IV   THE TRAJECTORY OF U.S./EC AIR SERVICES
             NEGOTIATIONS 2003-2007

A   Toward a U.S./EC Agreement I: Political Stalemate

At the U.S./EU Summit in June 2003, President George W. Bush and his EU political counterparts announced the formal start of comprehensive U.S./EU air transport negotiations.[170] The U.S. delegation, in what later seemed a tactical (if not strategic) error, offered to defy the Chicago system by accepting a new ownership and control clause that would have authorized every Community air carrier to operate to any and all U.S. points from any and all points in the EU.[171] This concession in theory would have reduced the legal impediments to transborder intra-Union mergers or acquisitions among EU carriers operating transatlantic services.[172] But that merger/acquisition possibility (which would allow, for example, British Airways to buy Iberia)[173] would risk a withdrawal of traffic rights by countries (other than the United States) which would continue to apply the Chicago ownership and control restrictions.[174] The other significant U.S. proposal

---

169. *See infra* Chapter 5, Part II(E).
170. *See* Byerly, *Charting the Course, supra* note 18, at 2 (noting that the joint declaration predicted 'an historic opportunity to build upon the framework of existing agreements with the goal of opening access to markets and maximizing benefits for consumers, airlines, and communities on both sides of the Atlantic'). The negotiations commenced in Oct. 2003. At U.S. urging, industry representatives (from airlines, airports, labor, and computer reservations system associations) were included in the negotiating sessions alongside the usual array of government departmental officials. *See id.* at 6-7. Byerly claims that the Commission initially opposed this approach, although private stakeholder inclusion is established U.S. practice, and that this opposition 'soured somewhat [the Commission's] relationship with European stakeholders.' *Id.*
171. Thus, as chief negotiator John Byerly perceived the offer, British Airways could operate seventh freedom services from Frankfurt, Lufthansa from Warsaw, Virgin Atlantic from Brussels, or easyJet from Paris. *Id.* at 7.
172. European Transport Commissioner Loyola de Palacio had argued prior to the talks that transborder consolidation and rationalization of the EU air transport industry was a 'pressing need.' *Id.*
173. This precise combination of carriers was in fact announced in late Jul. 2008. In light of rising fuel costs and an increasingly competitive market, the two carriers proposed to establish a joint holding company and to divide ownership shares according to their respective market values. Daniel Michaels, *British Air, Iberia in Talks to Combine*, Wall St. J., Jul. 20, 2008, at B1. The merger would not affect each carrier's branding and both would operate relatively independently of the other. *Id.* In addition to the merger proposal, both carriers planned to deepen their working relationship with American Airlines as part of the oneworld alliance. *Id.*
174. *Pace* U.S. negotiator John Byerly's claim that the U.S. proposal would have 'eliminated immediately, fully, and permanently all legal barriers in a comprehensive agreement to the merger of [EU] carriers,' the proposed agreement would only have had bilateral effects on the U.S./EC relationship. Byerly, *Charting the Course, supra* note 18, at 8.

was to seek Congressional approval for an initiative, considered 'primarily symbolic' by the European side, to increase foreign ownership limits for U.S. airline voting stock from 25% to 49%.[175] In return, the principal U.S. objective was to extend open skies to all of the Member States of the EU.[176]

On June 11, 2004, less than a year later and after six formal rounds of talks, the EU Council of Transport Ministers rejected a tentative U.S./EC air transport agreement presented to them by Commissioner de Palacio. Casting its decision in highly political terms, the Council regressed to an earlier Commission theme and considered that it was impossible to defend a situation where U.S. airlines could exercise traffic rights within the EU but European airlines were shut out of comparable opportunities inside the United States.[177]

In a speech to the International Aviation Club in Washington, D.C., just after the Council's vote, chief U.S. negotiator John Byerly, U.S. Deputy Assistant Secretary of State for Transportation Affairs, indicted his EU counterparts for failing to appreciate the improbability of a first-stage agreement that would revoke U.S. foreign ownership and cabotage laws. As to cabotage, Byerly once more

---

175. Calleja, *supra* note 25, at 16-17 (suggesting that U.S. change to 49% would have 'little or no value' to EU carriers, but that its symbolic power would be to bring U.S. and EC rules into alignment in a putative first-stage agreement, even though the proposal fell short of the 100% foreign investment sought by the Commission); *see also* Byerly, *Charting the Course, supra* note 18, at 8 (mentioning other, less dramatic U.S. proposals including ending formal designation as well as inaugurating a new era of airline competition cooperation between U.S. and EU authorities). The second Bush Administration, it should be noted, had favored the 49% proposal from an early stage, but especially when Jeffrey Shane became U.S. Under Secretary of Transportation for Policy. In 2003, in fact, the Administration had intended to include this proposal in its Federal Aviation Administration 're-authorization' legislation, but, according to Shane, 'delays in the interagency clearance process prevented us from transmitting it in time for consideration as part of what became Vision 100 [the popular name assigned to the eventual re-authorization legislation].' Shane, IAC Remarks, *supra* note 152, at 3. The proposal then found its way into Bush's re-election campaign. *See* Calleja, *supra* note 25, at18. Later, Bush officials asked Congress to consider the proposal as a freestanding bill, 'but without success.' Shane, IAC Remarks, *supra* note 152, at 3. One might fairly attribute to Shane the view that the 2005 proposed rulemaking to modify the control requirement of the U.S. nationality rule, *see* Chapter 3, Part V(B), was in a direct line of descent from those earlier Bush Administration initiatives on the numerical stock ownership requirement. As Shane recalled it in 2006, the Department of Transportation tried 'a different tack,' switching focus from numerical limits to what he and other DOT officials believed to be 'the wholly administrative constraints that, by our assessment, unnecessarily and excessively restrict the activities even of those foreign investors who fully *comply* with the stringent statutory limits.' *Id.* (emphasis in original). Shane and his colleagues 'thought that [they] were pursuing a far more moderate and evolutionary approach,' in effect proposing a more *au courant* regulatory interpretation of the control test that would not offend those members of Congress who dislike tampering with well-established statutes. Shane's optimism, as noted earlier, was seriously misplaced. *See supra* note 154.

176. *See* Byerly, *Charting the Course, supra* note 18, at 9. The United States saw a number of beneficial consequences for EU Member States which had hitherto abstained from open skies: Spain's Iberia could apply for antitrust immunity and Ireland's Aer Lingus could offer more U.S. services. The benefits to the United Kingdom were less specifically articulated. *Id.*

177. *See* Calleja, *supra* note 25, at 15.

disputed the Commission's perception of an imbalance between the existence of U.S. traffic rights among EU Member States and the absence of EU traffic rights in the domestic U.S. market. To Byerly, the EU is not a genuine 'cabotage' jurisdiction but a network of fifth freedoms connecting sovereign States, each of which enjoys a separate vote in ICAO.[178] Moreover, EU airlines have not sought cabotage access to the U.S. domestic market, just as U.S. passenger airlines do not use their EU fifth freedoms, preferring to exploit code-shared alliance relationships with EU carriers.[179] On foreign ownership, including the right to establish subsidiaries, Byerly again invoked commercial unreality, arguing that expansive code-sharing satisfies today's commercial needs.[180] But a right of establishment, in any event, was 'simply not doable in a first-step agreement.'[181]

But Byerly also concluded that the opposition of some EU Member States and airlines to a more limited first-stage agreement 'had little to do with the sufficiency of the U.S. offer and much more to do with relationships within the European Union itself.'[182] His most astringent remarks related to the reported behavior of some EU carriers which enjoy protected positions on international routes to third

---

178. Byerly, *Charting the Course, supra* note 18, at 11. Despite its ever-enlarging role over civil aviation in the EU and even beyond the Union's borders, the European Commission is only afforded observer status at ICAO. This has not stopped the Commission from pursuing full membership status, however. In 2002, it recommended to the EU Council of Ministers that it be allowed to enter formal negotiations with ICAO with a view to ensuring a single representative of the EU to the organization. *See* European Commission, *Recommendation from the Commission to the Council in Order to Authorise the Commission to Open and Conduct Negotiations with the International Civil Aviation Organization (ICAO) on the Conditions and Arrangements for Accession by the European Community*, SEC (2002) 381 final (Apr. 9, 2002). Such representation, in the view of the Commission, ought to include 'voting rights . . . equivalent to those of Member States represented in the relevant ICAO body and bound by the Community instruments from which external competence arises.' *See id.* sec. 6. However, admitting the European Union (*qua* European Community) would require an amendment to the Chicago Convention's Article 92 requirement permitting only States to have membership status in ICAO.

179. Only a few U.S. carriers operate a modest number of all-cargo flights using their fifth freedom privileges in the EU. In an era of code-sharing with their EU partners, no U.S. carriers have provided intra-Union air passenger services since at least 2002. *See* ATW, *Not Cabotage, supra* note 126; *see also* Byerly, *Turbulent Times, supra* note 35 (mentioning a handful of U.S. all-cargo services such as UPS operations out of Cologne and FedEx from Paris).

180. *See* Byerly, *Charting the Course, supra* note 18, at 11.

181. *Id.* On the right of establishment, *see supra* note 91.

182. Byerly, *Charting the Course, supra* note 18, at 12. What did Byerly mean? His speech speaks darkly of 'many rumors of wheeling and dealing' among the Member States on the eve of the Jun. 11 EU Council of Transport Ministers meeting. In orthodox EU fashion (but surprisingly to aviation officials), some Member States may have traded their support for a first-step agreement in return for other Member States' support on other issues, such as controversial trucking regulations. *See id.* at 13; *see also* John R. Byerly, Deputy Assistant Secretary for Transportation Affairs, U.S. Department of State, *U.S.-EC Aviation Relations: Success Today and Potential for the Future*, Remarks to the International Aviation Club, Washington, D.C., at 1 (Apr. 24, 2007) (commenting on 'alleged backroom deals to thwart approval of the Commission's proposals') [hereinafter Byerly, *U.S.-EC Aviation Relations*].

countries. These carriers are believed to have lobbied their governments (despite the official support of their trade association, the AEA, for the mandate) to oppose an agreement which would have removed their protection and given the European Commission a significant market-opening victory.[183] Breaking (or at least bending) his own code of diplomatic discretion, he branded the United Kingdom as leader of 'the naysayers.'[184] Byerly's speech is remarkable, therefore, for its candid *Realpolitik* assessment of the political reasons – as perceived from one side of the negotiations – for a disappointing diplomatic failure. The speech closed with a short litany of 'lessons' for future negotiations, built around the common theme of a more realistic and nuanced understanding of what can be achieved.[185]

Byerly's EU counterpart in the first negotiations, the late Michel Ayral, Director of the Air Transport Directorate of the European Commission, subsequently stepped down and was succeeded by Spaniard Daniel Calleja. As a newcomer to the negotiating table, Calleja's remarks were as interesting for their positive tone as for their actual content. Defying the exceptionalism of the airline industry, he identified the U.S./EC aviation talks as part of a larger process of transatlantic economic integration, forecast that the negotiations would lead inevitably and necessarily to a new model for global aviation, and argued that an agreement was 'achievable' in 2005. With a Hegelian flourish, Calleja asserted that aviation, a global industry, would inevitably achieve the kind of globalized open regulatory

---

183. To break the code of Byerly's speech, one only has to inspect his carefully phrased refusal to 'denigrate the commitment to competition of our European Open Skies partners and their airlines.' Byerly, *Charting the Course, supra* note 18, at 14. The largest non-open skies carrier was British Airways, imperium of London Heathrow.

184. *See id.* at 2. The masked ball character of the negotiations is thus revealed in the most polemical moments of Byerly's speech. Using a loaded reference to Machiavelli, Byerly sketches a hypocritical strategy that on the one hand called for a radical change in international aviation, including unlimited traffic rights, while recognizing on the other hand that the United States would not deliver that kind of end-stage agreement. The British flag carrier has subsequently emerged from the shadows to make explicit its view that cabotage is a 'key issue' for European carriers. *See* ATW, *Not Cabotage, supra* note 126 (reporting the following combative public remarks of British Airways managing director for airports and air transport control contracts Simon Cox, delivered at the May 2007 Baltimore/Washington International Airport Air Service Symposium:

    Whether [the right to serve cabotage routes] is used or whether it isn't, BA wants that opportunity.... What are you afraid of? If it's not a big deal, then it's not a big deal to drop [the prohibition against] it. Let's get to the open aviation area. Why are we in this halfway house?

185. Thus, for example, stakeholders which demand cabotage or the right of establishment 'with no near-term intention of making use of such rights' are pointing the negotiations toward failure. Byerly, *Charting the Course, supra* note 18, at 15. Additionally, Byerly stated that for future negotiations to be successful government and private sector stakeholders would need to work more closely together and with greater openness. *Id.* at 14. The EC would also have to guarantee rights normally included in air services agreements (e.g., fifth freedom rights outside the Union) and work toward building a new agreement based on the existing system of U.S./EU Member State bilateral agreements rather than denouncing those agreements and starting over. *See id.* 15-16.

environment that other industries already enjoy.[186] He examined the history of EC aviation liberalization, which in his view remained incomplete without a so-called 'external dimension.'[187] The U.S. and EU aviation markets, he noted, together account for 60% of global civil aviation output, so that the negotiations had 'the potential to set the benchmark for the future regulation of the international air transport industry.'[188]

Calleja did not moderate EU demands for unrestricted access to the U.S. domestic market, including abolition of all foreign ownership restrictions. Nor, departing from Byerly's pragmatic approach, did he frame his analysis in terms of a 'staged' agreement. Rather, he argued that these EU demands must be part of a necessary rethinking of the regulatory model for an industry in crisis.[189] More idealistically, therefore, he thought of the negotiations as leading to a completely new model for global aviation.[190] Since 'the status quo is not an option,'[191] Calleja predicted that a U.S./EC aviation agreement could be 'achievable' in 2005, although he did not speculate about its content or degree of liberalization.

B   Toward a U.S./EC Agreement II: Breaking the Impasse

The Dublin U.S./EU Summit on June 26, 2004, hard on the heels of the rejection by the Council of the European Union of the first Byerly-Calleja draft agreement, saw an executive effort to reignite the stalled negotiations. President Bush and his counterparts in the Irish Government and the European Commission jointly summoned the two sides' negotiators to continue efforts toward a comprehensive aviation accord.[192] Although informal contacts were maintained, however, it was not until October 2005 that John Byerly returned to Brussels to restart formal

---

186. Calleja stated the EC's basic objective to be to 'foster safe, affordable, convenient and efficient air service for consumers,' relying on 'the marketplace and unrestricted, fair competition to determine the variety, quality and price of air service.' Wryly, he pointed out that these words were taken directly from the Statement of U.S. International Air Transportation Policy. Calleja, *supra* note 25, at 10. 'Let the market decide.' *Id.* at 11.

187. *Id.* at 6.

188. *Id.* at 9.

189. *Id.* at 18 (describing as 'unsustainable' an airline industry model that subordinates impressive growth potential, a fundamentally international character, and high capital needs, to regulatory restrictions on access to international capital).

190. *Id.* at 19 (noting that the Commission-sponsored economic report on the benefits of transatlantic liberalization did not calculate the resonance of a U.S./EC agreement that could potentially attract third countries into its orbit and eventually eliminate restrictions worldwide). As will be noted elsewhere in this study, the European Commission often speaks in visionary terms as part of its mission to transcend the embedded conservatism of national regulation. Calleja's progressivism, therefore, should be understood within the context of such Commission initiatives as the Cecchini Report which calculated the cost of 'non-Europe,' *i.e.*, of not completing the common market. *See* Paolo Cecchini, The European Challenge, 1992: The Benefits of a Single Market (1988).

191. Calleja, *supra* note 25, at 20 (predicting a 'global future' for an airline industry that would not, understood in those terms, 'be condemned to endless bankruptcies').

192. *See* Byerly, *Charting the Course*, *supra* note 18, at 3.

negotiations for a first-stage agreement.[193] As anointed guardian of the treaties, meanwhile, the European Commission remained conscious of the unresolved legal consequences of the 2002 open skies rulings by the European Court of Justice, and was determined if necessary to adhere to the rule of law by forcing Member States to terminate all of the offending agreements (including, it has to be assumed, all bilaterals with all third countries, and not just with the United States).[194] The stakes for the major carriers on both sides of the Atlantic were now clear: if deprived of the soft power of its negotiated open skies agreements, the U.S. Government would retaliate by withdrawing antitrust immunity from the big transatlantic alliances.[195]

The 2005-2007 negotiations reprised the critical bargaining points of the earlier rounds. In return for allowing Community carriers to connect any point in the United States to any point in Europe for any purpose (passenger, combination, or cargo), thereby allowing the Commission to decontaminate the discriminatory nationality clauses condemned by the European Court of Justice,[196] the United States would add an open skies relationship with the (then) ten Member States, including the United Kingdom, which remained unmoved by post-1992 U.S. aeropolitical diplomacy. As well as opening London Heathrow to multicarrier competition, the open skies precedent would also offer full intra-Union and beyond-Union fifth freedom rights to U.S. carriers.[197]

Both Byerly and his European Commission negotiating partner, Daniel Calleja, expressed confidence that a new 'vision' of transnational aviation relations could emerge from their second parley.[198] A broad menu of additional topics of mutual interest – public subsidies, security, safety, environmental regulation,

---

193. *See* John Byerly, Deputy Assistant Secretary for Transportation Affairs, U.S. Department of State, *Liberalizing Transatlantic Aviation: The Case for Stability, Expansion, and Vision*, Speech to the USA-BIAS Conference, Washington, D.C. (Oct. 14, 2005) [hereinafter Byerly, *Liberalizing Transatlantic Aviation*].

194. *See* European Commission, *Consequences*, *supra* note 20, para. 38.

195. *See id.* (a prospective situation that Byerly described as a 'gathering storm'). On the meaning of antitrust immunity and its significance as the bonding agent for transatlantic aviation, *see supra* Chapter 1, Part II(C).

196. This offer to treat was characterized by U.S. Under Secretary of Transportation for Policy Jeffrey Shane as an unprecedented and transformational grant of rights, since it displaced the 'entire morass of nationality-based restrictions' across all EU Member States. Jeffrey N. Shane, U.S. Under Secretary for Transportation Policy, U.S. Department of Transportation, *Liberalization: More Important Than Ever*, Remarks to the 13th Annual International CEO Conference, Miami, FL, at 4 (May 9, 2005).

197. *See* Byerly, *Liberalizing Transatlantic Aviation*, *supra* note 193. If the EC negotiators were contemplating any strategy of once again equating intra-Union fifth freedom rights with U.S. cabotage rights, Byerly disabused them immediately of such destructive thoughts: 'Any other result – some quirky concoction one might call Open Skies Lite Plus – makes no sense and is an absolute non-starter.' *Id.* The mandate to the Commission did not (apparently) embrace fifth freedom rights for U.S. carriers to serve points *beyond* the European Union, although these rights eventually formed part of the final agreement. For further discussion of the political background to this fifth freedom issue, *see supra* note 35.

198. *See supra* Part IV(A).

consumer protection, cooperation in competition investigations, wet leasing, some kind of joint steering group, as well as the agenda for a second stage agreement – were identified by Byerly on the eve of his departure to Brussels for the resumed negotiations.[199] All of these topics had been inserted into the earlier failed draft agreement, but collectively they now expressed a sense, however inchoate, that a U.S./EC agreement could vault beyond the conventional 'open skies' template.

Surprisingly, Byerly's eve-of-departure address also raised a tantalizing promise of forthcoming adjustments to federal rules on inward investment in U.S. airlines, an issue that the Washington negotiators had always signaled to their Brussels colleagues would be deferred to the second stage. He indicated, cryptically but emphatically, that the U.S. administration was actively considering, 'at a senor level and as a matter of priority among all interested agencies in the Executive Branch,' what he called 'options to increase the opportunities for U.S. carriers to obtain foreign capital and to have greater involvement with citizens of countries with which we have an Open Skies [*sic*] relationship.'[200] In explicit terms, Byerly warned that 'this issue' was being considered by the Bush Administration 'on its own merits' and that it could not be 'linked to air services negotiations.'[201] Chapter 3 will tell the story of how Deputy Assistant Secretary Byerly's 'straw in the wind' evolved into a plenary bureaucratic proceeding of the U.S. DOT designed to liberalize the DOT interpretation of the statutory requirement that U.S. citizen-managers must 'control' the operations of U.S. airlines,[202] of how the EU

---

199. *See* Byerly, *Liberalizing Transatlantic Aviation, supra* note 193. Byerly also mentioned a potential area of friction – the longstanding principle, rooted in the Chicago Convention, ICAO rulings, and bilateral agreements, that fuel used for international aviation should not be taxed locally. (As noted, *infra* Chapter 6, note 181, the EC has lately embraced a tough environmental agenda that seeks to reduce aviation hydrocarbon and other emissions through policies that include stiffer tax regimes. The U.S. approach, in contrast, looks more to reductions through technological and traffic management improvements. *See* Andrew B. Steinberg, Assistant Secretary for Aviation and International Affairs, U.S. Department of Transportation, Remarks before the ICAO Colloquium on Aviation Emissions, Montreal, Canada (May 16, 2007). There were also some menu items that featured in the final agreement and that Byerly did not signal in his talk. In particular, certain provisions would be negotiated to improve EU carriers' access to U.S. Government-financed air travel and with respect to their use of branding and franchising opportunities in the U.S. market.

200. Byerly, *Liberalizing Transatlantic Aviation, supra* note 193.

201. *Id.* The naiveté of Byerly's statement was implicitly accepted by U.S. Under Secretary of Transportation for Policy Jeffrey Shane when he later conceded that the Europeans had done precisely the opposite by linking the foreign investment issue to the U.S./EC negotiations. *See* Jeffrey N. Shane, Under Secretary for Policy, U.S. Department of Transportation, *Aviation Deregulation: A Work in Progress*, Speech at the International Aviation Club, Washington, D.C., at 7-8 (Nov. 8, 2005).

202. In essence, the DOT rulemaking aimed to encourage foreign investment in U.S. airlines by expanding the permissible scope of foreign citizen participation in the commercial management of those airlines while protecting legitimate U.S. interests in security, safety, national defense, and the rule of law. *See* Byerly, *Turbulent Times, supra* note 35. The clever premise of these changes was that areas that U.S. law had deregulated (*i.e.*, commercial operations such as pricing, capacity, and fleet management) could be juristically and pragmatically separated

institutions insisted upon linking the outcome of that proceeding to the U.S./EC negotiations despite Byerly's explicit disavowal of any intended linkage, and of how the proceeding collapsed through misfortunes of timing (including the eruption of the Dubai Ports controversy)[203] and the work of a factional but well-marshaled Congressional opposition.[204]

U.S. lead negotiator John Byerly's conceptual framing of the 2007 agreement requires separating the draft as it existed in November 2005, just a month after the resumption of negotiations, from the 'enhanced' final draft submitted to the Council of the European Union nearly 18 months later.[205] The November 2005 version was 'tabled' (in the U.S. sense of subjected to deferred consideration) by the Transport Ministers Council at their meeting on December 5, 2005, signaling the importance (in European eyes) of a satisfactory resolution of the U.S. DOT's controversial rulemaking on liberalizing the interpretation of 'control' under the U.S. airline nationality laws.[206] By early 2006, the rulemaking proceeding became ensnared in the wider Dubai Ports controversy on foreign investment

---

from those areas where the government retains control (*i.e.*, security, safety, defense, and corporate governance). Late in the day, through a Supplemental Notice of Proposed Rulemaking issued in May 2006, the DOT displeased European watchers of the draft rule by adding a 'revocability' requirement that would allow any delegation of authority to foreign investors to be withdrawn by U.S. citizens. *See* U.S. Department of Transportation, *Actual Control of U.S. Carriers: Withdrawal of Certain Proposed Amendments*, Dkt. No. OST-2003-15759 (Dec. 5, 2006), at 4 [hereinafter U.S. DOT, *Withdrawal*].

203. The controversy involved the sale of British-based Peninsular & Oriental Steam Navigation (P&O) to the United Arab Emirates-owned enterprise, Dubai Ports (DP) World. The sale, which would have resulted in the transfer of operating rights over six U.S. ports, was approved by the U.S. Government's foreign investment review process. *See supra* note 104. Despite strong support from the Bush Administration, a Congressional outcry against control of critical infrastructure by an Arab State which had reputed links to some of the 9/11 terrorists compelled the Dubai company to divest P&O's U.S. holdings. *See generally* Deborah M. Mostaghel, *Dubai Ports World Under Exon-Florio: A Threat to National Security or a Tempest in a Seaport?*, 70 ALB. L. REV. 583 (2007); Stephanie Kirchgaessner et al., *Stinging Defeat for Bush as DP World Gives Up U.S. Ports*, FIN. TIMES, Mar. 10, 2006, at 1. The DP World controversy was described by John Byerly as a 'typhoon of xenophobia that pummeled the United States.' Byerly, *Turbulent Times*, *supra* note 35. For more on the impact of the controversy on U.S. aviation policy, *see infra* Chapter 3, Part V.

204. *See infra* Chapter 3, Part V(B). For an introductory overview of the so-called Notice of Proposed Rulemaking, *see supra* note 202.

205. *See* Byerly, *Turbulent Times*, *supra* note 35; *see also* European Commission, *Air Transport Agreement between the EU and U.S.*, at 1, Information Note (Mar. 6, 2007) [hereinafter European Commission, *Air Transport Agreement*].

206. *See supra* text accompanying note 200 (explaining the genesis of this rulemaking procedure). The Council expressed general satisfaction with the regulatory tenor of the draft agreement, calling it a significant improvement on the draft submitted to it in Jun. 2004, but indicated that improvements in the field of ownership and control – *i.e.*, adoption of the proposed rule changes by the DOT – were 'essential' to a stage one resolution. European Commission, *Air Transport Agreement*, *supra* note 205, at 1 & 3. Compounding the challenge to the U.S. team, the Council began to use a tough verbal formula to describe its expectations for the new rule: it would have to be 'clear, meaningful, and robust.' *Id.* at 3.

in U.S. essential infrastructure.[207] EU Transport Commissioner Jacques Barrot provided a series of baleful reports to the Council in June and October, 2006.[208] When the proposed U.S. rule, despite modifications,[209] finally succumbed to mounting Congressional pressure in late 2006,[210] a chastened Council of Transport Ministers expressed disappointment and regret, reaffirmed its commitment to a first-stage agreement, and called for the negotiators to begin 'urgent consultations... to seek elements that could be used to restore a proper balance of interests.'[211]

In the void opened up by the failed rulemaking, U.S. Deputy Assistant Secretary of State John Byerly and his U.S. negotiators began three rounds of discussions with the Calleja team in early 2007. The Americans offered a series of 'enhancements' (primarily concerning the thresholds for foreign investor control, extension of EU investor rights to carriers in countries with which the EU has special aviation relations, and franchising)[212] to meet the Council's condition of a 'balance' of

---

207. *See supra* note 203.
208. *See* European Commission, *Air Transport Agreement, supra* note 205, at 4. After four years as Commissioner for Transport, Barrot became the EU Commissioner for Justice in May 2008. *See* Press Release, European Parliament, European Parliament Approves Jacques Barrot as Justice Commissioner and Antonio Tajani as Transport Commissioner (Jun. 23, 2008).
209. *See supra* note 202 (discussing the 'revocability' requirement, which was added by a Supplemental Notice of Proposed Rulemaking in May 2006).
210. The formal withdrawal of the rule in Dec. 2006 followed an intensive campaign by members of Congress representing labor and some carrier management opposition to its adoption. The Dubai Ports imbroglio had offered a useful public policy context for this opposition. *See infra* Chapter 3, Part V.
211. European Commission, *Air Transport Agreement, supra* note 205, at 1.
212. The first enhancement was, in effect, an assurance that the U.S. Department of Transportation would apply to EU investors its emerging interpretive rule that non-U.S. investor ownership of 50% or more of the total (voting and nonvoting) stock in a U.S. airline would not automatically imply foreign 'control' over that airline. A new Annex on ownership, investment, and control contains certain commitments with respect to EU airlines and investors, including confirmation that the new agreement would enable EU airlines to apply for antitrust immunity for alliances with U.S. airlines. *See infra* Chapter 3, Part VIII. The second enhancement extended the sense of the 'Community carrier' concept to almost 30 non-Member countries with which the EU has developed special aviation relations allowing EU investors to buy carriers in those countries without triggering U.S. revocation of their carrier designations because of a noncitizen ownership and control profile. It is important to note that these concessions were non-reciprocal with respect to the third countries involved (in other words, they did not acquire similar rights for their carriers with respect to EU carriers or EU designations). Relatedly, EU carriers also won seventh freedom passenger rights to fly directly to the United States from countries in the evolving European Common Aviation Area (*see supra* note 20). The third significant enhancement clarified that 'franchising' of EU airline brand identities to U.S. corporate entities would be permitted provided that the foreign control rules were respected. *See supra* note 199 & *infra* Chapter 3, Part V(B) discussing the Virgin America brand. In addition to these three concessions, the U.S. negotiators made non-specific pledges to 'strengthen' the proposed steering (or 'joint') committee under the agreement and to 'bolster' the commitment to second stage negotiations. A final concession promised a small and mostly symbolic increase in EU carrier access to U.S. Government civil air transportation revenues. *See* Byerly, *Turbulent Times, supra* note 35.

rights and to prevent the Commission backsliding to its rearguard position that 'intra-Union fifth freedoms equal U.S. cabotage.'[213] It is unlikely that these enhancements, even in gross, were conceptually substitutable for the lost cause of the rulemaking,[214] but by March 2007 the political will on the part of most of the Community Member States to complete an agreement trumped doubts about the overall 'balance' struck in the second draft.[215] Moreover, the adoption of a specific time-scale for the second stage seems to have impressed the EU institutions that the first-stage deal would not be, in Byerly's incomparable phrasing, 'a clever foxtrot to the side.'[216] Accordingly, the American and European negotiators initialed the second draft U.S./EC Air Transport Agreement on March 2, 2007.[217] The 'step change' agreement, as it was characterized by EU Transport Commissioner Jacques Barrot, was unanimously approved by the Council of Transport Ministers in Brussels on March 22, 2007, and signed on behalf of the United States and the EU at their Summit in Washington, D.C., on April 30, 2007.[218]

From the outset, it should be noted, it was clear that the fruits of any Commission-led negotiation would have to be approved by the Member States

---

213. *See supra* text accompanying note 37. Byerly evidently felt a high level of frustration that the EC's rearguard position on 'balance,' especially because of U.S. carriers' virtually total indifference to intra-Union fifth freedom rights meant that the Commission would be returning its gaze to an issue 'in one corner' of the Nov. 2005 draft agreement that might implicate 5% of its value. Byerly, *Turbulent Times, supra* note 35. Similarly, any EC attempt to scale back U.S. carrier rights to serve fifth freedom points beyond Europe, again in the name of 'balance,' would have unmoored any possibility of an agreement. *See id.*

214. Although the Commission, exhibiting its bureaucratic *mentalité*, chose to present the outcome as precisely substitutable, arguing that the enhancements 'ensure a proper balance of interests,' and that the proposed Annex on ownership and control 'now provides greater security in this area than would have been the case under a policy reform by the [United States] that would have been outside the scope of the agreement and subject to possible changes.' European Commission, Information Note, *supra* note 2, at 5.

215. Somehow the United States persuaded the political constituencies within the EU Council of Transport Ministers of its *bona fides* in pursuing further investment liberalization in a second stage. But an element of *faute de mieux* may also have entered the Ministers' calculations. By early 2007, after the collapse of the rulemaking to liberalize foreign control, the prevailing reaction in the U.S. Congress to the possibility that the U.S./EC talks would collapse in the absence of a new rule, was (in the American vernacular) 'too bad.' Byerly, *Turbulent Times, supra* note 35. Also, U.S. negotiators pointed out that virtually all of the new rights acquired by the United States under the draft agreement resulted from adding additional Member States to its directory of 'open skies' agreements. *See id.* Of course, one of those new rights was the single biggest commercial concession in the agreement – the scrapping of Bermuda II and its oligopolistic chokehold on London Heathrow. John Byerly has branded Bermuda II as 'one of the greatest crimes in the history of aviation.' *Id.* at 4.

216. Byerly, *Liberalizing Transatlantic Aviation, supra* note 193; *see also* European Commission, Information Note, *supra* note 2, at 1.

217. *See* Byerly, *Turbulent Times, supra* note 35; *see also* European Commission, *Air Transport Agreement, supra* note 205.

218. *See* Byerly, *Turbulent Times, supra* note 35.

sitting in the Council of the European Union.[219] Further, it quickly became apparent that the open skies jurisprudence of the European Court of Justice would determine, based on its cautious slicing of sovereignty between the 'Community' and the Member States with respect to bilateral air services negotiations, that each Member State would then have to approve separately the final agreement in accordance with its domestic ratification procedures.[220] Ultimately, in fact, the 2007 U.S./EC Air Transport Agreement came into *provisional* effect on March 30, 2008, precisely and explicitly in anticipation of 27 separate domestic ratifications.[221] Finally, the negotiation needed to be seen in the context of the general recasting

---

219. *See* Henri Wassenbergh, Historic Decision by the EC Council of Transport Ministers 1 (Jun. 5, 2003) (unpublished paper, on file with author) (noting that the European Community/Union is not a sovereign State and that the Commission is not its government). Because the Court's ruling portrays areas of shared EC competence as well as exclusive EC competence, Wassenbergh expects Member States to join with EC representatives in creating so-called 'mixed' agreements. *See id.* For Wassenbergh, '"exclusive competence" only means that only the [EC] can *regulate* the subject concerned, *i.e.* the [EC] has to approve the result of negotiations by a [Member State] on such subject; it does not mean that only the [EC] may *negotiate* the subject.' *Id.* at 4 (emphasis in original). 'Mixed competence,' on the other hand, 'means that the [EC] and the [Member State] together may regulate, and therefore also together negotiate on the subject(s) of the mixed competence,' and here the EC 'has to co-approve the result of negotiations,' 'while all the [Member States] have to ratify the result.' *Id.* Wassenbergh takes the view that there will be two steps to bring third-country agreements into effect: Council approval followed by 'ratification in conformity with the national legislations [sic] of the Member States.' *Id.* at 5.
220. Thus, facing (at the time) 26 potential negotiators instead of one, chief U.S. representative John Byerly criticized the mandate for not being a 'unitary' grant of authority to the European Commission. Each Member State would (and ultimately did) have a veto over the final agreement. To this extent, the outcome of negotiations would be, in Community parlance, a 'mixed agreement.' Byerly, *Charting the Course*, *supra* note 18, at 6; *see also* Wassenbergh, *supra* note 219. Byerly's critique extended also to what he perceived as an incompleteness in the mandate, which denied the Commission authority to negotiate fifth and seventh freedom rights outside the U.S./EU market. According to U.S. officials with whom the author has spoken, the incomplete mandate was likely the result of a general sense of unhappiness which permeated Commission/Member State relations after the Commission won a U.S. negotiating mandate because of its ECJ legal proceedings against several Member States. Political tensions between the Member States and then-Transport Commissioner Loyola de Palacio and conspicuous ill-will concerning the expanded aviation dossier of the Commission were also contributing factors. Nevertheless, although the mandate was never formally amended to include extra-EU fifth freedom rights for U.S. carriers (or seventh freedom cargo rights), the Council of Ministers tacitly accepted U.S. intransigence on the matter and demonstrated its approval of the fifth/seventh freedom concessions by approving the final agreement in 2007. (Seventh freedom rights for U.S. carrier *passenger* services between or from EU Member States, however, do not appear to have been part of the negotiations at any time.)
221. *See* 2007 Air Transport Agreement, *supra* note 8, arts. 25 (discussing 'provisional' application of the Agreement) & 26 (referring to the completion of 'all necessary procedures for entry into force' of the Agreement). The retained sovereignty of the Member States is reflected further in the Conclusions of the Council of Ministers which explicitly preserve the right of each Member State, in the event that a so-called 'second stage' agreement is not reached after the textually-anticipated next round of negotiations, to suspend traffic rights in relation to its own territory. *See infra* text accompanying note 254.

of the structure of the EU airline industry, including the social and economic consequences of a new Community external aviation policy.[222]

V   AN EXECUTIVE BRIEFING ON THE 2007 U.S./EC
                 AIR TRANSPORT AGREEMENT[223]

Before imagining the future regulatory landscape for global air transport, we should pause to reflect on the actual achievements of the second and decisive round of transatlantic air transport negotiations that culminated in the April 2007 agreement. The U.S./EC Air Transport Agreement, signed in April 2007, came into provisional effect in March 2008.[224] The 2007 treaty represents only a 'first stage' accomplishment and the most recalcitrant political and legal challenges of the Chicago system – notably liberalization of the foreign ownership rules and, potentially, of the cabotage embargo – have been postponed to a second stage negotiation that is now in progress. The second stage, which is previewed in this briefing, may well become the political site for establishing what new dispensation, if any, lies 'beyond open skies.'

---

222. *See* ECA, Contribution, *supra* note 67 (containing the evolving position of the European Cockpit Association, the leading pilot representative organization in the Community). The ECA called for a 'social dialogue' on the potentially disruptive social and economic consequences of an EC external aviation policy, including bankruptcies following the loss of the protection afforded by the nationality clauses. *See id.* The ECA also criticized a lack of harmonization in the social, fiscal, and safety fields, which had created obstacles to the smooth functioning of the internal single aviation market. *See id.* Some 'transnational' airlines, for example, had been able to reduce operating costs by being registered and establishing employment contracts in a country other than their place of permanent operations. 'Given the existing differences in relation to fiscal and social costs, but also certain operational requirements across European Union countries, there are clearly possible disruptions to competition between airlines.' *Id.* Thus, 'two operators registered in two different countries can operate today from the same European airport under different flight and duty time limitation schemes for aircrews.' *Id.* In cautiously welcoming the 2007 U.S./EC Air Transport Agreement, the ECA noted that the 'social effects' of liberalization are foreseen in the Agreement and the creation of a Joint Committee on which it would be represented, but focused as much attention on the economic effects of the Agreement, for example criticizing a continued imbalance between U.S. access to the EU market and EU access to the closed domestic U.S. market. *See* ECA, *EU-U.S. Draft Air Transport Agreement*, Position Paper (Jan. 31, 2006), <www.eurocockpit.be/media/OAA_ECA_Position_PP_06_0131-F.pdf>; *see also* Press Release, ECA, EU-U.S. Agreement: Step in the Right Direction – But Concerns Remain (Mar. 5, 2007). Importantly, the ECA emphasized that the Agreement is only a first stage and that it is, at bottom, a 'very political decision' for the Member States; given its unpredictability, therefore, its withdrawal of rights provisions should be used 'robustly.' *See* ECA, *EU-U.S., For Better? Or For Worse?*, Online Article (Mar. 7, 2007), <www.eurocockpit.be/content/view/509/428/>.

223. While the European Community, *not* the European Union *qua* Union, is a signatory to the 2007 air transport agreement with the United States, the EC terminology continues to predominate here in accordance with my earlier expressed preference. *See supra* Chapter 1, note 10.

224. This provisional effect is to allow national ratification procedures to take place in the 27 EU Member States. *See* 2007 Air Transport Agreement, *supra* note 8, art. 26; *see also supra* note 221.

A   THE 17 KEYNOTE IDEAS OF THE 2007 AGREEMENT

The 2007 U.S./EC agreement, by its own express terms, is only a staging-post on the journey to (true) liberalization.[225] Despite its apparent multilateral provenance (at least on the European side), in most respects the 2007 agreement is effectively a further iteration of an existing, well-understood *bilateral* model – the open skies agreements that the United States has been pursuing both before and since the Clinton Administration's statement of U.S. international air transport policy in 1995.[226] Nonetheless, whether one agrees or not with Andrew Charlton's caustic 'calling a spade a spade' assessment of the agreement,[227] or Allan Mendelsohn's suggestion that the new agreement does not 'accomplish[] all that much of practical importance,'[228] it is important to take stock of certain features of the 2007 agreement that go *beyond* the conventional open skies template. (It will also be useful, in the next Part, to position the incremental advances of the U.S./EC Agreement within the context of an ambitious new bilateral agreement between the United Kingdom and Singapore.[229]) Here, in headline form, are the 17 key features of the U.S./EC Agreement:

　　1.　Creation of a 'Joint Committee'[230]
　　2.　Self-identification as a 'plurilateral' agreement[231]

---

225. For an assessment of what 'true' liberalization might mean in this context, *see infra* Chapter 6, Part IV.
226. *See supra* note 7.
227. *See* Andrew Charlton, Principal, Aviation Advocacy, Speech to ABA Air and Space Law Forum, Memphis, Tennessee (Oct. 4, 2007). Actually, Charlton used the more forceful variant (calling a spade a 'shovel'). The phrase, of course, means to call something by its real name: in this case, therefore, Charlton meant that the 2007 Agreement was, indeed, 'just another' open skies treaty.
228. Allan I. Mendelsohn, *The United States and the European Union in International Aviation*, [May 2008] ISSUES AVIATION L. & POL'Y ¶ 25,421, at 13,273 (2008).
229. *See* Agreement Between the United Kingdom of Great Britain and Northern Ireland and the Government of the Republic of Singapore Concerning Air Services, Nov. 21, 2007, U.K.-Sing., Gr. Brit. T.S. No. 4 (2008), (Cm. 7362) [hereinafter U.K./Singapore Agreement].
230. The European Commission has some experience in the establishment and operation of such bodies as an institutional tool to implement various forms of cooperation and international economic cooperation. *See, e.g.*, text accompanying *supra* note 20 (discussing the establishment of a Joint Committee for the EC/Switzerland agreement); European Commission, Information Note on ECAA (Dec. 2005), <http://ec.europa.eu/transport/air_portal/international/pillars/common_aviation_area/doc/2006_05_30_annexe1_ecaa_en.pdf> (noting the establishment of a Joint Committee under the ECAA agreement to resolve questions related to its interpretation). The 2007 U.S./EC Air Transport Agreement speaks to areas of U.S./EC cooperation that will include expert-level exchanges on new legislative or regulatory initiatives, as well as cooperation on potential areas for further development of the agreement. *See* U.S./EC Air Transport Agreement, *supra* note 8, art. 18. One year from Mar. 30, 2008, the Joint Committee is charged to develop 'approaches to regulatory determinations with regard to airline fitness and citizenship, with the goal of achieving reciprocal recognition of such determinations.' *Id.* art. 18(4)(f). The charge also includes developing a 'common understanding' of the criteria used by each party for airline control. *Id.* art. 18(4)(g). The Joint Committee will operate by consensus. *Id.* art. 18(6).
231. *See id.* art. 18(5) (extending the Agreement to third parties following the development of conditions and procedures and necessary amendments). For more on the nature of plurilateral agreements in international law, *see supra* note 121.

3. Second stage negotiations explicitly contemplated[232]
4. Unrestricted reciprocal third, fourth, and fifth freedom rights contained in the body of the Agreement and not in a traditional bilateral 'Annex'[233]
5. Unrestricted reciprocal seventh freedom all-cargo rights, except that U.S. rights will be limited to the Czech Republic, France, Germany, Luxembourg, Malta, Poland, Portugal, and the Slovak Republic[234]
6. Recognition of the internal EC construct of the 'Community air carrier' by the United States; all Community (EU) carriers are eligible for designation by all Member States for seventh freedom passenger/cargo combination services from both EU and European Common Aviation Area States[235]
7. Clarification of current ownership and control rules, allowing up to 49.9% foreign ownership of total equity in U.S. airlines without deeming that level to be 'control,' but allowing European Union to impose stricter 25% cap on U.S. investment in EU airlines; also allowing each party's nationals to own majority stake in third country airlines without suspension of relevant bilateral agreements[236]
8. Open pricing protocol without approval or filing requirements or any emergency measures, except that U.S airlines cannot be price leaders on intra-EU routes[237]
9. No unilateral capacity or 'change of gauge' restrictions

---

232. *See* U.S./EC Air Transport Agreement, *supra* note 8, art. 21.
233. On the inclusion of fifth freedom rights for U.S. carriers beyond the EU, *see supra* note 185.
234. *See supra* Chapter 1, note 58.
235. This statement merits some further explanation, for which I am grateful to the chief U.S. negotiator, U.S Deputy Assistant Secretary of State John Byerly. Under the 2007 Agreement, EU airlines can fly combination (passenger and cargo) service to the United States from any point in the EU as well as any point in the States of the European Common Aviation Area (ECAA), *see supra* note 20, as of the date of the Agreement. Thus, Lufthansa could fly a free-standing (seventh freedom) service from Trondheim (Norway) to New York, with no connection to Germany or anywhere else in the Union. But ECAA airlines, in contrast, have only the rights that the relevant bilaterals grant them (typically cargo seventh freedom but not combination seventh freedom). Thus, for example, Icelandair does not have the right to operate combination seventh freedom services from Madrid to the United States.
236. Under Annex 4 of the Agreement, ownership and control of an EU airline by an ECAA national does not put in jeopardy the EU airline's right to fly under the U.S./EC Agreement. *See* U.S./EC Air Transport Agreement, *supra* note 8, annex 4, art. 1(3). An Icelander could own and control Lufthansa, and Lufthansa could still fly to the United States under the Agreement. Moreover, the United States waived its right under its bilateral agreements with ECAA States (as well as Switzerland, Liechtenstein, and a number of African countries) to object to their airlines' operations to the United States on the ground that effective control is vested in nationals of EU Member States. *See id.* Annex 4, art. 2(2). Thus, a U.K. citizen could buy and control Icelandair and the United States would not object to Icelandair's continuing to fly to the United States under the U.S./Iceland open skies agreement. (The Annex 4 waiver with respect to ownership by itself – without control – is much broader and covers all third-country airlines in which EU carriers invest. *See id.* Annex 4, art. 2(1). This provision is modeled on the existing MALIAT Agreement. *See supra* note 76.)
237. *But see infra* Chapter 5, note 129 (indicating that this restriction may now be in the course of elimination).

10. Franchising provisions that will allow closer business relationships and cooperative arrangements between the airlines of each party and foreign businesses[238]
11. Reciprocal wet-leasing arrangements, except in domestic transportation
12. Recognition of the importance of minimizing regulatory divergence and 'working towards' compatible practices and standards in security, as well as affirmation that each party will 'evaluate' and 'take into account' possible adverse effects on international air transportation when considering security measures
13. Novel provisions on government subsidies and support (allowing 'observations' to be submitted to the Joint Committee on adverse effects of grants and other supports on 'fair and equal opportunity to compete')
14. Novel provisions on competition law (replacing classical 'market share' provisions by U.S. doctrinal formula on protecting competition rather than competitors, advocating a minimization of differences in application of competition laws to intercarrier agreements, and promoting generalized 'cooperation' between competition authorities – to discuss developments, to reach mutual understanding, to consult, and to notify – as outlined in Annex 2 and the MOU)[239]
15. Novel provisions on environmental matters (conditioning adoption of proposed environmental measures on evaluation of 'possible adverse effects on the exercise of rights' contained in the agreement)
16. Novel provisions on consumer protection
17. Novel provisions on traffic uplift preferences, in particular access by EU airlines to U.S. Government procured transport, except that 'city-pair contract fares' and transportation obtained or funded by the Secretary of Defense or the Secretary of a military department are excluded

Other than the generous seventh freedom concession by the United States, most of the provisions of the 2007 U.S./EC Air Transport Agreement are not startlingly innovative. Liberalization of the cabotage and nationality rules is not addressed. The Agreement respects the U.S. Government's desire to pull back from regulatory harmonization (the so-called 'level playing field') of the kind previously advocated by the European Commission and also by the AEA in its momentous September 1999 policy statement, 'Towards a Transatlantic Common Aviation

---

238. *See infra* Chapter 3, Part V(B) (discussing a franchising relationship between Virgin America and the U.K. Virgin Group).
239. *See infra* Chapter 6, Part III(E) (placing the provision against a broader backdrop of U.S./EC cooperation in the field of competition enforcement). In Mar. 2008, the European Commission announced that it had joined with the U.S. Department of Transportation to launch a study aimed at looking at the effects of airline alliances on competition, along with potential changes to their role following the 2007 U.S./EC Air Transport Agreement. A final report is expected in mid-2009. *See* Press Release, Europa, Competition: European Commission and U.S. Department of Transportation Launch Joint Research Project on Airline Alliances, IP/08/459 (Mar. 18, 2008).

Area.'[240] Thus, while a number of important regulatory issues are included (security, safety, the environment, competition, subsidies, consumer protection, and wet leasing), the focus under each rubric is on consultations and cooperation rather than formal harmonization. Under subsidies, for example, EU airlines have already criticized a list that does not include Chapter 11 bankruptcy protection, and the procedure contemplates exchanges of 'observations' between the parties rather than a World Trade organization (WTO)-like system of red light/yellow light/green light prohibitions and permissions.[241]

On the other hand, the Agreement does bring the United States and EC competition authorities into consensus on the U.S. mantra that antitrust law supports competition rather than competitors, and includes a major U.S. concession that will permit wet leasing (although only for international routes). The Agreement creates one institutional structure, a Joint Committee, to be formed by officials from both sides, but the Committee has no supervisory or enforcement authority. In one respect, the existence of the Committee may prove a marginal disimprovement on the present system of bilateral arbitration, since the additional step of a reference to the Joint Committee will be required before a dispute can proceed to conventional arbitration.[242]

B   THE SECOND STAGE AGENDA AND TIMETABLE

For post-Chicago regime change, therefore, industry stakeholders will look to the second stage of U.S./EC negotiations which began in Ljubljana, Slovenia, in May 2008. The agenda for the second stage[243] will implicate certain 'priority' issues that include further liberalization of traffic rights, additional foreign investment opportunities, the effect of environmental measures and infrastructure constraints on the exercise of traffic rights, further access to Government-financed air transportation, and wet leasing by foreign airlines in the U.S. domestic market.[244] John Byerly, the lead U.S. negotiator, has promised that in the second stage the United States will 'fairly assess decades-old policies to determine whether they serve our long term interests.'[245] That pledge of open-mindedness – primarily directed to the twin redoubts of nationality and cabotage – may run counter to political reality, however. According to a recent business briefing by the U.K.-based *Guardian* newspaper, 'with Congress now [since 2006] controlled by protectionist Democrats . . . it would be a surprise if restrictions on internal flights

240. *See supra* Part II(D).
241. *See generally* Final Act Embodying the Results of the Uruguay Round of Multilateral Trade Negotiations, Apr. 15, 1994, 33 I.L.M. 1125 (1994).
242. For a discussion of dispute settlement in international air transport and how the U.S./EC provisions mesh with prevailing practice, *see infra* Chapter 6, Part III(E).
243. *See* U.S./EC Air Transport Agreement, *supra* note 8, art. 21.
244. *See id.* art. 21(2).
245. Byerly, *U.S.-EC Aviation Relations, supra* note 182.

and ownership rights were lifted.'[246] Moreover, it has been observed that the second-stage negotiations have opened and will proceed against the backdrop of a U.S. presidential election and a new presidential administration, rarely ideal times for bold international initiatives that have a domestic commercial resonance.[247]

1　　　　The Second Stage Timetable

The 2007 Agreement went into effect provisionally on Sunday, March 30, 2008.[248] A specific timetable now governs the second stage of the U.S./EC open skies process. Negotiations began in Slovenia, which held the rotating presidency of the EU, on May 15, 2008.[249] Thereafter the parties will review progress no later than 18 months after the start of negotiations, and if no second stage agreement can be reached within 12 months after the review of progress, either party will be entitled to suspend any or all of the rights specified in the Agreement, but suspension would not come into effect until the IATA traffic season that begins no less than 12 months from the date of providing the notice of suspension.[250] For the

---

246. Dan Milmo, *Open Skies Q & A*, GUARDIAN UNLIMITED BUSINESS, Mar. 22, 2007.

247. Further evidence of a rising tide of protectionism comes from the recent collapse of the Doha Round of World Trade Organization negotiations. Despite strong backing by the second Bush Administration to close a deal for countries such as China and India to lower their tariffs on industrial goods in exchange for U.S. and European reductions of tariffs and subsidies on agricultural goods, domestic opposition from agricultural lobbies proved insurmountable. *See* John W. Miller, *Global Trade Talks Fail as New Giants Flex Muscle*, WALL ST. J., Jul. 30, 2008, at A1. As one editorial writer framed it, the question now is whether the collapse of the Doha Round marks 'a temporary setback' or an 'end [to] the post-World War II free-trade era that has done so much to spread prosperity.' *See* Editorial, *The End of Free Trade?*, WALL ST. J., Jul. 31, 2008, at A14.

248. The date was colorfully dubbed 'Super Sunday,' with Dallas/ Fort Worth International Airport running a clock to count down the launching of new services between DFW and Europe's London Heathrow and Amsterdam Schiphol. *Open Skies is Here – DFW International Airport Celebrates New International Services*, PR NEWSWIRE, Mar. 30, 2008. The European Commission has made the benefits accrued under the agreement part of its own latest P.R. campaign to promote its air transport policy. *See* EUROPEAN COMMISSION, FLYING TOGETHER: EU AIR TRANSPORT POLICY 9 (2007).

249. While the Agreement mandates that the United States and European Community 'shall begin negotiations not later than 60 days after the date of [its] provisional application,' *i.e.*, Mar. 30, 2008, it also states that a review process on negotiations is to begin 'no later than 18 months after the date when the negotiations are due to start.' *See* U.S./EC Air Transport Agreement, *supra* note 8, arts. 21(1) & 21(3). On the premise that the negotiations had a 'floating' due date for commencement, the timetable for calculating their review has been adjusted in the main text to reflect the date when negotiations actually began. This adjustment would also hold true for any notice of suspension of rights under the Agreement. *See infra* text accompanying note 253. However, it is important to keep in mind that the date for initiating the review process is also 'floating' and may in turn alter the date on which a suspension notice may be given. *See* U.S./EC Air Transport Agreement, *supra* note 8, art. 21(3).

250. *See id.*

reader's convenience, here is a chart of the treaty-enshrined timetable that focuses on the most likely dates:[251]

March 30, 2008 – Agreement goes into provisional effect
May 15, 2008 – Parties start negotiations[252]
November 15, 2009 – Review of progress begins
November 15, 2010 – If no second stage agreement, notice of suspension
March 2012 – Next IATA season begins, suspension takes effect

It appears, therefore, that up to four years may elapse from the time the U.S./EC Agreement went into effect before any rights could or would actually be suspended.

2   A Threat of EU Member State Unilateralism

On its face, the fact that the parties stitched a lengthy timetable into the U.S./EC Agreement would suggest, at least in part, an intention to accustom States and their carriers to a new status quo and to deter any unscrambling of vested and useful rights. But the political reality is that November 15, 2010, will represent the outside date by which the EU, and notably the Commission and a skeptical U.K. Government, would expect to have negotiated a pledge of legislative reform of the U.S. foreign ownership laws (if not also the cabotage laws).[253]

Behind the literal and linear form of the timetable, however, lies a unilateral European reservation of rights, evidently inspired by U.K. dislike of the first-stage deal, that threatens a sudden and disruptive undoing of specific route privileges apparently granted and used pursuant to the Agreement. Thus, it has been widely confirmed that the minutes of the Council of the European Union meeting that approved the Agreement reflect what would be a significant variation from the suspension protocol in the main Agreement. According to the Agreement, either 'party' may suspend any rights specified in the Agreement.[254] The Agreement defines 'party' as either the United States or 'the European Community and its Member States.'[255] It is not immediately clear, therefore, whether the Community as a whole, or individual Member States acting unilaterally in addition to or in lieu

---

251. *See supra* note 249 (explaining why the earlier start of the second stage negotiations caused some adjustment in these dates).
252. This was the actual date on which negotiations began. Under the 60-day window in the Agreement, the negotiations could have started any time until May 30, 2008. *See supra* note 249.
253. According to former U.K. Transport Secretary Douglas Alexander, withdrawal of traffic rights would occur if 'the Americans [fail] to act in relation to stage two.' Michael Harrison & Stephen Castle, *Heathrow Scramble Starts as EU Agrees to Historic 'Open Skies' Deal*, INDEPENDENT (London), Mar. 23, 2007, at 54. In response to a query on the likelihood of a U.K. suspension of rights under the Agreement should the U.S. not deliver full liberalization by 2010, Alexander stated that '[i]t is for that reason that I have worked with colleagues to ensure that the [United Kingdom] has the ability to take unilateral action.' On the issue of Member State unilateral suspensory action, *see infra* in the main text.
254. *See* U.S./EC Air Transport Agreement, *supra* note 8, art. 21(3).
255. *See id.* art. 1(6).

of the Community, would have the right to suspend. Nevertheless, it is clear that any suspension must be in accord with the terms of the Agreement.

Irrespective of how a right of suspension would be invoked formally by the EC side, however, the Council minutes indicate that any Member State could ultimately withdraw rights granted in the first stage *with respect to its own territory*. This language was (reportedly) insisted upon by the United Kingdom as the price for its support for the Agreement, and in the view of some reflects U.K. uneasiness with the introduction of open skies at Heathrow. Thus, at a future time the United Kingdom could withdraw rights awarded under the 2007 Agreement to Continental Airlines to compete at Heathrow alongside the legacy incumbents American Airlines and United Airlines,[256] but (arguably, but not definitively) could not unilaterally affect, for example, United's code-share access to Spain nor indeed United's own incumbency rights to Heathrow (which are vested under the former U.S./U.K. air services agreement, and therefore should not be treated as 'new' rights granted under the 2007 Agreement).[257] The U.K. position is, apparently, that traffic rights could be withdrawn after the second stage (whether unilaterally by an individual Member State or through suspension of the Agreement as a whole) if U.S. domestic market access through cabotage rights or reform of the airline ownership and control laws has not been achieved.

3   The Second Stage Agenda: Toward an OAA?

A comprehensive agenda for the second stage negotiations (bearing in mind the principles presented in Chapter 1) could be constructed using three categories: those 'priority' issues which are explicitly identified in Article 21 of the U.S./EC Air Transport Agreement[258] (these issues, as noted earlier, include further liberalization of traffic rights, additional foreign investment, the traffic effects of environmental measures and infrastructure constraints, increased access to Government-financed air transportation, and wet leasing);[259] certain additional issues which feature in the European Commission's vision of an 'OAA' (sustained regulatory convergence, including special labor provisions, for example);[260] and some innovative features of the 2007 bilateral open skies agreement between the United Kingdom and Singapore (reciprocity in both cabotage and seventh freedom rights, for example).[261]

---

256. *See infra* Chapter 3, note 464 (explaining how American and United replaced TWA and Pan Am, respectively, to acquire access to London Heathrow).

257. *See id.*

258. Although the treaty language is more circumspect than the main text suggests, since the issues are said to be 'of priority interest to *one or both* parties.' U.S./EC Air Transport Agreement, *supra* note 8, art. 21 (emphasis added).

259. *See id.* art. 21(2).

260. For further discussion of the OAA, *see infra* Chapter 6, note 249.

261. In Oct. 2007, the United Kingdom and Singapore signed a bilateral giving each party unfettered access into each other's domestic aviation markets. The agreement is noteworthy in that it goes beyond standard open skies agreements to extend cabotage and also seventh freedom rights to both sides. *See* U.K./Singapore Agreement, *supra* note 229, art. 3.

To a large extent, Article 21 of the U.S./EC Agreement does address some of the issues raised by the OAA and the U.K./Singapore bilateral, explicitly or implicitly ('further liberalization of traffic rights,' for example, could certainly implicate a discussion of cabotage, and regulatory convergence is encompassed in tracking the effects of environmental measures and infrastructure constraints on the exercise of traffic rights). Some of these issues, especially access to infrastructure, have been spoken of disparagingly in the past as 'soft' rights (in contrast to 'hard' rights such as traffic rights and the right of investment).[262] Yet these 'soft' rights will be, in the view of many, of 'hard' importance in the years to come.[263] The following presentation highlights a series of issues that could be considered in the second stage, accompanied by commentary on some of the aeropolitical challenges to which they will likely give rise:

1. *Further liberalization of traffic rights, including unlimited seventh freedom rights for cargo and passenger airlines of both parties, as well as reciprocal cabotage rights (although not excluded on an ex-bilateral basis subject to local laws)*[264]

The absence of any explicit reference to cabotage in Article 21 does not mean that this highly disputed issue will not return once again as a significant flashpoint in – and impediment to – the unfolding of the second stage negotiations. If some European carriers aim to unravel the rights awarded to U.S. carriers under the first stage, then cabotage has a proven record as a silver bullet. British Airways, for example, has always contested an 'open skies' template that completely excludes the huge U.S. domestic market and wraps U.S. carriers in '100% protection from foreign carriers when it comes to serving points behind their gateways in

---

262. For the implications of this hard/soft rights distinction, *see infra* Chapter 6, Part III(C).
263. Thus, for example, a recent doctoral thesis proposal by Paul Fitzgerald, former senior policy adviser to the Canadian Minister for Transport, offers the following perspective:

    Under the guises of airline security, airport infrastructure management, aviation safety, passenger rights, environmental initiatives, and secure borders, we see that the often unintended consequence of regulatory decisions in various jurisdictions is to have governments dictate to airlines the very practices that open skies policies want to leave to boards of directors.

    Paul Fitzgerald, LL.D. Thesis Proposal, McGill University Institute of Air and Space Law, Jun. 2008 (copy on file with author).
264. Reciprocal exchange of cabotage rights is part of the OAA blueprint and the new U.K./Singapore bilateral agreement. Certain U.S. airlines, however, have concluded collective bargaining agreements with their labor unions, in particular pilots' unions, that prevent these airlines from supporting liberalization of the cabotage laws. The prevailing U.S. view (among both government and industry officials) is that cabotage is a 'red herring' floated by those who publicly endorse liberalization but who seek in reality to maintain the status quo (or to return to the current system using the renunciation option enshrined in the U.S./EC Agreement). In U.S. eyes, it makes more commercial sense for airlines to gain access to the U.S. domestic market through relaxation of foreign investment and right of establishment restrictions.

the U.S. domestic market.'[265] Senior U.S. negotiators like John Byerly have publicly articulated their suspicion that some European carriers' 'high-minded rhetoric,' insisting on a 'better deal' or a 'truly open' agreement, is merely a masquerade that disguises a deep-seated commercial desire to halt or reverse the process of liberalization.[266]

2. Reciprocal inward investment rights[267]

The European Commission, reflecting the intense political pressure it must feel from aggressive flag carriers like British Airways,[268] has placed a strong marker with respect to future progress on the foreign investment issue. Within a few months of the signing of the Agreement, a proposed restrictive amendment to the U.S. nationality rule had provoked European Commission Vice President and Commissioner for Transport, Jacques Barrot, to send a strongly-worded letter to the new U.S. Secretary of Transportation, Mary Peters, emphasizing that this amendment, the initiative of James Oberstar, the powerful Chairman of the

---

265. *See* Broughton, *supra* note 158 (drawing the usual commercial comparison between U.S. domestic cabotage and intra-European routes, the latter available to U.S. carriers under the prevailing current 'open skies' template); *see also supra* text accompanying note 35 (discussing European Commission insistence on this equivalency).

266. *See* Byerly, *Turbulent Times, supra* note 35, at 4; *see also* Byerly, *U.S.-EC Aviation Relations, supra* note 182, at 1.

267. Investment liberalization is currently part of the OAA agenda only. It seems clear that U.S. Government negotiators and many U.S. industry leaders in principle favor full relaxation of the foreign investment restrictions on a reciprocal basis. A main focus (if not *the* main focus) of the second stage discussion will be how to overcome strong Congressional opposition typified by the proposed Oberstar amendment to the stillborn Federal Aviation Administration Reauthorization Act, which would prohibit foreign citizens from having any degree of business control over a U.S. airline. *See* H.R. 2881, 110th Cong. sec. 801 (2007) (as passed by the House Sept. 20, 2007); *but see* FAA Reauthorization Act of 2009, H.R. 915, 111th Cong. sec. 801 (2009) (reintroducing Rep. Oberstar's 2007 amendment). As noted previously, the right of investment would, in the view of most commentators, be structured as a 'right of establishment' that would require the foreign-owned enterprise (whether an acquired U.S. corporation or a newly created subsidiary of a foreign airline) to have its principal place of business in the inward jurisdiction as well as to operate in accordance with that jurisdiction's laws and policies on incorporation, taxation, labor, immigration, environment, national security, and other matters. All of this compliance, however, would require a nondiscriminatory national treatment regime that would give foreign investors equal standing with their domestic counterparts (for example, with respect to tax rates and access to the national judicial system). Moreover, the recently revised U.S. national security procedures for strategic inward investments could form part of a more liberal regime for foreign investment in U.S. airlines. *See supra* note 104. It remains unclear, however, whether the OAA intends ultimately to create a truly 'open' investment regime that would allow inward investment in OAA airlines by non-OAA nationals, or whether it would continue to insist that ownership and regulatory control must be vested in OAA nationals (whether U.S. or EU). The U.K./Singapore agreement, incidentally, breaks no new ground on reciprocal investment: the traditional caps remain, leaving Chicago system notions of cabotage and seventh freedom rights as the agreement's most impressive innovation. *See* U.K./Singapore Agreement, *supra* note 229, arts. 4-5.

268. *See supra* note 184 (discussing British Airways public statements on U.S. cabotage access).

Committee on Transportation and Infrastructure of the U.S. House of Representatives, would 'dangerously impair our ability to enter into a meaningful dialogue during the second stage negotiation, which should aim to establish a reciprocal investment regime based on mutual confidence establishing new opportunities between the European Union and the United States.'[269]

The U.S. DOT is well aware, even in the face of interventions like that of Congressman Oberstar, that the foreign investment issue is critical to the second-stage negotiations. Despite its failed rulemaking on foreign control, the DOT concluded from public comment in its rulemaking docket that 'the current regime is so unduly complex and burdensome that it needlessly inhibits the movement of capital that otherwise would flow into the U.S. airline industry,' thus diminishing the capacity of U.S. carriers to attract strategic investors from overseas capital markets.[270] The Department's *apologia pro vita sua* is striking, since it targets both the substance and procedure of DOT administrative review of citizenship requirements: in withdrawing its proposed amendments, the DOT questioned the 'antiquated notions' it must apply to the airline industry because of its administrative interpretations of the current statute, as well as its 'archaic and time-consuming administrative practices.'[271] The Department was not shy about admitting that its test of 'no semblance of actual control' by foreign citizens has introduced criteria extraneous to the statutory requirements.[272] Unfortunately, Congress amended the U.S. airline citizenship statute in 2003 to add a formal 'actual control' test and arguably to lock in the DOT's evolving interpretation, so that the Department has been, as it were, hoist on a petard of its own manufacture.[273] Nevertheless, it is significant that the leading U.S. administrative agency is persuaded that its citizenship tests are obsolete and counterproductive and serve 'no discernible interest' of the United States.[274]

---

269. *See* Letter from Jacques Barrot, Vice President of the European Commission, to Mary Peters, U.S. Secretary of Transportation, Brussels, FLM/ad D(2007) 1961 (Jul. 9, 2007) (indicating that failure to clarify the legal implications of the Oberstar amendment could disrupt ratification of the Apr. 2007 Agreement). Congressman Oberstar's proposed amendment clearly held the potential to derail the branding and franchising opportunities in the Apr. 2007 Agreement. In May 2008, however, the FAA bill was pulled from Senate consideration after attempts to end a filibuster related to non-aviation provisions in the bill failed.
270. U.S. DOT, *Withdrawal, supra* note 202, at 2; *see infra* Chapter 3, Part V(B).
271. U.S. DOT, *Withdrawal, supra* note 202, at 2.
272. *Id.* at 3.
273. On the 2003 amendment, *see infra* Chapter 3, Part V(B). The Department, it should be added, does not feel itself to have been hamstrung by the statutory change, believing that it has the delegated authority to change its interpretation 'when the past interpretation has become inconsistent with commercial developments and the public policy goals' of the statute. U.S. DOT, *Withdrawal, supra* note 202, at 9. It also disputes the argument that either the statutory change or its legislative history indicated that Congress intended to 'freeze' the DOT's earlier interpretations of 'actual control.' As will be seen, this is not an uncontested proposition.
274. U.S. DOT, *Withdrawal, supra* note 202, at 12. *See infra* Chapter 6, Part III(E) (proposing a new inward investment protocol to supersede the nationality rule).

3. *Effect of environmental measures and infrastructure constraints on the exercise of traffic rights*

This rubric comprises a basket of intertwined regulatory issues – runway construction,[275] slot congestion,[276] aircraft noise and carbon emissions,[277] and related

---

275. With the inclusion of the United Kingdom in the new transatlantic open skies agreement, of principal concern will be the construction of a third runway at London Heathrow. Environmental groups have been particularly vocal in their opposition to any expansion at Heathrow, while others have gone so far as to label forecasts for positive economic benefits that a third runway could bring as 'a sham.' *See* John Bingham, *Third Heathrow Runway a Step Closer*, DAILY TELEGRAPH, Jul. 15, 2008, at 12. Despite the opposition, U.K. Business Secretary John Hutton stated that the U.K. Government was ready to 'make the difficult decisions on air expansion' and further noted that 'British businesses, and ultimately the British people, would not forgive [the government] if we shirked our responsibility to do what's right because we wanted an easy ride from lobby groups.' *Id.* On Jan. 15, 2009, the Government announced that it was going forward with the third runway and a sixth terminal. *See Gordon's Heathrow Gamble*, ECONOMIST, Jan. 15, 2009. The expansion could increase air traffic over London from 480,000 to 700,000 flights a year. *Id.*

276. With Heathrow slots allegedly commanding over $40 million a pair, the future allocation of EU airport slots is of major concern to U.S. operators. *See* Adrian Schofield, *US Airways Joins Heathrow Rush*, AVIATION DAILY, Nov. 21, 2007. The Air France-KLM partnership has already begun leasing slots to U.S. carriers, including its U.S. SkyTeam partners, and has recently been cleared to begin code-sharing on transatlantic routes with Delta and Northwest Airlines. *See* Susan Carey, *Delta, Northwest Cleared for Pact with Europe*, WALL ST. J., May 23, 2008, at B4; Alister Osborne, *Skyteam Duo Take on BA to Seattle*, DAILY TELEGRAPH (London), Dec. 11, 2007, at 2; *see also supra* Chapter 1, note 65. It has been suggested that American negotiators may ask for slots to be freed up for U.S. carriers at Europe's big business hubs as part of the second stage talks, 'an unpleasant prospect for those already holding them.' Mark Pilling, *Slot Machines*, *in* AIRLINE BUS., Oct. 2007, at 74. The prospects for slot confiscation of this kind are unclear in a system historically based on the sanctity of grandfather rights. Nonetheless, change seems inevitable. The Commission's own expert study recognizes that price-based slot trading may be needed to cope with saturation capacity and the constraints on expansion imposed by environmental concerns. *See* MOTT MACDONALD, STUDY ON THE IMPACT OF THE INTRODUCTION OF SECONDARY TRADING AT COMMUNITY AIRPORTS (2006).

277. The subject of aviation emissions has lately become a fierce aeropolitical battleground. The major public and private international air transport organizations, ICAO and IATA, support a *global* aviation emissions trading scheme (ETS) (although the EU Member States have filed a reservation to the ICAO proposal), provided that it is properly designed, consensual, multilateral, and in lock-step with infrastructure enhancements, technological improvements, and research and development into alternative fuels. *See* International Civil Aviation Organization, *Consolidated Statement of Continuing ICAO Policies and Practices Related to Environmental Protection*, *in* Assembly Resolutions in Force, ICAO Doc. 9848 (Oct. 4, 2004); *see also* INTERGOVERNMENTAL PANEL ON CLIMATE CHANGE, AVIATION AND THE GLOBAL ATMOSPHERE (1999). The EC proposal, controversially, is both regional and unilateral in scope and does not prioritize technological and infrastructure improvements and research and development. *See generally* European Commission, *Proposal for a Directive of the European Parliament and of the Council Amending Directive 2003/87/EC So As to Include Aviation Activities in the Scheme for Greenhouse Gas Emission Allowance Trading Within the Community*, COM (2006) 818 final (Dec. 20, 2006). Through promotion of an ETS, however, the European

government taxing and charging strategies[278] – that will consume as much public policy attention in the years ahead as the signature negotiating issues of traffic rights and investment liberalization.

Community appears to acknowledge that its antiquated Air Traffic Management (ATM) system causes some percentage of greenhouse gas emissions. In the U.S. perspective, the EC proposal to include aviation (including all international aviation serving EU airports) in the existing ETS does not give the airlines credit for emissions caused by ATM inefficiencies that are beyond the industry's control. There is also a fundamental difference of interpretation between the United States and European Community as to the compatibility of the ETS with the Chicago Convention. *See* Press Release, Air Transport Association, ATA Says European Aviation Emissions Trading Scheme Illegal, Decries Legislation as 'Tax Grab' (Jul. 8, 2008). The Single European Sky (SES), incidentally, would enhance ATM in the EU by rationalizing the fragmented system that exists today. It would also have a positive environmental impact: IATA calculates that 12% of fuel burn in Europe is directly attributable to ATM and infrastructure inefficiencies (the same percentage attributed to the same problems in the United States). *See generally* VAN ANTWERPEN, *supra* note 25. It has been argued that unions and national pride are slowing progress towards SES implementation. Finally, night noise restrictions, subject in the main to local Member State regulations, are an important issue for U.S. cargo carriers. *See* Jeffrey N. Shane, Under Secretary for Policy, U.S. Department of Transportation, Statement Before the Aviation Subcommittee of the House Transportation and Infrastructure Committee (Feb. 8, 2006), <www.dot.gov/affairs/jeffshane020806.htm>.

278. The growing incidence of 'environmental' taxes and charges obviously increases the cost of doing business. As the price for approving a proposed third runway at Heathrow, *see supra* note 275, for example, the U.K. Government has imposed a number of taxes and charges wrapped in environmental labeling, including an increased tax meant to replace the Air Passenger Duty (APD) that it claims is necessary to ensure that Heathrow will comply with EC environmental laws if and when the third runway is constructed. *See* Rob Davies, *Trade Minister Attacks Air Taxes*, DAILY TELEGRAPH (London), Jul. 14, 2008, at 10. The new tax is projected to raise £2.5 billion annually for the Treasury. *Id.* There are also nitrogen oxide (NOx) charges in the United Kingdom and Switzerland. Germany has proposed the introduction of NOx charges (albeit on an allegedly revenue neutral basis). *See* Robert Wall, *Germany Tests NOx-Based Charges*, AVIATION DAILY, Sept. 28, 2007. Also, the Netherlands Government has introduced a ticket tax for passengers departing from Dutch airports. The tax, which became effective in Jan. 2008 and which increases the existing passenger service charge by euro 45 for transatlantic passengers, has withstood two court challenges. *See Dutch Ticket Tax Proposal Breaches International Obligations*, IATA Euro. News, Dec. 2007, at 2; Press Release, European Low Fares Airline Association [ELFAA], ELFAA Condemns Verdict on Dutch Travel Tax (Jul. 17, 2008). It is extremely difficult to combat these taxes. The governments attract political support by attaching an 'environmental' label even though the monies collected are not earmarked for environmental purposes (as noted above, the British APD, for example, flows to the general treasury.) It also appears that governments frame the taxes in a manner calculated to benefit the home carrier. In recent proposals to revise the current APD that will be subject to a consultation process, the U.K. Government hinted that special treatment should be accorded to transit passengers, with obvious benefits for carriers with hubs in Britain. The Dutch ticket tax proposal does not appear to apply to connecting passengers at all, even though their environmental footprint is arguably larger (because they both are taking off and landing) than passengers originating in the Netherlands who will be subject to the tax. *See* Press Release, ELFAA, *supra*. Legally, in this author's view, the Dutch tax appears to violate the Chicago Convention's prohibition on fees, dues, or other charges being imposed on aircraft solely for the right of entry or exit from the territory of a State party to the Convention. *See* Convention on International Civil Aviation art. 15(3), 61 Stat. 1180, 15 U.N.T.S. 295 (Dec. 7, 1944); *see also* Brian F. Havel, Legal Opinion of Professor Brian F. Havel to the Schiphol Group and Barin (Feb. 26, 2008) (copy on file with author).

4. Further access to government-financed air transportation

A liberalization philosophy would justify further EU carrier access to the so-called Fly America program.[279] To address U.S. Department of Defense concerns about the abolition or contraction of Fly America, it has been suggested by U.S. interests that all U.S. and EU carriers which seek U.S. Government business should be required to subscribe to the military airlift support obligations of the Civil Reserve Air Fleet (CRAF) program.[280] Such a contractual agreement, backed by appropriate penalties including loss of operating certificates by noncompliant carriers, would ensure that U.S. military requirements would not be compromised by full or partial elimination of Fly America. No comparable government-financed program formally exists in the EU.[281]

To ensure, however, that U.S. carriers suffer no discrimination under an *informal* government policy favoring EU airlines, it has been proposed that language should be included in a second stage agreement to guarantee equality of treatment in the procurement of government-financed international traffic. The WTO Plurilateral Agreement on Government Procurement provides a useful starting point for guaranteeing nondiscrimination.[282] Parties to that agreement are required to give the products, services, and suppliers of any other party to the agreement treatment 'no less favorable' than the treatment accorded to their domestic products, services, and suppliers (the 'national treatment' principle), and are further obligated not to discriminate among the goods, services, and suppliers of other parties (the 'most-favored-nation' principle).[283]

5. Provision of aircraft with crew (wet leasing)

The 2007 U.S./EC Agreement permits U.S. and EU carriers to wet-lease aircraft of the other party or a third country for international transportation. An extension of this right to transportation in the U.S. domestic market, which was not agreed in the

---

279. The Fly America Program was established by federal statute and requires individuals receiving U.S. federal funding to limit their air travel arrangements (in most circumstances) to U.S. carriers. *See* 49 U.S.C.A. § 40118 (West 2008). However, an exception to this rule is allowed for foreign carriers under a bilateral or multilateral agreement when the exception is 'consistent with the goals for [U.S.] international aviation policy' established by statute, *see* 49 U.S.C.A. § 40101 (West 2008), and in the context of an 'exchange of rights or benefits of similar magnitude.' § 40118(b); *see also* BRATTLE GROUP, *supra* note 81, ch. 1, at 7-8.

280. The Civil Reserve Air Fleet was established in 1952 as a means of augmenting the U.S. military's aircraft inventory. BRATTLE GROUP, *supra* note 81, ch. 7, at 1. The CRAF is made up of more than 900 U.S. commercial aircraft which the U.S. Department of Defense may utilize in a defense emergency. *Id.* It is funded largely through the Fly America Program, *see supra* note 279, which 'pays back' U.S. carriers for making parts of their fleet available. *Id.* ch. 7, at 17-18. Without Fly America, the U.S. Department of Defense believes it will not be able to sustain CRAF effectively. *Id.* ch. 7, at 18-19.

281. *See generally id.* ch. 7.

282. *See* Agreement on Government Procurement, Apr. 15, 1994, Marrakesh Agreement Establishing the World Trade Organization, Annex 4, Plurilateral Trade Agreements (1994).

283. For a fuller treatment of this fundamental structural principle of international trade, *see infra* Chapter 6, Part III.

first stage, would arguably be deemed to constitute cabotage operations and would therefore require a statutory change.[284]

6. *Expanding safety cooperation to include 'ramp' inspections*[285]

7. *Full embrace of the ECAA States*[286]

8. *Special labor provisions including social protections for airline workers and amendment of immigration laws to allow exercise of cabotage, wet leasing, and other operations (potentially part of the OAA's regulatory convergence ethos)*[287]

9. *Deeper agreements on convergence and harmonization*[288]

---

284. *See* PABLO MENDES DE LEON, CABOTAGE IN AIR TRANSPORT REGULATION 53-57 (1992) (discussing the development of U.S. cabotage statutes).

285. This feature is part of the U.K./Singapore Agreement only. *See* U.K./Singapore Agreement, *supra* note 229, art. 11.

286. This feature occurs only in the Open Aviation Area (OAA) proposal. For more analysis of the OAA, *see supra* text accompanying note 166.

287. An OAA could – but need not – require any general liberalization of the labor market, liberalization of outsourcing beyond wet leasing, modification of current employee social protections, or changes in the rights of labor organizations to represent employees. According to a major study on EU Member State labor regulation prepared for the European Commission, neither American nor European employees enjoy a more favorable position under law and regulation, so that it will be the performance of individual companies rather than differences in levels of social protection that will more decisively shape the prospects and welfare of employees of U.S. and EU airlines. *See infra* Chapter 6, Part III(E) (considering possible labor provisions of a 'beyond open skies' agenda).

288. As we will consider in Chapter 6, ultimately the European Commission is not interested in a series of incremental agreements. The Commission's air transport lexicon continues to include the concept of a future 'single market for air transport' between the European Union and the United States where the salient characteristic is the free flow of investment and unrestricted rights to provide air services (including cabotage). European Commission, *Air Transport Agreement, supra* note 205, at 2. But the Commission also expects that governments should work together efficiently and constructively in areas like aviation security, facilitation of international travel, and harmonization of technical standards in safety-related areas as well as in creating clarity and business certainty with respect to regulation of the competitive framework. Of course, a great deal more could be done on competition harmonization and convergence, but considerations of confidentiality because of separate regimes set limits that Annex 2 of the U.S./EC Air Transport Agreement and its accompanying Memorandum of Understanding explain and respect. As we will see, *infra* Chapter 6, Part III(E), some commentators, such as Rutger Jan toe Laer, propose that the second stage could embed a more integrated mechanism that would take advantage of the consumer-driven philosophy of U.S. and EC antitrust laws and their respective application. Replacement of the present 'double-approval' system by a 'one-stop approval' system for airline alliances would assign approval of new alliances to the jurisdiction which (to borrow U.S. jurisprudential parlance) has the greatest 'center of gravity' relationship with the transaction under review. This would be, for example, the jurisdiction where the alliance partner with the largest city-pair network or the largest contribution to alliance revenues is established. It is unclear whether this kind of 'substantive positive comity' would require legislative action (in the United States) or whether

The second stage issues presented in this Part have been harvested from three major emanations of international aviation public policymaking – the 2007 U.S./EC Air Transport Agreement, the 2006 U.K./Singapore bilateral air services agreement, and the European Commission's broad conceptualization known as the OAA. These issues are all likely to be considered in the coming negotiations, but they should also be understood as products of the specific aeropolitical circumstances of the U.S./EU relationship. Although the 2007 agreement anticipates its evolution into a plurilateral settlement that is open to third States, the parties will probably continue in the second stage to seek the kind of balancing of concessions that marked their earlier rounds of bargaining. The issues discussed here, therefore, may be resolved by conventional aerodiplomacy and bilateral compromises. This book, in Chapter 6, will propose a more cohesive second stage agenda – a select list of principles of liberalization – that seeks to transcend the specificity of U.S./EU aeropolitics and to generate an authentic transnational and plurilateral treaty designed to attract adherents from all regions of the globe. Many of the issues synthesized in this Part will feature in this re-imagined second stage framework, where they will support a more ambitious vision for the law and policy that determines the future of international air transportation.

VI   CONCLUSION: VISIONARIES, PRAGMATISTS, AND THE SHAPING OF A POST-CHICAGO GLOBAL AVIATION ORDER

The European Commission's vision of an 'OAA' is a vision that projects well beyond the current U.S. open skies template. The United States saw its goal in the first stage of U.S./EC transatlantic negotiations as the completion of its open skies program throughout the EU, and in effect negotiated for (although conceded more than) a multilateral version of its standard open skies bilateral instrument. Non-tariff barriers, therefore, such as access to the London Heathrow mega-complex, were uppermost in the minds of the U.S. negotiators. For the European Commission, however, its credibility as an external negotiator was in the balance, as well as its capacity to sustain its vision of achieving a settlement that would be greater than an amplified version of the U.S. open skies template. In the Commission's understanding, the most powerful strategy for market-opening would switch from

---

indeed the ouster of U.S. appellate procedures (in situations where the European Community becomes the 'one-stop' jurisdiction) would even be constitutionally valid. One of the assumptions of these proposals is that the alliance system will survive for the moment (and, consequently, that full freedom of transnational investment will not be a part of the second stage). Moreover, EU commentators such as Erwin von den Steinen believe it to be illogical, not just from a safety perspective, that there should be divergent rules under an OAA governing persons operating the same types of aircraft over the same routes and under the same operating conditions. For a fuller treatment of the challenges of antitrust convergence posed by U.S./EC airline liberalization, *see infra* Chapter 6, Part III(E).

incrementally adding traffic rights along the continuum of the traditional freedoms toward the negotiation of improved reciprocal investment opportunities.

Similarly, in the Commission's view, the markets would necessarily have to become more structurally alike in order to suppress competitive distortion, and that would mean promotion of regulatory harmonization and even convergence with regard to the economic conditions governing the operation of the markets (enforcement of competition laws, disfavor of subsidization, common standards for services such as groundhandling), as well as social (including labor) laws, and regulations covering the environment, security, safety, and air navigation reliability.[289] To the U.S. Government, according to one acerbic European observer, 'the terms harmonization and convergence are foreign jargon.'[290] A contrast between the Commission's idealistic vision and the business-driven pragmatism of the Americans was implicit in former U.S. Under Secretary of Transportation for Policy Jeffrey Shane's promotion of a cautiously tailored interpretive rule, in place of a legislative makeover, as a means to introduce flexibility into his Department's ongoing assessment of the degree of permissible foreign control over U.S. airline operations.[291] I will return to these ideological and philosophical contrasts between the U.S. and EC negotiators, which will shape the eventual outcome of the present transatlantic talks, in the closing Chapter.

In the introduction to Chapter 1 of *In Search of Open Skies*, I predicted a 'grand aerodiplomatic chess game' between the United States and Europe that was just beginning when the book was published in 1997.[292] That choice of metaphor

---

289. A sustainability issue now clouds the future expansion of EU air transport: in the view of some observers, the political imperatives of climate change within the Union have allowed the Commission's environmental officials to trump the deregulators of the Transport Directorate-General. *See* Gabriel S. Sanchez, *European Unilateralism*, NAT'L L.J., Mar. 31, 2008, at 23.

290. Woll, *supra* note 6, at 15. As has been evident throughout this Chapter, the U.S. and EC negotiators still do not agree on the issue of regulatory harmonization. A mantra of EC negotiating policy is that opening up market access is not sufficient to maximize commercial benefits, and that States must have comparable levels of safety, security, and other essential regulatory standards in order to ensure a truly level playing field. Calleja, *supra* note 25, at 6. The Commission also advocates strict application of competition and public subsidy (State aid) policies. *Id.* As will be considered further in Chapter 5, aviation within the European Community is subject to the same competition rules that apply to other industries, and in 2004 the Community adopted legislation that gives the Commission the same powers that it applies to intra-Union air transport in respect of international aviation on routes to and from the Union. *Id; see also* Press Release, Europa, Commission Welcomes New Powers to Apply the Competition Rules to Air Transport Between the EC and Third Countries, IP/04/272 (Feb. 26, 2004). For full discussion of the new legislation, *see infra* Chapter 5, Part II(D).

291. Pragmatism is a recurring feature of U.S. international aviation policy. The Department of Transportation has indicated, for example, that the restrictions on foreign ownership that appear in all U.S. bilateral air services agreements (*i.e.*, requiring the designated airlines of other States to be owned and controlled by the citizens of those States) can be waived if such a waiver is 'not inimical to U.S. interests.' For more on this point, *see* Havel, *supra* note 12 (proposing reforms to U.S. ownership and control rules).

292. BRIAN F. HAVEL, IN SEARCH OF OPEN SKIES 14 (1997).

was almost certainly naive. Victory in competitive chess presumes that one or other of the players has attained informational, conceptual, and cognitive advantages over an opponent. The U.S. and EC negotiators (and their advisers and cohorts) have not and will not confront that kind of asymmetry. In my background discussions with both U.S. and EC officials, I have encountered much more flexibility in approaching the reorganization of international aviation relations at a multilateral level, with fewer specific preconditions, than can sometimes be gleaned from official public rhetoric. But aeropolitical forces – including the declared resistance of U.S. and EU labor unions, the conservative impulses of political leadership, and lately the rise of national security and trade protectionism as paramount policy concerns – are inherent in the Chicago system and will frequently compress the scope for flexibility. Switching metaphorical fields, therefore, I now anticipate the beginning of a grand aeropolitical *Agora*.

Beyond Open Skies explores how the world's two aviation superpowers have arrived at this moment of impending transformation. It attempts not only to predict the outcome of their search for a new multilateral *modus vivendi*, but to present a specific blueprint, charged more with principle than detail (and consequently with a different emphasis from the TCAA model), to maximize the reciprocal benefits of abandoning the Chicago system. Through the powerful lens of the comparative method, I will show how these facially opposite air transport systems, a unitary federal airspace and a confederation of competing sovereign air powers, evolved to a point of legal and policy symmetry that allowed them to create a transformative open skies treaty and that will allow them, in the second stage of their ongoing negotiations, jointly to anchor a new kind of multilateral agreement, a *plurilateral* agreement, open to the gradual accession of all States and regional groupings that wish to accept a post-Chicago liberalized air transport system. The choice of the EC as a 'model jurisdiction' for comparative study is quite deliberate. Although the current U.S. international aviation policy speaks of 'building aviation relationships between the United States and "potential growth areas" – in Asia, South America, and Central Europe'[293] – the EC remains the largest aviation trading partner of the United States,[294] the closest to the United States in general economic philosophy,[295] and a compelling (and unique) precedent for the scrapping of restrictive bilateral air treaties in favor of truly open skies.[296]

---

293. 1995 Policy Statement, *supra* note 7, at 21,844. And, indeed, the United States has concluded a multilateral agreement with a select group of Asian countries. *See supra* note 76.

294. The United States and European Union together account for almost 60% of global air transport output. Calleja, *supra* note 25.

295. *See generally* DAVID HARVEY, A BRIEF HISTORY OF NEOLIBERALISM (2007); KARL POLANYI, THE GREAT TRANSFORMATION (Beacon Press 2001) (1957); MONICA PRASAD, THE POLITICS OF FREE MARKETS: THE RISE OF NEOLIBERAL ECONOMIC POLICIES IN BRITAIN, FRANCE, GERMANY AND THE UNITED STATES (2006).

296. *See* Shane, *Open Skies Agreements, supra* note 133 ('. . . an essential prerequisite [to a new liberalization] is a likeminded partner on the other side of the negotiating table that represents an airline industry and an aviation market comparable to our own. . . . The [EU] airline industry, taken as a whole, and the [EU] aviation marketplace, taken as a whole, certainly satisfy that test').

Chapter 3

Airspace Sovereignty: The Ontology of the Chicago System of International Air Transport Regulation

I   INTRODUCTION: THE CONCEPTUAL FRAMEWORK OF THE CHICAGO SYSTEM

This Chapter takes a closer look at the fundamental elements of the Chicago system in order to structure both the book's comparative analysis and the cogency of its final recommendations. Here, eight industry-specific features are used to establish the structural faults and contradictions of a long-prevailing regime that has been approaching its moment of legal and commercial entropy. The features, and associated themes, introduced here will appear throughout our later comparative studies of U.S. and European Community (EC) air transport deregulation, and in the elaboration of the principles of a 'beyond open-skies' plurilateral agreement in Chapter 6. The eight selected features are presented now in brief summary and more elaborately discussed in the balance of the Chapter:

(1) the doctrine of national airspace sovereignty, sanctified in the Chicago Convention as the juridical predicate for government control of the world airline industry for over 60 years;

(2) the piecemeal, negotiated exchange of air traffic rights and other conditions of airspace access through bilateral treaties as opposed to free multilateral grant;

(3) the doctrine of cabotage, which peremptorily excludes foreign airlines from traffic rights on domestic point-to-point routes;

(4) the nationality rule, by which each State reserves its domestic cabotage routes, and designation under its bilateral treaties to serve international routes, to carriers that are owned and controlled by the State or its citizens;

(5) the practice of public ownership of national (or 'flag') carriers, supported by incidents of State patronage that include subsidy programs and protection from market competition;

(6) government efforts to fine-tune regulatory control of the tremendous power of global distribution technology, including computer reservations systems, and to ensure a fair distribution of access to scarce airport slot and gate facilities;

(7) the evolution of levels of strategic cooperation among airlines of different national affiliation, including the device of code-sharing, all of which reflect a partial entrepreneurial evasion, with varying levels of official government complicity, of the Statist precepts of cabotage and nationality; and finally,

(8) confinement of authentic multilateral cooperation to technical and logistical matters such as ticket interlining, with the striking exception of the discredited practice of collective price-setting through the tariff conferences of the International Air Transport Association (IATA).

This critique of the Chicago system will identify signs of a perceptible transition, which has recently gathered pace, from a State-dominated system toward future *private* governance of the international airline industry. Despite the enduring 'specificity' of the Chicago system,[1] initiatives such as U.S. airline deregulation, the open skies program, and the EC single aviation market, have begun a gradual displacement of the State's primary role in the international airline industry in favor of independent managements and the market system. As airlines receive greater autonomy to define their markets through freedom to price, to determine capacity, and to enter specific city-pair routes, these governments are seeking to replace *a priori* State control with supervision of the market *a posteriori* through competition policy, and (in the EU) by rolling back traditional ownership stakes in so-called 'flag' carriers. But efforts to 'export' the U.S. deregulatory model, or to expand the European model of multi-State liberalization beyond the outer borders of the Union, must still contend with the restrictions of the Chicago bilateral order. There is, after all, a basic systemic incompatibility between the Chicago idea of zero-sum diplomatic exchanges and a free market system which, if one may borrow the vocabulary of the deconstructionists, presumes the 'death' of the State.[2]

---

1. Michael G. Folliot uses the terms 'specificity' and 'universality' to describe two opposing principles at work in the international air transport system: expressions of supranational tendencies apply the principle of 'universality' (the European Community's liberalization policy being the prototypical instance), while expressions of national tendencies (the 'zero-sum' strategies of the bilateral system) apply the principle of 'specificity.' Michael G. Folliot, *La Communauté Économique Européenne et Le Transport Aérien*, 32 R. Fr. D. Aérien 137, 140 (1978).

2. While the large air carriers of the future will continue to be 'international' in their operations, there is no early evidence that any of them will deliberately break free of their home territories while doing so. For many of them, in fact, the home territory is the locus of their primary passenger, cargo, and mail traffic. The 'legacy' EU flag carriers, for instance, have rarely taken advantage of the opportunity to escape their home markets and to establish a significant presence in other States. A few unusual exceptions exist, such as the Hungarian State carrier

Indeed, despite the deregulatory enthusiasm of American and European administrators, vestiges of the Chicago regulatory 'complex' continue to influence their treatment of new developments in the air transport industry, such as global distribution systems, the explosion in demand for scarce airport facilities, and even passenger rights, that were not foreseen by the designers of the Chicago system but which have important implications for competition in a future globalized industry. On the other hand, this very same deregulatory enthusiasm has inspired two initiatives by airline managements to moderate, although not entirely to disapply, the rigid nationality and cabotage rules. These initiatives, the emergence of strategic alliances between carriers of different national affiliations and the related device of code-sharing, have created an uneasy cohabitation of State and management interests within an industry historically ruled solely by sovereign prerogative. States have nevertheless tolerated these developments to the point where they have become part of the trade agenda at bilateral air negotiations. Government complicity in the use of artifices that have destabilized the sovereignty moorings of the Chicago system are a sure portent of its eventual demise.

II   AIRSPACE SOVEREIGNTY

We begin with the most elemental principle of the Chicago system, the doctrine of airspace sovereignty. The customary international law principle of exclusive sovereignty of States over the use of their airspace (traceable to the Roman axiom *cujus est solum, ejus est usque ad coelum et ad inferos)*[3] was enshrined in Article I

Malev, operating Dublin/Athens and Helsinki/Athens. *See* Malev Hungarian Airlines, <www.malev.hu>. Low-cost carriers, in contrast, have flourished in the EU since liberalization using a business model that includes large bases operating so-called stand-alone operations outside a carrier's home territory. *See, e.g.*, Ryanair, Where We Fly, <www.ryanair.com/site/EN/dests.php?flash=chk> (showing how low-cost carrier Ryanair's route map includes multiple operations from Frankfurt and Brussels that have no route connection to the carrier's home territory of Ireland). In this study, a 'globalized' airline is simply one that is commercially free to operate internationally on any routes (including cabotage routes) that it chooses to enter, not necessarily a carrier that has (somehow) engineered autonomy from all national territorial or governmental affiliations.

3. I.H. PHILEPINA DIEDERIKS-VERSCHOOR, AN INTRODUCTION TO AIR LAW 5 (8th rev. ed. 2006). The Roman axiom translates into English as 'for whomsoever owns the soil, it is theirs up to the sky and down to the depths.' The boundaries where airspace ends and outer space begins have not been clearly defined. The Outer Space Treaty, quite differently from aviation law, specifies that no nation can assert sovereignty claims over outer space. As one commentator has recently noted, '[w]hile outer space activities have continued to develop without significant restrictions . . . there are important practical reasons why a clear legal distinction between "commercial aviation flights" and "commercial space flights" should now be properly determined, given the impending advent of space tourist activities – particularly involving suborbital flights. This is even more appropriate as the fundamental premises upon which air law and outer space law are respectively based are wholly divergent.' Steven Freeland, *Up, Up and . . . Back: The Emergence of Space Tourism and its Impact on the International Law of Outer Space*, 6 CHI. J. INT'L L. 1, 6 (2005).

of the 1919 Paris Convention on the Regulation of Air Navigation.[4] 25 years later, this philosophy of 'closure' was affirmed as the international legal standard at the International Civil Aviation Conference (the Chicago Conference) of 1944.[5] Cued by the Paris text, Article 1 of the Convention on International Civil Aviation (the Chicago Convention)[6] provides that '[t]he contracting States recognize that every

---

4. 'The High Contracting Parties recognize that every Power has complete and exclusive sovereignty over the air space [*sic*] above its territory [including its territorial waters].' Convention Relating to the Regulation of Aerial Navigation (*Convention Portant Réglementation de la Navigation Aérienne*), Oct. 13, 1919, 11 L.N.T.S. 173, *reprinted in* 30-1 ANNALS AIR & SPACE L. 5 (2005). By the outbreak of World War II, 34 States had ratified this Convention (the United States signed, but did not ratify). Since the Chicago Convention came into force on Apr. 4, 1947, *infra* note 6, the Paris Convention of 1919, 11 L.N.T.S. 173, *reprinted in* [Aug. 2000] 3 Av. L. Rep. (CCH) ¶ 26,011, at 21,092 (May 31, 1920) (and the Havana Convention of 1928, 47 Stat. 1901, *reprinted in* [Apr. 2000] 3 Av. L. Rep. (CCH) ¶ 26,012, at 21,097 (Feb. 20, 1928), its analogue in the Americas, ratified by the United States) have been ineffective except for historical purposes or comparison with the Chicago Convention.
5. The Chicago Conference, which opened on Nov. 1, 1944, was convened by President Roosevelt, responding to a British initiative. All of the Allied Powers, and some neutral states, participated – a total of 54 countries. *See* DIEDERIKS-VERSCHOOR, *supra* note 3, at 13-14 (noting that Saudi Arabia declined, and Russia did not participate at the last minute). The purpose of the Conference was to make arrangements for the establishment of provisional world air routes and services and to set up an interim council to collect, record, and study data concerning international aviation. The participants arrived at the conference with different agendas. The Americans, supreme in civil air transport, advocated open competition. The British proposed an international organization to coordinate air transport, to apportion the world's air routes and to decide on frequencies and tariffs. *See id.* at 13. Australia and New Zealand offered the most imaginative solution – which Professor Michael Levine branded (with evident alarm) as a harbinger of 'international socialism' – the creation of a single world airline. Michael Levine, *Scope and Limits of Multilateral Approaches to International Air Transport*, *in* OECD, FORUM FOR THE FUTURE: NEW POLICY APPROACHES TO INTERNATIONAL AIR TRANSPORT 87 n.6 (1993); *see also* DIEDERIKS-VERSCHOOR, *supra* note 3, at 9.
6. Among the documents adopted by the Chicago Convention, the centerpiece was the Convention on International Civil Aviation, *opened for signature* Dec. 7, 1944, 61 Stat. 1180, 15 U.N.T.S. 295 (entered into force Apr. 4, 1947) [hereinafter Chicago Convention]. The ninth and latest edition of the quadrilingual text (English, French, Spanish, and Russian), with amendments and annexes, is available from the International Civil Aviation Organization (ICAO). *See* International Civil Aviation Organization [ICAO], *Convention on International Civil Aviation*, ICAO Doc. 7300/9 (9th ed. Nov. 26, 2007). As of Jul. 2008, ICAO reported 190 contracting States. *See* ICAO, ICAO Documents, Doc 7300 Status, <www.icao.int/icaonet/dcs/7300.html>. In addition to the Chicago Convention, the Chicago Conference also adopted two other documents establishing the first five freedoms: International Air Services Transit Agreement, *opened for signature* Dec. 7, 1944, 59 Stat. 1693, 84 U.N.T.S. 389 (entered into force Jan. 30, 1945) (122 State parties as of 2006) [hereinafter Two Freedoms Agreement] and the International Air Transport Agreement, *opened for signature* Dec. 7, 1944, 59 Stat. 1701, 171 U.N.T.S. 387 (entered into force Jan. 30, 1945) (11 State parties as of 2006) [hereinafter Five Freedoms Agreement]. The United States entered into both the Two Freedoms and Five Freedoms Agreements, but withdrew from the latter, effective Jul. 25, 1947. The Chicago Convention established ICAO, as discussed *infra* Part IX. The Conference also adopted several resolutions and recommendations, including a standard form bilateral agreement for the exchange of air routes. The Chicago Convention was amended in 1962 and 1974 to adopt certain institutional or procedural modifications to ICAO's administrative structure. On Sept. 24, 1968, a Protocol was concluded at Buenos Aires, and attached to the Convention, which declared the English, French, and Spanish

State has complete and exclusive sovereignty over the airspace[7] above its territory.'[8] Article 6 perfects the logic of this restrictive proposition – which was inspired by defense considerations[9] – by ordaining that '[n]o scheduled international air service[10] may be operated over or into the territory of a contracting State, except with the special permission or other authorization of that State, and in accordance with the terms of such permission or authorization.'[11]

---

texts of the Convention to be of equal authenticity (although this equality had been declared in the original Convention, only an English text was ever opened for signature). *See* Protocol on the Authentic Trilingual Text of the Convention on International Civil Aviation, 19 U.S.T. 7693. A 1977 Protocol, agreed at Montreal, added Russian to the texts deemed authentic. *See* ICAO, *Convention on International Civil Aviation, supra*, at 48.

7.   Variations exist in treaty texts as to whether 'airspace' should be one or two words (the Paris and Chicago Conventions diverge, the latter preferring one word). This book adopts the Chicago usage.

8.   Chicago Convention, *supra* note 6, art. 1. In a German language study of the Chicago system, Jürgen Basedow refers to an international air transport market that exists 'against a background of international law sovereignty dogma' (*'im Zeichen des völkerrechtlichen Souveränitätsdogmas'*) (this author's translation). Jürgen Basedow, *Verkehrsrecht und Verkehrspolitik als Europäische Aufgabe ('Transport Law & Policy as a European Task'), in* EUROPÄISCHE VERKEHRSPOLITIK 7 (Gerd Aberle ed., 1987); *see also* 49 U.S.C.A. § 40103(a) (West 2008) (stating that '[t]he United States Government has exclusive sovereignty of airspace [*sic*] of the United States'). As formerly enacted, this provision stated more grandiloquently that '[t]he United States of America is hereby declared to possess and exercise complete and exclusive national sovereignty in the airspace of the United States, including the airspace above all inland waters and the airspace above those portions of the adjacent marginal high seas, bays, and lakes, over which by international law or treaty or convention the United States exercises national jurisdiction . . . .' *See* Federal Aviation Act of 1958, 72 Stat. 731, 798.

9.   Governments wanted to limit access to the airspace over their territories to prevent activities such as unauthorized photographing of military installations. In the intervening decades, satellites and high-resolution photography have made aerial photography less important. Websites such as Google Earth have made global satellite imagery free and easily accessible to anyone with an Internet connection. *See* Google Earth, <earth.google.com/index.html>. Air traffic control also has proven sophisticated enough to keep aircraft away from sensitive areas. *See generally* General Accounting Office [GAO], *Airline Competition: Impact of Changing Foreign Investment and Control Limits on U.S. Airlines*, at 14-15, GAO/RCED-93-7 (Dec. 1992, at 14-15) [hereinafter GAO, *Airline Competition*].

10. Article 5 of the Chicago Convention deals generally with rights of charter (*i.e.*, nonscheduled) traffic.

11. Chicago Convention, *supra* note 6, art. 6. Comparison with the international regime for outer space is instructive. Article 1 of the Outer Space Treaty of 1967 provides that '[o]uter space, including the moon and other celestial bodies, shall be free for exploration and use by all States . . . .' Outer Space Treaty, Jan. 27, 1967, 18 U.S.T. 2410, T.I.A.S. No. 6347; *see also* Henry A. Wassenbergh, *Regulatory Reform: A Challenge to Inter-Governmental Civil Aviation Conferences*, 11 AIR L. 31, 31 (1986). In an international legal system replete with emergency, safeguard and exception provisos to *pacta sunt servanda*, it is unsurprising to find that Article 9(b) of the Chicago Convention contains an emergency exception: 'Each contracting State reserves also the right, in exceptional circumstances or during a period of emergency, or in the interest of public safety, and with immediate effect, temporarily to restrict or prohibit flying over the whole or any part of its territory . . . ' The need for this precautionary language is unclear: in the schema of the Convention, scheduled air services overfly or land on sovereign territory (Article 1) solely by sovereign edict (Article 6). The rights reserved in Article 9 would

Thus, *States*[12] rather than airlines retained exclusive control of the air columns above their territories,[13] the consensus at Chicago having been that only State authorities could secure operational and economic regulation of public air services to secure what were perceived (other than by the United States) as the core values of a new world aviation system: financial stability, operational safety, regularity, and continuity.[14] Accordingly, whether within their domestic provinces, or in the

be exercisable whether or not Article 9 existed. But note the diminution of sovereignty implicit in the concept of 'no-fly orders' that forbid States to use airspace above parts of their territory in order to safeguard civilian populations from aerial aggression. The United Nations Security Council indicated that UN military aircraft would be allowed to enforce no-fly orders imposed by the Council in 1991 and 1992 after the cessation of hostilities in Iraq. *See generally* Michael Milde, *Aeronautical Consequences of the Iraqi Invasion of Kuwait*, 16 AIR L. 63 (1991); *see also* Scott L. Silliman, *Symposium: Responding to Rogue Regimes: From Smart Bombs to Smart Sanctions; The Iraqi Quagmire: Enforcing the No-Fly Zones*, 36 NEW ENG. L .REV. 767 (2002) (questioning the legal predicate under UN resolutions for the no-fly orders). The fundamental legal basis for the UN-sanctioned orders against Iraq, it must be noted, was ultimately the UN Charter, not the Chicago Convention. *See* DIEDERIKS-VERSCHOOR, *supra* note 3, at 19. In 2006, former British Prime Minister Tony Blair advocated a new UN no-fly zone over the war-wracked Darfur region of the Sudan. *See* Guy Dinmore, *Blair Backs No-Fly Zone Over Darfur*, FIN. TIMES (London), Dec. 13, 2006, at 1.

12. Diederiks-Verschoor notes how the Convention assumes the 'equality' of States in international aviation. DIEDERIKS-VERSCHOOR, *supra* note 3, at 16. The preamble, indeed, specifically mentions a system based on 'equality of opportunity.' *Id.* But the doctrine of air sovereignty turned this principle into a protectionist shibboleth, as each State sought to maximize its own airline's 'opportunity' by imposing restrictions on foreign airlines concerning capacity, frequency, and pricing. *Id.*

13. Article 2 of the Chicago Convention deems the 'territory' of a State to be 'the land areas and territorial waters adjacent thereto under the sovereignty . . . of such State.' Nothing is said about sovereignty over the airspace above the high seas. Since treaty and custom portray the high seas themselves as being 'free,' it would be reasonable to suppose that the airspace above those seas enjoys a similar regime of freedom. This last principle was inserted into Article 2 of the 1958 Convention on the High Seas, Apr. 29, 1958, 13 U.S.T. 2312, 450 U.N.T.S. 82, to which the United States is a party, and adopted into Article 87(1)(b) of the 1982 UN Convention on the Law of the Sea, U.N. Doc. A/Conf.62/122, 21 I.L.M. 1261 (1982) [hereinafter UNCLOS]. UNCLOS, which entered into force on Nov. 16, 1994 (but without U.S. participation) also includes traditional coastal navigation and overflight freedoms in its 200 nautical mile 'exclusive economic zone.' UNCLOS, *supra*, art. 58; *see also generally* Jonathan I. Charney, *Entry into Force of the 1982 Convention on the Law of the Sea*, 35 VA. J. INT'L L. 381 (1995); John A. Duff, *The United States and the Law of the Sea Convention: Sliding Back from Accession and Ratification*, 11 OCEAN & COASTAL L.J. 1 (discussing background to U.S. recalcitrance on UNCLOS). For a comparison between the traditional freedom of the high seas and the principles of the Chicago Convention, *see* R.M. Forrest, *Is Open Competition Preferable to Regulation?*, 6 AIR LAW 7, 8 (1981); *see also generally* Major Stephen M. Shrewsbury, *September 11th and the Single European Sky: Developing Concepts of Airspace Sovereignty*, 68 J. AIR L. & COM. 115 (2003) (exploring how airspace sovereignty doctrines will be modified through example of proposed EC integration of air navigation services).

14. The United States, although it did not try to rupture the emerging consensus, advocated a system of free competition to determine fares, frequencies, schedules, and capacity, and sought a multilateral exchange of privileges of friendly passage (the so-called 'freedoms of the air'). BETSY GIDWITZ, THE POLITICS OF INTERNATIONAL AIR TRANSPORT 49-50 (1980); *see also* Shrewsbury, *supra* note 13, at 132 (noting how U.S. negotiators 'campaigned for "freedom of the air"

regulation of their international services, States traditionally kept air transport as a concessionary activity, where market access was not the product of individual entrepreneurial initiative but depended on a right of access conceded by the State.[15] Henry A. Wassenbergh refers to this exclusionary State control, the 'closed' system designed at Chicago, as a public international law enshrinement of the so-called 'gateway policy.'[16]

III	AT THE HEART OF THE CHICAGO SYSTEM: THE FREEDOMS OF THE AIR AND BILATERALISM

A   THE NINE FREEDOMS

To recall the axiom introduced in Chapter 1, a corollary of the doctrine of airspace sovereignty is that all commercial international air passenger transport services are forbidden except to the extent that they are permitted.[17] Despite U.S. lobbying at Chicago, there is no general 'freedom of the air' to foster free international competition in the supply of air services.[18] The system crafted at Chicago is that States will only allow the general principle of *non-freedom* to be modified in order to accommodate a bundle of narrowly-defined access

---

in a commercial sense'). The Europeans feared that a competitive market would decimate their infant aviation industries. *See* Gloria J. Garland, *The American Deregulation Experience and the Use of Article 90 to Expedite EEC Air Transport Liberalization*, EUR. COMM. L. REV. 193, 194 (1986); *see also* Andras Vamos-Goldman, *The Stagnation of Economic Regulation under Public International Air Law: Examining its Contribution to the Woeful State of the Airline Industry*, 23 TRANSP. L.J. 425 (1996) (noting how commercial aviation has evolved apart from military aviation and toward emphasis on precisely the trend to liberalized trade that the United States championed in 1944).

15. Bastiaan van der Esch, *Main Issues of Community Law Governing Access to Air Transport and Member States' Control of Fares*, in TOWARD A COMMUNITY AIR TRANSPORT POLICY: THE LEGAL DIMENSION 40 (Pieter J. Slot & Prodromos D. Dagtoglou eds., 1989). A concessionary status, which contemplates (but often does produce) multiple recipients of the state's favor, is distinguished from straightforward 'service-monopolies' such as the postal service. *Id.* Perhaps the best example of a regulated service monopoly is the supply of electricity. *See* Robert Kuttner, *Plane Truth: The Case for Re-Regulating Airlines*, NEW REP., Jul. 17, 1989, at 21-23.

16. Henry A. Wassenbergh, *New Aspects of National Aviation Policies and the Future of International Air Transport Regulation*, 13 AIR L. 18, 19 (1988). 'In virtue of their sovereignty States control the access to the international air traffic market to/from and via their territory, which territory includes the national airspace, and they control the international access to/from their domestic markets.' *Id.* 'Gateways,' in other words, are the *terminal* points of international point-to-point route service. New York and London are gateways to the United States and the United Kingdom, respectively. The Chicago system does not permit pick-up of new passengers at a gateway point for onward travel *within* the jurisdiction. The doctrine of cabotage will be considered in greater detail at *infra* Part IV.

17. *See* Colin Thaine, *The Way Ahead from Memo 2: The Need for More Competition a Better Deal for Europe*, 10 AIR L. 90, 91 (1985).

18. Jacques Naveau, *Bilateralism Revisited in Europe*, 10 AIR L. 85, 86 (1985).

rights – incongruously dubbed 'freedoms of the air'[19] – that governments typically exchange on a bilateral basis. These freedoms, incorporated into the 'Two Freedoms' and 'Five Freedoms' Agreements at Chicago,[20] are formulated in an ascending order of liberality of market access. The first and second freedoms are 'transit' rights which involve passing through the granting State's territory.[21] They permit, respectively, overflight and non-commercial landing (for example, for a refueling stop).[22] Despite their technical nature, these rights can sometimes have substantial economic consequences. Without overflight, for example, countries that control large amounts of airspace (such as Canada or Russia) could otherwise block direct international routes.[23] The third, fourth, and

---

19. In view of the sovereignty principle of Article 1 of the Chicago Convention, it would be more accurate to speak of 'privileges' rather than 'freedoms,' and indeed both the Two Freedoms and Five Freedoms Agreements use the term 'privilege' for each of the prescribed access rights. Nonetheless, the expression 'freedoms of the air' has attained wide currency in the law of international air transport. *See* PETER P. C. HAANAPPEL, RATEMAKING IN INTERNATIONAL AIR TRANSPORT: A LEGAL ANALYSIS OF INTERNATIONAL AIR FARES AND RATES 11 (1978) [hereinafter HAANAPPEL, RATEMAKING]; *see also* ICAO, Chicago Conference, Introduction, <www.icao.int/ icao/en/Chicago_Conf/intro.html> (explicitly referring to the sequential granting of reciprocal air rights as 'freedoms'). Professor Lowenfeld pronounced himself 'offended' by the application of the word 'freedoms' to the Chicago system, 'because the freedoms of international civil aviation seemed to be available for sale or barter, not what one thinks of as a characteristic of freedom.' Andreas F. Lowenfeld, *Competition in International Aviation: The Next Round*, Address to International Conference on Air Transport and Space Application in the New World, Tokyo (Jun. 1993), *in Airline Commission Documents*, Dkt. No. 000384 [hereinafter Lowenfeld Address]. For an explanation of the citation format for the proceedings of the 1993 Airline Commission, *see* Chapter 1, note 11.
20. *See supra* note 6. The Five Freedoms Agreement restates the two freedoms proclaimed in the Two Freedoms Agreement. Five Freedoms Agreement, *supra* note 6, art. I, §§ 1(1)-(2).
21. For a useful graphic representation of the all of the freedoms discussed in the main text, *see* U.S. Department of Transportation [U.S. DOT], Freedom Rights, <http://ostpxweb.dot.gov/aviation/ Data/freedoms.htm> [hereinafter Freedom Rights]. The freedoms should not be regarded as archaisms. They remain indispensable to the structure of Chicago system of exchanges of rights, and continue to be deployed even in the most advanced iteration of the Chicago bilateral, the new U.S./EC Air Transport Agreement. *See* 2007 O.J. (L 134) 4 (May 25, 2007) [hereinafter U.S./EC Air Transport Agreement]. The first and second freedoms appear in Article 3(1)(a) and (b) of the Agreement, respectively.
22. Two Freedoms Agreement, *supra* note 6, art. I, § 1. Although many States have ratified the Two Freedoms Agreement, *supra* note 6, 'a commercial enterprise . . . would not get very far if . . . limited to the exercise of these two privileges.' Forrest, *supra* note 13, at 8.
23. Overflights could be a source of fee income to national governments (or national airlines, in the case of Russia's Aeroflot), but are highly susceptible to abuse if the territory of transit is aeronautically significant . Russia's overflight charges stemming from its jurisdiction over the shortest air routes from Europe to East Asia (the trans-Siberia corridor) have been a vexed question for decades. Overflight charges (or 'royalties') imposed by Russia on EU airlines, which in 2006 caused a transfer of over 300 million euro into Aeroflot's coffers, were the subject of a formal sunsetting agreement between the European Community and the Russian Federation in November 2006. *See* Press Release, Europa, EU and Russia Agree to Abolition of euro 300 Million Siberian Overflight Payments, IP/06/1626 (Nov. 24, 2006) (indicating that normal navigation charges in accordance with Article 15 of the Chicago Convention would become the only charges imposed after Dec. 31, 2013; meanwhile, no new overflight charges would be introduced and existing overflight royalties would be grandfathered but subject to a sliding scale of reductions after 2010). Earlier, in 2005, the United States also reached an

fifth freedoms are called 'traffic' rights, because they grant permission to pick up and discharge passengers, cargo, and mail.[24]

For purposes of explanation, it will be helpful to take the example of two notable aviation rivals, the United States and the United Kingdom, and two of their signature carriers, United Airlines (United) and British Airways (BA). The third freedom bestows upon United, as a designated U.S. carrier, the right to carry passengers from the United States to the United Kingdom.[25] The mirror image of this right is the fourth freedom, which permits United to enplane passengers in the United Kingdom for transit back to the United States.[26] BA, in turn, carries passengers to the United States using U.K. third freedom rights, and flies passengers back to the United Kingdom employing the fourth freedom. The fifth freedom, the network-building freedom, allows United to enplane passengers in the United Kingdom for further transit to a third State (France or Germany, for example) with which the United States also shares bilateral exchange rights.[27] This is known as 'beyond' fifth freedom traffic,[28] and requires the United States to have the permission of *both* the United Kingdom *and* the third State, France or Germany.[29]

---

agreement with Russia to improve U.S. access to trans-Siberian overflights. Like a similar agreement signed almost a decade earlier, this new agreement still does not provide U.S. airlines with an *open* right of first freedom access, since the new protocol continues to impose numerical caps on U.S. overflight frequency. But it does provide that U.S. airlines will only have to pay user fees for air navigation services rather than overflight charges as such. *See* Protocol between the Government of the United States of America and the Government of the Russian Federation to Amend the Jan. 14, 1994 Air Transport Agreement between the Government of the United States of America and the Government of the Russian Federation, annex IV, secs. 5-6, *reprinted in* [Nov. 2005] 3 Av. L. Rep. (CCH) ¶ 26,474d, at 22,977-5 & 6 (Oct. 5, 2005) (not yet in force).

24. *See* Freedom Rights, *supra* note 21.
25. Five Freedoms Agreement, *supra* note 6, art. I, § 1(3) (stating '[t]he privilege to put down passengers ... taken on in the territory of the State whose nationality the aircraft possesses'); *see also* U.S./EC Air Transport Agreement, *supra* note 21, art. 3(1)(c)(i)-(ii).
26. Five Freedoms Agreement, *supra* note 6, art. I, § 1(4) (stating '[t]he privilege to take on passengers ... destined for the territory of the State whose nationality the aircraft possesses'); *see also* U.S./EC Air Transport Agreement, *supra* note 21, art. 3(1)(c)(ii).
27. Five Freedoms Agreement, *supra* note 6, art. I, § 1(5) (stating '[t]he privilege to take on passengers ... destined for the territory of any other contracting State and the privilege to put down passengers ... coming from any such territory'); *see also* U.S./EC Air Transport Agreement, *supra* note 21, art. 3(1)(c)(i)-(ii). *See generally* PAT HANLON, GLOBAL AIRLINES: COMPETITION IN A TRANSNATIONAL INDUSTRY 99 (2d ed. 2002) (discussing how access to fifth freedom rights allows air carriers to establish 'fairly large hubs' in foreign countries; examples include British Airways and Qantas in Singapore and formerly British Airways/Air Liberté in Paris, where the latter was a subsidiary). For a general statement on how the EC views U.S. airlines' access to intra-Union fifth freedom routes (e.g. London/Paris) as functionally comparable to access to the U.S. domestic market, as well as the importance of EC fifth freedom rights to U.S. cargo carriers' parcel-shipment networks, *see* European Commission, *Communication from the Commission on the Consequences of the Court Judgments of 5 November 2002 for European Air Transport Policy*, para. 14, COM (2002) 649 final (Nov. 19, 2002).
28. HANLON, *supra* note 27, at 88.
29. If United enplanes no additional passengers in the United Kingdom, but merely carries its U.S.-origin passengers to additional beyond points, this is usually treated as 'blind sector' transit

When United carries passengers from the United States to the United Kingdom with an *intermediate* stop in France or Germany, discharges some U.S. passengers and picks up new passengers in France or Germany bound for the United Kingdom, this carriage, known as 'intermediate' fifth freedom traffic, also requires the United States to have the permission of *both* the United Kingdom *and* the intermediate third State, France or Germany.[30]

Again, fifth freedom rights exercised by BA replicate those of United: BA might pick up passengers in the United States for onward transit to Canada, for example, or make an intermediate stop in Canada en route to the United States to discharge passengers from the United Kingdom and to enplane new passengers bound for the United States. As Gertler properly emphasizes, the exchange of fifth freedom rights at a strictly bilateral level 'may become entirely valueless if traffic rights are not also granted by the third country concerned' (France, Germany, or Canada in these examples).[31] A more colorful gloss was offered by former U.S. Civil Aeronautics Board (CAB) chairman John Robson, in remarks to his fellow Airline Commission members in 1993:[32] '[B]eyond rights are essentially prisoner to whatever arrangements can be made with the second, the beyond point.'[33] Inevitably, this 'network' precondition to the exercise of fifth freedom rights causes most complications in practice, and was a major cause of the failure of the Five Freedoms Agreement to attract State adherents.[34]

---

and does not require negotiated permission (unless the beyond point is a *second* destination in the United Kingdom, a so-called coterminalization right). In fact, U.S. and U.K. carriers possess unlimited 'blind sector' rights beyond each other's territory. *See* Agreement Between the United States of America and the United Kingdom of Great Britain and Northern Ireland Concerning Air Services annex 1, sec. 5, para. 5 [March 1999] 3 Av. L. Rep. (CCH) ¶ 26,540c, at 23,251 (Jul. 23, 1977) (indicating, in an explanatory note to the text of the expiring U.S./U.K. air services agreement, known as Bermuda II, *see infra* note 66, that U.S. and U.K. airlines have the right to carry online connecting traffic to countries that are not listed in the agreement's specific route-pair columns).

30. *See* HANLON, *supra* note 27, at 88. This alignment is simply fifth freedom beyond traffic viewed from a different 'holographic' perspective, that of the third State, France or Germany. The movement of passengers from the United States to the intermediate State, France or Germany, takes place under the U.S./France bilateral or U.S./Germany bilateral, respectively, each of which includes beyond fifth freedom rights for the U.S. carrier to pick up passengers in France or Germany (as the case may be) bound for the United Kingdom.

31. *See* Z. Joseph Gertler, *Order in the Air and the Problem of Real and False Options*, 4 ANNALS AIR & SPACE L. 93, 119 (1979).

32. *See infra* note 33.

33. *Airline Commission Proceedings*, Testimony of John E. Robson, Former Chairman, Civil Aeronautics Board (May 26, 1993), at 95.

34. The Five Freedoms Agreement is not without precedential force, however. It can be portrayed as a precursor to the plurilateral model developed in the final Chapter of this book. Thus, Article I proposes a multilateral grant of the five freedoms to all contracting States, without the need for separate bilateral treaties. But only a few countries have ever signed or ratified the agreement. *See supra* note 6. The United States withdrew from the agreement in 1946, declaring that its poor adoption record made it an unreliable medium for the establishment of international air routes. Withdrawal of the United States of America, [U.S.] Dept. of State Press Release No. 510, *reprinted in* [Oct. 1998] 3 Av. L. Rep. (CCH) ¶ 26,016, at 21,117 (Jul. 25, 1946).

The route-building potential of the Chicago system is circumscribed still further by the general rule that the exercise of the rights in the Two Freedoms/ Five Freedoms Agreements must be tied to specific 'route' patterns between the home State and any foreign State with which it is contracting bilaterally. Thus, the third, fourth, and fifth freedoms as described above relate only to through-service 'on a route constituting a reasonably direct line out from and back to the home territory of the State whose nationality the aircraft possesses.'[35] The practical consequence of this proviso is to ensure that United and BA, for example, do not use fifth freedom rights to create long chains of intermediate connections that have only incidental (or theoretical) origin and termination points in their home territories.

In counterpoint to this prevailing philosophy of closure, State practice has introduced some nuances into the Chicago routing system that increase airline flexibility (although they are not usually part of the formal bilateral agenda). It is possible, for example, for air passenger traffic to originate from a country *other than* the United States, to transit through the United States, and to continue to the United Kingdom, where those passengers are set down. This complex of access rights is known as the 'sixth freedom:' in effect, fourth freedom (inbound) traffic is moved from (say) Mexico to the United States (United's State of nationality or 'home' State) under the U.S./Mexico bilateral. Some of the U.S./Mexico passengers then continue as third freedom (outbound) traffic from the United States to the United Kingdom under the U.S./U.K. bilateral. From BA's point of view, passengers in France flying to New York via London on BA flights would be sixth freedom traffic, combining two streams of fourth and third freedom traffic (*i.e.,* Paris/London and London/New York).[36]

In sixth freedom scenarios, the 'home' State (the United States or the United Kingdom) is itself an intermediate or swivel point between two other origin and destination States (Mexico/United Kingdom or France/United States); put another way, the home State's carrier exercises fifth freedom rights out of *its own* territory. Some commentators go further and distinguish a seventh freedom, namely, sixth freedom traffic as in the above examples, but *without* a stop at the transit point in the home State, the United States or United Kingdom.[37] Thus, United could offer direct

---

35. Five Freedoms Agreement, *supra* note 6, art. I, § 1. *See generally* Frank D. Hall, *Development of the International Framework of Air Transportation,* 5 NORTHROP U. L.J. AEROSPACE, ENERGY & ENV'T 1, 6 (1984).

36. Sixth freedom traffic is very difficult for the destination State (the United Kingdom and the United States, in these examples) to control, and effectively requires the cooperation of the sixth freedom carrier (or its government) for bilateral regulation. *See* DANIEL A. KASPER, DEREGULA- TION AND GLOBALIZATION: LIBERALIZING INTERNATIONAL TRADE IN AIR SERVICES 53 (1988). Where sixth freedom traffic *is* carried with the knowledge and consent of the third State (here, Mexico or France) under the Mexico/U.K. or U.S./France bilaterals, the term 'anterior fifth freedom' traffic should be substituted for 'sixth freedom.' *See* HANLON, *supra* note 27, at 87 (noting controversial nature of the sixth freedom, which is nonetheless supported by some States – those whose locations give their airlines good opportunities to carry sixth freedom traffic – on the ground that it is 'implicit in the grant of a pair of third/fourth freedoms'). *See also* 2007 Air Transport Agreement, *supra* note 21, art. 3(1)(c)(i)-(ii).

37. *See* HANLON, *supra* note 27, at 89 (mentioning now-expired U.S. privilege for services between Tokyo and Seoul). As part of a U.S./U.K. mini-agreement in 1991, under which United Airlines and American Airlines replaced Pan Am and TWA, respectively, as the designated Heathrow

service from Mexico to the United Kingdom, or BA could operate a Frankfurt/New York route, without transiting through their respective home countries.[38]

Finally, under the rubric of 'cabotage,' an eighth and a ninth freedom can be identified. Eighth freedom traffic gives a foreign carrier so-called 'fill-up' rights as it transits between two or more gateways in the home State. BA, on a coterminalized London/New York/Los Angeles route, for example, would be permitted to board new passengers in New York for the New York/Los Angeles segment only. Ninth freedom traffic is cabotage in its pure form, the right to pick up and set down passengers between two domestic points (New York and Chicago or London and Glasgow Prestwick), neither of which is the end-point of a flight sequence that began in a foreign State.[39] By the terms of the new 2007 U.S./EC Air Transport Agreement, for now the most broadly liberal iteration of a Chicago bilateral agreement, the eighth and ninth freedom freedoms are explicitly excluded.[40]

---

carriers, U.K. authorities believed that the United States granted the United Kingdom seventh freedom rights to pick up passengers at a restricted series of European points served by British Airways or other U.K. airlines with U.S. route authority (including points in Luxembourg, The Netherlands, Ireland, Belgium, France, and Germany), and to fly them to the United States without transiting through the United Kingdom. *See* Government of the United States of America and the Government of the United Kingdom, Memorandum of Consultations, ¶ 12 (Mar. 11, 1991) (copy on file with author). Demonstrating again the network limitations of the bilateral system, these rights remained unexercised because of resistance from the European governments whose airports would be affected (but seventh freedom rights are now accorded to all EC-licensed airlines under the 2007 U.S./EC air services agreement, *see supra* note 21). Although the point was mooted by State practice, DOT officials contended that the United States did not concede 'stand-alone' seventh freedom rights to the British. In fairness to the Americans, the plain meaning of the Memorandum of Consultations and of the master bilateral agreement, *see* Agreement Amending the Agreement of Jul. 23, 1977, as Amended, [Mar. 1999] 3 Av. L. Rep. (CCH) ¶ 26,540f, at 23,266-68 (Dec. 4, 1980), certainly suggests that the rights granted were predicated on flights that would originate in the United Kingdom. *See generally* HANLON, *supra*, at 90-93 (discussing future exercise of seventh freedom services from the European Union to the United States, and acquiescing in the U.K. interpretation of the 1991 Memorandum of Consultations).

38.   As will be seen, *infra* Chapter 5, Part II, seventh freedom traffic is part of the EC single aviation market. *See also* U.S./EC Air Transport Agreement, *supra* note 21, art. 3(1)(c)(ii) (providing for mutual all-cargo 'sevenths' and, for the first time, *pace* the U.K. position reflected in *supra* note 37, according seventh freedom rights to all EC-licensed scheduled air passenger carriers with respect to U.S.-bound services from all EU points, U.S./EC Air Transport Agreement, *supra* note 21, art. 3(1)(c). All-cargo seventh freedoms are an optional part of the DOT's open skies model agreement. *See* U.S. Department of State, Air Transport Agreement Between the Government of the United States of America and the Government of [country] (Jan. 1, 2008), <www.state.gov/documents/organization/19622.pdf> [hereinafter Model Open Skies Agreement].

39.   Cabotage, domestic traffic carried by foreign aircraft, is discussed *infra* Part IV. *See generally* HANLON, *supra* note 27, at 89-90 (observing that 'sovereign States have steadfastly refused to trade cabotage rights,' but clarifying how this resistance has broken down within the EC single aviation market); *see also* HAANAPPEL, RATEMAKING, *supra* note 19, at 11-12. On the distinction between eighth and ninth freedom cabotage, *see* George Petsikas, *'Open Skies' – North America*, 17 ANNALS AIR & SPACE L. 281, 288 (1992); *see also* Fred Lazar, *Turbulence in the Skies: Options for Making Canadian Airline Travel More Attractive*, C.D. HOWE INST. COMMENT., Apr. 2003, at 3.

40.   *See* U.S./EC Air Transport Agreement, *supra* note 21, art. 3(6)(a)-(b).

B   TRADING THE FREEDOMS: THE RISE OF BILATERALISM

After the failure of the Five Freedoms Agreement to prompt a multilateral exchange of rights of access,[41] the bilateral treaty developed as the principal diplomatic and political vehicle for these trades. As objects of purely bilateral exchange, however, the freedoms of the air were conceded only on the basis of defensive reciprocity. As Professor Bin Cheng has written, 'every newborn "freedom of the air" is in reality an additional shackle on the right to fly of foreign carriers, to be removed only at a price.'[42] A State could choose from among the so-called 'freedoms' a bundle of permissions that would open its national airspace to a greater or lesser extent depending on how generously it and its bilateral partners wished to exchange international air services.[43]

In fact, the bilateral method of exchange was not embodied in the Convention at all,[44] but rather in the text of a collateral resolution adopted by the Chicago Conference. Resolution VIII, captioned 'Standard Form of Agreement for Provisional

41. This was the U.S. proposal to the Chicago Conference. *See* ANDREAS F. LOWENFELD, AVIATION LAW: CASES AND MATERIALS 2-7 & 2-8 (2d ed. 1981) (analyzing various diplomatic positions at the Conference).

42. BIN CHENG, THE LAW OF INTERNATIONAL AIR TRANSPORT 322 (1962). *See generally* F. Allen Bliss, *Rethinking Restrictions on Cabotage: Moving to Free Trade in Passenger Aviation*, 17 SUFFOLK TRANSNAT'L L. REV. 382 (1994).

43. The U.S./Ireland agreement (now disapplied by the 2007 U.S./EC Air Transport Agreement), for example, permitted U.S. carriers a very limited fifth freedom right of picking up passengers in Shannon or Dublin for onward transit. Only one fifth freedom point beyond Dublin could be selected by the U.S. Government. Agreement Between the United States of America and Ireland on Aviation Transport Services Amending the Agreement of Feb. 3, 1945, as Amended, Sept. 6, 1990, T.I.A.S. 11,739 [hereinafter U.S./Ireland Agreement]; *but see* Ireland, [Apr. 2008] 3 Av. L. Rep. (CCH) ¶ 26,354, at 22,449 (noting that civil air transport between the U.S. and Ireland is now governed by the 2007 U.S./EC Air Transport Agreement). The outgoing bilateral agreement also included the unusual 'Shannon stopover' requirement that mandated that for every flight to or from Shannon Airport in the west of Ireland, an airline could then operate one flight to or from Dublin. (The stopover was a longstanding reflex of public policy, designed to support a weak regional economy.) *See* U.S./Ireland Agreement, *supra*. The new U.S./EC Air Transport Agreement phased out the Shannon stopover over an 18-month transitional period. During the transition, the ratio of Dublin/Shannon flights moved from 1:1 to 3:1 (the ratio could be averaged out over the period of the transition). *See* Steven Lott, *U.S., Ireland Sign Agreement: EU Open-Skies Deal May Slip*, 362 AVIATION DAILY, Nov. 15, 2005, at 1. Had the new U.S./EC Agreement collapsed, the Shannon phase-out likely would not have occurred because of U.S. insistence that it would not negotiate a replacement bilateral with Ireland (despite the urging of the then Irish Minister for Transport, Martin Cullen). *See* Honor Mahoney, *U.S. Wants EU-Wide Flight Deal*, IRISH TIMES, Jan. 10, 2007, at 17.

44. *See* COMITÉ DES SAGES, EXPANDING HORIZONS: CIVIL AVIATION IN EUROPE, AN ACTION PROGRAMME FOR THE FUTURE 48 (1994) [hereinafter Report of the *Comité des Sages*]. The *Comité* describes how the Chicago Convention, having failed to achieve a multilateral framework to share the freedoms of the air, was effectively displaced by bilateral agreements that contain principles and rules not found in the Convention (including the nationality principle, predetermination of capacities, etc.). The *Comité* asserts that the Convention does not *explicitly* oppose multilateral arrangements for the exchange of traffic rights (in fact, it contains provisions to facilitate joint operating organizations and pooled services). *Id.* (as discussed in the final Chapter of this book, *infra* Chapter 6, Part III). While this argument has some merit, its practical consequence seems

Air Routes,' recommended a model non-exclusive bilateral agreement[45] which States were free to adopt during a transitional period (the immediate postwar period) 'in order to obtain practical experience for giving effect to more permanent arrangements at a later date.'[46] Just as the subsidiary General Agreement on Tariffs and Trade (GATT) survived the stillborn International Trade Organization,[47] the bilateral focus of provisional Resolution VIII vitiated the multilateral grant of rights proposed in the Five Freedoms Agreement. Indeed, in the absence of any 'permanent arrangements,' bilateralism persisted long past the transitional period expected by Resolution VIII.[48]

The so-called 'air services agreements,'[49] and their related confidential memoranda of understanding,[50] have become the 'prime source of norms for the

---

merely to be that the existing Convention need not be formally denounced by parties to a new plurilateral agreement.

45. The notion that 'exclusive' rights should not be awarded to any one State, a prototypical non-discrimination or 'most favored nation' principle, also appears in Article 7 of the Chicago Convention, which sets conditions for the grant of cabotage rights. For the discussion, *see infra* Part IV.

46. Resolutions of the Final Act of the International Civil Aviation Conference, Dept. of State Pub. No. 2282, *reprinted in* 3 Av. L. Rep. (CCH) ¶ 28,012, at 25,061 (Dec. 7, 1944). The text of Resolution VIII appears at 25,063-66.

47. *See* discussion in JOHN H. JACKSON, SOVEREIGNTY, THE WTO AND CHANGING FUNDAMENTALS OF INTERNATIONAL LAW 92-98 (2006). The GATT was the 'default' successor to the planned International Trade Organization (ITO). U.S. Congressional antipathy doomed the ITO project in 1950. *Id.* at 94.

48. On the nature and scope of bilateral air transport agreements generally, *see* CHENG, *supra* note 42, at 231-46. *See also* Org. Econ. Coop. & Develop. [OECD], *Background Document*, Workshop on Regulatory Reform in International Air Cargo Transportation, Paris, at 54-63 (Jul. 5-6, 1999) (including an excellent treatment of how air cargo is dealt with in bilateral air services agreements); INTERVISTAS, THE ECONOMIC IMPACT OF AIR SERVICE LIBERALIZATION (2006) (placing bilateral agreements in their economic and political context); Z. Joseph Gertler, *Bilateral Air Transport Agreements*, 42 J. AIR L. & COM. 779 (1976); Whitney Gilliland, *Bilateral Agreements, in* THE FREEDOM OF THE AIR 140-158 (Edward McWhinney & Martin A. Bradley eds., 1968); Oliver J. Lissitzyn, *Bilateral Agreements on Air Transport*, 30 J. AIR L. & COM. 248 (1964).

49. *See generally* David J. Bederman, Note, *Prospects for European Air Deregulation*, 21 INT'L LAW. 561, 563 (1987). In the United States, incidentally, air services agreements are merely 'executive agreements,' not 'treaties' in the precise meaning of Article II of the United States Constitution (*i.e.*, for which Senate ratification is required). *See* discussion in Barbara A. Bell, *The Extraterritorial Application of United States Antitrust Law and International Aviation: A Comity of Errors*, 54 J. AIR L. & COM. 533, 540 (1988). The practice in U.S. foreign policy, however, has been to submit multilateral instruments (such as the World Trade Organization Charter and attached agreements and the treaty to enlarge the North Atlantic Treaty Organization) to the Senate for Article II ratification, and it is to be expected that the plurilateral agreement proposed in the final Chapter of this book would require that this kind of Congressional sanction. This is particularly so because the plurilateral will require amendments to domestic U.S. legislation. Nonetheless, the new U.S./EC Air Transport Agreement (which is technically a bilateral agreement, however) was not submitted to the Congress for ratification. For the criteria used in selecting the constitutional basis for domestic approval of U.S. international treaties, *see* U.S. Dept. of State, Circular 175, § 721.3, *reprinted in* BARRY E. CARTER ET AL., INTERNATIONAL LAW 203-204 (1995).

50. In its 1979 memorandum, *Air Transport: A Community Approach*, the European Commission observed that '[t]hese bilateral agreements do not always state precisely the real content of the

economic regulation of international civil aviation.'[51] The result, a massive case-by-case negotiation and exchange of literally thousands of international air routes, has been picturesquely described by Professor Cheng as a 'labyrinthine legal grotto.'[52] Indeed, in an assertion at odds with the arguments made in this book, European air law specialist Jacques Naveau wrote that the 'narrow commercial interests' that pervade air transportation mean that 'bilateralism is there to stay.'[53]

1	*Ex Post Facto* Flexibility: The Moderate Liberalism of Bermuda I

It would be impossible, in a work of this size, to trace all of the negotiated idiosyncrasies of the world's present stock of air service bilaterals. Yet some guideposts as to content will be helpful. Chapter 1 considered the typical features of what might be called the late-model U.S. open skies liberal bilateral (the open skies model will again feature in an analysis of U.S. international aviation policy in the next Chapter). For now, however, the pre-liberalization phase of the Chicago system can be represented through two paradigmatic agreements concluded some 30 years apart between the same contracting parties, the United States and the United Kingdom. The first treaty, the U.S./U.K. Air Transport Agreement of 1946, popularly known as the Bermuda I agreement in tribute to the place of its negotiation and signature, became the prototype for all subsequent bilateral agreements on the international exchange of air services.[54] Somewhat paradoxically, this earlier agreement revealed several conceptual affinities with the later open skies

---

decisions. They are often supplemented by confidential letters of understanding exchanged between the aeronautical authorities of the [S]tates concerned.' BULL. EUR. COMM'N, Supp. 5/79, annex II, at 27-28, ¶ 35. *See generally* Oliver J. Lissitzyn, *The Legal Status of Executive Agreements on Air Transport* (Parts I and II), 17 J. AIR L. & COM. 436 (1950) & 18 J. AIR L. & COM. 12 (1951).

51. L. Gilles Sion, *Multilateral Air Transport Agreements Reconsidered: The Possibility of a Regional Agreement Among North Atlantic States*, 22 VA. J. INT'L L. 155, 159 (1981). *See also* HANLON, *supra* note 27, at 87 (commenting that the traditional concept of bilateral agreements also suggests that these agreements 'should result in an equitable exchange of economic benefits').

52. CHENG, *supra* note 42, at 491. *See also* Cornelia Woll, *The Activism of the European Commission in the Case of International Aviation* 6 (AICGS/DAAD, Working Paper Series, 2003) (stating that, if one takes account of all informal exchanges, amendments, additions, and writings, the global number of extant bilateral air services agreements may be as high as 10,000).

53. Naveau, *supra* note 18, at 87.

54. Agreement Between the Government of the United States of America and the Government of the United Kingdom Relating to Air Services Between Their Respective Territories, *reprinted in* [Apr. 2008] 3 Av. L. Rep. (CCH) ¶ 26,540a, at 23,219 (Feb. 11, 1946) [hereinafter Bermuda I]; *see also* Jacques Naveau, *Away from Bermuda? An Arbitration Verdict on Capacity Clauses in the Belgian/Ireland Air Transport Agreement*, 8 AIR L. 44 (1983). Following the 2007 U.S./ EC Air Transport Agreement, Bermuda I now only governs aviation relations between the United States and Guyana and between the United States and Zambia.

philosophy, which cannot be said of any feature of its protectionist successor in 1977. Thus, while sponsorship of competition was certainly not the driving purpose of the 1946 Bermuda conference,[55] by the standards of many later agreements, which locked in a predetermined 50/50 capacity split among competing airlines on designated routes,[56] Bermuda I's provisions on *ex post facto* capacity adjustments might even qualify as 'liberal.'[57]

In 1980, the ICAO Panel on Regulation of Air Transport Services identified three basic capacity management philosophies[58] for use in a bilateral context: the Bermuda I *ex post facto* method, the 50/50 predetermination method adopted in later bilaterals, and a third approach that the panel labeled the 'free-determination' method, in which governments rely almost exclusively on competitive pricing and responses of airlines to market forces (in effect, the U.S. open skies approach).[59] While not a wholesale suppression of State intervention, Bermuda I's omission of rigid anterior controls over capacity reflected the flexibility sought by the Bermuda

---

55. *See* Wassenbergh, *supra* note 11, at 31.
56. Many countries have traditionally insisted on equal division of capacity. *See* Praveen Singh, *Some Aspects of Australia's Bilateral Air Services Agreements*, 9 Air L. 160 (1984). The long-held U.S. view is that its air carriers have the primary claim to 'U.S. generated traffic.' While the principle of primacy over national traffic seems destined to be diluted by the liberalizing spirit of current U.S. international aviation policy, the statutory mandate for *any* U.S. international aviation policy (as contained in the International Air Transportation Competition Act of 1979 and *infra* Chapter 4, Part III) requires the Secretaries of State and Transportation to strengthen the competitive position of U.S. air carriers 'to ensure at least equality with foreign air carriers, including the attainment of the opportunity for air carriers to maintain and increase their prof-itability in foreign air transportation.' 49 U.S.C.A. § 40101(e) (West 2008). It is not hard to extrapolate a principle of formal and substantive equal capacity from these words. On this point, *see also* F. Loy, *Bilateral Air Transport Agreements: Some Problems of Finding a Fair Route Exchange*, *in* The Freedom of the Air, *supra* note 48, at 174-189.
57. Like many bilateral treaties, Bermuda I's provisions are scattered among several acts of the contracting parties, including a manifesto of general principles which is the 'Agreement' proper, an 'Annex' describing the routes being exchanged, and a Final Act, or resolution, of the conference delegates to which the Agreement and Annex are formally appended. The Agreement and Annex are reprinted in 3 Av. L. Rep. (CCH) ¶ 26,540a, at 23,219-23,227. For the text of the Final Act, *see* Agreement Between the Government of the United States of America and the Government of the United Kingdom of Great Britain and Northern Ireland Relating to Air Services Between Their Respective Territories, Final Act, Feb. 11, 1946, T.I.A.S. 1507 [hereinafter Bermuda I Final Act].
58. 'Capacity' is output or supply. In the context of air passenger transportation, capacity refers to the number of passengers per day that can be carried on a particular route. 'Capacity restrictions' are limits to the number of flights (and thus available seats) permitted between two points. 'Excess capacity' means empty seats – too many flights chasing too few passengers to result in efficient carriage. 'Capacity determination' in an international bilateral air services agreement means the setting of the total traffic volume or payload that an airline can carry on an international air route over a given period. It can be expressed in terms of available passenger seat kilometers, flight frequencies, or type of aircraft. *See generally* Haanappel, Ratemaking, *supra* note 19, at 1.
59. In its draft 'predetermination' clause, the ICAO panel opted for a formula of equal sharing of the total capacity. *See* Ralph Azzie, *Second Special Air Transport Conference and Bilateral Air Transport Agreements*, 5 Annals Air & Space L. 3, 7-9 (1980).

negotiators, who hoped to accommodate both American expansionism and British protectionism in the same regulatory formula.[60]

At the same time, however, the 'liberalism' of the Bermuda I capacity rules was arguably also accidental, the product of over-artful draftsmanship. Hence, for example, Paragraph 5 of the Final Act of the Bermuda conference[61] provided that, 'in the operation by the air carriers of either Government of the trunk services described in the Annex to the Agreement, the interest of the air carriers of the other Government shall be taken into consideration so as not to affect unduly the services which the latter provides on all or part of the same routes.'[62] Paragraph 6 of the same instrument amplified this vague invocation of 'interest' by providing that the agreed services should retain 'as their primary objective the provision of capacity adequate to the traffic demands between the country of which [the air carrier operating the service was] a national and the country of ultimate destination of the traffic.' The net effect of these twin paragraphs was an unintelligible compromise. Their elliptical structure, deliberately avoiding any predetermined traffic shares for either party's carriers, appeared capable of leaving decisions regarding flight frequency (and change of gauge[63]) to the airline managements, with *ex post facto* adjustment by the two governments through consultation.[64] The United States tended to interpret these provisions liberally, although other countries understood the text to sanction capacity controls where the contracting parties so agreed.[65]

In other aspects of market regulation, too, the original Bermuda I could be scored as a modestly liberal agreement, at least on paper. Under Article 2 of the Agreement proper, the parties granted each other the right to designate one or more air companies which were allowed to operate regular international air services between and beyond the contracting States.[66] Thus, multiple designation (a core

---

60. DIEDERIKS-VERSCHOOR, *supra* note 3, at 60-62.
61. *See supra* note 57.
62. *Id.*
63. Bermuda I permitted a change of aircraft along a route to fit the size of the passenger load being carried. This is commonly called a 'change of gauge' provision. Bermuda I, *supra* note 54, annex, sec. V.
64. Professor Lowenfeld condemned the drafting of Bermuda I, including Article 6, as an 'only partly articulate compromise.' Lowenfeld Address, *supra* note 19, at 2. A second, more complex formula governed fifth freedom traffic rights, which were '{subject to the general principle that capacity should be related: (a) [t]o traffic requirements between the country of origin and the countries of destination; (b) to the requirements of through airline operation; and (c) to the traffic requirements of the area through which the airline passes after taking account of local and regional services.' Bermuda I Final Act, *supra* note 57. This vague language produced much inter-governmental controversy and was consciously abandoned in the U.S. open skies regime. *See* James R. Atwood, *International Aviation: How Much Competition, and How?*, 32 STAN. L. REV. 1061, 1066 (1980) (book review).
65. Albert W. Stoffel, *American Bilateral Air Transport Agreements on the Threshold of the Jet Transport Age*, 26 J. AIR L. & COM. 119, 129-30 (1959).
66. *See* Bermuda I, *supra* note 54, art. 2. The specific routes to be followed were set out in the Annex. *Id.* annex, sec. III. In the first paragraph of the Annex, the designated air carriers of each of the contracting parties were granted access to all of the airports that were designated for international air services. This market flexibility is in sharp contrast to the 1980 restrictive

element of open skies) was at least contemplated, although the particular routes to be served by the designated carriers, using the Chicago freedoms, was the object of rigid codification in the Annex.[67] Article 6 of the Agreement was an early specimen of the restrictive rule of national ownership and control, but was drafted to allow the possibility that designated airlines might be under the 'substantial ownership and effective control' of nationals of *either* party.[68] This rather less restrictive phrasing, which was superseded in later Bermuda I agreements by a requirement of ownership and control by nationals of the *designating* party (or by the party itself), reflected U.S. 'aero-colonization' in Latin America after World War II. (A number of South American carriers, such as Panagra, were owned and controlled by one or more U.S. carriers in the immediate postwar years.)[69] But Bermuda I did not adopt any measures to liberalize the setting of prices. On the contrary, the agreement included the least liberal form of official fare supervision, the so-called 'double approval' system. While airlines were allowed to negotiate and agree fares through the tariff conferences of the IATA,[70] all fare modifications required advance filing with and approval by the aeronautical authorities in both countries.[71]

The hundreds of Bermuda I-type agreements varied in details, but the foregoing describes their common essential structure.[72] Although, as seen earlier, the

---

amendments to Bermuda I's successor, styled Bermuda II, 28 U.S.T. 5367, *reprinted in* [Mar. 1999] 3 Av. L. Rep. (CCH) ¶ 26,540c, at 22,234 (Jul. 23, 1977) [hereinafter Bermuda II], allowing only particular U.S. carriers to operate from U.S. points to London's Heathrow Airport. *See* Agreement Amending the Agreement of Jul. 23, 1977 [Bermuda II], as Amended, Dec. 4, 1980, *reprinted in* [Mar. 1999] 3 Av. L. Rep. (CCH) ¶ 26,540f, at 23,271.

67. *See* Bermuda I, *supra* note 54, annex. A discussion of the route sequences permitted under Bermuda II is contained *infra* in the main text. Moreover, States typically agreed to restrictions on the number of permitted air carriers. *See* Stoffel, *supra* note 65, at 127-30.

68. Bermuda I, *supra* note 54, art. 6.

69. Panagra, for example, was part-owned by Pan Am for over 30 years and was eventually absorbed into Braniff in 1967. *See generally* WILLIAM A. KRUSEN, FLYING THE ANDES: THE STORY OF PAN AMERICAN GRACE AIRWAYS (1997). Eventually these arrangements were seen as much too cozy, giving U.S. airlines a large say in the competitive structure of the airline systems of foreign countries.

70. *See* discussion of the IATA tariff-setting mechanisms, *infra* Part IX. In its heyday, IATA's regional traffic conferences set airline fares by unanimity, although States retained the right to review and approve the established rates. The practice of State aviation authorities, however, was to concur in the rates struck at IATA conferences *See* Stoffel, *supra* note 65, at 134.

71. Bermuda I, *supra* note 54, annex, sec. 2. Although the terms are often used interchangeably, strictly speaking a 'fare' is a price to be paid for the air transportation of passengers and their baggage, while a 'rate' is the air transportation price for cargo. The broader term 'tariff' comprises the price to be paid for the air transportation of passengers, baggage, and cargo, and the conditions under which that price applies, often including prices and conditions for agency and other auxiliary services. *See generally* HAANAPPEL, RATEMAKING, *supra* note 19, at 1.

72. In 1959, the European Civil Aviation Conference (ECAC) promulgated a set of model clauses, known as the 'Strasbourg Clauses,' which was recommended for use among ECAC members. For the text of the Strasbourg Clauses, *see* JAMES R. FOX, THE REGULATION OF INTERNATIONAL COMMERCIAL AVIATION: THE INTERNATIONAL REGULATORY STRUCTURE, Booklet 1, Treaties, 30-35 (1993). The ECAC model differed from Bermuda I only in its omission of any explicit capacity clauses, although periodic bilateral consultation, which would presumably include review of capacity shares, was required by Article 9. *See id.*

ex post facto capacity clauses in Bermuda I could be read as devolving a certain amount of discretion to airline managements, the more authentic managed trade philosophy of Bermuda I-style bilateralism was best expressed in Paragraphs 4 and 9 of the Final Act.[73] The first of these provisions established that each contracting State should have a 'fair and equal opportunity' to operate the agreed international services.[74] The second announced the intention of both governments 'that there should be regular and frequent consultation between their respective aeronautical authorities... and that there should thereby be close collaboration in the observance of the principles... in the Agreement and its Annex.'[75] Accordingly, Bermuda I sought to create a fairly stable 'equal' opportunity between the appointed ('designated') air carriers of each contracting party, so that neither State, irrespective of the market success of its carriers, could keep more than a guaranteed segment of its negotiating partner's market.[76] In Colin Thaine's evocative phrase, the contracting parties, through consultation and collaboration, wished to ensure that 'blood [would not be] drawn.'[77]

---

73. *See* Bermuda I Final Act, *supra* note 57, paras. 4 & 9.
74. *Id.* para. 4.
75. *Id.* para. 9.
76. GAO, *Airline Competition, supra* note 9, at 44. An international arbitration between Belgium and Ireland in 1981 – one of very few arbitrations in international air transport – revealed the working of this delicate balancing of sovereign rights. *See* Jacques Naveau, *A New Arbitration Verdict Involving a Bilateral Agreement: Arbitration on the Belgium/Ireland Capacity Clause*, 38 IATA Weekly Bull. 975 (1981) [hereinafter Naveau, *A New Arbitration*]; Jacques Naveau, *Arbitral Award in the Dispute between the Belgian and Irish Civil Aviation Authorities over Services between Brussels and Dublin by Sabena and Aer Lingus, given at Dublin July 17, 1981*, 8 Air L. 50 (1983) [hereinafter Naveau, *Arbitral Award*]. The Bermuda I-style capacity clause in the Belgium/Ireland bilateral provided that air transport capacity 'shall be adapted to traffic needs.' Naveau, *Arbitral Award*, at 45. Belgium argued that the route was subject to excessive capacity because of the higher number of flights operated by the Irish carrier, Aer Lingus, and that the average load factor (*i.e.* seats filled on each flight) on the route was only 40%. Belgium therefore requested the arbitrator to assign both Sabena and Aer Lingus four round-trips per week on the route. Ireland countered that Aer Lingus had developed the route and that 60% of the route's traffic originated in Ireland. In any event, there was no international law requirement of 'equality.' Arbitrator Winberg stated that 'the airlines should take their mutual interests into account,' and that meant that 'an airline may not provide excessive capacity likely to endanger the viability of the other carrier's operations on a given route.' Naveau, *A New Arbitration, supra*, at 975. Finding overcapacity to be proven by the unusually low load factors, Winberg cut the frequencies of both carriers on the route, although he did not insist on formally equal capacity. Naveau, *Arbitral Award, supra,* at 57. Thus, Sabena's competitive weakness on the route was compensated by reducing the capacity of the more successful competitor, Aer Lingus, thereby checking the play of market forces that would have sent Sabena 'into the red,' as the arbitrator commented. Sabena, incidentally, was eventually forced into liquidation in 2001.
77. Thaine, *supra* note 17, at 91. While this is generally the case, examples of bilateral conflict – where one State retaliates against a prior restrictive action by the other – abound in the international airline system. For a recent analysis of the inadequacies of dispute resolution under existing bilaterals, *see* Brian F. Havel, *International Instruments in Air, Space and Telecommunications Law: The Need for a Mandatory Supranational Dispute Settlement Mechanism*, *in* The International Bureau of the Permanent Court of Arbitration, 4 Peace Palace Papers: Arbitration in Air, Space, and Telecommunications Law 11 (2002) (noting that ad hoc arbitration

2   **Treaty-Based Rigidity: Bermuda II**

The Bermuda I archetype endured unchallenged into the 1970s. As the United States moved toward domestic airline deregulation in the latter part of that decade, its aviation officials began to explore ways to inject more competition into the Chicago/Bermuda system. Predating by 15 years U.S. Secretary of Transportation Federico Peña's 'new' international aviation policy, in 1979 the Carter Administration unveiled a model agreement designed to trade 'liberalization for liberalization' in place of 'restriction for restriction.'[78] The times had not been auspicious, however, for U.S. international aviation policy. Just two years before, the restrictive potential of the Chicago system had been dramatically reaffirmed when U.S. negotiators conceded a trophy protectionist agreement, immediately dubbed 'Bermuda II,' to their U.K. diplomatic counterparts meeting (once again) on the eponymous Caribbean island.[79] The circumstances of the negotiation foretold its outcome: in 1976, the United Kingdom had denounced Bermuda I following U.S. refusal to maintain previously-agreed capacity controls in the wake of the 1973 oil crisis.[80]

As a result of the new dispensation, Bermuda I-style *ex post facto* consultation and compromise gave way to a new regulatory architecture where virtually all of the restrictions were negotiated and codified in the treaty itself. In the telling words of former U.S. Civil Aeronautics Board Chairman Marvin S. Cohen, 'Bermuda II included terms that were so contrary to our fundamental competitive principles

---

is the most prevalent dispute resolution mechanism in U.S. bilaterals, and arguing that 'all air, space, and telecommunications disputes with an international character should be subject to mandatory mechanisms of settlement before permanent arbitral tribunals'). *See also* Craig Canetti, *Fifty Years after the Chicago Conference: A Proposal for Dispute Settlement under the Auspices of the International Civil Aviation Organization*, 26 LAW & POL'Y INT'L BUS. 497 (1995) (surveying various mechanisms for bilateral dispute settlement, including consultations, *ad hoc* arbitration, and, in older bilaterals, designation of ICAO; in documenting a growing practice of unilateral State action, Canetti proposes a revival of ICAO resolutions, and mentions a little-known ICAO sanction that allows the Member States, when the ICAO Council concludes that an airline is not conforming to a final decision, to prohibit the carrier from passing through their airspace). In the WTO/GATT dispute settlement system established in 1995, incidentally, retaliation is explicitly a remedy of last resort. JACKSON, *supra* note 47, at 197-98. *See generally* Sion, *supra* note 51, at 187-92. Chapter 4 of this book will examine two U.S. aviation statutes that permit unilateral retaliatory action outside the ambit of any bilateral agreement to 'protect' U.S. carriers' interests against anticompetitive actions by foreign governments.

78. For an economic study of the maiden open skies initiatives, *see* Jose Gomez-Ibanez & Ivor P. Morgan, *Deregulating International Markets: The Examples of Aviation and Ocean Shipping*, 2 YALE J. ON REG. 107 (1984)

79. *See supra* note 66.

80. More precisely, the United Kingdom invoked the termination provision in Article 13 of the Bermuda I Agreement, which provided for formal termination one calendar year after receipt of notice by the other contracting party. *See* Bermuda I, *supra* note 54, art. 13. The United States (acting through its Civil Aeronautics Board) had previously agreed to temporary capacity restrictions on flights to and from the United Kingdom as a fuel conservation measure. *See* Gomez-Ibanez & Morgan, *supra* note 78, at 112.

that many of the U.S. airlines were astounded.'[81] The agreement recapitulated the single most restrictive feature of Bermuda I, making airline fares again subject to the 'double approval' system of unilateral veto by either government.[82] Capacity on many named routes was specifically capped, and some routes were configured as monopolies or duopolies in place of multiple designation.[83] Annex I to the 1977 Agreement, which dealt with route exchanges, illustrates very clearly how the Chicago system promoted 'closure.'[84] With respect to passenger traffic, the Annex divided into two broad categories, U.S. outward traffic to the United Kingdom and U.K. outward traffic to the United States. Within each category, the Annex prescribed permitted combinations of points on Atlantic, Pacific, Caribbean, and 'round-the-world' air routes. To plot the combinations, a four-column matrix was used: column A listed the 'gateway' airports from which service originated; column B listed any permitted points for 'intermediate' fifth freedom service; column C named the permitted destination points in the other party's territory; and column D identified the allowed 'beyond' points to third countries. Entries in columns B and D, as discussed earlier, required collateral negotiations with the third countries whose airports were named. At the foot of each matrix, detailed notations explained special limitations on designation, capacity, and frequency.

The *a priori* content of Annex I, coupled with the bureaucratic airline designation procedures of the contracting States, displaced the dynamic market-driven

---

81. Marvin S. Cohen, *U.S. International Transportation Policy: Reflections and Objectives*, Address to the International Aviation Club, Washington, D.C. (Jan. 16, 1981) (copy on file with author).

82. *See* Bermuda II, *supra* note 66, art. 12.

83. *See id.* arts. 3 & 11. For example, in the Annex as originally agreed, the New York/Frankfurt and Washington Dulles/Frankfurt fifth freedom routes (via London) were jointly restricted to a total of no more than two designated U.S. airlines. *See id.* annex I. Some routes were configured so that an additional designation would be triggered beyond a certain capacity threshold, *e.g.*, 600,000 passengers per annum on the duopolized Chicago/London route. Accusations that the U.S. incumbent (American Airlines) was deliberately suppressing capacity in order to keep below the threshold for that route (by using smaller aircraft or withdrawing frequencies) surfaced during Congressional hearings in 1995 on a so-called U.S./U.K. 'mini-deal' that ultimately added United as a new carrier to London from Chicago's O'Hare Airport. *International Aviation Policy: Hearing Before the Subcomm. on Aviation of the Senate Comm. on Commerce, Science and Transportation*, 104th Cong., 1st Sess. 68-71 (1995) [hereinafter 1995 Aviation Hearings]. In an irony of bilateral diplomacy, United had previously been foreclosed from operating *any* flights to London from its primary world hub at Chicago. *See* Memorandum of Consultations and Draft Exchange of Notes Concerning Modifications to the U.S./U.K. Air Services Agreement, Jun. 5, 1995, Part II, ¶ 1 , at 3 (copy on file with author) (further specifying, until Jan. 1997, that there would be numerical caps on seasonal roundtrip frequencies and that the new service be operated using aircraft with a capacity of 211 seats or lower) [hereinafter 1995 U.S./U.K. Agreement].

84. *See* Bermuda II, *supra* note 66, annex I. The discussion in the main text focuses on the Annex as *originally* negotiated. The minutiae of the Annex (route combinations, flight frequencies, and so forth) have been under continual renegotiation. *See* 3 Av. L. Rep. (CCH) ¶¶26,540d-26,540j, at 23,257-23,294.

choices that private (or privatized) airline managements might make.[85] Indeed, in the form in which it existed for the 30 years of its duration,[86] Bermuda II met *none* of the open skies criteria proposed by U.S. international aviation policy.[87] Article 11, for example, postulated that when a carrier of one of the parties inaugurated service on a route already served by designated airlines of the other party, the incumbents must 'refrain from increasing the frequency of their services to the extent and for the time necessary to ensure that the airline inaugurating service may fairly exercise its rights [to have a fair and equal opportunity to compete].' The Article set an outside limit on this restraint of two years or the point when the inaugurating airline would *match* the frequencies of any incumbent, whichever occurred first. In other words, the Article appeared to interpret 'fair and equal' competition as normally meaning *exactly* equal competition. This is an example of the so-called 'Bermuda II 50/50 capacity' rule.[88]

While the system just described might display a Cartesian elegance if designed in a laboratory, in the crude reality of State practice it became – as the Bermuda II annex so vividly displays – a haphazard, unpredictable, and cumbersome farrago of sovereign prerogatives, artificial access rights, and diplomatic posturing. Bermuda II, which has now been superseded by a comprehensive U.S./EC open skies concordat,[89] was the defining example of what the European Commission's *Comité des Sages* described as the 'directive, protectionist and competition-restrictive policies' that undermined the international law of air transport through the agency of bilaterals.[90]

---

85. The route maps of U.S. carriers fall into two shapes – conventional point-to-point (third and fourth freedom traffic) or a patchwork of 'beyonds' (fifth freedom routes). This dichotomy of routing interests has created tensions for U.S. negotiators in bilateral talks. *See Airline Commission Proceedings*, testimony of James R. Tarrant, Deputy Assistant Secretary for Transportation Affairs, U.S. Dept. of State (May 26, 1993), at 120-21.
86. Until its supersession by the 2007 U.S./EC Air Transport Agreement signed in Apr. 2007.
87. *See supra* Chapter 1, Part II(C).
88. *See* Bermuda II, *supra* note 66, art. 11.
89. *See supra* note 21. Bermuda II was the high-water mark for U.K. protectionism. Subsequently, under Conservative prime ministers Thatcher and Major, the United Kingdom endeavored to ease some of the restrictive features of Bermuda II, especially its limited designations on many high-traffic routes. Amendments to the Agreement were typically achieved by exchange of diplomatic notes between the British Ambassador to the United States and the U.S. Secretary of State. Fox, *supra* note 72, Booklet 1, at 111-85. Moreover, after the privatization of British Airways in the mid-1980s, the United Kingdom itself adopted a program of offering liberal bilateral agreements. *See* U.K. Civil Aviation Authority, *CAA Statement of Policies On Route and Air Transport Licensing*, annex 6, para. 2 of Official Record Series 1 (Aug. 8, 2008) (advocating removal of all bilateral restrictions 'so that the airline industry can compete on the same footing as other industries,' and expressing the Authority's aim to make the United Kingdom's international aviation markets 'as contestable as possible by eliminating all unnecessary restrictions within its licensing and other regulatory processes'). The most recent amendment of Bermuda II was in Mar. 1997, removing Hong Kong from the Bermuda II agreement just prior to the handover of that territory to China. *See* Agreement Amending the Agreement of Jul. 23, 1977 [Bermuda II], as Amended, Mar. 27,1997, *reprinted in* [Jan. 2007] 3 Av. L. Rep. (CCH) ¶ 26,540j, at 23,293.
90. Report of the *Comité des Sages*, *supra* note 44, at 48.

After some mildly moderating amendments to its designation provisions in 1995,[91] further efforts in 2000 and 2002 to liberalize Bermuda II deadlocked over U.S. demands for additional access to London Heathrow for U.S. carriers other than United Airlines and American Airlines, while British negotiators insisted on rollbacks to restrictive U.S. laws on foreign ownership and cabotage.[92] The U.S./U.K. negotiations were subsequently absorbed into the larger U.S./EC air transport talks that followed the 'open skies' rulings by the European Court of Justice in November 2002.[93] The final chapter of this book, building on the post-Bermuda II momentum of the new transatlantic air transport treaty that emerged from those talks, will propose scrapping the entire 'archaic system of air service agreements'[94] in favor of a new *plurilateral* solution, a multinational treaty whose price of admission would be a regime of open competition, superseding the managed trade ethos of the bilateral era.[95]

IV   THE VENERABLE DOCTRINE OF CABOTAGE

A   A PRINCIPLE OF EXCLUSION

A further symptom of the sovereignty complex that ultimately swayed the hearts and minds of the Chicago Convention delegates, is 'cabotage.' The word has a venerable pedigree: it is a phenomenon of the history of trade, invented with the deliberate mercantilist purpose of protecting domestic commerce from foreign competition. Originally, cabotage was a creature of maritime law, and described a State reserving to itself the right to restrict all coastal navigation between two points within its territory for the exclusive use of its own subjects.[96] In the

---

91. See *supra* note 83.
92. Revealing the downward trajectory of the U.S./U.K. negotiations, *see* Kevin Done, *U.S. Hopeful of Liberalising Flights Across Atlantic*, FIN. TIMES, Jun. 2, 2000, at 12; Kevin Done, *Over and Out for Marathon Talks on Open Skies Accord: U.S.-UK Aviation Position of 'Heathrow Four' Airlines Remains Entrenched*, FIN. TIMES, Sept. 12, 2002, at 11.
93. See *supra* Chapter 2, Part III.
94. From Remarks of the Honorable Gerald L. Baliles, Chairman, National Airline Commission, before the International Air Transport Association Symposium, Cairo, Egypt, *in Airline Commission Documents*, undocketed, (Sept. 6, 1993), at 6. Governor Baliles noted the 'political appeal' of the Chicago Convention, '[whose] defining logic, "one for you, one for me," is difficult to refute.' *Id. See also* Remarks of Gerald L. Baliles Before the Aero Club of Washington, *in Airline Commission Documents*, undocketed, Feb. 23, 1993, at 4-7. Chapter 6 of this study will also weigh the political resistance to what would be, in effect, a recast Chicago Convention. *See infra* Chapter 6, Part IV.
95. 'We are dealing with bilaterals, which by definition mean managed trade.' *Airline Commission Proceedings*, statement of Commissioner Charles M. Barclay, President, Air Line Pilots Association, May 24, 1993, at 230. The Commission heard testimony on the distinctions between 'managed trade,' where each country controls the terms of access to its aviation market on a strictly bilateral basis, and the more open-ended WTO/GATT regime, in which 'most favored nation' and nondiscrimination principles generalize any favorable treatment extended to a bilateral partner. *See, e.g., Airline Commission Proceedings*, testimony of James R. Tarrant, Deputy Assistant Secretary for Transportation Affairs, U.S. Department of State (May 26, 1993), at 49-52.
96. DIEDERIKS-VERSCHOOR, *supra* note 3, at 23-24.

international aviation milieu, cabotage has been defined neutrally as the carriage of passengers, cargo, and mail between two points within the territory of the same State for compensation or hire,[97] but also peremptorily as a sovereign right that has traditionally been reserved to the exclusive use of that State's national carriers.[98] It is in this *preceptive* sense that Article 7 of the Chicago Convention acknowledges the right of each State 'to refuse permission to the aircraft of other contracting States to take on in its territory passengers, mail, and cargo carried for remuneration or hire and destined for another point within its territory.'[99]

In this book, as in the Chicago Convention itself, the term cabotage carries its peremptory, exclusionary connotation instead of its purely descriptive denotation as carriage between domestic points. As was implicit in our presentation of the five freedoms, cabotage restrictions are so universal that the idea of an eighth and ninth freedom, granting access to domestic routes on a fill-up or autonomous basis, emanated from the glosses of commentators and did not appear in the official classification systems of the Two Freedoms and Five Freedoms Agreements.[100] Despite strong European lobbying from the outset of U.S./EC negotiations for a

---

97. W.M. Sheehan, *Air Cabotage and the Chicago Convention*, 63 HARV. L. REV. 1157 (1950). *See also* Douglas R. Lewis, *Air Cabotage: Historical and Modern-Day Perspectives*, 45 J. AIR L. & COM. 1059 (1980); ISABELLE LELIEUR, LAW AND POLICY OF SUBSTANTIAL OWNERSHIP AND EFFECTIVE CONTROL OF AIRLINES 77 (2003). According to Professor Cheng, aerial cabotage 'applies to air transport between any two points in the same political unit, that is to say, in the territory of a State as the term is used in air law.' CHENG, *supra* note 42, at 314. Matte's definition echoes the same principle, but more precisely: 'Le terme "cabotage" comprend, en général, toute activité commerciale de transport, caractérisée par le fait que le transporteur embarque des passagers, du courrier, ou des marchandises à un certain endroit, à destination d'un autre point, tous les deux points (de départ et de destination) se trouvant à l'intérieur du même pays' ('The term cabotage means, in general, all commercial transport activity, characterized by the fact that the transporting entity embarks passengers, mail, or goods in a certain place, destined for another place, the two places (of departure and of destination) being found within the same country'). NICOLAS M. MATTE, TRAITÉ DE DROIT AÉRONAUTIQUE ('TREATISE ON AERONAUTICAL LAW') 173 (1980) (this author's translation). For a more pragmatic view, *see* Judith M. Trent, *Cabotage Rights: Politics, Policy and Economics*, paper prepared by Global Aviation Associates, Ltd., *in Airline Commission Documents*, undocketed, (May 1993) ('[T]he term "cabotage" in aviation refers to traffic that is carried between two cities, both of which are within the territory of one State').
98. *See* analysis in GAO, *International Aviation: Measures by European Community Could Limit U.S. Airlines' Ability to Compete Abroad*, at 54, GAO/RCED-93-64 (Apr. 1993) [hereinafter GAO, *International Aviation*].
99. A precursor to Article 7 appears in Article 22 of the superseded Paris Convention of 1919, which, rather than formulating a general cabotage prohibition, grants a permissive authority to each State 'to establish reservations and restrictions in favor of its own national aircraft in regard to the commercial transportation of passengers . . . between two or more points in its territory.' *See supra* note 4.
100. *See* Pieter J. Slot, *Civil Aviation in the Community: An Overview, in* TOWARD A COMMUNITY AIR TRANSPORT POLICY, *supra* note 15, at 8. For a discussion of the eighth and ninth cabotage freedoms, *see supra* Part III(A). These most commercially elusive privileges are further considered in PETER P.C. HAANAPPEL, PRICING AND CAPACITY DETERMINATION IN INTERNATIONAL AIR TRANSPORT: A LEGAL ANALYSIS 12 (1984) [hereinafter HAANAPPEL, PRICING].

new air transport agreement, the cabotage exclusion was locked into the final U.S./ EC text as agreed in April 2007.[101]

Considerations of national security, national prestige, and public interest underlay the adoption of cabotage as a governing principle of the international aviation system.[102] Security, however, was initially the paramount concern. Both the United States and the Soviet Union wished to screen sensitive defense installations from roving foreign air traffic.[103] Secondly, national prestige, and the rise of national 'flag' airlines, prompted a clamp-down on foreign competitive incursions.[104] Finally, public interest objectives required assuring safety standards and service levels (particularly as to unprofitable peripheral routes).[105]

While national security reasons may have had rhetorical resonance among the delegates at Chicago in 1944, those reasons have much less validity in a globally integrated economy.[106] The reasons for the continued insistence on aviation cabotage are now wholly economic and protectionist, as was evident from testimony elicited by the Airline Commission in 1993 and in the arguments presented in the

---

101. Article 3 (the 'Grant of Rights' provision) of the 2007 U.S./EC Air Transport Agreement provides that '[n]othing in [the Agreement] shall be deemed to confer,' with respect to the airlines of one contracting party and with respect to the territory of the other contracting party, 'the right to take on board . . . passengers, baggage, cargo, or mail carried for compensation and destined for another point' in such territory. U.S./EC Air Transport Agreement, *supra* note 21, art. 3(6).
102. *See generally* Sheehan, *supra* note 97.
103. Dr. Pablo Mendes de Leon, at the very outset of his encyclopedic analysis of cabotage, comments that the military aspects of aviation may explain why the subject 'has been dealt with as part of the principle of sovereignty in international civil aviation at a multilateral level from the very beginning.' PABLO M. J. MENDES DE LEON, CABOTAGE IN AIR TRANSPORT REGULATION 5 (1992).
104. *See* Trent, *supra* note 97, at 1.
105. The Canadian Government, for example, feared that U.S. carriers would fail to serve sparsely-populated cabotage routes in its northern territories. Being able to require public obligations of one's own carriers accordingly has much appeal. Trent, *supra* note 97, at 4. Transport Canada's new international aviation policy statement, 'Blue Sky,' confirms that '[u]nder no circumstances will the policy approach include cabotage rights.' Transport Canada, *Blue Sky: Canada's New International Air Policy* (Dec. 2006). It is not clear from the policy statement, however, whether maintenance of regional air services (rather than protectionism) remains a key driver of Canada's adherence to traditional cabotage principles. (For a more neutral analysis of the legal and commercial effects of conceding cabotage rights in Canada, *see* Armand de Mestral, *Canadian-EU Bilateral Air Service Agreements* (Institute for European Studies Working Paper No. 05/05, 2005) 26 (conspicuously omitting damage to regional air services in calculating 'unfavorable' consequences of foreign carriers serving cabotage routes in Canada). A prototypical solution for this problem may be the Essential Air Service Program in the United States, which permits carriers to compete for specific low-traffic routes on the basis of best service proposals and lowest subsidy levels. A special regime for underserved routes is also part of the EC liberalization program. *See infra* Chapter 5, Part II(C).
106. The United States, for example, can assure civil airlift capacity through its Civil Reserve Air Fleet program. *See infra* note 247 and accompanying text. On the subject of cabotage at the Chicago Convention, *see generally* Lewis, *supra* note 97, at 1059; *see also* Vamos-Goldman, *supra* note 14, at 430.

European Commission's study of the potential economic effects of a U.S./EC air transport agreement, the so-called 'Brattle Report,' almost a decade later.[107]

B   CABOTAGE IN A MULTILATERAL AIRSPACE ENVIRONMENT

A number of threshold issues of law and policy must be addressed in examining cabotage at the twilight of the Chicago system. In the context of the EC, where the airspace of the Member States was transformed in 1997 into what is arguably a single cabotage area,[108] the question arises as to the legal compatibility between this kind of regional arrangement (and any broader arrangement, including the merger with U.S. airspace that is proposed in this book) and the sovereignty precepts of the Chicago Convention. Must the Convention now be modified or renegotiated to permit States to 'pool' their sovereign airspaces, or can the EC project proceed in accordance with the existing terms agreed at Chicago? For the United States, consideration of how cabotage is preserved in federal and treaty law

---

107. *See* BRATTLE GROUP, THE ECONOMIC IMPACT OF A U.S.-EU OPEN AVIATION AREA, ch. 1, 14-15 (2002) (arguing that, as a policy matter, there is a 'strong case for eliminating' restrictions on fill-up (*i.e.*, eighth freedom) cabotage as part of a U.S./EC Air Transport Agreement because 'although the restrictions are sometimes defended on safety grounds, in fact, they appear designed to protect domestic jobs.' *See also* Trent, *supra* note 97, at 2-3 (suggesting certain *status quo* interests in cabotage as a job protection device). In addition to the procompetition arguments marshaled in the main text, it is important to recognize the economic wastefulness that cabotage creates. As former CAB Chairman Marvin Cohen told the Airline Commission, governments 'ought to have a very good reason' to justify the enormous waste of resources, and collateral environmental damage, when, for example, a Japan Air Lines 747 flies from Tokyo to Honolulu, deplanes half of its passengers in Honolulu, and is then forced to fly half-empty from Honolulu to Los Angeles simply because of the cabotage restriction. *Airline Commission Proceedings* (Jun. 24, 1993), at 111-12. As the Brattle Report diagnosed, one antidote to this specific problem would be the grant of so-called 'eighth freedom' fill-up rights.

108. Political union, the elimination of political boundaries, is not (yet) a feature of the European Union's economic integration (nor even of the broader EU political enterprise). Air transport within the Union, even with the creation of a 'common' air transport market and mutual cabotage privileges, will remain *international* air transport as defined in Article 96(b) of the Chicago Convention ('an air service which passes through the air space [*sic*] over the territory of more than one State'). *But see* Shrewsbury, *supra* note 13, at 147-150 (discussing the potential shift in the legal framework of airspace sovereignty in light of the EU's 'Single European Sky' (SES) project to integrate air navigation services throughout the airspaces of the 27 Member States). For this reason, it is strictly speaking incorrect to speak of a Community-wide 'cabotage area' as though it were a legal mirror image of the U.S. federal system. Indeed, 'true' EU cabotage routes (Rome/Milan, London/Prestwick) are not available under the present regime to non-EU carriers (and only became available to EU carriers in 1997). Within the common air transport market, however, existing fifth freedom rights of non-EU carriers (*e.g.*, London/Frankfurt, Paris/Rome) can be considered as 'quasi'-cabotage because these routes are now freely accessible to all EU carriers, without specific bilateral negotiation, as 'intra-Union' routes. *See infra* Chapter 5, Part II. The European Commission, as surrogate negotiator for all Member States, has sought without success to deploy this transformed status of fifth freedom rights as a negotiating lever to open the U.S. 'true' cabotage market. *See supra* Chapter 2, Parts II & III. On the impact of EC air transport liberalization on U.S. aviation policy, *see* Paul S. Dempsey, *Aerial Dogfights over Europe: The Liberalization of EEC Air Transport*, 53 J. AIR L. & COM. 615 (1988).

also requires weighing some preliminary policy implications of trading away all domestic traffic rights as part of a future multilateral air transport settlement. The compatibility between the EC's common aviation area and the Chicago Convention will be addressed first.

1 Pooling Airspaces in the EC: Can Cabotage Be Traded Away?

All 27 Member States of the EC have ratified the Chicago Convention.[109] Article 1 of that Convention, as noted previously, recognizes that 'every State has complete and exclusive sovereignty over the airspace over its territory.'[110] At first reading, this categorical declaration might point to a Convention bias against agreements that would partition a State's sovereign control of its airspace or, as in the EC enterprise, surrender it (or at least its commercial exploitation) to a supranational entity.[111] And yet, on at least three levels, the Chicago Convention does not seem to block this 'regionalization' of sovereign interests. First, in general terms, the Convention does not appear to have envisaged a grand-scale pooling of airspace at all, having confined its treatment of shared sovereignty to a discussion of so-called joint operating organizations under Articles 77 to 79.[112] According to Jürgen Erdmenger, '[n]othing within the Chicago Convention prevents a regional grouping of states from organizing its internal air transport partly or totally on a multinational basis.'[113]

---

109. *See* ICAO, ICAO Documents, Doc 7300 Status, *supra* note 6 (listing of 190 ratifying States (as of 2008) based on information received from the depositary, the Government of the United States of America). For the Convention's cite coordinates, *see supra* note 6.
110. Chicago Convention, *supra* note 6, art. 1. Article 1 of the Chicago Convention propounds a rule of customary international law. *See* Ludwig Weber, *External Aspects of EEC Air Transport Liberalization*, 15 Air L. 277, 280 (1990).
111. The European Community has not itself acceded to the Convention. For an analysis of the international treatymaking powers of the EU institutions, *see infra* Chapter 5, Part II(E).
112. *See* van der Esch, *supra* note 15, at 33. Article 77 of the Chicago Convention provides scope for creating 'joint air transport operating organizations' and 'international operating agencies.' The prototypical Article 77 entity is the Scandinavian Airline System (SAS), a consortium of the national flag carriers of Sweden, Norway, and Denmark. For more detailed information about cooperative arrangements, *see* ICAO, *Scandinavian Airline System: Consortium Agreement and Related Agreements*, ICAO Circular 99-AT/20 (1970). As of Jan. 1, 1995, Sweden followed Denmark into membership of the European Union, but Norway did not. SAS as a whole was specifically made subject to the new Community legislation on faresetting and capacity-sharing by widening the definition of 'Community air carrier' to include air carriers that had been providing scheduled air services between Member States on the basis of third and fourth freedoms of the air during the 12 months prior to adoption of the inaugural 1987 liberalization package. *See* G.O. Zacharias Sundström & Bo Ståhle, *Regulation of Civil Aviation in Scandinavia*, in Slot & Dagtoglou, *supra* note 15, at 285, 287. More formal arrangements subsequently brought Sweden and Norway within the ambit of the single aviation market in preparation for the 'European Economic Area' project and (in Sweden's case) eventual accession. *See infra* Chapter 5, Part II.
113. Jacques Naveau, *Bilateralism Revisited in Europe*, 10 Air L. 85, 88 (1985) (quoting Jürgen Erdmenger, *The Regional Framework as a Solution?*, Lecture to 8th International ITA Symposium (May 20-22, 1980).

Second, Article 6 of the Convention, which provides for access to airspace only by sovereign grant, contains no determination of the *form* in which a State may permit or authorize scheduled service in or over its territory. In other words, although States elected after 1944 to trade access rights through a complex web of bilateral agreements, bilateralism need not have been the *exclusive* mode of exchange.[114] Subject to the discussion below of Article 7 of the Convention, in fact, there would appear to be no *a priori* principles of international law that would deprive the EC of the right to consider its combined territory and the airspace above it as a single subject of international law, with one 'air sovereignty,' one new Community 'nationality,' one Community nationality register for aircraft, and one Community statute to regulate the air carrier corporations: in sum, a regime governed by the general principles of Community law and the relevant secondary legislation.

Third, and finally, Article 7 of the Convention clearly implies that cabotage can form the subject of sovereign barter. In its first sentence, the text acknowledges cabotage in its peremptory, exclusionary meaning ('[e]ach contracting State shall have the right to refuse permission to the aircraft of other contracting States to take on in its territory passengers, mail and cargo carried for remuneration or hire and destined for another point within its territory').[115] In its second sentence, Article 7 then contemplates that States may not 'specifically grant any such privilege *on an exclusive basis* to any other State or an airline of any other State' (nor obtain any such exclusive privilege from any other State).[116] One clear implication of the Convention language is that cabotage *can* be traded, but that such arrangements cannot be offered or obtained '*on an exclusive basis.*'[117] But the full consequences of this 'unconditional most favored nation' language are not easy to fathom.[118]

---

114. This was precisely the argument in the Report of the *Comité des Sages*, *supra* note 44, at Appendix. *See also* Peter P.C. Haanappel, *The External Aviation Relations of the European Economic Community and of EEC Members into the Twenty-First Century, Part II*, 14 Air L. 122, 141 (1989) (asserting that States, not the Chicago Convention, created the bilateral system).

115. Chicago Convention, *supra* note 6, art. 7. For some implications of the Convention's reference to 'aircraft' as opposed to 'airlines' or 'air carriers,' *see infra* note 160.

116. Chicago Convention, *supra* note 6, art. 7. Article 7 is made applicable to nonscheduled (charter) services by the terms of Article 5 of the Convention. *Id.* art. 5. In practice, charter flights tend to be international point-to-point operations that do not implicate cabotage traffic.

117. *Id.* art. 7 (emphasis added). Indeed, Article 17 of the Paris Convention, 1919, *see supra* note 4, specifically countenanced bilateral trading of cabotage rights. *See* discussion in Bliss, *supra* note 42, at 382, 384-86. No distinction is made in the present discussion between *eighth* and *ninth* freedom cabotage; nothing in the Convention suggests that fill-up rights on coterminalized international services would somehow fall outside the reach of Article 7. *See, e.g.*, Mendes de Leon, *supra* note 103, at 185-86.

118. For a partial 'most favored nation' (MFN) reading of Article 7, *see* Pablo M. J. Mendes de Leon, *Euro-Cabotage: A Lever for Liberalization of International Civil Aviation, in* EEC Air Transport Policy and Regulation and Their Implications for North America 196-197 (Peter P.C. Haanappel et al. eds., 1990). Under unconditional MFN treatment, when State A grants a privilege to State C while owing unconditional MFN to State B, A must grant the equivalent privilege to B, without necessarily receiving any reciprocal concession from B. This kind of MFN inherently excludes a policy of 'exclusivity.' *See generally* Mitsuo Matsushita et al., The World Trade Organization: Law, Practice, and Policy 143-154 (2003).

Thus, Article 7 does not evidently prohibit the mutual exchange of cabotage privileges on a *non-exclusive* basis only, so that according to one interpretation, cabotage may be granted to *no* other State, or to *all* other States which request such rights.[119]

Yet this seems an overly strict limitation on State sovereign power, and perhaps even *contra legem*. Consistently with the exegetical rules in Article 31 of the Vienna Convention on the Law of Treaties,[120] Article 7 can be read nonrestrictively to allow the Member States to exchange (or 'pool') cabotage among each other, and this multilateral exchange would be a 'non-exclusive' grant simply because it is extended to more than one State. Even if that were not so, the literal reading of Article 7 also suggests that, as long as the arrangement does not *specifically* stipulate its exclusivity *vis-à-vis* non-Member States, its compliance with Article 7 should not be in doubt.[121] (But EU Member States might not be prepared to put such an open-ended clause into binding Community legislation.[122]) Ultimately, while the creation of a common economic airspace[123] means that Member States have surrendered their preciously-guarded rights of *intra-State* air transport to a supranational authority (and consequently to each other), the EC has not felt compelled to harmonize this comprehensive transmission of sovereign rights with the poorly-conceived (and outmoded) 'exclusivity' proviso

---

119. *See* Sheehan, *supra* note 97, at 1160.
120. Vienna Convention on the Law of Treaties, *opened for signature* May 23, 1969, 1155 U.N.T.S. 331. *See also* BARRY E. CARTER & PHILIP R. TRIMBLE, INTERNATIONAL LAW: SELECTED DOCUMENTS 58-59 (2001). Article 31(1) of the Vienna Convention accords primacy to a good faith interpretation in accordance with the 'ordinary meaning to be given to the terms of the treaty in their context and in the light of its object or purpose.' Article 31(2) posits that the 'text' shall be the principal determinant of 'context.' The object or purpose of the Chicago Convention was to create a *closed* system which States could open up by exercise of their sovereign discretion. A blunderbuss unconditional MFN provision would have been wholly inconsistent with the deference to sovereignty evidenced in Articles 1, 2, and 6 of that treaty.
121. *See* various commentators cited in Bliss, *supra* note 42, at 387 n.18. This reading also accords with the interpretation offered by the U.S. Department of State: '[Article 7] does not intrude on the rights of a State that makes a cabotage grant to exercise its sovereign, unilateral judgment whether, and under what circumstances, it will make additional grants.' *International Air Transportation Competition Act of 1979: Hearings on S. 1300 Before the Subcomm. on Aviation of the Senate Comm. on Commerce, Science, and Transportation*, 96th Cong., 1st Sess. 90-91 (1979).
122. *See* Mendes de Leon, *supra* note 118, at 197 (suggesting a more subtle phrasing, whereby EU States would not exclude the possibility that domestic traffic rights would never be 'the object of negotiations' with third States). On the other hand, if the creation of a common air sovereignty is held logically to *precede* the pooling of traffic rights, it would appear that those rights *could* be exchanged on an exclusive basis, because in that event all the intra-Union air carriers would have become domestic carriers for that purpose. Some of these issues are analyzed in Henry A. Wassenbergh, *EEC – Cabotage After 1992?*, 13 AIR L. 282 (1988).
123. *But see* Shrewsbury, *supra* note 13, at 147-150 (discussing a common airspace sovereignty in the safety and navigational spheres, which would be the projected outcome of the EC 'Single European Sky' project to integrate air navigation services throughout the airspaces of the 27 Member States).

of Article 7.[124] Not coincidentally, there have been proposals within the International Civil Aviation Organization (ICAO) to delete the second sentence of Article 7, but those proposals have not been accepted.[125]

2   Cabotage and U.S. International Aviation Policy

a   The Legal Foundations of U.S. Cabotage

Keeping faith with the Chicago Convention, the United States has enforced the exclusionary principle of cabotage in its domestic law and international treaty law since the advent of modern aviation, even though the word itself has never been used in a federal aviation statute.[126] It is one of the basic legal premises of the system that permits foreign air carriers to ply their trade in U.S. skies. Thus, the Federal Aviation Administration (FAA) is vested with broad powers to permit foreign aircraft to engage in commercial operations in the United States, provided the country of registration of the foreign carrier grants reciprocal privileges to U.S. carriers,[127] and provided the foreign carrier's activities would be in the 'public interest.'[128] Designation of a foreign carrier under a bilateral air services agreement typically satisfies the test of 'public interest,' and the foreign carrier will then be authorized by official certification to navigate in the United States.[129] This permission to navigate is abridged *a priori*, however, by a specific statutory bar against the grant of domestic service privileges to foreign carriers.

Until 1994, the legislative language expressed this abridgement using the simple formula of a grant of navigation rights subject to the domestic services exception.[130] Code revisions in 1994, intended to enhance simplicity, actually

---

124. Weber, *supra* note 110, recommends deleting the second sentence of Article 7, while leaving the first sentence unchanged: 'It is submitted that Article 7, second sentence, does not contain a rule which is in any way essential for today's air transport system. In view of its unclear and ambiguous wording, its usefulness may indeed be questioned.' *Id.* at 283.
125. *See* Peter P.C. Haanappel, *International Aviation Framework and Implications for Canadian Policy: Research Conducted for the Canada Transportation Act Review,* at 19, Can. Transp. Act Rev. Research Paper (Mar. 2001). The Haanappel report notes that the grant of intra-EU cabotage rights has not resulted in any 'formal reaction or protest' from non-Member States. To explain this forbearance, Haanappel invokes both the ontology of EC lawmaking in public international law and the realities of aeropolitical diplomacy: as to the former, Haanappel seems to think that the EC rules have received a benign reception because they emanate from an entity which acts as a supranational organization of independent States rather than a federalized State; as to diplomacy, he surmises that protest by non-EU Member States could have led to withdrawal of the fifth freedom rights that some non-EU States enjoy on intra-Union international air routes. *See id.* at 20. In any event, this juristic discourse will not need to be sustained if the Chicago Convention is eventually displaced by the kind of plurilateral settlement considered in Chapter 6 of this study.
126. *See generally* Nicky E. Hesse, *Some Questions on Aviation Cabotage,* 1 McGILL L.J. 129, 133 (1953).
127. 49 U.S.C.A. § 41703(a)(1) (West 2008).
128. 49 U.S.C.A. § 41302 (West 2008).
129. *See infra* text accompanying note 218.
130. The statutory language provided that '[f]oreign civil aircraft permitted to navigate in the United States . . . may be authorized by the [Civil Aeronautics] Board to engage in air

produced a more elliptical formula: instead of a grant of navigation rights narrowed by a specific cabotage exception, the replacement text instead grants cabotage privileges to foreign carriers in two very specific circumstances (emergencies and 'dry'-leasing of foreign-registered aircraft by U.S. carriers[131]), with the presumed statutory intent that only these exceptions will be tolerated to what is now an implied general prohibition of cabotage privileges.[132] The first exception, interestingly, empowers the Secretary of Transportation, in emergency circumstances (such as labor strikes, severe weather conditions, or unavailability of U.S. airlift capacity) to authorize departures from strict cabotage in renewable short-term increments of up to 30 days.[133]

---

commerce within the United States *except that they shall not take on at any point within the United States, persons, property, or mail carried for compensation or hire and destined for another point in the United States.'* 49 U.S.C. § 1108(b) (emphasis added) (a re-enactment of previous sections) (repealed 1994). See Lewis, *supra* note 97, at 1068.

131. A 'dry' lease means an aircraft without crew. 'Wet' leases involve leasing both aircraft and crew from the foreign carrier.) A third type of aircraft lease arrangement is the ACMI lease (Aircraft, Crew, Maintenance and Insurance), which is effectively a wet lease with maintenance and insurance added. *See, e.g.,* the lease arrangements offered by Air Universal on its website, <www.airuniversalltd.com/Services.htm>.

132. The purpose of the 1994 code revision was to restate the transportation laws in a comprehensive form, without substantive change, substituting simple language and making 'technical' improvements. *See* 1994 U.S.C.C.A.N. 818-819. Revised Title 49 permits foreign aircraft to provide air commerce in the United States, but the aircraft may take on for compensation, at a place in the United States, passengers or cargo destined for another place in the United States only if –

(1) specifically authorized under section 40109(g) of this title; or
(2) under regulations the Secretary prescribes authorizing air carriers to provide otherwise authorized air transportation with foreign-registered aircraft under lease or charter to them without crew.

49 U.S.C.A. § 41703(c) (West 2008). Paragraph (1) refers to an emergency provision authorizing a short-term cabotage exemption (in renewable periods of 30 days) where U.S. air carriers are unable (for example, because of labor disputes) to accommodate traffic in designated interstate markets. The 1994 code consolidation still includes a cluster of 'cabotage-implicit' definitions, borrowed from the old statute, which further support the 'implicit' general prohibition noted in the main text. Thus, a 'foreign air carrier' is defined as a non-U.S. citizen providing 'foreign air transportation,' and this term in turn is defined as 'the transportation of passengers . . . between a place in the United States and a place outside the United States when any part of the transportation is by aircraft.' 49 U.S.C.A. §§ 40102(a)(21) & (23) (West 2008).

133. 49 U.S.C.A. § 40109(g) (West 2008). The DOT has activated this authority in a few, closely circumscribed instances. *See, e.g.,* U.S. DOT, *In the Matter of Foreign Air Carriers: Facilitation of Air Services in Support of Hurricane Rita Evacuation and Relief Efforts*, Dkt. No. OST-2005-22553, Order 2005-9-18 (Sept. 22, 2005) (granting all foreign air carriers holding permit and/or exemption authority from the DOT permission for seven business days to participate on behalf of the Federal Emergency Management Agency and relief agencies in airlift to provide evacuation/relief services responding to Hurricane Rita); *see also* U.S. DOT, *Antonov Design Bureau*, Dkt. No. OST-2006-26568 (Dec. 8, 2006) (granting Ukrainian carrier Antonov Design Bureau permission to transport up to four aircraft engines to the Boeing Commercial Airplane Company in Washington State from General Electric Aircraft Engines in Columbus, Ohio, due to lack of available U.S. aircraft to transport this type of cargo, time-sensitivity of shipment, and unsuitability of surface transportation).

The route grant provisions of U.S. aviation bilaterals reflect the cabotage interdiction. Article 2(4) of the Bermuda II agreement, for example, excluded from any general grant of traffic rights 'the rights to take on board, in the territory of the other Contracting Party, passengers, cargo or mail carried for compensation and destined for another point in the territory of that other Contracting Party.'[134] Under the 1977 text, BA had authority to fly passengers from London to New York, from London to Los Angeles, and even for continuing 'coterminal' service from New York to Los Angeles,[135] but under Article 2(4) of the Agreement, and U.S. federal law, the U.K. carrier was blocked from enplaning *new* passengers in New York for the onward segment to Los Angeles.

b   *The Durability of U.S. Cabotage Restrictions*

Although U.S. federal aviation legislation mandates a procompetitive policy for air transport negotiations, the legislative prohibition on cabotage has effectively quarantined this concept as a potential element in U.S. bilateral treaty bargaining.[136] Similarly, the current U.S. international aviation policy makes no reference to cabotage as part of its 'plan of action' for liberalized markets.[137] The model liberal bilateral developed initially in President Bill Clinton's Administration, and also the new U.S./EC Air Transport Agreement, use a cabotage clause that is a standard component of all earlier Bermuda I and II bilaterals, whatever their shading of 'liberality.'[138] Here, for purposes of comparison with the Bermuda II text quoted earlier, is Article 3(6) of the new air transport agreement:

Nothing in this Article shall be deemed to confer on:

a. U.S. airlines the right to take on board, in the territory of any Member State, passengers, baggage, cargo, or mail carried for compensation and destined for another point in the territory of that Member State;

---

134. Bermuda II, *supra* note 66, art. 2(4).
135. *See* discussion of 'coterminalization' rights *supra* note 29.
136. A statutory statement of U.S. policy in international aviation negotiations appeared for the first time in the International Air Transportation Competition Act of 1979. The statement, which was retained unamended in the consolidated code at 49 U.S.C.A. § 40101(e) (West 2008), is analyzed in some detail, *infra* Chapter 4, Part III(B). It calls *inter alia* for 'the greatest degree of competition compatible with a well-functioning international air transportation system,' § 40101(e), including 'strengthening the competitive position of [U.S.] air carriers to ensure at least equality with foreign air carriers, including the attainment of the opportunity for [U.S.] air carriers to maintain and increase their profitability in foreign air transportation.' § 40101(e)(1). Given the cabotage-implicit statutory definitions of 'foreign air carrier' and 'foreign air transportation,' *see supra* note 132, Congress evidently did not foresee cabotage as a constituent of any negotiations.
137. *See* U.S. International Air Transport Policy Statement, 60 Fed. Reg. 21,841, 21,844-45 (May 3, 1995) [hereinafter 1995 Policy Statement].
138. The latest version of the U.S. Department of State's model open skies agreement, released in Jan. 2008, retains the cabotage clause. *See* Model Open Skies Agreement, *supra* note 38, art. 2(4).

b. Community airlines the right to take on board, in the territory of the United States, passengers, baggage, cargo, or mail carried for compensation and destined for another point in the territory of the United States.[139]

The elimination of cabotage has emotive connotations for the U.S. airline industry, particularly its labor sector.[140] When the Airline Commission held hearings to polish the text of its final report, Captain J. Randolph Babbitt, the then President of the Air Line Pilots Association,[141] cautioned his colleagues not to recommend cabotage as a constituent of any putative multilateral aviation negotiation.[142] Babbitt asserted that no other country (not even the combined EU Member States) can generate air traffic comparable in magnitude to the U.S. share of approximately 30% of global aviation passenger and cargo traffic.[143] Accordingly, he could conceive of no equitable mutual abolition of cabotage restrictions that the United States could accept.[144]

---

139. *See* U.S./EC Air Transport Agreement, *supra* note 21, art. 3(6) ('Grant of Rights').

140. '[T]o air carriers cabotage . . . is a swear word.' *Airline Commission Proceedings*, remarks of Commissioner John F. Peterpaul, Vice-President for Transportation, International Association of Machinists and Aerospace Workers (Aug. 2, 1993), at 78. In the succeeding decade, union opposition to granting cabotage rights to foreign carriers has not softened. The largest and most powerful airline employees' organization, the Air Line Pilots Association (ALPA), has recently expressed itself as 'strongly opposed to any changes in the U.S. law prohibiting cabotage.' Air Line Pilots Association [ALPA], Crewroom: Cabotage, <www.alpa.org/Default.aspx?tabid=236>. In that document, as well as contending that opening up cabotage routes to non-U.S. carriers would be bad economic policy (and that low-cost carriers provide sufficient additional competition in the domestic U.S. market), ALPA argues that 'allowing a foreign airline to operate in the U.S. domestic market (and presumably [to] remain subject to its national laws) is at odds with a wide range of U.S. laws such as labor, immigration, safety, and tax laws.' *Id.* This last argument appears to conflate the consequences of a regime of cabotage rights with the quite separate consequences of abolishing the so-called nationality rule, *see infra* Part V, through a 'right of establishment,' under which foreign carriers would be able to buy U.S. airlines or to set up subsidiary airlines under U.S. law on the same terms as U.S. corporations. In those circumstances, a foreign airline would be subject to exactly the same legal regime as a U.S. airline. *See* BRATTLE GROUP, *supra* note 107, ch. 1, at 14. If ALPA is suggesting, however, that granting cabotage rights to non-U.S. airlines would not *per se* carry this consequences of legal parity with U.S airlines, that contention is probably correct under the Chicago Convention regime.

141. Babbitt is now the Chairman and Chief Executive Officer of Eclat – an airline industry consulting firm.

142. *Airline Commission Proceedings*, remarks of Commissioner J. Randolph Babbitt, President, Air Line Pilots Association (Aug. 2, 1993), at 70-73.

143. *Id.* at 73. According to 2007 statistics, Europe (without the States of the Commonwealth of Independent States) accounted for 30.5% of world passenger traffic carried (both domestic and international departures). *See World Airline Report*, AIR TRANSP. WORLD, Jul. 2008, at 77 & 98. The North American region generated 34.6% the global total. For comparison purposes, Asia/Pacific airlines carried 25.8% of the world total, and Latin American/Caribbean operators carried 5.3%. *Id.* at 64 & 93.

144. *Airline Commission Proceedings*, remarks of Commissioner J. Randolph Babbitt, President, Air Line Pilots Association (Aug. 2, 1993), at 73. Similarly, Professor Paul Stephen Dempsey maintained in his submission to the Airline Commission that an exchange of rights of 'similar

Babbitt's statistical perception certainly reflects obvious imbalances at the bilateral level. But it does not measure shares of exclusively *international* traffic, which accounts for at least 50% of the European carriers' business, as opposed to approximately 20% for U.S. airlines.[145] Moreover, at the level of a U.S./EC agreement, Babbitt's assessment does not embrace the radiating *network* effects of a truly open system of airline competition.[146] Even if he is correct that the cumulation of intra-Union fifth freedom rights flown by U.S. carriers was only 29 pairs in 1993 (and is trending toward zero in 2008 as a result of transnational alliances),[147] those connectors could have a far greater *network* potential to enable U.S. carriers to compete with EU airlines for traffic to beyond points (for example, in the Asia/Pacific region).[148] That potential is unrealized because of the limitations

---

magnitude' would be 'a practical impossibility .... The disproportionate size of the U.S. market vis-à-vis foreign markets ... suggests that no foreign market would be of comparable size to justify an exchange of cabotage rights.' Paul S. Dempsey, *Airlines, Aviation & Public Policy – The Need for Regulatory Reform*, Submission to the Airline Commission, *in Airline Commission Documents*, Dkt. No. 000044 (Jun. 1, 1993), at 83. In remarks to a 'media roundtable' convened before a recent round of U.S./EC negotiations in Jan. 2007, John R. Byerly, U.S. Deputy Assistant Secretary of State for Transportation Affairs and lead member of the U.S. negotiating team, indicated that the United States would not be 'in a position to offer' any concessions on cabotage rights to EC carriers, emphasizing that cabotage 'is an established principle of the international civil aviation world' as well as being 'an enormously controversial issue.' Byerly implied that this U.S. reluctance was also based on the fact that U.S. carriers have no practical use for cabotage rights within the EU Member States. He noted that intra-Union fifth freedom rights – which EC officials have regarded as analogous to cabotage within a unified EC airspace, *see, e.g.*, Brattle Group, *supra* note 107, ch. 1, 12 n.25, – are now hardly used at all by U.S. airlines, which prefer to rely on alliance partners for intra-Union service beyond their transatlantic gateways. United States Mission to the European Union, *U.S's Byerly Reaffirms Commitment to Finalizing Transatlantic Air Services Accord*, Transcript of Media Roundtable (Jan. 11, 2007), <http://useu.usmission.gov/Dossiers/Open_Skies/Jan1109_Byerly_Roundtable.asp>. U.S. air cargo carriers, in contrast, exploit all of the network potential of their fifth freedom access to Union routes. *See supra* Chapter 2, Part II(C).

145. *See* Caroline Brothers, *European Airlines Reap Benefits of Oil Hedging*, N.Y. Times, Jun. 12, 2008. While conceding distortions created by the fact that *intra*-Union traffic is considered 'international' for this purpose (but recalling, however, that the EU is not a federalized State but a supranational organization), the figures stand in stark contrast to the domestic focus of the U.S. industry.

146. *Airline Commission Proceedings*, testimony of Marvin S. Cohen, former Chairman, Civil Aeronautics Board, Jun. 24, 1993, at 112.

147. *Airline Commission Proceedings*, testimony of Commissioner J. Randolph Babbitt, President, Air Line Pilots Association (Aug. 2, 1993), at 86. Captain Babbitt may in fact have overstated the actual number. In 1991, for example, there were only 20 intra-EU international city-pairs served by U.S. carriers (based on a threshold of at least 100 flights per year). U.S. carriers had additional unexercised fifth freedom rights. Operations occurred in both directions. *See* GAO, *International Aviation, supra* note 98, at 48 (citing DOT sources). In the following decade, the creation of transatlantic air carrier alliances caused U.S. scheduled air passenger carriers to withdraw virtually completely from beyond-gateway fifth freedom services within Europe, relying instead on their EU partners to provide those services. *See supra* Chapter 2, Part II.

148. Indeed, the 29 city-pairs mentioned by Captain Babbitt did not nearly exhaust the potential intra-EU fifth freedom rights that were *not* granted (or that were granted by only one of the two

of bilateralism: indeed, even though U.S. carriers have secured comprehensive extra-Union beyond points as part of the new U.S./EC Air Transport Agreement, those rights will be mere surplusage unless beyond destination States grant concomitant inbound traffic rights. (This impediment has always been present in the 'open skies' model, which typically exchanges a so-called 'starburst' array of fifth freedom beyond rights.)[149] Those beyond rights would be triggered *automatically* if the centrifugal influence of a U.S./EC plurilateral (transcending the 2007 U.S./EC Agreement by grants of cabotage and open investment rights) lured an East Asian air consortium, including protectionist Japan, to accede.

Within U.S. territory, most foreign airlines would presumably use eighth freedom cabotage for the limited purpose of generating new traffic on 'tag-end' segments, the so-called fill-up rights mentioned in the earlier example of British Airways' continuing service from New York to Los Angeles.[150] Even if true (ninth freedom) cabotage were allowed, foreign carriers would still face the challenges of new entrant status and the powerful incumbency of the U.S. airlines at their hubs, and may prefer to have an opportunity to invest in or to purchase a domestic carrier operation.[151] Adding another layer of complexity to the cabotage argument, this Chapter will later examine a transitional feature of the modern Chicago system, the

---

States required to complete the traffic connection) under bilateral treaties preceding the new U.S./EC Air Transport Agreement, *see supra* note 21. The new agreement will allow full intra-Union fifth freedom rights for U.S. carriers (as well as full fifth freedom beyond rights to points outside the Union). *See* U.S./EC Air Transport Agreement, *supra* note 21, art. 3(1) ('Grant of Rights'). *But see supra* Chapter 2, note 220 (indicating that the grant of extra-Union fifth freedom rights was not in fact contemplated under the European Commission's negotiation mandate from the EU Council of Ministers).

149. *See* 1995 Aviation Hearings, *supra* note 83, at 96 (testimony of Robert L. Crandall, President, American Airlines). Another recent open skies innovation is the exchange of reciprocal code-share privileges on all fifth freedom (beyond) routes. *See* Model Open Skies Agreement, *supra* note 38, art. 8(7).

150. *See supra* text accompanying note 39.

151. *See* TRANSPORTATION RESEARCH BOARD, SPECIAL REPORT 255: ENTRY AND COMPETITION IN THE U.S. AIRLINE INDUSTRY – ISSUES AND OPPORTUNITIES (1999). The inward investment required to establish and develop full hub operations would be enormous. On the other hand, even 'tag-end' rights, mentioned in the main text, might not be economically valuable to EU carriers: 'Not only would they be competing with established U.S. airlines offering many more flights, they may only be able to attract 10 to 15 additional passengers to "fill-up" the domestic segment of a flight. . . .' GAO, *International Aviation*, *supra* note 98, at 57. As will be seen in Chapter 4, however, predictions as to the future competitive patterns of U.S. domestic air services are difficult to make. As the GAO study recognized, some U.S. transcontinental routes (at the time of the study, for example, Philadelphia/Los Angeles and Boston/Los Angeles) are not as frequently served by U.S. airlines, so that a flight originating in London or Paris would have a good chance of winning a competitive market share on these domestic segments. *See id.* There is also the intangible of predicting consumer response to a perceived higher quality of service provided by some EU brand-name carriers. *But see* Air Line Pilots Association, *supra* note 140 (arguing that weak U.S. airline industry finances could be negatively affected by overcapacity resulting from the grant of cabotage rights and that 'the growth of domestically-based low-cost carriers has already provided consumers with increased choices in service and pricing').

concept of code-sharing, which some analysts have portrayed as a subterfuge that already allows foreign carriers to elude the strict cabotage exclusion.[152]

Despite the perceived *theoretical* value of U.S. cabotage rights, however, studies indicate that the termination of the rules on national ownership and control would be a greater boon to foreign carriers.[153] As the 2002 Brattle Report observed, 'For sound business reasons, most foreign-owned air carriers operating in purely domestic commerce would opt to do so as a domestic corporation.'[154] Using the prototype of Sir Richard Branson's attempt to establish Virgin America as a

---

152. *See infra* Part VIII. Indeed, some airline executives claim that code-sharing is a superior means of market access to traditional cabotage. *See* Graeme Leach, *Air Warfare*, at 22, Inst. of Directors (U.K.) Policy Paper (Dec. 2000) (observing how code-sharing agreements have diminished the need for a U.K. airline to have a physical presence in the U.S. marketplace, and bmi Chairman Sir Michael Bishop's related skepticism that British Airways and Virgin Atlantic were motivated solely by economic considerations when arguing for U.S. cabotage rights during U.S./U.K. bilateral talks). *See also* former American Airlines President Bob Crandall's apodictic confidence that '[c]abotage is less valuable than code-sharing, so I cannot imagine why anybody would want to substitute cabotage for code-sharing.' 1995 Aviation Hearings, *supra* note 83, at 111. The views of Sir Michael and Mr. Crandall (as will be seen, *infra* Chapter 6) are tenable only within the existing Chicago system (and its nationality stipulations). In a plurilateral environment, code-sharing would be only one of several 'doing business' options. Quite apart from the implications of code-sharing, however, the rigidity of the traditional Chicago system of freedoms actually has the potential to undermine cabotage. A 2006 opinion of the Canadian Transportation Agency, for example, illustrates the murkiness of sixth freedom rights and stopovers. *See* Canadian Transportation Agency, *In the Matter of a Complaint Filed by Air Canada that Northwest Airlines, Inc. is Offering for Sale Air Services between Points in Canada*, Decision No. 24-A-2006 (Jan. 13, 2006) (finding that 'tour' passenger traffic carried by Northwest from Japan to the United States and then flown to Canada using sixth freedom rights with stopovers at various Canadian points, and finally flown to a point in the United States prior to returning to Japan, did not involve services to passengers originating their travel in Canada and carrying them only to another point in Canada; the term 'stopover' in this context meant a deliberate interruption of a journey agreed to in advance, and no limit on the number of such stopovers existed in the U.S./Canada air transport agreement). The case does, however, illustrate how circumvention of strict cabotage could become a valuable economic right. Canadian carriers, for example, have been lobbying for so-called 'modified sixth freedom' traffic to be included in the U.S./Canada air transport agreement, which would allow a Canadian airline like Air Canada to sell (with one ticket and a 24-hour stopover) a connecting service, for example, between Seattle and New York via Toronto. *See* Vern Kakoschke & David Dubrovsky, Canada: Taking Flight: Expanded Canada/ U.S. Open Skies to Begin September 2006, Mondaq Website (Aug. 29, 2006), <www.mondaq.com/i_article.asp_Q_articleid_E_42438>. A more recent (and bizarre) example of how to circumvent strict cabotage restrictions may be the establishment of Virgin Galactic – the world's first spaceline – which will originate and terminate its suborbital flights in U.S. airspace. *See* Virgin Galactic Homepage, <www.virgingalactic.com>.

153. *See Air Transport: Do Europeans Need Cabotage Rights in the US?*, EUROPEAN REPORT, no. 2032, Apr. 12, 1995 (cabotage is 'not very interesting' to EU airlines, which have a preference for clearly defined commercial agreements with U.S. partners); Bliss, *supra* note 42, at 401 (stating that '[a] policy of unrestricted ownership of a United States carrier would render any cabotage laws meaningless and permit the investor to assume all the routes and market advantages of the target carrier').

154. BRATTLE GROUP, *supra* note 107, ch. 1, at 14.

domestically incorporated airline, the report observed that 'other foreign airline officials have said that they would never try to compete on any scale in the U.S. market except as a U.S.-incorporated carrier.'[155] Combined with the fact that responsibility for safety compliance, at least under the present Chicago Convention regime, remains with the carrier's home State, the prospects for a surrender of the U.S. cabotage proscription look decidedly bleak.[156]

V   SOVEREIGNTY AND CITIZENSHIP PURITY: THE
           NATIONALITY RULE

A   THE SUBSTANTIAL OWNERSHIP/EFFECTIVE CONTROL DYAD

The nationality rule was deliberately embraced by the governments at the Chicago Conference in 1944. At the urging of the United States, they sought to ensure that the exchange of rights to designated carriers would not allow third party airlines, representing States that were strangers to the specific bilateral agreement under which traffic rights were conceded, to gain control of these operations. The U.S. delegation championed this proposal because of fears that route privileges could slip into the hands of foreign airlines controlled by ex-enemy or enemy States or nationals. In the portentous language of the U.S. State Department, '[r]ights and permits are conceded by a country or countries to another country or countries as part of friendly relations and not for the purpose of being peddled.'[157] Accordingly, the Chicago Conference debated numerous standards to ensure that no State would concede route and access privileges to foreign airlines in which ownership and control was not substantially vested in nationals of its bilateral partner.[158] Ultimately, the delegates decided not to

---

155. *Id.*
156. [U.K.] Civil Aviation Authority, *Ownership and Control Liberalisation: A Discussion Paper*, at 6, CAP 769 (Oct. 2006) (discussing options for remote exercise of safety compliance procedures where a State permits cabotage access to foreign carriers).
157. U.S. Dept. of State, Proceedings of the International Civil Aviation Conference (1948), at 556. *See* Z. Joseph Gertler, *Nationality of Airlines: A Hidden Force in the International Air Regulation Equation*, 48 J. AIR L. & COM. 51, 57 (1982). The U.S. laws on ownership and control of domestic airlines have existed since 1926, initially to protect the 'heavily subsidized fledgling airline industry.' *See* GAO, *Airline Competition, supra* note 9, at 12.
158. As with cabotage, the original national security justification for the nationality principle has worn away with time. Here, too, it can be argued that the reasons for its continued survival are largely economic. It is true that the U.S. Department of Defense (DOD) continues to express concerns about terminating the nationality rule, believing that removal of the rule could potentially threaten the economic viability of the Civil Reserve Air Fleet (CRAF) program, an important part of U.S. national security that *inter alia* assures supplementary airlift capacity in wartime from U.S. commercial airlines. The European Commission's Brattle Report in 2002 was skeptical of the DOD's reluctance to tamper with the nationality rule, concluding that 'an EU-U.S. Open Aviation Area would not jeopardize the CRAF program and it might enhance it.' BRATTLE GROUP, *supra* note 107, at x-xi. For further discussion of the CRAF system, *see infra* note 247. On the U.S. security implications of terminating the nationality rule, *see infra* note 288.

incorporate any provision on the nationality or ownership of airlines into the Chicago Convention itself, but instead to include such provisions in the two subsidiary accords reached at the Conference, the Two Freedoms and Five Freedoms Agreements.[159] The relevant text in each instrument is identical:

> Each contracting State reserves the right to withhold or revoke a certificate or permit to an air transport enterprise of another State in any case where it is not satisfied that *substantial ownership and effective control* are vested in nationals of a contracting State.[160]

The 1944 Conference did not intend the standard of 'substantial ownership and effective control' to veto *all* foreign investment in a national air carrier. Rather, it established a double-pronged citizenship purity test,[161] quantitative ('substantial ownership'[162]) and qualitative ('effective control'), such that only investments of a size and nature to meet both of those tests would trigger forced revocation of a certificate or permit.[163] Virtually all post-Chicago bilateral agreements, including both Bermuda models, the liberal bilaterals of the U.S. open skies program, and the new U.S./EC Air Transport Agreement, include the citizenship purity protocol (known as the 'nationality clause').[164] As Jürgen Basedow has written, 'who

---

159. *See supra* note 6.
160. Two Freedoms Agreement, *supra* note 6, art. I, § 5; Five Freedoms Agreement, *supra* note 6, art I, § 6 (emphasis added). The Chicago Convention itself, incidentally, settled only the issue of nationality of *aircraft*, not of *airlines*. Thus, Article 17 of the Convention provides that '[a]ircraft have the nationality of the State in which they are registered,' Convention on International Civil Aviation, *supra* note 6, 15 U.N.T.S. at 308, and Article 20 requires every aircraft engaged in 'international air navigation' to bear 'its appropriate nationality and registration marks.' *Id.* Aircraft registration is a separate subject that is treated only collaterally in this study. One liberalizing change with respect to U.S. registration laws has already been noted which has no analogue in the law requiring citizen ownership of airlines. The International Air Transportation Competition Act of 1979, current version at 49 U.S.C. § 41703(c) (2003), permits U.S. carriers to use foreign-registered 'dry leased' aircraft (aircraft minus crew) in U.S. domestic operations.
161. *See* Brian F. Havel, *A New Approach to Foreign Ownership of National Airlines*, [2001-2004 Transfer Binder] Issues Aviation L. & Pol'y ¶ 25,201, at 13,201 (2003).
162. No specific numerical benchmarks are provided in the treaties. Domestic legislation, as will be seen, varies on this point, but 'substantially' surely implies more than 50% (and probably at least 75% based on the U.S. implementing legislation).
163. *See* discussion in Bernard Wood, *Foreign Investment in National Airlines and the Significance of the SAS/BCAL Decision*, 13 Air L. 138, 140 (1988).
164. *See* the 2007 U.S./EC Air Transport Agreement, *supra* note 21, art. 4, which provides as follows:

Authorization

On receipt of applications from an airline of one Party, in the form and manner prescribed for operating authorizations and technical permissions, the other Party shall grant appropriate authorizations and permissions with minimum procedural delay, provided:
a. for a U.S. airline, substantial ownership and effective control of that airline are vested in the United States, U.S. nationals, or both;
b. for a Community airline, substantial ownership and effective control of that airline are vested in a Member State or States, nationals of such a State or States, or both.

can perform transport services most efficiently is secondary; what matters is whether [that person] is a foreigner or a national.'[165]

This chauvinistic preference for national ownership and control has had a significant corollary that sets airlines apart from most other transnational economic enterprises: they have not become multinational corporations.[166] In terms of ownership and organization, they have been owned and controlled by their sponsoring States or by the individual or corporate citizens of the State in which they provide domestic services or by which they are designated to fly negotiated international routes.[167]

B   PROSCRIBING MULTINATIONAL AIRLINES: THE NATIONALITY RULE
IN DOMESTIC LAW

The nationality rule is not just a treaty obligation, it is also part of each State's domestic law. In effect, the bar on foreign ownership and control is a double-bolted legal lock. The lock's external bolt is the nationality clause included in all air services agreements to ensure that only airlines bearing the nationality of the States

---

As discussed, U.S. air services bilaterals must comply with federal law on ownership and control of airlines, which is based on the international treaty provisions considered in the main text.

165. 'Hier geht es also nur sekundär darum, wer eine Verkehrsleistung am effizientesten erbringen kann; vorrängig stellt sich vielmehr die Frage, ob er Ausländer oder Inländer ist.' (author's translation). Basedow, *supra* note 8, at 7. According to Cheng, the bilateral provisions on substantial national ownership have the effect of enabling the contracting States 'to bar flags of convenience from international air transport.' CHENG, *supra* note 42, at 377. *See also* DIEDERIKS-VERSCHOOR, *supra* note 3, at 16-17 ('[In international air transport law] due to the Chicago Convention's strict provisions and also to bilateral agreements stipulating the requirements of "substantial ownership and effective control..." complications...from... "flags of convenience" do not occur...because it is governed by a system of permits containing strict rules for all flights.'); *But see* MENDES DE LEON, *supra* note 103, at 26 (noting that flags of convenience 'cannot be excluded' because of weakness in control of registration by international law).

166. *See* Havel, *supra* note 161, at 13,101-05 (noting how the citizenship purity test excludes U.S. airlines from foreign capital markets, disqualifies them from mergers or acquisitions involving foreign airlines, and forces them to enter artificial 'alliances' with foreign airlines instead of becoming the kinds of strong multinational corporations that have developed in virtually all other transnational industries).

167. *See* Havel, *supra* note 161, at 13,201-05. As Gazdik has observed, the philosophy that prevailed at Chicago was to treat international air routes and traffic as a specialized commodity subject to granting, acquisition, or exchange. *See* J.G. Gazdik, *Nationality of Aircraft and Nationality of Airlines as Means of Control in International Air Transportation*, 25 J. AIR L. & COM. 1 (1958). Commerce in this commodity would be the exclusive patronage of the national governments. Moreover, these 'rights' would remain the sovereign property of the States, not of the airlines that used them. Indeed, as Dr. Pablo Mendes de Leon has observed, the 'closed' Chicago system necessarily implied that the 'freedoms of the air' would be *privileges* rather than *rights*. *See* MENDES DE LEON, *supra* note 103, at 44 (observing that 'in a world divided into closed airspaces, the grant of any transit or traffic right must be viewed as a *privilege*').

negotiating each bilateral treaty serve the routes awarded under the treaty. The internal bolt, which ensures compliance with the nationality clause, is each country's domestic legislation requiring national ownership and control of its air carriers. Although, as we have seen, the treaty-based nationality clause has been the object of highly creative reform proposals,[168] the Chicago system truly cannot be reformed unless and until the internal bolt is disabled by significant aeropolitical powers such as the United States and the EU.

Thus, the internal measures that States have taken to promote compliance with the nationality clauses in their air services agreements have an indirectly restrictive impact on the potential for transnational ownership of airlines – and hence for evolving a multilateral system of authentically liberalized airline competition. The prospectus for the BA privatization in 1987, for example, proclaimed that the rights of BA to operate on international routes could be forfeited if the company ceased to be 'substantially owned and effectively controlled' by U.K. nationals.[169] Similarly, long before the tortuous legal infrastructure put in place to facilitate KLM's recent quasi-merger with Air France, KLM officials admitted that the ownership/control dyad was 'the main reason the Dutch government retains a stake in the airline.'[170]

In the United States, the fountainhead jurisdiction of airline deregulation, an airline cannot commence business without satisfying the government that it has an acceptable citizenship profile, and the government has statutory powers to ensure continuing fidelity to that profile.[171] Indeed, one U.S. carrier challenged

---

168. *See supra* Chapter 2, Part II. *See infra* text accompanying note 280 (discussing post-nationality rule test of 'establishment').

169. The U.K. Civil Aviation Act of 1982, however, does not prescribe any level of permitted foreign share ownership. *See* [U.K.] Civil Aviation Authority, *supra* note 156, at 3. The British Airways Articles of Association contain powers that might be used to limit the number or voting rights of shares in which non-U.K. nationals own interests or, if necessary, to require their compulsory disposal, or to restrict the transferability of shares. The prospectus pointed out that, although there was no accepted international agreement as to the precise level of ownership or control that must be retained by U.K. nationals, the Articles included a power to impose an overall limit of not less than 25% on the number of shares owned by non-U.K. nationals. In the absence of intervention from a foreign government or large interests of single or associated non-U.K. nationals, the directors would not expect to have to implement this procedure unless the proportion of non-U.K. owned shares approached 35%. BRITISH AIRWAYS PROSPECTUS (1987). In fact, foreign ownership of the company grew after flotation, when some 17% of the shares were owned by foreign nationals. In Dec. 2007, 40% of the issued capital was held outside the United Kingdom, with just under half of those shares held in the United States. British Airways, Investor Relations, 2007 Factbook: Shareholder Information, <http://media.corporate-ir.net/media_files/irol/69/69499/bafactbook/2007/ShareholderInformation_March2007.pdf>. The U.K. policy on foreign investment was evidently considerably more liberal than that of the United States even before the application of the EC laws on transnational Community ownership.

170. GAO, *Airline Competition*, *supra* note 9, at 43. For an analysis of the legal structure of the Air France/KLM alignment, *see infra* Chapter 5, Part III(B).

171. *See* U.S. DOT, *Application of Virgin America Inc., For a Certificate of Public Convenience and Necessity Under 49 U.S.C. § 41102 To Engage in Interstate Scheduled Air Transportation of Persons, Property, and Mail*, Dkt. No. OST-2005-23307, Final Order (May 18, 2007)

the U.S. Department of Transportation (DOT) on the inconsistency of a deregulated industry that is forced to meet citizenship purity tests. In a submission in support of a capital injection from British Airways,[172] US Airways (formerly known as USAir) argued that deregulation 'took the government out of the business of second-guessing airline management decisions with respect to investments and capital structure.' The DOT, however, disagreed that its 'citizenship responsibilities [had been reduced] to a *de minimis* level. Deregulation did nothing to reduce our concerns, or those of Congress, regarding foreign control of U.S. air carriers; indeed, much of our precedent in this area has been generated since deregulation.'[173]

States do expend much legal brainpower and ingenuity in defense of the nationality rule. Yet, as the U.S. experience shows, the restrictions hardly lend themselves to clarity or certainty.[174] Investors are entitled to know what governments will permit or will not permit, but prediction of these essential standards is fouled up by the very fact that the rule is almost never applied in its pure form, being tempered in U.S. practice, for example, by provisions allowing *some* foreign investment, and a measure of foreign influence, when it can be politically supported.[175]

[hereinafter U.S. DOT, *Virgin America,* Order to Show Cause] (indicating that an applicant for a certificate to be a U.S. carrier must show, as part of its 'fitness' prerequisites, that it meets the statutory requirements of U.S. citizenship). Under 14 C.F.R. § 204.5, U.S. air carriers which undergo or propose to undergo a change in ownership or management are required to file updated 'fitness' information that will be subject to informal review and that may or may not also be subject to a public docketed proceeding. *See* Actual Control of U.S. Airlines, 70 Fed. Reg. 67,389, 67,389-90 (proposed Nov. 7, 2005) [hereinafter NPRM]. For a survey of the historical antecedents to the present U.S. legislation, *see* John T. Stewart, Jr., *United States Citizenship Requirement of the Federal Aviation Act – A Misty Moor of Legalisms or the Rampart of Protectionism?,* 55 J. AIR L. & COM. 685, 688-97 (1990).

172. *See infra* note 194.
173. In the Matter of USAir and British Airways (Various Applications), Order No. 93-3-17, *reprinted in* [1992-1994 Transfer Binder] Av. L. Rep. (CCH) ¶ 22,907, at 14,139 (Mar. 15, 1992) [hereinafter Various Applications of BA/USAir]; *see also* Statement of Seth Schofield, President and CEO of USAir, Inc. on the Importance of Foreign Equity Investment in U.S. Airlines, *in Airline Commission Documents,* undocketed, Jun. 3, 1993, at 12 [hereinafter Statement of Schofield].
174. 'The process is so uncertain, so unpredictable and so unreasonable that its mere existence is a barrier to foreign investment in U.S. airlines.' Statement of Schofield, *supra* note 173, at 7.
175. Typically, that political support will depend on whether the foreign investors are nationals of countries with which the United States has an open skies bilateral relationship. *See* Air Carrier Fitness Div., U.S. DOT, How TO BECOME A CERTIFICATED AIR CARRIER 13 (May 2005) [hereinafter U.S. DOT, CERTIFICATED AIR CARRIER]. For earlier, more general comments on foreign investment, *see,* for example, DOT pronouncements in Application of Discovery Airways, *reprinted in* [1989-1992 Transfer Binder] Av. L. Rep. (CCH) ¶ 22,526, at 15,206, 15,354. In that case, the DOT stated that it 'regard[ed] the free flow of investment capital as a vital force in the international business environment,' *id.* at 15,211, and was therefore 'committed to a policy of fostering new entry in the airline industry, and welcome[d] lawful foreign investment as a part of that process,' *id.* at 15,354.

1   **Case Studies in the Nationality Rule and the Unmaking of a U.S. Government Rulemaking**

a   *Airline Citizenship: Law and Policy in the United States*

U.S. administrative supervision of foreign investment begins with the definition of 'air carrier' in the Federal Aviation Act.[176] The Act requires that persons wishing to provide scheduled or charter air transportation within the United States first apply for a 'certificate of public convenience and necessity' from the DOT.[177] This certificate can only be issued to an 'air carrier,' which the legislation defines as 'a citizen of the United States undertaking by any means, directly or indirectly, to provide air transportation.'[178] Completing the definitional chain, the Act declares that a 'citizen of the United States' means

- (A) an individual who is a citizen of the United States;
- (B) a partnership each of whose partners is an individual who is a citizen of the United States; or
- (C) a corporation or association organized under the laws of the United States or a State, the District of Columbia, or a territory or possession of the United States, of which the president and at least two-thirds of the board of directors and other managing officers are citizens of the United States, which is under the actual control of citizens of the United States, and in which at least 75% of the voting interest is owned or controlled by persons that are citizens of the United States.[179]

Applying the interpretive principle, *expressio unius est exclusio alterius,*[180] sub-paragraph (C) establishes a definite upper limit of 25% on foreign investment in the *voting* securities of U.S air carrier corporations. (The law is silent, however, on how much *nonvoting* equity capital, *i.e.,* nonvoting common and preferred stock and debt, that a foreign entity can invest in a U.S. airline.[181]) Notwithstanding the

---

176. As of Jul. 5, 1994, all U.S. transportation laws were consolidated and codified as Title 49, U.S.C. All statutory references in this book are to the newly-consolidated code, where appropriate.
177. 49 U.S.C.A. § 41101(a) (West 2008).
178. § 40102(a)(2). A 'charter air carrier' is separately defined as an air carrier holding a certificate of public convenience and necessity that authorizes it to provide charter air transportation. § 40102(a)(13).
179. § 40102(a)(15).
180. *See* Leatherman *v.* Tarrant County Narcotics Intelligence & Coordination Unit, 507 U.S. 163, 168 (1993).
181. There is nothing in the statutory language to suggest that a 25% cap also applies to nonvoting stock, and the DOT has continued to take the position that it does not – most recently in the context of the U.S./EC air transport negotiations. Previously, the Department insisted on a 49% maximum for total equity (voting and nonvoting stock). According to a 2003 letter from the DOT's Inspector General, Kenneth M. Mead, to Congressman Don Young, Chairman of the House Transportation and Infrastructure Committee, 'the maximum total foreign-equity ownership of an air carrier typically permitted by the Department may be up to 49%.' DOT,

surprising use of the disjunctive 'or' to separate the words 'owned' and 'controlled' in the statute (the Chicago instruments, as shown above, use 'and'), U.S. officials have always read the words conjunctively to require 'control' of at least 75% of the voting interest also to remain with U.S. citizens,[182] thereby implicating the Chicago/Bermuda test of 'effective control.'[183]

Until 2004, however, the statutory language itself did not expressly mention the *qualitative* dimension of the Chicago control test, which looks beyond objective numerical benchmarks to evaluate the actual degree of influence exerted by foreign ownership interests, even if their numerical voting strength falls within the statutory requirements.[184] For instance, a foreign investor's combined voting and nonvoting ownership interests may, perhaps because of the magnitude of its

---

Office of Inspector General, Letter to The Honorable Don Young, Chairman, House Transportation and Infrastructure Committee, Mar. 4, 2003, at 8, <www.oig.dot.gov/Stream File?file=/data/pdfdocs/dhl_complete.pdf> [hereinafter DOT Inspector General Letter]. *But see* U.S./EC Air Transport Agreement, *supra* note 21, which mentions a cap of 49.9% (annex 4, art. 1(1)(a)(ii)), as well as indicating explicit tolerance for over 50%, *id.* art. 1(1)(b).

182. There was some ambiguity in the original version of the statute, since the 'control' test did refer, literally, to the same objective concept – interest in voting stock – as the ownership test (and there was no separate test of U.S. managerial control). The U.S. authorities, however, have never applied that distinction so literally and have considered 'control' to be a much broader concept than mere stewardship over voting rights. As the 2004 amendment to the statute now appears to crystallize, *see infra* in main text, control includes many other indicia of corporate governance and influence and multiple benchmarks have evolved to determine its presence.

183. The disjunctive language suggests that Congress assumed, although did not make explicit, that control would simply follow ownership. The disjunctive reading allows the conclusion, however, that an air carrier could be 75% owned by foreign citizens but not necessarily *controlled* by them to that extent. (For example, a group of U.S. citizens might hold a single block of 25% of the voting equity which might be the largest single ownership stake and thereby be most strongly positioned to influence the decisions of the holders of the balance. But this reading would surely violate the object and purpose of the nationality rule. The Civil Aeronautics Board decided that the words must be read conjunctively, and required that air carriers be owned *and* controlled by citizens of the United States. The CAB preferred this interpretation as more consistent with the Congressional intent that there be 'actual control' by U.S. citizens. *In re* Daetwyler, Order No. 71-10-114, 58 C.A.B. 118, 121 (Sept. 17, 1971). As the DOT noted in 2005 in its proposed rulemaking procedure on the future interpretation of 'actual control,' the phrase 'actual control' was specifically encoded in 2004 into the statutory definition of a citizen of the United States. *See infra* in main text. This was a change 'reflecting Departmental precedent, but it remains for the Department to interpret that requirement.' NPRM, *supra* note 171, at 67,390.

184. It is difficult to assign fixed benchmarks for control, and the DOT has never attempted to do so. For that reason, the qualitative test has necessarily tended to be subjective and case-specific. Witnesses at the Airline Commission, and members of the Commission itself, agreed that *a priori* benchmarks would not work. Commissioner Herbert D. Kelleher, then Chairman of Southwest Airlines, noted that '[t]here are very few publicly held companies in the world that would not [be] under the control of the 25 percent owner.' *Airline Commission Proceedings*, Jun. 24, 1993, at 122. *See also Airline Commission Proceedings*, remarks of Commissioner Felix G. Rohaytn, Senior Partner, Lazard Frères & Co., May 24, 1993, at 221-22, May 26, 1993, at 121-22; Jeffrey D. Brown, Comment, *Foreign Investment in U.S. Airlines: What Limits Should be Placed on Foreign Ownership of U.S. Carriers?*, 41 SYRACUSE L. REV.

equity investment or its mere presence on the board of directors, trump the U.S. interests, or at least subordinate the U.S. carrier's interest to the needs of the participating foreign investor. As a senior U.S. aviation official commented, '[a] voting interest in a corporation is a particular kind of corporate involvement and is not necessarily identical to economic ownership or economic participation in the corporation.'[185]

In sum, therefore, the benchmarks in the U.S. statute may indicate the presence of 'substantial ownership and control' by U.S. citizens of 75% or more of voting equity, but not *necessarily* the absence of 'effective control' by foreign stake-holders. That apparent 'gray area' explained the DOT's historical approach of calibrating U.S. citizenship through the *de facto* or 'actual' control that resides in foreign citizens – whether through ownership of nonvoting stock, debt, or even the 'aura' of likely interference conveyed by the foreign citizen during live testimony before a DOT administrative law judge.[186] The qualitative standard, previously 'read into' the statute by DOT regulators, was explicitly inserted into U.S. law through a statutory amendment that became effective in 2004.[187] Thus, the

---

1269, 1275 (1990). In support of these insights, *see* the following explanation by the CAB of its approach to issues of foreign influence:

> In examining the control aspect for purposes of determining citizenship, we look beyond the bare technical requirements to see if the foreign interest has the power – either directly or indirectly – to influence the directors, officers or stockholders. We have found control to embrace every form of control and to include negative as well as positive influence; we have recognized that a dominating influence may be exercised in ways other than through a vote.

In re Page Avjet Corp., Order No. 83-7-5, Dkt. No. 40905, 102 C.A.B. 488, at 5-6 (Jul. 1, 1983) (citations omitted).

185. FAA Deputy Chief Counsel Edward P. Faberman, in letter to private law firm, Oct. 21, 1982, *quoted in* Stewart, *supra* note 171, at 703 n. 59.

186. *See infra* text accompanying note 199 (discussing recent DHL/ASTAR case). The substance over form argument has likewise been applied by the U.K.'s Civil Aviation Authority (CAA), but its application was made necessary by an open-ended statutory requirement of 'effective control.' Thus, in its 2006 discussion paper on ownership and control in the airline industry, the Authority noted that U.K. law, prior to its supersession by EC regulations, differed from that of the United States in that it did not prescribe any level of permitted share ownership, nor the proportion of nonqualifying nationals that could serve on an airline's board. [U.K.] Civil Aviation Authority, *supra* note 156, ch. 2, at 3. As discussed, *infra* Chapter 5, Part II, EC law now specifies both majority share ownership *and* effective control (by EU citizens), although it still does not place restrictions on the number of non-EU citizens who may serve on an EU airline's board. The CAA continues to monitor indirect influence that may amount to *de facto* control. *See* [U.K.] Civil Aviation Authority, *supra* note 156, ch. 2, at 4.

187. *See* Vision 100 – The Century of Aviation Reauthorization Act, sec. 807, Pub. L. 108-176, 117 Stat. 2490. The legislation amends 49 U.S.C. § 40102(a)(15) by adding the words 'which is under the actual control of citizens of the United States' to the definition of U.S. air carrier citizenship. Thus, the test of managerial control is now conceptually separated from the statutory requirement that 75% of the voting interest in a U.S. carrier must be 'owned or controlled' by U.S. citizens. There is virtually no statutory history to explain why Congress made this change. The revision reflects not only a more cautious security environment after 9/11, but it may also be assumed that the legislation intended to influence

wider qualitative assessment, referred to in 2006 by Jeffrey Shane, then DOT Under Secretary for Policy, as the 'it's for us to know and for you to find out' standard, has evolved from a staple of DOT practice into a statutory obligation.[188] Application of a *de facto* control test, moreover, is consistent with the CAB's prior practice of interpreting the citizenship restrictions in substantive, not formalistic, terms.[189]

Even though the legal standards for determining U.S. citizenship of carriers may be broadly established, the application of these standards remains, in the words of one commentator, 'unsettled.'[190] Some of this uncertainty emanates

---

events in the DHL/ASTAR citizenship proceeding considered *infra* in the main text. Thus, in addition to modifying 49 U.S.C. § 40102(a)(15), the legislators adopted a *lex specialis* imposing a citizenship test for Department of Defense airlift contracts. The nature of that test tracked the particular circumstances of the DHL/ASTAR commercial relationship. Section 2710 of the Emergency Wartime Supplemental Appropriations Act 2003, sec. 2710, Pub. L. No. 108-11, 117 Stat. 559, directed the DOT to use an administrative judge in the DHL/ASTAR proceeding and established a foreign revenue test with respect to qualification as a U.S. citizen (barring from defense airlift contracts any carrier receiving more than 50% of its operating revenue over the most recent three-year period from a non-U.S. citizen which has a direct or indirect voting interest in the carrier or which is a foreign State agency or instrumentality). The 'bill of attainder' nature of these provisions seems not to have raised jurisprudential eyebrows. In any event, neither the administrative law judge nor the DOT found that this special foreign revenue test could have any application in the DHL proceeding.

188. Jeffrey N. Shane, Under Secretary for Policy, U.S. Department of Transportation, *Aviation Deregulation: A Work in Progress*, Speech at the International Aviation Club, Washington, D.C., at 4 (Nov. 8, 2005). As Shane elaborated in later testimony to Congress, the subjective test of 'no semblance of foreign control' is now 'buttressed by a long list of subjective criteria that have appeared over the years in CAB and DOT case law, which does not make it easy to predict how DOT might rule in any given foreign control case.' Jeffrey N. Shane, Under Secretary for Policy, U.S. Department of Transportation, Statement Before the Aviation Subcommittee of the House Transportation and Infrastructure Committee (Feb. 8, 2006), <www.dot.gov/affairs/jeffshane020806.htm> [hereinafter Shane, Statement]. Prior to its statutory incarnation in 2004, the actual control rule attracted airline criticism that reflected Shane's wryly accurate 'it's for us to know and for you to find out' comment. US Airways (then-USAir), in its submission to the Airline Commission opposing foreign investment restrictions, lambasted the government's statutory interpretation: '[T]he larger problem comes from a barrier *not* in the statute .... *De facto* control is not a clear concept in the legal or business community, but the DOT apparently knows it when it sees it. [We] do not understand how the regulators get from the statute to that point.' Statement of Schofield, *supra* note 173, at 6 (emphasis in original). *See also* Daniel P. Kaplan, Foreign Investment in Domestic Airlines, in *Airline Commission Documents*, Dkt. No. 001018 (Jul. 2, 1993), at 34.

189. *See* the CAB's discussion of its analytical method in the quoted extract from *In re* Page Avjet Corp., *supra* note 184. For summaries of current DOT interpretive practice, *see* DOT Inspector General Letter, *supra* note 181, at 8-10; DOT, CERTIFICATED AIR CARRIER, *supra* note 175, at 13-15. *See also* the discussion of applicable factors *infra* note 190. Similar restrictions are in place in virtually all air transportation markets which conduct bilateral negotiations under the Chicago system. *See generally* [U.K.] Civil Aviation Authority, *supra* note 156, ch. 2, at 4. The EC rules also require that the airline's headquarters must be located within the Community.

190. Brown, *supra* note 184, at 1271. More colorfully, one commentator compared examining U.S. government policy on airline ownership to 'traversing a misty moor of legal uncertainty.'

from the political overtones that accompany certain high-profile transactions. In the mid-1990s, when foreign equity still flowed into U.S. airlines as an expected part of transatlantic alliance-making, representative transactions included a weak domestic carrier, shut out of traditional sources of indigenous capital, which was seeking a foreign 'white knight' to finance (and prolong) its survival,[191] and a domestic carrier, in a weak but not desperate condition, falling to a takeover bid that was partly financed by foreign capital.[192] Facing an unpalatable choice between rebuffing the benefactor or starving the domestic carrier of needed financial support, the DOT tried to cut the Gordian knot by both upholding the citizenship requirement and preserving some accessibility to foreign capital.

The result, inevitably, was a compromise that made application of the law seem impressionistic in its application, and consequently unpredictable. Unilateral admission of foreign investment, without any offer of or demand for reciprocity from the foreign investor's home government, also jeopardized a powerhouse bargaining chip that could be placed in the service of future liberalization. The DOT was evidently aware of these difficult systemic tensions. In reluctantly renewing code-sharing authority to BA and USAir (now US Airways) as part of the U.K. carrier's $300 million investment in USAir,[193] the Department brooded that '[w]e remain extremely dissatisfied with our existing aviation agreement with the United Kingdom and the lack of progress to date toward achieving liberalization. We will continue to review our options for dealing with our overall aviation relationship with the United Kingdom.'[194]

Stewart, *supra* note 171, at 687. Moreover, new inflections in DOT policy have revealed themselves constantly. The Department has shown concern, for example, with the minutiae of quorum, proxy, committee, and supermajority provisions of corporate bylaws that could, in some circumstances, operate in a manner creating both positive and negative control by the noncitizen directors over board actions. *See generally* DOT, CERTIFICATED AIR CARRIER, *supra* note 175, at 13-15. A disallowable 'supermajority' provision would occur, for example, if a foreign investor had the right to name one-third of the directors, and important corporate actions required 75% approval by the board. In those circumstances, the foreign interest would have a right to veto major decisions of the rest of the board. *See id.* at 14.

191. *See* British Airways' investment in the former USAir, discussed *infra* in the main text, which was accompanied by an *apologia* submitted to the Airline Commission by USAir 'on the importance of foreign equity investment in U.S. airlines.' USAir, *Submission to the [Airline Commission]*, undocketed. *See also* Statement of Schofield, *supra* note 173.

192. *See* KLM's investment in Northwest Airlines, discussed *infra* in the main text.

193. *See supra* text accompanying note 172.

194. *See* Application of British Airways plc for Exemption from Section 402 of the Federal Aviation Act of 1958, as Amended, and Application of USAir, Inc. for Statement of Authorization to Code-Share with British Airways plc, Order No. 94-3-31, *reprinted in* [1992-1994 Transfer Binder] Av. L. Rep. (CCH) ¶ 23,164, at 14,746 (Mar. 17, 1994) [hereinafter Applications of BA/USAir for Exemption/Authorization]. The need for reciprocity remains a constant of DOT citizenship jurisprudence. Thus, in a Supplemental Notice of Proposed Rulemaking issued during its controversy-studded NPRM foreign ownership proceedings, the Department insisted that

We would only apply our updated interpretation [of the actual control test] . . . in cases where the foreign investors' home countries have an open-skies agreement with the United States

A decade later, intercarrier equity investments across the Atlantic have given way for the moment to code-sharing and route collaboration, more pragmatic and less risky coins of exchange. But the administrative *acquis* of the DOT's earlier decisions on foreign investment is still being applied against a political backdrop. The following sections will consider an extraordinary confluence of recent events that saw the DOT attempting (in Sarkozian terminology) a *rupture* with its existing administrative practice, while simultaneously retrenching to traditional positions in examining the citizenship of U.S.-based airline corporations alleged by U.S. rivals to be under the direct control of EU nationals. Each of these events (a proposed rulemaking procedure that would have abandoned most of the DOT's existing 'actual control' jurisprudence, a challenge by cargo express integrators FedEx and UPS to the citizenship of the U.S. affiliate of DHL, their German-owned rival, and the attempt by Sir Richard Branson's Virgin corporation to establish a U.S. franchise) occurred in the long aeropolitical shadow of the negotiations leading to the 2007 U.S./EC Air Transport Agreement.

b   *DHL/ASTAR and Virgin America: Citizenship as a Competitive Weapon*

The preceding Part characterized as 'unsettled' the application of the U.S. Government's ownership and control requirements prior to the 2004 revision of the ownership and control law. A more recent commentator preferred the word 'uncertain.'[195] The deceptive simplicity of the black-letter law (U.S. citizens must comprise two-thirds of the board and other managing officers, with 75% of the voting interest being owned or controlled by U.S. citizens) produced a jurisprudence where the factors pointing toward foreign control could ultimately be trumped by an impressionistic, *gestalt*-driven, and therefore inherently unpredictable jurisprudence.[196] By adding an explicit requirement of 'actual control,' the 2004 amendment in effect *endorsed* the DOT's accumulated jurisprudence with all

---

and offer U.S. carriers and other U.S. investors a comparable ability to invest in their own airline industries, or where it is otherwise appropriate to ensure consistency with U.S. legal obligations.

[Supplemental Notice] Actual Control of U.S. Air Carriers, 71 Fed. Reg. 26,425, 26,4528 (supplement proposed May 5, 2006) [hereinafter Supplemental NPRM]. The proposed rule's 'reciprocity condition,' the DOT hoped, 'should encourage market liberalization that would create new opportunities for U.S. airlines and other U.S. investors to take advantage of similar opportunities overseas.' *Id.*

195. Kirsten Bohmann, *The Ownership and Control Requirement in U.S. and European Union Air Law and U.S. Maritime Law – Policy; Consideration; Comparison*, 66 J. Air L. & Com. 689, 706 (2001).

196. This is not to say that regulators are operating entirely without evaluative rudders. There have been several official and even judicial efforts to classify appropriate benchmarks for foreign control, most recently by the DOT Inspector General in the *DHL/ASTAR* dispute (considered

if its attendant uncertainty.[197] The opportunity to assess what effect the 2004 amendment would have (if any), arose in the very dispute which precipitated its adoption – an attempt by FedEx and UPS to use the citizenship law to disqualify an affiliate of their German rival, DHL, from providing cabotage services in the United States.[198]

i   DHL/ASTAR

FedEx, UPS, and DHL are the world's 'Big Three' providers of express package delivery services.[199] The facts of their U.S. citizenship controversy are probably

---

infra in this Section). The Inspector General identified and defined a total of seven factors, of which only the final four were relevant to the *DHL/ASTAR* case itself:

- *Control via Super-Majority or Disproportionate Voting Rights* – minority foreign owners must not have disproportionate influence with their voting rights
- *Negative Control/Power of Veto* – minority foreign owners cannot possess veto rights over major corporate decisions
- *Buy-Out Clauses* – a foreign entity must not be entitled to exercise buy-out clauses that, if exercised, would jeopardize the air carrier's financial or operational ability to continue in business . . . .
- *Equity Ownership* – the maximum total foreign-equity ownership of an air carrier typically permitted by the Department may be up to 49% . . . .
- *Significant Contracts* – contracts with foreign entities may not be used to control the U.S. air carrier . . . .
- *Credit Agreement/Debt* – debt-instrument clauses or bankruptcy agreements cannot allow a foreign entity to control the air carrier . . . .
- *Family Relationships/Business Relationships* – a foreign citizen may not exert control over an air carrier through a U.S. citizen family member or business associate

DOT Inspector General Letter, supra note 181, at 7-8.

197. For the (astonishingly attenuated) legislative history of the amendment, *see* 149 Cong. Rec. at 7813 (2003). In a brief colloquy, Senator Ted Stevens (R.-Alaska), observed that the amendment 'codifie[d] the existing requirement that U.S. air carriers be effectively controlled by U.S. citizens,' but that 'it [left] the interpretation of effective control up to DOT.' *Id.* According to Senator John McCain (R.-Ariz.), in the DOT's view the amendment 'accurately reflect[ed] the current state of law regarding citizenship,' and would not 'in any way affect [DOT's] determination of what constitutes a citizen of the United States.' *Id.* These comments (probably unwittingly) portray the amendment as surplusage, in that it merely entrenched a preexisting set of practices. But Senator Stevens's additional comments illuminate the amendment's true purpose. Noting that, at the time, a DOT administrative law judge was deciding whether the 'actual control' standard should be applied in a particular proceeding (*see* discussion of the DHL/ASTAR controversy in the main text, *supra*), he stated that, if the amendment were *not* adopted, the DOT would 'set a precedent which allows foreign governments to compete with U.S. companies for business which, by statute, is reserved to U.S. carriers.' *Id.* The practical purpose of the amendment, beyond codifying the existing standard, was to require application of the 'actual control' benchmark in *all* proceedings.
198. *See supra* note 197 (explaining the political background to the adoption of the amendment).
199. (An ontological distinction should be made between the narrow universe of global integrators engaged in express delivery services from the multiplicity of other players which are part of the field of global air transport, including combination (air passenger/air cargo) carriers.) The potency of broader system goals in assessing foreign control was evident from the DOT's disposition between 1989 and 1992 of various proceedings concerning an evolving courtship

the most complex of any DOT citizenship review proceeding and undoubtedly there has never been a more politicized dispute in the annals of DOT citizenship

between the Dutch flag carrier, KLM, and the then fifth-ranking U.S. carrier, Northwest Airlines (Northwest) *See* In the Matter of the Acquisition of Northwest Airlines by Wings Holdings, Inc., Order No. 89-9-51, *reprinted in* [1989-1992 Transfer Binder] Av. L. Rep. (CCH) ¶ 22,513, at 15,159. In Aug. 1989, KLM offered equity support totaling $400 million to a $3.65 billion mixed debt/equity leveraged buyout of NWA by Wings Holdings, Inc. (Wings). KLM's participation represented 56.74% of the equity capital, but only 19% of the voting stock, in the transaction. A large equity stake alone would not have voided Northwest's citizenship under the numerical test in the Federal Aviation Act, because the bulk of KLM's interest would be in nonvoting stock. In a consent order dated Sept. 29, 1989, however, the DOT found that KLM's high equity interest could place it in a position to exert 'actual control' over Northwest even though the Dutch carrier would fall substantially shy of owning 25% of the voting stock of Wings (two-thirds of which was owned or controlled by individuals and entities associated with a prominent U.S. businessman, Alfred Checchi). The DOT empha-sized that *nonvoting* stock was nonetheless *equity* and as such represented a genuine own-ership interest: 'The fortunes of KLM's investment will follow Northwest's more closely than those of creditors, will not be as secure as those of creditors, and will accordingly provide KLM with more incentive to participate in the airline's business decisions.' *Id.* at 15,161. Combined with other negotiated 'links' between these direct transatlantic competitors (a KLM financial 'advisory committee,' a KLM nominee on Northwest's board, and plans for joint marketing, sales, schedules, operations, and customer services), the deal was simply undoable. *See id.* at 15,162. The consent order scaled back KLM's equity investment to a maximum of 25%, with any excess placed in a U.S.-administered voting trust, abandoned the advisory committee and imposed recusal obligations on the lone KLM director with respect to matters affecting KLM's finances as well as the competitive relationship between KLM and North-west. *See id.* at 15,164-65. The DOT, lacking any tangible evidence of how the deal would work in practice, ultimately fell back on a hypothetical, *gestalt* analysis of how it *might* work if KLM sought to leverage its equity stake and management links into a more robust role in Northwest's corporate governance. Yet, when Northwest petitioned in 1991 for modifications to the original order, the subjectivity of the DOT's effective control test was colored by an entirely new factor, the aeropolitics of bilateral open skies discussions between Washington and The Hague. *See* U.S. DOT, *In the Matter of the Acquisition of Northwest Airlines, Inc. by Wings Holdings, Inc.*, Dkt. 46371, Order Modifying Conditions (Jan. 23, 1991) [hereinafter Northwest/Wings Petition]. By an order issued in Jan. 1991, the DOT allowed KLM to retain its entire equity interest, with only the excess over 49% of total equity required to continue in an independent voting trust. (Moreover, this concession was generalized in the order so that the DOT would henceforth interpret the law to allow a foreign investor to hold as much as 49% of a U.S. airline's total equity (including both voting and nonvoting stock), so long as foreign investment did not exceed the statutory limit of 25% of voting stock and unless other control factors were present.) *See id.* at 20-21. The DOT also allowed expansion of KLM's represen-tation on Northwest's board when the number of directors was increased, and continued the various recusal provisions. Finally, the order loosened or abandoned many of the financial reporting requirements imposed in 1989. The Department stated explicitly that all of these modifications were made in the context of a 'liberalized aviation relationship' between the United States and the Netherlands, KLM's homeland. *Id.* at 16. Given that the original restric-tions were imposed deliberately to obstruct KLM's influence over Northwest, there was an unsettling paradox in the government's new generosity. As a number of submissions to the DOT by competing carriers argued, KLM's interest in scaling back the restrictions could only have been with the intent to achieve (or would at the very least facilitate) an extension of its influence on Northwest's financial and corporate affairs. The Department, caught in the vortex of international air diplomacy, did not (and could not) agree. Moreover, in 1993, following

review.[200] The outcome, favoring DHL's U.S. domestic airlift supplier, ASTAR, amply sustains the assertion in the preceding discussion that the citizenship review

signature of the new U.S./Netherlands open skies accord, the DOT granted unprecedented authorization to KLM and Northwest 'to integrate their services and operate as if they were a single carrier.' Joint Application of Northwest Airlines, Inc. and KLM Royal Dutch Airlines for Approval and Antitrust Immunity of an Agreement pursuant to sections 412 and 414 of the Federal Aviation Act, as amended, Final Order No. 93-1-11; In the Matter of the Acquisition of Northwest Airlines, Inc. by Wings Holdings, Inc., *reprinted in* [1992-1994 Transfer Binder] Av. L. Rep. (CCH) ¶ 22,876, at 14,056 (Jan. 11-12, 1993) [hereinafter Joint Application of KLM/Northwest Airlines for Antitrust Immunity]. As part of this remarkable concession, achieved through a blanket grant of antitrust immunity under the DOT's special international authority, *see infra* in the main text, the Department restructured the 1989/91 recusal conditions to embrace only decisions by Northwest on maintenance or termination of the entire relationship, and (consistently with the nature of bilateral treaty diplomacy) the conduct of U.S./Netherlands and U.S./EC negotiations. The DOT agreed to cancel existing recusal safeguards concerning financial and potential competition matters, on the novel premise that 'with the implementation of the [integration agreement], KLM and Northwest *will no longer be competitors.*' *Id.* at 14,065 (emphasis added). It was the Department's conceit that the two airlines could fuse as one operational vehicle even while maintaining the incidents of separate citizenship reflected in the statutory tests of ownership and control. While that conceit may indeed be sustainable if one looks only to numerical benchmarks, it is much more difficult to perceive how KLM's rising influence over Northwest could have been construed as compatible with the qualitative test of 'effective' or 'actual' control presented in the original consent order in 1989. For example, as Delta Air Lines argued in its submitted comments on the revised KLM/Northwest application, to insist on a recusal condition solely with respect to Northwest's continued participation in or termination of the integration agreement would be 'meaningless' because KLM would still participate in board discussions of matters relating to its financial interest. The *gestalt* of the entire agreement, given KLM's high equity holding, its increased presence on the Northwest board, and its prospective future investments in its U.S. partner, all pointed to manifest error by the Department in deciding not to re-examine Northwest's citizenship. Ultimately, the government appears to have trusted that Northwest's future ability to assert its independence, through voting down the agreement unencumbered by a KLM veto, would be the truest guarantor that KLM could never exercise 'effective control.' But it is surely form over substance, and a reversal of the DOT's own precedent, to suggest that the mere *right* to vote down the agreement necessarily means that Northwest would ever have the fiscal *power* to do so, especially in light of Northwest's volatile economic performance and likely reliance on KLM for further infusions of capital. In any event, as an economic matter the alliance *as a marketing device* proved generally successful. But the appeal of equity investment, as with other transcontinental airline alliances of that era, proved ephemeral. Following litigation arising from Northwest's adoption of a takeover defense to prevent KLM from boosting its stake to a previously agreed 25%, Northwest gradually repurchased KLM's ownership stake between 1997 and 2000. Despite the withdrawal of equity, however, as of 2007 KLM (itself now part of an evolving merger relationship with Air France), continues to have one representative on Northwest's board (KLM's former CEO Leo van Wijk). *See* Daniel Michaels, *Clear Skies: Behind Easing of Airline Rules, KLM's 20-Year Urge to Merge–Dutch Carrier's Various Links Pushed Legal Boundaries*, WALL St. J., Sept. 5, 2006, at A1; *see also* Martin du Bois, *Northwest Will Pay $1.17 Billion to Buy KLM's 19% Stake*, WALL St. J., Aug. 11, 1997, at A11; Susan Carey & Shailagh Murray, *Northwest Airlines, KLM Agree on Plan to Expand Their Alliance*, WALL St. J., Jul. 31, 1997, at C18.

200. *See supra* note 197 (discussing Congress's thinly-veiled statutory intervention in the controversy). Demonstrating the formidable lobbying might of FedEx and UPS, the legislation also formally mandated the use of an administrative law judge (ALJ) (as opposed to continuing

process is not only a lawyer's evidentiary playground but is also clouded by the unpredictability of the ad hoc, impressionistic – and unabashedly aeropolitical – analysis which DOT regulators have continued to apply.

The facts presented here are a liberal summarization of the very detailed facts presented in the hearing. FedEx and UPS own 80% of the parcel and express delivery market in the United States, while DHL is their major competitor in foreign markets. The ultimate owner of DHL is the German mail monopolist Deutsche Post. Up to July 2003, DHL was conducting express delivery operations in United States domestic (cabotage) markets using its wholly-owned air carrier called DHL Airways.[201] In April 2003, a Congressionally-mandated administrative law judge was appointed to examine the citizenship of DHL Airways. During the course of the proceedings, DHL sold DHL Airways to a group of U.S. investors headed by former Burger King chief executive John Dasburg. Dasburg had previously become chief executive officer of DHL Airways. He renamed the company ASTAR Air Cargo, Inc. ('ASTAR') and became its president. The issue in the proceeding, therefore, was whether ASTAR, which received 90% of its U.S. express delivery package business under a non-exclusive wet-lease agreement[202] with DHL (a similar arrangement to the one which DHL previously had with DHL Airways), was (and is) a citizen of the United States under the airline ownership statute, 49 U.S.C. § 40102(a)(15).[203] Only an air carrier with U.S. citizenship can provide domestic (cabotage) services inside the United States.

The administrative law judge, Burton S. Kolko, who characterized the proceeding as a disguised private lawsuit (ASTAR *v.* FedEx/UPS), found that ASTAR is, and continues to be, a U.S. citizen. In his Recommended Decision served on December 19, 2003,[204] he found that not only does ASTAR meet the stock

---

informal review) in the DHL/ASTAR proceeding. *See* Emergency Wartime Supplemental Appropriations Act of 2003 sec. 2710, Pub. L. No. 108-11, 117 Stat. 559 (directing the DOT to appoint an ALJ for the DHL case); U.S. Department of Transportation, *Order Instituting Formal De Novo Review*, Dkt. No. OST-2002-13089 (Apr. 17, 2003) (official transfer of the case before an ALJ).

201. In 2001, DHL was purchased by Deutsche Post, leading to a restructuring and subsequent change of ownership for DHL Airways. This change was challenged by UPS and FedEx, leading to an informal review process which culminated in a finding that DHL Airways met the citizenship requirements. *See* U.S. DOT, In re *Compliance with U.S. Citizenship Requirements of DHL Airways, Inc.*, Dkt. No. OST-2001-8736, Order Dismissing Third Party Complaints (May 11, 2001). This informal finding led to an independent investigation by the DOT Inspector General and the passing of a legislative provision by Congress requiring the appointment of an administrative law judge to reevaluate the matter.

202. A wet lease means that the lessee receives the benefit of both aircraft and crew from the lessor. Under current U.S. regulatory practice, U.S. domestic wet-leasing must be provided by U.S. citizens. *See* 14 C.F.R. § 119.53 (2008). Dry-leasing (aircraft without crew) by foreign airlines for U.S. domestic purposes is permissible, however.

203. Thus, the DOT limited the issues and discovery in the proceeding to that of ownership structure alone. *See* U.S. Department of Transportation, *In the matter of the citizenship of DHL Airways, Inc. Under 49 U.S.C. Sec. 40102(a)(15)*, Dkt. No. OST-2002-13089, Order 2003-7-36 (Jul. 30, 2003).

204. U.S. DOT, *Recommended Decision of Administrative Law Judge in Docket No. OST-2002-13089* (Dec. 19, 2003), at 12 [hereinafter ALJ Decision]. Under the initial review of DHL Airways, the

ownership requirements of the statute (100% of its voting rights are now owned by U.S. citizens), but that the preponderance of reliable, credible, and probative evidence indicated that ASTAR is 'actually controlled' by U.S. citizens. On May 13, 2004, the DOT issued an order declining review of the administrative law judge's Recommended Decision.[205]

FedEx and UPS had argued that ASTAR was so beholden to its wet-lease agreement with DHL, its dominant supplier, that DHL would be in a position to exercise 'actual control' over ASTAR. At both levels of review, a stacking of the huge quantities of evidence advanced by each side led inescapably to the classic *gestalt* approach that has characterized prior DOT decisions on citizenship. On the one hand, ASTAR's business profile – 90% of its express delivery business (by revenue) supplied by DHL under a wet-lease agreement – was virtually identical to that of DHL Airways. [206] Arguably, ASTAR could still be regarded, like DHL Airways before it, as merely a 'creature of the DHL network,' a so-called 'cost center,' as FedEx and UPS maintained.[207] Alternatively, as Judge Kolko ultimately

---

DOT had relied upon the unamended statute which simply required a formal analysis that a company '[b]e incorporated in the United States'; '[h]ave a president and two-thirds of the board of directors who are U.S. citizens'; and '[e]nsure that no less than 75% of its voting stock is owned by U.S. citizens.' The DOT Inspector General (who recommended the ALJ appointment to Congress) readily admitted that DHL Airways had met those formal require-ments, though noting that the DOT also looked to 'the totality of the circumstances to determine whether [a] carrier is, in fact, under "actual control" of U.S. citizens.' *See* DOT Inspector General Letter, *supra* note 181, at 2-3. The 'actual control' requirement passed into law in 2004 and was the basis upon which the ALJ rendered his decision in the DHL Airways/ASTAR case.

205. U.S. DOT, *In the matter of the citizenship of DHL Airways, Inc. n/k/a ASTAR Air Cargo, Inc.*, Dkt. No. OST-2002-13089, Order 2004-5-10 Declining Review (May 13, 2004) [hereinafter Order Declining Review].

206. With the important qualification that, under the new agreement, DHL guaranteed a payment to ASTAR of $15 million annually whether or not DHL used ASTAR's airlift capacity. In Judge Bolko's view, this guarantee would act as a disincentive to DHL to cut off ASTAR's supply of business. Even if DHL terminated the contract or moved its business elsewhere, DHL would remain obligated to pay the guarantee and ASTAR would be free to develop alternative business sources. Any threat of termination would also be illusory, the judge found, because DHL would need the coherence of ASTAR's U.S. network. FedEx and UPS also called attention to the fact that under the Agreement, not only was DHL to be notified by ASTAR prior to any change in control, but that DHL could modify the Agreement to the detriment of the new owners in the event of such a change. Discounting any claim for a rational basis to these provisions, FedEx and UPS asserted that they effectively handcuffed ASTAR's owners from selling their stake in the company. ASTAR responded (and won the day) by pointing to the narrow scope of the restric-tions. Under the Agreement, ASTAR owners could still sell equity in ASTAR so long as they did not give up 50% of the voting rights. Further, they could also sell both equity and voting rights to new investors so long as they did not acquire more than 50% of the voting rights. *See* U.S. DOT, *ASTAR Air Cargo, Inc.'s Post Hearing Brief in the Matter of DHL Airways, Inc.*, Dkt. No. OST-2002-13089 (Oct. 31, 2003), at 49-52; ALJ Decision, *supra* note 204, at 23.

207. Here is how Judge Kolko put it: 'ASTAR *arguendo* was formed at the instance of a foreign entity; a foreign entity is backing the loan financing over 80% of its purchase price; its dominant customer is a foreign entity; and without that customer, ASTAR probably would not exist – certainly not in a form resembling its form today.' ALJ Decision, *supra* note 204, at 32. Thus, FedEx and UPS argued, summarizing this line of argument, that ASTAR's owners

found, it could be said that in a dynamic marketplace for express delivery services the non-exclusivity of the wet-lease agreement would allow enough flexibility to ASTAR to cultivate discretionary business relationships other than with DHL.[208] In choosing between these two possible interpretations, however, what precisely would be the determinative factor suggesting either the presence or absence of a substantial risk of foreign control? How could the DOT regulators intuit what they have previously called 'the shadow of substantial foreign influence?'[209] Merely stacking the evidence would not incontrovertibly point one way or the other. The resolving factor, as it has been in the past, was *gestalt*.

Judge Kolko, for his part, seemed dazzled by the pugnaciousness of the alleged servants of DHL (Dasburg and his ASTAR comrades): 'They are not as numerous as "The Magnificent Seven," but I suspect that one messes with this trio at his peril.'[210] Accordingly, he characterized Dasburg and his associates as a 'client' of DHL, not a dominated subordinate.[211] Nevertheless, the DOT, in adopting the judge's Recommended Decision,[212] made two key observations (responding to FedEx and UPS submissions) that transcended the evidentiary details of what the wet-lease agreement actually provided and of how aggressive the ASTAR executives might have appeared to the judge in live testimony. First, the Department took note of ASTAR's assertion that American consumers benefit from the competition (with FedEx and UPS) provided by ASTAR's presence in the U.S. market as part of the DHL network.[213] Second, as a matter of international aviation policy, the DOT rejected the FedEx/UPS contention that accepting ASTAR's

---

were assuming no risk, and therefore could not enjoy true control. *See* U.S. DOT, *Post Hearing Brief of FedEx and UPS in the Matter of the Citizenship of DHL Airways*, Dkt. No. OST-2002-13089 (Nov. 10, 2003), at 51.

208. Thus, the fact that ASTAR could still 'procure and develop [a] meaningful air freight business independent of [DHL] demonstrates in itself that [DHL] does not control it. Control rests in the hands of [ASTAR] because it maintains the power of choice to pursue the business model it crafts.' ALJ Decision, *supra note 204*, at 25.

209. *Uraba, Medellin and Central Airways, Inc. – Certificate of Public Convenience and Necessity*, 2 C.A.B. 334, 337 (1940).

210. ALJ Decision, *supra* note 204, at 21.

211. In summarizing his assessment and disposal of the FedEx/UPS claims, the ALJ stated that while the 'facts and suppositions' raised in the dispute 'suggested an inquiry into the question of its actual control, they do not determine the answer.' He reiterated that ASTAR ought to be viewed independently of DHL. The fact that ASTAR's relationships were global, that it was 'part of a greater, foreign-operated integrated system,' and that it 'can be viewed as a unit of a venture larger in conception and scope' did not, in effect, place it under the control of that grander enterprise. At bottom, '[t]o determine the citizenship question at the core of [the ASTAR] proceeding, the salient question is who has the power to direct or dominate ASTAR. The answer is ASTAR.' *See* ALJ Decision, *supra* note 204, at 31-33.

212. Following the conclusion of the ALJ that ASTAR was a citizen under the meaning of 49 U.S.C. § 40102(a)(15), the DOT supported his ruling by denying FedEx and UPS's request that the Department review the decision and affirming that the ALJ had thoroughly analyzed the evidence and correctly applied the statute. *See* Order Declining Review, *supra* note 205, at 29.

213. *Id.* Citing the adverse economic climate, DHL planned to discontinue its U.S. domestic services in January 2009 to focus solely on international services. *See* Press Release, DHL, DHL Express to Focus U.S. Business on International Services (Nov. 10, 2008).

citizenship would undermine a significant U.S. bargaining chip in international aviation negotiations. On the contrary, the Department found, denying citizenship to ASTAR could lead to retaliation against U.S. express delivery companies which use similar dominant-customer arrangements with local air carriers in foreign markets.[214]

Reading the psychological state of the challenged company's officers (or potential foreign masters), and assessing the challenge within the context of international aviation policy, represent separate *gestalt* approaches detected in the leading DOT precedents, *Daetwyler*[215] and *KLM/Northwest*,[216] respectively. The *ASTAR* case articulates an additional *gestalt* factor, that of consumer welfare. *ASTAR*, therefore, represents yet another shift in the mood of DOT investment control interpretation. But it is surely unwise, as a matter of law and policy, to allow unpredictable impressionistic criteria – the perceived braggadocio of a domestic or foreign citizen, the likely impact of the Department's determination on doing-business issues in foreign markets, or the projected competitive effects in the marketplace of allowing or disallowing citizenship, to trump simple examination of any restrictions on the voting powers of the voting equity held by the majority owner (or any other collateral restraint on the voting powers of the voting equity held by the majority owner).[217] That sense of uneasiness with the transparency of its own citizenship process, moreover, would prompt the DOT to open a later rulemaking that attempted precisely to replace 'it's for us to know and for you to find out' subjectivity with a core group of objective standards of assessment.[218]

ii   Virgin America

The DHL/ASTAR decision related to players in the air cargo sector (and, in particular, the highly profitable just-in-time segment of that sector). A different (or at least differently-nuanced) set of impressionistic criteria could have been expected to emerge in a proceeding that concerned the more contentious air passenger and combination sectors. In fact, the most heralded recent decision in those sectors, deciding the fate of Sir Richard Branson's hoped-for air carrier affiliate

---

214. *Id.* at 28.
215. *See In re* Daetwyler, Order No. 71-10-114, 58 C.A.B. 118 (Sept. 17, 1971). 58 C.A.B. 118 (1971). In *Daetwyler*, the CAB examined whether or not Swiss citizen Peter Daetwyler exercised 'foreign' control over Interamerican Airfreight. Despite meeting the formal citizenship requirements, *id.* at 119, the CAB found that Daetwyler did exercise control over the airline and that it was 'reflected by the fact that [Interamerican] is the direct successor of [Daetwyler's] forwarding company and [was] created wholly at the instance of Daetwyler,' *id.* at 120. Also relevant for the CAB was the fact that Daetwyler held the statutory maximum of 25% stock ownership in Interamerican and controlled one-third of the airline's board of directors. *Id.* Further evidence of ties with Daetwyler, including the fact that Interamerican was to continue operating within Daetwyler's previously established network of companies, tipped the scale toward the CAB finding that Interamerican was under foreign control. *See id.*
216. *See supra* note 199.
217. For further discussion of the perils of impressionistic criteria, *see* Havel, *supra* note 161, at 13,204-08.
218. *See infra* in the main text (discussing the NPRM proceeding).

(Virgin America) in the United States, turned out to be quite a dry and technical affair that seemed preoccupied with more traditional (and more objective) criteria of foreign control, such as the citizenship of Board members. It fell to the media to point out that, a mere 48 hours after the DOT's final decision was released, the EU Council of Transport Ministers met in Brussels to decide the fate of the U.S./EC Air Transport Agreement.[219]

Certainly, based on its prior jurisprudence, it would have been unsurprising had the DOT nodded to the ongoing U.S./EC negotiations in its *Virgin America* decision; in its recent ruling on antitrust immunity for the SkyTeam alliance, for example, it acknowledged without dissimulation that it was seeking to catch the mood of the new U.S./EC agreement.[220] Nevertheless, the DOT's reasoning in *Virgin America* was politically inspired in its way. Apart from its curious timing, it was a decision that needed to be anchored in legal positivism – and shorn of the impressionistic policy factors of *DHL/ASTAR* – in order to mitigate the disapproval of U.S. industry stakeholders, including worried rival carriers as well as labor unions protesting Virgin's antipathy to unionization. Early on, once Virgin America's plans to commence operations in 2006 had been announced, the project became embroiled in controversy as the Air Lines Pilots Association and several carriers, including American Airlines, Continental, Delta, and US Airways, alleged that Virgin America would not satisfy U.S. ownership and control rules.[221]

By the close of 2006, matters did not look favorable for Virgin. In its December 2006 order, the DOT determined that the new carrier was not a citizen as required by 49 U.S.C. § 40102(a)(15).[222] In making that determination, the DOT applied its ownership and control benchmarks with special rigor. The Department found that Virgin's majority stakeholder, a complex limited partnership dubbed 'VAI LLC,' could not satisfy its traditional analysis requiring not only that the controlling entity must be a U.S. citizen under the statute, but that each 'layer' of that controlling entity – in this case, the partners and their various investing partnerships – must also satisfy the citizenship test.[223] With VAI disqualified, Virgin America

---

219. *See* Jeff Bailey & Nicola Clark, *An American Version of Virgin Atlantic is Tentatively Approved for Service*, N.Y. TIMES, Mar. 21, 2007, at C3 (noting the close proximity of the decision to the EU Council of Ministers vote and the opinion of the Association of Flight Attendants that the 'tentative approval was aimed at winning European support for the open skies [agreement]' with the United States); Dan Reed & Ben Mutzabaugh, *Virgin America Gets Provisional OK to Operate in USA*, USA TODAY, Mar. 21, 2007, at 2B (stating that the approval came two days before the Council of Ministers vote).

220. *See infra* discussion in the main text.

221. *See* U.S. DOT, *Application of Virgin America Inc. for a Certificate of Public Convenience*, Dkt. No. OST-2005-23307, Order 2006-12-23 to Show Cause (Dec. 27, 2006), at 6-8 [hereinafter Virgin Order to Show Cause I].

222. *Id.* at 21.

223. *Id.* at 14. 49% or more of the total equity of each of the constituent partnerships was in the hands of either Cayman Island or other foreign partnerships. *See id.* at 14-15. In attempting to satisfy the DOT with respect to the ownership structure of VAI, Virgin had maintained that the latter was structured 'to allow only U.S. investment managers the ability to control the entity and therefore, the investment in the airline.' *Id.* at 14.

itself was subsequently determined also to fall short of the statutory mark.[224] While the DOT had at its disposal a more 'liberal' approach of disaggregating citizenship in instances where foreign interests are genuinely and obviously passive and none of the foreign investors shows an incentive or ability to exercise any actual control over the carrier, it opted not to exercise this discretion on the ground that Virgin America's foreign ownership interests were simply too extensively involved in the company.[225]

Thus, while failure to pass the ownership threshold was enough to bounce Virgin America's application, the 'actual control' test was also dispositive against it. In concluding that Virgin America was actually controlled by Branson and the Virgin Group, the DOT undertook a five-part analysis that *inter alia* found foreign control of Virgin America's management (putative CEO Frederick Reid was beholden in his position to the U.K.-based Virgin Group[226] and VAI had the power to appoint six of the nine Virgin America board members);[227] foreign control of Virgin America's strategic and business operations (Virgin Group provided its U.S. affiliate with the initial funding to develop a business plan, recruited and hired its executives, and solicited its investors);[228] foreign control of Virgin America's financing (with a preponderance of debt financing supported by the Virgin Group);[229] foreign control of Virgin America's trademark licensing (the restrictions in the licensing agreement between Virgin America and the Virgin Group to use the 'Virgin' trademark too tightly cramped Virgin America's commercial decisions);[230] and a residual foreign control that enabled Virgin

---

224. *Id.* at 15. A tangential citizenship analysis was also conducted by the DOT with respect to the ties of Virgin America's president, officers, and directors to Richard Branson and the Virgin Group. While the DOT found these parties to be U.S. citizens under the statute, it indicated that their undeniable links to Branson and the Virgin Group were relevant for the 'actual control' analysis. *See infra* in the main text.

225. Virgin Order to Show Cause I, *supra* note 221, at 14.

226. Virgin America's objection that Reid's position was solidified only after receiving approval from VAI failed to satisfy the DOT since it had already determined that VAI itself was not a U.S. citizen.

227. Virgin Order to Show Cause I, *supra* note 221, at 16-17.

228. *Id.* at 17-18. The DOT was not persuaded by Virgin America's assertion of independence from the Virgin Group. The reliance of the former on agreements entered into or funded by the latter, as evidenced by Virgin America's accession to such agreements without modification, added weight to the DOT's concerns over foreign control.

229. *Id.* at 18-19. The DOT found that, contrary to Virgin America's detailed funding plan which consisted of a combination of debt and equity financing (with $88.9 million out of $177.3 million supposedly coming from VAI), $131.9 million of debt financing for the carrier actually came from the Virgin Group. These facts led the DOT to find that Virgin America's survival hinged on the Virgin Group's financing and that the Virgin Group, not U.S. investors, would bear the risk of the airline's success or failure. The conclusion to be drawn from this arrangement, according to the DOT, was that U.S. investors were only brought in to satisfy the statutory requirements while leverage for control remained in substantial part with the Virgin Group.

230. Even though that is precisely the point of trademark franchising; under U.S. law, a trademark owner which does not adequately police use of its trademark by its licensee can forfeit its rights in the mark. *See* 15 U.S.C. Section 1127 (2008) (definition of 'abandoned').

Group to block or influence Virgin America's commercial decision-making despite its minority (25%) interest.[231] When combined with the DOT's negative appraisal of VAI's – and subsequently Virgin America's – citizenship, these manifestations of control vitiated Virgin America's claim to have satisfied 49 U.S.C. § 40102(a)(15). The DOT gave Virgin America 14 days to respond.[232]

Having filed substantial revisions to its financial arrangements, management, and corporate structure, Virgin America was back under the DOT spotlight in March 2007 – with much more favorable results.[233] On citizenship, Virgin America made it clear that it was willing to provide the DOT with affidavits confirming that VAI, an entity largely supported by hedge funds, satisfied the statutory citizenship requirement on the ground that the foreign investors in the hedge funds were diffuse and passive.[234] Virgin America further promised that such investors would be segregated from the carrier itself and that the large 25% voting interest of the Virgin Group would be placed in an irrevocable voting trust in order to protect U.S. investor interests in instances of conflict.[235] In addition to Virgin America's own pledges, the DOT imposed three additional conditions: first, all non-U.S. investors in VAI would have to be completely walled-off from investing in Virgin America; second, all investors must be able to meet the statutory citizenship requirement; and third, that Virgin America had to provide the DOT with a detailed diagram of VAI's ownership structure, including the nationality and percentage of foreign investment in VAI.[236] Subject to these conditions being met, and the continuing obligation of Virgin America to provide the DOT with any notice should the Virgin Group seek an additional equity interest in the carrier, the DOT was satisfied that Virgin America complied with the ownership test of the statute.[237]

The DOT's separate 'actual control' analysis also yielded positive results for Virgin America. On management, the carrier was willing to concede substantial overhauls in its officer corps, including the removal of Reid as CEO. Additionally, the Virgin Group's board representation was cut from three to two and the U.K.

---

231. Virgin Order to Show Cause I, *supra* note 221, at 19-20. Thus, the Virgin Group had entered into a number of agreements arranged to facilitate the sale of Virgin America to VAI, which nevertheless still gave the U.K. investor the power to block or influence commercial decisions.
232. *Id.* at 20.
233. *See* U.S. DOT, *Application of Virgin America Inc. for a Certificate of Public Convenience*, Dkt. No. OST-2005-23307, Order 2007-3-16 to Show Cause (Mar. 20, 2007) [hereinafter Virgin Order to Show Cause II].
234. *Id.* at 47-48.
235. *Id.* at 48. The DOT imposed certain conditions on Virgin America's offer to establish a voting trust to govern the Virgin Group's equity interest. Specifically, it stated that Virgin America board members who were U.S. citizens must confirm any voting trust nominee named by the Virgin Group and that the Virgin Group could remove the trustee only if the U.S. board members confirmed the removal. Any changes to the identity of the voting trustee must also be reported to the DOT and, in instances of conflict between the Virgin Group and Virgin America's board, the trustee would be subject to certain limitations. *See id.* 57-59.
236. *Id.* at 49.
237. *Id.* at 50.

entity lost all of its special voting powers. As for Virgin America's board as a whole, the DOT determined that only after VAI had reorganized itself to wall off foreign investors could its power to approve board members be deemed compliant with the statute.[238] Finally, with respect to its licensing agreement with the Virgin Group, Virgin America offered amendments to allow it more latitude in its use of the 'Virgin' trademark, including the freedom to code-share with any other (non-U.K.) carrier. The DOT also insisted, in an echo of Judge Kolko's recommendation in DHL/ASTAR, that Virgin America should be at liberty to enter into operating agreements with any other carrier, even competitors of Virgin Atlantic, so long as it foregoes using the 'Virgin' name in those instances. The Department deemed these changes to be consistent with its overarching requirement that the licensing agreement should afford Virgin America full freedom to operate independently, with restrictions being imposed in only the narrowest of circumstances.[239] As a final assurance to the DOT regulators, Virgin America provided documentation that it had secured $10 million in additional U.S. investment as well as $20 million in debt financing from U.S. investors prior to launch.[240]

The DOT granted operational clearance to Virgin America without once invoking (or even hinting at) the imminence of the decision by the EU Council of Transport Ministers on the fate of the U.S./EC Air Transport Agreement.[241] Given the DOT's history in past administrative proceedings of openly expressing its pique at the troubled state of U.S./U.K. aviation relations,[242] it is interesting (although, as noted above, politically understandable) that the DOT failed explicitly to offer its *Virgin America* decision as a salve for the troubled spirits of the EU

---

238. Virgin Order to Show Cause II, *supra* note 233, at 52-53.

239. *Id.* at 55-57.

240. *Id.* at 60-61 & 64. In addition to the parts of the DOT's 'actual control' analysis discussed above, the DOT also examined Virgin America's proposals to revise its loan agreements in order not to trigger further control issues. *Id.* at 54-55. The DOT also looked at the power of U.S. investors to 'put' their interest to the Virgin Group and found that, given the overall changes proposed by Virgin Group regarding management and financing, this was no longer problematic. *Id.* at 60. Following the Mar. 2007 decision, Virgin America was deemed fit to begin operations and launched its service in August of that year. In the interim, the DOT determined that Reid could stay with the carrier for nine months after the final issuance of the operating order – six as CEO and three more as a consultant. *See* U.S. DOT, *Application of Virgin America Inc. for a Certificate of Public Convenience*, Dkt. No. OST-2005-23307, Order 2007-5-11, Final Order (May 18, 2007) (allowing Reid to temporarily remain with Virgin America); Order 2007-8-17, Order Confirming Oral Actions and Issuing Effective Certificate (Aug. 17, 2007) (allowing Virgin America to begin selling tickets).

241. *Cf.* Reed & Mutzabaugh, *supra* note 219, at 2B (containing a statement from Rep. John Mica that the timing of the decision with the Council of Ministers vote was 'coincidental').

242. In 1999, for example, the DOT rebuffed an American Airlines/British Airways application for antitrust immunity and alliance approval following the collapse of negotiations for a new air services agreement to replace Bermuda II. *See* U.S. DOT, *Joint Application of American Airlines, Inc., and British Airways, plc*, Dkt. No. OST-97-2058, Order Terminating Proceedings (Jul. 30, 1999). The DOT emphasized that it was unwavering in its policy 'requiring an Open-Skies agreement as an essential predicate to any decision approving and granting antitrust immunity to an alliance operation.' *Id.* at 2.

Ministers as they gathered in Brussels. After all, the decision was always likely to be interpreted, in the specific aeropolitical context in which it appeared, as a limited compensation for the DOT's failed rulemaking proceeding to dramatically liberalize its interpretation of actual control under the citizenship statute. We turn now to consider the Department's proposal – which, in resting on a kind of intuitive separation between the commercial and regulatory control of an airline, may fore-shadow the eventual displacement of the nationality rule by a so-called 'right of establishment' for foreign air carriers.[243]

c   *The DOT's Noble Failure: The 2005/06 Rulemaking*

The U.S. DOT is aware that its citizenship review proceedings have an aeropoli-tical resonance (explicitly, as in *DHL/ASTAR*, or implicitly, as in *Virgin America*), and that the intrusion of unpredictable elements of policy into the review process has led to charges of even greater impressionism, subjectivism, and *gestalt* than a determination of 'foreign control' already risks.[244] In 2005, the DOT surprised industry stakeholders by proposing a radical liberalization of the U.S. actual control test that could have objectified the review criteria and increased the role of foreign investors in the management of U.S. airline corporations. Adoption of the proposal, which was a unilateral initiative by the United States made in the midst of U.S./EC air transport negotiations evidently *pour encourager les eur-opéens*, became an EC precondition to acceptance of the draft treaty.[245]

The DOT announced its plans to modify the 'actual control' rule by publishing a Notice of Proposed Rulemaking (NPRM) in November 2005 and inviting feed-back.[246] As it had to for statutory reasons, the proposal left the statutory 25% investment ceiling unaltered, and also the statutory control indicia which mandate that the president and two-thirds of the Board of Directors of a U.S. airline must be U.S. citizens. Given the fact that the 'actual control' standard is now also a stat-utory requirement, the DOT could not propose simply to abolish the test. Instead, it laid out a new protocol for how it would apply the test. Except for certain ring-fenced areas such as the documents of corporate organization, participation in the Department of Defense Civil Reserve Air Fleet (CRAF),[247] and issues concerning

---

243. The right of establishment has been mentioned already in this study, *see supra* Chapter 2, Part II(D). and will be the subject of further analysis, *see infra* in the main text & Chapter 6, Part III(E).

244. *See also supra* Chapter 2, Part IV.

245. *See supra* Chapter 2, Part IV (noting, however, that the treaty was accepted by the EU Council of Ministers despite the failure to adopt the DOT proposal).

246. NPRM, *supra* note 171, at 67,389.

247. The Civil Reserve Air Fleet Program (CRAF) opens up the use of civil aircraft to the military in times of emergency. CRAF was created under authority of the Defense Production Act 1950, 50 U.S.C. app. §§ 2061-2170 (1982). *See* Brattle Group, *supra* note 107, ch.7, at 1-4. This program provides over 90% of the passenger air transportation required by the military during an activation, and nearly 40% of the cargo transportation. CRAF was activated during the 1990/91 Desert Shield/Storm campaign, when civilian airlines carried 63% of the passengers and 25% of the cargo transported by air to the Gulf. Stage 1 of CRAF was also activated

safety and security,[248] a foreign investor in a U.S. airline would be able to exercise actual control over the commercial aspects of the airline's operations, including sales, marketing, pricing, route selection, and scheduling. DOT Under Secretary for Policy Jeffrey Shane, incidentally, had suggested this 'tweaking' of the DOT's interpretive rule on control as early as 1992, when BA was planning to invest $750 million in a struggling USAir and wanted DOT officials to take a more flexible view of its level of involvement in the U.S. airline's operations.[249]

---

between Feb. and Jun. 2003 during the early phase of the Iraq War, when the U.S. Department of Defense requested 47 widebody aircraft and associated flight support and mechanical crews. *See U.S. Military Ends CRAF Missions Related to Iraq War*, 352 Av. DAILY, Jun. 19, 2003, at 2. The U.S. Congress's General Accounting Office (GAO) reported in 1992 that the CRAF system would not be compromised by unlimited foreign investment. *See* GAO, *Airline Competition*, *supra* note 9, at 15. The Brattle Report echoed the GAO's findings that CRAF dependability would not be threatened by foreign ownership and control of U.S. airlines. *See* BRATTLE GROUP, *supra* note 107, ch. 7, at 7-17. While participation is optional for U.S. airlines, it is a prerequisite to eligibility for significant military business and for doing business with civilian government agencies. *See generally* GAO, *Civil Reserve Air Fleet Can Respond as Planned, But Incentives May Need Revamping*, GAO 03-278 (Dec. 2002). One of the key objections to allowing inward foreign investment in U.S. airlines is that it would place aircraft formerly under U.S. control in the hands of foreign owners who would not have to abide by U.S. rules to remain available for CRAF. Concern focused on the disincentive a foreign investor would have to making aircraft available to the U.S. military. These concerns prompted the DOT to affirm in its NPRM proposal that any U.S. airline's involvement in the program would remain in the actual control of U.S. citizens. That is, 'the carrier could not allow foreign investors to make decisions that would make participation in CRAF or other national defense airlift operations impossible as a practical matter.' The DOT also stated that it retained investigatory power over the airlines and that it would look into any alleged incidence of foreign control over an airline's participation in CRAF. The DOT also answered concerns over the potential for foreign investors to alter the nature of an airline's fleet by pointing to market incentives for not doing so; choices over types of aircraft would remain controlled by commercial needs, not concerns over CRAF. The DOT also reminded its critics that CRAF remained a voluntary program and that the Department of Defense could offer whatever economic incentives it saw fit to maintain steady participation in CRAF. *See* Supplemental NPRM, *supra* note 194, at 26,434.

248. Under the proposal, the following criteria would have been used to determine 'actual control:'

(1) All necessary organizational documentation, including such documents as charter of incorporation, certificate of incorporation, by-laws, membership agreements, stockholder agreements, and other documents of similar nature. The documents will be reviewed to determine whether U.S. citizens have and will in fact retain actual control of the air carrier through such documents. (2) The carrier's operational plans and actual operations to determine whether U.S. citizens have actual control with respect to:

(A) Decisions whether to make and or continue Civil Reserve Air Fleet (CRAF) commitments, and, once made, the implementation of such commitments with the Department of Defense;
(B) Carrier policies and implementation with respect to transportation security requirements specified by the Transportation Security Administration; and
(C) Carrier policies and implementation with respect to safety requirements specified by the Federal Aviation Administration.

NPRM, *supra* note 171, at 67,396.

249. *See supra* in the main text.

To justify such a dramatic break with its own interpretive practice, however, the DOT relied not on critiques of its past jurisprudential record of citizenship review but on 'changes in the global economy and [the] evolving financial and operational realities in the airline industry itself.'[250] The DOT found that U.S. carriers were unduly handicapped by being blocked from soliciting foreign capital to expand their operations.[251] As addressed in the NPRM, the DOT had become convinced that the idea of allowing a foreign investor to have operational control over commercial decisions would yield investment opportunities beyond the 'portfolio' stake tolerated under the current 25% cap on foreign ownership.[252] In short, the agency concluded, ' "actual control" should [not] be interpreted in a way that needlessly restricts the commercial opportunities of U.S. carriers and their ability to compete.'[253]

We have previously mentioned the political firestorm (of protectionist sentiment in Congress) that derailed the NPRM.[254] But the proposal, which involved (as Jeffrey Shane indicated) throwing out a lot of law,[255] also presented intriguing questions of law and policy that held the attention of the many industry constituencies which responded to the NPRM docket. On the juristic side, commentators queried whether the proposal would be an impermissible reach of authority – an action *ultra vires*, as it were.[256] After all, the 2004 amendment to the citizenship

---

250. Shane, Statement, *supra* note 188.
251. At the very least, the current low asset prices of U.S. carriers would be boosted as domestic buyers faced greater competition. *See* Michael G. Whitaker, Vice President, International and Regulatory Affairs, United Airlines, Address, *Liberalizing U.S. Foreign Ownership Restrictions: Good for Consumers, Airlines and the United States*, Seminar Prior to the ICAO Worldwide Air Transport Conference: Challenges and Opportunities of Liberalization (Mar. 22-23, 2003).
252. In this regard, it worth quoting the following remarks by the chief U.S. negotiator in the U.S./ EC treaty conclaves, John Byerly, Deputy Assistant Secretary of State for Transportation Affairs, in response to a question at a May 11, 2006 press briefing:

    [T]he investment that airlines outside the United States would be interested in pursuing is what we call 'strategic investment,' that is not trying to put some money in and hope the stock rises and pull it out and make some money. That is not the nature of the investment – a short term, for capital gains approach. But rather investing in an enterprise in which you have expertise, aviation, airlines, having some say in the business so your own views are represented in the commercial decisions of the American airline in which you have invested, and then making a wise and prudent economic bet, wager, that is going to yield a positive result for you and maybe a positive result that goes beyond stock market gains.

    Press Briefing, United States Mission to the European Union, U.S.'s Byerly, EU's Calleja Hope Air Services Accord Could Be Applied by Mar. 2007 (May 11, 2006), <http://useu. usmission.gov/Dossiers/Open_Skies/May1106_Byerly_Calleja.asp>.
253. NPRM, *supra* note 171, at 67,393-96. As the DOT noted, a well-crafted final rule would enable U.S. airlines to adapt to a better regulatory climate that allows them to 'pursue whatever strategies they believe will enhance their ubiquity, competitiveness and profitability in the global airline industry.' *See* Supplemental NPRM, *supra* note 194, at 26,427.
254. *See supra* Chapter 2, Part IV(B).
255. *See* Shane, Statement, *supra* note 188.
256. Challengers to the proposal did indeed claim that the DOT was attempting to circumvent Congress's authority. According to Continental Airlines, one of the proposal's leading

statute[257] converted the normative status of the actual control test, which was previously a DOT interpretive gloss on the ambiguous words of the statute, into a formal element of the statute. Moreover, as noted previously, it was clear from the Congressional record that the control requirement was inserted at least in part because of the pending DHL/ASTAR proceeding in which the DOT's insistence on requiring an 'actual control' test under the statute was being challenged (and not for the first time).[258] Arguably, however, the legislative record reveals that the insertion of an explicit actual control test was also intended to incorporate the existing interpretive practice of the DOT – a practice which, as the NPRM itself demonstrates, includes constant reinterpretation of the actual control criteria to reflect changing market and aeropolitical circumstances.[259] The recent decision of the Court of Appeals for the District of Columbia in *Sabre, Inc. v. DOT* [260]seems to confirm that deference will be accorded, in the event of a judicial challenge, to an administrative agency's broad reading of a broadly-worded statute.[261]

---

opponents, Congress's establishment of 'actual control' in 49 U.S.C. § 40102(a)(15) represented a codification of longstanding DOT practice and precedent. Thus, the DOT had no right under the statute to reinterpret the meaning of those words. *See* U.S. DOT, *Comments of Continental Airlines* [on the NPRM], Dkt. No. OST-2003-15759 (Jan. 6, 2006).

257. *See supra* in the main text.
258. *See supra* text accompanying note 173.
259. *See* 149 Cong. Rec. S. 7757, 7813 (Jun. 12, 2003). Supporters of the NPRM, in fact, called attention to the vagueness of the 'actual control' language in the statute and argued that it would always be necessary for the DOT to interpret it. *See* U.S. DOT, *Comments of United Airlines* [on the NPRM], Dkt. No. OST-2003-15759 (Jan. 6, 2006); *Comments of Delta Airlines*, Dkt. No. OST-2003-15759 (Jan. 6, 2006); *Comments of Federal Express*, Dkt. No. OST-2003-15759 (Jan. 6, 2006).
260. 429 F.3d 1113 (D.C. Cir. 2005). The case involved a challenge by the computer reservations system company Sabre, Inc., to the DOT's authority to regulate it as a 'ticket agent' within the meaning of 49 U.S.C. § 40102(a)(45). *Id.* at 1115. In deciding the case, the court applied 'the familiar two step analysis' (commonly referred to as the *Chevron* doctrine) found in Chevron U.S.A., Inc. v. Natural Resource Defense Council, 467 U.S. 837 (1984). Under this analysis, 'the court must first give effect to the unambiguously expressed intent of Congress,' *Sabre Inc.*, F.3d at 1121 (quoting *Chevron*, 467 U.S. at 842-43), and, should the statutory language prove 'silent or ambiguous,' then it must uphold the administrative agency's 'interpretation of a statute it administers, as developed in a rulemaking, if it is 'based on a permissible construction of the statute,' *id.* (quoting *Chevron*, 467 U.S. at 843). As *Chevron* goes on to state, an administrative agency's 'legislative regulations are given controlling weight unless they are arbitrary, capricious, or manifestly contrary to the statute' they elucidate. 467 U.S. at 844.
261. *Sabre Inc.*, F.3d at 1125 (citing PGA Tour, Inc. v. Martin, 532 U.S. 661 (2001) (stating that 'statutes written in broad, sweeping language should be given broad, sweeping application'). In a subsequent modified version of its proposal, the DOT attempted to counter claims that it did not have the legal authority to interpret and apply the statute. The argument relied in part on the Department's longstanding history of developing and applying the 'actual control' test prior to its legislative codification; no direction had come from Congress mandating that once the test was codified the DOT was relieved of interpretive latitude. Further, the DOT relied on the legislative history of the statute itself, which appeared to recognize the DOT's competence to freely interpret and apply its past interpretive practice and, more importantly, that the codification itself would 'not affect [the DOT's] determination of what constitutes a citizen

Was the proposal workable (a key factor in its significance)? Some likened the DOT's plan to a centrifuge. When the centrifuge revolves it throws off corporate organizational documents, CRAF, security, and safety, leaving all other aspects of operations still spinning within the center. No doubt there are aspects of the normal commercial operations of an airline which overlap with the elements spun off by the centrifuge – fleet planning, for example, must surely take place with an eye toward future CRAF participation and revenues. Nonetheless, courts examining a pre-enforcement challenge to the NPRM may have appreciated the logic of the DOT's argument – to eliminate actual control scrutiny for areas where there has been a renunciation of significant government regulation, namely, in routes, pricing, fleet selection, capacity, marketing, and so on. And whether or not critics were correct that the proposal was premised on an unrealistic model of airline operations,[262] the DOT could have moderated this criticism, and better served industry stakeholders, had it avoided using the exclusionary criteria listed in the NPRM (*i.e.*, that foreign control will not be permitted with respect to organizational documentation, CRAF participation, security, and safety).

---

of the United States.' Supplemental NPRM, *supra* note 194, at 26,436-37 (quoting 149 Cong. Rec. S. at 7813 (Jun. 12, 2003)). The DOT proposal, incidentally, would likely also have survived a judicial challenge because it was in substance a regulation and therefore protected by the Supreme Court's so-called *Chevron* doctrine. *See supra* note 260 (laying out the *Chevron* doctrine). The administrative law argument runs as follows. Despite the fact that the DOT decided that the outcome of its rulemaking procedure would be a 'Statement of General Policy' – and, as such, nonbinding, discretionary, and unilaterally rescindable – the Department chose to adopt its new proposal through the means of a formal notice of rulemaking, which is not a required procedure for policy statements. Courts have found that a policy statement adopted by an agency after a formal NPRM procedure has a reduced level of 'alterability' by the agency. In fact, the use of the NPRM procedure, coupled with the level of specificity in the language of the proposal, suggested that the Department was actually on track to create a 'regulation' rather than a mere statement of policy. As such, it would carry the force of law (as though it were a statute), would bind the courts, and would not be discretionary in each case where it is applied. In addition, regulations attract the operation of the so-called *Chevron* doctrine, *see supra* note 260, which requires courts to give complete deference to regulations and to enforce them without permitting a challenge to the validity of the underlying policy (or requiring the agency, in this case the DOT, to mount a justification for the policy). The *Chevron* doctrine is especially applicable where the underlying legislative history (*i.e.*, the Congressional debates on the legislation under which the agency has acted) support the notion that the agency has a delegated power to enact regulations.

262. Continental Airlines, a leading industry skeptic on the NPRM, attacked 'the unworkable nature of bifurcating control of a corporation.' Press Release, Continental Airlines, Continental Airlines Statement on D.O.T. Proposal to Allow Foreign Control of U.S. Airlines (May 3, 2006). The Air Line Pilots Association argued that certain business decisions, such as fleet composition, markets served, schedules, and fares, could not be surrendered without yielding true control. The Association also castigated what it saw as the DOT's undue narrowing of its evaluation to four areas of control rather than placing its evaluative emphasis upon the individual or entity making the critical determinations over the airline's operations. The pilots' union also raised concerns over the adverse impact the proposal would have on domestic airline jobs. *See* U.S. DOT, *Comments of the Air Line Pilots Association International* [on the NPRM], Dkt. No. OST-2003-15759 (Jan. 6, 2006); Press Release, ALPA, ALPA President Blasts Proposal to Loosen Foreign Control Rules, Release #06.004 (Feb. 8, 2006).

Instead, the proposal could have made an explicit statement that the 'actual control' factors previously considered by the Department would no longer include any factor (other than the factors specifically mentioned in the NPRM) previously considered by the DOT in any citizenship proceeding.[263] Thus, for example, a foreign investor could reasonably predict from such a statement that its business relationships with a U.S. airline (for example, that the foreign investor supplies 90% of the cargo revenues of the U.S. carrier[264]) would not indicate 'actual control' by that foreign airline. Such an explicit reference to the DOT's past precedents on 'actual control,' in fact, would more properly have conformed the NPRM to the Congressional intent described earlier.[265]

Setting aside the *ultra vires* question and operational doubts, as a policy matter the proposal was unquestionably a significant step in the direction of regime change. It was not the New Jerusalem of abolishing all inward restrictions on ownership and control, but it did represent a substantial liberalization of the existing approach to determining control. Simply stated, 25% ownership *with* control is better than 49% ownership (the Bush Administration's now-defunct proposal[266]) *without* control. Under the DOT proposal, a foreign investor with 25% ownership could presumably also own far more than 50% of the nonvoting equity, insist on supermajority voting, and gain control over the scheduling operations of a U.S. airline. And, after all, other industry innovations such as code-sharing and alliances have evolved despite a regulatory environment that remains several steps behind the collaborations created in the marketplace, and the marketplace could have been

---

263. See, for example, U.S. DOT Under Secretary for Policy Jeffrey Shane's recent observation that '[r]ather than the long list of subjective tests created by years of case law, we would seek only four objectively verifiable answers' [*i.e.*, with respect to corporate documents, CRAF participation, safety, and security]. Shane, Statement, *supra* note 188.

264. This, of course, is the DHL/ASTAR paradigm. *See supra* in the main text.

265. It is worth noting, incidentally, that the DOT would have limited access to the benefits of its proposed change of policy to those countries which offered 'reciprocity' in terms of investment opportunities to U.S. carriers. NPRM, *supra* note 171, at 67,396. The DOT's two requirements would be 'evidence of an Open Skies agreement, or where it is otherwise appropriate to ensure consistency with U.S. international legal obligations.' Technically, the EC was not offering a reciprocal modification of its own 'effective control' test, but the United States might well have taken the view that reciprocity does not have to mean *identical* treatment. The European Community's 49.9% ownership ceiling, for example, could have been broadly interpreted as sufficiently reciprocal, and EC negotiators did indicate that they would examine their own rules to consider whether greater flexibility could also be introduced into EC effective control determinations. Although the EU Council of Ministers accepted the U.S./EC Air Transport Agreement despite the NPRM's collapse, one provision of the agreement's annex on ownership, investment, and control reveals that the EC negotiators appeared to have retained some residual resentment towards their U.S. colleagues on this matter. The agreement reserves the right of the Community and its Member States to limit investments by U.S. nationals in the voting equity of an EU airline to the 25% limit specified for foreign investors in U.S. carriers. In other words, if this provision is ever applied, U.S. investor rights could be (considerably) less than those accorded to all other non-Member State investors. U.S./EC Air Transport Agreement, *supra* note 21, annex 4, art. 1(4).

266. *See infra* note 287 and accompanying text.

trusted to use the DOT's proposed rule to invent new modes of cooperation and investment. In practical terms, the proposal could well have served its avowed purpose (as portrayed by Under Secretary for Transportation Policy Shane) of prising open access to foreign equity investment.[267]

Other than opening a spigot for greater foreign investment, the ongoing business effects of the NPRM proposal, had it been adopted, are harder to gauge. Although the proposal was heralded as possibly allowing a corporation like the Virgin Group, for example, to enforce brand identity standards on a related U.S. operation in which it took up to a 25% interest, in fact the U.S./EC Air Transport Agreement made about as much provision for inward franchising and branding *simpliciter* as the NPRM could have done.[268] There were also suggestions that the new proposal would have encouraged deeper integration of transnational alliances such as Star and oneworld and perhaps a return to the abandoned era of equity investments.[269]

---

267. *See* Shane, Statement, *supra* note 188. The DOT did modify its original NPRM in response to criticism from certain sections of the airline industry and from Congress. *See* Supplemental NPRM, *supra* note 194, at 26,425. It should be noted that the supplemental NPRM changed little of the actual wording of the proposed final rule and was really intended as an interpretive commentary to the NPRM. In its 'supplemental' proposal, the Department stated that it 'would be requiring all delegations to foreign interests ultimately to be revocable by the board of directors of voting shareholders,' thus maintaining 'actual control.' This revocability condition would likely have deterred strategic investors. Had it actually been adopted, ideally the wording would have reflected typical corporate practice by allowing a foreign investor to insist contractually on the payment of penalties (in an amount not out of proportion to the value – both strategic and financial – of the investment) if its ability to control particular commercial operations were compromised or revoked. In any event, all of that is now speculative. In the wake of the Dubai Ports controversy, *see infra* note 294, as well as strong labor opposition, both the House and Senate introduced bills to prevent the DOT from rendering a final decision on the NPRM for one year and providing also that 180 days prior to any enactment, the DOT would have to issue a report to Congress on the potential effect the enactment might have on aviation. *See* H.R. 4542, 109th Cong. (2006); S. 2135, 109th Cong. (2006). A second effort to prohibit the DOT from enacting and enforcing the proposed rule came in a bill for appropriating funds for the 2007 fiscal year. The bill's language expressly prohibited the DOT from using the 'funds made available by [the] Act . . . to finalize or implement the policy proposed.' H.R. 5576, 109th Cong. § 104 (2d Sess. 2006). Although this language never made it into law, the DOT's efforts to enact its revised rule were ultimately thwarted by strong bipartisan pressure on the President not to let the agency proceed. In Dec. 2006, the DOT announced that it was withdrawing the rule, though it stated that it would continue its efforts to open up U.S. airlines to more foreign investment. Press Release, U.S. DOT, U.S. Department of Transportation Withdraws International Investment Rule - Commits to Working on Open Skies Agreement, DOT 110-06 (Dec. 5, 2006).

268. *See* U.S./EC Air Transport Agreement, *supra* note 21, annex 5 (permitting reciprocal franchising and branding in compliance with applicable laws on control, cabotage, and consumer protection, while insisting – without further clarification of what this might mean – that the franchisee must have 'the ability to exist outside of the franchise').

269. *See supra* in the main text. On the other hand, the introduction of a delegation revocability condition under the DOT's supplemental proposal, *see supra* note 267, would surely have deterred further strategic investments in U.S. airlines.

A caveat, of course, is that the U.S. Supreme Court's *Copperweld* doctrine only extends antitrust immunity on pricing and market division collaboration to related entities,[270] and not to independent competitors such as the members of airline alliances. To deepen their integration lawfully, therefore, U.S./EU alliance partners would have continued to need the special privilege of antitrust immunity for international operations that the U.S. DOT, by historical accident, can still confer.[271] And mention of that strange artifact of antitrust immunity reminds us, surely, of the wisdom of moving to a 100% foreign investment regime.[272]

C   A Future Without the Nationality Rule?

1   **Alliances: From Code-Sharing to Contract**

For the airlines, the current caps on cross-border investment mean that *ersatz* merger and acquisition methods have to be tried. Thus, large-scale transcontinental alliances have become more stable and can be expected to persist as a workable business model so long as the nationality rule itself persists as the governing legal standard. While airlines are still prepared to invest in each other transnationally,[273]

---

270. Copperweld *v.* Independence Tube, 467 U.S. 752 (1984). In *Copperweld,* the Court found that the requirement of § 1 of the Sherman Antitrust Act requiring two or more entities to contract, combine, or conspire is not satisfied by 'an internal "agreement" to implement a single, unitary firm's policies.' *Id.* at 769. Given that 'officers of a single firm are not separate economic actors pursuing separate economic interests' and that '[i]n the marketplace, such co-ordination may be necessary if a business enterprise is to compete effectively,' the 'officers or employees of the same firm do not provide the plurality of actors imperative for a § 1 conspiracy.' *Id.* For a critical history of the Sherman Antitrust Act, *see* Robert L. Bradley, Jr., *On the Origins of the Sherman Antitrust Act,* 9 Cato J. 737 (1990).
271. *See infra* Chapter 4, Part III(C).
272. British Airways, for example, complained that the NPRM had not gone nearly far enough in loosening strictures on foreign investment. *See* Martin Broughton, Chairman, British Airways, Speech to the Wing's Club, New York (Jan. 19, 2006).
273. The new U.S./EC Air Transport Agreement, *see supra* note 21, is expected to ignite a number of long-expected transborder investments, and has already encouraged a potential British Airways takeover of Spain's Iberia. *See supra* Chapter 2, note 173 and accompanying text. Prominent recent examples of transnational investment (where less than 100% of the target carrier was acquired) include Air France/KLM, *see infra* Chapter 5, Part III(B), and cross-ownership stakes taken in each other by Cathay Pacific and Air China. *See* U.S. DOT, *Comments of United Airlines, supra* note 259, at 2. Lufthansa, meanwhile, has taken a 49% stake in Swiss International Air Lines and plans for eventual 100% ownership once negotiations to secure traffic rights have been concluded and the relevant agreements are in place. *See* Press Release, Lufthansa, Squeeze-Out Procedure Successfully Completed (Jan. 20, 2006). Barring a block from EC competition authorities, Lufthansa is poised also to take an 80% stake in British carrier bmi. *See* David Wighton, *Will bmi Take Off or Stall Under Lufthansa?,* Times (London), Jan. 13, 2009, at 39. If the deal goes through, Lufthansa will also acquire 12% of Heathrow's much-coveted slots, giving the German carrier the potential to compete with British Airways on long-haul routes out of London. *Id.* The pattern of investment seems almost predictable: a large carrier buys into a smaller flag carrier and adds 'route synergies' to its

over the last decade they have generally preferred to avoid substantial equity investments altogether and to outflank government restrictions using the device of code-sharing and extensive cross-border alliances based on code-sharing. Some code-sharing alliances have secured the boon of U.S. antitrust immunity for their collaborative operations.[274]

While all of these arrangements must stop short of an international corporate merger, they do provide access to additional passenger traffic for international routes that participating airlines are authorized to serve.[275] Moreover, while alliances were justifiably criticized in the 1990s as transitory,[276] incapable of creating genuine operating efficiencies,[277] anticompetitive, and generally uneven in their performance,[278] a more stable, contract-based system of global alliances

---

network. Past examples included Air France/Sabena, BA/Qantas, and BA/USAir. *See generally* U.S. DOT, *U.S. International Aviation Issues in a Global Perspective*, Issues Papers, *in Airline Commission Documents*, Dkt. No. 001207 (May 1993). Some aspects of these collaborations are explored further *infra* in the main text.

274. *See infra* in the main text.
275. *See generally* Karel van Miert, former EU Transport Commissioner, *European Air Transport Policy in the Perspective of the Achievement of the Internal Market: What Next?*, Speech at the Aviation Club of Great Britain, London (Mar. 30, 1992) (on file with the Library of the EU Delegation, Washington DC) (discussing strategic importance of alliances) [hereinafter van Miert, *European Air Transport Policy*].
276. As the GAO pointed out, 'these alliances can be dissolved at any time.' GAO, *International Aviation, supra* note 98, at 57. Even the most bonded of the early relationships, that between KLM and Northwest, included a mutual right of withdrawal upon one year's notice. *See* Carey & Murray, *supra* note 199.
277. 'The only way to get operating efficiencies that make sense and a structure that makes sense, is to allow two carriers to merge.' *Airline Commission Proceedings*, remarks of Commissioner Felix G. Rohaytn, Lazard Frères & Co., Chairman of Financial Issues Team (May 24, 1993), at 221.
278. In 1996, the DOT awarded antitrust immunity to two notable transcontinental alliances (Lufthansa/United and Delta/Swissair/Sabena/Austrian). Neither of these pioneering arrangements involved substantial equity or debt investment by a foreign carrier in a U.S. airline, and the DOT did not address issues of ownership and control in the immunity proceedings. More recently, the Department granted immunity to a major transcontinental alliance (allowing United Airlines and its Star Alliance partners to add Swiss International Air Lines, LOT Polish Airlines, and TAP Air Portugal to their network of immunized partnerships and permitting extended cooperation between United Airlines and Air Canada). *See* Press Release, U.S. DOT, DOT Tentatively Approves Antitrust Immunity for Expanded Star Alliance, DOT 120-06 (Dec. 19, 2006). The government, however, initially rejected immunity for a broad code-sharing alliance involving SkyTeam members Delta Air Lines, Northwest, Air France, KLM, Alitalia and CSA Czech Airlines, *see* Press Release, U.S. DOT, DOT Proposes Broad Code-sharing Authority to Skyteam Alliance Members, Tentatively Denies Antitrust Immunity, DOT 186-05 (Dec. 22, 2005), before taking a more indulgent stance in the light of the U.S./EC Air Transport Agreement, *see infra* Chapter 4, note 297. Again, neither the Star Alliance nor the SkyTeam arrangements included any transfusions of equity among any of the participating carriers. It remains true, therefore, that agreements to engage in joint marketing, sales, schedules, and operations – extending even to blending control over prices and capacity – will not trigger a citizenship review of the U.S. partner. Without some evidence that instruments of corporate governance are affected (board membership, for example), it appears that the DOT will regard nonequity marketing alliances as dissoluble contractual arrangements. But this view, if correct, is unarticulated in the DOT's published opinions.

(comprising Star Alliance, oneworld, and SkyTeam) had emerged by the middle of the first decade of the new century.[279] But alliances will always be a second or third-best option. They are an accidental product of the nationality rule, not of optimal strategic planning.

2   Reforming the Nationality Rule in Domestic Law

The pace of reform of the nationality rule at the international level, unlike in domestic law, has acquired an appreciable momentum. As we saw in Chapter 2, many participants in aviation's global webs of influence have staked out liberal positions. And other initiatives are set to continue. The European Commission is undertaking a massive country-by-country renegotiation of EU Member States' bilateral agreements to require third countries to accept the designation of 'Community air carriers' by each Member State.[280] The new U.S./EC Air Transport Agreement offers U.S. recognition of multinational ownership that spills well over the existing borders of the EU. And, at the opening of the U.S./EC second stage negotiations in Ljubljana in May 2008, the United States made an unanticipated offer to join the EU in agreeing to waive all traditional nationality objections with respect to many common U.S./EU third-country bilateral relationships.[281]

---

279. *See* Keith Johnson, *Airline Deal May Spur Carriers to Find Savings from Alliances*, WALL ST. J., Dec. 17, 2003 (noting airline managers' enthusiasm, despite KLM/Air France merger model, for evolving alliances beyond marketing and scheduling into 'cost-cutting machines that can offer merger-style benefits' including joint fuel purchasing, joint aircraft orders, and joint maintenance-and-repair operations).

280. European Commission, *Communication from the Commission on Relations Between the Community and Third Countries in the Field of Air Transport*, paras. 36-41, COM (2003) 94 final (Feb. 26, 2003); *see also infra* Chapter 5, Part III(C).

281. According to U.S. Deputy Assistant Secretary for Transportation Affairs John Byerly, the second stage should include 'an ancillary multilateral agreement that will be open to accession by other countries that are prepared to enter into reciprocal obligations to lift barriers to cross-border investment by pledging to forego recourse to the nationality clause.' *The U.S.-EU Air Transport Agreement: Making the Most of the Second Stage*, Remarks to the European Aviation Club, Brussels, Belgium (May 13, 2008). The U.S. initiative is consistent with the historic inclination of U.S. international aviation to grant waivers of the nationality clause in U.S. bilateral air services agreements. *See* Jeffrey N. Shane, Associate Deputy Secretary of Transportation, *Open Skies Agreements and the European Court of Justice*, Remarks to the American Bar Association's Forum on Air and Space Law, Hollywood, Florida (Nov. 8, 2002) (emphasizing that the U.S. external bolt is 'permissive'). Typically, because of the domestic legislation that virtually all countries have adopted, mere 'designation' by another country tends to satisfy the U.S. authorities. Other countries also typically inform the United States of any change in ownership and control (given the preponderance today of privatized, publicly-quoted airline corporations, this information could hardly be hidden). Yet it appears that this information, even if it reveals a shift to foreign ownership, will not necessarily cause the United States to withdraw or suspend traffic rights. The reasons why the United States has granted waivers of the nationality restriction are both juridical and aeropolitical. Juridically, there is in fact no statutory requirement in the Federal Aviation Act or elsewhere in U.S. law requiring that substantial ownership and control be in the hands of the designating foreign country or its citizens. It is solely a treaty-based requirement. With respect to aeropolitics, the

But, while efforts are under way to liberalize the nationality clause at treaty level, major aeropolitical powers like the United States and the EU Member States still require their own national airlines to satisfy citizenship purity tests created under domestic (or EC) legislation. As long as the major aviation powers keep their nationality restrictions in place, other countries will rarely be tempted unilaterally to abolish their own internal restrictions and to risk a loss of negotiated and valuable traffic rights. Thus, the prisoner's dilemma of the bilateral system will remain a powerful deterrent. For the airline industry, unless the major powers unlock what has been called the 'internal' bolt of the nationality lock,[282] reform efforts to free airlines from the shackles of national ownership will remain largely theoretical, the stuff of well-intentioned position papers but not of commercial reality. Occasional politically inspired waivers of the nationality clause, and support for global reform initiatives, will not substitute for the predictability that airlines need in order to begin a serious process of cross-border restructuring of their industry.

The case of Australia is instructive.[283] Australia, in fact, has made the most eye-catching change to the traditional domestic nationality rule. Responding to

---

United States makes waiver determinations based on whether a change in the ownership/control composition of a foreign airline affects U.S. aviation policy or interests (and typically it will not). *See* Allan I. Mendelsohn, *The United States, the European Union and the Ownership and Control of Airlines*, [2001-2004 Transfer Binder] Issues Aviation L. & Pol'y ¶ 25,151, at 13,172 (2003). For example, when the European Court of Justice applied EC anti-discrimination rules to declare illegal the nationality clauses in EU Member States' air services agreements with third countries, the United States responded almost immediately by proposing an amended form of the nationality clause that would, for example, accept designations of airlines by France even if those airlines were owned and controlled by other EU States or their nationals – be they Germans or Dutch or Italians. *See id.* at 13,180. (This concession was subsequently made part of the 2007 U.S./EC Agreement.) Similarly, the United States did not suspend the traffic rights of Aerolineas Argentinas when that company fell under primarily Spanish ownership and control. Most remarkably, the DOT relied on a preexisting open skies relationship to accept a Luxembourg-designated cargo airline, Cargo Lion, in which no Luxembourg national had *any* ownership interest (a German national owned 49%, a Swiss national owned 41%, and a U.K. and Canadian national each owned 5%). *See* U.S. DOT, *Translux International Airlines (a/k/a Cargo Lion)*, Dkt. No. OST-98-4329, Notice of Action Taken (Nov. 25, 1998). But ad hoc escapes from the ownership and control restrictions are not likely to create the regulatory certainty and predictability needed for airlines to assume that they can engage in cross-border investment activity without concern about losing traffic rights. Even if the United States recognizes a German-owned French airline, will Japan also do so? What about Brazil? The tolerance of the bilateral network for change is itself unpredictable. Although the worldwide airline trade group, the International Air Transport Association (IATA), in 2001 and again in 2003 invited governments to issue unilateral generalized waivers with respect to the foreign ownership (but not control) restriction in bilateral agreements, the best that can be expected is for the grant of piecemeal waivers. And that is a poor substitute, as far as most air carriers are concerned, for knowledge-based forward planning.

282. The 'external' bolt, as we have noted, *supra* Chapter 2, Part V, is the provision in every bilateral treaty requiring each State's designated airlines to be owned and controlled by nationals of that State.

283. For a fuller account of the Australian experiment described here, *see* [U.K.] Civil Aviation Authority, *supra* note 156, ch. 3, at 7.

high fares and declining competition in its domestic air transport markets (and Singapore Airlines' professed interest in buying Australia's weakest carrier, Ansett), Australia amended its domestic airline legislation in 1999 to enable non-nationals to own up to 100% of any Australian airline with exclusively domestic operations. While Australia's concession is dramatic, it is limited in effect because it deliberately avoids any problematic third-country designation issues.[284] As applied, the legislation also generally permits foreign investors to establish a new aviation business in Australia, provided that the airline remains incorporated and headquartered in Australia and (again) serves only internal routes. IATA, representing most of the world's international carriers, recently complimented Australia's 'evolution in thinking.'[285]

In the United States, consistent with U.S. international aviation policy on the nationality clause, a constituency has been forming to press for reform of the domestic legislative tests for citizenship. The reformist constituency now includes many of the U.S. airlines that often sheltered behind the nationality clause in the contented years when the U.S. domestic market was flourishing. United Airlines, for example, has undergone a dramatic conversion since its bankruptcy, calling liberalization of the foreign ownership restrictions 'a promising policy option whose time is ripe.'[286] The U.S. DOT, as it showed in its daring NPRM gambit, wishes to tweak the prevailing system to dilute some of its preconceived notions of sinister foreign control. The outgoing Bush Administration kept faith with earlier liberal initiatives by asking Congress to follow Europe's lead by raising the foreign voting stock ownership cap to 49% from 25% (with all of the implications for the control test that such an increase would involve).[287] It remains to be seen whether these perceptible movements in the *Zeitgeist* have survived the Dubai Ports controversy and its aftermath,[288] but the consequences of soaring oil prices in 2007/08

---

284. *See generally* [Australian] Foreign Investment Review Board, Civil Aviation: Domestic Services, <www.firb.gov.au/content/other/sensitive/aviation.asp?NavID=51>.

285. PETER VAN FENEMA, INTERNATIONAL AIR TRANSPORT ASSOCIATION, OWNERSHIP AND CONTROL: REPORT OF THE THINK TANK – WORLD AVIATION REGULATORY MONITOR 24 (2000).

286. Whitaker, *supra* note 251. The British, following suit, have spoken in more provocative language. Virgin Atlantic Airways' external affairs director, Barry Humphreys, told the same ICAO conference at which Whitaker spoke that retention of the nationality restrictions 'borders on madness.' Barry Humphreys, Director of External Affairs and Route Development, Virgin Atlantic Airways, Address, *Liberalised Airline Ownership and Control*, Seminar Prior to the ICAO Worldwide Air Transport Conference: Challenges and Opportunities of Liberalization (Mar. 22-23, 2003).

287. The Bush Administration's proposed change was defeated in Congress. *See* Christopher Furlan, Air Cargo Foreign Ownership Restrictions in the United States 16 (Unpublished Paper, University of Miami School of Law), <http://www.tiaca.org/images/tiaca/PDF/Air%20Cargo%20Foreign %20Ownership%20Restrictions%20in%20the%20United%20State.pdf>. The change was a component of Vision 100 – The Century of Aviation Re-authorization Act. *See* GAO, *Foreign Investment in U.S. Airlines*, at 3, GAO-04-34R (Oct. 2003) [hereinafter GAO, *Foreign Investment*]. The legislation, in fact, ultimately tightened the nationality rule by adopting an explicit 'actual control' requirement. *See id.*

288. *See supra* Chapter 2, note 203 (discussing outcry against acquisition of U.S. port facilities by an Arab State allegedly connected with the 9/11 attacks). The controversy left behind a slew of more than 20 proposed bills that would restrict or entirely foreclose foreign investment in

have prompted U.S. airlines and the industry commentariat to intensify calls for abrogation of the nationality rule.[289]

3   Liberalizing the U.S. Domestic Rules on Ownership and Control

Given the powerful worldwide impact of U.S. air transport law and policy, what kinds of changes should the United States make to liberalize the nationality restrictions in the Federal Aviation Act? Congress could (but apparently will not for the moment) accede to former U.S. Transportation Secretary Norman Mineta's call to raise the ceiling of foreign voting stock ownership to 49%.[290] Given the persistence of the 'control' requirement in DOT citizenship review procedures, however, accentuated by the failure of the NPRM, as well as the commercial uncertainties associated with less than a majority shareholding, this change would be unlikely to spur any sizeable new foreign investment in the U.S. airline industry.

The most productive strategy, therefore, would be to respond to the international consensus – forged among airlines, airline organizations, and government and non-government international organizations – to abolish the ownership and control tests and require instead that U.S. airlines continue to demonstrate an 'establishment,' 'strong link,' or 'corporate affinity,' in or with the United States. Replacement of the citizenship test by a so-called 'right' (or, more accurately, 'obligation') of establishment or corporate affinity test[291] would involve making a clear conceptual separation between commercial and regulatory control of an airline. For a private investor, 'control' means a majority of the voting equity and also probably some measure of managerial or strategic influence. If the U.S. Government were to decide to concede that kind of *commercial* control to a foreign investor, while seeking to

---

critical infrastructure (including the airline industry). Reflecting the sentiment of the times, ten members of the House Aviation Subcommittee sent a letter to President Bush emphasizing, in light of the then-pending Dubai Ports takeover and NPRM on foreign control of U.S. airlines, that foreign government ownership of U.S. airlines also posed a 'security risk' for the United States. *See* Press Release, U.S. Congressman Peter DeFazio, Lawmakers Urge Administration to Drop Proposed Foreign Ownership of Port Operations & U.S. Airlines (Mar. 3, 2006).

289. *See e.g.*, *The Need to Shrink*, Economist (U.S. Edition), Feb. 16, 2008 (noting that the U.S. airline industry 'shelters behind a deeply inefficient ban on foreign ownership' which exacerbates its current troubles); *Pie in the Sky*, Economist, Dec. 1, 2007 (stating the irony that '[f]or all the brave talk of liberalisation, the airline business has yet to escape the bane of economic nationalism'); Dean Foust et al., *Fly the Shrinking Skies*, Bus. Wk., Jun. 9, 2008, at 29 (discussing rising fuel costs as a means to lower Congressional resistance to increasing foreign ownership caps); Holman W. Jenkins, Jr., *The Second Death of U.S. Airlines*, Wall St. J., Jun. 18, 2008, at A13 (calling for a removal of foreign ownership limits as a means of staving off potential bankruptcies brought about by soaring fuel costs).

290. *See* Press Release, U.S. DOT, Proposal Would Make It Easier for Airlines to Raise Money, DOT 158-05 (Nov. 2, 2005).

291. For the juristic source in EC law of the concept of the right of establishment, *see supra* Chapter 2, note 91; *see also infra* Chapter 6, Part III(E) (further analyzing how this concept can supersede the nationality rule).

retain the incidents of *regulatory* control with the federal and state governments, it would need to settle three critical questions of law and policy:

First, how would the U.S. Government ensure that an airline remains under effective U.S. *regulatory* control for safety and security standards (as indeed it must do under international treaty law[292])?

Second, while the Chicago system persists, how would the U.S. Government ensure that other countries would accept its designation of an airline as a U.S. carrier for service on international routes?

Third, how would the U.S. Government ensure that the foreign investor did not simply engage in regulatory arbitrage by maintaining a shell identity in the United States and moving the airline's true commercial operations to a low-regulation, low-wage third country (the 'flag of convenience' problem notorious in the global maritime industry[293])? U.S. airline labor unions fear that foreign-owned airlines will locate themselves in flag of convenience countries and then cherry-pick the most profitable domestic ('cabotage') and international U.S. routes using foreign crews and foreign-registered aircraft.

As to the first question – regulatory control – the use of a right (or obligation) of establishment amplifies well-understood corporate law criteria such as place of incorporation and principal place of business. Any airline (including a subsidiary of a foreign-owned airline) that operated domestic (cabotage) services in the United States, or that wished to be designated by the United States to serve its international routes, would have to legally 'establish' itself in the United States by incorporating under the law of one of the 50 states, by having a principal place of business in the United States, and by holding current economic and operational certifications granted by the U.S. aeronautical authorities (the DOT and the FAA). These requirements would apply both to existing U.S. airlines acquired by foreign investors (including foreign airlines), and also to U.S. subsidiaries or new ventures created by foreign airlines.[294]

---

292. *See* Boaz Moselle et al., The Economic Impact of an EU-US Open Aviation Area 9-3 (2002).

293. On the issue of flags of convenience, *see supra* Chapter 2, note 81.

294. While the dynamic proposed in this book would trade away the anachronism of the nationality rule so that *any* kind of foreign investment scrutiny would be mooted, in the U.S. political climate that has followed 9/11 and the more recent Dubai Ports controversy, it seems inevitable to expect that, as a counterweight to the abrogation of the nationality rule, there could be some kind of special pre-transaction review before a foreign takeover of a U.S. airline would be permitted. The United States already has a trans-sectoral review process in place in the guise of the Committee on Foreign Investment in the United States (popularly known as 'CFIUS'). *See supra* text accompanying Chapter 2, note 100. *See generally* Edward M. Graham & David M. Marchick, U.S. National Security and Foreign Direct Investment (2006). At present, because of the nationality rule, airline industry transactions potentially covered by CFIUS review (*i.e.*, mergers, acquisitions, or takeovers by or with any foreign airline which could result in foreign control of a U.S. airline engaged in interstate commerce) are not technically within the CFIUS remit. (*But see* the DOT's proposed relaxation of the foreign control standard, *supra* in the main text, which potentially could have created investment events that might trigger CFIUS review.) CFIUS was originally established by executive order in 1975 to monitor inward

A principal place of business can be determined based on such details as the amount of capital invested in U.S.-based physical facilities, payment of U.S. corporate income tax, U.S. registration of aircraft, amount of localized managerial and technical employment in the United States, and so forth.[295] Here, in fact, a DOT checklist (of affiliating factors) would actually make sense.[296] Moreover, to maintain a principal place of business in the United States, an airline must be in full compliance with all applicable federal and state laws, including taxation, environmental, immigration and labor measures, as well as federal safety and security oversight and participation in the military CRAF program.[297] The term should be

---

investment in the United States. It was not until 1988, however, amid concerns about the impact of rising investment from Japan, that Congress and the President gave CFIUS 'real teeth.' David Marchick, National Foundation for American Policy, *Swinging the Pendulum Too Far: An Analysis of the CFIUS Process Post-Dubai Ports World*, at 21 n.2, NFAP Policy Brief (Jan. 2007). Congress passed the Omnibus Trade and Competitiveness Act of 1988 and, through the Exon-Florio Amendment to that bill, gave the President the right to block foreign acquisitions of U.S. companies that 'threaten to impair' U.S. national security. President Reagan later delegated significant authority for implementing Exon-Florio to CFIUS. *See id.* CFIUS was heavily criticized in the aftermath of its approval of the Dubai Ports transaction. In 2007, new legislation for the first time gives formal statutory status to CFIUS, which continues to be a multiagency screening body chaired by the Secretary of the Treasury but which now includes for the first time, *ex officio*, the Director of National Intelligence. Notably, since Dubai Ports there has been a substantial increase in the CFIUS workload, but more significantly the more politicized environment has made review procedures longer, more uncertain and, if clearance is granted, more burdensome, even for acquiring companies established in trusted ally States. *See* Marchick, *supra*, at 1-3. (Marchick's policy brief sets forth a strong case for more foreign investment in the United States, and warns against the chilling effect of the CFIUS process.) While the Department of Transportation is not a designated agency under the new CFIUS legislation, it is conceivable that a mandatory 'special CFIUS' protocol could be developed for the airline industry requiring not only CFIUS clearance under existing procedures but also a certification by the Secretary of Transportation that a covered purchase (merger, acquisition, or takeover) would not threaten either the financial fitness of the target U.S. airline or its safety. The Brattle Report, incidentally, considered CFIUS review to be adequate to alleviate national security concerns, since foreign acquirors could be required to continue to participate in the CRAF system. *See* BRATTLE GROUP, *supra* note 107, ch. 7, at 15-16; *see also* GAO, *Foreign Investment, supra* note 287, at 7-8 (implicitly confirming the tenor of its 1993 observations on the CRAF system and its implications).

295. *See* ICAO Secretariat, *Liberalizing Air Carrier Ownership and Control*, Paper Presented to the ICAO Worldwide Air Transport Conference, at 6, ATConf/5-WP/7 (Oct. 21, 2002).

296. The European Commission, in seeking to enhance uniformity in standards of air carrier licensing by Member States, continues to promote stronger links in the principal place of business requirement to the location of the airline's operations. *See* European Commission, Proposal for a Regulation of the European Parliament and of the Council on Common Rules for the Operation of Air Transport Services in the Community, COM (2006) 396 final (Jul. 18, 2006). For a further discussion and analysis of the final changes brought about by the proposal, *see infra* Chapter 5, Part II.

297. American military security interests present a related issue of regulatory control. As noted earlier, the U.S. Department of Defense has expressed concern that foreign-owned U.S. airlines would not provide supplemental airlift support through the voluntary CRAF system during emergencies such as the Iraq war. U.S. airlines, all the while beating their patriotic breasts, have consistently ranked the importance of peacetime economic incentives of CRAF

flexible enough to accommodate the new forms of airline enterprise that will arise. A multinational airline corporation – such as a unified United/Lufthansa – could have a multinodal principal place of business.[298]

As to the second question – acceptance of U.S. designations on international routes – American aeropolitical power is such that third countries would very probably accept designations based on the right of establishment/corporate affinity test so long as the United States maintained its regulatory control over the airline. This is even more likely because of a perceptibly more liberal U.S. attitude to third-country ownership and control of airlines designated by other countries to serve routes into the United States.[299]

The third question – avoidance of shell identity and flag of convenience abuses – should be resolved by the stringency of the establishment/affinity test. With respect to domestic (cabotage) routes, a foreign entity serving those routes would have to 'establish' itself (as a subsidiary of a foreign airline, or in the form of an entirely new airline venture as originally envisaged by Virgin Group chairman Richard Branson). The same establishment/affinity test would apply for airlines wishing to serve U.S. international routes, with the added safeguard that (unlike in maritime transport) access to international air routes requires not only a designation by one country but also an acceptance by the other country at the end of each route. The United States could simply refuse designations by countries to which a foreign-owned U.S. airline has attempted to 're-flag.'[300]

participation more highly than the contingent risks of emergency activation. *See* GAO, *Airline Competition, supra* note 9, at 51. As a general matter, foreign ownership would not alter this calculus of economic self-interest either in peace or war. Also, annulment of the foreign ownership laws could be accompanied by measures to make CRAF a compulsory obligation for all U.S.-certificated carriers or at least a precondition for foreign investment.

298. *But see* [U.K.] Civil Aviation Authority, *supra* note 156, ch. 5, at 5 (describing multiple licensing for airlines operating in equally important markets as having 'a certain counter-intuitive aspect'). Certainly, regulators will have to develop tools for oversight of airlines which increasingly will operate in more distant markets, and these tools may involve regional and international collaboration or even new multilateral oversight authorities such as the EU's evolving safety agency. The CAA study discusses one dimension of this situation in the context (still hypothetical) of a New Zealand airline choosing to invoke the right to operate cabotage services in the United Kingdom that is granted to New Zealand air carriers under the 2005 U.K./New Zealand bilateral air services agreement. Given that a designated New Zealand carrier is explicitly required to be under the 'effective regulatory control' of its government, how would that control be exercised? The study canvassed a number of alternative scenarios (aircraft returning to New Zealand for regular inspection; a New Zealand regulatory outpost in the United Kingdom; 'contracting-out' by New Zealand of safety over-sight to the U.K. authorities; 'contracting-out' of safety oversight to third-country authorities); while seeming to favor a fifth scenario – Air New Zealand establishing a U.K. subsidiary (Air New Zealand (U.K.) Limited) which would have a significant amount of operations and its principal place of business in the United Kingdom and would operate as a discrete U.K. airline subject to U.K. and EC safety regulation. This final scenario, it should be noted, is precisely the 'right of establishment' that is presented *supra* in the main text. *See id.* Ch. 5, at 5-6.

299. An attitude reflected in the U.S. opening move at the Ljubljana negotiations. *See supra* text accompanying Chapter 2, note 243.

300. This scenario assumes, of course, the persistence of some formal methodology of 'designation.'

The regime change of abolishing the citizenship purity test is not yet part of the U.S./EC negotiations, but the second stage may proceed in that direction. A broader vision of the 'right of establishment' (much broader, for example, than Article 43 of the EC Treaty[301]) would still regard an airline's 'nationality' as important, but would (as the NPRM implicitly tried to do) de-link commercial and regulatory nationality. Commercial nationality (the right of private investors, regardless of citizenship, to own 51% or more of a foreign airline and to manage it without restriction) would be entirely deregulated. But an airline would still have (and must have) a regulatory nationality, a State in which it is incorporated, where it has its principal place of business, where it pays taxes, employs local management and employees, obeys local laws, and is subject to safety, security, and fiscal supervision.[302] The NPRM, through its creative splitting of commercial operations from operations that must be controlled by citizens, implicitly hinted at this distinction between commercial and regulatory nationality.

D   CONCLUSION: THE SUPERIOR NORM OF NATIONALITY

In remarks to the Airline Commission over 15 years ago, former CAB chairman John E. Robson described present U.S. open skies bilaterals, lacking 'some kind of regime on cross-ownership,' as 'a narrow sky.'[303] The nationality and cabotage rules both spring from the Chicago genuflection to sovereignty. Both are fixtures in the bilateral order, but nationality is ultimately the superior norm. If that regulatory tripwire were eliminated, and foreign citizens could invest freely to merge with or acquire U.S. carriers – or, for that matter, to establish their own U.S. subsidiaries – the doctrine of cabotage would be deprived of meaning. For now, the nationality rule is the prime indicium of the 'specificity' of the Chicago system of bilateral air services agreements, and as such it is no mere technicality. In designing a replacement for the Chicago system, the fate of the nationality rule will be a pivotal concern.

---

301. *See supra* Chapter 2, note 91.
302. One could posit, of course, that a foreign airline could simply 'operate' in the United States and retain its existing regulatory link to its home State. Or that, in a future with no foreign ownership and control restrictions, an airline need never touch down at all in its licensing State. *See* [U.K.] Civil Aviation Authority, *supra* note 156, Executive Summary, at 3. The Chicago Convention presumes such a nexus when it provides that an airline which provides cabotage operations in a foreign State remains regulated solely by its home State. The European Union appears to condone the same attenuated link between an airline and its licensing State when the airline is providing services in or from another Member State. In sum, a migration to offer services in a foreign State without a change in nationality is conceivable, but unlikely to gain international support.
303. *Airline Commission Proceedings*, remarks of John E. Robson, former CAB Chairman, May 26, 1993, at 95-96.

VI   FETISHIZING SOVEREIGNTY: THE PUBLIC STAKE
            IN AIR TRANSPORT

A   Public Airlines and Public Subsidy

The Chicago system's stipulation of citizenship, as expressed in the nationality rule, was responsible for the fusion of sovereignty, economic, and public service interests that gave the international airline industry one of its most visible commercial symbols: the trademarked liveries of the so-called 'flag carriers.' In the EU, brand-name flag carriers have included Aer Lingus, Air France, Alitalia, British Airways, Iberia, KLM, Lufthansa, and SAS. The 'flag' connection was much more than a patriotic reflex, however. In most cases, the State-to-airline bond was cemented by the State itself holding a majority or exclusive ownership stake in the airline company. Of the airlines just mentioned, only British Airways, Lufthansa, and Iberia have completely severed their ownership link with their former sponsor governments, but several EU governments have reduced their stakeholdings in their national carriers or have plans to do so.[304]

As well as serving somewhat intangible goals of national identification and prestige,[305] State control of flag carriers left governments at liberty to press their

---

304. The privatization process is a moving target, but as of mid-2008 a clear pattern of government withdrawal from ownership had emerged over the preceding decade. As of the time of writing, the following airlines had the following remaining public stakes (in parentheses): Aer Lingus (25.35%, down from 100% in 1997), Air France-KLM Group (French Government stake of 18.6%, down from 98.6% in 1997), Austrian Airlines (39.7%, down from 51.9% in 1997), Finnair (55.78%, down from 70% in 1997), KLM (Netherlands Government stake of 6%, down from 38.2% in 1997), and Luxair (23% owned by the State of Luxembourg, down from 36.5% in 1997, with 13% owned by partly-private, partly-public Luxair Group). SAS continued to be 50% owned by the three Nordic governments (14.3% by the Danish and Norwegian Governments and 21.4% by the Swedish Government). Neither Icelandair nor Swiss International Airlines (successor to the partly-public Swissair) has any public ownership. *See infra* Chapter 5, Part I (further documenting information on the ownership profiles of these and other EU-based airlines). Alitalia, a long-underperforming traditional flag carrier, relaunched in January 2009 as a privately-owned airline with KLM-Air France taking a 25% stake. *Business This Week,* Economist, Jan. 15, 2009. In 2007 also, the Portuguese Government indicated that it might float a minority stake in TAP, still 100% government-owned, and to sell an additional portion of the carrier to a strategic partner. *See* Peter Wise, *Portugal, High-flying Flotations: Planned Privatizations Including Galp Energia and Air Portugal Should Spur Capital Markets and Lower Public Debt,* Fin. Times Bus. Ltd., May 1, 2006. The Greek Government's longstanding efforts to privatize 100% government-owned Olympic Airlines appear to be stalled until the carrier resolves its State aid issues with the European Commission. *See* AFX International Focus, *Greece's Karamanlis Says EU Talks Hold Up Olympic Airlines Privatization,* Sept. 10, 2006. *See infra* Chapter 5, Part III(F).

305. Betsy Gidwitz, in her book, quotes the satirical comment of historian Walter Laqueur, who wrote in a 1980 article in the *New York Times* that a viable modern State must have four attributes: 'operation of a television system, a police force of at least 100 men, a budget sufficient to maintain at least one delegate at the United Nations – and a national airline.' Gidwitz, *supra* note 14, at 21.

home airlines to provide peripheral or unprofitable transport services,[306] or to perform as instruments of national employment policy,[307] 'without regard to the economic implications or commercial significance' of those demands.[308] In the United States, a complex balance of political and economic forces supposedly justified regulatory supervision of a system with multiple competing – and privately-owned – airlines.[309] For Europe, in contrast, beyond the Chicago precepts of sovereignty and nationality, and a European tradition favoring *le système étatique*, there does not appear to have been any overarching economic principle that accounts for the long preservation of the European States' controlling stakes in their flag carriers.[310]

In becoming (in effect) part of the national patrimony, the European airlines were awarded economic shelter in the form of a generalized preemption of competition from potential rivals. Internal airline competitors were kept at bay through monopoly licensing of domestic route systems, or through toleration of apparently

---

306. *See* OECD, Committee on Competition Law and Policy, *Deregulation and Airline Competition* 35 (1988) [hereinafter OECD Report]. The 'public service' nature of air transport, ensuring a regular and reliable provision of air services to all parts of a country at the lowest cost consistent with a reasonable return to the operating carriers, has been advanced as the principal reason for the national regulation of entry, capacity, and fares. *See id.* The Essential Air Service (EAS) program in the United States is a clear example of the drawbacks inherent in the 'public service' approach. A 2006 GAO study determined that the Program is not cost-effective. *See* GAO, *Commercial Aviation: Programs and Options for the Federal Approach to Providing and Improving Air Service to Small Communities*, at 17, GAO-06-398T (Sept. 14, 2006) [hereinafter GAO, *Commercial Aviation*] (noting that 'most EAS flights operate with aircraft that are largely empty').

307. *See* [U.K.] Civil Aviation Authority, *The Single European Aviation Market: Progress So Far*, at 5, CAP 654 (Sept. 1995) [hereinafter [U.K.] CAA Report]. That policy trope continues even in the era of privatization. Alitalia's initial privatization tender offer included the condition that any new owner 'must protect Alitalia's "national identity" and employment levels.' Lex Column, *Alitalia*, FIN. TIMES, Jan. 31, 2007, at 16.

308. Report of the *Comité des Sages*, *supra* note 44, at 5.

309. Although criticized by Stephen Breyer and others today as 'incoherent,' prevention of unreasonably low prices among competitors – 'excessive competition' – has been advanced as at least one rationale for the early U.S. experiment in airline regulation. STEPHEN BREYER, REGULATION AND ITS REFORM, 29-30 (1982). Breyer also canvassed other plausible economic justifications for the coming of regulation in the 1930s, including modulation of the supply/demand cycles that have notoriously disrupted the airline industry. *See id.* at 30-35. As Breyer concludes, *many* rationales probably contribute to the regulation of a particular industrial sector. *See id.* at 34. Indeed, two of Breyer's suggestions, 'informational defects' in the market and the 'paternalistic' view that consumers do not understand certain market risks, helped to explain the latter-day intrusion of the government into the market for computer reservations systems.

310. *See* European Parliament, *Report of the Committee on Transport and Tourism on the [European] Commission's Report to the Council and the European Parliament on the Evaluation of Aid Schemes Established in Favor of Community Carriers*, at 17, PE 203.392 (Feb. 25, 1993), describing the traditional model of 'flag carrier' airlines as 'more politically than economically justified.' The European Parliament reaffirmed this belief in May 2000, when it 'welcomed the end, as announced by the [European] Commission, of the transition period for State aid for airlines, and put forward the view that State airlines should be made to exist within an entirely *commercial* environment.' European Parliament, European Parliament Fact Sheets, Air Transport: Competition and Passenger Rights, <http://www.europarl.europa.eu/ftu/pdf/en/FTU_4.6.6.pdf> (emphasis added).

anticompetitive agreements or takeovers.[311] Restrictions on foreign carriers were put in place by means of the bilateral orthodoxy of managed competition through negotiation.[312] Competition from other modes of transportation was modulated through national infrastructural policy.[313]

311. Domestic protection in Europe also involved shelter from charter air traffic, which enjoyed a flexible tariff structure that might otherwise have created serious economic competition for the scheduled flag carriers. *See generally* ELMAR GIEMULLA ET AL, *Introduction, in* EUR. AIR L. (Kluwer) 19-23 (1995). This competitive paradigm is now reversing in Europe, as charter carriers struggle to compete with low-cost scheduled carriers such as Ryanair and easyJet. The chief of the large European travel services group TUI noted recently that '[t]he traditional charter business in Germany has been shrinking in absolute terms over the past five years . . . . [t]he clear winners have been the low-cost [scheduled] carriers.' Gunter Endres, *Groupstrategy*, AIRLINE BUS., Nov. 21, 2006 (noting that the era of the glossy travel brochure and three-week annual family holidays had been displaced by 'two-digit' or 'one-digit' air fares, with customers bypassing the 'package' concept and going directly to the airline website).

312. *But see* the U.K. open skies initiatives inaugurated in the early 1980s, *infra* Chapter 5, Part II. Moreover, apart from the most visible markers of restrictive competition (prices, capacity, access to routes), a State's relationship with its flag carrier can also provoke substantial indirect discriminatory treatment of foreign carriers operating into that State's territory. Air carriers in the international competitive system are therefore not necessarily placed in equal positions, since an artificial comparative advantage can be created despite the formal 'equality of opportunity' expressed in bilateral agreements and in the Preamble to the Chicago Convention. Areas of discriminatory behavior include laws, policies, and practices of governments in such matters as airport and navigation charges, access to facilities, availability and pricing of fuel, taxation, remittance of funds, and currency exchange rates. *See*, for example, retaliatory measures taken by the U.S. Department of Transportation in response to Aerolineas Argentinas paying user charges at Buenos Aires International Airport (Ezeiza) that were one-third as much as those levied on U.S. competitors. The DOT conditioned the Argentine carrier's U.S. operating certificate on the airline paying into escrow, on a per-flight basis, the difference between its Buenos Aires charges and the amount paid by U.S. carriers. *See* U.S. Department of Transportation, *In the Matter of Aerolineas Argentinas*, Dkt. No. OST-2003-15092 (Nov. 25, 2003). Aerolineas lost a 2005 U.S. court of appeals challenge to the DOT's authority to issue the escrow order. *See* Aerolineas Argentinas S.A. *v.* U.S. Department of Transportation, 415 F.3d 1 (D.C. Cir. 2005) (finding that it is sufficient to show a disparate impact in order to condemn an alleged discriminatory practice and not necessarily an intent to discriminate). *See also* Gertler, *supra* note 31, at 81-82. Many unilateral protective measures of this kind contravene the Chicago Convention, which seeks to ensure the 'national' treatment of aircraft of other contracting States with respect to charges for the use of airports and navigation facilities. Chicago Convention, *supra* note 6, art. 15.

313. The EU, in contrast, has bolstered moves by railway companies to run high-speed train services in competition with air transport. *See* Press Release, Europa, Inauguration of the TGV High-Speed Line, IP/07/329 (Mar. 15, 2007) (noting the euro 241 million investment the European Union has made in establishing a new high-speed rail link between France and Germany). It might be expected that air transport growth would be less supported – with a corresponding shift to rail networks – because of government attention to climate change strategies. But even EC policy planners, in an age when airline carbon emissions have become a key target of environmental lobbyists, anticipate that the proposed inclusion of airlines in the EC emissions trading scheme, rather than shifting mass passenger demand to rival forms of transportation as the airline industry has argued, 'would have only a small effect on forecasted demand growth from business-as-usual levels of 142% to a minimum of 135%.' European Commission,

In addition to these assorted regulatory bounties, the European States often expunged their flag carriers' weak fiscal results by liberal transfusions of public aid in the form of direct subsidies.[314] Cumulatively, these various protections tended to curtail incentives for productive efficiency or profit maximization even further.[315] This 'public utility' view of airlines, as primarily a nationalized 'service' or 'system' provider within the domestic and international transport infrastructure, has been the dominant economic approach in the Chicago system.[316] The rise of low-cost carriers such as Ryanair and easyJet, however, has forced the EU flag carriers – most of them engaged in a sometimes painful depoliticization through sale of government ownership stakes[317] – increasingly to make decisions based on 'rational choices that are driven by a strictly commercial view of the network.'[318]

      Summary of the Impact Assessment, para. 5.3.1, SEC (2006) 1685 (Dec. 20, 2006). Indeed, in its 2005 environmental impact statement, the European Commission specifically ruled out encouraging rail as a substitute for short-haul air travel as a way to curb aircraft emissions – preferring an economic model that reduced and taxed those emissions efficiently within the existing airline industry paradigm. *See* European Commission, *Annex to 'Reducing the Climate Change Impact of Aviation'*, para. 3.4.5, SEC (2005) 1184 (Sept. 27, 2005).

314.   *See infra* Chapter 5, Part III(F) (discussing EC policy on subsidies, known generically in the common market system as 'State aids').

315.   While the economic performance of most of the major EU flag carriers was notoriously poor in the 1990s, by 2006 most European airlines (and most of those undergoing privatization or already privatized), were maintaining a trend that saw strong improvements in their operating profits in the first decade of the new century. *See European Airlines: A Gradual Ascent*, Bus. Wk., Dec. 5, 2005. Lufthansa, now 100% private-owned, capped a decade of recovery with full-year earnings up by 30% to $750 million. *See id.* Exceptions included old-line publicly-owned carriers such as Alitalia (with a projected 2006 operating loss of $490 million), *see Alitalia Set to Report Massive Operating Loss as AF KLM Declines to Bid*, ATW Daily News, Jan. 30, 2007), and Olympic Airlines, still revising its 2005 financial accounts as of Dec. 2006 to reflect a $162 million loss, *see Olympic Airlines Reports Increased Loss for 2005*, M2 Airline Industry Information, Dec. 11, 2006. But the outlook has declined in Europe, as elsewhere, in 2008. The latest operating environment, driven largely by oil price increases, has been described by Willie Walsh, CEO of British Airways, as 'the worst trading environment the industry has ever faced.' David Prosser, *This Time, Even Sir Richard Branson May Not Be Able to Ground His Big Enemy*, Independent (London), Aug. 15, 2008, at 44.

316.   The term 'public utility' as an object of regulatory endeavor typically embraces large-scale supply of infrastructural services such as energy (electricity, oil, and gas), water and sanitation, telecommunications, and transportation (including, for example, airport landing rights). For an interesting look at how deregulation of many of these industries has evolved over the past 25 years, and arguing for further deregulation in telecommunications and electricity, *see* Robert W. Crandall, *An End to Economic Regulation?*, in Competition and Regulation in Utility Markets (Colin Robinson ed., 2003). As Crandall notes, economists distinguish 'economic' and 'social' regulation. The former is the control of prices, service quality, and entry conditions in specific sectors such as transportation, communications, and energy. The latter is the regulation of risks to health, safety, and the environment. *See id.* at 162-66. The present book deals primarily with economic regulation (and deregulation), although aviation safety and environmental issues appear in the context of the desirability of transnational harmonization of regulatory policies.

317.   *See supra* note 304 (discussing privatization of EU airlines).

318.   Emre Serpen & Kevin O'Toole, *Flag Bearers*, Airline Bus. Oct. 2002. A leading airline consulting group recommends that flag carriers abandon the 'public utility' mindset and

U.S. regulation of the airlines (although its origins predated Chicago) was not dissimilar: the CAB sought to maintain relatively stable market shares, and profitability, among a fixed constellation of privately owned incumbent airlines (the United States has never had a flag carrier as such).[319] The U.S. approach, echoing its European counterparts, featured systemic preemption of the general antitrust laws, allowing the CAB to confer 'immunity' upon carriers that entered anticompetitive capacity limitation agreements, or to sanction mergers that saved weak carriers at the cost of substantially reducing competition. The Board carefully shepherded access to routes so that existing shares could be maintained, and even resorted to a wholesale moratorium on new route awards when the industry became blighted by overcapacity.[320] The CAB regime also included a program to subsidize essential air operations for underserved communities (a true public utility dimension that survived in both the U.S. and EC air transport regimes even after deregulation).[321]

So visibly benevolent was the CAB's stewardship, in fact, that critics accused the agency of having been 'captured' by the airlines,[322] an ironic measure of the pervasive influence of the Chicago protectionist model even in a system without

---

separate out those parts of the network that are commercially viable (an airline's 'natural market') from services run as a social or political obligation. If it is not politically acceptable to excise the unprofitable social obligations, these operations should be 'ring-fenced' and the government stakeholder asked to compensate the airline for losses suffered directly or because of consequential inefficiencies caused to the rest of the operation. *Id.*

319. The closest aspirant to the title of official U.S. airline was Pan American World Airlines (Pan Am). Pan Am never had official flag carrier status from the U.S. Government, but airlines such as American and United (the former of which bought many of the defunct carrier's Pacific and Latin American routes) inherited Pan Am's global profile as U.S. flagships. Although the original Pan Am airline corporation dissolved in 1991, its name was briefly resurrected from 1996 to 1998 to designate a charter service with a focus on low-cost long-haul flights between the United States and the Caribbean. *See* Ina Paiva Cordle, *Pan Am Emerges Again From Bankruptcy Court*, Miami Herald, Jun. 29, 1998. The famous name was reincarnated for the third time in 1998 by Guilford Transportation, which rebranded itself as Pan Am Systems in 2006 and now operates Pan Am Railways (with several thousand rail cars emblazoned with the Pan Am logo), and the Pan Am Clipper Connection, a small regional airline based in Portsmouth, New Hampshire. *See* Tom Spoth, *Pan Am has landed on the rails in Billerica*, Lowell Sun, Apr. 5, 2006 (suggesting that Pan Am is one of the five most recognized brand names in the world).

320. *See infra* Chapter 4, Part II(B).

321. *See infra* Chapter 4, Part II(D).

322. *See, e.g.,* Michael E. Levine, *Why Weren't the Airlines Reregulated?*, 23 Yale J. on Reg. 269, 274 (2006) (positing that regulation transferred benefits from a 'consuming majority' to an 'organized industry minority'). For that purpose regulation required what Levine calls 'slack,' *i.e.*, the effect of information and monitoring costs that shield the actions of a regulator from observation by a rational electorate. *Id.* at 273. Slack, however, is destroyed by the gaze of an intense public scrutiny where the costs to a citizen of becoming informed on a matter drop to nearly zero (*id.* at 273-74), precisely how Levine views the experience of airline deregulation in the mid-1970s. *See also* the discussion in Dominick T. Armentano's sustained attack on the U.S. antitrust establishment, Antitrust and Monopoly: Anatomy of a Policy Failure (1990) in which he notes, with respect to increasing regulation in the 1930s, that '[t]here is now solid historical evidence that a number of American industries welcomed governmental intervention

flag carriers or State sponsorship.[323] As will be seen, bilateralist pressures prevented the United States from withdrawing from full regulatory control of its *international* airline industry, so that vestiges of the pre-1978 public utility ethos prevail still within this regime (including some fare-filing formalities, retention of antitrust immunity authority, and administrative hearings to select carriers for negotiated international routes where open skies agreements do not apply).[324] Indeed, some influential U.S. voices, dismayed by the sour financial performance of U.S. domestic carriers in recent years, have called on Congress to declare formally that the U.S. airline *system* (as opposed to its constituent airlines) is a public utility.[325] Such a pronouncement would undoubtedly prefigure

---

in an attempt to restrict and restrain competition, and in order to preserve positions of wealth and power within the industrial order . . . [including] the airlines [*sic*] industry.' *Id.* at 273. These comments fit with economist George Stigler's comment that, as a rule, 'regulation is acquired by the industry and is designed and operated for its benefit.' *Preface, in* REGULATION: ECONOMIC THEORY AND HISTORY (Jack High ed., 1991).

323. Regulation of the domestic airline industry in the United States did in fact exhibit features of the Chicago bilateral system: it encompassed an *ex ante* regulatory mechanism to set fares (although capacity and frequency were never regulated), and, at the core of the system, a franchise or licensing program to police access to specific routes. *See* James W. Callison, *Airline Deregulation – Only Partially a Hoax: The Current Status of the Airline Deregulation Movement*, 45 J. AIR L. & COM. 961 (1980). It is possible, though hardly intellectually satisfying, to define 'regulation' as merely the sum of these various incidents of regulatory control in any industry. A general definition of the term, in fact, is elusive. Even United States Supreme Court Justice Stephen Breyer, in his landmark work, REGULATION AND ITS REFORM, admits that he makes 'no serious effort . . . to define "regulation." ' BREYER, *supra* note 309, at 7; *see also* Levine, *supra* note 322, at 271-72 (insisting that 'the economic theory of regulation purports to be a positive rather than a normative theory'). Instead, Breyer posits a broad swathe of regulatory activity, included in the term 'economic regulation,' that covers not only prices and entry, but also other regulatory action that is usually entrusted to the central government (notably in health, safety and environmental matters). *See* BREYER, *supra* note 309, at 7. *But see* *supra* note 316 (drawing a distinction between 'economic' and 'social' regulation, and noting that the focus in the present study is primarily on 'economic regulation' in its more narrow scope, and specifically the terms of economic access (fares, capacity, route licenses, and so forth) to the airline industry). *See generally* Levine, *supra* note 322, at 270, n.1 (differentiating between the 'public choice' theory of regulation (where regulation comes into being to create and/or transfer rents from politically weak groups to politically stronger groups) and the 'public interest' theory of regulation (positing that regulation is driven by public-spirited government actors to serve as a public corrective for inefficiencies and/or injustices brought about by market imperfections or the failure of market outcomes to conform to social norms)). For Levine, the public choice theory 'doesn't account very well for the enactment and persistence of airline deregulation.' *Id.* at 270.

324. *See infra* Chapter 4, Part III.

325. *See, e.g.*, Press Release, Jay Rockefeller, Senator for West Virginia, Senate Commerce Subcommittee: Statement at the Hearing 'The State of the Airline Industry: The Potential Impact of Airline Mergers and Industry Consolidation' (Jan. 24, 2007) (indicating his belief that 'regulating the airline industry again is necessary,' at least with respect to making sure that small communities are not harmed by consolidation, while conceding that 'the industry is far too changed and far too global for us to return to a completely regulated environment'). Recent security concerns about critical infrastructure, including the airline 'system,' could also trigger reregulatory efforts. *But see* GAO, *Airline Deregulation: Reregulating the Airline Industry*

reregulation of the domestic industry, an option that is considered (and opposed) in Chapter 4.[326]

B THE RETREAT OF THE STATE: THE AGE OF DEREGULATION

1 New Models of Airline Regulation in the United States and EC

The public utility theory, whether applied using the U.S. or EC regulatory models, has been under assault on both continents from a broad prescription of law and policy known as 'deregulation.'[327] The United States abolished CAB-style regulatory control of prices and entry in its domestic airline industry, and even sought a partial 'export' of this idea through negotiation of bilateral open skies

---

Would Likely Reverse Consumer Benefits and Not Save Airline Pensions, at 36, GAO-06-630 (Jun. 2006) (arguing that reregulation of airline entry and rates would undo the lower fares that have characterized deregulation). Moreover, the GAO noted that reregulation – to the small extent it has occurred in the U.S. economy – has focused on situations of inadequate competition (the cable television industry, for example), whereas 'lack of competition has not been the case in the airline industry.' *Id.*

326. *See infra* Chapter 4, Part IV(C).
327. *See generally*, Jack High, *Introduction, in* REGULATION: ECONOMIC THEORY AND HISTORY, *supra* note 322, at 12-13 ('Deregulation is itself part of a broader issue in the history and economics of regulation: Why do some industries fall under the regulatory umbrella while others do not?'). For an analysis of deregulation as a reform option in a globalizing economy, *see* Alfred C. Aman, Jr., *A Global Perspective on Current Regulatory Reforms: Rejection, Relocation, or Reinvention?*, 2 GLOBAL LEGAL STUD. J. 429 (1995). On the successes of deregulation in the airline and (to a lesser extent) telecommunications industries, *see* ALFRED E. KAHN, LESSONS FROM DEREGULATION: TELECOMMUNICATIONS AND AIRLINES AFTER THE CRUNCH 2 (2004) (extolling what the author calls 'the superiority of open competition over direct comprehensive regulation'). For a look at how different countries use regulatory policy (both regulation and deregulation) as part of a strategy for economic development, *see* RICHARD H. K. VIETOR, HOW COUNTRIES COMPETE: STRATEGY, STRUCTURE, AND GOVERNMENT IN THE GLOBAL ECONOMY (2007) (arguing that business executives have a self-regarding responsibility to inform, and to be informed about, the macroeconomic strategies – including regulatory policy – used by governments). Deregulation, along with other policy reforms aimed at fostering free markets, fiscal discipline, and privatization, comprised what came to be known as the 'Washington Consensus.' *See* John Williamson, *From Reform Agenda to Damaged Brand Name: A Short History of the Washington Consensus and Suggestions for What to Do Next*, FIN. & DEV., Sept. 2003, at 10. This consensus (or, rather, its very name) has, in the words of one observer, 'bec[o]me a lightning rod for those disenchanted with globalization and neoliberalism or with the perceived diktats of the U.S. treasury.' Jeremy Clift, *Beyond the Washington Consensus*, FIN & DEV., Sept. 2003, at 9. Yet, amidst the criticism, and although the full regulatory implications of the 2008 banking sector crisis remain to be understood, the consensus has continued to maintain currency, in recent years absorbing further policy positions aimed at tempering the social 'aftershocks' associated with rapid liberalization and combating corruption. *See* Dani Rodrik, *Goodbye Washington Consensus, Hello Washington Confusion? A Review of the World Bank's Economic Growth in the 1990s: Learning from a Decade of Reform*, 44 J. ECON. LIT. 973 (2006).

agreements.[328] In the EU, the Member States first dismantled Chicago-type controls of their *international* inter-State airline system and, with the abolition of intra-Member State cabotage in 1997, have achieved a wholly unified commercial airspace.[329]

But beyond the EU's borders, to the chagrin of European Commission policy-makers, the bilateral system prevails even as the Commission continues to re-engineer the nationality clause in Member State bilaterals with third States (including, in 2007, with the United States)[330] to implement European Court of Justice rulings that such bilaterals must recognize ownership and control of EU air carriers by EU nationals other than the nationals of the designating Member State.[331] While the next two Chapters will examine the specific legal processes used in each jurisdiction to accomplish air transport deregulation, as a general matter it can be said that the prescriptive shift to deregulation appealed to U.S. and EC authorities by

---

328. The mixed results of this experiment are considered *infra* Chapter 4, Part III. *See, e.g.*, ANGELA CHENG-JIU LU, INTERNATIONAL AIRLINE ALLIANCES 70 (2003) (noting how 'anti-competitive practices' of airline alliances are the result of an open skies regime that operates within 'the grey area of public international law' rather according to the principles of antitrust and competition law).

329. *See infra* Chapter 5, Part II. Importantly, however, the Community has not yet achieved its ambition of a unified *navigational* airspace, although EC legislation to establish (incrementally) a so-called 'Single European Sky' (SES) has been in place for some years. *See* Niels A. van Antwerpen, *The Single European Sky*, [2001-2004 Transfer Binder] ISSUES AVIATION L. & POL'Y ¶ 20,251, at 10,301 (2002). Progress on creating airspace 'blocks' in the SES has been slow. *See* European Commission, *Building the Single European Sky Through Functional Airspace Blocks: A Mid-Term Status Report*, sec. 3, COM (2007) 101 final (Mar. 15, 2007) (noting the uneven progress made across the EU and disparities among Member States' individual contributions).

330. With respect to the United States, however, a comprehensive air services agreement replaced the Member States' separate bilaterals. *See supra* Chapter 2, Parts III & IV; Chapter 5, Part II(E).

331. *See* European Commission, *Developing the Agenda for the Community's External Aviation Policy*, para. 1.2, COM (2005) 79 final (Mar. 11, 2005) (discussing the 'horizontal mandate' from the EU Council of Ministers, conferred to implement the terms of the 2002 open skies judgments of the European Court of Justice, *see infra* Chapter 5, Part II(E), which authorizes the Commission to negotiate insertion of the standard clause on Community nationality into the bilateral agreements concluded between the Member States and a given third country). Since 2002, also, the EU Council has granted the Commission a series of mandates to negotiate comprehensive air services agreements with neighboring States as part of a planned European Common Aviation Area (ECAA) that applies the full Community *acquis* in aviation law. *See* European Commission, *supra*, para. 2.1. This project implicates a much deeper integration than that envisaged or accomplished in the 2007 U.S./EC Air Transport Agreement. *See* Press Release, Europa, EU & South East Europe: First Steps Towards an Extended Single Aviation Market, IP/06/764 (Jun. 9, 2006) (announcing the opening for signature of an ECAA agreement linking the Union with its South-East European neighbors Albania, Bosnia and Herzegovina, Bulgaria, Croatia, the Former Yugoslav Republic of Macedonia, Romania, Serbia, Montenegro, and the United Nations Mission in Kosovo; note that Bulgaria and Romania became full members of the European Union on Jan. 1, 2007). Other mandates, requiring varying degrees of integration (and hence of adjustment to Chicago system principles) continue to be awarded. *See* European Commission, *supra*, para. 2.1-2.2. For a more detailed discussion of the European Community's external aviation relations policy and its implications for the bilateral system, *see infra* Chapter 5, Part III(D).

eliminating *a priori* government interference in management and market decisions,[332] and allowing the government to withdraw from economic control over
route entry and exit, prices, capacity, consolidation, and profitability.[333]

Nevertheless, because of the danger that wholly unpoliced firms will substitute a 'private' regulatory structure through collusion or unchecked predatory
behavior, an Edenic condition of *total* deregulation is rarely attempted. Although
the U.S. and EC bureaucracies have withdrawn from intervention in the economic
decisions of the airline industry, *ex ante* controls have largely been replaced by *ex
post* discretionary regulation (sometimes assisted by private enforcement), in the
form of the general body of the antitrust or 'competition' laws.[334]

---

332. *See* Wassenbergh, *supra* note 16, at 20.

333. For a 'pendular' view of this process of regulation and deregulation, *see* Richard D. Cudahy,
      The Coming Demise of Deregulation, 10 YALE J. ON REG. 1 (1993). Judge Cudahy's argument
      at that time was resolutely synchronic, however. Written in the midst of the 1991-93 downturn
      in the domestic airline industry, he uses the crisis to suggest that 'the time may be coming when
      market forces alone will not be trusted to carry the whole burden of the public interest in basic
      infrastructure industries.' *Id.* at 14. In light of this embrace of the 'public utility' school, it is
      scarcely surprising that Cudahy forecasts a reregulation of the airline industry. In an article
      published in 2006, however, Judge Cudahy appears to have softened his position. Rather than
      advocating a 'full-blown pattern of regulation,' he now suggests targeting the specific problem
      of excessive competition in the industry – perhaps with agreed limitations on the total number
      of aircraft in use at any particular time (a capacity agreement that would need antitrust
      immunity), or through 'experimentation with procedures for setting and announcing fares'
      that could cause prices to remain at or above costs. Richard D. Cudahy, *The Airlines: Destined
      to Fail?*, 71 J. AIR L. & COM. 3, 34 (2006) [hereinafter Cudahy, *Airlines*]. But, despite this more
      measured approach, Cudahy's philosophical leanings are always toward public intervention.
      In his view, air travel is a mass transportation system that, like other such systems, is 'not
      destined to be profitable in the long run,' and deregulation has created a public resistance to
      fare increases that systemically jeopardizes airlines' profitability. In those circumstances,
      public support and subsidies become necessary. *Id.* at 34-35. The rising cost of fuel, coupled
      with decreases in capacity, have resulted in higher fares from most U.S. and European airlines
      in 2008. *See* Michelle Higgins, *Fewer Flights, Fewer Bargains*, N.Y. TIMES, Aug. 10, 2008, at
      7. Early analysis of the trend indicates that both vacationers and business travelers have begun
      to scale back their travel plans, while very cheap tickets and package vacation deals are less
      readily available. *See* Gary Stoller, *Will Fares Go So High That Only the Rich Can Fly?*, USA
      TODAY, Aug. 4, 2008, at 8A. As one industry analyst put it with regard to nearly 30 years of
      cheap air fares, '[T]he party is over . . . . [N]ow it is time to pay the bill.' *Id.* What remains to be
      seen is whether 'paying the bill' in the wake of a decades-long cheap fare extravaganza is more
      than consumers (and regulators) can endure.

334. This book adopts the Breyer thesis that classical regulation and the antitrust laws (to the extent
      that they turn unregulated markets into competitive ones), are alternative modes of managing
      the competitive process. *See* the analysis in BREYER, *supra* note 309, at 156 *et seq.* In Justice
      Breyer's view, classical regulation 'ought to be looked upon as a weapon of last resort.' *Id.* at
      185. He urges 'reliance upon an unregulated market in the absence of a significant market
      defect.' *Id.* at 185-86 (noting some of the economic efficiencies of competitive markets).
      Breyer, one of the architects of U.S. airline deregulation, unsurprisingly finds a 'mismatch'
      between classical regulation and the 'structurally competitive' airline industry. *Id.* at 197. *But
      see* Cudahy, *Airlines*, *supra* note 333, *passim* (arguing that there have been significant recur-
      ring structural market defects in the deregulated U.S. airline industry, including a tendency to
      overcapacity and excessive price competition).

Under this approach, governments (or their supranational surrogate, in the case of the EC) 'regulate' the target industry through the standard rules of competition law that seek to maintain the *conditions* of a competitive marketplace in all sectors of the economy,[335] and cease to apply a specific set of rules designed for the industry in question.[336] The intensity of official intervention then becomes a factor of the government's 'enforcement' attitude: most of competition law comprises negative mandates, reaching both market *conduct* (companies must not fix prices, split markets, or indulge in predatory below-cost price wars), and market *structure* (companies must not enter mergers that give them undue dominance in the marketplace).[337] Sometimes officialdom takes a more proactive role to compel the observance of these prohibitions, as when it requires the parties to file advance notice of impending merger transactions.[338] In the American antitrust tradition (though not very much in what until recently was the more centralized culture of EC competition law[339]) private lawsuits serve as an auxiliary to, and may sometimes exceed, the level of official enforcement.[340]

---

335. *See* John C. Reitz, *Legal and Administrative Problems of Airline Deregulation*, 42 Am. J. Comp. L. 419-20 (1994) (describing deregulation – paradoxically – as reregulation by the antitrust laws, or 'indirect' regulation).

336. Robert L. Thornton, *Airlines and Agents: Conflict and the Public Welfare*, 52 J. Air L. & Com. 371, 371 (1986). Professor Dennis Swann, in a study of the dual phenomena of regulation and deregulation, recognizes that a *laissez faire* economy does not necessarily inspire the play of healthy competitive energies. On the contrary, businesses may display strong collusive forces that tend toward the suppression of competition in their mutual interest. Swann's premise leads to the perception, similar to that held by Reitz, *supra* note 335, that antitrust or competition laws are in themselves a species of regulation (though they operate *ex post facto*) because their purpose is to *force* businesses to practice competition. Dennis Swann, The Retreat of the State: Deregulation and Privatization in the U.K. and U.S. 16 (1988). For a similar *aperçu* concerning EC law, *see* David J. Gerber, *Constitutionalizing the Economy: German Neoliberalism*, 42 Am. J. Comp. L. 45, 50 (1994) ('Competition law would "enforce" competition by creating and maintaining the conditions under which it would flourish!'). *See also* Breyer, *supra* note 309, at 156-57. It is well-known, incidentally, that the U.S. airlines and airline unions vigorously opposed deregulation in 1978. *See* Levine, *supra* note 322, at 282-84 (noting unanimity of airlines – and labor interests – concerning their preferred policy of CAB regulation).

337. Agreements between competitors to fix prices or divide markets are presumptively (that is to say, *per se*) unlawful in both the U.S. and EC competition codes. Predatory pricing, however, is subject to more refined tests of intent and likelihood of success that make it more hazardous to allege (and to prove). Breyer, *supra* note 309, at 157; *see also* K. Craig Wildfang, *Symposium, The Antitrust Enterprise: Principle and Execution: Predatory Conduct Under Section 2 of the Sherman Act: Do Recent Cases Illuminate the Boundaries?*, 31 Iowa J. Corp. L. 323, 351 (2006) (discussing U.S. Government's failed 2001 civil predatory pricing action against American Airlines); *see also infra* Chapter 4, Part IV(B). For a conspectus of U.S. antitrust prohibitions, *see* Breyer, *supra* note 309, at 157-58. *See also* Reitz, *supra* note 335, at 430.

338. Advance notice of certain proposed mergers is now a feature of both U.S. and EC administrative practice. *See infra* Chapter 4, Part III & Chapter 5, Part II(D). This requirement disrupts the neat dichotomy in the main text between *ex ante* and *ex post* supervision, because a bureaucratic green flag is needed to proceed to consummation of the notified transaction.

339. *See infra* Chapter 5, Part II(D) (discussing recent decentralizing reform of EC competition law enforcement).

340. *See generally* E. Thomas Sullivan & Jeffrey L. Harrison, Antitrust and Its Economic Implications 41-52 (5th ed. 2009).

In the EC, a competition regime driven by the dictates of economic 'natural selection' was hardly compatible with the traditional invulnerability of the flag carriers, kept aloft by transfers from the State treasury as part of the public endowment. In light of the volatile performance of the U.S. airline industry in the decade after deregulation, the European Commission engaged in what seems to have been a largely rhetorical effort to deflect suspicion that its deregulatory ambitions for air transport would amount only to a warmed-over appropriation of the U.S. experiment.[341] Accordingly, 'liberalization,' the European Commission's first conceptual wrapping for its new air transport policies, posited initially a more modest deregulatory program.[342] Using this supposedly temperate approach, government (or the European Commission, *in loco parentis*) established preset limits on the use by airline managers of any grant of commercial freedom.[343]

For example, the EC modified the system that allowed airlines to collaborate on tariff-setting subject to governmental oversight, using a series of price bands

---

341. 'We do not opt for a totally unregulated market. Rather our philosophy is to have a market free from unnecessary red tape but at the same time maintaining such rules as are necessary to ensure a fair, efficient system, benefiting all sides of the industry alike – operators, employees and users.' Karel van Miert, former EU Transport Commissioner, in speech to the 'Eurofreight' Conference, *The European Transport Policies*, Brussels, Apr. 9, 1990, at 3 (copy on file with the Library of the EU Delegation, Washington, DC). Although the rise of the Ryanair/easyJet paradigm suggests a more aggressive deregulation project than van Miert's benign language expected to call forth, the Commission's current self-assessment of its air transport policy remains – even allowing for a frank acknowledgement of the now-monarchical position of the consumer – not dissimilar to van Miert's of over 15 years ago. The emphasis is still on a peculiarly European view of what the Commission calls 'regulated competition' rather than deregulation:

    European policy has profoundly transformed the air transport industry by creating the conditions for competitiveness and ensuring both quality of service and the highest level of safety. Consumers have been the principal beneficiaries as this policy has led to more routes, greater choice and an increased overall quality of service.

    This is the original, European way of liberalizing: opening markets, unleashing the industry's potential and developing a regulated competition model. There will be a need for policy evolution in order to strengthen this success. This will have to be discussed with all interested parties, in order to consolidate an open, innovative, safe and sustainable market which may also be a model to our partners.

    European Commission, Air Transport Portal of the European Commission, Internal Market, <http://ec.europa.eu/transport/air_portal/internal_market/index_fr.htm>.

342. Although a scan of more recent Commission materials suggests that phobic avoidance of the term 'deregulation' has ended, the Commission seems inclined to prefer the phrase 'regulated competition' in relation to the air transport market. That is not true, however, of other sectoral markets. *See, e.g.,* Neelie Kroes, European Commissioner for Competition Policy, *Key Developments in European Competition Policy Over the Past Two Years,* Speech to the European American Press Club, Paris, Speech/07/2 (Jan. 8, 2007) (commenting, in the context of competition policy generally, that '[d]eregulation may be justified in areas where competition policy is sufficient to make markets function directly').

343. Wassenbergh, *supra* note 11, at 35, n.12.

(in airline deregulation parlance, 'zones of pricing flexibility') within which prices could fluctuate without any official interference.[344] Similar bands were created for capacity determination and for opening access to formerly duopolistic air routes.[345] Arguably, the incremental EC program could be characterized as 'regulatory reform' rather than deregulation *or* liberalization, although at some late moment in the continuum of change the shift to *ex post* control was so pervasive that deregulation became the more appropriate juridical label.

Indeed, in its 2006 proposed revisions to the EC code for air transport, the European Commission finally dropped some of the interventionist safeguards built into the original laws (for example, to combat below-cost pricing strategies).[346] But the Commission maintained special provisions for public service functions on Member State-designated routes, a program which in its original design for air transport liberalization helped (along with safeguards) to create a middle-of-the-road approach between unbridled U.S. deregulation and the cartelized behavior of the Chicago system.[347] Certainly, liberalization was a helpful term to describe the successive phases of EC deregulation, but in fact it *also* accurately portrays the staggered dismantling of regulatory barriers that characterized U.S. airline deregulation after 1978.[348] In that gradualist sense, the labels 'liberalization' and 'regulatory reform' function as cognates, conceptual staging posts on the journey to full deregulation (including competition policy). Indeed, as will be seen in the next two Chapters, each of this book's model jurisdictions eschewed the kind of instantaneous deregulation sought by the most ardent free market zealots.[349] Contrary to

---

344. *See* SWANN, *supra* note 336, at 31.
345. *See infra* Chapter 5, Part II.
346. European Commission, *Proposal for a Regulation of the European Parliament and of the Council on Common Rules For the Operation of Air Transport Services in the Community (recast)*, Explanatory Memorandum, para. 6, COM (2006) 396 final (Jul. 18, 2006), at 9 [hereinafter European Commission, *Common Rules*] (explaining that experience with the existing regime 'has shown that there has not been any market failure' justifying pricing safeguards in addition to the general competition rules).
347. *See* European Commission, *The Way Forward for Civil Aviation in Europe*, paras. 20-25, COM (94) 218 final (Jun. 1, 1994); *see also* European Commission, *Common Rules*, *supra* note 346, Explanatory Memorandum, para. 3 (maintaining Community rules on public service obligations while 'lighten[ing] the administrative burden,' but also introducing rules to avoid 'excessive recourse' by Member States to these procedures). The Commission's assertion with respect to U.S./EC conceptual differences on deregulation will be considered in light of more recent developments, *infra* Chapter 5, Part III(C).
348. *See* discussion *infra* Chapter 4, Part II.
349. There is clearly much shared substantive (and even procedural) ground between the competition laws of the two jurisdictions. *See* Neelie Kroes, European Commissioner for Antitrust Policy, *Developments in anti-trust policy in the EU and U.S.*, Speech to the Council on Foreign Relations, New York, Sept. 15, 2006, Speech/06/494, noting how, for example, EC anti-monopoly law 'broadly equates' to its U.S. counterpart and that 'there is no doubt that the competition systems in Europe and the [United States] have more similarities than differences.' These similarities, moreover, will form the basis of the proposal advanced in Chapter 6 of this study for a common U.S./EC airline competition code. *See infra* Chapter 6, Part III(E).

popular myth, for example, airline deregulation was not introduced in the United States by means of a 'big bang.'[350]

2   Airline Privatization in the EU

As the EU's *Comité des Sages* noted almost a decade and a half ago, the economic consequence of the European State-based public utility model – fragmentation into smaller, weaker airlines and systemic inefficiencies – was a heritage from which Europe 'still suffer[ed].'[351] In his introduction to the Report of the *Comité*, Chairman Herman De Croo chastised Europe's governments for allowing 'mentality changes' to lag behind technological, economic, and regulatory changes: 'This change of mentality is . . . more important than the accumulated wisdom of any [c]ommittee.'[352]

One of the most significant 'mentality changes' for the Member States in the years since the Comité reported, and emblematic of the end of ideological *dirigisme* in the airline industry, has been the economic phenomenon of 'privatization,' a term used here to mean the sale of government corporate assets into partial or full private ownership.[353] In the EU's industry generally, the pace of this transformation has accelerated in recent years: 'What is unique about the 1980s and early 1990s is that the sporadic and limited phenomenon of the 1960s has become widespread and almost routine.'[354] As recognized in a major OECD study published in 1992, privatization emerged as a signal of a much wider restructuring of the relationship among State, market, and society that characterized the States of the EU and their neighbors since the early 1980s.[355] Moreover, while privatization

---

350. *See infra* Chapter 4, Part II.
351. Report of the *Comité des Sages, supra* note 44, at 5.
352. *Id.* at 7.
353. In the United States, in contrast, 'privatization' means the transformation of publicly-held (*i.e.*, share-owned) corporations into closely held or 'private' entities. In the U.S. airline industry, for example, at certain times the now-defunct Trans World Airlines and also Northwest Airlines were 'privatized:' shares in these companies were then no longer traded on public exchanges. Prior to the global financial turmoil of late 2008, there was recent interest in U.S. (as well as non-U.S.) airlines from the cash-rich 'private equity' buyout firms that came to prominence in the global economy of the mid-2000s. *See, e.g., Private Equity Eyes U.S. Airlines*, REUTERS, Feb. 16, 2007 (indicating that a stabilizing U.S. airline industry, despite substantial debt and traditionally difficult labor relations, may attract interest from more than a dozen private equity firms). *But see* Enda Curran, *Airlines Predicted to Lose Billions More*, WALL ST. J., Aug. 21, 2008, at B2 (reporting IATA's estimate that airlines could lose $6.1 billion in 2008 due to rising fuel costs and geopolitical instability); Bill Lindsay, *Quantas Posts Record Net, But Warns About Outlook*, WALL ST. J., Aug. 22, 2008, at B4 (reporting that Australian flag carrier Qantas' record full-year earnings could be offset by the uncertain fuel market and economic conditions).
354. Vincent Wright, *Industrial Privatization in Western Europe: Pressures, Problems and Paradoxes, in* PRIVATIZATION IN WESTERN EUROPE 1 (Vincent Wright ed., 1994).
355. *See* Committee on Competition L. & Pol'y, OECD, *Regulatory Reform, Privatization, and Competition Policy* (1992). For a more recent assessment, *see* PRIVATIZATION EXPERIENCES IN THE EUROPEAN UNION (Marko Köthenbürger et al, eds., 2006) (distinguishing among changes in

in the United Kingdom during the Thatcher-Major premierships concededly had an early odor of political ideology,[356] the 'demonstration effect' of the British model, and specifically of BA as a paradigm for the airline industry,[357] transcended mere ideological scorekeeping. To mention just one example of the substantial technical benefits of Anglo-style privatization in the airline industry, with massive capital purchases becoming necessary to replace ageing aircraft fleets in the 1990s, converting airlines to private ownership offered new sources of capital to finance these

---

ownership or 'simple' privatization, changes in the rules of market participation and conduct, *i.e.*, liberalization (a situation where public ownership of a market player may persist), and changes in public regulation, also called deregulation). In the EC, liberalization frequently occurred without a concomitant privatization (especially in network industries such as telecommunications). *See id.*, *Introduction*, at xi.

356. Yet Major's Labor Party successor, Tony Blair, continued what his critics labeled a 'neo-Thatcherite' approach to free market reforms. *See, e.g.*, John Gray, *Essay: From Churchill to Macmillan on to Thatcher and Blair, British Leaders Have Encouraged the Idea That We Can Still Be a Global Player. It is a Fantasy. . .*, NEW STATESMAN, Jun. 6, 2005 (arguing that privatization produces better coffee but inferior railway services, but noting critically that policy responses to both of those sectors – which should allow in appropriate cases for tax-funded State services – are nowadays doctrinally governed by the sanctity of consumer choice in a free market).

357. The economic success of a privatized British Airways contained some troubling implications, however. Was it a true privatization or did BA benefit from a new 'national champion' policy that required the government to stand guard over the airline's international monopolies and to tolerate its absorption of healthy domestic competitors? *See, e.g.*, [U.K.] Department for Transport, Air Service Agreements Between the UK and the US – Government Response, <www.dft.gov.uk/pgr/aviation/international/airserviceagreementsbetweent2962> (stating that 'it is a simple statement of fact that [British Airways] is our largest airline, in terms of route network and employment, and that must be given due weight when considering the balance of interests'). In the negotiations leading to the 2007 U.S./EC Air Transport Agreement, *supra* note 21, the U.S. representatives suspected that BA's transformation into a 'protected' privatized carrier was fueling the U.K. Government's resistance to change of the existing bilateral order. From late 2006, however, the views of the U.K. Government and of British Airways began to diverge publicly on the fate of the U.S./EC transatlantic air transport negotiations. *See* Rt. Hon. Douglas Alexander, U.K. Secretary of State for Transport, Speech to the International Aviation Club, Washington, DC (Oct. 4, 2006) (declaring the United Kingdom in favor of liberalizing the North Atlantic market through a comprehensive U.S./EC agreement). *But see* Steve Goldstein, *UK Government May Oppose Open-Skies Deal: BA Chairman*, MARKETWATCH, Mar. 5, 2007 (quoting BA Chairman Martin Broughton's inaccurate prediction that the U.K. Government would oppose the 2007 U.S./EC Air Transport Agreement in the EU Council of Ministers out of 'sympathy' with the position of British Airways). There seems little doubt that BA will suffer a material loss of profits as a result of the ending of restricted access to London Heathrow envisaged in the new agreement. *See* Aude Lagorce, *British Airways Hit Over 'Open-Skies' Deal: Transatlantic Rival Virgin Welcomes Tentative U.S.-EU Pact*, MARKETWATCH, Mar. 5, 2007; David Robertson, *British Airways Faces £250m Threat to Profits as Open Skies Era Takes Off*, TIMES (London), Mar. 29, 2008, at 64 (noting that despite British Airways' insistence to the contrary, stiffer competition at Heathrow may force the airline to change its high fare model out of Heathrow after the investment bank BNP Paribas estimated a £273 million loss to projected profits for British Airways over the next year).

giant outlays, and concurrently released the airlines from the imperatives of the so-called 'public sector borrowing requirement.'[358]

Even where privatization has not occurred or is not planned in the future, or has occurred in a mixed private/public mode, the force of competition law should be unaffected: the Treaty of Rome, the wellhead of the EC's norms of competition law, declares itself indifferent to whether capital is publicly or privately owned.[359]

---

358. Ray Rees, *Economic Aspects of Privatization in Britain, in* PRIVATIZATION IN WESTERN EUROPE, *supra* note 354, at 50-53; *see also* Wright, *supra* note 354, at 4-5; ROBERT HEBDON & HAZEL DAYTON GUNN, THE COSTS AND BENEFITS OF PRIVATIZATION 2 (1995) (arguing that labor costs under privatization are lower because labor productivity tends to be higher in the private sector while wages and benefit costs are lower); PAUL S. DEMPSEY, LAW AND FOREIGN POLICY IN INTERNATIONAL AVIATION 83 (1987). Another significant benefit of privatization is the control of labor costs as employee participation schemes flourish. *See generally* Prodromos D. Dagtoglou, *Air Transport and the European Community*, 6 EUR. L. REV. 335, 336 (1981); Wright, *supra* note 354, at 3 (noting a 'backlash against the prevailing neo-corporatism – that comfortable, collusive and costly institutionalized relationship between the State, the employers and the trade unions'). On the 'ideological' mission of privatization, *see* SWANN, *supra* note 336, at 11.

359. Article 295 of the EC Treaty provides that '[t]his Treaty shall in no way prejudice the rules in Member States governing the system of property ownership.' Note, however, that where States retain substantial *minority* rights (and sometimes even a blocking right known as a 'golden share') in privatized firms, it is difficult to predict when these rights will be exercised and for what purpose, creating 'an element of uncertainty.' Wright, *supra* note 354, at 39. While 'golden shares,' in particular, became an accepted part of 1990s European capitalism, allowing governments to retain influence over vital economic sectors even while privatizing strategic companies, they came under attack from EC regulators because of their propensity to block cross-border takeovers through discrimination against foreign bids. In 2007, the European Court of Justice ruled that Germany had failed to fulfill its obligations under Article 56 of the EC Treaty (free movement of capital) by maintaining provisions found in a 1960 law privatizing the equity in the Volkswagenwerk limited company (Volkswagen). *See* Case C-112/05, Comm'n *v.* Germany, 2007 E.C.R. I-8995. Relying on its decision in Case C-367/96, Comm'n *v.* Portugal, 2002 E.C.R. I-4731, the Court held that the German provisions allowing the State to have a blocking minority to oppose decisions with a lesser share (20%) than normally required under general corporate law and to cap investor voting rights at 20% ran afoul of Article 56 by possibly deterring foreign investors 'from acquiring a stake in the capital of that company in order to participate in it with a view to establishing or maintaining lasting and direct economic links with it which would make possible effective participation in the management of that company or in its control.' *See* Comm'n *v.* Germany, *supra*, para. 55. Another provision in the German law, granting federal and local authorities the right to each appoint two members to Volkswagen's supervisory board so long as the authorities held shares in the company, was also found incompatible with Article 56 because it gave those authorities the capacity to influence the company beyond the level of their actual investment while depriving other shareholders of the possibility of exercising influence commensurate with their own. *See* Comm'n *v.* Germany, *supra*, para. 64. While the Court recognized that EU Member States may restrict the free movement of capital for certain tax purposes enumerated in Article 58 of the EC Treaty and 'for overriding reasons in the general interest to the extent that there are no Community harmonising measures providing for measures necessary to ensure the protection of those interests,' *see* Comm'n *v.* Germany, *supra*, para. 72 (citing Comm'n *v.* Portugal, *supra*, para. 49) – so long as they are proportionate, *i.e.*, 'appropriate to secure the attainment of the objective which they pursue and not [going] beyond what is necessary in order to attain it, *id.* para. 73 (citing Comm'n *v.* Portugal, *supra*, para. 49) – the Court was not convinced that

Member State governments are required in either circumstance to be guided by the principles of fair competition and to refrain from applying the balm of public subsidy, directly or indirectly, to ease the financial travails of the flag carriers.[360] This conflict between free market principles and public aid bedeviled the EC deregulatory program through the 1990s and was seen as a threat to the future of the entire project.[361] As a U.S. study noted, 'the trend toward privatization may cause [Member State] governments to increase subsidies and capital assistance to their airlines in the short-term in an effort to put them on a sound financial footing, thereby making them more attractive to private investors.'[362] Given that governments differ in their resources and public spending priorities, the drafters of the Treaty of Rome probably hoped that the Commission '[could] hold the ring and decide, on the basis of criteria laid down in the Treaty, which subsidies should be granted and which should not.'[363] As will be seen in Chapter 5, a subsidy race among the Member State governments dominated the first years of EC air transport liberalization, forcing the European Commission into a triangulated strategy that sought to mollify both the donor governments and their opponents (other governments and rival airlines).[364]

Germany's asserted primary justification – the protection of workers' rights – required the local and federal governments to maintain disproportionate control over the company, *see id.* paras. 74-76.

360. As Wright notes, 'there are aspects of the open market – monetary convergence, competition policy, public procurement policy – which logically prevent *dirigiste* governments from fully exploiting their public enterprises as instruments of industrial [or] regional policy or of purely political patronage.' Wright, *supra* note 354, at 4.

361. *See infra* Chapter 5, Part III(F). *see also* Swann, *supra* note 336, at 2.

362. GAO, *International Aviation, supra* note 98, at 41. The GAO's forecast of events proved accurate, although the agency did not return subsequently to the issue of EC State aids.

363. Sir Leon Brittan, Vice-President of the Commission of the European Communities, *A Framework for International Competition*, Speech to the World Economic Forum, Davos, Switzerland, at 9 (Feb. 3, 1992) (copy on file with the Library of the EU Delegation, Washington DC). Elevating subsidy surveillance to the pan-Community level may have been intended to avoid the conflicts that national governments would have in asking government departments to monitor (or to adjudicate on) each other's industrial aid programs, especially when the aid was intended to help the national firm compete with rivals from other Member States.

364. Among the European Commission's criteria for examining State aids is the so-called 'market investor' principle, which requires an initial review to determine whether the funding is being given under conditions that would be acceptable to a hypothetical private investor evaluating the risk and potential of a similar investment (for example, in the context of a proposed rights issue by a privatized airline). The artificiality of this test is immediately obvious. If it were a genuine predictor of likely private investor response, the weak Italian flag carrier Alitalia could have been recapitalized without State involvement in 2005. Instead, the Berlusconi government won controversial approval from the Commission to subscribe to 489 million euro (just under half) of the capital increase, leaving its stake in the carrier at 49.9%. *See* European Commission, Press Release, Conditional Go-Ahead for the Recapitalization of Alitalia, IP/05/678 (Jun. 7, 2005). *See* discussion of earlier aid to Alitalia and to other flag carriers, and of the State aids issue generally, *infra* Chapter 5, Part III(E).

VII   THE REGULATORY REFLEX: COMPUTER
                   RESERVATIONS SYSTEMS AND AIRPORT ACCESS

When Professor Jack High asked why some industries fall under the regulatory
umbrella while others do not, he omitted an even more puzzling supplementary:
why might some *aspects* of some industries fall under the umbrella, while others
escape it?[365] Although this Chapter has traced the desire of U.S. and EU authorities to liberate their aviation industries from prior regulatory supervision, the
switch to a seamless *ex post* competition policy is occasionally blocked by
unusual regulatory challenges that are unique to the industry being deregulated.
The challenge that regulators face is to draw the outer boundaries of regulatory
intervention as narrowly and precisely as possible, including only situations
where the consumer demonstrably lacks reliable factual and statistical (as
opposed to anecdotal) feedback, and no competing sources of information are
available.

    Thus, neither travel agents nor the airlines themselves will typically supply
accident or safety history information to ticket purchasers, nor could the average
consumer be expected to process the variables (aircraft type, meteorological risks,
pilot performance, and so forth) that comprise the profile of a carrier's safety
record. Government involvement in safety regulation, therefore, appears inescapable as a matter of rational regulatory policy: unsafe carriers should simply not be
allowed to compile *any* kind of safety 'record,' and there has indeed been no
deregulation of this government supervision in either model jurisdiction.[366]
A similar argument, based also on consumer protection principles, has been
used to justify microregulation to prevent deception by code-sharing.[367]

    Within the U.S. and EU air transport industries, two developments presented
challenges with special resonance for the reform of international aviation: the rapid
diffusion in the industry of computer reservations systems (CRS) (now frequently
referred to as global distribution systems (GDS),[368] and the distribution of scarce
airport runway and terminal resources (the slot and gate problem).[369] The predicate
for invasive government regulation of these two apparently unrelated aspects of air

---

365. *See* High, *supra* note 327, at 12-13.
366. *See* GRA, Inc., *Aviation Safety Data Accessibility Study Index: Public Access to Safety Infor-
      mation*, Report to the Federal Aviation Administration, <www.faa.gov/library/reports/
      aviation/media/pub_access.pdf> (finding no evidence in accident data that would support
      the ranking of individual airlines based on their safety records; infrequent but catastrophic
      nature of air accidents cannot be predictive of future safety performance and rankings would
      provide no information to consumers seeking to make safety-enhancing comparisons).
367. *See infra* Part VIII(C).
368. Actually, CRS and GDS are synonymous terms, but a GDS is more accurately a globalized
      CRS (as the major systems have become). *See* Timothy M. Ravich, *Deregulation of the Airline
      Computer Reservation Systems (CRS)*, 69 J. AIR L. & COM. 387, 412, n. 2 (2004). The term
      'CRS,' because of its historical usage in U.S. and EC regulatory instruments, is preferred here.
369. For a more detailed analysis of the U.S. and EC regulatory response to the competitive
      challenges of computer reservations systems and congested airport facilities, *see infra*
      Chapter 4, Part IV(B) & Chapter 5, Part III(C).

transport was that of competition policy: each is allegedly capable of foreclosing the entry of new airlines, or of forestalling system expansion by existing carriers, in both cases to the detriment of a competitive marketplace. The solutions proposed, in the main, have reflected the persistence of a Chicago regulatory 'reflex' in international aviation,[370] even among governments otherwise committed to an open skies philosophy. In both spheres of regulation, the administrative authorities returned to *ex ante* controls to 'load' the market structure in favor of weaker players (nonowners of CRS or start-up carriers seeking airport space). While CRS and slot congestion problems were unknown to the drafters of the Chicago Convention, in light of the multilateral reform proposed in this book it is important to note the apparent ease with which administrators in both model jurisdictions resorted to traditional regulatory oversight in place of the new competition ethos – and later, in the case of CRS in the United States, just as readily abandoned regulatory meddling when the marketplace for distribution services changed utterly.[371]

A   CRS: From Regulation to Deregulation in 20 Years

As originally defined by a U.S. Government agency, a CRS was an electronic system offered by a carrier to subscribers (typically travel agents) that contained information about that carrier's schedules and fares, and frequently about the availability of other carriers' services, and that provided its subscribers with the ability to issue tickets.[372] As an information system, granting travel agents (and more recently the private computer user) instant power to scroll through an elaborate inventory of airline pricing and scheduling information, and to compare carrier prices virtually at a glance, it suggested conditions of almost 'perfect' competition in the airline industry.[373] As a product distribution system for the

---

370. A similar reflex can be observed within the U.S. and EC jurisdictional boundaries in commercial areas where the systemic effect on international aviation is less discernible, for example with respect to the protection of passenger rights. On EC regulation of passenger rights, *see infra* Chapter 5, Part III(C).

371. Like the issue of passenger rights, CRS regulation may reflect a paternalistic reflex on the part of governments in their decision to regulate rather than to trust the play of market forces, and the likelihood that the market will deliver what Ravich, calls 'qualitatively-sound service.' Timothy M. Ravich, *Re-Regulation and Airline Passengers' Rights*, 67 J. Air L. & Com. 935, 963 (2002). Some kinds of regulatory intervention are intended to correct – or at least to alleviate – an objective structural deficiency in the marketplace (lack of airport slot access, for example), but CRS and passenger rights' regulation suggests intervention merely to improve the industry standard for customer service or, as one aviation consultant noted, to promote 'care . . . feeling and empathy.' Ravich, *supra*, at 963. While not the same kind of control as regulation of fares and routes, the *conduct* of a supposedly deregulated industry is nonetheless being subjected to regulation. *See id.*

372. *See* Economic Regulations, 14 C.F.R. § 255.3. For a brief account of the emergence of the CRS phenomenon, *see* Michael J. Durham, *The Future of SABRE*, in The Handbook of Airline Economics 485 (Darryl Jenkins ed., 1995).

373. *See* Statement of Robert L. Crandall, President, American Airlines, Inc., Before Economic and Commercial Law Subcomm. of the House Committee on the Judiciary, *in Airline Commission*

airlines, the CRS enabled maximization of revenue yields in a segmented demand environment, allowing constant adjustment of the distribution of passengers between discounted-fare vacationers and full-fare business travelers.[374] This functional duality created unique problems of regulatory oversight in both model jurisdictions.

While CRS appeared facially to enhance consumer choice,[375] correcting asymmetries of information in air transport between suppliers and consumers of air transport services,[376] system ownership became increasingly concentrated in a handful of

---

Documents, undocketed (Jun. 9, 1993), at 1 (commenting also on lack of brand loyalty in airline industry). The Internet has been viewed similarly as a system of almost perfect transparency. *See* Ravich, *supra* note 371, at 399-402 (describing the Internet as a 'direct channel' distribution system with minimal transactional expenses); *see also* Martha Brannigan et al., *First-Class Mutiny; Fed Up with Airlines, Business Travelers Start to Fight Back – Already Hurt by Slowdown, Carriers Are Now Facing Technology-Savvy Fliers – Almost Perfect Information*, WALL ST. J., Aug. 28, 2001, at A1 (quoting Delta Air Lines Chairman Leo F. Mullin's statement that '[a]nyone who has a modicum of Internet capability and wants to take what is now a modest amount of time can very rapidly find out [airfares] and comparison shop... There is almost perfect information out there'). *See also* Transportation Group International, *Consumer Attitudes and Use of the Internet and Traditional Travel Agents*, A Report for the National Commission to Ensure Consumer Information and Choice in the Airline Industry (Sept. 19, 2002) (discussing the rise of the Internet and the concomitant decline in travel agents' business, emphasizing that 'the government as a rule does not intervene in how suppliers distribute their products' nor does the government shield private businesses from downward swings in the business cycle or from marketplace shifts in demand for their services).

374. *See generally In Re* Air Passenger Computer Reservations Systems Antitrust Litigation, 694 F. Supp. 1443, 1449 (C.D. Cal. 1988); *see also* American Airlines, Inc. *v.* KLM Royal Dutch Airlines, Inc., 114 F.3d 108 (8th Cir. 1997) (discussing the complex algorithmic basis for fare construction using CRS databases). Thus, CRS programs divided aircraft seats into sub-units to be sold on different terms to different market segments. Since demand varies flight-by-flight, day-by-day, and season-by-season, a simple two or three-level, peak/off-peak fare structure proved insufficiently sensitive in most markets. The airlines, through their CRS networks, could perform detailed analyses of profiles of thousands of different flights to determine the optimal mix of discount and full fare tickets an airline should sell to maximize yields. *See* Michael Levine, *Airline Competition in Deregulated Markets: Theory, Firm Strategy and Public Policy*, 4 YALE J. ON REG. 393, 449-50 (1987). This phenomenon was originally known in the airline industry as 'yield management,' although 'revenue management' is probably the more common usage today. *See* Michele McDonald, *Yielding to the LCCs*, 43 AIR TRANSP. WORLD, Mar. 1, 2006; *see also* Ronald Katz, *The Impact of Computer Reservation Systems on Air Transport Competition, in* OECD Report, *supra* note 306, annex I, at 92. As will be considered later, the rise of the Internet and of low-cost carrier competition each posed considerable challenges for the major airlines' traditional yield management.

375. *See* Donald J. Boudreaux & Jerome Ellig, *Beneficent Bias: The Case Against Regulating Airline Computerized Reservation Systems*, 57 J. AIR L. & COM. 567, 593 (1992) (discussing dramatic lowering of airline and travel agent costs, and hence airline fares, caused by CRS).

376. From a consumer welfare perspective, any reduction of asymmetrical access to information in the air transport industry may indeed be warranted (and welcomed). Given the biases inherent in the original CRS market structure, however, an authentic reduction of asymmetry had to await the era of Internet travel services and, concomitantly, the eventual erosion of CRS market power. *See infra* Chapter 4, Part IV(B) (discussing market-based – as opposed to regulatory – solutions).

major carriers,[377] and the network reached a virtual saturation point that made new entry into the CRS industry highly unlikely.[378] At the distribution level, a perception developed that large carrier-owners such as American (SABRE) or United (Apollo) would be able to use their CRS market power to stifle or extinguish new entry and to facilitate informational manipulation and distortion that arguably harmed consumer welfare. Undoubtedly, these systems had some potential for manipulation by system owners (if the owners were also airlines, as they typically were) as instruments of anti-competitive abuse.[379] As the market structure appeared to the regulators, carriers like American and United, which were also owners of systems (known as 'hosted' systems[380]), could try to ensure that their flights, and the flights of airlines associated with them in code-share alliances or joint CRS ownership, were preferentially listed on the early (and presumably most heavily-consulted) screen displays.[381]

The U.S. and EC regulatory responses, as later comparative studies will reveal, imposed direct behavioral constraints on the system owners in the CRS industry. Regulators in both jurisdictions sought removal of so-called 'architectural' bias in the listing of flights on-screen displays, and prescribed nondiscriminatory terms of contract between system owners and subscribers, as well as between owners and their competitor airlines.[382] It was not always clear, however,

---

377. *See* the competitive concerns expressed by the General Accounting Office, in GAO, *Airline Competition: Weak Financial Structure Threatens Competition*, GAO/RCED-91-110 (Apr. 1991). The GAO was particularly troubled by a transfer of excess revenues to United and American from their weaker competitors through CRS charges. *Id.* at 5. At the time of the GAO report, the major U.S. systems were American Airlines' SABRE and United Airlines' Apollo, which accounted for about 55% of ticket sales, down from nearly 80% in 1980. SABRE was then the only CRS still owned by a single airline (American). Apollo became part of a consortium (Galileo International) jointly owned by United, the then-USAir, and several European airlines. Delta, Northwest, and TWA (together with a 12-airline Asian consortium, Abacus) owned Worldspan, which had a market share of 20%. Continental Airlines' System One, co-owned by a U.S. data processing company, entered a joint venture with Galileo's largest EU rival, Amadeus. For the subsequent history of these systems, *see infra* note 387.

378. In the early 1970s, the U.S. airline industry tried without success to establish a single industry-wide computerized reservations service for its (also regulated) travel agent representatives. The last such failure, in 1976, prompted United, American, and TWA to offer their own systems. *See* Richard J. Fahy, *The Applicability of the Antitrust Laws to a Deregulated Airline Industry*, 10 AIR L. 152, 158 (1985). For an interesting, 'journalistic' account of the invention of the CRS concept, *see* BARBARA STURKEN PETERSON & JAMES GLAB, DEREGULATION AND THE SHAKEOUT IN THE AIRLINES: RAPID DESCENT 61 (1994).

379. *See infra* Chapter 4, Part IV(B).

380. *See infra* note 381.

381. This 'bias' might be reinforced by incentives to travel agents to book ticket buyers onto these preferred flights. Other recognized anticompetitive strategies included exclusive use contracts that bound subscriber agents to use only the hosted system, and system participation fees charged to rival airlines that varied according to the host's assessment of each airline's competitive threat to its market share.

382. Micromanagement of screen displays, in particular, produced subtle differences of approach in the two jurisdictions. Unlike the U.S. regulations, for example, EC rules still rank flights (other than nonstop direct flights) based on elapsed travel time for the passenger, and therefore prioritize interline (two or more carriers) over online (single carrier) connecting service, if the total

that pervasive micromanagement of screen content was either necessary or useful when several systems existed in the marketplace, run by a multiplicity of thinly-margined travel agent outlets, which were in turn shadowed by the existence of the airlines' own in-house reservations abilities.[383] Although 'localized' dominance remained a risk in an industry with few competitors, U.S. courts were never persuaded, despite the regulators' zeal for rulemaking, that any individual system had actually acquired 'market power,' the benchmark standard for anticompetitive activity in both model jurisdictions.[384] Nevertheless, with so many potential anticompetitive risks awaiting discovery as global distribution technologies developed, in both the United States and EU the regulators continued to sponsor new CRS rulemaking efforts, unconvinced of the effectiveness of their solutions but persuaded as a threshold matter, it seemed, that system ownership would always incite some preferential treatment of the host carriers.[385]

Private initiative is sometimes a catalyst – intentionally or not – for regulatory change in the international aviation marketplace. Ultimately, the U.S. DOT conceded, in its 2004 regulatory package abolishing CRS behavioral scrutiny, that 'the major predicate for the [CRS] rules [was] always . . . the systems' control by airlines.'[386] As the U.S. airlines divested their control over CRS networks beginning

---

travel time is shorter. *See* Council Regulation 2299/89, Code of Conduct for Computerized Reservation Systems, annex I, paras. 1-2, 1989 O.J. (L 220) 1; *see also infra* Chapter 5, Part III(C). The U.S. rules, in contrast, required screen display criteria that were neutral as to carrier identity, but did not more precisely specify the order in which flights should appear according to the selected criteria. The DOT took the position that the marketplace would decree the most efficient schedule displays. *See* Richard J. Fahy, Jr., Esq., *The Cutting Edge of Technology and Regulation, in* THE HANDBOOK OF AIRLINE ECONOMICS, *supra* note 372, at 504. Also, the spreading practice of code-sharing implicated issues of screen content. The possibility that a flight would be operated by a carrier *other than* the carrier whose code appeared on the screen was a classic instance of the kind of asymmetrical information that a CRS was supposed to correct. Some on-screen notation of the code/operator discrepancy was therefore required under both U.S. and EC rules. *See infra* Chapter 4, Part IV(B) & Chapter 5, Part III(C). *But see* Ed Perkins, *The Pros and Cons of Code-Sharing* (Jul. 12, 2006), <www.smartertravel.com/travel-advice> (noting that fares on code-shared flights may vary depending on the participating airline on which the passenger books and may also involve connecting flights on different airlines using different terminals and requiring multiple security processing).

383. *See* Cindy R. Alexander & Yoon-Ho Alex Lee, *The Economics of Regulatory Reform: Termination of Airline Computer Reservation System Rules*, 21 YALE J. ON REG. 369, 413-14 (2004) (noting, for example, how the CRS rules only selectively prohibited display bias – displays for corporate travel departments and displays prepared by travel agents for advising individual consumers were exempted).

384. *See infra* Chapter 4, Part IV(B) & Chapter 5, Part III(C).

385. *See, e.g.,* European Commission, *Report of the Application of Articles 4(a) and 6(3) of Council Regulation No. 2299/89 as Amended by Regulation Concerning a Code of Conduct for CRS*, at 3, COM (95) 51 final (Mar. 7, 1995).

386. U.S. Department of Transportation, *Computer Reservations System (CRS) Regulations*, Dkt. No. OST-97-2881, Final Rule, 14 C.F.R. Part 255, 69 Fed. Reg. 976, 977 (Jan. 7, 2004) [hereinafter DOT, Final CRS Rule]. The Final Rule, as the DOT's regulatory adieu to the CRS industry is commonly called, was 'the culmination of a highly controversial and protracted regulatory review proceeding that lasted more than six years.' David Heffernan, *Sabre, Inc. v. DOT: The D.C. Circuit Affirms DOT's Broad Authority to Regulate CRSs and Other Air*

in the middle of the last decade,[387] it must have seemed rational to expect that independent networks should be able to use the precise targets of behavioral regulation, such as display bias, as profit-maximizing strategies.[388] In fact, the relatively speedy end to the 20-year CRS regulatory cycle (from regulation to deregulation) in the United States was precipitated by two major entrepreneurial developments: as the airlines divested their 'hosted' systems,[389] the Internet (pioneered as a travel conduit by low-cost carriers) was transforming the business model for airline ticket distribution.[390] The DOT credited both developments for its decision to promulgate its Final Rule abolishing regulation of CRS networks.[391] The EC, meanwhile, has concluded that U.S. airlines, enjoying

---

    Travel Intermediaries, Paper Presented to the American Bar Association Forum on Air & Space Law, at 1 (Feb. 2, 2006).

387. Since the mid-1990s, three domestic CRS networks have evolved from vertical integration with major airlines into independent entities that now dominate the U.S. travel agent market: Sabre (formerly owned by American Airlines until 1996), Galileo (formerly owned by a consortium of U.S. and EU airlines, but which became fully divested after its sole remaining airline shareholder, United Airlines, sold its stake in 2001), and Worldspan (sold by joint owners Delta Air lines, Northwest Airlines, and American Airlines in 2003). In 2007, Travelport – the current owner of Galileo – acquired Worldspan for a reported $1.4 billion. Doug Tsuruoka, *Travelport Acquisition Ups Reservations Ante*, INVESTORS BUS. DAILY, Oct. 9, 2007, at A04. For further details on the 'national' structure of the European CRS markets and on some of the vestigial airline ownership stakes in those structures, *see infra* Chapter 5, Part III(C).

388. And whatever gains a CRS might obtain from such a bias would have to exceed the cost of its potential loss of travel agents who prefer an unbiased system. *See* Alexander & Lee, *supra* note 383, at 415-16.

389. Thus, as the DOT pointed out in abolishing the CRS rules, '[t]he U.S. airlines' divestiture of their ownership interests has eliminated [the] basis for the rules.' *Id.* Under 49 U.S.C. § 41712 (Section 417 of the Federal Aviation Act), the DOT has a general surveillance authority to prohibit airlines and 'ticket agents' from engaging in unfair competition and deceptive practices in the sale or provision of air transportation. Given U.S. airlines' divestiture of their ownership in CRS networks, it was unclear whether the DOT could enforce this provision against non-airline owned, *i.e.* independent, systems. In Sabre, Inc. *v.* Department of Transportation, 429 F.3d 1113 (D.C. Cir. 2005), a recent decision of the United States Court of Appeals for the District of Columbia Circuit, the court found as a matter of statutory construction that the definition of 'ticket agents' includes independent CRS networks. *See supra* note 261.

390. Thus, the DOT also recognized in dissolving its CRS regime that '[a]irlines are selling an increasingly large share of their tickets through their Internet websites and a diminishing share through travel agents using a system.' The agency must have expected, therefore, that the new marketplace would discipline the competing CRS networks. *See* DOT, Final CRS Rule, *supra* note 386, at 977. For a recent conspectus of the shifting parameters of airline distribution, *see* GAO, *Airline Ticketing: Impact of Changes in the Airline Ticket Distribution Industry*, GAO-03-749 (Jul. 2003) . *See also* Ravich, *supra* note 371, at 399 (describing the Internet as a 'second generation CRS').

391. *See* Alexander & Lee, *supra* note 383, at 430 (concluding that the CRS rule termination occurred because technological advances made entry profitable for innovative suppliers – using electronic commerce – which were not subject to CRS regulation (despite calls from the CRS industry to include the new suppliers)). The authors describe the CRS regulatory cycle as a classic case of regulation under an 'interest group' theory, in which the gradual dissipation of rents from the beneficiaries of regulation (the incumbent systems) ultimately triggers

reduced CRS booking fees since deregulation, have lowered their distribution costs compared with their EU competitors.[392] The European Commission has reacted to virtually identical market changes by signaling that it, too, foresees the demise of formal behavioral command-and-control.[393]

B   THE COMPETITIVE QUANDARIES OF AIRPORT ACCESS

A quite different – and much more intractable – problem is presented by regulation of access to congested airport facilities. Air transport, after all, 'rides' on the public way: not only each State's sovereign airspace, but also its capital investment in airport runway, apron, and terminal infrastructure and in air traffic control systems.[394] But there is obviously only a finite amount of gate and runway access at any airport at any given time. Control of the choicest space, and the premium high-density landing and take-off times, obviously creates competitive advantages. Again, questions of regulatory intervention are presented when incumbents can choke off competition by their historic quasi-proprietary control over the airport gate and terminal space[395]

---

reform. *Id.* at 428. They argue also that the DOT's decision not to extend CRS-style regulation to the new electronic ticket distribution channels – which enable travelers to book tickets without a travel agent – was 'good policy since it prevents regulation from inadvertently impeding the advance of technology.' *Id.* at 412.

392. *See* European Commission, *Consultation Paper on the Revision of Regulation 2299/89 on a Code of Conduct for Computerised Reservation Systems*, paras. 61-64, Consultation Paper (2007) [hereinafter European Commission, *CRS Consultation Paper*].

393. *See infra* Chapter 5, Part III(C). *See also* European Commission, *CRS Consultation Paper, supra* note 392 (following U.S. precedent in citing the rise of alternative distribution channels and change of control of CRS providers as predicates for regulatory reform). The EU still has one important CRS network with an airline ownership interest: the Amadeus network is indirectly minority-owned by three European carriers (Lufthansa, Air France-KLM, and Iberia). *See* Heffernan, *supra* note 386, at 2. The U.S. Department of Transportation judged Amadeus' U.S. market share to be too small to present a risk of abuse. *See* European Commission, *CRS Consultation Paper, supra* note 392, para. 51.

394. The breadth of public interest concerns presented by airports is evident in the official statutory declaration on U.S. airport development, 49 U.S.C.A. § 47101(a) (West 2008) (mentioning *inter alia* safety, noise, environmental protection, technological progress, reasonableness of fees and rates, and avoidance of revenue surpluses).

395. A structural barrier to new airline entry is the degree to which certain airlines hold long-term leases of gates, counter space, and even entire terminal facilities, which give the incumbent carriers considerable leverage in negotiating to rent unused gates and other facilities to potential rivals. In 2003, 89% of the domestic gates at 30 U.S. large-hub airports were leased to airlines under either exclusive or preferential arrangements, and 48% were leased under exclusive use terms. *See* Press Release, Airports Council International/North America, Highlights of the 2003 General Information Survey (2003) (noting, however, that international gates tend to be largely 'common use' since flights are less frequent and sharing gates is not problematic). Majority-in-interest clauses in airport leases grant incumbent tenant airlines a right of veto over new capital improvements. *See* Gail F. Butler & Martin R. Keller, *Airports and Airlines: Analysis of a Symbiotic, Love-Hate Relationship, in* THE HANDBOOK OF AIRLINE ECONOMICS, *supra* note 372, at 87. Under so-called 'residual use and lease agreements,' signatory airlines agree to assume the financial risk of running an airport, assuring that the airport will break even by paying fees that

and runway slots.[396] While privatization has lessened the public stake in some airports in both the United States and EU,[397] there remains a systemic incongruity between the lowering of barriers for market entry and increased competition on the one hand, and a scarcity of access at many airports to take-off and landing slots, as well as terminal apron and gate space, on the other.[398]

As with CRS, governments in both model jurisdictions have sought a regulatory solution to this dilemma of scarcity. The United States adopted so-called 'high density' rules for a few chronically congested airports, and slots at these airports could be freely bought and sold among carriers, supplemented by a rudimentary allocation system that attempted to capture surrendered slots for new

---

generate revenues equal to the remaining ('residual') costs of operations once all (or a specified percentage of) non-airline sources of revenue have been taken into account. In 1998, 84% of U.S. residual use and lease agreements had a majority-in-interest clause, with an average length at large-hub airports of 28 years. The potential for disapproving or delaying projects that would benefit new entrants is obvious. But majority-in-interest carriers are legally barred from exercising veto rights over projects financed through U.S. federally-mandated 'passenger facility charges.' *See* FAA/OST, *Airport Business Practices and Their Impact on Airline Competition*, at 7-8, Task Force Study (Oct. 1999).

396. The U.S. Federal Aviation Administration, in its Federal Aviation Regulations, § 93.213(a)(2), defines a slot to mean 'the operational authority to conduct one [Instrument Flight Rules] landing or take-off operation each day during a specific hour or 30-minute period at one of the High Density Traffic Airports.' On the meaning of 'High Density Traffic Airports,' *see infra* note 399. The Federal Trade Commission, in comments before the FAA in 1984, defined a slot more generically as the 'right to use the navigable airspace for a take-off or landing at a particular airport during a particular hour of the day.' Comments of the Bureau of Economics, Competition, and Consumer Protection of the Federal Trade Commission Before the FAA, Dkt. No. 24,110 (Aug. 3, 1984), at 2 n.1. Thus, a carrier possessing all or a large percentage of slots at a constrained (*i.e.*, 'high density') airport may have market power. *See* David Starkie, *The Economics of Secondary Markets for Airport Slots*, in A Market in Airport Slots 51, 66 (Keith Boyfield ed., 2003).

397. Airport privatization efforts have been slow to develop in the United States, a notable exception being Chicago's recent decision to pursue a leasing of Midway Airport. *See* Robert Poole, Reason Foundation Commentary, *Will Midway Lease Re-Start U.S. Airport Privatization?: Like Toll Roads, Other Countries Are Far Ahead of the U.S. in Airport Privatization*, Public Works Financing, Jan. 2007. Poole compares the United States unfavorably with other countries' airport privatizations – beginning with Margaret Thatcher's disposal of the British Airports Authority in 1987. *See id.* (calculating that over 100 world airports have been privatized in the intervening two decades, including Brussels, Copenhagen, Frankfurt, Hamburg, Mexico City, Rome, Sydney and, imminently, Hong Kong and Tokyo). Macquarie has even created a privatized airports mutual fund for global investors. *See id.* Under the statutory 1996 Airport Privatization Pilot Program, up to five U.S. airports could apply to be leased into private control without being required to repay prior federal grants, provided the Federal Aviation Administration and 65% of the user airlines concurred. *See* Ben Wear & Kate Alexander, *City Ponders Leasing Airport*, Austin American-Statesman, Feb. 21, 2007, at A1. According to Poole, the 65% airline approval threshold was responsible for the lack of privatizations in the succeeding 10 years but now, as U.S. carriers have become more risk-averse and less willing to operate as s 'joint venturers' with airports, the Pilot Program may be reactivated. *See* Poole, *supra*.

398. *See* van Miert, *European Air Transport Policy*, *supra* note 275, at 5. Apron capacity is the available parking space for aircraft. *See id.* at 4.

entrants.[399] Persistent delays and overscheduling have prompted a need for more regulation to limit operations, even if the precise nomenclature of 'high density' is no longer used when restrictions are restored.[400] The EU, where airport congestion is a much more endemic challenge, opted for a more invasive administrative procedure, which authorizes Member States themselves to microregulate slot allocation through airport coordinators at congested airports and using lotteries, preset quotas for new entrant applicants, and some preservation of the vested rights of incumbent carriers.[401]

---

399. *See infra* Chapter 4, Part IV(B). The High Density Rules originally placed limits on hourly operations at five congested U.S. airports – Chicago O'Hare, LaGuardia, John F. Kennedy International, Newark International, and Washington Reagan. Outside these Rules (or their successors, *see infra* in this note), there is no regulatory authority that allocates specific slots to air carriers at U.S. airports and 'slot allocation' is largely a question of airplanes lining up to land or take off. *See* EUROPEAN COMMISSION, STUDY ON THE IMPACT OF THE INTRODUCTION OF SECONDARY TRADING AT COMMUNITY AIRPORTS, VOLUME I ch. 5, at 8 (2006) [hereinafter EUROPEAN COMMISSION, SLOT TRADING STUDY I]. Moreover, the U.S. Federal Aviation Administration was legislatively charged to study moderation or elimination of the Rules whenever possible, assertedly on the basis of improvements in technology and air traffic control procedures. *See* 49 U.S.C.A. § 41714(e) (West 2008). Thus, after FAA proceedings, the Rules were statutorily terminated for O'Hare after Jul. 1, 2002, and for LaGuardia and JFK after Jan. 1, 2007. 49 U.S.C.A. § 41715 (West 2008). Nonetheless, the FAA retains a general power to prescribe appropriate operations to limit congestion and delay. In May 2008, in a bold effort to exercise this authority, the Bush Administration proposed to auction slots at Kennedy and Newark airports in an effort to reduce congestion over the New York region. *See* Matthew L. Wald, *U.S. Plans Steps to Ease Congestion at Airports*, N.Y. TIMES, May 17, 2008, at B1. While the auction plans were tweaked for each hub, with airlines being allowed to keep up to 20 daily slots with a percentage of the remainder to be put up for bid, both plans would ultimately take slots away from larger carriers for potential redistribution to others. Political opposition stalled the plan, and the U.S. airlines' primary trade organization, the Air Transport Association, filed suit to permanently stop FAA implementation, arguing that the Administration lacks statutory authority to mandate the auctions. *See* Press Release, ATA, ATA Files Lawsuit Against Federal Aviation Administration (Aug. 11, 2008). In December 2008, pursuant to an order from the U.S. Court of Appeals for the D.C. Circuit, the FAA announced that it was suspending the auction until final resolution by the court. *See* Press Release, U.S. FAA, New York Airports Slot Auction (Dec. 9, 2008).
400. *See* § 41715(b); *see also* U.S. DOT & Federal Aviation Administration [FAA], 14 C.F.R. Part 93, Congestion and Delay Reduction at Chicago O'Hare International Airport, Final Rule, 71 Fed. Reg. 51,382 (Aug. 20, 2006); *see also* U.S. DOT & FAA, 14 C.F.R. Part 93, Congestion Management Rule for LaGuardia Airport, Proposed Rule, 71 Fed. Reg. 51,360 (Aug. 29, 2006). The potential severity of these issues is demonstrated by a general power conferred on the FAA in 2003 to host 'scheduling reduction meetings' at a severely congested airport (which may not necessarily be one of the 'high density' group of airports). *See* 49 U.S.C.A. § 41722 (West 2008).
401. *See infra* Chapter 5, Part III(C). Notably, despite these regulatory artifacts, the European Union tolerates a 'gray market' in slot trading at congested hub airports. *See* EUROPEAN COMMISSION, SLOT TRADING STUDY I, *supra* note 399, ch. 5, at 7. The European Commission has come to accept some commercial slot trading as consistent with EC law. *See* Press Release, Europa, Airport Slot Allocation: The Commission Clarifies Existing Rules, IP/08/672 (Apr. 2008).

Both regulatory approaches have serious drawbacks. One of the challenges for regulators in the United States is that, precisely because they created a synthetic marketplace at critical national airports, slot prices became prohibitively expensive for new entrants. A peak period slot in a major U.S. slot-managed airport has an estimated market value of more than three-quarters of a million dollars.[402] EC regulators, fearing (with some justification) that premium slot prices would actually diminish new competition, allowed governments to be more involved in the mechanics of allocation 'even if this seems to be contrary to the deregulation process.'[403]

The EC solution illustrates a major obstacle to integration of national commercial (and, indeed, navigational) airspaces, one which has already proven troublesome to the EC deregulation enterprise. All Member States have agreed to a multilateral exchange of the nine freedoms of the air:[404] the authenticity of the exchange is compromised, however, if a Member State is able to resist operations by carriers from other Member States into and out of its airspace on grounds of infrastructural shortcomings, while the resisting State's own airlines are freely operating to and from other States that have invested in airport facilities.[405] As long as these infrastructural discrepancies exist, it will be difficult to propose that governments ought not, as a matter of policy, intervene to limit slot and gate access at heavily-trafficked airports.[406] Neither can a multilateral reform proposal ignore the dangers of a 'safeguard' system, built into the EC slot allocation regime in order to accommodate serious infrastructural inadequacy, but which governments may be tempted to use pretextually to limit competition from foreign carriers.[407]

---

402. Bankruptcy appraisals can give a sense of how slots are valued in the marketplace. For example, US Airways controls 250 slots at LaGuardia and 334 at Washington Reagan. An appraiser in the US Airways' 2004 bankruptcy assigned a collective value to these slot treasuries of $462.2 million. That calculation would yield a per-slot price of approximately $800,000. *See* Dan Fitzpatrick, *U.S. Airways' parts may hold most value*, PITTSBURGH POST-GAZETTE, Sept. 16, 2004. On the question of the 'property' status of slots, *see infra* Chapter 4, Part IV(B).

403. Van Miert, *European Air Transport Policy*, *supra* note 275, at 5. *But see infra* Chapter 5, Part III(C) (indicating that the European Commission is rethinking its cautious attitude to creating a regulated marketplace for slot trading).

404. *See infra* Chapter 5, Part II.

405. Thus, principles of 'transparency, neutrality, and non-discrimination' become critical to the operation of slot allocation systems in an open market. *See* EUROPEAN COMMISSION, STUDY ON THE IMPACT OF THE INTRODUCTION OF SECONDARY TRADING AT COMMUNITY AIRPORTS, VOL. II, appendix 17, sec. 5 (2006); *see also* NERA ECONOMIC CONSULTING, STUDY TO ASSESS THE EFFECTS OF DIFFERENT SLOT ALLOCATION SCHEMES 109 (2004) (concluding that the use of market mechanisms to allocate slots would greatly enhance the effectiveness of other market liberalization measures such as a transatlantic open aviation area).

406. *See generally* 1995 Policy Statement, *supra* note 137, at 4.

407. *See infra* Chapter 5, Part III(C).

VIII   THE LATE-MODEL CHICAGO SYSTEM: STRATEGIC
              ALLIANCES AND CODE-SHARING

A   ENTREPRENEURIAL CIRCUMVENTIONS OF THE NATIONALITY RULE

'Globalization' of the economic conditions of international air transport is an industry
watchword that manifestly lacks any secure foundation in international or municipal
law. The nationality rule in its pure form creates insuperable legal obstacles to transborder mergers and acquisitions and out-of-State subsidiary operations, while the
imperatives of bilateral diplomacy, including the cabotage exclusion, frustrate
commercial development of international route networks. Nevertheless, competition-minded airline managements, both of flag carriers and of privately-owned operators, have for at least a decade pursued strategies for cooperation and integration that
seek to loosen the grip of the legal restraints imposed by the Chicago system.

    Two of those industry innovations will be examined here, the construction of
transnational *non-merger* alliances of varying levels of collaborative magnitude,
and the related contrivance of code-sharing between U.S. and foreign carriers.[408]
While there has been a large degree of official toleration for these entrepreneurial
innovations, the U.S. administrative response to code-sharing demonstrates that
governments have also felt a need to reconcile them with the demands of Chicago-
style bilateral trade diplomacy.

B   GLOBAL MARKETING ALLIANCES

1   **Strategies for Alliance-Building**

The nationality rule, with its twin benchmarks of majority ownership and effective
control by citizens, implicitly prohibits conventional corporate mergers and acquisitions among airlines of different States.[409] Accordingly, the primary instrument

---

408. Code-shares between trunk carriers and their regional 'feeders' have existed in the United
     States since the 1960s, however. The first service was offered by US Airways (then Allegheny
     Airlines). *See* Disclosure of Code-Sharing Arrangements and Long-Term Wet Leases, 59 Fed.
     Reg. 40,836 (Aug. 10, 1994) (also noting existence of international code-shares 'at least since
     the early 1980s').
409. *But see* the structure of the Air France/KLM quasi-merger, which functions with full legality
     within the frame of the common nationality rules of the European Community, but had to be
     tailored to meet the exigencies of the Chicago nationality rule with respect to third countries.
     As of May 2005, eight U.S. airlines had established 108 arrangements to place their designator
     codes on services provided by 85 different foreign carriers, up from six U.S. airlines that had
     established 39 arrangements with 38 different foreign carriers in fiscal year 2000. *See* GAO,
     Aviation Safety: Oversight of Foreign Code-Share Safety Program Should be Strengthened, at
     7, GAO-05-930 (Aug. 2005) [hereinafter GAO, *Code-Share Safety*]. The majority of U.S.
     airlines' code-share arrangements are with European airlines. *See id.* at 8. Some arrangements
     embrace selected routes only, while others cover all routes served by the foreign partner. *See
     id.* at 7 n.9.

of transborder carrier cooperation is the so-called 'marketing alliance,' a many-faceted business vehicle that now exists among several U.S. and EU airline partners (as well as among airlines in most regional aviation markets).[410] An alliance can include almost any aspect of delivering service to passengers, from fairly rudimentary joint operations in ticketing and baggage handling or reciprocal participation in frequent flier programs to the most sophisticated network collaboration in code-sharing and scheduling operations at international hubs (the Star, oneworld, and SkyTeam global alliances, for example) and even (as with the original KLM/Northwest concept) the promotion of a global brand identity.[411]

---

410. The General Accounting Office and the U.S. Department of Transportation have had international alliances in their analytical sights since 1995. In that year, the GAO published a major study of the competitive impact of selected international alliances. *See* GAO, *International Aviation: Airline Alliances Produce Benefits, But Effect on Competition is Uncertain*, GAO/RCED-95-99 (Apr. 1995) [hereinafter GAO, *Airline Alliances*]. The GAO concluded generally that the larger and more integrated the alliance, the more the airline partners benefited in terms of revenue enhancement. *See id.* at 5. Consumers also gained from conveniences such as shorter layover times, but it was not possible to determine the short-term or long-term impact on competition and fares. *See id.* Enough anecdotal and statistical information from rival airlines existed, however, to indicate that the alliances in their early years poached business from competitors more than they stimulated new traffic through competition. *See id.* at 20; *but see* U.S. DOT, *International Aviation Developments (First Report): Global Deregulation Takes Off*, at 8 (Dec. 1999) [hereinafter U.S. DOT, *International Aviation Developments*] (suggesting that much if not most of the new traffic generated through the three biggest alliances from 1992 through 1998 'represents traffic that is new to the system'). This trend was confirmed in a follow-up DOT study. *See* U.S. DOT, *International Aviation Developments (Second Report):Transatlantic Deregulation: The Alliance Network Effect*, at 4-5 (Oct. 2000) [hereinafter U.S. DOT, *Second International Report*]. In 2004, returning to the alliance theme in the context of U.S./EC air transport negotiations, the agency concluded that open skies had facilitated the formation of more integrated U.S./EU international alliances, allowing the airlines to expand their networks and to provide competitive service for more passengers to more locations at cheaper fares. U.S. passengers, accordingly, pay less to reach most EU destinations, causing a significant increase in passenger traffic. *See* GAO, *Transatlantic Aviation: Effects of Easing Restrictions on U.S.-European Markets*, at 12, GAO-04-835 (Jul. 2004). The GAO, incidentally, had a less sanguine view of alliances in 2001 when it scrutinized the projected competitive impact of a mooted American Airlines/British Airways alliance in the North Atlantic air corridor. *See* GAO, *American Airlines/British Airways Alliance*, at 3, GAO-02-293R (Dec. 21, 2001) (noting that, without 'some regulatory remedy,' the alliance could dominate markets, and therefore exercise market power to raise fares and limit service, between major U.S. cities and London's two major international airports). Finally, DOT reports in 1999 and 2000 generally saw alliances as positive emanations of private initiative. *See* U.S. DOT, *First International Report, supra,* at 5 (arguing that economic realities, infrastructure constraints, restrictions in bilateral agreements, and the Chicago nationality rule have combined to make alliances the only practical way to build competitive global systems); U.S. DOT, *Second International Report, supra,* at 5 (predicting that the 'Alliance Network Effect' of transatlantic price reductions and traffic gains will play a 'key role' in the future economic and competitive environment for aviation).

411. Worldwide, as of Sept. 2007, there were close to 500 alliances among around 120 mainline passenger airlines. *See Airline Alliance Survey*, AIRLINE BUS., Sept. 21, 2007. The GAO's 1995 study ranked alliances by degree of network integration through code-sharing, although the greater that element of network linkage the greater will be the operating and marketing

Although 'cross-shareholdings' and mutual representation on boards of directors were originally thought helpful in anchoring a partnership,[412] the rigor of the
nationality rule has convinced carriers that there is no sound reason to buy minority
stakes in one another for any reason *other than* to deter a dissolution of a marketing
alliance.[413] As the partners develop separate relationships with airlines in other

integration that accompanies it. *See* GAO, *Airline Alliances, supra* note 410, at 15. The GAO's
ranking remains useful and applicable today. The agency described the KLM/Northwest and
Lufthansa/United relationships as 'strategic alliances' involving code-sharing on a vast
number of routes so as to strategically link the participants' flight networks. *Id.* at 6. Lesser
alliances would focus on regional or even point-to-point code-sharing. *See id.* at 15. DOT
policy does not require official approval for simple marketing arrangements (such as linking
frequent flier programs or sharing airport facilities). *See id.* at 12-13. *But see* 49 U.S.C.A.
§ 41720 (West 2008) (establishing filing requirements for, *inter alia*, significant code-share
initiatives between major air carriers within the domestic U.S. market); *see also infra* note 417
(discussing Delta/Northwest/Continental agreement).

412.   A rare example of representation by one carrier on another's board of directors was mentioned,
supra, note 199.

413.   Thus, examples of the sale or purchase of minority stakes now require looking outside the
model jurisdictions considered in this book. *See* Nicolas Ionides, *Garuda Looks for Strategic
Partner*, AIRLINE BUS., Jan. 1, 2007 (discussing Indonesian Government's hope to bring a
strategic equity partner into Garuda Indonesia in order to rescue the ailing national carrier;
the government would continue as the majority shareholder). *See also* Professor Dempsey's
classic reference, made in the early 1990s era of cross-national airline investments, to foreign
airlines' 'dumb equity,' invested despite suboptimal returns in order to achieve 'synergistic
revenue' from the U.S. partner's 'passenger feed.' Dempsey Submission to the Airline
Commission, *supra* note 144, at 89. In addition to the prominent collaboration of KLM and
Northwest, *see supra* note 199, airline alliances of note in recent years have included the
following: (i) *United Air Lines/Lufthansa.* In Jun. 1994, these giant carriers implemented a
marketing alliance that uses code-sharing to link their route networks. GAO, *Airline Alliances,
supra* note 410, at 24. Initially, Lufthansa code-shared on United's flights between Frankfurt
and 25 U.S. interior cities via two of United's hubs, Chicago O'Hare and Washington Dulles,
while United in turn code-shared on Lufthansa flights between Frankfurt and 30 European and
Middle Eastern cities. *See id.* A deepening of the parties' relationship, including the formal
establishment of their global Star Alliance, followed the signing of a new U.S./Germany open
skies agreement and the accompanying award of antitrust immunity to the alliance. In 2003,
the partners began 'Atlantic Plus,' a revenue-sharing program – costs are not shared – encompassing all transatlantic flights and feeder segments in transatlantic itineraries. The program
purportedly removes the desire of front-line personnel to push their own company's service.
See BTN Online Business Travel News, Special Report: *Airline Alliances – International
Airline Alliances: The Tango Continues*, Apr. 28, 2003. Lufthansa ruled out any direct financial assistance to United during the latter's recent bankruptcy. *See Lufthansa and United Seek
to Take Advantage of New Freedoms*, AIRLINE BUS., Feb. 1, 2003, at 9; *see also supra* note 278
(discussing grant of expanded antitrust immunity for Star Alliance); (ii) *American Airlines/
Canadian International Airlines.* In 1994, American invested $182 million to acquire 33% of
Canadian International Airlines' equity and two out of eight board seats as part of a
20-year agreement for American to provide services and training in planning, pricing, accounting, passenger services, and other areas. This alliance, too, won antitrust immunity in 1996,
following signature of the U.S./Canada open skies pact. When Air Canada acquired Canadian
in late 1999, it bought out American's equity stake. In 2000, the two former partners also
terminated their code-share agreement. *See* Extel Company News, *Canadian Airlines Terminated Their Code-Share Relationship With American Airlines* (May 19, 2000); (iii) *Delta*

continental systems, a 'network' feasibility arises in which some participants (usually smaller flag carriers) act as feeder carriers while the major players serve the long-haul intercontinental routes.[414]

In the United States in the early 1990s, second-tier airlines, notably US Airways and Northwest, adopted the tactic of trading a marketing alliance – with the marquee attraction of access to behind-gateway U.S. traffic using code-sharing[415] – in return for substantial equity investment by a foreign partner. As these kinds of equity-based alliances withered away,[416] larger carriers began to enter into extensive marketing alliances without the same precondition of investment transfers.[417]

Airlines/Swissair/Singapore Airlines. These carriers formed a tripartite arrangement in 1989, magisterially titled the 'Global Excellence Program,' whereby Swissair and Singapore Airlines invested $193 million and $180 million, respectively, in Delta; each received 5% of equity and Delta and Swissair entered into a code-sharing, marketing, and cargo handling agreement including sharing of terminal facilities at several airports. The Program dissolved in Nov. 1997, paving the way for Singapore in turn to join the Star Alliance; (iv) *Delta Airlines/ Swissair/Sabena/Austrian Airlines.* In late 1994, Delta, Swissair, and Austrian Airlines entered into an unusual 'trilateral' code-share and block-space agreement on Austrian Airlines' Washington/Geneva/Vienna service. *Delta Air Lines, Austrian and Swissair Sign Trilateral Code-share Agreement,* PR Newswire, Nov. 10, 1994. With the addition of Sabena, an integrated marketing and code-share alliance developed among the partners under the title 'Atlantic Excellence Alliance', which received U.S. antitrust immunity in 1996 following new U.S. open skies agreements with Switzerland, Belgium, and Austria. The Alliance ended in 1999 when Delta opted to enter a new global partnership with Air France – the new SkyTeam alliance. Austrian had already withdrawn to join the Star Alliance. Sabena linked up with American Airlines to create a new immunized transatlantic alliance that survived until Swissair and Sabena collapsed in the aftermath of the 9/11 attacks. *See* Simon Warburton, *Sabena Regrets End of Atlantic Excellence Pact,* AIR TRANSP. INTELLIGENCE, Dec. 14, 1999. Following the revival of Swissair (as 'Swiss') in 2001 and the merger of the revived company into the Lufthansa Group, Swiss became part of the Star Alliance. Jens Flottau, *Wishing on the Star,* AVIATION WK. & SPACE TECH., Apr. 10, 2006, at 38.; (v) *Air Canada/Continental Airlines.* Finally, in 1993 Air Canada invested $235 million in Continental in return for a 27.5% equity interest, six out of 18 board seats, and certain contractual arrangements for cooperation and synergies. In 2008, the two carriers entered into a code-sharing agreement in anticipation of Continental's announcement of its intention to join the Star Alliance (of which Air Canada is a member). John McRank, *Air Canada, Continental Sign Code-Sharing Deal,* REUTERS, Jul. 24, 2008.

414. Prior to the SkyTeam reconfiguration, for example, Northwest and KLM were thought likely to extend their evolving alliance by seeking an Asian partner to access traffic originating from beyond their gateway points. *See* Tae Hoon Oum et al., *Strategic Airline Policy in the Globalizing Airline Networks,* 32 TRANSP. J. 14, 17 (1993). Neither airline, in fact, has developed a strong Asian connection. Northwest has limited code-sharing with Korean Air and KLM has code-shares with China Southern and Malaysia Airlines. *See* AIRLINE BUS., *Alliance Survey, supra* note 411. The most artful practitioners of this form of 'synthetic globalization' are United Airlines and Lufthansa, leading an extensive global network of code-shares secured by extensive grants of U.S. antitrust immunity.

415. *See infra* in the main text.

416. *See supra* note 278.

417. The Lufthansa/United alliance was the most prominent example of the 1990s. *See supra* note 413. As previously observed, even during United Airlines' recent bankruptcy Lufthansa never considered a transfer of funds to its ailing partner. Since 1998, all of the major U.S. carriers at

The U.S. DOT, statutorily compelled to monitor the 'citizenship' profiles of U.S. airlines, has thus far detected no diminution of national U.S. control as a consequence of any of the marketing alliances that have emerged in the transatlantic corridor,[418] and granted sweeping antitrust immunity to the deeply-integrated KLM/Northwest combination.[419]

---

various times have also entered alliance 'reciprocity' agreements (principally involving code-sharing and frequent flier programs) with one or more of their peers. *See* 49 U.S.C.A. § 41720 (West 2008) (enacted in 2000, now requiring certain kinds of joint ventures among U.S. passenger airlines to be submitted to the DOT at least 30 days before implementation, but not expressly requiring DOT approval of such agreements). The very existence of these domestic agreements caused the DOT, in one recent proceeding, to echo Justice Department concerns about immunizing a global alliance that included two major U.S. airline competitors and could therefore have anticompetitive 'spillover' effects in the domestic market. *See supra* note 278 (discussing denial of immunity to the Delta-led SkyTeam alliance). Unlike those international alliances which have been blessed with U.S. antitrust immunity, domestic agreements are governed by the antitrust laws which prohibit agreements on fares, routes, and capacity. *See, e.g.*, Press Release, U.S. DOT, DOT Ends Review of Alliance Carriers' Agreement, DOT 26-03 (Mar. 31, 2003) (announcing approval of Delta/Northwest/Continental code-sharing and frequent flier reciprocity agreement, conditioned *inter alia* on surrender of specified gates at Boston Logan and New York LaGuardia airports and restriction of joint bids to corporations and travel agents, including a prohibition against making joint bids for domestic travel originating at a corporation or travel agency's headquarters city if the company has its principal place of business in a city where the alliance carriers' market share exceeds 50%). *See also* U.S. DOT, Termination of Review Under 49 U.S.C. 41720 of Delta/Northwest/Continental Agreements, 68 Fed. Reg. 16,854 (Apr. 7, 2003). A similar agreement between United Airlines and US Airways has also been implemented without DOT opposition. *See* U.S. DOT, Review Under 49 U.S.C. § 41720 of United/US Airways Agreements, 67 Fed. Reg. 62,846 (Oct. 8, 2002) (noting that the joint venture would not be the equivalent of a merger, and that each airline would independently establish fare and capacity levels in its city-pair markets). Two recent studies have concluded that domestic alliances can yield consumer benefits (lower fares). *See* Gustavo E. Bamberger, Dennis W. Carlton, & Lynette R. Neumann, *An Empirical Investigation of the Competitive Effects of Domestic Airline Alliances*, 47 J. L. & Econ. 195 (2004) (noting that average fares fell by about 5-7% and total traffic increased by 6% on affected city-pairs, in part because rivals responded to the increased competition); GAO, *Aviation Competition: Effects on Consumers from Domestic Airline Alliances Vary*, GAO/RCED-99-37 (Jan. 1999) (focusing on the original Northwest/Continental alliance). In mid-2008, United Airlines and Continental Airlines agreed to enter into an expansive marketing alliance set to take effect sometime in 2009. As part of the agreement, Continental will terminate its membership in SkyTeam in order to join United as a member of the Star Alliance. *See* Susan Carey, *UAL and Continental Pair, But Won't Merge*, Wall St. J., Jun. 20, 2008, at B1.

418. The Department did serve a warning notice on British Airways and USAir, however, that further capital tranches, which would have ratcheted up the U.K. carrier's stake in the U.S. carrier, would require ongoing surveillance of USAir's ownership structure and citizenship compliance. The DOT took umbrage at USAir's suggestion that 'deregulation has reduced [the DOT's] citizenship responsibilities to the *de minimis* level.' Various Applications of BA/USAir, *supra* note 173, at 14,139-141. BA announced in Jan. 1996 that it did not propose increasing its investment in its U.S. partner, *see Complaint of USAir Inc.*, para. 33, 96 Civ. 5724 (July 30, 1996) [hereinafter USAir Complaint]. For more information on the troubled story of this pioneering transnational partnership, *see supra* text accompanying note 249.

419. *See supra* note 199. For an interesting policy analysis of globalization through alliances, *see* Oum et al., *supra* note 414 (noting strong consumer bias in favor of large airlines with

2   KLM/Northwest and Its Progeny: The Immunity Artifice

The original KLM/Northwest 'Cooperation and Integration Agreement,' in fact, may have represented the ultimate strategic assault on the late-model Chicago system. In January 1993, brushing aside furious protests by Northwest's U.S. competitors, the U.S. DOT used its vestigial authority over intercarrier agreements between U.S. and foreign air carriers to grant a sweeping renewable five-year antitrust immunity to this agreement.[420] KLM and Northwest sought authority to integrate their services so completely that they would be operating 'as if they were a single carrier.'[421] Indeed, given this corporate presumptuousness, there was some merit in the argument of Delta Air Lines that the transaction was a *de facto* merger, rather than an ordinary business venture between two carriers, and therefore could not qualify for antitrust immunity because the DOT's merger immunity power had ended on January 1, 1989.[422]

The Department's benign response – that the two carriers 'would remain separate and independent corporations and would not be merged into one'[423] – might have been accurate as a matter of technical corporate law, but the anticipated degree of fusion of the parties' operational identities suggested that the agency was neglecting the teaching of its own 'substance over form' test for U.S. citizen control of U.S. carriers.[424] In *substance*, the parties contemplated total coordination of marketing and scheduling, shared revenues on joint

---

extensive international networks). The authors' discussion presumes that the existing system of 'synthetic alliances' will survive; thus, the authors define a 'global alliance network' as a 'global airline network formed by a group of affiliated airlines which offer seamless services to consumers through a joint use of computer reservations systems, through-fares and ticketing, automatic baggage transfer, coordinated flight schedules, code-sharing of flights, joint marketing, sharing of a frequent flier program, etc.' *Id.* at 15. The authors offer a choice of models for the new international alliances: one mega-carrier aligning with several junior 'feeder' partners, or an alliance among large senior partners, one from each continent, supported by regional feeder carriers. In whichever form, they predict the emergence of four to six of these global alliances. *See id.* at 18; *see also* DAWNA L. RHOADES, EVOLUTION OF INTERNATIONAL AVIATION: PHOENIX RISING 118 (2003) (observing that, 'by and large,' Oum's predictions on the shape of alliances are proving accurate).

420. The U.S. Secretary of Transportation, as will be seen, has inherited an old Civil Aeronautics Board power to privilege certain intercarrier agreements in international air transportation from the reach of the U.S. antitrust laws. *See* 49 U.S.C.A. § 41308 (West 2008). The exemption can only be awarded if certain public interest criteria are satisfied. *See* 49 U.S.C.A. § 41309 (West 2008). *See infra* Chapter 4, Part III(C).

421. Joint Application of KLM/Northwest for Antitrust Immunity, *supra* note 199, at 14,056. For an account of how the alliance unraveled from an equity-based transaction into a more conventional joint marketing arrangement, *see supra* note 199. Following the announcement of Northwest's plans to merge with Delta Air Lines in 2008, KLM – now in a quasi-merger relationship with Air France – has sought to deepen its relationship with both carriers on the transatlantic market as part of SkyTeam. *See infra* Chapter 4, Part III(C).

422. Delta did not mention, although it must have realized, that neither the CAB nor the DOT ever had authority to bless mergers in *international* air transportation: the federal rules on ownership and control would not allow a foreign air carrier to merge with a U.S. airline.

423. Joint Application of KLM/Northwest for Antitrust Immunity, *supra* note 199, at 14,063.

424. *See supra* text accompanying note 186.

services,[425] a unified travel agency commission program, and unified inventory management. Most significantly from an antitrust perspective, the grant of immunity would allow them literally to consult on and set prices on all shared routes, and even to compete jointly for corporate accounts using common pricing packages.[426] Moreover, the Department anticipated that the parties might foreseeably lodge a later request for approval of operation under a common name.[427]

The U.S. General Accounting Office, reporting on international aviation alliances in 1995, attached the label 'merger model' to the KLM/Northwest alignment, specifically to distinguish it from the (now-defunct) 'investor model' (BA/USAir) in which cooperative strategies were the recipient's cost for transfer of foreign carrier capital,[428] and the 'marketing agreement + code-sharing' model (Lufthansa/United) that describes most of the noninvestment alliances in the international air transport industry.[429] Since the GAO study, United and Lufthansa have ramped up their partnership to include revenue-sharing on the North Atlantic

---

425. Airlines that enter code-sharing alliances typically decide among themselves how to divide revenues earned on code-shared routes. A prorated formula, adopted at arm's length (absent antitrust immunity), will account for the miles each airline flies under the alliance and is necessary to avoid the risk that the parties are 'revenue-pooling' to compensate the weaker airline for a failure to achieve its internal capacity targets. *See* Christopher P. Wright, et al., *Dynamic Revenue Management in Airline Alliances* (Tuck School of Bus. Working Paper No. 2008-46, Feb. 11, 2008) (discussing a variety of revenue-sharing mechanisms including static proration – *i.e.*, predetermined shares – and more dynamic market-sensitive schemes such as 'free sale').

426. The DOT now refers to these and other enhanced forms of cooperation (such as joint purchasing of equipment) as 'second stage' commercial agreements, *i.e.*, agreements that transcend code-share and marketing agreements. They include revenue and benefit-sharing arrangements that create a greater risk of antitrust litigation and potential antitrust liability. *See* U.S. DOT, *Joint Application of The Austrian Group, British Midland Airways Limited, Deutsche Lufthansa AG, Polskie Linie Lotnicze S.A., Scandinavian Airlines System, Swiss International Air Lines Ltd., TAP Air Portugal, and United Air Lines, Inc., and of United Air Lines, Inc. and Air Canada, , under 49 U.S.C. §§ 41308 and 41309 for Approval of and Antitrust Immunity for Commercial Alliance Agreements*, Dkt. Nos. OST-2005-22922 and OST-96-1434, Show Cause Order (Dec. 19, 2006), at 17 [hereinafter U.S. DOT, *Star Alliance Show Cause Order 2006*].

427. Joint Application of KLM/Northwest for Antitrust Immunity, *supra* note 199, at 14,057. For more on franchising and branding, *see* U.S./EC Air Transport Agreement, *supra* note 21, annex 5 (stating that U.S. and EU airlines 'shall not be precluded from entering into franchise or branding agreements') & *supra* Part V(B) (discussing the licensing agreement between Virgin America and the U.K.-based Virgin Group).

428. *See* GAO, *Airline Alliances*, *supra* note 410, at 21; *see also U.S. Airlines Can Find Capital for Right Deal*, Reuters, Dec. 6, 2006 (charting the demise of foreign airline equity injections into U.S. airlines, attributed primarily to U.S. investment and control restrictions). Only one recent cross-national investment is notable, a $75 million investment by Canadian-based ACE Aviation Holdings in the merged US Airways/America West carrier in 2005. The investment was conditional on the merged carrier outsourcing its maintenance to an ACE-related entity, Air Canada Technical Services. The agreement included cooperative arrangements between Air Canada and the merged airline. *See* Press Release, Air Canada, ACE Aviation Announces Planned Investment in Merged US Airways-American West Carrier (May 19, 2003).

429. *See* GAO, *Airline Alliances*, *supra* note 410, at 23.

corridor and projected initiatives such as joint purchasing of aircraft,[430] a collaborative escalation that approaches the 'merger model.' The alliance between American Airlines and British Airways, denied antitrust immunity, remains a member of the genus 'marketing agreement + code-sharing.'

The DOT did scrutinize the competitive implications of allowing KLM and Northwest to merge their operations and identities, if not their corporate structures, but found that they were not significant competitors on most routes served by the alliance.[431] Paradoxically, therefore, antitrust immunity was granted precisely because the Department concluded that it was not needed.[432] (The DOT's competitive analysis of global alliances – which has scarcely altered in the course of three significant sets of immunity requests decided between 2002 and 2006 – will be critiqued in the treatment of U.S. airline merger policy in Chapter 4.)[433] Clearly, the intensity of integration between the two carriers, oriented toward *intentional* establishment of a single-brand identity, would normally have led to consummation of a formal legal merger in place of a joint venture or intercarrier agreement, and to rigorous screening under Department of Justice premerger clearance procedures.[434] The nationality predicate of the Chicago system, however, forecloses the structural stability, corporate synergies, and allocative efficiencies that a genuine merger would allow. Instead, the government decreed an entirely artificial bond between the parties through the grant of antitrust immunity, thereby creating the further paradox of seeking to enhance competition in the international airline market by risking potentially anticompetitive behavior (including price-fixing).[435]

---

430. *See supra* note 413.
431. *See infra* text accompanying Chapter 4, note 251.
432. KLM and Northwest believed that immunity *was* necessary, and would not have completed the transaction without it. (Price-setting alone would have raised competitive concerns.) A similar posture – a refusal to proceed without immunity – by applicant airlines has become routine in immunity proceedings. *See, e.g.,* U.S. DOT, *Star Alliance Show Cause Order 2006, supra* note 426, at 16.
433. *See infra* Chapter 4, Part III(C) (discussing applications by British Airways and American Airlines (begun in 2001), by two existing international alliances integrating into the new SkyTeam network (begun in 2004), and by incoming members of the Star Alliance for an expansion of immunity (begun in 2005)). The DOT initially denied immunity for the SkyTeam alliance, but had a change of heart in 2008 following the U.S./EC Air Transport Agreement.
434. But, in any event, the U.S. Department of Justice usually intervenes in proceedings related to DOT grants of antitrust immunity. *See, e.g.,* U.S. DOT, *Alitalia-Linee Aeree Italiane-S.p.A., Czech Airlines, Delta Air Lines, Inc., KLM Royal Dutch Airlines, Northwest Airlines, Inc., & Société Air France for Approval of and Antitrust Immunity for Alliance Agreements under 49 U.S.C. §§ 41308 and 41309,* Dkt. No. OST-2004-19214, Order to Show Cause (Dec. 22, 2005), at 15 [hereinafter U.S. DOT, *SkyTeam Order to Show Cause 2005*] (reminding the DOT that an important goal of airline deregulation was to make the airline industry subject to the same competitive and antitrust standards applicable to other industries, so that fears of antitrust litigation would be an insufficient basis for a grant of immunity).
435. Countering the enthusiasm of the DOT and GAO for the perceived consumer benefits of alliances, other voices have been raised in dissent. *See, e.g.,* U.S. DOT, *SkyTeam Order to Show Cause 2005, supra* note 434, at 12-13 (citing the conclusions of the Brattle Group that

DOT agency officials have in the past asserted that they have 'no policy' on the award of antitrust immunity, and that applications would be considered on a case-by-case basis.[436] Officials seemed inclined toward an industrial policy view that a few strong alliances (shielded, if need be, by an antitrust exemption) would create more competition in international aviation markets than a market comprising many weaker competitors. They insisted that interlining (which focuses on particular gate-to-gate markets) was simply not an effective competition-inducing device compared with the aggressive rivalry in thousands of city-to-city connections made possible through alliances. This reasoning has clearly continued to influence the disposition of recent immunity proceedings. And, to the extent that the DOT has provided any written expression of immunity policy, it tends to be couched more neutrally as supportive of open skies agreements with the homelands of foreign applicants, of procompetitive, proconsumer agreements, and, in rather circular terms, of 'our international aviation competition policy.'[437]

Nonetheless, a strategic policy *is* discernible from three significant immunity proceedings concluded between 2002 and 2006 that have each broadly conformed to the Department's KLM/Northwest analytical paradigm.[438] As will be seen, the DOT has underplayed the pervasive unease of the Department of Justice with the very idea of antitrust immunity.[439] Despite the DOT's professed ideological commitment to open skies and enhanced competition, its apparent willingness to prioritize liberalized open skies relationships over specific competitive concerns arguably had the further paradoxical consequence (initially, at any rate) of tending to *diminish* competition between the United States and the signatory countries.[440] In fact, antitrust immunity became such a prized attribute of large code-share alliances (even with little empirical quantification of the 'added value' that immunity offers a strong code-share network)[441] that other governments conditioned

---

immunized alliances have exercised market power – including raising rivals' interlining costs – to maintain higher fares, evidenced by fare increases in transatlantic open skies markets that have not been reflected in non-open skies markets).

436. As expressed in interviews with the author.
437. U.S. DOT, *SkyTeam Order to Show Cause 2005*, *supra* note 434, at 3.
438. *See supra* in the main text.
439. *See* U.S. Transportation Research Board [TRB], *Effects of Airline Alliances and Partnerships on Competition*, *in* ENTRY AND COMPETITION IN THE U.S. AIRLINE INDUSTRY, *supra* note 151, at 147 (noting that the Department of Justice, as party to the public review of carrier requests for antitrust immunity, has emphasized the potential adverse effects on travelers in mainline, gateway markets where the partner airlines had been rivals).
440. *See infra* Chapter 4, Part III(C). *See* 1995 Aviation Hearings, *supra* note 83, at 44 (statement of Kenneth M. Mead, Director, Transportation Issues, Resources, Community and Economic Development, GAO) (noting dissenting view that 'it does not make sense' to remove U.S. antitrust protection of consumers in the hope of increasing competition).
441. In fact, it was the inability of the SkyTeam members to articulate this 'added value' that most clearly doomed their quest for immunity in 2004. *See* U.S. DOT, *SkyTeam Order to Show Cause 2005*, *supra* note 434, at 34 (finding that the applicants had not demonstrated the benefits of immunity – especially for the public – beyond those made possible by arm's-length code-sharing or other lawful forms of collaboration, and had provided 'little information' about implementation of immunity).

their consent to open skies on immunization for partnerships involving their home carriers.[442]

But the DOT's relentless logic of trading immunity for open skies has also had recent strategic success, despite the competitive compromises that clearly have been made. In the final round of U.S./EC negotiations, one of the trump cards credibly played by the U.S. negotiators – merely through a closing codicil in a speech by U.S. Under Secretary of Transportation for Policy Jeffrey N. Shane – was that the DOT might move to rescind all transatlantic immunities in the absence of a comprehensive open skies settlement.[443]

The European Commission, meanwhile, affected early on to have taken a similarly 'casuistic' approach to the whole alliance phenomenon, treating each application 'within the whole framework of discussions on competition rules and antitrust questions.'[444] But in fact EC competition review of these alliances has been permissive, a reflex of an underlying industrial policy that has encouraged European flag carriers (at least while the Chicago system persists) to pursue global partnerships.[445] There was some surprise in 1996 – in the aftermath of the announcement of the first proposed British Airways/American Airlines joint venture[446] – when the Commission initiated a retroactive antitrust investigation of all U.S./EU carrier alliances.[447] Nonetheless, after several years of apparent

---

442. As evidenced, for example, by the German Government's position in 1996. *See* Press Release, U.S. Department of Transportation, DOT News, DOT 45-96 (Feb. 29, 1996).

443. Jeffrey N. Shane, Under Secretary for Policy, U.S. Department of Transportation, Remarks to the International Aviation Club, Washington, D.C., at 5 (Sept. 12, 2006). For a proposal favoring a similarly strong gambit with respect to the Chicago nationality rule, *see supra* Part V(B).

444. EUROPEAN COMMISSION, PANORAMA OF EU INDUSTRY '94 8 (1994). Until 2003, in fact, the Commission lacked formal enforcement powers to rule on air transport between the EU and third countries. Instead, it applied general Community competition law and its power to have Member States put an end to infringements of EC law. *See* Press Release, Europa, Commission Closes Probe into KLM/Northwest and Lufthansa/SAS/United Airlines Transatlantic Air Alliances, Press Release, IP/02/1569 (Oct. 29, 2002) [hereinafter Press Release, Alliances]; *see infra* Chapter 5, Part II(D). *See* Neelie Kroes, European Commissioner for Competition Policy, *Competition in the Aviation Sector: The European Commission's Approach*, Address to the Conference Celebrating the 20th Anniversary of the International Institute of Air and Space Law, Leiden, Speech/06/247 (Apr. 24, 2006) (indicating the Commission's 'generally positive attitude' to industry restructuring which enhances efficiency and competitiveness).

445. The European Commission has recently emphasized its 'broadly positive approach' to airline alliances (and mergers) in order to allow European carriers to compete effectively on a global level. *See* European Commission, *Competition: Commission Confirms Sending Statement of Objections to Members of SkyTeam Global Airline Alliance*, Memo/06/243 (Jun. 19, 2006) [hereinafter European Commission, *Confirmation of Objections*]. *See also* Kroes, *supra* note 342 (suggesting that EC policy encourages European airline competitors to become 'global winners,' while (perhaps secondarily, the speech appears to suggest) ensuring consumer welfare).

446. *See supra* note 410.

447. The Commission was unusually forthright in its press statement on the investigation, offering a preliminary view that 'these agreements will substantially restrict competition on the routes

inactivity, the Commission either closed its investigations without further challenge[448] or reached amicable agreements with the alliance partners to improve the competitive conditions affecting specific city-pairs.[449]

C   CODE-SHARING AS 'PSEUDO-CABOTAGE'

1   A Code-Share Taxonomy

The cornerstone of most airline alliances, as the prior discussion has revealed, is also the most notorious marketing device in the international air transport market, namely, code-sharing.[450] Indeed, code-sharing usually, although not invariably, accompanies a wider marketing partnership that combines advertising, ticketing, and baggage handling operations on the 'shared' routes.[451] The two participating airlines list their separate connecting flights in CRS and on e-tickets under a single two-letter code identifier,[452] as though the same carrier were providing the entire flight[453]

---

between the United States and Europe, as well as on some intra-[Union] routes.' European Commission, *Airline Agreements*, Background File for the Press, at 3 (Jul. 3, 1996) (copy on file with the Library of the EU Delegation, Washington D.C.) (mentioning the following target 'cooperation agreements': Lufthansa and United, SAS and United, British Airways and American Airlines (pending), Delta with Swissair, Sabena, and Austrian Airlines, KLM and Northwest, and British Airways and USAir).

448. For example, with respect to the KLM/Northwest alliance the Commission concluded that. although the parties had very high market shares on the Amsterdam/Detroit and Amsterdam/ Minneapolis St. Paul routes, the alliance would face competition from substitutable indirect services. *See* Press Release, Alliances, *supra* note 444.

449. *See id. But see* the Commission's somewhat stricter scrutiny of the recent SkyTeam alliance, which foundered initially in the United States. *See* European Commission, *Confirmation of Objections, supra* note 445 (broadly supporting the alliance while identifying a number of routes on which the alliance may have negative competitive effects). For further treatment of EC enforcement policy on alliances, *see infra* Chapter 5, Part III(B).

450. Code-sharing has a poor image in the popular media. *See, e.g.*, Linda Burbank, *Terminal case of confusion*, USA TODAY, Aug. 18, 2006, at 8D (presenting a case study of a passenger confounded by code-sharing practices between US Airways and United Express, and noting that '[c]onsumer advocates have long criticized code-sharing as confusing for customers, who buy tickets from one airline only to discover they're flying another').

451. *See* GAO, *Airline Competition, supra* note 9, at 35. Code-sharing, in fact, is an intensification of the long-established practice of interlining, by which airlines mutually accept each other's passenger tickets, baggage checks, and cargo waybills on multiple connections. *See* GAO, *Airline Alliances, supra* note 410, at 12-13.

452. The International Air Transport Association assigns air designator codes to individual airlines and these codes are used in reservations, schedules, and ticketing. *See id.* at 13. For a listing of all IATA airline codes, *see* Airport City Codes Homepage, <www.airportcitycodes.com/ airlinescodes.html>.

453. 95% of U.S. airline tickets issued today are electronic (and typically include a printable itinerary), but only 70% of tickets issued worldwide. E-tickets and itineraries tend to clearly show the operating airline. *See infra* note 499 (stating the applicable government regulations). Paper tickets have caused problems for passengers because of lack of specificity as to the operating as opposed to the selling carrier. *See* James Gilden, *The Code-Share: When Your*

(incidentally elevating their profile in typical CRS displays that list all direct nonstop flights and other direct flights before connecting flights[454]). Importantly, however, participating airlines are not combining to offer a single service: on the contrary, the code-share is simply a device to allow each airline to *pretend* that it is offering an integrated service that is in fact partly operated by its partner.[455]

Airline's Not Your Airline, CHI. TRIB. ONLINE ED., Feb. 11, 2007. For a recent discussion of the growing number of U.S. carriers placing their codes on flights operated by foreign carriers, *see* GAO, *Code-Share Safety*, *supra* note 409, at 7.

454. Thus, a flight jointly operated by two airlines can be displayed on the screen near flights offered by a single airline for the same pair of cities, making the jointly operated flight easier for travel agents to find. GAO, *Airline Competition*, *supra* note 9, at 34. Code-sharing in international air transport is fundamentally different from its most common domestic (U.S.) equivalent, where a regional 'commuter' airline commits to an exclusive feeder relationship with a single major airline (in many cases, the feeder carrier is also owned by the major). Since 1998, also, all of the major U.S. carriers have also entered domestic code-share arrangements with one or more of their peers. *See supra* note 417; *see also* U.S. TRB, *supra* note 439, at 135. In its 1999 study of the U.S. airline industry, the U.S. Transportation Research Board considered that, in contrast to airlines in a typical 'commuter' code-share arrangement, *international* code-sharing arrangements, precisely because many of them involve airlines that compete with each other in the same gateway-to-gateway markets, may cause a decline in rivalry on overlapping routes. *See id.* at 136-37.

455. '[E]ach airline partner is able to market the flight as its own product.' GAO, *Airline Alliances*, *supra* note 410, at 39. Current practice also recognizes two variants of the code-sharing principle, wet-lease agreements ('renting' another airline's aircraft and crew) and 'block-space' agreements. Under the latter, one airline provides another with a certain number of seats on flight segments that the second airline does not operate. The second airline purchases these seats – and therefore bears the economic risk – and then independently markets and sells the 'space' under its own two-letter designator code. In Feb. 1998, Continental Airlines and Virgin Atlantic Airways began a code-sharing agreement in the form of a mutual block-space arrangement. *See Virgin Atlantic Airways and Continental Airlines Commence Code-share Flights*, BUS. WIRE, Jan. 30, 1998. In 2004, following evolving industry practice, Continental converted its blocked-space deal into a 'free sell' code-share operation, where the marketing carrier sells seats on the operating carrier's flights from the operating carrier's inventory, but takes no inventory risk. *See* Continental Airlines, 10-K Filing (2004), <www.continental.com/web/en-US/content/company/investor/docs/continental_10k_2004.pdf>. Until 1997, Virgin had a similar arrangement with Delta Air Lines under which Delta was authorized to buy seats on Virgin's nonstop services from its U.S. gateways to London Heathrow, an airport which Delta was not designated to serve under Bermuda II. Virgin obtained no new access to U.S. routes; it benefited solely from additional revenues it received from services it already operated. As this arrangement requires, Delta carried the risk of any unsold seats. *See* U.S. DOT, *Joint Application of Delta Air Lines, Inc. and Virgin Atlantic Airways, Ltd., for an Exemption under 49 U.S.C. § 40109 and for a Statement of Authorization under 14 C.F.R. Part 212 to Engage in Code-share and Blocked-Space Operations (United States/London)*, Dkt. No. 95-2-28, Order No. 95-2-28 (Feb. 10, 1985) (based on Delta's London Heathrow access, finding public benefit from enhanced inter-gateway and intra-gateway competition for U.S. passengers traveling to London). *See* Delta's advertising campaign for its London service, headlined 'Delta & Virgin Atlantic to Heathrow/Think of it as Delta Service with a British Accent,' in which the copy underscored the paradox of code-sharing arrangements: 'Delta Air Lines offers daily non-stops to Heathrow, operated by Virgin Atlantic Airways, a Delta Worldwide Partner.' N.Y. TIMES MAGAZINE, Feb. 25, 1996, at 33. For discussion of the extra-bilateral provenance of the Delta/Virgin authority, *see* 1995 Aviation Hearings, *supra* note 83, at 65 & 171. (Delta's

According to DOT aviation officials, U.S. agency practice recognizes two principal types of code-sharing authority.[456] The first type is linked exclusively to international services and simply combines each carrier's existing international route authority. Consequently, it involves no access to cabotage routes and is readily conceded under bilateral agreements. British Airways, for example, might advertise a London/Cancún service under its own airline code, even though the service requires a Miami connection that involves changing to a Miami/Cancún segment operated by the BA U.S. carrier-partner, American Airlines. This coding device makes use of the fact that U.S. and U.K. carriers possess unlimited 'blind sector' rights (*i.e.*, non-traffic beyond rights) from each other's territory.[457] In effect, the BA Cancún service combines a preexisting privilege (to fly from Miami to Cancún, without picking up new passengers in Miami) with a code-share. Similarly, United Airlines can place its code on service from Chicago to Amsterdam and Brussels, connecting with bmi's London operations to these cities.[458] These assorted code-shares allow airlines to connect traffic to and from foreign cities, to which they do not fly themselves, with their own flights. The code-share permits a U.S. airline, for example, to create a commercial impression that it is offering online service to destinations that would otherwise be uneconomical to serve with its own aircraft and crew.[459] This practice is also a means by which to circumvent some of the route access restrictions that pepper non-open skies bilateral agreements.[460]

President, Ronald W. Allen, described the arrangement as a 'commercial response to an untenable regulatory situation.') *Id*. at 65.

456. The U.S. Department of Transportation regulates code-share and long-term wet-lease arrangements under Parts 207 (for U.S. carriers) and 212 (for foreign carriers) of its Economic Regulations. *See* 14 C.F.R. §§ 207 & 212 (West 2008). Since 1987, the DOT has required code-sharing arrangements between U.S. and foreign carriers to be filed for approval. *See* GAO, *Airline Alliances, supra* note 410, at 13. (A special statutory waiting period – with approval not expressly required – applies to domestic code-sharing among major carriers.) The U.S. Air Carrier Licensing Division of the DOT maintains a useful and extensive (though unofficial) code-share list online at <http://ostpxweb.dot.gov/aviation/X-40%20Role_files/coderpt.pdf>.

457. *See supra* note 29. As already seen, the United Kingdom might also negotiate separate fifth freedom rights between Miami and Cancún, combining traffic rights under its U.S. and Mexico bilaterals that would enable British Airways to bypass the American Airlines code-share segment if it saw an economic opportunity in doing so.

458. As seen, *supra* Chapter 2, Part IV. EC negotiators were unable to treat all such intra-Union flights as 'cabotage' in the negotiations with the United States that led to the 2007 U.S./EC Air Transport Agreement.

459. *See* GAO, *Airline Alliances, supra* note 410, at 12. Northwest's alliance with KLM, for example, has allowed Northwest to market services to around 94 cities in Europe, Africa, the Middle East, and India, when it actually flies to only eight of those cities using its own metal. *See* Northwest Airlines, Alliances ('Northwest Airlines Global Alliance Partners'), <www.nwa.com/corpinfo/allia/>. Thus, Northwest lists KLM's flights ex-Amsterdam to 94 beyond cities as its own and connects these flights with Northwest's flights between the United States and Amsterdam (as well as with KLM-operated U.S.-Amsterdam flights that carry the Northwest code). *See id.* Northwest can thus more effectively attract passengers who wish to travel between the 94 cities and the United States than through use of a standard interline agreement. *Id.*

460. GAO, *Airline Alliances, supra* note 410, at 12. Under current U.S. open skies agreements, U.S. carriers enjoy unlimited 'starburst' code-share privileges to all third-country points beyond the bilateral partner's territory. As with ordinary fifth freedom privileges, however, there is no

The second type of code-share authority, however, clearly implicates the cabotage doctrine because it allows *internal* U.S. points to be connected to a foreign carrier's international system and thereby potentially provides feeder traffic to the foreign carrier for its long-haul services.[461] As with the first type, the foreign carrier must have the economic authority *independently of the code-share* to serve the entire code-shared itinerary (for example, through the use of 'coterminal' rights – or through the open routing provisions of an open skies agreement[462]). This is a sensible restriction, since both carriers to a code-share will be applying their respective codes to the service as if they were actually performing the service with their own aircraft. The U.S. DOT can grant any additional economic authority that a carrier needs to close the code-sharing deal.[463]

The most generous code-share accommodation of the second type, far surpassing economic authority based solely on coterminal rights and which has become standard fare for open skies agreements, was originally made to BA as a result of the 1991 Heathrow succession negotiations.[464] The British carrier was

---

assurance that the third countries concerned – influenced by prevailing aeropolitical considerations – will concede the application of the code-share to inbound or outbound services. *See,* for example, the objection lodged by American Airlines to granting of foreign air carrier permit to Virgin Nigeria Airways until the Nigerian Government approved an American Airlines code-share on British Airways flights between London Heathrow and Lagos (in alleged violation of the U.S.-Nigeria open skies agreement). *See* U.S. DOT, *Application of Virgin Nigeria Airways Limited for a Foreign Air Carrier Permit Under 49 U.S.C. § 41301,* Dkt. No. OST-2005-23461, Answer of American Airlines (Jan. 6, 2006).

461. Similarly, other countries may grant this 'quasi'-cabotage privilege to U.S. carriers. United Airlines, for example, puts its code on All Nippon Airways flights to three interior Japanese cities (Fukuoka, Sapporo, and Sendai) that connect to United's transpacific operations at Nagoya. *See* Darren Shannon, *ANA, United Seek Limited Code-Share Expansion,* AIR TRANSP. INTELLIGENCE, Feb. 9, 2005.

462. *See supra* Chapter 1, Part II(C) for a brief discussion of these provisions.

463. *See* BRIAN F. HAVEL, IN SEARCH OF OPEN SKIES 112, n. 400 (1997) (indicating how open skies agreements expand foreign carrier authority – and consequently code-share privileges – to embrace all U.S. points). Under its Economic Regulations, the U.S. Department of Transportation will normally issue a Statement of Authorization to the extent consistent with the applicant's underlying economic authority, if the proposed arrangement is 'in the public interest.' In determining the public interest, the DOT considers, among other things, the extent to which the authority requested is consistent with the applicable bilateral aviation agreement and the benefits to U.S. carriers, passengers, and shippers under the proposed arrangement. *See generally* U.S. DOT, *Joint Application of American Airlines, Inc. and British Airways plc for Statements of Authorization under 14 C.F.R. Part 212 to Conduct Reciprocal Code-Sharing,* Dkt. No. OST-2002-13861, Final Order (May 30, 2003) (holding that opponents of code-sharing must show 'compelling competitive reasons' to disapprove a request, but that here, in the absence of an associated request for antitrust immunity, such a showing had not been made) [hereinafter U.S. DOT, *BA/AA Final Order 2003*]. Bilateral restrictions on third-country code-share services, however, had earlier caused the DOT to deny code-share approval for particular international routes requested by British Airways and American Airlines. *See* U.S. DOT, *U.S.-UK Alliance Case,* Dkt. No. OST-2001-11029, Order to Show Cause (Jan. 25, 2002) (for example, denying approval for the U.S.-Istanbul and U.S.-Cairo markets).

464. Memorandum of Consultations and Draft Exchange of Notes concerning Modifications to the U.S./U.K. Air Services Agreement, *reprinted in* [Jan. 2007] Av. L. Rep. (CCH) ¶ 26,540j, at 23,293 [hereinafter 1991 U.S./U.K. Agreement]. Under this amendment to Bermuda II by

granted a (then unique) privilege to apply its code to and from all of its authorized U.S. gateways in combination with *any* internal points served by the then-USAir. As it operates at the time of writing (in the oneworld alliance with American Airlines), this form of code-sharing enables BA, for example, to advertise a London (Gatwick)/Austin, Texas service even though the actual BA-operated flight terminates at Dallas-Fort Worth and American Airlines provides the service (on a separate aircraft) between its hub at Dallas-Fort Worth and Austin.[465] There is no one-on-one restriction for connections beyond Dallas: BA has developed a so-called 'starburst' route pattern by putting its code on almost *all* American Airlines services operating through Dallas (in effect, making them 'feed' flights) that will ultimately terminate at London.[466] Because open skies agreements award foreign carriers direct third and fourth freedom access at all U.S. airports, these carriers already have the requisite authority, *independently of code-sharing*, to implement a BA-style 'starburst' network in association with their U.S. partner airlines.[467]

---

exchange of diplomatic notes, British negotiators won a generic liberal code-sharing arrangement for British Airways and a U.S. partner in exchange for approving substitution of Pan Am and TWA by United Airlines and American Airlines on transatlantic services to London Heathrow. The economic impact on BA of replacing the old U.S. international carriers with two giant domestic carriers, with their vast feeder operations, resulted in a tough British bargaining position to try to provide some compensatory shift of benefits to British Airways. Under a further U.S./U.K. Memorandum of Consultations initialed in Jun. 1995, the number of domestic U.S. points available for code-sharing was dramatically increased to include virtually all points beyond the British Airways U.S. gateways listed in Bermuda II. *See* U.S. Department of Transportation, *Joint Application of American Airlines, Inc. And British Airways plc under 14 C.F.R. Part 212 and 49 U.S.C. § 40109 For Statements of Authorization and Related Exemption Authority*, undocketed (Nov. 18, 2002), at 3-5.

465. The number of 'simulated' online links that British Airways can offer is impressive: choosing at random from the DOT-approved lists, a passenger might fly 'BA' from Lubbock, Texas to Dallas-Fort Worth (the American Airlines-operated segment) and onward to London (the British Airways-operated segment) or under similar operating conditions from Peoria, Illinois to Chicago and onward to Pisa, Italy.

466. Incidentally, the 'starburst' privilege – as operated between British Airways and the then-USAir – was contested by the 'Big Three' U.S. carriers, American, United and Delta, based on their exegesis of the 1991 U.S./U.K. Agreement, *supra* note 464. The DOT, however, read the instruments of amendment to provide not only conventional code-share authority (using existing traffic rights granted elsewhere), but also a more expansive variant that did not require the British carrier to show that Bermuda II *otherwise* authorized it to serve points beyond its gateways: '[T]he relevant paragraph] effectively grants, *by its own terms*, the bilateral route authority to serve on a code-sharing basis any points meeting its criteria [and contains no condition] limiting the number of flights that may be operated beyond the gateway.' Various Applications of BA/USAir, *supra* note 173, at 14,137 (emphasis added).

467. *See* U.S./EC Air Transport Agreement, *supra* note 21, art. 10(7) (authorizing code-sharing arrangements on the basis that all airlines in such arrangements hold the appropriate authority and meet the requirements normally applied to such arrangements). These vague conditions were adapted from Article 8(7) of the DOT's Model Open Skies Agreement, *see supra* note 38. That this language will support a foreign carrier's claim to exercise unrestricted code-sharing privileges inside the United States seems to flow from the fact that, under the new Agreement, EU carriers now have operating authority *in their own right* to serve every U.S. airport from every EU airport. *See* U.S./EC Air Transport Agreement, *supra* note 21.

The choice of code, incidentally, is up to the carriers, provided they comply with DOT disclosure regulations,[468] and normally each will apply its own code for as much of the total service as possible. For a London/Austin service, for example, BA may cover the Dallas/Austin segment under its own code used from London, and American Airlines will also list the flight under its carrier code as a regular domestic connection (the two flight numbers may appear in multiple listings on CRS screens, crowding out competing flight options to lower screens, and also consecutively on airport departure/arrival screens[469]). KLM/Northwest and Lufthansa/United Airlines, for example, which have overlapping international designations, may use *both* codes and *both* airline names.

2   Does Code-Sharing Violate Cabotage?

The theoretical inconsistency between these internal U.S. route privileges and the cabotage exclusion is readily apparent. BA and KLM use their two-letter codes to offer an apparently seamless passage from London to Austin or from Amsterdam to Minneapolis, respectively, although U.S. law prohibits BA and KLM from operating either the Dallas/Austin or Chicago/Minneapolis cabotage segments, which in reality are services provided by American Airlines (over Dallas) and Northwest Airlines (over Chicago). No *legal* inconsistency is apparent, however. Both arrangements honor the technical requirements of Article 7 of the Chicago Convention, as well as U.S. federal cabotage law, because domestic point-to-point traffic is carried by the domestic carrier, in these examples American Airlines and Northwest Airlines.[470]

---

468. *See infra* note 497.
469. *See generally* GAO, *Airline Alliances, supra* note 410, at 37-39. USAir was not a designated carrier on any transatlantic services and accordingly the DOT authority referred to in the main text permitted only a BA code to be applied to those flights. After the unraveling of its code-share arrangements with British Airways, in 1998 USAir – renamed US Airways – relaunched its London services (beginning with Philadelphia/Gatwick, where British Airways was operating as a monopoly supplier). *See US Airways launches Philadelphia-London route,* M2 PRESSWIRE, Apr. 3, 1998.
470. *See generally* MENDES DE LEON, *supra* note 103, at 115-17. This form of code-sharing also raises another intriguing question about the theoretical scope of the cabotage doctrine. Both the federal cabotage exclusion and Article 7 of the Chicago Convention define cabotage in terms of prohibiting foreign air carriers (*in casu,* foreign 'aircraft') from taking on passengers 'destined for another [point or place] within' the home State's territory. But the passengers boarding American Airlines and Northwest Airlines at Dallas or Minneapolis are not technically 'destined' for another U.S. city; they actually comprise transfer traffic connecting at the U.S. gateways of British Airways and KLM, respectively, for onward transit to European destinations. The true cabotage operation is the segment that transits passengers *inbound* from the British Airways and KLM gateways, who transfer to American Airlines and Northwest for terminal destinations within the United States. Arguably, therefore, the Austin/Dallas or Minneapolis/Chicago segments are not true cabotage, since the passengers travel beyond their U.S. transfer points; if that is so, why do British Airways or KLM need a code-sharing artifice in order to provide these services? The only counterpoint is an old U.S. Civil Aeronautics Board ruling which indicates that a foreign air carrier cannot circumvent cabotage by carrying

In fact, the second type of code-share authority, to the extent that it carries passengers *inbound* from Europe, is essentially a variant of existing coterminal rights that BA or KLM already possessed for continuing service to U.S. points beyond the primary gateway. The real incentive for these foreign carriers to win code-sharing privileges within the United States is to capture traffic that is *outbound* to London or Amsterdam, using the American Airlines and Northwest domestic services as feeder carriers in the same way that United, American, and Delta use their domestic networks to funnel traffic to their international operations.[471]

3   Code-Sharing: A Costly Compromise for U.S. International Aviation Policy – and for the Airline Industry

In its 1995 statement of U.S. international aviation policy the U.S. DOT expressed broad support for international code-sharing alliances as a way to enhance global service options.[472] But code-sharing, while at least offering a mechanism for second-tier U.S. airlines to compete with the 'Big Three' internationally, never

---

passengers between two U.S. points, if those passengers then change aircraft and airline at the second point for onward transit to foreign destinations. *See* Application of Qantas Empire Airways for Interpretative Rule, Order No. E-13710, 29 C.A.B. 33 (Apr. 6, 1959). But if the carriage remains online, and passengers do not leave the aircraft at the gateway (or even if they do, but only briefly), exercise of these rights does not appear theoretically distinct from existing coterminal rights for inbound traffic or from intermediate stops at other gateways (for example New York/San Francisco en route to Japan) for outbound traffic. (Mendes de Leon disagrees with the CAB finding on the more specific basis that physical separation from the aircraft could only qualify as cabotage if the passenger makes a definite 'stopover' at the gateway point. *See* MENDES DE LEON, *supra* note 103, at 35-37. There is no evidence, however, that foreign carriers are challenging the need for code-sharing authority in both directions. Moreover, the U.S. Department of Transportation continues to treat the *Qantas* ruling as sound law. *See* U.S. DOT, *In the Matter of Expanded Air Services at Northern Mariana Islands International Airports*, Dkt. No. OST-2006-25663, Order No. 2007-2-23 (Feb. 23, 2007), at 10 n.17 (finding *inter alia* that cabotage operations 'would include the carriage by a foreign air carrier of cargo between the [Commonwealth of the Northern Mariana Islands, a political dependency of the United States] and other U.S. points for transfer to either a U.S. air carrier, or another foreign air carrier for carriage between the [Commonwealth] and a foreign point, *in either direction*') (emphasis added). Consistently with the view of *inbound* cabotage taken earlier in this note, *see* the recently-enacted statutory provisions allowing foreign aircraft to trans-ship *inbound* international cargo deposited in Anchorage, Alaska, to any point in the lower 48 States. Even though the cargo technically originates in a foreign State, the transportation that takes place within the United States is essentially U.S. traffic (just as U.S.-produced supplies would be) – and therefore classifiable as eighth freedom cabotage since it is an extension of international service. *See* Robert Andriulaitis, Opinion, *Cargo Capers*, INTER-VISTAS CONSULTING INC., Dec. 2003, at 17.

471. *See generally* U.S. DOT, *Second International Report*, *supra* note 410, at 9 (showing how U.S. 'behind-gateway' feeder traffic for all alliances increased exponentially over the six-year period ending in 1999).

472. *See* 1995 Policy Statement, *supra* note 137, at 4-5.

proved effective *in its own right* as a tactic to apply pressure to foreign governments to open their markets to U.S. airlines. To the contrary, bilateral partners are more apt to visualize code-sharing as a surrogate for granting direct access to their markets.[473] Moreover, as noted earlier, it appears to have been the incentive of broad antitrust immunity, not the Lufthansa/United code-share alliance itself, that prompted German participation in the open skies initiative and that seems to have been a significant driver in reconciling the Europeans – including the British – to the terms of the 2007 U.S./EC Air Transport Agreement.[474]

Far from revealing a fluent strategy for market enhancement, in fact, DOT code-sharing applications regularly draw fire from disadvantaged rival carriers disappointed by the Department's readiness to grant this authority despite a lack of progress in bilateral aviation talks;[475] or conversely, to grant it where the Department *does* see progress but the U.S. airlines believe that stronger leverage should have been exerted.[476] BA's extraordinary reach into U.S. cabotage points, first with USAir and later with American Airlines, was a negotiating coup; the British, on the other hand, were able to continue for another 17 years to limit to two (United and American) the number of U.S. airlines that could serve London Heathrow and to tightly restrict those airlines' fifth freedom rights for destinations beyond London.[477] The KLM/Northwest integration agreement, with its price-fixing immunity, was anointed despite arguments that a wider agreement with the EC, or a broader agreement on investment opportunities, could have been negotiated.[478]

---

473. *See* 1995 Aviation Hearings, *supra* note 83, at 32, 36 (statement of Kenneth M. Mead, Director, Transportation Issues, Resources, Community and Economic Development, GAO) (also criticizing lack of economic analysis by the DOT prior to award of code-share authority, *e.g.* with respect to the 1991 U.S./U.K. Agreement, *supra* note 464).

474. *See supra* text accompanying Chapter 1, note 62.

475. *See, e.g.*, U.S. DOT, *BA/AA Final Order 2003*, *supra* note 463, at 2 (summarizing responsive pleadings by rival U.S. airlines which argued that there had been no developments in the U.S./U.K. bilateral relationship warranting approval of extensive code-sharing approval for British Airways and American Airlines).

476. *See infra* note 480.

477. Indeed, in the recent U.S./EC negotiations these were precisely the reasons that U.S. officials believed that the United Kingdom no longer had any incentive to open its highly-restricted market to U.S. carriers. British Airways, after all, already enjoyed significant access to the behind-gateway U.S. market through code-sharing. *See* GAO, *Airline Alliances*, *supra* note 410, at 33.

478. *See* Joint Applications of KLM/Northwest for Antitrust Immunity, *supra* note 199, at 14,059. Similar arguments surfaced in earlier applications involving German, Italian, and Canadian airlines. *See* Joint Applications of United Air Lines, Inc., and Lufthansa German Airlines, Inc., [1992-1994 Transfer Binder] Av. L. Rep. (CCH) ¶ 23,120, at 14,635; Various Applications of Continental Airlines, Inc. and Alitalia-Linee Aeree Italiane-S.p.A., Order 94-9-4 (Sept. 3, 1994); Joint Application of United Airlines, Inc. and Air Canada, Order No. 92-10-29 (Oct. 16, 1992). In the KLM/Northwest proceeding, United Airlines called for postponement of final action on antitrust immunity until the United States received 'a formal and binding commitment from the Netherlands to support and secure an open skies regime between the United States and other European Community members.' Joint Applications of KLM/Northwest for Antitrust Immunity, *supra* note 199, at 14,059. The Memorandum of Consultations between

And even in the same circumstances where the DOT will willingly play its toughest card to promote market liberalization – refusing antitrust immunity to an alliance where the foreign carrier's homeland has not engaged in an open skies relationship with the United States[479] – code-sharing arrangements between the U.S. and foreign carriers involved in that alliance will still win approval despite the vociferous complaints of U.S. rivals that the open skies agenda is not thereby advanced.[480] Although the special concessions made in earlier U.S./U.K.

---

the two countries contemplated 'fair and expeditious consideration' of antitrust immunity, but did not require or guarantee that it would be awarded. *Id.* at 14,062. Northwest Airlines, in a statement to the Airline Commission, argued that code-sharing allowed KLM and Northwest to blend their 'complementary networks' and avoid the investment and resources needed for independent assembly of such networks. This possibility, in Northwest's view, would prompt other countries to seek open skies agreements to allow their national carriers to achieve similar 'strategic linkages.' Statement of Richard B. Hirst, Senior Vice-President and General Counsel, Northwest Airlines, *in Airline Commission Documents*, Dkt. No. 000069 (Jun. 3, 1993), at 2-3. *But see* U.S. DOT, *Joint Application of American Airlines, Inc. and Iberia Lineas Aereas de España, S.A., for an Amended Statement of Authorization*, Dkt. No. OST-2001-11037, Department Action (Mar. 14, 2002), in which United Airlines successfully protested an American Airlines/Iberia Airlines code-share that would have required extra-bilateral approval, arguing that Spain's policy against approval of extra-bilateral U.S. carrier code-share services deprived United of reciprocal treatment of its own proposed code-shares. In denying the application, the DOT took note of 'the overall state of our aviation relationship with Spain, including the absence of progress toward an open-skies regime,' which informed the Department's policy of not granting authority for code-share services outside the aviation agreement. *Id.* at 2.

479. DOT policy awards antitrust immunity only for alliances where the participating foreign carriers represent homelands which have open skies agreements with the United States. *See* U.S. DOT, *U.S.-UK Alliance Case*, Dkt. No. OST-2001-11029, Order to Show Cause (Jan. 25, 2002), at 34 [hereinafter U.S. DOT, *U.S.-UK Alliance Show Cause Order 2002*] (conditioning antitrust immunity on the conclusion of an open skies agreement with the United Kingdom, homeland of the applicant foreign carriers, British Airways and bmi, each of which sought separate alliance arrangements with U.S. carriers, *see infra* note 480). The restrictive conditions of Bermuda II therefore governed. Moreover, both applications expressly acknowledged that their immunity would be premised on conclusion of a U.S./U.K. open skies treaty. *See supra* in the main text.

480. In the so-called U.S.-U.K. Alliance Case that began in 2001, *see supra* note 463, applications for antitrust immunity 'blanket' (open-ended) code-sharing were made respectively by the combination of British Airways and American Airlines on the one hand, and by United Airlines and British carrier bmi on the other (the latter application was part of a broader 'expansion' application within the Star Alliance membership that included four other European airlines). *See* U.S. DOT, *U.S.-UK Alliance Show Cause Order 2002*, *supra* note 479, at 1-2. The two applications, both of which confronted the same DOT regulatory policy of refusing immunity where the foreign carriers' home State did not have an open skies agreement with the United States seem to have been collapsed into the same docket by the DOT for obvious political reasons. *See* U.S. DOT, *U.S.-UK Show Cause Order 2002*, *supra* note 479, at 1; U.S. DOT, *U.S.-UK Alliance Case*, Dkt. No. OST-2001-11029, Final Order (Apr. 4, 2002) [hereinafter U.S. DOT, *U.S./UK Alliance Final Order 2002*]. U.S. carriers Continental, Delta, Northwest, and US Airways strongly opposed the requested authorizations for antitrust immunity and code-sharing. Tentative immunity of the British Airways/American Airlines partnership was nevertheless granted subject to the 'public interest' condition that the award would only take effect upon – and hopefully would facilitate – the anticipated conclusion of a U.S./U.K. open

negotiations made it problematical to deny extensive code-sharing to the BA/ American Airlines and United Airlines/bmi alliances,[481] it remains difficult to appreciate conceptually why, if the political intent of denying immunity is indeed to leverage an open skies agreement, that intent is then set aside when code-sharing is freely granted to the very same applicants.

These politically-tinged disputes, however, are part of the inescapable logic of the Chicago system, which requires that code-sharing and marketing alliances, designed initially as informal techniques among airlines to gain some route or network leverage in the closed bilateral order, have gradually been reabsorbed into the making of official aviation policy at the bilateral level.[482] The consequence, as already seen with determinations of airline citizenship, is an unsatisfactory inter-jection of foreign policy criteria and significant bilateral dilution of two powerful bargaining strategies, the cabotage and nationality rules, that should be traded *solely*

---

skies agreement (which did not happen). *See* U.S. DOT, *U.S.-UK Alliance Show Cause Order 2002, supra*, at 48. Moreover, the DOT, as a matter of international aviation policy, also expressed the hope that a U.K. open skies agreement would 'enhance the ability of the United States' to conclude a later U.S./EC agreement. *Id.* at 51. The tentative approval included additional conditions of substantial slot divestiture (*see id.* at 1), and in those circumstances the parties subsequently chose to abandon their integrated 'merger-model' alliance. *See* U.S./ U.K. Alliance Final Order 2002, *supra*, at 8. Their arrangement was repackaged as a more straightforward marketing alliance based on extensive behind-gateway code-sharing in U.S. and European markets (but not on overlapping nonstop U.S.-London route segments) and the immunity request was dropped. The DOT approved this renewed application while rejecting other U.S. carriers' protests that no recent developments in U.S./U.K. aviation relations war-ranted this treatment and despite the DOT's own admission of 'dissatisfaction' with the state of those relations. U.S. DOT, *BA/AA Final Order 2003, supra* note 463, at 2-3. Similar code-share approval was awarded to the United/bmi alliance. With respect to United/bmi, tentative immunity was also made contingent on a U.S./U.K. open skies agreement, but proposed code-sharing arrangements once again were not explicitly affected by this condition. *See* U.S. DOT, *U.S./U.K. Alliance Final Order 2002, supra*, at 11. The parties' subsequent formal application for code-sharing was granted subject to a carve-out for code-share services between any points in the United States and London. *See* U.S. DOT, *Joint Application of United Air Lines, Inc. And British Midland Airways Limited d/b/a bmi*, Dkt. No. OST-2003-15758, Notice of Action Taken (Dec. 3, 2003), at 1-2 [hereinafter U.S. DOT, *United/bmi Final Action 2003*]. These operations would in part have required extra-bilateral authority (bmi was not designated under Bermuda II to serve U.S. points ex-Heathrow, for example) that the DOT would not concede 'given the current state of our aviation relationship with the United Kingdom.' *Id.* at 3. To this limited extent, the Department finally used code-sharing authority as a lever for liberalization (although, by this time, as the applicants pointed out, the catalyst for negotiations was no longer U.S./U.K. relations but the conduct of the European Commission's mandate).

481. *See supra* note 480.
482. The authority to code-share has been assimilated to the bilateral bargaining process and may sometimes be regulated in the bilateral air services agreement or even by means of 'comity and reciprocity.' *See* Kaplan, *supra* note 188, at 18. In reviewing code-sharing proposals, the DOT early on announced that it would examine the applicable bilateral air services agreements, and the existence of reciprocity and benefits to U.S. carriers, passengers, and shippers. *See* U.S. DOT, *Joint Application of American Airlines, Inc. and Lufthansa German Airlines, Inc., for Statements of Authorization Under Parts 207 and 212 of the Department's Regulations to Engage in Blocked-Space and Code-Share Operations (Chicago-Munich/Dusseldorf)*, Dkt. No. 47475, Order 91-4-13 Granting Statements of Authorization (Apr. 5, 1991), at 2-3.

as part of an authentic multilateral liberalization of the international system.[483]
Bilateral compromise has given carriers like KLM and BA a quasi-cabotage
privilege (through code-sharing) that has not been 'paid for' through a specific
bilateral concession of inward investment by U.S. airlines in the Netherlands or
the United Kingdom, or until March 2008 even with expanded access for U.S.
airlines to and beyond London Heathrow.[484]

The cost to U.S. international aviation policy has been that continued tolerance
of KLM/Northwest-type combinations, by applying a lesser standard of legal scrutiny (through antitrust immunity or a more benevolent competition analysis conditioned by foreign policy goals),[485] sacrifices the vital tactical advantage of
explicitly associating any deeper integration of foreign carriers with U.S. airlines –
whether by merger, acquisition, or even by the creation of new subsidiaries – with the
establishment of a new, genuine, multilateral air services framework. Indeed, even
at the beginning of the last decade open skies penetration of the Netherlands, as
negotiated in the pioneering 1992 U.S./Netherlands air services agreement, was
greeted skeptically by Airline Commission witnesses as a poor trade-off for
KLM's enhanced access to behind-gateway traffic in the United States. Earlier,
former United Airlines Chairman Stephen Wolf warned in Congressional hearings
that 'foreign carriers should not be allowed to circumvent the reciprocity inherent in
the negotiating process simply by purchasing access to our markets.'[486]

---

483. *See infra* Chapter 4, Part III(D).
484. The effective date of the new U.S./EC Air Transport Agreement.
485. The U.S. Department of Transportation unapologetically invoked 'foreign policy reasons'
      (notably, a 'strong demonstration' of U.S. commitment to open skies) to explain its readiness
      to award an antitrust immunity that was only contingently expected under the pending U.S./
      Netherlands bilateral. Joint Application of KLM/Northwest for Antitrust Immunity, *supra*
      note 199, at 14,061-62. Foreign policy reasons were also used to justify immunity in the
      2002 conditional approvals in the applications of British Airways/American Airlines and
      United Airlines/bmi. U.S. DOT, *U.S./U.K. Alliance Final Order, supra* note 480, at 9 (repris-
      ing its statement in the earlier show-cause order, the DOT declared that 'replacing the
      restrictive Bermuda [II] aviation agreement with an open skies agreement would provide
      important public benefits. We believe that our final decision in this proceeding could help
      the United States achieve open skies with the United Kingdom').
486. Testimony of Stephen M. Wolf, Chairman and CEO, United Airlines, Inc., *Before the Sub-
      comm. on Aviation of the Comm. on Public Works and Transportation.* (Feb. 17, 1993), *in
      Airline Commission Documents*, Dkt. No. 001040, at 15. Ironically, in 1995 Mr. Wolf took
      over the presidency of the then-USAir, which had a rather different corporate view of foreign
      code-sharing alliances. And United itself changed policy after Mr. Wolf's departure with the
      birth of the United/Lufthansa alliance, the forerunner of the globalized Star Alliance. Lufth-
      ansa's enhanced access to behind-gateway U.S. traffic is an important part of this relationship,
      and code-share access to United's large U.S. domestic network is part of the inducement to
      attract new European airline members of Star. *See* U.S. DOT, *Joint Application of Polskie
      Linie Lotnicze S.A., Scandinavian Airlines System, Swiss International Air Lines Ltd., TAP Air
      Portugal, and United Air Lines, Inc., under 49 U.S.C. §§ 41308 and 41309 for Approval of and
      Antitrust Immunity for Commercial Alliance Agreements*, Dkt. No. OST-2005-22922, Final
      Order (Feb. 13, 2007) (approving antitrust immunity for United Airlines and a coterie of new
      European partner airlines).

Airlines are evidently anxious to persuade the public that their marketing agreements (especially now that the cement of equity investments has disappeared) reveal a commitment to a long-term relationship.[487] Yet, as Dawna Rhoades has argued, these alliances are put together by competitors, entities which possess an 'inalienable *de facto* right to pursue their own interests.'[488] There is, in fact, an economic literature of 'instability' that describes the syndrome of airline alliance failure.[489] The empirical data suggest the price to be paid for sustaining these counterfeit partnerships: BA, unable to 'control' its USAir partner, watched a progressive deterioration in the U.S. carrier's financial position and domestic competitiveness.[490] Relationships of this kind can appear ephemeral, merely short-term arrangements of convenience that are displaced by fresh marketing strategies as the travel seasons pass.[491] Many airline alliances, after all, have simply failed.[492]

---

487. *See* RHOADES, *supra* note 419, at 70-71 (noting that the 'business model' of alliances necessarily cannot involve control through ownership and therefore includes (again, in the absence of equity stakes) active participation in management, withholding or threatening to withhold some vital resource or capability (e.g., access to frequent flier programs or to codified knowledge such as CRS)).

488. *Id.* at 71 (quoting another source).

489. *Id.* Even the great global alliances are not immune to this syndrome. *See, e.g.,* the speculation surrounding the exit of Thai Airways from the Star Alliance, which centered on calculations of the benefits (or losses) that Thai might expect in a grouping that includes Singapore Airlines. *See* RHOADES, *supra* note 419, at 91. *See also* Jens Flottau, *Falling Star: Airline Alliance Parts Ways with the 'New' Varig,* 166 AV. WEEK & SPACE TECH. No. 2, at 41 (Jan. 8, 2007) (recounting bankrupt Brazilian carrier Varig's expulsion from the Star Alliance).

490. Indeed, following the planned British Airways/American Airlines link-up revealed in Jun. 1996, the British carrier's partnership with USAir was irretrievably soured by antitrust litigation commenced by USAir against British Airways in U.S. federal court. Among other allegations, the lawsuit accused British Airways of attempted monopolization of U.S./U.K. air routes. *See* USAir Complaint, *supra* note 418, paras. 88-91. *See* RHOADES, *supra* note 419, at 91 (reporting an analysis of the British Airways/USAir partnership which concluded that BA gained additional profit of $27.2 million while USAir gained only $5.6 million during the first quarter of 1994, a 'lopsided' benefit that over time could strain any alliance).

491. Daniel Kaplan, in his study of inward investment, described code-sharing (and other strategic nonequity arrangements) and foreign investment as 'discrete acts' that should be treated accordingly by U.S. policy. Thus, Kaplan would unilaterally increase inward investment rights by foreign carriers as a spur to gaining their support for liberal bilateral arrangements including code-sharing and other cooperative devices. Kaplan, *supra* note 188, at 29-30. Kaplan's strategy appears to be a variant of existing open skies policies. But raising the ceiling for permissible investments (which is presumably what Kaplan favors), without changes to the existing bilateral system, merely heightens concerns about forfeiting 'control' by U.S. nationals, and is unlikely to occur in any event without concessions on the proposed business alliance. Most importantly, as argued in the main text, *supra,* this strategy would surrender a critical bargaining tool in the search for a multilateral successor to the current open skies approach.

492. *See* the generally unsuccessful alliance histories presented *supra* in the main text. *See also* RHOADES, *supra* note 419, at 83-93 (offering a disconsolate *tour d'horizon* of many failed alliances). *See,* for example, Rhoades's conclusion that the number of alliance failures between 1997 and 2000 was equivalent to the number of new alliances (24% of the annual total). *See id.* at 83. Leo Mullin, CEO of Delta Air Lines, was thought to have accurately gauged industry opinion when he called alliances 'an inevitable but not hazard-free step in the evolution of the airline industry.' *Id.* at 83. There are many variables at work in

And carrier enthusiasm for code-sharing cannot – almost by definition – substitute for reform of the bilateral regime. Code-sharing, as already discussed, is not a *right* that airlines enjoy in the conduct of their commercial aviation relations; like all international traffic 'rights' under the Chicago system, it is in substance a *privilege* granted by sovereign States and, as such, ultimately revocable.[493]

4   Code-Shares and the Consumer

Given the fundamentally deceptive nature of code-sharing, it is not surprising that it has caught the attention of regulators. The U.S. DOT's official policy on 'airline designator code-sharing' betrays an unsettling ambivalence, especially in light of the agency's apparent support for the practice in its 1995 international aviation policy statement. On the one hand, although some carriers represent code-sharing as a way to 'simplify connecting service,'[494] which undoubtedly has consumer appeal,[495] the Department has clearly perceived the consumer deception that is inherent in this device: '[T]he holding out or sale of scheduled passenger air transportation involving a code-sharing arrangement . . . is prohibited as unfair and deceptive in violation of 49 U.S.C. § 41712.'[496]

---

alliance-making, including the relative financial health of each partner, the complexity of streamlining route structures, and decisions about which airline's ticket offices must close to make way for the joint one. *See* AIRLINE BUSINESS: THE SKIES IN 1993 (annual rev. ed.), at 14, *in Airline Commission Documents*, undocketed (1993). A spectacular fizzle was the so-called 'European Quality Alliance' (the Alcazar project) among KLM, Swissair, SAS, and Austrian Airlines, which would have achieved a combined European market share of 20%. *See* Kenneth P. Quinn & Nicholas J. Radell, Restoring the Health of the Airline Industry, Submission of Mercer Management Consulting, *in Airline Commission Documents*, Dkt. No. 000277 (Apr. 28, 1993), at 2.

493. For example, against a background of difficult bilateral negotiations with the British, the DOT displayed impatience, if not actual petulance, in its consideration of bmi's request for extra-bilateral authority to code-share with United Airlines on U.S. routes ex-London Heathrow. *See U.S. DOT, United/bmi Final Action 2003, supra* note 480, at 2-3 (rejecting even the appeal of United Airlines, facing bankruptcy, that it would benefit financially from a favorable decision, and insisting that 'the grant of such extra-bilateral authority to bmi is beyond what we are prepared to grant to a carrier of the United Kingdom at this time').

494. *See*, for example, British Airways' defense of this practice in its media packet on the USAir alliance in British Airways, Media Materials on USAir Investment, *in Airline Commission Documents*, undocketed.

495. The DOT and others have shown that consumers generally prefer online over interline connections, believing that same-carrier connections involve quicker gate transfer at terminals, and are less likely to cause lost luggage. GAO, *Airline Alliances, supra* note 410, at 14.

496. 14 C.F.R. § 257.4 (West 2008). 49 U.S.C. § 41712, a/k/a Section 411 of the Federal Aviation Act, as will be seen, *infra* Chapter 4, Part IV, specifically empowers the DOT to investigate and order termination of unfair or deceptive practices or unfair methods of competition in air transportation *or the sale of air transportation*. The text has been recodified as 49 U.S.C.A. § 41712 (West 2008). Professor Mendes de Leon agrees that code-sharing arrangements do not infringe upon the international law of cabotage, but may very well offend civil law provisions on consumer deception, since the passenger is served by a carrier other than the one apparently selected at the point of ticket purchase. *See* MENDES DE LEON, *supra* note 103, at 117.

In contrast, under 1999 amendments to the DOT regulations, U.S. and foreign carriers that offer timely notice of the existence of code-sharing arrangements[497] can expect approval of a specific code-sharing proposal, provided that four forms of notice are observed: code-share flights that are operated by a carrier other than the carrier whose code is used must be *asterisked* or otherwise marked in written or electronic schedule information (and must disclose the corporate name of the transporting carrier),[498] notified to consumers in oral communications prior to ticket purchase, notified to consumers in written communications at the time of ticket purchase,[499] and announced in print, broadcast, and Internet advertisements[500] – all of which will presumably protect the traveling public from the bait-and-switch characteristic of international code-sharing.[501] Since 1999, also, ticket agents (including Internet travel sites such as Expedia and

---

497. The rules apply also to the marketing of 'foreign air transportation' within the meaning of the U.S. aviation statutes, *i.e.*, excluding transportation between two foreign points, whether the service is offered by a U.S. carrier or a foreign carrier. The rules are limited, however, to sales and calls made in the United States, consistent with the DOT's 'overall policy of limiting this type of rule to transactions that take place in the United States.' U.S. DOT, Disclosure of Code-Sharing Arrangements and Long-Term Wet Leases, Dkt. Nos. OST-95-179 & OST-95-623, Final Rule, 64 Fed. Reg. 12,838, 12,845 (Mar. 15, 1999) [hereinafter DOT Code-Share Final Rule 1999]. Application of the rules to overseas sales 'might conflict with foreign consumer protection measures' and would therefore make implementation impractical. *Id.*
498. The revised rules require disclosure of both the 'corporate name' and the 'network name' of the transporting carrier. *See* DOT Code-Share Final Rule 1999, *supra* note 497, at 12,842. Knowledge of the former is especially significant in domestic U.S. air transportation, where commuter airlines share the code of major airline partners and use a 'network' name that is often similar to a major airline partner. Passengers who wish to avoid a commuter service because of prior bad experience, or special needs (for example, disability access) or a preference for jet service, may be attracted by the goodwill of the network name yet will fly on an undesired carrier and may be subject to a different contract of carriage under which the major carrier bears no legal responsibility for the flight. *See id.*
499. For ticketless travel, the written notice can be provided at the time of check-in for the first flight of the itinerary. 14 C.F.R. § 257.5(c)(3) (West 2008). Interestingly, nowhere do the rules require actual notice on the face of the ticket. While this may seem counterintuitive, the DOT decided to defer further consideration of such a rule 'until standards for ticketing, evolution of ticketless travel, and the effectiveness of other disclosure measures' can be better evaluated. DOT Code-Share Final Rule 1999, *supra* note 497, at 12,839.
500. Some obliqueness seems to have been tolerated with respect to radio and television advertisements, which in the revised 1999 rules permit the generic tag-line 'Some services are provided by other airlines.' 14 C.F.R. § 275.5(d) (West 2008). In a 2005 amendment, the genericness exemption was extended, although not quite so expansively, to print media (including the Internet). *See* U.S. DOT, Disclosure of Code-Sharing and Long-Term Wet Lease Arrangements, Dkt. No. 2004-19083, 70 Fed. Reg. 44,848 (Aug. 4, 2005) (easing notice requirements in print advertisements to remove need for complex footnotes that evidently increased consumer confusion).
501. 14 C.F.R. § 257.5 (West 2008). Foreign carriers were not included in the original rules, but it is now agency policy, when a code-sharing arrangement involving a foreign air carrier is approved, to require explicitly that the foreign carrier must adhere to the requirements of Section 257. *See, e.g., United/bmi Final Action 2003*, *supra* note 480, appendix C.

Travelocity) have been covered by these precautionary rules.[502] The DOT's experience under the original rules had been that compliance was 'haphazard,' that airlines and travel agents failed to disclose code-sharing arrangements at least 30% of the time, and that public advertisements routinely included 'general and often uninformative language.'[503] The agency rulemaking that led to the 1999 revisions was intended to strengthen the consumer disclosure requirements of the rules (and, as noted, to extend their application to ticket and travel agents).[504]

The EC Code of Conduct on CRS facilities requires flights involving a change of aircraft to be treated and displayed as connecting flights, so that code-shared flights should be listed as connecting flights; the now-defunct U.S. regulations, which did not require a specific display order as between nonstop and connecting flights, required only that code-share arrangements be flagged electronically to system users and consumers.[505] As seen earlier, EC regulations prohibit repeated listings of the same code-share flights on computer screen displays, which risk crowding out competing services.[506]

As a final comment, it is perhaps worth noting that it might have been expected that the more airlines are compelled to disclose the true 'interline' nature of their code-shared services, the less powerful code-sharing might appear as a marketing tool. On the contrary, however, as the U.S. DOT presciently remarked in its 1999 rulemaking, the economics of code-sharing have magnified the utility of this device, making it likely to become more complex, more likely to involve chains of connected partners, and more global in scope.[507] And, in the view of the U.S. regulators, the more expansive and complex code-sharing becomes, the more complaints from consumers can be expected.[508]

---

502. *See* 14 C.F.R. § 257.2 (West 2008). In 1999, ticket agents sold about 80% of all airline tickets sold in the United States. *See* DOT Code-Share Final Rule, *supra* note 497, at 12,844. Previously, regulation of ticket agents occurred using the DOT's general statutory and agency surveillance powers over unfair and deceptive practices. *See* 49 U.S.C.A. § 41712 (West 2008). Misrepresentations with respect to the quality of service being sold by ticket agents were (and still are) covered under 14 C.F.R. § 399.80 (West 2008).

503. *See* Notice of Proposed Rulemaking: Disclosure of Code-Sharing Arrangements and Long-Term Wet Leases, 59 Fed. Reg. 40,836, 40,838-39 (Aug. 10, 1994). For the outcome of the rulemaking, *see* 14 C.F.R. § 257 (West 2008), 'Disclosure of Code-Sharing Arrangements and Long-Term Wet Leases.' Industry observers expected that travel agents would eventually be expected to comply, although not quite with the *Sturm und Drang* predicted by industry analyst Ed Perkins: 'When a travel agent hands you a ticket, it's going to sound like a Miranda warning.' *Quoted in* David Field, *Getting The Agreement To Take Wing*, WASH. TIMES, Jun. 16, 1996, at A13.

504. *See* 59 Fed. Reg. 40,836, 40,838-39. The DOT reported consumer confusion about whether service was being offered by jet or turboprop aircraft, loss of frequent flier miles of the airline whose code was on the ticket, and check-in procedures. *See id.* at 40,837.

505. *See supra* Part VII(A).

506. *See id.*

507. *See* DOT Code-Share Final Rule 1999, *supra* note 497, at 12,842. Thus, a well-regarded annual survey of alliances shows a steady increase in the number of code-share agreements over the five years ending in 2007. *See Airline Alliance Survey*, *supra* note 411.

508. *See id.* The DOT imposes a further regulatory hurdle on code-share arrangements through its Code-Share Safety Program. Established in 2000, the program requires U.S. carriers to

IX   MULTILATERALISM AND REGIONALISM IN THE CHICAGO SYSTEM

There is no doubt that the most striking feature of the international air transport system has been its profusion of individually-negotiated bilateral concessions. At another level of perception, however, there has been a remarkable degree of worldwide systematic integration and homogenization of technical and administrative activities, particularly with respect to the so-called 'interlinability' of air transport documents.[509] In contrast, of the three principal *economic* incidents of air transport (fares, capacity, and route access), only fares have ever been regularly settled multilaterally, by a global syndicate of the world's airlines meeting regularly to fix fares, but doing so with government approval as an extension of the typical bilateral diplomacy of the Chicago system.

Throughout most of its history, the airlines' private trade association, IATA,[510] combined these aspects of technical cooperation and faresetting cartelization. Its 'clearing house,' for example, is based in Geneva and acts as a conduit for settlement of accounts between airlines.[511] Through its 'traffic conferences,'[512] joint meetings of

---

conduct safety audits of their foreign code-share partners as a condition for DOT authorization. *See* U.S. DOT, *Code-Share Safety Program Guidelines*, Revision 1 (Dec. 21, 2006). An initial audit – using ICAO safety benchmarks – must be completed prior to the U.S. carrier placing its code on flights operated by a foreign airline. *Id.* at 11. The U.S. carrier must conduct 'renewal audits' of its foreign code-share partners within 24 months of the initial audit or previous renewal audit. *Id.* Each audit report must be made available to the FAA for review. *Id.* at 14.

509.   Interlining is a technical arrangement between air carriers of different nationalities whereby an air passenger can travel on the services of several airlines using successive route connections, transiting many States with one ticket paid for in one currency (usually, the currency of the State in which the ticket is purchased). *See* Press Release, Europa, Competition: Commission Proposes to Revise Block Exemption for IATA Passenger Tariff Conferences, IP/05/1432 (Nov. 16, 2005) (classifying the traditional interlining system as just one of four types including also global airline alliances, code-sharing agreements, and bilateral interlining agreements). Traditional interlining operated through the airline collaboration procedures of the International Air Transport Association. *See id.*; *see also* main text, *supra*.

510.   *See* IATA, Annual Report 2007 (2007). The IATA was a resuscitated version of the former International Air Traffic Association, a trade organization set up in 1919 by six European airlines. *See* J.W.S. Brancker, IATA and what it does 6 (1977). By 1939, the group had grown to 33 members, including carriers from North and South America, Asia and Africa, as well as Europe. *See generally* Stanley B. Rosenfield, The Regulation of International Commercial Aviation 4 (1984); Diederiks-Verschoor, *supra* note 3, at 11. As of the time of writing, the IATA consists of some 230 scheduled airlines, representing 93% of all international scheduled traffic. *See* IATA Fact Sheet, Jan. 2009, <http://www.iata.org/pressroom/facts_figures/fact_sheets/iata.htm>; U.S. DOT, *International Air Transport Association Tariff Conference Proceeding*, Dkt. No. OST-2006-25307 & U.S. DOT, *Agreement Adopted by the Board of Governors of the International Air Transport Association*, Dkt. No. OST-2006-26404, Final Order (Mar. 30, 2007), at 1 [hereinafter U.S. DOT, *IATA Final Order 2007*].

511.   *See* Diederiks-Verschoor, *supra* note 3, at 50.

512.   *Provisions for the Regulation and Conduct of Air Traffic Conferences*, Art. IV, International Air Transport Association, Oct. 1945. (At the 1978 IATA general meeting, the name was changed to *Provisions for the Conduct of the IATA Traffic Conference*.) *See* Rosenfield, *supra* note 510, at 5. Resolutions of the IATA traffic conferences, despite their multilateral

airlines serving defined geographical regions, IATA was the most significant player in the emergence of an officially-sanctioned, quasi-cartelized system of establishing binding international air fares, since virtually all bilateral air services agreements negotiated between the Bermuda I model[513] and the later U.S. liberal models (which shun IATA ratemaking procedures)[514] adopted IATA's traffic conference and ratesetting machinery,[515] thereby incorporating the air carriers' own self-regulated ratemaking procedures in State-to-State sovereign negotiations as part of the Chicago system.[516] IATA's activation of faresetting procedures at the multilateral level was a result of the failure of the Chicago Conference to agree on a mechanism to regulate international airfares (and the consequent 'default' mechanism, the bilateral system).[517] The typical Bermuda I bilateral required that the rate struck by the appropriate IATA traffic conference should then be subject to the approval of both governments in the bilateral nexus (*i.e.*, double approval pricing),[518] but governments typically rubber-stamped the results

---

provenance, were always at the heart of the bilateral system. These conferences – first nine and later three – encompassed different geographical regions, and comprised IATA members operating scheduled commercial international air transport service either entirely within the region or to one or more points within the region. *See* Sion, *supra* note 51, at 182-83; *see also* LOWENFELD, *supra* note 41, at 2-121 ('A Closer Look at IATA: How a Traffic Conference Works').

513. Annex II to Bermuda I referenced the decision of the U.S. Civil Aeronautics Board to 'approve the rate conference machinery' of IATA. All rates struck by the conference would, however, require CAB approval. The ratesetting structure of the bilateral was built on this IATA foundation. *See* ANDREAS F. LOWENFELD, AVIATION LAW: DOCUMENTS SUPPLEMENT 375-76 (1981).

514. The 2007 U.S./EC Air Transport Agreement, *supra* note 21, makes no mention at all of IATA ratemaking procedures.

515. *See* U.S. Department of Transportation, *International Air Transport Association Tariff Conference Proceeding*, Dkt. No. OST-2006-25307, Initial Comments of the International Air Transport Association (Oct. 20, 2006), at 2 [hereinafter U.S. DOT, *IATA Comments 2006*] (discussing requirement that air carriers designated to serve bilaterally negotiated international routes operate with IATA-agreed fares and rates, which was written into – and continues in – numerous bilateral agreements). A standard clause to this effect was adopted by the European Civil Aviation Conference in Strasbourg in 1954: 'Such agreement [respecting tariffs] shall, where possible, be reached through the rate-fixing machinery of the International Air Transport Association.' *See* A. Salzman, *IATA, Airline Rate-Fixing and the EEC Competition Rules*, 2 EUR. L. REV. 409, 410-12 (1977). Innovative pricing primarily developed where government bilaterals – such as those of the U.S. open skies program – so provided. *See* Stephen Wheatcroft & Geoffrey Lipman, *Air Transport in a Competitive European Market*, at 105, Economist Intelligence Unit (1986).

516. IATA's traffic conferences, in their prime, were said to constitute an extraordinary transnational 'cartelization' of the airline industry, albeit with government approval (which J.W.S. Brancker, *supra* note 510, regarded as an absolving fact). Needless to say, the basic premise of IATA conference ratemaking in its original incarnation, as Lowenfeld emphasized, was that 'every participant in the market [would] match the fares offered by each of the others . . . rather than letting the lowest fare, or the competitor with the lowest costs, in effect determine the fares charged by all . . . ' LOWENFELD, *supra* note 41, at 5-44.

517. *See* ROSENFIELD, *supra* note 510, at 5.

518. *See* Bell, *supra* note 49, at 536. *See also* Paul S. Dempsey, *The Role of the International Civil Aviation Organization in Deregulation, Discrimination and Dispute Resolution*, 52 J. AIR L. & COM. 529, 541-47 (1987).

of the airlines' joint conferences, so that in effect the airlines were engaged in an enduring government-supported price-fixing conspiracy.[519]

Nevertheless, as the international airline system became more cartel-shy, and U.S. and EC antitrust regulators fixed the conferences in their surveillance sights, the IATA conferences lost much of their aura of unanimity. The 'canary in the mine' for government-sanctioned IATA rate-fixing appeared in the North Atlantic region in the late 1970s, where airlines began to charge airfares filed directly with governments in an effort to meet the competition from new, cut-rate transatlantic tariffs offered by carriers such as Laker Airways.[520] In June 1978, a revised IATA structure split the organization into separate 'trade association' and tariff coordinating systems. Within the latter, traffic conference procedures were recast as optional and unilateral, and efforts were made to redefine the conferences to allow greater flexibility for innovative fares.[521] Gradually, the conferences focused virtually in their entirety on lubricating the interline system, allowing airlines to agree prices for multi-leg flights on the same ticket that use more than one carrier.[522] In addition, IATA proceedings, hitherto conducted *in camera*, were opened to

---

519. *See* Naveau, *supra* note 18, at 88. Such concerted ratemaking does, of course, resemble price-fixing, which is illegal *per se* under the antitrust code of the United States. United States *v.* Socony-Vacuum Oil Co., 310 U.S. 150 (1940). To shield the IATA mechanism from antitrust attack, Congress provided that under 49 U.S.C. § 41308 (formerly Section 412 of the Federal Aviation Act of 1958), all IATA rate agreements were required to be filed with the U.S. Civil Aeronautics Board, and the CAB would then use its antitrust immunity powers under 49 U.S.C. § 41309 (formerly Section 414 of the Federal Aviation Act of 1958) to approve such agreements unless they were 'adverse to the public interest.' *See* U.S. DOT, *International Air Transport Association Tariff Conference Proceeding*, Dkt. No. OST-2006-25307, Order to Show Cause (Jul. 5, 2006), at 28-32 (discussing standards by which immunity was first granted and then conditionally withdrawn) [hereinafter U.S. DOT, *IATA Order to Show Cause 2006*].

520. In 1982, the United States signed a Memorandum of Understanding with the European Civil Aviation Conference, a regional intergovernmental organization discussed *infra* in the main text. The Memorandum established a price band (*i.e.*, 'zone of reasonableness') around a reference fare level within which carriers were free to set fares without governmental interference. Outside the band, the zone pricing provisions of the relevant bilaterals remained in force. *See* Memorandum of Understanding Concerning Transatlantic Scheduled Air Fares with Annexes, Washington D.C., May 2, 1982. *See generally* Civil Aviation Authority (London), *Airline Competition on European Long Haul Routes* (CAP 639), Nov. 1994, at 35 [hereinafter CAA Report, *Airline Competition*]. The Memorandum lapsed in 1991, as the open skies era was beginning and liberal tariff approval regimes were being concluded between the United States and its European bilateral partners. *See* EUROPEAN CIVIL AVIATION CONFERENCE [ECAC], 50 YEARS OF ECAC 23 (2005); *see* LOWENFELD, *supra* note 41, at 5-48 (offering a concise history of the impact of Sir Freddie Laker's upstart transatlantic service).

521. *See* Sion, *supra* note 51, at 184-85. *See also* HAANAPPEL, *supra* note 19, at 3. Prior to recent DOT activity, the most serious assault on the IATA tariff-fixing mechanism came from one of its early champions, the U.S. Civil Aeronautics Board. The CAB's 'show cause' proceeding, commenced in 1978, was designed to remove the grant of antitrust immunity in which IATA's ratesetting activities had been cocooned since the time of Bermuda I. C.A.B. Dkt. No. 32851, Order 78-6-78 (Jun. 9, 1978), *reprinted in* LOWENFELD, *supra* note 41, 5-72.

522. *See* U.S. DOT, *IATA Comments 2006, supra* note 515, at 3, tracing how the traffic conference methodology evolved into one of unilateral carrier development and implementation, while maintaining the boon of interlining. Thus, all IATA enforcement activity was terminated.

government observers and to representatives of ICAO.[523] Both the United States and the EC shielded the redefined tariff conferences from attack on antitrust or competition law grounds.[524]

With the upsurge of faresetting flexibility accorded to air carriers by open skies liberal bilaterals, as well as the signing of the U.S./EC Air Transport Agreement of 2007 with its cooperative agenda for antitrust enforcement, IATA's durability as a tariff-setting force in the international air transport economic order is likely in terminal decline.[525] One of the critical questions that an antitrust regulator might pose – 'have IATA tariff conference discussions actually caused fares to be higher than they would otherwise be?'[526] – does not seem to have been adequately answered for either the U.S. or EC competition hierarchies by IATA's efficiency arguments.[527] In March 2007, the U.S. DOT terminated antitrust immunity for

---

See id; *see also* Press Release, Europa, Competition: Commission Ends Block Exemption for IATA Passenger Tariff Conferences for Routes Between the EU and Non-EU Countries, IP/07/973 (Jun. 29, 2007) [hereinafter Press Release, IATA 2007].

523. *See* ROSENFIELD, *supra* note 510, at 6.

524. *See* Civil Aeronautics Board, IATA Traffic Conferences Board Review, 89 C.A.B. 468 (1981), Order No. 85-5-32 (May 6, 1985) (granting antitrust immunity based on foreign policy considerations). *See also* Press Release, IATA 2007, *supra* note 522 (noting that, since 1993, the Commission had granted a so-called 'block exemption' from the competition rules for IATA tariff conferences). *See infra* Chapter 5, Part II(D). As will be seen, the European Commission also became an official IATA observer in order to safeguard the price-setting freedoms of *intra-Union* airline liberalization.

525. A definitive obituary would be premature, however. According to IATA, 124 airlines currently participate in the passenger tariff conferences and 90 in the cargo conferences. IATA insists that the coordination that takes place relates only to 'establish[ing] the fare conditions and prices for fully-flexible interline travel.' IATA, Multilateral Interline System – Today, <www.iata.org/whatwedo/passenger/irms/multilateral-interline-system-today.htm> [hereinafter IATA, Multilateral Interline System]. *See also* U.S. DOT, *IATA Order to Show Cause 2006*, *supra* note 519, at 3-14 (explaining and criticizing IATA tariff conference procedures for setting 'normal' and 'special' fares for interlining and finding that attractive, flexible interline fares are available outside IATA conference system). IATA claims that over three million passengers annually use its 'Interline Product' on transatlantic routes alone. *See* U.S. DOT, *IATA Comments 2006*, *supra* note 515, at 13; *see also* Affidavit of Brian Pearce, IATA Chief Economist, *id.* paras. 5-7. Most low-cost carriers – many of which eschew the costs inherent in interlining – do not participate in IATA's multilateral interline system. *See* [U.K.] Civil Aviation Authority, *UK Regional Air Services*, CAP 754 (2005), at 53 (noting that low-cost and 'no-frills' airlines' schedules are designed to maximize point-to-point traffic and to make best use of the aircraft, rather than to ensure convenient connections onto other flights).

526. *See* U.S. DOT, *IATA Comments 2006*, *supra* note 515, at 9. Concededly, the U.S. Department of Transportation felt that it did not need to prove that this state of affairs existed, *see id.*, – but if fares were not in fact any higher, IATA would have a *prima facie* argument of efficiency.

527. IATA has submitted numerous arguments supporting a curtailment of its traffic conference procedures in the name of antitrust law, including limiting geographic area tariff coordination activity to interlinable fares and rates and foreclosing the exchange of cost information. *See* U.S. DOT, *IATA Comments 2006*, *supra* note 515, at 10. The U.S. authorities, however, asked skeptically whether IATA interlining principally serves the rarer breed of travelers who have relatively complex itineraries that involve multiple airlines and a number of stopovers. *See id.* at 13. For IATA's self-interpretation of its current interline product, *see* IATA, Multilateral

IATA passenger and cargo tariff conferences for the transatlantic and U.S./ Australia markets.[528] Similarly, in September 2006 the EC adopted a regulation which ended the exemption from EC competition laws for IATA passenger and cargo tariff conferences for markets within Europe, for transatlantic markets, and for Australia.[529]

Nevertheless, IATA is an enduring institution. As the airline industry was convulsed by external shocks in the last few years, IATA shape-shifted to emphasize its trade association credentials and reinvented itself as the industry's indispensable agenda-setter and implementer.[530] IATA's safety audit program,[531] as well as its leadership services on climate change,[532] challenges to airport

---

Interline System, *supra* note 525 (indicating that meeting competition concerns is now 'crucial' to the success of IATA interlining).

528. The phase-out of immunity took effect on Jun. 30, 2007. *See* U.S. DOT, *IATA Final Order 2007, supra* note 510, at 2. The DOT found that airline travelers could already obtain interline services that are largely comparable with those established through the tariff conferences. *See id.* Thus, the tariff conferences were found to be 'inherently anticompetitive' and not to provide important public benefits or meet a serious transportation need. *Id.* Moreover, the original justification for the immunity – foreign policy – was no longer tenable because the European Union and Australia were phasing out the tariff conferences' exemptions from their own competition laws. *See id.*

529. *See* Commission Regulation 1459/2006, On the Application of Article 81(3) of the Treaty to Certain Categories of Agreements and Concerted Practices Concerning Consultations on Passenger Tariffs on Scheduled Air Services and Slot Allocation at Airports, 2006 O.J. (L 272) 3. In this block exemption, the European Commission made clear that an exemption for the IATA tariff conferences would only be prolonged at a later stage if the air carriers could provide data showing that passenger tariff conferences continue to benefit consumers. *See* Press Release, IATA 2007, *supra* note 522. However, the limited data suggested that less than 5% of tickets sold for journeys between the European Union and third countries are issued at an IATA interlinable fare for an interline journey. *See id.* Thus, the Commission seemed to premise its termination of exemption primarily on a decline in use of the IATA system by EU carriers, thus preserving a system that no longer delivered consumer benefits while continuing to pose a significant risk to competition. *See* European Commission, *Revision of Block Exemption from Competition Rules for IATA Conferences – Frequently Asked Questions*, at 1, Memo/ 06-359 (Oct. 2, 2006). The exemptions ended on a rolling basis – Dec. 31, 2006, for markets within Europe; Jun. 30, 2006, for transatlantic markets; and Jun. 30, 2008, for the Australian market. Similar terminations were applied to the relevant cargo markets. *See* U.S. DOT, *IATA Final Order 2007, supra* note 510, at 3.

530. *See*, for example, IATA's newest mantra, 'At the Air Transport Industry's Side.' *See* <www.iata.org>.

531. *See* INTERNATIONAL AIR TRANSPORT ASSOCIATION, IATA OPERATIONAL SAFETY AUDIT: DESIGNED FOR THE AVIATION INDUSTRY (2004) (discussing the success of IATA's single common airline safety standards, which evolved from a voluntary to a self-committed process by IATA member airlines and that includes registration with IATA as an audited operator). The IATA audit can replace most of the code-share audits required, for example, under U.S. regulations and can also be used as a public mark of quality. *See* IATA, *IATA Operational Safety Audit: Commonly Asked Questions* (2004) (noting that the U.S. Federal Aviation Administration has recognized that IATA audits comply with U.S. requirements that foreign code-share partners be safety-audited).

532. IATA has become a global advocate for the airline industry's position on aviation carbon emissions. *See* IATA, Industry Priorities for 2009, <http://www.iata.org/about/priorities.htm>.

charges, the abrogation of the Chicago nationality rule, and ticketless travel[533] have all been effective initiatives that have persuaded its airline funders to maintain their support. With a revised logo and a more contemporary motto – 'to represent, lead, and serve the airline industry' replaced the quasi-governmental mission of 'promoting safe, reliable, secure, and economical air transportation'[534] – IATA is seeking to be more business-oriented and more 'relevant.'[535]

ICAO[536] is a creature of the Chicago Convention and was formally established in 1947 (after a two-year 'interim' status[537]) as a specialized agency of the United Nations.[538] As a public international organization, it is quite distinct from the privately-created IATA.[539] Montreal-based ICAO, to which States send permanent diplomatic representatives, claims to be dedicated virtually entirely to *technical* cooperation among its contracting Member States (of which there are 190, making it one of the most universal of international organizations).[540] This cooperation takes many forms, including the mundane work of collecting statistics as well as the development of common standards for navigation aids and techniques, weather reporting, equipment and crew certification, security compliance, insurance, and so forth.[541] Nevertheless, ICAO has endeavored to find a role also in the

---

533. *See* <www.iata.org> for details of IATA's 'Simplifying the Business' initiative.
534. IATA's leaders like to coin mottoes. *See supra* note 530 for an even more recent example.
535. Reported in 31 AIR TRANSP. WORLD, Dec. 1994, at 80.
536. The organization has definite issues of self-confidence with an acronym that is commonly pronounced 'AI-KAY-OH.' *Cf.* IKEA, <www.ikea.com>. Perhaps to ICAO's chagrin, the present author (citing an earlier article by Professor Michael Milde) drew attention to this fact at the Organization's Apr. 11, 2008 Symposium on Regional Organizations.
537. The 'Interim Agreement on International Civil Aviation' was adopted at the same time as the Chicago Convention, and established the 'Provisional International Civil Aviation Organization' ('PICAO'). *See* Interim Agreement on International Civil Aviation, 59 Stat. 1516, *reprinted in* [Mar. 2001] Av. L. Rep. (CCH) ¶ 28,011, at 25,051 (Dec. 7, 1944). The Interim Agreement required 'acceptance' rather than ratification or accession so that it quickly came into force. Fox, *supra* note 72, at 3. The first meeting of the PICAO 'Assembly' took place on Jun. 6, 1945. *See id.* Headquartered in Montreal, the PICAO set up the structure for the permanent ICAO organization.
538. Part II of the Chicago Convention comprises the 'constitution' of ICAO. Article 65 provides the authority for the ICAO 'Council,' its permanent steering body, to enter into 'arrangements' with international organizations such as the United Nations. Chicago Convention, *supra* note 6, art. 65. Echoing the tenor of the times, Article 44 of the Convention (listing ICAO's 'objectives') commits the organization to 'prevent economic waste caused by unreasonable competition.' For a discussion of the institutional profile of ICAO, *see* DIEDERIKS-VERSCHOOR, *supra* note 3, at 45-50.
539. *See* DIEDERIKS-VERSCHOOR, *supra* note 3, at 10.
540. *See* ICAO, ICAO Documents, Doc 7300 Status, <http://www.icao.int/icaonet/dcs/7300.html>.
541. *See* RUWANTISSA I. R. ABEYRATNE, AVIATION IN CRISIS (2003) (offering the perspective of ICAO's senior legal officer on his organization's work in the arenas of airline security, commercial transactions, and insurance); *see also Annual Review of Civil Aviation 2005*, 61 ICAO J., No. 5 (2006) (discussing ICAO initiatives on safety oversight and auditing; aviation security and auditing, including identification of and development of legal responses to new threats such as the misuse of aircraft as weapons; environmental protection including noise abatement, carbon emissions, and airport land-use; technical cooperation with developing States including

economic regulation of the air transport industry,[542] and has convened a series of policy conferences on airline liberalization and the reform of the Chicago nationality rule.[543]

Aviation's response to the political imperatives of global climate change has given ICAO an opportunity to significantly enhance its self-appropriated 'global leadership role' role in economic regulation and liberalization.[544] As the EC unveils unilateral climate change laws, including the inclusion of all international air transport to and from the Community into its carbon emissions trading scheme,[545] the United States insists that a future regulatory regime for aviation's carbon footprint

---

worldwide deployment of experts and supply of equipment for air traffic-related field projects; and technical advances in air navigation including satellite-based systems).

542. *See Annual Review of Civil Aviation 2005, supra* note 541, at 28.

543. ICAO's incursions into economic regulation have not been greeted with unalloyed praise. Lowenfeld early on argued that ICAO was 'ill-adapted' to a future role in economic regulation of the industry. LOWENFELD, *supra* note 41, at 5-112. Indeed, not surprisingly for an intergovernmental organization, ICAO long acted in vigorous defense of the Chicago system. In 1994, for example, ICAO sponsored a worldwide Air Transport Conference at which delegates loyally endorsed the prevailing bilateral order. ICAO, *Report of the Conference on Air Transport*, ICAO Pub. No. 9644, AT Conf./4, 53-54 (Nov./Dec. 1994). By the time of ICAO's Worldwide Air Transport Conference in 2003 (AT Conf/5), however, the 'sense of ICAO' has moved toward greater acknowledgment of the liberal orthodoxy of the U.S. open skies program. *See* ICAO, *Consolidated Conclusions, Model Clauses, Recommendations and Declarations*, ATConf/5 (Jul. 10, 2003) [hereinafter ICAO, *Conclusions 2003*] (accepting the empirical reality of a decade of 'dynamic' commercialization and liberalization and recognizing the emergence of 'widespread support' by States for these processes, especially with respect to the limitations of the nationality rule). (For commentary on ICAO's specific textual proposals for liberalization of the nationality rule, *see supra* Chapter 2, Part II(D)). The 2003 Conference also adopted a 'Declaration of Global Principles for the Liberalization of International Air Transport' that called for giving international air transport 'as much economic freedom as possible while respecting its specific characteristics and in particular the need to ensure high standards of safety, security, and environmental protection.' ICAO, *Conclusions 2003, supra*, at 19. The Declaration, however, anticipated that States would liberalize flexibly, through bilateral as well as regional and sub-regional instruments. *See id.* at 21. This evolution in thinking – while still framed by cautious government-friendly language about stability, efficiency, safety, and labor protection – continued at the 2006 conference, ATConf/6, in Dubai. *See* Taïeb Chérif, Secretary-General of the International Civil Aviation Organization, *Open Statement to the ICAO Global Symposium on Air Transport Liberalization*, Dubai (Sept. 18, 2006) (describing liberalization (in the specific context of open skies agreements) as the 'cornerstone' upon which to build the future of the air transport industry). *See* ICAO, *Strategic Objectives for 2005-2010*, Consolidated Vision and Mission Statement (2005) (committing ICAO to developing guidance for and facilitating States in the process of 'liberalizing the economic regulation of international air transport,' although with 'appropriate safeguards').

544. ICAO, *Conclusions 2003, supra* note 543, at 21.

545. In Jul. 2008, the European Parliament adopted legislation to include aviation in the Community's Emissions Trading Scheme (ETS). *See* Press Release, European Parliament, Aviation to be Included in the European Trading System from 2012 as MEPs Adopt Legislation, 20080707IPR33572 (Jul. 8, 2008). Commenting on the legislation, European Parliament Rapporteur on Emissions, Peter Liese, stated: 'Of course, a global agreement is our final goal, but the inclusion of third country flights starting and landing in Europe is a major step for the global fight against climate change.' *Id.*

must be the product of ICAO consensus.[546] Some cynicism has been expressed about the authenticity of this U.S. deference to the sometimes creaking machinery and incremental outcomes of ICAO intergovernmental deliberation.

A regional analogue of ICAO – and an explicit regionalized auxiliary of ICAO – is the European Civil Aviation Conference (ECAC).[547] ECAC, the offspring of the Council of Europe, was in fact convened as an ICAO-sponsored conference in Strasbourg in 1954 (although it was never a 'subordinate air transport commission' to ICAO in the sense envisaged in Article 55 of the Chicago Convention[548]). Like ICAO, Paris-based ECAC comprises only its participating member States (typically represented through their Directors-General for Civil Aviation) and is not an IATA-like consortium of airline companies. Although much of ECAC's work is derivative of ICAO's areas of concern,[549] its standing committees include ECO-I, the committee for 'scheduled transportation,' which embraces economic regulatory issues such as tariffs and conditions (*e.g.*, travel agency commissions, baggage handling, overbooking, denied boarding, and so forth).

In fact, ECAC historically played a much larger role in economic regulation than its ICAO foster parent, but not necessarily in pursuit of liberalization.[550] One of its earliest achievements was the 1967 European Agreement on the Procedure for the

---

546. At the 36th General Meeting in 2007, the ICAO Assembly adopted a new resolution identifying ICAO as the lead international organization to address the impact of aviation emissions on the environment. *See* ICAO, *Consolidated Statement of Continuing ICAO Policies and Practices Related to Environmental Protection*, app. A, Assemb. Res. A36-22 (2007), *compiled in Assembly Resolutions in Force*, at I-54, ICAO Doc. 9902 (Sept. 28, 2007). Although the resolution calls upon 'States to refrain from environmental measures that would adversely affect the orderly and sustainable development of international civil aviation' and 'to continue to cooperate closely with international organizations,' *see id.*, Portugal, acting on behalf of the EU Member States and other States of the ECAC, entered a reservation with respect to the resolution's call for States 'not to implement an emissions trading system on other Contracting States' aircraft operators except on the basis of mutual agreement between those States,' *id.* app. L. *See* ICAO, *Assembly Resolutions in Force*, *supra*, app. A, at A-1 (noting Portugal's reservation to Appendix L of Assembly Resolution A36-22).

547. *See* Constitution of the European Civil Aviation Conference, art.1(2)(c) (committing ECAC to 'making an effective contribution to the normal work of [the] ICAO'). ROSENFIELD, *supra* note 510, at 39.

548. Convention on International Civil Aviation, *supra* note 6, 15 U.N.T.S. at 336. ICAO does, however, provide secretariat services to ECAC. *See* ROSENFIELD, *supra* note 510, at 5; *see also* ICAO, *Relationship of ICAO with the European Civil Aviation Conference*, Assemb. Res. A10-5, *superseded by Relationship Between ICAO and Regional Aviation Bodies*, Assemb. Res. A27-17, *compiled in Assembly Resolutions in Force*, *supra* note 546.

549. *See* ECAC, *supra* note 520 (noting ECAC's involvement in issues of aviation safety and security, including a Europe-wide ramp inspection of aircraft landing in ECAC Member States that complements ICAO audit programs; an aviation security audit program; initiatives on aircraft noise abatement; recommendations on good leasing practices; and work on air traffic management).

550. The powerful role of the European Commission as Europe's principal economic regulator for aviation has diminished ECAC's capacity (and reason) for maneuver in this area. In fact, it appears that ECAC's most recent contributions have been to cosponsor so-called 'Dialogues' among ECAC, the European Union, and airline industry representatives on economic issues such as passenger rights. *See* ECAC, *supra* note 520, at 27.

Establishment of Tariffs for Scheduled Air Services.[551] This agreement sought to insert into bilateral negotiating relationships the IATA fare-fixing mechanisms utilized by the airlines (but did recommend the liberal 'double disapproval' model for fares).[552] Diederiks-Verschoor notes ECAC's pioneering contribution to third-country aviation relations, in particular the ECAC/U.S. Memorandum of Understanding (MOU) relating to transatlantic fares and tariffs.[553] The MOU introduced the concept of price-banding that later formed the basis for the European Commission's tariff liberalization program. In exchange for these guaranteed zones of flexibility, the U.S. CAB eventually agreed to suspend its IATA 'show cause' proceeding,[554] allowing U.S. airlines to participate once again in multilateral tariff coordination procedures.[555]

X   THE CHICAGO SYSTEM ON THE CUSP OF REFORM

So long as the bilateral system persists, even with the emergence of regional cabotage systems such as the EC single aviation market and the open skies enhancements introduced by the EC's 'Community clause' initiative and the 2007 U.S./EC Air Transport Agreement, international aviation will be hostage to the competition-depleting compromises that flow from a system based on protected sovereign rights rather than freely-exchanged service 'commodities.' As Chapter 6 will explore, various commentators have promoted further multilateral initiatives that would inject greater measures of competitive energy into the international air transport environment than can be achieved through continuing to apply the Chicago-based methodology of the open skies regime. A working group within the World Trade Organization, for example, is considering how the Air Transport Annex to the General Agreement on Trade in Services (GATS) can be expanded beyond its present narrow focus on 'soft' rights (aircraft repair and maintenance, selling and marketing of air transport services, and CRS)[556] to extend the international trade principles of transparency, most favored nation, nondiscriminatory market access, and national treatment to international air transport.[557]

---

551. Paris, Jul. 10, 1967. *See generally* DIEDERIKS-VERSCHOOR, *supra* note 3, at 53.
552. *See* ROSENFIELD, *supra* note 510, at 34-35.
553. *See supra* note 520. *See* DIEDERIKS-VERSCHOOR, *supra* note 3, at 53; *see also* ROSENFIELD, *supra* note 510, at 36.
554. *See supra* note 521.
555. *But see supra* note 528 (discussing the ending of antitrust immunity for these procedures). By the mid-1990s, in any event, the major U.S. airlines were already withdrawing from multilateral tariff coordination. *See* 31 AIR TRANSP. WORLD, Dec. 1994, at 80.
556. *See infra* Chapter 6, Part III(C).
557. The Uruguay Round of the General Agreement on Tariffs and Trade (GATT) introduced 'trade in services' onto the GATT world trade agenda for the first time. This approach for air transport was originally launched in the Air Transport Commission of the International Chamber of Commerce in Paris in Oct. 1986. *See* Wassenbergh, *New Aspects, supra* note 16, at 32. But, as will be seen, skepticism is rife; States that are accustomed to the equipoise of the bilateral system, which assumes a qualitatively as well as quantitatively balanced exchange of

In this juristic setting, the old classification of traffic rights into 'freedoms of the air' would be displaced by new criteria based on the 'import of air services.'[558]

And well before the 2007 U.S./EC air transport concordat, commentator L. Gilles Sion called for a new U.S./EC North Atlantic multilateral compact, which would independently develop a full competitive regime and include a 'plurilateral' mechanism to allow other groups of likeminded States to adhere to the pact as their economic circumstances (or the force of outside economic circumstances) evolved.[559] The second stage of U.S./EC negotiations, which began in May 2008, contemplates potential relaxation – if not yet complete abolition – of inward investment rules.[560] As I will argue in Chapter 6, such an agreement could itself be established on a plurilateral platform that offers 'the international template for air service agreements.'[561]

---

rights, would not likely accept unqualified national treatment standards that would extend to foreign carriers the rights of establishment and traffic rights (*i.e.*, 'hard rights') enjoyed by the host country's own carriers. *See infra* Chapter 6, Part III(C).

558. *See generally* BRIAN HINDLEY, TRADE LIBERALIZATION IN AVIATION SERVICES: CAN THE DOHA ROUND FREE FLIGHT? (American Enterprise Institute 2004) (considering the implications of applying GATS principles to air transport services as well as the alternative of forming a transcontinental aviation area outside the GATS). For an analysis of how liberalizing GATS disciplines might be adapted to the 'laboratory' conditions of aircraft-intensive express delivery services, *see* Brian F. Havel, *Rethinking the GATS As A Pathway to Global Aviation Liberalization: A 'Lead Sector' Strategy for the GATS – Express Delivery Services as a Model for Global Air Transport Reform*, Presentation to the Air Transport Research Society 2005 World Conference, Federal University of Rio de Janeiro, Brazil (Jul. 3, 2005) (copy on file with author). For earlier considerations of this topic, *see* Henry A. Wassenbergh, *The Application of International Trade Principles to Air Transport*, 12 AIR L. 84 (1987); Paul V. Mifsud, *New Proposals for New Directions: 1992 and the GATT Approach to Trade in Air Transport Services*, 13 AIR L. 154 (1988). Trade in services also embraces such diverse sectors as banking, telecommunications, information services, insurance, tourism, and transportation.

559. *See generally* Sion, *supra* note 51; *see also* Mifsud, *supra* note 558, at 170; KASPER, *supra* note 36, at xvii.

560. *See* U.S./EC Air Transport Agreement, *supra* note 21, art. 21(2) (also placing on the agenda for the second stage further liberalization of traffic rights, environmental and infrastructural constraints on traffic rights, access to government-financed air transportation, and wet-leasing). Importantly, U.K. foreboding about the 2007 Agreement resulted in a species of unilateral sunset provision which allows either party to suspend rights in the Agreement if a second stage agreement fails. *See id.* art. 21(3).

561. A. L. C. de Mestral and H. Bashor, *International Air Transport Agreements and Regionalism: The Impact of the European Union Upon the Development of International Air Law* 18 (Jean Monnet/Robert Schuman Paper Series. Vol. 5, No. 20, Jul. 2005). De Mestral and Bashor also take note of around 10 other multilateral air services agreements among 'likeminded' economies but detect a more general 'unevenness' in approaches. *Id.* at 30. Other commentators are supportive of extending the U.S./EC model to other jurisdictions. *See, e.g.*, Haanappel, *supra* note 125, at 22 (suggesting that accession of Canada to a U.S./EC common aviation area would be an interesting policy development); Pablo M.J. Mendes de Leon, Presentation to ICAO Global Symposium on Air Transport Liberalization, Dubai, at 10 (Sept. 18-19, 2006) [hereinafter Mendes de Leon, ICAO Presentation] (proposing possibility of accession by third States or regional organizations to a future U.S./EC agreement, giving it a 'plurilateral' rather than a 'multilateral' dimension).

Although these ideas have been extremely slow to take root,[562] the 2007 Agreement points to a political readiness to consider further and deeper integration in the future. This study, therefore, offers a plurilateral strategy that builds on the recent reappraisals that have occurred in both U.S. and EC international aviation policy, and that reflects the juridical symmetry that these two continental systems have now attained.[563]

The international air transport system established at Chicago, with its rigid notions of sovereignty, nationality, and cabotage, strikes jarringly anachronistic notes in an era that still, despite convulsions in the global financial markets, professes to support international free trade, competition, and consumer choice. In the next two Chapters, this study will focus its attention on the United States and the EC as the two 'model jurisdictions' that are ideally positioned to build a future plurilateral successor to the Chicago aviation order. These next Chapters will examine how kindred jurisdictions replaced highly-bureaucratized models of public airline regulation with regimes of *ex post* competition law surveillance, and will offer a critical evaluation of the legal and policy implications of their separate experiments. By a comparative study of the U.S. and EC programs of airline deregulation, including U.S. efforts to 'export' its deregulation initiative, insights will be gained for the construction of a new treaty for the post-2008 era in international aviation.

---

562. Thus, the most recent U.S. free trade agreement to win Congressional approval, the Central American Free Trade Agreement (CAFTA) specifically excludes 'air services, including domestic and international air transportation services,' with some primarily GATS-related exceptions. *See* Central American Free Trade Agreement ch. 11, art. 11.1.4(a). For the U.S. implementing legislation, *see* Dominican Republic-Central America-U.S. Free Trade Agreement Implementation Act, Pub. L. 109-53, 119 Stat. 462. Exclusion of air transport services from U.S. free trade pacts – another marker of the industry's 'specificity' and 'exceptionalism' – has been a consistent feature of such pacts. *See* Mifsud, *supra* note 558, at 167 (noting that air transport was not included in either of the free trade agreements (Canada/U.S. and North American Free Trade Agreement, NAFTA) between Canada and the United States, 'the most liberal trade agreement[s] between the most cordial trading partners').

563. *See* Mendes de Leon, ICAO Presentation, *supra* note 561, at 10.

Chapter 4

Model Jurisdiction I: The United States

Airline Deregulation Within and
Beyond a Unitary Airspace

I   INTRODUCTION

This Chapter will trace the historical and juridical sources of the airline deregulation enterprise in the United States, analyze the structural profile of the domestic air transport industry in the aftermath of deregulation, and critically examine the U.S. open skies policy which was influenced and shaped by the new domestic competitive environment. As will be seen, the initial burst of deregulatory lawmaking (in 1978) reached only to the peripheral borders. The domestic experiment, nevertheless, forms a conceptual bridge to this book's primary focus on the international dimension of U.S. air transport law and policy. That discussion will explore how successive U.S. administrations attempted, through a bilateral open skies policy, to resolve the contradiction between liberated domestic air markets and the tightly wound restrictions of the Chicago bilateral system.[1] A worldwide economic downturn interrupted the initial enthusiasm of U.S. airlines for open skies, and the first generation of 'liberal' bilaterals soon disappeared. Only in the last decade or so, as seen in Chapters 1 and 2, has official U.S. policy sought to restore that early promise of liberalization outside domestic frontiers.

Even in 2007, however, after the signing of the most liberal of all open skies agreements, the U.S./EC Air Transport Agreement,[2] the twin redoubts of cabotage and national ownership have not yet been surrendered. These traditional markers of

---

1. Virginia J. Clarke, *New Frontiers in EEC Transport Competition*, 8 J. Int'l L. Bus. 455, 460 (1987).
2. *See* U.S./EC Air Transport Agreement, 2007 O.J. (L 134) 4 (May 25, 2007) [hereinafter U.S./EC Air Transport Agreement].

Chicago bilateralism would be the coin of exchange in any proposal to merge U.S. federal airspace into a larger transcontinental regime of open competition. As Chapter 3 revealed, tolerance of code-sharing alliances, and an associated willingness to concede antitrust immunity, have compromised the potential strength of the U.S. negotiating position by allowing foreign competitors unprecedented surrogate access to behind-gateway traffic without fundamental concessions toward a multilateral regime of free market access. Chapter 6 will develop a proposal to correct this strategic slippage within the framework of the second stage of U.S./EC air transport negotiations, to the mutual advantage of the United States and its aviation trading partners in the EU.

To provide context for this discussion, a brief introductory note on the composition of the modern U.S. airline industry is appropriate. The industry has developed a characteristic 'tiered' profile, reflected in U.S. DOT statistical reports which classify U.S. carriers by size of annual operating revenues.[3] Twenty-two passenger carriers, led by the familiar triad of American Airlines, United Airlines, and Delta Air Lines, post annual revenues in excess of $1 billion and are termed Group III (formerly 'major') carriers.[4] In 1997, this top-tier list comprised only nine carriers, but it now includes a bevy of fiercely competitive low-cost airlines like Air Tran, JetBlue, and Frontier. (To put the magnitude of the U.S. passenger fleet in its global setting, six Group III carriers are among the world's ten largest airlines.)[5] Airlines with revenues from $100 million up to $1 billion qualify as 'Group II' (formerly 'national') carriers. This list of over 30 carriers includes such stalwarts as Air Wisconsin, Hawaiian Airlines, and Midwest Airlines, but also relatively recent start-ups such as Allegiant Air, Spirit Airlines, and USA3000, all of which have grown dramatically as lower-cost alternatives to the established network carrier incumbents.[6] Three dozen or so lesser carriers with revenues between $20 million

---

3. *See* U.S. Department of Transportation [DOT], Bureau of Transportation Statistics, *Air Carrier Groupings*, Accounting & Reporting Directive No. 284 (Oct. 31, 2007) (effective Jan. 1, 2008) [hereinafter U.S. DOT, *Air Carrier Groupings 2008*]. The carriers are grouped according to the operating revenue boundaries in Part 241.4.

4. *See* U.S. DOT, *Air Carrier Groupings 2008, supra* note 3 (also including for reporting purposes the huge express delivery carriers FedEx and UPS). In order of total passenger operating revenues for the third quarter of 2006, the top seven network majors also comprise Continental Airlines, Northwest Airlines, Southwest Airlines, and US Airways. *See* U.S. DOT, Bureau of Transportation Statistics Data, *Third -Quarter 2006 System Airline Financial Data*, BTS 60-06 (Dec. 18, 2006).

5. Ranked by scheduled passenger kilometers flown, Air France-KLM is fifth, Lufthansa is sixth, British Airways is seventh, and Japan Airlines is tenth. *See* INTERNATIONAL AIR TRANSPORT ASSOCIATION [IATA], WORLD AIR TRANSPORT STATISTICS 103 (52nd ed. 2005) [hereinafter IATA, WORLD STATISTICS].

6. *See* U.S. DOT, *Air Carrier Groupings 2008, supra* note 3, at 2. Price competition, which accompanies the recognition that air travel can be viewed as a commodity, reflects what has happened in other industries where traditional full-service, high-quality providers have been squeezed by low-cost, 'no-frills' competitors. *See* David Gillen, *Airline Business Models and Networks: Regulation, Competition and Evolution in Aviation Markets*, 5 REV. OF NETWORK ECON. 366 (2006) (discussing gradual 'commoditization' of air travel as more consumers fly, air travel becomes an 'A to B' proposition, and flying has forfeited its association with exoticism, luxury, and wealth; in this setting, price-sensitive consumers are ready to trade elements of service for lower prices).

and $100 million or less than $20 million occupy the remaining 'Group I' category (an amalgam of the former 'large regional' and 'medium regional' categories). Among these airlines are sizeable operations like GoJet, Republic Airlines, and Shuttle America.[7]

In the supply of international services, the past decade has seen a number of intriguing trends.[8] Facing febrile competitive conditions at home (stoked in large part by the rise of low-cost carriers), the big U.S. incumbents (notably American, United, Delta, Northwest, and Continental) have increasingly focused on their network strengths in international air travel.[9] But brand new entry into international services has been limited to some marginal activity in the low-cost and premium markets: Spirit and JetBlue, two ambitious low-cost carriers, have pushed into the U.S./Caribbean tourist sector,[10] but premium end providers EOS, Maxjet, and more recently Silverjet, were unable to defy predictions that the incumbents' scale and scope advantages (including passenger loyalty programs) would be difficult to overcome.[11] Whether low-cost international services will expand beyond narrow slices of the tourist market remains uncertain.[12] The conventional model for international service reflects a different logistical dynamic, requiring the airline to 'gather' passengers from a supporting behind-gateway domestic route network. Here the

---

7. *See* U.S. DOT, *Air Carrier Groupings 2008, supra* note 3, at 3. Republic Airlines, for example, has built up extensive code-sharing relationships with four major domestic partners (American, Delta, United, and US Airways). Shuttle America, in fact, is one of a number of Republic subsidiaries, created to allow compliance with the major partners' labor union scope clauses. *See* Sandra Arnoult, *Three Heads Are Better Than One: Subsidiaries of Republic Airways Holdings*, AIR TRANSP. WORLD, Jan. 1, 2006, at 60.

8. Testifying to how the giant U.S. domestic market contributes to U.S. carrier magnitude, in terms of *international* passenger kilometers flown, only two U.S. carriers – American and United – make the top 10. British Airways (in pole position), Lufthansa, Air France-KLM, Singapore Airlines, Cathay Pacific, Japan International Airlines, and Emirates all feature on this list. *See* IATA, WORLD STATISTICS, *supra* note 5, at 103.

9. Delta, for example, which initiated 15 new international routes in 2006, has repositioned itself so that 35% of its revenues are now derived from international services as opposed to only 20% in 2005. The airline, traditionally viewed as a domestic carrier, expects that share to escalate to 40%. One interesting (and risky) aspect of Delta's strategy is to target second-tier destinations such as Venice, Italy, and Nice, France, known for tourism rather than corporate travel. *See* Evan Perez and Melanie Trottman, *Going Global*, WALL ST. J., Sept. 26, 2006, at A1 (noting that U.S. carriers, after a decade of cost-shaving, have per-seat costs that are very competitive with European rivals).

10. *See* Bruce Mohl, *Carriers Making Caribbean Even More Alluring*, BOSTON GLOBE, Oct. 30, 2005, at M8.

11. The bankruptcy of all three carriers was compounded by rising oil prices. *See Silverjet Sacks Entire Workforce*, BBC News, Jun. 13, 2008, <http://news.bbc.co.uk/2/hi/business/7453108.stm>. *See also Analysis: Eos and Maxjet: Transatlantic survivors*, TRADE GAZETTE UK & IRELAND, Oct. 20, 2006 (speculating that, while these airlines could not compete with the incumbents on frequency, their pricing strategy could attract budget-conscious business travelers and leisure travelers seeking greater comfort).

12. Although to some extent JetBlue broke another mold when it inaugurated transcontinental U.S. flights. *See Long-haul Low-cost*, AIRLINE BUS., Dec. 1, 2004, at 7.

hub-and-spoke network structure of the majors still plays a critical role that low-cost competitors cannot match with a simple point-to-point system.[13]

Deregulation in the United States attempted a redistribution of industry wealth from the airlines (the protected constituency under regulation) to the passenger/consumer (the new post-regulation protected constituency). This is, arguably, the net consequence of an increase in routes served, in air carriers serving these routes, and of an aggregate reduction, or stabilization, in prices.[14] The impact on the airlines themselves has been much more problematic, as certain carriers have succumbed to the new dynamic of ferocious price competition and returns to shareholders and bondholders have sometimes collapsed.[15] And, compounding the challenging effects of this new competitive environment, the U.S. airline industry has been tormented by wholly exogenous events such as cyclical weakness in the national economy, the impact of escalating aviation taxes, fees and insurance costs, sustained oil price rises, embargoes created by disease epidemics, the radiating effects of war and terrorism, and, most appallingly, the terrorist attacks of September 11, 2001.[16] Indeed, the industry seems to have been fated

---

13. There is a lively industry debate on the 'holy grail' economics of low-cost long-haul passenger air transport, especially without the cross-subsidy potential of premium classes. *See id.* High aircraft utilization, high density seating, and high load factors, all hallmarks of low-cost service, are difficult to exploit in long-haul contexts. *See id.* Among the potential models being touted is the new Airbus 380 mega-carrier in an all-economy configuration of 760 (and, in a stretched version, 870) seats. *See* Tim Clark, *Low-cost Set for Long-haul*, AIRLINE BUS., Apr. 1, 2005. In Asia, meanwhile, several medium/long-haul point-to-point low-cost carriers are already operating, although no-frills services on true long-haul routes like Asia/Europe have only been attempted by industry veteran Stephen Miller's now-failed Oasis Hong Kong Airlines (to London Gatwick). *See* Andrea Crisp, *Dream or Reality*, AIRLINE BUS., May 1, 2006 (discussing incumbents' competitive advantages through cargo and cross-subsidization from premium classes, fleet size, and natural behind-gateway feed). Most recently, speculation has centered on the plans of AirAsia entrepreneur Tony Fernandes to start Kuala Lumpur/U.K. services that would evolve sales and marketing links with giant EU low-cost carriers like Ryanair and easyJet. Fernandes envisages low-cost carriers around the world partnering in a loose network to package flights rather than entering interlining or alliance arrangements.

14. *See* AIR TRANSPORT ASSOCIATION [ATA], BALANCING THE AVIATION EQUATION: 2007 ECONOMIC REPORT 12 (2007) [hereinafter ATA, 2007 REPORT] (summarizing the positive consumer welfare effects of regulation).

15. *See Airline Commission Proceedings*, Remarks of Robert F. Daniell, Chairman and CEO, United Technologies Corp. (Jun. 16, 1993), at 13-16.

16. The Air Transport Association (ATA), the U.S. industry's principal trade association, published a number of studies analyzing what it has called the 'tenuous' financial profile of much of the industry in the aftermath of the events mentioned in the main text. *See, e.g.*, ATA, AIRLINES IN CRISIS: THE PERFECT ECONOMIC STORM (2003); ATA, 2007 REPORT, *supra* note 14. Before the twin specters of surging oil prices and economic recession presented themselves in 2008, signs of improvement, however, had also been documented. *See* John Heimlich, ATA Vice President & Chief Economist, *2007 Outlook: 'Reaching for the Skies?'*, <www.airlines.org/economics/review_and_outlook/ATA2007EconOutlookOpEd.htm> (rejoicing in a 2006 industry earnings report of $2 billion to $3 billion, in contrast to $35 billion in net losses, and numerous bankruptcies, over the preceding five years). For a longer-term prognosis, *see* U.S. FEDERAL AVIATION ADMINISTRATION [FAA], FAA AEROSPACE FORECASTS FY 2007-2020 (2007) (forecasting a return to significant growth, with one billion passengers being carried by 2015 by U.S. commercial

to experience a very complex and difficult adjustment to the loss of its regulatory cushion.[17] While some aspects of the changing structural profile of the post-regulation airline industry will be examined in some depth later in this Chapter, it is time now to turn to the currents of history.

II THE LEGAL AND HISTORICAL BACKGROUND

A PROLOGUE: AN APT QUOTATION

In 2006, speaking to an audience of U.S. airline industry executives, Jeffrey Shane, the then U.S. Under Secretary for Policy at the U.S. DOT, reminded them of how tenuous were the prospects for enacting airline deregulation when it suddenly appeared as a public policy issue in the 1970s. Although this book does not start its Chapters and Parts with quotations, Shane's astute remarks on the political will that achieved deregulation merit this single exception:

> At a time when deregulation is so widely accepted a public policy objective, it is all too easy to forget how immense an achievement it was. I think of it as the public policy equivalent of the bumble-bee flying. Just as it's not supposed to be physically possible for a bumble-bee to fly, it shouldn't have been politically possible to deregulate the airline industry. In the mid-1970's deregulation was little more than a fashionable idea among a few academic economists. The process whereby an arcane economic proposition was placed on the national policy agenda with such prominence that it simply had to be addressed is one of the most interesting stories in the annals of Congress. It had every indication of turning into one of those quixotic non-contests that we see so often in the legislative process: The public's interest in deregulation was marginal and diffuse; the industry's opposition intense and focused. And yet, in 1978 Congress passed the Airline Deregulation Act. Building further on that historic public policy choice, Congress went on to deregulate trucking, railroads, financial services, energy, and so on. Deregulation today is rapidly taking its place as the default economic policy around the world. But we shouldn't forget that the deregulation of U.S. airlines came first.[18]

---

aviation – up from a record 741 million in 2006, and international traffic significantly outpacing domestic).

17. To set beside the consumer welfare gains of deregulation, the industry has generated a marginal producer surplus, never posting a net profit margin higher than that of the average U.S. corporation (and in fact typically posting a much lower one). *See* Heimlich, *supra* note 16. According to the ATA, U.S. airline profits for 2008 could be as low as $3.5 billion – a substantial drop-off from the $5 billion they posted in 2007. *See Trade Groups See U.S. Airline Profits Falling,* Associated Press, Jan. 4, 2008.

18. Jeffrey N. Shane, Under Secretary for Policy, U.S. Department of Transportation, Remarks to the International Aviation Club, Washington, D.C., at 1 (Sept. 12, 2006).

B   THE REGULATORY ERA: THE *KITTY HAWK* IRONY

The following Parts of Chapter 4 will trace the principal legal and historical themes in the emergence of the inclination to deregulate in U.S. aviation policy. Professor Andreas Lowenfeld spoke of the 'intellectual bankruptcy' of the U.S. Civil Aeronautics Board (CAB),[19] which commanded the airline economy for four decades until the Ford/Carter deregulatory program took wing. A similar unease with regulatory processes animated the hearings held in 1978 by the Subcommittee on Aviation of the Committee on Public Works and Transportation of the U.S. House of Representatives, which preceded the adoption of deregulation legislation.[20] Members of Congress pointed disdainfully to the 'Kitty Hawk irony' of air transport regulation – even while the CAB routinely suppressed new entry through unfavorable administrative rulings and expensive legal proceedings, the agency displayed on its logo 'the image of the airplane which made the first manned flight at Kitty Hawk in 1903.'[21]

In 1938, President Franklin D. Roosevelt signed the Civil Aeronautics Act (which was re-titled in 1958, though basically unchanged, as the Federal Aviation Act[22]). This legislation established the CAB (known until 1940 as the Civil Aeronautics Authority[23]) as an independent agency charged to provide classic public

---

19. Andreas F. Lowenfeld, *Competition in International Aviation: The Next Round*, Address to International Conference on Air Transport and Space Application in the New World, *in Airline Commission Documents*, Dkt. No. 000384 (Jun. 10, 1993), at 1. As evidence of bureaucratic underachievement, Professor Lowenfeld specifically mentioned the Domestic Passenger Fare Investigation, on which the CAB 'labored in ten phases over five years without coming to any intelligible result, except possibly that it was unfair to permit a discount fare for the wife accompanying the full-price paying passenger, but not for the girlfriend, or for the 21-year-old student but not for the worker of the same age.' Lowenfeld also criticized the 'sterile' nature of the CAB's route grant proceedings, which showed, to his ironic viewpoint, that 'due process of law was an entry barrier.' *Id.* at 2.

20. *See generally* LEGISLATIVE HISTORY OF THE AIRLINE DEREGULATION ACT OF 1978, compiled by the Committee on Public Works and Transportation, U.S. House of Representatives, May 1979 [hereinafter LEGISLATIVE HISTORY 1978].

21. *See* REPORT OF SENATE COMM. ON COMMERCE, SCIENCE AND TRANSPORTATION, U.S. House of Representatives, *Amending the Federal Aviation Act of 1958* (Feb. 6, 1978), *reprinted in* LEGISLATIVE HISTORY 1978, *supra* note 20, at 168.

22. In 1958, when Congress established the Federal Aviation Administration, the legislation was re-titled the 'Federal Aviation Act.' 49 U.S.C. §§ 1301-1551 (1979) (recodified in scattered sections of 49 U.S.C.A. beginning at § 40101 (West 2008)). The 1958 Act preserved the economic regulatory system introduced under its predecessor. The Airline Deregulation Act of 1978, discussed at various points in this study, was not a separate body of legislation but instead amended several pieces of existing legislation, most notably the Federal Aviation Act. In 1994, Congress formally integrated these texts as part of a comprehensive consolidation (without substantive changes) of the various federal transportation statutes.

23. The Civil Aeronautics Authority had a comprehensive regulatory remit, covering both economic and safety matters. In 1940, Congress amended the 1938 Act, transferring safety regulation to the Commerce Department and rechristening the Authority as the Civil Aeronautics Board. Under the 1958 amending legislation, responsibility for safety (including air traffic control) became the province of the Federal Aviation Administration, where it remains.

utility-type regulation over the nascent air transportation industry.[24] In 1938, and again in 1958, the agency was assigned to promote 'adequate, economical and efficient service . . . at reasonable charges' and, secondarily, to encourage '[c]ompetition to the extent necessary to assure the sound development of an air transportation system properly adapted to the needs of the foreign and domestic commerce of the United States . . .'[25]

While the quotidian operations of the CAB regulatory system lie outside the scope of this book,[26] certain archetypal features of public utility regulation should be noted. Echoing the linguistic formula used in Chapter 1 to convey the restrictiveness of the Chicago system of international air transport, it can be stated, in summary, that all U.S. interstate domestic air passenger transport was forbidden

---

24. For an excellent account of the reasons behind the passage of the 1938 legislation, *see* Paul S. Dempsey, *The Rise and Fall of the Civil Aeronautics Board – Opening Wide the Floodgates of Entry*, 11 Transp. L.J. 91, 95-107 (1979). As Professor Dempsey explains, Congress was especially concerned that excessive competition was undermining the financial stability of carriers, particularly in the post-Depression era of business fatalities. *See id.* The new Act was patterned on the activist regulatory scheme included in the Motor Carrier Act of 1935, which established federal regulation of motor carrier entry and rates under the jurisdiction of the (now defunct) Interstate Commerce Commission. 49 U.S.C. app. §§ 301-327 (1970), *recodified as* 49 U.S.C.A. § 10101 (West 2008). *See also* Dempsey, *supra*, at 99; Steven Morrison, *Airline Service: The Evolution of Competition Since Deregulation, in* Industry Studies 226 (Larry L. Duetsch ed., 1993). Under the 'public welfare' school of transportation regulation, competition would not be unbridled; it would be controlled competition, in the public interest. But Congress rejected the concept of a European-style national transportation monopoly, even while encouraging the certification of additional carriers to compete with the existing carriers. *See* Dempsey, *supra*, at 105. *See also To Create a Civil Aeronautics Authority: Hearings Before the House Comm. on Interstate and Foreign Commerce*, 75th Cong., 3rd Sess. (1938).
25. 49 U.S.C. § 1302(c)-(d) (1970). Competition under this regulatory apparatus was subordinated to the logistical and technical efficiency of the transportation 'system.' *See supra* note 22. The recodified 49 U.S.C., *see supra* note 22, shows a post-regulation consumer bias in using recast language that refers to 'the availability of a variety of adequate, economic, efficient, and *low-priced services* without unreasonable discrimination or unfair or deceptive practices.' 49 U.S.C.A. § 40101(a)(4) (West 2008) (emphasis added). Much more substantial linguistic surgery – and a manifest change of emphasis – altered the second part of the language quoted in the main text: in effect, a system of air transportation supported by 'managed' competition gave way to a system of competition supporting a system of air transportation. Thus, the new text calls for 'maximum reliance on competitive market forces and on actual and potential competition (A) to provide the needed air transportation system; and (B) to encourage efficient and well-managed air carriers to earn adequate profits and attract capital . . . ' § 40101(a)(6).
26. Nor will this book attempt an economic analysis of the pre-deregulation performance of the U.S. airline industry. It is worth noting, however, that the existence of a regulatory umbrella did not necessarily shelter U.S. airlines from the impact of national recessions. *See Airline Commission Proceedings*, testimony of John E. Robson, former Chairman, Civil Aeronautics Board (Jun. 30, 1993), at 39. For perspectives on the economic behavior of the U.S. airline industry before and after deregulation, *see* Government Accountability Office [GAO], *Airline Deregulation: Re-regulating the Airline Industry Would Likely Reverse Consumer Benefits and Not Save Airline Pensions*, at 10-11, GAO-06-630 (Jun. 2006) [hereinafter GAO, *Re-regulating the Airline Industry*] (showing that industry revenues and expenses have tripled since deregulation, but without the regulatory stability of fares based on costs plus a fixed rare of return).

except to the extent that it was specifically permitted by the CAB.[27] This system of official permissions regulated three broad areas of economic activity by the privately owned airlines:[28] entry (including route assignments), prices, and antitrust, each of which will be considered below. As a pending matter, it is important to notice that the system of regulatory control was quite *open* in its mandate: conceivably, a competition-minded CAB could have used the imprecise bounds of discretionary authority in the 1938/58 codes to enhance, rather than constrict, competitive entry and faresetting. And, as will be seen, that is precisely what the CAB's leadership resolved to do in the immediate prelude to the deregulation statute.

1   CAB Route Authority: The 'Grandfather' Syndrome

As to entry, the CAB prescribed which routes were to be flown, which communities would receive air service, and designated the specific carrier or carriers that would serve those markets. The first regulatory encounter between a carrier and the CAB involved application for a certificate of 'public convenience and necessity' under Title IV of the 1958 Act.[29] This procedure applied both to systemic expansion by existing carriers as well as to new entry application.[30] The Board had a broad authority to impose 'such reasonable terms, conditions, and limitations as the public interest may require' on air carrier certificates.[31] Sixteen carriers operating when the 1938 statute was passed were 'grandfathered' into the new system, receiving certificates for the routes they already served.[32] Of the 10 largest

---

27. *See* the acerbic survey of the CAB's cumbersome operating procedures by John E. Robson, its former Chairman, in *Airline Commission Proceedings*, testimony of John E. Robson (Jun. 30, 1993), at 31.
28. On the parallels between European State participation in airline ownership and the U.S. system of public regulation of private carriers, *see supra* Chapter 3, Part VI.
29. *See* 49 U.S.C. § 1371 (1970). In order to grant the certificate, the Board had to find the applicant 'fit, willing, and able' to perform such transportation properly, and that such transportation was 'required by the public convenience and necessity.' 49 U.S.C. § 1371(d)(1). (These statutory criteria survived into the deregulation era: both the 'fit, willing, and able' and 'public convenience and necessity' formulas are found in recodified 49 U.S.C. § 41102(b)(1) and (2), respectively.) While neither the 1938 nor the 1958 statute defined any of the terms 'fit, willing, and able,' the CAB traditionally selected three primary factors – the existence of an organizational basis for the conduct of air transportation, the presence of a plan for the conduct of the service made by personnel shown to be competent in such matters, and the availability of (or access to) adequate financial resources. *See* Additional Service to Latin America, Dkt. No. 525 et al., 6 C.A.B. 857, 899-900 (May 17, 1946). Congress intended that only those carriers which could convincingly demonstrate minimum financial strength and sufficient stability to protect the public from abuse or risk should be authorized to perform air transport operations. *See* Supplemental Air Service Proceeding, Order Nos. E-24237/8/9, 45 C.A.B. 231, 267 (Sept. 27, 1966). The CAB subsequently relaxed its requirement as to adequate financial resources, requiring only the existence of a plan for financing. *See generally* Chicago-Midway Low-Fare Route Proceeding, Order No. 780-8-208, 78 C.A.B. 454 (Aug. 31, 1978).
30. *See* Legislative History 1978, *supra* note 20, at 220.
31. 49 U.S.C. § 1371(e)(1) (recodified as 49 U.S.C.A. § 41109(a)(2)(B) (West 2008)).
32. In other words, the CAB issued certificates of public convenience and necessity authorizing the incumbents to operate their existing routes. This select group comprised American, Braniff,

domestic U.S. airlines operating in 2008, five had been beneficiaries of grand-fathering in 1938. Indeed, the CAB's conservatism in granting new route awards was notorious. Despite the wide discretion implied in the new statutory framework, it chose to preserve in amber the basic route/carrier configuration that it had inherited in 1938. Thus, in the agency's 40-year history, it never granted a single major ('trunk') route to a new entrant.[33] Moreover, until 1977 the Board prohibited entry on any route that already had two or more carriers.[34]

As Congress noted in 1978, the 1938 legislation was passed with repeated assurances from its sponsors and from carriers that 'competition from capable innovative new airlines would be increased rather than stifled,' but the historical administration of the statute, and its of successor, showed otherwise.[35] Finally, carriers not only had to plead for entry, but also for permission to exit, or 'abandon,' a previously served route.[36] A carrier could not simply suspend service on a route; it required CAB approval to do so. The most common form of 'exit' was

---

Chicago & Southern (later merged into Delta), Colonial (which merged into Eastern), Continental, Delta, Eastern, Inland (also merged into Eastern), Mid-Continent (subsequently merged with Braniff), National, Northeast, Northwest, Penn Central (later, as Capital Airlines, merged with United), Transcontinental and Western (later combined as Trans World Airlines), and United. *See* James W. Callison, *Airline Regulation – A Hoax?*, 41 J. AIR L. & COM. 747, 758 (1975).

33. *See* Morrison, *supra* note 24, at 226. Although subsidiary routes were gradually authorized, these were not allowed to interfere with the route spread of the trunk line carriers. These lesser categories included 'local service' carriers feeding the trunk operators (authorized from 1943), which would grow to become regional carriers such as Allegheny (now US Airways), Air West, Hughes, Frontier, North Central, Ozark, Piedmont, Texas International, and Southern; air taxi and commuter airlines operating aircraft with fewer than 20 seats (from 1952), and various charter operators (after 1962). *See id.* The Senate Committee on Commerce, Science, and Transportation heard testimony that, between 1950 and 1974, the CAB received 74 applications from new firms desiring to enter the domestic airline industry and granted none. *See* LEGISLATIVE HISTORY 1978, *supra* note 20, at 222.

34. *See* Morrison, *supra* note 24, at 226. From 1969 to 1974, the Board enforced an unwritten policy of refusing even to consider applications to compete with incumbent carriers on any given route. *See* LEGISLATIVE HISTORY 1978, *supra* note 20, at 168.

35. *See* LEGISLATIVE HISTORY 1978, *supra* note 20, at 167-68. The Report commented further that

Board regulation of fares and rates has discouraged price competition at every turn. New entrants have been singularly unsuccessful in gaining new route authority, and in the entire [40]-year history of the CAA and CAB, not one airline has been successful in obtaining government permission to enter the domestic trunk industry, despite repeated attempts.

Id. at 168.

36. 49 U.S.C. § 1371(j). To concede 'abandonment,' the CAB had 'to find such abandonment to be in the public interest.' *Id.* A vestigial trace of this power can be found in 49 U.S.C.A. § 41734 (West 2008), which relates to abandonment of routes under the Essential Air Service Program. *But see* the Air Transportation Safety and System Stabilization Act of 2001, H.R. 2926, 107th Congress (2001), the U.S. Government's regulatory response to the airline industry's woes in the wake of Sept. 11, 2001, which conditioned federal credit arrangements to airlines *inter alia* on preserving scheduled service to any points served prior to Sept. 11, 2001. 'On its face, this is reregulation.' Brian F. Havel & Michael G. Whitaker, *The Approach of Re-Regulation: The Airline Industry After September 11, 2001,* [2001-2004 Transfer Binder] ISSUES AVIATION L. &

through mergers, which (often with CAB prompting) allowed healthy carriers conveniently to extend their route authority.[37]

2   CAB Rate Authority: The 'Pullman' Effect

With respect to faresetting, carriers had to file 'tariffs' with the Board, including prior notice of any change in fares.[38] The Board's power was not to determine fares as such, but it had various supervisory and suspensory powers that allowed it to re-calibrate those fares it deemed to be 'unjust or unreasonable,'[39] or to prevent a fare going into effect pending agency investigation of the proposed fare, which frequently resulted in cancellation or alteration of that fare.[40] Despite its lack of *original* ratemaking authority, the Board conducted two ratemaking proceedings designed to develop a general domestic fare policy that would enable it to 'standardize' its consideration of tariff filings. Indeed, the Board's confessed priority in setting fares was the global one of maintaining carrier profitability, and it did not probe the relationship between fares and costs in particular markets.[41]

It is hard to imagine today, but initially the Board simply replicated first-class, 'Pullman,' rail fares.[42] Later, the agency contrived various standardized industry formulas based on serving markets of a given distance on the basis of aircraft configured with an assumed number of seats. In the Domestic Passenger Fare Investigation (DPFI), for example, which began in 1969, the Board calculated a fare level that would provide the carriers with a 12% return on investment, assuming that 55% of the seats on the standard-configuration aircraft would be filled at this fare level. Thus, tariffs filed above the DPFI level were rejected as unlawfully

---

POL'Y ¶ 10,051, at 4109 (2001) (noting that the Act arguably foreclosed all discretionary route exit for any U.S. airline accepting financial relief for direct losses incurred as a result of the federal ground stop order issued on Sept. 11, 2001 and for any incremental losses to the end of 2001 that were the result of the terror attacks).

37. *See* Morrison, *supra* note 24, at 227.
38. 49 U.S.C. app. §§ 1373 & 1482 (1970). Today, only tariffs for international air transportation are in principle required to be filed. *See* 49 U.S.C.A. § 41109(a)(2)(B) (West 2008).
39. 49 U.S.C. § 1482(d) (repealed).
40. 49 U.S.C. § 1482(g) (repealed). The Board had a statutory window of up to 180 days to review any proposed fare. *See id.*
41. *See* Civil Aeronautics Board [CAB], *Report to Congress on Implementation of the Provisions of the Airline Deregulation Act of 1978, in Airline Commission Documents*, Dkt. No. 000462, Jan. 31, 1984, at 16 [hereinafter CAB, *Report to Congress*]. Although the Board allowed some discounting in the 1960s, after 1969, as it embraced greater uniformity in faresetting, it ordered their availability sharply reduced. *See id.* at 17.
42. *See id.* at 16. The CAB maintained in 1978 that this original fare structure was 'probably not seriously out of line' with the cost of providing air transportation in the pre-jet era. *Id.* The parity with first-class rail fares, which persisted into the 1950s, helped perpetuate the regulatory era notion of flying as a 'rich man's club.' *See* BARBARA STURKEN PETERSON & JAMES GLAB, RAPID DESCENT: DEREGULATION AND THE SHAKEOUT IN THE AIRLINES 28 (1994). *See also* International Airline Passengers Association, Submission to Airline Commission, *in Airline Commission Documents*, Dkt. No. 000490, at 3 (stating: 'Those of us who remember the days of the Civil Aeronautics Board remember a very simple fare structure – one high fare for everyone').

excessive, and those below DPFI were rejected as uneconomically low.[43] Support for Professor Lowenfeld's charge of 'intellectual bankruptcy' is most available from the process that generated this rigid distance-based formula: former CAB chairman Robson witheringly depicted the DPFI, which Lowenfeld deplored, as the 'baroque' period of fare regulation.[44]

Another obvious flaw in the CAB's regulatory ratemaking, as the DPFI vividly illustrated, was the forced need for consistency. Coach fares in all markets were generally adjusted in unison.[45] The system had no built-in tolerance for different markets or market segments (the relative lack of time-sensitivity in leisure travel, for example).[46] Instead, by restraining fare flexibility, the system forced airlines to engage in wasteful, nonprice competition – flight frequency and scheduling, airplane equipment, inflight cabin service, or ergonomic seating configurations, none of which the CAB explicitly controlled.[47] Carriers naturally sought the premium that the CAB allowed in long-haul markets, adding equipment and flights in these markets while shaving service to less profitable short-haul markets.[48] What the CAB would *not* do, until almost the eve of deregulation, was even to

---

43. *See* LEGISLATIVE HISTORY 1978, *supra* note 20, at 169; CAB, *Report to Congress, supra* note 41, at 17. In the belief that cross-subsidization of short-haul routes by long-haul routes would increase aviation services, making markets of less than 400 miles more competitive with surface modes, the formulas were fixed to allow long routes to be more expensive than cost and short routes to be below cost. *See id.*

44. *Airline Commission Proceedings* (Jun. 30, 1993), at 36. *See* CAB, *Report to Congress, supra* note 41, at 17 (containing the Board's institutional *mea culpa* for the DPFI). Since the DPFI was explicitly distance-based, the fares in many markets were seriously out of line with actual costs. The average cost of service falls as the number of passengers traveling in a market rises, yet the DPFI did not consider market density in establishing fares. *See id.*

45. *See* CAB, *Report to Congress, supra* note 41, at 16.

46. The Board 'never formally considered the advantages of peak-load pricing.' *Id.* at 16. In addition, although earlier CAB-approved discounting focused on particular passenger segments (youth fares, for example), the post-regulation pricing structure differentiates discretionary and time-sensitive passengers generically, often using advance-purchase and minimum stay requirements. (This differentiation was ingeniously harnessed in the carriers' yield management technologies, discussed *supra* Chapter 3, Part VII.)

47. The CAB did not regulate flight capacity or frequency. 'No term, condition, or limitation of a certificate shall restrict the right of an air carrier to add to or change schedules, equipment, accommodations, and facilities for performing the authorized transportation and service as the development of the business and demands of the public shall require.' 49 U.S.C. § 1371(e)(4) (1970). This language has survived, virtually unaltered, into recodified 49 U.S.C.A. § 41109(a)(2)(B) (West 2008).

48. There was no *legal* compulsion on the CAB to restrain price competition. It simply chose to do so, in exercise of its regulatory discretion. Since many routes had only one or two authorized carriers, and free entry was excluded, price competition did not appear to be a sensible tactic. The system had 6,000-7,000 monopoly routes and about 2,500 markets in which there were two or more carriers. *See Airline Commission Proceedings,* remarks of Commissioner John E. Robson, former Chairman, Civil Aeronautics Board (Jun. 30, 1993), at 37. Post-regulation, according to a recent Government Accountability Office study, the average number of effective competitors (an airline that carries at least 5% of the traffic in that market) in any city-pair increased from 2.2 in 1980 to 3.5 in 2005. By 2005, 76% of city-pair markets analyzed by the

consider the argument, in deciding route cases, that lower fares would create new traffic, thereby allowing additional carriers into active competition.[49]

3   CAB Antitrust Authority: Regulatory Omnipotence

Finally, in the sphere of antitrust, the regulated airline industry lived a charmed life: the Board had, and exercised, plenipotentiary powers to immunize inter-carrier mergers and agreements that might otherwise violate the U.S. antitrust laws.[50] The sweep of this immunizing authority has been unmatched in U.S. regulatory history.[51] In fact, the Board held Janus-like powers over airlines' business transactions. In one guise, it could second-guess the wisdom of carrier managements by disapproving mergers and acquisitions that it found 'not ... consistent with the public interest'[52] or intercarrier agreements it found 'adverse to the public interest.'[53] Changing its countenance, however, it could use its power to immunize approved transactions to permit carriers to engage in seriously anticompetitive behavior without peril from antitrust exposure, and indeed without any attempt by the CAB to measure that behavior against the principles and policies of the antitrust laws.[54] The 1971-75 capacity reduction agreements between United

---

GAO (*i.e.*, all markets with greater than 1180 flying passengers per quarter) had three or more carriers, compared with 34% of all city-pair markets in 1980. Only 5% of city-pair markets had one carrier by 2005, compared to 20% in 1980. *See* GAO, *Re-regulating the Airline Industry, supra* note 26, at 26-28 (noting that small markets – less than 250 miles – have not done as well as longer-distance markets which allow more options for connecting over hubs).

49. *See* LEGISLATIVE HISTORY 1978, *supra* note 20, at 169; CAB, *Report to Congress, supra* note 41, at 18.

50. 49 U.S.C. § 1384 (1970). The language of Section 414 of the Federal Aviation Act purported to 'relieve' from the operations of the antitrust laws 'any person' affected by a CAB order (granted under other sections) to approve *inter alia* a merger or acquisition, an interlocking board relationship, or an intercarrier agreement. The recodified text, found in 49 U.S.C.A. § 41308 (West 2008), applies only to agreements that do not involve 'interstate transportation,' *i.e.*, agreements involving international transportation.

51. See the comments of the Senate Committee on Commerce, Science, and Transportation, *in* LEGISLATIVE HISTORY 1978, *supra* note 20, at 241-51.

52. 49 U.S.C. § 1378(b) (1970) (repealed). The only explicit check on the Board's discretion to approve *any* transaction was that the applicable transaction should not create a monopoly. *See* 49 U.S.C. § 1378(b) (repealed).

53. 49 U.S.C. app. § 1382(b) (1970) (repealed).

54. *See* comments in the REPORT OF THE SENATE COMMITTEE ON COMMERCE, SCIENCE, AND TRANSPORTATION, *in* LEGISLATIVE HISTORY 1978, *supra* note 20, at 241. The CAB's record in assessing mergers was to use them as a tool for resuscitating ailing carriers, and not to investigate the potential or actual competitive nexus between the merged airlines. In one instance, the Board approved a merger that created a monòpoly in a given market upon the mere promise of the carriers not to reduce service. *See id.* at 245. *See* the observations of Administrative Judge Joseph J. Saunders, North Central-Southern Merger Case, C.A.B. Order Nos. 79-6-7, 79-6-8, 82 C.A.B. 1 (May 15, 1979): 'While acknowledging from time to time that national antitrust policy was an important public interest consideration, the Board also took the position that it was 'not an antitrust court,' and that 'concepts and specific criteria developed by the courts in interpreting the provisions of the Clayton Act in the context of free market conditions are not necessarily

Airlines, American Airlines, and Trans World Airlines, for example, were blatantly anticompetitive but obtained incontestable CAB approval and immunity.[55] Indeed, this decision to allow major carriers to improve their profitability by the expedient of agreeing to capacity limitations on major routes was cited by proponents of deregulation as a classic instance of ill-conceived regulatory meddling.[56]

None of this vast regulatory oversight, it should be stated, occurred by the mere exchange of polite letters between the applicant and the CAB. In what former CAB Chairman John Robson described as *'overdue* process . . . an attempt to judicialize the marketplace decisions,'[57] the CAB conducted lengthy (and expensive) proceedings to dispose of its route, fare, and antitrust exemption applications. Thus, each time a carrier wished to serve a new city-pair, it had to prosecute a separate application through formal evidentiary hearings.[58] Congressional testimony showed that the CAB used the device of granting a 'motion for expedited hearing' to give preference to certain route applications and to consign others, lacking this privileged status, to a limbo that led to their eventual dismissal as 'stale.' The Senate was highly critical of this procedural chicanery.[59] In sum, the

---

determinative of whether a proposed action meets . . . the overall public interest considerations deemed relevant by the framers of the Federal Aviation Act . . . 'Under this interpretation . . . the Board's antitrust resolve was erratic; and with the broad discretion afforded by the "public interest" test, antitrust policy was often ignored. . . .' (citations omitted).

55. Anomalous as they now appear in the age of deregulation, these capacity reduction agreements, and the powers by which the CAB immunized them, have returned to public debate in 2008 as the airline industry struggles to cope with the pincer effects of high capacity and volatile fuel prices. *See infra* Part IV(C) (discussing recent arguments for reregulation of the U.S. airline industry). Under its antitrust immunity powers, the CAB approved a wide variety of agreements affecting domestic air transportation, covering such routine and unobjectionable matters as uniform procedures for ticketing, interlining baggage, and the recognition of tickets issued by one carrier for transportation on another carrier, as well as efficiency-enhancing solutions such as joint provision of ground facilities, including maintenance. *See* Legislative History 1978, *supra* note 20, at 247. The European Commission preserved similar 'technical' exceptions through the 'block exemption' feature of its liberalization program. *See infra* Chapter 5, Part II.

56. *See, e.g.*, Morrison, *supra* note 24, at 227. According to evidence presented to Congress, the capacity limitation agreements were largely attempts to increase the profits of carriers by market-sharing arrangements with select competitors. The carriers were shielded from price competition by regulation; the capacity agreement provided shelter from service competition also. Passengers received high load factor service without the benefit of the lower prices that could be expected in a competitive environment. *See* Report of the Senate Committee on Commerce, Science, and Transportation, *in* Legislative History 1978, *supra* note 20, at 247-48.

57. *Airline Commission Proceedings* (Jun. 30, 1993), at 31 (emphasis added).

58. *See* Legislative History 1978, *supra* note 20, at 168.

59. *Id.* at 222. 'Staleness' dismissals usually occurred after three years. There is much anecdotal evidence of the CAB's tardiness, whether accidental or contrived, in processing new route applications. For example, in 1967 Continental Airlines applied to serve the San Diego/Denver route. Although the Administrative Law Judge found that Continental should be permitted to offer service in that market, the Board refused authority due to the overall weak state of the industry (after 1969, it had imposed an informal moratorium on all major routes for this reason). In late 1975, a court of appeals sent the case back to the Board for additional hearings, and

omnipotence of the CAB, both procedurally and substantively, caused airline executives to focus not on the competitive demands of particular routes, but on the legal and technical arguments and supporting data required to persuade the CAB to exercise its plenary authority to grant a new route, to alter an existing fare, or to permit some form of cooperative activity with another carrier. Since the CAB, in other words, assumed the 'managerial prerogative' for the industry,[60] a regulatory mindset enveloped both the CAB itself and its airline supplicants.[61]

C   DEREGULATION: THE INTELLECTUAL PREMISES

The political, economic, and (in fairness) academic catalysts for airline deregulation in the United States have been widely canvassed. The existing regulatory system, while it displayed certain obvious inefficiencies, was not in any danger of early breakdown. Equally obvious, however, was that the CAB and its byzantine procedures could take little credit for the industry's growth: that outcome was the product of surging demand for air travel in a huge and affluent domestic market, a demand that could be nurtured and gratified by advanced new jet technologies.[62] And even with this sustained expansion, carrier profits continued to be modest.[63] Accordingly, there was no broad fealty to regulation, nor any noticeable rejection of it. But other possibilities for operating the industry began to be considered.[64] For example, extensive analysis by professors of economics, who held that

Continental received its authority to serve the route nearly 10 years after it first filed its application. *See id.* at 223.

60. *Airline Commission Proceedings*, remarks of Commissioner Herbert D. Kelleher, President, Southwest Airlines, Jun. 16, 1993, at 70.

61. An incidental consequence of the CAB's supremacy was its ability to prevent airline bankruptcies, by gently folding ailing carriers into other carriers when a crisis threatened. The resulting combination, even if it had anticompetitive effects, could be immunized from antitrust challenge. *See Airline Commission Proceedings*, remarks of Commissioner John E. Robson, former Chairman, Civil Aeronautics Board, Jun. 30, 1993, at 34.

62. From the beginning of regulation in 1938 to 1974, the number of revenue passenger-miles flown per year had increased from 476 million to 120 billion, while investment increased from $30 million to more than $8 billion. *See* STEPHEN BREYER, REGULATION AND ITS REFORM 198 (1982).

63. *See* LEGISLATIVE HISTORY 1978, *supra* note 20, at 170.

64. In a 1951 study, Lucile Sheppard Keyes suggested three possible alternatives to the CAB regulatory apparatus: full-scale nationalization, abolition of all 'the present specific regulation of the air transport business (except that involving safety),' and a mixed system of regulatory control and decontrol. LUCILE SHEPPARD KEYES, FEDERAL CONTROL OF ENTRY INTO AIR TRANSPORTATION 331, 338 (1951). The second and third options would actually differ little in practice, since they would both confine government intervention to the antitrust sphere. *See also* Lucile Sheppard Keyes, *National Policy Toward Commercial Aviation – Some Basic Problems*, 16 J. AIR L. & COM. 280 (1949); RICHARD E. CAVES, AIR TRANSPORT AND ITS REGULATORS 447-48 (1962) (recommending a staged deregulation of the air transport industry, initially opening up large city-pair markets to free entry and pricing).

transportation modes were in no sense public utilities[65] and that air carriers had no inherent tendencies toward monopoly,[66] was supposedly confirmed by the early experience of unregulated intrastate carriers in California and Texas.[67] In other

---

65. Traditional public utility industries (telephone services, electrical grids) have obvious characteristics of large-scale investment in fixed, immobile assets. Airplanes, the 'hardware' of the airline industry, require large investments. Otherwise, however, very little airline capital is invested in fixed, immobile assets. The principal asset, the aircraft, is mobile and is capable of competitive deployment in many types of market. The airspace 'grid' is a fact of nature, and public investment has created a network of accessible airport facilities. For a discussion of public utility regulation, *see supra* Chapter 3, note 316 and accompanying text.

66. At the dawn of airline deregulation in the United States, the notion of competition was virtually synonymous with an appealing economic theory known as the 'contestable markets hypothesis' or 'contestability.' Contestability was assumed to be an unappreciated characteristic of airline markets: ease of entry (airplanes are inherently mobile and use publicly-owned airports and airspace) would allow potential competitors to discipline the prices charged by actual competitors in any given city-pair market. The result, a systemic market discipline, would presumably thwart monopoly pricing behavior. Thus, even though a city-pair market might have high concentration (one or two dominant carriers), the *in terrorem* effect created by the existence of other potential competitors who could quickly mobilize the route would deter price-gouging (or 'supranormal profits,' in economic parlance) or other market abuses by the dominant players. *See* KEYES, *supra* note 64, at 344; CAVES, *supra* note 64, at 429, both of whom analyzed the theoretical implications of contestability even before it was named as such in the economic literature (a post-deregulation event). The theory had superficial allure: its key assumption was that a new entrant would have the same costs as existing incumbents, and could theoretically enter the market, undercut the incumbents' price by a small margin, and costlessly exit the markets if the incumbents moved their prices below the entrant's cost (so-called 'hit-and-run' entry). However, the assumption of porous entry and exit in airline markets has only been intermittently accurate in post-1978 experience. In particular, the theoretical assumption that producers would face costless and instantaneous entry and exit, implying a conceptual separation between market structure and market power, did not accurately portray the post-1978 marketplace. *See* Michael E. Levine, *Price Discrimination Without Market Power*, 19 YALE J. ON REG. 1, 10 n.27 (2002). For an economic analysis of the contestability theory, *see* WILLIAM BAUMOL ET AL., CONTESTABLE MARKETS AND THE THEORY OF INDUSTRY STRUCTURE (rev. ed. 1988).

67. Because the Civil Aeronautics Act regulated 'interstate air transportation,' airlines operating exclusively within one state were not subject to federal regulation. Price comparisons could therefore be made, at least crudely, between fares on intrastate routes and comparable interstate routes. It was not unusual to find that certificated carriers charged over 50% more than their intrastate brethren to cover comparable distances. *See* Morrison, *supra* note 24, at 227. *See generally* Michael E. Levine, *Is Regulation Necessary? California Air Transportation and National Regulatory Policy*, 74 YALE L.J. 1416 (1965); Simat, Helliesen & Eichner, Inc., *The Intrastate Air Regulation Experience in Texas and California, reprinted in* REGULATION OF PASSENGER FARES AND COMPETITION AMONG THE AIRLINES 40 (P. Macavoy & J. Snow eds., 1977). Levine wrote a wistful revisit of his 1965 article in 1987. *See* Michael E. Levine, *Airline Competition in Deregulated Markets: Theory, Firm Strategy, and Public Policy*, 4 YALE J. ON REG. 393 (1987) [hereinafter Levine, *Airline Competition*]. For a further, more assertively 'deregulationist' dissection of the state of the U.S. airline industry after its 'perfect economic storm' in the early 2000s, *see* Michael E. Levine, *Why Weren't the Airlines Reregulated?*, 23 YALE J. ON REG. 269 (2006) [hereinafter Levine, *Reregulation*] (including recollections of the opposition of organized airline interests to calls for deregulation that Lucile Sheppard Keyes first put on the national agenda as early as 1949, *see id.* at 276). The rationale for the intrastate/interstate comparison is disputed by Richard J. Fahy in his article, *Deregulation in the United*

words, the airline industry did not have the characteristics that made economic (as opposed to safety) regulation desirable or necessary.[68]

In addition, various Congressional players shaped a legislative strategy for deregulation. Of critical significance was Senator Edward Kennedy's Subcommittee on Administrative Practice and Procedure of the Senate Committee on the Judiciary, which held widely publicized hearings in 1976 to consider arguments on airline deregulation.[69] The Kennedy Report[70] concluded that:

> The airline industry is potentially highly competitive, but the [CAB's] system of regulation discourages the airlines from competing in price and virtually forecloses new firms from entering the industry. The result is high fares and security for existing firms. But the result does not mean high profits. Instead the airlines – prevented from competing in price – simply channeled their competitive energies toward costlier service: more flights, more planes, more frills. . . . The remedy is for the [CAB] to allow both new and existing firms greater freedom to lower fares and . . . to obtain new routes.[71]

States: Success or Failure?, 16 INT'L BUS. LAW. 272 (1988), where he noted that 21 out of 23 carriers went bankrupt in California's free marketplace. Similar skepticism was expressed by some CAB staff officials. Memorandum of Julien R. Schrenk, *Evaluation of Report of CAB Special Staff: Regulatory Reform 1975, in Airline Commission Documents*, Dkt. No. 000462, at 2 & 4 [hereinafter CAB Schrenk Memorandum].

68. For an opportunity to see and hear Professor Michael Levine's personal recollections of his pioneering work on California's intrastate airlines in the 1960s, *see A Conversation with Michael E. Levine* (Apr. 17, 2006), the first in a series of webcast 'Conversations with Aviation Leaders' produced by the International Aviation Law Institute of DePaul University College of Law. (The series is creating an oral history of the legal, political, and economic events surrounding U.S. airline deregulation in the 1970s.) The entire conversation may be found online at <www.law.depaul.edu/centers_institutes/aviation_law/webcast.asp>.

69. *See generally* James W. Callison, *Airline Deregulation – Only Partially a Hoax: The Current Status of the Airline Deregulation Movement*, 45 J. AIR L. & COM. 961, 962 (1980). Although senior CAB officials would later support deregulation, in the mid-1970s the agency was divided on the issue of regulatory reform. *See, e.g.*, CAB Schrenk Memorandum, *supra* note 67. Shrenk deplored 'the near term (and possibly long-term) disruption in the air transportation system such a basic change would create,' and questioned whether a shift to market-oriented systems would be 'in the public interest.' *Id.* at 1.

70. *See* REPORT OF THE SUBCOMM. ON ADMINISTRATIVE PRACTICE AND PROCEDURE OF THE SENATE COMM. ON THE JUDICIARY, 94th Cong., 1st Sess. 3 (1975) [hereinafter KENNEDY REPORT].

71. *Id.* at 3. *See also* Gloria J. Garland, *The American Deregulation Experience and the Use of Article 90 to Expedite EEC Air Transport Liberalization*, 7 E.C.L.R. 193, 218 (1986). Thus, starved of the opportunity to compete through lower fares or by invading new routes, carriers in the CAB-style regulated system were forced to promote costly 'service' competition oriented toward the business traveler (the marks of differentiation tended to be flight frequency, in-flight food and beverage services, flight equipment, and advertising). It has been suggested that this nonprice competition was actually cost-enhancing competition, which could be paid for by ever-increasing CAB-approved fare increases. *See* KENNEDY REPORT, *supra* note 70, at 25, 29; Garland, *supra*, at 221; Herbert D. Kelleher, *Deregulation and the Troglodytes – How the Airlines Met Adam Smith*, 50 J. AIR L. & COM. 299, 314 (1985).

Tellingly, the report stopped shy of recommending abolition of the CAB. It confined its recommendations to broadening entry, scrapping fare regulation, and revamping the agency to respond better to consumer needs.[72]

D   DEREGULATION: A POLITICAL ACT OF WILL

A political act of will – which, in U.S. governance, had to implicate the full attention and support of the President – carried into effect the 'immense achievement' of U.S. airline deregulation.[73] Moreover, airline deregulation was a *bipartisan* presidential achievement.[74] A draft deregulation bill was submitted to Congress in October 1975, by the Republican administration of President Gerald R. Ford.[75] By 1978, committees of both the Senate and the House of Representatives were working on draft versions of bills to reform airline regulation.[76]

---

72. The report did not reach consensus on what a post-regulation industry structure would look like, with estimates varying from 'more than six' carriers to as many as from 200 to 400. *See* KENNEDY REPORT, *supra* note 70, at 63, n.128. Ironically (in view of the steady concentration the industry has experienced since deregulation began), the CAB staff reports assumed 100 to 200 separate carriers, and some officials feared chronic *fragmentation* of the industry as a result. *See* CAB Schrenk Memorandum, *supra* note 67, at 3. For a first-hand account of the Kennedy hearings and of their significance in building political support for airline deregulation, *see A Conversation with Michael E. Levine, supra* note 68.

73. Returning to Jeffrey Shane's clever assessment of the political will behind deregulation, Shane and Professor Michael Levine would agree on the indispensability of executive leadership to the coming of deregulation, but Levine would probably dispute Shane's observation that the public's interest was 'marginal and diffuse.' In fact, for a brief but critical window of time, the public (and their avatars in the media) became immensely intrigued by the supposedly esoteric domain of airline deregulation. Thus, Levine explains airline deregulation as a coincidence of (1) an inflationary period that made the public interested in any policy that promised lower prices, (2) an 'academic story' that supported lower consumer prices and that could be translated into something newsworthy for the media and 'striking for policy entrepreneurs,' (3) a combination of political ideology (the Ford Administration) and jockeying between Jimmy Carter and Edward Kennedy for the support of centrist Democrats as the 1980 election approached, and (4) unfavorable publicity 'in suspicious times' for widespread direct contact between the regulators and the industry (and even a whiff of scandal related to the Watergate affair). The issue became 'politically salient,' Levine argues, and thus eliminated the protective veil of 'slack,' Levine's term for the collusion that allows regulators and their industries to cohabit outside the gaze of public scrutiny. Levine, *Reregulation, supra* note 67, at 277.

74. *See Airline Commission Proceedings*, comments of John E. Robson, former Chairman, Civil Aeronautics Board (Jun. 30, 1993), at 30.

75. Callison, *supra* note 69, at 963, n.3.

76. As noted in the main text, the terminological mindset of the legislators was instructive. The initial Senate bill, S. 2493, as reported out of the Committee on Commerce, Science, and Transportation on Feb. 6, 1978, proposed enactment of the 'Air Transportation Regulatory Reform Act of 1978.' LEGISLATIVE HISTORY 1978, *supra* note 20, at 6. The House version, H.R. 12611, reported out of the Committee on Public Works and Transportation on May 19, 1978, envisaged an 'Air Service Improvement Act of 1978.' *Id.* at 509. Only after the House/Senate Conference Report, which issued on Oct. 12, 1978, did the title 'Airline Deregulation Act of 1978' win bicameral endorsement. *See id.* at 843.

On October 24, 1978, in the closing hours of the 95th Congress, Ford's successor, Democrat Jimmy Carter, signed into law the Airline Deregulation Act (ADA), which proposed a gradual shutting-down of the airline industry's regulatory incubator, including the demise of the CAB itself in 1985.[77]

It is important to recognize, in comparing the U.S. and European deregulatory endeavors, that despite growing academic and legislative fervor for airline deregulation in the United States, there was no so-called *big bang* to launch deregulation of the U.S. airline industry.[78] The 'specificity' of this industry, a 50-year-old regulated oligopoly where route and rate competition was blockaded, and new routes were awarded by the CAB in a manner calculated to stabilize existing market shares, meant that an instantaneous deregulation was no more plausible in the United States than it was later inside the EC.[79] To allow time for the behemoth incumbents to adjust to the new conditions of *post hoc* competitive scrutiny,

---

77. President Carter's executive leadership was indispensable to the deregulation project, but no less critical was the strong advice he received on the subject from one of his young aides, lawyer Mary Schuman (later Mary Boies). Ms. Boies' role was saluted by former CAB Chairman Alfred E. Kahn in his webcast interview for the DePaul International Aviation Law Institute's 'Conversations with Aviation Leaders' series. *See A Conversation with Alfred E. Kahn*, <www.law.depaul.edu/centers_institutes/aviation_law/kahn_interview.asp>.

78. *See* Kelleher, *supra* note 71, at 300. The expression 'big bang' comes from the Thatcher Government's deregulation of the London Stock Exchange in 1986. The fixed minimum scale of brokerage commissions and the single capacity broker/jobber system helped to sustain the Exchange's near-monopoly of securities trading. In Oct. 1986, brokerage commissions became negotiable, and on the same day firms were permitted to act in a dual capacity as both principals and agents in the marketing of securities. The combination of dual capacity and brokerage competition was referred to as the 'Big Bang.' *See generally* ANDREW MARR, A HISTORY OF MODERN BRITAIN 427 (2007); *see also* DENNIS SWANN, THE RETREAT OF THE STATE: DEREGULATION AND PRIVATIZATION IN THE U.K. AND U.S. 280 (1988). For a favorable 20-year retrospective on the contribution of the 'Big Bang' to exposing London's creaking investment houses to international competition and, until recently, in any event, restoring the city's fortunes as a global financial center, *see* Peter Thai Larsen, *Hats off: Big Bang Still Brings Scale and Innovation to Finance in London*, FIN. TIMES ONLINE, Oct. 26, 2006.

79. The view has persisted in EC liberalization literature that U.S. airline deregulation *did* happen with sudden force. *See* Eugenie Kalshoven-van Tijen, *The EEC Commission as the European Version of the CAB?*, 15 AIR L. 257 (1990) (stating that '[d]eregulation in the USA happened almost overnight'); *see also* Pat Hanlon, *Book Review: Kenneth Button et al., Flying into the Future: Air Transport Policy in the European Union*, 109 ECON. J. F843 (1999) (describing how the authors 'contrast the more gradual, incremental process of liberalization in Europe with the essentially 'big bang' type of deregulation that took place in the United States'); *but see* Kenneth Button, *Airlines*, Paper Presented to the Meeting of STELLA/STAR Focus Group 5: Institutions, Regulations and Markets in Transportation, Athens (Jun. 4-5, 2004) (describing U.S. airline deregulation as a 'big bang', but only in the sense that 'a single act radically changed the way the domestic aviation market was regulated . . . the move was not to an immediate free market but rather a time schedule for the relaxation of price and entry regulations established'). Curiously, the European Commission recently appropriated the term 'big bang' to refer to the accession of 10 Eastern European countries to the European Union in 2004. *See* European Commission, Myths and Facts About Enlargement, <http://ec.europa.eu/enlargement/questions_and_answers/myths_en.htm>.

and to the disappearance of the regulatory safety net that protected even the most cost-inefficient carriers, the 1978 Act ushered in a 'staggered' approach to deregulation that was more like the later EC phases of gradual liberalization than the revolutionary assault on the regulation barricades that it may appear (or have been made to appear) in retrospect. This deliberately piecemeal approach was attacked as 'a supreme philosophical contradiction,'[80] and at least partially a 'hoax.'[81]

If indeed some deception or imposture was contemplated, it could be discerned from the manner in which Congress chose to structure its new deregulation statute. Rather than a *de novo* recodification, the ADA instead comprised a lengthy procession of amendments to the original Federal Aviation Act. Partly because of intense lobbying by most of the airlines, which publicly endorsed competition but privately preferred the 'steady-state' CAB regime,[82] Congress did not have the appetite for a sudden Smithian lurch to a free market. Indeed, the initial draft bill reported out of the Senate Committee on Commerce, Science, and Transportation was conservatively designated the 'Air Transportation Regulatory Reform Act of 1978.'[83] Given the legislators' vestigial 'regulatory' complex, which envisaged only a 'moderate, controlled release of some regulatory fetters,'[84] it is also unsurprising that the House and Senate legislators did not propose the immediate abolition of the CAB and all its works. Instead, they elected to limit the agency's lifespan through a series of rolling sunset provisions, under which it would gradually forfeit its authority in each of its traditional spheres of regulatory control.[85]

---

80. Wesley G. Kaldahl, *Let The Process Of Deregulation Continue*, 50 J. Air L. & Com. 285, 286 (1985).

81. Callison, *supra* note 69, at 965.

82. *See* Levine, *Reregulation, supra* note 67, at 282 (explaining how the preferred policy of the large airlines was CAB regulation, a unanimity that ended when United Airlines publicly endorsed deregulation in 1977). Nonetheless, widespread industry opposition continued until the passage of the ADA. *See id.* In Levine's assessment, neither the airline industry nor its labor unions was likely to embrace a policy that would destroy the value of CAB certificates (including their value as implicit loan collateral); destroy the industry's ability to suppress fare competition in concert with the CAB; remove a 40-year moratorium on new entry; dramatically revise the route network, making some fleets and facilities obsolete; and expose labor contracts that were well above market in wages and work rules to competitive pressure. *Id.* at 276.

83. Legislative History 1978, *supra* note 20, at 172.

84. *See* Rep. of House Comm. On Public Works and Transportation of the House of Representatives, May, 19, 1978, *in* Legislative History 1978, *supra* note 20, at 512. *See* Paul S. Dempsey, *Airlines, Aviation and Public Policy, the Need for Regulatory Reform*, Submission to the Airline Commission, *in Airline Commission Documents*, Dkt. No. 000044 (Jun. 1, 1993) [hereinafter Dempsey, *Airlines, Aviation and Public Policy*]. Professor Dempsey distinguished deregulation from regulatory reform, construing the latter as a 'modest political agenda for improvement of the regulatory process.' *Id.* at 16.

85. The original draft bill reported to the full Senate from the Committee on Commerce, Science, and Transportation (S. 2493) did not propose sunsetting the CAB. *See* Legislative History 1978, *supra* note 20, at 165-217. Senators envisaged that the work of deregulation, begun in the new statute, would be completed at some unspecified future time if 'exposure to new conditions of less regulation' were successful. *See* comments of Senator Schmitt, *id.* at 379. The 'sunset' option first appeared in H.R. 12611, reported out of the House Committee on Public Works and Transportation on May 19, 1978. *See id.* at 509. It was the brainchild of Rep. Elliot Levitas of

Congress did consider the much simpler option of investing this suddenly temporal CAB with wide discretion to implement a broad Congressional mandate for increased competition. This option failed, partly because legislators recalled that the 1938 legislation similarly anticipated (in vain) that the new Board would exercise its apparent discretion to welcome innovative new entrants to the industry, and partly because of a perceived identity of interest between the Board and the air carriers, who played a much greater role in the CAB's traditional decisionmaking process than the 'muted and distant' public.[86]

In defiance of this comfortable and complacent history, Congress believed, nevertheless, that 'the heavy hand of CAB economic regulation' could now be replaced by 'the creative hand of carrier management.'[87] The ADA's preambular goal sought 'to encourage, develop and attain an air transportation system which relies on competitive market forces to determine the quality, variety, and price of air services.'[88] The 'Declaration of Policy' in the Federal Aviation Act (which, as seen earlier, promised competition only 'to the extent necessary to assure the sound development of an air transportation system'[89]) was deliberately reformulated to place 'maximum reliance on competitive market forces.'[90] And the U.S. Senate Committee on Commerce, Science, and Transportation, reporting on the draft bill, adopted (but without explicit attribution) the Supreme Court's doctrinal position that U.S. competition law (the antitrust code) 'protect[s] competition, not competitors.'[91]

Georgia, 'the staunchest advocate of real deregulation on either side of Congress.' Callison, *supra* note 69, at 961, 964 n.4. Section 31 of the draft bill proposed that the CAB would terminate on Dec. 31, 1982. The legislative intent of that provision, as expressed in the Committee's report, was to 'force the Congress to undertake a thorough review of the CAB and the functions it performs, and to determine whether the agency should be continued in the same or modified form.' LEGISLATIVE HISTORY 1978, *supra* note 20, at 513. The prospect that the CAB would leave the stage entirely had not yet captured the legislative imagination. Interestingly, H.R. 12611 also required the CAB to submit reports and recommendations on the need for its own continuance, an assignment that survived into the final draft of the new statute. Under the House/Senate conference substitute for S. 2493 and H.R. 12611, as discussed in the main text, Congress established a 'rolling' sunset schedule, commencing with route authority on Dec. 31, 1981, followed by tariff authority on Dec. 31, 1983, and leading to full sunset (subject to any action Congress might take on foot of the Board's assessment of its own future viability) as of Jan. 1, 1985. *See id.* at 969-70.

86. LEGISLATIVE HISTORY 1978, *supra* note 20, at 170. *See* Levine, *Reregulation, supra* note 67 (noting widespread, nearly unanimous industry opposition to deregulation); *see also supra* note 82 (discussing Levine's assessment of the reasons for this unanimity of opposition). *See generally* Michael E. Levine, *Regulatory Capture, in* 3 NEW PALGRAVE DICTIONARY OF LAW AND ECONOMICS 267 (Peter Newman ed., 1998).
87. LEGISLATIVE HISTORY 1978, *supra* note 20, at 171.
88. *Id.* at 1. The text of the ADA is reprinted also in JEFFREY MILLER, THE AIRLINE DEREGULATION HANDBOOK 29-78 (1981).
89. 49 U.S.C. app. § 1302(d) (1970).
90. 49 U.S.C. app. § 1302(a)(4) (1980).
91. LEGISLATIVE HISTORY 1978, *supra* note 20, at 218. *See* Brown Shoe Co. *v.* United States, 370 U.S. 294, 320 (1962); *see also* Brooke Group Ltd. *v.* Brown & Williamson Tobacco Corporation, 509 U.S. 209, 224 (1993) (finding that, although below-cost pricing may impose 'painful losses'

Accordingly, the whole thrust of the new legislation was intended to pare back the regulatory discretion of the CAB and its assorted operating bureaus, transferring economic decisionmaking authority to both incumbent and new entrant airline managements.[92]

1   CAB Route Deregulation: The Fruits of Dormancy

New *entry* was the first sphere of application of the gradualist approach to deregulation. The ADA continued to require a CAB certificate of public convenience and necessity for new route entry, granted only after a public hearing, but relieved the applicant of the burden of showing that the transportation was 'consistent' with the public convenience and necessity.[93] Instead, the statute imposed the burden of demonstrating *inconsistency* with that standard upon any 'opponent' who challenged the application.[94] This procedural burden-shifting had an important substantive consequence: route access was now effectively opened to any carrier that could show itself 'fit, willing, and able' to perform the requested transportation, the same standard that governs U.S. DOT treatment of start-up applications in

---

on its target, such a consequence is 'of no moment' to the antitrust laws if competition is not injured – 'it is axiomatic that the antitrust laws were passed for the "the protection of competition, not competitors."' In an interesting postscript, this cardinal precept of U.S. antitrust law made a recent reappearance in the 2007 U.S./EC Air Transport Agreement. *See* U.S./EC Air Transport Agreement, *supra* note 2, art. 20(1).

92. The CAB was historically organized into operating bureaus, or divisions. Following its most recent reorganization in 1976, the CAB comprised the Bureau of Domestic Aviation, performing route and rate regulation; the Bureau of International Aviation, which worked with the State Department in bilateral negotiations; and the Bureau of Consumer Protection. Other CAB components included the Office of the General Counsel, Bureau of Administrative Law Judges, the hearing officers, and some smaller staff offices. *See* MILLER, *supra* note 88, at 4-5. The CAB itself included five full-time members, serving staggered six-year terms, who were appointed by the President subject to Senate confirmation. Each December, the President appointed one of the members Chairman for the following year. The Chairman appointed the bureau directors, general counsel, and managing director, who was the day-to-day manager of the agency. *See* 49 U.S.C. § 1321 (1970-79) (repealed).

93. The standard with respect to *foreign* air transportation was different: there, the transportation had to be '*required* by the public convenience and necessity.' 49 U.S.C. app. § 1371(d)(1) (1970) (the discussion in the main text covers only domestic interstate transportation). Under current law, a U.S. carrier need only be 'fit, willing, and able' to provide domestic transportation, while for foreign transportation the former language that applied to domestic air transport (the requirement of 'consistency' with the public convenience and necessity) has superseded the old language that the transport be 'required' by the public convenience and necessity. *See* 49 U.S.C.A. § 41102 (West 2008).

94. 49 U.S.C. app. § 1371(d)(9)(B) (1970). The recast language of this Section now applies only to applications for foreign air transportation: an opponent must show that the requested transportation 'is not consistent with the public convenience and necessity.' The evidentiary standard is 'preponderance of the evidence' that the transportation is not so consistent. 49 U.S.C.A. § 41108(c)(2) (West 2008).

domestic air transport today.[95] And having moderated the CAB's traditional gate-keeper role in route admissions, the legislation also carved out certain *a priori* categories of 'dormant' and 'automatic' entry that the CAB was supposed to facilitate with a lesser degree of administrative intervention, including (in most cases) *no* required finding with respect to the public convenience and necessity. 'Dormant' (or 'unused') authority allowed the CAB, upon application, to award certain underutilized routes to new entrants.[96] The Board was required to grant the applications expeditiously, in as little as 15 days (and without notice or hearings requirements) if only one other carrier served the route.[97]

The dormancy provisions proved to be one of the most publicized aspects of the new statute. There was wide media coverage of the lines that formed outside the Board's Washington, D.C. offices to become the 'first applicant,' in accordance with the statute's requirements,[98] to seek entry on each route that had fallen dormant.[99] 'Automatic' entry was another statutory effort to minimize CAB discretion. The ADA offered open entry, without the requirement of a formal hearing, by certificated and some intrastate carriers on one new route selected by each carrier in January

---

95. *See* § 41102(b)(1) & (c)(1); *see also* MILLER, *supra* note 88, at 12. For commentary on the burdens of proof of fitness (which remained on the applicant) and of public convenience and necessity (burden of inconsistency with public convenience and necessity moved to opponent of application), as set forth in 49 U.S.C. app. § 1371(d)(9)), *see* JOINT EXPLANATORY STATEMENT OF THE COMM. OF CONFERENCE, *in* LEGISLATIVE HISTORY 1978, *supra* note 20, at 907-08.

96. *See* 49 U.S.C. § 1371(d)(5) (repealed). On a one-time basis only, the Act allowed the 'dormant' carrier to preclude reassignment of the route by reactivating service. The required minimum of service, to prevent 'dormancy,' was five roundtrips per week for at least 13 weeks during any 26-week period. 49 U.S.C. § 1371(d)(5)(A) (repealed). Otherwise, the Act required the CAB to suspend the route authority of the 'dormant' carrier (unless it found that suspension was not necessary to encourage continued service between such points by the applicant air carrier). *See* 49 U.S.C. § 1371(d)(5)(J) (repealed).

97. *See* 49 U.S.C. § 1371(d)(5) (repealed). Where two or more other carriers served the route, the Board could take up to 60 days to make its decision. Here, the Board had discretion to find that the issuance of the certificate would be 'inconsistent with the public convenience and necessity.' Moreover, in making that determination, it had to give notice and an opportunity to file written evidence and argument (although oral hearings would be at the Board's option). *See* 49 U.S.C. § 1371(d)(5)(F) (repealed).

98. The dormancy privilege was only awarded to the 'first applicant' who applied within 30 days after the last day of the 26-week qualifying period for dormancy. 49 U.S.C. § 1371(d)(5) (repealed). All applicants had to satisfy the CAB, of course, of their fitness to undertake the proposed transportation. *See id.*

99. *See* MILLER, *supra* note 88, at 12. Braniff, one of the most aggressive carriers, received several routes. United, then the largest U.S. carrier, applied for (and received) only one route, Buffalo/Florida (Miami). *See id. See* Michele McDonald, *Changed Forever: The Transition from Total Government Control of the Airline Industry to Open Competition Has Been a Wild Ride That Some Enjoyed and Some Did Not*, AIR TRANSP. WORLD (40th Anniversary Issue), Summer 2004, which includes Michael Levine's recollection of the so-called 'Great Route Grab,' during which (as the CAB-designated supervisor of the lines outside the agency's offices) his first official act in the deregulated era was to adjudicate whether the 'airline men' could leave the line to go to the men's room without losing their places. For further Levine recollections of the moment of deregulation, *see A Conversation with Michael E. Levine, supra* note 68.

1979, 1980, and 1981.[100] Congress was somewhat timid about this new authority. In a regulatory throwback, each certificated carrier was also able to shelter one *existing* nonstop route from the automatic entry provisions,[101] and the Board was empowered to modify the program if it were found to be causing 'substantial public harm' to the national air transportation system.[102] In fact, the automatic entry provisions had little impact on competitive conditions in most domestic markets.[103]

The CAB continued to administer this route regulation regime until its route authority was forced to sunset on December 31, 1981.[104] Technically, demise of this authority was accomplished by declaring certain provisions of the amended Federal Aviation Act, and the Board's authority thereunder, to 'cease to be in effect' as of the sunset date. The substantive result of this slate of sunsetting provisions was to end the requirement for a determination of consistency with the public convenience and necessity,[105] to end the Board's power to grant temporary route certificates,[106] to end specification of terminal and intermediate points on route certificates,[107] to end the requirement for CAB permission to abandon or exit a route,[108] and to end the requirement that a carrier had a *duty* to provide the transportation authorized by its certificate.[109] This composite

---

100. *See* 49 U.S.C. § 1371(d)(7) (repealed). The Board had a 60-day window to issue the certificate, which it was required to do unless it determined that the applicant was 'not fit, willing, and able' to provide the transportation. *Id.* The Act permitted a second round of applications each year for carriers not receiving a route because more than one carrier had applied in the previous year. *See* 49 U.S.C. § 1371(d)(7)(B) (repealed).
101. 49 U.S.C. § 1371(d)(7)(c) (repealed).
102. 49 U.S.C. § 1371(d)(7)(D) (repealed).
103. *See* MILLER, *supra* note 88, at 12. Finally, the ADA removed an anomalous feature of prior law and CAB policy that excluded some U.S. international carriers, but notably the signature U.S. global airline Pan American, from serving cabotage routes within the United States. Pan Am, for example, had been awarded certificates to serve several U.S. cities on an international route, but not to carry passengers traveling only *between* these cities. It had route authority for Chicago/New York/London, but could not transport Chicago passengers bound only for New York, or vice versa. The ADA awarded these 'eighth freedom' (or 'fill-up') rights to U.S. international carriers. *See* 49 U.S.C. § 1371(d)(6) (repealed). Again, notice the legislators' caution. To ensure that the fill-up authority did not have 'a severe impact on other carriers in these markets,' the Act limited the authority to *one* roundtrip flight per day unless the Board authorized additional flights. *Id. See also* LEGISLATIVE HISTORY 1978, *supra* note 20, at 907. Pan Am was able to introduce some highly competitive discounts as a result of this concession. *See* MILLER, *supra* note 88, at 13.
104. *See* 49 U.S.C. app. § 1551(a) (1979). By then, the CAB had certificated 10 new air carriers. Four were newly established – Midway, New York Air, People Express, and Muse Air. Four others – PSA, Air Cal, Air Florida, and Southwest – were formerly intrastate carriers. The remaining two, Capitol and World, were formerly charter airlines. *See generally* William A. Jordan, *Airline Entry Following U.S. Deregulation: The Definitive List of Startup Passenger Airlines 1979-2003*, Transportation Research Forum (2005).
105. *See* 49 U.S.C. § 1551(a)(1)(A) (1979) (recodified as 49 U.S.C.A. § 41102 (West 2008)).
106. *See* 49 U.S.C. § 1551(a)(1)(B) (recodified as 49 U.S.C.A. §§ 41102 & 41110 (West 2008)).
107. *See* 49 U.S.C. § 1551(a)(1)(C) (recodified as 49 U.S.C.A. § 41109 (West 2008)).
108. *See* 49 U.S.C. § 1551(a)(1)(D) (recodified as 49 U.S.C.A. § 41312 (West 2008)).
109. *See* 49 U.S.C. § 1551(a)(1)(F) (repealed).

termination of CAB authority, centered on abolition of the agency's regulatory lodestar of 'public convenience and necessity,' meant that carriers would be free to enter and exit markets at their own discretion, subject only to an initial demonstration of fitness to provide transportation (which, as noted above, is a continuing requirement in domestic U.S. air transportation).[110]

2   CAB Fare Deregulation: Zones of Flexibility

The ADA also sought to dismantle the regulatory barriers that denied pricing freedom to airline carriers. The technical approach chosen by Congress was to continue the Board's existing rate regulation authority, but to establish *a priori* that the Board would not have authority to find a fare 'unjust or unreasonable' (on the basis of being too low or too high) where that fare was constructed to comply with certain statutory price ranges within which carriers could, generally speaking, price freely without agency intervention. This 'zone of reasonableness' artifice was later incorporated in the multilateral U.S./ECAC understanding on transatlantic tariff-setting,[111] and also found favor with the European Commission as a central mechanism of its program of airline liberalization.[112] Thus, rather than legislating an instantaneous end to the blockading of independent fare fluctuations, the ADA established a 'standard industry fare level'[113] that had a 5% flexibility zone for unregulated fare increases, and a 50% flexibility zone for unregulated fare decreases, and which was to be adjusted semi-annually by the percentage change from the last previous period based on the actual operating costs per available seat mile for combined interstate and overseas air transportation.[114]

---

110. (And, as noted earlier, the fitness requirement, along with a public convenience and necessity prerequisite, also exists for certification in foreign air transportation, *see supra* note 93.) The ADA neglected to specify how this initial fitness review authority would be discharged after the CAB's demise in 1985. There were other legislative gaps, too, notably the future disposition of the Board's authority to protect consumers and to prevent unfair competitive practices. Congress corrected these omissions, concluding that the CAB's assorted regulatory authorities should continue and should henceforth be the province of the Department of Transportation, in special sunset legislation enacted in 1984. *See* REP. OF HOUSE COMM. ON PUBLIC WORKS AND TRANSPORTATION (May 21, 1984), *reprinted in* LEGISLATIVE HISTORY OF THE CIVIL AERONAUTICS BOARD SUNSET ACT OF 1984, 1984 U.S.C.C.A.N., at 2857, 2859 [hereinafter LEGISLATIVE HISTORY 1984]. The Committee found that 'the fitness test as administered by [the] CAB has not been a substantial barrier to entry and we do not intend to have [the] DOT turn it into one in the future. The public should not be denied the benefits which flow from CAB fitness evaluations.' *Id.* at 2863.

111. *See* Chapter 3, note 520.

112. *See* BRIAN F. HAVEL, IN SEARCH OF OPEN SKIES § 4.4.2.1 (1997).

113. The ADA defined the 'standard industry fare level' as 'the fare level . . . in effect on July 1, 1977, for each interstate or overseas pair of points, for each class of service existing on that date, and in effect on the effective date of the establishment of each additional class of service established after July 1, 1977.' 49 U.S.C. § 1482(d)(6) (1979) (repealed).

114. *See* 49 U.S.C. § 1482(d)(4) (repealed). *See also* Jerry L. Beane, *The Antitrust Implications Of Airline Deregulation*, 45 J. AIR L. & COM. 1001, 1018 (1980). In practice, as noted in the main text, the CAB had already established noninterference fare zones that in some respects were

The carriers' pricing flexibility within the zone of reasonableness was not entirely untrammeled, however. First, the Act retained the requirement to post proposed tariff changes with the CAB, although the advance time was reduced to 30 days (from 60) in the case of zonal fares.[115] It is surprising that Congress adhered to this regulatory relic, since it obviously created ideal conditions for 'phony' competition, enabling carriers to signal their future pricing intentions to each other considerably in advance of the effective dates.[116] Second, the statute reserved power to the Board to suspend fares above the standard industry level which were 'unduly preferential, unduly prejudicial, or unjustly discriminatory,' and to suspend fares below that level that the CAB determined to be 'predatory.'[117] The ADA's sunset provisions called for termination of the CAB's fare regulation authority effective January 1, 1983. Again, the legislative technique was to declare that the applicable provisions of the amended Federal Aviation Act, and the Board's powers thereunder, would 'cease to be in effect' after the sunset date. Thus, the entire tariff-filing structure dissolved,[118] along with the investigative apparatus employed by the Board to monitor, suspend, and alter proposed tariffs.[119]

3   CAB Antitrust Deregulation: The Longest Sunset

With antitrust, too, Congress ensured that its regulatory 'complex' persisted after 1978. Although the anchoring feature of the prior statute – the CAB's power to

---

      broader than the statutory zones. *See* C.A.B. Policy Statement PS-80, C.A.B. Dkt. Nos. 31290 & 30891 (Aug. 25, 1978), published at 43 Fed. Reg. 39,522 (1978). *See* Callison, *supra* note 69, at 978.

115. *See* 49 U.S.C. § 1482(d)(4) (repealed).

116. Indeed, the Act appeared to anticipate this behavior. It permitted the Board to establish an alternative advance filing requirement of 25 days to enable other carriers to file matching fares in advance of the effective date of the first carrier's proposed new fares. 49 U.S.C. § 1373(c)(1) (1979) (recodified as 49 U.S.C.A. 41504(b)(1) (West 2008), but only applying to foreign air transportation). Price signaling through electronic reservations systems, allowing competitors to view proposed price increases before they take effect (and avoiding the risk of losing sales to those competitors) has been a continuing concern under *ex post* scrutiny of airline competitive behavior. The U.S. Department of Transportation continues to enforce a 1994 consent decree on price signaling that in effect requires immediate availability of fare information to consumers. *See* U.S. *v.* Airline Tariff Publishing Company et al., 1994 U.S. Dist. LEXIS 11,904 (D.D.C. 1994) (in which the court approved a final judgment that would *inter alia* prohibit the defendant airlines from disseminating first or last ticket dates); *see also* U.S. *v.* American Airlines, Inc., 2004 U.S. Dist. LEXIS 27,053 (D.D.C. 2004) (enforcing 1994 consent order against American Airlines for attaching certain future travel dates to advanced purchase fares, a practice that the U.S. Department of Justice alleged had 'little or no meaning to consumers'). *See* Eric Torbenson, *American Pays Fine to Settle Dispute Over Ticketing Policies*, DALLAS MORNING NEWS, Aug. 7, 2004.

117. 49 U.S.C. § 1482(d)(4) (1979) (repealed). Similar provisions appeared in later EC legislation. *See infra* Chapter 5, Part II(D).

118. *See* 49 U.S.C. app. § 1551(a)(2)(A) (1979) (repealed).

119. *See* 49 U.S.C. § 1551(a)(2)(B)). In fact, as discussed *infra* in the main text, the Civil Aeronautics Board had ceased *de facto* regulation of industry fares as early as 1981. *See*

award antitrust immunity – was diluted by requiring a new finding of 'public interest,' the new legislation maintained administrative policing of all industry mergers and acquisitions, and made it a precondition for winning antitrust immunity for intercarrier agreements.[120] The only significant reform was that the CAB would now be mandated to use a conceptual framework, borrowed largely from the antitrust laws, to measure the anticompetitive effects of all proposed transactions before granting its approval. As discussed below, the new framework was immediately compromised by a grant of broad waiver authority to the Board. Remarkably, too, although the Act envisaged sunsetting the CAB's 'antitrust' authority in 1985, it did not contemplate a reversion to conventional *post hoc* antitrust scrutiny of the industry. On the contrary, the sunset provision initially decreed a staged transfer of the CAB's authority, with no change in content, to the Department of Justice, beginning January 1, 1985.[121] As will be seen, later legislation would be needed to roll back the government's industry-specific control of airline transactions.

As noted above, the ADA sought to modify the CAB's analysis of industry transactions to meet antitrust concerns. The new provisions on merger review showed the typical technical features of the revised approach. The Board was again directed not to approve mergers that would 'not be consistent with the public interest,' but the potential antitrust exposure was broadened to include not only the prior standard of monopolies and conspiracies to monopolize the business of air transportation (literally, the *Sherman Act* test),[122] but any transaction whose effect 'may be substantially to lessen competition, or to tend to create a monopoly, or which in any other manner would be in restraint of trade' (again, in literal terms, the *Clayton Act* test).[123] While a clearly monopolistic merger could still not be saved, a new composite 'public interest' exception allowed the Board to approve a transaction that fell within the Clayton Act criteria if it specifically found that (a) the anticompetitive effects of the proposed transaction were outweighed in the public interest by the probable effect of the transaction in meeting 'significant transportation conveniences and needs of the public;' and that (b) such significant conveniences and needs would not be satisfied by 'a reasonably available alternative

---

CAB, *Report to Congress, supra* note 41, at 18. Even in 1978, the agency anticipated the new ADA ranges of pricing flexibility by granting automatic approval to fares that were up to 10% above the DPFI formula and 70% below it. *See id.*

120. *See* 49 U.S.C. §§ 1378 (repealed), 1379 (repealed), 1382 (1979). 49 U.S.C. § 1379 appears in a recodified form as 49 U.S.C.A. §§ 41309 & 42111 (West 2008).

121. *See* 49 U.S.C. § 1551(a)(3), (b)(1)(C) (repealed).

122. Specifically, Section 2 of the Sherman Act, which makes it a crime to 'monopolize, or attempt to monopolize, or combine or conspire with any other person or persons, to monopolize any part of the trade or commerce among the several States, or with foreign nations....' 15 U.S.C.A. § 2 (West 2008).

123. Specifically, Section 7 of the Clayton Act, which concerns mergers between corporations engaged in commerce or in any activity affecting commerce 'where in any line of commerce or in any activity affecting commerce in any section of the country, the effect of such transaction may be substantially to lessen competition, or to tend to create a monopoly.' Clayton Act, 15 U.S.C.A. §§ 12-27 (West 2008).

having materially less anticompetitive effects.'[124] The Congressional intent behind this opaque and convoluted statutory construction (inherited from earlier bank merger legislation[125]), was to test mergers in the air carrier industry by 'the antitrust standards traditionally applied by the courts to unregulated industries.'[126] Of course, that is precisely what the new Section did *not* do, since an arguably anticompetitive merger could nonetheless win CAB approval as meeting transportation conveniences, *and*, having been thus approved, could be garlanded with full antitrust immunity (provided the CAB took the small additional step of finding that the exemption was required 'in the public interest').[127]

Some notice has earlier been taken of the legislative confusion that surrounded the demise of the CAB's variegated antitrust authority. Merger approval authority was originally transferred to the Department of Justice effective January 1,

---

124. 49 U.S.C. § 1378(b)(1)(B) (1979) (repealed). Similarly, during what might be called the 'liberalization' phase after 1978, the Act recognized that certain types of intercarrier agreements that arguably might be held to violate the antitrust laws were necessary to the smooth and efficient operation of the air transportation system. These agreements could be approved under the same 'public benefits' test as that applied to mergers. This so-called 'immunity' power has now lapsed with respect to domestic air transport. However, the CAB was at all times absolutely prohibited from approving any agreement controlling capacity or fixing rates, fares, or charges between air carriers. A special latitude for efficiency-enhancing intercarrier agreements also occurred in the first phase of the European Community's airline liberalization package as promulgated in 1987. See HAVEL, *supra* note 112, at 327-28.

125. This is an 'efficiencies' defense, commonly referred to as the 'Bank Merger' defense. An analogous provision appears in the Bank Merger Act of 1966 (codified at 12 U.S.C.A. § 1828 (West 2008)).

126. *See* JOINT EXPLANATORY STATEMENT OF COMM. OF CONFERENCE, *in* LEGISLATIVE HISTORY 1978, *supra* note 20, at 914. CAB supervision of intercarrier agreements was also adapted to the new formula. The Act made filing of these agreements permissive, which had the important consequence that unfiled agreements could not receive the CAB's imprimatur of antitrust immunity. *See* 49 U.S.C. §§ 1382(c)(1), 1384 (1979). If filed, the Board could approve any agreement that it did not find to be 'adverse to the public interest,' but not any agreement that substantially reduced or eliminated competition. 49 U.S.C. app. § 1382(c)(2)(A). *See* the recodification of these cited provisions in 49 U.S.C.A. §§ 42111 & 41308 (West 2008). As with mergers, however, the statute allowed the Board to recuperate even anticompetitive agreements that satisfied the double-pronged test of meeting a serious transportation need, without alternative less anticompetitive means, that applied to mergers. *See id.* As a precaution, however, the Act prohibited Board recuperation of fare-fixing or capacity-sharing agreements between domestic carriers. *See id.* Agreements that were not filed with the CAB, and did not therefore receive antitrust immunity, became subject for the first time to the general antitrust laws concerning price-fixing, capacity-sharing and market allocation. *See* Barry E. Hawk, *United States Regulation Of Air Transport, in* TOWARD A COMMUNITY AIR TRANSPORT POLICY: THE LEGAL DIMENSION 255, 257 (Pieter J. Slot & Prodromos D. Dagtoglou eds., 1989).

127. 49 U.S.C. app. § 1384 (1979); *see supra* note 22 (containing the recodification reference). Indeed, this is precisely how the CAB (and later the Department of Transportation) administration of ADA merger review powers unfolded in practice. In the decade-long history of the Section's operation, only one proposed merger was rejected despite the continuous stream of merger proposals with which both bodies were confronted. *See* FTC BUREAU OF ECONOMICS REPORT, THE DEREGULATED AIRLINE INDUSTRY – A REVIEW OF THE EVIDENCE 29 (Jonathan Ogur et al., 1988) [hereinafter FTC REPORT].

1985;[128] before the transfer took effect, however, the authority was reassigned to the DOT, with the same effective date, by Section 3(a) of the Civil Aeronautics Board Sunset Act of 1984.[129] According to the DOT, both it and the Justice Department 'generally opposed' the transfer.[130] The original ADA provisions envisaged an eventual bipartite assignment, with the DOT generally responsible for foreign transportation, which was not deregulated, while the Justice Department assumed control over antitrust review (and immunity) for both domestic and foreign air transportation.[131] Both Departments were concerned that DOT antitrust jurisdiction could lead to 'reregulation,'[132] but it was noted without apparent irony in Congressional testimony that the statutory criteria for approval and antitrust immunity of mergers and intercarrier agreements were not necessarily based on antitrust considerations.[133] Under the 1984 sunset legislation, the DOT's inherited power to confer antitrust exemptions, as well as the general regime providing for special treatment of airline mergers and similar intercarrier transactions, finally

---

128. 49 U.S.C. § 1551(b)(1)(C) (1979). *See also* the recodified versions in 49 U.S.C.A. §§ 41308-41309 (West 2008).
129. *See* Civil Aeronautics Board Sunset Act of 1984, Pub. L. No. 98-443, 98 Stat. 1703. *See generally* Legislative History 1984, *supra* note 110.
130. U.S. DOT, *Report to Congress: Administration Of Aviation Antitrust Functions* 4 (May 1987) [hereinafter DOT Report]. For an analysis of the reasons why the DOT retained what would normally have been a Justice Department competence in the post-regulation period, *see* Legislative History 1984, *supra* note 110, at 2863-64; *see also* Patricia M. Barlow, Aviation Antitrust: The Extraterritorial Application of the United States Antitrust Laws and International Air Transportation 34-36 (1988); Patricia M. Barlow, *Aviation Antitrust – International Considerations After Sunset*, 12 Air L. 68, 77-78 (1987) [hereinafter Barlow, *International Considerations*].
131. *See* 49 U.S.C. app. § 1551(b)(1)(B)-(C) (1979) (recodified in 49 U.S.C.A. §§ 40105, 41308, & 41309 (West 2008)). *See also* Legislative History 1984, *supra* note 110, at 2859.
132. Legislative History 1984, *supra* note 110, at 2864. Fearing a *de facto* continuation of the CAB within its own portals, the DOT itself suggested to Congress that it would be better to give the CAB's antitrust authority to the Department of Justice and its consumer protection powers to the Federal Trade Commission (which has a general consumer protection mission under the Federal Trade Commission Act). The Committee's response to this argument was more pragmatic than analytical: it noted that CAB personnel dealing with antitrust and consumer protection issues would represent only a small number of the agency's employees who would move to DOT (indeed, by 1984 the vast majority of CAB employees worked on international aviation and community air service matters). Also, the CAB's institutional commitment to deregulation, discussed in the main text, *infra*, was now a matter of some acclaim. *See id.*
133. *See* Barlow, *International Considerations, supra* note 130, at 78. Congressional sanguineness was evident from the deliberations of the House Committee on Public Works and Transportation, which based its decision to assign these responsibilities to the DOT on the premise that even transactions found to be inconsistent with the antitrust laws (except outright monopolies) could be sanctioned by the CAB using the so-called Bank Mergers test. *See supra* note 125. The Committee felt that the DOT, as 'the lead transportation agency,' would be 'in the best position to evaluate whether a proposed transaction or relationship would provide substantial transportation benefits ... [or] evaluate whether a proposed alternative is practical or just a theoretical exercise.' Legislative History 1984, *supra* note 110, at 2863-64.

expired with respect to domestic air transportation on January 1, 1989.[134] Thus, as of that year, proposed airline mergers and agreements became subject to the general antitrust laws,[135] which now include (in the case of merger and acquisition activity) the notice and review procedures of the so-called Hart-Scott-Rodino legislation.[136]

4   A Regulatory Vestige: The Essential Air Service Program

Some CAB officials, resisting the deregulatory impulse, warned Congress that the airline industry served basic transportation and communication functions that could be disrupted by switching to a market rather than 'system' orientation.[137] Accordingly, a final philosophical inconsistency, or perhaps hesitation, in the 1978 legislation can be divined from the establishment of the 'Essential Air Service' (EAS) Program, which guaranteed air service (in effect, subsidized service) to city-points that Congress feared might lose vital air service if left to what some legislators saw as the 'whim' of competitive market forces.[138] Interestingly, despite the Program's legislative intent to help small communities maintain air connections, the statutory language was composed to allow literally *any* point in the United States, and not solely small or isolated communities, to become eligible for subsidized service: the key determinant was service by only one (or no) air carrier.[139]

---

134. *See* Section 3(c) of the Civil Aeronautics Board Sunset Act, *supra* note 129. *See* Barbara A. Bell, *The Extraterritorial Application Of United States Antitrust Law And International Aviation: A Comity of Errors*, 54 J. Air L. & Com. 533, 534 (1988). With respect to the survival of an antitrust immunity power in foreign air transportation, *see supra* Chapter 3, Part VIII and *infra* in the main text.

135. '[T]here appears to be no valid argument for applying a specially tailored antitrust policy to mergers between airlines.' Lucile Sheppard Keyes, *The Regulation of Airline Mergers by the Department of Transportation*, 53 J. Air L. & Com. 737, 740 (1988).

136. *See* Title II, Hart-Scott-Rodino Antitrust Improvements Act of 1976, 15 U.S.C.A. § 15(a) (West 2008), which created a new Section 7A of the Clayton Act. The advance notification proposals of this legislation were deemed by the DOT to be 'more effective and less burdensome' than the regime established by the Federal Aviation Act. DOT Report, *supra* note 130, at 22. 'Experience has demonstrated that application of the antitrust laws is far better suited to the dynamic needs of a competitive industry than the prior approval requirements imposed by the Federal Aviation Act.' *Id.*

137. *See* CAB Schrenk Memorandum, *supra* note 67, at 7.

138. *See* 49 U.S.C. § 1389 (1979). (The EAS Program is now codified in 49 U.S.C.A. §§ 41731-41742 (West 2008).) One of the Congressional purposes behind EAS was to enhance the growing commuter airline industry. *See* Legislative History 1978, *supra* note 20, at 254.

139. This curious result follows from the definition of the operative term 'eligible point' in the first two subsections of Section 419 of the revised Federal Aviation Act. 49 U.S.C. app. § 1389(a), (b) (1979) (recodified as 49 U.S.C.A. § 41731 (West 2008)). The statute effectively divided all eligible points into those being served by one certificated carrier on the date of its enactment, and those that had been deleted from air carrier certificates since 1968 (and were therefore receiving no service). The Act also placed some restrictions on subsidy payments to carriers that the Board classed as 'trunks' (the current DOT classification is Group III carriers). *See* 49 U.S.C. app. § 1389(a)(7)(B) (recodified as 49 U.S.C. § 41731 (West 2008)). (The original

In a familiar regulatory reflex, air carriers serving cities which were guaranteed air service were required to give notice before reducing service below the level defined by the Board for those cities as 'essential air transportation,' or entirely abandoning the routes.[140] Although the EAS Program was placed under DOT stewardship as of January 1, 1985,[141] it has never been sunsetted. In fact, the initial 10-year transition period was renewed for an additional 10 years in 1988,[142] and the Program was renewed indefinitely through elimination of the sunset provision in 1998.[143]

E   SCRAMBLING THE SYSTEM: ALFRED KAHN'S REGULATED
                DEREGULATION

A memorable feature of U.S. airline deregulation was the willing complicity of (at least some) mandarins of the CAB in their own demise as regulators. As early as April 1976, then-CAB chairman John Robson testified on the Board's behalf to the U.S. Senate that 'economic regulation should be redirected so [that] domestic air transportation is essentially governed by competitive market forces. We believe [that] this will provide a more efficient, lower-cost system responsive to the public needs for air travel.'[144] In the view of some critics, complicity turned to anarchy

---

Senate bill did not restrict the subsidies payable to the major airlines.) *See* LEGISLATIVE HISTORY 1978, *supra* note 20, at 255.

140.   49 U.S.C. app. § 1389(a)(3) (1979) (recodified as 49 U.S.C.A. § 41731 (West 2008)). The standard period of notice for certificated carriers was 90 days. *See id.* The statute also empowered the CAB to compel withdrawing carriers to maintain subsidized service for 30-day increments (without definite limit) while the Board sought replacement service. *See* 49 U.S.C. app. § 1389(a)(6) (recodified as noted, *supra*). For a striking recent example of how the imposition of route exit regulation still finds favor with Congress, *see supra* note 36 & *infra* Part IV(C).

141.   *See* 49 U.S.C. app. § 1551(b)(1)(A) (1979).

142.   *See* 49 U.S.C. § 1389(1) (1987). *See also* 49 U.S.C.A. § 41742 (West 2008).

143.   *See* 49 U.S.C.A. § 41742 (West 2008). The EAS budget endured serious funding cuts in the 1990s. Funding now comes from a combination of permanent and annual appropriations. The Federal Aviation Authorization Act of 1996 (P.L. 104-264) permanently appropriated the first $50 million of such funding (for EAS and safety projects at rural airports) from the collection of overflight fees from foreign aircraft overflying the United States. Congress can appropriate additional funds from the general fund on an annual basis. *See* GAO, *Commercial Aviation: Programs and Options for the Federal Approach to Providing and Improving Air Service to Small Communities*, at 5, GAO-06-398T (Sept. 2006) [hereinafter GAO, *Small Communities*]. In 2000, in the Wendell H. Ford Aviation Investment and Reform Act for the 21st Century, Pub. L. No. 106-181 (popularly known as AIR-21), Congress established the Small Community Air Service Development Program (SCASDP), an experimental grantmaking program that funds specific air service development projects including incentives to carriers, feasibility studies, marketing efforts for air service, subsidizing an airline start-up, subsidizing bus service to hub airports, and so forth. For assessments of the actual performance of EAS and SCASDP, as well as proposals for future improvement of these programs, *see* GAO, *Small Communities, supra*, at 8-14 & 16-22.

144.   As cited *in Airline Commission Proceedings*, testimony of John E. Robson, former Chairman, Civil Aeronautics Board (Jun. 30, 1993), at 29. As noted earlier, however, not all CAB staff members agreed with the Chairman's optimistic prophecy. *See* CAB Schrenk Memorandum,

with President Carter's appointment of Alfred E. Kahn, an outspoken academic economist, to chair the CAB in the immediate pre-deregulation period. Kahn sought to hasten the transition to deregulation by acting ostensibly within the compass of the CAB's existing powers to promote a kind of 'regulated deregulation' – a display of presumptive agency authority that caused some acceleration of the phased timetable intended by Congress in the ADA and found echoes in the tactical pursuit of more rapid airline liberalization by the European Commission nearly ten years later.[145]

Specifically, and without awaiting Congressional action, Kahn introduced wholesale grants of new route authority on a multiple/permissive basis in various underserved markets,[146] intending to allow airline managers to fathom market forces and to decide whether to enter particular routes and in which ones they would remain.[147] Before deregulation, the CAB had limited the number of carriers that could serve any given route,[148] although flight frequency remained at the

---

supra note 67. *See also* McDonald, *supra* note 99 (recalling political amazement that bureaucrat Robson had turned his back on his own bureaucracy).

145. *See* FTC REPORT, *supra* note 127, at 3. Critics charged that competition on the basis of fares was nowhere included in the CAB's legislative mandate. *See* Dempsey, *supra* note 24, at 121. Neither, however, was it *excluded*. CAB, *Report to Congress, supra* note 41, at 16. Kahn, an economics professor at Cornell University who was later named as President Carter's inflation 'czar,' was a strong advocate of the prevailing deregulation philosophy. The regulation-killing frenzy that he inspired within the pre-deregulation CAB led at least one commentator to muse that the Federal Aviation Act, coupled with 'enlightened enforcement,' was already a pro-competitive statute. Callison, *supra* note 69, at 961. Kahn, incidentally, gave unstinting praise to Robson, his predecessor, for smoothing the path to deregulation, stating that Robson really 'cleared the field' so that Kahn himself could spearhead economic deregulation of the airlines. For this and many other observations of the former Chairman on his stewardship of airline deregulation, *see A Conversation with Alfred E. Kahn, supra* note 77.

146. Kahn granted 'operating authority by the bushel basket,' according to Dempsey, *supra* note 24, at 119.

147. One of Kahn's strategies was to target underserved airports such as Oakland in California and Midway in Chicago for low-fare entry. Kahn credited Michael Levine, his General Director of International and Domestic Aviation, for conceiving this 'politically palatable pretext' for deregulation. *See A Conversation with Alfred E. Kahn, supra* note 77. *See, e.g.,* Oakland Service Case, Order Nos. 78-4-121, 78-9-96, 78 C.A.B. 593 (Apr. 19, Sept. 21, 1978). In *Oakland*, the CAB granted permissive nonstop subsidy-ineligible authority to virtually every carrier that applied for it, between Oakland and 16 other cities. *See id.*; Callison, *supra* note 69, at 964. Levine himself described the *Oakland* proceeding as 'the turning point in airline deregulation.' *See A Conversation with Michael E. Levine, supra* note 68. Levine added that the same logic he had used to target underutilized airports for unrestricted new entry was slated to be applied to all airports with a million or more passengers annually – before deregulation made this strategy unnecessary. *See id.*

148. The Board very early established a policy of discriminating against new entrants in favor of grandfathered carriers. Under the original statutory provisions, if a carrier could prove that, during the grandfather period (May 14, 1938-Aug. 22, 1938), it was an air carrier continuously operating over the segment for which operating authority was sought, it was entitled to a certificate of public convenience and necessity to serve that route. *See* Dempsey, *supra* note 24, at 109. But between 1950 and 1974, the CAB received 79 applications to commence new operating authority on scheduled domestic routes, and *not one* was granted. *See* KENNEDY

carrier's option.[149] The Board decided to grant multiple authority to all qualified carriers by nonhearing show-cause proceedings, putting an end to cumbersome comparative selection proceedings and the restriction of entry to a single carrier.[150] Indeed, Kahn's economic design seemed to propose the creation of so-called 'contestable' markets by sheer administrative forbearance: the agency asserted that establishing opportunities for dormant (*i.e.*, permissive) authority would keep the potential of new entry alive and thereby apply a 'competitive stimulus' to incumbent carriers.[151] The CAB also approved individual carriers' applications for discount and promotional fares, including the 'Peanuts' fare offered by Texas International and the American Airlines 'Super-Saver' fare from New York to Los Angeles.[152] By the late fall of 1977, the CAB was allowing airlines to implement their own pricing strategies.[153]

Although the legal soundness of summarily jettisoning a 40-year history of regulatory policy was questioned,[154] Kahn had nevertheless set in motion what he

---

REPORT, *supra* note 70, at 78. Indeed, citing excess capacity in the industry, the CAB imposed a moratorium on *all* grants of new route authority between 1969 and 1974. *See* KENNEDY REPORT, *supra* note 70, at 6. In 1938, United Airlines, for example, controlled 22.9% of the national market, and in 1975 it still controlled 22%. *See id.* at 79-80. In addition, not a single new domestic trunkline carrier was authorized under the pre-Kahn CAB regime. The 16 domestic trunkline carriers of 1938 merged into the 10 that existed at the time the ADA became law in 1978. *Id.* at 6.

149. *See* FTC REPORT, *supra* note 127, at 5.

150. Despite criticism that it was engaged in a hasty and 'instant' deregulation of the routing system, the CAB used the procedural vehicle of the 'show cause' orders to issue a plethora of 'boiler-plate orders' setting applications for show cause disposition, and explicitly adopting a policy of multiple permissive entry in these proceedings. *See, e.g.*, Multiple Permissive Authority, CAB Order to Show Cause No. 78-12-106, 79 C.A.B. 391 (Dec. 14, 1978), Final Order No. 79-2-26, 80 C.A.B. 402 (Feb. 7, 1979); Application of United Air Lines, Inc., C.A.B. Order No. 78-11-54 (1978); *In re* Western Air Lines, Inc., C.A.B. Order No. 78-11-53 (1978). *See also* the dissent of CAB member O'Melia in Milwaukee Show-Cause Proceeding, C.A.B. Order No. 79-3-13, at 1-6 (1979).

151. Oakland Service Case, 78 C.A.B. 593, at 610, n. 26. *See* discussion by Committee on Public Works and Transportation of the House of Representatives, *in* LEGISLATIVE HISTORY 1978, *supra* note 20, at 509.

152. *See* Kelleher, *supra* note 71, at 302 (citing the Texas International Airlines, 'Peanuts' Fares Proceeding, Order No. 77-2-133, 72 C.A.B. 868 (Feb. 25, 1977) and the American Airlines, 'Super-Saver' Fares Proceeding, Order No. 77-3-80, 73 C.A.B. 1066 (Mar. 15, 1977)). *See* CAB, *Report to Congress, supra* note 41, at 18. Kahn's new ethos called for according significant, even determinative, weight to low-fare proposals of particular applicants. *See* Midwest-Atlanta Competitive Service Case, Order No. 78-4-13, 76 C.A.B. 336 (Apr. 6, 1978). *See also* Oakland Service Case, 78 C.A.B. 593 (1978); Kelleher, *supra* 71, at 302; and Callison, *supra* note 69, at 971.

153. Thus, by the time the CAB delivered its farewell report to Congress in 1984, discount fares accounted for over 80% of coach revenue passenger miles in the U.S. airline industry. *See* CAB, *Report to Congress, supra* note 41, at 104.

154. In the view of the U.S. Supreme Court, however, the mere fact that an agency departs from an earlier regulatory approach has not been (in itself) grounds for judicial rejection of the new approach. *See* FCC *v.* WOKO, 329 U.S. 223 (1946). The key to judicial tolerance would appear to be the advancement of statutory objectives. *See, e.g.*, National Air Carrier Ass'n. *v.* Civil

called the 'scrambling' of the air transportation system.[155] A Delta Air Lines executive challenged Michael Levine, then CAB General Director of International and Domestic Aviation, with the question 'why do we need you if you are going to let everyone serve everywhere?' To which Levine replied, 'Precisely.'[156] And, as the Board itself predicted, prospective new entrant carriers – low-cost, low-fares, low-frills challengers to the lumbering holdover incumbents – would have their first favorable window of opportunity in these early years of deregulation, before the older carriers brought labor costs into line, expanded their networks, or consummated their various mergers.[157]

The CAB expired, pursuant to statutory mandate, on January 1, 1985.[158] Its expectation of new competitive entry had proven initially accurate, as a proliferation of start-up carriers delighted the traveling public during the post-1978 period of graduated regulatory liberalization. The rise of new entry would all but cease, however, when the Reagan Administration pitched the industry into a state of virtual *non*-regulation (ironically, in light of the manifest Congressional ambivalence toward deregulation that is reflected in the structure of the ADA), allowing the larger incumbent carriers to benefit from a bystanding government, unmoved to

---

Aeronautics Bd., 442 F.2d 862, 874 (D.C. Cir. 1971). To that extent, presumably, Kahn's unorthodoxy gained from the ADA's amendment of the goals of the Federal Aviation Act to place 'maximum reliance on competitive forces.' *See supra* in the main text. *See also* Chapter 3, notes 260 & 261 (discussing the so-called *Chevron* doctrine of judicial review of agency interpretations of statutes).

155. *See* Callison, *supra* note 69, at 969. Professor Dempsey, *supra* note 24, at 94, observed that 'Chairman Kahn's explicit philosophy was to "so scramble the eggs that no one will ever be able to get them back into their shells again." '

156. *See A Conversation with Michael E. Levine, supra* note 68.

157. '[I]ncreased competition by new, low-fare entrants is likely to continue and spread. Reliance on market forces rather than an artificial ratemaking system has enabled carriers to attune their fares more closely to costs and market conditions than was hitherto possible, to the long-term benefit of consumers.' CAB, *Report to Congress, supra* note 41, at 104. *See* Melvin A. Brenner, *Airline Deregulation – A Case Study In Public Policy Failure*, 16 TRANSP. L.J. 179, 194 (1988).

158. *See* Section 3 of the Civil Aeronautics Board Sunset Act, *supra* note 110. *See* Edward A. Morash, *Airline Deregulation: Another Look*, 50 J. AIR L. & COM. 253 (1985). In the matter-of-fact words of ex-CAB Chairman John Robson, 'the [CAB] sunsetted and its earthly remains were transferred to the Department of Transportation.' *Airline Commission Proceedings*, testimony of John E. Robson, former Chairman, Civil Aeronautics Board, Jun. 30, 1993, at 30. As already discussed, the U.S. Department of Transportation continues to exercise the CAB's regulatory control over the economic licensing process for new carriers, as well as its consumer protection authority. *See supra* note 110. Moreover, airlines are still subject to extensive safety regulation by the DOT's Federal Aviation Administration. *See* FTC Report, *supra* note 127, at 1. '[T]he U.S. Airline Deregulation Act took the government out of the business of telling airlines where to fly and what to charge, but it in no way deregulated airlines from a safety, operational and technical standpoint.' Michael E. Levine, *quoted in* Stephen Wheatcroft & Geoffrey Lipman, *Economist Intelligence Report, Air Transport in a Competitive European Market* 91 (1986) [hereinafter EIU Report]. *See also* SWANN, *supra* note 78, at 31; *Airline Commission Proceedings*, statement by Commission Chairman Gerald L. Baliles (Jun. 23, 1993), at 321-22.

antitrust enforcement, to rebuild much of their lost hegemony. Some of the economic events of the immediate post-regulation period will appear later in this Chapter. Now, however, the study focuses once more on the international air transportation system, and will evaluate the legislative and policy tools selected by Congress and the DOT in their efforts, beginning in 1980, to introduce the ADA's objective of 'maximum reliance on competitive market forces' into an international aviation marketplace still in thrall to the Chicago system.

III   EXPORTING DEREGULATION: PROBING THE LIMITS
                  OF BILATERALISM

A   THE EMERGENCE OF AN OPEN SKIES INTERNATIONAL
                  AVIATION POLICY

U.S. domestic airline regulatory reform was within the unilateral competence of Congress. Although there were enough Congressional misgivings about the new policy to delay its complete implementation until as late as 1989, the United States nonetheless now enjoys deregulation of the economic incidents of airline travel. As Congress turned its focus outward to international aviation, however, the deregulators understood that some of their reformist ardor would necessarily be cooled by the protectionist role of most other governments, and by the existence of the byzantine patchwork of bilateral air transport agreements that comprised the Chicago system.[159] For Congress in the early 1980s, the path to international airline liberalization promised uncertain diplomacy with trading partners grown accustomed to the old economic compromises of bilateralism.

     In the context of the Chicago system, the burden of U.S. international aviation policy has been (and must be) to direct the Departments of State and Transportation concerning the play of permissible demands and concessions that accompanies every bilateral negotiation which they conduct on behalf of the United States.[160]

---

159. *See* Daniel P. Kaplan, *Study on Foreign Direct Investment, in Airline Commission Documents,* Dkt. No. 001018, Jul. 2, 1993, at 12.

160. *See* GAO, *International Aviation: Measures by European Community Could Limit U.S. Airlines' Ability to Compete Abroad,* at 19, GAO/RCED-93-64 (Apr. 1993) [hereinafter GAO, *European Community*]. Because air transport negotiations are truly intergovernmental, and have political as well as economic implications, the head of the U.S. delegation has traditionally been a State Department official. *See Airline Commission Proceedings,* remarks of Judge Abraham D. Sofaer, Chairman of the International Aviation Issues Team (Jun. 15, 1993), at 99-100. But Judge Sofaer, while conceding the State Department's need to gauge 'national interest' implications in any negotiation with foreign powers, questioned whether the *leadership* of the delegation should be so obviously politicized. *Id.* Yet it is hard to discount the political imperatives that rule Chicago system treatymaking. During the negotiations culminating in the U.S./EC Air Transport Agreement of 2007, *supra* note 2, the head of the U.S. delegation was State Department career official John R. Byerly, Deputy Assistant Secretary of State for Transportation Affairs. For Byerly's insider account of the insistently political U.S./EC negotiation process, *see* John R. Byerly, U.S. Deputy Assistant Secretary for Transportation Affairs, *Turbulent*

The evolution of U.S. government policy can be traced through a series of magisterial pronouncements by successive presidential administrations, culminating in the DOT statement published under President Clinton in 1995.[161]

During the regulatory prime of the CAB, a number of official guidelines on international policy appeared, most recently during the first year of the Nixon Administration in 1970.[162] The Nixon document, consolidating earlier efforts, assumed the continuity of bilateral regimentation of the world airline system in accordance with the pricing and capacity protocols of Bermuda I.[163] Within that system, the rights exchanged by the United States were expected 'to assure [U.S.] air carriers the opportunity to achieve no less than [under rights] available to the foreign air carriers.'[164] 'Competition,' though frequently intoned in the statement, was to be encouraged on a 'case-by-case' basis and had not yet been elevated to its later primacy as a systemic goal.[165] Indeed, the kind of competitive activity most encouraged in the statement was among domestic carriers competing for international route designations.[166] As to the volume of competition between domestic and foreign carriers, a matter which was understood to be a matter of intergovernmental consensus, the statement contented itself with generally disapproving unfair and discriminatory violations of bilateral commitments.[167]

The Nixon formulation appeared during the relatively stable (and complacent) primacy of Bermuda I. By the late 1970s, however, a transformation had occurred. The perceived U.S. capitulation in the Bermuda II negotiations in 1977, accepting a restrictive regime that seemed at odds with the emergence of domestic regulatory

---

Times: Regulation, Security and Profitability in the Airline Industry, Address to the Chatham House Conference on Air Transport, London (Mar. 5, 2007) (discussing *inter alia* the challenge of finding a 'balance' between U.S. and EC expectations, particularly with respect to the consequences of the 'typhoon of xenophobia' in the United States that doomed the 2005 Notice of Proposed Rulemaking on the foreign ownership laws, *see supra* Chapter 2, note 203 & Chapter 3, Part V(B).

161. *See supra* Chapter 1, note 7.
162. *See International Review, Statement of International Air Transportation Policy*, Jun. 22, 1970, *reprinted in* 36 J. AIR L. & COM. 651 (1970) [hereinafter *1970 Policy Statement*].
163. *See id.* at 654. On the other hand, foreshadowing the DOT's 1995 policy, the statement made a vague recommendation of 'further studies' as to the 'feasibility of exchanging rights on a multilateral basis.' *Id.* The Bermuda I mechanisms, discussed *supra* Chapter 3, Part III(B), included reliance on IATA tariff conferences for fare regulation as well as *ex post* capacity adjustment procedures to balance market share.
164. *Id.*
165. *Id.* at 653. Thus, the 'Declaration of Policy' in the Federal Aviation Act, prior to being draped in the colors of the new deregulatory ethos, in 1970 simply called for '[t]he encouragement and development of an air-transportation system properly adapted to the present and future needs of the foreign and domestic commerce of the United States...' 'Competition,' although mentioned in the Declaration, was encouraged only 'to the extent necessary' to achieve this utilitarian objective. 49 U.S.C. app. § 1302 (1970). Competition is integral to the successor section to § 1302, 49 U.S.C.A. § 40101 (West 2008), which speaks of 'maximum reliance on competitive market forces and on actual and potential competition.'
166. *See 1970 Policy Statement, supra* note 162, at 656-57.
167. *See id.* at 657.

reform, provoked strong Congressional reaction.[168] The Carter Administration's response to the Bermuda II firestorm was an interagency protocol entitled *United States Policy for the Conduct of International Air Transportation Negotiations*, issued on August 21, 1978.[169] The new policy, obviously influenced by the consumer welfare philosophy of the impending airline deregulation legislation, similarly extolled 'reliance on competitive market forces to the greatest extent possible.'[170] While the Carter approach acknowledged the limitations imposed by the sovereignty constraints of Chicago-type bilateralism,[171] it sought also to reject what it labeled 'the self-defeating accommodation of protectionism.'[172] Under this reworked aeropolitical outlook, the policy proposed to transfer some of the liberalizing features of domestic reform, notably greater route entry and pricing freedom, to the international plane, and, in addition, to eliminate capacity and frequency barriers (which were never part of the U.S. domestic regulatory framework).[173] Route entry, as interpreted by the United States, would also embrace 'designation of new U.S. airlines in international markets that will support additional service.'[174]

The diplomatic sweetener for bilateral partners – to discourage backsliding into a raft of new Bermuda II-style renegotiations[175] – would be an increase in the number of 'gateway cities' for nonstop or direct air service.[176] As previously seen, the choice of the term 'gateway' has carried a specific cabotage-excluding message in U.S. international aviation policy, and the 1978 statement nowhere intimated any change in the legal status of cabotage.[177] Finally, the new policy included warning signals

---

168. 'In this [Bermuda II] negotiation, the United States put together a makeshift negotiation structure and came away with an agreement which is a major step backward in 40 years of attempting to bring market-oriented competition to international aviation.' See SENATE REP. NO. 96-329, *reprinted in* LEGISLATIVE HISTORY, INTERNATIONAL AIR TRANSPORTATION COMPETITION ACT OF 1979, at 54-55 [hereinafter LEGISLATIVE HISTORY (IATCA)]. For an analysis of the Bermuda I and II agreements, *see supra* Chapter 3, Part III(B).

169. *See Airline Commission Papers*, undocketed [hereinafter *1978 Policy Statement*]. The policy was the product of the Interagency Committee on International Air Transportation Policy, chaired by the Department of Transportation, and including representatives of the Departments of State, Justice, Defense, and Commerce, the CAB, the Council of Economic Advisors, White House domestic policy staff, the National Security Council, and the Office of Management and Budget.

170. *Id.* at 1.

171. Crude aeropolitical reality was frankly admitted in the 1978 statement: 'Bilateral aviation agreements, like other international agreements, should serve the interests of both parties. Other countries have an interest in the economic prosperity of their airline industries, as we do in the prosperity of ours.' *Id.*

172. *Id.* at 4.

173. *Id.* at 2-3. The statement advocated devolution of pricing decisions to individual airlines, with minimal regulatory supervision over predatory pricing practices. A particular concern was price distortion because of foreign government subsidy. *See id.*

174. *Id.* at 3.

175. *See Airline Commission Proceedings*, testimony of Marvin S. Cohen, former Chairman, Civil Aeronautics Board (Jun. 24, 1993), at 28-30.

176. *See 1978 Policy Statement, supra* note 169, at 4. For discussion of the typical agenda points in international air services negotiations, *see supra* Chapter 1, Part II(B).

177. *See supra* Chapter 3, Part IV(B).

about U.S. unhappiness with 'unfair or destructive competitive practices' (such as discriminatory airport costs) imposed on U.S. airlines by other countries, and referenced 1974 legislation (the International Air Transportation Fair Competitive Practices Act or IATFCPA) that gave government officials wide powers to implement retaliatory charges against countries that sanction such practices.[178]

Beginning in 1978, the Carter administration began to test-market its new 'open skies' policy among its bilateral aviation partners.[179] Liberal agreements

---

178. *1978 Policy Statement, supra* note 169, at 3. The International Air Transportation Fair Competitive Practices Act of 1974, Pub. L. No. 98-443, 98 Stat. 1706 (signed into law on Jan. 3, 1975) [hereinafter IATFCPA], *inter alia* authorized the Secretary of Transportation to monitor airport charges imposed on U.S. airlines by foreign countries, and to report all instances of discriminatory charges to the Civil Aeronautics Board and the Secretary of State. If the Secretary of State could not eliminate the discrimination by negotiations, the Secretary of Transportation was empowered, with the Secretary of State's approval, to impose compensating charges on air carriers of the countries concerned for access to similar facilities in the United States. *See* 49 U.S.C. app. § 1159(b) (1975). The IATFCPA legislation has been recodified in 49 U.S.C.A. § 41310 (West 2008). This statute, and subsequent U.S. unfair competition legislation in the international air transport sector, will be considered *infra* Part III.

179. The phrase 'open skies' has circulated in the international air transport milieu since at least the mid-1970s, and was used, for example, to reflect the concerns of scheduled carriers that charter operators might be permitted to provide limited scheduled services; scheduled carriers, sensing a need to reconfigure the nature of their services, called for equal access to 'on demand' charter traffic. *See* statement of Knut Hammerskjöld, former Director-General of the International Air Transport Association (IATA), *quoted in North Atlantic Price War Looms*, AV. WEEK & SPACE TECH., Nov. 14, 1977. *See also Carriers Grappling with New Problems*, AV. WEEK & SPACE TECH., Dec. 20, 1976. 'Open skies' gained its present, much broader conceptual profile, which embraces a series of procompetitive adjustments to the bilateral system that governs scheduled international air carrier operations, after the Carter Administration moved in 1977 to undermine the IATA's multilateral ratemaking conferences. The Administration wished to return tariff negotiations to the bilateral agenda, consolidating route, capacity, and fare issues in one forum. In fact, by 1977 there were as many so-called 'open rate' routes as those still operating under 'closed rate,' cartel-like conditions, and IATA executives felt constrained to announce a moratorium on all traffic conference activity at their annual general meeting of that year. *See North Atlantic Price War Looms, supra.* Paradoxically, in light of the dialectic of the present study, the U.S.-led assault on IATA's traffic conferences pitted unilateral State intervention in the service of price competition against the abuse by the airline corporations of their managerial prerogatives, admittedly with State consent, in pursuit of a stable, cartel-like fare structure governing worldwide interline operations. Director-General Hammerskjöld was skeptical about government intentions, arguing that the bilateral system inevitably centered on 'market share, protectionism and power politics:' 'I personally believe that a completely free market providing equal opportunities for all is the last thing governments want.' *Id.* Restoration of the airlines' plenary managerial prerogatives in international air transport, but within a framework of open and fair competition, is the intent of the proposal presented in Chapter 6 of this book. The U.S. open skies agenda, while it continues to advance the pricing revolution begun by President Carter, cannot accommodate the competitive discipline that would be imposed by a multilateral antitrust enforcement system. The present agenda, as clarified by the George H. W. Bush Administration in 1992 and adopted by Presidents Clinton and George W. Bush, is described *supra* Chapter 1, Part II(C).

on wider gateway access and greater managerial freedom to frame pricing and frequency strategies were reached with small, free trade-advocating countries like South Korea and the Netherlands.[180] To justify extending open skies privileges to these relatively small markets, the Administration touted the creation of competitive alternatives to established intercontinental gateways like Tokyo and London. The strategic assumption, which also underscored the renaissance of open skies initiatives in later presidencies, was that the threat from upstart alternatives would tempt larger markets to liberalize.[181] It was, in a sense, an intriguing application of the domestic theory of market contestability to the aviation relations of States.[182] The new policy quickly attracted Congressional support as a means to redeem the unpleasant legacy of Bermuda II. Indeed, the draft International Air Transportation Competition Act of 1979 (IATCA),[183] according to its Senate sponsors, sought 'to institutionalize the progressive policy and cooperation which the United States is today practicing.'[184]

B   THE IATCA: AN AMBIVALENT CHALLENGE TO BILATERALISM

The ADA left international air transportation virtually untouched. In the domestic interstate system, of course, the statute could exercise the full might of the

---

180. *See* U.S. DOT, Issues Paper, *U.S. International Aviation Issues in a Global Perspective, in Airline Commission Documents*, Dkt. No. 001207 (May 1993), at 2 & 21 [hereinafter U.S. DOT, Report to Airline Commission]. *See* Protocol Relating to the United States-Netherlands Air Transport Agreement of 1957, Mar. 31, 1978, 29 U.S.T. 3088 [hereinafter U.S./ Netherlands Protocol], stating the desire of both governments 'to promote an international aviation system based on competition among airlines in the marketplace with minimum government interference.' *Id.* preamble. Capacity was unrestricted, although air services were required to 'bear a close relationship to the requirements of the public for such services.' *Id.* Article 11, amending Article 10 of the 1957 agreement, 12 U.S.T. 837, 840. Government intervention on prices was limited to 'prevention of predatory or discriminatory practices, protection of consumers from abuse of monopoly power, and protection of airlines from prices that were artificially low because of direct or indirect governmental subsidy or support.' *Id.* art. 6(a). *See also* Air Transport Agreement between the United States and the Republic of Korea, Amending the Agreement of Apr. 24, 1957, Mar. 22, 1979, 30 U.S.T. 3823. Seoul is a secondary hub for transpacific services by U.S. carriers, Tokyo being the primary hub. The agreement with South Korea was amended in Jun. 1991 to increase the number of points Korean carriers may serve in the United States, provided Korea fulfilled certain obligations to improve the 'doing business' conditions for U.S. carriers serving Korea. The Korean government attempted to meet these obligations, and aviation relations with Seoul remained relatively stable, *see* U.S. DOT Report to Airline Commission, *supra*, at 21, leading to a full open skies agreement in 1998. *See* Air Transport Agreement Between the Government of the United States of America and the Government of the Republic of Korea, [Oct. 2006] 3 Av. L. Rep. (CCH) ¶ 26,375a, at 22,571 (Jun. 9, 1998).
181. *See* U.S. DOT Report to Airline Commission, *supra* note 180, at 2.
182. *See* Chapter 2, Part II(B) (discussing the encirclement strategy).
183. The Act became law on Feb. 15, 1980. *See* Pub. L. No. 96-192. The Act has since been incorporated into various parts of 49 U.S.C.
184. LEGISLATIVE HISTORY (IATCA), *supra* note 168, at 55.

Congressional commerce power to create a paradigmatic shift from regulation to a phased deregulation.[185] The legislative impact of the IATCA, in contrast, would be unavoidably one-dimensional, since it could only mandate the terms of U.S. engagement in the international bilateral system, and would therefore constitute only a kind of 'unilateral declaration of deregulation.' The structure of the IATCA reflected the paradox of legislating for greater competition in a system that depends so much on foreign concurrence: although the statute grants permissive authority

---

185. *See* U.S. CONST. art. I, § 8, cl. 3 (granting Congress 'the power [t]o regulate commerce with foreign nations, and among the several States'). *See* Jeffrey A. Berger, *Phoenix Grounded: The Impact of the Supreme Court's Changing Preemption Doctrine on State and Local Impediments to Airport Expansion*, 97 Nw. U. L. REV. 941 (2003) (stating that '[t]he national air transportation system may be the most national of all federal regulatory schemes, as the chief capital of the industry – the aircraft – are by nature divorced from any single locality'). The pervasive (and hence permissible) nature of federal air transport regulation has been ratified by the U.S. Supreme Court, and rests on the conceptual bedrock of what the U.S. legal system understands as 'preemption,' the displacement of local (State) regulatory authority by federal control where uniformity is required for the smooth functioning of the national economy. *See* Berger, *supra*, at 949. In this context, federal power operates through the Supremacy Clause. *Id.*; U.S. CONST. art. VI, cl. 2; *See, e.g.*, City of Burbank *v.* Lockheed Air Terminal, 411 U.S. 624, 625 (1973) (observing that '[w]hatever subjects of this [interstate commerce] power are in their nature national, or admit only of one uniform system, or plan of regulation, may justly be said to be of such a nature as to require exclusive legislation by Congress'). The *Lockheed* Court approved the scope of this use of the commerce power *inter alia* by invoking U.S. sovereignty over national airspace and the safety and 'efficient utilization' authority of the Federal Aviation Administration. As Justice Jackson stated in his concurrence in Northwest Airlines, Inc. *v.* State of Minnesota, 322 U.S. 292, 303 (1944), '[f]ederal control is intensive and exclusive. Planes do not wander about in the sky like vagrant clouds. They move only by federal permission, subject to federal inspection, in the hands of federally certified personnel and under an intricate system of federal commands. The moment a ship taxis onto a runway it is caught up in an elaborate and detailed system of controls.' *See also* United States *v.* Helsley, 615 F.2d 784, 786 (9th Cir. 1979) (stating: 'We think the federal power to regulate the airspace is as complete and as valid as the federal power, to the extent it rests upon the commerce clause, to regulate navigable waters'). Allowing for the remodeling of the federal 'command' after 1978, these principles are essentially sound. *But see* Texas International Airlines, Inc. *v.* Civil Aeronautics Board, 473 F.2d 1150 (D.C. Cir. 1972), rejecting as 'untenable' complaints by Braniff and Texas International that 'Air Southwest' [*sic*, the name used by the court in referring to Southwest Airlines], a Texas intrastate carrier, required CAB certification on the ground that its services connecting various Texas cities 'affected' interstate commerce. *Id.* at 1152. It is inconceivable, nonetheless, that Texas could license, for example, Air France, to provide Dallas/Houston roundtrip air service without running afoul of the Federal Aviation Act provisions on cabotage, even though *technically* the service – though not the service supplier – would be entirely intrastate in nature. Air France, in any event, can only operate within U.S. airspace by *federal* permission, and its operations would certainly not be localized in Texas. Moreover, it would also be necessary to consider the impact of the explicit preemption clause in the Airline Deregulation Act that denies states the authority to adopt laws or regulations *inter alia* affecting air carrier routes. *See* 49 U.S.C.A. § 41713(b)(1) (West 2008). *See also* American Airlines *v.* Department of Transportation, 202 F.3d 788 (5th Cir. 2000) (applying express preemption clause, and the 'air route' exclusion, to deny enforcement of a joint ordinance agreed between Dallas and Fort Worth, upon the federally-mandated creation of a single Dallas-Fort Worth airport, to close aircraft operations at Love Field, the original Dallas airport).

for a more flexible route/rate regime, it could not follow the ADA model of decreeing a phased elimination of regulatory control.[186]

1   The IATCA's 'Soft Law' Approach to the Chicago System

Accordingly, a striking difference between the ADA and the International Air Transportation Competition Act was the latter's much greater reliance on program-matic goal-setting, what might be called 'soft' legislation, as opposed to the 'hard' provisions that predominate in the ADA. At the most abstract level, that of the initial 'Declaration of Policy,' the IATCA was faithful to its domestic predecessor, as well as to the terms of the 1978 policy statement, in superseding the old reg-ulatory standard of 'competition to the extent necessary to assure the sound devel-opment' (of air transportation) with the recast ADA directive of 'maximum reliance on competitive market forces and on actual and potential competition.'[187] The IATCA Declaration of Policy also inserted a new coda, originally found in the House version of the draft bill, advocating '[t]he strengthening of the competitive position of United States air carriers to at least assure equality with foreign air carriers, including the attainment of opportunities for United States air carriers to maintain and increase their profitability, in foreign air transportation.'[188]

These twin objectives – reliance on competition and enhancement of the competitive position of U.S. air carriers – are facially contradictory. To have confidence in the marketplace is necessarily to exclude the prospect of official intervention to shore up the competitive position of individual carriers. Yet the objective of 'strengthening' U.S. carriers resurfaces *expressis verbis* later in the statute, as the first element in a recital of ten 'goals' that the Departments of State and Transportation must observe in their formulation of U.S. international aviation policy.[189] Given that the common purpose of all of these goals is to encourage a policy 'emphasiz[ing] the greatest degree of competition that is compatible with a

---

186. Consequently, although the ADA eventually repealed (through its 'sunset' provisions) most of the Civil Aeronautics Board's economic regulatory power, and abolished the agency itself, it transferred the CAB's authority in foreign air transportation to the Department of Transpor-tation: the IATCA, in turn, merely reconfigured, but did not supersede or 'sunset,' this area of governmental responsibility. Accordingly, the IATCA's legislative structure remains in place, and the text refers, when appropriate (noting changes), to the current version of the U.S. code following the last major nonsubstantive revision and codification of the U.S. federal trans-portation laws that took effect on Jul. 5, 1994. *See* 1 Av. L. Rep. (CCH) ¶ 1000 *et seq.*

187. 49 U.S.C. app. § 1302(a)(4) (1980) (now recodified in 49 U.S.C.A. § 40101(a)(6) (West 2008)). The Act does accept that the domestic and international systems are not truly comparable, and speaks of the need to consider 'material differences, if any, which may exist between inter-state . . . transportation, on the one hand, and foreign air transportation, on the other.' *Id.*

188. 49 U.S.C. app. § 1302(a)(12) (now recodified in 49 U.S.C.A. § 40101(e)(1) (West 2008)). As noted in the main text, *infra*, the House draft language explicitly included a policy of main-taining (and increasing) U.S. air carriers' *market share* in foreign air transportation. *See Joint Explanatory Statement of the Committee of Conference, in* Legislative History (IATCA), *supra* note 168, at 79.

189. 49 U.S.C. § 1502(b) (1980) (now recodified in 49 U.S.C.A. § 40101(e) (West 2008)).

well-functioning international air transportation system[,]'[190] it is reasonable to inquire whether the true Congressional understanding of the scope of the phrase 'greatest degree of competition,' and of the level of its compatibility with a 'well-functioning international air transportation system,' meant only competition that preserved, or at the very least did not *endanger*, the international market share of U.S. airlines.

This interpretation is supported by the original House version of the text, which spoke explicitly of strengthening the competitive position of U.S. international air carriers, 'including the attaining of opportunities...to maintain and increase their market share in foreign air transportation.'[191] The language substituted in conference (quoted above), which calls for assuring 'equality' with foreign carriers,[192] reveals more legislative finesse but is undoubtedly inspired by the same conservative impulses. Moreover, the eighth policy 'goal' is also couched in terms that suggest concern for maintaining the existing competitive position of U.S. carriers, since it offers opportunities for foreign carriers to increase access to U.S. points *only* 'if exchanged for benefits of similar magnitude [for U.S. carriers]...with permanent linkage between rights granted and rights given away.'[193] The Act's other stated goals betray little of this sharp ambivalence toward the consequences of genuine competition. In fact, they merely reprise the procompetitive components that featured in the 1978 policy statement, focusing on freedom of pricing to meet 'consumer demand,' multiple and permissive international authority for U.S. air carriers, and increases in nonstop U.S. gateway cities, as well as the goal of eliminating unfair competition that, as noted earlier, Congress transformed into the IATFCPA legislation in 1974.[194]

2 Protecting U.S. Carriers: The IATCA's 'Hard Law' Approach

The 'hard' provisions of the Act bear out the sense of legislative vacillation detected in its goal-setting agenda. Indeed, much of the substance of the IATCA is concerned with equipping U.S. administrators to impose tough retaliatory discipline in response to foreign competitive infractions against U.S. airlines. As shown by the passage of the IATFCPA in 1974, and by the sentiments of the 1978 policy statement, leeriness of such foreign anticompetitive practices had emerged as an important reflex of U.S. international aviation policy. The CAB had previously developed procedures for disallowing or discontinuing foreign air carrier schedules, subject to presidential disapproval within 10 days, in the event of

---

190. *Id.*
191. LEGISLATIVE HISTORY (IATCA), *supra* note 168, at 79.
192. 49 U.S.C. app. § 1502(b)(1) (1980) (now recodified in 49 U.S.C.A. § 40101(e)(1) (West 2008)).
193. 49 U.S.C. app. § 1502(b)(8) (1980) (now recodified in 49 U.S.C.A. § 40101(e)(8) (West 2008)). The unhelpful broadness of the IATCA's policy goals was the subject of criticism at the Airline Commission hearings. *See, e.g., Airline Commission Proceedings*, remarks of John E. Robson, former Chairman, Civil Aeronautics Board (Jun. 15, 1993), at 61.
194. *See supra* note 178.

foreign government 'impairment' of U.S. carrier operating rights over the objections of the U.S. Government.[195] While useful, these procedures could only affect implementation of foreign carriers' schedules.[196]

The IATCA drafters inserted a much more expansive power, supposedly comparable to powers already available to foreign governments, summarily to suspend or modify foreign air carrier *permits*, without a hearing (but subject to presidential approval), whenever the CAB (and later the DOT) found that a foreign government or air carrier, over the objections of the U.S. Government, had 'impaired, limited, or denied the operating rights of United States air carriers, *or* engaged in unfair, discriminatory, or restrictive practices with a substantial adverse competitive impact upon United States carriers, with respect to air transportation services to, from, through or over the territory of such country.'[197] To maximize diplomatic pressure, permissible retaliation would extend to restricting the operations of third-country airlines serving fifth freedom routes from the offending State into the United States.[198] The Senate Committee on Commerce, Science, and Transportation, in reporting on the legislation, was at pains to emphasize that such wide powers would only be triggered after failure of diplomatic intercession (although the Act does not say so), and were subject in any event to White House veto.[199]

The blunderbuss quality of these so-called 'Section 9' powers of the CAB was mitigated, to some degree, by the more measured provisions of Section 23 of the statute. Although this section was intended to bolster the 1974 IATFCPA legislation by expanding its substantive scope beyond discriminatory airport charges to encompass, like Section 9, literally *any* species of discriminatory or anticompetitive action by a foreign government or carrier,[200] it also introduced a formalized

---

195. This regulatory authority, now exercised by the Department of Transportation, appears in Filing and Approval of Schedules, 14 C.F.R. § 213.3(c)-(d) (West 2008).

196. *See id.* But the sanction could nonetheless be a powerful one, explicitly denying permission to operate proposed schedules or to discontinue existing ones. CAB/DOT orders could be flexibly applied, selecting particular routes for disapproval or discontinuance. *Id.*

197. 49 U.S.C. app. § 1372(f) (recodified as 49 U.S.C.A. § 41304(b) (West 2008)) (emphasis added).

198. *See id.*

199. The CAB (and now the DOT) would also be subject to the general Federal Aviation Act proscription against acting inconsistently with obligations assumed by the United States under an air transport agreement. *See* 49 U.S.C.A. § 40105 (West 2008). Citing international law precedent, the Senate Report on the IATCA excepted U.S. countermeasures against a prior violation from this proscription. Such countermeasures would be permissible under general international law principles of retorsion (*i.e.*, self-defense) even if they would, in themselves, comprise a breach of the parties' agreement. *See* LEGISLATIVE HISTORY (IATCA), *supra* note 168, at 58-59.

200. *See supra* text accompanying note 178 (briefly discussing the International Air Transportation Fair Competitive Practices Act of 1979 (IATFCPA)). The new statutory language in Section 23 of the IATCA spoke in blanket terms of 'unjustifiable or unreasonable discriminatory, predatory, or anticompetitive practices against a United States air carrier,' or the imposition of 'unjustifiable or unreasonable restrictions on access of a United States air carrier to foreign markets.' 49 U.S.C. app. § 1159(b)(1) (1980) (recodified as 49 U.S.C.A. § 41310 (West 2008)).

complaint and investigation procedure.[201] Unlike Section 9, therefore, Section 23 was 'judicialized' to give U.S. air carriers a forum through which to prompt intergovernmental negotiations to resolve disputed competitive practices.[202]

Ironically, in view of its stereoscopic assault on anticompetitive practices, the IATCA gave a renewed statutory voice to the controversial Fly America program that had also been introduced in the 1974 legislation.[203] Reviled by foreign airlines as being itself a blatantly unfair and discriminatory practice, the program instructed the Comptroller General of the United States to deny reimbursement for official U.S. Government overseas airline travel that did not utilize U.S. national carriers (assuming that they provided appropriate scheduled service). While the IATCA did

---

201. *See id.* Under these provisions, however, a hearing is *stricto sensu* optional at the discretion of the U.S. agency. The Section grants the CAB (and now its successor, the DOT) plenary authority simply to approve or dismiss the complaint. The section *is* drafted in hortatory prose, proclaiming a legislative preference that the CAB/DOT proceed by careful diplomatic negotiations, though not actually requiring this to happen. *See id. See* Complaint of Northwest Airlines, Inc. Against the Government of Australia, [1992-1994 Transfer Binder] Av. L. Rep. (CCH) ¶ 22,904, at 14,119 (Feb. 5, 1993) [hereinafter Northwest Complaint].

202. *See* LEGISLATIVE HISTORY (IATCA), *supra* note 168, at 66. Section 23 conferred no special enforcement powers beyond those already provided in the IATFCPA with respect to foreign carrier permits and tariffs. IATCA/IATFCPA complaints by U.S. air carriers continue to feature on the DOT's docket, especially in cases where relationships with larger foreign markets have come under strain through high U.S. carrier penetration. *See, e.g.,* U.S. DOT, *In the Matter of Aerolineas Argentinas, S.A., under Section 41310(c)(2) International Air Transportation Fair Competitive Practices Act, as Amended,* Dkt. No. OST-2003-15092, Final Order (Nov. 25, 2003). For a more strategic use of this forensic channel by a U.S. airline, *see* U.S. DOT, *Complaint of United Air Lines, Inc., against The European Commission and National Implementing Authorities under 49 U.S.C. § 41310,* Dkt. No. OST-98-4030-2, Order (Jul. 27, 1998) (asserting that proposed actions by the Commission and some Member States, including limitations placed on United's alliance arrangements with Lufthansa, SAS, and other carriers affecting service levels, slot availability, pricing and CRS displays, would preclude United from exercising rights specifically provided for under open skies agreements with the United States, and that sanctions would be appropriate to ensure the 'continued viability of the U.S. Government's open skies policy in Europe'). Following the European Commission's decision to close its investigation of the United/Lufthansa/SAS alliance, and the resolution of the issues raised therein, United moved successfully for a voluntary dismissal of its Complaint. *See* U.S. DOT, *Complaint of United Air Lines, Inc., against The European Commission and National Implementing Authorities under 49 U.S.C. § 41310,* Dkt. No. OST-98-4030-2, Order Dismissing Complaint and Terminating Proceeding (Nov. 27, 2002).

203. *See* Section 5 of the IATFCPA, *supra* note 178, which added a new section to the Federal Aviation Act, 49 U.S.C. app. § 1117 (1975) (recodified as 49 U.S.C.A. § 40118 (West 2008)). The statutory preference for U.S. air carriers had existed, however, since the International Travel Act of 1961. *See* IATFCPA, *supra* note 178, sec. 6. For discussion of the origins of the Fly America program, and its relationship with the U.S. Department of Defense Civil Reserve Air Fleet program for U.S. air carriers, *see* BRATTLE GROUP, THE ECONOMIC IMPACT OF AN EC-U.S. OPEN AVIATION AREA ch. 7, at 4 (2002); *see also* Institute for Defense Analyses, *Sustaining the Civil Reserve Air Fleet (CRAF) Program* (May 2003) (concluding that the legislative history of Fly America does not reveal any express intent to use these restrictions as an incentive for U.S. carriers to participate in CRAF, even though major U.S. carriers perceive the existence of Fly America preferences as precisely such an incentive).

preserve the central premise of the program – U.S. federal agencies should prefer U.S. 'flag' services – it inserted a procompetitive blandishment authorizing the U.S. Government to offer bilateral negotiating partners the right to carry official U.S. passenger traffic (but without guaranteeing specific dollar amounts) as an incentive to encourage more liberal air transport agreements.[204]

The legislation requires, however, that U.S. concessions be matched by 'rights or benefits of similar magnitude.'[205] In the recently completed 2007 U.S./EC Air Transport Agreement,[206] the United States has agreed to grant to EU air carriers certain 'Fly America' rights[207] that have not been (and cannot be) reciprocated in kind, since EU Member States do not have similar programs.[208] While the concessions are limited and although their scope remains unclear, it can be assumed that the U.S. Government believes that the *general* level of reciprocal exchanges of rights in the Agreement (most notably, the creation of a 27-member 'open skies' relationship with the United States) trumps any legislative implication that U.S. concessions should be limited solely to those necessary to secure concessions affecting other governments' must-fly programs. In any event, the U.S. concessions

---

204. Section 21(c) of the IATCA authorized inclusion of the right to transport U.S. official passenger traffic under the terms of a bilateral agreement that is consistent with the IATCA's goals for international aviation policy. *See* 49 U.S.C. app. § 1117(c) (1980) (recodified as 49 U.S.C.A. § 40118(b) (West 2008)). It is interesting that the Senate Report on IATCA declined to authorize a dollar figure: if it had, a right or benefit of 'similar magnitude' might not be available from any U.S. bilateral aviation partner. *See* LEGISLATIVE HISTORY (IATCA), *supra* note 168, at 65-66.

205. 49 U.S.C. app. § 1117(c) (1980) (recodified as 49 U.S.C.A. § 40118(b) (West 2008)). *But see* the discussion in main text, *supra*, on the 'Fly America' concessions offered in the recent U.S./EC Air Transport Agreement. *See* Institute for Defense Analyses, CRAF Report, *supra* note 203, at B-38 (concluding that 'such rights have been exchanged exceedingly rarely,' and evidently assuming, based on the two examples cited – bilateral agreements with Saudi Arabia and Brazil – that reciprocity in kind is in fact intended by the statute).

206. *See supra* note 2.

207. *See* U.S./EC Air Transport Agreement, *supra* note 2, annex 3 (entitled: 'Concerning U.S. Government Procured Transportation'). Annex 3, as interpreted in the parties' Memorandum of Consultations, grants EU carriers the right to carry U.S. Government personnel (other than defense and military personnel) or cargo between the United States and the European Union, or between two points outside the United States. Exceptions would exist for city-pair contracts awarded by the U.S. General Services Administration (these contracts change from year to year but clearly introduce unpredictability into the availability of the concession). *See id.*, Memorandum of Consultations, para. 21. Also, the U.S. delegation affirmed that, under the current interpretation of U.S. law, the carriage of 'Fly America' traffic by a U.S. carrier includes transportation sold under the code of a U.S. carrier pursuant to a code-share agreement, but carried on an aircraft operated by a foreign air carrier. *See id.*, Memorandum of Consultations, para. 20. The pertinent regulations are contained in 41 C.F.R. §§ 301-3. *See* Federal Travel Regulation; Use of Commercial Transportation, Fly America Act, 63 Fed. Reg. 63,417-421 (Nov. 13, 1998) (stating the position of the U.S. General Services Administration and the relevant Fly America rules for U.S. Government personnel, including a special exception allowing code-shared flights). *See id.* at 63,419.

208. *See* U.S./EC Air Transport Agreement, *supra* note 2, Memorandum of Consultations, para. 22. Whether this is factually correct or not is an interesting question. There may be 'unofficial' pressure to use national carriers. *See* Institute for Defense Analyses, *supra* note 203, at B-39.

helped to mollify some of the most intense opposition to the Agreement, at least on the part of the U.K. Government if not the U.K. mainline carriers.[209] In prior jousting over a U.S./U.K. bilateral to replace Bermuda II, the British repeatedly cited the 'Fly America' program as a serious obstacle to further liberalization.[210]

C   THE IATCA AND THE CHICAGO SYSTEM: ENDURING REGULATION

1   International Designation: Public Franchises and Private Profits

Aside from its 'soft' goal-setting agenda and its strengthening of the government's antidiscrimination authority, the IATCA's other changes were regulatory and technical, designed to improve the administrative procedures still required by a 'regulated' international air transportation system. The IATCA's regulatory changes did not displace the bedrock requirement that both U.S. and foreign international air carriers need specific authorization by the U.S. DOT to operate all air routes to and from the United States – unless the bilateral relationship is one of 'open skies.'[211] U.S. carriers do so by 'designation' of the U.S. Government

---

209. Further possibilities for enhancing access to government-procured (*i.e.*, U.S.) air transportation are scheduled for discussion in the second stage of U.S./EC negotiations. *See* U.S./EC Air Transport Agreement, *supra* note 2, art. 21 & Memorandum of Consultations, para. 23. *See also* Martial Tardy and Madhu Unnikrishnan, *Transport Ministers' Nod Paves Way for Second Phase of Open-Skies Talks,* 367 AV. DAILY, Mar. 23, 2007 (discussing the second stage agenda, including Fly America).

210. As late as 2000, the U.K. Government was still pressuring the United States to lift the Fly America restrictions as part of any open skies deal. *See* [U.K.] Department of Transport, *Air Service Agreements Between the UK and the U.S.–Government Response,* Cmd 4907 (2000) (describing U.S. 'intransigence' on cabotage, airline ownership, and Fly America, while noting that removal of Fly America would not 'necessarily' require U.S. domestic legislation). The U.K. Government has not directly criticized the modifications to Fly America in the new U.S./EC Air Transport Agreement – unlike U.K. carriers British Airways and Virgin Atlantic as well as other interested groups. *See* United Kingdom Parliament, House of Commons Transport Committee, *Open Skies – The Draft EU-U.S. Air Transport Agreement,* Minutes of Oral Evidence, Hansard (Mar. 13, 2007) (including testimony by U.K. airline executives questioning practical value of Fly America concessions because of likely U.S. restrictions); *see also* Martin Broughton, Chairman, British Airways, Speech to Chatham House Conference on Open Skies (Mar. 5, 2007) (noting contrast between U.S. Fly America program, on which the United States had made 'minuscule concessions,' and U.K. policy 'to fly the most economic way possible, even if it's on a subsidized U.S. carrier enjoying Chapter 11 bankruptcy protection').

211. In open skies bilaterals, there are no limitations in principle on the number of carriers that may be authorized ('designated') by either party. Approval from the DOT to fly a route will therefore be expected if the U.S. air carrier holds the requisite certificate of public convenience and necessity. *See supra* text accompanying Chapter 3, note 177. As part of an initiative to streamline the regulatory burden on carriers, the DOT may now grant 'blanket' open skies authority to carriers that request it. *See* U.S. DOT, *Notice on Streamlining Regulatory Procedures for Licensing U.S. and Foreign Air Carriers,* Dkt. No. OST-2005-22228 (Aug. 26,

under its numerous bilateral agreements.[212] The opportunity to acquire new designations is subject to an arduous administrative law procedure,[213] and the DOT

<hr>

2005). *See also* U.S. DOT, *Application of Spirit Airlines, Inc. For Blanket Open-Skies* [*sic*] *Certificate Authority*, Dkt. No. OST-2007-27790 (Apr. 13, 2007) (seeking blanket authority to serve all existing and future U.S. open skies partners). *See also* U.S. DOT, *Application of American Airlines, Inc. for Certificate of Public Convenience and Necessity Pursuant to 49 U.S.C. 41101*, Dkt. No. OST-2000-8516, Order Issuing Certificate (Apr. 3, 2007), at 1 (granting applicant American Airlines certificate authority to provide combination – passenger/ cargo – service to 'all of our foreign aviation partners that have entered into an open-skies [*sic*] agreement with the United States where that agreement is being applied'). The decision also awards automatic authority with respect to all future open skies agreements 'without the need for further action by the Department or the carrier.' *Id.* at 3.

212. Rep. James Oberstar, now Chairman of the House Transportation Committee of the U.S. House of Representatives, charged in a written submission to the Airline Commission that the DOT had 'adopted policies favoring large carriers both in the initial award and in the transfer of international routes,' leading to 'concentration of international routes' among these carriers. Rep. James Oberstar, *Submission to Airline Commission, in Airline Commission Documents*, Dkt. No. 000928 (Jun. 11, 1993), at 7 [hereinafter Oberstar]. Of course, the availability of new entrant carriers for international routes outside the small circle of major carriers has, at least until now, been negligible. Nonetheless, even within the circle, this criticism has resurfaced on other occasions. For example, with respect to proceedings for the award of routes to the People's Republic of China, the DOT has been accused of allowing United and Northwest to consolidate their positions in the U.S./China market over the past decade, to the point where these carriers now control over 75% of U.S./China air services – squeezing out other potential competitors such as American Airlines and Continental Airlines. *See* Julie Johnson, *United Awarded New Route to China*, Sun-Sentinel.com, Jan. 10, 2007 (describing the United/Northwest market lead as 'virtually insurmountable' in the approach to the 2008 Beijing Olympic Games).

213. These designations require a 'public interest' determination by the Department of Transportation under Section 401(c) of the Federal Aviation Act, 49 U.S.C. app. § 1371 (1979) (now recodified as 49 U.S.C.A. § 41108 (West 2008)), based upon oral or written submissions by interested carriers. *See also* 14 C.F.R. § 302.210 (West 2008) (setting forth procedures for show-cause proceedings to designate air carriers). Oral evidentiary procedures, provided for under the regulations, involve hearings before an administrative law judge, with final decision by a senior DOT official (subject to acceptance or remand by the Assistant Secretary). Under show-cause procedures, typically no oral hearing is held and administrative law judges are not involved. *See id. See also* U.S. DOT, *In the Matter of 2007 U.S.-China Combination and All-Cargo Frequency Allocation Proceeding*, Dkt. No. OST-2006-25275, Order Instituting Proceeding and Inviting Applications (Jul. 10, 2006), at 3 (using 'written, non-oral show-cause proceedings' to establish 'a complete evidentiary record,' with reduced costs and delay, in order to allocate a new U.S.-China route to one of four incumbent combination carriers and one of four incumbent cargo carriers). On occasion, the Department can determine *ex ante* that the public interest will be served by U.S. carrier designations, as it has recently done in response to the availability of additional frequencies (*i.e.*, daily round-trips) under the U.S./People's Republic of China bilateral agreement. *See id.* at 2 (finding that the new routes offered a valuable resource for travelers and shippers and would enhance competition in the U.S./China market). The DOT criteria for a route award (developed through precedent and rulemaking) include implications for market structure (level of competition), route integration, fare and service proposals, incumbency, ability to enter quickly, passenger and cargo data forecasts, relevant code-share agreements, willingness to accept partial grant of a frequency allocation, efficient integration with behind-gateway traffic, and although (rarely in the era of

has declined to substitute open competitive bidding (or even an auction or lottery system).[214]

Somewhat incongruously, but responding to the cash needs of ailing carriers such as Pan Am and more recently United Airlines, the DOT *has* allowed a 'secondary market' in acquired designation rights to develop, in which U.S. carriers buy and sell such designations among themselves.[215] With the spread of open

---

deregulation) effect on competition in the domestic industry. *See id.* app., Evidence Request, at 2-6; U.S. DOT, Limited Entry-Markets: Certificate Duration, Notice Requirements for Carriers Leaving During a Selection Case, and Procedures and Criteria for Selecting Carriers, Notice of Proposed Rulemaking, Dkt. No. 43403, 50 Fed. Reg. 38,539 (Sept. 23, 1985) (enumerating carrier selection criteria and rejecting possible use of lotteries and auctions as opposed to conventional criteria) [hereinafter U.S. DOT, Limited-Entry Markets Rule-Making]. A foreign government's possible response to particular fare or service proposals is not an acceptable factor to consider, nor (again because of deregulation) is the extent to which addition of the authority at issue would strengthen any applicant. *See id. See also* U.S. DOT, Certificate Duration in Limited Entry-Markets: Requirements for Carriers Leaving Limited-Entry Markets During a Selection Case; Procedures and Criteria for Selecting Carriers for Limited-Entry Markets, Final rule and policy statement, Dkt. No. 43403, 51 Fed. Reg. 43,181 (Dec. 1, 1986) (noting that selection criteria vary in weight depending on the particular circumstances of each proceeding).

214. *See* U.S. DOT, Limited-Entry Markets Rule-Making, *supra* note 213 (deciding against using lotteries or auctions to distribute authority for limited-entry routes, preferring to assign 'valuable aviation rights, which the U.S. Government has secured through bilateral negotiations,' in 'the most reasoned and rational way possible'). One advantage of open-designation bilaterals – the open skies model – is that carrier selection hearings become unnecessary. *See also* comments of Mary Street, former Chief, Europe Division (now Assistant Director for Negotiations), DOT Office of International Aviation, Interview (Dec. 4, 1995) [hereinafter Street Interview] (stating that '[t]he more "open skies" agreements that exist, the less the need for these [designation] procedures') (copy on file with author).

215. *See Airline Commission Proceedings*, testimony of Jeffrey N. Shane, former U.S. Department of Transportation Assistant Secretary for Policy and International Affairs (Jun. 24, 1993), at 84. The 'specificity' of the Chicago system intrudes into this so-called 'secondary' market. First, the DOT must by statute approve a transfer as consistent with the public interest. *See* 49 U.S.C.A. § 41105 (West 2008). *See* Andrew B. Steinberg, Assistant Secretary for Aviation and International Affairs, U.S. Department of Transportation, Statement Before the Senate Committee on Commerce, Science, and Transportation (Jan. 24, 2007) (noting that transfers require a formal record and an opportunity to comment by all interested parties). Moreover, unlike in new route proceedings, in transfer cases the Department *does* consider effects on domestic competition (as well as effects on the viability of the carriers involved and on the trade position of the United States in the international air transport market). *See* U.S. DOT, *Delta Airlines, Inc. and United Air Lines, Inc.*, Dkt. No. OST-2006-25517, Order Approving Route Transfer (Aug. 25, 2006), at 2-4 [hereinafter U.S. DOT, *Delta/United Route Transfer Proceeding*]. Second, the U.S. Government must still negotiate the consent of its bilateral partners when U.S. carriers transfer international route authority in the secondary market. Sometimes, as in the absorption of Pan Am's transatlantic route network by United, the request for consent enables a foreign government to obtain windfall benefits in return for its acceptance of the new designation. *See Airline Commission Proceedings*, testimony of Jeffrey N. Shane, *supra* (*see* discussion of the Heathrow succession agreement, *supra* Chapter 3, note 464). There have been allegations of route trafficking, *i.e.*, applying for routes with the intention of immediately selling them in the 'secondary' market. For example, American Airlines claimed that America West and Hawaiian Airlines negotiated the sale to Northwest of their Honolulu/Japan awards

skies and open-route designations, fewer of these sales take place.[216] It is a notable regulatory paradox, nonetheless, that international route sales enable carriers to earn windfall income from the award of what is legally a public franchise.[217]

Foreign air carriers, designated by *their* countries of origin under bilateral agreements with the United States, need a DOT permit that finds them 'fit, willing, and able' to provide the foreign transportation and also that the foreign carrier 'is qualified and has been designated by [its] government,' *or* that the proposed transportation is 'in the public interest.'[218] While this latter 'public interest' requirement, if applied, would appear to interpose the U.S. Government's discretion into the designation decisions of its foreign negotiating partners, it would be 'unusual' to protest a foreign country's designation.[219] In practice, the 'designation' and 'public interest' requirements are fused, so that a foreign government's designation

'well before the route award was finalized.' The U.S. Airline Industry, American Airlines, Inc., *in Airline Commission Documents*, Dkt. No. 000085 (May 1993), at 11-12 [hereinafter American Airlines Submission].

216. Between 1986 and 1992, the sales prices in the 'secondary market' for international routes totaled $2.8 billion (all but $74 million of which represented route purchases by American, United, and Delta). *See* Oberstar, *supra* note 212, at 6; Department of Justice, submission to Airline Commission, *in Airline Commission Papers*, undocketed, at D [hereinafter Department of Justice Submission]; U.S. DOT, *International Award and Transfers of International Route Authority, in Airline Commission Documents*, Dkt. No. 000000, at 72 [hereinafter U.S. DOT, *International Route Authority*]. While open designations under open skies bilaterals have greatly reduced these sales, from time to time they figure in the trade press. *See* U.S. DOT, *Delta/United Route Transfer Proceeding, supra* note 215 (approving United's sale to Delta of U.S./U.K. route rights between JFK International Airport and London for a reported $21 million; because of Bermuda II restrictions, Delta nevertheless had to limits its acquired service to London Gatwick, whereas United was one of the anointed carriers serving Heathrow). *See also* Steven Lott, *United to End International JFK Service, Sells London Rights*, 365 Av. Daily, Jul. 31, 2006. Another recent example was the 2001 transfer of an extensive bundle of foreign route rights from TWA (Trans World Airlines) to American Airlines as part of a bankruptcy court auction of TWA's assets. *See* U.S. DOT, *Joint Application of American Airlines, Inc. and TWA Airlines LLC for transfer of certificate and other authorities under 49 U.S.C. 41105*, Dkt. Nos. OST-01-9027 et al. (Apr. 4, 2001) (finding *inter alia* that the transfer would advance U.S. international aviation policy objectives by providing consumers with new competitive options and would also improve the 'trade position' of the United States through American's strengthened competitiveness against foreign carriers).

217. A practice condemned by Rep. James Oberstar, Aviation Subcommittee Chairman (now Chairman of the House Transportation Committee), in his submission to the Airline Commission, *supra* note 212, at 6. As Oberstar recognized, however, airlines have relied on their inventory of routes as collateral to obtain financing, and extinguishing the market in these routes could inflict serious financial damage. *See id.* Concerned about large carrier dominance of route sales, in 1993 Oberstar sponsored a House bill, H.R. 472, to require the DOT to solicit counter-bids for each route sale. The agency would have to weigh a number of 'public interest factors' in making its selection, including the need to strengthen smaller air carriers to enhance competition. *Id.* at 7. The bill did not progress beyond the Aviation Subcommittee. The DOT's practice, incidentally, has been to consider applications for the sale of international routes after a carrier has served a new market for at least one year. U.S. DOT, *International Route Authority, supra* note 216, at 73.

218. 49 U.S.C.A. § 41302 (West 2008).

219. Street Interview, *supra* note 214.

will usually be of determinative significance.[220] The statecraft of the Chicago system, after all, makes the grant or conditioning of foreign air carrier permits more a matter of foreign policy than of economic selection.[221]

2   International Fares: Zonalism and Unilateralism

For air carriers operating wholly in domestic transportation, faresetting discretion was completely deregulated from 1983. For U.S. and foreign airlines engaged in foreign air transportation, however, the antique regulatory protocol of 'filing' tariffs, which are then subject to government suspension, rejection, or cancellation 'in the public interest,' continues to apply if the relevant bilateral agreement does

---

220. 'The negotiation of a bilateral agreement itself represents a determination by the Government of the United States that the grant of route authority provided for under the bilateral is in the "public interest." ' SENATE REPORT NO. 96-329, LEGISLATIVE HISTORY (IATCA), *supra* note 168, at 57. This genuflection to *pacta sunt servanda* has a statutory source in the Federal Aviation Act itself, which has always required the CAB (and now the DOT) to act consistently with obligations assumed by the United States under an air transport agreement. 49 U.S.C. app. § 1502(a) (1979), *recodified as* 49 U.S.C.A. § 40105(b) (West 2008). *See* PAUL S. DEMPSEY, LAW AND FOREIGN POLICY IN INTERNATIONAL AVIATION 122 (1987). The DOT does, however, make a specific determination with respect to whether a foreign airline is 'fit, willing, and able' to operate in the United States. For this purpose, the airline must provide information about its license (operating authority) from its homeland government and its designation by its government, its ownership and management personnel, its financial condition, its operating plan, and the ability of its company and personnel to comply with laws and regulations. This determination is known as 'economic' authority. *See* 49 U.S.C.A. §§ 41301-41302 *et seq.* (West 2008). As part of its determination, the DOT asks the Federal Aviation Administration (FAA) whether any safety concerns about the airline exist (*i.e.*, 'safety' authority). *See id. See also* 14 C.F.R. § 129 (West 2008). The FAA since mid-1991 has adopted a much more proactive screening process for foreign airlines proposing service to the United States, including visits to foreign countries. The purpose of the International Aviation Safety Assessments Program (IASA) is to ensure that all of the 600 or so foreign carriers that operate to or from the United States are properly licensed and with safety oversight provided by a competent civil aviation authority in accordance with ICAO standards. *See* U.S. Federal Aviation Administration, International Aviation Safety Assessments (IASA) Program, <www.faa.gov/safety/programs_initiatives/oversight/iasa/>. The FAA's findings, positive or otherwise, are a matter of public record. *See id.* The Foreign Air Carrier Licensing Division in the DOT's Office of International Aviation processes these applications and maintains a list of licensed foreign air carriers. U.S. DOT, Office of International Aviation, <http://ostpxweb.dot.gov/aviation/intla-viationprog.htm>. Foreign designations are submitted initially to the Department of State, not to the DOT. *See* Street Interview, *supra* note 214.

221. Indeed, for this very reason, the IATCA applies the ADA's simplified procedures for certificate applications (notice, written evidence, and no requirement of an 'oral evidentiary hearing') to foreign carrier permit applications. Previously a public hearing had been required. *See* 49 U.S.C. app. § 1372(d) (1980), *recodified as* 49 U.S.C.A. § 41305 (West 2008); *see also* 49 U.S.C.A. § 41306. In another foreign policy intrusion, the President has statutory authority under Section 801(a) of the Federal Aviation Act, 49 U.S.C. app. § 1461(a) (recodified as 49 U.S.C.A. § 41307), to review all DOT decisions with respect to award or transfer of route authority or permits, but may *disapprove* a DOT action only on grounds of 'foreign relations or national defense considerations.' Disapproval for economic reasons or for reasons related to carrier selection is explicitly prohibited. *See id.*

not substitute a more liberal provision.[222] In a unilateral U.S. gesture of liberalization, the IATCA did adopt the ADA 'zone of reasonableness' artifice to create a general nonintervention zone for fares in foreign air transportation.[223] The IATCA's pricing methodology for the zone also replicated the ADA: fares could float up to 5% above and 50% below a 'standard foreign fare level.'[224] The magnanimity of the gesture, however, was compromised by sweeping Board authority (now vested in the DOT) to suspend, reject, or cancel fares which were in some measure 'unreasonable or unreasonably discriminatory' or predatory, or as retaliation for 'unreasonable' foreign government regulatory actions affecting U.S. air carrier fares.[225]

The rate regulation provisions illustrate another of the IATCA's recurring intersections with foreign policy. The most liberal Bermuda I-style pricing approval mechanism in the Chicago system is called 'double disapproval,' where *both* parties to the bilateral must disapprove a fare in order to prevent it going into effect.[226] While a unilateral statutory power to reject, cancel, or suspend

---

222. *See* 49 U.S.C.A. §§ 41504 & 41509 (West 2008). Although the Department of Transportation's Model Open Skies Agreement no longer includes an optional 30-day filing requirement, this protocol had already been dispensed with in more recent open skies agreements. *See* U.S. Department of State, Air Transport Agreement Between the Government of the United States of America and the Government of [country] art. 12 (Jan. 1, 2008), <www.state.gov/documents/organization/19622.pdf> [hereinafter Model Open Skies Agreement]. *See also* Air Transport Agreement Between the Government of the United States of America and the Government of Canada art. 6(2), [Apr. 2008] 3 Av. L. Rep. (CCH) ¶ 26,246a, at 21,977 (Mar. 12, 2007) [hereinafter 2007 U.S./Canada Agreement]. The new U.S./EC Air Transport Agreement, *supra* note 2, dispenses with all filing requirements. *See id*, art. 13(1). Note, however, that the Model Open Skies Agreement and the U.S./EC Air Transport Agreement each mandates immediate access, on request by the other party's authorities, to information on historical, existing, and proposed prices. *See* Model Open Skies Agreement, *supra*, art. 13(2); U.S./EC Air Transport Agreement, *supra* note 2, art. 13(2)(b).
223. In accordance with ADA terminology, the Civil Aeronautics Board would be precluded from finding intra-zone fares 'unjust or unreasonable' on the basis of being either too high or too low. *See* 49 U.S.C. app. § 1482(j)(6) (1980) (recodified as 49 U.S.C.A. § 41509(e)(2) (West 2008)).
224. *Id.*
225. *See* 49 U.S.C. § 1482(j)(1) (1980) (recodified as 49 U.S.C.A. § 41509(a)(1) (West 2008)). Strong echoes of this approach appear even in the DOT's revised Model Open Skies Agreement, *supra* note 222, which approves State party 'intervention' to prevent 'unreasonably discriminatory' prices or practices, protection of consumers from prices that are 'unreasonably high or restrictive due to the abuse of a dominant position,' or prices that are artificially low because of government subsidy. *Id.* art. 12(1)(a)-(c).
226. *See* Peter P.C. Haanappel, Pricing and Capacity Determination in International Air Transport: A Legal Analysis 148 (1984). Under 'country of origin' pricing, which was featured in the 1978 U.S./Netherlands agreement, jurisdiction to veto fares is divided according to the origin of the traffic: only the United States could veto the fares proposed for traffic originating in its territory, and only the Netherlands could object to rates originating in Dutch territory. *See* U.S./Netherlands Protocol, *supra* note 180, art 6(c). A similar agreement with Belgium, also signed in 1978, introduced the ultimate in liberalization (short of total price decontrol), the concept of 'double disapproval pricing.' Protocol Between the Government of the United States of America and the Government of Belgium Relating To Air Transport Agreement

fares obviously violates the double disapproval principle and also potentially compromises the liberal pricing protocols of the open skies era,[227] Section 1102(a) of the Federal Aviation Act requires the CAB (and now the DOT) generally to exercise its powers and duties 'consistently with' U.S. bilateral obligations.[228] Thus, U.S. administrators should defer to an open skies agreement that offers more restrained conditions of unilateral intervention (for example, to combat monopoly or predation).[229] Indeed, at the Senate's urging, Section 25 of the IATCA included an even more specific provision subordinating the CAB's numerous investigation and enforcement powers to Section 1102(a).[230] This precaution, while supererogatory, underscores the IATCA's 'contingent' existence in the shadow of the Chicago bilateral system.

3   International Antitrust Regulation: Wielding the Wand of Immunity

a   *Avoiding the Sunset*

To the extent that merger and acquisition activity can occur in foreign air transportation (current law confines it to transactions among U.S. air carriers which have international operations[231]), antitrust review passed to the Department of Justice on January 1, 1989.[232] With respect to so-called 'intercarrier agreements'

---

of 1956, Dec. 14, 1978, 30 U.S.T. 617, art. 6(4)-(5). This requires the agreement of *both* governments to suspend a proposed price, even where the price charged by a government's own originating traffic is concerned. *See id.* art. 6. For the most protean of protocols, *see* the pricing mechanism in the new U.S./EC Air Transport Agreement, discussed *supra* note 222.

227. Although these powers are intended to be applied against 'filed' tariffs, even in open skies agreements the U.S. Government can request tariff information (and, presumably, apply these tariff surveillance powers in appropriate circumstances).

228. 49 U.S.C. app. § 1502(a) (1979) (recodified as 49 U.S.C.A. § 40105(b)(A) (West 2008)).

229. *See* Article 12 of the revised Model Open Skies Agreement, *supra* note 222, which, as noted, limits intervention 'by the Parties' to actions to combat discriminatory prices, abuses of a dominant position, and predation caused by government subsidy (a species of 'dumping'). While this regime may appear to be, on its face, merely a modest reduction in the sweep of powers in the federal legislation, the notion of 'intervention' as used in the Model Agreement seems to exclude *any* unilateral action even if the conditions for intervention are met. Thus, while a complaining party is required to proceed to WTO/GATT-type consultations and reasoned resolution, *see id.* art. 12(3), 'intervention' seems limited to invoking and participating in this conciliatory process – any disputed tariff will go into effect (or continue into effect), *by default*, if no agreement is reached. This is a quite surprising 'automaticity,' given the typical reticence of international enforcement procedures, but it has existed since the inauguration of 'double disapproval' pricing in the U.S./Belgium air services protocol of 1978. *See supra* note 226. As noted, *supra* note 222, the 2007 U.S./EC Air Transport Agreement is even more liberal in its application to prices than the Model Open Skies Agreement.

230. *See* 49 U.S.C. app. § 1482(c) (1980) (recodified as 49 U.S.C.A. § 46101(a)(4) (West 2008). *See* Legislative History (IATCA), *supra* note 168, at 68-69.

231. *See supra* Chapter 3, Part V(B) (discussing restrictions on foreign ownership in U.S. law).

232. As provided in Section 3 of the Civil Aeronautics Board Sunset Act of 1984, *supra* note 129.

affecting foreign air transportation (including agreements between U.S. air carriers and foreign airlines), the IATCA abandoned the rigid ADA procedures of compulsory filing and CAB approval subject to the 'public interest.'[233] Instead, the new legislation simply assimilated intercarrier agreements in foreign air transportation (for example, cooperative marketing alliances or code-sharing arrangements) to the optional filing procedures, and the 'Bank Merger' standard for agency approval, that the ADA applied to domestic agreements until 1989.[234] The Senate Report noted that *unfiled* agreements in foreign air transportation (as well as *all* domestic agreements) would henceforth be subject to the general antitrust laws.[235]

Although the ADA's regulatory control of domestic intercarrier agreements was forced (in explicit terms) to sunset in 1989, foreign air transportation was, implicitly, not affected.[236] Thus, the extraordinary CAB/DOT antitrust immunity power, which ended for domestic agreements on January 1, 1989, continues to apply to intercarrier agreements involving foreign air transportation.[237] As discussed earlier, airline managements have seized upon these vestigial regulatory artifices – but especially the immunity power – to try to dilute the full force of the Chicago nationality principle, including its implied prohibition on international merger activity in the airline industry.[238] Inspired by an extraordinary episode of entrepreneurial ingenuity,[239] antitrust immunity was first sought by and accorded

---

233. *See supra* note 126.
234. Section 11 of the IATCA, *amending* Section 412 of the Federal Aviation Act, 49 U.S.C. app. § 1382 (recodified in 49 U.S.C.A. § 41309 (West 2008)). *See* SENATE REPORT, LEGISLATIVE HISTORY (IATCA), *supra* note 168, at 73. Reflecting foreign policy concerns, the standard was modified in the IATCA to add the words 'including international comity or foreign policy considerations' to the phrase 'important public benefits' that governs the Board's (and now the Department's) unusual discretion to approve anticompetitive agreements. *Id.* As the Senate Report noted, inter-carrier agreements might very well reflect policy compromises that the U.S. Government has reached with another sovereign nation. The 'public benefits' test therefore required somewhat greater latitude to allow reviewing officials to find that agreements implementing intergovernmental accommodations would be in the public interest. *See id.* at 61. Examples of such accommodations would surely include intercarrier agreements allowing for code-sharing arrangements between airlines that are also competitors.
235. *See* SENATE REPORT, LEGISLATIVE HISTORY (IATCA), *supra* note 168, at 73.
236. The sunset legislation scheduled only the extinction of the CAB/DOT immunity power for interstate transportation. *See* Section 3 of the Civil Aeronautics Board Sunset Act of 1984, *supra* note 129. Section 6 of the Act contemplated that Congress might, acting on the basis of reports from the DOT, retain the immunity power in interstate air transportation, *explicitly* retain it in foreign air transportation, or repeal it for both. In the end, the legislated sunset target, repealing the power for domestic air transportation only, took effect without change.
237. *See* Section 414 of the Federal Aviation Act, 49 U.S.C. app. § 1384, *recodified as* 49 U.S.C. § 41308 (2003). This provision *inter alia* authorizes the grant of an antitrust exemption to an otherwise anticompetitive agreement '[w]hen the Secretary of Transportation decides it is required by the public interest.'
238. *See supra* Chapter 3, Part VIII.
239. *See* Rutger Jan toe Laer, *Kick Starting Cross-Border Alliances*, 32 AIR & SPACE L. 287, 288 (2007) (evocatively describing a joint KLM/Northwest Airlines executive meeting in 1992 as culminating in 'the metaphoric triumphant cry: the concept of antitrust immunity for cross-border airline alliances had been born – and life would never be the same').

to the KLM/Northwest combination.[240] At its inception, the two airlines were proposing to operate for all intents and purposes as a single carrier.[241] After a hiatus during which this combination remained the sole exemplar of a legally privileged international alliance, the U.S. DOT wielded its wand of immunity for a series of nonequity carrier partnerships.[242]

<table>
<tr><td>b</td><td>Two Case Studies in Alliance Approval and Antitrust Immunity: The Force of Bilateral 'Specificity'</td></tr>
</table>

A major paradox of present U.S. air diplomacy, as noted previously, is that U.S. national law and regulatory policy can permit, and even immunize, cooperative agreements between U.S. and foreign airlines that may not only create anticompetitive risks, but may also be manifestly harmful to an effective U.S. strategy to create true – in other words, *multilateral* – open skies.[243] These aeropolitical tensions have been present in all of the immunity proceedings considered by the U.S. DOT since its first alliance immunization proceeding, the KLM/Northwest application for approval of a comprehensive quasi-merger agreement. Building on that precedent and on the more recent order in American Airlines/British Airways,[244] it can be seen that the agency tended to allow the goal of bilateral open skies to drive its analysis of antitrust concerns, in the process yielding

---

240. *See supra* Chapter 3, Part VIII(B).
241. *See id.*
242. *See supra* Chapter 3, Part VIII (analyzing the shifting fortunes of these partnerships and the emergence of global alliances built on the antitrust immunity power). In U.S. DOT, *Joint Application of Northwest Airlines, Inc. and KLM Royal Dutch Airlines for Approval and Antitrust Immunity of an Agreement Pursuant to Sections 412 and 414 of the Federal Aviation Act, as Amended,* Dkt. No. 48342, Order 92-11-27 to Show Cause (Nov. 16, 1992) [hereinafter U.S. DOT, *Joint Application of KLM/Northwest for Antitrust Immunity*], the DOT determined that approval *and* antitrust immunity should be accorded the KLM/Northwest agreement based on its 'important public benefits,' including operating efficiency and better service to American travelers. Moreover, as indicated *supra* Chapter 3, Part VIII(B) the DOT sent a wider policy signal by explicitly linking its approval to the newly-signed 1992 open skies agreement with the Netherlands, which was intended to encourage other European countries to enter into liberalized aviation agreements. In a reflection of the diplomatic quandary created for U.S. negotiators by the prize of antitrust immunity, the German Government indicated that a similar open skies pact, initialed between Germany and the United States in Mar. 1996, would not take effect unless the United States granted immunity to allow expansion of an existing Lufthansa/United Airlines strategic alliance. Thus, in the cases of the Netherlands and Germany, approval of antitrust immunity for alliances between airlines of the respective parties only came *after* the open skies agreement was signed. With respect to alliances involving U.K. carriers (American Airlines/British Airways and United Airlines/bmi), the DOT agreed to grant immunity (albeit in the former case with steep conditions which the parties rejected) conditionally without an open skies agreement, with the expectation that the conditionality would spur conclusion of an open skies agreement with the United Kingdom.
243. *See supra* Chapter 3, Part VIII.
244. *See supra* Chapter 3, Part VIII(B).

decisions that were neither good for competition law nor satisfying as international aviation policy.[245]

Because of the nationality principle there is, strictly speaking, no true concept of 'merger' in international air transportation.[246] The IATCA provides that these intercarrier agreements may be filed for the agency's approval at the option of the carriers. Even if an agreement fails to satisfy the Clayton Act test because it threatens a substantial reduction or elimination of competition,[247] it can still be recuperated if the Secretary of Transportation finds that it is necessary to meet a serious transportation need, or to achieve important public benefits (including 'international comity and foreign policy considerations,' a phrase which, as noted earlier, was added by the U.S. Senate to reflect policy accommodations with foreign governments),[248] and where no materially less anticompetitive alternatives are available: the so-called Bank Merger Act escape clause.[249] In both

---

245. The DOT's preliminary and continuing 'fitness review' jurisdiction does not encompass competition issues. For example, the DOT lacks power to require a U.S. airline to divest itself of an international route as a condition for approval of financing and management changes. *See* GAO, *Airline Competition: Impact of Changing Foreign Investment and Control Limits on U.S. Airlines*, at 17, GAO/RCED-93-7 (Dec. 1992) [hereinafter GAO, *Foreign Investment*]. Accordingly, foreign investments in U.S. airlines are also subject to the general antitrust scrutiny of the Department of Justice. The Antitrust Division can consider, for example, whether an investment by a foreign airline 'would tend to reduce competition in markets in which the U.S. and foreign airline compete' and could order the U.S. airline to divest itself of international routes in order to green-light the investment. GAO, *Foreign Investment, supra*, at 17. In a marker of the 'specificity' of international air transportation, however, the Division's authority can be blindsided by the DOT's continuing power to bless intercarrier agreements (short of 'mergers') between domestic and foreign carriers with full antitrust immunity. (Indeed, the grant of immunity could even be made to intercarrier agreements among domestic competitors, provided they related exclusively to foreign air transportation. *See* 49 U.S.C.A. §§ 41308-41309 (West 2008). At the international level, as the KLM/Northwest controversy first revealed, this vestigial DOT dominion produced an unruly intermixture of competition policy and broader goals of international aviation policy.

246. The DOT, however, considered the KLM/Northwest intercarrier agreement to be, in its intended effects, 'equivalent to a merger of the two carriers,' U.S. DOT, *Joint Application of KLM/Northwest for Antitrust Immunity, supra* note 242, at 13, and that the American Airlines/British Airways Alliance Agreement would position the two carriers 'to operate as if they were a single entity,' U.S. DOT, *U.S.-UK Alliance Case*, Dkt. No. OST-2001-11029, Order to Show Cause (Jan. 25, 2002), at 5 [hereinafter U.S. DOT, *U.S.-UK Alliance Case*], or 'as if there had been an operational merger between the partners,' *id.* at 33.

247. Section 412 of the Federal Aviation Act, recodified in 49 U.S.C.A. § 41309 (West 2008), provides that the Secretary of Transportation shall approve an intercarrier agreement that is not adverse to the public interest, but shall disapprove an agreement that 'substantially reduces or eliminates competition' *unless* the Secretary makes a further finding in accordance with the dual test, *infra* note 249.

248. *See supra* note 234.

249. This test, as restated in Section 412 of the Federal Aviation Act, recodified in 49 U.S.C.A. § 41309(b) (West 2008), requires rejection of an anticompetitive agreement *unless* the Secretary of Transportation finds that the agreement 'is necessary to meet a serious transportation need' or to achieve 'important public benefits (including international comity and foreign

of the alliances under scrutiny here, the DOT did apply the standard Clayton Act test to examine whether the carriers' proposals for cooperative operation of their services would 'substantially reduce competition by eliminating actual or potential competition [between the applicants] so that they would be able to produce supra-competitive pricing or reduce service below competitive levels.'[250]

Critically in both proceedings, once the Department focused on specific sets of city-pair combinations, the potential anticompetitive effects of each alliance were magnified. Thus, while the impact of these collaborations on the U.S./Europe market generally would not have attracted challenge under prevailing antitrust guidelines,[251] the focus of the Department's analysis was (in the case of KLM/ Northwest) the individual gateway markets of Minneapolis-St. Paul/Amsterdam and Detroit/Amsterdam, where competition would not merely be reduced, but entirely *eliminated*,[252] by the projected joint operations of KLM and Northwest,[253] and (with respect to American Airlines/British Airways) the structural overlap affecting the applicants' air services between major U.S. points and London. The U.K. capital city captures 90% of all travelers in the flagship U.S./U.K. market, and the combined carriers would command 51% of that market – including lucrative nonstop services for five U.S./Heathrow city-pairs (Boston, Chicago, Los Angeles, Miami, and New York).[254] The proposed alliance would effectively

policy considerations),' *and* that the transportation need cannot be met or those benefits cannot be achieved by 'reasonably available alternatives that are materially less anticompetitive.'

250. U.S. DOT, *U.S.-UK Alliance Case, supra* note 246, at 34. For an explanation of how the Department established a shared docket to consider this alliance and an alliance proposed between United Airlines, bmi, and other foreign airlines, *see supra* Chapter 3, note 480. For analysis of the scope of the KLM/Northwest Commercial Cooperation and Integration Agreement, *see supra* Chapter 3, Part VIII(B).

251. In the U.S./Europe market, the combined KLM/Northwest market share would make them (at the time of the application) the fifth largest transatlantic carrier. *See* U.S DOT, *Joint Application of KLM/Northwest for Antitrust Immunity, supra* note 242, at 15. In the American Airlines/British Airways proceeding, the applicant alliance would hold 26% of scheduled passenger traffic between U.S. and European gateways, but competitive discipline existed from the Star and SkyTeam alliances as well as from other non-allied U.S. and U.K. carriers. *See* U.S. DOT, *U.S.-UK Alliance Case, supra* note 246, at 37.

252. The language of the Clayton Act, incorporated in Section 412 of the Federal Aviation Act and now recodified as 49 U.S.C.A. § 41309 (West 2008).

253. *See* U.S. DOT, *Joint Application of KLM/Northwest for Antitrust Immunity, supra* note 242, at 15-16. In fact, an early trend showing substantial increases in fares between the partners' hub airports appears to have been sustained. *See* U.S. DOT, *Joint Application of Alitalia-Linee Aeree Italiane-S.p.A. et al. for Approval of and Antitrust Immunity for Alliance Agreements Under 49 U.S.C. 41308 and 41309*, Dkt. No. OST-2004-19214, Public Answer of American Airlines, Inc., at 31, A12 (detecting high Northwest fares ex-Amsterdam far exceeding the average fare paid by a U.S. to Europe passenger).

254. U.S. DOT, *U.S.-UK Alliance Case, supra* note 246, at 38. American Airlines and British Airways were also major competitors in the Dallas-Fort Worth/London Gatwick market. *See id.* at 44.

eliminate the parties' competition in those city-pair markets.[255] Moreover, the legacy of Bermuda II, as considered in Chapter 3, has been a privileged status for the four airlines designated to serve U.S./Heathrow.[256] Two of those airlines were now applying to orchestrate their privileges into an integrated code-sharing alliance enjoying antitrust immunity.

A typical agency solution to these problems might be to condition approval on surrender of an airline's certificate authority on one or more of the threatened routes and the selection of a new U.S. carrier to serve them. But the 'specificity' of the bilateral relationships, one characterized by open skies and the other by a highly restrictive designation protocol, militated against a conventional remedy. Under the open-designation provisions of the U.S./Netherlands open skies agreement, *any* U.S. carrier could freely serve those routes.[257] The Department speculated, however, that other carriers would not be 'interested' in providing the same nonstop service as KLM and Northwest on either route.[258] Nonetheless, even though fares concededly might rise in these newly uncompetitive markets, the DOT concluded that 'the [a]greement *overall* will benefit competition' by enabling the two carriers to 'operate more efficiently and to provide the public with a wider variety of online services.'[259]

---

255. Thus, the alliance would significantly increase concentration in those markets and provide the new partnership with a dominant position in markets serving more than five million passengers annually. The alliance's share of nonstop frequencies would be more than 60% in all of the overlap markets except Los Angeles. *See id.* at 44.

256. *See supra* Chapter 3, Part III(B). Under Bermuda II (superseded in Mar. 2008 by the U.S./EC Air Transport Agreement, *see supra* note 2), only American Airlines, United Airlines, British Airways, and Virgin Atlantic could serve U.S. points to and from London Heathrow. Continental, Delta, Northwest, and US Airways could only serve London Gatwick with their own aircraft under the entry restrictions imposed by Bermuda II. *See* U.S. DOT, *U.S.-UK Alliance Case, supra* note 246, at 38. The DOT found that Heathrow and Gatwick constituted separate antitrust markets for time-sensitive (*i.e.*, primarily business) passengers. *See id.* at 40.

257. *See* U.S. DOT, *Joint Application of KLM/Northwest for Antitrust Immunity, supra* note 242, at 15-16.

258. Although some price discipline would flow from fares offered for connecting service to Amsterdam over rival carriers' U.S. hubs. *See id.*

259. *Id.* (emphasis added). While it is true that the U.S. Department of Justice has moderated its skepticism about 'efficiencies' defenses to otherwise doubtful mergers (as reflected, for example, in comparison of its 1989 and 1992 horizontal merger guidelines), it is still the case that '[t]he expected net efficiencies must be greater the more significant are the competitive risks....' 57 Fed. Reg. 41,552 (1992). Nonetheless, the Department now expects efficiencies to be a significant factor in refraining from challenge of mergers that are likely to have only 'slight anticompetitive effects.' U.S. DEPT. OF JUSTICE & FEDERAL TRADE COMM'N, COMMENTARY ON THE HORIZONTAL MERGER GUIDELINES 55 (2006) [hereinafter DOJ/FTC, COMMENTARY]. Economic analysis of the interplay between the assumed efficiencies of the KLM/Northwest and American Airlines/British Airways alignments revealed the demonstrable disappearance of competition in a number of important international markets. In fact, U.S. airline executives have been troubled by the DOT's history of creating international aviation policy without benefit of full economic inquiry: 'We have seen no indication at DOT of robust, intellectually defensible economic analyses of prospective bilateral transactions.' Robert L. Crandall, President, American Airlines, *Hearing on International Aviation Policy,*

With respect to American Airlines/British Airways, the Department confronted the reality that no other U.S. carrier would have the right to replace one of the four treaty-sanctified carriers at Heathrow. And, while acknowledging that the U.S./U.K. carrier combination would yield 'significant public benefits,' the Department appeared to define these public benefits not within the KLM/Northwest analytical framework of improved efficiencies and online services but rather in the conceptually distinct context of international aviation policy – as a spur to the achievement of an open skies agreement with the United Kingdom and ultimately with the EC.[260]

In other words, although the Department performed a competition analysis that imposed swingeing slot divestiture requirements on the alliance partners,[261] the analysis focused explicitly on carving out a so-called '*de facto*' open skies relationship with the United Kingdom that would provide other U.S. airlines with useable slots and facilities at Heathrow once the *de jure* situation became resolved.[262] The Department proposed, therefore, to artificially project future new entry onto a hypothetically liberalized bilateral relationship. As the partners contended with some bitterness, the analysis in this sense betrayed more of an inclination toward 'notions of industrial planning under the rubric of "public policy"' than a determination to tackle all of the immediate competitive problems threatened by the alliance.[263] In fact, even with the required divestitures, the alliance concededly would eliminate one competitor in the Los Angeles/London market and immunity carve-out conditions would probably not compensate for

---

104th Cong. 1st Sess. 168 (May 24, 1995) [hereinafter 1995 Aviation Hearings]. In Nov. 1994, the DOT established an Office of Aviation and International Economics (now the Office of Aviation Analysis). Data trends and forecasting models for alliance applications are developed by the Competition Policy and Analysis Division of this Office. *See* U.S. DOT, Office of Aviation Analysis, <http://ostpxweb.dot.gov/aviation/aviatanalysis.htm>. Foreign carriers participating in alliances with U.S. partners are required to submit enhanced traffic statistics to the Office of Aviation Analysis. *See* U.S. DOT, *Joint Application of The Austrian Group, British Midland Airways Limited, Deutsche Lufthansa AG, Polskie Linie Lotnicze Lot S.A., Scandinavian Airlines System, Swiss International Air Lines Ltd., TAP Air Portugal, and United Air Lines, Inc., Under 49 U.S.C. §§ 41308 and 41309 for Approval of and Antitrust Immunity for Alliance Expansion Agreements and an Amended Coordination Agreement*, Dkt. No. OST-2005-22922, Final Order (Feb. 13, 2007) (directing foreign participants to report full-itinerary Origin-Destination Survey of Airline Passenger Traffic for all itineraries including a U.S. point). (In the multilateral market proposed in this study, airlines would perform their own economic investigations of market opportunities.)

260. *See* U.S. DOT, *U.S.-UK Alliance Case, supra* note 246, at 36, 48, & 51. Thus, a new U.S./U.K. agreement would mean that the United States had open skies treaties with all but three EU Member States, 'thereby substantially enhancing [the U.S.] negotiating position.' *Id.* at 51.

261. Thus, the partners would be required to provide other U.S. airlines with 224 weekly slots, to support 16 daily round-trips. *See id.* at 1 & 35.

262. *See id.* at 34 (stating preexisting DOT policy that no American Airlines/British Airways alliance agreement would receive immunity without adequate provision for new and expanded U.S. carrier service through London airports, particularly Heathrow).

263. *Id.* at 29 (summarizing alliance partners' submission).

loss in competition in the Chicago/Heathrow and Dallas-Fort Worth/Heathrow city-pairs.[264]

Having found a threat of substantially reduced competition, the IATCA requires the Department to take two further analytical steps, assessing either transportation needs or public benefits, as well as the unavailability of any materially less anticompetitive alternative to meet those needs or benefits, before any doubtful agreement can win agency approval and proceed to seek antitrust immunity. In KLM/Northwest, although the DOT referred initially to this double-pronged Bank Merger Act analysis, it appears to have dispensed with it in light of the perceived 'overall' competitive balance of the agreement.[265] In American Airlines/British Airways, on the other hand, the Department had already fused its competition and public benefits analysis, establishing a 'new entry' standard that depended on the negotiation of a new U.S./U.K. open skies agreement, so that a separate, independent 'public benefits' step could not authentically take place other than in circular logic: public benefits required *de facto* access to Heathrow; *de facto* access to Heathrow would provide public benefits.

Both opinions proceeded to consideration of the carriers' associated requests for a Section 41308 antitrust exemption. The DOT immunized the entire KLM/Northwest transaction on the grounds that its implementation would serve the public interest and that it would be 'impracticable' to exclude the operations in the markets where competition was being eliminated.[266] With respect to American

---

264. *See id.* at 48. Thus, the DOT conceded that no new entry was 'likely' in either the Chicago/Heathrow or DFW/Heathrow markets. American hubs at both U.S. gateways and British Airways hubs at London Heathrow. It appears from the opinion that DFW/Heathrow was considered a *potential* overlap market for the alliance partners; as indicated, *supra* note 254, the two airlines already operated a DFW/Gatwick overlap operation. U.S. DOT, *U.S.-UK Alliance Case, supra* note 246, at 48. United Airlines, which also hubs at Chicago, is already in the Chicago/Heathrow market. *See id.* at 47. For these reasons, the Department proposed the additional remedial step of an immunity 'carve-out' with respect to pricing, inventory, yield management coordination, or pooling of revenues with respect to unrestricted coach-class fares or any business or first-class fares for local U.S. point-of-sale passengers in the nonstop Chicago/DFW-London Heathrow overlap markets. *See id.* For two other overlap markets (New York/Heathrow and Boston/Heathrow), however, other U.S. airlines would likely only enter the market if they could obtain the necessary slots and facilities at Heathrow (assuming, of course, the overarching juristic fact of a new U.S./U.K. open skies treaty). For these markets, as noted in the main text, the DOT targeted prospective slot divestiture to Continental Airlines (for service out of Newark), Delta Air Lines (for service out of JFK International and Boston), Northwest (for service out of whichever hub it chose) and US Airways (also out of any hub of its choice). *See id.* at 49. In the Department's view, the alliance did not threaten competitive harm in either the Los Angeles/Heathrow or Miami/Heathrow markets even though, as the agency acknowledged, no other U.S. airline was poised to enter the Los Angeles market. *See id.*

265. *See* U.S. DOT, *Joint Application of KLM/Northwest for Antitrust Immunity, supra* note 242, at 16.

266. *See id.* The 'impracticability' stemmed from the carriers' stated intent to integrate all of their services and the dependence of their service in those markets on the flow of connecting traffic. *See id.* A curiosity of the proceeding was that the applicants argued that their agreement did not *require* antitrust immunity but that they would not proceed without it. The DOT willingly

Airlines/British Airways, the Department also approved immunity 'in the public interest.'[267] But the agency surely missed a beat in terms of intellectual coherence when it based its finding on the 'public benefits' of efficient operational integration advocated by the alliance partners – the very notion of 'public benefits' which the agency had earlier displaced in favor of its own ambitions for international aviation policy.[268]

c   *Immunity Proceedings: The Conflict of Competition and Aviation Policy*

Whether one regards the KLM/Northwest and AA/BA decisions (respectively) as examples of regulatory forbearance or of regulatory churlishness, both orders can certainly be considered as official amplifications of the international aviation *rapprochement* that began with the 1992 open skies agreement with the Netherlands. As part of that agreement, both parties signed a Memorandum of Consultations on September 4, 1992, consenting to give 'sympathetic consideration'

> to the concept of commercial co-operation and integration of commercial operations between airlines of the United States and the Netherlands through commercial agreements or arrangements, provided that such agreements or arrangements are in conformity with the applicable antitrust and competition laws[, and] to provide fair and expeditious consideration to any such agreements or arrangements filed for approval and antitrust immunity.[269]

Pragmatically, this language was deliberately crafted with the earlier KLM investment in Northwest Airlines firmly in mind.[270] In approving the agreement despite its competitive infirmities, the DOT took note of the Memorandum's

---

accepted this somewhat disingenuous position as reflecting past agency practice, whereby the DOT denies antitrust immunity to agreements that do not violate the antitrust laws unless the immunity is required by the public interest and the parties will not go ahead without immunity. Contradictorily, however, the Department accepted that a potential anticompetitive exposure existed (the two Midwestern markets), yet discounted this exposure in apparently immunizing based on public interest and the parties' reluctance to proceed without immunity. All subsequent immunity decisions, including American Airlines/British Airways, have included in the record that the applicants would not proceed without antitrust immunity. The rationale for this position, of course, is precisely its conceptual incompatibility with the competition rules: integration of services, notably with respect to pricing, scheduling, and route planning, carries inevitable antitrust risk. *See* U.S. DOT, *U.S.-UK Alliance Case*, *supra* note 246, at 54.

267.   *Id.*
268.   *See id.* at 54.
269.   U.S. DOT, *Joint Application of KLM/Northwest for Antitrust Immunity*, *supra* note 242, at 3 (quoting the Memorandum of Consultations to the air services agreement between the United States and the Netherlands).
270.   *See supra* Chapter 3, Part VIII(B).

language and explicitly found approval and immunity to be 'consistent with the [open skies] accord' with the Netherlands.[271]

Further, the DOT confidently declared that 'we would expect [that] our willingness to take such action might well encourage other countries to seek similar liberal aviation arrangements with the United States.'[272] Accordingly, although the lack of a second major Dutch carrier would prevent United and American, for example, from exactly duplicating Northwest's covenant with KLM, the DOT anticipated that other integration opportunities would evolve from future liberal bilaterals.[273] Finally, in weighing the 'public interest' requirements in both Sections 41308 and 41309, the agency coupled the language of the Memorandum with tendentious tributes to 'the spirit of the [U.S./Netherlands] accord' and the '[o]pen [s]kies spirit,' concluding that the agreement was 'likely to benefit the public interest by encouraging a further liberalization of transatlantic airline service agreements.'[274]

In this setting, the overtly politicized language and tone of the later American Airlines/British Airways opinion can be appreciated as a reiteration rather than a transformation of the DOT's policy toward immunity applications. From the perspective of competition rules, the KLM/Northwest combination had significant but not extensive route overlap, whereas the American Airlines/British Airways partnership featured a deep tapestry of overlapping services. Yet ultimately both applications passed the immunization test, explicitly for political reasons – *in nomine* open skies. Immunity proceedings, in fact, were colored from the outset by the Department's open skies policy agenda. In KLM/Northwest, the agency inserted an opening reference to a Carteresque 'encirclement' theory,[275] illustrating how its order was intended for a much wider public than the two applicant carriers.[276]

---

271. U.S. DOT, *Joint Application of KLM/Northwest for Antitrust Immunity, supra* note 242, at 2.
272. *Id.* at 12.
273. *See id.* at 3.
274. *Id.* at 18.
275. 'Since the price and service quality of U.S./Netherlands airline service will be determined by market forces, not restrictive agreements, U.S./European travelers will have an incentive to choose the airline services available on routes from the United States to the Netherlands and beyond instead of other U.S./Europe routes. Such a shift in demand *may persuade other countries to agree to less restrictive bilateral agreements with the United States.*' U.S. DOT, *Joint Application of KLM/Northwest for Antitrust Immunity, supra* note 242, at 3 (emphasis added). For a comprehensive analysis of the background, proceedings, and ultimate collapse of the proposed AA/BA alliance, *see* James L. Devall, *American Airlines/British Airways: An Alliance That Was Not Meant to Be?*, [2001-2004 Transfer Binder] ISSUES AVIATION L. & POL'Y ¶ 10,101, at 4151 (Mar. 2002).
276. The value of the policy, as will be seen, was ultimately questionable. In return for unlimited gateway access to all points in the Netherlands (in effect, to Amsterdam), the United States surrendered open gateway access to all points in its territory and immunized from the reach of U.S. competition laws a highly artificial corporate linkage, with demonstrable anticompetitive risks, between two potential competitors. *See supra* note 275 (discussing the true 'benefit' of the Netherlands open skies arrangement – a cluster of unrestricted beyond (fifth freedom) rights – which were themselves subject to additional negotiations with the beyond destination States).

Indeed, as noted earlier,[277] the DOT reprised its KLM/Northwest analysis in 1996, rewarding the flag carriers of several EU countries – and most prominently, Germany's flag airline, Lufthansa – with comparable immunity for their nonequity partnerships with U.S. carriers.[278] In each instance, the applicant U.S. and EU airlines had previously engaged in price and frequency competition over many of their proposed code-share routes.[279] Nevertheless, the DOT either discounted antitrust objections by the Department of Justice, or imposed mild conditions that provisionally 'carved out' certain routes (or types of fares on specific routes) from the scope of immunity, while insisting that immunization would yield procompetitive and consumer benefits in an emerging *worldwide* aviation market.[280] The Department assumed that any diminution of transatlantic competition between the country-pairs would be quickly reversed as new competitors felt tempted by open skies.[281] In keeping with its KLM/Northwest precedent, the DOT explicitly tied its determination of the statutory 'public interest/public benefits' issues to the conclusion of an open skies agreement with the home State of each U.S. applicant's foreign partner.[282] The DOT's scrambled accommodation of

---

277. *See supra* Chapter 3, Part VIII(B).
278. *See id.*
279. Even on routes where they already code-shared, the applicants coordinated only on a service and marketing basis but priced their seats independently in competition with each other in order to maximize their revenue on these routes. *See* U.S. DOT, *Joint Application of United Air Lines, Inc. and Lufthansa German Airlines for Approval of and Antitrust Immunity for an Alliance Expansion Agreement*, Dkt. No. OST-96-1160, Order 96-5-12 to Show Cause (May 9,1996), at 19 [hereinafter U.S. DOT, *Joint Application of Lufthansa/United 1996*]. Code-sharing also tends to reduce or eliminate overlapping direct service. Delta, for example, used to compete with Sabena (the Belgian flag carrier) on the Brussels/New York route; following their code-share agreement, only Sabena operated the route. The successor to Sabena, SN Brussels Airlines, signed a code-share agreement with American Airlines in 2003 (which received immunity from the DOT in 2004) to provide the Belgian carrier with feed into Brussels from U.S. destinations. *See American Airlines 'Pleased' With Grant of Antitrust Immunity With SN Brussels Airlines*, PR NEWSWIRE, Apr. 15, 2004.
280. *See* U.S. DOT, *Joint Application of Lufthansa/United 1996, supra* note 279, at 23-24 (indicating the DOT's perception at that time that traditional antitrust analysis of city-pair markets must give way to the perspective of a worldwide aviation market).
281. *Id.* at 24. As TWA submitted to the DOT in the initial Lufthansa/United proceeding, the existence of 'an abstract legal right' (of market access) could not validate the claim that entry into the U.S./Germany market would be easy (given German market dominance by Lufthansa, with beyond traffic flow over its European hub, which would in turn create strong systemic advantages for United on transatlantic services). *Id.* at 21-23. *See also* evidence of lack of new long-haul entry in EU international markets, *infra* Chapter 5, Part I.
282. This explicit connection continues to be DOT policy, as noted earlier in the American Airlines/ British Airways proceeding. *See supra* Chapter 3, note 242. *See also* U.S. DOT, *Joint Application of The Austrian Group, British Midland Airways Limited, Deutsche Lufthansa AG, Polskie Linie Lotnicze Lot S.A., Scandinavian Airlines System, Swiss International Air Lines Ltd., TAP Air Portugal, and United Air Lines, Inc., Under 49 U.S.C. §§ 41308 and 41309 for Approval of and Antitrust Immunity for Alliance Expansion Agreements and an Amended Coordination Agreement*, Dkt. No. OST-2005-22922, Show Cause Order (Dec. 19, 2006), at 20 (indicating that 'the predicate for [DOT] consideration of a grant of global antitrust immunity is the existence of an "open-skies" framework') [hereinafter U.S. DOT, *Joint Application*

divergent law and policy interests was voiced (with considerable ambivalence) in its final order in the 1996 Delta-led alliance proceeding. While conceding that there will 'necessarily be a diminution of competition' in the subject markets, the agency insisted that its decision was 'based *alternatively* on both our economic analysis of the significance of any minor loss of competition *and our long-term international aviation policy.*'[283]

What was striking in these decisions was the Department's recurring candor as it faced the consequences of reducing nonstop competition in major transatlantic markets, and of transforming competitors into partners empowered to coordinate prices and capacity with legal impunity (under the U.S. laws, at any rate).[284] Evidently aware of these effects, including the serious risk of *inter-alliance* collaboration,[285] the DOT responded with generic appeals to unspecified future

---

of Lufthansa/United 2006]. Earlier proceedings showed an even more unapologetic linkage between competition and aviation policy. In its preliminary findings in the Delta/Swissair/ Sabena/Austrian Airlines proceeding, the DOT described impairment of competition on four New York/Europe routes as a 'close issue' that was ultimately counterbalanced by 'important strategic U.S. objectives in international transportation policy regarding the promotion of aviation liberalization.' U.S. DOT, *Joint Application of Delta Air Lines, Inc., Swissair, Sabena S.A., and Austrian Airlines for Approval of Antitrust Immunity*, Dkt. No. OST-95-618, Order 96-5-26 to Show Cause (May 20, 1996), at 22. (The four markets were New York to Brussels, Zurich, Geneva, and Vienna.) In its grant of final approval, however, the DOT backtracked somewhat on the boldness of its earlier assertion, noting that the prospect of an open skies agreement, while a 'critical element enabling us to proceed with an evaluation of the competitive impact of an application for antitrust immunity,' was 'in no way dispositive of an affirmative finding on the competitive issues involved in a particular case.' U.S. DOT, *Joint Application of Delta Air Lines, Inc., Swissair, Sabena S.A., and Austrian Airlines for Approval of Antitrust Immunity*, Dkt. No. OST-95-618, Final Order 96-6-33 (Jun. 14, 1996), at 15 n.39 [hereinafter U.S. DOT, *Joint Application of Delta/Swissair*]. There were no more orders in this proceeding, and the alliance collapsed in 1999. *See supra* Chapter 3, note 413.

283. U.S. DOT, *Joint Application of Delta/Swissair, supra* note 282, at 15-16 (emphasis added). The DOT even conceded Delta's hub dominance at Cincinnati and Atlanta, and the alliance's likely power over prices and capacity in these markets.

284. *See infra* Chapter 5, Part III(B) (discussing the European Commission's investigation of the competition effects of transatlantic alliances).

285. Thus, for example, the DOT has made it an express condition of granting immunity to each alliance approved since 1996 that the partners withdraw from IATA tariff coordination activities affecting through-prices between the U.S. and the foreign partner's home State, as well as between the United States and any other country that has designated a carrier whose alliance with a U.S. carrier has been or is subsequently given immunity. *See* U.S. DOT, *U.S.-UK Alliance Case, supra* note 246, at 55-56. Why was this condition imposed? In the Department's candid admission, '[T]he issue of competition between [an immunized] alliance and other carriers, *particularly other alliances*, is pressed upon us by *the need to mitigate the potential anticompetitive effects of the immunity* provided for the alliance's internal integration and to make it as likely as possible that the economic efficiencies of the alliance can be passed on to consumers.' Joint Application of United Airlines and Lufthansa German Airlines for Approval of and Antitrust Immunity for an Alliance Expansion Agreement, Dkt. No. OST-96-1116, Final Order 96-5-27, *reprinted in* [1994-1999 Transfer Binder] Av. L. Rep. (CCH) ¶ 23,375, at 14,412 (May 20, 1996) (emphasis added). In other words, the DOT conceded that immunity creates potentially anticompetitive alliance activity, both within the partnership (because competitive service will end in many markets), but also *among* immunized alliances, a risk

new entry and to the importance of a 'worldwide' view of air transport competition,[286] but primarily to the overarching importance of the open skies program, as inoculating compensations.

d　　　　　*The SkyTeam Proceedings: Slouching Toward Regulatory Incoherence*

The Department's complex policy objectives of incubating an open skies philosophy, while also creating integration efficiencies and limiting market power, produced measurable consumer benefits in the 1990s.[287] But the delicate balance necessarily required by this triple-pronged approach has been upset by evidence suggesting that immunized alliances have used their market power to impose higher fares and to limit capacity growth and to fight back nonaligned competitive

---

of oligopolistic collaboration that looks uncomfortably similar to the very cartel (IATA) that the U.S. Government has for years challenged as destructive of international airline competition. By excluding IATA tariff coordination, the Department has hoped that inter-alliance competition 'will, on balance, outweigh any potential anticompetitive effects of price coordination within the alliance itself.' U.S. DOT, *Joint Application of Lufthansa/United 1996, supra* note 279, at 28. This language has become incantatory. *See also* U.S. DOT, *U.S.-UK Alliance Case, supra* note 246, at 56 (expressing confidence that potential price competition with rival airlines will outweigh anticompetitive effects of intra-alliance price coordination). The DOT, in its Jul. 2006 'show cause' order in the IATA antitrust immunity proceedings, *see supra* Chapter 3, Part IX, revealed that the condition of withdrawal from IATA tariff conferences has not been 'as effective as hoped,' U.S. DOT, *International Air Transport Association Tariff Conference Proceeding*, Dkt. No. OST-2006-25307, Order 2006-7-3 to Show Cause (Jul. 5, 2006), at 25. Although, in the DOT's view, immunized alliance partners do not 'need' to engage in IATA conferences in order to coordinate their fares, *see id.*, they have done so with respect to non-alliance markets and 'the decisions on fares and rates in alliance markets reflected the decisions for non-alliance markets.' *Id.* Through this attempted IATA-proofing arrangement, in fact, the DOT has tolerated one form of potentially serious anticompetitive activity in order to contain the risk of another, scarcely the kind of analysis that typically accompanies U.S. merger investigations under the Clayton Act. *See generally* Harold Shenton, *New Open Skies Equals Old IATA*, 13 AVMARK AV. ECON. 3 (1996) (noting potential of immunized alliances to destroy smaller airlines through a network of openly-concluded partnerships, thereby increasing domination of world markets).

286.　In this respect, the Department still views global alliances as ideally offering a higher order of integration that transcends conventional city-pair and even country-pair analysis (and overlapping routes within those pairs) and covers broader geographic areas. *See* U.S. DOT, *Joint Application of Lufthansa/United 2006, supra* note 282, at 9. *But see infra* note 292 (noting DOT disfavor of a 'worldwide' immunity grant, suggesting a policy bias for global alliance-making that is more rhetorical than actual).

287.　*See* U.S. DOT, *Joint Application of Alitalia-Linee Aeree Italiane-S.p.A., Czech Airlines, Delta Air Lines, Inc., KLM Royal Dutch Airlines, Northwest Airlines, Inc., and Société Air France for Approval of and Antitrust Immunity for Alliance Agreements Under 49 U.S.C. §§ 41308 and 41309*, Dkt. No. OST-2004-19214, Answer of American Airlines, Inc. (Jun. 24, 2005), at 5 [hereinafter U.S. DOT, Answer of American Airlines] (citing DOT reports issued in 1999 and 2000).

challenges at their hubs.[288] While this evidence has been contested,[289] in the 2005 SkyTeam I proceeding[290] the Department confronted (and, for the moment, nimbly sidestepped) a more fundamental jurisprudential challenge to the integrity of the whole contrivance of immunity-backed alliances. Accepting as dogma that the antitrust laws 'represent a fundamental national economic policy,' and that any species of immunity from those laws 'should be the exception, not the rule,'[291] the Department rejected a bold attempt by SkyTeam members Northwest Airlines and Delta Air Lines to throw a common cloak of comprehensive immunity over their two separate transatlantic alliances (KLM/Northwest and Delta/Air France).[292]

To justify their application, the U.S. carriers offered the pretext of a 'gap in immunity' that allegedly opened when their respective alliance partners, KLM and Air France, agreed a quasi-merger that incidentally, but not intentionally, yoked both of these immunized relationships together.[293] Taking its cue from the

---

288. *See id.* at 6-7. Stricter scrutiny of competition among globalized immunized alliances (as evidenced in the SkyTeam immunity proceeding) has been prompted in part by the increased level of concentration at EU airports that alliances have engendered: SkyTeam has a market share of 50% or more in over 480 U.S./Europe city-pairs, with no competitor having more than 10%; Star enjoys that kind of share in 279 city-pairs, and oneworld in 104. These incumbency statistics reveal the specter of market power and the challenge posed to DOT policy by the limited number of transcontinental alliances – and by immunity itself, which is now enjoyed by all three alliances. For the complete statistical survey, *see id.* at 5-6.

289. *See* U.S. DOT, *Joint Application of Alitalia-Linee Aeree Italiane-S.p.A., Czech Airlines, Delta Air Lines, Inc., KLM Royal Dutch Airlines, Northwest Airlines, Inc., and Société Air France for Approval of and Antitrust Immunity for Alliance Agreements under 49 U.S.C. §§ 41308 & 41309*, Dkt. No. OST-2004-19214, Order to Show Cause (Dec. 22, 2005), at 10 *et seq.* [hereinafter U.S. DOT, SkyTeam I Show Cause Order] (summarizing a 'battle of the experts' on measurement of changes in fare and capacity levels affecting both open skies and non-open skies markets).

290. SkyTeam II followed the failed SkyTeam I application in 2007. *See infra* note 297.

291. U.S. DOT, SkyTeam I Show Cause Order, *supra* note 289, at 33.

292. *See id.* at 2. The immunity request was unusual in that, for the first time, it involved two U.S. air carriers ('[t]his case is one of first impression,' *id.* at 31). The proposed alliance combination represented a merger of two existing immunized alliances: KLM/Northwest, first created in 1993, and the alliance among the early SkyTeam members Delta, Air France, Alitalia, and ČSA (Czech Airlines). *See id.* Moreover, the initial application was bolder still: it requested a worldwide grant of immunity to include cooperation also in transpacific and North American markets. *See id.* at 6. The U.S. Department of Justice strongly objected to this unprecedented claim for global immunity, and the parties relented. *See id.*

293. U.S DOT, SkyTeam I Show Cause Order, *supra* note 289, at 4. The U.S. carriers' rationale for immunity was grounded on concern that Air France-KLM would have to forego certain collaborative activities with Northwest or Delta, in order to avoid claims that Northwest and Delta were somehow colluding through the combined Air France-KLM entity. Thus, both U.S. carriers would be unable to participate simultaneously as full, immunized partners as Air France-KLM continues to integrate operations and centralize decisionmaking. One or other of the U.S. partners would therefore be forced to withdraw from its immunized relationship, to the detriment of both the affected carrier and consumers. *See id.* at 7 & 23. On the *sui generis* jurisprudence of the Air France/KLM 'merger,' *see infra* Chapter 5, Part III(B).

comments of the Department of Justice (although without making a final determination on the matter), the DOT expressed concern that allowing two U.S. carriers, Northwest and Delta, to coordinate prices and schedules (and other commercial decisions) within a fully immunized SkyTeam alliance would risk anticompetitive 'spillover' coordination in those airlines' domestic markets (where the normal antitrust rules apply without mercy).[294]

The DOT opinion, in fact, displays irritation as it surveys an incomplete record with respect to the parties' likely future agreements or behavior, particularly because the applicant U.S. carriers evidently assumed that immunity has become such an expectation of right that, although they possess overlapping domestic and international networks, they could seek it based merely on speculative promises of the future 'public benefits' required to be demonstrated under the statute.[295] The Skyteam application was flawed as a matter of competition policy because it sought immunization for an alliance that broke from the previous template of combining end-to-end networks.[296] More dramatically, however, as a weathervane

---

294. Thus, the Department of Justice argued (in its submission on the proposed expanded SkyTeam immunity) that immunity could harm competition in domestic markets 'by providing cover for competitors [Northwest and Delta] to discuss competitive matters outside the immunity and [by] shielding anticompetitive conduct from antitrust enforcement.' U.S. DOT, SkyTeam I Show Cause Order, *supra* note 289, at 41; *see also id.* at 16 (noting Department of Justice concern that immunity for activities involving international air transportation could not (in the absence of more detailed agreements) preclude the possibility that the U.S. carriers might collusively exchange competitive information relating to domestic markets or engage in behavior that would undercut domestic competition). Excessively broad grants of immunity could enable carriers such as Northwest and Delta, by providing a 'pretextual' reason to discuss nonexempt matters, to discuss competitive information relating to domestic competition. *Id.* at 42. In the submission of United Airlines, immunizing such potentially collusive behavior would act as an unintended 'substitute for domestic mergers.' *Id.* at 23. The DOT, as it turned out, chose to deny the application because of 'insufficient public benefits' (the proposed jumbo alliance did not promise the kind of major expansion of online service that resulted from the creation of earlier transatlantic combinations, *see id.* at 35), and not to 'reach' the question of 'domestic spillover.' *Id.* at 43. The spillover issue has probably been mooted by the subsequently announced Delta/Northwest merger. *See infra* note 422.
295. *See supra* in the main text (discussing the statutory public benefits requirement). *See* U.S. DOT, SkyTeam I Show Cause Order, *supra* note 289, at 30 & 33. Thus, in the DOT's view, the enlarged alliance offered little that could not be obtained by arm's-length code-sharing. *See id.* at 34. Otherwise, the projected benefits were 'theoretical and attenuated,' and the applicants had provided the agency with 'so little information about their plans' that it was appropriate to recall the words of the Civil Aeronautics Board that 'it is often difficult to predict the competitive effects of an agreement which has not yet been implemented and we have no assurance that we could always do so accurately.' *Id.* at 34. The SkyTeam partners nevertheless sought reconsideration of the DOT's rejection after the signing of the U.S./EC Air Transport Agreement.
296. *See* U.S. DOT, SkyTeam I Show Cause Order, *supra* note 289, at 35. The partners in those prior proceedings had some overlapping routes (sometimes with enormous competitive effects, as in American Airlines/British Airways), but the nub of the partnership was the ability to connect the behind-gateway and beyond-gateway traffic of a U.S. airline and one or more foreign airlines to offer online services in many markets that no individual alliance member could serve online (as noted in the main text, KLM/Northwest, for example, enabled service

of international aviation policy the application (and its disposition) exposed the risk of conceptual incoherence that results from using antitrust immunity as a juristic proxy for the DOT's open skies agenda. When two U.S. airlines saw an opportunity to test the limits of its regulatory benevolence, the Department withdrew in fear from its own creation.[297]

---

over Minneapolis-St. Paul and Amsterdam from Spokane to Warsaw). *See id.* Here, further immunizing an existing alliance that included the international elements of the overlapping networks of Northwest and Delta would create little new online service at a potentially serious cost to competition. *See id.* at 31.

297. The flaws identified in the SkyTeam I application have not been obviated merely because of the recent success of the SkyTeam II request for approval. Aeropolitics, once again, seems to have motivated the disposition of that second application. The six-carrier SkyTeam application was renewed in 2007 following the signing of the U.S./EC Air Transport Agreement. Again, the application sought immunity for the first attempted 'merger' of two immunized alliances, KLM/Northwest and Delta/Air France/Alitalia/Czech Airlines. In its Apr. 2008 SkyTeam II Show Cause Order, the DOT seemed untroubled by its prior finding in SkyTeam I that the alliance did not promise the kind of major expansion of complementary end-to-end networks of earlier transatlantic combinations – and in fact, remained what the Show Cause Order described as 'a merger of overlapping networks.' U.S. DOT, *Joint Application of Alitalia-Linee Aeree Italiane-S.p.A., Czech Airlines, Delta Airlines, Inc., KLM Royal Dutch Airlines, Northwest Airlines, Inc., & Société Air France for Approval of and Antitrust Immunity for Alliance Agreements Under 49 U.S.C. §§ 41308 and 41309*, Dkt. No. OST-2007-28644, Show Cause Order (Apr. 9, 2008), at 5 [hereinafter U.S. DOT, SkyTeam II Show Cause Order]. By the time of SkyTeam II, however, two major aeropolitical events evidently colored the DOT's assessment of what was, for all practical purposes, virtually the same integrated alliance proposal (but with more attention to revenue and cost pooling in place of markups for each carrier's code-share segments). First, following the signing of the 2007 agreement (now referred to in DOT opinions and press releases as 'Open Skies-Plus'), all of the home States of the applicant carriers were presumptively in the open skies family. *See* Press Release, U.S. DOT, DOT Approves Expanded Transatlantic Alliance Involving Delta, Northwest, DOT 73-08 (May 22, 2008); *see also* SkyTeam II Show Cause Order, *supra*, at 2 (noting that the existence of an open skies agreement is a 'predicate' for immunity requests). Second, and probably more importantly, in addition to the existing Air France/KLM quasi-merger, the Department was aware at the time of its final decision that Delta and Northwest had announced their intention to merge. *See* U.S. DOT, *Joint Application of Alitalia-Linee Aeree Italiane-S.p.A., Czech Airlines, Delta Airlines, Inc., KLM Royal Dutch Airlines, Northwest Airlines, Inc., & Société Air France for Approval of and Antitrust Immunity for Alliance Agreements Under 49 U.S.C. §§ 41308 and 41309*, Dkt. No. OST-2007-28644, Final Order (May 22, 2008), at 1 [hereinafter U.S. DOT, SkyTeam II Final Order]. In these circumstances, the knotty point of having two U.S. carriers within the same immunized alliance stood a reasonable chance of being effectively neutralized. Notably, the DOT did not explicitly refer to the prior opposition of the Department of Justice in SkyTeam I to worldwide immunity for the alliance, suggesting only the imprudence of immunity outside the transatlantic market while Delta and Northwest remained separate. *See* U.S. DOT, SkyTeam II Final Order, *supra*, at 2. But the Department made sure, at least for the time being, that as long as Delta and Northwest remained separate they would observe a strict antitrust protocol with respect to their competition in U.S. markets (except, however, with respect to travelers engaged in the so-called 'Domestic Portion of International Journeys,' *i.e.*, behind-gateway passengers who connect at Delta or Northwest hubs for travel to foreign destinations). *See id.* at 11.

e   *Mixing Competition Policy and Politics: The Instability*
                     of Immunity Jurisprudence

Thus, as revealed in the case studies of KLM/Northwest and American Airlines/
British Airways, and also in the conceptual slippage evident in the SkyTeam
decisions, the DOT's immunity proceedings have proved to be an unstable mix
of competition analysis and the overt politicization of its open skies agenda. If the
narrow competitive objective of DOT policy is (as its decisions still assert[298]) to
increase behind-gateway and beyond-gateway opportunities for passengers who
otherwise lack convenient online service (for example, a Spokane passenger flying
over Minneapolis-St. Paul to Amsterdam and onward to Warsaw), the ideal *procompetitive* solution is not to encourage artificial and unsystematic alliances
among partners which court each other *faute de mieux*, in the process consciously
choking off otherwise viable competition. A much more radical solution presents
itself: to enable all airlines to build whatever route connections they wish, direct or
indirect, with or without code-share partners, in a multilateral liberalized environment. Iterations of antitrust immunity, like toleration of the code-share device, are
doubly unconvincing as a matter of policy. Competition is reduced, it seems inevitably, but without a countervailing assurance that bilateralist governments will
advance toward a comprehensive liberalization.

As the immunity proceedings reveal, U.S. policymakers have repeatedly lost
opportunities to leverage multilateral negotiations, for example through a *genuine*
open skies agreement that requires full *reciprocal* liberalization of inward investment. Ironically, at the very moment when the EC was itself ready to embrace such
an agreement, U.S. negotiators were more concerned to threaten the Europeans
with termination of the existing flawed paradigm of 'open skies plus immunity'
than to reach for the kind of transformative regime that is presented in this book.[299]
In this context, the 2007 U.S./EC Air Transport Agreement remains, after all,
largely a conflation of the existing open skies protocols with EU Member States
and is factually the result of adventitious juristic events within the EC that had no
direct involvement by the United States. U.S. unilateralism, the *deus ex machina* of
global aviation policy in the 1990s, finds itself muzzled by opposition to foreign
ownership in Congress and unable to leap conceptually beyond the strategy that has

---

298. With the conspicuous exception of the American Airlines/British Airways proceeding, the
     creation of new online service lies at the heart of the DOT's 'public benefits' analysis in
     immunity proceedings. *See supra* in the main text (discussing the statutory provenance of this
     analysis). The DOT typically emphasizes the multiple thousands of city-pair markets that will
     receive online service from an approved alliance. *See, e.g.,* U.S. DOT, *Joint Application of
     Lufthansa/United 1996, supra* note 279, at 18 (noting that the alliance would bring online
     service to over 52,000 city-pair markets). *See also* SkyTeam I Show Cause Order, *supra*
     note 289, at 31 (noting that, collectively, the addition of small numbers of passengers in a
     huge number of markets, with through fares that are lower than fares otherwise available, will
     result in a large increase in total traffic, well beyond 'mere interlining').
299. *See supra* text accompanying Chapter 3, note 443 (referencing speech by Jeffrey Shane).

been pursued, with uncertain results, in the immunity proceedings reviewed in this Part. For the DOT, the open skies/alliance immunity paradigm represents the current frontier of new policymaking, even as its frailties – in the realms of both competition policy and aviation policy – have become increasingly manifest. Accordingly, this study turns now to a much broader critique of the open skies strategy, which was repositioned at the center of U.S. international aviation policy by the Netherlands agreement in 1992.

D   Moving Beyond Open Skies: The Need to Reconceptualize
                U.S. International Aviation Strategy

1   **Open Skies and Retrenchment: U.S. Bilateral
                Relations 1978-92**

Despite expectations raised by the International Air Transportation Competition Act of a new diplomatic paradigm in international aviation relations, and initial successes such as the Netherlands and South Korean open skies protocols,[300] by 1982 the U.S. airline industry was in the grip of a fierce recessionary onslaught and the major U.S. carriers prevailed upon Reagan Administration officials to dispense with its campaign for bilateral liberalization. As Professor Dempsey related, the carriers specifically protested that the new liberal agreements conceded too many 'hard rights,' namely, access to U.S. interior city hubs, in exchange for so-called 'soft rights,' including increased theoretical access to smaller markets (such as the Netherlands and Belgium) that would have limited growth potential for U.S. operators but whose large national carriers, brand names such as KLM or Sabena, would have a disproportionate capacity to capitalize on foreign traffic opportunities.[301]

---

300. During the period 1978 to 1982, the United States signed 'liberal' protocols to existing air services agreements with the Netherlands, Belgium, the Federal Republic of Germany, Israel, Jamaica, South Korea, Papua New Guinea, and Singapore. *See* L. Gilles Sion, *Multilateral Air Transport Agreements Reconsidered: The Possibility of a Regional Agreement Among North Atlantic States*, 22 Va. J. Int'l L. 155, 193 (1981). As well as pricing liberalization, these protocols also relaxed (indeed in many cases eliminated) restrictions on capacity and frequency and expanded 'gateway' access to the United States for foreign carriers. *See* discussion of the 1978 U.S./Netherlands agreement, *supra* note 180, in Peter P.C. Haanappel, *Deregulation Of Air Transport In North America And Western Europe, in* Air Worthy 91, 101 (J.W.E. Storm van's Gravesande & A. van der Veen Vonk eds., 1985). Foreign carriers did not get unlimited ('cabotage') access to points in the United States, only *increased* access to a number of additional and existing U.S. gateways. *Id.*

301. The U.S. airlines were suspicious also of what they perceived as imprecise pledges of liberal pricing opportunities and unspecific prohibitions against discrimination and unfair competitive practices. *See* Dempsey, *supra* note 24, at 77. *See* Association of Flight Attendants, AFL-CIO, *Comments to the Airline Commission, in Airline Commission Documents*, Dkt. No. 000046 (Jun. 1, 1993), at 3-4 (stating that '[o]ur first concern is that a general goal was applied, mistakenly, in our judgment, to a bilateral with a single small country. What was lost in the U.S.-Netherlands Open Skies bilateral was any sense of *real* rights for rights and values for values. . . .') (emphasis in original).

For the next decade, until the resuscitation of open skies in the U.S./Netherlands agreement of 1992,[302] the United States repressed its international deregulatory zeal and practiced a more or less traditional protectionist aerodiplomacy within the international bilateral system.

Nevertheless, even without an open skies crusade, there was a widespread perception within other aviation trading blocs, notably the EU, that U.S. airlines since the early 1980s managed to garner more valuable rights in bilateral aviation agreements – which were modeled on Bermuda I, with *ex post facto* capacity adjustment clauses[303] – than their foreign competitors.[304] This was partly a function of the U.S. Government's patient bilateral negotiation of fifth freedom interconnections among EU Member States (and equally among major Asian hub cities),[305] but it also reflected the consequence of substituting the (then) lower-cost U.S. competitors like the 'Big Three,' American, United, and Delta,[306] which have impressive behind-gateway domestic route systems, in many international markets formerly served only by the traditional American 'flag' carriers, Pan American and Trans World Airlines.[307]

---

302. Agreement between the United States of America and the Netherlands, amending the Agreement of Apr. 3, 1957, as Amended, and the Protocol of Mar. 31, 1978, as Amended, Oct. 14, 1992, T.I.A.S. No. 11976.
303. *See supra* Chapter 3, Part III(B).
304. *See* GAO, *European Community, supra* note 160, at 46-48; U.S. DOT Report to Airline Commission, *supra* note 180, at 2.
305. Although these EC rights later fell into desuetude (among air passenger carriers), they did initially have commercial value to the major U.S. airlines. For example, Delta Air Lines, hubbing at Frankfurt, provided service from New York to Frankfurt and also from Frankfurt to Athens and multiple other internal EU city-pairs. EU carrier resentment of such operations was understandable: Lufthansa, in contrast, could serve Frankfurt to New York but was (and is) prohibited by federal law from picking up passengers in New York for onward transit to Miami or any other internal U.S. city-point. *See* GAO, *European Community, supra* note 160, at 47. *But see* the discussion of code-sharing, *supra* Chapter 3, Part VIII(C) (explaining Lufthansa's camouflaged access to U.S. points that became possible through a strategic alliance with United Airlines). Delta pulled down its Frankfurt hub for intra-Union operations in 1997. *See* James P. Woolsey, *On Top of the World; Delta Airlines Company Profile*, 34 AIR TRANSP. WORLD, Jul. 1997, at 30 (noting that the Frankfurt hub was a legacy of the Pan Am North Atlantic system that Delta acquired in 1991, and had been a major lossmaker – and was therefore jettisoned in favor of alliance-based routing strategies). *See also supra* Chapter 2, note 35 (mentioning how U.S. negotiators viewed the volume of intra-Union fifth freedoms as little more than 'decimal dust').
306. In the early 1990s, U.S. airlines' average costs ranged between 20 and 30% less than for major competitors such as Japan Air Lines, British Airways, Air France, and Lufthansa. *See* DOT Report to Airline Commission, *supra* note 180, at 3. IATA's cost performance report in Jul. 2006 suggested that the U.S. majors, after painful restructuring, were retaining an appreciable cost advantage. IATA, *Airline Cost Performance*, IATA ECON. BRIEFING No. 5, Jul. 2006.
307. *See* U.S. DOT Report to Airline Commission, *supra* note 180, at 2. Neither Pan Am nor TWA had developed substantial domestic route systems. In part, this was a result of deliberate CAB policy, as seen, *supra* note 103. For Robert Crandall, then President of American Airlines, the hubbing potential of the new U.S. megacarriers 'level[ed] the playing field' with EU carriers, which had built a strong European hubbing system. *See Airline Commission Proceedings* (Jun. 3, 1993), at 246. In one sense, however, the playing field *could not* be leveled,

European and Asian airlines, blocked by federal cabotage laws, could not assemble equivalent 'transborder' networks among the states of the United States, and were therefore foreclosed from direct access (*i.e.,* other than through code-shares) to the assured competitive premium the U.S. megacarriers enjoyed through their huge domestic feeder network.[308] Thus, from 1979 to 1992, as Pan Am and TWA withdrew from most of their international operations, the successor generation of U.S. flag carriers increased its share of the available capacity from 45% to 70% in the U.S./France market, from 29% to 61% in the U.S./Germany market, and from 49% to almost 60% in the U.S./U.K. market.[309] Moreover, as U.S. carriers'

---

at least not in what was then the incarnation of the U.S. and European industries: the United States had many more players and potential players in most of its major bilateral markets. Canada, France, Japan and the United Kingdom, for instance, each had only one or at most two scheduled passenger carriers serving the United States, while eight or more U.S. carriers could serve each of those markets. *See* U.S. DOT Report to Airline Commission, *supra* note 180, at 3. The low number of foreign carriers, of course, reflected deliberate government policy to enhance the competitive position of the 'flag' carrier. *Id. (See also* the discussion of the privileged status of flag carriers, *supra* Chapter 3, Part VI.) Today, only the United Kingdom has increased the number of its carriers available to serve the transatlantic marketplace (three now do so), while there are still around eight U.S. airlines with equipment and sufficient connecting traffic to ensure profitable international service to these four States.

308. As discussed *supra* Chapter 3, Part VIII(C). This is an enduring complaint of EU governments and their carriers.

309. *See* Stephen S. Stirton & Victoria L. Vettergren, American Airlines (1993) (unpublished MBA thesis, Harvard University), Ex. 1, *in Airline Commission Documents*, Dkt. No. 001039 (Dec. 17, 1992), at 3 [hereinafter Harvard Thesis]; Submission of U.S. Airports for a Better International Air Service (USA-BIAS), *in Airline Commission Documents*, undocketed (May 26, 1993) [hereinafter USA-BIAS Submission]. (These three countries, with Japan and Canada, accounted for almost 70% of all U.S. international air traffic in the early 1990s, *see Airline Commission Proceedings*, testimony of Jim Tarrant, then Deputy Assistant Secretary for Transportation Affairs, Department of State (May 26, 1993).) By 2006, air passenger market share patterns had shifted considerably to the European side of the ledger: U.S. carriers had 41.8% of the U.S./U.K. market, 41.6% of the U.S./France market, and 42.2% of the U.S./Germany market. *See* U.S. DOT, Office of the Assistant Secretary for Aviation and International Affairs, *U.S. International Air Passenger and Freight Statistics: March 2008*, tbl. 3, International Aviation Development Series (Jul. 2008) [hereinafter U.S. DOT, *Statistics*]. A caveat must be entered with respect to these newer statistics, however. As recently as the mid-1990s, the operating carrier was likely to be the same as the marketing carrier. U.S. capacity shares in the age of code-sharing alliances, however, may significantly undercount actual U.S. capacity (for example, United's code may be placed on a Lufthansa Chicago O'Hare/Frankfurt service). Thus, some part of the drop in U.S. capacity may also be due to better coordination within the alliances (and consequently reduced overlap) with respect to operation of transatlantic services. *See id.* at 1 (discussing counting anomalies produced by code-sharing). Some counterweight to the high U.S. shares in the early 1990s emerged from the higher market share of *cargo* traffic that several States secured under their bilateral agreements with the United States. *See Airline Commission Proceedings*, testimony of Paul L. Gretch, Director, DOT Office of International Aviation (May 26, 1993), at 69-70. Air France, for example, carried 69% of the cargo tons on U.S./France routes in the year ending Oct. 1992. (The more recent figures are also revealing: as U.S. air passenger shares dropped, freight shares rose. The French carrier share of the U.S./France air freight market, for example, dropped to 49.2% for the year ending Mar. 2008, *see* U.S. DOT, *Statistics, supra,* tbl. 5.)

shares of bilateral capacity rose under traditional bilateral regulation, their success set off a wave of protectionist retaliation.[310]

2   U.S./Europe: A Continuing Story of Aeropolitical Discord

In the midst of the sometimes vertiginous reaction to the 2007 U.S./EC Air Transport Agreement, it should not be overlooked that this agreement incorporates conventional denunciation provisions that are common to Chicago system bilaterals.[311] In this specific sense, the 2007 transatlantic agreement holds the potential to revisit some of the aeropolitical volatility that beset some of its bilateral antecedents in the 1990s. Moreover, precisely because the 2007 agreement must still be classified as a Chicago-style bilateral agreement, aeropolitical posturing – including unilateral denunciation – will be an inescapable contingency of its future existence. In this and the following parts, we will consider some earlier controversies in U.S. bilateral aviation relations, and in the final Part we will evaluate how current U.S. international aviation law and policy has failed to manage, much less obviate, the aeropolitical risks that are endemic to the Chicago system. To circumvent these risks, this book proposes a plenary settlement that would replace the Chicago bilateral system with a plurilateral-based open aviation regime.

The typical Chicago system reflex of governments confronting falling market share for their carriers is to insist, as France did in its relations with the United States in the early 1990s, on bilateral artifices such as frequency caps, schedule limitations, and fifth freedom quotas.[312] While technically compatible with Bermuda I-type *ex post* capacity adjustment, this insistence on limiting capacity is really a return to managed trade, designed to favor proportionally the weaker foreign competitor.[313] The French tactic for forcing the United States to accept capacity restrictions, however, was nothing less than a total denunciation of the U.S./France bilateral.[314] The sequence of events was swift. In late 1991, the French

---

On a revenue basis, however, the freight market is only about one quarter of the passenger market. *See* U.S. DOT Report to Airline Commission, *supra* note 180, at 15.

310. With many domestic industrial and sectoral constituencies to appease, protectionist impulses appear to be an inescapable reaction to disequilibria in international trade. Compare the response of U.S. automakers, for example, to Japanese import penetration of only 20%. *See Airline Commission Proceedings*, testimony of Bernard Attali, President of Air France (Jun. 3, 1993), at 201. In the aviation sector, a private aviation consulting group referred in 1993 to '[a]n emerging trend of retrenchment' in U.S. bilateral air transport relations. Update on the Global Airline Industry, Mercer Management Consulting, *in Airline Commission Documents*, Dkt. No. 000277 (Apr. 27, 1993), at 50. Escalating the U.S. carriers' threat to foreign markets, their rising market penetration occurred (ironically) against a broader backdrop of worldwide recession and depressed demand. *See* U.S. DOT Report to Airline Commission, *supra* note 180, at 3.

311. *See supra* Chapter 2, Part V(B) (offering a fuller account of the suspension/denunciation protocols that form part of the U.S./EC agreement).

312. *See* GAO, *European Community, supra* note 160, at 48-49.

313. Comments of United Air Lines, Inc. on the Commission's Draft Report, *in Airline Commission Documents*, Dkt. No. 001019 (Jul. 26, 1993), at 2.

314. The U.S./France bilateral was originally signed in 1946, although like most bilaterals it was amended many times since then. *See* Industry Brief, International Aviation: Unrealized

Government refused to approve the summer schedules of U.S. airlines serving France that would take effect on April 1, 1992.[315] When the United States declined a French request to order a substantial reduction in proposed capacity increases by the U.S. fleet, France formally denounced its U.S. bilateral on May 4, 1992.[316] In place of the agreement, U.S./France aviation relations converted (until a new, more liberal agreement was reached in 1998) to the unpredictable basis of 'comity and reciprocity,'[317]

Opportunity, *in Airline Commission Documents*, Dkt. No. 000267 (Apr. 1993), at 7. In 1998, with Air France resurgent and its transatlantic market share no longer in serious disequilibrium, the United States signed a more liberal bilateral with France that was followed by a full open skies agreement (removing all restrictions on service to intermediate and beyond countries) in Oct. 2001. *See* Press Release, U.S. DOT, United States, France Reach Open-Skies [*sic*] Aviation Agreement, DOT 111-01 (Oct. 19, 2001). In 2007, the U.S./France open skies bilateral was superseded in accordance with Article 22(1) of the U.S./EC Air Transport Agreement, *supra* note 2.

315. The French argued that the proposed 42% increase in air services to France, as the U.S. airlines proposed, exceeded the projected demand on those routes. The French Government sought a 15% capacity increase. *See* GAO, *European Community, supra* note 160, at 48-49.

316. *Id.* The term 'denunciation,' which carries a loaded, antagonistic connotation, is nonetheless recognized as a synonym of the less inflammatory term 'termination' in RESTATEMENT (THIRD) OF FOREIGN RELATIONS LAW OF THE UNITED STATES § 332 (1987) (distinguishing denunciation or termination of an agreement according to its terms from termination because of supervening events or fundamental change of circumstances, *id.* § 335-336). The French Government did not seek to escape its treaty obligations on any premise of *rebus sic stantibus*, although the Bermuda I capacity clauses included in the treaty, with their implication of rough parity between the competing national carriers, might have served as a predicate for such a declaration. Rather, denunciation occurred in accordance with Article XII of the Agreement between the Government of the United States of America and the Provisional Government of the French Republic Relating to Air Services between their Respective Territories, Jun. 18, 1946, 139 U.N.T.S. 114 (as amended), which provided for termination by either contracting party upon one year's notice to the other party (after an initial consultations phase). All U.S. bilaterals contain a denunciation clause; when triggered, it collapses the entire treaty regime. With rare exceptions, the United States has not negotiated specialized termination clauses targeted to specific treaty provisions. In the now-superseded U.S./Ireland bilateral of 1945, however, Article 9 allowed termination of the agreement '*or any of the rights for air transport services granted thereunder*' upon one year's notice by either party. Exchange of Notes Constituting an Agreement between the United States of America and Ireland Relating to Air Transport Services, Feb. 3, 1945, 122 U.N.T.S. 305. And a similar 'suspension of rights' feature appears to have been stitched into the 2007 U.S./EC Air Transport Agreement. As previously discussed, Article 23 of that agreement, *supra* note 2, which contains standard termination language (except that the post-notification period of one year until termination is extended by reference to the next succeeding IATA traffic season), must be read conjunctively with Article 21(3), which allows either party to 'suspend rights specified in the [a]greement.' This provision, as noted in the prior discussion, may also be subject to autonomous Member State suspensive action in accordance with an extra-agreement understanding reached within the Council of the European Union. *See supra* Chapter 2, Part V(B).

317. 'Comity and reciprocity' literally freezes the parties' relationship as of the date of denunciation: for example, France did not authorize a new U.S. carrier on the Boston/Paris route subsequently abandoned by Northwest. Street Interview, *supra* note 214.

with flight schedules agreed from season to season on what was described by one DOT official as a *comme il faut* basis.[318]

Germany, disturbed by Lufthansa's loss of market share, went to the very brink of denunciation, but called instead for Bermuda I-type consultations on capacity adjustment.[319] The bilateral agreement with Germany was the most liberal with a European partner other than the first-wave open skies agreements with the Netherlands and Belgium. It included multiple permissive designation for both participating governments, as well as a so-called 'open route description' granting U.S. carriers access to all points in Germany, as well as all beyond points.[320] In November 1992, as Lufthansa's financial shape continued to worsen, the United States and Germany signed an interim arrangement to freeze capacity pending negotiation of a replacement bilateral.[321] The Italian Government, too, has always elevated the

---

318. In English, 'as necessary.' *See Airline Commission Proceedings*, testimony of Paul L. Gretch, Director, DOT Office of International Aviation (May 26, 1993), at 128. As a technical matter, since the terms of the agreement required one year's notice of denunciation, the U.S./France bilateral formally expired a year after that event, on May 4, 1993. *See* U.S. DOT, *Report to Airline Commission, supra* note 180, at 15. As the experience with France demonstrated, a regime based on comity is inherently unpredictable. Fifth freedom 'beyond' rights guaranteed under the bilateral, for example, could easily be denied by the French Government in the absence of a treaty obligation. *See Airline Commission Proceedings*, testimony of Paul L. Gretch, Director, DOT Office of International Aviation (May 26, 1993) & testimony of Patrick V. Murphy, DOT Acting Assistant Secretary for Policy and International Affairs (May 24, 1993), at 208-09. In Mar. 1996, the United States announced that it would accept only half of Air France's requested increase in flights for the 1996 summer season, prompting a French in-kind retaliation affecting proposed U.S. carrier schedules. There was immediate speculation – which was confirmed by subsequent events – that the United States would link any moderation of its stance to a new open skies framework with France, modeled on recent agreements with Germany and a cluster of smaller European states. *See* David Buchan, *France Hits Back at US Flight Cuts*, FIN. TIMES, Mar. 23-24, 1996, at 2; *see also* Greg Steinmetz & Brian Coleman, *US Finds Unfriendly Skies Over Europe*, WALL ST. J., Jul. 17, 1995 (quoting a comment by DOT senior official Murphy that, unless France were to strike an open skies deal, the United States would 'block' any proposed alliance between Air France and a U.S. airline).
319. The German Government sought a floor of 40% on its domestic carriers' capacity. *See* U.S. DOT Report to Airline Commission, *supra* note 180, at 13. *See also Change, Challenge and Competition, The National Commission to Ensure a Strong Competitive Airline Industry: A Report to President and Congress* (Aug. 1993), at 21 (referencing letter of former German Chancellor Helmut Kohl to then-U.S. President George H. W. Bush) [hereinafter *Airline Commission Report*].
320. *Airline Commission Proceedings*, testimony of Paul L. Gretch, Director, DOT Office of International Aviation, (May 26, 1993), at 129-34. The U.S./German protocol of 1978, which amended the parties' original 1955 air services agreement, was one of the early successes of the Carter administration's open skies policy. *See* Protocol Relating to the United States of America/Federal Republic of Germany Air Transport Agreement of 1955, Nov. 1, 1978, 30 U.S.T. 7323 (1978-79).
321. *See* U.S. DOT, *Joint Application of Lufthansa/United 1996, supra* note 279, at 22 n.47; GAO, *European Community, supra* note 160, at 49; U.S. DOT Report to Airline Commission, *supra* note 180, at 14. In Mar. 1996, much sooner than negotiators had originally forecast, the United States and Germany agreed a draft open skies framework, the full implementation of which was subject to a German precondition of U.S. antitrust immunity for an expanded

economic survival of its troubled flag carrier, Alitalia, to a level of high policy principle.[322] In the unquiet U.S./EC aeropolitics of the early 1990s, Italy also signaled to U.S. officials that denunciation of its U.S. bilateral would be 'thinkable.'[323]

France and Germany, and even Italy, eventually subscribed to the U.S. open skies ideology.[324] Germany, indeed, claimed credit for steering the EU Council of Transport Ministers toward approval of the 2007 open skies capstone agreement between the United States and the EC, and German Federal Minister of Transport, Wolfgang Tiefensee, signed the agreement in Washington, D.C. on April 30, 2007.[325] Although the United Kingdom is also a signatory to that agreement, continued British ambivalence about an open skies relationship with the United States may be an instance of coming events casting their shadow before. While the deadlock that characterized U.S./U.K. aviation relations for the past three decades has now been broken,[326] U.K. aviation officials and industry leaders, including the U.K. Secretary of State for Transportation, have signaled that failure to abrogate U.S. restrictions on inward aviation investment will (at the least) persuade

---

Lufthansa/United strategic alliance. The impetus for the sudden acceleration of the negotiation schedule, and the signing of a new agreement in May 1996, was likely a rapid improvement in Lufthansa's financial performance during 1995, Aviation Europe, Nov. 30, 1995, at 3, but this fact merely serves to emphasize the mercurialness of bilateral treaty arrangements. In 2007, the U.S./Germany open skies bilateral was superseded in accordance with Article 22(1) of the U.S./EC Air Transport Agreement, *supra* note 2.

322. This emphatic policy, which seemed to be in retreat as foreign suitors were solicited to bid for Alitalia after 2006, has been revived by the recent return to power in Apr. 2008 of Prime Minister Silvio Berlusconi's conservative administration. *See infra* Chapter 5, Part III(F).

323. *See* U.S. DOT Report to Airline Commission, *supra* note 180, at 16. The then-applicable U.S./ Italy agreement, signed in 1970, was very restrictive in terms of carrier entry and route allocation. Indeed, until 1991, only Delta (as successor to Pan Am) and TWA held designations. *See* Air Transport Agreement between the Government of the United States of America and the Government of the Italian Republic, Jun. 22, 1970, 21 U.S.T. 2096, as amended 1988, 1990, 1991). This agreement was amended by a new open skies protocol initialed on Dec. 6, 1999. The trigger for the new protocol – as commonly occurs in open skies negotiations – was Alitalia's request for antitrust immunity for its proposed transatlantic alliance with KLM/Northwest. *See* Press Release, U.S. DOT, U.S. Transportation Secretary Slater Signs U.S.-Italy Open Skies Agreement, DOT 206-99 (Dec. 6, 1999). In 2007, the U.S./Italy open skies bilateral was superseded in accordance with Article 22(1) of the U.S./EC Air Transport Agreement, *supra* note 2.

324. *See supra* notes 314, 321, & 323.

325. *See* Press Release, German Embassy, Washington, D.C., Tiefensee: European-U.S. Open Skies Agreement is Milestone in Transatlantic Relationship, Washington, D.C. (Apr. 30, 2007). Tiefensee's speech in Washington warned, consistently with the European approach to the next stage of negotiations, that an agreement to remove reciprocal ownership and control restrictions would be critical to the success of those negotiations. *See also* the remarks given by the Federal Minister of Transport, Building and Urban Affairs, Wolfgang Tiefensee, President of the EU Council of Ministers for Transport, Statement to the International Aviation Club, Washington, D.C. (Feb. 5, 2007) (reiterating EU ambition of an 'Open Aviation Area' that removes all restrictions on reciprocal investment in air carriers).

326. The 'game-changer,' as it were, was U.K. participation in the 2007 U.S./EC Air Transport Agreement, 30 years after the signing of the highly restrictive Bermuda II agreement. *See supra* Chapter 3, Part III(B) (discussing origins and impact of Bermuda II).

the United Kingdom to invoke a unilateral power – granted under an extra-agreement compromise approved by the EU Council of Transport Ministers in order to secure U.K. support[327] – to suspend the open skies rights granted in U.K. airspace to U.S. air carriers under the 2007 agreement.[328]

Indeed, it remained a persistent irony of the bilateral order that the United States and United Kingdom, dedicated to evangelizing other markets on behalf of open skies, were themselves yoked together in one of the most *illiberal* aviation regimes, the Bermuda II bilateral of 1977.[329] The U.K. Government, despite its flattering self-portrayal as a 'committed liberalizer,'[330] proved itself an adroit and uncompromising negotiator under Bermuda II, winning a stipulation in 1980 that only Pan Am and TWA could serve routes to London Heathrow and then, in 1991, forcing new concessions from the United States as the price of buying back those rights of designation for transfer to American and United.[331]

Nevertheless, despite the mutually provocative history of Anglo-American aviation relations, and U.S. suspicions that the United Kingdom's 'all or nothing' approach to the 2003-2007 transatlantic air transport negotiations was a Machiavellian ploy to sabotage the European Commission's dearly won mandate,[332] as a public matter the U.K. Government has consistently favored the kind of 'Open Aviation Area' which is the ultimate goal of the Commission's aerodiplomacy.[333] Thus, in its submissions to the Clinton Airline Commission in 1993, the United Kingdom questioned the value of a U.S. open skies philosophy that still sacralized the cabotage and foreign investment inheritances of the Chicago order.[334]

3   Resisting Open Skies: The U.S./Asia/Oceania Market

Bilateral turmoil has affected non-European markets also. The perennially unsteady U.S./Japan bilateral relationship,[335] for example, remains unperfected by open skies. Nevertheless, both sides have moved beyond their clashes in the

---

327. *See supra* Chapter 2, Part V(B) (presenting a more complete discussion of this compromise, which supposedly clarifies an ambiguity inherent in Articles 1 and 21 of the U.S./EC agreement). According to one plausible reading of these two provisions, they appear to limit exercise of the suspension power solely to the European Community and its 27 Member States acting as a single 'party.'
328. The U.K. Government publicly signaled such an intention in a statement by former U.K. Transport Secretary Douglas Alexander. *See supra* Chapter 2, note 253.
329. *See* the analysis of Bermuda II, *supra* Chapter 3, Part III(B).
330. Submission Prepared by the U.K. Government, British Embassy, Washington, D.C., *in Airline Commission Documents*, Dkt. No. 001166 (Jul. 19, 1993), para. 3 [hereinafter U.K. Submission].
331. *See supra* Chapter 3, note 464.
332. *See* the remarks of John Byerly, Deputy Assistant Secretary for Transportation Affairs at the U.S. Department of State, discussed *supra* Chapter 2, Part IV(A).
333. *See supra* Chapter 2, Part V(B) (discussing content of the Open Aviation Area, which would offer full capital mobility and full airspace freedoms including cabotage).
334. *See* U.K. Submission, *supra* note 330, at para. 7-9.
335. As of 1992, U.S. airlines carried 64% of the bilateral air passenger traffic between the United States and Japan. *Id.* at 3. By 2008, the figure remained steady at 64.4% (a number that has been more or less constant for a decade). *See* U.S. DOT, *Statistics, supra* note 309, tbl. 3.

early 1990s, when hubbing power at Tokyo was important primarily because of technological limitations on nonstops to Asia.[336] At that time, Japan expressed continuing discontent that fifth freedom beyond rights were enabling U.S. carriers to combine at Tokyo traffic flows from a variety of U.S. cities for onward transit to multiple destinations in the Asia/South Pacific market.[337] The matter was not resolved until 1998, when the 1952 U.S./Japan agreement[338] was amended through reciprocal concessions *inter alia* granting the two primary ('incumbent') carriers from each side unlimited third and fourth freedom rights and an orderly expansion in beyond fifth freedom rights.[339] But the negotiations were tortuous and replete with political gamesmanship, not least the widely circulated charge by Northwest Airlines, the leading U.S. incumbent in the U.S./Japan market, that Japan's refusal to accept open skies – and its quest for 'equalization' of traffic rights for each party's carriers – reflected the broader protectionist instincts of Japanese international trade policy.[340]

Other Asia/Oceania markets have shown similar patterns of discord. Australia, for example, maintains a striking conceptual separation between its highly

---

336. Hubbing power in Tokyo is not as important as it was 10 or 15 years ago because airlines have evolved polar routings that enable them to fly routes as long as Newark/Hong Kong and JFK/Bangkok on a nonstop basis. Thus, whether or not to hub in Tokyo is now more a matter of strategic choice. United Airlines, for example, which succeeded Pan Am as a privileged incumbent under the U.S./Japan bilateral, has pulled down its service from Tokyo Narita to China and Hong Kong in favor of nonstop service from the United States. United however, does maintain fifth freedom service from Narita to secondary Asian destinations such as Taipei and Bangkok. *See* United Airlines, *Worldwide Timetable*, May 1-Jul. 15, 2007, at 134-135. Northwest Airlines, the bilateral market leader, still prefers to flow the majority of its trans-pacific/United States traffic over its Tokyo hub.

337. *See* U.S. DOT Report to Airline Commission, *supra* note 180, at 19. These fifth freedom services, of course, compete directly with overseas operations of domestic Japanese carriers.

338. The U.S./Japan agreement, originally negotiated in 1952 and since substantially amended, remains one of the most restrictive in the U.S. bilateral directory and includes limited designation and limited city-pair combinations. *See* Civil Air Transport Agreement Between the United States and Japan, Aug. 11, 1952, 4 U.S.T. 1948 (entered into force Sept. 15, 1953). Japan's expected tactical posture in the new bilateral talks discussed in the main text, according to the DOT, would be to exchange broader third and fourth freedom ('gateway') rights between the United States and Japan in return for a scaling-back of U.S. carriers' fifth freedom traffic rights. *See Airline Commission Proceedings*, testimony of Paul L. Gretch, Director, DOT Office of International Aviation (May 26, 1993), at 136. Notably, Northwest and United are the only U.S. carriers which enjoy 'grandfathered' fifth freedom rights under the U.S./Japan agreement; other U.S. carriers, more recent entrants to the market, could serve only U.S./Japan routes. *Id. See also* U.S. DOT Report to Airline Commission, *supra* note 180, at 19-20.

339. *See* Robert Matthews, *The New U.S.–Japan Bilateral Aviation Agreement: Airline Competition Through the Political Process*, 3 J. AIR TRANSP. WORLD WIDE 1, 13 (1998). The agreement also extended increased third and fourth freedom frequencies, and for the first time beyond fifth freedom authority, to the so-called 'non-incumbent' carriers which were added through memoranda of understanding after the original 1952 text. *Id.* The agreement and its subsequent amendments may be found in 3 Av. L. Rep. (CCH) ¶¶ 26,366a *et seq.*

340. *See* Matthews, *supra* note 339, at 8-9 (contrasting open skies with Japanese negotiators' advocacy of 'controlled expansion'). The fraught nature of the U.S./Japan aviation relationship stems from the Japanese perception that U.S. carriers were able to exploit the postwar political environment to their considerable advantage, notably their hugely disproportionate enjoyment of fifth freedom

deregulated and denationalized domestic aviation marketplace and the classic bilateral aerodiplomacy through which it aggressively stewards its international markets to safeguard the interests of its privatized flag carrier, Qantas.[341] Until 2008, the U.S./Australia bilateral (like its Japanese counterpart, in fact), was of the Bermuda I genotype and memorialized the so-called 'primary reliance doctrine,' which holds that capacity operated under a bilateral should be geared primarily to meeting traffic demands between the two contracting States, with third country (fifth freedom) traffic having a secondary, supporting role.[342]

This formula, which survived the 1998 liberalizing of the U.S./Japan bilateral,[343] has been a sure recipe for aeropolitical confrontation. One such example common to both Australia and Japan was the Osaka/Sydney fifth freedom dispute in the early

rights. *See* Matthews, *supra* note 339, at 2. 'Equalization' of beyond rights, therefore, was of far greater importance to the Japanese negotiators than a commitment to what they dismissively called 'U.S.-style' open skies, which still excluded access to the huge U.S. domestic market and under which their less cost-efficient airlines would continue to lose market share to trimmer U.S. competitors. *See id.* at 3-4 (noting that 'equalization' probably also meant eliminating the market share disparities that gave U.S. carriers over 60% of the bilateral market). Ultimately, in the view of the U.S. Department of Transportation, Japan's concessions were prompted by fear that U.S. carriers' hubbing operations in Japan would shift to rival East Asian airports. *See id.* at 11. U.S. efforts in mid-2007 to further liberalize the U.S./Japan bilateral, including ending double disapproval pricing, were evidently unavailing. *See* Madhu Unnikrishnan, *U.S., Japan Negotiators Go Home Empty-Handed*, 368 Av. DAILY, Apr. 9, 2007, at 2.

341. *See* Brian F. Havel, Moderator's Briefing Paper for the 2007 ABA Forum on Air & Space Law, *Beyond Open Skies: Liberalization after the U.S.-EC Agreement* (Oct. 4, 2007) (on file with author). Qantas has not been shy about expressing its view that the U.S. open skies policy does not include access to government business or to liberalized foreign investment opportunities. *See* Katherine Murphy, *Australia Pushes U.S. for Open Skies*, THE AGE, Aug. 10, 2006. There has been some easing of Australia's general policy in recent years, notably the conclusion of an all-cargo open skies agreement with the United States in 1999, *see* Press Release, U.S. DOT, United States, Australia Agree to Open Skies for Cargo, DOT 215-99 (Dec. 14, 1999), followed by a full open skies agreement with the United States in February 2008, *see* Press Release, U.S. Dept. of State, U.S. Reaches Open Skies Accord with Australia, 2008/115 (Feb. 15, 2008). National ownership and control of Qantas is a matter of special statutory provision in Australia and was policed scrupulously by the Australian Government in the face of opportunistic trading by international investors during 2006 and 2007. *See* Geoff Easdown & Gerard McManus, *Bellyflop: Qantas in Disarray as Multibillion Dollar Bid Fails*, HERALD SUN (Australia), May 7, 2007, at 1. The Qantas takeover fiasco, an $11 billion bid that included substantial foreign equity, illustrated the perils of defending strict citizenship profiles against the hyperventilated strategic behavior of contemporary global finance markets and investors. Concern over the citizenship purity of Qantas was central to the collapse of merger talks between the carrier and British Airways in December 2008. *See* Reuters, *Qantas, British Airways Merger Talks Grounded* (Dec. 18, 2008).

342. *See* Air Transport Agreement between the Government of the United States of America and the Government of Australia, Dec. 3, 1946, 7 U.N.T.S. 201. Amendments to the agreement may be found in 3 Av. L. Rep. (CCH) ¶¶ 26,207b *et seq.* (superseded by Air Transport Agreement Between the Government of the United States and the Government of Australia [Feb. 2008] 3 Av. L. Rep. (CCH) at 21,850 (Feb. 14, 2008)). *See also* Article 12 of the U.S./Japan agreement, *supra* note 338. This notional allocation is described in the text of the bilateral as one of the 'general principles of orderly development' of air services to which each contracting party is expected to subscribe. *Id.*

343. To circumvent the vagueness of the Bermuda I language, Part I of the 1998 protocol includes explicit numerical formulae that govern capacity on fifth freedom routes. *See* [U.S.-Japan]

1990s. Relying partly on the primary reliance doctrine, both the Australian and Japanese Governments attempted to impose strict numerical limits on U.S. carrier traffic on the Osaka/Sydney route. This route represents 'primary' third and fourth freedom traffic for Australian and Japanese domestic carriers and fifth freedom ('secondary') traffic for U.S. competitors, which serve these routes as extensions of U.S./Australia or U.S./Japan third freedom traffic rights.[344] The Australian dimension of the Osaka/Sydney dispute led to a protracted controversy that fell along the typical bilateral 'eye for an eye' continuum of threats of route withdrawal or suspension.[345]

4   The U.S. Response: Aerodiplomacy Trumps Retaliation and Denunciation

Although we earlier referred to a 'judicialization' of U.S. air carrier remedies under the IATCA/IATFCPA complaint procedure,[346] in the relatively few instances of an

---

Agreement Relating to and Amending the Civil Air Transport Agreement of Aug. 11, 1952, as Amended, *reprinted in* [Nov. 1999] 3 Av. L. Rep. (CCH) ¶ 26,366i, at 22,546 (Apr. 20, 1998).

344. *See* U.S. DOT Report to Airline Commission, *supra* note 180 at 5 & 19. Canberra proposed capacity caps on fifth freedom service by U.S. carriers serving Australian points from other Far Eastern hubs. The Japanese maintained, as a general principle, that fifth freedom traffic should be limited to no more than 50% of local fifth freedom traffic based on passengers on board, but did not formally enforce this requirement – which the United States contested as an inaccurate reading of the notoriously vague and ambiguous Bermuda I capacity provisions.

345. A 1993 DOT order, following a complaint by Northwest Airlines that the Australian Government imposed 'strict numerical limitation' on its fifth freedom services between Osaka and Sydney, was another powerful illustration of the zero sum outcome of these bilateral disputes. *See* Complaint of Northwest Airlines, Inc. against the Government of Australia, [1992-1994 Transfer Binder] Av. L. Rep. (CCH) ¶ 22,904, at 14,120 [hereinafter Northwest Complaint Australia]. On Dec. 31, 1992, the Government of Australia proposed that Northwest terminate one flight on the Osaka/Sydney sector, and on the other two flights that it may not carry more than 50% Osaka/Sydney (fifth freedom) passengers. Northwest filed its complaint seeking U.S. retaliatory countermeasures against the U.S. operations of Australia's privatized flag carrier, Qantas Airways Limited (Qantas), including suspension of authority to operate nonstop service in the Los Angeles/Australia market. Although the DOT initially deferred imposing sanctions pending intergovernmental consultations, it later announced its intention to terminate three weekly Los Angeles/Sydney flights by Qantas (if the Australian Government persisted with its curtailment of Northwest's services). On Apr. 1, 1993, Australia formally requested international arbitration of the dispute. *See* U.S. DOT Report to Airline Commission, *supra* note 180, at 19. By order of May 24, 1993, the DOT finalized its tentative findings regarding retaliatory sanctions on Qantas. *See* U.S. DOT, *Complaint of Northwest Airlines, Inc. against the Government of Australia*, Dkt. No. 48611, Final Order 93-5-31 (May 24, 1993). Thus, despite a Bermuda I-type air transport agreement calling for joint government consultations on capacity, each party engaged in a series of unilateral retaliatory strikes against the other's carrier under which each airline would be forced to forfeit accumulated (and wholly unrelated) market shares. In Jun. 1993, however, following a U.S./Australia 'accommodation' by exchange of letters, the DOT terminated the Northwest proceeding and vacated its notice regarding termination of the authority of Qantas to serve the Los Angeles/Sydney route. *See* U.S. DOT, *Complaint of Northwest Airlines, Inc. Against the Government of Australia*, Dkt. No. 48611, Order Terminating Proceeding (June 18, 1993).

346. Thus, it is a peculiarity of the IATCA/IATFCPA investigation process, shown in the various decisions discussed here and in the next Part that the U.S. Government provides a forum for a

actual formal complaint the outcomes have been tempered by broader aeropolitical concerns and the desire for amicable compromise in place of unilateral U.S. retaliation. Although the U.S. DOT has willingly placed its statutory powers at the disposal of U.S. carriers facing threats to suspend, modify, or outright refuse particular route authority,[347] the DOT has been inclined, when contemplating or making a finding against a foreign government, to suspend any enforcement action if aeropolitical bilateral discussions are envisaged or in progress with that government. Moreover, the advent of liberalized open skies relationships has made little if any difference either to the likelihood that an IATCA/IATFCPA complaint might be filed, or to its eventual disposition. The one unilateral remedy that the United States has not applied, despite provocation, is denunciation of a foreign bilateral agreement. This discussion considers a non-open skies dispute (the U.S./ Japan fifth freedom controversy previously mentioned), and a more recent dispute over code-sharing privileges that arose under the now-superseded U.S./Italy open skies agreement.

The trade management instincts of Japan, under its Bermuda I-model 1952 bilateral agreement with the United States, have made it a regular target of IATCA/IATFCPA investigation. As well as the Osaka/Sydney complaint which it filed in 1992,[348] in 1996 U.S. carrier Northwest Airlines protested Japan's refusal to authorize its proposed Seattle/Osaka/Jakarta fifth freedom service.[349] As is typical in these disputes, Northwest argued for a specific retaliatory action, in that case suspension of what was then Japan's only permitted regular fifth freedom service through the United States (Japan/Los/Angeles/Brazil), as well as a third/fourth freedom service connecting Hiroshima and Honolulu.[350] The DOT approved Northwest's complaint essentially on the ground of legitimate expectations,

---

private air carrier directly to challenge the sovereign action of a foreign government under an agreement that confers 'bilateral rights' on the U.S. Government.

347. 'We have consistently viewed denial of U.S. carrier rights to operate services provided for in our aviation agreements as a most serious violation of this country's bilateral rights.' *See* U.S. DOT, *Complaint of Northwest Airlines, Inc., Against the Government of Japan, Under 49 U.S.C. Section 41310*, Dkt. No. OST-96-1500, Order Approving Complaint (Feb. 13, 1997) [hereinafter U.S. DOT, *Northwest Complaint Japan*]. For a past perspective that still merits consideration, *see* American Airlines report, *Unenforced Bilateral Agreements, in Airline Commission Documents*, Dkt. No. 000267 (Jul. 1, 1993), which catalogued a series of restrictive unilateral actions, taken under 'liberal' Bermuda I-type capacity/designation agreements with the United States, by the governments of Chile, Guatemala, Panama, Costa Rica, and Japan. The pattern identified in that report was stereotypical: a U.S. carrier proposed a frequency increase on a particular service, which was then unilaterally blocked by the aviation authorities (and sometimes by the highest political officials) of the affected foreign government. U.S. carrier responses comprised either capitulation or invoking the IATCA/IATFCPA complaint procedures (which, as considered in the main text, may ultimately yield only zero-sum retaliatory action).

348. *See supra* note 345.

349. *See* U.S. DOT, *Northwest Complaint Japan, supra* note 347.

350. *See id.* at 2. U.S. carriers (as well as other stakeholders in IATCA/IATFCPA proceedings such as cities and airports) do not necessarily share similar goals or objectives as to optimal outcomes. In this instance, United Airlines, for example, argued that its third and fourth freedom

performing a close exegesis of treaty and MOU texts, as well as invoking nego-tiating history, to conclude that a later expansion of third and fourth freedom services was never intended to affect the fifth freedom rights acquired by North-west as one of the two U.S. designated 'incumbent' carriers under the original 1952 bilateral treaty.[351] More interesting than its straightforward decision on the merits, however, was the Department's readiness to forego immediate sanctions (for example, restrictions on services by Japanese carriers in the U.S./Japan market) because of ongoing 'formal and informal' discussions with the Japanese Govern-ment.[352] The public interest, according to the DOT, would be best served by subordinating retaliation against Japan's 'unjustifiable and unreasonable restric-tion' to the prospect of resolving Northwest's complaint within a broader settle-ment of U.S. carrier fifth freedom rights.[353]

The 2004 American Airlines/United Airlines joint complaint against Alitalia and the Government of Italy revealed that changing the bilateral aeropolitical context to open skies may yield virtually the same outcome in an IATCA/IATFCPA dispute.[354] The complaint grew out of Italy's reconfiguration of air services between Milan's Linate and Malpensa airports. Malpensa, the newer field, was designated for international ex-EU air services, while Linate became prioritized for intra-Union point-to-point air traffic.[355] Italy then excluded the complainant U.S. carriers from code-sharing with their European alliance partners in transatlantic flows through to Linate on the ground that those services did not qualify as solely intra-Union flights for purposes of access to Linate under the new configuration. Alitalia, however, continued to code-share with its U.S. and EU partners through its Air France/Delta alliance intercontinental connections over Rome and Paris – although, sinking the complainants' primary case, it was

---

rights with Japan should not be jeopardized in the context of what was essentially a fifth freedom dispute. *Id.* For more on the political interests that color international aviation nego-tiations, *see* Matthews, *supra* note 339.

351. *See* U.S. DOT, *Northwest Complaint Japan, supra* note 347, at 5-6. This conclusion seemed uncontroversial, given that the original 1952 provisions were amplified and confirmed in a 1965 exchange of diplomatic notes which included the open-ended provision that 'where the word "beyond" appears in an air route . . . without specification of a subsequent geographical direction, air services on such beyond portion of the route may be operated to any point or points, including points in the home territory.' *Id.* at 4 n.13.

352. *Id.* at 6.

353. *See id.* United's suggestion that the DOT make findings with respect to similar Japanese actions on United's proposed San Francisco/Osaka/Jakarta service was met with a similar response – setting aside what the Department viewed as the inappropriateness of dealing with that question within the ambit of Northwest's complaint, it nonetheless confirmed that Uni-ted's grievance would also be raised with Japan in forthcoming talks. *See id.*

354. U.S. DOT, *Joint Complaint of American Airlines, Inc., United Airlines, Inc., against Alitalia-Linee Aeree Italiane-S.p.A. and The Government of Italy, Under Section 2(b) of the International Air Transportation Fair Competitive Practices Act, as Amended,* Dkt. No. OST-2004-19790, Order (Jul. 25, 2005) [hereinafter U.S. DOT, *American/United Complaint*].

355. *See id.* at 3.

revealed that the Italian carrier had ceased placing its own code on Linate origin and destination fifth freedom transatlantic services by the time the DOT took jurisdiction.[356]

The only remaining contested use of a code by Alitalia, display of Air France's code on the Alitalia-operated Linate/Paris flights that passengers could use to connect with Air France-operated transatlantic services to the United States,[357] concerned flights that did not operate under the U.S./Italy agreement. Rather, these services concerned rights *inter se* of carriers operating under 'other air services regimes' (including, presumably, France/Italy).[358] The DOT concluded (as in the Japan proceeding) that the 'public interest' militated against making findings under the U.S./Italy agreement that would affect 'positive aviation relations' with third countries.[359] Accordingly, although the DOT considered that 'a situation in which U.S. carriers are denied the right to provide code share-only services into Linate that can be and are provided by EU carriers to be contrary to the spirit of an open skies agreement,' the matter would be pursued aeropolitically through 'our ongoing dialogue with the [European Union].'[360] Simply put, all EU carriers could provide intra-Union code shares to Linate but U.S. carriers could not do so as extensions of their transatlantic services.

The new U.S./EC Air Transport Agreement may provide a natural legal procedural framework to address this problem, since France and Italy are now both parties to the same agreement with the United States, but it remains unclear how the intercontinental implications of confining Linate to intra-Union traffic might be resolved. Code-sharing privileges, in a fully open skies environment, should not be conceptually dependent on the territorial situs of the EU airport through which a transatlantic service flows. Whatever one may say about the timorousness of the DOT's finding, its final order offers a particularly telling example of the Procrustean rigidity of bilateral aerodiplomacy even in an era of open skies. The Department's plaintive coda – regretting that the outcome violated the 'spirit' of open skies – could not be a more persuasive recognition of the inherent limitations of an open skies policy that has been consciously engineered to fit within the limitations of the Chicago system.[361]

---

356. *Id.*
357. *See id.* at 6.
358. *See id.*
359. U.S. DOT, *American/United Complaint, supra* note 354, at 6.
360. *Id.*
361. Indeed, the U.S. carriers subsequently filed a petition for reconsideration, charging that DOT officials had 'struggled to find an appropriate remedy directed at Alitalia and the Italian Government.' U.S. DOT, *Joint Complaint of American Airlines, Inc. and United Airlines, Inc. Against Alitalia-Linee Aeree Italiane-S.p.A. and the Government of Italy Under Section 2(b) of the International Air Transportation Fair Competitive Practices Act, as Amended*, Dkt. No. OST-2004-19790, Joint Petition of American Airlines, Inc. For Reconsideration of Order (Aug. 15, 2005), para. 2. The U.S. airlines also warned that the DOT's finding of a violation of the 'spirit' of the U.S./Italy open skies agreement was equivocal and could be misconstrued as an acquiescence in a violation of its letter. *Id.* paras. 3 & 6. The U.S. complainants argued that they held appropriate authority for the code-share services, since the route annex to the U.S./

As noted earlier, the United States has not imposed the draconian penalty of suspending a foreign carrier permit (as the IATCA/IATFCPA procedures clearly allow), nor has it resorted in recent times to denunciation of a disputed bilateral agreement,[362] even though it has itself been the target of precisely this remedy.[363] Clearly, U.S. denunciation, accompanied by a refusal to continue air service exchanges on a basis of comity and reciprocity, would be a formidable weapon to apply against any foreign air power.[364] In the cases of Air France or British

---

Italy agreement allowed U.S. carriers to offer services between all points in the United States and all points in Italy (including Linate) via all intermediate and beyond points. *See id.* at para. 3. They also argued, as a matter of commercial reality, that business travelers prefer the 'closer-in' Linate airport to Malpensa, creating a competitive handicap for Alitalia's U.S. competitors in violation of the 'fair and equal opportunity to compete' language of the bilateral. *Id.* at para. 4. Other recent IATCA/IATFCPA complaints have been considered earlier. *See supra* note 202 (considering DOT actions involving Argentina and the European Union).

362. In 1995, the United States officially contemplated denunciation of its Bermuda II bilateral with the United Kingdom. A senior airline executive testified to Congress that denunciation would be 'an effective strategy' because of the disproportionate importance to British Airways of access to U.S. skies. *See* 1995 Aviation Hearings, *supra* note 259, at 104 (testimony of Robert L. Crandall, President, American Airlines). United Airlines Chairman Gerald Greenwald, noting France's denunciation of its U.S. bilateral, rejected denunciation because 'it simply confirms the status quo.' *Id.* Greenwald doubted the political feasibility of a 'true' denunciation *Id.* In 2000, after British Airways withdrew from its London/Pittsburgh route and the U.K. Government refused to authorize a replacement U.S. carrier on the route or to renegotiate Bermuda II, frustrated airline industry leaders in Congressional testimony again called for denunciation (or 'renunciation,' as they somewhat inaccurately labeled it) of the U.S./U.K. air transport agreement. *See also* Stephen M. Wolf, Chairman, US Airways Group, Inc. & Frederick W. Smith, Chairman, President and CEO, FedEx Corporation, *The Recent Breakdown of Aviation Negotiations Between the United States and the United Kingdom*, Testimony Before the U.S. House of Representatives, Committee on Transportation and Infrastructure, Subcommittee on Aviation (Feb. 15, 2000) (discussing options for finding a successor to Bermuda II).

363. *See, e.g., supra* Chapter 2, note 152 and accompanying text (discussing the European Commission's call for denunciation of all U.S./EC bilateral open skies treaties after the rulings of the European Court of Justice in 2002). The United States last formally denounced an air transport agreement (with Peru) in 1978. *See Airline Commission Proceedings*, testimony of James R. Tarrant, Deputy Assistant Secretary for Transportation Affairs, Department of State (May 26, 1993), at 152. DOT witnesses described U.S. denunciation as 'very rare.' *Id.* In addition to France and the United Kingdom, incidentally, Thailand denounced its aviation bilateral with the United States in 1990, citing figures showing that the majority of passengers flown into Bangkok by U.S. carriers were from Asian points. *See id.* at 60. The most significant denunciation of a bilateral agreement with the United States, of course, was by the United Kingdom in 1976. DOT Report to Airline Commission, *supra* note 180, at 15. As a general comment, U.S. airlines have expressed displeasure at the perceived slowness of the IATCA/IATFCPA procedures and seeming unwillingness of the Departments of State and Transportation to escalate the level of reprisal.

364. While the focus of this Part is on responses to discriminatory and protectionist interference with the exercise of air traffic rights by U.S. carriers, it is evident that U.S. bilateralist policy may provoke controversies with foreign governments – and therefore potential disruptions of traffic rights – premised on other aeropolitical issues, including the consequences of the

Airways, for example, passenger airline operations to and from the United States are a much more significant component of revenues than U.S./France or U.S./U.K. traffic is for any individual U.S. airline. The ready availability of the expedient of bilateral denunciation to *all* governments, with the consequent disruption of private management expectations and planning, is one of the most profoundly anachronistic features of the Chicago system.[365]

For instance, a deliberate trend in recent U.S. legacy carrier route planning has been a refocusing of capacity on more profitable international sectors as yields in the domestic market declined.[366] That shift has been projected, monitored, and attained using rights in place under a complex directory of U.S. bilateral arrangements. The planning process for new route entry involves advance ordering of new aircraft, and obviously a time-lag exists between commissioning aircraft

---

oversight exercised unilaterally by the U.S. Federal Aviation administration (FAA) over the safety standards of other States since 1992. (The FAA's International Aviation Safety Assessment Program applies ICAO standards to other States' civil aviation safety regimes and authorities, while the European Community's infamous 'blacklist' targets specific air carriers.) *See generally* U.S. Federal Aviation Administration, *supra* note 220; Council Regulation 2111/2005, 2005 O.J. (L 344) 15. In Feb. 2006, for example, the Venezuelan President, Hugo Chávez, threatened to stop most U.S. flights to and from his country because of the FAA's a decade-old failing assessment of Venezuela's air safety regime. The FAA finding meant that Venezuelan airlines had to wet-lease aircraft from other countries to fly to the United States. *See* Jim Landers, *When the FAA Goes Abroad, It Returns with New Baggage: Spat with Venezuela Illustrates Political Consequences*, DALLAS MORNING NEWS, Jun. 2, 2006, at 1D. Notably, the existence of an open skies relationship with the United States is immaterial to the pursuit or outcomes of these FAA assessments. *See id.* While both sides in the U.S./Venezuela dispute threatened denunciation of the bilateral treaty, neither in fact did so and the matter was eventually resolved following the FAA's elevation of Venezuela's safety rating. *See* Press Release, U.S. FAA, FAA Raises Safety Rating for Venezuela, Release No. AOC 10-06 (Apr. 21, 2006). *See also* Government of Venezuela, *Venezuela Recategorization Process by the Federal Aviation Administration (FAA)*, Paper Presented to the [ICAO] Directors General of Civil Aviation Conference on a Global Strategy for Aviation Safety, DGCA/06-IP/19 (Mar. 15, 2006) (discussing Venezuela's actions taken under its bilateral air services treaty with the United States following the FAA's initial categorization).

365. The availability of the denunciation remedy has been unaffected by the conclusion of bilateral open skies agreements, including the recent U.S./EC Air Transport Agreement. *See supra* Chapter 2, Part V(B) (discussing special circumstances that have added a more specific 'suspension' remedy to the conventional treaty termination clause in this agreement). *See also* Model Open Skies Agreement, *supra* note 222, art. 15; *see also* 2007 U.S./Canada Agreement, *supra* note 222, art. 20.

366. United Airlines, for example, reduced its capacity in the North American market by nearly 14% between Aug. 2004 and Aug. 2005, and increased its international capacity over the same period by about 10% (to a total of 40% of the airline's entire capacity). American Airlines showed a similar pattern. *See* Andrew Compart, *Spanning the Globe: Will Adding International Service Save U.S. Airlines?*, TRAVEL WKLY., <http://travelweekly.com/multimedia/TWSURVEY2005/going_interna.htm>. This trend is set to continue in tandem with the need to connect North America with other quickly developing regions, so that flows will increase to the Asia-Pacific, Commonwealth of Independent States, and Middle East markets. *See* Airbus Global Market Forecast 2006-2025, North America, <www.airbus.com/store/mm_repository/pdf/att00009261/media_object_file_Airbus_NA_GMF.pdf>.

production and deployment of the aircraft into actual service.[367] Accordingly, unilateral modification or withdrawal of negotiated route (and capacity) opportunities, as could have occurred if the 2003/2007 U.S./EC open skies talks had ultimately failed[368] – and as the U.K. Government warns may happen with respect to new rights awarded under the 2007 U.S./EC Air Transport Agreement[369] – will merely frustrate airline planning and transfer avoidable (and substantial) costs to the air transport industry and ultimately to the traveling public.[370]

5   A Reconceptualization of Open Skies – Some Preliminary Thoughts

Given the unpredictable consequences of quasi-political judicialized enforcement of the IATCA/IATFCPA complaint procedure, as well as the pusillanimous approach of U.S. aviation officials to the weapon of denunciation, it is unsurprising that U.S. air carriers have been dissatisfied with the contingent nature of the present system. Moreover, the aeropolitical interests represented in this system force U.S. airlines to pursue goals and objectives that may be in conflict not only with their direct competitors but also with other stakeholders such as airports and municipalities. And even liberalized open skies agreements do not address, much less remove, the unpredictability of foreign government (or foreign airline) action. Reconceptualization, therefore, has become an imperative not only of the classical Chicago system, but of the open skies model as well.

Notwithstanding the recidivist disenchantments of bilateral aerodiplomacy, the Clinton and second Bush Administrations chose to pursue the concept of liberal bilateral agreements. Beginning with the September 1992 agreement with the Netherlands,[371] reached in the final months of the first Bush Administration,

---

367. Indeed, a chronic misalignment of the business and capital cycles has been a fundamental challenge to the air passenger industry throughout the world. *See* Havel, *supra* note 341.

368. *See* Byerly, *supra* note 160 (forecasting, in the event of failure of the U.S./EC talks, possible termination of existing U.S./Member State bilateral agreements and consequent 'destabilization' of the transatlantic market, including dissolution of U.S/EU air carrier alliances through forfeiture of antitrust immunity).

369. *See supra* note 328 (noting the U.K. Government's publicly-stated position with respect to suspension of rights under the U.S./EC Air Transport Agreement).

370. *See* Submission of United Airlines to Airline Commission, *in Airline Commission Documents*, Dkt. No. 00059 (Jun. 14, 1993), at 5.

371. As previously noted, the Bush Administration authorized an experimental open skies policy in 1992, which led to a new liberal bilateral agreement with the entrepreneurially-inclined Netherlands. *See* GAO, *European Community, supra* note 160, at 52. In addition to the expanded open skies initiative announced in 1994, the U.S. Department of Transportation undertook other pioneering initiatives to liberalize and improve aviation relations with EU Member States, including expanding the rights of EU airlines to operate U.S./EU routes under the 'Underserved Cities Program.' This program, initiated by the DOT in 1989, was basically an exercise of federal discretion that allowed foreign airlines to provide extra-bilateral international service to and from U.S. city-points that did not otherwise receive the identical

U.S. officials ended the practice of 'bean-counting' of gateways in favor of mutually unrestricted route access for each party's carriers to the other's territory.[372] In June 2008, the U.S. Department of State reported over 90 open skies agreements, 34 of which were with countries in the European sector (including the EU and a number of its associated States and geographical neighbors).[373] In addition, Argentina had signed a cargo-only open skies agreement with the United States.[374] Notably, these agreements mostly continued a longstanding U.S. practice of modernizing an existing agreement (by protocol or exchange of notes) rather than adopting a new text, so that the 'liberal' agreements have principally comprised the preexisting bilaterals overlaid with open skies amendments.[375] A 1995 agreement with Canada (and obviously a separate initiative from the European market-opening approach), was textually a new agreement based on a template developed by the U.S. DOT as part of its revamped open skies strategy.[376] Another

---

      international nonstop service from U.S. airlines. Lufthansa, for example, was awarded Frankfurt/Charlotte, N.C. in 1990. A procompetitive bilateral (*i.e.*, one that offered simple reciprocity to U.S. airlines which might wish to provide direct service) with the foreign airline's home country was a precondition to admission to the program. The 'new generation' bilaterals, offering unrestricted gateway access, eliminated the need for (although not the technical existence of) the program.

372.   The expression 'bean-counting' was used by Mary Street, *see* Street Interview, *supra* note 214.
373.   The 2007 U.S./EC Air Transport Agreement, *see supra* note 2, effectively superseded open skies agreements with EU Member States Austria, Belgium, the Czech Republic, Denmark, Finland, France, Germany, Italy, Luxembourg, Malta, the Netherlands, Poland, Portugal, Romania, Slovak Republic, Slovenia, and Sweden. For a complete listing of U.S. open skies bilateral relationships, *see* U.S. Department of State, Open Skies Partners (Jun. 12, 2008), <http://2001-2009.state.gov/e/eeb/rls/othr/2008/22281.htm>.
374.   *See id.* For Australia's recent signing of a full open skies agreement, *see supra* note 341.
375.   *See* Street Interview, *supra* note 214. The EU Member State exceptions have included France, Luxembourg, Malta, Poland, Portugal, Romania, and the Slovak Republic.
376.   As previously noted, *see supra* Chapter 2, note 21, the 1995 Canada/U.S. agreement was further liberalized in 2005, pursuant to which a full open skies regime entered into effect in 2007. Neither the 1995 agreement nor the 2005 amended agreement modified either party's cabotage or nationality restrictions. The Canadian transport agency appears to foresee no relaxation of either restriction. *See* Transport Canada, *A New International Air Transportation Policy*, Consultation with Stakeholders, at 4 (2006) (stating that '[u]nder no circumstances would the proposed approach [to international air transport policy] include cabotage rights'). *See also id.* at 7 (proposing a reconsideration of the ownership regime governing *foreign* airlines, for example by allowing a principal place of business basis for foreign carrier designations, but omitting any reference to modification of Canada's domestic nationality laws). The new treaty and its 2005 upgrading did, however, ease the competitive anomaly of a highly restrictive aviation bilateral existing side-by-side with the North American Free Trade Agreement. *See Airline Commission Proceedings*, comments of James R. Tarrant, Deputy Assistant Secretary for Transportation Affairs, Department of State (May 26, 1993), at 143-46. In some ways, the superseded U.S./Canada Agreement was more restrictive than Bermuda II, with many major Canadian cities having no direct nonstop service by U.S. carriers. *See id.* An extraordinary vacuum, for example, was the absence of *any* direct air link between the two capitals, Washington, D.C. and Ottawa. *Id. See also* U.S. DOT Report to Airline Commission, *supra* note 180, at 10. Before 1995, Canada had originally proposed an 'asymmetrical' route phase that would give Canadian carriers immediate open skies access to U.S. points, while reciprocal access for U.S. carriers would have been phased in over 10 years. The competitive

conspicuous exception to the amendment overlay procedure is the newly minted 2007 U.S./EC Air Transport Agreement.[377]

The transcendent challenge that faces U.S. international aviation policy planners, however, is that each iteration of their open skies policy, like the International Air Transportation Competition Act itself, has assumed the continuity of the bilateral order. While the DOT's most recent formal statement of U.S. policy (in 1995) broke with its precursors in openly predicting a transition to multilateralism,[378] substantively it was designed only to stretch the inherent conceptual elasticity of the traditional bilateral negotiating topics of route selection, airline designation, capacity, and pricing.[379] In other words, open skies expanded the traditional bilateral marketplace through unrestricted gateway service,[380] multiple permissive designation, full pricing and capacity freedom,[381] and full exercise of 'beyond' fifth freedom rights and other traffic rights.[382] Moreover, once the 'grand design' strategy of encircling and luring

environment changed in mid-1992, however, when Canadian carriers entered equity relationships with U.S. carriers in preparation for open skies. On the recently concluded Canada/EC Air Transport Agreement, *see* Chapter 2, note 21.

377. *See supra* note 2.
378. *See* U.S. International Air Transport Policy Statement, 60 Fed. Reg. 21,841 (May 3, 1995) [hereinafter 1995 Policy Statement].
379. For this analysis, *see supra* Chapter 1, Part II(C).
380. The 'first generation' liberal bilaterals of the Carter Administration did not offer unrestricted access, but rather an expanded choice of 'gateway' points. *See generally* Daniel C. Hedlund, Note, *Toward Open Skies: Liberalizing Trade in International Airline Services*, 3 MINN. J. GLOBAL TRADE 259 (1994).
381. The pricing protocols are not entirely unrestricted; apart from the continued availability of unilateral U.S. 'intervention' under the IATCA/IATFCPA legislation, safeguard procedures in the model bilateral would allow a unilateral call for consultations in the event of 'unreasonably discriminatory prices,' monopoly practices, or price predation. *See* Model Open Skies Agreement, *supra* note 222, art. 13. As discussed earlier, however, the 'double disapproval' mechanism would allow a contested price, even if one party regards it as predatory, to go into effect if consultations deadlock. (No doubt, in those extreme circumstances, the United States could invoke its unilateral antidiscrimination authority under the IATCA/IATFCPA procedures.) In contrast, the pricing language in the U.S./EC Air Transport Agreement does not include any of these safeguard procedures – the only qualification to the general principle of pricing freedom is that, pursuant to applicable EC law, U.S. airlines do not enjoy the right of price leadership on intra-Union routes. *See* U.S./EC Air Transport Agreement, *supra* note 2, art. 13; *but see infra* Chapter 5, note 129 (questioning whether this restriction remains valid).
382. These are, in fact, the elements of the U.S. Department of Transportation's definition of an 'open skies' program as conceived during the *first* Bush Administration in 1992. Coterminal rights were also envisaged. *See* In the Matter of Defining 'Open Skies,' final order issued by Jeffrey N. Shane, Assistant Secretary for Policy and International Affairs, [March 2001] 3 Av. L. Rep. (CCH) ¶ 26,960, at 23,901 (Aug. 5, 1992). *See also* GAO, *European Community, supra* note 160, at 53. The grant of rights in the 2007 U.S./EC Air Transport Agreement has removed the possibility, always present under the classical bilateral model, that a U.S. carrier would encounter resistance in securing third State approval to operate intra-Union fifth freedom services. *See* U.S./EC Air Transport Agreement, *supra* note 2, art. 3. For example, under the superseded U.S./Greece and U.S./France bilateral agreements, Greece could object to a fifth freedom service by a U.S. carrier (*e.g.*, Chicago O'Hare/Paris Charles de Gaulle/Athens) even though the U.S./France bilateral permitted fifth freedom services beyond Paris.

larger players was exhausted,[383] a certain historical logic led to the first stage 2007 U.S./EC Air Transport Agreement that included both the smaller players to which the grand design was originally targeted as well as all of the larger players which followed (as well as some, like the United Kingdom and Spain, which did not). Even the 1995 statement's apparent readiness to contemplate further cohabitations modeled on the pilot KLM/Northwest agreement, but only within an open skies framework, merely repeated what had been the DOT's working policy since 1992.[384]

None of this is intended to suggest that the 2007 agreement lacks the stamp of innovation. To the contrary, as shown in the executive briefing in Chapter 2, the agreement extends the reach of open skies in directions that were not contemplated by the existing open skies template. Most striking has been the creation of a standing Joint Committee, an institutional channel for collaboration that far transcends the ad hoc availability of emergency 'consultations' under the existing model.[385] Moreover, the aeropolitical (and aeroeconomic) climates have altered substantially in Europe's favor since the early open skies era when U.S. carrier growth always risked protectionist retaliation. As German Transport Minister Wolfgang Tiefensee intimated in a February 2007 speech to the International Aviation Club (timed to boost the fortunes of the ongoing U.S./EC negotiations), Europe's enthusiasm for market access to the United States, and for an end to ownership and control restrictions, has largely displaced its former skepticism about the free market economic premise of open skies.[386]

Nevertheless, although the U.S. international aviation policy has assumed (at least in part) the virtual exhaustion of traditional bilateralism, the U.S. DOT's open skies strategy, even in its most robust manifestation in the 2007 U.S./EC Air Transport Agreement, still does not contemplate liberalization of the cabotage and nationality

---

(For discussion of how U.S. carrier exploitation of intra-Union fifths has fallen into desuetude, as well as the aeropolitical implications of the existence of these rights, *see supra* Chapter 2, note 35 and accompanying text.

383. *See supra* text accompanying note 27.
384. *See* 1995 Policy Statement, *supra* note 378, at 21,842-843. The 1995 statement, incidentally, omitted any reference to antitrust immunity, the 'sweetener' that entered U.S. aerodiplomacy through the exigencies of practical negotiation – and as such surely reflected U.S. admission that the 'encirclement' strategy was poised to fail.
385. *See* U.S./EC Air Transport Agreement, *supra* note 2, art. 11(6); *cf.* Model Open Skies Agreement, *supra* note 222, art. 13.
386. *See* Tiefensee, *supra* note 325. Europe's 'old thinking' was reflected in the following statement from the British Airways submission to the Airline Commission:

The combination of nationalism and economics has made the traditional [U.S.] definition of ["open skies"] (*i.e*, focused on greater access to international routes, gateways, capacity and pricing) highly unattractive to a number of the United States' major bilateral partners[,] particularly France, Australia, Germany and Japan. Given the acknowledged strength of the U.S. majors, the present vision of the open skies proposition understandably creates the fear of bilateral rape and pillage, leading to calls from these quarters for further protectionism and subsidy to prevent the premature demise of the national airline industry.

British Airways, Submission to the Airline Commission, *in Airline Commission Documents*, Dkt. No. 000124 (June 1993) at 3.

principles, the twin keystones of the Chicago system.[387] It is one of the premises of the present study that the United States *must* put these regulatory artifacts into play in as part of a specific multilateral aviation strategy, because open skies and bilateralism are in fundamental conceptual misalignment: the result is merely a contingently open marketplace, still dominated by nationalistic aeropolitical and aeroeconomic concerns, which can be narrowed or closed upon the unilateral calculation of any bilateral partner (or, in the case of the 2007 U.S./EC agreement, a consortium of bilateral partners).[388]

a   *IATCA and the 2007 U.S./EC Air Transport Agreement*

As noted above, the IATCA was designed to insinuate some regulatory reform into the Chicago bilateral system, which makes it (almost by definition) an inadequate platform for broader multilateral liberalization. Indeed, even in the existing bilateral context, at least one DOT official has publicly contested the proposition that the IATCA's recitation of policy desiderata (in Section 17)[389] steers the U.S. Government's conduct of bilateral treaty negotiations.[390] It is instructive, nevertheless, to examine some key IATCA principles in the context of the 2007 U.S./EC Air Transport Agreement and the U.S. negotiation posture.

While the IATCA calls for greater pricing and entry freedom in bilateral agreements, the first element of its prescribed agenda for U.S. international aviation policy is the strengthening of the competitive position of U.S. carriers 'to ensure at least equality with foreign air carriers,' an opaque formulation that appears to elevate conservation of market share to the highest priority in U.S. strategic aviation policy.[391] The opacity deepens in the IATCA eighth stated goal, which pledges increased (non-cabotage) access for foreign air carriers in exchange for 'benefits of similar magnitude for air carriers *or the traveling public*.'[392] Focusing solely on the term 'air carriers' in that phrase, the Airline Commission's international aviation issues team interpreted 'similar magnitude,' with little advance in clarity, to mean 'a balanced arrangement but not necessarily an identical exchange.'[393]

387. *See supra* Chapter 3, Parts IV & V.
388. *See* the political cynicism reflected in British Airways' 1982 testimony before the House Subcommittee on Investigations and Oversight, quoted in John A. Nammack Associates, Inc., Memo to USA-BIAS Members re: British View of US 'Free Market' Practices, *in Airline Commission Documents*, Dkt. No. 001029, Mar. 24, 1993, at 2-3, in which the Carter/Reagan open skies program was viewed as an attempt to help stronger U.S. airlines, with protected home markets, to loosen the shackles of the IATA pricing regime.
389. *See* Section 17 of the IATCA, amending Section 1102 of the Federal Aviation Act of 1958, in 49 U.S.C. app. § 1502(b) (1980) (recodified as 49 U.S.C.A. § 40101(e) (West 2008)).
390. *See* Paul L. Gretch, Director, Office of Int'l Aviation, U.S. DOT, *The EU-U.S. Agreement: Prospects for the New Transatlantic Market*, Speech to the Future of Air Transport Conference, Institute of Economic Affairs (Dec. 2007) (presentation on file with author). The normative status of the IATCA goals was not always so readily questioned. *See Airline Commission Proceedings*, testimony of Edward J. Driscoll, President and CEO, National Air Carrier Association (May 26, 1993), at 195.
391. 49 U.S.C. app. § 1502(b) (recodified as 49 U.S.C.A. § 40101(e) (West 2008)).
392. *Id.* (emphasis added).
393. Comments on Specific Issues as Identified by the International Aviation Issues Team, *in Airline Commission Documents*, Dkt. No. 000096, at 1.

Failing accomplishment of this ideal, the team suggested, the United States should content itself with the 'pragmatic approach' of managed competition, even if that means consenting to a limitation on capacity in order to retain open provisions on carrier designations or pricing, for example.[394] Other submissions to the Commission pressed for emphasis on the second component of the statutory phrase, calling for benefits to the 'traveling public.'[395]

Given the natural biases (and stakeholder identity) of bilateral air transport negotiations, however, it is hard to imagine that this calculus of interests could ever have been reversed in favor of the public. The IATCA, in fact, speciously seeks to protect the public while also requiring U.S. carrier market share to be maintained and benefits of equal magnitude to be exchanged with foreign carriers. These goals could be accomplished either in compliance with a policy of increased competition or, as the Airline Commission appeared to think, in derogation from such a policy. The assumption of U.S. antitrust law, that competition is good for consumers, is therefore not indisputably the assumption made by the IATCA principles.

Whichever way the language is parsed, it is virtually axiomatic that the United States, with its colossal domestic market, cannot achieve a *literal* balance of economic opportunities for its carriers – opportunities of 'similar magnitude,' in the IATCA parlance – within a purely bilateral negotiating framework, and even with the combined markets of its 27 EU partners.[396] In that sense, in fact, even with a 'multilateralized' understanding of bilateralism in the U.S./EC agreement, the open skies program – which has regularly traded open gateway access to the United States in exchange for open access for U.S. carriers to much smaller foreign markets – has literally violated the terms of the applicable statute. But the 2007 agreement, which (in its crudest interpretation) opens London Heathrow to all U.S. carriers in return for recognition of intra-Union seventh freedom rights for EU carriers, is much more *intuitively* the result of a 'balanced' negotiation than any of its conventional predecessors. As we will see in Chapter 6, the European Commission does not necessarily accept that an authentic balance can exist without

---

394. *Id.* at 2.
395. For example, *see* Airports Council International, North America, Comments on International Aviation Issues to Airline Commission, *in Airline Commission Documents*, Dkt. No. 000131 (Jun. 24, 1993), at 2; *Airline Commission Proceedings*, testimony of Diane Peterson, Airports Council International, North America (May 26, 1993), at 196. Former CAB chairman Marvin Cohen testified about a decades-long habit of seeing the U.S. Government as 'representing airlines at the bargaining table [and] looking at the American traveling public as the property of U.S. carriers.' *Airline Commission Proceedings*, testimony of Marvin S. Cohen, former Chairman, Civil Aeronautics Board (Jun. 24, 1993), at 12. There has undoubtedly always been a tension between the IATCA's broad emphasis on competition and the narrow focus of the actual negotiating conditions of bilateral air transport agreements. The IATCA does, however, require the Secretaries of State and Transportation to consult a wide range of air transportation constituencies (in addition to the air carriers) on both 'broad policy goals *and* individual negotiations.' 49 U.S.C. app. § 1502(c) (1980) (recodified as 49 U.S.C.A. § 40105(c) (West 2008)) (emphasis added). Named tribunes of the industry include airport operators, airline labor groups, consumer interest groups, travel agents, and tour organizers. *See id.*
396. *See Airline Commission Proceedings*, remarks of Judge Abraham Sofaer, Chairman, International Issues Team (Jul. 19, 1993), at 406-07.

further progress on abolition of the nationality/cabotage rules, but in fact the first stage agreement allowed the U.S. Government for the first time to approximate, if not literally to achieve, the balance of economic opportunities for its carriers that IATCA requires and that was largely unattainable under the more modest directory of strictly bilateral agreements that preceded the 2007 breakthrough.[397]

Even if U.S. officials were not ready to acknowledge explicitly the long shadow of the IATCA in their negotiations with the EC, they were still forced to operate within the boundaries of the IATCA's legislative encoding of the mercantilist view of air transport that has been critical to the functioning of the Chicago bilateral system. As in all prior open skies negotiations, therefore, U.S. negotiators were using the negotiating process strategically as a way to secure competitive advantages for U.S. carriers against foreign airlines.[398] But, without a U.S.

---

397. Again, it seems safe to suggest that the benefits to the 'traveling public,' as mentioned in the IATCA, were assumed to be incidental to the benefits secured for U.S. carriers. That there are tensions created by the IATCA's uncertain blending of protectionist and liberalizing language is plain from Airline Commission testimony. Captain J. Randolph Babbitt, then President of the Air Line Pilots Association, confronted U.S. Department of Transportation aviation negotiators at the Airline Commission with the consummate diplomatic paradox that lay at the heart of open skies. As Babbitt noted, the 1992 open skies agreement with the Netherlands implemented several IATCA liberalizing goals, including unrestricted U.S. gateway access for the large Dutch carrier KLM. In return, as one DOT panelist conceded in reaction to knavish prodding by Babbitt's fellow Commissioner, former CAB Chairman John Robson, U.S. carriers won the right 'to go anywhere in the Netherlands.' *Airline Commission Proceedings*, testimony of John E. Robson, former Chairman, Civil Aeronautics Board; *see also* testimony of Paul L. Gretch, Director, DOT Office of International Aviation (May 26, 1993), at 94-95. Babbitt queried how this manifestly imbalanced negotiation, an exchange of hugely disparate airspaces, could nevertheless achieve the IATCA's protectionist goals, which are highlighted in the statute, of 'profitability' and 'an equal footing' for U.S. carriers. *Airline Commission Proceedings*, testimony of Capt. J. Randolph Babbitt, President, Air Line Pilots Association (May 26, 1993), at 75-76. The DOT's response, articulated by Gretch, demonstrated the muddled policy analysis that the IATCA made necessary. While asserting that Section 17 of the IATCA provided only 'fairly lofty guidance in individual cases,' Gretch nonetheless took refuge in the empirical facts that a weakened U.S. carrier, Northwest, had been helped by the code-sharing elements of the agreement, while underserved U.S. communities might receive new KLM service. On the other hand, the rest of Gretch's reply, ascending once more to the 'lofty,' sought to place the Dutch agreement in a 'broader perspective,' as a means to support the so-called 'encirclement strategy.' *See supra* in the main text. *See also Airline Commission Proceedings*, testimony of Paul L. Gretch, Director, DOT Office of International Aviation (May 26, 1993), at 77-80. Gretch faced an insurmountable task in expounding the true premise of the Dutch agreement to the Commissioners: the vocabulary of the IATCA, with its apparent emphasis on a piecemeal doling-out of improved gateway access while 'managing' the negotiation to preserve U.S. carriers' market share and profitability, has been wholly inadequate to describe or embrace the task of assessing the *network* consequences of initiatives like the U.S./Netherlands open skies pact. The rhetoric of the IATCA, its required search for 'balance,' or even for a 'pragmatic' compromise, is the rhetoric of bilateralism. The true value of the Dutch agreement, as Gretch later admitted almost casually, was the enhancement of fifth freedom rights (as well as alliance code-share opportunities) for U.S. carriers *beyond* Dutch territory, enabling them to use Amsterdam, for instance, as an efficient collection-point, or 'hub,' for onward traffic.

398. *See* Kaplan, *supra* note 159, at 13.

readiness – or, more accurately, legal ability – to renounce the nationality and cabotage principles, an open skies policy framed only within the IATCA's inconsistent embrace of both liberalization and protectionism will not break away from a perceived disequilibrium (encouraged by the IATCA's language) between the rights that can be granted under open skies agreements and the need to secure 'comparable benefits' for U.S. carriers.[399]

b   *The Risks of More Bilateralism*

In sum, therefore, U.S. confidence in its present open skies initiative is surely misplaced. Even though the refurbished campaign eventually produced a first stage U.S./EC air transport agreement in 2007, the historical evidence shows irrefutably that governments will ultimately feel little hesitation in denouncing or renegotiating their bilateral commitments should their national carriers' market shares fall into jeopardy or, as in the case of a future British suspension of rights awarded under the 2007 agreement, should the United States fail to deliver the 'balance' which the European Commission and certain EU Member States appear to find missing from the first stage agreement. As former CAB chairman Marvin Cohen cautioned the Airline Commission, the limits of the bilateral system, and of its artificial imperatives of 'balance' and 'equality' in air transport negotiations, appear to have been reached.[400]

If those principles are pursued into the second stage of U.S./EC negotiations, whichever side asserts them, they will assuredly block any substantial progress. The international aviation system is poised for a radical new U.S. initiative, just as it was after the British denounced Bermuda I in 1976 and the Carter Administration responded by inventing the open skies liberalization strategy. A proposal for a dramatic new multilateral initiative, which will reconceptualize the interpretation of 'balance' in the IATCA principles and in the exhausted policy of open skies, will be presented in Chapter 6.[401]

---

399. *See, e.g., Airline Commission Proceedings*, remarks of Judge Abraham Sofaer, Chairman, International Aviation Issues Team (Jun. 15, 1993), at 65-68.

400. *Airline Commission Proceedings*, testimony of Marvin S. Cohen, former Chairman, Civil Aeronautics Board (Jun. 24, 1993), at 31-32. Cohen gave as an example of dissonance between market forces and bilateral open skies agreements the 1980 U.S./Thailand bilateral, which the Thai Government eventually denounced when U.S. carriers developed six times as much capacity as the Thai flag carrier. *See id.* at 31. Just as with the EU Member States, however, aeropolitical and aeroeconomic changes transformed the Thai view of open skies: in 2005, the U.S. and Thailand signed an open skies air services agreement. *See* Press Release, U.S. Department of State, U.S. Signs Open Skies Aviation Agreement with Thailand, 2005/857 (Sept. 12, 2005). Thailand has become an export-driven economy (which led to an all-cargo open skies agreement in 2003), and has significantly expanded its tourist industry (leading to passenger open skies). *See* Norman Y. Mineta, U.S. Secretary of Transportation, Remarks to the American Chamber of Commerce, Bangkok, Thailand (Apr. 18, 2005) (noting Thailand's ambition to become a full regional aviation hub to serve its cargo export and tourism industries).

401. The bilateral ethos, indeed, has always assumed the distribution of airline routes and rights as an end in itself. Yet the task ahead for U.S. negotiators is not merely to trade airline services, but to create the infrastructure on which the rest of trade rides. One witness at the Airline

IV   A CRITIQUE OF U.S. FEDERAL AIRLINE
              DEREGULATION

A   Lessons from the U.S. Experience

The last two Parts traced the evolution of the legal and policy foundations of U.S. airline deregulation. From tentative beginnings as a project for regulatory reform, the U.S. airline industry saw the emergence of a full-fledged withdrawal of official rate, capacity, and route controls. There followed an ambitious (if flawed) attempt to implant similar reforms in the *dirigiste* international air transport system. Yet the true deregulatory enterprise has been stymied, both domestically and internationally, by persistent fidelity to the Chicago system doctrines of cabotage and airline nationality. Even U.S. domestic airline deregulation, despite the roll of trumpets in 1978, never broke free of the Chicago interdictions on foreign airline competition in domestic inter-city markets and foreign ownership of U.S. air transport providers. The plurilateral proposal in Chapter 6, therefore, implicates an organic link between domestic and international deregulation: the abolition of these anachronistic controls inside the U.S. federal system is connected to a genuine liberalization of the major international markets served by U.S. carriers.

In proposing a deregulated international system that 'looks like America,' it is intimated that U.S. airline deregulation (and its EC derivative, for that matter) may be worthy of emulation. On this question, some preliminary contextual observations are appropriate. The paradigm shift toward U.S. airline deregulation in the 1970s assumed certain fundamental economic dogmas: that the existing system of statutory regulation was inefficient, that it protected incumbent air carriers against a mass of potential new entrants, and that the free marketplace would generate an efficiency that would drive fares down.[402] A similar evaluation can be made of today's international regulatory system: broadly speaking, fares remain relatively high, service opportunities too limited, and inefficient carriers too protected by direct government subsidy or indirect government economic patronage. Is a similar 'paradigm shift' justified at the international level? Or, as some commentators have argued, has the U.S. deregulatory experience, including successive rounds of wrenching carrier losses and bankruptcies since 2001, damaged the case for unleashing free market competition among the world's airlines?

Commission hearings drew a striking analogy with the construction of the interstate highway system, postulating that

[I]f we had tried to build [that system] by letting each two communities negotiate a bilateral between them, there would have been a lot of equity issues that each city would have had with the other city [and] we never would have gotten an interstate highway system which has created wealth. The rest of . . . trade rides on that infrastructure, and creates wealth for the entire economy.

Airline Commission Proceedings, remarks of Commissioner Charles M. Barclay, President, American Association of Airport Executives; Staff Member, Aviation Subcomm. of the U.S. Senate Comm. on Commerce, Science, and Transportation, 1977-1983 (May 24, 1993), at 212.

402.   *See* Submission of Federal Express Corp. to the Airline Commission, *in Airline Commission Documents*, Dkt. No. 000143 (Jun. 29, 1993), at 1. Little remembered today, the deregulation of the scheduled airline passenger industry was preceded by the Airline Cargo Deregulation

While economic analysis is outside the scope of this study,[403] advocacy of a plurilateral deregulated airline market would be incomplete without an analysis of some critical issues of competition law and policy presented by the structural dynamics of the U.S. airline system after 1978. Some of these canonical features emerged through industry innovation; some were directly the responsibility of government policymakers. All have allegedly created impediments to the 'maximization' of reliance on competitive forces that the ADA/IATCA statutes were supposed to herald. It is important in this discussion, however, also to evaluate these alleged 'impediments' in the broader context of a new internationalized industry, in which U.S. airlines would engage their foreign competitors on both domestic and international routes. Finally, as the aeroeconomic hazards of oil price rises and recession continue to threaten the U.S. airline industry, it is important, also, to evaluate some of the arguments for 'reregulation' that have lately crept back into U.S. public policy discourse.

B   Securing Competition in a Deregulated Airline Industry

1   The Structural Unpredictability of U.S. Deregulation

The U.S. domestic experiment, looking back after three decades, held many surprises. While consumer welfare has undoubtedly been enhanced,[404] only in the last ten years or so has the entrepreneurial spirit that launched Ryanair and easyJet in Europe been reflected – though not in such a pronounced utilitarian style – by a clutch of new U.S. low-cost point-to-point carriers alongside Southwest Airlines, the Ur-practitioner of this business model.[405] To that limited extent, the hopes of would-be deregulators in the 1970s that the California intrastate point-to-point

---

Act of 1977, Pub. L. No. 95-163, 91 Stat. 1284 (signed into law on Nov. 9, 1977) (recodified as various sections of 49 U.S.C.).

403. *But see, e.g.*, Fred L. Smith, Jr. & Braden Cox, *Airline Deregulation*, in The Concise Encyclopedia of Economics, <http://www.econlib.org/library/CEETitles.html>.

404. *See* GAO, *Re-regulating the Airline Industry, supra* note 26, at 18-19 (concluding, based on analysis of DOT ticketing data from 1980 to 2005, that there had been 'substantial decreases' in median fares since 1980, with an overall decrease of nearly 40% for median roundtrip fares since that time; the advantage was more marked for passengers flying long distances or in medium to large markets – in part because regulation had encouraged cross-subsidization of shorter routes by these markets).

405. The so-called LCC (low-cost carrier) business model may be inherently finite: of the approximately 50,000 city-pairs in the United States, only 8% generate enough traffic to warrant point-to-point service. That 8%, however, accounts for almost 80% of airline passengers. The LCCs 'have figured this out and are "cherry-picking" the legacy carriers' networks with their fleets of narrow-body 737s and smaller regional jets.' Boston Consulting Group, *New Metrics for Market Share: Lessons from the Airlines*, at 5, Opportunities for Action in Consumer Markets (Feb. 2006) (noting that, by 2007, 80% of all passengers could choose to fly an LCC on a given route – almost the same number of passengers in the city-pairs that offer point-to-point service). But, as observers, including Tom Haughey, Director of the Dublin Airport Authority, are increasingly questioning: is the U.S. domestic airline industry experiencing aggregate growth or just a redistribution of existing (or, at best, marginally incremental) traffic, as a result of LCC incursions?

model would add competitive spice to the post-regulation industry have been partially realized.[406] This more differentiated structure, which includes low-cost subsidiaries spun off from the big incumbent carriers,[407] has emerged despite the obvious concentration of the marketplace (after a brief burst of entrepreneurial initiative in the early 1980s)[408] that followed deregulation.

But recent differentiation does not necessarily mean that the industry is substantially less concentrated.[409] In 1978, the top eight U.S. airlines were all full-service carriers serving both domestic and international routes. These large 'legacy' carriers (so-called because they predate the rise of low-cost carriers except Southwest Airlines)[410] – American, United, Delta, Continental, Northwest, Trans World Airlines, Pan Am, and Eastern Air Lines – commanded an 80.9% share of total U.S. revenue passenger miles.[411] That figure climbed to near 94% in 1994 (by which time USAir and Southwest Airlines had supplanted Pan Am and Eastern, both defunct), while the market share for the top three airlines (American, United, and Delta) reached almost 58%.[412] In 2007, after an unprecedented multi-year economic battering of the legacy carriers, the top eight U.S. airlines (now comprising American, United, Southwest, Delta, US Airways,[413] Continental, Northwest, and new low-cost carrier, JetBlue) commanded 77.8% of total U.S. revenue passenger miles, while American, United, and Delta still retained almost 40% of the

---

406. *See* KLM, *Submission to Airline Commission, in Airline Commission Documents,* Dkt. No. 000384 (Jun. 10, 1993), at 2.

407. *See infra* note 433 (discussing broad lack of success of these efforts).

408. As seen earlier, *see supra* note 72, forecasts of 100 to 200 new airlines were routinely made before deregulation occurred.

409. As of 2008, however, the large network carriers were more troubled by excess capacity than by concentration. According to a Sept. 2008 IATA analysis, passenger demand growth fell to 1.9% between Jul. 2007 and Jul. 2008 while capacity increased by 3.8%. *See* Press Release, IATA, Airlines to Lose US$5.2 Billion in 2008 – Slowing Demand and High Oil to Blame, No. 41 (Sept. 3, 2008). Though service cuts have not been keeping with demand, according to *The Wall Street Journal's* travel web-log, U.S. airlines planned to dramatically cut domestic capacity during the fourth-quarter of 2008: AirTran Airways (7-8%); Alaska (5%); American (12%); Continental (10%); Delta (13%); JetBlue (10%); Northwest (7-8%); United (16%); US Airways (6-8%). *See* Posting of Matt Phillips to The Middle Seat Terminal, <http://blogs.wsj.com/middleseat/2008/09/03/after-labor-day-a-look-at-airline-capacity-cuts/> (Sept. 3, 2008, 10:00 EST).

410. Legacy airlines are considered to be those carriers which were in operation before deregulation and whose goal is to provide service from 'anywhere to everywhere.' GAO, *Commercial Aviation: Legacy Airlines Must Further Reduce Costs to Restore Profitability,* at 5, GAO-04-836 (Aug. 2004) [hereinafter GAO, *Legacy Airlines*]. Thus, these airlines support large, complex hub-and-spoke operations with thousands of employees and hundreds of aircraft. *See id.*

411. *See* GAO, *Airline Competition – Strategies for Addressing Financial and Competitive Problems,* GAO-RCED-93-52 (Kenneth M. Mead, Director, Transp. Issues, Resources, Community, and Economic Development Division), *in Airline Commission Documents,* Dkt. No. 000045 (Feb. 18, 1993), at 5 [hereinafter GAO Submission].

412. The next largest carrier was America West, which had about half the total market share of Southwest Airlines. Industry market share is again expressed here in revenue passenger miles.

413. US Airways' market share now includes the contribution of its 2005 merger partner, the former America West.

total. Factoring out point-to-point carriers Southwest and JetBlue, the legacy carriers still held 65.7% of the U.S. *domestic* market.[414]

The evolving U.S. market structure reflects some retrenchment by the legacy carriers, but it is also reflects their durability in the marketplace. Other than Southwest, which has offered both direct and multinodal point-to-point ('bus service') routes since deregulation began, the only low-cost carrier to break into the top tier in 30 years of open competition is New York-based JetBlue.[415] As low-cost competition has diluted brand premiums and helped to commodify air travel, driving down industry revenues in an era of Internet price transparency, what has accounted for the staying power of the legacy carriers?[416] To answer that question, a long view is needed. Looking back to the economic arguments that presaged deregulation, the focus on *intrastate* routes (such as California) did enable observers to understand the general price reductions that the end of the CAB's artificial uniformity would make possible. What they missed, however, was how deregulation would allow firms to restructure their operations to create new service offerings and marketing practices that would raise the barriers to new entry and pose an unanticipated challenge to the real-world performance of the 'contestability' theory.[417]

---

414. For the most up-to-date figures, *see* the U.S. DOT's Bureau of Transportation Statistics, <http://transtats.bts.gov/>. The next largest carrier is Alaska Airlines, which has about two-thirds of the total domestic share of number eight carrier JetBlue. *See id.*

415. Note that, in contrast to 'no frills' low-cost carriers such as Ireland's Ryanair, JetBlue has not foregone comfort features such as reclining seats, head rests, window blinds, or snack and beverage service. *See* Cath Urquhart, *Ryanair Says That Sick Bags on No-Frills Flights Will be Handed Out Only on Demand, So Do Not Try to be Ill When Staff are Busy*, TIMES (London), Feb. 21, 2004, at 16; Ben Webster, *Airline Draws Bottom Line on Fatter Passengers*, TIMES (London), Feb. 25, 2004, at 1.

416. This is not to suggest that the legacy carriers have not seen a sustained decline in market share after 2000, only that the present iteration of low-cost carrier competition has once again not caused a major displacement of carrier rankings and market presence. The fall in demand, particularly from premium-fare business travelers, caused huge dislocations in the cost structures of the legacy carriers and forced some of them into bankruptcy. Their rebuilding of their cost structures (including shedding pension liabilities and terminating expensive labor contracts through bankruptcy), added to the inherent advantages of incumbency discussed later in this Part, suggest that they will ultimately contain the low-cost challenge. *See* GAO, *Re-regulating the Airline Industry, supra* note 26, at 16-18.

417. This is an appropriate point to mention a contrarian view on the nature of 'barriers to entry' as a matter of general antitrust policy. *See generally* DOMINICK T. ARMENTANO, ANTITRUST AND MONOPOLY: ANATOMY OF A POLICY FAILURE (1990). Armentano argues that 'barriers to entry,' so-called, are simply 'market efficiencies' that serve ultimately to improve consumer welfare. 'When and if dominant firms failed to provide such improvements, rivals would inevitably enter markets and compete. Thus, superior economic performance ought not to be attacked prematurely in the name of removing "barriers" to competition.' *Id.* at 1. Not surprisingly, Armentano's view of the market behavior of large corporations is benign: 'Large corporations in open markets – regardless of their size – must earn their market positions each day through voluntary exchange. They are continually accountable to consumers and owner-investors, and their fortunes depend upon their competitive performance.' *Id.* at 277. While I would dispute what appears to be Armentano's unconditional embrace of Smithian principles, and his confidence that the market will eventually overwhelm all positions of economic power, his argument does suggest the need for a more nuanced analysis of barriers to entry. In the

Thus, the prognosticators did not foresee the emergence of hub-and-spoke air-line networks, computer-driven reservations systems, domestic (and even global) code-sharing alliances,[418] consumer loyalty programs such as the 'frequent flier' concept, or a market for landing slots at the nation's busiest airports.[419] All of these market features reveal deregulation as a protean concept, where the ingenuity of the airline entrepreneurs remains pivotal but where competition policy must always hold the ring. What observers also could not have imagined, however, was the degree to which antitrust enforcement policy, and in particular the application of the CAB/DOT special merger review procedures (artificially preserved until 1989 by the CAB sunset legislation),[420] could systematically approve intercarrier combinations that posed a clear risk of anticompetitive effects. At a time when some industry leaders identify excess capacity rather than excess concentration as the leading market weakness,[421] the lessons of that laissez-faire era should not be forgotten.[422]

---

airline industry, for example (as discussed in the main text), computerized yield management technology and the rise of the Internet have created a remarkably transparent system of price information that, in helping to commodify air travel, has undoubtedly diluted the brand premium of the legacy carriers. Armentano also appreciates, I believe correctly, the elemental failure of antitrust law to understand competition as a *process*, not an equilibrium condition, and the instability of synchronic market structures. *Id.* at 2. And he continues to criticize what he sees as antitrust's misconceived stasis. *See* DOMINICK T. ARMENTANO, ANTITRUST: THE CASE FOR REPEAL 53 (3d ed. 2007) (arguing that 'the actual competitive process is one of discovery and adjustment; it is not a static state of affairs.... [t]he economic problem is not one of allocating resources efficiently when everything is known and constant, but of learning how to allocate and reallocate resources in an uncertain and changing world'). In any event, the search for clear and simple antitrust methodology continues. *See* Michael S. Jacobs, *The New Sophistication in Antitrust*, 79 MINN. L. REV. 1 (1994) (criticizing the emergence of an empirical doctrine of super-rational corporate sophistication, transcending traditional assumptions of uniform rationality – for example, profit-maximization – as a basis for evaluating corporate actions in antitrust cases).

418. These alliances and their competitive effects are discussed *supra* Chapter 3, Part VIII.
419. *See generally* GAO Submission, *supra* note 411, at 4.
420. *See supra* Part II(D).
421. *See supra* note 409.
422. This admonition holds even deeper resonance for an industry that may have begun a new round of consolidation among its biggest carriers. *See, e.g.*, Lou Whiteman, *Strong Travel Demand Has Quelled the Urgency of Carrier Consolidation, But a Souring Economy Could Spur Deals*, DAILY DEAL, May 31, 2007 (discussing rumors surrounding potential suitors for Northwest Airlines, including a possible equity investment in Northwest and Delta Air Lines by their European SkyTeam alliance partner, Air France-KLM). In 2008, Northwest and Delta announced plans to merge. The deal quickly received approval from the European Commission. *See* Paulo Prada, *Delta's Purchase of Northwest is Cleared by EU Regulators*, WALL ST. J., Aug. 7, 2008, at B3. Following the close of a six-month investigation, the Department of Justice announced in October 2008 that the merger was likely to benefit U.S. consumers and not lessen competition. *See* Press Release, U.S. Dept. of Justice, Statement of the DOJ's Antitrust Division on Its Decision to Close Its Investigation, 08-963 (Oct. 29, 2008).

2   An Enduring Business Model: Complex, Costly Hub-and-Spoke Networks

The so-called 'hub-and-spoke' system has been described as a 'pure artifact of private regulation.'[423] As Professor Michael Levine has written, '[t]he word "hub" is virtually absent from pre-deregulation theoretical comment on the industry.'[424] Deregulation transformed the airline route maps of the major carriers from linear ('point-to-point') arrangements to 'hub-and-spoke' (or 'sunburst') networks that can converge and connect passengers arriving on subsidiary 'feeder' lines.[425] For a system of 25 cities, for example, point-to-point requires 300 roundtrips for complete coverage; hub-and-spoke requires only 24.[426] In an undistorted competitive system, hubbing conduces to efficient airport usage, improved scheduling, and better equipment deployment.[427] It allows frequent jet service in many city-pair markets where traffic density would not otherwise support it.[428]

---

423. Robert Kuttner, *Plane Truth: The Case for Re-Regulating Airlines*, NEW REPUBLIC, Jul. 17, 1989, at 21 & 23. *See also* the comments of industry gadfly Theodore P. Harris, in *In the Wake of Airline Deregulation: New Departures in Air Transportation Policy for the 21st Century, in Airline Commission Documents*, Dkt. No. 000302 (Oct. 29, 1992), at 5 (remarking that ['hub-and-spoke' systems] are hardly innovative – merely reincarnations of sixteenth century freight transportation systems. The initial objective of hub systems was survival in the early turbulence of deregulation. Today they provide market control and domination by *blocking out* competition, *tying up* gates and slots, and *controlling* feed through code-sharing' (emphasis in original)).

424. Levine, *Airline Competition, supra* note 67, at 413.

425. As seen earlier, under CAB regulation an airline could only expand its network by petitioning for authority to serve a new route. *See* analysis of CAB regulatory procedures, *supra* Part II(B). The major ('trunk') airlines served primarily transcontinental routes or north-south routes, and new route authority tended to be 'tacked on' to the end of an existing flight, creating multistop flights reminiscent of bus or train trips that make intermediate stops between origin and destination – a system that remains one of Southwest's route models.

426. *See* ALFRED E. KAHN, LESSONS FROM DEREGULATION: TELECOMMUNICATIONS AND AIRLINES AFTER THE CRUNCH 52 n.13 (2004) (briefly illustrating the workings of the hub-and-spoke system). In general, hub-and-spoke reduces the number of roundtrips by the number of cities in the network divided by two. *See* Economic Strategy Institute, *The Future of the Airlines, in Airline Commission Documents*, Dkt. No. 001150 (Jul. 20, 1993), at 6 [hereinafter Economic Strategy Institute].

427. The ultimate 'fly-anywhere' deployment of airlines would be a system having nonstop flights from each airport to every other airport, the so-called 'kaleidoscope' network. Given the wide variations in consumer demand, such a system would be highly inefficient. Even if the airspace and airports could support tens of thousands of additional flights, 'the large unit costs associated with flying small aircraft in congested space would raise fares to unpalatable levels.' Stephen Still, *Fortress Defense*, AIRLINE BUS., Sept. 1, 2002, at 97. The point-to-point model also generates certain efficiencies through increased aircraft utilization, lower costs from serving less-congested airports, and avoiding aircraft waiting on the ground as part of a hub bank. *See* DEUTSCHE BANK, THE FUTURE OF THE HUB STRATEGY IN THE AIR TRANSPORT INDUSTRY 5 (2006) (noting that point-to-point service disfavors 'bundling' of traffic).

428. *See generally* Kelleher, *supra* note 71, at 316. *See* Still, *supra* note 427, at 97 (stating that the U.S. domestic market features 115,000 origin-and-destination pairs, but that only 18% of these markets are large enough to support nonstop service (at least 75 passengers per day)).

The hubbing innovation had a more problematical side, however, both for the carriers which operate them and for the passengers who use them. For the airlines – the network legacy carriers – hubs naturally require a very high degree of complexity and high costs to maintain the service.[429] For travelers, fare premiums prompted ascription of the epithet 'fortress' to describe some of the larger complexes. Levine, an apostle of deregulation who moved somewhat toward apostasy in later years, noted the huge competitive effort that would be required to displace the incumbent (or even to attempt duopolistic cohabitation with the incumbent) at a large hub, dominated by a national brand airline. Levine argued that 'a large, better-known, multi-hub incumbent can attract more traffic at any given price level than [any] new entrant.'[430]

While the effect of their operational and marketing leverage at hubs remains relevant,[431] the severe demand shocks that hit the legacy carriers after 2000 caused some shifting in the industry's profit-earning structure toward the so-called

---

(In Europe, Still notes, a similar market distribution exists, since only 15,000 of 110,000 O&D markets transport more than 75 passengers per day.)

429.   *See* DEUTSCHE BANK, *supra* note 427, at 5. The legacy carriers are constantly seeking to tweak their hubs' efficiency output and also to rationalize hub usage. *See* Philipp Goedeking et al., *Breaking the Bank*, AIRLINE BUS., Sept. 1, 2003, at 93; Philipp Goedeking et al., *Peak Performance*, AIRLINE BUS., Jun. 1, 2004, at 68 (analyzing American Airlines' decision to spread out flights at major hubs during the day instead of arranging them in the 'peaked' connecting banks used previously – increasing aircraft, employee, and gate utilization but with some sacrifice of connectivity – and how that practice has spread to Europe); *see also* Richard Pinkham, *Capped Hubs*, AIRLINE BUS., Jun. 1, 2003, at 57 (predicting vulnerability of some of U.S. Midwest's 14 connecting complexes for traffic between the two coasts).

430.   Levine, *Airline Competition, supra* note 67, at 445. This does not mean, however, that better-known incumbents could not compete vigorously against *each other*, either at inter-hub level or simply by entering a rival's hub and connecting it to an established hub network. *See* Economic Strategy Institute, *supra* note 426, at 8. Hubs that are a thousand miles apart can compete for connecting ('flow') traffic. For example, Dallas-Fort Worth, Denver, Salt Lake City, Phoenix, and Chicago compete for much of the same coast-to-coast traffic. Levine's sentiments continue to echo. *See* Still, *supra* note 427, at 98 (noting how low-cost carriers 'avoid fights with entrenched majors').

431.   The fortress hub phenomenon is still manifest at highly-concentrated legacy hubs such as Delta's at Cincinnati, where DOT figures support a continuing 'hub effect' of higher fares. *See* U.S. DOT, Office of Aviation Analysis, *Domestic Airline Fares Consumer Report* (Feb. 2007) (ranking fare premium data across 100 U.S. airports, and showing Cincinnati as the highest-premium facility with a 40-68% fare premium and with no access to low-cost competition in all short-haul and long-haul markets). In addition to Cincinnati, Charlotte, Minneapolis, and Pittsburgh rank high on the DOT's list of hub premium airports. The DOT has repeatedly excoriated the network carriers for maintaining hub premiums ('pockets of pain') in the absence of price discipline from low-cost competitors. *See* U.S. DOT, Office of the Assistant Secretary for Aviation and International Affairs, *Domestic Aviation Competition Series: Dominated Hub Fares* (Jan. 2001) [hereinafter U.S. DOT, *Dominated Hub Fares*] (rejecting network carriers' claims that high fares at hubs were the result of fewer discretionary travelers, higher quality of service, higher costs of serving business passengers, and the unrealistic expectations of the 'Southwest effect' – the depressive effect of Southwest's entry into a market on that market's fare levels – rather than sheer market power). Premiums, however, are a natural result of the barriers to competitive entry at hubs. *See* Still, *supra* note 427, at 98.

Southwest model[432] – nimbler point-to-point services in high-density markets that showed significant cost advantages over the legacy carriers' expensive network infrastructure and high labor costs.[433] To the extent that the low-cost model now claims 30% of so of the domestic marketplace (although Southwest, itself a 'legacy' low-cost carrier, accounts for a large portion of that figure),[434] this result is precisely because low-cost carriers target high-density routes[435] – including,

---

432. The U.S. Department of Transportation maintains that there is a 'Southwest effect,' whereby the entry of Southwest Airlines into a market 'virtually always' has a profound depressive effect on prices and simultaneously boosts traffic. DOT, *Dominated Hub Fares, supra* note 431, at 10. *See also* U.S. DOT, Office of Aviation and International Affairs, *Southwest Expands to Philadelphia – Third Quarter 2004*, Domestic Aviation Competition Issues Brief Number 26 (noting, *inter alia*, an 80% drop in fares and tenfold increase in traffic in Southwest's three largest Philadelphia short-haul markets after service began in 2004). Southwest's own explanation of the 'Southwest Effect' appeared on a website it set up to challenge the restrictions on service at Dallas Love Field airport. *See* <http://www.setlovefree.com> (now defunct).

433. *See* GAO, *Legacy Airlines, supra* note 410, at 47-48 (suggesting, on present evidence, that the recent low-cost incursion may represent some of the 'most significant changes' in industry structure since airline deregulation was introduced). *But see* Still, *supra* note 427 (indicating that over 30% of Southwest's traffic is 'connecting'). The legacy carriers themselves spun off a number of low-cost subsidiaries, but making two organizations operate independently and successfully under a single corporate umbrella has proven difficult to achieve. The last of these experiments, United's 'Ted,' was shut down in 2008. *See* Press Release, United Airlines, United Streamlines Operations to Compete in Unprecedented Fuel Environment (Jun. 4, 2008) (stating United's plans to eliminate Ted and reconfigure its 56 aircraft to begin operating United services in 2009). *See also* Peter J. Howe, *Swan Song*, BOSTON GLOBE, Apr. 5, 2006, at C1 (describing demise of Delta's 'Song' offshoot, its second attempt at a spin-off discount airline); *see also* David Field, *Trustseeker*, AIRLINE BUS., Aug.1, 2006 (indicating that Song's contribution to Delta was more stylistic than substantive). *See also* United Airlines, *Investor Briefing* (2007) (presenting Ted as an all-coach carrier, designed for leisure markets, that would fit into a network product structure that includes premium transcontinental service between New York and Los Angeles/San Francisco and more typical first class/coach services).

434. *See supra* text accompanying notes 411 & 412.

435. *See* GAO, *Legacy Airlines, supra* note 410, at 40-41 & 44 (discussing how low-cost carriers have become effective, and sometimes dominant, competitors in nearly 85% of the 5,000 largest city-pair markets in the United States). Point-to-point travel is more efficient on very high-volume city-pairs where there is enough business to support frequent jet service. Southwest has captured high shares on high-volume short-haul routes such as Phoenix/Los Angeles. The problem is that high-density point-to-point routes (such as New York/Los Angeles) are already highly competitive and these markets, which are finite, have largely matured. *See* Economic Strategy Institute, *supra* note 426, at 8. Arguments have been made, for example, that Virgin America, by starting transcontinental service connecting points like San Francisco/New York, is targeting markets that already have robust competition. *See* Press Release, Virgin America, Virgin America Identifies First Six Destinations, Announces Further 40 Cities Under Consideration (Jan. 31, 2007). New and creative business models, however, surface all the time. Allegiant, a new-entrant carrier, has developed a niche by linking smaller cities, where it is often the only large-jet service, to leisure destinations such as Las Vegas and Orlando. *See* Allegiant Travel Company, *Investor Presentation*, Merrill Lynch Global Transportation Conference (Jun. 18, 2008) (claiming to 'leverage otherwise "unwanted" customers, cities, and assets'). Another niche entrant is ExpressJet, which operates point-to-point 'regional jet' service to medium-size communities that have lost service from larger carriers or that have

since 2003, some U.S. transcontinental services.[436] They compete effectively in, and sometimes dominate, fewer markets than the legacy carriers,[437] but those markets tend to be denser and more profitable than many of the legacy airlines' 'hub markets,' *i.e.*, markets where travel originates or terminates in one of the legacy airline's hubs, and where those airlines still show dominance.[438] Where the legacy and low-cost carriers do compete (at least at the city, if not the airport, level), one procompetitive consequence has been prevention of the kinds of fare maintenance that can occur when major carriers stay out of each other's dominant hubs or do not seek to undercut their competitors at shared hubs.[439]

Nonetheless, travelers appear to accept both hub and point-to-point models and there is no economic reason why the two systems cannot coexist in the future.[440] An escape valve for large-hub legacy incumbents – where the existence

---

service only into major hubs. *See* David Field, *ExpressJet Strays into Scheduled Territory*, AIRLINE BUS., Feb. 19, 2007 (contrasting ExpressJet's strategy with the failed attempt by former United Airlines feed carrier Independence Air to operate a regional jet hub operation at United's Dulles hub; United quickly replaced Independence with other feeders and the smaller airline could not match the marketing and pricing power of United).

436.   *See* GAO, *Legacy Airlines, supra* note 410, at 42 (mentioning service by JetBlue from Fort Lauderdale to Long Beach and by Southwest between Baltimore and California, both inaugurated in 2003).

437.   For an interesting attempt to categorize U.S. low-cost carriers, both successful and unsuccessful, by their product and route structures and relationship with labor, *see* Nancy Brown Johnson, *Airline Industry Council Report, Low-Cost Competition in the United States, in* LABOR & EMPLOYMENT RELATIONS ASSOCIATION, PROCEEDINGS OF THE 58TH ANNUAL MEETING 69 (2006) (noting that the two most successful U.S. LCCs, AirTran and Southwest, have contrasting business models for challenging the hub system – AirTran has some hub activities (*e.g.*, Atlanta), whereas Southwest operates a more pure-form point-to-point system that favors secondary airports but with high connectivity opportunities between flights; both have higher labor productivity than the legacy carriers, which allows them to charge lower fares but still yield a profit (although the gap has narrowed after recent legacy carrier bankruptcies)).

438.   'Dominance,' in this context, means a single airline carrying more than half of the total passenger traffic. *See* GAO, *Legacy Airlines, supra* note 410, at 45. Nearly 85% of dominated markets are dominated by legacy carriers, but the nature of hub-and-spoke networks tends to mean that their dominated markets are much less dense than markets where low-cost carriers dominate. *See id.* at 47.

439.   The primary reason why legacy carriers stay out of each others' hubs, however, is that there are very few markets with a strong enough local traffic base to support two hub carriers. Chicago's O'Hare is one of the handful of dual hubs in the United States, supporting both American Airlines and United Airlines. Southwest's Midway Airport operations appear to be providing some price discipline for the O'Hare majors, and indeed Southwest has been recently pushing aggressively into dominant hubs of legacy carriers at Philadelphia (US Airways), Dulles International (United Airlines), and Denver (also United). The U.S. Department of Transportation's Bureau of Transportation Statistics, incidentally, classifies U.S. hubs as large, medium, and small. *See* U.S. DOT, Bureau of Transportation Statistics, *Air Traffic Hubs 2008*, <http://www.bts.gov/programs/geographic_information_services/maps/hub_maps/2008/pdf/2008_Hubs.pdf>.

440.   *See* DEUTSCHE BANK, *supra* note 427, at 5, suggesting that the hub-and-spoke strategy is 'widely accepted' by customers as providing the clear advantage of a variety of connections, while the low-cost point-to-point segment, which is described as a 'market niche,' generates extra demand through lower fares.

of the hub-and-spoke infrastructure will always provide network advantages – continues to be the internationalization of traffic flow. As discussed in Chapter 3, the desire of carriers to increase traffic through their networks (thereby adding 'spokes' to an existing hub) motivated the development of strategic alliances with foreign carriers to create a kind of *ersatz* 'online' (single-carrier) service.[441] These alliances of convenience, which seek to elude the fine print of the cabotage/nationality restrictions through code-share strategies and other cooperative arrangements, achieved their *ne plus ultra* in the KLM/Northwest agreement discussed at various places in this study.[442] As considered previously, the cost structure of the point-to-point model has tended to militate against its transferability to long-haul service, particularly for the premium traveler.[443]

3   CRS: Adjusting to a Post-Regulatory Environment

Hubbing was a logistical reconfiguration that *might* have been predicted; the technological marvel of CRS could not.[444] The nature of allegedly competition-

---

441. *See* Kaplan, *supra* note 159, at 5; *see also* Deutsche Bank, *supra* note 427, at 6 (again, noting customer acceptance of the network effects of hub-and-spoke in international air transport; the members of the Star Alliance, for example, fly to almost 850 cities in over 150 countries via their interconnected hubs – 'in a pure-play point-to-point system, it would not be economically feasible to offer customers such a comprehensive range of options').

442. As airline network consultant Stephen Still has argued, *supra* note 427, at 99, '[c]arriers should not scrap their powerful, interconnected, worldwide networks. . . . These are their sources of strength.' For foreign competitors generally, the profile of the U.S. hub network is one of protected fiefdoms that pour passengers into the U.S. international route network. *See* British Airways, Toward Open Skies: British Airways' Views Concerning International Aviation Policy, *in* Airline Commission Documents, undocketed (May 21, 1993), at 2 [hereinafter BA, Toward Open Skies]. As noted, *supra* Chapter 3, Part VIII, the DOT's practice of awarding immunity to large carrier alliances has certainly depleted the pool of potential foreign challengers – and added a safety margin for the U.S. partners as they defend their domestic hubs. The elimination of the cabotage and nationality rules, in contrast, could stimulate a major procompetitive realignment of hub activity. *But see supra* note 409 (discussing the view of some legacy carriers that excess capacity, not rising concentration, is the primary cause of post-2000 industry weakness). Some U.S. hubs, however, have conspicuously declining capacity. *See* Gary Stoller, *St. Louis' Airports Aren't Too Loud: They're Too Quiet*, USA Today, Jan. 9, 2007, at 1B (reporting that St. Louis, the 18th largest U.S. metropolitan area, has excess capacity at Lambert Airport in the wake of American Airlines pulling down the hub it inherited from bankrupt Trans World Airlines; American already has a powerful Midwest hub at Chicago).

443. Indeed, there seems to be some evidence that the growth potential of the low-cost segment, in both the United States and Europe, is nearing maturity. *See* Deutsche Bank, *supra* note 427, at 7; Still, *supra* note 427, at 97 (observing that unless low-cost carriers such as Ryanair change their business models and confront major carriers in their hubs, their growth prospects 'are bound to be constrained').

444. For an analysis of the nature and function of CRS (now known by the acronym GDS, for 'global distribution systems'), and the persistence of a Chicago regulatory 'complex' that has led to *ex ante* regulatory controls over this sector of the air transport industry, *see supra* Chapter 3, Part VII(A). Where CRSs (at least initially) helped individual airlines to sell and manage their own seat inventory, the GDS consolidates information from many airlines,

reducing tactics in the CRS industry – preferential listing biases, travel agent incentivization, exclusive-use contracts, discriminatory participation fees[445] – was weighed by government agencies, in private litigation, and by commentators. As previously considered, certain structural features of the *parvenu* CRS industry incited an official regulatory response; others merely provoked continuing anxiety that competition might be harmed. The regulators focused principally on the 'architectural' components of reservations systems – how the information could be manipulated on a travel agent's desktop computer. The fact that the huge CRS internal inventory reduced to a mere screen load of information accentuated the importance of the priority criteria that would determine the order of appearance of flights.[446] To discourage preferential listing of the carrier-owner's flight schedules, CAB/DOT behavioral rules were promulgated in 1984 and 1992 to counter so-called 'display bias.'[447] (At the marketing level, to combat a perception that carrier-owners were selectively charging variable 'booking fees' matched to the perceived competitive threat posed by participating carriers to the 'host,' the rules also prohibited charging discriminatory booking fees among the participating airlines.[448])

Nevertheless, the system became such a moving target, with so much potential for novel forms of architectural bias, that the task of devising effective legislative controls was probably too formidable.[449] But it was not the unequal battle against

---

allowing travel agents, businesses, and individuals to shop in a single electronic marketplace. *See* Barry C. Smith et al., *E-Commerce and Operations Research in Airline Planning, Marketing, and Distribution*, 31 INTERFACES 37 (2001).

445. *See supra* Chapter 3, Part VII(A).

446. For a good, nontechnical description of computer reservations systems, *see* Chris Lyle, *Computer-Age Vulnerability In The International Airline Industry*, 54 J. AIR L. & COM. 161 (1988).

447. The Federal Aviation Act of 1958, Section 411 (unchanged by the Airline Deregulation Act) granted the Civil Aeronautics Board (and now the Department of Transportation, pursuant to the Civil Aeronautics Board Sunset Act of 1984, 49 U.S.C. app. § 1551(e)), the power to investigate problems and issue orders whenever it found an 'unfair or deceptive practice or an unfair method of competition in air transportation *or the sale of air transportation.*' 49 U.S.C. § 1381(a) (Supp. 1984-85) (recodified as 49 U.S.C.A. § 41712 (West 2008)) (emphasis added). The CAB put 'display bias' on the regulatory agenda. In its view, this kind of manipulation could distort consumer preference by occluding access to lower fares and by matching the consumer to less convenient connections. *See* C.A.B., REPORT TO CONGRESS ON AIRLINE COMPUTER RESERVATIONS SYSTEMS, *in* U.S. Cong., *Review of Airline Deregulation and Sunset of the Civil Aeronautics Board (Airline Computer Reservations Systems): Hearings Before the Subcomm. on Aviation of the House Comm. On Public Works and Transportation,* 98th Cong., 1st Sess. 73.

448. As a result, booking fees remained uniformly higher than a competitive market would have provided. On the ending of this practice, *see infra* note 450.

449. Derek Saunders, for example, described a built-in 'structural bias' that exists in any system, and which is determined by the choice of system parameters, but argued that even the choice of structural bias can be competitively motivated. Derek Saunders, *The Antitrust Implications of Computer Reservations Systems*, 51 J. AIR L. & COM. 157, 181 (1985). Even tardy information processing, though supposedly prohibited under the rules, could generate bias. Delaying input of information on fares, especially when a competitor's new low fare was involved, or displaying available flights as full, even neglecting to discontinue a competitor's low-fare offer so

bias that caused the end of CRS deregulation in 2004: rather, as noted in Chapter 3, it was the exogenous fact that U.S. airlines divested their ownership stakes in the leading systems.[450] Due to the ownership changes and technological changes in the CRS business (including the rise of competitive Internet sites and fares), the U.S. DOT concluded in 2004 that 'competition between the systems is no longer a direct form of airline competition.'[451]

Nonetheless, as considered in the earlier treatment of this subject in Chapter 3, computer reservations systems presented a challenging exercise in finding the correct regulatory tempo in an era of deregulation.[452] Although competitive

---

that extra, but unwanted, low-fare passengers are added, are all examples of database bias that probably could be pursued even within the CAB/DOT bias rules. *See Review of Airline Deregulation and Sunset of the Civil Aeronautics Board: Hearings before the Subcomm. on Aviation of the House Comm. on Public Works and Transportation,* 98th Cong., 1st Sess. 91 (1983); *see also* Saunders, *supra,* at 183; *see also* Submission of new entrant UltrAir to Airline Commission, *in Airline Commission Documents,* Dkt. No. 000523 (May 28, 1993), at para. 3 [hereinafter UltrAir Submission] (complaining of 'mistakes' or omissions in depiction of critical information).

450. *See* Computer Reservations System (CRS) Regulations: Final Rule, 14 C.F.R. Part 255, 69 Fed. Reg. 976, 977 (Jan. 7, 2004) [hereinafter CRS Final Rule] (finding that all of the U.S. airlines that had controlled a CRS had divested their ownership interests and, indeed, were selling an increasingly large share of their ticket inventory through Internet websites and a diminishing share through travel agencies). Given that 'the major predicate' for the CRS rules had always been airline control of systems, the airlines' divestiture of ownership had 'eliminated' that basis for the rules. *Id.* By action of the Department's so-called 'Final Rule,' all extant CRS regulation (including of display bias and of discriminatory booking fees) sunsetted after short transition periods. *See id.* at 977-78. For a discussion of the consequences for airlines and CRS vendors of the end of the discriminatory booking rule, *see* European Commission, *Consultation Paper on the Revision of Regulation 2299/89 on a Code of Conduct for Computerised Reservation Systems,* paras 51-60, Consultation Paper (2007) [hereinafter European Commission, *CRS Consultation Paper*] (noting that, with the introduction of free bargaining and the availability of alternative distribution outlets, booking fees paid by airlines had dropped 20-30%). Moreover, some of the largest travel agencies are now implementing technology that allows them to obtain bookings directly from the airlines, bypassing CRS channels altogether. *See id.* para. 59. *See also* CRS Final Rule, *supra,* at 1017 (finding that CRS 'no longer obtain contracts that will keep travel agents from using other electronic channels for obtaining information and making bookings').

451. *See id.* at 1010. Thus, in a real-world manifestation of Armentano's 'process' theory of market behavior, *see supra* note 417, the DOT found in 2004 that, 'while each [CRS] system still has market power over most airlines, this power is diminishing. Moreover, the record does not show a likelihood that the systems would use that power to distort airline competition except potentially through the sale of bias.' CRS Final Rule, *supra* note 450, at 977. *But see infra* note 461 (indicating that Canadian authorities chose to regulate against bias even while eliminating almost all other CRS regulatory surveillance). Among the market facts contributing to the decline of CRS market power is airlines' control over access to their webfares. *See* CRS Final Rule, *supra* note 450, at 989.

452. The CRS rules were interesting in that they represented an outcome where *behavioral* rules were chosen over *structural* relief (such as forced divestiture) as a mechanism for dealing with the competitive issues raised by the vertical integration of a firm with market power at one level of an industry into a second and otherwise competitive level of that industry. *See* the discussion in Lyle, *supra* note 446, at 175; *see also* Levine, *Airline Competition, supra* note 67, at 482. Ultimately, the market itself generated divestiture.

innovation may be dampened by excessive regulation, CRS so transformed the airline industry that the innovators evidently amassed a degree of market power that could threaten new competition.

On the other hand, there was merit in the major system owners' contention that their invention of the CRS, with all of its bias-inherency, should be treated simply as a valid competitive weapon by the large carriers who developed it, just as upstart new entrants use their low-cost, low-price profile as a competitive weapon against the incumbents.[453] Indeed, some commentators suggested that the compelled neutrality of the rules was wrongheaded, arguing that the best way to diminish the carrier-owners' appetites for awarding themselves the premier listings was to incentivize the owners by allowing rival carriers to bid against each other for those listings.[454] While the potential competitive barriers imposed by refusing to list, or de-listing, an airline (particularly a new entrant), deliberately 'mis'-listing its services, or (in the DOT's view) returning to past patterns of display bias,[455] will require the private and public antitrust watch to continue even after

---

453. *See, e.g., Airline Commission Proceedings,* testimony of Robert L. Crandall, President, American Airlines (Jun. 3, 1993), at 164-65 (specifically mentioning frequent flier programs as a valid form of 'major carrier' competition). *See also* the discussion of Dominick Armentano's view of barriers to entry, *supra* note 417.

454. *See* Donald J. Boudreaux & Jerome Ellig, *Beneficent Bias: The Case Against Regulating Airline Computerized Reservation Systems,* 57 J. Air. L. & Com. 567, 584-85 (1992). These authors also suspected (without empirical evidence) that display bias deception was unlikely given a 'highly competitive' travel agent industry and the desire of agents to compete away business from other agents who did not take the time for multiple screen searches. *Id.* at 577. *See also* Andrew N. Kleit, *Computer Reservations Systems: Competition Misunderstood,* 37 Antitrust Bull. 833, 856-59 (1992) (also questioning whether potential for display bias deception actually existed, given wide dissemination of pricing information and travel agent desire to maintain customer relationships). *See also* European Commission, *CRS Consultation Paper, supra* note 450, at paras. 51-60 (confirming that free negotiation with CRS providers over content since 2004 has led to reduced booking fees for airlines in the U.S. market; and that 'content fragmentation' has not occurred because airlines have generally offered the same content in each CRS system in which they participate). Moreover, none of the CRS systems was ever judicially dubbed an 'essential facility' that would permit the exercise of monopoly power in a downstream market (*i.e.,* air transportation) if not shared with other airlines (*see* Robert Pitofsky, Donna Patterson, and Jonathan Hooks, *The Essential Facilities Doctrine Under U.S. Antitrust Law,* 70 Antitrust L.J. 443 (2002) (describing application of the doctrine as 'rare and exceptional' outside intellectual property). Nor did lawsuits alleging CRS dominance fare well in U.S. courts. *See* Cindy R. Alexander & Yoon-Ho Alex Lee, *The Economics of Regulatory Reform: Termination of Airline Computer Reservation System Rules,* 21 Yale J. on Reg. 369, 384-86 (2004).

455. Listing (and de-listing) strategies are variants of display bias. The DOT remains convinced that creeping display bias could be a future competitive problem, even after airline CRS divestiture. In the agency's view, booking system vendors could offer special preferences to specific airlines, especially in markets where an airline is locally dominant (such as hub markets), thereby engendering consumer deception but also potentially harming competition as disfavored airlines reduce services or exit markets. *See* CRS Final Rule, *supra* note 450, at 993. The DOT's evidence-gathering for its final CRS rules showed that vendors want to sell bias and airlines are willing to buy it. *See id.* But, for the moment, the agency accepts that 'ongoing developments' (the Internet, in the first instance) will reduce CRS market power and deter

divestiture, the DOT correctly gauged that the sustained erosion of CRS market power shows that there is no compelling case for further *ex ante* regulatory interference.[456]

The legacy carriers' continued use of CRS no longer assures them the unalloyed competitive boon that these systems provided in the pre-Internet era. Arguably, a higher dependence on CRS booking systems has migrated into a competitive disadvantage in discretionary markets, since the low-cost carriers are capturing these bookings primarily through direct (and therefore cheaper) distribution channels such as their own Internet sites, telephone bookings, and so on.[457] For business travel, however, it is apparent that CRS booking systems retain a 'concentration of content' advantage that still appeals to corporate travel managers.[458] Moreover, the legacy carriers have long experience in using CRS technologies to support yield management programs that predict and manage market share.[459] Presumably, these 'sunk advantages' will continue to prove strategically useful in the competitive wars to come.[460]

---

recurrences of bias. *See id.* at 994 (discussing of the scope of the DOT's competition enforcement powers under Section 411 of the Federal Aviation Act (recodified as 49 U.S.C.A. § 41712 (West 2008)) – *i.e.*, the powers used to regulate and deregulate CRS).

456. *See* CRS Final Rule, *supra* note 450, at 977 & 989-90.

457. *See id.* at 988 (finding that leisure travelers are more likely to book through the Internet without using a 'brick-and-mortar' *or* online travel agency) & 990 (noting claims of several low-cost carriers that their ability to obtain most of their revenues from direct sales 'gives them a great cost advantage over other airlines'). Further, as the DOT has pointed out, the legacy carriers operate more complex hub-and-spoke route systems and that complexity limits their ability to obtain direct sales, unlike low-cost carriers which operate point-to-point services. There are, however, significant sunk costs in maintaining the hub-and-spoke system – and its use of CRS technologies. *See id.* In response to the changing marketplace, five major U.S. airlines – Continental, Delta, Northwest, United, and American – pooled financial resources to launch Orbitz, an online travel company offering direct ticket sales to travelers.

458. David Jonas, *Southwest Adds Galileo Distribution*, Travel Mgmt., May 23, 2007 (reporting that Southwest Airlines, which has historically spurned any attempts by third parties to access its inventory, has entered a long-term distribution agreement with the Galileo global distribution system in order to improve its access to corporate travel accounts).

459. Yield management is particularly important to an industry which operates with fixed capacity. By monitoring consumer behavior, airlines can react by offering discounts in order to fill unsold seats and thus avoid wasted or 'dead' capacity.

460. The major carriers continue to exhibit entrepreneurial flexibility as distribution systems have evolved, recognizing that global distribution systems combined with the Internet's growth and consumer relevance have bridged the gap between airlines and consumers once filled by travel agents. In addition to operating their own direct airline-to-customer websites, in Nov. 1999, United, Continental, Delta, and Northwest established a travel website to rival the big online discount sites Travelocity and Expedia. American Airlines eventually participated in this new enterprise, dubbed 'Orbitz.' More than 40 foreign and domestic airlines later became 'charter associates.' Low-cost carriers Southwest Airlines, JetBlue, AirTran, and ATA are the most notable holdouts in the domestic industry. The Orbitz site gives users instantaneous access to the member airlines' latest fares. In 2001, the U.S. Department of Justice investigated Orbitz to determine whether it might facilitate price-fixing or price-signaling. *See infra* note 575 for analysis of an earlier price-signaling investigation. The Department concluded that the venture had not reduced competition or harmed consumers, In fact, the airlines had used Internet

Finally, as noted in Chapter 3, the EC also is scaling back its CRS regulations to reflect the widening of distribution channels through divestiture and new Internet-based technologies.[461] Although, in the past, the definitional specifications of the CAB/DOT rules embraced 'foreign air carriers' who either owned or participated in a computer reservations system,[462] and complaints of bias were made *against* U.S. carrier-owners by their foreign competition, the DOT has recently confined its treatment of CRS in bilateral agreements to general policy guidelines, addressed to the contracting States, calling for national treatment for each party's foreign CRS vendors.[463]

**4   Loyalty Programs and Slot/Gate Scarcity: Enduring
            Non-Price Entry Barriers**

Market power accumulation, and incremental elevation of non-price entry barriers, can also be tied to certain other structural features of the U.S. airline industry that helped to support the hub incumbency of legacy carriers in many markets. First, there is the advent of a series of marketing devices which these carriers have used to attract customers, including frequent flier incentives,[464] corporate travel programs

---

marketing to exert competitive pressure on travel agencies and CRS to reduce the costs of distribution through traditional channels. *See* R. Hewitt Pate, Assistant Attorney General, *Investigation Concludes Orbitz Joint Venture Has Not Harmed Consumers or Reduced Competition*, Statement Regarding the Closing of the Orbitz Investigation (Jul. 21, 2004). The Orbitz case amounted, in the view of one analyst, to another 'example of antitrust being used to suppress competition rather than promote it.' *See* James V. DeLong, *Online Travel Services: The Antitrust Assault on Orbitz – and on Consumers*, at 1, CATO Policy Analysis No. 441 (Jun. 6, 2002).

461.   The Canadian Government has also ratcheted back its CRS regulations in explicit response to market forces. The revised rules dropped the 'obligated carrier' requirement which forced owner-airlines or airlines with over 10% of the domestic market to participate in all four Canadian systems (and thereby forced carriers to choose CRS-based distribution), and also removed the nondiscrimination rule that required vendors to charge the same fees to all airlines (driving up participation costs). *See* Regulations Amending the Canadian Computer Reservation Systems (CRS) Regulations, 137 Canada Gazette No. 43 (Oct. 25, 2003). Unlike the U.S. comprehensive sunset, however, the Canadian legislation retains a requirement of unbiased and neutral display of fares provided by participating carriers. *See id.*

462.   14 C.F.R. § 255.3 (West 2008).

463.   *See, e.g.*, U.S./EC Air Transport Agreement, *supra* note 2, art 17. The latest (2008) revision of the U.S. Model Open Skies Agreement, *supra* note 222, in contrast, adheres to the spirit of the 2004 sunset legislation and omits all references to CRS. The DOT has insisted that, even though it has abolished its antidiscrimination rules for CRS, it will take action to ensure that foreign airlines have 'a fair opportunity to compete for travelers in the United States.' CRS Final Rule, *supra* note 450, at 1023.

464.   At first, the notion of a frequent flier program was greeted dubiously inside the house of its inventor, American Airlines. *See* PETERSON & GLAB, *supra* note 42, at 59-60. Derided initially as a marketing gimmick, its usefulness in creating brand loyalty in a 'commodified' industry is now well-understood. Virgin Atlantic Airways Ltd. *v.* British Airways plc, 872 F. Supp. 52, 57 (S.D.N.Y. 1994). As Michael Levine has written, the core attraction of these programs is that they reward business travel on behalf of a principal with free travel that will most regularly be used by the agent. *See* Levine, *Airline Competition, supra* note 67, at 452-53. As reported by

(discount pricing to large institutional customers), and travel agent commission overrides, collectively portrayed in a U.S. federal court decision as 'loyalty programs.'[465] Thus, new carrier entry is presumably hurt by the incumbents' network advantage of offering 'frequent flier' programs.[466] Nevertheless, although the U.S. DOT as early as 1989 was investigating whether frequent flier programs constitute a marketing tool or a true barrier to entry,[467] the Airline Commission concluded four years later that 'no action' was required on this issue and the DOT has never taken any regulatory action directed at these programs.[468]

Another oft-cited competitive obstacle, the payment of travel agency 'commission overrides,' could be described as frequent flier programs for travel agents.[469] By booking a certain percentage of their business with a particular airline, agents can earn bonuses that compensate to some extent for the fact that airlines no longer pay ordinary travel agent commissions.[470] Overrides (in tandem

---

American Express Business Travel's 2005 Global Business Traveler Survey, <http://home3. americanexpress.com/corp/pc/2005/travel_prefs_print.asp>, and the Yesawich, Pepperdine, Brown & Russell/Yankelovich Partners 2007 National Leisure Travel Monitor (copy on file with author), respectively, over 80% of business travelers participate in airline frequent flier programs (up from just over 70% in 1993, *see* U.S. DOT, Report to Airline Commission, *supra* note 180), as do over half of leisure travelers (up considerably from under a quarter in 1993, *see id.*).

465. *Virgin Atlantic Airways*, 872 F. Supp. at 57 (this case was an early episode in a series of antitrust litigations pursued by Virgin Atlantic against British Airways in the U.S. courts; for a further example, *see infra* note 574).

466. To use an antitrust concept, frequent flier plans *tie* the customer to the brand name carrier. Levine noted some anticompetitive potential, for example assigning large bonuses to segments that have been subjected to new entry. For a general analysis of the economic impact of frequent flier plans, *see* Levine, *Airline Competition, supra* note 67, at 452-54. But, while it is not proven that frequent flier programs are indispensable for market penetration, it is noteworthy that Southwest Airlines and JetBlue, two of the most consistently profitable U.S. low-cost carriers, no longer compete solely on price-points and have each introduced frequent-flier incentives.

467. *See U.S. Agency Seeks Frequent-Flyer Data From 9 Big Airlines*, WALL ST. J., Jun. 21, 1989, at A10.

468. *See Airline Commission Report, supra* note 319, at 3. *See also* U.S. DOT, Aviation Consumer Protection Div., Frequent Flyer Programs, <http://airconsumer.ost.dot.gov/publications/ frequent.htm> (stating unequivocally that the DOT 'does not regulate frequent flier programs').

469. *See Virgin Atlantic Airways*, 872 F. Supp. at 57 (describing travel agency commission override (TACO) programs as 'incentive programs designed to encourage travel agents to book their customers on a particular airline. Typically, a TACO pays a travel agent a bonus when he or she has sold a specified number of tickets'). Airlines award both volume-based and market share overrides; the latter are viewed by new entrant carriers as especially pernicious, because they reward agents based on the *comparative* sales of the carrier with respect to other carriers. Even if a travel agency increases its sales on the carrier paying the override, its override commission may actually disappear if it increases sales on other carriers at a greater rate. *See* Statement of David G. Neeleman, President of Morris Air Corporation to the Airline Commission, *in Airline Commission Documents*, Dkt. No. 000140 (Jun. 3, 1993), at 5. (The Virgin Atlantic opinion, *supra*, does not draw a conceptual distinction between volume-based and market share-based overrides.)

470. By Mar. 2002, following the lead of Delta Air Lines, eight of the 10 largest U.S. airlines (except Southwest Airlines and Alaska Airlines) had reduced their base commissions to travel

with electronic booking systems) tend to give the large legacy airlines an advantage over smaller airlines, creating an artificial economy of scale.[471] A proposed regulatory solution would be to outlaw all commission overrides, but the U.S. DOT seems disinclined to unveil fresh regulatory initiatives on the distribution side of the airline industry so soon after abrogating its CRS rules.[472] To the extent that overrides may prove damaging to competition, therefore, they will be policed through the general antitrust laws.[473]

A second, much more intractable set of potential barriers to competitive entry – and also part of the critique in Chapter 3 of surviving regulatory intervention in air transport[474] – concerns the finite number of infrastructural facilities, particularly use of gates and access to runway 'slots' for take-off and landing, that exists at any airport at any given time.[475] Despite the manifold increase in air traffic since

agents to zero. Adjusting to the fierce economics of the post-9/11 industry, airlines saw this action as part of a reduction in distribution costs made possible by Internet accessibility and price transparency. A Wharton analysis at the time predicted that, as a result, agents would have to change from being 'commission-dependent retail clerks' into 'service-focused professionals with knowledge that leisure travelers are willing to pay for.' Wharton Communications, *Will Commission Cuts Kill the Small Travel Agent?* (May 8, 2002), <http://knowledge.wharton.upenn.edu/article.cfm?articleid=554>. In these circumstances, performance bonuses to travel agents (which are not required to be disclosed to the consumer) clearly encourage traffic-steering and consequently still have commercial appeal to the large carriers. *See id.*

471. *See* Morrison, *supra* note 24, at 245.
472. *Id.* Levine noted the symbiosis between the CRS phenomenon and the relationship between the airlines and the travel agent industry. After deregulation of commissions, the newly-open system began to reward airlines that were adept at paying high incentive commissions to travel agents for business that was 'truly incremental,' successfully distinguishing business that would have come to the airline anyway. 'This required a highly developed capability for monitoring the total market,' and clearly the CRS tie-in was the most prominent weapon in the armory for that purpose. Levine, *Airline Competition, supra* note 67, at 454-58.
473. Virgin Atlantic, in its antitrust complaint, alleged that when the TACO commission or bonus increased more than proportionally to the revenue generated with a particular airline, the travel agent had 'very significant economic incentives to steer consumers to a particular airline in order to reach the target that trigger[ed] the TACO.' *Virgin Atlantic*, 872 F. Supp. at 57. Virgin characterized this practice as a form of 'exclusive dealing arrangement' – in violation of § 1 of the Sherman Act – that foreclosed competition in a substantial share of the market for air transportation (the court declined to dismiss this charge on the defendant's summary judgment motion, citing the need for a factual inquiry). *Id.* at 58-59 & 66.
474. *See supra* Chapter 3, Parts VI-VIII.
475. Slot and gate scarcities can also be described as 'non-commercial' entry barriers, since they are not rooted in the supply and demand characteristics of the industry's product: thus, 'commercial' barriers would include high initial investment requirements ('sunk costs'), or large marketing expenditures to establish 'identity.' Lucile Sheppard Keyes, *A Preliminary Appraisal of Merger Control Under the Airline Deregulation Act of 1978*, 46 J. AIR L. & COM. 71, 96 (1980). Some commentators have suggested that the 'essential facilities' doctrine, *supra* note 454, could be applied to challenge the gate and slot incumbency of established airlines. *See* Marvin S. Cohen, *The Antitrust Implications of Airline Deregulation*, 28 ANTITRUST BULL. 131, 143-44 (1983). Continental Airlines and United Airlines, both of which hub at Denver, opposed the building of the new multibillion dollar Denver International Airport that opened in Feb. 1995 to replace Stapleton, since it would nearly double the available gate and landing

deregulation, U.S. airport resources (with the singular exception of Denver's new international airport) have expanded only marginally.[476] Ironically, the federal government, under statutory command both to maintain airspace safety and to encourage market competition among air carriers, has found itself largely responsible for turning the concept of slot apportionment into an appreciable entry barrier at some of the nation's busiest airports. Describing 'slots' as 'an operating privilege' subject to its absolute control,[477] the U.S. FAA originally adopted so-called *high density* rules to limit the number of airplanes allowed to fly into and out of the five most congested U.S. airports during peak business hours.[478]

As with international route awards, the U.S. DOT (with the blessing of the Department of Justice) engineered a 'secondary market' in awarded slots at these key airports, which could be bought, sold, or leased for any consideration and any

---

space and therefore cut into their joint market share. Eric Weiner, *Voters in Denver Approve a New $2.3 Billion Airport*, N.Y. TIMES, May 17, 1989, at A20. In 1990, Congress enacted the Passenger Facility Charge ('PFC') law to authorize airports controlled by public agencies to impose a user charge of up to $3.00 on each passenger enplaning or connecting at the airport. Congress raised the cap to $4.50 effective Apr. 1, 2001. The PFC is a local charge that can be imposed at the option of the local airport authority, with FAA approval, solely to finance projects that enhance capacity and safety, reduce noise, or promote airline competition. Congress clearly intended that PFCs would not be subject to the control and approval of the airlines. New facilities built with PFCs cannot be leased on long-term, exclusive-use leases. *See* GAO Submission, *supra* note 411, at 17. As of Jun. 1, 2007, 367 locations were using PFCs, including 94 of the top 100 airports. *See* Air Transport Association, Update on Passenger Facility Charges, <www.airlines.org/economics/taxes/PFCs.htm>. Another emerging public policy solution is simply to sell airports to private operators, who would run them to make a profit. *See* Morrison, *supra* note 24, at 244.

476. *See* discussion in AIRPORT REGULATION, LAW, AND PUBLIC POLICY 47-48 (Robert M. Hardaway ed., 1991). Denver is only the second new major commercial service airport opened in the United States in the past 40 years. The other is Dallas-Fort Worth. *See* FAA, CAPACITY NEEDS IN THE NATIONAL AIRSPACE SYSTEM 2007-2025: AN ANALYSIS OF AIRPORTS AND METROPOLITAN AREA DEMAND AND OPERATIONAL CAPACITY IN THE FUTURE 22 (2007). Since 2000, 14 new runways have opened at U.S. airports, but capacity constraints (*i.e.*, unacceptable levels of delay) are likely to persist for a decade or more. *See id.* at 2. Chicago's O'Hare International Airport, one of the busiest in the world, is currently in the process of reconfiguring its airfield to avoid runway incursion by expanding the length and overall number of runways. *See* O'Hare Modernization Program, City of Chicago, <http://egov.cityofchicago.org/>. As the FAA has emphasized, however, the limiting capacity for operations may be more than runway capacity by itself and can include taxiway congestion and terminal gate scarcity. *See* FAA, *supra*, at 6.

477. 14 C.F.R. § 93.223(a) (West 2008). On the 'property' value of slots, *see* Dario Maffeo, *Slot Trading in the Reform of the Council Regulation (EEC) No. 95/93: A Comparative Analysis with the United States*, 66 J. AIR L. & COM. 1569 (2001) (noting FAA position, confirmed in the federal regulations, that slots do not represent a 'property right,' but discussing a bankruptcy court ruling, resting precisely on the notion of 'marketability,' that slots are part of the proprietary estate of debtor airlines). Slot values at controlled airports can be astounding. In 2001, peak hour slots at Chicago O'Hare sold for an average of two million dollars, a figure that is scarcely surprising given the multimillion-dollar daily revenue potential of these privileges. *See id.* at 1579.

478. The affected airports were New York's JFK International and LaGuardia, Newark International, Chicago's O'Hare and Washington's Reagan National. Of these, only O'Hare was a 'hub' airport. *See generally* 14 C.F.R. § 93.121 (West 2008). The original rules were

time period.[479] Curiously, the rules prohibit any market (other than a one-for-one trade) for international slots.[480] For reasons of cost and competition deterrence, the

promulgated in 1969; restrictions were lifted at Newark in the early 1970s. *See* Notice of Proposed Rulemaking, Operation of Jet Aircraft in Commuter Slots at O'Hare Int'l Airport, 58 Fed. Reg. 280 (Jan. 5, 1993). As noted, *supra* Chapter 3, note 399, in 2000 the U.S. Congress modified its legislation to remove flight caps for all airports except Washington Reagan. *See* 49 U.S.C.A. § 41715 (West 2008) (adopted as part of 'AIR-21,' the Wendell H. Ford Aviation Investment and Reform Act of the 21st Century). The ostensible reason for the removal was concern with collateral effects on airport access and competition. *See* Operating Limitations at New York LaGuardia Airport; Notice of Order, 71 Fed. Reg. 77,854 (Dec. 27, 2006) [hereinafter FAA LaGuardia Rule 2006]. In the FAA's view, however, Congress's action has not affected the agency's claimed 'plenary authority,' premised on 49 U.S.C.A. § 40103(b) (West 2008), to manage the safe and efficient use of the navigable airspace and the 'National Airspace System' and, therefore, to limit flight operations where it deems necessary. Congestion and Delay Reduction at Chicago O'Hare International Airport; Final Rule, 71 Fed. Reg. 51,382, 51,386 (Aug. 29, 2006) [hereinafter FAA Chicago Rule 2006]; *see also* Congestion Management Rule for LaGuardia Airport; Proposed Rule, 71 Fed. Reg. 51,360 (Aug. 29, 2006) [hereinafter FAA LaGuardia Proposed Rule 2006]. Accordingly, the agency has been acting to reinstitute flight caps at severely congested airports where the high density rules have lapsed or are scheduled to lapse. *See, e.g.*, FAA Chicago Rule, *supra* (imposing temporary flight caps at O'Hare, using 'plenary authority' and also relying on 2004 federal legislation, 49 U.S.C.A. § 41722 (West 2008), that included a flight reduction mechanism to help reduce delays) & FAA LaGuardia Proposed Rule 2006, *supra* (instituting similar controls temporarily at LaGuardia airport in anticipation of likely long-term structural caps to be imposed after rulemaking process). This broad exercise of agency power, which for LaGuardia will include an unprecedented minimum size of aircraft serving the airport, has not been uncontested. *See, e.g.*, Air Transport Association, *FAA's Proposed Rule on Demand Management at LaGuardia Airport*, Issue Brief (Jan. 2007) (noting that the FAA's proposed rule 'goes beyond limiting operations and contains several features that raise significant policy and legal issues'). The FAA has recently sought to introduce slot auctions at high-volume airports in the New York area. The auctions were set to begin in fall 2008 but have encountered strong opposition from airlines and political leaders. The program has been suspended. *See supra* Chapter 3, note 399.

479. *See* 14 C.F.R. § 93.221(a) (West 2008). *See* David Starkie, *The Economics of Secondary Markets for Airport Slots*, *in* INSTITUTE OF ECONOMIC AFFAIRS, A MARKET IN AIRPORT SLOTS 51, 68 (Keith Boyfield ed., 2003) (noting that the high density rule itself did not prescribe a method for allocating runway operations between airlines, and that trading markets were introduced after trial and error with other methodologies).

480. *See* 14 C.F.R. § 93.217(a)(2) (West 2008). To the chagrin of domestic airlines, the FAA has in the past transferred slots to foreign competitors to honor bilateral treaty commitments. *See* 14 C.F.R. § 93, *passim*. *See*, for example, the general power conferred in 14 C.F. R. § 93.217(d) (stating that 'slots may be withdrawn at any time to fulfill the [DOT's] operational needs, such as providing slots for international . . . operations'). Regulatory provision is also made, however, to restrict allocation to a foreign carrier 'of a country that provides slots to U.S. air carriers . . . on a basis more restrictive' than that provided in the FAA rules. *See id.* at § 93.217(9)(d). A modification introduced in 1994, under the Federal Aviation Administration Authorization Act of 1994, forbids slots to be withdrawn at Chicago's O'Hare airport to accommodate international services. *See* 49 U.S.C.A. § 41714(b)(2) (West 2008). The intended beneficiaries of the change were the largest incumbents at O'Hare, United and American. United, in particular, has lobbied intensively to alter DOT practice. *See* Notice of Proposed Rule-Making, High Density Traffic Airports Allocation of International Slots at O'Hare International Airport, 55 Fed. Reg. 9090 (Mar. 9, 1990).

large incumbent slot-holders have always been disinclined to sell or lease slots to new entrants (or to existing slot-holders seeking network expansion).[481] To enable the FAA to accumulate unused slots for new entrants, it created a lottery for surrendered slots.[482] Some of this slot pool came from a 'use or lose' provision introduced in 1992, which generally required that airlines fly planes in their allocated slots 80% of the time.[483] There is little evidence that these buy/sell and lottery measures dislodged substantial additional slots for new entry.[484] The

---

481. The gradual abolition of high-density rules led to much reduced activity in the slot markets, however. *See* Starkie, *supra* note 479, at 69. Moreover, the FAA was subject to continuous lobbying on behalf of new entrants and small communities, causing a raft of exemptions which compromised the efficacy of the rules and encouraged Congress eventually to abolish them. *See id.* Without slots in place (which has always been the case for most of the nation's airports), airlines tend to schedule excessively in peak times, a source of chronic traffic delays and congestion.

482. 14 C.F.R. § 93.225 (West 2008). 25% of the first selection of slots are reserved for selection by new entrants. If new entrants do not select all of these, 'limited incumbent carriers' (holding 12 or fewer slots at the airport) can select from the remainder. *Id.*

483. 14 C.F.R. § 93.227 (West 2008) (a two-month period is provided for calculation of slot utilization). Airlines criticized this provision as market-insensitive, since it appeared to disallow temporary frequency reductions to match a short-term decline in demand. Testimony of Stephen Wolf, Chairman and Executive Officer, United Airlines, Inc., *Before the Subcomm. On Aviation of the House Comm. on Public Works and Transp.* (Feb. 17,1993), *in Airline Commission Documents*, Dkt. No. 001040 (Jun. 3, 1993), at 3. The FAA does, as a matter of policy, permit applications for short-term waivers of the 'use or lose' rule in 'a highly unusual and unpredictable condition which is beyond the control of the slot-holder and which exists for a period of nine or more days.' 14 C.F.R. § 93.227 (2007). In Sept. 2005, for example, in the aftermath of the destructive effects of Hurricane Katrina on New Orleans and its region, the agency granted a request from American Airlines for a four-month waiver of its slot usage requirements for four slots that it was scheduled to use between New York LaGuardia and New Orleans. But the FAA denied a subsequent request from the Regional Airlines Association for a blanket waiver of the use or lose rule at the (then) three high density traffic airports. The request was premised on a number of adverse systemic conditions, including high fuel costs caused in part by supply disruptions after Katrina. Hewing closely to the narrowly-drawn waiver provision, the FAA found that many of the circumstances in the petition went to 'longstanding and fundamental obstacles to airline profitability,' and were not specific to Katrina. *See* Notice of Denial of Request for Waiver of the Minimum Slot Usage Requirement, 70 Fed. Reg. 57,350, 57,351 (Sept. 30, 2005).

484. New entrants, incidentally, migrated to smaller hub airports (Chicago's Midway, for example), where slots are uncontrolled, as one means to overcome the escalating cost of slots at high density facilities. *See, e.g.,* U.S. FAA, *In the Matter of Proposed Congestion Management Rule for LaGuardia Airport*, Dkt. No. FAA-2006-25709, Comments of the Air Carrier Association of America (Dec. 29, 2006) [hereinafter U.S. FAA, ACA Comments 2006] (arguing, in relation to LaGuardia, that the high density regulations led to a serious lack of competition as a few legacy carriers increased their dominance of slot holdings (including a practice of using the buy/sell rule to trade only with other legacy carriers)). Noting that redistribution of slot authorizations after expiry of the high density rule at LaGuardia would not begin until 2010, the Air Carrier Association, a lobbying group for U.S. 'low-fare' carriers, called for immediate withdrawal of 10% of slots from legacy carriers holding over 75 slots and redistribution of these authorizations to 'limited incumbents.' *Id.* at 6; *see also infra* note 488 (commenting on the proposed new rules for LaGuardia).

evidence, indeed, has been to the contrary – that incumbent airlines, collectively hoarding their slot treasuries through such maneuvers as buying, selling, leasing, and trading slots solely with other legacy carriers,[485] have impeded their competitors' access to the marketplace.[486]

The Airline Commission recommended removal of the high-density slot rules because they place 'artificial limits' on competition,[487] and it appears that the current FAA quest for alternative market-based and administrative mechanisms is a response to that perspective. For example, the FAA's proposed post-High-Density Rules for Chicago O'Hare and New York LaGuardia suggest that the agency will continue to rely on a slot-based infrastructure (with the 'slot' now re-imagined as an 'operating authorization'), but one that is configured to avoid the incumbent-to-incumbent bias of the existing buy/sell arrangements.[488] As will be

---

485. *See* U.S. FAA, ACA Comments 2006, *supra* note 484, at 3. According to the U.S. Department of Justice,

> . . . an incumbent with market power may well be able to outbid a more efficient entrant, simply because maintaining market power is more profitable than entering a competitive market . . . once a potential buyer's identity is known to the seller, the seller has every incentive to seek out an incumbent airline that would be willing to offer more money to maintain its market power than the entrant would be willing to apply to erode it.

U.S. FAA, *Notice of Alternative Policy Options for Managing Capacity at LaGuardia Airport and Proposed Extension of Lottery Allocation*, Dkt. No. FAA-2001-9854, Comments of the United States Department of Justice (Jun. 20, 2002), at 6.

486. Moreover, when large blocks of slots did become available, for example in an airline bankruptcy or liquidation, the Department of Justice frequently intervened to prevent acquisitions that would enhance market power.

487. *Airline Commission Report, supra* note 319, at 9. Alternatively, the Report recommended raising the limits 'to the highest practicable level consistent with safety requirements.' *Id.* The competitive value of holding slot treasuries is evident from the role that voluntary (or forced) divestiture of these privileges can play (in both the United States and the European Union, *see infra* Chapter 5, Part III(C)), in persuading antitrust regulators to approve otherwise challengeable mergers. A recent U.S. example was the attempt by United Airlines and US Airways to divest (by sale or transfer of leases) assets including over 200 slots at Ronald Reagan National Airport in Washington, D.C. The divested assets would be assembled to allow a newly-created independent carrier, DC Air, to maintain all of US Airways' services from Reagan National. *See* General Accounting Office, *Aviation Competition: Issues Related to the Proposed United Airlines-US Airways Merger*, at 7, GAO-01-212 (Dec. 2000). The strategy failed, however, because the U.S. Department of Justice announced that it would file a civil complaint to stop the acquisition. *See* Press Release, U.S. Department of Justice, Department of Justice and Several States Will Sue to Stop United Airlines From Acquiring US Airways (Jul. 27, 2001) (predicting that the transaction would reward United with a monopoly or duopoly on nonstop service on over 30 routes, and rejecting the proposed DC Air remedy as inadequate to replace the competitive pressure that US Airways brings to the marketplace).

488. *See* FAA LaGuardia Proposed Rule 2006, *supra* note 478, at 51, 363-364. Unlike Chicago, where a massive airport expansion program has begun, LaGuardia's physical site permits no foreseeable capacity expansion (other than through more efficient air traffic control technology). The FAA's proposed new primary market rules for LaGuardia, therefore, will depart from the High-Density Rule 'slot' precedent by creating finite operating authorizations that will be returned on a rolling basis to the market pool. The average life of an authorization under this system (once the initial grandfathered allocations start to expire at the rate of 10% each

seen, the issue of airport congestion is particularly acute in the European airport system, and indeed, all hopes for authentic international liberalization must be contingent upon the hard realities of sufficient infrastructural access.[489] As one airline consultant commented, '[w]e don't have enough capacity to have a totally free market.'[490]

5 The Death and Life of A Merger Policy for the U.S. Airline Industry

The drafters of the deregulation statutes made a clear judgment that the airline industry would be susceptible to the kinds of anticompetitive activity that the antitrust laws are intended to check. The Declaration of Policy in the ADA contains an explicit competition law charter – with a strong consumer welfare bias – for U.S. air transportation.[491] Section 102 of the Act charges the U.S. DOT to prevent 'unfair, deceptive, predatory, or anticompetitive practices' in air transportation, and to avoid 'unreasonable industry concentration, excessive market domination, monopoly powers, and other conditions that would tend to allow at least one air carrier or foreign air carrier unreasonably to increase prices, reduce services, or exclude competition' in air transportation. The statutory objectives also embrace 'actual and potential competition... to provide efficiency, innovation and low prices,' and encouragement of entry into air transport markets by new and existing air carriers, as well as the strengthening of small air carriers 'to ensure a more effective and competitive airline industry.'[492]

---

year after the first three years) is expected eventually to be 10 years. FAA LaGuardia Proposed Rule 2006, *supra* note 478, at 51,364. A new stock of authorizations would be available each year after 2010, which the agency would prefer to be allocated using a secondary buy/sell market (rather than relying on an administrative mechanism such as a lottery). *See id.* at 51,366. In its rulemaking, the FAA seems to favor a secondary market system of 'blind' or 'non-transparent' auctions of the authorizations in order to counter the incumbents' ability under the (highly transparent) existing secondary market to 'fence out' new entrants or other airlines that could pose a competitive threat. *Id.* at 51,372. During summer 2008, the FAA imposed flight caps during peak hours at New York City area airports in an effort to reduce congestion. *See* Scott McCartney, *Buckle In: It's Going to be a Rough Summer for Flying,* WALL ST. J, Apr. 22, 2008, at D1. The FAA has, however, lifted the 88-per-hour flight cap at Chicago's O'Hare airport to coincide with its runway expansion project. *See* Susan Carey, *FAA Restrictions to End at O'Hare,* WALL ST. J., Jun. 17, 2008, at D3. On recent FAA efforts to introduce slot auctions for New York airports, *see supra* Chapter 3, note 399.

489. Genuine logistical impediments must be accommodated in any proposed multilateral system. Too often, however, governments use the congestion issue as a kind of all-purpose escape clause to reduce access to its airports by foreign competitors of its national carriers.

490. Quoted in Harvard Thesis, *supra* note 309.

491. *See Airline Commission Proceedings,* testimony of Marc Schechter, Chief, Transportation, Energy and Agriculture Section, Antitrust Division, Department of Justice (Jun. 23, 1993), at 55.

492. Section 102 of the Federal Aviation Act, as amended by both the Airline Deregulation Act and the International Air Transport Competition Act and now recodified as 49 U.S.C.A. § 40101(a) (West 2008).

Normally, federal competition law enforcement (both civil and criminal) is the bailiwick of the Antitrust Division of the Department of Justice, although the Federal Trade Commission enjoys some concurrent civil jurisdiction and provides important auxiliary support in consumer protection and premerger screening.[493] But, as previously seen, a peculiarity of the 'phased' unfolding of airline deregulation was that the holdover domestic merger review authority of the CAB, recast to include new Clayton Act/Bank Merger Act standards, was retained until 1989 (and exercised after the Board's sunset by the DOT).[494] Further, the Department also inherited a generalized authority originally granted to the Board in Section 411 of the Federal Aviation Act, to investigate and issue 'cease and desist' orders with respect to 'unfair or deceptive practice[s] or . . . unfair method[s] of competition' in air transportation.[495] The Department retains some latitude under Section 411 to proscribe practices that would not, strictly speaking, violate the Sherman Act.[496]

a   *Mergers in the Reagan Era: Laissez-Faire under*
           CAB/DOT Review

The CAB/DOT administrators evaluated airline mergers through the prism of 'contestability.'[497] They consistently accepted the economic analysis that

---

493. *See generally*, on the subject of 'public' enforcement of the U.S. antitrust laws, HERBERT HOVENKAMP, FEDERAL ANTITRUST POLICY: THE LAW OF COMPETITION AND ITS PRACTICE 592-601 (3d ed. 2005).

494. *See supra* note 234 and accompanying text.

495. Section 411 of the Federal Aviation Act, 49 U.S.C. § 1381 (1979), *recodified as* 49 U.S.C.A. § 41712 (West 2008). Section 411 is enforceable through administrative proceedings that would result in industry-wide rules (*e.g.*, the CRS rules) or in an order to an airline to cease and desist from a deceptive or unfair or anticompetitive practice. This authority is analogous to similar powers given to the Federal Trade Commission under Section 5 of the Federal Trade Commission Act, 15 U.S.C.A. § 45(a) (West 2008) (and, indeed, the Senate declined in 1984 to transfer this residual CAB authority to the FTC: LEGISLATIVE HISTORY 1984, *supra* note 110, at 2861-62).

496. The Sherman Act is notorious for its laconic expression of proscribed corporate behavior: '[T]he Sherman Act condemns "every contract, combination . . . or conspiracy in restraint of trade," or every person who shall "monopolize," without giving a clue about what those phrases mean.' HOVENKAMP, *supra* note 493, at 49. Section 411's reach has been interpreted by the Seventh Circuit, in an airline suit protesting the CAB bias rules, as empowering the Board to forbid anticompetitive practices '*before* they become serious enough to violate the Sherman Act.' United Air Lines, Inc. *v.* Civil Aeronautics Board., 766 F.2d 1107, 1114 (7th Cir. 1985) (emphasis added). A deceptive practice is one that will tend to deceive a significant number of consumers. *See id.* at 1113. An unfair method of competition is a practice that violates antitrust laws or antitrust principles. *See id.* at 1114. The agency may therefore prohibit some airline conduct that is otherwise permitted under the antitrust laws. *See* CRS Final Rule, *supra* note 450, at 994. Thus framed, the DOT's power could be exercised *before* the occurrence of an antitrust injury. *See United Air Lines*, 766 F.2d at 1114. The DOT continues to cite the *United* case in support of its authority. *See* CRS Final Rule, *supra* note 450, at 994. Supplementing Section 411, the DOT also has extensive administrative authority to conduct investigations of anticompetitive activity, including the authority to compel production of reports, documents, and, testimony. *See generally* Procedural Regulations, 14 C.F.R. § 300 *et seq.* (West 2008).

497. 'Contestability,' *see supra* note 66, assumes the constant presence of 'potential' competitors in airline markets to discipline would-be price gougers. *See* Keyes, *supra* note 475, at 80. The

prevailed in the immediate pre-deregulation period, namely, that '[a]irline markets are nearly always concentrated by traditional antitrust standards, yet most are competitive in performance.'[498] Anticipating but not quite adopting the 'integrated approach' of the later Department of Justice antitrust guidelines,[499] the CAB/DOT looked beyond actual market share data to focus on other factors, notably the ease or difficulty of entry into the affected markets,[500] to determine whether a proposed transaction would confer market power upon the surviving carrier.[501] The administrators generally took the view that the elimination of specific potential competitors would not be a critical factor, so long as barriers to entry were not so high that other cost-efficient competitors could not quickly penetrate the relevant market

---

level of market concentration should not, therefore, have a direct impact on fares; the threat of entry means that markets with only *one* incumbent will price competitively. Although this scenario may seem unrealistic, it was thought that at least an imperfect version would hold in the airline industry, where assets (*i.e.*, airplanes and air routes) are highly mobile. *See, e.g.*, Elizabeth E. Bailey & John C. Panzar, *The Contestability of Airline Markets During the Transition to Deregulation*, 44 J.L. & CONTEMP. PROBS. 125 (1981). *See*, for an exhaustive economic analysis of contestability, BAUMOL, *supra* note 66. A counterpoint to this theory is that there are certain costs in terms of time and capital that a carrier must incur to establish reputation (advertising, for example), and incumbents will have certain advantages of scale and scope, including a large network and a frequent flier program. *See* OECD, COMMITTEE ON COMPETITION LAW & POLICY, DEREGULATION AND AIRLINE COMPETITION 110-11 (1988). Critics have been quick to note that the laxity of CAB/DOT merger control largely coincided with the passive nature of official antitrust enforcement that characterized the Reagan Administration (1981-89). *See* Fahy, *supra* note 67, at 274.

498. *See, e.g.*, Northwest Airlines, Inc.-Republic Airlines, Inc. Acquisition Case, Order No. 86-7-81, [1979-1989 Transfer Binder] Av. L. Rep. (CCH) ¶ 22,390, at 14,540 (Jul. 31, 1986). *See also* Joseph F. Brodley, *Antitrust Policy Under Deregulation: Airline Mergers and the Theory of Contestable Markets*, 61 B.U. L. REV. 823, 825 (1981).

499. *See, e.g.*, U.S. DEPT. OF JUSTICE & FEDERAL TRADE COMM'N, HORIZONTAL MERGER GUIDELINES 1-3 (rev. ed., 1997) [hereinafter HORIZONTAL MERGER GUIDELINES] (noting that the separate elements of antitrust review – market definition and concentration, potential adverse competitive effects, entry analysis, efficiencies, and failing and exiting assets – do not follow any analytically significant order, so that, for example, the presence of likely early entry could displace anticompetitive effects and allow termination of review without considering other analytical elements).

500. The focus on ease of entry was emphatic. *See*, for example, the DOT analysis in Texas Air-People Express Acquisition, Order No. 86-10-53, [1979-1989 Transfer Binder] Av. L. Rep. (CCH) ¶ 22,396, at 14,606 (Oct. 24, 1986): '[T]he basic question to be analyzed in airline merger cases remains the ease with which entry can occur.' *Id.* at 14,614. Despite the fact that the would-be merger participants accounted for roughly 60% of the service in the crowded northeastern corridor markets (New York/Washington and New York/Boston), the DOT concluded that the merger would not substantially reduce competition because expansion or entry was possible in at least one airport in each of the three cities. *See id.* at 14,611. Overall, the analysis relied heavily on 'entry barrier' concepts, but the defining characteristic of an entry barrier that made it sufficiently 'high' to compel rejection of an airline merger was not at all clear. *See* Keyes, *supra* note 135, at 743.

501. 'The core concern of the antitrust laws, including as they pertain to mergers between rivals, is the creation or enhancement of market power.' DOJ/FTC, COMMENTARY, *supra* note 259, at 1. Market power is commonly defined as the ability profitably to maintain prices above competitive levels for a significant period of time. *See id.*; *see also* Keyes, *supra* note 135, at 743.

and discipline the remaining participants.[502] Nevertheless, critics of this conjectural approach to *future* market performance noted its inconsistency with general Clayton Act standards.[503]

The CAB/DOT fixation with contestability[504] ensured a string of merger successes for the legacy incumbents. In the ten-year history of CAB/DOT jurisdiction, only one proposed merger was rejected (in 1979, by the CAB), although in the Texas Air/Eastern Air merger the DOT required the sale of take-off and landing slots by the merged carrier in order to permit a rival shuttle service at the key northeastern corridor airports.[505] The Department of Justice intervened in vain to oppose several mergers that were subject to DOT review procedures:[506] the Antitrust Division objected without success to the acquisition by Northwest Airlines of Republic Airlines, which gave Northwest a hub dominance in Minneapolis,[507] to

---

502. *See* the competition analysis in U.S. DOT, *Piedmont-Empire Acquisition Show Cause Proceeding*, Dkt. No. 43518, Order No. 85-12-17 (Dec. 9, 1985).

503. *See, e.g.*, Brodley, *supra* note 498, at 825. Nonetheless, the Department of Justice has not been troubled by the need to make guesses about future market performance, and routinely expects this kind of hypothesizing as part of its merger analysis work (for example, with respect to projection of the efficiencies that might result from a corporate combination). *See* DOJ/FTC, COMMENTARY, *supra* note 259, at 2-3.

504. Through the 1980s, however, contestability theory as applied to airlines 'took repeated blows' from studies that found that the number of *actual* competitors significantly affected price levels on a route. Severin Borenstein & Nancy L. Rose, *How Airline Markets Work, or Do They? Regulatory Reform in the Airline Industry* 44 (NBER Working Paper Series, Working Paper No. 13452, Sept. 2007). As summarized by Borenstein and Rose, '[p]otential competition in general had a modest effect [on] disciplining pricing.' *Id.* (noting, however, that some studies suggested an exception when the potential competitor was Southwest Airlines). Fares were demonstrably higher on routes with only one airline than on routes with more active competitors, and declined significantly with entry of a second or third competitor. *See id.* 'By the end of the 1980s,' the authors conclude, 'the theory was seldom raised in the context of airlines.' *Id.*

505. Texas Air Corporation-Eastern Acquisition, Order No. 86-8-77, [1979-1989 Transfer Binder] Av. L. Rep. (CCH) ¶ 22,391, at 14,555 (Aug. 28, 1986). The DOT held that, unless adequate facilities for a competitive shuttle service were provided, the merger would 'substantially reduce competition' in two critical northeastern corridor markets. The DOT analysis carved out a special status for the market niche afforded by shuttle services, which in its view were unique for business travelers and for that precise reason were unaffected by fare levels at other competing metropolitan airports. A purchase of a large block of slots to create a competitive service appeared 'impracticable,' in the agency's opinion. *Id.* at 14,557. Accordingly, Texas Air entered into an agreement with Pan Am to spin off the necessary slot and gate facilities at the New York, Washington, and Boston airports. *See* Texas Air Corporation and Eastern Air Lines, Inc., Order No. 86-10-2, [1979-1989 Transfer Binder] Av. L. Rep. (CCH) ¶ 22,393 (Oct. 1, 1988), at 14,581.

506. JOHN E. KWOKA & LAWRENCE J. WHITE, THE ANTITRUST REVOLUTION 100 (1988).

507. Northwest Airlines, Inc.-Republic Airlines, Inc. Acquisition Case, *supra* note 498, at 14,537. The DOT did, however, disagree with the administrative law judge's assertion that, under deregulation, there is a theoretical *presumption* of unlimited entry which makes it nearly impossible for opponents of an airline merger to show that the merger would substantially reduce competition. *See id.* at 14,540. Nonetheless, given that the combined share of Northwest/Republic enplanements at Minneapolis-St. Paul in 1986 was 80%, the burden on airlines opposing the transaction – to show anticompetitive effects – was high indeed. *See id.* at 14,538-539. Ultimately, the DOT found that 'a combination of all the disciplining factors'

Trans World Airlines' takeover of its only St. Louis competitor, Ozark Airlines,[508] and to the acquisition by United Airlines of Pan Am's battery of lucrative Pacific routes.[509] According to internal studies by the Justice Department, the Northwest/ Republic and TWA/Ozark mergers both resulted in creation of some market power in their respective hubs.[510]

As noted above, the 1978 deregulation legislation advocated avoidance of industry concentration and the encouragement of vigorous new entry. A more sanguine note was sounded soon after deregulation in an article by Professor Almarin Phillips in the University of Pennsylvania Law Review. Commenting that '[a]irline mergers are nearly inevitable in the deregulated environment,'[511] Phillips detected an inconsistency between the 1978 Act's purpose of making available 'a variety of adequate, economic, efficient, and low-price services by air carriers' and the practical economics of a dynamic, differentiated industry.[512] The ADA, Phillips contended, 'largely ignores the near-inevitability that the rivalry engendered in unregulated markets will induce structural changes.'[513]

(competing connecting service, a relatively unconstrained airport, and the ability of carriers to move quickly to establish efficient hubs at new locations) would prevent reduction of competition. *Id.* at 14,547. In other words, despite the two carriers' joint dominance, the DOT was confident that supracompetitive pricing would attract not only new point-to-point entry, but new *hub* entry. *See id.* at 14,544-545.

508. Trans World Airlines-Ozark Airlines Acquisition, Order No. 86-9-29, [1979-1989 Transfer Binder] Av. L. Rep. (CCH) ¶ 22,392, at 14,570 (Sept. 12, 1986). The DOT recognized the similarity of the competitive conditions here with the Northwest/Republic merger, and again concluded that another carrier could timely obtain the facilities necessary to establish a large-scale hub at St. Louis. *See id.* at 14,571 & 14,575. Even if this should not occur, non-hub services could provide adequate competitive discipline. *Id.* at 14,577.

509. The DOT approved the acquisition of the International Pacific Division of Pan American World Airways by United Airlines, Inc., in 1985. *See* Pacific Division Transfer Case, Order No. 85-11-87, [1979-1989 Transfer Binder] Av. L. Rep. (CCH) ¶ 22,382, at 14,465 (Oct. 31, 1985). The DOT rejected the Justice Department's recommendation that approval be conditioned on the spin-off of a U.S./Tokyo route to a viable competitor. *See id.* at 14,495. The Department of Justice, in a brief filed with the DOT, stated that the proposed acquisition could substantially reduce competition for air passenger services between the United States and Tokyo. *See id.* at 14,472. The acquisition would transform United from a 'disruptive force to a major incumbent' with both the incentive and ability to maximize profits by cooperating with IATA's efforts to fix fares and restrict output. *Id.* at 14,490. Taking note of the regulatory environment for the award of transpacific routes, the Antitrust Division also identified 'high barriers to entry.' *Id.* at 14,473. In response, the DOT stated that it would consider designating a new carrier to replace United on the Seattle/Portland-Tokyo route. *See id.* at 14,468. The DOT conceded the increased concentration of the market, but believed that the transpacific market was growing rapidly enough to offset this concern. *See id.* at 14,483.

510. *See* Gregory J. Werden et al., *The Effects of Mergers on Price and Output: Two Case Studies from the Airline Industry*, 12 Managerial & Decision Econ. 341, 342 (1991); *see Airline Commission Proceedings*, comments of Marc Schechter, Chief, Transportation, Energy and Agriculture Section, Antitrust Division, Department of Justice (Jun. 23, 1993), at 39.

511. Almarin Phillips, *Airline Mergers in the New Regulatory Environment*, 129 U. Pa. L. Rev. 856, 876 (1981).

512. *Id.* at 858.

513. *Id.*

While Phillips was surely correct that structural change must be anticipated, the fact remains that the CAB/DOT merger policy favored the incumbent legacy carriers by moving the industry to a tighter concentration than existed even when the CAB regulatory system held sway.[514]

b   *After 1989: Stronger Surveillance by the Antitrust Division*

As of January 1, 1989, however, the ADA's protracted 'liberalization' of merger control ended,[515] and the Department of Justice (through its Antitrust Division) unseated the DOT as the watchdog of domestic airline industry concentration.[516] Mergers between or among U.S. airlines are now subject to the general body of the antitrust laws, including the prophylactic merger review procedures of the Hart-Scott-Rodino Act.[517] Although the Department of Justice did not have, and

---

514. The General Accounting Office (as it then was), reviewing the DOT's implementation of its merger authority as of 1989, concluded that the DOT had not adequately taken into account the effects of mergers on competition when it reviewed the proposed transactions. *See* GAO, *Airline Competition: DOT's Implementation of Airline Regulatory Authority*, at 37, GAO/ RCED-89-93 (Jun. 1989). In a separate study of the TWA/Ozark merger, for example, the GAO found substantial fare increases at St. Louis on routes where the two airlines had been competitors. GAO, *Airline Competition: Fare and Service Changes at St. Louis Since the TWA/Ozark Merger*, at 16-20, GAO/RCED-88-217BR (Sept. 1988). This study led to a broader review of airline fares at airports where one or two airlines handled most of the traffic. The analysis showed a 'hub premium' of more than 20% at concentrated airports. *See* GAO, *Airline Competition: Higher Fares and Reduced Competition at Concentrated Airports*, at 32-63, GAO/RCED-90-102 (Jul. 1990) [GAO, *Reduced Competition*]. The study defined 'concentrated airports' as those where one airline enplaned 60% of passengers or two airlines enplaned 85%. The 'hub premium,' incidentally, has remained a favorite target of official scrutiny. *See* GAO, *Aviation Competition: Challenges in Enhancing Competition in Dominated Markets*, GAO/01-518T (Mar. 13, 2001) (noting that major airlines 'dominated' – *i.e.*, carried more than 50% of passengers – at 16 of the 31 largest U.S. airports and that these airports showed a discernible premium of up to 41% in the absence of low-fare competition); *see also* DOT, *Secretary's Task Force on Competition in the U.S. Domestic Airline Industry: Pricing*, at 12, Executive Summary (Feb. 1990); GAO, *Reduced Competition, supra*, at 3. *See generally* GAO, *Airline Deregulation: Changes in Airfares, Service, and Safety at Small, Medium-Sized, and Large Communities*, GAO/RCED-96-79 Report (Apr. 1996) (noting endurance of hub premium factor at large airports colonized by one or two of the 'established' carriers). Nonetheless, it is worth observing that the increasing spread of low-fare competition – and consequent effects on legacy carrier pricing – is reflected in the absence of new hub premium investigations since 2001.
515. *See supra* Part II(D).
516. As noted, previously the Justice Department participated as a party to DOT domestic merger review proceedings, frequently in vain opposition to a proposed transaction. *See Airline Commission Proceedings*, testimony of Marc Schechter, Chief, Transportation, Energy and Agriculture Section, Antitrust Division, Department of Justice (Jun. 23, 1993), at 40-41.
517. Under the Hart-Scott-Rodino Antitrust Improvements Act of 1976, 15 U.S.C.A. § 18a (West 2008), as amended in Dec. 2000 (with effect from Feb. 2001), the parties to an acquisition of voting stock or assets of a U.S. corporation must notify the Justice Department before completing the transaction when the transaction exceeds $50 million in value and when one of the

still does not have, a merger policy that is specific to the airline industry (or to any other industry),[518] the Antitrust Division announced almost immediately that it would seek to block major airline mergers that involved a combination of carriers with major transfer points or hubs in the same city, or that would allow the acquisition of international routes by a carrier that already held authority to provide competing international service on those routes.[519]

---

parties has $100 million or more in total assets or net sales and the other has $10 million or more in total assets or net sales. Transactions valued at more than $200 million are reportable without regard to 'size of person.' *See* Press Release, Federal Trade Commission, Major Changes to Hart-Scott-Rodino Premerger Notification Requirements to Take Effect February 1, 2001 (Jan. 25, 2001). All dollar thresholds are now adjusted to reflect changes in the gross national product during the previous year. *See id.* After a filing, the responsible federal agency (either Justice or the Federal Trade Commission, depending on the industry in question) then performs a premerger review of the transaction to determine if it is likely to have anticompetitive effects. The rules are complex and time-consuming; airline mergers since 1989 have been handled by the Department of Justice. On the respective roles of the Departments of Justice and Transportation in airline mergers, *see* Steinberg, *supra* note 215 (indicating that, in a realignment of these agencies' pre-1989 roles and indeed of the roles they play currently in the review of international alliances, the Department of Justice determines whether a transaction will be challenged under the antitrust laws and the Department of Transportation conducts a competitive analysis of the proposed merger – including public interest factors within the Department's purview such as international route transfers, economic fitness, codesharing, and possible unfair or deceptive practices – 'and by practice will submit its views and findings to the Antitrust Division privately').

518. *See* J. Bruce McDonald, Deputy Assistant Attorney General, Antitrust Division, U.S. Department of Justice, *Antitrust for Airlines*, Remarks to the Regional Airline Association, President's Council Meeting (Nov. 3, 2005) [hereinafter McDonald Remarks 2005]. According to McDonald, 'the organizing principle is competition.' *Id. See also* Horizontal Merger Guidelines, *supra* note 499.

519. *See* Paul M. Barrett, *Airline Mergers May Be Harder, U.S. Aide Warns*, Wall St. J., Mar. 8, 1989, at 8. *See also* McDonald Remarks 2005, *supra* note 518 (confirming that this approach remains valid and explaining the Division's focus on specific origin/destination city and airport pairs, as well as on passenger demand segmentation (nonstop versus connecting, business versus leisure). The Division may also look at markets in which the merger partners are *potential* competitors. *See id. See generally* Robert D. Willig, *Antitrust Lessons from the Airline Industry: The DOJ Experience*, 60 Antitrust L.J. 695, 696-97 (1992) (analyzing and airline merger review by Antitrust Division as requiring identification of relevant product markets, typically city-pair routes; relevant participants, including potential new entrants; and ease of entry, as shaped by what Willig calls the 'hub-and-spoke network architecture'). *See also Airline Commission Proceedings*, testimony of Marc Schechter, Chief, Transportation, Energy and Agriculture Section, Antitrust Division, Department of Justice (Jun. 23, 1993), at 30-32 (noting, on the demand side, that consumers ordinarily do not switch origin/destination as a result of a price increase, confirming that the typical product market is the 'city-pair'). As a general principle, mergers between carriers with overlapping hub-and-spoke networks are likely to raise concerns about diminution of competition, while mergers between carriers that only compete on routes where feed is unimportant (freestanding origin-and-destination routes such as New York/Los Angeles) are more likely, other things being equal, to be viewed as benign. *See* Willig, *supra*, at 701. Finally, although the concept of 'contestability' is no longer in explicit favor, the Antitrust Division still seeks to determine whether new entry will occur to discipline a proposed merger. *See* McDonald Remarks 2005, *supra* note 518.

And, in signals of greater activism after 1989, the Department later averted the merger of the computer reservations systems owned by American and Delta,[520] the acquisition by American Airlines of all of TWA's routes between London and the United States, Eastern's sale of its assets at the Philadelphia hub to (the then) USAir, which already had 56% of Philadelphia's air passenger departures, and United's proposed acquisition of Eastern's 67 slots at Washington National Airport.[521] The Division also filed suit to require USAir to divest its London authority in the wake of its ill-fated investment and marketing alliance with British Airways.[522]

More recently, the Division twice threatened lawsuits to block the acquisition of US Airways (the successor airline to USAir) by United Airlines. Both threats (in

---

520. In 1989, the Department of Justice responded to Congressional concern about CRS market domination by threatening to seek an injunction to block a proposed merger between what was then the American Airlines-owned giant SABRE network and the much smaller (7% national share) Delta Air Lines-owned DATAS II system. *See* J.H. Cushman, *Airlines Won't Link Computers*, N.Y. TIMES, Jun. 23, 1989, at 1. The Department stated that the proposed link-up would reduce competition in both the market for air travel and the sale of computer services to travel agents. The airlines agreed not to proceed with their planned merger. *See id.* At the time, Charles Rule, then chief of the Antitrust Division, commented that major airlines '[had] used tools such as computer reservations systems and frequent flier programs to make new entry almost impossible.' Bridget O'Brian & Paul M. Barrett, *Delta Bid On Reservations Under Scrutiny*, WALL ST. J., Mar. 22, 1989, at 4. The American/Delta combination would have reduced the players in the CRS industry from five to four, and would have increased SABRE's national market share to 46%. In 2007, the Federal Trade Commission considered a proposed merger between Travelport (owner of the EU-based Galileo system) and Worldspan, granting final approval in July. *See* Jennifer Michels, *Travelport Completes Acquisition of Worldspan*, AVIATION DAILY, Aug. 22, 2007. This is the first CRS merger considered after the airlines divested themselves of their ownership stakes in these systems, *see supra* Chapter 3, Part VII, a factor that the Department of Justice has mentioned as an important marketplace change in its commentary on recent CRS rule revisions in the United States. *See id.*; *see also* U.S. DOT, *Notice of Proposed Rulemaking – Computer Reservation Systems Regulations*, Dkt. Nos. OST-97-2881 *et seq.*, Reply Comments of the Department of Justice (Jun. 9, 2003), at 13 (stating that 'perhaps the most significant change that has occurred in this industry since the last review of the rules is the divestiture of the CRS by their domestic airline owners').

521. *See* James F. Rill, Assistant Attorney General, Antitrust Division, Department of Justice, *The Agenda for Antitrust: Developments at the Department of Justice*, Remarks at 25th Annual New England Antitrust Conference, Cambridge, Mass. (Oct. 25, 1991) (quoted in Willig, *supra* note 519, at 697). As to the Eastern/USAir matter, the DOJ felt that it would be unlikely that another carrier would be able, within a reasonable period, to assemble a block of gates sufficiently large to operate a hub in competition with USAir. *See* Paul M. Barrett & Bridget O'Brian, *U.S. Plans Lawsuit To Block Eastern's Asset Sale To USAir*, WALL ST. J., Jun. 8, 1989, at 4. USAir withdrew from its proposed Eastern contract, and was replaced by the growing Chicago regional, Midway Airlines. *See* Carl Lavin, *Upstart Airline is Coming of Age*, N.Y. TIMES, Jul. 13, 1989, at 1. On the United/Eastern slot purchase, from which United withdrew after a Justice Department challenge, *see Airline Commission Proceedings*, comments by Marc Schechter, Chief, Transportation, Energy and Agriculture Section, Antitrust Division, Department of Justice, Jun. 23, 1993, at 29.

522. *See id.* For further analysis of the USAir/British Airways transaction, *see supra* Chapter 3, Part V.

1995 and again in 2000-2001)[523] were premised on the implications of United's acquisition of major US Airways hub operations at high-use East Coast airports.[524] While the wave of mergers and acquisitions in the 1980s was approved under a doctrine of contestability,[525] that doctrine appeared facile in an era of hub dominance. Thus, the 1995 investigation focused on US Airways operations at Washington's National Airport and LaGuardia Airport in New York, destinations already heavily serviced by Chicago-based United. And, in its 2000-2001 review, the Division questioned the reduction in significant competition for nonstop service from the Washington area that would flow from a combination of United's Washington Dulles hub with US Airways' large bases of operations at Washington Reagan and Baltimore Washington International.[526]

Until the Delta/Northwest combination announced in mid-2008,[527] there had only been one completed (and approved) merger between large U.S. domestic carriers since the handover of merger review authority in 1989 – the 'end-to-end' combination of the US Airways and America West route networks in 2005.[528] Most recently, Delta and Northwest announced a proposed merger on

---

523. In May 2000, United, at the time the nation's largest airline, offered $11.6 billion to buy US Airways, then the sixth largest. United argued that the combination would synergize its east-west network with US Airways' north-south operations. *See Hearing Before the Comm. on Transp. and Infrastructure on Proposed United-US Airways Merger*, 106th Cong., 2nd Sess. (Jun. 13, 2000).

524. *See* Michael E. Levine, Professor, Harvard Law School, Testimony Before the United States Senate Committee on Commerce, Science, and Transportation Hearing on Airline Mergers (Feb. 1, 2001) (stating that '[the proposed merger] will [build] a wall of scarce East Coast infrastructure around a fortress occupied by a Big Two, who will use the protection of that fortress to attack their pursuers').

525. *See supra* note 504 and accompanying text.

526. *See* McDonald Remarks 2005, *supra* note 518. Under the terms of the merger, United planned to divest some US Airways assets at Reagan and to create a new spin-off airline called DC Air. *See* Jay Etta Hecker, GAO Director of Physical Infrastructure Issues, Testimony before the U.S. Senate Committee on Commerce, Science, and Transportation (Feb. 1, 2001). There were other warning signs of potentially reduced competition, of course. In 2000-2001, for example, the Antitrust Division was also troubled by the fact that United and US Airways were the most significant carriers in a number of hub-to-hub markets, including Philadelphia/Los Angeles, Philadelphia/San Francisco, Philadelphia/Denver, and Pittsburgh/Washington. With their strong East Coast hubs, they were also the only two (or two of three) carriers connecting some northeastern cities such as Burlington and Albany with some southeastern cities such as Greensboro and Roanoke. More generally, the merger would increase concentration in large East Cost business centers, possibly affecting bidding for corporate and government contracts and would also have lessened competition in several transatlantic markets. *See id.*

527. *See supra* note 422.

528. Thus, America West operated primarily in the western United States, with hubs in Phoenix and Las Vegas, while US Airways was principally an eastern U.S. carrier, with hubs in Philadelphia, Pittsburgh, and Charlotte, and substantial presences in Washington, D.C., and New York City. *See* McDonald Remarks 2005, *supra* note 518. As McDonald notes, a clever investment banker code-named the deal 'Project Barbell.' *Id.* The Department of Justice, which announced after a short investigation that it would not take any action against the merger, found that integration of airlines with complementary networks (and few nonstop overlaps) could achieve efficiencies that benefit consumers. *See id. See also* Press Release, U.S. Dept. of

April 14, 2008[529] which won regulatory approval six months later. Unlike their predecessors in the pre-1989 laissez-faire era, it is to be hoped that government regulators will view the latest round of potential mergers and consolidations through a more sophisticated interpretive prism: not just examining the facts of market power and concentration (the market, as discussed at the outset of this Chapter, is already concentrated), but also considering 'sophisticated predictions' of a larger vision for the future of the industry.[530]

Justice, Statement by Assistant Attorney General R. Hewitt Pate Regarding the Closing of the America West/US Airways Investigation, *End-to-End Merger Cleared*, 05-338 (Jun. 23, 2005). Projected combination efficiencies are part of the DOJ's horizontal merger analysis. *See supra* note 503. *See also* Roger W. Fones, former Chief, Transportation Section, U.S. Department of Justice, *Panel Contribution: Building a National Policy to Restore American Competitiveness in Air Transport, in* International Aviation Law Institute, DePaul University College of Law & Chicago Council on Global Affairs, *Sustainable Aviation Policies for America and the World: A Leadership Summit*, at 9, Synopsis of the Proceedings (Oct. 19, 2006) (arguing that 'network extensions' such as the US Airways/America West merger create efficiencies of both scope and scale, whereas mergers of two carriers involving 'significant horizontal overlap' have historically not led to lasting cost efficiencies. Fones suggests that merger candidates with a horizontal overlap profile should try to demonstrate how the industry has changed over the past ten years (the rise of low-cost carriers and regional carriers, cheaper distribution, and the commoditization of the airline product) and show how the merger will eliminate redundancy. *See id.*; *see also supra* note 422 (discussing the Delta/Northwest merger announcement). The American Airlines acquisition of the assets of TWA in 2001 was not so much a merger as a forced liquidation of a failing firm which could not have successfully reorganized in bankruptcy or obtained another solvent buyer. *See* Fones, *supra*. Again, a 'failing firm' rationale is contemplated in the DOJ's merger analysis guidelines. *See supra* note 499.

529.   Delta/Northwest merger rumors began when the two airlines filed for Chapter 11 bankruptcy on Sept. 15, 2005. The rumors were reinvigorated when then U.S. Secretary of Transportation Norman Mineta indiscreetly informed an audience of business executives in Shanghai that he sometimes wondered whether or not 'Delta and Northwest will come out as a merged carrier.' He added that he was just 'thinking out loud.' *U.S. Transport Chief Ponders Delta-Northwest Merger*, USA TODAY, Jan. 10, 2006. *See also supra* note 422.

530.   Albert A. Foer, *On Behalf of the American Antitrust Institute Concerning Airline Mergers*, Testimony Before the Commerce, Science, and Transportation Committee (Jun. 21, 2000). Press reports at the time of the first United/US Airways merger attempt suggested that the DOT retained residual merger review jurisdiction for domestic transactions that involved international route authority, but the DOT's oversight of that authority is not, strictly speaking, a merger control mechanism: the DOT's merger review jurisdiction (which embraced only transactions between domestic carriers) was scrapped by the legislation sunsetting the Civil Aeronautics Board. *See supra* Part II(D). If a proposed transaction, however, involves the acquisition of international routes, and the transfer of certificate authority for those routes, the DOT must by statute find the transfer consistent with the public interest. *See* 49 U.S.C.A. § 41105 (West 2008). As part of that determination, the Department could find that the transfer would be contrary to the public interest on competitive grounds or because of the trade position of the United States in the international air transportation market, and could disapprove the transfer in whole or in part or condition its approval on requirements to protect the public interest. A disapproval of route certificate transfers would not technically prevent the merger, but might make the merger undoable in practice. To that extent, the news reports had more than

6   **Finding the Proper Regulatory Tempo: A Case Study of the 1998 Predatory Pricing Guidelines**

a   *The DOT Enters a Jurisprudential Minefield*

This discussion of U.S. competition policy offers a vivid and difficult lesson for international airline deregulation: the competitive enhancements of deregulation can be compromised through inadequate competition law enforcement but also through excessive regulatory meddling.[531] '[A] competitive airline business, free of counterproductive regulation, is a desirable goal but one that requires attention by the antitrust authorities on many fronts.'[532] The antitrust laws, as they are currently written, allow an enforcement-minded administration ample power to block competitively problematical mergers, acquisitions, and agreements (including transactions involving the 'secondary markets' in slots and international route authority),[533] and to prosecute and punish hard-core price-fixing and market-division offenses.[534] On the other hand, regulatory micromanagement of the industry (which still pervades international air transportation) makes the government a kind of universal ombudsperson, mediating not just consumer complaints[535] but

---

a scintilla of accuracy. *See generally* Steinberg *supra* note 215. It is a matter of no little irony, as we have seen, that the DOT retains the authority to grant antitrust immunity to intercarrier alliances in international air transportation. Despite serious competition misgivings by the Antitrust Division of the Department of Justice, the DOT granted virtually every one of the immunity requests it received. In a further irony, the DOT's antitrust analysis in its immunity proceedings might be characterized as contestability *redux*: in each case, the agency has adhered to a macroeconomic assumption that open skies agreements, which reduce regulatory barriers to entry, will necessarily encourage new entry that will compensate for the diminution of competition caused by the alliance.

531. *See Airline Commission Proceedings*, testimony of Dr. Frank Mulvey, former Research Associate, GAO (Jun. 1, 1993), at 82-83.
532. Willig, *supra* note 519, at 703.
533. *See Airline Commission Proceedings*, testimony of Marc Schechter, Chief, Transportation, Energy and Agriculture Section, Antitrust Division, Department of Justice (Jun. 23, 1993), at 29.
534. *See id.* at 43. As noted at various places in this discussion, the competition law authority of the U.S. Department of Justice encompasses Section 1 of the Sherman Act (agreements in restraint of trade, *e.g.*, price-fixing), Section 2 of the Sherman Act (monopolization, *e.g.*, predation) and Section 7 of the Clayton Act (mergers and acquisitions). In addition, the Department has extensive authority to conduct both civil and criminal investigations, including the ability (for example, by subpoena or civil investigative demand) to compel the production of both testimony and documents. If the Department concludes that the antitrust laws have been *or are about to be* violated, it may bring civil or criminal charges in a U.S. federal district court. In civil cases, the agency may seek declaratory or injunctive relief. *See generally* HOVENKAMP, *supra* note 493, at 592-601.
535. *See* James C. May, President and CEO, Air Transport Association of America, *Hearing on Aviation Consumer Issues*, Statement Before the Subcommittee on Aviation of the House Committee on Transportation and Infrastructure (Apr. 20, 2007) (resisting government efforts to adopt passenger rights legislation by arguing that regulation is only justified when market forces do not cause an industry to conform to social norms or to protect the health and safety of workers and the public; in May's view, market forces were driving improvements to customer

intercarrier disputes that might be better left to the marketplace and the 'antitrust injury' standard.[536] Dismantling some of the architectural bias of computer reservations systems, for example, involved lengthy official rulemaking proceedings with ambivalent results that were largely vitiated by structural events in the industry.[537]

The balance to be struck between the impulse to regulate and the impulse to trust the marketplace is nowhere more difficult to gauge than in the wars between new entrant or low-cost carriers and the incumbent legacy carriers. Should the government's role be to 'regulate' the playing field in favor of new entry (as the European Commission has sometimes sought to do) or to let the antitrust injury standard correct perceived imbalances? Crystallizing this policy dilemma, the U.S. DOT announced in 1998, after intense lobbying by the low-cost carriers, that it would consider the establishment of an Enforcement Policy Regarding Unfair Exclusionary Conduct in the Air Transportation Industry.[538] While exclusionary conduct could take many forms,[539] the main focus of interest was so-called

---

service and U.S. airlines had responded to passenger complaints through voluntary codes of conduct and other measures).

536. An antitrust plaintiff must prove (1) injury causally linked to a violation of the antitrust laws, and (2) that the injury is of the 'type' the antitrust laws were intended to prevent. *See* Cargill, Inc. *v.* Montfort of Colo., Inc., 479 U.S. 104, 113 (1986) (*quoting* Brunswick Corp. *v.* Pueblo Bowl-o-Mat, Inc., 429 U.S. 477, 489 (1977)). Not all forms of injury caused by antitrust violations are compensable. Plaintiff must show that the injury was caused by a reduction, rather than increase, in competition flowing from the defendant's acts, since 'the antitrust laws . . . were enacted for the protection of competition not competitors.' *Brunswick Corp.*, 429 U.S. at 489. *See* American Airlines Submission, *supra* note 215, at 13 (commenting that the many investigations of CRS systems and Congressional calls for even more 'micro-regulation' are 'the consequence of intense lobbying by airlines which avoided the expense and risk inherent in creating this entirely new business. . . . ').

537. The Airline Commission, having heard a bewildering array of testimony and points of view, decided that CRS and frequent flier programs 'required no action' by the Commission. *See Airline Commission Report, supra* note 319, at 3. While allegations of hard-core anti-competitive activity in the CRS industry – attempted monopolization, for example – met with scant judicial favor, the Department of Justice did successfully avoid a further pruning of the industry when it threatened to enjoin the Apollo/System One merger.

538. *See* Enforcement Policy Regarding Unfair Exclusionary Conduct in the Air Transportation Industry, Dkt. No. OST-98-3713, 63 Fed. Reg. 17,919 (Apr. 10, 1998) [hereinafter DOT Enforcement Policy]. In adopting the policy, the DOT indicated that it was acting 'on the basis of informal complaints.' *Id.*

539. As an example of the kind of conduct it proposed to police, the DOT mentioned the alleged retaliation by Northwest Airlines against new entry by Reno Air ('Reno'), based in Reno, Nevada, at Northwest's Minneapolis hub. Northwest allegedly 'blanketed' all of Reno's routes, including the Minneapolis/Reno market (which it had previously exited after substantial losses) and three short-haul Reno/West Coast markets, and applied exceptionally low fares to each route. Reno believed that the timing of Northwest's entry and the signaling of its pricing decisions demonstrated an attempt to forestall Reno Air's entry into Minneapolis. Northwest's retaliatory strategy, called 'route overlay' in industry parlance, led to Department of Justice action in 1993 following a complaint by Reno against Northwest. *See* Statement of Reno Air, Inc., *in Airline Commission Documents*, undocketed (Jul. 2, 1993), at 3 [hereinafter Reno Air Submission]. The Department's response, which evidently prompted Northwest's

predatory pricing as a possible violation of the antitrust laws.[540] Under the arche-typal facts, a dominant carrier would apply reduced rates that were specific to the routes and flight times of a new entrant.[541] By reducing sales of its higher-priced tickets, the incumbent would likely experience substantial self-diversion and an opportunity cost.[542] The upstart entrant may quit the market (or be forced to raise prices as part of a disciplined oligopoly). If the new entrant were to quit the market, the dominant carrier would recoup its opportunity cost by raising prices.[543]

Supplementing traditional Department of Justice antitrust enforcement,[544] the DOT proposed to use its Section 411 statutory powers to prohibit unfair compet-itive practices, such as incipient predation, even if they did not yet escalate to a violation of the antitrust laws.[545] Among the scenarios triggering enforcement

---

decision *not* to overlay Reno's West Coast routes, reflected an informal enforcement power that the government could deploy merely by the issue (or threat of issue) of civil investigative demands. According to Marc Schechter, the responsible Justice official who testified before the Airline Commission on the Reno Air dispute, 'conduct aside from pricing can form the basis of a predatory conduct case.' Thus, the Department queried whether the route overlay made commercial sense for Northwest outside the strategy of driving Reno Air out of the market. *See Airline Commission Proceedings*, testimony of Marc Schechter, Chief, Transpor-tation, Energy and Agriculture Section, Antitrust Division, Department of Justice (Jun. 23, 1993), at 65. *See also* U.S. DOT, *Enforcement Policy Regarding Unfair Exclusionary Conduct in the Air Transportation Industry*, Dkt. No. OST-98-3713, Findings and Conclusions on the Economic, Policy, and Legal Issues (Jan. 17, 2001), at 62 [hereinafter U.S. DOT, *Enforcement Policy Findings and Conclusions*] (discussing Northwest/Reno affray as example of unfair competitive practice that posits an airline's entry into one or more markets served by a second airline in order to force the latter to exit a market served by the first airline). A route overlay unsupported by price predation, however, would seem to represent conventional head-to-head competition. Northwest did not, in fact, withdraw its new Minneapolis/Reno service. Setting the scene for the DOT's eventual announcement of proposed guidelines, Reno Air also called on the Department of Transportation to use its own Section 411 jurisdiction, considered earlier, to 'prohibit efforts by incumbent carriers to duplicate service patterns and initiate fare reduc-tions when those actions, taken together, clearly are calculated or are likely to impede entry by a new carrier in a city-pair market, or to place the new entrant in economic jeopardy.' Reno Air Submission, *supra*, at 8. Northwest Airlines has been the object of other private enforcement proceedings alleging predation. *See infra* note 569.

540. Technically, predatory conduct is alleged to violate Section 2 of the Sherman Act, 15 U.S.C. § 2, which proscribes monopolization and attempted monopolization through exclusionary conduct such as predation.
541. The DOT used the term 'new entrant' in this context to mean an independent airline that had started jet service within the previous 10 years and was pursuing 'a competitive strategy of charging low fares.' DOT Enforcement Policy, *supra* note 538, at 17,920.
542. *See id.* at 17,921. According to the DOT, incumbents (or 'major carriers' as the Department described them in its enforcement policy) maximized revenues through price discrimination, and fare premiums at local hub markets could mean revenues of tens of millions of dollars. *Id.*
543. *See* U.S. DOT, *Enforcement Policy Findings and Conclusions, supra* note 539, at 75. Section 411 has been recodified as 49 U.S.C.A. § 41712 (West 2008). *See* DOT Enforcement Policy, *supra* note 538, at 17,920.
544. *See supra* note 539.
545. Notably, these Section 411 powers can be exercised in pursuance of a policy that differs from Sherman Act standards. 'Congress specifically gave [the DOT] the authority to prohibit

action would be the classical predatory scenario where the number of passengers carried by the incumbent airline at low fares exceeded the total number of seats operated by the entrant (if the incumbent then obtained less local revenue than it would have obtained by using a reasonable alternative response to the new entrant).[546]

By January 2001, however, DOT officials had concluded that this slide-rule approach to pricing and capacity competition had serious defects. After receiving thousands of responses during its public comment period,[547] the Department reversed course and accepted that the development of standards on a case-by-case basis would be a more effective way of proceeding than publication of formal *a priori* guidelines.[548] The Department found that the issues in each case would reflect the complexities inherent in airline competition and market differences, so that the nature of individual markets and market participants would better determine whether consumers were being denied competitive service and fares.[549] In an age of deregulation, the DOT felt uneasy about adopting prescriptions for carrier behavior in the marketplace in a way that could discourage legitimate competition. On the other hand, the Department had to tread carefully to dispel any impression that, *as a matter of public policy*, an incumbent airline is entitled to respond to new competitors in a way that keeps all of its traffic and even its market share in nonstop hub markets (which have demonstrable monopolistic tendencies).[550]

Most significantly, however, the rhetoric of the low-cost carriers masked a significant anomaly in competitor behavior, and in antitrust law and theory, that the Department ultimately felt compelled to accommodate. Predatory behavior, as many commentators have remarked, is 'generally difficult to distinguish' from the kind of competition that benefits consumers,[551] precisely the kind of vigorous

---

conduct that violates antitrust principles, even if [that conduct] does not violate the antitrust laws.' U.S. DOT, *Enforcement Policy Findings and Conclusions, supra* note 539, at 74.

546. *See id.* at 75-76.

547. *See id.* at 4. The Air Line Pilots Association, for example, sidestepped any analysis of the legal and policy content of the guidelines and directly faulted the DOT for giving 'undue protection' to carriers whose low fares were allegedly based on substandard wages and working conditions. U.S. DOT, *Policy Statement Regarding Unfair Exclusionary Practices – Statement of Enforcement Policy Regarding Unfair Exclusionary Conduct*, Dkt. No. 98-3713-822, Comments of the Air Line Pilots Association, International (Jul. 24, 1998), at 2.

548. Typical of legacy airlines' objections, for example, was United Airlines' submission that the DOT proposed its enforcement policy because it 'found that network airlines "systematically" engaged in predatory-type conduct.' U.S. DOT, *Enforcement Policy Findings and Conclusions, supra* note 539, at 52. The DOT response to that argument was not, in a technical sense, to deny it. Rather, in rebuffing United's insistence that a rational policy required a 'system-wide review' of the industry, the Department declared that it 'never intended to generally regulate responses to entry.' *Id.* More accurately, the Department's policy foray seemed intended to regulate specific cases through general guidelines. The difference is not entirely trivial.

549. *See id.*

550. *Id.* at 48.

551. *Id.* at 11 (citing authorities).

competition that deregulation is supposed to encourage. As the U.S. Supreme Court itself observed in *Brooke Group Ltd. v. Brown & Williamson Tobacco Corp.*,[552] because '[t]he mechanism by which a firm engages in predatory pricing – lowering prices – is the same mechanism by which a firm stimulates competition,' mistaken inferences drawn from competitor activity, even if that activity imposes 'painful losses' on a competitor, would chill the very conduct that the antitrust laws are designed to protect.[553] While the low-cost carrier sector advocated some degree of official oversight during the formative period of a new entrant's operations, the Department had to bear in mind that passengers in many apparently predatory pricing scenarios realize a short-term windfall, a 'boon' as the Supreme Court has called it,[554] albeit with the risk that they later lose the benefit of competition on the route altogether.[555]

Distinguishing predatory actions from situations where vigorous competition motivates incumbents to offer broad-based fare cuts in several markets, including those served by a new entrant, or where an incumbent simply matches the low-fares of an new entrant,[556] sets up an enforcement tripwire that may simply not be worth

---

552. 509 U.S. 209 (1993).
553. *See Brooke Group Ltd.*, 509 U.S. at 226. The prohibitive cost of pursuing a 'mistaken inference,' in fact, brings to mind the remark of prominent securities attorney Stephen D. Susman that antitrust has become 'the playground of big companies.' 67 Antitrust & Trade Reg. Rep. (BNA) 631 (Dec. 1, 1994). It must be conceded, moreover, that *private* enforcement – despite its attendant windfalls of treble-damages and attorney's fees – not only involves complex factual analysis in prolonged and costly lawsuits, but is frequently used itself as a tactic to rein in a strong competitor. (*See* comments of the U.S. Supreme Court in *Brooke Group Ltd.*, 509 U.S. at 209.) In the mergers and acquisitions area, it is very rare for private parties to seek injunctive relief to block impending transactions (as the Department of Justice routinely does). The inducement of treble damages does not exist in injunction cases. *See Airline Commission Proceedings*, testimony of Marc Schechter, Chief, Transportation, Energy and Agriculture Section, Antitrust Division, Department of Justice (Jun. 23, 1993), at 42. *See infra* note 569 (discussing recent private enforcement activity).
554. *Brooke Group Ltd.*, 509 U.S. at 224. Intoning its 'axiom' that the antitrust laws 'protect . . . competition, not competitors,' *Brown Shoe Co. v. United States*, 370 U.S. 294, 320 (1962), the Court cautioned that 'unsuccessful predation is in general a boon to consumers' so that the standards for predatory pricing liability should not be set 'so low that antitrust suits themselves became a tool for keeping prices high.' *Id.*
555. *See DOT Enforcement Policy, supra* note 538, at 17,921. Yet this may not happen, precisely because recoupment of losses from below-cost pricing is likely to be difficult. As the U.S. Supreme Court recently observed, '[w]ithout successful recoupment, 'predatory pricing produces lower aggregate prices in the market and consumer welfare is enhanced.' *Weyerhaeuser Co. v. Ross-Simmons Hardwood Lumber Co.*, 549 U.S. 312 (2007). But in some quarters there is always anxiety about corporate motives. Hence, no doubt, the specter of reregulation implicit in the argument by the Transportation Research Board, in its submission on the DOT's proposed enforcement guidelines, that incumbents be compelled to make a commitment to maintain fare reductions for a specified number of seats for a period of two years, regardless of whether the new entrant remains in the market. *See* U.S. DOT, *Enforcement Policy Findings and Conclusions, supra* note 539, at 79 (citing authorities).
556. Even if those fares are well below the incumbent airline's original fares. *See* U.S. DOT, *Enforcement Policy Findings and Conclusions, supra* note 539, at 68. Note, however, that

the time and energy of government enforcers. This broadly abstentionist approach, though initially resisted by the DOT,[557] is well-supported in legal precedent and scholarship, despite the existence and longevity of the doctrine.[558] The Supreme Court, for example, has continued to confirm its earlier skepticism about the 'implausibility' of predation[559] (which also tilts the odds considerably against private pursuit of this kind of litigation).[560]

b   *The Rational Side of Predation*

The conceptual instability of predation, however, should not mean (and has not meant) that occasionally the alleged fact patterns cannot become sufficiently pervasive to merit closer scrutiny, either through public or private enforcement.[561] It would be entirely rational, for example, that an incumbent airline could wish to

---

because of the other service features that incumbents can offer (a frequent flier program, for example), the price-match *could* in effect *undercut* the new entrant's fare, again leading to possible regulatory scrutiny. *See id.*

557. Thus, the Department suggested in its initial announcement of the guidelines that the nature of the air transport industry would allow 'unfair exclusionary practices' to succeed, since major air carriers, in comparison with major players in other industries, can price-discriminate to a much greater extent, adjust prices much faster, and shift resources between markets much more readily. DOT Enforcement Policy, *supra* note 538, at 17,921.

558. *See Brooke Group Ltd.*, 509 U.S. at 209; *see also Weyerhaeuser*, 549 U.S. at 325 (reaffirming *Brooke Group* rule requiring 'dangerous probability' that firm engaged in predation can recoup its investment in below-cost pricing); *see, e.g.*, Frank H. Easterbrook, *Predatory Strategies and Counterstrategies*, 48 U. Chi. L. Rev. 263, 264 (1981) (arguing that 'there is no sufficient reason for antitrust law or the courts to take predation seriously'); Jonathan B. Baker, *Predatory Pricing After Brooke Group: An Economic Perspective*, 62 Antitrust L. J. 585, 586 (1994) (noting two necessary but uncertain events needed to make predation rational, namely, the victim of the alleged predation would have to exit, and the predator would have to generate profits in excess of its initial losses). In the Chicago School view, successful predation would be rare because it requires ceasing to engage in economically rational behavior in the present – by suffering short-term losses – in an effort to drive a rival from the market and to reassert monopolistic control in the future. *See Weyerhaeuser*, 549 U.S. at 323 (stating that 'a rational business will rarely make this sacrifice'); *see also* Spirit Airlines, Inc. *v.* Northwest Airlines, Inc., 431 F.3d 917, 953 (6th Cir. 2005) (Moore, J., concurring). *But see* Baker, *supra*, at 590 (also noting that some 'post-Chicago' economists have theorized that price predation is not only plausible but profitable, especially in a multimarket context where predation can occur in one market and recoupment can occur rapidly in other markets).

559. *See* Matsushita Electric Industrial Co. *v.* Zenith Radio Corp., 475 U.S. 574, 588-90 (1986).

560. *But see infra* note 569 (discussing recent private enforcement action against Northwest Airlines by low-cost rival Spirit Airlines).

561. Private enforcement remains to evolve as a significant source of competition surveillance in the EC system. *See* Paul Csiszar, Directorate-General for Competition, European Commission, Economist, May 31, 2008, at 24 (noting that recourse to private action in the United States explains why U.S. authorities bring fewer cases against allegedly abusive behavior by large companies; in the European Community, 'private antitrust action is still in its infancy,' creating a greater risk of potential underenforcement if Europe's competition authorities do not act). On recent private enforcement proceedings against Northwest Airlines, *see infra* note 569.

develop a reputation for 'fierce' responses to new entry.[562] The DOT itself recognized, for example, that the allegedly anticompetitive actions of American Airlines at Dallas-Fort Worth (DFW) justified the filing of an antitrust lawsuit by the Department of Justice in 1999.[563] According to the government's complaint in that case,[564] American sought to defend its monopoly power (and its supracompetitive pricing) at DFW against new entrant, low-cost competition by saturating routes with enough additional capacity at low fares to keep the entrant from operating profitably. The incumbent would also drain traffic from its rivals by matching their connecting fares with its own nonstop fares.[565]

The proposed evidentiary record suggested that these actions were neither transitory nor spontaneous, but rather flowed from (and were intensified in accordance with) American's deliberate business strategy to 'investigate' the financial

---

562. *Spirit Airlines, Inc.*, 431 F.3d at 937 n.5 (quoting a remark by former Northwest Airlines executive Michael Levine, now a faculty member at New York University School of Law, mentioned in an article in the *DePaul Business Law Journal*; Levine called this reputational information 'the predatory investment in deterrence' (citation omitted)). The Court of Appeals also quoted the following remarks of former CAB Chairman Alfred Kahn, made in reference to Northwest Airlines' alleged 'scorched-earth' policy toward upstart rivals like People Express: 'If predation means anything, it means deep, pinpointed, discriminatory price cuts by big companies aimed at driving price cutters out of the market, in order then to be able to raise prices back to their previous levels. I have little doubt that is what Northwest was and is trying to do.' The original quote appears in Paul Stephen Dempsey, *Predation, Competition, and Antitrust Law: Turbulence in the Airline Industry?*, 67 J. AIR L. & COM. 685, 702 (2002).

563. *See* United States v. AMR Corp. et al., D. Kans. Civil Action 99-1180-JTM (filed May 13, 1999) [hereinafter Complaint Against American Airlines]. In another high-profile instance of the vagaries of predation jurisprudence, this time involving a 1993 private lawsuit against American Airlines, Continental Airlines and Northwest Airlines charged – unsuccessfully – in federal court that American Airlines unleashed a titanic predatory price war in 1992 that was calculated to drive both of them out of business The issue of predation had been freshly considered by the U.S. Supreme Court just weeks before the so-called 'Antitrust Dogfight' began in federal court in Galveston, Texas. Amidst uncertainty about the scope of the 'recoupment' theory articulated in the high court's opinion, the jury returned a verdict in American's favor. Ironically, Continental itself had been sued by a smaller competitor, UltrAir, on a virtually identical predation theory. The Galveston case evolved from American's 1992 'value pricing' program, a simplified four-tier pricing plan that contained only first-class, unrestricted-coach and 14-day and 30-day advance-purchase tickets, eliminated all special discounts, and slashed first class and coach seats by 20 to 50%. The plan was estimated by American to be likely to cause the airline an initial revenue loss of over $100 million in its first three months. American's calculations included forecasts of how much its rivals might lose as they responded to American's action (some of them offered even deeper fare cuts). Continental and Northwest alleged that American's preoccupation with how much its weaker rivals would lose showed that 'value pricing' was intended to debilitate or destroy them. American responded that any prudent company would estimate the impact of such a program on competitors. 'Value pricing,' as it turns out, produced no winners. American repeatedly moved its whole pricing structure downward to meet new rival promotions, intending to prevent the re-emergence of fare proliferation. *See* Transportation News Digest, Department of Transportation, *in Airline Commission Documents*, undocketed (1993) (with extract from WALL ST. J., Jul. 12, 1993, at A1).

564. *See* Complaint Against American Airlines, *supra* note 563.

565. *See id.* para. 28.

resources of its low-cost competitors, to 'determine' their break-even load factors, and to 'conduct' head-counts at the departure gates to monitor their passenger loads.[566] Most significantly, the American strategy overrode its own internal capacity-planning models and was arguably 'not profitable except as a means of excluding or stifling competition.'[567] Critically, the strategy allegedly succeeded in preserving the incumbent's monopoly power not only by evicting competitors but by allowing subsequent substantial fare increases and service reductions.[568] In the ensuing litigation, however, the government's case foundered on its inability to provide a reliable (rather than speculative) measure of American's opportunity costs.[569]

---

566. *Id.*
567. *Id.* para. 48.
568. *See id.* para. 7.
569. *See* U.S. *v.* AMR Corp., 140 F. Supp. 2d 1141 (D. Kan. 2001) (awarding summary judgment in favor of defendant), *aff'd*, U.S. *v.* AMR Corporation, 335 F.3rd 1109 (10th Cir. 2003) (noting that the Supreme Court has declined to state which of the various cost measures for calculating predatory recoupment is definitive). For a recent example of private enforcement of the predation standard, *see Spirit Airlines Inc.*, 431 F.3d at 917, in which the United States Court of Appeals for the Sixth Circuit reversed a district court grant of summary judgment to defendant Northwest, holding *inter alia* that a reasonable jury could find that a separate and distinct low-fare or leisure passenger market existed on the contested routes, and that Northwest successfully used its market power to engage in predation in that market and on those routes, as plaintiff Spirit contended. Ironically, it was in this case that the court deployed Northwest executive Michael Levine's past professorial declamation of a 'new competitive equilibrium analysis' to illustrate a strategy of 'fierce' predation. Here is Levine's analysis from his original article (the court's quotation, 431 F.3d at 929, somewhat mangles the actual language):

> The essence of the strategy is simple. Match, or better yet, beat the new entrant's lowest fare with a low fare restricted to confine its attractiveness to the leisure-oriented, price-sensitive sector of the market. Match business-oriented fares and offer extra benefits to retain the loyalties of travel agents and frequent fl[i]ers. Add frequency where possible, to 'sandwich' the new entrant's departures between one's own departures. Make sure enough seats are available on your flights in the market in order to accommodate increases in traffic caused by the fare war. In short, leave no traveler with either a price or a schedule incentive to fly the new entrant.

> Levine, *Airline Competition, supra* note 67, at 476. Is this kind of targeted market manipulation (the Levine 'script') predatory? Or is it just the language of market competition and bold capitalism delivered in Levine's characteristically aggressive register? The Sixth Circuit, in quoting the language, clearly thought it could be a predatory script. To that end, the court also quoted Levine's conclusion that 'the incumbent will not operate profitably under such conditions especially if, as is usually the case, it is a higher-cost airline than its competitor.' *Spirit Airlines Inc.*, 431 F.3d at 929. For other Levine comments that caught the court's attention, *see supra* note 562. Finally, while the information and travel agent advantages that legacy carriers enjoyed in the 1980s have been blunted somewhat in the Internet age, frequent flier programs are still effective as competitive weapons to bleed traffic from new entrants. *See also* R. Bruce Wark, *A Review of Airline Predatory Pricing Cases*, AIR & SPACE LAW., Spring 2006, at 1 (criticizing the *Spirit* decision); *but see* Mark S. Kahan, *Discovering the Unicorn: Spirit v. Northwest*, AIR & SPACE LAW., Spring 2007, at 1 (responding to Wark's critique).

c   *The DOT Abandons Regulatory* a Priorism

In sum, the DOT has abandoned generic guidelines for the application of its enforcement discretion to incipient cases of airline predation or other potential unfair competitive practices.[570] The sheer variety of potential practices militated against this kind
of *a priori* 'managed' approach to enforcement.[571] Moreover, as the Department
concluded in its findings on the legal and policy issues, the guidelines 'would
have protected only one class of airlines against only one type of unfair competitive response, the use of fare reductions and capacity increases to eliminate
competition.'[572] Such a narrow approach, preempting the enforcement process rather
than evolving from it, was ultimately rejected as bad policy.[573] In the end, the DOT
retreated to the safest harbor in enforcement policy, the one that most naturally com-
forts all antitrust enforcers – the high-profile deterrent proceeding (as in the American
Airlines matter discussed above) that targets 'the more egregious cases.'[574]

---

570. There were other reasons for the DOT's abandonment of its predatory pricing guidelines
     besides its own intellectual tergiversation. The pervasiveness of government, and the repeated
     pressures to restrict their economic liberties, make it hardly surprising that airlines have a
     strong lobbying presence in Washington, D.C. (a 'mighty' lobby, according to a New York
     Times headline, *see* Leslie Wayne & Michael Moss, *Bailout for Airlines Showed the Weight of
     a Mighty Lobby*, N.Y. TIMES, Oct. 10, 2001, at A1). And there is no doubt that airline lobbying
     efforts to repel reregulation have been largely successful. A glance at the opensecrets.org
     website, which monitors political campaign financing, reveals that airlines are not among
     the top ten industries engaged in Congressional lobbying activities. This is curious; the top
     of the list is dominated by utility industries that have historically attracted intense public
     regulation (electricity, oil and gas, telecommunications). The airlines, in contrast, have had
     the complex status of a deregulated 'public utility' still cocooned in a giant web of regulation.
     Public choice theory provides at least one paradigm to help explain this outcome. James
     Buchanan (winner of the Nobel Prize in Economic Science in 1986) and Gordon Tullock
     are credited as the primary architects of public choice theory. Their book, THE CALCULUS OF
     CONSENT: LOGICAL FOUNDATIONS OF CONSTITUTIONAL DEMOCRACY (1962), is still considered the
     seminal work in this field. As Gary Libecap has written, 'all things being equal, those interest
     groups with great wealth, size, and homogeneity will have more resources to influence poli-
     ticians regarding the assignment of property rights, more votes to attract attention to their
     demands, and more cohesion to be effective lobbyists.' John E. Richards, *Toward a Positive
     Theory of International Institutions: Regulating International Aviation Markets*, INT'L ORG.,
     Winter 1999, at 10. Diffuse interests (individual consumers, for example) have little incentive
     to spend time and money to organize or become informed and therefore have very limited
     effective influence. *See id.* Concentrated interests (that is, producers or service providers), on
     the other hand, face lower organizational costs and have larger incentives to become organized
     and informed about regulations and therefore tend to have much higher effective influence.
     See id. To some extent, the airlines' influence over future regulatory initiatives may have been
     compromised by the surrender of financial power implied in the 2001 bailout. *See infra*
     Part IV(C).
571. *See* U.S. DOT, *Enforcement Policy Findings and Conclusions, supra* note 539, at 63.
572. *Id.* at 71.
573. *See id.*
574. *See id.* at 63. This approach, along with a calculated leniency toward whistleblowers, has been
     the most cost-effective way to deal with the government's inevitable resource limitations. For

Of course, these proceedings will be prosecuted not by the DOT but by the Department of Justice.[575]

---

more pervasive, 'industry-wide' action, the existing procedures of public and private enforcement seem adequate. A conspicuous recent example is the U.S. DOJ investigation (also being pursued by the Office of Fair Trading (OFT) in the United Kingdom) into alleged price-fixing of transatlantic fuel surcharges by British Airways and Virgin Atlantic executives. BA has already admitted breaching competition laws and set aside a $700 million reserve to cover legal contingencies. *See* David Leppard, *BA Chiefs Face Extradition Over 'Price-Fixing'*, CHI. SUN. TIMES, May 27, 2007, at 3. The alleged conspiracy was 'whistle-blown' when Virgin opted to notify the OFT in 2006 under the U.K. Enterprise Act of 2002, which grants possible immunity to companies that notify authorities of alleged offenses and provide evidence to support a prosecution. *See id.* BA was punished with a combined $524 million fine from the OFT and the DOJ. *See* Kaveri Niththyananthan, *Charges Are Filed in BA Price-Fixing Case*, WALL ST. J., Aug. 8, 2006, at B2. Additionally, the OFT has brought charges against one current and three former BA executives alleging price-fixing under the U.K. Enterprise Act. *See id.* If found guilty, the four could face up to five years' imprisonment and/or an unlimited fine. *Id.* Whether convicted or acquitted, all four defendants are protected under U.K. law from being charged again for the crime in the United States. *Id.* Meanwhile, the European Commission continues to pursue its investigation into a suspected air freight cartel in the United States that implicates BA, SAS, Japan Airlines, and Air France-KLM. *See Air-Freight Cartel Inquiry Advances*, WALL ST. J., Dec. 22, 2007, at A6A. In Jun., 2008, the U.S. DOJ imposed over $500 million in fines on airlines participating in the cartel. *See* Press Release, U.S. Dept. of Justice, Major International Airlines Agree to Plead Guilty and Pay Criminal Fine Totaling More Than $500 Million for Fixing Prices on Air Cargo Rates, 08-570 (Jun. 26, 2008).

575. In another example of 'pervasive, industry-wide action,' in late Dec. 1992 the Antitrust Division of the Department of Justice filed a civil antitrust action involving the airlines' alleged use of a computerized 'clearinghouse' for air fare information in order to fix prices and to implement a species of oligopolistic predation. The suit sought court action to prohibit the airlines' historical practice of providing advance notice of fare increases and discount sales, ostensibly for the benefit of travel agents and the public but in reality, the government contended, facilitating a price consensus among the airlines. The Airline Tariff Publishing Company (ATPCO) is a joint venture created by a number of airlines that acts as an electronic clearinghouse for all airline fares. Airlines have access through ATPCO to each others' current and proposed fares. The Justice Department's lawsuit charged that the airlines used the ATPCO system to negotiate fare increases and the elimination of discount fares with one another. Certain features of the system allowed this coordination to occur. For example, airlines could signal proposed first ticket dates for future fare increases, subject to indications of concurrence from other participants. A similar signaling process applied to withdrawal of discount fares. The Department also uncovered the existence of non-public 'footnote designators' intended to highlight fare proposals and to tie proposed fare actions in one market to those in other markets, facilitating trading of fare increases across markets and fare types as well as the punishment of competitors who fail to cooperate (for example, by indicating that a discount fare has been initiated to counter – and to deter – a competitor's discount or refusal to join a fare increase). *See Airline Commission Proceedings*, testimony of Marc Schechter, Chief, Transportation, Energy and Agriculture Section, Antitrust Division, Department of Justice (Jun. 23, 1993), at 33-34 ('The ATP system allows the airlines to tell each other what prices they would like to charge in the future and then allows them to negotiate a consensus price increase'). *See* U.S. *v.* Airline Tariff Publishing Co., 836 F. Supp. 9 (D.C. 1993) (approving proposed final judgment as in public interest). The ATPCO system still exists, although now with remedial safeguards in place to avoid the price signaling violations

The safe harbor approach still leaves unresolved what the DOT itself should or should not do with its Section 411 enforcement powers.[576] The DOT's abandoned enforcement policy was premised on the idea that Section 411 jurisdiction might be pressed into service as a rapid-response mechanism to deter conduct that could impede competition but which may not, for example, technically rise to being predation under the antitrust laws.[577] On balance, however, the Supreme Court's judicial skepticism ought to give pause: the government's role should not be to serve as a kind of paternalistic corporate hand-holder for new entrants,[578] and as a general proposition notorious acts of predation can always be deterred in their incipiency by the *in terrorem* issue of a civil investigative demand.[579]

that provoked DOJ enforcement. *See* ATPCO, <www.atpco.net/atpco/set_corpinfo.htm> (containing a description of the corporate business). For an example of a private antitrust enforcement action with industry-wide ramifications, *see* Continental Airlines, Inc. et al. *v.* United Airlines, Inc. & Dulles Airport Airline Management Council, 277 F.3d 499 (4th Cir. 2002) (vacating summary judgment in favor of plaintiff on the ground that challenged bag templates installed by defendants, limiting carry-on bag size, would not necessarily be an intercompetitor restraint of trade – and could even have positive competitive effects *inter alia* through greater efficiency and better flying experiences – given the unique architectural configuration of Dulles International Airport).

576. The incumbent airlines' dislike of Section 411, and their resilience in challenging not only its application but its very legality, has been a feature of a number of DOT proceedings. In attacking the proposed predation enforcement guidelines, for example, Continental Airlines and Delta Air Lines contended that Section 411 would not allow consideration by the DOT of an airline's capacity decisions. *See* U.S. DOT, *Enforcement Policy Findings and Conclusions, supra* note 539, at 108. 49 U.S.C.A. § 41109(a)(2) (West 2008), an anchor of deregulation, proscribes the issuance of air operator certificates with limitations on capacity. The DOT takes the view that this provision is part of the statutory scheme for defining its power to grant and condition certificates for operation of passenger airline operations and does not affect its authority under Section 411. Similarly, the DOT may address pricing behavior under Section 411 even though it cannot condition certificates with respect to tariffs. *See* U.S. DOT, *Enforcement Policy Findings and Conclusions, supra* note 539, at 108. The Department must of necessity take this view – otherwise its discretionary power of market correction would be compromised by the basic pricing and capacity freedoms of deregulation – but many industry stakeholders find Section 411 an unpredictable and intrusive instrument that risks unwarranted reregulation of airlines' commercial behavior.

577. A rapid-response mechanism to halt and then investigate suspected predatory fares has long been included in the DOT's general *international* regulatory powers. Just how 'rapid' the response could be is itself problematic. Section 411 requires the DOT to hold a hearing before determining that a party has engaged in an unfair method of competition. Preliminary relief is not available. *See* U.S. DOT, *Enforcement Policy Findings and Conclusions, supra* note 539, at 69.

578. But the urge to meddle in airline competition is never far from some Congressional minds. During the 2000-2001 United/US Airways merger investigation, for example, Congressman James Oberstar (later Chairman of the House Transportation Committee) introduced the 'Airline Competition Preservation Act of 2001' to allow regulators to force airlines to roll back fares and to prevent discrimination against new entrant airlines if three or fewer airlines controlled 70% or more of an airport's flight movements as of Jan. 3, 2001.

579. The DOT did not decide to vacate the field of enforcement and to defer entirely to the Department of Justice. It considered that such an outcome would be inconsistent with its role under Section 411 to 'complement' DOJ enforcement of the antitrust laws. U.S. DOT, *Enforcement Policy Findings and Conclusions, supra* note 539, at 71. Moreover, the DOT also

C   PORTENTS OF REREGULATION: AN INDUSTRY IN PERPETUAL
                TRANSITION

1   **The Lessons of the September 11, 2001 'Stabilization'**
                Package

As noted earlier, reregulation of the airline industry has been touted as a possible remedy for its vulnerability to cyclical economic variations, and that call has found fresh resonance in the current era of volatile oil prices – which may yet turn out to be structural rather than cyclical.[580] The political durability of the deregulatory experiment, which celebrated its 30th anniversary in 2008,[581] was certainly compromised in the aftermath of the September 11, 2001 terrorist attacks on the United States. In the next Part, we will look more closely at what this government assistance, and the conditions which attached to it, may have portended for airline deregulation. We will then consider some of the arguments favoring, and disfavoring, a return to a reregulated airline industry in the United States.

---

rejected the view that enforcement action under Section 411 would entail 'a general regulation of airline fares and services.' *Id.* at 89. The prospect of reregulation was discounted at two levels: the enforcement authority is to be used in aid of the consumer benefits of deregulation, and reregulation would require 'a radical expansion' of statutory authority and would in any event be too expensive and resource-intensive. *Id.* The real threat to deregulation, according to the government, is 'the use by dominant airlines of their market power to end competition.' *Id.*

580. No commentator has been more stalwart in his advocacy of reregulation than the Director of the McGill University Institute of Air and Space Law, Professor Paul Stephen Dempsey. *See, e.g.,* Paul Stephen Dempsey, *The Cyclical Crisis in Commercial Aviation: Causes and Potential Cures,* Submission to the ICAO Worldwide Air Transport Conference (2003), *reprinted in* 28 ANNALS AIR & SPACE L. 1 (2003) [hereinafter Dempsey, *The Cyclical Crisis*] (conditionally suggesting government intervention in a failing marketplace in order to compress the impact of market cycle swings, while acknowledging the absence of a homogeneous cost structure and the 'prevailing political correctness' that refuses to blame deregulation for the financial woes of the industry). Professor Dempsey's position has been consistent, as evident from his submission to the Airline Commission 15 years earlier. *See* Dempsey, *Airlines, Aviation and Public Policy, supra* note 84, at 108-14 (supporting 'managed competition' to police what he called 'excesses at the margin,' Professor Dempsey proposed, *inter alia,* 'immunized' capacity agreements to cure airport congestion and overcapacity, prior review of airline buyouts and continuing review of debt/equity targets, pricing simplification and standardization, price ceilings in monopoly or duopoly markets, new controls on predatory pricing and other forms of unfair competition, and all of these revived regulatory powers to be wielded by a new, independent intermodal transportation commission). To be fair to Professor Dempsey, the recent oil price crisis has provoked similar responses, particularly with respect to capacity coordination, from within the industry itself. For another perspective on cyclicality in air transport and its implications for regulation, *see* Richard J. Cudahy, *The Airlines: Destined to Fail?,* 71 J. AIR L. & COM. 3 (2006).

581. Although the air traffic controllers' strike in 1981, which put a cap on capacity expansion, effectively hobbled deregulation for two years. *See Airline Commission Proceedings,* testimony of Herbert D. Kelleher, former President, Southwest Airlines (Jun. 16, 1993), at 70-71.

a   *The First Approach of Reregulation: The September 11,*
                       2001 'Stabilization' Package

On the morning of September 11, 2001, terrorists hijacked four commercial
passenger airliners. Two of the planes crashed into the World Trade Center in
New York City, killing nearly 3,000 people and causing the collapse of both
towers. A third plane crashed into the Pentagon in Washington, D.C., killing
nearly 200 people. The fourth plane, likely heading to another target, crashed in
western Pennsylvania, killing its crew and dozens of passengers. Responding to
these attacks, the Federal Aviation Administration issued a federal ground stop
order on September 11, 2001, prohibiting all flights to, from, and within the
United States. Airports did not reopen until September 13 (except for Ronald
Reagan National Airport, which partially reopened on October 4). Consumer
demand for airline services, already in apparent recession, plummeted dramat-
ically after the attacks. To address the financial survival of U.S. airline carriers
in the aftermath of September 11, Congress passed and President Bush signed
into law a package of measures to assist the airline industry to recover.

The terse wording of the statutory preamble to the Air Transportation Safety and
System Stabilization Act (the 'Stabilization Act') was chilling: the purpose of the
legislation, signed by President Bush on September 22, 2001, was '[t]o preserve
the continued viability of the United States air transportation system.'[582] Before
September 11, 2001, the airlines, and more specifically the major carriers that comprise the Air Transport Association, clearly held what public policy theorists would
describe as the concentrated producer/provider advantage.[583] Neither the smaller,
lower-cost carriers nor the disparate elements of the passenger rights lobby, nor for
that matter any motivated and cohesive group of legislators, presented a sufficiently
persistent countervailing influence in favor of (some) economic reregulation.

The severely weakened financial condition of the airlines after September 11,
2001, has probably shifted the balance of influence for the foreseeable future. It is
not enough to make the glib assertion, as some commentators have done, that
securing an assistance package in the immediate backwash of the terrorist attack
was itself an awesome demonstration of the power of the airlines' lobbyists.[584] If
the airlines have built their lobbying efforts to resist reregulation, then their pitch
for federal assistance was a conspicuous defeat for those efforts. To succeed as a
concentrated set of interests, the airlines needed at least the appearance of financial
stability; without that, they faced a newly concentrated Federal Government
and could not expect to wield their former preponderance of influence. In these
circumstances, even if winning the assistance package was a 'master stroke,'[585]

---

582. Air Transportation Safety and System Stabilization Act, Pub. L. No. 107-42, 115 Stat. 230
      [hereinafter Stabilization Act].
583. *See supra* note 570 (explaining the airlines' influence over regulatory initiatives in terms of
      their concentrated advantage as a lobbying power in Congress).
584. *See* Wayne & Moss, *supra* note 570 (quoting commentators).
585. *Id.*

the outcome of the stabilization package carried the inevitable risk of invading the industry's zones of regulatory freedom. The industry was able to pry open the federal purse, but certain reregulatory encroachments could be expected in response. Given the short time available to craft the legislation, the encroachments were necessarily limited. But their presence signals concerns for the future of a deregulated industry. We turn now to consider the recent assistance package in greater detail.

The Stabilization Act of 2001 was an intensive and occasionally highly confidential collaborative effort among Congress, the Bush Administration, and airline executives.[586] Cobbled together in less than two weeks after September 11, 2001, the Act demonstrated a reactive resilience that many did not expect of the Federal Government, but also exposed the pathology of U.S. airline finances even before the attacks.[587] Crippled by airport closures, flight stand-stills, and a massive sapping of public confidence, the already weakened condition of the airlines prevented them from subsidizing their own economic model of flying above break-even capacity. Compounded by insurance woes and the likelihood of multibillion dollar tort claims many times the value of even the largest airlines, a resurgence of the statist philosophy of *l'état capitaliste* seemed necessary to maintain the integrity of the mobile air transport system.[588]

The Stabilization Act, coupled with two derivative orders of the DOT and one derivative order of the Office of Management and Budget (OMB), formed the core of the Federal Government's regulatory response to 9/11.[589] The opening title, providing for disaster relief, attracted the most notoriety.[590] The two-thirds of the

---

586. Organized labor played no part in the negotiations once it became clear that the assistance package would not extend to protection for airline employees. *See id.*

587. *See* Michael Arndt et al., *Suddenly Carriers Can't Get off the Ground*, Bus. Wk., Sept. 3, 2001, at 36 (discussing the precarious state of airline finances before the attacks).

588. The irony of these developments was not lost in Europe. The European airlines made their own requests for public financial support, citing the U.S. experience to show that the American antitrust philosophy of supporting 'competition' but not competitors (borrowed by the European Union in its airline liberalization program) had been sidelined by a European-style statist industrial policy of subsidization and bailout. On Oct. 10, 2001, the European Commission decided to allow EU Member States to compensate carriers for revenue lost immediately after the Sept. 11 terrorist attacks. However, the incumbent Transport and Energy Commissioner, Loyola de Palacio, explicitly rejected any other government aid to carriers within the EU. Paulo Prada et al., *Airlines Praise EU Opposition To Financial Aid For the Industry*, Wall St. J., Oct. 11, 2001, at A14.

589. The Act had five titles, each responsive to a particular dimension of the prevailing crisis: disaster relief to support the industry, aviation insurance assistance, certain taxation adjustments, victim compensation measures, and a brief closing title (to be developed in subsequent legislation) committing the government to enhancing airline safety and security. *See* Stabilization Act, *supra* note 582.

590. The Act's financial assistance was a two-pronged instrument: five billion dollars to be disbursed as aid for 'direct losses' incurred as a result of the federal ground stop order (issued Sept. 11, 2001) and for any incremental losses to Dec. 31, 2001, that were the result of the terror attacks; an aggregate of ten billion dollars to be furnished in the form of federal credit instruments 'subject to such terms and conditions as the President deems necessary.' *Id.* sec.

aid that was allocated in the form of federal credit instruments was administered through a newly created Air Transportation Stabilization Board.[591] The creation of an official financial oversight council, even one with a limited and specific mandate, was obviously a dramatic turnabout in the long march to a fully deregulated free market airline industry. It was hardly surprising, in the political context of a desperate and unloved industry making a Chrysler-esque appeal to the coffers of the central government, that members of Congress would make intrusive re-regulatory demands on the industry. In the days preceding the final version of the Act, Congressional hearings were filled with siren calls for 'de-monopolization' of hub airports and price caps on hub airport tickets, and the rhetoric of the stalled passenger rights campaign once again took the airlines to task for their perceived past arrogance.[592] In the end, time prevented the kind of detailed trade-offs that normal political lobbying produces. The intervention of former Goldman Sachs partner Jon Corzine, then a New Jersey freshman Democratic Senator and later Governor of New Jersey, did, however, spark a reprise of one of the key elements of the Chrysler rescue of 1975: in return for credit assistance, airlines could be required to enter contracts with the Board under which the government, contingent on the financial success of the assisted airlines, would 'participate in the gains of the participating [airlines] through the use of such instruments as warrants, stock options, common or preferred stock, or other appropriate equity instruments.'[593]

101(a)(1). The direct aid was dispensed mechanically, allocating the monies according to recorded available seat miles for Aug. 2001. *See id.* sec. 102(b).

591. The Board comprised the voting triumvirate of the Secretary of Transportation (or his designee), the Chairman of the Board of Governors of the Federal Reserve (or his designee), and the Secretary of the Treasury (or his designee), with the nonvoting addition of the Comptroller General of the United States (or his designee). *See id.* sec. 102. To qualify for federal credit assistance, an airline had to convince the Board that credit was 'not reasonably available' at the time of the proposed 'transaction', that the intended 'obligation' (presumably the 'transaction') was one that was 'prudently incurred,' and that the proposed 'agreement' (presumably the 'transaction' or 'obligation') was 'a necessary part of maintaining a safe, efficient, and viable commercial aviation system in the United States.' *Id.* at sec. 102(c)(1). The drawbacks of hasty draftsmanship were manifest in statutory writing that used three distinct terms (transaction, obligation, and agreement) to capture whatever it was, within the bounds of 'prudent' spending, that airlines would be doing with the borrowed money. Moreover, the use of these terms suggested specific commercial events such as aircraft leasing or purchase; in reality, the airlines wanted to use the aid merely to sustain daily operations. *But see* Office of Management and Budget, *Regulations For Air Carrier Guarantee Loan Program under Section 101(a)(1) of the Air Transportation Safety and System Stabilization Act,* Final Rule (codified at 14 C.F.R. § 1300.17(b) (West 2008)) (indicating that continuing debt service would not qualify for Federal credit assistance).

592. *See* David Phinney, *Airlines Plead for Billion [sic] Relief Package,* STATES NEWS SERV., Sept. 19, 2001 (noting that Senator Fritz Hollings (D-S.C.) was a particularly vocal proponent of these reregulatory issues).

593. H.R. 2926, *supra* note 36, at tit. 1 § 102(d). The notion of a government-mandated stakeholding in exchange for credit assistance was clarified under Section 1300.10 of the OMB implementing Regulations, which provided that 'the Board shall not accept an equity interest in an air carrier that gives the Federal Government voting rights.' This apparent reluctance to have blocks of voting stock in the hands of the government, however, did not vitiate the Act's explicit expectation that the Board may participate in the financial success of the air carrier

The second signal of a tilt toward reregulation was potentially more intrusive and unsettling. Economic deregulation, as conceived by the architects of the 1978 legislation, removed government control of prices, capacity, and route selection. Carriers, which previously had to apply for permission to serve all domestic routes and competed primarily on the basis of inflight service, could now choose which routes to fly, how often, and at what fare.[594] If a route proved unprofitable, inefficient, or otherwise fell outside a matrix for successful business operations, the airline could discontinue service unilaterally and without the former regulatory precondition of an official certificate of discontinuance from the CAB.[595]

Route flexibility could be said to be the nub of deregulation, since complex and expensive route proceedings were so much the heart of the old regulatory apparatus.[596] If a carrier wanted federal aid to serve smaller underserved communities, it could opt into the EAS program established under the ADA. As a program participant, the carrier would then subject itself to certain continuing restrictions on entry and exit.[597] Section 105(a) of the 2001 Stabilization Act, *as least as it written,* represented another apparent regulatory turnabout. The Section prescribed that the DOT Secretary 'should take appropriate action to ensure that all communities that had scheduled air service before September 11, 2001, continue to receive adequate air transportation service and that EAS to small communities continues without interruption.' Although the draftsmanship was confusing,[598] this provision

---

through warrants, stock options, common or preferred stock, or other equity instruments. *See also* Greg Hitt et al., *Airline Bailout May Become Boon for U.S,* WALL ST. J., Oct. 9, 2001, at A2. As indicated *infra* note 623, these conditions prompted Professor Dempsey to describe the bailout as a 'forced nationalization.' As well as making the government a potential stakeholder in private airline corporations, the first title of the Stabilization Act featured two other harbingers of a new paradigm of official intrusiveness. The first, contained in Section 104 of the Act, conditioned federal credit arrangements to airlines on a 'legally binding agreement with the President' that, for the two years beginning Sept. 11, 2001, capped the compensation (or severance pay) of officers or employees of the recipient carriers at 2000 levels if their total compensation package was in excess of $300,000 during that year.

594. *See generally supra* Part III(C)-(D).
595. The requirement for CAB permission to abandon or exit a route was formally abolished when the agency's route authority sunsetted on Dec. 31, 1981. *See* 49 U.S.C. app. § 1551(a)(1)(D) (1979).
596. *See supra* Part II(B) (discussing lengthy CAB route proceedings).
597. For further discussion of the EAS program, *see supra* Part II(D).
598. Thus, the statutory language was either an attempt to preserve the operating terms of the existing EAS program, in which case it was a complete redundancy (although there is no reference in Section 105(a) to the formal title of the program, Section 105(b) of the Stabilization Act does, however, appropriate an additional $120 million to the EAS program (using its correct statutory reference) for fiscal year 2002, evincing a clear understanding that the EAS program was indeed implicated in the Act's arrangements); or it was a poorly-written conflation of a *general* restriction on route exit with the specific (and statutory) restriction on route exit that has always characterized the EAS. That the latter may be the correct reading was apparent from subsection (c) of Section 105, which stated that, '[n]otwithstanding any other provision of law, the Secretary is authorized to require an air carrier receiving direct financial assistance under this Act to maintain scheduled service to any point served by that carrier before Sept. 11, 2001,' and to enter into agreements to ensure that outcome.

certainly implied that discretionary route exit would be foreclosed to U.S. airlines if they accepted 'direct' financial assistance under the Stabilization Act[599] *regardless of whether any given route was part of the EAS infrastructure.* Moreover, the generality of the Secretary's power to 'ensure that all communities' continue to have air service, *regardless of whether any given airline has received 'direct' financial assistance under the Act,* appeared to be conferred without restriction. On its face, this was reregulation.[600]

b   *Lessons of the Stabilization Act*

According to correspondent Laurence Zuckerman of *The New York Times*, the perceived impact of the Stabilization Act, and particularly of the creation of the Stabilization Board, was that 'the federal government [was] taking on its biggest role in shaping the nation's airlines since the industry was deregulated a generation ago.'[601] The creation of the new Stabilization Board, for however limited a duration and however defined a purpose, did permit the federal government to become involved in a task that advocates of deregulation assigned solely to the marketplace: to pick winners and losers.[602] On the strength of the evaluative criteria in the OMB Regulations (including indications of how closely the government could benefit from future airline gains through stock or warrant participation), the Board could help a weakened carrier to survive or doom its prospects in the near-term. The Comptroller General of the United States, David M. Walker, a

---

599. Meaning presumably, only assistance granted under the first prong of the Federal Government's relief instrument. *See supra* main text.
600. Given the applicability of the venerable 'last-in-time' doctrine, under which the Supreme Court has ruled that the most recent legislation prevails over any prior enactments in the event of inconsistency (*see, e.g.,* The Head Money Cases, 112 U.S. 580 (1884)), the Stabilization Act manifestly trumps the 1978 Deregulation Act on the subject of route exit. The DOT's Services Reduction Order, however, resisted these ambiguities of the statute and instead rested most of its entire regulatory authority on the scope of the small community service program created by 49 U.S.C. § 41731 *et seq.* The Order also speaks in vague terms of the DOT's 'overall responsibility to monitor industry conditions, advise [C]ongress on industry developments, and implement Congressional legislation [including the Stabilization Act].' No specific provision of the Stabilization Act is cited. It seems, therefore, that the powers claimed in the Stabilization Act to restrict route exit were only contingently exercised through the Order. Nonetheless, while the text of the Order suggests that the DOT believed that it is carrying out its conventional and circumscribed functions under the EAS program, Congress, which enacted the Secretary's general exit power 'notwithstanding any other provision of law,' evidently contemplated a broader (and more intrusive) mandate.
601. Laurence Zuckerman, *U.S. Takes Big Role in Airline Crisis*, N.Y. TIMES, Oct. 4, 2001, at A1.
602. This was almost certainly going to happen. The OMB Regulations, for example, clearly discouraged a condition of bankruptcy protection or receivership and put pressure on airlines in bankruptcy to ensure that the Board's guarantee and the underlying financial obligation were part of a bankruptcy court-certified reorganization plan. *See* 14 C.F.R. § 1300.11(a)(2) (West 2008). The eligibility criteria, and the obvious disfavor of insolvency, may have prompted some carriers to forego bankruptcy in the hope of using the credit assistance program to preserve their viability. That fact alone would distort the play of market forces.

nonvoting Board member, stated that it was 'clear' that 'the Board would have a considerable amount of discretion.'[603] If this was a kind of postmodern industrial policy, it was highly unpredictable in its implications. The government, through its sudden largesse, could assert itself as an industry 'czar,' in the characterization used by former Secretary of Labor Robert Reich,[604] making endless numbers of big and small decisions that would affect the financial and operational destiny of all of the airlines.[605]

This extended treatment of the Stabilization Act should remind the reader of the incontrovertible potentiality of the power of the federal government over all dimensions of commercial life.[606] Some commentators, of course, deny that the post-September 11, 2001 assistance package prefigured any economic reregulation of the industry. In this view, the psychology of Congress, although plainly containing an element of irritation with perceived past arrogance, has not evolved into a new regulatory mindset that would undo the accomplishments of the 1978 Act and its subsequent history. That is certainly the optimistic view.[607] The psychological consequences could also cut the other way: the industry became in thrall to federal beneficence, and Congress (and the administrators) may feel that other interventions to 'correct' the perceived imbalances of deregulation may be warranted before the government again departs the stage. This is especially so in light of continuing concerns about the infrastructural security of air carriers and airports that have entered public consciousness in the years since the Stabilization Act.[608]

2   2008: The Reregulation Debate Redux

The stabilization package suggests, ominously, that even in the birthplace of airline deregulation rate, route, and even capacity reregulation can no longer be deemed an exhausted cause. In mid-2008, at what appeared to be the crest of the oil price crisis, two stalwarts of the industry, Robert L. Crandall (former Chairman and CEO of American Airlines) and Michael Levine (now a senior lecturer at New York University School of Law)[609] used the fora of the Wings Club and the International

---

603. Zuckerman, *supra* note 601.
604. *Id.* at C5.
605. Congress did, however, make clear that it did not intend the rescue package to act as a lifeline for carriers that were already in financial jeopardy before Sept. 11, 2001. *See* Zuckerman, *supra* note 601.
606. Consider, for example, the Office of Thrift Supervision's freezing of the entire assets of the law firm Kaye, Scholer during the savings and loan crisis of the early 1990s. For a critique of the statutory interpretation which authorized the freeze, *see* Keith R. Fisher, *Statutory Construction and the Kaye, Scholer Freeze Order* (MSU Legal Studies Research Paper No. 03-17, 1992).
607. And perhaps appears even more optimistic when viewed in the light of the U.S. Government's $700 billion bailout of the Wall Street financial industry in late 2008.
608. *See supra* Chapter 3, Part V(B) (considering the Dubai Ports controversy and its aftermath).
609. In addition to distinguished academic appointments, Michael E. Levine has held several key positions both as a U.S. aviation regulator and as an airline industry executive. He is best

Aviation Club,[610] respectively, to offer contrasting prescriptions for the industry's future.[611] Neither proposed a wholesale return to government-controlled regulation, but their ideological compasses pointed in diametrically opposed directions.

Crandall seemed prepared to saddle deregulation – with its strong bias for consumer benefits produced through 'competition of any stripe in every market'[612] – with responsibility for the cumulative failure of the post-1978 industry.[613] Levine (in a viewpoint that is shared in this book)[614] saw the solution to current challenges in deregulation's freedom to innovate and to allow the industry continually to re-invent itself.[615] For Levine, in fact, all industries have fixed and common costs and all industries face the risk of being unable to sustain these costs as competition

---

known in the industry, probably, for his pioneering work in influencing and shaping the industry's transition to deregulation. *See supra* Part II(D) for more discussion of Levine's role.

610. Both clubs hold their meetings in Washington, D.C.

611. *See* Robert L. Crandall, former Chairman, President and CEO, AMR Corp., Remarks to the Wings Club, Washington, D.C. (Jun. 10, 2008); Michael E. Levine, Distinguished Research Scholar and Senior Lecturer, New York University School of Law, *Airline Survival in a Tough World*, Remarks to the International Aviation Club, Washington, D.C. (Jul. 29, 2008) [here-inafter Levine, *Airline Survival*].

612. *See* Crandall, *supra* note 611.

613. Rejecting 'unfettered competition' for an industry that serially fails to capture its full costs, Crandall offered a mix of new regulatory interventions including a mandated 'sum-of-segments' pricing policy (to encourage nonstop flights, and discourage airline connecting complexes, by charging the full price for each segment of a connecting itinerary), required binding arbitration for labor disputes, tougher bankruptcy laws that would oust managements more quickly, stringent flight caps, tighter financial standards for new airlines, massive investment in infrastructure, and 'a more accommodating stance toward industry collabora-tion' on capacity-sharing. *See id.* Crandall also took a swipe at supporters of liberalizing inward investment, arguing that foreign investors would seek only to augment their own feeder traffic and to 'discourage the creation of incremental competitive capacity by resurgent U.S. competitors.' Crandall professed himself 'mystified by the apparent willingness of U.S. nego-tiators to further weaken the domestic system by turning over control to people without any stake in making our domestic system work.' *Id.* As we have seen, *supra* Chapter 3, Part V(C), and will revisit in Chapter 6, the right of establishment offers significant protections against the kind of injury to the U.S. airline system that Crandall forecasts as the result of greater foreign investment. His criticism that foreign airlines will seek only 'feeder traffic,' however, reflects a Chicago system mentality that U.S. carriers (or carriers in any sovereign State) have a 'right' to local traffic. This is a conceptual premise that would disappear in the plurilateral replace-ment proposed in Chapter 6. As in the U.S. auto industry, therefore, adaptation to new mac-roeconomic circumstances may involve the presence of foreign brands in the U.S. aviation marketplace. *See* Levine, *Airline Survival, supra* note 611, at 9.

614. *See* discussion *infra* Part IV(D).

615. 'What is essential is that we generate multiple competing predictions, along with the freedom for firms to innovate using them and see which innovations flourish and which ones die. Only a deregulated market can do that.' *Id.* at 7. Levine also responded to a number of Crandall's specific proposals. He rejected a sum-of-segments pricing policy, for example, because it pays no regard to the true economic cost of seats that are more valuable when produced together with those serving other itineraries or that might otherwise go to waste. Id. at 4. The govern-ment which would implement all of Crandall's changes, Levine concluded tartly, 'is the government that has been unable for twenty-five years to modernize the [air traffic control] system.' Levine, *Airline Survival, supra* note 611, at 7.

drives down prices. Crandall's ideological position, in Levine's estimation, amounts to a 'picking-winners' industrial policy that would justify economic regulation of virtually every industry when a structural shift in costs is combined with a slowing of the business cycle.[616]

And yet, *pace* Crandall and Professor Paul Stephen Dempsey, the incidents of deregulation are likely to survive any industry restructuring that flows from current macroeconomic conditions.[617] A return to the expired rate regulation system seems inconceivable, for instance, given the challenges of determining reasonable cost levels in the heterogeneous conditions of the 2008 industry,[618] as well as the difficulty of integrating into a general fare formula the much more widespread practice of discounting, which now embraces 90% of all traffic.[619] In addition, the CAB's fare formula was distance-based and did not differentiate between non-stops, onestops, or connections. And that was before the hub-and-spoke system and the emergence of hub connection itineraries.[620] Despite the exit restrictions noted

---

616. *Id.* at 4 & 10. Levine, like Sir Leon Brittan, condemns industrial policy as unresponsive to market changes and hostage to political pressures and interest groups. Levine, *Airline Survival, supra* note 611, at 10. And reregulation, as Levine points out, 'won't affect the price of oil or the fragility of the economy.' *Id.* at 5. Nor could CAB regulation prevent overcapacity, oil shocks, or weak earnings. *Id.* at 8. Levine's speech recites a long list of speculative future structural changes that may occur in the U.S. air transport industry as a result of 2008 economic conditions, including adoption of the EC business model of producing travel for price-sensitive customers separately from business travel networks. *See id.* at 6.

617. Or to put the matter in the somewhat unkind words of Michael Levine, 'Let's not break the concentration of airline managements by saving them from grisly contemplation.' *Id.* at 12.

618. The post-regulation cost variables include the (fluctuating) number of new carriers entering and exiting operations, resort to bankruptcy protection by ailing carriers, the evolution of the domestic 'majors' into significant international carriers, the shifting policies of carriers toward their hub operations, commissions to travel agents, and even traveler amenities. In general, there are wide variations in costs among the carriers. *See Airline Commission Proceedings,* testimony of Robert L. Crandall, President, American Airlines (Jun. 3, 1993), at 70.

619. Even Professor Dempsey concedes that the lack of a 'relatively homogeneous cost structure among new entrant vis-à-vis incumbent airlines' could be prohibitive in organizing reregulation. Dempsey, *The Cyclical Crisis, supra* note 580, at 13.

620. The Airline Commission, presented with a menu of faresetting measures including mandated floors and ceilings, rejected any return to official ratemaking. *See* Airline Industry Pricing Behavior, Domestic Aviation Issues Team, *in Airline Commission Documents,* Dkt. No. 000093, at 15. Other options included a mandated simplified fare structure and a prohibition on charging fares below a carrier's fully allocated costs. *See id. See also Airline Commission Report, supra* note 319, at 14. Similar definitional problems would result from a scaled-back proposal, which has sometimes been advanced, to limit government regulation of fares to predatory pricing. To be workable as an *a priori* procedure, this would require official establishment of minimum fares. To determine those fares, in the heterogeneous market conditions that now prevail, would the government have to set minimums for every route in the system? On what type and level of service would those minimums be calculated? Inevitably, 'zones of reasonableness' would tend to be based on the cost structure of the larger airlines, but that cost structure is not shared, even after the majors' years of cost-paring, by the more efficient point-to-point carriers. On predation generally, *see supra* Part IV(B).

in the stabilization legislation,[621] route regulation, too, would appear to be an unworkable anachronism, given that the major carriers have expanded far beyond the geographical compartments to which the regulators confined them, and have used hub-and-spoke networks to become significant participants in thousands of routes beyond the direct, point-to-point bias of the Board's route matrix. The industry, moreover, has advanced beyond the CAB's routing policy objective of bringing the carriers into closer balance in their relative strength and profit potential, so that average industry costs would not be a meaningful mechanism of price control.[622]

With all of that said, the 2001 stabilization intervention, and the kind of governmental control over airline destiny that it implicated,[623] makes it problematical to assert today – as the Clinton Airline Commission was able to conclude in 1993 – that the regulation/deregulation debate is 'an argument about a past that can never be recreated.'[624]

---

621. *See supra* in the main text.
622. Monitoring of airline financial health, however, continues as part of the U.S. Department of Transportation's certification procedures for new carriers. As discussed, the DOT operates an air carrier fitness program that certifies new carriers as 'fit, willing, and able' to provide air transportation. In reviewing domestic start-ups, the DOT examines financial plans and managerial adequacy and considers the more nebulous concept of 'compliance disposition.' In a further throwback to the regulatory era, new certificates are frequently limited by the DOT as to aircraft size, or route entry, or duration, depending on how the applicant performs in the fitness tests. Expansion beyond those limits would require DOT approval. *See, e.g.*, U.S. DOT, *Application of Virgin America Inc., For a Certificate of Public Convenience and Necessity Under 49 U.S.C. § 41102 To Engage in Interstate Scheduled Air Transportation of Persons, Property, and Mail*, Dkt. No. OST-2005-23307, Final Order (May 18, 2007) (conditioning Virgin America's certificate, if the airline proposes to operate more than 17 aircraft, on written notification to the DOT and demonstration of fitness to conduct such operations before their commencement). Given the consumer protection and safety issues in the airline industry, however, the fitness procedure, and some initial limitations on carrier freedom, would appear unavoidable. Moreover, as we noted in Chapter 3, DOT fitness surveillance continues even after certification. There are no emergency powers to revoke economic authority, however, and declaring an airline 'unfit' (which would surely put it out of business) requires at least an oral evidentiary hearing. Some commentators have called for preset minimum financial ratios that would trigger a DOT financial review if an airline failed to meet or exceed them (similar to the powers given to the Federal Deposit Insurance Corporation under the post-bailout FDIC Improvement Act of 1991). *See* Dempsey, *Airlines, Aviation and Public Policy, supra* note 84, at 109. There is, of course, great potential for commercial damage to an airline that is haled before official scrutineers because of 'fitness' deficiencies, as the DOT has itself recognized.
623. *See* Dempsey, *The Cyclical Crisis, supra* note 580, at 11 (arguing, based on the post-9/11 bailout, that 'a forced nationalization' of the airline industry is conceivable – and indeed partly occurred when the U.S. Government demanded sizeable warrants for the purchase of stock as part of the stabilization rescue (a development that Dempsey refers to, perhaps ironically, as 'socialism')).
624. 'Until the Commission began its work, much of the aviation debate in this country revolved around the old deregulation versus reregulation argument. The Commission saw this argument for what it was . . . an argument about a past that can never be recreated.' Statement of Hon. Gerald L. Baliles, Chairman, U.S. Airline Commission, before the Subcommittee on Aviation of the Senate Committee on Commerce, Science and Transportation, 104th Cong. (Mar. 1, 1995) (1996), at 6.

D   U.S. AIRLINE DEREGULATION: AN UNFINISHED EXPERIMENT

After 40 years of regulation, the industry has enjoyed almost as long in the free market. Undoubtedly, expectations for this new environment soared, and disappointments have been legion.[625] The majors declared and fought a war of attrition, believing that a critical mass, developed quickly, would be the only way to survive the Darwinian fallout after regulation ended. Gaining market share became the paramount economic objective, even at the expense of profitability (and consequent indebtedness).[626] The push for market share was accompanied by an expectation that the industry must inevitably consolidate, scaling back the number of players in order to boost the profit margins of the survivors.[627] And, in 2008, the majors continue to blame their competitive difficulties on systemic overcapacity, now compounded by oil price spikes, and continue to covet potential merger partners.[628]

Yet, as the past decade of new entry has shown, it remains premature to judge the experiment on its experience thus far, particularly when that experience was gained during repeated exogenous setbacks (and, in the early years, an unexpected laxity in federal antitrust enforcement).[629] The structure and business environment of the airline industry appears to be in relative flux, a fact that competition law enforcement must endeavor to accommodate[630] and to which all stakeholders must continuously adapt their expectations of deregulation. Historical facts – for

---

625. But, as Steven Morrison has written, '[c]omparisons of perfect regulation with actual deregulation are as empty as comparisons of perfect deregulation with imperfect regulation.' Morrison, *supra* note 24, at 246.

626. *See Airline Commission Proceedings*, testimony of Herbert D. Kelleher, former President, Southwest Airlines, Jun. 16, 1993, at 71.

627. *Id.* at 71-72. Looking much further into the future, 'modular' airline companies will likely develop, featuring comprehensive outsourcing. *See* Furman Selz Inc., 1993 Airline Industry Outlook, *in Airline Commission Documents*, Dkt. No. 001213 (Mar. 3, 1993), at 9 (observing that 'capital-intensive behemoths' are a legacy of the regulatory era of in-house control of all phases of airline operation, with costs passed on to the consumer through regulated fare increases. Under the Furman Selz scenario, 'airlines could become "assetless" entities, contracting out most functions and operating only as service companies that bring a customer into contact with a seat, and then moving that seat.' *Id.* This is, of course, already the model being pursued by global consumer brands such as Nike.

628. *See supra* in the main text.

629. The serial bankruptcies of major U.S. carriers in recent years (including Continental Airlines, Delta Air Lines, Northwest Airlines, United Airlines, and US Airways) have led to complaints, including quite vocally from the Europeans, that these airlines are maintained by seemingly limitless life support and compete with solvent carriers at artificially low costs. *See* Julius Maldutis, *Airline Bankruptcies Have Run Amok*, 165 Av. WEEK & SPACE TECH., Aug. 21, 2006, at 62. Economists dispute whether bankruptcy is the result of 'exogenous' (macroeconomic) or 'endogenous' (management-related) events, but undoubtedly both have played a part in the record number of U.S. airline bankruptcies. Recent changes in U.S. bankruptcy law, including reduction of the time period during which a corporation retains the exclusive right to file a reorganization plan, may discourage future resort to these 'strategic bankruptcies.' *Strategic Bankruptcy Less Appealing, Moody's Says*, CREDIT INVESTMENT NEWS, Mar. 17, 2006.

630. *See* the comments of Armentano, *supra* note 417, on the enduring failure of antitrust law and policy to comprehend the diachronic nature of competition.

example, that price information can be manipulated on travel agents' screens[631] or that low-cost new entry is likely to remain feasible in an era of oil price volatility[632] – do not necessarily persist either to ensure future market power or to force its dilution.[633]

The new dispensation proposed in Chapter 6 would undoubtedly cause further structural convulsion: the end of the cabotage and nationality privileges must inevitably create new competitive configurations, reshuffling the gainers and losers with perhaps more dramatic consequences that at any time since the launch of the deregulation experiment. As we move to our second model jurisdiction, the EC, and plan a further transition toward a post-bilateral order in international air transportation, we need to recognize the U.S. experiment, in both its domestic and global initiatives, as a rich source of legal and policy analysis and, as it faces up to the ever-present threat of regulatory rollbacks, a trove of real-world experience.

---

631. *See* discussion of changes in CRS regulation, *supra* in the main text. Travel agents have borne the brunt of the technological shifts of the past decade and a half. The first warning sign appeared suddenly in 1994 when Delta Air Lines unilaterally reduced travel agency commissions as part of a cost-reduction plan. Other carriers quickly followed suit. *See Agents Face Future Cuts*, AIRLINE BUS., Dec. 1994, at 9. The travel agency business actually brought a lawsuit – which was later settled – alleging unlawful collusion by the major carriers in adopting the commission terminations. *See In re* Travel Agency Commission Antitrust Litig., 898 F. Supp. 685 (D.C. Minn. 1995) (denying summary judgment to defendant airlines); Edwin McDowell, *Lawsuit by Travel Agents Against Airlines is Settled*, N.Y. TIMES, Sept. 4, 1996, at D2. But a more ominous development was yet to come. Driven by Internet capabilities, airlines across the globe have evolved the concept of ticketless travel. 'E-tickets' make it possible for airlines to issue tickets directly to customers without ticket stock (potentially cutting travel agents out of the distribution chain). The International Air Transport Association (IATA) has recently met its goal of having the world's airlines becoming 100% 'e-ticket' capable by 2008. *See* Press Release, IATA, Industry Bids Farewell to Paper Ticket, No. 25 (May 31, 2008).

632. The oil price rises will exacerbate problems already being encountered by low-cost carriers in the face of mounting costs and aggressive competition from the slimmed-down and more cost-aware major carriers. Increasingly, also, they are competing against each other. *See* Chris Walsh, *Low-Cost Airlines Hit Ceiling*, ARIZ. DAILY STAR, May 20, 2007 (mentioning how Northeast-based JetBlue has been forced to scale back growth plans in the face of operational problems).

633. *See In re* Air Passenger Computer Reservations Systems Antitrust Litigation, 694 F. Supp. 1443, 1457 (C.D. Cal. 1988). Moreover, airlines must continuously devise business strategies to resist a pervasive 'commodification' of air travel generated by years of declining ticket prices. *See* NAWAL TANEJA, AIRLINE SURVIVAL KIT: BREAKING OUT OF THE ZERO SUM GAME 17-18 (2003) (discussing airline seat as a commodity); *see also* American Express 2005 Global Business Survey, <http://home3.americanexpress.com/corp/pc/2005/travel_prefs.asp> (finding that even global business travelers rank price almost as highly as flight schedules in selecting air transport). Air Canada, for example, has recently pioneered a number of ticket price innovations that allow the consumer to purchase 'à la carte,' unbundling its fares to allow the carrier to be treated as a low-cost or all-frills supplier depending on the selected services. In addition, Air Canada offers an innovative flight pass and subscription service which sells bulk travel (by number of trips or elapse of time) to individual consumers. *See* Barbara De Lollis, *A Blueprint for Airline Industry?*, USA TODAY, May 7, 2007, at 1B. Some of Air Canada's innovations are migrating into U.S. airline business models, especially those of low-cost carriers. *See id.*

Chapter 5

Model Jurisdiction II: The European Community

An Experiment in Multilateral Airline Liberalization

I   INTRODUCTION: AN OVERVIEW OF THE EU AIR TRANSPORT INDUSTRY

In beginning an analysis of EC airline liberalization, it is important to emphasize once again the signature legal distinction between the evolution of the U.S. and EC deregulatory models. In the United States, as noted in the preceding Chapter, deregulation of the interstate airline system was a matter of Congressional fiat. The old dispensation, regulatory controls over prices and entry by an independent official agency, was similarly the product of a Congressional diagnosis of what troubled the industry and how to treat it. When Congress attempted reform of international aviation, however, it had to trim its exercise of unilateral powers to accommodate a multiplicity of competing sovereigns which regulate the conditions of entry to each other's skies. In those circumstances, Congress merely enacted a broad manifesto of desirable competitive change, while the regulatory agencies, the Civil Aeronautics Board and later the Department of Transportation, evolved an 'open skies' strategy to promote incremental, treaty-by-treaty, liberalization of the patchwork of bilateral compromises that today constitutes the international air transport system.

EC liberalization, in contrast, reveals a complete inversion of the U.S. dialectic of reform. Here, the liberalization project *begins* with multiple sovereigns and their interconnected bilateral aviation treaties. Prodded by international institutions of their own creation, and pursuing an agenda of market integration ordained by international treaty, the EU Member States gradually liberalized intra-Union scheduled air passenger and cargo transport – not just as a matter of prudent policy, but under compulsion of supranational law – in three discrete phases between 1987 and 1997. The EC reform program culminated in the reciprocal abolition of domestic (ninth freedom) cabotage among the Member States, transforming the Union into a legal analogue of the unitary 'federalized' airspace in the United States. Chapter 6 of this book proposes a plurilateral confederation of the U.S. and EU airspaces that seeks to leverage this new systemic symmetry to attain the goal of a complete transnational airline liberalization – a goal that seemed immeasurably distant when President Carter signed the International Air Transportation Competition Act in 1980.[1]

As in the prior U.S. inquiry, this Chapter opens with some brief contextual remarks on the composition of the airline industry in the model jurisdiction. The most immediate point of contrast with the United States is that of geographical distance. It is unsettling for Europeans to reflect on the huge disparity between the physical size of their continent and that of the United States. The entire land territory of the 27 EU Member States, from Brittany to the Russian frontier, from northern Sweden to the toe of Italy, is only about 40% of the land mass of the United States, fractionally larger than the corridor of southwestern and western states from Texas to California. Whatever the psychic consequences of this disparity on the average European, for Europe's airline industry it has meant a system that features considerably shorter average stage lengths (720 km) than the United States (1,220 km)[2] and that faces much more intense intermodal high-speed rail and automobile competition than U.S. carriers.[3] Moreover, although

---

1. *See supra* Chapter 4, Part III(B).
2. Longer stage lengths, all other things being equal, allow lower airline unit costs and, consequently, lower prices. *See* Institute of Air Transport, *Air Transport Markets in Europe and the United States: A Comparison*, Jun. 2001, at ii [hereinafter ITA Report]. The densest population centers in the United States are on the eastern and western seaboards, some 4000 km apart, compared with the average length of the densest routes linking EU States of less than 700 km. Europe's population and most intensive economic activity is highly concentrated in an arc extending from London to Milan and including Amsterdam, Brussels, Frankfurt, and Zurich. London and Paris are only 365 km apart, compared with the 4000-km separation of New York and Los Angeles. *See* ITA Report, *supra*, at 3-4.
3. In Europe, over one-half of trips of distances up to 700 km are made by road – in the United States, road transport accounts for one-half of trips up to 1,200 km. Air transport represents more than 50% of distances over 1,200 km in both the United States and Europe, but on medium distances (400 to 1,000 km) passenger rail carries more than a quarter of traffic in Europe while U.S. rail services carry fewer than 1% of passengers traveling distances over 100 km. *See* ITA Report, *supra* note 2, at 21. Over medium distances, intermodal competition is especially felt in the relationship between Europe's High Speed Train (HST) systems and air transport, and indeed some airlines have begun to 'code-share' with HST connections over the shorter routes such as Paris/Brussels. *See* American Airlines, Codeshare Partners – SNCF, <www.aa.com/content/aboutUs/codesharePartners/SNCF.jhtml>. When HST services replace conventional trains, they 'capture market share primarily from air transport, while taking very little from road transport.' ITA Report, *supra* note 2, at 21. Thus, whenever a new HST service begins, the market share of rail transport has risen above that of air transport for distances under 600 km (the distance covered by an HST in three hours or less). *Id.* Historically, EU rail services have logged nearly 25 times as many passenger miles as the publicly-subsidized US National Railroad Passenger

intra-European routes represent the second-largest 'domestic' market in the world for scheduled air travel, the U.S. home market is more than twice as large in terms of revenue passenger kilometers flown.[4] Europe's long-haul intercontinental output, however, is proportionally much larger than its confined domestic market, and Europe is involved either as an origin, destination, or connecting point in about *two-thirds* of the world's total airline travel between the major continental regions.[5] Finally, as explored in Chapter 3, unlike the assortment of multiple competing private carriers in the United States, the European airline system was historically atomized among the various national markets, which were dominated (both domestically and on international routes) by jealously-protected, publicly-financed flag carriers.[6] Privatization of these carriers, as well as legal and policy disincentives to cross-border mergers and acquisitions, has not displaced the market strength of their home 'silo' markets.

Comparable to the 'tiered' structure of the modern U.S. industry, until the late 1990s the EU's commercial airline businesses also formed a hierarchical profile crowned by the national carriers – 'instruments for advancing national air policy,' according to two leading British commentators.[7] From the perspective of sheer size (in this instance, the annual number of scheduled passengers carried),[8] the group of

---

Corporation (commonly known as Amtrak). General Accounting Office [GAO], *International Aviation: Measures by European Community Could Limit U.S. Airlines' Ability to Compete Abroad*, at 16, GAO/RCED-93-64 (1993) [hereinafter GAO, *European Community*]. Amtrak passenger traffic between 1975 and 2004 grew only marginally, from 3.9 million to 5.5 million revenue passenger miles, as compared with air transport's increase from 136 million to 556 million revenue passenger miles. Department of Transportation, Bureau of Transportation Statistics, Table 1-37: US Passenger-Miles, <http://www.bts.gov/publications/national_transportation_statistics/2006/html/table_01_37.html>. While a long series of stringent Congressional budget cuts had led to expectations that this figure was probably the high-water mark of U.S. passenger rail service, in Mar. 1996 Amtrak announced an ambitious $600 million plan to acquire a new fleet of 'Acela' high-speed trains for its most heavily-traveled northeastern routes. Amtrak officials anticipated 'giv[ing] the airlines a run for their money' on the New York/Boston and New York/Washington airline shuttle routes. Matthew L. Wald, *Builder Is Chosen For Speedy Trains on Northeast Run*, N.Y. TIMES, Mar. 16, 1996, at 1. Funding for the new trains will come from a combination of federal subsidies and borrowing. *Id.* Cracks in Acela's braking system caused an embarrassing interruption of service for all 20 high-speed trains in the winter of 2004/2005. *See Acela Trains Back on Track to Boston*, PHILADELPHIA INQUIRER, Jul. 22, 2005, at A17.

4. *See* ITA Report, *supra* note 2, at 28. The larger U.S. air traffic figure is at least partly a factor of the country's larger land mass and consequent greater availability of long-haul routes. *See id.*

5. *See generally* International Civil Aviation Organization [ICAO] Secretariat, *Industry Situation and Airline Traffic Outlook*, ATConf/5-WP/23 (Feb. 24, 2003).

6. *See generally* Elmar Giemulla et al., *The Road to Liberalization*, in 1 Eur. Air L. prelims, at 19, paras. 3-26 (Sept. 2006). Unlike in the United States, postwar Europe adopted the economic vehicle of the 'public enterprise.' Kenneth Button & Dennis Swann, *Transatlantic Lessons in Aviation Deregulation: EEC and U.S. Experiences*, 37 ANTITRUST BULL. 207, 208 (1992). Indeed, as we will see, the Union's foundational treaty, while considerably narrowing each Member State's freedom to shelter economic sectors from market competition, does not call into doubt the right of Member States to conduct economic activity through the agency of public enterprise.

7. Button & Swann, *supra* note 6, at 216.

8. There are various statistical methodologies used to portray airline 'size'; the lists referred to in the main text reflect number of passengers carried in 2007. *See World Airline Report*, AIR TRANSP. WORLD, July 2008, at 39. *But see infra* note 25 (discussing alternative methods of evaluation).

large airlines now includes not only the traditional national titans – Air France,[9] Alitalia, British Airways, Iberia, KLM, Lufthansa, and SAS – but also an increasingly powerful pair of carriers which operate as low-cost, low-fare specialists, Ryanair and the easyJet component of the easyGroup companies. Using the ranking indicium of scheduled passengers carried, Ryanair and easyJet place among the world's top 15 carriers (based on 2004 figures), whereas of the traditional flag carriers only the EU's 'Big Four,' Air France, British Airways, Lufthansa, and Iberia are in this group. Of the seven top-tier flag airlines, only British Airways, Iberia, and Lufthansa have been fully converted to private ownership.[10] The French State still holds a 15.7% stake in the Air France-KLM Group,[11] and the Dutch State continues to hold 6.9% of KLM.[12] The French Government adopted legislation in December 2002 to ensure that Air France could not be fully taken over by a foreign competitor and that France's air routes would remain under French control. Alitalia, until late 2008, was 49.9% State-owned,[13] while the Danish, Norwegian, and Swedish States collectively own 50% of SAS,[14] although for each of these airlines the amount of State ownership has been progressively scaled back from 100% in the last several years. This discernible trend toward privatization shows no sign of abating.[15] Ryanair and easyJet are both publicly traded independent companies with no State ownership stakes.

The relatively high rank of the seven big flag carriers is largely the result of their successful development of international operations, using the managed trade perquisites of the Chicago system (guaranteed duopolistic competition, market share and price stability, revenue pooling arrangements), to surmount the drawback of a relatively modest domestic feeder system.[16] While the next level of EU legacy carriers comprises a number of smaller flag lines – Aer Lingus,[17] Austrian

---

9. Although Air France and KLM have entered a species of merger, *see infra* Part III(B), they are still operating as separate airline corporations and are so treated here.
10. Goldman Sachs, *Evaluation of Ownership Options Regarding Aer Lingus Group plc, Appendices*, Report to the Department of Transport of Ireland (Oct. 6, 2004).
11. Air France-KLM, Capital Structure: Breakdown of the Shareholding at 31 Jan. 2009, <http://www.airfranceklm-finance.com/share-capital-shareholding.html>.
12. *See* KLM, Annual Review 07-08: Towards Smart Leadership 45 (2008). The Kingdom of the Netherlands still retains a 'golden share' which could give the State an option to take an interest of up to 50.1% of the issued capital in KLM in certain circumstances. *See id.*
13. For a discussion of the recent relaunch of Alitalia, *see infra* Part III(F).
14. As of 2007, the Danish Government owned 14.3% of SAS, the Norwegian Government owned 14.3%, and the Swedish Government owned 21.4%. *See* Association of European Airlines, Yearbook 07 54 (2007) [hereinafter AEA Yearbook].
15. *See supra* Chapter 3, Part VI(B).
16. *See also* Jürgen Basedow, *Symposium on U.S./E.C. Legal Relations: Airline Deregulation in the EC*, 13 J. Air L. & Com. 247, 251 (1994).
17. After its conversion to private ownership in 2006, Aer Lingus was quickly pursued by Irish low-cost carrier Ryanair, which sought control of the company. Although the European Commission blocked the takeover, Ryanair was allowed to keep its 25% stake in the Irish flag carrier (a stake which has since climbed to just below 30%). *See EU Lets Ryanair Keep Stake in Aer Lingus*, Wall St. J., Oct. 10, 2007, at D12. Other substantial stakeholders in Aer Lingus include the Employee Share Ownership Trust, comprising airline staff (12.5%) and the Irish Government

Airlines,[18] Czech Airlines,[19] Finnair,[20] Luxair,[21] Malev,[22] Olympic Airlines,[23] and TAP Air Portugal[24] – even the 'Big Four' EU airlines are overshadowed, in terms of fleet size, scheduled passengers carried, and scheduled passenger kilometers flown, by the domestic leverage enjoyed by the 'Big Three' U.S. megacarriers.[25]

(25%). *Id.* A more recent bid by Ryanair for Aer Lingus collapsed after the Irish Government blocked it on competition and valuation grounds. *EU Says Ryanair Drops Bid for Aer Lingus Merger,* Reuters News Service, Jan. 27, 2009.

18. As of 2007, the Austrian Government, through its privatization and investment agency, owned a 39.8% minority stake in Austrian Airlines. *See* AEA Yearbook, *supra* note 14, at 36.

19. As of 2007, Czech Airlines is effectively 100% owned and controlled by the Czech Government through a network of State-controlled institutions. *See* AEA Yearbook, *supra* note 14, at 42.

20. As of 2007, the Finnish State's controlling stake in Finnair is 55.78%. *See* AEA Yearbook, *supra* note 14, at 44.

21. As of 2007, the State of Luxembourg owns 23.1% of the Luxair shares, with 13.2% owned by the partly-private, partly-public Luxair Group. *See* AEA Yearbook, *supra* note 14, at 51.

22. Following Malev's brief flirtation with private ownership starting in 1992, the Hungarian State property agency, Állami Privatizációs és Vagyonkezelo Zrt., acquired 99.95% control of the airline in 1999. *See* Malev Hungarian Airlines, Corporate Info, <http://ww2.malev.hu/BP/ENG/I_CORPORATE_ENG/>. In 2007, however, the Hungarian Government sold its stake in the airline to AirBridge, a holding company of the Russian Air Union alliance. The sale prompted the European Commission to examine whether Malev still qualifies (on citizenship grounds) as a Community air carrier. *See* Cathy Buyck, *EC Questions Malev's Russian Ties,* ATW Daily, Dec. 10, 2007.

23. Olympic Airlines, formerly Olympic Airways, is 100%-owned by the Greek State. *See* AEA Yearbook, *supra* note 14, at 53. On the Olympic State aids controversy, *see infra* Part III(F).

24. As of 2007, TAP Air Portugal remained 100% in the ownership of the Government of Portugal. *See* AEA Yearbook, *supra* note 14, at 57.

25. In 2008, for example, American Airlines' fleet size (including American Eagle) was as large (895 aircraft) as Air France, British Airways, and Lufthansa combined (844 aircraft). *See* American Airlines, Fleet Profile (Jan. 2009), <www.aa.com/content/amrcorp/corporateInformation/facts/fleet.jhtml>; Lufthansa, Lufthansa Fleet, <http://konzern.lufthansa.com/en/html/ueber_uns/flotte/index.html>; British Airways, Fleet, <http://media.corporate-ir.net/media_files/irol/69/69499/Fleet_210508.pdf>; Air France, Fleet, <http://corporate.airfrance.com/en/strategy/fleet/a-modern-and-rationalized-fleet/index.html>. Notably, however, the rankings of the big EU carriers improve dramatically if one scores only *international* passenger kilometers flown rather than combined domestic/international, since the huge U.S. home market is then discounted in assessing the size of the largest U.S. airlines. In that revised list, in 2007 Air France held the top position, with Lufthansa and British Airways in second and third positions respectively. American Airlines, United, and Delta were in sixth, seventh, and 10th positions, respectively. Lufthansa, IATA Rankings: 2007 IATA International Rankings in Scheduled Services, <http://www.lufthansa-financials.de/servlet/PB/menu/1015966_l2/index.html?pbanker=table-11-28-29_08-03-2006#table-11-28-29_08-03-2006>. Moreover, as an indicium of comparative financial health, operating revenues for Air France-KLM, British Airways, and Lufthansa were one-third higher than American Airlines, United, and Delta. Each group of three airlines, in fact, grossed a total of between $62.23 billion (the three U.S. carriers) and $88.55 billion (the three EU carriers) in operating revenues in 2007. *See World Airline Report, supra* note 8, at 39. And Air France-KLM has become the largest global scheduled passenger airline by revenue, grossing almost $38.1 billion in 2007 compared with $32.9 billion for the next largest player, Lufthansa. *See* IATA Rankings, *supra.* The next rank of carriers in both regions is also broadly comparable in revenue terms. *See id.* Another cross-vector of comparison should be mentioned. FedEx and UPS Airlines, the world's two largest all-cargo air carriers, had operating revenues in 2007 of $22.6 billion and $4.9 billion, respectively. *See World Airline Report, supra* note 8, at 44-45.

But these varied ranks of the flag carriers no longer represent a complete profile of the EU air transport sector. The competitive contours of this sector were thrown into flux following the completion of the deregulation process in 1997.[26] A number of privately-owned low-cost, no-frills airlines, including Ryanair, easyJet, Germanwings, and Hapag Lloyd Express, have emerged (or expanded beyond local or charter operations) to challenge the flag carriers in their domestic markets, and to a more limited extent on international routes within the EU (as in the United States, there remains little new competition on long-haul routes to other continental regions).[27] Expanding beyond a domestic or regional focus to capture inter-State traffic (as in the United States), these carriers have eroded the advantages of the one-country, one-flag carrier system. [28] We will revisit some of these emergent trends during a closing assessment of the EC deregulation program.[29] The analysis turns now, however, to a brief conspectus of the unique constitutional and legal structure within which EC air transport liberalization was conceived and implemented.

II   THE SUPRANATIONAL LEGAL AND POLICY FOUNDATIONS OF EC AIRLINE DEREGULATION

A   GENERAL PRINCIPLES OF THE COMMUNITY LEGAL ORDER

The central purpose of the Treaty Establishing the EC, simply put, is to enhance economic prosperity by integrating the economies of the Member States.[30] The Treaty system rests on a premise of free competition that is inherently opposed to the notion of protected national air carriers. Indeed, the principles of economic regulation in the Treaty underscore this antinomy: Article 3(g), located among the 'Principles' of the Treaty, states that the activities of the EU (*in casu*, the EC),[31]

---

26. *See infra* Part II(C).

27. *See generally* EUROPEAN COMMISSION, ANALYSES OF THE EUROPEAN AIR TRANSPORT MARKET: ANNUAL REPORT 2007 (2007).

28. *See* David Jarach, *Future Scenarios for the European Airline Industry: A Market-Based Perspective*, 9 J. AIR. TRANSP. 23, 30 (2004) (describing the low-cost carriers as 'flexible, dynamic, and innovative players' which make 'healthy profits').

29. *See infra* Part III(G).

30. Article 2 states that the objectives of the Treaty are to promote throughout the Community a harmonious, balanced and sustainable development of economic activities, a high level of employment and of social protection, sustainable and non-inflationary growth, a high degree of competitiveness and convergence of economic performance, a high level of protection and improvement of the quality of the environment, the raising of the standard of living and quality of life, and economic and social cohesion and solidarity among Member States. All references to the Treaty Establishing the European Community (EC Treaty) are taken from the consolidated version, available at 2006 O.J. (C 231E) 1, 37 (Dec. 29, 2006).

31. For a note on nomenclature (and in particular the alternating use of the politico-geographic term 'European Union' and the juristic term 'European Community'), *see supra* Chapter 1, note 10.

shall include 'a system ensuring that competition in the internal market is not distorted.'[32] The mandate of Article 3(g) is given expression in Articles 81 and 82, which prohibit the cartelization of EU industry.[33] This supranational 'competition policy' forms part of the medley of juridical and economic ideas – also including free movement of goods (the customs union) and of workers, freedom of establishment of corporations and trained persons, freedom to provide services, and free movement of capital – that comprises the so-called 'internal market.'[34] These rules, often phrased as specific provisions with time limits, were designed to dismantle obstacles to free circulation of the factors of production within the EC.[35]

There is another level of common economic action within the EC, however, that is sector-specific. Here, the EC Treaty applies a *lex specialis*, featuring varying degrees of regulatory intrusion, to three areas of economic activity – agriculture,[36] fisheries,[37] and transport[38] – where concerted action was thought to be desirable or essential. Transport is a complex, investment-intensive service sector, studded with cross-border and extra-Union entanglements through international agreements and regulations, such as the Chicago bilateral air transport treaty system which has historically regulated the international aviation relations of the Member States *inter se* and with non-EU countries. It is also a sector, as we have seen at various points in our discussion, in which State ownership has historically played a significant role, in part because a transport *system* must (at least in traditional European thinking) satisfy diverse and often unprofitable public requirements that commercial operators might neglect.[39] Aligned with the market integration implications of the fact that commerce moves along the road, rail, pipeline, waterway and air infrastructures, the Treaty drafters saw transport as a conspicuous target for Member State coordination.[40]

---

32. EC Treaty art. 3(g).
33. EC Treaty arts. 81-82.
34. While close analysis of these concepts is outside the scope of the present study, excellent treatments of their substance and application can be found in TREVOR HARTLEY, THE FOUNDATIONS OF EUROPEAN COMMUNITY LAW (6th ed. 2007) and TAKIS TRIDIMAS, THE GENERAL PRINCIPLES OF EU LAW (2d ed. 2007).
35. *See generally* P.S.R.F. MATHIJSEN, A GUIDE TO EUROPEAN UNION LAW ch. 13 (9th ed. 2007). In 2008, at the behest of French President Nicholas Sarkozy, competition was conspicuously downgraded as a main objective of the yet-to-be-ratified Lisbon Treaty. *See* The Enforcer, ECONOMIST, Jan. 8, 2008. For more on the Lisbon Treaty, *see supra* Chapter 1, note 10.
36. EC Treaty arts. 32-38.
37. EC Treaty art. 32(1) defines 'agricultural products' to include 'fisheries.'
38. *Id.* arts. 70-80.
39. Report of the *Comité des Sages, Expanding Horizons: Civil Aviation in Europe, an Action Programme for the Future*, at 45 (1994) [hereinafter Report of the *Comité des Sages*].
40. While these sectoral policies by no means exhaust the present scope of common EC 'policies' (for example, economic and monetary as well as social), a complete taxonomy lies beyond the scope of the present work.

B   THE COMMUNITY INSTITUTIONS AND EC AIR TRANSPORT
             LIBERALIZATION

The distribution of legislative powers among the EC institutions is in flux. With each adjustment, the balance of power has shifted in relatively modest increments toward the popularly-elected European Parliament. Conceptually, the Community's most centralized institutions, the Commission and the Council of the European Union, accept sovereignty and power in a direct transfer from the Member States.[41] Further, despite the Parliament's elected status,[42] the appointive, executive Commission has the exclusive right to initiate new legislative proposals[43] and the Parliament is only exceptionally empowered to veto the passage of new legislation.[44]

1   The Council of the European Union

Formerly labeled the Council of Ministers, the dominant political organ of the EC now styles itself (despite the absence of any such nomenclature in existing or proposed treaty language[45]) the 'Council of the European Union.' The Council is comprised of government ministerial (*i.e.*, 'cabinet') representatives in various sectors – including foreign affairs, agriculture, finance, and transport, for example – who directly represent their States' interests. Unlike the Commission, therefore, the Council *qua* Council is not a permanent presence in Brussels (or Luxembourg).[46] Its membership rotates in different 'configurations,' determined by the sectoral issues it is addressing. It is in the configuration of the Council of Transport Ministers, comprising ministers of transport of the member governments, that it has pursued its airline liberalization initiatives.[47] The Council has both legislative

---

41. *See* the reasoning of the European Court of Justice in Case 6/64, Costa *v.* ENEL, 1964 E.C.R. 585.
42. The European Parliament has been elected by direct universal suffrage since 1979.
43. This principle is not explicitly stated in any of the constitutive treaties; it is implicit, however, in the absence of any Treaty provisions where the Council is authorized to act *without* a Commission proposal. Moreover, the Commission's power of initiation is cemented by Article 250, which requires the Council to act unanimously to amend a proposal from the Commission.
44. *See* EC Treaty art. 251.
45. The EC Treaty, laconic as always, refers only to a 'Council.' *See* EC Treaty art. 7. The Treaty of Lisbon, discussed *supra* Chapter 1, note 10 & *infra* note 63, would delete this article from the EC Treaty and transfer it to Article 13 of the Treaty on European Union. *See* [Post-Lisbon Treaty] Consolidated Version of the Treaty on European Union art. 13, 2008 O.J. (C 115) 13; Table of Equivalences, 2008 O.J. (C 115) 361, 367.
46. The Council is, however, served in Brussels by a permanent body of senior bureaucrats (holding ambassadorial rank) known as COREPER, the *Comité des Représentants Permanents*, Committee of Permanent Representatives. EC Treaty art. 207. Additionally, the Council has a resident General Secretariat. *See id.*
47. In the 1990s, the number of configurations was 22. That number was reduced to 16 in Jun. 2000 and to only nine in Jun. 2002. The Transport Ministers continue to meet as a defined group, but they are now technically part of the 'Transport and Energy' configuration. *Cf.* Council of the European Union, Transport, Telecommunication and Energy Council (TTE), <www.consilium.

and executive powers and is charged in Article 202 of the EC Treaty with ensuring that the 'objectives' of the Treaty are attained and with coordinating the general economic policies of the Member States.[48] The Council exercises its legislative power, in compliance with significantly revamped procedures, in association with the European Parliament.[49]

2   The European Commission

The European Commission is the executive arm of the EC, charged by Article 211 of the EC Treaty with ensuring that the broad economic aims of Article 3 are

---

europa.eu/cms3_fo/showPage.asp?id=413&lang=en>. The 'specificity' of the Chicago bilateral system has compelled the EU Member State governments to assume a paradoxical role. Through the Council of Transport Ministers, the governments participate in the constitutional rulemaking activities of the European Community concerning air transport; but each government is also a participant, in the sphere of air transport, in the Chicago Convention system that predates the establishment of the original European Communities. Thus, the ministerial delegates who championed airline liberalization were simultaneously committing their governments to severance of connections previously established among the Member States on a bilateral intergovernmental basis, and were also forcing a recontextualization, in both legal and policy terms, of bilateral aviation relations among each of the Member States and the rest of the world.

48. EC Treaty art. 202.
49. The Community uses three species of final legal act that are borrowed from French administrative practice. The plenary form, the *regulation*, has immediate force of law in the Member States upon promulgation. In EC Treaty parlance, it is 'directly applicable;' in the more traditional vocabulary of international law, it is 'self-executing.' EC Treaty art. 249. *See also* MARK W. JANIS, AN INTRODUCTION TO INTERNATIONAL LAW 87-88 (2003). Regulations enter into force on the date specified in them or, in the absence of a date, on the twentieth day following the date of their publication in the *Official Journal of the European Communities. See* EC Treaty art. 254(2). A *directive*, in contrast, mixes supranational and national legislative authority, since it is addressed to Member States and is binding upon them, but it also gives the Member States a discretion, to be exercised within a specified time frame, as to what domestic legislative procedures they will use to transform the directive into national law. EC Treaty art. 249. A *decision*, finally, is binding on only those to whom it is specifically addressed, a universe of potential recipients that encompasses classifications as diverse as all of the Member States (in which case, it behaves with much the same effect as a regulation) or a single private individual. *See id.* In applying the competition law rules, the Commission usually acts by decision, as for example when it imposes fines on private corporations for violations of the competition code in Articles 81 or 82. The relevant Treaty provision also mentions *recommendations* and *opinions*, but neither of these forms of action possesses what the Treaty calls 'binding force.' EC Treaty art. 249. Moreover, while the language of the Treaty speaks only of regulations as 'directly applicable,' the European Court of Justice has invented a quite distinct, more generalized extra-Treaty doctrine of 'direct effects,' which determines whether *any* given act of the Community, irrespective of its nominal designation, may be relied upon directly by litigants in national court litigation. The selection of which form of act to use will frequently depend on the political crosswinds buffeting the ministers assembled in Council: a regulation (or a decision addressed to all Member States) suggests a high degree of conciliar solidarity about the need for immediate action, while directives, with their built-in scope for procrastination, are preferred if minority displeasure is to be appeased. Most of the Community's air transport program has been enacted using the plenary device of the regulation (with, on occasion, a decision addressed to all Member States). On the contentious issue of air fares, however, the Council retreated to the use of directives.

achieved.[50] As noted above, the Commission vaults beyond the conventional boundaries of executive power by having a monopoly over initiation of new legislative proposals.[51] Moreover, although the Council (with the Parliament) is the usual adopting authority for final legislation, the Treaty drafters foresaw that the ministers' intermittent presence in Brussels (or Luxembourg) required some delegation of administrative competence to the Commission. Accordingly, Article 202 of the EC Treaty provides for the grant of 'implementing powers' to the Commission under Council legislation.[52] Among the functional portfolios routinely assigned to members of the Commission are transport and competition, both of relevance to the present study. Below this political level, there is an administrative/secretariat apparatus which comprises 41 Directorates-General.[53] The pertinent 'DG' operations in the airline liberalization program are Energy and Transport as well as Competition.[54]

The right of legislative initiative, though highly important, does not completely situate the star of the Commission in the Community's institutional constellation. As the only 'permanent' sitting supranational institution in the legislative process, the Commission has taken seriously its broadly-sketched Treaty mandate to 'formulate recommendations or deliver opinions on matters dealt with in this Treaty, if it expressly so provides *or if the Commission considers it necessary*.'[55] In the view of one European commentator, this general license to innovate makes the Commission 'the guardian of the Treaty, the possessor of rights of its own,'[56] and a steady stream of discussion documents – sometimes called, to grand effect, 'White Papers' – issues from the Berlaymont[57] as the Commission seeks to influence and shape the contours of EC economic and social policy from its broadly 'integrationist' perspective.[58] The emergence of a common policy in the notoriously State-centered

---

50. EC Treaty art. 211.
51. In traditional parliamentary democracies, the executive arm, the 'government,' does enjoy an effective monopoly over legislative initiative precisely because of its secure parliamentary majority. Nevertheless, the Commission is not formed from the members of the European Parliament; to the contrary, membership of both bodies appears to be incompatible. EC Treaty art. 213(2) (commissioners may not hold any other occupation, gainful or not, during their terms of office).
52. EC Treaty art. 202.
53. *See* European Commission, Directorates-General and Services, <http://ec.europa.eu/dgs_en.htm>.
54. *See id.*
55. EC Treaty art. 211 (emphasis added).
56. Robert Espérou, *Commentary: A Europe Full of Suspicions?*, 15 Air L. 273, 273 (1990).
57. The name of the Commission headquarters building in Brussels. In fact, the Commission spent most of the last decade dispersed throughout the city as a result of an asbestos reconditioning of the Berlaymont. Many Commission offices returned there only in 2004.
58. In its inaugural White Paper published in 1979, *Air Transport: A Community Approach*, Bull. Eur. Comm. Supp. 5/79, the Commission posited the achievement of full freedom of market access in air transport on a 'phased' basis, although it also proposed that more flexible tariff procedures could be introduced rapidly. The Commission also recommended legislation akin to the Community's then-current Regulation 17 (which had established a pansectoral competition enforcement regime) to apply the competition rules to air transport. In 1984, the European

air transport sector, while certainly helped by a continuum of Court of Justice intervention over the past two decades, was inspired and advanced primarily by the Commission's White Paper productivity.[59]

3 The European Parliament

The European Parliament has been directly elected since June 1979[60] and yet, as has been seen earlier, it has always been denied the conventional parliamentary

---

Commission advanced beyond the desiderata expressed in Memorandum 1 toward more tangible liberalization proposals. In its second air transport encyclical, *Progress Towards the Development of a Community Air Transport Policy*, Civil Aviation Memorandum No. 2, COM (84) 72 final [hereinafter Memorandum 2], the Commission sought to inspire Member State regulatory authorities, in effect, to replicate the final two years of Alfred Kahn's pre-deregulation stewardship of the Civil Aeronautics Board, *see supra* Chapter 4, Part II(E), permitting the maximum degree of competition that the system could absorb without unraveling the basic fabric of intergovernmental consensus and industry cooperation. As in the United States, the acolytes of European airline deregulation focused on price competition as a central benefit of breaking open the protectionist and monopolistic shell in which the airlines then operated. Thus, in addition to proposals to relax capacity restrictions, drastically slash revenue pooling on routes and open more routes to smaller airlines, the Commission sought to evolve beyond the rigid and cumbersome double-approval pricing regime of existing bilaterals, and suggested preset 'zones of reasonableness' within which tariff adjustments could fluctuate in response to market conditions, without joint (or, preferably, *any*) government approval. *See* Memorandum 2, *supra*, at 34. Memorandum 2 was not intended directly to lay siege to the Chicago bilateral system, but to analyze and suggest remedies for its competitive dysfunction. Illustrating what Button and Swann have called the 'international demonstration effect' sparked by acts of deregulation elsewhere, Button & Swann, *supra* note 6, at 220 & 227, the Memorandum saluted the innovativeness of U.S. air transport deregulation policy. *See* Memorandum 2, *supra*, at 12-13. The Commission also pleaded for the establishment of a unified Community posture toward international organizations and non-Member countries. *Id.* at 12-13. Further, the European Commission was anxious that the Council should understand the Commission's proposals as interdependent, and that therefore the eventual legislative implementation should occur as a 'package deal.' *Id.* 'Summary' at III. (The word 'package' became a phrasemaker in EC airline liberalization, describing the legislative elements of each of the three phases of the liberalization process. *See infra* Part II(C); *see generally* Paul S. Dempsey, *Aerial Dogfights Over Europe: The Liberalization of EEC Air Transport*, 53 J. Air L. & Com. 615, 659 (1988)).

59. As its various initiatives since 1992 to create integrated markets in various modes of transport (road, rail, air, sea, inland waterway) have taken shape, the Commission has sought to project a broader vision of economic, social, and environmental sustainability for transport. The Commission's thinking is incorporated in a lengthy White Paper issued in 2001: *European Air Transport Policy for 2010: Time to Decide*, COM (2001) 370 final (Sept. 12, 2001) (describing a 'new imperative' of sustainable development for the common transport policy – including the integration of environmental considerations and a reshifting of the balance of use among modes, redistributing cargo and passenger traffic toward rail and waterway transport and away from the congestion and pollution issues that, in the Commission's view, bedevil road and air transport).

60. By the time of the Jun. 2004 elections, the Parliament had swollen to 732 members, making it the largest elected representative assembly in the world.

prerogative of initiating new legislation.[61] Its role in its first 15 years or so was typically advisory and consultative,[62] except where two intricate procedural contrivances – the cooperation procedure (introduced in the Single European Act but now rarely used in practice) and the codecision procedure (a 1992 Maastricht Treaty innovation extended in the Treaty of Amsterdam in 1999) – mandate the Council actually to consider and vote upon parliamentary amendments.[63] The codecision procedure, which now covers two-thirds of EC legislative activity including transport, ultimately gives the Parliament a final veto. The path to its exercise, however, is littered with procedural arcana.[64] Only the default

---

61. The Parliament, in common with the Council, has a discretionary power to request the Commission to submit any proposal on matters on which it considers that a Community act is required to implement the EC Treaty. *See* EC Treaty art. 192. In an interesting self-conception, the Parliament's official website describes this manifest inversion of the conventional legislative process as the 'power of political initiative.' *See* European Parliament, Powers: Legislative Power, <http://www.europarl.europa.eu/parliament/public/staticDisplay .do?id=46&pageRank=2&language=EN>. In fairness to the Parliament, it has worked to gain access to and input into the Commission's proposed annual legislative program and to suggest elements it would like to see included – but this process is a matter of interinstitutional cooperation and is not mandated in the Treaty (which provides only an ex post facto power to review the Commission's annual general report). EC Treaty, art. 200.

62. *See, e.g.*, EC Treaty art. 192 (prescribing that the Parliament shall participate in the legislative process by 'delivering advisory opinions'). The so-called 'consultation' procedure still applies in a number of sensitive areas where the Council retains plenary control (notably agriculture, competition, taxation, and negotiation of treaties). *See, e.g.*, EC Treaty art. 83 (in relation to legislation for a competition policy, laying down the classic formula that the Council acts by a qualified majority 'on a proposal from the Commission and after consulting the European Parliament').

63. These procedures have survived despite institutional awareness that they render the legislative process overly complex. For a highly critical presentation of the technical operation of both devices, *see* European Commission, *Report for the Reflection Group*, at 28-33, Office for Official Publications of the European Communities (1995) [hereinafter Report of the Commission for the Reflection Group] (condemning the procedures as so complex as '[to render] the Union's *modus operandi* extremely obscure.' *Id.* at 32). The codecision procedure, the dominant legislative mechanism used by the Community institutions, is maintained under the Treaty of Lisbon (in which it is called the 'the ordinary legislative procedure'). *See* Treaty of Lisbon Amending the Treaty on European Union and the Treaty Establishing the European Community (EC) art. 2a, 2007 O.J. (C 306) 1, 42 (Dec. 17, 2007) (listing the 'horizontal amendments' to the treaties).

64. *See* EC Treaty art. 251. According to commentators' glosses, the codecision procedure involves three 'readings' of a matter of proposed legislation (or 'act'). In the first reading, the Commission submits a proposal to the Parliament and the Council. The Council obtains the opinion of the Parliament and then, acting by a qualified majority, adopts the act including any amendments proposed by the Parliament or, if it dislikes what Parliament has done, adopts a 'common position' which is retransmitted to the Parliament. Within no more than three months, if the Parliament does nothing the act is adopted in accordance with the common position. The Parliament can also reject the proposed act by an absolute majority of its component members (the first veto) or propose amendments to the common position by the same majority. Within another three months, if the Council likes all of the Parliament's amendments it can (by qualified majority) adopt the amended common position as final. If the Commission has given a negative opinion on any amendment, the Council must act unanimously. If the Council opposes any amendment, the President of the Council and the President of the Parliament have six weeks

'consultation' procedure in Article 192 of the EC Treaty, whereby the Parliament delivers an advisory opinion and the Commission and Council are free to ignore its opinion *provided* that they obey the ritual of consultation,[65] was used to adopt the phases of airline liberalization until 1997.[66]

4   The European Court of Justice

The task of the European Court of Justice is defined in the EC Treaty, in words described by one European jurist as 'short and sibylline,' to be to 'ensure that in the interpretation and application of [the] Treaty the law is observed.'[67] The activist role of the Court has been of periodic, but galvanic, significance in air transport liberalization. The discussion of the specific judgments from which the program gathered its momentum will disclose a broad teleological lexicon that the Court has typically employed in its treatment of the law of competition.[68] Indeed, the drafting style of the 314 Articles of the EC Treaty invites precisely this kind of judicial creativity: a broad collection of general rules and procedures has prompted repeated resort by the Court (at least in its first decades[69]) to invocation of the 'objectives of

---

to convene a Council/Parliament Conciliation Committee (reminiscent of the House/Senate bill reconciliation procedures in the United States) to try to agree a joint text. The Committee has six weeks to deliberate. If it agrees on a joint text, the Council (by qualified majority) and the Parliament (by absolute majority of votes cast) have a further six weeks in which to adopt the text (otherwise it lapses). If the Committee does not approve a joint text, the act fails to be adopted. There is a possibility of increasing the time periods referred to in the Article. These arcana would be little changed by the proposed Treaty of Lisbon.

65. *See* Case 138/79, SA Roquette Frères *v.* Council, 1980 E.C.R. 3333 (voiding legislation adopted without obtaining the Parliament's 'opinion' as required by the applicable Treaty provision).

66. The cooperation procedure was the procedure for transport legislation until the Treaty of Amsterdam. Although amendments introduced in the Maastricht Treaty require the cooperation procedure for future legislative action in the transport sector, the Council remains able to override parliamentary opposition provided it acts unanimously. The cooperation procedure, laid down in EC Treaty art. 252, was criticized as really 'just a more elaborate consultation procedure.' MATHIJSEN, *supra* note 35, at 64.

67. EC Treaty art. 220. The characterization of the text is by MATHIJSEN, *supra* note 35, at 114. 'The law' referred to in Article 220 includes all of the so-called *acquis communautaire* (literally, 'Community patrimony'), *i.e.*, the provisions of the constitutive treaties and the secondary legislation adopted thereunder, as well as, self-referentially, the judicial and quasi-judicial decisions of the various EC institutions including the Court.

68. *See generally* Bastiaan van der Esch, *The Principles of Interpretation Applied by the Court of Justice of the European Communities and their Relevance for the Scope of the EEC Competition Rules*, 15 FORDHAM INT'L L.J. 366 (1992).

69. Professor David Gerber detected an evolution in the Court's methodology away from the teleological reasoning of its earlier periods ('an appropriate tool for an aggressive court'), to a preference for 'manipulation of narrower principles drawn largely from its own previous decisions.' David J. Gerber, *The Transformation of European Community Competition Law?*, 35 HARV. INT'L L.J. 97, 127 (1994). While this evolution may be inevitable in a maturing jurisprudence, it does suggest, as Gerber argues, a 'more cautious role.' *Id.* The Court may well be modulating its tone, as post-Maastricht constitutional changes are considered, to deflect the kinds of harsh political criticism that has led in Britain, for example, to Euroskeptic support for a Council override power with respect to Court judgments. The Commission has been broadly

the Community' and other general doctrines of intent-based interpretation.[70] In Daniel Goyder's apt phrase, the Court's use of this methodology provided 'windows of opportunity' for the Council and Commission to apply the Community's competition code to the air transport sector.[71]

The ultimate enforcement of EC law is entrusted to the Court. Thus, for example, while the European Commission would rarely challenge a Member State's dereliction of its obligations under EC law without preliminary, informal consultations to promote voluntary compliance, the Commission does have power to bring the matter before the Court under Article 226 of the EC Treaty, as observed in Chapter 2 in connection with the Commission's successive challenges to Member State engagement with the U.S. open skies policy.[72] A special enforcement regime applies when the Commission proceeds against a Member State for violation of the Treaty rules on unlawful public subsidies (so-called 'State aids').[73]

The Court's catalytic effect on the emergence of an EC common aviation policy, both internally and (through its open skies rulings) externally, has been extraordinary. We will consider the Court's role in shaping a Community external aviation policy later in this Chapter. But its role in the creation of the internal Community market in air transport was equally powerful. In a sequence of judgments between 1974 and 1986, the Court sealed the juridical union between the

---

supportive of the Court's review function: 'It is thanks to the decisions of the Court of Justice, and its dialogue with national courts, that the internal market has been consolidated, that the common policies have been encouraged, that the [Union's] identity has been affirmed, and that discriminatory and nationalistic temptations have been resisted.' Report of the Commission for the Reflection Group, *supra* note 63, at 33.

70. Thus, in Case 6/64, Costa *v*. ENEL, 1964 E.C.R. 585, 593-94, the Court fashioned the principle of the supremacy of Community law from the 'terms and spirit' and 'objectives' of the Treaty, which made it 'impossible' for the Member States 'to accord precedence to a unilateral and subsequent measure over a legal system accepted by them on a basis of reciprocity.'

71. DANIEL G. GOYDER, EEC COMPETITION LAW 413 (1988).

72. EC Treaty art. 226. Under Article 228, the Court has jurisdiction to 'find' whether or not a Member State has failed to fulfill an obligation under the Treaty. EC Treaty art. 228. The Commission's Article 226 authority finds further normative support in Article 10 (requiring Member States to take all measures to fulfill their Treaty obligations). For a discussion of the Commission's formal use of this procedure to challenge the cluster of Member States that contracted open skies agreements with the United States after 1995, *see supra* Chapter 2, Part III(A).

73. Similarly, under certain defined conditions, a Member State may bring a challenge in the Court against the validity of any Council (or Council/Parliament) or Commission legislative act, and a private corporation or individual may institute proceedings in the Court against a decision (or against a regulation or a decision addressed to another entity) that is of 'direct and individual concern' to the complainant. Each of these grounds of standing is found in EC Treaty art. 230. Much procedural law attaches to the content of this Article, including a series of 'grounds' for challenge that the Treaty drafters borrowed from French administrative law governing *actions en recours pour excès de pouvoir*. A successful challenge under Article 230 usually leads to annulment of the act by the Court. EC Treaty art. 231. The latter procedure is frequently the recourse of corporations that have been fined by the Commission for a violation of the competition laws. Initial jurisdiction to hear challenges to competition law fines has been transferred to a new auxiliary tribunal, the Court of First Instance, since 1989. EC Treaty art. 225. Decisions of the Court of First Instance are appealable to the Court of Justice 'on points of law only.' EC Treaty art. 225(1).

EC's transport and competition policies, and emboldened the Commission to upset a legislative stasis in the Council of Ministers that had led the then European Commissioner for Competition, Peter Sutherland, to describe his role as being 'to play Vladimir to the Council's Godot.'[74]

The sequence of rulings is iconic to aviation lawyers. In *Commission of the European Communities v. French Republic*,[75] the so-called *French Sailors* case, the Court declined to interpret the opacity of Article 80(2) of the EC Treaty, with its apparent omission of sea and air transport from the ambit of a required common transport policy, to mean that the 'general rules' of the Treaty were disapplied in those sectors unless the general rules contained a specific exception for transport.[76] In *European Parliament v. Council of the European Communities* (*Obligations of the Council* case),[77] the European Parliament brought an action for a declaration that the Council of Ministers had infringed various provisions of the EC Treaty, including Articles 3(f) (calling for a common policy 'in the sphere of transport') and 51 (dealing with free movement of services in the transport sector), and various Articles of the Transport Title, by failing to introduce or adopt a common policy for transport.[78] While the Court concluded that the absence of a policy did not in itself

---

74. Peter D. Sutherland, European Commissioner for Competition [1985-89], *Civil Aviation in the European Community – Competition Without Frontiers, in* INTERNATIONAL CONFERENCE PROCEEDINGS, DEVELOPING EUROPEAN REGIONAL AIR TRANSPORT – THE NEXT TEN YEARS 1-2 (1986). In fairness to the Commissioner, he stated explicitly that he would be 'unwilling' to play such a role. *Id.*

75. Case 167/73, Commission *v.* France (*French Sailors*), 1974 E.C.R. 359.

76. *Id.* at 371. For example, Article 51(1) provides that freedom of services in the transport sector shall be governed by the Treaty provisions on transport itself. EC Treaty art. 51(1). The freedom of establishment provisions (Articles 43-48) *do* apply directly to air transport, but this freedom is useless without the freedom to provide services. *French Sailors*, 1974 E.C.R at 371. The expression 'general rules' has never appeared in any iteration of the Treaty and arguably embraced only former Parts One and Two ('Principles' and 'Foundations' of the supranational order). Whether, therefore, the Council might be required to adopt a specific act under Article 80(2) to apply what was then Part Three of the Treaty – including in particular, its competition rules – to maritime or air transport was left unresolved in the judgment. According to the Commission's reading, expressed in Memorandum 2, while the Court concededly applied only the Treaty's general rules on the free movement of workers, EC Treaty arts. 39-42, and then only to maritime transport, the composite effect of its ruling was to find that air transport must be subject to the Article 81 prohibition of concerted practices that restrain competition. *See* Memorandum 2, *supra* note 58, at 17.

77. Case 13/83, Parliament *v.* Council (*Obligations of the Council*), 1985 E.C.R. 1513.

78. *Obligations of the Council*, 1985 E.C.R. at 1583. The Council protested that the policy concerned an extremely complex subject matter loaded with the variables of infrastructure, prices, conditions of transport, intermodality, freedom of establishment and freedom to provide services, social welfare problems, and competition. *See id.* at 1594-95. The Parliament's action, incidentally, was based procedurally on EC Treaty art. 232, one of the least commonly-used enforcement provisions of Community law. In essence, it grants a remedy against the supranational institutions for a 'failure to act.' EC Treaty art. 51(1) provides that '[f]reedom to provide services in the field of transport shall be governed by the provisions of the Title relating to transport.' The general removal of restrictions on freedom to provide intra-Community services is mandated by Article 49.

constitute a failure to act 'sufficiently specific in nature' to form the subject of a declaratory proceeding under the EC Treaty, it did discern one 'sufficiently specific' fetter on the Council's discretion: the Council's repeated failure to devise a transport policy setting forth the 'the conditions under which non-resident carriers may operate transport services within a Member State.'[79] The Court found that the requirement for that substantive element of the policy *was* specific in the Treaty through Article 51(1), enclosed within the chapter on freedom of services, which provides that freedom to provide services in the field of transport is to be governed by the Title on Transport.[80] 'It follows,' the Court reasoned, 'that in that respect [*i.e.*, introducing freedom of services in transport] the Council does not have the discretion on which it may rely in other areas of the common transport policy.'[81] While the Court did not explain whether its decision on Article 51(1) also encompassed the aviation sector,[82] an opportunity to apply its ecumenical principles of interpretation specifically to air transport would come just a few years later.

The *French Sailors* and *Obligations of the Council* cases reflected the incrementalism that sometimes marks the rulings of the European Court of Justice when it is seeking to slice more thinly the margins of Member State autonomy in a supranational legal order. The Court articulates a general principle – in the *French Sailors* case, that the 'general rules' of the EC Treaty trump the discretionary powers of the Council of Ministers to implement, or delay the implementation of, a common transport policy – but gives it an initially specific application, free movement of workers in the maritime industry.[83] In *Obligations of the Council*, the Court, while paying effusive homage to the Council's discretionary powers in Title V, simultaneously narrowed those powers across *all* transport sectors by application of a second

---

79. *Obligations of the Council*, 1985 E.C.R. at 1600.
80. *See id.* at 1599.
81. *Id.* at 1600. The Council would retain a measure of discretion only as regards the means employed to obtain the result (freedom to provide services). *Id.* The Court's textual explication did betray a puzzling circularity: one reading of the language of Article 51(1) is surely that it was designed as an *exception* to the general freedom to provide services, suspended in the transport sector pending exercise of the Council's discretion to frame a common policy taking account of the 'distinctive' features of transport (the qualifying epithet used in Article 71(1)). Why then should the mere existence of that exception have imposed the very obligation in Article 71 that was purposely avoided in Article 51? In fact, the Court's interpretive fusion of transport services in the Transport Title with a separately-treated component of the common market (freedom of services) in the Title on free movement of persons, services, and capital, thereby forcing an abridgment of the Council's apparent discretion under the Transport Title, would logically foreshadow a further exegesis (in the *Nouvelles Frontières* case, *infra*) to read Article 80(2) subject to the competition rules in Articles 81 and 82. In any event, the Court had given Europe's supranational transport policy what one German jurist described at the time as 'a new impulse.' Jürgen Basedow, *Vorwort* ('Foreword'), *in* EUROPÄISCHE VERKEHRSPOLITIK ('European Transport Policy') (Gerd Aberle ed. 1987).
82. Thus, this part of the judgment, which makes no reference to Article 80(2), appears to encompass only international inland (rail, road and inland waterway) transport.
83. *See* generally HARTLEY, *supra* note 34, at 192-235 (using the lines of cases concerning the Community's treatymaking powers and the doctrine of direct effects to trace this process).

'general rule' of the Treaty, the freedom to provide services.[84] More than 20 years ago, in its 1986 ruling in *Ministère Public v. Lucas Asjes*[85] (best known by its apt sobriquet, *Nouvelles Frontières*),[86] the Court breached the ramparts of the most protected and protectionist European transport sector, the airline industry, subordinating it to the Treaty's competition rules notwithstanding the Council's apparently unbounded discretion in Article 80(2) as to 'whether' and 'to what extent' air transport services should be encased within a common policy.

The local controversy that prompted the Article 234 reference in *Nouvelles Frontières*[87] involved a number of mixed civil and criminal proceedings against the executives of domestic French airlines and travel agencies (including the eponymous Nouvelles Frontières) who had been charged with infringing certain articles of the French Civil Aviation Code, when selling air tickets, by applying tariffs that had not been submitted to the French Minister for Civil Aviation for approval (or which were different from the approved tariffs).[88] *Nouvelles Frontières*, in other words, presented a direct challenge to the prevailing tariff protocol in bilateral air-services agreements, under which the designated airlines of both parties fixed their fares by common accord (and usually within the framework of an IATA tariff conference[89]), thereafter submitting the agreed fares to their respective aviation authorities for 'double approval.'[90] Citing to the Chicago Convention and various international tariff protocols, the French Government invited the Court to recognize the international treaty underpinnings of its municipal fare approval statute.[91] The Court of Justice responded sharply that the government 'has not claimed that the said international agreements obliged the Member States which signed them not to respect the competition rules in the EC Treaty.'[92]

---

84. The judgment does not *explicitly* state that its application excludes sea and air transport.
85. Joined Cases 209 & 213/84, Ministère Publique *v.* Lucas Asjes (*Nouvelles Frontières*), 1986 E.C.R. 1425.
86. Nouvelles Frontières, one of the principal defendants before the Paris court, is one of France's largest tour operators.
87. The Court of Justice has a specialized jurisdiction to render 'preliminary rulings' on issues of EC law referred to it by national courts. EC Treaty art. 234. While there has been little private litigation of Community antitrust law in the national courts, a reference made under this specialized jurisdiction from a minor French administrative tribunal in *Nouvelles Frontières* was – in one vital sense – the catalyst for the entire Community airline liberalization program. Although the Court pronounces only in the context of the lawsuit in which the reference is made, its opinion is said to have '*de facto* effect *erga omnes.*' MATHIJSEN, *supra* note 35, at 99. Municipal courts are free to resubmit questions already considered by the Court in Luxembourg, which is not bound by precedent, but 'it can be assumed that parties in subsequent cases involving provisions which have been interpreted by the Court will not lightly contest that interpretation.' *Id.*
88. *See Nouvelles Frontières*, 1986 E.C.R. at 1459. The French Civil Aviation Code, in keeping with the Chicago system, required standardization of air fares and prohibited the sale of tickets at prices below the government-approved price.
89. *See supra* Chapter 3, Part IX.
90. *Nouvelles Frontières*, 1986 E.C.R. at 1462-63. Signatory states usually indicated that use of the IATA mechanism would make subsequent official approval a formality.
91. *See id.* at 1462-63.
92. *Id.* at 1463.

Unlike in its earlier decisions in *French Sailors* and *Obligations of the Council*, the Court rooted its exegetical analysis squarely in Article 70 of the Treaty, the opening provision of the Transport Title, which announces that '[t]he objectives of this Treaty shall, in matters governed by this [t]itle, be pursued by Member States within the framework of a common transport policy.'[93] In the Court's teleological reasoning, this choice of language made the *objectives* of the Treaty, particularly the institution of a system ensuring that competition in the internal (common) market is not distorted (Article 3(g)[94]), 'equally applicable to the transport sector.'[95] Where the Treaty *intended* to except certain activities from the dominion of the competition rules, 'it made an express derogation to that effect.'[96] In the Transport Title, however, there is no provision that would suspend the application of the competition rules to transport, or condition their application upon specific Council acts.[97] In the absence of any explicit gatekeeper exception, therefore, the Court concluded that the competition rules, in particular Articles 81 through 86, must apply directly to the domain of transport.[98]

Turning to the air transport sector, the Court addressed the implications of its earlier interpretations in *French Sailors* and *Obligations of the Council*. Focusing on Article 80(2) itself, with its notional optionality as to Council action on appropriate provisions for sea and air transport, the Court ruled that the wording, coupled with its position in the Treaty, indicated an intention on the part of the drafters 'merely to define the scope of [Article 70] *et seq.* [the transport Articles] as regards different modes of transport, by distinguishing between transport by rail, road, and inland waterway, covered by paragraph (1), and sea and air transport, covered by paragraph (2).'[99] Accordingly, the Court's earlier decision in *French Sailors* excluded sea and air transport only from the rules of the *Transport Title* relating to the common transport policy, at least pending Council action to the contrary.[100] 'Air transport remained, on the same basis as the other modes of transport, subject to the general rules of the Treaty, *including the competition rules.*'[101]

---

93. EC Treaty art. 70.
94. *See supra* in the main text.
95. *Nouvelles Frontières*, 1986 E.C.R. at 1465.
96. *Nouvelles Frontières*, 1986 E.C.R. at 1465. Article 36, for example, disapplied the competition rules with respect to production and trade in agricultural products except 'to the extent determined by the Council' within the framework of Article 37(2) and (3). *Id.*
97. *See id.* at 1466.
98. *See id.*
99. *Nouvelles Frontières*, 1986 E.C.R. at 1466.
100. *See id.*
101. *Id.* (emphasis added). Given that no formal legislation existed to apply the Treaty competition rules to air transport, the Court's judgment had the practical effect of a *renvoi* to the 'competent national authorities' of the Member States and to the Commission. The Court clearly felt that the absence of any implementing regulations conferring powers of enforcement in respect of air transport did not *per se* entail that there was no Article 81 infraction. Either a 'national authority' for competition enforcement, or the Commission, could have acted against the challenged fare approval protocol and decided that it infringed Article 81, under their basic enforcement powers in Article 84 (national authority) or Article 85 (Commission). Because no such action or decision had been taken so far, however, the price-fixing was presumptively

The Court supplied no guidance as to whether all existing tariff agreements were now presumptively void, or whether Member States had an obligation to report themselves or each other with respect to such agreements, or as to the continued endurance of the IATA tariff apparatus under which the challenged ticket prices had been determined.[102] Indeed, just as after the Court's landmark open skies rulings in 2002,[103] a risk existed that the Court's complicated judgment would be received merely as 'tokenism,' especially if flag carriers could lobby their governments to secure Article 81(3) or Article 86(2) exemptions.[104]

But the European Commission, sensing a psychological breakthrough in the heretofore indolent treatment of air transport competition in the Community, was ready to ride the momentum of the judgment using *its* Court-validated competence under Article 85.[105] The activist Commissioner for competition matters, Irish lawyer Peter Sutherland, immediately threatened the issuance of a reasoned decision declaring, under Article 85(2), that concerted air fare agreements constituted an infringement of Article 81(1) of the EC Treaty. In a bold display of the Commission's presumptive authority under Article 81, at Sutherland's behest the Commission in 1986 sent letters to ten major EU air carriers alleging violation of the Treaty's competition rules by price-fixing, capacity limitation, revenue pooling, and restricted market entry.[106] The Irish flag carrier, Aer Lingus, for example, was cited for a six-year agreement to pay KLM not to fly to Dublin, thereby illegally eliminating competition on the Dublin/Amsterdam route.[107] The

---

legal for the time being. Thus, as a result of the judgment, both the national authorities and the European Commission were conceded original powers under Articles 84 and 85 to enforce Article 81 with respect to international, intra-Community, air and maritime transport.

102. In fact, the Court made no specific finding that the French statutes *did* violate Community law, although to do so would have been inconsistent with the 'interpretive' analysis preferred under Article 234.

103. *See supra* Chapter 2, Part III.

104. *See* Virginia Clarke, *New Frontiers in EEC Transport Competition,* 8 J. INT'L L. & BUS. 455, 466 (1987). Similarly, Member State administration of the competition laws would lead to inconsistent application. *Id.* at 469. On Article 86 of the EC Treaty, *see infra* text accompanying note 110.

105. *See* David J. Bederman, *Prospects for European Air Deregulation,* 21 INT'L LAW. 561, 569 (1987). In an earlier discussion document, European Commission, *Completing the Internal Market,* at 30, White Paper from the Commission to the European Council, COM (85) 310 final (Jun. 14, 1985) [hereinafter White Paper on the Internal Market], the Commission had warned that '[i]f the Council [of Ministers] fails to make progress towards the adoption of proposed Regulations concerning the application of the competition rules to air transport, the Commission intends to take decisions regarding existing infringements . . . according to [Article 85] of the [EC] Treaty.'

106. *See* the Commission's *Seventeenth Report on Competition Policy* (1988), point 46, at 47-48. There being no precedent for a pure 'general powers' procedure under Article 85, the Commission adopted the device of sending nonbinding letters to the carriers involved. David L. Perrott, *Regional Developments, European Communities,* 21 INT'L LAW. 1205, 1206 (1987).

107. STEPHEN WHEATCROFT & GEOFFREY LIPMAN, ECONOMIST INTELLIGENCE UNIT, AIR TRANSPORT IN A COMPETITIVE EUROPEAN MARKET 60 (1986). Also cited were revenue and capacity sharing pacts between Aer Lingus and British Airways, and between Air France and SAS. *See id.* The airlines involved were Alitalia, Lufthansa, Olympic, Aer Lingus, Air France, British Airways, British Caledonian, KLM, Sabena, and SAS. *See* Press Release, European Airlines, 1 E.C.L.R. 202-203 (1987).

Commission's threat formally to record an infringement by all of the airlines under Article 85(2) – and to test the limits of Article 85's enforcement powers[108] – was forestalled by the Council's adoption of a first liberalization package in 1987.[109]

Even without the intervention of the Court of Justice,[110] the Commission might have been able to attack aspects of the airlines' monopolistic incumbencies using its freestanding Article 86 powers to challenge anticompetitive activities by public monopolies.[111] The historical evidence suggests, however, that the Commission had not considered Article 86 as an available resource,[112] and also that a purely hortatory campaign, waged by means of White Papers and discussion documents, was unlikely to pose a serious threat to the aviation prerogatives of the

---

108. *See supra* note 106.

109. The Commission, incidentally, originally attempted Article 85 enforcement against the airlines as early as 1981 when it sent questionnaires to the governments of the Member States and the airlines established in those territories. *See Eleventh Report on Competition Policy* (1982), point 5, at 21. These proceedings were slow and inadequate because at the time the Commission lacked Regulation 17-type compulsory powers of investigation. The characteristics uncovered by the Commission, shared by most agreements other than a handful of more 'liberal' bilaterals, were familiar: an equal split of route capacity, seasonal coordination of schedules, IATA tariff consultations, required official blessing of both governments for all capacity, schedule and fare agreements, and revenue pooling. Nicholas Argyris, *The EEC Rules of Competition and the Air Transport Sector*, 26 COMMON MKT. L. REV. 5, 6 (1989). The last element is a curiosity in a rigid bilateral arrangement of 50/50 capacity, because it is a revenue transfer mechanism that only operates when one carrier (presumably through the fortuitous play of competitive selection) gains more than the agreed capacity share. *See id.* The existence of the pool, of course, acts itself as a disincentive to compete. *See id.* at 9-10.

110. One additional seminal opinion of the Court of Justice bears mention. Airline competition beyond the borders of the European Union attracted the scrutiny of the Court of Justice in the *Ahmed Saeed* case, Case 66/86, Ahmed Saeed Flugreisen *v.* Zentrale zur Bekämpfung Unlautern Wettbewerbs e.V., 1989 E.C.R. 803. In that case, the Court considered the difficult and contentious subject of extraterritorial assertions of jurisdiction over international air transport. The Court ruled that Article 82, which contains an unvarnished prohibition from which no Article 81(1)-style derogation or exemption was possible, is a competition rule which is directly applicable before national jurisdictions and is subject to no territorial limitation, either in the domestic sphere or in air transport relations with non-Member States. Bilateral or multilateral tariff agreements, for example, could bring Article 82 into play if one of the carriers abused its dominant position, forcing other carriers to apply excessively high or low fares or the exclusive application of only one tariff on a particular route. *Id.* at 851. Under the Court's ruling, therefore, in the absence of action by the Commission pursuant to its treaty powers, national courts were empowered to apply Article 82 *directly* to air transport to and from the EU. *Id.* The Court's expansive view of Article 82 would appear to have allowed any of the transatlantic alliances – despite the absence at the time of EC implementing procedural legislation – to be challenged in a Member State national court, relying on EC competition law, by an aggrieved competitor. As a result of recent legislative changes, the Community competition policy now applies without geographical restriction to all extra-Union air transport.

111. *See infra* text accompanying note 224.

112. *See* Remarks of Commissioner Sutherland, *in* REGIONAL AIR CONFERENCE PROCEEDINGS, *supra* note 74, at 2-3 (regretting disapplication of Commission's competition enforcement powers by virtue of Regulation 141).

Member States or their flag carrier clients.[113] In contrast, beyond providing occasional checks on Civil Aeronautics Board or Department of Transportation (DOT) administrative discretion, the U.S. federal courts did not assume a direct doctrinal role in the execution of the U.S. deregulation experiment. The legal panoply of airline deregulation was imposed by a kind of self-referential Congressional edict, emendations of a system that Congress had itself previously decreed. The common market, with the Commission as program manager and the Court of Justice as exegete-in-chief, displayed a striking example of institutional cross-fertilization as it made its approach toward liberalizing the airline industry.

C   THE LEGISLATIVE FOUNDATIONS OF THE SINGLE AVIATION MARKET: A 'PACKAGE' DEAL

Between 1987 and 1992, the EC institutions collaborated in three stages of legislation designed to create among the Member States *inter se* a (legal) replica of the deregulated environment accomplished within the United States by the Airline Deregulation Act.[114] The concept of 'phasing' change, related to the specificity of the airline industry,[115] was endorsed by the industry itself. A senior lawyer at the IATA warned (ironically) after the 1987 package, for example, that other industries had benefited from very long transitions,[116] and that ground transport had enjoyed

---

113. *See generally* SELECT COMMITTEE ON THE EUROPEAN COMMUNITIES, EUROPEAN AIR TRANSPORT POLICY, H.L. (5th ser.) 115 (1985), noting that many scheduled airlines (like their American counterparts in the late 1970s) were opposed even to the limited ideas proposed by the Commission: 'Clearly, there is a battle ahead.' *Id.*

114. The selected juridical approach, despite some Member State misgivings, was to overlay the existing inter-State air services bilaterals with an entirely new structure of common rules adopted under EC Treaty powers, a kind of uniform multilateral replacement for each Member State's separate bilateral network with its fellow Members, and to which all the Member States would immediately subscribe. In principle, the Member States were not called upon formally to renounce their existing bilaterals with each other, nor did the adopted legislation include any provision (of the kind later inserted into in the EC/Switzerland special civil aviation agreement) to cancel or terminate the preexisting bilaterals. Nevertheless, in conformance with the Member States' obligations in Article 10 of the EC Treaty to comply with action taken by the Community institutions, whenever the new regime imposed greater liberality than an existing agreement, the later instrument would presumably prevail as a matter of supranational law. *See* Jürgen Basedow, *Symposium on US-EC Legal Relations: Airline Deregulation in the European Community,* 9 EUR. COMPETITION L. REV. 247, 253-54 (1994) (noting that preexisting bilaterals contained provisions which 'clearly violated basic principles of Community law,' including the prohibition of discrimination on the basis of nationality and the prohibition on agreements in restraint of trade. Conversely, existing liberal bilaterals (for example, between the United Kingdom and the Netherlands) initially outpaced the gradational establishment of the new Community order.

115. Recognition of the industry's 'specificity' continues to resonate in Community policy. *See, e.g.,* EUROPEAN COMMISSION, AVIATION WORKING GROUP, EUROPEAN CLIMATE CHANGE PROGRAMME II: FINAL REPORT (2006) (discussing what might be done to reduce the effects of aviation emissions on the environment).

116. Article G(9) of the Maastricht Treaty renumbered EC Treaty art. 8 as Article 7. The original article provided for a general transition period of 12 years for establishment of the common market, divided into three stages of four years each.

an effective transition period of 25 years; air transport, therefore, 'should be allowed sufficient time for all necessary adaptations, and the overall well-functioning of the industry should not be sacrificed for an abstract principle.'[117] The sequence of deregulatory packages, padded with exception and safeguard clauses and so-called block exemption privileges, to some extent provided the measured transition for which the industry had lobbied.

Viewed as an exercise in intergovernmental cooperation, the European grand design ultimately vaulted beyond its U.S. antecedent in its systematic integration of independent sovereign airspaces through provisions for eighth freedom (consecutive) cabotage and (after 1997) the multilateral demise of traditional cabotage.[118] The culminating 1992 reform 'package,'[119] now consolidated into a single regulation that incorporates a number of revisions and clarifications,[120] included legislation in three target areas of liberalization: the tariff approval regime, market (route) access and capacity,[121] and a common licensing code for carriers owned and controlled by EU Member State nationals. (In this survey, reference is made primarily to the text of the 2008 consolidated regulation.)[122] In parallel with these market-opening initiatives, the European Commission leveraged the *Nouvelles Frontières* jurisprudence of the Court of Justice to introduce the kind of post hoc competition surveillance for the airline industry that had long existed for almost all other sectors of EU industry.[123]

---

117. Ludwig Weber, *Effect of EEC Air Transport Policy on International Cooperation*, 24 Eur. Transp. L. 448, 452 (1989). Weber indicated in his article that his views did not necessarily reflect those of the Association.

118. *See supra* Chapter 3, Part IV (discussing cabotage).

119. *See supra* note 58 for a comment on this 'phrasemaker' term. The term 'package' to describe each iteration of the liberalization program was adopted, according to an *obiter dictum* remark of the European Court of Justice, 'on account of the fact that [each package] consisted of several documents.' Case C-361/98, Italian Republic *v.* Comm'n, 2001 E.C.R. I-385.

120. *See* Common Rules for the Operation of Air Services in the Community, Council Regulation 1008/2008, 2008 O.J. (L 293) 3 [hereinafter Common Rules]. On Jul. 9, 2008, the European Parliament adopted a legislative resolution approving the EC interinstitutional common position on the European Commission's *Proposal for a Regulation of the European Parliament and of the Council on Common Rules for the Operation of Air Transport Services in the Community*, COM (2006) 396 final (Jul. 18, 2006) [hereinafter European Commission, *Common Rules*]. The new rules went into effect on Nov. 1, 2008. For further discussion, *see* Gabriel S. Sanchez, *The Total Package? On the New Common Rules for Air Transport in the European Union*, 8 Issues Aviation L. & Pol'y 105 (2008).

121. In the United States, as already considered, only fares and routes had been regulated, while capacity and scheduling (in a system with no competitive 'sovereigns') always devolved to airline management discretion. *See supra* Chapter 4, Part II(B).

122. *See supra* note 120.

123. The system of competition enforcement is considered in some detail *infra* Part II(D). In a notable development, also, the final package of reforms in 1992 ended the formal distinction between scheduled and charter airline services within the European Union, indicating how the *raison d'être* of separate scheduled and nonscheduled industries was undercut by expansion of liberalization in the scheduled sector.

On fares and pricing, Article 22 of the 2008 regulation articulates the deregulatory ideal: 'Community air carriers . . . shall freely set air fares and air rates for intra-Community services.'[124] The 2008 regulation abandons the vestigial advance filing mechanism for tariffs that had been preserved in the 1992 legislation[125] as well as an IATCA (International Air Transportation Competition Act of 1979)-like 'no hearing' intervention authority which it awarded to Member States to monitor outbreaks of alleged price predation or excessive pricing that, in their estimation, could cripple their domestic operators.[126] A later amendment to the

---

124. Common Rules, *supra* note 120, art. 22 ('pricing freedom'). Bernardine Adkins noted that the regulation status of the 1992 air fares legislation, Council Regulation 2409/92, 1992 O.J. (L 240) 15, opened up the possibility of reliance on the text in national courts by interested third parties (Member States, other airlines, or even a motivated private citizen), to challenge any suspected price collusion practices (in addition to any causes of action under Articles 81 and 82 of the EC Treaty). BERNARDINE ADKINS, AIR TRANSPORT AND EC COMPETITION LAW 232 (1994). As one analyst pointed out, the 1992 'Regulation brought price competition to the [EU] airline market but contained the seeds of its own destruction if Member States chose to challenge fares subjectively deemed improper.' Susan Beth Farmer, *Chapter 9: Competitive Policy and Merger Analysis in Deregulated and Newly Competitive Industries* 39 (Dickinson School of Law Legal Studies Research Paper No. 05-2008, Jun. 2, 2008). But such interference never came to pass. *See id.*

125. The advance filing period, if a Member State chose to retain it (the 1992 made a filing requirement optional for Member States) had been progressively compressed from 60 days in 1987, to 45 days in 1990, and to merely 24 hours in the final 1992 package. Council Regulation 2409/92, *supra* note 124, art. 5(2). No filing at all could be required, however, if a carrier were simply matching an existing fare (only 'prior notification' was needed). *Id.* U.S. law continues to require the filing (with the Secretary of Transportation) of tariffs for transportation between the United States and non-U.S. points. *See* 49 U.S.C.A. § 41504 (West 2008).

126. For a discussion of the IATCA authority to intervene in international faresetting, *see supra* Chapter 4, Part III(C). Having consulted industry stakeholders on the 2008 revised regulation, the Commission found that air carriers were opposed to 'anything that might jeopardize the freedom to set fares,' including the safeguard mechanism for Member State intervention. European Commission, *Common Rules, supra* note 120, at 4. In any event, these prophylactic mechanisms were never invoked by any Member State. *See* [U.K.] Civil Aviation Authority, *Response to European Commission Consultation for Revision to Third Package* para. 61 (Jun. 16, 2003) (contending that this lack of enforcement indicated that Member States concluded that 'either there is not a problem with air fares or that government intervention may be more costly than the market imperfection it is designed to eliminate'). In its consultation on the third package, the Commission floated the idea that it should have a power, analogous to the power which the 1992 legislation awarded to the Member States, to intervene on its own initiative to prevent the development of extremely high or extremely low fares unrelated to the operating costs of the services in question. European Commission, *Consultation Paper With a View to Revision of Regulations 2407/92, 2408/92, and 2409/92 of 23 July 1992 ('The Third Package' For Liberalization of Air Transport)* (2003) [hereinafter European Commission, *Third Package Consultation Paper*]. Most national authorities considered that, in a free market economy, 'all factors concerning the calculation of air fares should remain in the hands of the carriers' – and consequently disfavored regulation in this area. European Commission, *Summary of Contributions Received by the Commission Following the Consultation Paper With a View to Revision of Regulations No. 2407/92, 2408/92 and 2409/92 of 23 July 1992 ('The Third Package' For Liberalization of Air Transport)*, at 9 (2003) [hereinafter European Commission, *Summary of the Third Package Contributions*]. The national authorities argued that current rules of Community competition law, which prohibit predatory pricing by

1987 competition regulations granted an analogous intervention power to the Commission to police route as well as price predation. This power, which expired in 2004, could be applied on an interim basis pending deployment of the Commission's full competition enforcement apparatus.[127]

Although the 2008 regulation has implicitly withdrawn a prior provision granting Community-licensed air carriers exclusive rights to 'introduce new products or lower fares than the ones existing for identical products,'[128] this explicit prohibition on price leadership by non-Community airlines was the object of vexed attention in recent transatlantic air diplomacy.[129]

---

companies in a dominant position, were adequate. Finally, the authorities also emphasized (as the Commission itself had conceded implicitly in its 1992 guidelines) that the complexity of air fares presents great practical difficulties for reviewing methods. *See id.* In the end, the new rules only contain provisions mandating full transparency for fares while prohibiting price discrimination based on a consumer's nationality or place of residence. *See* Common Rules, *supra* note 120, art. 23.

127. *See* Council Regulation 1284/91, 1991 O.J. (L 122) 2 (amending the now repealed Council Regulation 3975/87, 1987 O.J. (L 374) 1). The Commission had grown concerned that, as had happened under U.S. deregulation, the removal of regulatory controls – and consequent enhanced freedom of market action – might coax air carriers into adopting strategies to eliminate competitors other than by what might be called 'competition on the merits.' This unusual derogation from normal enforcement procedures was reinforced by the Commission's preexisting power to impose periodic penalty payments which has been retained under Article 24 of Council Regulation 1/2003, 2003 O.J. (L 1) 1. Although the interim enforcement article intercalated into the competition legislation in 1991 did not expressly state that airlines had standing to request this kind of emergency action, they did have a direct right of complaint under Article 3(1) of Regulation 3975/87, *supra*, to begin normal investigation steps and it seemed logical that they should have access to both procedures. Indeed, the recent competition modernization regulation (Regulation 1/2003), which now applies to air transport and ultimately superseded Regulation 3975/87, *supra*, in its entirety, continues also to provide standing to lodge a complaint to 'natural or legal persons who can show a legitimate interest.' Regulation 1/2003, *supra*, art. 7(2). In the Commission's consultation paper on revisions to the 'third package,' it noted that it received a number of 'reports' of fares considered 'abnormally high on routes on which, in practice, there is a quasi-monopoly,' or 'abnormally low or non-existent ("free" tickets).' Since these cases 'raise[d] the question' of the link between the rate charged and the production costs for the service provided, the paper initiated thinking on whether, in examining these phenomena (notably the extremely low fares that have become integral to the low-cost carrier business model), the Commission should be allowed to act 'on its own initiative.' European Commission, *Third Package Consultation Paper, supra* note 126, at 7 & 8. Where did the 'reports' (in effect, complaints) come from? Some may have come from Member States, which (as discussed in the main text) enjoyed their own power of intervention in faresetting under Regulation 2409/92. There was no evidence, however, that any Member State has ever used this power against another Member State's air carrier. Association of European Airlines [AEA], *AEA Comments on the EC Consultation Paper* (Jul. 2003) [hereinafter AEA, *Consultation Paper*]. The preferred approach, it would seem, is for Member States (perhaps at the behest of national carriers) to forward *sub rosa* 'reports' to the Commission.

128. Council Regulation 2409/92, *supra* note 124, art. 1(3).

129. The 1992 article was intended to prevent competitive advantages to non-Community airlines when there was (as is typical in the bilateral system) no reciprocity and Community carriers could not price-lead in the home markets of the non-Community airlines. *See* [U.K.] Civil Aviation Authority, *supra* note 126, para. 62 (proposing that the article should be removed, although suggesting that the article may provide some – but 'questionable' – leverage in negotiating with third countries). Assuming that the Community will keep its commitment

The preamble to the 1990 (second-phase) Council regulation on market access and capacity[130] declared an ambition in its final recital that was without precedent in public international aviation law, namely, that the Council should adopt 'further measures of liberalization *including cabotage* in respect of market access and capacity sharing by June 30, 1992.'[131] The Commission envisioned that the final package in 1992 would complete the liberation of traffic rights from bilateral bureaucratic control, finally breaking the canonical bond between each State's airspace sovereignty and the award of access rights to its air transport markets. Full seventh freedom rights (unconnected to a compulsory home segment[132]), coupled with abolition of *intra*-State cabotage, would yield a comprehensive, uniform, open route network across the entire airspace of the EC. Provided they were registered under a new common system of 'Community' licensing, also introduced in the 1992 package,[133] Member State airlines could freely provide services between any two airports between or within the national territories of the Community. The Council reacted favorably to the Commission's bold design, but political compromises forced postponement of the full cabotage initiative until 1997.[134] The Council also insisted upon the usual safeguard measures dictated by airport capacity and infrastructural limitations.

Thus, the definition of traffic rights in Article 2(14) of the 2008 consolidated regulation – 'the right to operate an air service between two Community airports' – is a panoramic grant of authority that is now so widely-drawn after the iterations of the three legislative packages that it also embraces intra-Member State cabotage.[135] Also, Article 16 of the 2008 regulation lays down amplified criteria

---

under Article 13(2) of the 2007 U.S./EC Air Transport Agreement, 2007 O.J. (L 134) 4, and using the language embedded in that provision, the European Commission does appear to have conceded that this latest iteration of the regulation is 'not more restrictive' than its predecessor and therefore that the price leadership embargo will be inoperative. According to the U.K. Civil Aviation Authority, the price leadership provision was difficult to enforce in practice and there were 'numerous examples where non-Community air carriers [were] ignoring the article.' [U.K.] Civil Aviation Authority, *supra* note 126, para. 62 (noting that where the article was honored, Community air passengers may in fact have been disadvantaged).

130.   Council Regulation 2343/90, 1992 O.J. (L 217) 8 (repealed by Council Regulation 2408/92 on Access for Community Air Carriers to Intra-Union Air Routes, 1992 O.J. (L 240) 8).

131.   Council Regulation 2343/90, *supra* note 130, pmbl. (emphasis added).

132.   *See supra* Chapter 3, Part III(A).

133.   *See infra* Part III(E).

134.   Though the actual date, when it arrived in 1997, had an anticlimactic feel because it was conspicuously out of step with the actual dynamics of the EU airline industry in the mid-1990s. Although a few routes were already receiving consecutive cabotage service, full cabotage remained a theoretical prospect in an industry where the majors were still in the grip of restructuring and early recovery, while the low-cost carriers had yet to ramp up the kinds of multiple point-to-point services that would subsequently alter the landscape of intra-Union air transport. In sum, unlike the U.K.'s Big Bang in 1996, Apr. 1, 1997, was more like a 'Big Fizz.' Joan M. Feldman, *For 1997, The Big Fizz: European 'Open Skies' Arrived on April 1 with a Few Changes But Without the Foreseen Air-Services 'Revolution,'*, 34 AIR TRANSP. WORLD, Apr. 1997, at 26.

135.   Article 3(2) of the 1992 regulation foreclosed this extraordinary market access until Apr. 1, 1997, but did immediately concede what the Chicago system (with its home connection bias) understands as 'eighth freedom' or 'consecutive' cabotage, namely, domestic traffic rights

intended to curb 'excessive recourse' by Member States to the 'public service obligation' (PSO) exception introduced in the earlier packages to encourage subsidized air service to peripheral or development regions.[136] Finally, given the EU's air facilities crunch, it is unsurprising that the 2008 consolidated regulation reproduces some of the restrictive 'infrastructural' conditions of its predecessor, in particular (in Article 19(1)) subjecting the exercise of traffic rights between Community airports to 'published Community national, regional, or local operational rules relating to safety, the protection of the environment and the allocation of slots.'[137] For airlines, one of the most problematic components of Article 19 is likely to be the continued permissive authority of Member States to regulate the distribution of air traffic between airports which serve the same city or conurbation.[138]

---

exercised on a service 'which constitutes . . . an extension of a service from, or as a preliminary of a service to' the home State of the carrier. Thus, subject to certain capacity formulas in the 1992 legislation, British Airways could serve the Rome/Milan route as an extension of a London/Rome route, picking up passengers in Rome for service to Milan after flying from London, *or* taking passengers from Milan to Rome before flying onward to London.

136. European Commission, *Common Rules, supra* note 120, at 8. Among the methods incorporated in the 2008 regulation to avoid 'excessive recourse' is a power granted to the Commission, as part of its already existing power to investigate and even terminate PSO designations, to require production by a Member State of an economic report justifying the need for a PSO and its compatibility with the criteria laid down in the regulation. *Id.*; *Common Rules, supra* note 120, art. 18.

137. *Common Rules, supra* note 120, art. 19(1). Again, the imposition of these rules is subject to a Commission examination after compulsory notification by the Member State intending to impose the measures. *See id.* art. 19(3). The 2008 regulation reduces to incremental periods of 14 days (accompanied by Commission surveillance) a potentially very broad emergency procedure in the 1992 legislation which could be exercised initially to a maximum of three years. *Id.* art. 21. The 2008 legislation is an interesting reductive adaptation of what was originally (in the 1992 regulation) an implied Member State 14-day window of autonomy for 'sudden problems of short duration' before the Commission could become involved, either *sua sponte* or on complaint of another Member State. Council Regulation 2408/92, *supra* note 130, art. 9(5). Despite its tempting scope, the emergency powers in Article 9 of the 1992 regulation were never actually applied. *See* Commission Decision of 5 December 2003, German Measures Relating to the Approaches to the Zurich Airport para. 24, 2004 O.J. (L 4) 13. Also, it should be noted that Article 6 of Commission Directive 2002/30/EC of Mar. 26, 2002 on the Establishment of Rules and Procedures with Regard to the Introduction of Noise-Related Operating Restrictions at Community Airports, 2002 O.J. (L 85) 40, replaced Article 9 of Regulation 2408/92 in connection with the movement of 'marginally compliant aircraft.' Notably, in none of these oversight procedures is there any provision for a direct complaint by air carriers concerning Member State emergency action (unlike the U.S. oversight procedures in the IATCA, which are *normally* triggered by air carrier complaints).

138. Under Council Regulation 2408/92, *supra* note 130, art. 8(1), the relevant language applied to the distribution of traffic 'between the airports within an airport system,' but the regulation defined airport 'system' as two or more airports grouped together as serving the same city or conurbation, precisely the formula used in 2008. *Common Rules, supra* note 120, art. 19(2). Exercise of a Member State's right to distribute airport traffic within a city or conurbation involves balancing the legitimacy of an active airport planning policy with a need to restrict access to the individual airports in the system, a dichotomy which is likely to continue to cause commercial tension between officials and carriers. Perhaps the most prominent example of

As the final component of the third liberalization package, the Council adopted a new regulation 'on licensing of air carriers.'[139] Motivated in part by Commission concerns about variations in Member State application of common requirements introduced in 1992 for the grant of a Community operating license by

these kinds of disputes has been the battle among Italy, non-Italian Community carriers, and the Commission with respect to the Italian Government's plan (ironically to execute one of the approved 'priority projects' in the Community's trans-European transport network) to develop Milan's new airport, Malpensa, into a hub at the expense of its predecessor, Linate. The Commission in a 1998 decision analyzed both the issue of discrimination – which is explicitly mentioned in Article 8(1) of the 1992 regulation and in Article 19(2) of its 2008 successor – and the issue of proportionality of the official action (which, though not explicitly mentioned in Article 8(1), has been found by the European Court of Justice to be a requirement of the Community doctrine of freedom of services in Article 49 of the EC Treaty, *see, e.g.*, Case C-76/90, *Säger*, para. 12, 1991 E.C.R. I-4221, and which is now incorporated in Article 19(1) of the 2008 regulation). *See* Commission Decision 98/810/EC, 1998 O.J. (L 337) 42. As a result of a government decree setting a high annual traffic threshold of two million passengers using Linate that only Alitalia could satisfy (because the threshold was met solely by Alitalia's Rome/Milan service), the Commission found indirect discrimination between Alitalia and the other Community carriers serving Linate. Secondly, in applying the principle of proportionality the Commission found that the legitimate objective of developing a Malpensa hub could have been achieved less restrictively and did not require the transfer of a volume of traffic which was incompatible with Malpensa's existing level of airport structures and access infrastructures. Both elements of the Commission's analysis were upheld by the European Court of Justice in Italian Republic *v.* Comm'n, *supra* note 119 (confirming that the principle of proportionality applies even if a regulatory action applies without distinction to national and nonnational providers). The case illustrates both the advantages and drawbacks of the Commission's regulatory watchdog role. Positively, it enabled non-national Community carriers to obtain a Commission intervention that modified the discriminatory and restrictive effects of a massive publicly-funded airport project; on the other hand, the exercise of the Commission's authority through formal proceedings was repeatedly overtaken by events as the transition to Malpensa evolved. Thus, even before the Court of Justice had ruled on the Italian Government's appeal against the Commission's original decision, the Commission had taken a further decision in late 2000 in response to non-national carrier complaints of continuing discrimination in the Malpensa transition following a revised traffic distribution decree issued by the Italian Minister for Transport. The carriers opposed the Minister's plan that would restrict Linate exclusively to a series of volume-capped intra-Union point-to-point services – which they argued would still preserve an indirect discrimination on the Rome/Milan route in favor of Alitalia – and sought a declaration that all European carriers must be allowed to operate at Linate without restriction. Commission Decision 2001/163/EC, 2001 O.J. (L 26) 1 (finding that infrastructural improvements at Malpensa had removed any discriminatory effects in favor of Alitalia, and accepting that the objectives of transforming Malpensa into a fully operational hub and promoting Linate as a 'privileged infrastructure for point-to-point connections' might require rules establishing access thresholds based on traffic volumes; amendments proposed to these rules by the Italian Government would satisfy the condition of proportionality). The Malpensa/Linate transition, nonetheless, still stokes controversy, even outside the EU. The U.S. Department of Transportation refused to authorize Italian-based carrier Eurofly's proposed Milan/New York service out of Linate unless U.S. carriers were allowed to use Linate for equivalent long-haul services. The DOT was well aware that Linate is closed for all long-haul services since the Malpensa transition plan took effect. Eurofly, which operates an all-business class service, switched to Malpensa and won DOT approval. *See Eurofly Launches Milan – New York Service as Dispute is Resolved*, FLIGHT INT'L, Jun. 6, 2006.

139. Council Regulation 2407/92, 1992 O.J. (L 240) 1.

a Member State, the 2008 regulation strengthens the requirements for granting and revoking operating licenses with an eye to greater consistency.[140] The licensing legislation, as a general proposition, supplements the opening of traffic rights in the EU with a pan-Community licensing system that allows a carrier licensed in any Member State to operate without discrimination as though licensed in any other Member State.[141] It does not, as such, legislate for the right of freedom of establishment, which remains in technical conflict with individual State licensing legislation (and the maze of third-country bilaterals).[142]

At the core of the 2008 regulation is the concept of the 'operating license,' an authorization granted by a Member State to carry passengers (and also mail or cargo) for remuneration.[143] An air carrier meeting the technical requirements of the regulation *shall* receive such a license and therefore be allowed to operate air services within the EU as a 'Community air carrier.'[144] The legislation defines the conditions for the grant of an operating license (in effect, a 'new entrant' license).[145] Here a hallmark feature of the Chicago system is converted into a general principle of EC law through the insertion of EU-wide (as opposed to *national*) restrictions on ownership and control. The regulation requires the would-be licensee to have its principal place of business located in the licensing Member State,[146] and then (as it were) '*multilateralizes*' the Chicago nationality rule by requiring that 'Member

140. European Commission, *Common Rules, supra* note 120, at 2.
141. The Commission also regarded the 1992 licensing regulation, with its common criteria on effective control and financial and economic fitness, as an adequate safeguard against the emergence of 'flags of convenience' in international civil aviation. European Commission, *The Way Forward for Civil Aviation in Europe*, at 24, COM (94) 218 final (Jan. 6, 1994) [hereinafter European Commission, *The Way Forward*].
142. The juristic and practical implications of the failure to coordinate the Community licensing laws with exercise of the right of establishment, especially with respect to the grant of seventh freedom rights awarded to Community carriers under the 2007 U.S./EC Air Transport Agreement, *see supra* note 129, are considered in more detail *infra* Part III(E). The preamble to the 1992 legislation confirmed only the applicability of the regulation to the 'principle of the freedom to provide services' and the need to take account of the 'specific characteristics' of the air transport sector. Council Regulation 2407/92, *supra* note 139, pmbl., recital 3. While this preamble is no longer part of the proposed consolidated rules, nothing in the new Common Rules legislates for a right of establishment. *See generally* Common Rules, *supra* note 120.
143. *Id.* art. 3(1).
144. *Id.* arts. 3(1) & 15. Interestingly, the 1992 rules specifically stated that an operating license 'does not confer in itself any rights of access to specific routes or markets.' *See* Council Regulation 2407/92, *supra* note 139, art. 3(2). While this language has been dropped from the 2008 regulation, the revision does retain provisions allowing a Member State in a non-discriminatory manner to distribute and regulate the exercise of traffic rights for logistical, environmental, safety, security, and other reasons. Common Rules, *supra* note 120, art. 19.
145. *Id.* art. 4. The common rules referred to here concern the grant of an operating license on grounds of *financial* fitness and good business repute. *Id.* arts. 5 & 7. The regulation also provides that the grant of an operating license shall be dependent upon possession of a valid 'air operator's certificate' (AOC), issued by the same State that issues the operating license. The AOC certifies professional ability and organization to ensure safe operation of aircraft. *Id.* art. 6.
146. *Id.* art. 4(1). The 1992 rules also required the would-be licensee to have its registered office located in the licensing Member State as well. *See* Regulation 2407/92, *supra* note 139, art.

States and/or nationals of Member States own more than 50% of the undertaking and effectively control it.'[147] The 'control' requirement, as we have seen, attempts to deny corporate power to a blocking minority of third-country nationals.[148] Similar to the practice of the U.S. DOT, a 'Community air carrier'[149] is under a continuing obligation to demonstrate (on request by the licensing State) that it is abiding by the citizenship requirements of the licensing regulation.[150]

The actual technical requirements of licensing, which virtually mirror the 'financial fitness' criteria developed by the DOT,[151] are much more explicit in the EC legislation than in its U.S. analogue on the question of the *continuing* nature of financial scrutiny. Under EC rules, licensing authorities may investigate a carrier's financial fitness *at any time*, and in any event whenever there are 'clear indications that financial problems exist or when insolvency or similar proceedings are opened against' a carrier licensed by them.'[152] The sanction provided is

---

4(1)(a). This requirement was apparently dropped for reasons of clarity. *See* European Parliament, Committee on Transport and Tourism, *Draft Report for a Regulation of the European Parliament and of the Council on Common Rules for the Operation of Air Transport Services in the Community (Recast)* amend. 9, Provisional 2006/0130 (COD) (Feb. 7, 2007).

147. Common Rules, supra note 120, art. 4(f). The licensing rules do, however, state an exception to this ownership and control rule where provided for in agreements between the European Community and a third country. *Id.*

148. *See generally* FRANKY DE CONINCK, EUROPEAN AIR LAW: NEW SKIES FOR EUROPE 108 (1994). Article 2(9) of the Common Rules, like the predecessor regulation, contains a definition of 'effective control' borrowed from Notice 90/C 203/06 where the Commission interprets 'control by other undertakings' in connection with the concentrative and cooperative operations under the merger regulation. In summary, 'effective control' means a relationship (formed by rights, contracts, or otherwise) which confers the possibility of directly or indirectly exercising a 'decisive influence' on an air carrier, in particular by (a) the right to use all or part of the carrier's assets, and/or (b) rights or contracts which grant a 'decisive influence' on the composition, voting, or decisions of the governing bodies of the air carrier or on the running of its business. *Cf.* Council Regulation 2407/92, *supra* note 139, art. 2(g).

149. While the term 'Community air carrier' was not used *per se* in the 1992 licensing regulation, it is defined in the Common Rules, *supra* note 120, as an air carrier with a valid operating licen[s]e granted by a competent licensing authority' as defined in the regulation. *Id.* art. 2(11).

150. *Id.* art. 8(1). On DOT citizenship review jurisdiction, *see supra* Chapter 3, Part V.

151. *See* Common Rules, *supra* note 120, art. 5. For example, a carrier must show a financial capacity to meet actual and potential obligations for a period of 24 months from the start of operations, as well to meet fixed and operational costs according to its business plan for three months from the start of operations – without taking into account any income from its operations. *Id.* art. 5(1)(a)-(b). To allow some gauging of this fiscal capacity, each applicant air carrier must submit a business plan for (at least) the first three years of operation. *Id.* art. 5(2). An annex to the regulation also requires submission by new entrants of a plethora of financial and business information, including management accounts, projected balance sheets, basis for projected income and expenditure figures, details of start-up costs, sources of finance, shareholders (including nationality and type of shares to be held), cash-flow statements and liquidity plans, and financing of aircraft purchasing or leasing.

152. *Id.* art. 9(2). Awareness of impending financial trouble might come, for example, from the requirement that an air carrier must provide the licensing authority with its annual audited accounts. *Id.* art. 8(4). In addition, the third part of the annex to the regulation lists several categories of financial information that might be requested in addition to the annual financials. *Id.* annex I.

suspension or revocation of the license if the authorities are not satisfied that the carrier can meet its actual and potential obligations for a 12-month period.[153] In addition, whereas the DOT has no inherent powers *per se* to preempt a foreign investment in an already-certificated carrier,[154] any intended mergers or acquisitions involving a 'Community air carrier' must be notified to the licensing State and may trigger a financial review.[155] Indeed, scrutiny of an EU airline's *citizenship* may also occur, as a matter of general prudence, when the carrier notifies the licensing State of an impending merger or acquisition transaction.

D   THE EC TREATY'S COMPETITION CODE: STILL LEADING
                   FROM THE CENTER

Until the Council finally acted through its decentralization initiative in late 2002 to further 'disseminate a competition culture within the Community,'[156] the intellectual dominance of the Commission, supported by its accessible jurisdiction under the famed Regulation 17,[157] had eclipsed virtually all private Treaty-based antitrust litigation in the Member States.[158] The Community's supranational competition law has been overwhelmingly developed through Commission decisions

---

153. Common Rules, *supra* note 120, art. 9(1). There is an option to grant a temporary license not exceeding twelve months pending financial reorganization. *Id.*
154. *See supra* Chapter 4, Part IV.
155. Common Rules, *supra* note 120, art. 8(5)-(6). Other 'triggering' situations include plans for (a) operation of a new scheduled service to a continent or world region not previously served, (b) changes in type or number of aircraft used, and (c) substantial change in the scale of a carrier's activities. *Id.* Moreover, the licensee must give 14 days' advance notice of any change in the ownership of any single shareholding which represents 10% or more of the total shareholding of the air carrier, its parent, or ultimate holding company. *Id.* Following the 1992 licensing regulation, the Council and Commission stated that information on the changes in shareholding would only be necessary in situations where majority shareholding and effective control would be in doubt as a consequence of such change. DE CONINCK, *supra* note 148, at 109. This is presumably still true under the revised regulation. The Commission's role in this licensing system when a license application is denied has been eliminated, however. Under the 1992 regulation, it could 'state its views on the correct interpretation of the Regulation' if it disagreed with a Member State's denial of the license (without prejudice to the Commission's rights under the EC Treaty to bring an enforcement action against a Member State). Council Regulation 2407/92, *supra* note 139, art. 13(3). Under the 2008 regulation, the Commission is no longer afforded this right. *See* Common Rules, *supra* note 120, art. 10 (which displaces the text of Regulation 2407/92, Article 13(3)). The Commission's own proposal that it be granted the power to revoke a license if it appeared that a national licensing authority had fallen short of the regulation's requirements was removed from the final version of the regulation. *See id.* art. 14.
156. Council Regulation 1/2003, *supra* note 127 (on the implementation of the rules on competition laid down in Articles 81 and 82 of the Treaty) (as amended by Council Regulation 411/2004, 2004 O.J. (L 68) 1).
157. *See infra* note 168.
158. The Court of Justice has been mindful of the absence of private party enforcement. *See generally* Case 127/73, BRT *v.* SABAM, 1974 E.C.R. 313, in which the Court applied its direct effects doctrine to Articles 81 and 82. On direct effects, *see supra* note 49.

on liability issued from Brussels, and appeals against those decisions before the twin tribunals of review in Luxembourg. The decentralization (or 'modernization,' as the Commission has called the recasting of Regulation 17), is so at odds with the Community's antitrust enforcement culture that even the Council, in enacting the Regulation, explicitly recalled that Regulation 17 had given 'a central role to the Community bodies,' and that '[t]his central role should be retained.'[159] As a result of the modernizing Regulation 1/2003, Member State competition authorities and courts are formally empowered to apply the Community competition code along with the Commission. Importantly, however, the Commission remains the primary enforcer – the Regulation explicitly provides that the competition authorities of the Member States are automatically relieved of their competence if the Commission initiates its own proceedings,[160] and both the Member State competition authorities and the national courts are required to follow Commission decisions.[161]

Articles 81 and 82 of the EC Treaty reach anticompetitive activity by private parties in the Member States, while the burden of Articles 87 through 89 is to restrain governmental action, through grants of public subsidy (or 'aids granted by States,' in Treaty parlance)[162] to certain preferred enterprises, that may hold even more insidious consequences for fair competition in the Community. Our brief discussion of the Community's antitrust law begins with the private suppression of competition that is proscribed by Articles 81 and 82.

1   **The Primary and Secondary Sources of EC Competition Law**

a   *Regulating Private Action: Articles 81 and 82, Regulation 1 of 2003*

The kernel of the EC's supranational competition law is contained in Articles 81 and 82 of the EC Treaty. Article 81(1), which seems consciously to evoke Section 1 of the U.S. Sherman Act, prohibits, as incompatible with the common market, all intercorporate agreements, decisions by associations of corporations, and concerted practices that 'may affect trade between Member States' and have 'as their object or effect the prevention, restriction or distortion of competition within the common market.'[163] Article 81(2) declares all practices prohibited under

---

159. Council Regulation 1/2003, *supra* note 127, pmbl., recital 33.
160. *See id.* art. 11(6) ('The initiation by the Commission of proceedings for the adoption of a decision under Chapter III [finding of infringement] shall relieve the competition authorities of the Member States of their competence to apply Articles 81 and 82 of the Treaty').
161. *See id.* art. 16(1)-(2) (providing that national courts and competition authorities, respectively, must not take decisions which would 'run counter' to Commission decisions already adopted with respect to agreements, decisions, or practices).
162. EC Treaty, tit. VI, ch. 1, sec. 2.
163. EC Treaty art. 81. The Article describes five types of prohibited agreement, which can be summarized (using U.S. antitrust vocabulary) as price-fixing; control or limitation of

Article 81(1) 'automatically void,' while Article 81(3) holds out an exemption (which will render Article 81(1) 'inapplicable') for agreements or practices that, in general, advance consumer welfare by improving the production or distribution of goods or promote technical or economic progress.[164] Article 82, which bears a partial similarity to Section 2 of the Sherman Act, attacks monopolization by prohibiting dominant undertakings from abusing their dominance to affect trade between Member States.[165] Importantly, however, Article 82 does not reproduce the Sherman Act's separate interdiction of 'attempted monopolization.' In the wake of World War II, the Treaty framers did not consider the mere acquisition, as opposed to unlawful manipulation and exercise, of market power to be offensive in a balkanized Continent bereft of large concentrations.[166]

Articles 81 and 82 (in their prior nomenclature) existed in a vacuum during the opening years of the new European order. In 1962, the Council of Ministers, as required by Article 83 of the EC Treaty,[167] adopted a framework instrument for actually applying both Articles to competitive activity. That instrument, Council Regulation 17/62[168] (which involved a wholesale delegation of implementing powers in accordance with Article 202 of the EC Treaty)[169] became the principal force behind the centralization of competition law enforcement in the Commission.[170] Regulation 17, which was repealed in 2003 by Regulation 1/2003,[171] conceptualized Article 81 as operating by a blanket prohibition that was remediable in part by the grant of an exemption. There were parallels between this now-defunct 'notification and exemption' procedure in Regulation 17 and the DOT's residual power in international air transportation to immunize intercarrier agreements against antitrust challenge.[172] It remains possible for corporations and

---

production, markets, technical development, or investment; market division; discrimination among competitors, and tying arrangements.

164. *Id.* art. 81(2)-(3). The exempted agreements must not, in U.S. antitrust terms, impose unreasonable ancillary restrictions or enhance market power in respect of a substantial part of the products in question.

165. *Id.* Such abuse may consist of imposing unfair sale or purchase prices, limiting production, markets or technical developments, discrimination among competitors at the same level of production, and tying arrangements.

166. René Joliet, Monopolization and Abuse of Dominant Position: A Comparative Study of American and European Approaches to the Control of Economic Power 8-13 & 131-33 (1970).

167. Article 83 instructs the Council to adopt 'appropriate regulations or directives to give effect to the principles set out in Articles 81 and 82.' EC Treaty art. 83. According to Article 83(2), the Council was charged to 'design' an implementing act *inter alia* that made provision for fines and periodic penalties and the exemption procedure required to operate Article 81(3). *Id.*

168. Council Regulation 17/62, 1962 O.J. (13) 204, *amended by* Council Regulation 59/62, 1962 O.J. (58) 1655; Council Regulation 118/63, 1963 O.J. (162) 2696; Council Regulation 2822/71, 1971 O.J. (L 285) 49, *repealed by* Council Regulation 1/2003, *supra* note 127, art. 43.

169. *See supra* text accompanying note 52.

170. An erudite analysis of this centralization, its effects, and possible further reforms of EC competition law may be found in Giorgio Monti, EC Competition Law (2007).

171. *See supra* note 127.

172. *See supra* Chapter 4, Part III(C).

individuals to seek exemptions, but the decentralization produced by Regulation 1/2003 ends the requirement of formal notification to the Commission[173] and creates instead a self-policing competition regime that gives the private sector autonomy to decide for itself whether an exemption applies to a proposed agreement or practice.[174] The new system, described in the recitals to Regulation 1/2003 as a 'directly applicable exception system,'[175] grants national competition authorities and courts power not only to apply Article 81(1) and Article 82[176] but also the exemption protocol of Article 81(3).[177]

Regulation 1/2003, like its predecessor, authorizes the Commission (but also national competition authorities and national courts) to investigate and, if necessary, to order termination of infringements of Articles 81 and 82. The Commission, as well as national entities, can levy substantial fines.[178] Investigations can be launched *sua sponte* by the Commission on its own initiative or upon complaint by a Member State or by individuals or corporations 'who can show a legitimate interest.'[179] And investigations can also now be initiative by a national competition authority or within the context of a national court proceeding.[180]

---

173. According to Article 4(1) of Regulation 17/62, *supra* note 168, the Commission 'must' be notified of agreements that might violate Article 81, and can grant an exemption from Article 81(1) based upon that filing.

174. As leading Community practitioner Ian S. Forrester, Q.C. wrote in relation to the Regulation 17/62 notification procedure, '[i]t [was] thus by the application of Article [81(1)] and not by the non-application of Article [81(1)] that most difficult competition choices [were] made.' Forrester, *Competition Structures, in* ANNUAL PROCEEDINGS OF THE FORDHAM CORPORATE LAW INSTITUTE, INTERNATIONAL ANTITRUST LAW & POLICY 472 (Barry E. Hawk ed., 1994). The exemption procedure was so lengthy and expensive (and exemption decisions so rare) that the Commission compromised its operation through more informal (and legally unstable) substitutes. Its operation was strongly criticized by the Commission itself in its White Paper on modernization of the rules implementing Articles 81 and 82, 1999 O.J. (C132), and in the recitals to Regulation 1/2003 (citing the 'centralized scheme' of Regulation 17 as inimical to national implementation of the competition rules, to the Commission's best use as an enforcer of the 'most serious infringements,' and to corporations which must bear the costs of the system, Council Regulation 1/2003, *supra* note 127, pmbl., recital 3).

175. *Id.* pmbl., recital 4.

176. Both of these Articles are in any case directly applicable (*i.e.*, have direct effects) in Member State courts by virtue of prior Court of Justice rulings. *Id.*

177. *See id.* arts. 5 & 6 (conferring a blanket power on national competition authorities and national courts, respectively, to 'apply Articles 81 and 82' of the Treaty). The decentralization of the exemption procedure is in part a response to the problem of the Commission's administrative inability to reach exemption decisions quickly. As Forrester noted over a decade ago, 'a structural discordance exists between the asserted jurisdictional reach of the Commission and its administrative capacity to deliver the legal certainty for which its theory creates a need.' Forrester, *Competition Structures, supra* note 174, at 469.

178. Council Regulation 1/2003, *supra* note 127, art. 23 (outlining a conspectus of penalties for intentional or negligent failure to cooperate with investigations as well as for infringements of Articles 81 and 82).

179. *Id.* art. 7(1)-(2). Complaining third parties are likely to be competitors. For a discussion of the right to file a complaint with the Commission under Article 3 of the former Regulation 17, *see* Case 125/78, GEMA *v.* Commission, 1979 E.C.R. 3173.

180. Council Regulation 1/2003, *supra* note 127, art. 3.

The Commission and national officials have extensive co-investigatory powers under Regulation 1/2003, including the 'dawn raid' provision retained from Regulation 17 despite its controversial history.[181] Thus, Articles 20 and 21 of the new Regulation vest authority in agents of the Commission to enter any premises (including the homes of company directors, managers, and other staff members) to examine books and records and to interview personnel.[182]

In 1965, as the notification procedures began to create an enormous administrative backlog, the Council granted the Commission quasi-legislative authority to issue collective or 'block' exemptions to corporations under Article 81(3), exempting them from liability for violation of Article 81(1) where the specific conditions of the group exemption were met in their separate transactional relationships.[183]

---

181. 'The Commission's powers of investigation of suspected competition law violations, principally contained in [Regulation 17/62], are well known to be wide; some might say, draconic.' David L. Perrott, *Regional Developments, European Communities*, 21 INT'L LAW. 569, 574 (1987). Notably, however, the revised legislation in 2003 was constructed to supplement rather than circumscribe the Commission's powers, on the premise that '[t]he detection of infringements of the competition rules is growing ever more difficult.' Council Regulation 1/2003, *supra* note 127, pmbl., recital 25. The visibility of the airline industry, and its demonstrable link to consumer welfare (especially as a marker for the political success of the European Union) are likely to continue to foster government activism in antitrust enforcement. In 2005, for example, the Commission started an air cargo price-fixing investigation in collaboration with the U.S. Department of Justice. In 2006, although the Commission was not immediately involved, the U.K. competition enforcement authority, the Office of Fair Trading, and the U.S. Department of Justice launched a high-profile investigation of a possible criminal conspiracy to fix the amount of fuel surcharges imposed on passengers on long-haul flights to and from Britain. *See supra* Chapter 4, note 574.

182. *See* Council Regulation 1/2003, *supra* note 127, arts. 20 & 21 (providing for a review of the lawfulness of the Commission's actions solely by the Court of Justice). Access to private homes is subject to authorization from the national judicial authority. *Id.* art. 21(3). On its face, Article 21(3) sets up a potential for conflict with national judicial authorities, since it empowers them to 'control' that the Commission decision is 'authentic' and that the coercive measures 'are neither arbitrary nor excessive,' while simultaneously proscribing them from calling into question 'the necessity for the inspection' or from demanding information in the Commission's file. The 'lawfulness' of the Commission's proposed inspection, as noted above, is subject to review only by the Court of Justice. *See id.* The seemingly unchecked reach of Article 14 of Regulation 17/62, the predecessor provision, was the subject of litigation before the Court, which has not been persuaded to rein in these wide powers. *See, e.g.*, Case 46/87R, Hoechst A.G. *v.* Comm'n, 1987 E.C.R. 1549. The Commission is sensitive to the 'dawn raid' perception, as is evident from its propagandist publication, *Competition Policy in the European Community*, at 5, European File Series, Directorate-General for Audiovisual, Information, Communication and Culture (1992) ('Unannounced early morning calls at a company's office by Brussels investigators is the traditional image of [EC] 'trust-busters' at work.... However, such cases only occur where firms are suspected of trying to hide evidence'). Regulation 1/2003 does not, however, grant these powers automatically to the national competition authorities, whose powers of investigation and inspection continue to be regulated by their national laws (although there is nothing to prevent the national legislatures from according such powers to national authorities). *See* Regulation 1/2003, *supra* note 127, art. 22.

183. Council Regulation 19/65, 1965 O.J. (36) 533. This practice is arguably contemplated in Article 83 of the EC Treaty, which speaks of regulations or directives designed *inter alia* 'to lay down detailed rules for the application of Article 81(3), taking into account the need to

That authority is retained in Regulation 1/2003.[184] A further holdover from the old centralized system is the mechanism of an Advisory Committee comprising Member State competition authority representatives.[185] This mechanism was also placed in the later legislation on competition in air transport, and was intended (particularly by France) as a political bottleneck to allow Member States to monitor – and, if necessary, to encumber – Commission actions against potential infringers. Regulation 1/2003, however, merely requires the Commission (or, in reality, its administrative investigating agency, the Directorate-General for Competition) to 'consult' the Committee before taking any decisions with respect to finding of an infringement or imposition of penalties.[186]

---

ensure effective supervision on the one hand, and to simplify administration to the greatest possible extent on the other.' EC Treaty art. 83(2)(b). The 'highly formalistic' process of writing block exemptions (as David Gerber has called it) has produced legislation of varying degrees of specificity, sometimes prescribing precisely-drafted clauses, sometimes (as in the case of the air transport exemptions) presenting a lengthy series of 'content-evaluative' criteria to test the restrictiveness of proposed agreements. *See generally* Gerber, *supra* note 69, at 134. Regulations adopted by the Commission to implement this authority have been quite specific in their detail. Transactions that qualified for block exemption included joint research and development agreements, especially among small and medium-sized companies.

184. Notice that the modernization of the competition code in 2003, despite its emphasis on 'dissemination' of the Community competition culture and of its enforcement, did nothing to disrupt the exclusivity of the Commission's block exemption authority under a suite of regulations (including Council Regulation 3976/87, 1987 O.J. (L374) 9, which applies to air transport, *see infra* in the main text). *See* Council Regulation 1/2003, *supra* note 127, pmbl., recital 10.

185. Technically, the 'Advisory Committee on Restrictive Practices and Dominant Positions.' Regulation 1/2003, *supra* note 127, art. 14.

186. *Id.* art. 14(1). The Commission does have to 'take the utmost account' of the Committee's opinion (which, *pro forma* as this language first appears, requires the Commission to append the opinion to the draft decision and even to publish a written opinion). *Id.* art. 14(5)-(6). Under Council Regulation 141/62, 1962 O.J. Spec. Ed. (124) 2751, air transport (along with transport in general) was specifically excluded from the ambit of Regulation 17/62. (Regulation 1/2003 repealed Regulation 141/62 along with Regulation 17/62, *see* Council Regulation 1/2003, *supra* note 127, art. 43(1)-(2)). Accordingly, the EC Treaty's transitional regime (Articles 84 and 85, ex-Articles 88 and 89, important in the context of the seminal *Nouvelles Frontières* judgment), continued to govern air transport. The Council adopted Regulation 141/62 on the ground that the 'distinctive features' of transport, acknowledged in the text of Article 71 of the EC Treaty, might require different rules for this sector. Regulation 141/62 exempted inland transport (road, rail, and inland waterways) for three (later extended to six) years, but air and sea transport were exempted *sine die*. The competition rules were applied to inland transport by Council Regulation 1017/68, 1968 O.J. (L 175) 1; 18 years later, in 1986, the rules were extended to maritime transport under Council Regulation 4056/86, 1986 O.J. (L 378) 4. *See generally* Argyris, *supra* note 109, at 9. (Both Regulations 1017/68 and 4056/86 were amended by Regulation 1/2003 to bring those competition regimes into conformity with the provisions of the later instrument: *see* Regulation 1/2003, *supra* note 127, arts. 36 & 38.) By the time the air transport program was being shaped in the late 1980s, the Council and Commission had jointly evolved a prototype competition enforcement system that they could readily superimpose upon a new economic sector. As will be seen, the fully armed enforcement mechanisms of Regulation 17/62 were gradually engineered into the common air transport policy during the 1987/97 liberalization program.

b   *Applying Competition Law to the Airlines*

The airline industry has now been assimilated to the recent revamping of the Community competition regime, and large parts of the 1987 'one package' deal that applied competition law to air transport have been abrogated.[187] Curiously, in an industry where (for carriers with services beyond EU territory) almost 70% of scheduled revenue passenger kilometers are produced to connect Europe to the rest of the world, the modernizing regulation adopted in 2003 (which repealed much but not all of the prior legislation), left intact its spatial restriction to intra-Union air services.[188] In February 2004, the Council adopted a regulation which repealed the entirety of the prior legislation, including by implication its spatial confinement to intra-Union air traffic.[189] Accordingly, both the procedural mechanisms enshrined in Regulation 1/2003 (the successor to both Regulation 17 and Regulation 3975/87), and the block exemption powers in the surviving Regulation 3976/87, now apply also to practices relating to air transport between the EU and third countries 'which may affect trade between Member States.'[190] In its enforcement of the competition rules under Regulation 1/2003, therefore, the Commission is expected to consider the competitive effects of bilateral air services agreements between Member States and third countries.[191]

---

187. *See supra* Part II(C) for discussion of the Community legislative 'packages' which created the framework for a single aviation market.

188. *See* Council Regulation 1/2003, *supra* note 127, art. 39. On the 'externality' of the EU international air transport industry, *see* the comments of the AEA, *Consultation Paper, supra* note 127, para. 1.2. Nor did the restriction any longer make sense in an industry where long-haul operations have evolved through the structuring of transnational alliances between and among strong competitors. *See supra* Chapter 3, Part VIII (discussing emergence of alliance phenomenon).

189. *See* Council Regulation 411/2004 art. 1, *supra* note 156; the applicable language in Regulation 3976/87 (the block exemption regulation), referring to the applicability of air services 'between Community airports,' was simply deleted instead of rephrased. Thus, Article 1 of the Regulation states simply that 'This Regulation shall apply to air transport.' Regulation 3976/87 art. 1, *supra* note 184 (as amended by Article 2 of Council Regulation 411/2004, *supra* note 156).

190. Council Regulation 411/2004, *supra* note 156, pmbl., recital 3.

191. *Id.* pmbl., recital 4. The Council pointed out, however, that the Commission's consideration of the bilateral agreements ought not to 'affect the rights and obligations of the Member States under the Treaty with respect to the conclusion and application of such agreements.' *Id.* The institutional anomaly whereby the Commission had to rely on Article 85 for the assessment of global airline alliances such as Star and SkyTeam has therefore been removed. Article 85 required the Commission to cooperate with the national competition authorities for investigations, since it had no direct enforcement powers. In case of infringement, the Commission could only suggest remedies, but these were left in the hands of the Member States to be implemented. In order to create a clear and coherent regulatory framework, the new Regulation allows the Commission to review and, if necessary, to take enforcement action to preserve competition with regard to international airline cooperation agreements (such as alliances) and air services agreements between Member States and/or the European Community and non-EU countries. In addition, the Commission can decide to grant block exemptions for air transport agreements involving, for instance, transatlantic routes, as is

Block exemptions were first applied to the air transport sector in 1987 in accordance with Council Regulation 3976/87 on the application of Article 81(3) to certain agreements and concerted practices in the air transport sector.[192] Strictly speaking, this regulation did not so much grant qualified exemptions under Article 81(3) as postpone the full impact of Article 81(1) upon certain established practices characteristic of the 'specificity' of the international airline system. The preamble, like that of its companion Regulation 3975/87, candidly records that the air transport sector has been governed by a network of international bilateral (and multilateral) agreements, and that changes to this regulatory order to ensure increased competition 'should be effected gradually so as to provide time for the air transport sector to adapt.'[193] Accordingly, the very next recital skips any pretense of Article 81(3) competitive justification and simply proposes that the Commission 'should be enabled [for the foregoing reasons] to declare . . . that the provisions of Article 81(1) do not apply to certain categories of agreements between undertakings.'[194]

Since Regulation 1/2003 subjected the air transport sector to the general Community competition regime as of May 1, 2004, eliminating the former notification process for individual exemptions under Article 81(3), air carriers must now assess for themselves whether their agreements and concerted practices satisfy the conditions of Article 81(1) and (3) of the EC Treaty. Accordingly, the Commission since 2003 has been more conservative in its assessment of broadly-applicable general exemptions issued under the authority of Regulation 3976/87. Indeed, with Regulation 1469/2006, the European Commission put its last standing block exemptions for air transport on the fast track to extinction.[195] Published in October 2006, the regulation phased out the block exemption for IATA's tariff conferences over the course of the year, beginning with tariff conferences for carriage of

---

already the case for air transport services between Community airports. (Operations that can be qualified as a merger, such as the Air France/KLM deal, will continue to fall under the merger regulation.)

192. Council Regulation 3976/87, *supra* note 184.
193. *Id.* pmbl., recital 3.
194. *Id.* Exercising its powers, the Commission sliced the exemptions much more thinly than the Council appears to have contemplated in its regulation, for example compacting open-ended references to 'joint planning and coordination of airline schedules' and 'consultations on tariffs' into much more narrowly-framed categories involving, respectively, cooperation to provide service at less busy times or on low-density routes, and nonbinding tariff consultations with observer status for the Commission. The Commission's recast categories also included limited revenue pooling, similarly imbued with the public service dimension of serving low-density markets, and slot allocation and airport scheduling, if procedures were transparent and participation voluntary. *See, e.g.,* Commission Regulation 2671/88, 1988 O.J. (L 239) 9. Other exemption targets that the Commission extrapolated from the regulation included the common purchase, development, and operation of computer reservations systems (on condition that air carriers of Member States have equal access to such systems and that services of participating airlines were listed on a nondiscriminatory basis) as well as technical and operational ground-handling at airports and services for the provision of in-flight catering. All of these exemptions have since expired or been repealed. *See generally* European Commission, Competition: Antitrust Legislation, <http://ec.europa.eu/comm/competition/antitrust/legislation/legislation.html>.
195. *See* Commission Regulation 1459/2006, 2006 O.J. (L 272) 3.

passengers within the EU on December 31, 2006, and culminating in the removal of the exemption for all routes between the EU and third countries on October 31, 2007.[196] Consonant with the decentralization ethos of Regulation 1/2003, here also it is now incumbent on individual carriers to demonstrate that their interlining agreements are compliant with EC competition rules. The 2006 regulation also terminated block exemptions for IATA's slot and scheduling conferences.[197] In the Commission's view, the evolved nature of these conferences had already made them compatible with EC competition rules and thus 'the legal certainty provided by a block exemption is therefore no longer needed.'[198] Under Regulations 3976/87 and 411/2004, however, the Commission retains its authority to issue block exemptions for air transport, now including air commerce with third countries outside the EU.[199]

c   *Merger Control in the EC*

After a long gestation, the EC's supranational merger control policy was formulated in a Council of the European Union regulation adopted in 1989 on the control

---

196. *Id.* arts. 1 & 4. *See supra* Chapter 3, Part IX, on the subject of the IATA tariff conferences and efforts to tailor them to competition law mandates. The question of whether the IATA interlining system is indispensable to consumer welfare (the principal argument of its proponents) has been questioned (*see, e.g.,* Submission of the U.K. Permanent Representative to the European Union, Consultation on a Draft Commission Regulation on the Application of Article 81(3), at 1 (Mar. 15, 2006); *see also* [U.K.] Civil Aviation Authority, *supra* note 126, para. 57 (asserting that the IATA system has shown evidence of 'anticompetitive effects' and encourages 'cartel-like behavior'). The Commission seems to share this skepticism: 'The intra-Community air transport market has evolved in such a way that the degree of assurance that consultations on tariffs will continue to meet all the criteria of Article 81(3) of the Treaty is declining.' Commission Regulation 1459/2006, *supra* note 195, pmbl., recital 11. On extra-Union routes (particularly across the North Atlantic), the development of alliances and comprehensive code-shares has undoubtedly caused a substantial diminution in reliance on IATA tariff coordination. *See* U.S. Department of Transportation [DOT], *U.S. Comments on Draft Commission Regulation Concerning Passenger Tariff Coordination* para. 4 (Apr. 3, 2006); *see also* European Commission, *Concerning the Revision and Possible Prorogation of Commission Regulation 1617/93*, paras. 15-17, DG Competition Discussion Paper (2004).
197. Commission Regulation 1459/2006, *supra* note 195, art. 2.
198. Press Release, Europa, Competition: Commission Revises Block Exemption for IATA Passenger Tariff Conferences, IP/06/1294 (Oct. 2, 2006). The Commission had even been accused of becoming an implicit party to anticompetitive activity through its powers to observe airline traffic and slot allocation conferences. For early criticism of the Commission's willingness to exempt traffic and slot conferences, *see* Basedow, *supra* note 114, at 263 (arguing that the Commission's power to participate in consultations on tariffs and slot allocation could implicate Commission officials in 'casual' approbation of cooperative activity that could bind them in later formal antitrust proceedings). *See also* the Commission's concession to the potentiality of Basedow's criticism, in European Commission, *The Way Forward, supra* note 141, at 12-13 (admitting that '[k]eeping the balance between safeguarding the interlining system and avoiding a price cartel has always been a delicate and difficult task.... Economically difficult times bring a temptation to shift this balance in favor of the interests of the airline industry').
199. *See* Council Regulation 411/2004, *supra* note 156 (repealing Council Regulation 3975/87 and amending Regulations 3976/87 & 1/2003).

of concentrations between undertakings.[200] The 'merger regulation,' as it has been commonly known since 1989,[201] was the first major pansectoral initiative by the Council under Article 83 of the EC Treaty, the implementation provision of the competition rules, since the now-superseded Regulation 17 in 1964.[202] Both it and its 2004 successor were explicitly designed to close a gap in the jurisdictional reach of the supranational competition policy[203] and to provide a one-stop review

---

200. Council Regulation 4064/89, 1990 O.J. (L 257) 14, *amended by* Council Regulation 1310/97, 1997 O.J. (L 180) 1, *repealed by* Council Regulation 139/2004, 2004 O.J. (L 24) 1.

201. In fact, the regulation (even after its 2004 recasting) prefers almost invariably to use the generic term 'concentration,' which carries the meaning associated in American antitrust jurisprudence with the practice of 'mergers and acquisitions.' *See* Sir Leon Brittan, Q.C., Vice-President of the Commission of the European Communities, *Competition Policy in the European Community: The New Merger Regulation*, Speech to the EC Chamber of Commerce, New York, at 4 (Mar. 26, 1990) (copy on file with the Library of the EU Delegation, Washington, D.C.) [hereinafter Brittan, *Competition Policy*]. Thus, Article 3(1) of the 2004 regulation declares that a 'concentration shall be deemed to arise' where a change of control on a lasting basis results from (a) the 'merger' of two or more previously independent undertakings or parts of undertakings, or (b) the acquisition, by one or more persons already controlling at least one undertaking, or by one or more undertakings (by purchase of stock or assets or by contract or other means) of direct or indirect control of the whole or parts of one or more other undertakings. The 2004 recasting removes the confusing taxonomic view of joint ventures taken by its predecessor, and provides simply that 'a joint venture performing on a lasting basis all the functions of an autonomous economic entity shall constitute a concentration' for purposes of Article 3(1)(b). *See* Council Regulation 139/2004, *supra* note 200, art. 3(4).

202. *See supra* note 168.

203. *See* Brittan, *Competition Policy, supra* note 201, at 3. The preamble to the regulation indicates that the Council relied 'principally' on Article 308 of the EC Treaty as the legal basis for both the original regulation and its recasting. Council Regulation 139/2004, *supra* note 200, pmbl., recital 7. This 'catch-all' Treaty provision empowers the Council (on a proposal from the Commission and after consultation with the Parliament) to take action to attain an objective of the 'Community' where 'the necessary powers' have not been provided in the Treaty. EC Treaty art. 308. Thus, the 2004 preamble repeats its predecessor's finding that the existing competition code – Articles 81 and 82 – does apply to certain concentrations, but is concededly insufficient 'to control all operations which may prove to be incompatible with the system of undistorted competition envisaged in the Treaty.' Council Regulation 139/2004, *supra* note 200, pmbl., recital 7. The implicit legal difficulty recognized in the 1989 and 2004 preambles is that the competition rules of the EC Treaty do not specifically mention the control of mergers and acquisitions *in their incipiency*. The scope of Article 81 would appear, on its face, to encompass such agreements where their consequence would be to prevent, restrict, or distort competition. A similar argument could apply to deployment of Article 82. In the *Philip Morris* case, for example, the European Court of Justice held that, in principle, the acquisition by one company of an equity interest in a competitor, where one company obtains control of the commercial conduct of the other, or where commercial cooperation between them might result, was capable of infringing Article 81(1). *See* Joined Cases 142 and 156/84, British & Am. Tobacco & R.J. Reynolds Indus., Inc. *v.* Comm'n, 1987 E.C.R. 4487, 4577. Similarly, in the *Continental Can* case in 1973, the Court provided an interpretation of Article 82 that indicated a possible application in merger control. *See* Case 6/72, Euroemballage Corp. *v.* Comm'n, 1973 E.C.R. 215. The Court held that Article 82 could apply to a merger if the position of an already dominant company is thereby enhanced so that the degree of control over the market substantially obstructs competition (*i.e.*, so that the only undertakings left in the market are those which are dependent on the dominant undertaking with regard to their

mechanism that would displace national supervision once certain quantitative thresholds were exceeded.[204]

The revised merger regulation in 2004[205] recognized that certain key macro-economic drivers – completion of the internal market and of economic and monetary union, enlargement of the EU, and the lowering of international barriers to trade and investment – 'will continue to result in major corporate reorganizations, particularly in the form of concentrations.'[206] Moreover, the arrival of the merger regulation displaced all other competition legislation across all economic sectors, reminiscent of how the domestic U.S. airline industry was returned to the jurisdiction of the general antitrust laws after 1989.[207] Article 22(2) of the 1989 regulation (recodified in Article 21 of the 2004 version),[208] suspended Regulation 3975/87 – the legislation that, until 2003, applied supranational competition law to the air transport industry – with respect to concentrations captured by the merger

---

market behavior). *See id.* at 245. The problem with these applications of Articles 81 and 82 is that market power must exist *before* it can be attacked, and clearly an effective merger law should be able to prevent market power from coming into existence. *See* Button & Swann, *supra* note 6, at 240-41. Prior to adoption of the regulation, the Commission had built up an administrative oversight practice under Articles 81 and 82.

204. The degree of transactional magnitude that signals a 'Community dimension' – the threshold levels – is a moving target that can be adjusted by the Council as competitive conditions require. At the time of writing, the 'Community dimension' is achieved whenever (i) the combined aggregate worldwide turnover (the Community term for 'gross revenues') of the companies concerned exceeds EUR 5000 million *and* the aggregate Community-wide turnover of each of at least two of the companies concerned exceeds EUR 250 million, *unless* each of the companies concerned achieves more than two-thirds of its aggregate Community-wide turnover within the same Member State. Council Regulation 139/2004, *supra* note 200, art. 1(2)(a)-(b). Article 5 of the regulation offers various technical formulas for calculation of turnover, including rules for treatment of revenues earned through parents, subsidiaries, or affiliates, *see id.*, and the Commission has issued several Notices giving further technical detail on calculation of turnover. The high thresholds of Commission scrutiny, maintained in the 2004 recasting, have been criticized. Sir Leon Brittan (who believed the thresholds were set too high) described the 'turnover threshold' as 'a necessarily arbitrary way of defining which concentrations have sufficient impact on the Community as a whole to merit decision by the Commission rather than by Member States.' Brittan, *Competition Policy, supra* note 201, at 5. Alternative tests were considered, but turnover '[was] the only one which [was] both reasonably certain in its application and not excessively complex.' *Id.* Given the small number of mergers in the EU airline industry, it may be queried whether the somewhat crude mathematical division of jurisdictions is appropriate in this sector. A case-by-case accommodation between the Community and national authorities, such as preceded the regulation, would have a greater likelihood of keeping the European Commission involved – and, consequently, of preserving competition against (for example) national carrier consolidation with competitors in the domestic market.

205. *See supra* note 201.

206. Council Regulation 139/2004, *supra* note 200, pmbl., recital 3.

207. In the case of the European Community, however, it was not until 2003, with the repeal of Council Regulation 3975/87, that the airline industry would become subject to the same competition enforcement procedures as EU industries generally.

208. Council Regulation 4064/89, *supra* note 200, art. 22(2); Council Regulation 139/2004, *supra* note 200, art. 21(1).

regulation.[209] Accordingly, the merger regulation applies to concentrations between undertakings in the air transport sector.

The merger regulation (in 1989 and in 2004) refrains from any advance judgment – which would be a statement of industrial policy, were it otherwise – as to the structural reconfiguration of specific industries that mergers and acquisitions can produce.[210] Nor is there any equivalent in the regulation to the statistical testing performed by the U.S. Department of Justice, which has typically used algorithmic ratios as an initial predictor of the competitive impact of planned transactions and tended to disfavor those that fall outside prescribed parameters.[211] Other than a recommendation in the 1989 preamble (retained in 2004) that a combined pan-Community market share of 25% or less is an 'indication' of compatibility with the common market,[212] the only computational baseline in the regulation concerns the distribution of jurisdiction between the Commission and the various Member State national antitrust authorities.[213]

---

209. Similarly, as clarified in Article 21 of the 2004 regulation, Council Regulations 1/2003 (the general competition enforcement legislation that replaced Regulation 17/62), 1017/68, and 4056/86 do not apply (the latter two have themselves been displaced by Council Regulation 411/2004, *supra* note 156), except in relation to joint ventures which do not have a Community dimension and have as their object or effect the coordination of the competitive behavior of independent undertakings. *See* Council Regulation 139/2004, *supra* note 200, art. 21(1).

210. As Sir Leon Brittan explained shortly after adoption of the original merger regulation, the Member States were divided on the *raison d'être* of a Community-wide merger enforcement policy. Some saw it as a tool of old-fashioned industrial policy, a way of shaping industrial structure and location and an opportunity to create large national champion enterprises more likely to be able to compete with U.S. and Japanese corporations. *See* Brittan, *Competition Policy, supra* note 201, at 3. Others saw it as a 'pure expression of competition principles': monopolization and market domination should be stopped, but everything else should be let proceed. *See id.* at 4. Sir Leon believed that the latter strain of analysis had prevailed, and that Community merger control was 'rooted in competition policy.' *Id.*

211. *See generally* HERBERT HOVENKAMP, FEDERAL ANTITRUST POLICY: THE LAW OF COMPETITION AND ITS PRACTICE 511-25 (3d ed. 2005) (describing measurement of market concentration using the so-called Herfindahl-Hirschman Index (HHI)). But the Commission is quite familiar with and 'often' applies the HHI as a 'useful proxy for the change in concentration directly brought about by the merger.' European Commission, Guidelines on the Assessment of Horizontal Mergers under the Council Regulation on the Control of Concentrations Between Undertakings para. 16, 2004/C 31/03, 2004 O.J. (C 31) 5 [hereinafter Horizontal Merger Guidelines].

212. Council Regulation 4064/89, *supra* note 200, pmbl., recital 15, restated in Council Regulation 139/2004, *supra* note 200, pmbl., recital 32; *but see* Horizontal Merger Guidelines, *supra* note 211, n.24 (indicating that, in cases of a 'collective dominant position,' the 25% indication does not apply). The 25% 'safe harbor' has not been reproduced in the main text of the regulation, indicating that it is not intended to bind the Commission's assessment of specific structural conditions in a given industry under Articles 81and 82. This is certainly the Commission's view. *See* Horizontal Merger Guidelines, *supra* note 211, para. 18.

213. The general evaluative principle in the regulation is that concentrations that 'are not liable to impede effective competition,' in particular as a result of 'the creation or strengthening of a dominant position,' 'shall be declared compatible with the common market.' Council Regulation 139/2004, *supra* note 200, art. 2(2). The Commission focuses in merger analysis on an increase in the market power of the merged entities, allowing them to act 'independently of their competitors, customers, and, ultimately, of consumers,' thereby threatening the

Enforcement of the merger regulation is entrusted solely to the Commission, subject to the unlimited jurisdiction granted to the European Court of Justice under Article 229 of the EC Treaty with regard to fines and periodic penalty payments.[214] While the precise enforcement model copies the blueprints of the Hart-Scott-Rodino Act in the United States, the U.S. Government's chief weapon in the arena of what is called 'premerger enforcement,' advance notification of impending business transactions was a Community practice during the entire lifetime of Regulation 17, the general competition enforcement regulation, from 1964 until its repeal in 2003.[215] Through this bureaucratic filtration process, the Commission undertakes the role of a supranational cartel authority, blending the merger oversight roles of both the Department of Justice and the Federal Trade Commission.

d   *Regulating Public Action: State Aids*

The vexed issue of the flow of public subsidies to Europe's troubled flag carriers will be treated later.[216] For now, a capsulized treatment of the applicable EC Treaty

---

'effective competition' that brings consumers low prices, high quality products, a wide selection of goods and services, and innovation. *See* Horizontal Merger Guidelines, *supra* note 211, paras. 2 & 8. 'By increased market power,' the guidelines say, 'is meant the ability of one or more firms to profitably increase prices, reduce output, choice or quality of goods or services, diminish innovation, or otherwise influence parameters of competition.' *Id.* para. 8. Based on Commission dissatisfaction with court practice in the Community, the 2004 regulation introduces a widening of the interpretive bandwidth of the phrase 'significant impediment to effective competition' to include what might be called 'collective dominance' in the context of an oligopolistic marketplace. Thus, under certain circumstances, concentrations involving the elimination of important competitive restraints that the merging parties had exerted on each other, *as well as* a reduction in competitive pressure on the remaining competitors – may, even in the absence of a likelihood of coordination between the members of the oligopoly, result in a significant impediment to effective competition. *See* Council Regulation 139/2004, *supra* note 200, pmbl., recital 25; *see also* Horizontal Merger Guidelines, *supra* note 211, para. 25. *See supra* note 212 (noting that the Commission will not apply the 25% 'safe harbor' indicator in cases of collective dominance). The interesting analytical notion of collective dominance might have been expected to (but did not) have some play in the Commission's investigations of transatlantic alliances.

214. *See* EC Treaty art. 229; Council Regulation 139/2004, *supra* note 200, art. 16.
215. Thus, the 2004 regulation lays down a procedure for prior notification to the Commission of concentrations 'with a Community dimension.' Notification must occur prior to implementation and following 'the conclusion of the agreement, the announcement of the public bid, or the acquisition of a controlling interest.' Council Regulation 139/2004, *supra* note 200, art. 4(1). Under Article 4(3), the Commission must publish the fact of the notification. *Id.* Two prenotification variations, instigated by the companies which would be obligated to notify, are envisaged in Article 4: if the companies inform the Commission that the merger may affect competition in a market within a Member State which is a distinct market that the Member State should examine, the Commission has the ultimate discretion to defer to the Member State's authorities. *Id.* art. 4(4). If a merger does not have a Community dimension but is capable of being reviewed under the national laws of at least three different Member States, the companies may so inform the Commission and the Commission may take jurisdiction in the absence of any Member State objection. *Id.* art. 4(5).
216. *See infra* Part III(F).

proscriptions and exemptions is appropriate. Article 87 of the Treaty, designed to promote transparency in public funding, outlaws aid granted by a Member State 'which distorts or threatens to distort competition by favoring certain undertakings or the production of certain goods.'[217] While it is difficult to conceive of any form of publicly-funded boon that would definitively *not* impede competition between undertakings, the prohibition in Article 87 is nonetheless modified to sanction certain classes of funding that either *shall* or *may* be 'compatible with the common market.'[218] These exceptions, directed chiefly to social welfare and developmental aid, are sometimes so imprecisely drawn they imperil the very principle they purport to qualify, magnifying the responsibility of the Commission to police rigorously their invocation by Member States.[219]

Inevitably, given the publicly-owned character of several EU flag carriers,[220] it is important to address how the Treaty might affect each Member State's authority to contribute additional capital to its own national enterprises. As a general matter, the Treaty system does not assume a completely privatized economy in the Member States, nor require its establishment.[221] This neutrality as to public ownership is implicit in the declaration that the EC Treaty 'shall in no way prejudice the rules in Member States governing *the system of property owner-ship*.'[222] Article 86(1) of the Treaty, in fact, speaks of 'public undertakings and undertakings to which Member States grant special or exclusive rights,' and binds the Member States (though not the undertakings directly) to obey the Treaty rules, including Article 12 prohibiting discrimination on grounds of nationality and

---

217. EC Treaty art. 87. The proscribed aid is declared 'incompatible with the common market,' rather than 'prohibited,' the term the drafters selected for Articles 81and 82.

218. EC Treaty art. 87(2).

219. The presumptively compatible categories include social welfare subsidies to consumers (provided they are applied without national discrimination) and disaster relief. EC Treaty art. 87(2). Categories that *may* be compatible include regional development aid, aid to promote 'execution of an important project of common European interest,' cultural and heritage conservation efforts, a catch-all category of aid 'to facilitate the development of certain economic activities or of certain economic areas, where such aid does not adversely affect trading conditions to an extent contrary to the common interest,' and a bodefully phrased license to the Council of the European Union to define 'other categories of aid' upon a proposal from the Commission. *Id.* The Commission has issued communications explaining the scope of some of these exceptions. *See* European Commission, Annual Reports on Competition Policy, <http://ec.europa.eu/comm/competition/annual_reports/>. As will be seen, Member States have attempted to grant airline subsidies under cover of the broad category of aid 'to facilitate the development of certain economic activities.' The Commission recognized in its 1984 discussion paper on air transport, *see* Memorandum 2, *supra* note 58, that State aids may be appropriate for airlines to fulfill public service obligations, or to compete with subsidized carriers from third countries, or to assist economically undeveloped regions. *Id.* at 37 & 38. Individual scrutiny of all 'normal commercial transactions' (loans, capital, or guarantees) would nevertheless be expected. *Id.* at 38. With Commission sanction, governments could also provide limited short-term subsidies or loans for specific airline adaptation problems. *See infra* note 588.

220. *See supra* Part I.

221. As was seen in Chapter 3, Part VI, much of the political impetus for privatization programs developed only in the 1980s.

222. EC Treaty art. 295 (emphasis added).

all of the competition rules in Articles 81-89 with respect to these undertakings.[223] Similarly, the second paragraph of Article 86 refers to '[u]ndertakings entrusted with the operation of services of general economic interest or having the character of a revenue-producing monopoly,' which are made subject to EC competition law – but conditionally, to the extent only that 'the application of [that law] does not obstruct the performance' of their assigned tasks.[224]

Article 86 appears, at face value, to represent a tailor-made 'national carrier' exemption from the application of the competition rules.[225] EU flag carriers have historically held special and exclusive rights to domestic and international air routes, serving the public interest and enjoying a monopoly of revenues from the supply of air services. Member States initially found it convenient to invoke Article 86(2) to justify, for example, the strict nationality-based licensing system for aircraft.[226] Had they adhered to their historical resistance to airline deregulation, however, the Commission may well have resorted to Article 86(3), one of the exceptional provisions that grants the Commission direct legislative power to adopt appropriate directives (and decisions) addressed to Member States, unmediated by Council – or parliamentary – involvement.[227] To the limited extent that the airline sector still exhibits public ownership profiles within the Union, it certainly falls within the domain recognized by Article 86. Yet the political consensus on airline liberalization that emerged in the Council of the European Union made it unnecessary for the Commission to launch a preemptive Article 86 strategy.

E   Toward Multilateralism: The EC's External
              Aviation Relations

1   **The Open Skies Rulings and the External Competence
              of the EC**

The cornerstone of a fully open, second stage plurilateral air transport agreement between the United States and the EC would be reciprocal sacrifice of each side's

---

223. *Id.* art. 86(1). *See* Case 41/83, Italian Republic *v.* Comm'n (British Telecommunications), 1985 E.C.R. 873.

224. EC Treaty art. 86(2). *See* Case C-320/91, Procureur du Roi *v.* Paul Corbeau, 4 C.M.L.R. 621 (1994).

225. This argument certainly gained some traction in the period prior to air transport liberalization. *See* Ludwig Weber, *Air Transport in the Common Market and the Public Air Transport Enterprises*, 5 ANNALS AIR & SPACE L. 283, 289 (1980) ('There has been widespread consensus that air transport enterprises are enterprises in the sense of [Article 86(2)] which are entrusted with tasks of "general economic interest" ').

226. Moreover, the Court of Justice, in Case 155/73, Italian State *v.* Sacchi, 1974 E.C.R. 409, supported this interpretation.

227. EC Treaty art. 86(3). The Commission, supported by strong Court of Justice rulings, did choose to use Article 86 aggressively as a sword to slice into State monopolies, for example in the telecommunications market, seeking to thwart Member States who might have tried to rely on the conditional language in Article 86(2) to shield powerful public corporations from competition.

cabotage and nationality restrictions.[228] In a strong signal of the 'specificity' of the air transport sector, however, neither the adoption of a common air transport policy, nor the legally unprecedented emergence of a 'de-cabotaged' single aviation market, persuaded the Member States to concede (as a political matter) the EC's[229] *exclusive* competence to negotiate and conclude extra-Union air transport treaties. Instead, in order to confirm what it interpreted to be the centrality of the Community's negotiating power, the Commission (as discussed in Chapter 2) felt compelled to bring a European Court of Justice challenge against the bilateral open skies agreements concluded by eight Member States with the United States.[230] Before looking once again at the specific rulings in that judgment and their implications, however, it is important to offer a brief consideration of the Court's pre-existing precedential framework within which it evaluated the integrity, under Community law, of the Chicago system and its network of bilateral agreements contracted separately by Member States.

The European Commission used a broad teleological argument to support its submission to the Court in the open skies cases that the Member States had infringed the external competence of the Community by concluding bilateral air transport agreements with the United States. Thus, the Commission contended that the Community has exclusive competence to conclude an international agreement even in the absence of Community provisions in the area concerned, 'where the conclusion of such an agreement is necessary in order to attain the objectives of the [EC] Treaty in that area, such objectives being incapable of being attained merely by introducing autonomous common rules.'[231] The Commission relied on Opinion 1/76 of the European Court of Justice,[232] as subsequently clarified by the Court's Opinion 1/94[233] and Opinion 2/92.[234] Opinion 1/94 was published as the second in time of these three opinions, and provides a framework for extrapolating the general principles of external competence.

In Opinion 1/94, upon a Commission reference under Article 300(6),[235] the Court explored the division of competence to conclude the package of treaty instruments required for admission to the new World Trade Organization (WTO).

---

228. *See infra* Chapter 6, Part III(E).
229. *See supra* Chapter 1, note 10; BRIAN F. HAVEL, IN SEARCH OF OPEN SKIES 268, n. 202 (1997) (containing other vexed observations on terminology).
230. As noted earlier, seven of these States (Belgium, Denmark, Germany, Luxembourg, Austria, Finland, and Sweden) signed 'open skies'-type agreements with the United States. The eighth country, the United Kingdom, had signed the more restrictive Bermuda II bilateral. *See supra* Chapter 3, Part III(B). *See also* European Commission, *Communication from the Commission on the Consequences of the Court Judgments of 5 November 2002 for European Air Transport Policy*, para. 27, COM (2002) 649 final (Nov. 19, 2002) [hereinafter European Commission, *Consequences*].
231. *Id.* para. 45.
232. Opinion 1/76 of Apr. 27, 1977, 1977 E.C.R. I-741.
233. Opinion 1/94 of Nov. 15, 1994, 1994 E.C.R. I-5267.
234. Opinion 2/92 of Mar. 24, 1995, 1995 E.C.R. I-521 (which was issued later than Opinion 1/94 despite its earlier date designation).
235. Article 300, which lays out a protocol for the interinstitutional conclusion of international agreements, makes available to the Council, the Commission, or a Member State, the

For present purposes, the central question faced by the Court was whether the supranational Community had exclusive competence to conclude the new General Agreement on Trade in Services (GATS),[236] or whether, because of areas of retained Member State competence with respect to services, both the EC *and* the Member States should become signatories – an outcome sometimes described in Community (though not Treaty) parlance as a 'mixed agreement' or 'mixity.'[237] The Commission argued that the entire service sector should be collapsed into the express (and exclusive) external competence of the common commercial policy in Article 133, hitherto understood to embrace only trade in goods.[238]

The Court was initially sympathetic to the Commission's contention that a narrow reading of Article 133 to include only 'goods' would be inconsistent with a dynamic, evolving international trade policy.[239] The Commission's jurisdictional reach exceeded its grasp, however: the Court declined to approve a comprehensive transmission of competence, unaffected by the specific definitions of trade in services in the GATS,[240] or by the sweeping scope of the GATS definition of the services sector – including transport, a sector where the Court had first unveiled its doctrine of 'implied' external competence in the famous *ERTA* judgment in 1971.[241]

---

opportunity to obtain the 'opinion' of the Court of Justice 'as to whether an agreement envisaged is compatible with the provisions of the [EC] Treaty.' EC Treaty art. 300(6). This power of interpretive review is unconnected to any specific adversarial contest.

236. *See infra* Chapter 6, Part III(C).
237. *See generally* INTERNATIONAL LAW ASPECTS OF THE EUROPEAN UNION 126-28 (Martii Koskenniemi ed., 1998).
238. Opinion 1/94, *supra* note 233, at I-5303 (setting forth views of Commission, Council and several Member States on the scope of the common commercial policy). The Commission has continued to argue that services in any form should be included in the common commercial policy. Thus, it has reasoned that the absence of an express provision in the EC Treaty for a comprehensive external system in respect of trade in services is explained by the relative unimportance of the sector when the Treaty was written. *See* Opinion 2/92, *supra* note 234, pt. C.
239. Opinion 1/94, *supra* note 233, at I-5399-401, para. 41.
240. As to the GATS definitions, the Court found that only one – the cross-frontier supply of a service where the supplier does not move to the consumer's country (or vice versa) – was 'not unlike trade in goods' and could 'fall within the concept of the common commercial policy.' *Id.* at I-5401. The Council of the European Union provided the example to the Court of a firm of architects established in country A that supplies an electrical installation project to a firm of engineers established in country B. *Id.* at I-5290. The other definitions – consumption abroad, (for example, services supplied in country A to tourists from country B, *id.* at I-5290) commercial presence of the foreign supplier through a subsidiary or branch (for example, the supply of banking services in country B by undertakings or professionals from country A, *id.* at I-5290-1), and the presence of natural persons from a foreign country (for example, where an undertaking from country A supplies construction services in country B by means of workers coming from country A, *id.* at I-5291) – could not form part of the common commercial policy because the EC Treaty contains separate specific chapters on the free movement of natural and legal persons (and their right of establishment). Opinion 1/94, *supra* note 233, I-5402. The Court pointed to the distinction between a 'common commercial policy' in Article 3(b) and 'measures concerning the entry and movement of persons' in Article 3(d). *Id.* Accordingly, the treatment of nationals of *non*-Member States on crossing the external frontiers of the Member States also could not form part of that policy. *Id.*
241. Case 22/70, *ERTA*, 1971 E.C.R. 263. As will be seen in Chapter 6, Part III(C), the GATS Annex on Air Transport Services specifically excludes most aspects of trade in air transport.

The Court noted the presence of discrete provisions in Title IV of the EC Treaty covering the particular services comprised in transport, in turn foreclosing the subsumption of transport services within the common commercial policy.[242] International agreements in the field of transport, therefore, fall within the scope of the common transport policy and not within the common commercial policy.[243]

Since most categories of trade in services, including transport, were therefore not subject to the express external competence in Article 133, the Court returned (at the Commission's prompting) to its earlier teaching in *ERTA* to evaluate whether the supranational entity could claim *any* external competence in these sectors. In *ERTA*, the Court had determined that not only are there *express* conferments of external competence in the Treaty, but that the competence of the Community to conclude international agreements 'may equally flow from other provisions of the Treaty and from measures adopted, within the framework of those provisions, by the supranational institutions.'[244] In other words, the Court in *ERTA*, true to its self-professed teleological mission, had carved out a doctrine of 'implied external powers' of the Community.[245] Such a doctrine, with its inevitable casuistic focus, naturally sets up the conditions for continuing legal contests between the Community, represented through the Commission, and the Member States, with which the Council of the European Union is institutionally allied.[246] Thus, the Commission, the Council, and several Member States each made separate submissions to the Court in the GATS proceedings concerning appropriate interpretive theories to determine an implied *ERTA*-type external competence in those aspects of the services sector that the Court held to lie outside the ambit of Article 133.

With respect to transport services, for example, the Commission grounded its claim to external competence on Article 71(1) of the EC Treaty, which provides for common rules 'applicable to *international transport* to or from the territory of a Member State or passing across the territory of one or more Member States.' Despite the Advocate-General's opinion in *ERTA* that 'international transport' really refers to 'intra-Union' transport in the context of the common market in

---

242. Opinion 1/94, *supra* note 233, at I-5402. Further segregating transport from a general commercial policy, a common transport policy is also included in the 'activities' of the Community laid down in Article 3 of the EC Treaty. *See* Opinion 1/76, *supra* note 232, para. 1. And the U.K. Government, in its submission to the Court in Opinion 1/94, indicated that whenever the Council has adopted external measures which have the predominant aim of regulating transport, it has done so on the basis of the Transport Title. *See* Opinion 1/94, *supra* note 233, at I-5308.
243. Opinion 2/92, *supra* note 234, para. 10 (summarizing paras. 48-52 of Opinion 1/94, *supra* note 233).
244. Opinion 1/94, *supra* note 233, at I-5402 (quoting Case 22/70, *ERTA*, para. 16, 1971 E.C.R. 263).
245. Opinion 1/94, *supra* note 233, at I-5411.
246. In the context of the GATS opinion, for example, the Council feared that the interpretation of the common commercial policy advocated by the Commission would lead to 'the transformation of that policy into a common policy on external economic relations,' including regulation of currency exchange rates – well beyond the trade and tariff issues conventionally thought to be part of the common commercial policy. *Id.* at I-5306.

transport, the Court in its final judgment accorded a wide reading to the provision to encompass 'transport from or to third countries,' and found an implied power, based on specific Treaty language, to enter appropriate international agreements relating to the subject matter of common rules previously adopted for the internal market.[247]

The Court's earlier observations in Opinion 1/76 seemed to suggest that the mere existence of internal powers for Community-level action for a specific objective could confer authority on the Community to enter into international commitments 'necessary for the attainment of that objective even in the absence of an express provision.'[248] As the Court emphasized with great force in its GATS opinion, however, the mere existence of a power to lay down common rules at internal level does not *automatically* deprive the Member States of their right to assume obligations with non-Member countries.[249] Only when common rules have been established, *and* those rules could be affected by a Member State's unilateral assumption of obligations to non-Member countries,[250] does supranational external competence become indisputably exclusive.[251] The Court thus sought to reel in its buccaneering language in Opinion 1/76 and to recast it in accordance with the more nuanced phrasing of its *ERTA* decision.[252]

The Commission's mixed success in the later open skies rulings, therefore, was foreshadowed by its failure in Opinion 1/94 to win an explicit ruling that the Member States' continuing freedom to conduct an external policy based on bilateral agreements with non-Member countries *must* inevitably distort the flow of services and undermine the internal market even in an area where the Commission has adopted common internal rules.[253] The Court in Opinion 1/94 rejected the attribution of competence based on the mere establishment of common internal rules in transport, particularly when not all transport matters were already covered

---

247. *ERTA, supra* note 241, at 275.
248. Opinion 1/76, *supra* note 232, para. 3. Moreover, according to the Court in that opinion, while this would be 'particularly so' when the internal power has *already* been used to adopt internal measures, the external exercise of power could not be 'limited to that eventuality.' *Id*. para. 4.
249. Or, as the Court would later summarize this jurisprudence in Opinion 2/92, 'the Community's exclusive external competence does not automatically flow from its power to lay down rules at internal level.' Opinion 2/92, *supra* note 234, sec. V, para. 3.
250. *See infra* in the main text.
251. Opinion 1/94, *supra* note 233, at I-5411. The possibility that common internal rules could be adopted that would *not* be affected by bilateral obligations is clearly left open in the Court's opinion. The burden would be upon the Commission, presumably, to demonstrate the incompatibility or distortion produced by the coexistence of common internal rules and bilateral external obligations.
252. The language which the Court used in Opinion 1/76, *supra* note 232 (that external competence did not require prior internal legislation) was qualified to relate solely to a situation 'where the conclusion of an international agreement is necessary in order to achieve Treaty objectives which cannot be attained by the adoption of autonomous rules.' Opinion 1/94, *supra* note 233, para. 85; Opinion 2/92, *supra* note 234, sec. V, para. 4.
253. The foreshadowing was embedded in the Commission's own arguments in the earlier case. Thus, the Commission suggested that travelers could choose to fly from airports in Member States which have concluded an open skies bilateral agreement with a non-Member country and its airline, enabling those Member States to offer the best quality/price ratio for transport

by common rules.[254] Critical to the future application of the Court's analysis, therefore, is to determine when (if ever) the scope of adopted common rules ('autonomous rules' in the Court's jurisprudential argot) may be 'affected or distorted' by international commitments undertaken by Member States.[255] For example, arguably if France were to award an exclusive permission to U.S. airlines to access cabotage routes within France,[256] this bilateral arrangement would affect the common rules contained in Regulation 2408/92, to the extent that those rules harmonize completely, from April 1, 1997, the conditions for air transport cabotage in the Member States of the EU. By reserving a right unilaterally to grant rights of access to U.S. carriers, outside the Community framework, France would necessarily infringe the exclusive external competence of the Community.[257] Here, the international commitment to the United States falls squarely within the scope of a common rule (a regulation providing for mutual cabotage among Member States), even if there is no necessary contradiction between the common rule and the commitment (granting cabotage rights to the United States does not *per se* preclude their full exercise by the other Member States).[258]

Even more specifically, however, the Court in its 'open skies' judgments provided a schema to predict when a set of internal rules necessarily displaces the autonomy of the Member States in their external relations. Thus, the Community's exclusive external competence prevails whenever the Community has expressly conferred on its institutions powers to negotiate with non-Member States, or whenever the Community has included in its internal legislative acts provisions relating to the treatment of nationals of non-Member States, or where the Community has achieved complete harmonization in a given area. In each of these three situations, the Court reasoned, the common rules could be 'affected' within the meaning of *ERTA* if the Member States retained freedom to negotiate with third countries.[259] It appears from the Court's later 2005 decision in *Commission v. Luxembourg*, considered below, that the elements of this schema

---

(and thereby, presumably, distorting the competitive relationships of EU airlines operating under the common air transport policy). Opinion 1/94, *supra* note 233, at I-5411.

254. The Court did find, however, that 'there is nothing in the treaty which prevents the institutions from arranging, in the common rules laid down by them, concerted action in relation to non-Member countries or from prescribing the approach to be taken by the Member States in their external dealings.' *Id.* at I-5411-12.

255. Case C-266/03, Comm'n *v.* Grand Duchy of Luxembourg, para. 42, 2005 E.C.R. I-4805 (discussed further *infra* in the main text).

256. Assuming, *arguendo*, that the exclusivity did not affect existing legal obligations to other Member States to allow cabotage services for their carriers within France, and also setting aside a probable violation of Article 7 of the Chicago Convention. *See supra* Chapter 3, Part IV.

257. This hypothetical is based on the facts in *Comm'n v. Luxembourg*, *supra* note 255 (upholding Commission's challenge to Luxembourg agreements with various Eastern European States on access to inland waterways in Luxembourg).

258. *See id.* para. 43.

259. *See* Comm'n *v.* Grand Duchy of Luxembourg [Open Skies], paras. 88-90, 2002 E.C.R. I-9741 [hereinafter Luxembourg Open Skies]; *see also* Comm'n *v.* Luxembourg, *supra* note 255, para. 45.

have a cascading effect, since they can be considered in sequence to decide whether a Member State's action has 'affected' a prior common rule.[260]

Nevertheless, the Court of Justice in its open skies rulings did not award the Commission the unalloyed exclusivity it claimed. Instead, the Court identified specific areas of exclusive external competence of the Community, leaving the balance of issues (implicitly, not explicitly) to Member State competence.[261] In strictly jurisprudential terms, therefore, the Court's suite of eight judgments hardly provided the 'legal clarity' claimed by the Commission with respect to the future management of Community external aviation relations.[262] The Commission was quick to apply a *mutatis mutandis* argument to the specific matters (airport slots, computer reservations systems, and intra-Community fares and rates) identified in the Court's judgment, purporting to sweep several additional areas of legislated Community action into the jurisdiction of exclusive supranational competence.[263] But the trio of exclusive Community competences that the Court identified, even when matched with the *mutatis* embellishments by the Commission, did not comprehensively displace Member State negotiating authority.[264]

---

260. Thus, in *Comm'n v. Luxembourg, supra* note 255, the Court held that the relevant regulation on access to Member State inland waterways covered only carriers *inter alia* established in and owned by nationals of a Member State, and did not govern the conditions of access by non-Community carriers. The contested bilateral agreements, accordingly, could not be regarded as 'affecting' the regulation. *Id.* at 46-49. The absence of these conditions of access also indicated that the harmonization achieved by that regulation was not complete. *Id.* at 50.

261. *See* Luxembourg Open Skies, *supra* note 259, para. 103 *et seq.* The Court found also that the eight bilateral agreements in question deprived 'Community air carriers' of their rights under the EC Treaty. Thus, the nationality clauses that are standard in all bilaterals between EU Member States and their non-EU negotiating partners, and which restrict traffic rights under each bilateral to air carriers owned and controlled by nationals of the parties to the agreement, violate the right of establishment in Article 43 of the EC Treaty. Community air carriers with Chicago system nationality affiliations to one Member State, but with an 'establishment' in another Member State, could not therefore avail of their Treaty-mandated right to service international (extra-Union) routes from both States. *See id.* para. 122 *et seq.* According to the Commission's legal construct, '[t]he beneficiaries of an international air transport agreement at Community level are "Community carriers." This is the sole definition of airlines within the Community and it is laid down in Regulation EC No. 2407/92 on the licensing of air carriers and Regulation EC No. 2408/92 on access for Community carriers to intra-Community air routes.' European Commission, *Consequences, supra* note 230, para. 37.

262. *Id.* para. 39.

263. *Id.* para. 31. These other matters, which the Commission indicates are 'typically' addressed in bilateral agreements, include Community legislation covering safety issues (and the new European Aviation Safety Agency), groundhandling and other 'commercial opportunities,' customs and excise charges, and environmental restrictions on aircraft including noise-related operating restrictions. *See id.* para. 30-31. Several additional matters also 'shape the trading environment in which international air transport takes place' without necessarily being within the scope of bilateral negotiations. These areas embrace Community legislation covering denied boarding compensation, air carrier liability, package vacations, and data protection. *See id.* para. 32.

264. Moreover, the Court's Article 43 analysis (concluding that a Member State could not grant the United States the typical bilateral right 'to withdraw, suspend or limit traffic rights' where

The dispute decided in 2005 in *Commission v. Luxembourg* concerned Luxembourg's unilateral action to negotiate a number of bilateral treaties between 1992 and 1994 with Eastern European States granting their residents access to the Duchy's inland waterways. Luxembourg's action was threatening because it took place against a backdrop of common Community action in the same field.[265] Prior to the first Luxembourg bilateral, the Council of the European Union adopted a decision (taken after a Commission recommendation made in June 1991) to authorize the Commission to negotiate a multilateral agreement applicable to the transport of passengers and goods by inland waterway between the Community and at least some of the same Eastern European States which had signed bilaterals with Luxembourg.[266] In a series of procedural steps, the Commission challenged Luxembourg's ratification of its bilateral agreements and ultimately initiated proceedings under Article 226 of the EC Treaty for failure to fulfill obligations.[267]

Using the schema from the open skies rulings, the Court in *Commission v. Luxembourg* suggested a sequential (and solecistic) pattern of reasoning that must have vexed the Commission: the regulation in question did not cover access by non-Community inland waterway carriers; because it did not do so, the regulation had not achieved complete harmonization and the Member States could retain external autonomy with respect to access to their inland waterways.[268] If this argument were dispositive, the Commission would have to make sure that every internal legislative act anticipated and incorporated the rights and obligations of non-Member States and their nationals, on the assumption that at least that level of incorporation (if not more) would be required to satisfy *ERTA*.

But the Commission in its proceeding against Luxembourg showed that it had learned its lesson from the 'open skies' judgments. Although the Commission continued to rely on *ERTA* to assert an exclusive external competence, it now proposed that the external actions of Member States in areas falling generally within Community competence could run afoul of Article 10 of the EC Treaty, which requires Member States positively to 'take all appropriate measures,

---

air carriers designated by a Member State were not owned by that State or its nationals), Luxembourg Open Skies, *supra* note 259, judgment, para. 1, finds only that the Member States have failed to fulfill their obligations under Article 43 and under Article 10 of the EC Treaty, but does not suggest that a remedy for that behavior lies in supranational rather than Member State action. If anything, the legal implication of Article 10 (stating, *inter alia*, that 'Member States shall take all appropriate measures . . . to ensure fulfilment of the obligations arising out of this Treaty') is that the Member States, not the Commission, will bear responsibility for correcting the violation of Article 43. *See* EC Treaty art. 10.

265. The Community has power to act in the sphere of inland waterway transport, although it lacks an explicit *external* competence in this sphere. Comm'n *v*. Luxembourg, *supra* note 255, para. 39. *See also* EC Treaty arts. 71(1) & 80(2).

266. Comm'n *v*. Luxembourg, *supra* note 255, paras. 16-17.

267. The Commission did negotiate a multilateral agreement on Community inland waterways with three of the States which had signed bilateral agreements with Luxembourg, but at the time of the Court's judgment no such multilateral agreement had been formally concluded. *See id.* paras. 21-22.

268. *See supra* note 265.

whether general or particular, to ensure fulfilment of the obligations' arising out of the Treaty or 'resulting from action taken by the institutions of the Community.'[269] Article 10 also imposes a corresponding negative obligation on Member States 'to abstain from any measure which could jeopardi[ze] the attainment of the objectives' of the Treaty.[270] This open-textured duty of loyalty to the Community decisionmaking process seemed at the very least inconsistent with Luxembourg's conclusion of bilateral agreements with its Eastern European partners on access to inland waterways in the Duchy. The Court declined to apply *ERTA* to find exclusive Community competence (reasoning that the internal Community legislation on inland waterways did not govern the conditions for access by non-Community carriers to the national transport of goods or passengers by inland waterway in a Member State).[271] But the Court nonetheless accepted that Article 10 frames a duty of genuine cooperation that is 'of general application' and 'does not depend either on whether the Community competence concerned is exclusive or on any right of the Member States to enter into any obligations towards non-Member countries.'[272]

Accordingly, the Court found that the decision of the Council authorizing the Commission to negotiate a multilateral agreement on behalf of the Community 'mark[ed] the start of a concerted Community action at international level.'[273] As such, the Member States faced 'if not a duty of abstention . . . at the very least a duty of close co-operation' with the Community institutions in order to achieve the Community tasks 'and to ensure the coherence and consistency of the action and its international representation.'[274]

2   A Synthesis of the Community's External Competence

From this series of cases, therefore, a jurisprudence of external competence has emerged that grants exclusivity to the Community not only in the traditional *ERTA*

---

269. EC Treaty art. 10.
270. *Id.*
271. Comm'n *v.* Luxembourg, *supra* note 255, paras. 48 & 50 (stating that 'the fact that [the relevant Regulation] does not govern the situation of carriers established in third countries operating within the Community demonstrates that the harmonization achieved by that regulation is not complete'). Thus, again, in the absence of a complete harmonization in a given area, *see id.* para. 45, the Court requires a conceptual nexus (whether implicit or explicit) between the internal Community legislation and an effect on non-Community nationals sufficient to trigger the exclusivity of the Community's external competence.
272. *Id.* para. 58.
273. *Id.* para. 60.
274. *Id.*. It was common ground, according to the Court, that Luxembourg negotiated, concluded, ratified, and implemented the contested bilateral agreements 'without cooperating or consulting with the Commission.' Comm'n *v.* Luxembourg, *supra* note 255, para. 61. Although the Luxembourg Government argued that its negotiations (at least with two of its target bilateral partners) had opened before the Council's decision to authorize the Commission to open negotiations, 'the fact remains that the contested bilateral agreements were all signed and ratified after that date.' *Id.* para. 63.

circumstances but also in situations where the Commission has successfully per-suaded the Council of the European Union to allow Community engagement in external negotiations (even if those negotiations have not produced a tangible agreement). This is quite a different outcome from the 1994 opinion, which con-ceded exclusive supranational competence to the Community only with respect to the traditional GATT sphere of international trade in goods (including cross-frontier supply of services, which the Court assimilated to trade in goods). With respect to most of the GATS, including transport services, the right of establish-ment, and the right to provide services, the Court treated the supranational author-ity as effectively *concurrent*, not exclusive, and required that the Member States should also sign the WTO instruments to preserve their rights in those areas where the Community had not yet established internal common policies (and thereby staked a claim to exclusive external competence to the extent that Member State bilateral – or multilateral – action could affect those common policies).[275]

Given the Community's undoubted international legal capacity, the direction of the Court's jurisprudence legitimizes the Commission's serial solicitation of exclusive mandates from the Council to negotiate air transport agreements on behalf of all of the Member States.[276] The Community *has* exercised its internal compe-tence to establish a common air transport policy. To the extent that the policy affects third-country nationals, the *ERTA* doctrine (as applied in the open skies judgments) has already displaced the separate negotiating competencies of the Member States. To the extent that the Council of the European Union has already granted negotiation mandates to the Commission for plenary treaty discussions with the United States and other countries, and (in respect solely of the nationality clauses) with the rest of the world,[277] Article 10 of the EC Treaty (as applied in *Commission v. Luxembourg*) establishes a duty of close cooperation between the Member States and the Commission in order to facilitate the Commission's discharge of these mandates.

The measuring standards used by the Commission in developing this juris-prudence date back to Neil Kinnock's tenure as EU Transport Commissioner in the mid-1990s. Long before the Court of Justice open skies rulings in 2002, Kinnock specifically cautioned Member States participating in the U.S. bilateral program that 'no one can seriously doubt' that there is exclusive Community competence 'where agreements with third countries affect *or potentially affect* [supranational] rules.'[278] The implications of a decade of this jurisdictional

---

275. *See* the Court's summary of its holding in Opinion 1/94, *supra* note 233, para. 96 (stating that provisions in EC internal legislative acts, or express conferment of powers, create exclusive competence; similarly, this exclusivity arises 'where the Community has achieved "complete harmonization" of the rules governing access to a self-employed activity, because the common rules thus adopted could be affected if the Member States retained freedom to negotiate with non-member countries').

276. *See infra* Part III(D).

277. *See id.*

278. *Commissioner Kinnock Takes Off on 'Open Skies,' Blasts Civil Aviation Deals with Member Countries*, 7 EuroWatch (Economics, Policy and Law in the New Europe), Apr. 21, 1995, at 12 (emphasis added).

sparring – which, if the Commission ultimately prevails in its quest for broad negotiating mandates, will involve the supersession of many hundreds of bilateral treaties[279] – will be revisited in the concluding Part of this Chapter.[280]

III   AN APPRAISAL OF MULTILATERAL AIRLINE DEREGULATION IN THE EC: GUIDEPOSTS FOR THE ERA BEYOND OPEN SKIES

A   THE DEMONSTRATION EFFECT OF THE EUROPEAN EXPERIMENT

Over 15 years after the adoption of the final package, and more than a decade after full achievement of a de-cabotaged single aviation market, it is appropriate to examine some key structural issues of the functioning single aviation market and the legal and policy tools being used by the EC to address them. This analysis will provide further 'demonstration' guidance in the search for a new code of plurilateral deregulation for the international air transport system. As an experiment in *international* airline deregulation, the EC offers an even more compelling precedent than the U.S. model, although, as will be seen, many of the conditions of competition that have emerged in the Community regime reflect phenomena already encountered in earlier discussions of the U.S. experience.

In its 1994 report, the *Comité des Sages* confidently proclaimed that '[t]he concept of the national carrier no longer fits into the regulatory pattern of the [t]hird [p]ackage.'[281] While this assertion accurately captured and foretold the *potential* of Community airline liberalization, after 15 years the industry is still in an uncertain transition from a motley assortment of large and small flagship airlines (virtually all of them sustained in the early years of deregulation by repeated trips to the well of public subsidy), toward a market-driven stratification of private transnationally-owned carriers serving regional or international networks under the discipline of both national and supranational competition laws. As the European Commission underscored in its own earliest assessment of the post-1992 airline industry, '[t]he single market [in aviation] is an economic process, not merely a legal act.'

---

279.   *See* the estimate of approximately 60 extra-Union treaties for each Member State (a grand total in 1995 of 900) made by KLM official Eugenie Kalshoven-van Tijen in her article, *The EEC Commission as the European Version of the CAB?*, 15 AIR. L. 257, 263-64 (1990). Why an 'estimate'? As the U.K. Civil Aviation Authority has noted, the 'openness' of most bilateral agreements with the United States is an exception in international aviation relations, and the Authority was unable in its study of long-haul international routes to analyze in detail the current state of bilateral relationships between EU Member States and non-EU countries other than the United States. *See* [U.K.] Civil Aviation Authority, *Airline Competition on European Long Haul Routes*, at 41-42, CAP 639 (Nov. 1994) [hereinafter [U.K.] CAA, *Airline Competition*].

280.   *See infra* Part III(G).

281.   Report of the *Comité des Sages*, *supra* note 39, at 22.

In anticipation of a design for a new international aviation order, this study inspected the present condition of the U.S deregulation experiment using a series of phenomena that have affected the idealized market system that deregulators hoped to unleash. In the EC's internal aviation market, although it has existed for only half the time of its U.S. predecessor, it is similarly possible to examine certain phenomena of law and policy that are continuing to shape this prototypical venture into international airline liberalization. Some of these phenomena – competition enforcement, alliances, allocation of scarce slot and gate capacity, global distribution systems, consumer protection – are challenges of deregulation that are substantially shared with the U.S. experience. But others, notably the organization of the EC's external aviation relations, the intra-Community 'de-nationalization' of Member State airlines, tailoring of a transnational merger policy to the strictures of the Chicago system, and the State subsidization of home carriers, have been unique to the European adventure in air transport reform.[282] Each set of issues will be examined in turn, beginning with the phenomena that have the clearest parallels with issues confronted in the period of U.S. reform.

B   REPRISING THE U.S. EXPERIENCE: PROTECTING COMPETITION IN A DEREGULATED ERA

1   **Europe's FTC: The Shifting Role of the European Commission**

As a general matter, the trio of legislative reform packages[283] viewed the European Commission as enforcer of last resort with respect to the fare and market access regimes, and of first resort with respect to application of supranational competition law to the Union's airline industry. The recent so-called 'modernization' of the Community's general competition regime[284] is intended to decentralize enforcement of Articles 81 and 82 of the EC Treaty, attempting to implant a more localized enforcement culture through the national judicial systems and national competition authorities. While it remains to be seen whether this ambitious attempt at subsidiarity can transform the competition enforcement culture in the Community, the transnational complexion of the airline industry, coupled with the catalytic role of the Commission in the air transport liberalization process – and its constitutional role as guarantor of the Treaty – will combine to assure its continued primacy in airline competition enforcement.[285]

---

282. For some observations on the antagonisms generated by U.S. airline bailouts after Sept. 11, 2001, as well as the availability of Chapter 11 bankruptcy relief to troubled U.S. carriers, *see supra* Chapter 4, Part IV(C).
283. *See supra* Part II(C).
284. *See supra* Part II(D).
285. Article 15(3) of Council Regulation 1/2003, *supra* note 127, requires Member States to forward to the Commission a copy of any written judgment of national courts deciding on the application of Articles 81 and 82 of the EC Treaty. Nonconfidential versions of these

Moreover, the persistence of a regulatory watchdog role for the Commission is unremarkable in the context of a multinational airline liberalization project: the U.S. DOT, as explored in Chapter 4, has retained custodial powers in international air transport that it long ago surrendered in the domestic arena. In Community competition law (and certainly as it affects the airlines), even after the modernization effort the Commission will continue to function as an international amalgam of the joint U.S. federal enforcement agencies, the Antitrust Division of the Department of Justice and the Federal Trade Commission. A decade and a half after adoption of the third package, however, there has been a visible recalibration of the Commission's airline competition enforcement agenda. At the beginning, the Commission was stewarding a new (and for some, painful)[286] economic order. It needed to keep track of Member State invocation of the various safeguard clauses[287] and to watch many microeconomic market variables, including the

---

judgments are filed and publicly available in the Commission's National Court Cases Database. *See* <http://ec.europa.eu/competition/elojade/antitrust/nationalcourts/>. As of mid-2008, it appears that no cases had been filed that concerned air transport competition.

286. The Commission unilaterally assumed the mantle of keeper of the deregulatory faith in order to counter what were recurrent outbursts of Member State (and flag carrier) fractiousness as the deregulation experiment took hold. Then-Competition Commissioner Karel van Miert cautioned the participants at a Council of Transport Ministers meeting in Sept. 1993 against 'a certain nostalgia for the co[z]y, state-bankrolled cartels' that preceded European airline deregulation, pledging that there would be 'no backtracking' on the supranational reform enterprise. David Gardner, *No Backtracking on 'Open Skies' Policy, Says Brussels*, FIN. TIMES, Sept. 28, 1993, at 20. Van Miert used this uncompromising language to repudiate a working paper from the Belgian presidency (Belgium then held the six-month rotating presidency of the Council of the European Union) calling for the reintroduction of capacity sharing and specific Community funding for ailing carriers. The meeting had been summoned to discuss the financial crisis in the EU civil aviation industry. Van Miert accused the airlines of lobbying Member States for new price and capacity cartels. A large majority of the Member States rejected a return to capacity collusion or joint price-setting, and the Commissioner himself ruled out any special EC funding to give succor to weakened carriers. Van Miert, who as Commissioner for Transportation had earlier approved large capital injections into Sabena, Air France, and Iberia, reaffirmed that these were 'last-chance' rescues. *See* Gardner, *supra*, at 20; *see infra* Part III(F) (discussing State aids).

287. Note, however, that because Member States could protest adverse Commission decisions to the Council of the European Union under the safeguard clauses (for example, in cases of alleged predatory pricing or infrastructural emergencies), it was only in 'pure' competition cases, such as general Article 81 enforcement, mergers, State aids, and alleged violation of the block exemptions, that the Commission's power was administratively unimpaired (subject, of course, to ultimate review by the judicial organs of the Community). *See generally* Valgerdur Bjarnadóttir, *Air Transport, European Economic Integration, Effects of '1992' on the Services Sectors of the EFTA Countries*, at 7, EFTA Occasional Paper No. 49 (Dec. 1994). As seen earlier, the safeguard clauses were virtually unused. Even in 1994, when Member States might have been expected to invoke them to stave off some of the full effects of deregulation on national carriers, the Commission reported that no State had requested the use of the safeguard clauses to correct downward spirals in air fares (Article 6 of Council Regulation 2409/92, *supra* note 124), or to impose temporary capacity freezes (Article 10 of Council Regulation 2408/92, *supra* note 130). The Commission also commented, evidently with some

power of dominant airlines to squeeze out new competitors through inflated capacity or frequency, to pay inflated override commissions to travel agents, to engage in predatory pricing behavior, or to refuse to interline.[288] And, finally, the Commission monitored airline cooperative practices under its various block exemptions.[289]

As the deregulated market has evolved, however, the Commission has seemed less concerned with flyspecking the details of how airlines are competing in the marketplace than with the broader competitive implications of airline behavior. Moreover, the Commission has increasingly identified airport access – at a premium because of congestion and slot scarcity – as critical to airline development.[290] Indeed, a review of the past decade of Commission competition reports discloses much more attention to the microeconomics of airport supply-side behavior, including decisions opening access to the groundhandling market[291] and overturning discriminatory landing charges.[292] With respect to inter-airline competition,

---

disappointment, that 'public debate' had ignored the presence of these specific safeguards in the third aviation package. European Commission, *The Way Forward, supra* note 141, at 11.

288. *See* Press Release, European Commission, IP/90/26, for a list of predatory practices that would have been expected to attract Commission attention under its now-defunct *prima facie* enforcement powers. In the past 15 years, there has been little published evidence (and almost no case law) concerning Commission scrutiny of airline anticompetitive behavior, notably control of predatory practices, including price dumping and unfair marketing devices. The predatory practice suit brought by British Midland against Aer Lingus in 1992 remains the most concrete illustration of Commission intervention. *See* ADKINS, *supra* note 124, at 96 (reporting two 'informal' price predation complaints to the Commission). *See also* ANGELA CHENG-JUI LU, INTERNATIONAL AIRLINE ALLIANCES 102 (2003) (noting paucity of airline price predation cases). Price predation, in any case, has become an example of a competition doctrine out of favor in a consumer-driven industry, and the Commission abandoned a recent suggestion that the 2008 consolidated regulation should award it renewed investigative powers with respect to very low prices charged by the industry's low-cost carriers. *See supra* note 126.

289. *See supra* Part II(D). *But see supra* note 194 (noting that all of the block exemptions have now expired).

290. *See* EUROPEAN COMMISSION, EUROPEAN COMMUNITY COMPETITION POLICY: XXVIITH REPORT ON COMPETITION POLICY 38 (1998).

291. *See, e.g.,* the Commission's decision under Article 82 of the EC Treaty requiring Aéroports de Paris (ADP) to introduce a nondiscriminatory system of commercial fees for groundhandling services. O.J. (L 230) 10-27. ADP lodged an application for annulment of that decision, which was dismissed on all grounds by the Court of First Instance in December 2000. *See* ADP *v.* Comm'n, 2000 E.C.R. II-3929. The court ruling is important for the Commission's efforts to ensure nondiscriminatory access to transport infrastructure, since it classifies the operation of an airport as a business and uses the Article 82 designation of an 'undertaking' to describe the airport operator. *See* EUROPEAN COMMISSION, EUROPEAN COMMUNITY COMPETITION POLICY: XXXTH REPORT ON COMPETITION POLICY 42 (2000).

292. As part of its trusteeship of a nondiscriminatory business environment in the Community, the Commission has been scrutinizing landing fees at all European airports since 1995 (when it ruled that the system of discounts at the main Brussels airport infringed Community law). *See id.* As part of a massive regulatory package for airports, the Commission has proposed a directive for airport charges 'requiring total transparency, user-consultation and the

the more broadly-focused perspective is best typified in the Commission's engagement with Ryanair in relation to that airline's receipt of public aid to establish air service at Charleroi airport, an underutilized facility some 60 miles east of the Belgian (and EU) capital, Brussels.[293] The Ryanair controversy was used by the Commission as an opportunity to clarify its thinking on the use of regional financial assistance to the airline sector to spur economic growth through creation of new services. In addition, the Commission (as it has in other industries) has occasionally opened a splashy antitrust investigation (for example, in 2005 it announced a price-fixing investigation of several EU and U.S. cargo carriers).[294]

2   Two Case Studies in Supranational Trusteeship: The Article 82 'Dominance' Factor

As the U.S. experience has amply demonstrated, genuine competition does not mean merely scrapping existing restrictions, but also using *ex post* regulatory powers to tackle discrimination targeted against new or expanding airlines seeking access to routes or airport facilities, or to exercise price or service leadership. Although enforcement may oscillate in intensity as a result of changing political or administrative priorities, these principles are enduring. Article 82 targets many types of abusive action designed to reinforce an undertaking's marketplace pre-eminence.[295] These actions must objectively influence the structure of the market by restricting the freedom of choice of other market participants (or aspiring participants).[296] Price predation, for example, has been viewed as *par excellence* an instance of monopolistic abuse and has been so found by the European Court of Justice.[297] The following case studies (one of a Commission decision, the other of

---

application of the principle of non-discrimination when calculating charges levied on [airport] users.' *See* Press Release, Europa, Commission Proposes Landmark Regulatory Package for Airports, IP/07/78 (Jan. 24, 2007). The proposal also seeks to establish a robust and independent dispute settlement and arbitration authority. *Id.*; *see also* European Commission, *Proposal for a Directive of the European Parliament and of the Council on Airport Charges*, COM (2006) 820 final (Jan. 24, 2007).

293. The Ryanair matter is considered at length in the discussion on State aids, *infra* Part III(F).

294. *See supra* note 181.

295. The abusive practices expressly cited in Article 82 are merely illustrative, 'not an exhaustive enumeration of the sort of abuses of a dominant position prohibited by the Treaty.' Case 6/72, Europemballage Corp. *v.* Commission (*Continental Can*), 1973 E.C.R. 215, 245; *see also* Case C-95/104, British Airways plc *v.* Comm'n, para. 57, 2007 E.C.R. I-2331 (this case is discussed *infra* in the main text) [hereinafter BA *v.* Comm'n (Judgment)].

296. *See*, for example, the Court's essay on 'dominance' in Case 85/76, Hoffman-La Roche *v.* Comm'n, 1979 E.C.R. 461, 520, which includes the following:

The dominant position thus referred to [in Article 82] relates to a position of economic strength enjoyed by an undertaking which enables it to prevent effective competition being maintained in the relevant market by affording it the power to behave to an appreciable extent independently of its competitors, its customers and ultimately of the consumers.

297. *See* Case C-62/86, Akzo Chemie B.V. *v.* Comm'n, 1991 E.C.R. I-3359, 3455, in which the Court found that '[p]rices below the average variable costs (that is to say, those which vary

an appellate review of a Commission decision), illustrate a movement toward greater sophistication in perceiving competition as not merely auxiliary to an *idée fixe* of what a competitive marketplace should look like, but also as an autonomous construct that preserves a 'system' of competition rather than any particular synchronic industry structure.

a   *An Early Example: British Midland v. Aer Lingus*

The first exemplar of Commission enforcement under Article 82, *British Midland Airways v. Aer Lingus,*[298] revealed that the Commission in its early period of airline competition enforcement was just as willing to employ considerations of industrial policy as to behave as an objective superintendent of the competitive structure. The case concerned the issue of a refusal to interline. Interlining is the oldest form of airline route cooperation, long antedating code-sharing and alliances, and provides passengers with the option of switching freely between airlines and alternative routings, a boon particularly for the business traveler.[299] It usefulness in an era of proliferating code-share, cooperation, and alliance agreements has been questioned, particularly when intra-EU traffic has become dominated by direct flights (the core of the low-cost business model) that require little or no interlining.[300] In 1992, however, interlining was by far the most prevalent form of inter-airline collaboration, and the Commission naturally saw the availability of

---

depending on the quantities produced) by means of which a dominant undertaking seeks to eliminate a competitor must be regarded as abusive. A dominant undertaking has no interest in applying such prices except that of eliminating competitors so as to enable it subsequently to raise its prices by taking advantage of its monopolistic position, since each sale generates a loss. . . .' The Court's attitude toward predation has not mirrored the skepticism that now informs the U.S. Supreme Court's doctrinal analysis, *see* discussion *supra* Chapter 4, IV(B).

298. Commission Decision 213/92, 1992 O.J. (L 96) 34 (*British Midland*).
299. *See* IATA, *Maintaining the Multilateral Interline System,* IATA Policy Paper (Jul. 2002) [hereinafter IATA Policy Paper]. The premise of 'interlining' (as explained in the Commission's decision, *British Midland, supra* note 298, at 35) is that airlines are authorized to sell each other's services. As a result, a single ticket can be issued which comprises segments to be performed by different airlines. The airline which issues the ticket collects the price for all segments from the passenger, and then pays the fare due to the carrying airline (less a service charge). Over 350 carriers participate in IATA's Multilateral Interline Traffic Agreement (MITA). *See* IATA, IATA Multilateral Interline Traffic Agreements (MITA), <www. iata.org/workgroups/mita.htm>. Because of interlining, passengers can buy a single ticket providing for transportation by different carriers, while airlines are enabled to complement their networks and frequencies. Interlining 'has been hailed as one of IATA's major achievements.' *Id.* In the past, the Commission repeatedly approved interlining as an exempted cooperative practice under its block exemption regulations. *See supra* note 198; *but see supra* note 196 (discussing the Commission's unwillingness to continue the block exemption as intra-Union interlining has decreased substantially in scope). On the distinction between interlining and the more recent phenomenon of code-sharing, *see supra* Chapter 3, Part VIII.
300. *See infra* note 310 (examining the practices of low-cost carriers with respect to interlining). *See generally* European Commission, DG Competition, *Concerning the Revision and Possible Prorogation of Commission Regulation 1617/93 on the Application of Article 81(3) to Certain Categories of Agreements and Concerted Practices Concerning Consultations on Passenger*

interlining relationships as a desirable accompaniment, if not a prerequisite, to a functionally competitive marketplace.

Acting on a complaint by the second-largest U.K.-based carrier, privately-owned British Midland Airways (known as bmi since early 2003), against the State-sponsored Irish flag airline, Aer Lingus,[301] the Commission examined whether the refusal of Aer Lingus to 'interline' its tickets with bmi on the London Heathrow/Dublin route constituted an abuse of the Irish airline's 'dominant position' on that route. Because of the recalcitrance of Aer Lingus, defying what was then customary industry practice,[302] travel agents could not issue tickets with an outward journey on bmi and a return journey on Aer Lingus (allowing the passenger to take advantage of an optimal mix of schedules, for example).[303]

Even in a competitive climate where interlining flourished, the Commission did not want to place itself in the position of *forcing* Aer Lingus to interline. Yet it also recognized the competitive disadvantage bmi faced as a new entrant on the London/ Dublin route, where Aer Lingus had the multiple advantages of a long incumbency protected by government warrant, national customer loyalty, high frequency of services, access to scarce slots at Heathrow, and a fairly stable 75% market share (unaffected, the Commission found, by demand substitutability of surface transport or supply substitutability of alternative airport connections).[304] The Commission found that the simultaneity of high market share and barriers to entry was 'indicative of dominance' (which, while not itself a violation of Article 82 of the EC Treaty, is nonetheless the legal predicate for a possible abuse of a dominant position).[305]

Tariffs on Scheduled Air Services and Slot Allocation at Airports, paras. 15 & 17, Discussion Paper (Mar. 2, 2005) (noting that 85% of tickets issued for travel within the EU are for direct flights and will not likely involve interlining, and that bilateral cooperation agreements provide viable alternatives to the IATA interlining system within the Union). Globally, however, IATA claims that interlining accounts for over $20 billion worth of passenger and cargo business for airlines worldwide. *See* IATA Policy Paper, *supra* note 299, annex, para. 3.

301. Beginning in Oct. 2006, the Irish Government floated Aer Lingus shares on the Dublin stock exchange, with Ryanair, Aer Lingus staff, and the government itself becoming the largest stockholders.

302. Traditionally, agreement or 'concurrence' to an application to interline was 'hardly ever refused,' the exception being where currency convertibility or the financial stability of the applicant were not assured. *Id.* But the Commission feared (largely correctly, as it turned out) that interlining as a standard practice might not survive liberalization of the air transport market. *See* ADKINS, *supra* note 124, at 35.

303. In the Commission's view, absence of interlinability would particularly disadvantage business travelers – the staple of an airline's business. *See British Midland, supra* note 298, at 35-36. The alternative to interlining, in the absence of intercarrier arrangements such as code-sharing, would be to purchase separate tickets for each flight, a less efficient option for passengers and a less remunerative one for travel agents. *Id.* at 36.

304. Over a decade later, the Aer Lingus market share on this route had been cut to 33%, primarily by the impact of Ryanair's low-cost service. Bmi, meanwhile, continued to capture a 15% share. *See* UK Airport News, *Ryanair is Top for Dublin to London Passengers* (Jun. 1, 2006), <www. uk-airport-news.info/stansted-airport-news-010606b.htm> (citing U.K. CAA statistics).

305. *British Midland, supra* note 298, at 39. *See infra* in this Part for another case study of the application of Article 82.

Indeed, the Commission noted that 'the mere fact that Aer Lingus was able to disregard the complaints of travel agents and business travelers suffering from the refusal to interline' demonstrated the airline's 'appreciable freedom of action' on the disputed route.[306]

Ultimately, the Commission found Aer Lingus in breach of *both* Articles 81 and 82 of the EC Treaty. The Article 82 violation was premised on the airline's 'abusive conduct' toward a new competitor. The Commission purposefully centered its analysis on competitive damage to *new entry*, rather than generalized damage to competition. In support, the Commission cited the definition of 'abusive conduct' established by the European Court of Justice in *Hoffman-La Roche v. Commission*:[307]

> practices which are likely to affect the structure of a market where, as a result of the presence of the undertaking in question, competition has already been weakened and which, through recourse to methods differing from those governing normal competition in goods or services based on traders' performance, have the effect of hindering the maintenance or development of the level of competition existing on the market.[308]

'Refusing to interline,' in the Commission's view, was 'not normal competition on the merits.'[309] The Commission discounted the unabashed plea of Aer Lingus that it had withdrawn interlining simply to avoid losing several points of market share to a new entrant, and held that refusal of new interlining and revocation of existing interlining could, depending on circumstances, each hinder the development of competition, whether by preventing a new service or disrupting an existing service. The only legitimate defense a dominant airline could offer for suspending interline privileges would be an objective commercial reason (such as concerns about creditworthiness[310]), but Aer Lingus could hardly propound such a justification

---

306. *British Midland, supra* note 298, at 39.
307. Case 85/76, 1979 E.C.R. 461.
308. *Id.* at 541.
309. *British Midland, supra* note 298, at 40.
310. As a general rule, the newer low-cost model of airline services eschews interlining (probably for efficiency and administrative reasons but also because, empirically, the typical low-cost passenger travels – and prefers to travel – on direct services to a specific destination point). A no-interlining policy, therefore, could be advanced by a low-cost carrier as a legitimate commercial reason for declining to interline in a given market (assuming that the policy is applied uniformly to other carriers in the same and other markets). *See* Ryanair, Making a Reservation, <http://www.ryanair.com/site/EN/faqs.php?sect=pnr&quest=connections> ('Can I book a connecting flight with Ryanair? No. Ryanair is strictly a "point-to-point" airline. We therefore do not offer, and cannot facilitate, the transfer of passengers or their baggage to other flights, whether operated by Ryanair or other carriers'); *see also* easyJet, Carrier's Regulations, <http://www.easyjet.com/EN/Book/regulations.html> ('...easyJet does not operate a connecting flight service [and] where you choose to book such an onward flight this will be considered to be a separate journey') For Aer Lingus at the time of the bmi dispute, however, interlining was a normal part of its business and a selective refusal to interline, coupled with the Irish carrier's dominance on the London Heathrow/Dublin route, gave rise to the anticompetitive effect.

when it singled out an airline with which it previously interlined, immediately after that airline started to compete on an important route.[311]

But the Commission delivered its strongest reproof with respect to using denial of interlining as a weapon against upstart entry. Travel agents and business travelers, under the then-prevailing market structure, would shun carriers that lacked interlining privileges, vastly increasing the task of building market share and profitability.[312] Passengers (and the agents acting on their instructions) would prefer to 'play safe' and to use the service of the airline with the highest frequency, in this instance the Dublin-based carrier.[313] Thus, by denying interlining privileges to bmi contrary to normal industry practice, the Commission found that Aer Lingus pursued a deliberate corporate strategy of imposing higher costs on bmi and depriving it of revenue.[314] Aer Lingus could point to no 'efficiencies' created by its refusal to interline, nor to any other 'persuasive and legitimate business justification.'[315] In these circumstances, the Commission concluded that Aer Lingus had breached Article 82 by abusing its dominant position in the London/Dublin air market.[316] The Commission's inculcation of new entry led it to impose a limited term obligation on Aer Lingus to interline with bmi on the contested route, although it felt uncomfortable with mandating Aer Lingus permanently to interline and indeed explicitly disavowed the existence of any such obligation.[317]

Yet the Commission's stated rationale for this reticence seems to have had less to do with competition policy than with an unarticulated sensitivity to a 1992 iteration of its industrial policy. If a refusal to interline were truly an anticompetitive act, it would likely remain so irrespective of the endurance of the act or the profile of the target (new entrant or established player). The Commission, however, appeared to suggest that only new entrants, and only at the commencement of their entry, could be victims of such a refusal. According to its reasoning, if a dominant airline develops a high frequency service, that is a legitimate competitive advantage which it need not necessarily share with rivals.[318] Nor should a new entrant be able to rely 'forever' on its competitors' frequencies and networks.[319] Clearly, according to the Commission, nonparticipation in interlining was *not* intrinsically perceived as an anticompetitive act; it would become so only

---

311. *British Midland, supra* note 298, at 40.
312. 'A new entrant without interlining facilities is likely to be considered . . . as a second-rate airline by travel agents and travelers alike, which will make it more difficult to attain the commercial standing required to operate profitably.' *Id.* at 40.
313. *Id.*
314. *Id.* at 41.
315. *Id.*
316. Four years earlier, in its *Sabena* decision, the Commission had delivered an equally skeptical reading of incumbent behavior toward new entry.
317. *British Midland, supra* note 298, at 44. The Commission's expression of caution has been justified by the rise of a low-cost carrier business model that abandons interlining. *See supra* note 310.
318. *British Midland, supra* note 298, at 44.
319. *Id.*

because of a Commission policy – voguish in the immediate aftermath of the third package – to encourage start-up entry. Thus, while new entry is always an expected corollary of successful competition enforcement, its encouragement in the circumstances of the *British Midland* decision was arguably more an application of a paternalistic *industrial* policy.[320] Hence the Commission's overt conclusion that the new entrant 'must' be encouraged to build up extensive networks and high frequencies by itself, and that bmi, for example, should be protected from 'an undue handicap imposed by its dominant competitor contrary to the industry's and that competitor's normal practice.'[321]

b   *Focusing on the Competitive Structure: The Travel Agency Incentives Case*

A recent set of judicial decisions in *British Airways plc v. Commission of the European Communities*[322] helpfully elucidates the current approach of the Community competition authorities to the 'abuse' condition of the Article 82 antimonopolization law. The Commission decision of July 14, 1999, prompted initially by a complaint by Virgin Atlantic Airways Ltd., a British Airways (BA) competitor, fined BA nearly 7 million euro for abuse of its dominant position on the U.K. travel agency market.[323] The judgment of the Court of First Instance (CFI) sought to determine under what circumstances the granting of certain kinds of

---

320. The Commission's most recent iteration of an industrial policy for air transport, however, has a quite different content. *See infra* Part III(G).
321. *British Midland, supra* note 298, at 44. The asserted breach of Article 85, in contrast, was manifestly technical. Aer Lingus had participated in an IATA tariff-coordinating conference in 1991. The Commission had granted a block exemption for consultations on passenger tariffs provided (*inter alia*) that those consultations contributed to the 'generalized acceptance of interlinable fares . . . to the benefit of air carriers as well as air transport users.' Aer Lingus attended and voted at the conference (including a vote on higher fares) while announcing that it would not participate in consultations concerning routes from Dublin to Amsterdam, London, and Paris. Nevertheless, the tariff consultations covered routes generally (including Dublin/Heathrow) as well as certain specific routes between Dublin and destinations served directly by Aer Lingus and indirectly by bmi. In these circumstances, the Commission found that Aer Lingus had not respected the conditions specified in the block exemption for tariff consultations, and that its participation in the consultations while refusing to interline with bmi was an infringement of Article 81(1). Perhaps the Commission additionally imposed a technical Article 81(1) violation to emphasize its concern with what it perceived as a much more blatant violation of Article 82. The Commission reserved the right to reconsider its order in light of changing market conditions. It imposed a substantial fine on Aer Lingus for its violations of Articles 81 and 82. *Id.* at 45.
322. British Airways appealed a European Commission decision enforcing Article 82 against the U.K. airline for abuse of a dominant position. Virgin Atlantic Airways, as the other complainant, was the other party to the proceedings. The 2003 Court of First Instance opinion (discussed in the main text) is at 2003 E.C.R. II-5917 [hereinafter BA *v.* Comm'n (CFI)]. The citation to the subsequent (2007) decision of the European Court of Justice appears *supra* note 295.
323. Travel agents supply airlines with services to promote their air transport operations. They help travelers to choose the services, issue tickets, collect money, and remit it to the airline. In

performance incentive bonuses by a dominant undertaking may be regarded as an abuse within the meaning of Article 82.

BA's various bonus schemes (part of its overall payments of travel agent commissions) had one significant common feature. Any travel agent which met BA's year-on-year target for sales growth would qualify for an increase in the commission paid on *all* tickets sold by the agent, not just on the tickets sold after the target had been reached. The marginal economic effects of this specific methodology disturbed the Commission's mind and later the Court's. Even relatively small changes (upwards or downwards) in sales of BA tickets could have disproportionate effects for the travel agent – by selling only slightly fewer tickets in comparison with a selected prior period, the agent would risk no longer coming, overall, within the benefit of a rebate or bonus, whereas selling slightly more tickets would earn a higher rebate or bonus retrospectively over the agent's entire sales volume and not just for future tickets sold. In that way, as Advocate-General Kokott later argued to the Court of Justice, the agent would be locked into a 'state of uncertainty' as to how high the profit margin with BA's tickets would finally be. The agent became incentivized not to switch to competitors, even in part.[324]

Neither Community law in general nor Article 82 in particular, however, demonizes bonus and rebate incentive schemes *per se*. Their operation, even when they are the brainchild of so-called dominant firms, will be viewed in the circumstances of each case and not through an a prioristic lens of disapproval. Nonetheless, a complex and highly differentiated bonus scheme operated by a dominant firm is bound to arouse suspicion (at the least from market competitors). Moreover, the opinion of the Court of First Instance, as amplified by the Advocate-General, demonstrates that the guiding principle of Article 82 is not so much the measurable empirical consequences of a bonus scheme as its potential (even in the absence of verified actual effects) to do further damage to a market that is already weakened by the presence of a dominant competitor. In other words, Article 82 is not designed only or even primarily to protect the immediate interests of individual competitors or consumers, but to protect the structure of the market and thus competition as such – 'as an institution.'[325]

The first step is to establish the existence of a dominant position in a given market. Applying a market definition analysis that would seem orthodox to

---

return, the airlines pay commissions to the agents based on sales of tickets made through those agents. Case C-95/04, British Airways plc *v.* Comm'n, Opinion of the Advocate General, para. 6, 2007 E.C.R. II-2331 [hereinafter BA *v.* Comm'n (AG Opinion)]. For an analysis of shifting patterns in airline ticket distribution, *see supra* Chapter 4, Part IV(B).

324. BA *v.* Comm'n (AG Opinion), *supra* note 323, para. 50. This is the so-called 'effect at the margin' also perceived by the Court of First Instance, *supra* note 322, paras. 272 & 273. Even a small decrease in BA ticket sales could, the Court found, lead to significant financial losses for a given travel agent. *See id.*

325. BA *v.* Comm'n (AG Opinion), *supra* note 323, para. 68 (noting that 'competition' in the market has already been weakened by the presence of a dominant firm). The Court of First Instance endorsed these arguments. *See* BA *v.* Comm'n (CFI), *supra* note 322, para. 86.

members of the U.S. antitrust priesthood, the Court of First Instance upheld the Commission's definition of the relevant product and geographic markets within which BA had gained dominance (*i.e.*, market power).[326] The Commission defined the product market as comprising the services which airlines purchase from travel agents for the purposes of marketing and distributing their airline tickets.[327] Rejecting BA's argument that the Commission should define the market as the supply of air transport services (and therefore analyze competition more conventionally on a route-by-route basis[328]), the Court held that BA's capacity to act independently of its competitors (a touchstone of dominant behavior) must be viewed more broadly in the context of the competitive conditions and the structure of supply and demand in the market (whatever that market might eventually prove to be).[329] Travel agents are independent intermediaries carrying on business in an independent competitive marketplace where they advise travelers, issue tickets, remit money to airlines, and provide airlines with advertising and commercial promotion services.[330] They provide an irreplaceable distribution service by offering a wider range of air routes, departure, and arrival times than any single airline could and by offering an information-filtering service to simplify (for the traveler) the complexity of airline real-time pricing systems.[331] Major travel agents individually negotiate agreements for the distribution of air tickets and are thus in a position to 'set the airlines in competition.'[332]

Within this market understanding, according to the Court, BA is not a supplier (or seller) at all, but a *purchaser* of air travel agency services – and it is possible both for a seller and a purchaser to hold a dominant position within the meaning of Article 82.[333] BA's proposed route-based product market definition would measure its economic strength as a provider of air transport services but not as a purchaser of travel agency services *on all routes to and from United Kingdom airports* (either in relation to all other airlines in the same purchaser capacity or in relation to United Kingdom travel agents).[334]

---

326. BA did not appeal the Court's delimitation of the market (product or geographic) to the Court of Justice. *See* BA *v.* Comm'n (AG Opinion), *supra* note 323, para. 22.
327. BA *v.* Comm'n (CFI), *supra* note 322, para. 89.
328. *Id.* para. 78 (*i.e.*, whether a single supplier of air transportation services on a particular route can profitably increase its prices).
329. *Id.* para. 91.
330. *Id.* paras. 92-93.
331. *Id.* paras. 95-98.
332. *Id.* para. 98 (a proposition, according to the Court, recognized by BA itself).
333. *Id.* para. 101-02.
334. BA *v.* Comm'n (CFI), *supra* note 322, para.104. As the Commission stated, *see id.* para. 87, it has previously classified travel agency services as a distinct market. *See* Commission Decision 91/480/EEC of Jul. 30, 1991 Relating to a Proceeding Pursuant to Article 81 of the Treaty (Case No. IV/32.659 – IATA Passenger Agency Programme), 1991 O.J. (L 258) 18. It has also sliced off other markets related to air travel as separate product markets. *See* Commission Decision 88/589/EEC of 4 November 1988 Relating to a Proceeding Under Article 82 of the

The Commission (and the Court) might have constructed an atomized geographic market definition (regionally biased, for example) that may or may or may not have affected the specification of BA's dominant position.[335] Instead, both bodies found that the distribution of airline tickets takes place at national level and that (consequently) airlines purchase the services for distributing those tickets on a national basis.[336]

In the second step of its analysis, the Commission examined whether BA's market share placed it in a dominant position in the relevant product and geographic markets.[337] The dominance referred to in Article 82, as the Court noted, relates to a firm's position of economic strength which enables it to prevent effective competition being maintained in the relevant markets by giving it the power to behave to an appreciable extent independently of its competitors, of its customers, and ultimately of its consumers.[338] BA, understandably, sought once again to shift the Court's attention to the intensity of competition in air transport services (a vain effort in view of the Court's embrace of the Commission's travel agency-based market definitions), contending that it is unable to act as an independent pricer in relation either to its route-by-route competitors or to travelers who have power to choose their carrier on each route.[339] The regulators, and the Court, advanced a simple but powerful statistical showing that BA's market share (of tickets sold through travel agents) constitutes a multiple of the market shares of each of its five main

---

Treaty (IV/32.318, London European – Sabena), 1988 O. J. (L 317) 47 [hereinafter *Sabena*]. In *Sabena*, the product market for the computer reservations system was immediately apparent: for the travel agent industry these systems have effectively superseded consultations of written schedules and tariffs and telephoned reservations through airlines. They have become 'an important feature of [a new airline's] marketing policy.' *Id.* at 49.

335. According to the Court, case law shows that the geographic market definition is the territory in which all traders operate in the same or sufficiently homogeneous conditions of competition in so far as concerns specifically the relevant products or services, without those conditions having to be perfectly homogeneous. BA *v.* Comm'n (CFI), *supra* note 322, para. 108.

336. *Id.* para. 111. Moreover, travel agents' handling of air tickets is carried out in the context of IATA's national plans for bank settlement and in this case through the Billing and Settlement Plan for the United Kingdom. *See id.* para. 112. Nor could BA dispute its own application of its bonus schemes in a uniform manner over the whole of the United Kingdom. *See id.* para. 113. In *Sabena, supra* note 334, the territory of Belgium constituted the product market in which the computer reservations system benefited Belgian consumers booking flights on the Brussels/Luton route. *Id.* at 50. As the decision notes, both the Commission and the Court of Justice have recognized that 'the territories of both large and medium-sized countries' constitute a substantial part of the common market. This satisfies the criterion of 'substantiality.' *Id. See* Case 127/73, BRT *v.* SABAM, 1974 E.C.R. 313. BA argued unsuccessfully that the relevant geographic market was broader than the United Kingdom, BA *v.* Comm'n (CFI), *supra* note 322, para. 83, given that many larger travel agents operated in several countries.

337. BA did not appeal the Court's assessment of its dominant position to the Court of Justice. *See* BA *v.* Comm'n (AG Opinion), *supra* note 323, para. 22.

338. BA *v.* Comm'n (CFI), *supra* note 322, para. 189 (citing Case T-128/98, Aéroports de Paris *v.* Comm'n, para. 147, 2000 E.C.R. II-3929).

339. BA *v.* Comm'n (CFI), *supra* note 322, paras. 175-76.

competitors in the national market for air travel agency services.[340] Pivoting back to the supply side, the Court reinforced BA's market power among travel agents through mention of its world rank in international scheduled passenger-kilometers flown, as well as its hub network (and hence its wider choice of routes and flight frequency).[341] The cumulative effect of BA's strength in services to and from the United Kingdom was to generate purchase by travelers of a preponderant number of BA air tickets through travel agents established in the United Kingdom.[342] Accordingly, these travel agents substantially depend on the income they receive from BA in consideration of their air travel agency services.[343]

As noted previously, Article 82 in no sense proscribes the mere *possession* of dominance,[344] and so there is, necessarily, a third step in the examination, which is to test for 'abuse' of dominance.[345] In Community law, abuse is an objective concept which expresses the likely effects of a dominant firm's actions to hinder competition in a market where, as a result of the very presence of the firm, the degree of competition is already weakened.[346] A dominant firm has a

---

340. *Id.* para. 211. In each market, the Commission needs to 'assess the degree of control in relation to the strength and number of competitors.' *Sabena, supra* note 334, at 52. *See* Case 27/76, United Brands Co. & United Brands Continental B.V. *v.* Comm'n, 1978 E.C.R. 207, 282. The Court of Justice has ruled that 'the ratio of market shares held by the undertaking concerned to those held by its competitors is also a reliable indicator.' *Sabena, supra* note 334, at 52. *See* Case 85/76, Hoffman-La Roche *v.* Comm'n, 1979 E.C.R. 461, 524. BA ticket sales by IATA travel agents represented 66% of the sales of the top 10 airlines handled by the Billing and Settlement Plan of the United Kingdom (BSPUK) in the same financial year. BA *v.* Comm'n (CFI), *supra* note 322, para. 206. In this respect the Court followed precedent by taking account of the 'highly significant indicator' that BA held large shares of the market and of the ratio between the market share held by BA and that of its nearest rivals. *Id.* para. 210 (citing Hoffman-La Roche, *supra*, paras. 39 & 48). This approach held particular validity, in the Court's view, because BA's nearest rivals held only marginal market shares. *Cf.* United Brands *v.* Commission, *supra*, para. 111.
341. BA *v.* Comm'n (CFI), *supra* note 322, paras. 212-13.
342. *Id.* para. 215.
343. *Id.* para. 216. The potential circularity of this argument (*i.e.*, a dominant position in travel agency services is caused by a dominant position in air transport services, which in turn causes abuse of a dominant position in travel agency services), *see id.* para. 120, is supposedly resolved by the Court's conceptual premise, well-supported in precedent, that an abuse of a dominant position committed on the dominated product market (here, air travel agency services), but the effects of which are felt in a separate market in which the firm concerned does not hold a dominant position (air transport services), may fall within Article 82 provided that the separate market is sufficiently closely connected to the first. But BA (by the Court's own analysis) *does* dominate in both markets. While the markets are indeed undeniably close, it is not clear that the Court demonstrated a nexus between the two markets sufficient to explain why BA's dominance in one logically and necessarily provokes abuse of dominance in the other.
344. *Id.* para. 242 (stating that 'the finding that a dominant position exists does not in itself imply any reproach to the undertaking concerned').
345. BA's unsuccessful appeal to the Court of Justice focused entirely on the statements of the Court of First Instance concerning abuse of its dominant position. BA *v.* Comm'n (AG Opinion), *supra* note 323, para. 22.
346. BA *v.* Comm'n (CFI), *supra* note 322, para. 241 (citing cases).

responsibility to ensure that its conduct does not undermine effective and undistorted competition in the common market.[347] Under Article 82, it is not necessary to demonstrate that the abuse has had a concrete effect on the markets concerned, only that the abusive conduct tends to restrict competition (in other words, that it is capable of, or likely to have, such an effect).[348] The Commission asserted that BA's bonus schemes engendered discrimination between travel agents established in the United Kingdom[349] and produced an exclusionary effect in relation to its airline competitors.[350]

As to the latter contention, the key structural finding by the Commission with respect to collateral effects on air transport competition, the Court impugned the bonus schemes as a 'fidelity-building' strategy[351] devoid of any economically justified consideration (such as efficiency gains or cost savings).[352] The

---

347. BA *v.* Comm'n (AG Opinion), *supra* note 323, para. 23. The Advocate General's opinion went on to state that '[n]ot every kind of price competition is therefore permissible under Article 82.' *Id.* para. 24 (citing cases).

348. BA *v.* Comm'n (CFI), *supra* note 322, para. 293. Instead, as the Advocate-General's opinion indicates, a 'line of conduct' of a dominant firm is abusive as soon as it 'runs counter to the purpose of protecting competition in the internal market from distortions.' BA *v.*Comm'n (AG Opinion), *supra* note 323, para 69. This understanding is consistent with a Community antitrust policy which treats competition as an *objective* concept which transcends the particular interests of individual competitors or even of consumers. *See also* BA *v.* Comm'n (AG Opinion), *supra* note 323, para. 86.

349. BA *v.* Comm'n (CFI), *supra* note 322, para. 227. Article 82(2)(c) of the EC Treaty provides that abuse of a dominant position may consist in applying dissimilar conditions to equivalent transactions with other trading parties, thereby placing them at a competitive advantage. The Court found that BA's bonus schemes could result in different rates of commission being applied to an identical amount of revenue generated by the sale of BA tickets by two travel agents, since their respective sales figures, and hence their rates of growth, would have been different during the previous reference period. BA *v.* Comm'n (CFI), *supra* note 322, para. 235.

350. *Id.* para. 227.

351. Fidelity-building strategies create a 'stickiness' or 'golden handcuff' connection between a firm and its customers. Competitors find it inordinately difficult to sell their products, so that the fidelity rebate or bonus has an exclusionary or 'foreclosure' effect. BA *v.* Comm'n (AG Opinion), *supra* note 323, para. 26. Community case law shows that a fidelity rebate by a dominant firm, granted in consideration of an agreement by the customer to take supplies exclusively or almost exclusively, violates Article 82. *See* Hoffman-La Roche, *supra* note 340, paras. 89 & 90. Here, BA's increased commission rates were capable of rising exponentially from one reference period to another, as the number of BA tickets sold by agents during successive reference periods progressed. BA *v.* Comm'n (CFI), *supra* note 322, para. 272. Conversely, the higher the revenues from BA ticket sales, the stronger was the penalty suffered by the travel agents concerned in the form of a disproportionate reduction in the rates of bonus awards, even in the case of a slight decrease in sales of BA tickets compared with the previous reference period. *Id.* para. 273.

352. *Id.* paras. 284 & 286. 'It is thus ultimately a question of balancing the advantages and disadvantages for competition and consumers against one another.' BA *v.* Comm'n (AG Opinion), *supra* note 323, para. 59 (noting that a rebate which is based on attainment of individually defined sales targets and which is primarily intended to bind the travel agent partner to the dominant firm – BA's scheme – is less likely to be explained by cost savings than a rebate based on objective sales quantities that apply uniformly to all partners and where the producer can achieve savings through producing larger quantities).

progressive nature of the bonus schemes, with their pronounced effect 'at the margin,'[353] restricted the freedom of travel agents to supply their services to the airlines of their choice and, in consequence, restricted the access of those airlines to the United Kingdom market for air travel agency services (and hence, indirectly, to the market for air transport services).[354] Although the Commission was not required to find any concrete effects of the abuse, the Court found that such effects had been demonstrated in a concrete way by the fact that travel agents sold 85% of all air ticket sales in the United Kingdom at the time of the complaint, so that BA's misconduct could not have failed to exclude competing airlines from United Kingdom air transport markets (by reason of the close nexus between the markets in question).[355]

The Court of Justice ruled in *Instituto Chemioterapico Italiano S.p.A. and Commercial Solvents Corp. v. Commission (Zoja)*[356] that Article 82 pursues practices that undermine a 'system of effective competition.'[357] To the Commission and the Court of First Instance, and ultimately to the Court of Justice on final appeal,[358] it was obvious that the structure of competition in the U.K. air travel agency and air transport services markets would have been different if BA had been free to pursue its complex reward system for travel agents. In addition to specific application of an Article 82 jurisprudence, the *British Airways* decision shows the value of the public enforcement power of the Commission both in opposing actual or threatened competitive infringements and in its 'demonstration effects' in support of a deregulated system of competition. The problem, as we examined

---

353. *See supra* in the main text; *see also* BA *v.* Comm'n (CFI), *supra* note 322, para. 272.
354. BA *v.* Comm'n (CFI), *supra* note 322, paras. 292 & 294. It is particularly difficult for competitors of the dominant firm to outbid a 'whole-turnover-based' rebate or bonus scheme such as that operated here by BA. BA *v.* Comm'n (AG Opinion), *supra* note 323, para. 52. These schemes will, in *absolute* terms, 'regularly weigh more strongly in the balance than anything which even more generous offers from competitors could normally achieve.... competitors would have to offer [travel agents] disproportionately higher rebates or premiums, which even for equally efficient competitors is often uneconomic.' *Id.*
355. BA *v.* Comm'n (CFI), *supra* note 322, paras. 294-95. Further, the Court found that the modest growth in the size of the market shares of some of BA's airline competitors did not suggest a lack of effect of BA's abusive scheme, since those market shares (absent the abuse) might have grown even more significantly. *Id.* para. 298.
356. Joined Cases 6 & 7/73, 1974 E.C.R. 223.
357. *Sabena, supra* note 334, at 53.
358. The European Court of Justice, in dismissing BA's appeal in 2007, confirmed that the Commission and the Court of First Instance had correctly applied EC competition law by examining the effects of the exclusionary conduct on 'an effective competition structure.' BA *v.* Comm'n (Judgment), *supra* note 295, para. 106. The Court of Justice held that there was no need, in pursuing that analysis, to examine actual consumer prejudice or even 'probable' effects. *Id.* paras. 98 & 107. *See also* European Commission, *Competition: Commission Welcomes European Court of Justice Judgment in the Virgin/British Airways Case*, Memo/07/103 (Mar. 15, 2007). In keeping with the Commission's contemporary regard for efficiencies, the Court ruled that exclusionary effects may be counterbalanced by 'advantages in terms of efficiency which also benefit the consumer.' BA *v.* Comm'n (Judgment), *supra* note 295, para. 86. But the Court found no objective economic justification for the BA loyalty scheme for its travel agents. *Id.* para. 69.

in our study of the U.S. system, is not so much the desirability of *ex post* regulatory surveillance of the marketplace as the efficiency and speed of the process by which it occurs.[359]

3   Airline Mergers and Alliances: A New Commission Activism

a   Europe's Airline Culture: Cooperation Trumps Merger

Chapter 3 looked at the *faux*-merger culture that currently represents how EU airlines have adjusted to their new regulatory environment.[360] As seen in that earlier discussion, the nationality rule has almost entirely suppressed transnational merger activity in international air transportation generally. But the 'Community air carrier' (considered below), a new legal escutcheon created in 1992, has already shown – notably in the Air France/KLM merger-in-fact[361] – that attempts at larger-scale transborder combinations between EU airlines can be expected to occur in future.[362] Indeed, the common licensing system[363] appears ideally crafted to promote merger activity: BA, for example, could acquire Ireland's Aer Lingus carrier,[364] and continue to operate as a 'Community air carrier' on all of the Irish

---

359. Thus, Virgin Atlantic's initial complaint against BA's marketing rebate agreements was lodged with the Commission on Jul. 9, 1993. BA *v.* Comm'n (CFI), *supra* note 322, para. 12. The Commission decided to initiate a proceeding in relation to BA's marketing agreements and adopted a statement of objections against BA on Dec. 20, 1996. *Id.* at 13. BA presented its oral observations at a hearing on Nov. 12, 1997, *id.*, and even introduced a new system of performance rewards as late as Jan. 1, 1998, *id.* para. 14 (leading to a supplementary complaint from Virgin, followed by a supplementary statement of objections from the Commission on Mar. 12, 1998, *id.* para. 19). The Commission adopted the contested decision on Jul. 14, 1999 (at which point BA for the first time withdrew its reward schemes). BA *v.* Comm'n (CFI), *supra* note 322, para. 314. The Court of First Instance ruled against BA's application to annul the decision on Dec. 17, 2003, and BA's appeal to the Court of Justice was finally decided in Mar. 2007 (Advocate-General Kokott's opinion was delivered on Feb. 23, 2006). Over the 14 years from initial complaint to the Court of Justice appellate ruling, the travel agency market was transformed by the rise of the Internet. While there is an undeniable (and effective) *in terrorem* benefit to the mere *initiation* of enforcement action, as shown in the Northwest/Reno matter, *see supra* Chapter 4, note 539, BA actually *intensified* its restrictive practices during the administrative procedure.
360. *See supra* Chapter 3, Part VIII.
361. *See infra* text accompanying note 404.
362. The signing and entry into provisional effect of the U.S./EC Air Transport Agreement, *supra* note 129, which essentially waives U.S. objections to the multilateralization of the nationality rule among the EU Member States, has already encouraged a fresh round of potential intra-Union merger activity, led by a new British Airways/Iberia announcement and the impending consummation of Lufthansa's control of U.K. carrier bmi.
363. *See infra* Part III(E).
364. Such an eventuality has been mooted for some time, especially since former Aer Lingus chief executive officer Willie Walsh migrated to a similar post with British Airways in 2005.

carrier's *intra-Union* routes, including cabotage routes within Ireland.[365] And, under the 2007 U.S./EC Air Transport Agreement, the U.K. airline's access to the *extra-Union* Aer Lingus network to and from the United States, for example, the densely-traveled Dublin/New York route, has been liberated from the archaisms of the Chicago nationality rule.[366]

Outside the U.S./EC aeropolitical relationship, the Chicago system remains in force and – given the economic importance to EU carriers of long-haul routes to the entire globe – there has been only modest evidence of a merger war among Europe's flagship airlines.[367] Nevertheless, as the Commission certainly recognizes, the array of nonmerger strategic contrivances that these airlines have developed among themselves and with non-EU, especially U.S., carriers – marketing alliances and cooperative arrangements, with or without the sealants of code-sharing and U.S. antitrust immunity, and occasionally (but rarely) accompanied by cross-shareholdings or minority shareholdings[368] – can produce anticompetitive effects similar to those anticipated to arise from disfavored mergers. This is because airlines that enter a working 'partnership,' or cross-invest capital in one another, are inherently less likely to compete directly with each other.[369]

---

365. *See supra* in the main text.

366. *See supra* Chapter 2, Part V(A).

367. The major EU carriers have been reluctant to engage each other at all on their respective home grounds. Following the signing of the 2007 U.S./EC Air Transport Agreement, *supra* note 129, British Airways announced the launch of OpenSkies, a subsidiary carrier, which currently operates business, premium economy, and economy class services between New York and both Paris and Amsterdam, *see* OpenSkies, Official Website, <www.flyopenskies.com/os/home>. Similarly, Air France also began services out of London Heathrow, including a new route from London to Los Angeles as part of its joint venture with Delta under the 2007 Agreement. (Less than seven months after launching Los Angeles/Heathrow service, Air France pulled down the route, blaming the 2008 economic downturn. *See* Press Release, Air France, Optimisation du Réseau Transatlantique de SkyTeam au Départ de Londres Heathrow (Oct. 8, 2008).) The 'specificity' of the international airline industry offers another possible reason for the virtual absence of transborder merger activity in the Union. Despite the change in legal operating conditions, it remains uncertain whether any EU Member State will allow its national airline to surrender its entire identity to another Member State's carrier. Indeed, the Air France/KLM merger explicitly contemplates the survival of the KLM brand within the combined entity. In the Irish Government's sale of Aer Lingus to the private markets the government retained a large enough stake that, under Irish corporate law, it could block takeover bids from foreign entities and thereby protect the brand. *See Aer Lingus: Plan to Privatize the Airline is Announced by Ireland*, WALL ST. J., Jul. 7, 2006.

368. As observed by the International Civil Aviation Organization (ICAO), strategic alliances (rather than acquiring majority stakes or pursuing full-scale mergers) have been the *'tao'* of the international airline industry because of the nationality rule. *See* International Civil Aviation Organization [ICAO], *Regulatory and Industry Overview*, para. 3.9, Information Paper (Aug. 15, 2006); *see also supra* Chapter 3, Part V(A)-(B) (discussing the history of the nationality rule and its impact on foreign ownership and control of airlines). As of Aug. 2006, only 74 of 1,020 airlines worldwide had shareholdings in foreign carriers, with only 278 airlines having equity of various levels in the hands of foreign investors. *Id.*

369. *See, e.g.*, doubts expressed by the Commission with respect to the 'appreciable' anticompetitive effects of a proposed bilateral cooperation agreement between Air France and Alitalia which was

But, while the Commission believes that flexibility should be the watchword in evaluating airline cooperation, its decision to investigate the SkyTeam alliance,[370] and to revisit its approval of the high-profile Star and oneworld alliances,[371]

---

notified to the Commission in 2001 under the now-obsolete process of *a priori* antitrust exemptions. *See supra* Part II(D); European Commission, Commission Decision of 7 April 2004 Relating to a Proceeding Under Article 81 (Case COMP/38.284/D2), *notified under* 2004 O.J. (C 305) 4 (Apr. 7, 2004) [hereinafter Air France/Alitalia Case]; *see also* Press Release, Europa, Commission Raises Competition Concerns About Co-Operation Agreement Between Air France and Alitalia, IP/02/966 (Jul. 1, 2002). The Air France/Alitalia partnership had a double aim, since it was also intended to integrate Alitalia into the worldwide SkyTeam alliance. *See* Air France/Alitalia Case, *supra*, para. 2. The bilateral agreement was comprehensive in scope (including cross-shareholdings, 'free-flow' (no pre-established limits) code-sharing, and price and schedule coordination), with the most intensive cooperation directed at the France/Italy market. As part of its analysis, the Commission examined both overlap and non-overlap routes in the France/Italy 'bundle,' finding seven overlap city-pair routes where competition would be degraded (through control by the parties of 'the quasi-totality' of traffic, *see* Press Release, *supra*), but concluding (with respect to non-overlap routes) that Alitalia's restructuring plan foreclosed re-entry on the single similar route (Paris/Turin) that could attract both Air France and Alitalia as competitors. *See* Air France/Alitalia Case, *supra*, paras. 109, 110-126, & 156. Applying the exemptions allowed under Article 81(3), the Commission accepted that the cooperative agreement would offer customers a more extensive network and increased flights, *see* Air France/Alitalia Case, *supra*, para. 132, but was skeptical as to whether (and on what routes) the parties' alleged efficiency-based unit cost reductions would be passed on to consumers. *See id.* para. 137. The parties' strong market position, coupled with high entry barriers (primarily slot scarcity but also including the parties' coordinated networks, high frequencies, and frequent flier programs) motivated the Commission to insist that the parties enter commitments to surrender slots at their major hub airports to encourage effective point-to-point competition on the seven overlap routes between France and Italy. *See id.* paras. 161-69. Other remedies imposed were participation for new entrants in the parties' frequent flier programs and a frequency freeze.

370. While the Commission has stated that it would 'not raise objections to the [SkyTeam] alliance as a whole,' it has continued to scrutinize the alliance's cooperation on certain routes in order 'to ensure that reduced competition in certain markets does not outweigh the benefits for customers of SkyTeam cooperation.' *See* European Commission, *Commission Confirms Sending Statement of Objections to Members of SkyTeam Global Airline Alliance*, MEMO/06/243 (Jun. 19, 2006). In response, SkyTeam members have offered to surrender slots at a number of key EU airports, to share their frequent flier programs, and to conclude interlining agreements with new entrants in order to increase competition on routes where alliance members hold a strong market position. *See* Press Release, Europa, Antitrust: Commission Market Tests Commitments From Eight Members of SkyTeam Concerning Their Alliance Cooperation, IP/07/1558 (Oct. 19, 2007). The investigation into SkyTeam did not prevent the Commission from approving the merger of its two key U.S. members, Delta and Northwest, in Aug. 2008. *See* Press Release, Europa, Mergers: Commission Approves Acquisition of Northwest Airlines by Delta Airlines, IP/08/1245 (Aug. 6, 2008). Commenting on their decision, the Commission stated that '[t]o the extent that [it] had previously found that members of the SkyTeam alliance could not be considered as effective competitors on transatlantic routes as a result of their membership . . . [the] assessment focused on the possible impact' of a Delta/Northwest structural link alone. *Id.*

371. A newly-hatched plan for British Airways, American Airlines, and Iberia to deepen their strategic relationship as part of the oneworld alliance prompted a fresh investigation by the European Commission into potential violations of EC cartel rules. *See Airlines' Deal is Probed by EU*, WALL ST. J., Aug. 30, 2008, at B5. A much more comprehensive investigation into the

suggests that Commission regulators remain troubled by the compromises of alliance engagement while simultaneously encouraging steps toward cross-border realignment among the major EU carriers.[372]

Case Studies in the Commission's Scrutiny
     of Transatlantic Alliances

By 2006, a decade after the European Commission announced that it would 'open procedures' to investigate the competitive impact of a series of six transatlantic airline cooperation agreements,[373] only one alliance – SkyTeam, the latest derivative of the various Delta-led partnerships[374] – remained under the Commission's scrutiny.[375] The corporate fates of the other original alliances

---

evolution and operations of airline alliances as a whole is currently in progress as part of a joint project – the first evidence of the greater transatlantic competition cooperation foreseen in the 2007 U.S./EC agreement – between the U.S. Department of Transportation and the Commission. *See* Press Release, Europa, Competition: European Commission and US Department of Transportation Launch Joint Research Project on Airline Alliances, IP/08/459 (Mar. 18, 2008).

372. Like the DOT, the Commission prefers not to take *a priori* positions on the competitive compliance of future emerging alliances. Its main concern, as it stated early on, is to ensure that projected combinations do not 'restrict the commercial freedom of other air carriers to enter the market or increase capacity as allowed by the third package.' European Commission, *The Way Forward, supra* note 141, at 12.

373. The named alliances were Lufthansa/United, SAS/United, British Airways/American Airlines, Delta/Swissair/Sabena/Austrian Airlines, KLM/Northwest, and British Airways/USAir. *See generally* Press Release, European Commission, Airline Agreements: Background File for the Press (Jul. 3, 1996) (copy on file with Library of the EU Delegation, Washington, D.C.) [hereinafter Airline Agreements]. The 1996 investigations were launched before the removal (in 2004) of the spatial restriction of the Community's air transport competition authority to intra-Community routes. Prior to 2004, only the potential effects of the alliances on *intra-Union* air transport fell within the scope of the Commission's trusteeship, and its existing powers of investigation and enforcement would protect these routes. *See* Airline Agreements, *supra*, para. 24. But, although the European Court of Justice had applied Articles 81 and 82 of the EC Treaty to air transport between the Community and third countries, the Council of Ministers had never equipped the Commission with the procedural machinery to implement these articles in international air transport markets outside the EU. Accordingly, the Commission proposed revisiting the imprecise (and intentionally transitional) enforcement procedures in the EC Treaty that it used in an *in terrorem* gesture prior to adoption of the 1987 liberalization package. *See supra* text accompanying note 105.

374. The original Delta/Swissair/Austrian Airlines alliance, into which the Commission opened its 1996 probe, had by 2000 (following the collapse of Swissair) been transmogrified into Sky-Team, a formation among Delta Air Lines, Air France, Alitalia, Aeromexico, CSA Czech Airlines, and Korean Air. In 2004, the alliance expanded to include Continental Airlines, KLM Royal Dutch Airlines (which subsequently entered a proposed merger with Air France), and Northwest Airlines. *See generally* Adam Cohen, *SkyTeam Gets Antitrust Warning*, WALL ST. J., Jun. 20, 2006, at A18. In the propitious aeropolitical context of a new U.S./EC air transport agreement, the SkyTeam alliance succeeded in reversing an earlier adverse decision and won antitrust immunity from the U.S. Department of Transportation in 2008.

375. *See supra* note 370.

can be synopsized quickly. The BA/USAir collaboration collapsed in acrimony and litigation.[376] The British Airways/American Airlines venture foundered on slot divestiture conditions imposed by the U.S. DOT and the Commission closed its case without further action.[377] Prior to that, KLM/Northwest (the 'Wings' alliance) became part of SkyTeam, and the United/Lufthansa and United/SAS combinations evolved into the global 'Star' alliance.

The Commission's evaluation of the remaining two integrated alliances (KLM/Northwest prior to its absorption into SkyTeam, and the Star grouping) seems to have shifted from the skepticism reflected in its initial announcement in 1996 – particularly with respect to the threat alliances might pose to new entry – to a more measured tolerance (what the Commission itself describes as a 'broadly positive approach')[378] over the intervening decade. This evolution in thinking may be in part an expression, once again, of the Commission's abiding reflex toward industrial policy, in this case the fitness of EU carriers 'to compete effectively on a global level.'[379] In sum, the Commission applied a consistent competitive metric to each alliance: the arrangements were approved under Community antitrust rules for their potential to generate economic benefits (including improved connectivity, costs savings, and synergies – with possible consumer price benefits), while the alliance was required to enhance entry on certain route pairs where alliance carriers previously competed but where the designated alliance carrier or carriers would not face any significant competitive pressure from rival airlines (or alliances).[380]

---

376. *See supra* Chapter 3, notes 466 & 490.
377. *See* Press Release, Europa, Commission Closes Probe into KLM/Northwest and Lufthansa/ SAS/United Airlines Transatlantic Air Alliances, IP/02/1569 (Oct. 29, 2002) [hereinafter Press Release, Alliances Probe] (mentioning the DOT's condition that 224 slots be divested in order to allay competition concerns). The planned BA/AA link-up subsequently became the oneworld alliance, although without benefiting from U.S. antitrust immunity. In 2008, American Airlines and British Airways, joined by BA's prospective merger partner, Iberia Airlines, filed a new request for immunity – requesting the unprecedented concession of global antitrust immunity, and prompting investigations from both the DOT and the European Commission. *See* Micheline Maynard, *American Defends Its Plan for Trans-Atlantic Alliance*, N.Y. Times, Sept. 4, 2008, at C3. The most vocal critic of the proposed alliance,, Sir Richard Branson, has condemned it as a 'monster monopoly,' alleging that the participating carriers would have nearly 60% of passengers traveling between the United States and London Heathrow, and command as much as 79% of the seats on some routes. *Id.* In December 2008, the U.S. Senate Committee on the Judiciary alerted the DOT of its strong reservations about granting antitrust immunity to international airline alliances, including the BA/AA proposal. *See* Alistair Osborne, *US Senate Warning Highlights Obstacles to BA-American Airlines Alliance*, Telegraph, Jan. 26, 2009.
378. Press Release, Alliances Probe, *supra* note 377.
379. *Id.* No doubt the Commission's benevolent temperament in examining transatlantic alliances has been informed, also, by the DOT's similar outlook.
380. It will be noted that SkyTeam includes a number of EU carriers which, in normal circumstances, would be competitors on intra-Union routes (Air France, Alitalia, and KLM). While the Commission could certainly address intra-Union competition in the context of its SkyTeam analysis, it has had an opportunity to examine competition on France/Netherlands and France/ Italy route pairs, respectively, in the Air France/KLM merger investigation and in its study of the Air France/Alitalia alliance.

Thus, in the case of Star[381] (into which the Commission closed its investigation in 2002[382]), the Commission warned the three founding partners in 1998 of serious concerns about significantly reduced competition on a target list of five transatlantic hub-to-hub 'origin and destination' routes on which they held combined market shares of between 55% and 95% (including Frankfurt/Chicago, Frankfurt/Washington, Frankfurt/Los Angeles, Frankfurt/San Francisco, and Copenhagen/Chicago).[383] By 2002, however, the Commission had concluded that Copenhagen/Chicago, a relatively thin route, had effective competition from indirect sixth freedom services (on which the Danish Government did not exercise price control), and that the airports would not be slot-constrained. Indirect (primarily sixth freedom) services through Frankfurt were hurt by government price control regulation, however,[384] and Frankfurt also suffered from a shortage of landing and take-off slots. The parties submitted 'undertakings' to surrender slots at Frankfurt to allow one or more prospective new entrants to provide new or additional competitive nonstop or indirect scheduled passenger air services.[385] In a parallel declaration, the German Government agreed not to exercise any control on fares of indirect services from Germany to the United States on the

---

381. For a description of the Star coordination agreements among Lufthansa, SAS, and United Airlines, *see* Commission Notice Concerning the Alliance Between Lufthansa, SAS, and United Airlines (Cases COMP/D-2/36.201, 36.076, 36.078 – Procedure under Article 85 (ex art. 89) EC) paras. 11-12, 2002 O.J. (C 181) 2 [hereinafter Star Alliance Notice] (noting retention of 'distinct corporate identities' in a framework of coordination that *inter alia* includes route and schedule planning, management of sales and distribution networks, travel agency and other commissions, cobranding, code-sharing, pricing, inventory and yield management, revenue-sharing, integration of information systems, frequent flier programs, and sharing of airport facilities and services).

382. *See* Press Release, Alliances Probe, *supra* note 377.

383. *See id.*; *see also* Star Alliance Notice, *supra* note 381, paras. 13-16.

384. *See id.* para. 31 (reporting that the German aviation authorities required filing of published fares for indirect services and could prohibit fares that undercut fares for nonstop services on the same route by a German or U.S. carrier providing third or fourth freedom services). Here is an interesting example of the sixth freedom at work – and of how national authorities can stymie competition by regulatory controls over its exercise. The German Government could support the economic performance of Lufthansa's third and fourth freedom (*i.e.*, direct) routes by imposing price controls (in effect, prohibition of price leadership) on EU (and third country) carriers whose service originated outside Germany but operated through their home States to Frankfurt. Thus, for example, Air France could use its fourth freedom privilege to fly passengers from New York to Paris (in its home State), and then use its third freedom privilege to fly some of those passengers to Frankfurt. A similar sequence operates in reverse to fly passengers from Frankfurt via Paris to New York. The Commission did not discuss fifth freedom services through Frankfurt – for example, Alitalia flying passengers to Frankfurt and onward to New York, combining third and fifth freedoms – presumably because operation of these kinds of services (at Frankfurt, at any rate) would be unlikely to lure effective competition and was not, in any case, proposed as an entry barrier by potential competitors.

385. *See id.* para. 28 (describing slot distribution among routes). An 'indirect' service, according to the Commission, would have a connecting time of not more than 150 minutes. *See id.* The parties also agreed to admit new entrants serving nonstop routes to their frequent flier programs and to interline with new entrants. *See id.* para. 29.

Frankfurt routes targeted by the Commission.[386] The Commission approved the alliance on the strength of these public/private commitments, but also because (bearing in mind the competition-boosting criteria in Article 81(3) of the EC Treaty)[387] the parties persuaded the Commission that their integration would enable them to offer a more competitive network for passengers traveling between Europe and the United States as a result of 'externalities' from a combination of three airline networks.[388]

The KLM/Northwest alliance won approval with broadly equivalent assurances about the consumer-friendly benefits of integration, while the Commission ultimately decided that the parties' high positions on the Amsterdam/Detroit and Amsterdam/Minneapolis-St. Paul routes (with combined market shares of 88% and 78% respectively) would be mitigated by competitors providing substitutable indirect service.[389]

Despite its initial concerns about oligopoly on the transatlantic marketplace, in both of these concluded alliance investigations the Commission focused its statements of objections on specific city-pair routes rather than on questioning the ontological premise for giant transnational collaborations. In that sense, the Commission seems to have bowed to the market reality that, by the time its investigations were closing, transatlantic air services were manifestly characterized by network competition among multimember airline alliances.[390]

i   The Nebulous World of Transnational EU
                Mergers: Air France-KLM

Despite revolutionary changes in the airline ownership rules within the EC, and although substantial restructuring of the EU airline industry can be expected, it may (at present) be politically difficult – and, because of the broader force of the nationality rule outside the EU, also legally impossible[391] – for a flag carrier to

---

386. *See id.* para. 32; *see also supra* note 384 (describing German control over sixth freedom services to Frankfurt).

387. *See supra* Part II(D).

388. *See* Star Alliance Notice, *supra* note 381, para. 20. Thus, the alliance would provide a larger number of direct and indirect routes (indirect routes would benefit from greater synchronization of schedules), a larger number of frequencies, greater capacity, and improved connections. Passengers would benefit directly from integrated flight services, as well as price savings from cost reductions through sharing of groundhandling facilities, elimination of duplicated marketing and distribution costs, joint purchasing of fuel, and so on. *See id.* paras. 22-23.

389. *See generally id.* para. 15 (noting absence of barriers to entry such as regulatory obstacles and slot shortages). The parties were also able to persuade the Commission that both target routes were relatively thin – 60,000 (Amsterdam/Detroit) and 36,800 (Amsterdam/Minneapolis-St. Paul) origin and destination passengers a year (compared, for example, with 306,000 for Frankfurt/Chicago) – and would not be likely to support two or more competitive nonstop services. *See id.*; *see also* Press Release, Alliances Probe, *supra* note 377.

390. *See* Star Alliance Notice, *supra* note 381, para. 9 (noting the parties' argument that traditional market definition should take the alliance phenomenon into consideration).

391. *But see supra* Chapter 2, Part V (discussing the grant of seventh freedom rights for EU carriers to fly from all EU airports to the United States, without risking a U.S. invocation of the nationality rule, under the 2007 U.S./EC U.S. Air Transport Agreement, *supra* note 129).

succumb to a 'foreign' acquisition by a carrier of another Member State.[392] But cracks in the Chicago edifice have been opening, nonetheless. In fall 2000, BA seriously contemplated an acquisition of Dutch flag carrier KLM, but may have been deterred by U.S. indications that it would suspend KLM's traffic rights if the carrier were majority British-owned.[393] A more momentous development followed in December 2003, when Air France and KLM orchestrated an elaborate cross-border transaction that might be described accurately as a merger-in-waiting. Billed as 'the first merger in [the aviation] sector between two national airlines with different cultures,'[394] the transaction involved the larger airline, Air France, making an exchange offer for all of KLM's common stock.[395]

The resulting legal structure is an Air-France-KLM 'holding company' which holds two publicly-traded air carrier subsidiaries, Air France and KLM.[396] In this 'one group/two air carriers/three businesses' organizational model,[397] the holding company owns 100% of the capital and voting rights in Air France, and 97.3% of the economic rights (including dividend rights) in KLM – but only 49% of that carrier's voting rights.[398] In order to protect KLM's traffic rights against a non-EU Member State objection[399] that the carrier is no longer majority-owned and effectively controlled by Dutch nationals, a safeguard provision (negotiated between the Dutch State and Air France-KLM and KLM) allows the Dutch State to exercise a renewable option to subscribe for KLM preferential shares that will automatically increase the State's stake to 50.1% of the capital and voting rights of KLM.[400]

---

392. This must be recognized as a separate question from the access that the new U.S./EC agreement promises to hubs located in other Member States for transatlantic services.

393. Adrianne Larson, *Cost, Control Issues Terminate British Airways-KLM Merger Plans*, 341 AVIATION DAILY, No, 57, Sept. 22, 2000, at 1. The critical issue for the United States was the absence of an open skies arrangement with the United Kingdom.

394. AIR FRANCE-KLM, REFERENCE DOCUMENT 2004-05 3 (2005) [hereinafter Air France-KLM Document].

395. *See id.* at 6. 96.3% of KLM's common stock was tendered in the offer. *See id.* The French Government subsequently concluded the privatization of Air France by reducing its equity interest in the airline from 44% to 23%. *See id.* at 6-7.

396. *See id.* at 6. KLM and its existing U.S. partners, Northwest and Continental, joined the Sky-Team global alliance (led by Air France and Delta) as part of the merger transaction. *See id.* at 52. On SkyTeam's current structure, *see supra* Chapter 4, Part III(C).

397. *See* the interview with Jean-Cyril Spinetta and Leo van Wijk in Air France-KLM Document, *supra* note 394, at 30 & 34 (the three businesses are air passenger transport, air cargo transport, and aircraft maintenance and repair).

398. *See id.* at 20. The balance (majority) of KLM's voting rights show an investor profile that mainly comprises Dutch foundations and the Dutch State. *See id.*

399. The objection must be from a State which represents a 'key market' served by KLM. *See id.* at 215.

400. After the option is exercised, the Dutch State has an obligation to hold discussions with the contesting State(s). *See id.* at 215. If the Dutch State establishes that KLM's key markets are no longer threatened, the agreement requires KLM to buy back the preferential shares with a view to canceling them. *See id.* The Reference Document incorrectly states that the Chicago system conditions KLM's operational rights on ownership and control by Dutch *or European*

Visibly, the Air France/KLM transaction – as well as the announced prospect of a future merger between BA and Iberia[401] – adds a dramatic political dimension to the traditional typology of the cooperative nonmerger relationship (which has included strategic alliances, cross-shareholdings, minority shareholdings, and even certain types of joint ventures). The technical details of the Air France/KLM transaction do not disguise the anomalous idea of a 'merger' that needs to contain a clause (the safeguard provision) that instantly nationalizes a major component of the merged business upon the political contingency of a foreign country's intervention. Moreover, despite the attempt by both airlines to project an authentic group identity, it is clear that the demise of a flag carrier remains culturally problematic in the EU. Thus, while it may well be that the two brand names within the merged entity are worth preserving for pure commercial reasons, the holding group has in any case been required to give to the Dutch State certain assurances about the maintenance of KLM's operations in the Netherlands (and at Schiphol),[402] and to give KLM itself a long series of assurances bottomed on the key premise of preserving KLM's separate brand identity ('for commercial and heritage reasons').[403]

---

nationals. Air France-KLM Document, *supra* note 394, at 214. The latter prerequisite (of EU ownership and control) accurately states Community law, but is not true as a matter of international law (which requires Dutch nationals to own and control an airline that exercises Dutch traffic rights).

401. *See supra* note 377.

402. The assurances to the Dutch State on maintaining KLM's operational activities in the Netherlands, including a multi-hub system based on Charles de Gaulle and Schiphol airports, run until May 2012. *See* Air France-KLM Document, *supra* note 394, at 215. A limited number of symmetrical destination transfers between the two airports (and two airlines) are covered in a separate assurance that expires in May 2009. *See id.* at 216.

403. The assurances to KLM include preservation of the CDG/Schiphol multi-hub concept and continued use of the separate Air France and KLM identifier codes. The assurances continue until May 2009. *See id.* at 217; *but see supra* note 402 (noting the parallel assurances to the Dutch State that appear to have a longer currency). In Mar. 2005, Lufthansa (through its holding company, Deutsche Lufthansa AG), signed an Integration Agreement for the absorption of Swiss International Air Lines into the Lufthansa Group. The Lufthansa/Swiss relationship bears important similarities to the Air France-KLM business model, once again tailoring a proposed merger to the exigencies of the Chicago system. Thus, while the ultimate goal is Lufthansa's takeover of Swiss, the acquisition will take place in several steps which involve transferring the Swiss shareholding to a new Swiss company (Air Trust) followed by Lufthansa's gradual accretion of up to 49% of Air Trust (after antitrust clearance). After negotiations 'in order to secure the air traffic rights,' Lufthansa will take 100% of Swiss. *See* Press Release, Swiss International Air Lines, Swiss Takes Off Into A New Future With Lufthansa (Mar. 22, 2005). An earlier announcement from Swiss predicted that traffic rights negotiations would conclude by the end of 2006 'at the latest,' although it did not specify what these negotiations would be. *See* Press Release, Swiss International Air Lines, Squeeze-Out Procedure Successfully Concluded (Jan. 20, 2006). In Jul. 2007, following the securing of all traffic rights, Swiss was fully integrated into Lufthansa. *See* Lufthansa, Monthly Report 07/2007, <http://www.lufthansa-financials.de/servlet/PB/menu/1023076_12/index.html>.

ii A Case Study in Community Merger Policy: The easyJet
Challenge to Air France-KLM

Despite all of the oversight artillery at the Commission's disposal under the revised merger regulation,[404] only a handful of 'true' airline mergers (as opposed to nonmerger alliances[405]) have qualified for Commission-level scrutiny under the merger regulation.[406] We have previously examined the Air France/KLM 'merger in-waiting'[407] (as well as the proposed acquisition of Swiss International Air Lines by Lufthansa)[408] and considered the innovative corporate structure designed for Air France-KLM.[409] Here, that transaction is inspected as a representative case study of Commission merger analysis.[410] Importantly, the Court of First Instance ruled in July 2006, in a challenge by EU low-cost carrier easyJet, that the Commission had not committed 'manifest error' in its February 2004 decision finding the Air France/KLM merger to be compatible with the common market.[411] The easyJet proceeding offered a rare occasion for a judicial excursus into the theory and practice of airline mergers under Community law.[412]

---

404. *See supra* in the main text.
405. *See supra* Chapter 3, Part VIII (discussing the special challenges posed by intercontinental airline alliances, some of which might be regarded as *de facto* mergers).
406. Ironically, the largest transaction reviewed prior to KLM/Air France concerned an acquisition involving two *U.S.* airlines with Community operations. In 1991, the U.S. carrier, Delta Air Lines Inc. ('Delta'), notified the Commission of its intention to acquire, by asset purchase, the North Atlantic air transport business of Pan Am Corporation Co. and its subsidiaries Pan American World Airways Inc. and Pan Am Shuttle Inc. ('Pan Am'). Among other assets, Delta would acquire 30 route authorities between New York and different European destinations, as well as the Detroit/London, Miami/London and Washington/Frankfurt routes, and 14 fifth freedom routes from Pan Am's Frankfurt hub to destinations in Europe and beyond. The Commission found that this transaction qualified as a 'concentration' (*in casu*, an acquisition of assets) with a 'Community dimension' created by the combination of the huge worldwide aggregate revenues of Delta and Pan Am with their aggregate Community-wide revenues. *See* Commission Decision of 13 Sept. 1991 (Case No. IV/M.130/91 – Delta Air Lines/Pan Am), 1991 O.J. (C 289). Despite concerns about combining Delta's huge domestic feeder network with Pan Am's international routes to and beyond Europe, the Commission ultimately found that Delta's competitive ascendancy was 'common to all the large American carriers;' given the 'present market structure,' the Commission therefore declined to find that Delta's augmented competitive potential created a 'dominant position' for that airline. *Id.*
407. *See supra* text accompanying note 394.
408. *See supra* note 403.
409. *See supra* notes 402-03 and accompanying text.
410. The Commission appears to have assessed the competitive implications of the Air France/KLM transaction using the premise that, despite its unusual technical attributes, it would ultimately operate conventionally as a matter of corporate law. A similar perspective has been adopted in the main text. Note also that, because of its timing, the merger was reviewed by the Commission under the original merger regulation, Council Regulation 4064/89, *supra* note 200. In this discussion, references to the equivalent provisions in the 2004 revised regulation, Council Regulation 139/2004, *supra* note 200, have been substituted where appropriate.
411. *See* Case T-177/04, easyJet Airline Co. Ltd. *v.* Comm'n, 2006 E.C.R. II-1931 (Ct. First Instance) [hereinafter easyJet *v.* Comm'n]; *see also* Commission Decision of 11 November 2004 (Case COMP/M.3280 – Air France/KLM), 2004 O.J. (C 60) 5.
412. Before reaching the merits the Court had to establish as a matter of admissibility that the applicant, easyJet, satisfied the requirement under Article 230(4) of the EC Treaty that a

Based on its analysis of 14 routes on which Air France and KLM had been direct competitors, the Commission had 'serious doubts'[413] about the merger's compatibility with the common market.[414] To 'dispel' these doubts,[415] the merging parties offered a series of commitments to resolve competition problems – a consensual practice encountered earlier in Commission review of transatlantic alliances.[416] With respect to mergers, however, the practice is formalized in the merger regulation as a mechanism to ensure competitive market structures,[417] and the Commission has issued detailed guidelines for the drafting of merger commitments.[418] The commitments offered by the parties related to both short-haul/European routes and long-haul/intercontinental routes. For each challenged bundle of routes, the parties pledged to make permanently available a number of slots, without financial compensation, in order to allow one or more new entrants to operate new or additional nonstop scheduled daily air passenger service.[419]

---

natural or legal person may only institute a proceeding against a decision addressed to other persons (here, Air France and KLM) which is 'of direct and individual concern' to the applicant. *See* easyJet *v.* Comm'n, *supra* note 411, paras. 30-39 (finding that easyJet satisfied the standing requirements since it was concerned directly – as a target of intentional imminent change in the relevant market, and individually – as an involved party in the Commission's predecision administrative procedure and a competitor of Air France and KLM on various direct routes). Community case law also requires that an action for annulment brought by a natural or legal person requires the applicant to have a present and vested 'interest' (and prospective advantage) in having the contested measure annulled. *See id.* para. 40 (citing cases). This ripeness test was satisfied by the applicant, which was challenging 'a concentration between two of its competitors which may affect its commercial situation,' *Id.* para. 41.

413. The phrase 'serious doubts' is not journalistic shorthand to describe the Commission's viewpoint on a proposed transaction. Rather, it is in fact the catalytic legal language incorporated into the merger regulation mandating the Commission (if it finds that such doubts exist) to initiate proceedings against a planned merger. *See* Council Regulation 139/2004, *supra* note 200, art. 6(1)(c).

414. Nine of the routes were in Europe, including major air corridors such as Paris/Amsterdam, Lyons/Amsterdam, and Marseilles/Amsterdam. *See* easyJet *v.* Comm'n, *supra* note 411, at para. 9.

415. *Id.* para. 16.

416. *See supra* in the main text.

417. Though the provisions are not conspicuous examples of drafting clarity, Article 6(2) of Council Regulation 139/2004 provides that, following 'modification' by the parties, the Commission may, if satisfied that it no longer raises 'serious doubts,' declare the merger to be compatible with the common market. The 'modification,' it appears from the second paragraph of Article 6(2), is to be in the form of 'commitments' entered into by the parties 'vis-à-vis' the Commission. Council Regulation 139/2004, *supra* note 200, art. 6(2).

418. *See* Commission Notice on Remedies Acceptable Under Council Regulation 4064/89 and Commission Regulation 447/98, 2001 O.J. (C 68) 3 [hereinafter Notice on Remedies] (indicating, *inter alia*, that the parties must show clearly that their remedy will restore effective competition in the common market on a permanent basis, and that it will be fully and timely implemented).

419. Bolstering these slot giveaways were some important additional concessions to new competition, including a six-season frequency freeze on the Paris/Amsterdam and Lyons/Amsterdam routes, a six-season cap of 14 frequencies per week on the Amsterdam/New York (JFK) route,

EasyJet's action sought to annul the Commission's acquiescence in the Air France/KLM commitments. The pertinent element of the standard for judicial review was to ensure the absence of 'manifest errors of assessment.'[420] EasyJet alleged an unbroken chain of errors by the Commission which would, if unchecked, authorize a concentration which would create or strengthen a dominant position as a result of which competition would be significantly impeded in the common market.[421] A focus on some of the applicant's arguments will help to illuminate the conceptual tools used by the Commission to examine mergers, including the technique of imposing commitments upon merging partners to preclude the creation or strengthening of a dominant position.

The device of slot surrender, typically pressed into service by the Commission as part of the commitments required in merger and alliance proceedings,[422] logically implies that the Commission perceives air transport markets in the binary terms that gives every slot its specific commercial value. Thus, the Commission defined the relevant product market for the Air France/KLM merger using point of origin/point of destination (O & D) city-pairs, any single combination constituting a separate market from the viewpoint of demand.[423] In response, easyJet, relying on its own customer profile, alleged that the Commission should have assessed the supply of 'leisure travel by air' on a broader basis than that of segmentation by city-pair route, in the context of the 'general leisure/holiday market.'[424] EasyJet was urging, in other words, an assessment of the broader, 'holistic' impact of the notified concentration in related markets beyond the area of direct overlap between Air France and KLM.

Problematically, easyJet (in the Court's view) failed to formulate a rival market definition that would go beyond the mere general assertion that, for some passengers wishing to travel for leisure purposes, various destinations were interchangeable.[425] The Court's reasoning, however, was paradoxical. On the one hand, it concluded that a market definition based on an O & D approach,

---

undertakings to interline with new entrants, and admission of new entrants to the parties' frequent flier program. *See* easyJet *v.* Comm'n, *supra* note 411, para. 16.

420. *Id.* para. 44 (citing cases) (also mentioning compliance with the rules governing procedure and the statement of reasons, as well as substantive accuracy of the facts and the absence of any misuse of powers).

421. *See id.* para. 45 (paraphrasing Article 2(3) of Council Regulation 139/2004, *supra* note 200).

422. *See, e.g., supra* note 370 (discussing the SkyTeam alliance).

423. *See* easyJet *v.* Comm'n, *supra* note 411, para. 47. The Commission's notice on market definition states that demand substitution (in simple terms, the availability of attractive consumer alternatives) constitutes the most immediate and effective force on the suppliers of a given product, in particular in relation to their pricing decisions. *See* Notice on Remedies, *supra* note 418, para. 14. Less potent sources of competitive constraint are supply substitutability and potential competition. *See id.*

424. easyJet *v.* Comm'n, *supra* note 411, para. 47.

425. *See id.* para. 59 (finding that the applicant had failed procedurally to make clear and precise arguments to support its alternative theory of the relevant market). Moreover, in what the Court apparently understood as a weakening of its position, easyJet did not challenge the merits of the O & D method itself. *See id.* para. 57.

which in substance includes routes characterized by the phrase 'leisure travel by air,' would allow analysis of 'all the competition problems' which the merger was likely to entail.[426] On the other hand, the Court was prepared to accept as a general premise that it is 'possible' that a merger could have the effect of creating or strengthening a dominant position – and significantly impeding competition – 'in markets in which there is no overlap between the activities of the parties to the merger.'[427] Although the applicant had failed to show such a potential effect, the Court held that the Commission is bound, where there are serious indications of a risk to competition (and even in the absence of any express request by third parties consulted during the predecision procedure) to assess the competition problems created by the merger *on all the markets which may be affected by it.* Ultimately, given the route-based nature of airline competition, even this widened scrutiny will likely resolve into city-pair analysis rather than the elusive metric of 'general' competitive effects advocated by easyJet.[428]

The easyJet lawyers also argued, rather solipsistically, that the Commission had erred in recognizing that a merger *qua* merger may allow the parties to reap competitive advantages that may benefit consumers (and, implicitly, divert customers from the merged entity's competitors).[429] The Court dealt brusquely with this contention, so demonstrably at odds with the consumer-oriented teleology of the competition laws. Merger control, according to the Court, is premised not on the prohibition of consumer advantages but on the aim of avoiding a dominance that impedes the common market. Thus, if the merger (through its efficiencies) offers passengers better service and price options, these consumer advantages ought to be encouraged unless they constitute 'evidence of the creation or strengthening of a dominant position.'[430] That evidence, the Court said, would only exist in limited cases (as, for example, in the probably unprovable event that the merged entity 'intends or has the capacity to operate a predatory pricing policy').[431]

---

426. *Id.* para. 61.
427. *See id.* para. 63. It must also be noted that the Court found that the applicant had not discharged its evidentiary responsibility either to demonstrate the incompleteness of the O & D method or the existence of a competition problem on non-overlapping markets. *See* easyJet *v.* Comm'n, *supra* note 411, paras. 61 & 64-67.
428. The 'general' argument advanced by easyJet reveals the evaluative difficulties presented by this kind of approach. EasyJet pointed out that Air France enjoys a monopoly on 27 of the 42 domestic routes from Paris, that it has 61.8% of the total capacity on routes from France, and that it has 53% of the total number of slots available at Paris-Orly and 74% of those at Paris-Charles de Gaulle. *See id.* para. 67. On its face, such contentions provide a synchronic snapshot of Air France's general competitive profile, but do not *in themselves* predict the patterns of a future combination with KLM or indicate the areas of competitive concern that need to be addressed. A route-by-route profile, on the other hand, offers a diachronic perspective that enables the degree of risk to competition to be more precisely identified – and, more importantly, to be addressed through appropriate commitments.
429. *See id.* para. 72.
430. *Id.*
431. *Id.* para. 72.

Relatedly, and in further pursuit of an inauspicious appellate strategy to establish a generalized threat to competition – rather than specific market disturbances – caused by the Air France-KLM concentration, easyJet raised the objection that the Commission had failed to consider what KLM might have done in the marketplace as an independent competitor to Air France. In other words, the Commission had not assessed whether KLM could have been a powerful potential competitor to restrain the dominance of Air France, especially at Paris, in light of the continued liberalization of the air transport sector and the Commission's mandates to negotiate liberal air services agreements with third countries.[432] The Commission dismissed the argument as speculative,[433] and the Court concurred with respect to KLM's *general* prospects in a liberalized environment (and, once again, in the absence of specific evidence).[434] But the Court did note 'settled case law' holding that an examination of the conditions of competition must be based on potential as well as existing competition.[435] In keeping with its preference for market specificity, therefore, the Court looked more closely at Air France's Paris stronghold and, in particular, to the arguments advanced by easyJet that KLM's limited domestic market would make separate operations by KLM at Paris, in part because of its proximity, a desirable strategic option. The Court, in rejecting the commercial premises of easyJet's contention, approved the reasoning of the Commission as to the strategic implications of KLM's centralized operations at Amsterdam (and those of Air France at Paris).

As a network carrier, KLM concentrates traffic into a specific hub and disperses passengers via hub connections to numerous spokes. City-pairs which are not connected to their hubs (*i.e.*, Paris to short-haul destinations within Europe) tend not to attract their commercial presence. New entrants in those markets tend to be the national carrier of the point of origin or destination or a low-cost carrier. KLM, therefore, would not be likely to operate in those markets if routes were not connected to Amsterdam.[436] Similarly, on long-haul routes, the non-duplicable viability of KLM's Amsterdam hub is based mostly on passengers in transit using feeder services from other routes in the KLM network.[437] As to easyJet's superficially plausible argument on the proximity of Paris and Amsterdam, the Court (focusing on long-haul services) concluded that passengers would not regard it as an advantage to be able to change at both Paris and Amsterdam, and that a Paris-based duplication of KLM's primary passenger throughput at Amsterdam (transit passengers from the United States and local passengers heading to the Far East) would merely cannibalize KLM's centralized operations at its hub airport.[438] Absent some demonstration of a 'commercial interest' by KLM in the substantial

---

432. *See generally id.* paras. 111-112.
433. *See* easyJet *v.* Comm'n, *supra* note 411, para. 113.
434. *See id.* para. 115.
435. *Id.* para. 116.
436. *See id.* paras. 118-19.
437. *See id.* para. 120.
438. *See id.* para. 123.

investment needed to create a second hub at Paris, easyJet failed to sustain its challenge based on potential competition.[439]

In the final part of its appeal, easyJet turned away from its macroeconomic assault and attacked the legitimacy of the Commission's assessment of the specific commitments given by Air France and KLM. In analyzing these challenges, the Court hewed to the basic proposition that, according to 'settled case law,' the Commission enjoys a 'broad discretion in assessing the need for commitments to be given in order to dispel the serious doubts raised by a concentration.'[440]

A quick summary of some of easyJet's arguments (all of which the Court rejected), and of the Court's responses, will help to elucidate how the Commission frames and defends commitments. First, the applicant complained that the affected markets were not sufficiently attractive to low-cost carriers. The Court rejected what it interpreted as easyJet's implicit premise that new entry should be effectively cost-free, noting that commitments 'cannot exempt new entrants from the costs attendant upon market entry, since those investments are logically inherent in any commercial activity.'[441] Second, easyJet argued that neither party had been forced to adopt more fundamental structural remedies such as divestiture of a viable business or surrender of market shares to a competitor. The Court agreed with the Commission that access to slots, rather than to a fleet of aircraft, was the most significant barrier to entry, and appeared to agree also that the parties did not have a viable business to divest.[442] As to the inadequacy of the proposed slot divestiture (a third easyJet argument), the court indicated a lack of empirical support for the allegation[443] and deferred to the Commission's discretion as to the appropriate commitments.[444]

---

439. easyJet *v.* Comm'n, *supra* note 411, para. 123.
440. *Id.* para. 128. Thus, the Court's review is not for purposes of substituting its own assessment but is 'limited to ascertaining that the Commission has not committed a manifest error of assessment.' *Id.* Moreover, the fact that other commitments might have been accepted, *or might even have been more favorable to competition*, will not prompt annulment of the decision in so far as 'the Commission was reasonably entitled to conclude that the commitments set out in the decision served to dispel the serious doubts.' *Id.* (citing case).
441. *Id.* para. 145. Nor would the presence of large companies on a route be considered 'an absolute barrier' to entry. *Id.* para. 147. The Court also cited with approval the Commission's argument that its framing of commitments is intended to maintain overall competition on the markets affected – which (as here) may include intermodal competition, for example from high-speed rail services. easyJet *v.* Comm'n, *supra* note 411, para. 147. The robust approach taken here to the challenges faced by new entrant competition has an interesting counterpoint in the Commission's then-unseasoned posturing in favor of new entrant competition in the early British Midland/Aer Lingus dispute. *See supra* text accompanying note 298.
442. *See* easyJet *v.* Comm'n, *supra* note 411, paras. 155-258. Divestiture, in fact, is the remedy preferred by the Commission, but it is not always practicable. *See id.* para. 154.
443. Moreover, numerous competitors and business customers supported the level of divestiture. *See id.* paras. 168-69.
444. Thus, the Commission had concluded that commitments should be offered on markets where the parties enjoyed a market share of almost 50% (respecting the 'presumption of dominance' established in AKZO *v.* Commission, para. 60, 1991 E.C.R. I-3359. *See* easyJet *v.* Comm'n, *supra* note 411, para. 174. Accordingly, the retention of sizeable market shares by the parties

The court rebuffed easyJet's fourth attack – on the inadequacy of accompanying behavioral remedies (including frequency freezes, interline agreements, blocked-space agreements, access to frequent flier programs, and obligations with respect to fares) – on the ground that these remedies, in combination with the irrevocability of the slot surrender commitments, could even be regarded as structural.[445] The Commission's margin of appreciation, therefore, was again respected.

Finally, on the objection that the Commission failed to identify a new entrant and to set a time limit for new entry, while it is certainly true (as the applicant alleged) that the Commission in past cases has required advance identification by the parties of potential new entrants on threatened routes, the Court once more emphasized the Commission's broad discretion in framing commitments and that there is no statutory requirement for the parties to identify a new entrant.[446] The Court did imply, however, that the Commission would have to identify a definite new entrant when *no* potential competitors express an interest in entering the affected markets[447] – which was not the case here.[448] Whether or not an identified or prospective entrant actually does enter the market, on the other hand, seems not to have troubled the Court as a normative matter. This is because, evidently, the Court of First Instance subscribes to the contestability theory of the disciplining power of potential new entry.[449] As empirical proof, the Court cited the emergence of new entry on Germany/Austria routes to constrain a Lufthansa/Austrian Airlines high-fare duopoly.[450]

The ruling of the Court of First Instance in easyJet's challenge to the European Commission's Air France/KLM merger decision reveals how the judicial branch

---

did not prove a manifest error by the Commission, in the Court's view, because of remedial measures (including slot divestiture) and intermodal competition. *See id.* para. 175.

445. Behavioral commitments can be viewed as weaker than structural ones, but are 'not by their nature insufficient to prevent' creation or strengthening of a dominant position. *See id.* para. 182. Here, a set of strong structural commitments (slot divestitures), in the Court's impression, imprinted a structural patina upon the other remedies. *See id.* para. 183.

446. *See id.* para. 197 (noting absence of such a requirement in the merger regulation). As a practical matter, new market entry takes time as carriers formulate and rework business plans. In the instant matter, the slot divestiture was unlimited in duration and permanent (the surrendered slots, if unused, would escheat to the local slot coordinators and not to the merging parties, *see id.* para. 183), enabling new entrants to enter the affected markets at any time and without a time limit. *See* easyJet v. Comm'n, *supra* note 411, para. 201.

447. *See id.* para. 206.

448. 'Concrete interest' was expressed by several competitors, including Meridiana, Virgin Express, and Volare. *See id.* paras. 191 & 198-99. The Commission also took an intriguing 'default' position on this argument, in the process revealing its current perspective on the shape of the EU aviation market: other competitors were likely to enter the markets affected, the Commission argued, 'since in Europe there are numerous low-cost airlines inclined to enter these markets, including Ryanair, Virgin Express, Smartwings, Sterling, Air Service and Sky-Europe.' *Id.* para. 200. That argument, if pressed to its logical end, would obviate any need ever to identify specific potential entrants.

449. *See id.* para. 202. On the nature of the contestability theory, *see supra* Chapter 4, Part IV(B).

450. *See* easyJet v. Comm'n, *supra* note 411, para. 202.

perceives the Commission's exercise of its merger control power. The ruling shows a pervasive judicial deference to the Commission's negotiation of commitments, whether the remedies applied are behavioral or structural.[451] It approves of the Commission's binary approach to market identification and evaluation, an approach which accentuates the effectiveness of slot surrender as a (structural) remedy.[452] For those who challenge the Commission merger determinations, the court expects marshaling of specific evidence targeted to specific markets rather than generalized 'macro' arguments about damage to competition (or to competitors).[453]

c   *Conclusion: When the Mergers Come*

Earlier this study examined the controversial record of the U.S. DOT during its run as the (temporary) cynosure of merger enforcement in the domestic

---

451. EasyJet roundly criticized the outcome of its appeal, regarding it as a false vindication of the Commission's 'cursory nod' to the interests of air passengers. Press Release, easyJet, Reaction to the Decision of the European Court of First Instance (Jul. 4, 2006). The merger was, the airline pointed out, 'the first tie-up of Europe's old national airlines,' and strict scrutiny was therefore demanded. *Id.* EasyJet executives accused the Commission of having bowed to political pressure (from France) to speed the merger through its review processes. *See id.*

452. It remains to be seen, however, whether the Commission's binary approach to market analysis survives as the EU market becomes more segmented. Other approaches could include a qualitative refinement of easyJet's rejected 'leisure travel market' metric or a zonal snapshot based not on sets of city-pairs but on travel patterns within a particular region or among regions. So far, in both U.S. and Community practice, the origin/destination binary pair has found most favor in merger (and alliance) analysis.

453. Following the flotation of Aer Lingus stock in Oct. 2006 its arch-rival Ryanair attempted a hostile takeover of the company. The move fell within Article 3(1)(b) of Regulation 139/2004, *see supra* note 200, and led to a preliminary investigation by the European Commission into the merger's likely impact on competition. *See* Prior Notification of a Concentration Case (Case COMP/M.4439), 2006 O.J. (C274) 45. At the close of its preliminary analysis, the Commission concluded that Ryanair's bid raised serious competition concerns, particularly in the area of consumer choice. *See* Press Release, Europa, Mergers: Commission Opens In-Depth Investigation into Ryanair's Takeover of Aer Lingus, IP/06/1867 (Dec. 20, 2006). Of particular significance to the Commission was the (conspicuous) fact that the two carriers were each other's closest competitors on a large number of routes and both were the main operators out of Dublin Airport. *See id.* The Commission reaffirmed these findings six months later when it ordered termination of the merger plan. *See* Press Release, Europa, Mergers: Commission Prohibits Ryanair's Proposed Takeover of Aer Lingus, IP/07/893 (Jun. 27, 2007). The Commission drew no comfort from Ryanair's public commitment to lower Aer Lingus short-haul fares by 10% (Ryanair gave no analogous commitment with respect to its own fares), and indicated that the commitment would in any case be difficult (if not impossible) to monitor. *See* European Commission, Mergers: Commission's Prohibition of Ryanair's Acqui-sition of Aer Lingus – Frequently Asked Questions, MEMO/07/258 (Jun. 27, 2007). Similarly, Ryanair's commitment to limited slot divestiture at Dublin Airport failed to assuage the Commission's fears because, following the *easyJet* ruling, the Commission demanded that 'remedies based on the divestiture of slots must be linked to the likelihood of entry.' *Id.* Following a close market analysis, the Commission found scant evidence that 'entry by one or more competitors on the basis of the [slot divestitures] would be sufficiently likely

airline industry.[454] Just a few years of minimal oversight, along with fortress hub entrenchment, allowed a partial (though not enduring) restoration of the comfortable oligopolistic configuration of the U.S. market that preceded deregulation. The single aviation market, similarly, could become the preserve of a coterie of aggressive mega-carriers if a certain kind of industrial policy trumps regulatory skepticism toward transborder (and large intra-border) mergers and acquisitions. Thus, the strategic challenge, recurrent in the history of EC policymaking, is to settle a critical question of industrial policy: is it not better to encourage broader alliances of airlines, including full-blown mergers or takeovers, particularly when so many of the EU's national carriers have such relatively modest domestic markets, in order to breed leviathans of the air that will better compete in a globalized aviation market?[455]

Possibly the Commission will countenance (if that could be the correct term in a deregulated environment) a 'tiered' system of carriers. In so doing, the Commission would be seeking to ensure (in concert with national antitrust authorities) that regional networks remain open to new entrant competition, while the major intra-Union international routes, and long-haul services outside the EU, are operated by larger, full-service mega-carriers (including, perhaps, more muscular versions of the post-liberalization low-cost carriers that collectively have captured a 19.5% market share in Europe)[456] that can better compete with U.S., Asian, and Middle Eastern rivals.[457] Given the relatively modest number of intra-Union

---

and of a sufficient scope to remove . . . competition concerns on the overlap routes.' *Id.* Ryanair's reluctance to adopt an 'upfront' solution whereby it would only take control of Aer Lingus *after* a suitable new entrant was found to operate 12 to 16 aircraft on routes to and from Dublin (in contrast to Ryanair's own proposal for a new entrant with eight aircraft) merely increased Commission incredulity about Ryanair's commitment to the EC competition ethos. *See id.* Following the decision, Aer Lingus requested the Commission to order Ryanair to divest itself of its then-25% stake in the airline (which has since climbed to nearly 30%). The request was denied, however, on the premise that Ryanair's stake remained a minority interest and a forced sale would only be ordered in cases of control. *See Regulator Can't Request Sale of Aer Lingus Stake*, WALL ST. J., Oct. 12, 2007, at A13. On Ryanair's latest bid to take over Aer Lingus, *see supra* note 17.

454. *See supra* Chapter 4, Part IV(B).

455. This is precisely the expression of 'industrial policy' that some major U.S. carriers have sought to have adopted as the motor of U.S. aviation policy. *See* the summary of the remarks made by Glenn F. Tilton, Chairman, President, and Chief Executive Officer, United Airlines, to the Aviation Leadership Summit, *in* International Aviation Law Institute, DePaul University College of Law & Chicago Council on Global Affairs, *Sustainable Aviation Policies for America and the World: A Leadership Summit*, Synopsis of the Proceedings (Oct. 19, 2006).

456. *See* EUROCONTROL, *Low-Cost Carrier Market Update: June 2007*, at 3, Doc 257 (Sept. 12, 2007).

457. Indeed, this hierarchy of service was already the expectation of the GAO in its 1993 study of the competitive threat from the liberalized EU airline industry. GAO, *European Community, supra* note 3, at 39. It was also manifest in the European Commission's own empirical survey of the post-1992 industry in its publication *Panorama of EU Industry '94 (Air Transport)*, at 3-8. The Commission then identified a 'tiered' system capped by the legacy national carriers providing a mix of intra-Union and global services, below which would be the mid-level

long-haul routes, a hierarchy of carrier operations would more likely conform to the structural reality of the EU air transport market.[458]

Greater consolidation may be expected (and is being attempted)[459] in the afterglow of the first-stage U.S./EC aviation treaty, although the list as of mid-2008 includes only Air France-KLM and BA/Iberia (as well as the special circumstance of Lufthansa's extra-Community bid for Swissair).[460] The larger EU airlines have so far adopted a cautious strategy during the liberalization years, which they have applied both within the EU and in their external relations with non-EU airlines, of 'sham' mergers, cooperative marketing alliances including code-sharing arrangements and other forms of non-permanent corporate association with other airlines.[461] Nevertheless, while only a very few significant (and still not fully consummated) transnational mergers have occurred in the single aviation market, the 2004 merger regulation provides the Commission with a flexible legal instrument to superintend the future formation of larger EU carriers.[462]

---

carriers operating reasonably large networks either within the European Union or internationally, or both (British Midland and Virgin Atlantic were named), a mix of 'regional carriers' operating on dense point-to-point routes, and finally the small 'niche' players operating specific, thinly-subscribed domestic or bilateral services. *Id.* To an appreciable extent, much of this prophesying has in fact come to pass, although the Commission clearly did not foresee the explosive growth of the low-cost sector (which it tamely characterized in 1994 as 'regional carriers' rather than the Union-wide operators they later became). The Transport Commissioner at the time, Karel van Miert, looked forward to a diversified industry, not just a coterie of dominant mega-carriers. Karel van Miert, former EU Transport Commissioner, *European Air Transport Policy in the Perspective of the Achievement of the Internal Market: What Next?*, Speech to the Aviation Club of Great Britain, at 8 (Mar. 30, 1992) (copy on file with the Library of the EU Delegation, Washington DC) [hereinafter Van Miert, *European Air Transport Policy*].

458.   *See, e.g.*, [U.K.] Civil Aviation Authority, *The Single European Aviation Market: Progress So Far*, at 53-61, CAP 654 (1995) (finding that new entrant competition had emerged on denser regional international routes and within domestic markets, but that the dominant flag carriers had not (with the rare exception of British Airways' incursions in France and Germany) attempted to break down existing barriers between national markets within Europe and to engage other major EU carriers in competition on their home ground. To the extent that this has happened in the intervening years, it has tended to be through low-cost subsidiary operations, but the 2007 U.S./EC Air Transport Agreement, *supra* note 129, promises that major EU carriers will confront each other at their respective hubs, at least for transatlantic traffic.

459.   *See supra* note 362.

460.   On Switzerland's special status vis-à-vis Community air transport, *see supra* Chapter 2, note 20. Lufthansa is also seeking to acquire majority control of U.K. carrier bmi. *See supra* Chapter 3, note 273.

461.   For a full discussion of the phenomenon of intercarrier alliances, and the associated practice of code-sharing, *see supra* Chapter 3, Part VIII. The Commission has also examined (but not challenged) a number of intra-Union carrier alliances, including Sabena/Swissair and Lufthansa/SAS. Airline Agreements, *supra* note 373, para. 18; *see also supra* note 369 (discussing the Commission's response to the recent Air France/Alitalia bilateral cooperation agreement).

462.   The original 1989 regulation was described by Professor David Gerber as 'the single most important addition to European Community competition law since its inception.' Gerber, *supra* note 69, at 135.

C REGULATORY CHALLENGES OF MULTILATERAL AIRLINE
LIBERALIZATION I: ISSUES COMMON TO THE U.S. EXPERIENCE

1 **Computer Reservations Systems in Europe**

We have already spent some time examining both the logistical versatility and
potentially subversive competitive traits of CRS, as well as the U.S. administrative
law response to this polarity.[463] The EC, like the United States until 2004, chose
regulatory supervision of the CRS phenomenon as a means to balance the procompetitive and anticompetitive effects of these systems, although initially with
no greater finesse in taming their apparent potential for bias and competitive exclusion than had been evident in prior U.S. DOT rulemaking.[464] Indeed, the original
CRS 'code of conduct' adopted by the Council in Regulation 2299/89,[465] which
proceeded from an explicit recognition that the 'useful' services of a CRS masked
serious competitive 'abuses,'[466] established behavioral criteria not dissimilar to
those promulgated by the DOT in 1984 to moderate perceived architectural bias
in CRS displays. The Regulation also established a master principle, present in its
defunct DOT counterpart, that air carriers shall be allowed to participate in all CRS
'on an equal and nondiscriminatory basis.'[467] More specifically, the code provides a
standard format for 'ranking' flight options in a system's 'principal display.'[468]

---

463. Although the relevant EC regulations (and the expired U.S. regulations) refer to 'CRS' systems, in the travel industry they are now more commonly called GDS, or 'global distribution
systems.' *See supra* Chapter 3, Part VII & Chapter 4, note 444. In the text we continue to refer
to CRS systems.
464. As the Commission has pointed out, part of the bias-inherency of CRS came initially from their
origin as *internal* reservations systems. European Commission, Reference Concerning a Code
of Conduct for CRS, at 3, COM (95) 51 final [hereinafter European Commission, *Reference on
CRS*]. This phenomenon has rapidly changed, however, as airlines have increasingly divested
themselves of CRS ownership. *See infra* in the main text.
465. Council Regulation 2299/89, 1989 O.J. (L 220) 1, *as amended by* Council Regulation 3089/93,
1993 (L 278) 1 *and* Council Regulation 323/1999, 1999 O.J. (L 40) 1. (All references here to
the original regulation include relevant amendments introduced in the 1993 and 1999 legislation.) The regulation is not an original EC law product. Its substantive provisions were
borrowed virtually entirely from the European Civil Aviation Conference (voluntary) code
of conduct adopted in Mar. 1989. DE CONINCK, *supra* note 148, at 56. Previously, EC regulatory
monitoring of CRS operated solely through the block exemption process.
466. Council Regulation 2299/89, *supra* note 465, pmbl. The abuses cited in the preamble included
denial of access to the systems or discrimination in the provision, loading, or display of data, or
unreasonable conditions imposed on participants or subscribers.
467. *Id.* art. 3(2).
468. *Id.* art. 5(1)-(2). Flights must be ranked not on the basis of carrier identity, but according to a
default hierarchy (which the customer may request to be altered for an individual transaction)
that gives priority to nonstop direct flights between the city-pairs concerned, followed by other
direct flights not involving a change of aircraft, and finally connecting flights. *Id.* annex I(1) &
art. 5(2). The DOT's former rule similarly prohibited identity-based ranking. *See supra*
Chapter 4, Part IV(B). As to time of departure, the default hierarchy ranks nonstop direct
flights by departure time and ranks other direct flights and connecting flights by elapsed
journey time. Council Regulation 2299/89, *supra* note 465, annex I(2).

These ranking criteria contrast with the 'permissive' criteria of the former DOT regulations, which required an 'integrated display' based on uniform display criteria but did not decree that vendors observe any specific ranking order in translating the principle of nondiscrimination into on-screen displays.[469]

One of the problems which spurred the Community to impose its CRS regulations is that the structural complementarity of the systems that comprise the CRS industry may award market power to system owners in their own markets, a tendency reinforced by the historic practice of 'tying' subscribers (primarily travel agents) to single systems.[470] Several provisions of the EC code of conduct, mirroring the former DOT rules, attempt to proscribe air carriers from 'tying' incentives or commissions to retail agents to the sale or issue of tickets from a specific CRS or from insisting that any specific CRS be employed for sale or issue of its tickets.[471] While the DOT's former rule contented itself with a hazy admonition to system owners not to 'impede' use of alternative systems, the EC regulation explicitly prohibits so-called 'exclusive contracts' that restrict users to a single system.[472]

For all of the likely positive effects of the CRS code on curbing competitive abuses, it is worth inquiring why the Community failed to follow the DOT's phaseout of CRS regulation. Nearly two decades ago, when the first CRS code was promulgated, the 'big four' systems – Amadeus, Sabre, Galileo/Apollo, and Worldspan – were in the hands of the airlines. Today, only a minority share of Amadeus remains in carrier ownership.[473] The deregulated CRS market in the United States has also given U.S. airlines and CRS providers a competitive advantage over their EU counterparts by allowing them to reduce fees and offer deeper discounts.[474] And, other structural changes to the distribution market,

---

469. *See* DE CONINCK, *supra* note 148, at 55; [U.K.] CAA, *Airline Competition, supra* note 279, at 54-55. *See supra* Chapter 4, Part IV(B).

470. *See supra* Chapter 4, Part IV(B).

471. Council Regulation 2299/89, *supra* note 465, art. 8(1)-(2).

472. *Id.* art. 9(2). As the U.S. experience taught, stiff contractual penalties for termination could serve as a surrogate for 'exclusivity' provisions, and accordingly the EC code also regulates the content of vendor/subscriber contracts, outlawing 'unreasonable conditions' and allowing users to terminate without penalty at the end of the first year with as little as three months' notice. *Id.* art. 9(4). Arguably, however, the protective coverage is just as incomplete as the old DOT rules were: while 'exclusivity' is blocked, there is no *explicit* prohibition of the kinds of liquidated damages clauses that once attracted a great deal of complaint in the United States. Article 10(1) of the CRS code insists only that subscriber fees shall 'be non-discriminatory, reasonably structured and reasonably related to the cost of service.' *Id. as amended by* Commission Regulation 3089/93, *supra* note 465.

473. *See* European Commission, *Consultation Paper on the Possible Revision of Regulation 2299/89 on a Code of Conduct for Computerised Reservation Systems*, at 11-12 (2007) [hereinafter European Commission, *CRS Consultation Paper*]. Prior to 2005, 47% of Amadeus's capital and 86% of the voting rights were owned by Air France, Iberia, and Lufthansa. Following the entry of two private equity firms, BC Partners and Civen, 46.4% of the capital is held by the airlines, with voting rights now proportional to ownership. *Id.* at 12. As for the ownership stake of the three airlines, Air France-KLM leads at 23.2%, with Iberia and Lufthansa each holding 11.6%. *Id.*

474. The European Commission found the freeing of the negotiation process in the U.S. post-regulation CRS market to be the source of this competitive advantage. Airlines in the

notably including direct ticket sales through the Internet, have dethroned CRS and the travel agents which use them from their dominance of consumer bookings.[475] Arguably, these shifts in the producer and consumer climates should have prompted EC regulators to follow the U.S. precedent. In place of exploitation through carrier control, economic incentives and competition from alternative booking channels have become the new 'ordering principles' of the CRS market. Yet, despite predictions of imminent total deregulation,[476] the European Commission decided only to loosen rather than release its regulatory fetters.[477]

Following an open consultation with stakeholders, a consensus emerged that the existing rules are outdated and market-distorting, but that continued carrier investment in certain large systems made it prudent to retain rules on neutral displays and fairness.[478] The Commission itself was unpersuaded that the rise of alternative booking channels sufficiently moderated fears that CRS abuse would no longer have a serious adverse impact on consumers, noting that '[m]any corporate travelers remain highly dependent upon the single distribution channel constituted of the travel agents and the CRS' and that this was equally 'true for travelers in Member States with low Internet penetration rates.'[479] Accordingly,

---

United States can offer full access to their fare inventory to a CRS in exchange for a reduction in fees. Travel agents may also opt into these full-access arrangements by paying a charge for each booking. The effect has been a 20-30% reduction in booking fees in the United States. *Id.* at 12-14. In the European Union, also, individualized discounts remain proscribed. *Id.* at 14.

475. The European Commission found that direct Internet bookings, when combined with call centers and airline office sales, accounted for nearly 40% of all ticket sales in the EU. Despite this, however, the Commission was not satisfied that the new distribution channels offset the market dominance of CRS, especially Amadeus, where its footholds in France, Germany, and Spain still gave it an appreciable advantage. *See* European Commission, *CRS Consultation Paper, supra* note 473, at 14.

476. *See* Kevin Mitchell, *Don't Break the Code*, AIRLINE BUS., Feb. 20, 2006.

477. *See* European Commission, *Proposal for a Regulation of the European Parliament and of the Council on a Code of Conduct for Computerised Reservation Systems*, COM (2007) 709 final (Nov. 11, 2007) [hereinafter European Commission, *CRS Proposal*]. The story of revising the CRS rules actually dates back five years to the Commission's selection of the Brattle Group economic consultancy and the Norton Rose law firm to conduct a study on CRS deregulation. While the study offered proposals to partially liberalize the CRS market (discussed below), it remained skeptical as to whether or not increased competitive pressure was an acceptable trade-off for potential market abuses. *See* BRATTLE GROUP & NORTON ROSE, STUDY TO ASSESS THE POTENTIAL IMPACT OF PROPOSED AMENDMENTS TO COUNCIL REGULATION 2299/89 WITH REGARD TO COMPUTERISED RESERVATION SYSTEMS 52 (2003). In particular, the study was concerned that the Amadeus CRS system – at the time still owned and controlled by Air France, Iberia, and Lufthansa – could be used by its parent carriers to engage in abuse in their home markets. *Id.* at xi. The study also expressed reservations about whether competition authorities could adequately redress potential abuses in light of the fact that they would be difficult to detect and enforcement could take years. *Id.* at xi & 47.

478. The Commission's 2007 consultation paper on CRS included a set of questions to elicit stakeholder feedback on the CRS rules. *See* European Commission, *CRS Consultation Paper, supra* note 473, at 22. A full archive of stakeholder contributions, along with a summary, may be found online at the Air Transport Portal of the European Commission, Public Consultations, <http://ec.europa.eu/transport/air_portal/consultation/2007_04_27_en.htm>.

479. *See* European Commission, *CRS Proposal, supra* note 477 at Explanatory Memorandum, sec. 2.

the Commission opted for continued safeguards that it hoped would not compromise the prospect of increased competition.[480]

Responding to claims of market distortion, the Commission has been reexamining the requirement that parent carriers – airlines which own or control a CRS – participate equally in all CRS ('mandatory participation') and that CRS treat all carriers alike with respect to their fees and services ('nondiscrimination'). The effect of these rules has been to stifle competition by preventing a parent carrier dissatisfied with a particular CRS's operation or fees from withdrawing or scaling back its participation. The CRS code has also inhibited CRS from freely competing with one another due to the prohibition on discriminating among carriers with respect to charges and contractual terms.[481] Some competitive clarity will enter the CRS market should the Commission's latest proposal, which would prune the nondiscrimination rule, come into effect. The outcome, of course, would be *partial* liberalization through making the market actors themselves responsible for the level and pricing of services they negotiate; carriers in particular would finally be able to procure competitive pricing for CRS services.[482] Where the Commission appears less 'libertine' in its thinking is in matters involving parent carriers. The Commission's proposal would still mandate a parent carrier, if requested, to furnish any competing CRS with the inventory it provides to its own system. And guidelines on display neutrality – a staple of the CRS code – would also be maintained.

The Commission, in sum, is still hesitating on CRS deregulation.[483] Surprisingly for an agency that has not been afraid to put itself in front of market development, the Commission seems to have discounted the rapid emergence of Internet distribution and may find that its code revisions appear ill-tuned to market realities by the time they are enacted. A number of stakeholders, in fact, recommended insertion of a 'sunset clause' that would allow the amended CRS code to lapse once all airlines have fully divested their remaining CRS ownership interests.[484]

---

480. *Id.* A largely understated goal of the Commission's CRS Proposal has been the promotion of rail transport in CRS displays.

481. *See* European Commission, *CRS Proposal, supra* note 477, at Explanatory Memorandum; European Commission, *CRS Consultation Paper, supra* note 473, at 4 & 6-7.

482. *See* EC, *CRS Proposal, supra* note 477, art. 10; *cf.* Commission Regulation 2299/89, *supra* note 465, art. 10 *as amended by* Council Regulation 323/1999, *supra* note 465, art. 10. Non-parent carriers would also remain free to negotiate separate arrangements with the CRS in which they participate, and with no requirement that they share identical data with each. They remain bound, however, to ensure that the information they do share is accurate. *See* European Commission, *CRS Proposal, supra* note 477, art. 9.

483. The Commission Proposal calls for other revisions to the CRS code. CRS vendors would be prohibited from identifying travel agents in their Market Information Data Tapes (MIDT), in order to prevent airlines from using such data to pressure travel agents to reduce bookings on rival airlines. *See id.* art. 7. Additionally, the revised regulations would increase safeguards for personal booking information and set fines for any violations to the CRS code. *See id.* arts. 11 & 13-14.

484. *See* European Commission, *Summary of the Contributions Received by the Commission Following the Open Consultation on the Possible Revision of Regulation 2299/89 Establishing a Code of Conduct for Computerised Reservation Systems (CRS)* (2007).

2 The Infrastructure Challenge

Federal airport slot regulation in the United States, as we have seen, has been confined to a select group of what used to be called 'high density' airports.[485] In the EU, in contrast, traffic congestion at major airports is an endemic structural problem that inevitably forecloses opportunities for potential new entrant competition,[486] and has been one of the most obstinate restraints on the European Commission's competition vocation.[487] Congestion is most notorious at two massive air complexes, London Heathrow and Frankfurt, that are the hubs for the most lucrative services on the continent.[488] In the 2008 consolidated version of the third liberalization package, as we have seen, Member State national and local authorities retain a vaguely-formed power to limit open market access rights that they may invoke *inter alia* on grounds of infrastructural overload.[489]

While issues of scarcity and congestion abound in the European airport system, the Commission's rulemaking has been most pervasive in the area of slot control. In addition to its former various block exemption provisions to allow airlines to consult on slot allocation under conditions of nondiscrimination,[490]

---

485. *See supra* Chapter 4, Part IV(B).
486. 'It is a fact that congestion at some key airports has reduced the possibility for new entrants to take advantage of new business opportunities offered by the Third Package. This means that rights which have been legally granted are in effect not available, thus negating the concept of equal treatment.' Report of the *Comité des Sages, supra* note 39, at 20. *See also* Basedow, *supra* note 114, at 258. *See also* NATIONAL ECONOMIC RESEARCH ASSOCIATES [NERA], STUDY TO ASSESS THE EFFECTS OF DIFFERENT SLOT ALLOCATION SCHEMES 15 & 51-52 (2004) (noting the 'operational link' between Council Regulation 2408/92 (now part of the 2008 consolidated regulation) and slot allocation because Member States are entitled to subordinate market access to slot allocation). The report also stated that new entrants would 'welcome the opportunity to compete directly with established carriers serving congested airports' and that slot availability and not traffic rights issues has the greatest potential for causing inefficiencies in the EU aviation market.
487. The Commission is still searching for what Button and Swann call a 'tractable policy' for slots. Button & Swann, *supra* note 6, at 252. Of the 32 Category One EU airports, a recent report found that seven had excess demand for slots which could not be accommodated throughout the day (*e.g.*, London Heathrow and Frankfurt), and 14 more had excess demand during peak flight times (*e.g.*, Brussels and Munich). NERA, *supra* note 486, at 23-30. Additionally, another recent study has found that unless significant infrastructural improvements are made at EU airports, nearly a fifth of potential demand for flights to and from EU airports – accounting for up to four million flights per year – will not be met. ECAC & EUROCONTROL, CHALLENGES TO GROWTH: 2004 REPORT 2 (2004). While competition from rail and road would restrict the average annual growth of intra-Union air travel to 3.4% between 2005 and 2025, Europe/Asia routes, to take one important example of extra-Union market potential, are projected to grow by an annual average of 5.5%. *See* BOEING COMPANY, CURRENT MARKET OUTLOOK: 2006 8 (2006).
488. *See* NERA, *supra* note 486, at 23-30 (noting that the capacity constraints at London Heathrow and Frankfurt reflect physical limitations of each's runway capacity).
489. *See supra* Part II(C).
490. The Commission, as already noted, has recently ended a series of block exemptions for airline joint planning, including slot allocation. *See supra* note 194; *see also* European Commission,

the Commission has made several efforts to create and strengthen a pan-Community 'code of conduct' on the allocation process.[491] An initial draft in 1990, proposing a U.S. FAA-style 'slot pool' of newly-created, unused, and surrendered slots, drew strong opposition from the larger incumbents.[492] Another code of conduct, once described by former Competition Commissioner Karel van Miert as a 'Pandora's box,' was adopted in the form of a Council regulation published in January 1993.[493]

The aim of the 1993 regulation was to develop 'neutral, transparent and non-discriminatory rules' that would support start-up carriers.[494] The marks of political compromise were present, however, in the bureaucratic slot control artifice chosen in lieu of direct Commission surveillance. In an exception to a deregulatory paradigm of entrepreneurial autonomy subject to Commission (and occasionally Member State) intervention, the regulation devolved directly to each *Member State* the right, and in certain exigent circumstances the obligation, to appoint an independent 'coordinator' for an airport which it considers to be congested.[495] Apart from a general monitoring function, the most important task of the coordinator is to act as a kind of micro-FAA, framing high-density slot allocation regimes at the 'coordinated' airport.[496] The principles for allocation appear in Article 8, and echo earlier FAA rulemaking (reserving a guaranteed block of slots for new entry, and even adopting the same 80% 'use-or-lose' benchmark for grandfather rights).[497]

Revision of Block Exemption from Competition Rules for IATA Conferences – Frequently Asked Questions, MEMO/06/359 (Oct. 2, 2006).

491. Report of the *Comité des Sages, supra* note 39, at 20.
492. GAO, *European Community, supra* note 3, at 51. And U.S. airlines with EU operations were concerned that the Commission proposals would allow some of their EU airport slots to be confiscated in the name of 'open entry' for Member State carriers. The proposals did not appear to envisage distribution of slots to non-EU carriers.
493. Council Regulation 95/93 on Common Rules for the Allocation of Slots at [EU] airports, 1993 O.J. (L 14) 1 *as amended by* Council Regulation 894/2002, 2002 O.J. (L 142) 3 *and* Council Regulation 1554/2003, 2003 O.J. (L 221) 1 *and* Council Regulation 793/2004, 2004 O.J. (L 138) 50. The 2002 and 2003 amendments concerned the temporary suspension of the regulation's so-called 'use or lose rule' following the terrorist attacks on 9/11, and the outbreak of the SARS epidemic, respectively. The 2004 amendment imposes technical changes on the regulation which are meant to presage a more fundamental revision of the slots allocation process.
494. Council Regulation 95/93, *supra* note 493, pmbl.
495. *Id.* art. 3(2). A Member State may reach this determination as a matter of its own government policy, but it can be prompted to action where more than 50% of the carriers at a particular airport (or the airport authority) consider that capacity is inadequate to meet actual or planned operations, *or* when new entrants encounter 'serious problems' in securing slots. *Id.* art. 3(3). The requirement that the coordinator act independently appears in Article 4(2); according to Article 5, the coordinator will be assisted by a coordination committee (which has carrier and airport authority representation). *Id.* art. 5.
496. Council Regulation 95/93, *supra* note 493, art. 4(5). The coordinator's mandate includes compilation (and dissemination) of data on the historical pattern of slot requests, allocations, and availability. *Id.* art. 4(8).
497. 'Grandfather' rights are preserved if slots are used at least 80% during the preceding season. *Id.* art. 10(2). Otherwise (unless certain mitigating factors apply) the slots must be surrendered

As with CRS regulation, the Commission has suffered another bout of regulatory hesitation in dealing with the EU facilities crunch. The slot control rules have been in place for a rather long time (over 15 years), and have faced continuing criticism that they have neither bolstered competition nor lowered infrastructural barriers for new entrants.[498] The Commission is undertaking a two-phase revision to the regulation, the first of which accomplished technical changes to the regulation which were intended as a precursor for more substantial revisions to the entire slot allocation process.[499] The second phase, however, has been derailed by critical feedback suggesting that the inaugural amendments had failed to increase competition while squandering scarce slots.[500] To address stakeholder

---

into a slot pool, which also comprises newly created slots and slots given up for any other reason. *Id.* art. 10(1), (4). Slots are freely exchangeable between carriers or by one carrier among its different routes. *Id.* art. 8. New entrants have priority in the slot allocation of up to 50% of slots in the slot pool. *Id.* art. 10(6). Press reports in summer 2008 indicated that, despite falling demand during the oil crisis peak, certain U.K. airlines were flying empty or near-empty planes in order to maintain compliance with their cumulative slot usage obligations at key complexes such as London Heathrow. *See, e.g.,* Helen Nugent, *Planes 'Fly Empty' to Keep Slots at Airport,* Times (London), Jul. 16, 2008, at 1; *MP Blasts Environmental Impact of 'Ghost Flights',* Eastbourne Herald, Jul. 23, 2008.

498. *See* Martin Staniland, A Europe of the Air?: The Airline Industry and European Integration 175-78 (2008). Numerous studies conducted in the 1990s found that the regulation's 'use or lose' rule was not effective in generating enough new slots for entrants and that incumbent airlines had engaged in 'hoarding,' even to the point of allegedly operating flights at a loss rather than risk losing slots to competitors. *Id.* at 177; *see also supra* note 497 (containing a recent example). Slot coordinators, too, came under scrutiny for failing to promote competition on routes. Staniland, *supra,* at 176-77.

499. *See* European Commission, *Commercial Slot Allocation Mechanisms in the Context of a Further Revision of Council Regulation (EEC) 95/93 on Common Rules for the Allocation of Slots at Community Airports,* at 4, Commission Staff Working Document (Sept. 17, 2004) [hereinafter European Commission, *Slot Allocation*]. The 2004 amending regulation offers a number of clarifications, perhaps most notably in definitively tying the formal definition of a slot to the existence and discretionary authority of the coordinator. Thus, in EC parlance, a slot is now defined as 'the permission given by a coordinator . . . to use the full range of airport infrastructure necessary to operate air services . . . at a specific date and time for the purposes of landing or take-off.' Council Regulation 793/2004, *supra* note 493, art. 1(a). In other words, slots are understood as permissions rather than property under the regulation. Other revisions include an expanded definition of what constitutes a new entrant, strengthening the requirements for slot coordinator neutrality, and strengthening the regulation's enforcement provisions. Interestingly, the 2004 revision also mandated that slot coordinators must also take into account industry scheduling guidelines such as those provided by IATA's Worldwide Scheduling Guidelines. *Id.* arts. 5-9.

500. *See* European Commission, *Communication on the Application of Regulation (EC) 793/2004 on Common Rules for the Allocation of Slots at Community Airports* (Nov. 15, 2007). Most of the criticism concerned what stakeholders saw as an overly complicated definition of a new entrant. Article 1 of Regulation 793/2004, *supra* note 493, defined a new entrant as 'an air carrier holding more than 5% of the total slots available' on a given day, 'or more than 4% of the total slots' on a given day 'in an airport system of which that airport forms a part.' Some Member States worried that the definition was not uniformly understood and therefore would not be applied consistently throughout the EU. European Commission, *Communication, supra,* at 2. Member States also expressed concern that the amended slot rules had the

grievances, the Commission has further tangled its regulatory agenda by announcing clarifications of the slot regulation, including the neutrality of the slot coordinator, the transparency of scheduling data, and the secondary trading of slots.[501]

But it is on this last point of secondary trading that the Commission has finally begun to yield to market principles in place of iterative regulation as the determinant of the most efficient allocation of slots.[502] The Commission has recognized that '[w]here there is no transparent market for the scarce resources of slots at congested airports, incumbent air carriers are often not aware of, or confronted with, the full opportunity costs of the slots they hold.'[503] The longstanding consequence of this imperfect market information has been that carriers in the EU were holding slots even when the market value of their holdings far exceeded the revenue generated from retention. The Commission's late embrace of the market principle contrasts strongly with its prior threat of enforcement proceedings against the U.K. Government for tolerating secondary trading at London Heathrow and other British airports.[504]

The Commission's new receptivity to slot trading is also a prudent acknowledgment not only that slot exchanges are and have been ongoing at EU airports for some years, but also that nothing in the original 1993 regulation expressly prohibits the practice.[505] It remains to be seen what effect this modestly liberalizing

---

effect of limiting competition by preferring new entrants over carriers with smaller-scale operations looking to expand and compete on routes with incumbent airlines. *Id.* at 2-3. Others were skeptical that the slot rules had any effect at all on new entrants, noting that the highly competitive nature of the EU aviation market likely accounted for new carrier penetration at primary and secondary EU airports. *Id.* Some stakeholders also urged that the Commission take a more proactive role to ensure slot coordinator neutrality and to establish a clear definition of efficient use of airport capacity. *Id.* at 4-5; *see also* European Commission, *Conclusions of the EC – Stakeholder Hearing on Slots of 29 January 2008* (2008).

501. European Commission, *Communication from the Commission to the European Parliament, the Council, [and] the European Economic and Social Committee of the Regions on the Application of Regulation (EEC) No 95/93 on Common Rules for the Allocation of Slots at Community Airports, As Amended*, COM (2008) 227 (Apr. 30, 2008) [hereinafter European Commission, *Slot Communication*]. With regard to the slot coordinator, the Commission reaffirmed 'that the coordinator should act autonomously from, not be instructed by, and not have a duty to report back to the airport managing body, a service provider or any carrier operating from the airport concerned.' On this point the Commission further stated that the slot coordinator's financing should be independent of any party affected by or having an interest in its activities. *Id.* sec. 1. On the mater of scheduling data transparency, the Commission called upon Member States to ensure its submission to an existing combined, freely-accessible, database open to all interested parties. *Id.* sec. 3. The Commission also provided some clarifications on local rules and the consistency between slots and flight plans. With respect to the former, however, no ground was gained on allowing the development of localized rules which would allow more latitude in distributing slots. *Id.* secs. 4 & 6.

502. *See id.* sec. 5. For discussion of secondary trading of slots in the U.S. context, *see supra* Chapter 4, Part IV(B).

503. *Id.*

504. STANILAND, *supra* note 498, at 183.

505. The Commission's clarification did note, however, that slot trading ought to be conducted in a transparent manner in accordance with all administrative requirements set forth in the applicable slots legislation. It also warned that should it 'become[] apparent that for competition or

clarification will have on EU airport and slot competition. While full deregulation in this area may be well-nigh impossible in light of the complexity of the capacity problems at EU airports, for the first time the Commission has shown confidence that the market also can spur air carriers to use or surrender their slots in a rational, economically beneficial manner.

3   Passenger Rights: Overexuberant Regulation?

While the U.S. airlines successfully staved off passenger rights legislation in the United States by substituting voluntary codes of conduct and amending their contracts of carriage,[506] their counterparts in the EU have faced a substantial regulatory burden (although one that applies also to all non-EU airlines departing EU airports). Council Regulation 261/2004, which took effect in February 2005, sets forth common rules for compensation and assistance in instances where air passengers are subject to cancellations, long delays, or denied boarding.[507] Rules governing compensation for denied boarding had in fact been in place in the EC since 1991,[508] but the Commission has recently made it a priority to strengthen passenger rights through a combination of legislation and voluntary initiatives undertaken by the airlines themselves.[509] In the words of former EU Transportation Commissioner Loyola de Palacio, '[P]assenger rights [legislation] is one of the major initiatives of [the] Commission in order to put the citizens at the heart of EU policies.'[510]

other reasons revision of the existing legislation is required,' the Commission will make an appropriate proposal. *See* European Commission, *Slot Communication, supra* note 501, sec. 5.

506. For a summary of the U.S. airlines' efforts to substitute voluntary customer service initiatives for passenger rights legislation, *see* Daniel H. Rosenthal, *Legal Turbulence: The Court's Misconstrual of the Airline Deregulation Act's Preemption Clause and the Effect on Passengers' Rights*, 51 DUKE L.J. 1857, 1859-61 (2002).

507. *See* Council Regulation 261/2004, 2004 O.J. (L 46) 1.

508. *See* Council Regulation 295/91, 1991 O.J. (L 36) 5. In the words of the Commission: 'This [legislation] gave passengers the right to financial compensation, to the choice between an alternative flight at the earliest opportunity, re-routing or reimbursement of the ticket . . . and to assistance to reduce the inconvenience of waiting for a later flight.' European Commission, *Proposal for a Regulation of the European Parliament and of the Council Establishing Common Rules on Compensation and Assistance to Air Passengers in the Event of Denied Boarding and of Cancellation or Long Delay of Flights*, Explanatory Memorandum, para. 3, COM (2001) 784 final (Dec. 21, 2001).

509. *See generally* European Commission, *Communication from the Commission to the European Parliament and the Council on the Protection of Air Passengers in the European Union*, COM (2000) 365 final (Jun. 21, 2000). Unlike in the United States, however, the Commission views voluntary self-regulation as 'an essential complement to legislation' rather than an end in itself. *Id.* para. 40.

510. *See* Press Release, Europa, New Rights for Passengers in the Whole EU, IP/04/98 (Jan. 26, 2004). Palacio sought to encapsulate the impetus behind the Commission's stance on passenger rights as follows: 'Too many times, air passengers are victims of practices which deserve that they receive a fair treatment and proper compensation: henceforth, they will all benefit from new strengthened rights.' *Id.* The trope of citizen rights is one that recurs and evolves in EC air transport policy. In a sense, the entire low-cost carrier phenomenon of the past decade

This 'putting at the heart' entails heightened compensation standards in instances of cancellations, delays, or denied boarding for all passengers within the territory of an EU Member State who have a confirmed reservation on either a scheduled or nonscheduled flight.[511] Passengers departing a third country for the territory of the EU are also entitled to compensation if they are flying on a Community air carrier and have not received benefits or compensation in that third country.[512] With respect to flights departing within the territory of the EU, the regulation pays no regard to either the nationality of the passenger or the flag of the carrier.[513] Should any of the three 'events' which trigger the legislation occur, the responsible airlines must take steps to compensate or accommodate passengers in accordance with the common rules.[514] Only in 'extraordinary circumstances' are

was, for EU elites, a demonstration of how the EU project bolsters citizen welfare. In reply to a BBC online panel question asking him to identify some of the benefits EU membership has conferred on U.K. citizens, former U.K. Transport Secretary Douglas Alexander pointed to cheaper flights as a direct result of the single market as one of them. BBC News, Cheap Flights Are Thanks to EU, Online Video Interview with Douglas Alexander, <http://news. bbc.co.uk/2/hi/uk_news/politics/4906358.stm>. Curiously, EU climate change policy, which aims to pull the airline industry into the Community emissions trading scheme, is now advanced by EU leaders as an enhancement of citizen environmental rights (thereby exhibiting a trope shift in EU consumer thinking). *Cf.* European Commission, Homepage for Stavros Dimas, Commissioner for Environment, <http://ec.europa.eu/commission_barroso/dimas/index_en.htm>; Charter of Fundamental Rights of the European Union art. 37, 2000 O.J. (C 364) 1 ('A level of environmental protection and the improvement of the quality of the environment must be integrated into the policies of the Union and ensured in accordance with the principle of sustainable development'); Press Release, Europeans Put the Environment Centre Stage, IP/08/445 (Mar. 13, 2008).

511. Council Regulation 261/2004, *supra* note 507, art. 3. The preamble to the regulation took notice of the waning distinction between scheduled and nonscheduled flights and stated that the protections afforded under the regulation ought to be extended to both, including flights which are part of package tours. *Id.* pmbl., recital 6.

512. *Id.* art. 3(1)(b). The application of the regulation to flights departing third countries is a notable extension of reach from the 1991 regulation, which only applied to flights departing EU Member States. *See* Council Regulation 295/91, *supra* note 508, art. 1.

513. Council Regulation 261/2004, *supra* note 507, art. 3(1).

514. The 'events' are the aforementioned occurrences of denied boarding, cancellation, or delay. For denied boarding, the regulations first anticipate a call for volunteers who are willing to travel on a later flight (with the amount of compensation being negotiated between the volunteer and the airline). If insufficient volunteers are found and a passenger is denied boarding, compensation must be paid at a 'dissuasive level' of between 250 and 650 euro depending on the length of the flight. Passengers are also accorded a right to further assistance from the airlines, including a choice between reimbursement of their ticket or an alternative flight and the provision of meals and hotels in relation to the time they are forced to wait. *See id.* arts. 4 & 7-9. The same rules apply for all cancellations not caused by 'extraordinary circumstances' unless the passengers were informed of the cancellation at least two weeks prior to the scheduled time of departure or are informed in less than two weeks and rerouted at a time close to their original flight. *Id.* art. 5. The regulations also provide for some compensatory payments and accommodations for delays which fall short of cancellations (the compensation provided being subject to the length of delay). *See id.* art 6. For any delay exceeding five hours, passengers may request full reimbursement of the purchase price of their ticket for the parts of their journey not made and for any part already made if the purpose of the journey

the airlines relieved from their compensation obligations,[515] and at all times they remain subject to 'effective, proportionate and dissuasive' sanctions for any failure to adhere to the new rules.[516]

The airline industry has vented strong opposition to the passenger rights regulation. IATA has estimated compliance costs alone to be in excess of $700 million a year.[517] But an attempt to nullify the regulation failed when the European Court of Justice upheld its validity in January 2006.[518] While petitioners on behalf of the airlines brought eight questions before the Court, the three most important were whether the regulation violated the Montreal Convention of 1999,[519] failed to

---

has been nullified by the delay, along with a return flight to their first point of departure. *Id.* art. 8(1)(a). This only applies, however, if the passenger elects not to continue the journey. *See generally* European Commission, Air Passenger Rights Information Leaflet (2007); Air Passenger Rights Poster (2007), <http://ec.europa.eu/transport/air_portal/passenger_rights/information_en.htm>.

515. Extraordinary circumstances under the regulation include those events 'which could not have been avoided even if all reasonable measures had been taken.' Council Regulation 261/2004, *supra* note 507, art. 5(3). According to the regulation's preamble, '[s]uch circumstances may, in particular, occur in cases of political instability, meteorological conditions incompatible with the operation of the flight concerned, security risks, unexpected flight safety shortcomings and strikes that affect the operation of an operating air carrier.' *Id.* pmbl, recital 14. *See infra* note 530 (discussing a new ECJ ruling on the definition of 'extraordinary circumstances').

516. *Id.* art. 16(3). Enforcement of the passenger rights legislation is entrusted to the Member States themselves through a designated National Enforcement Body (NEB). *Id.* art. 16(1). The European Commission maintains a website listing each Member State's NEB, along with understandings on procedures, a complaint form for passengers, and copies of leaflets and posters explaining the rights granted under the regulation. *See supra* note 514.

517. *See* Press Release, IATA, IATA Condemns Absurd European Court Ruling (Jul. 10, 2006). A smaller trade association, the European Regions Airline Association, projected a more subdued number of approximately $130 million annually. *See* Cathy Buyck, *A Right Mess*, AIR TRANSP. WORLD, Mar. 2006, at 33.

518. The case arose out of a petition by IATA and the European Low Fares Airline Association (ELFAA) for a preliminary reference to the ECJ on the legality of certain portions of the regulation. *See* Case C-344/04, The Queen on the Application of the International Air Transport Association, European Low Fares Airline Association v. Department of Transport, 2006 E.C.R. I-403 [hereinafter Passenger Rights Case].

519. The most substantive portion of the Court's decision focused on the incompatibility of the regulation with the Montreal Convention of 1999 and its predecessor. While the ECJ recognized that the Convention governed the conditions when, after a flight delay, passengers 'may bring actions for damages by way of redress on an individual basis,' there was nothing inherent in the Convention itself preempting the European Community from adopting regulations mandating 'standardized and immediate compensatory measures...[which] operate at an earlier stage than the system which results from the Montreal Convention.' *Id.* paras. 44-45. Thus, a passenger could utilize the protections of the passenger rights regulation and still bring an action to redress damages caused by the delay under the Montreal Convention. *Id.* para. 47. The decision of the Court on this aspect of the legal challenge to the regulation has met with stiff criticism. *See* Jorn L. Wegter, *The ECJ Decision of 10 January 2006 on the Validity of Regulation 261/2004: Ignoring the Exclusivity of the Montreal Convention*, 31 AIR & SPACE L. 133 (2006); Stephen Dolan, *EC Aviation Scene (No. 2: 2006)*, 31 AIR & SPACE L. 211, 226-28 (2006). According to international lawyer Wegter, Regulation 261/2004 undermines the intent of the Montreal Convention and its precursor instruments 'to

meet the appropriate standards of proportionality,[520] and discriminated against the low-fare sector in comparison with other airlines and in comparison with competing modes of transportation.[521]

Despite success in the courtroom, however, the Commission has encountered even greater difficulties in seeking uniform implementation of its rights legislation. Several Member States were initially hesitant to comply with the requirement to establish a National Enforcement Body (NEB)[522] and, even then, to enact national laws laying down appropriate sanctions for violators.[523] There were immediate concerns, also, that the NEBs were not sufficiently independent and lacked the resources necessary to carry out their mandate under the regulation.[524] Perhaps most damaging to confidence in a new epoch of passenger rights was an independent report issued in 2007 concluding that, after two years in effect, the legislation 'appears not to be working consistently well in practice, primarily as a result of a number of key elements of the [r]egulation being unclear, and ineffective enforcement.'[525]

---

provide *an exclusive cause of action* for passenger claims arising out of death, bodily injury, *delay* and damage to baggage in international air carriage.' Wegter, *supra*, at 147-48 (emphasis added). Stephen Dolan, DHL's legal counsel on aviation, echoes this criticism while drawing attention to the fact that the ECJ's attempt to distinguish the regulation from the Montreal provisions finds no support in case law precedent. Dolan, *supra*, at 227-28.

520. *See* Passenger Rights Case, *supra* note 518, paras. 78-92. Rebuffing the argument raised by the low-fare carriers that the regulation's compensation requirements bear no relation to the ticket price, the ECJ stated that 'the harmful consequences to which a delay gives rise and which [the regulation] seeks to remedy are in no way related to the price paid for a ticket.' *Id.* para. 88. The Court found that the compensation requirements were not manifestly inappropriate to the objective pursued because there also existed exemptions for exceptional circumstances, as well as conditions limiting the impact of the regulation on carriers if passengers are provided information about cancellations sufficiently early or offered rerouting. *Id.* para. 91.

521. As a matter of law, the principle of nondiscrimination requires that 'comparable situations not be treated differently and that different situations must not be treated in the same way unless such treatment is objectively justified.' *Id.* para. 95. In this instance, the ECJ determined that the situations of undertakings operating in different transport sectors (*e.g.*, air, bus, rail) are not comparable because the 'manner in which they operate, the conditions governing their accessibility and the distribution of their networks' make them non-interchangeable regarding the conditions of their use. *Id.* para. 96. Further, passengers who are inconvenienced by a delay or cancellation of their flight are in 'an objectively different situation from that experienced by passengers on other means of transport in the event of incidents of the same nature.' *Id.* para. 97. Finally, the Court determined that the regulation had to treat all of the airlines identically since damage suffered by passengers in the case of a cancellation or delay of a flight is similar regardless of which airline the passenger is using or what its pricing policies may be. Passenger Rights Case, *supra* note 518, para. 98.

522. Council Regulation 261/2004, *supra* note 507, art. 16(1).

523. *See* Press Release, Europa, European Commission Defends Air Passenger Rights, IP/05/858 (Jul. 6, 2005).

524. *See* Press Release, Europa, First Anniversary of Air Passenger Rights, IP/06/177 (Feb. 16, 2006).

525. Steer Davies Gleave, Review of Regulation 261/2004: Final Report 12 (2007).

The Commission, as with CRS and slot allocation, remains undaunted in its mission to find and enforce the correct regulatory tempo for air passenger rights in the EU. Even though it has been unable to measure the regulation's quantitative impact on reducing levels of denied boarding, delays, or cancellations, or on the reclassifying of cancellations to delays, the Commission claims credit for qualitative improvements prompted by raising airline consciousness about the treatment of inconvenienced passengers.[526] While this kind of self-congratulatory assessment is understandable in light of a zeal to put EU citizens (and, apparently, its noncitizens as well) at the 'heart' of its policies, the more pressing focus of policy must remain on the capacity and air traffic control challenges which are truly at the 'heart' of denied boarding, cancellations, and delays. In that sense, the passenger rights legislation does represent regulatory overexuberance: as a rational matter, the airlines ought not to be exposed to a battery of obligations and penalties when the true sources of passenger discomfort are infrastructural bottlenecks beyond the carriers' immediate control.[527] Nonetheless, within the narrower regulatory space occupied by its rights legislation, the Commission remains focused on improving enforcement through the NEBs[528] and clarifying ambiguous elements of the regulation, specifically the distinction between cancellations and delays[529] and the contested meaning of 'exceptional circumstances.'[530]

---

526. *See* European Commission, *Communication from the Commission to the European Parliament and the Council Pursuant to Article 17 of Regulation [EC] 261/2004 on the Operation and the Results of this Regulation Establishing Common Rules on Compensation and Assistance to Passengers in the Event of Denied Boarding and of Cancellation or Long Delay of Flights*, sec. 4.1.4, COM (2007) 168 final (Apr. 4 2007) [hereinafter European Commission, *Regulation Communication*].

527. The ELFAA, in particular, has been vocal in calling for air traffic control (ATC) service providers to be responsible for compensation to passengers for 'the vast number of delays due to ATC inefficiencies, failures and strikes.' *See* Press Release, European Low Fare Airlines Association, ELFAA Q & A's for Passenger Compensation Decision Negative Result (Jan. 10, 2006).

528. European Commission, *Regulation Communication, supra* note 526, sec. 7.1. As an early sign of its commitment to holding Member States responsible, the Commission issued an ultimatum to Member States in Apr. 2007 that they had six months to substantially improve their compliance with the regulation or risk having infringement proceedings brought against them. Press Release, Europa, Commission Gives Airlines and Member States Six Months to Make Air Passenger Rights Work, IP/07/471 (Apr. 4, 2007).

529. European Commission, *Regulation Communication, supra* note 526, sec. 7.3. The Commission took time in its Communication to discuss the lack of clarity which exists under the rules over what constitutes a 'delay' and what constitutes a 'cancellation.' With respect to a 'delay' in particular, the Commission stated unequivocally that its regulation provides no definition of delays and that confusion exists on what the airlines' obligations are in instances of delays lasting over 24 hours. *See id.* secs. 5.2 & 5.4.

530. *Id.* sec. 7.4. The Commission found that 70% of the resources of the NEBs were directed toward determining whether or not a flight had been cancelled in exceptional circumstances, even though only 30% of all complaints raised this issue. *Id.* The Commission chastised the NEBs for failing to challenge air carriers sufficiently when they invoked the 'exceptional circumstances' exception in the regulation. *Id.* sec. 5.2. The suspicion of the Commission is 'that the "exceptional circumstances" card is played too often by airlines in order to avoid paying compensation for which no payment deadline is foreseen in the [r]egulation.' *Id.*

D   REGULATORY CHALLENGES OF MULTILATERAL AIRLINE
               LIBERALIZATION II: ISSUES BEYOND THE U.S. EXPERIENCE

1   **Building the Community's External Aviation Policy I:**
               The Chicago Bilateral System After the ECJ Open
               Skies Rulings

The three airline reform packages effectively repealed the Chicago system among
the Member States of the EU. It was inevitable, therefore, that the Commission
would turn its focus to the continued existence of the Chicago system outside EU
borders and to the question of its own supranational competence to negotiate traffic
rights with third countries. Until the EU institutions acquired some form of
universal authority over bilaterals, third countries would be able to 'weigh the
comparative advantages' of the individual Member State bilateral agreements
and view them as 'alternative entry doors leading into the single European market'
(for example, through competition as to the regulations they include on inward
investment or fifth freedom privileges[531]). Marking the 'specificity' of the air
transport sector, however, few issues of transference of external competence
were so fiercely contested by the Member States.[532]

The European Commission, in fact, had lobbied for transfer of full external
negotiating competence in air transport since as early as 1990, when it submitted a
proposal for a Council decision on a consultation and authorization procedure
for agreements concerning commercial aviation relations between Member States
and third countries.[533] The Commission's proposal, which it resubmitted in
1992,[534] was blemished not only by inelegant draftsmanship but also (and perhaps

---

In December 2008, the European Court of Justice ruled that airlines could not cite technical
problems to avail themselves of the 'extraordinary circumstances' exception unless the
problems lay clearly beyond a carrier's control. *See* Case C-549/07, Wallentin-Hermann *v.*
Alitalia, 2009 E.C.R. 00 (publication pending).

531. Basedow, *supra* note 114, at 277. For example, an increase in the number of permissible carrier
designations on bilateral routes can dramatically increase the flow of passengers through a hub
airport; even though the increase exposes the home carrier to more intense competition, it also
enables that carrier to capture a larger volume of fifth freedom traffic circulating within the
EU. Lufthansa has competed with several U.S. airlines under the multiple designation provisions of the former U.S./Germany bilateral, but this additional competition also extended
Frankfurt's reach as an intra-continental hub (compared with London Heathrow under
Bermuda II, for example, which was restricted to service by only two or three U.S. airlines).
Id. at 268.

532. Before the compromise reflected in the 1996 'split mandate,' Member States had suggested
various alternatives, including a 'pragmatic' case-by-case approach. *See, e.g., Transport
Council: EC Ministers Agree on Allocating Slots at Airports*, TRANSP. EUR., Dec. 23, 1992
(setting forth miscellaneous Member State positions on the Commission's 1992 proposal for
external aviation competence).

533. European Commission, *Proposal for a Council Decision on a Consultation and Authorization
Procedure for Agreements Concerning Commercial Aviation Relations Between Member
States and Third Countries*, COM (90)17 final (Feb. 13, 1990).

534. European Commission, Commission Proposal COM (92) 434 final (Oct. 1993), 1993 O.J. (C
216) 15 (amending Commission Proposal COM (90) 17, *supra* note 533) [hereinafter Aviation
Relations Proposal].

relatedly) by conceptual irresolution as to the transitional life of existing bilateral agreements[535] and with respect to the juncture at which the Commission itself would intervene as the primary negotiating authority with non-Member States – and whether it would do so 'collectively' with each third State or simply negotiate each Member State's third-country bilaterals as they came due for renewal or renegotiation.[536] Ultimately, however, the Commission expected that, after an extended conversion period (the end of 1998, in its resubmitted proposal)[537] the negotiation and conclusion of *all* agreements, including extensions of existing agreements, would be supranationalized.[538]

In the aftermath of the European Court of Justice open skies rulings,[539] as we have seen in Chapter 2, the Council of the European Union awarded the Commission a so-called 'vertical' mandate for comprehensive air service negotiations with the United States. The Court's rulings, however, provided no legal premise for the Commission to resurrect its 1990/92 reach for exclusive supranational authority or for the Council to oust the Member States from at least partial involvement in negotiating their bilateral air services agreements with all other non-Member States.[540] Nevertheless, as a result of the Court's ruling, Member States' bilateral agreements with third countries were now juristically fragile, infected with illegal nationality clauses that made them vulnerable not only to further Commission challenges but also to the risk of private action – for example, by Community-licensed and owned air carriers excluded from operating out of rival markets in other Member States of the Community.[541]

In part to preempt these risks, the Council awarded to the Commission a second, more circumscribed mandate which would operate on a country-by-country basis to allow the Commission, when authorized by the Member States, to negotiate with a specific third country in a single negotiation *inter alia* to remove the traditional ownership and control clauses from all of that country's directory of

---

535. For example, the Proposal appeared to contemplate that Member States would be allowed to continue to negotiate and sign extensions of existing bilaterals, subject to certain conditions such as a 'Community reservation clause,' *i.e.*, a clause that requires the third country to concede the wider reach of Community ownership and control rules. The United States, in that era, was refusing to incorporate special 'Community'-sensitive provisions in its open skies negotiations.

536. Instead of a wholesale absorption of the existing bilateral treaty network, the Commission evidently envisaged a transitional case-by-case examination of each treaty prior to renewal to test its compatibility with a (hypothetical) common external aviation policy; should concerns arise, the Commission would request the Council for authority to negotiate with the third State partners. Aviation Relations Proposal, *supra* note 534, arts. 4 & 5.

537. *Id.* art. 6(1).

538. This was the implication of Article 6 of the Commission's proposal, which would have sunsetted Council and Commission approval of separate Member State bilateral negotiations of air treaties with non-Member States as of Dec. 31, 1998.

539. *See supra* Chapter 2, Part III(A).

540. *See id.*

541. 'In such a case, the European Commission would find itself obliged to request the denunciation of the bilateral air services agreement in question.' European Commission, *EU External Aviation Policy & 'Horizontal' Agreement – FAQs*, Question 1, Information Note (2006) [hereinafter European Commission, *FAQs*].

bilateral air services agreements with the 27 Member States.[542] These clauses would be replaced by a standardized clause giving all 'Community air carriers' nondiscriminatory access to traffic rights to and from that third country from each EU Member State. (Additional clauses would bring the agreements into conformity with other substantive provisions of Community aviation law.[543]) This parallel mandate – dubbed the 'horizontal' mandate because of its operative scope and also to distinguish it from the more substantial authority granted to conduct comprehensive 'vertical' negotiations with the United States and other countries – now implicates the Commission, whenever the Member States so direct,[544] in the formidable task of bringing all 1500 or so Member State bilaterals with third countries into compliance with the Court of Justice ruling.[545]

---

542. This Commission mandate would have to be seen as a 'second best' solution to a difficult aeropolitical problem (recognition of Community carrier designation by all non-Member States) that the Commission might have hoped to resolve in tandem with the United States. *See* Daniel Calleja, Director of Air Transport, European Commission, Speech to the International Aviation Club, Washington, D.C., at 8 (Nov. 16, 2004) (calling on U.S. and EC aviation administrators to 'jointly persuade' third countries to accept necessary changes in bilateral ownership and control provisions).

543. *See infra* notes 546 & 547.

544. The Member States are at liberty to conduct the negotiations themselves (subject to maintaining a cooperative relationship with the Commission required under Community legislation). If Member States anticipate significant aeropolitical complications with particular third countries, the Commission explicitly calls upon them to switch to the horizontal, Commission-driven pathway. *See* European Commission, Air Transport Portal, <http://ec.europa.eu/transport/air_portal/index_en.htm>. The simultaneous and alternative availability of Member State and Commission negotiating authority is not what the Commission forecast or desired in its 1990/92 proposals, *see supra* in main text, but it nevertheless represents more than the Commission might have expected from the Council following the ECJ's quite Solomonic division of labor between Member States and the Community institutions with respect to the conclusion of bilateral air services agreements.

545. Member States retain authority to negotiate with third countries on 'matters of national competence' (but presumably outside the framework of U.S./EC negotiations) pending a mandate 'for a full negotiation on a Community agreement.' European Commission, *Communication from the Commission on Relations Between the Community and Third Countries in the Field of Air Transport*, para. 45, COM (2003) 94 final (Feb. 26, 2003) [hereinafter European Commission, *Relations*]. While this is true in principle, the Commission persuaded the Council and Parliament to adopt legislation that requires Member States to cooperate with the Commission whenever bilateral negotiations spill over into areas of Community competence. *See* Council Regulation 847/2004, 2004 O.J. (L 157) 7. Although the Regulation does not explicitly identify the separate spheres of Community and Member State competence, its primary effect is to ensure that Member States conducting bilateral negotiations with third countries take account of the general principles of Community air transport law, in particular by including certain 'relevant standard clauses' that apply Community law. *Id.* art. 1. Thus, the Regulation is an effort to transform the mindsets of national authorities into a 'Community' interest mindset. Member States are required to provide information to the Commission on all planned aviation negotiations with non-Member States. *See id.* art. 1(2). If the Commission concludes that the negotiations are likely to 'undermine' the objectives of pending Community negotiations or lead to an agreement which is incompatible with Community law, it must so inform the Member State (although no sanction or further procedure is provided for that eventuality). *Id.* art. 1(4). In addition, each Member State must request 'expressions of interest'

The horizontal mandate, it will be noticed, preserves the existing patchwork of third-country bilateral air treaties, which continue in force as formally amended either by separate Member State negotiations to insert the standard clauses agreed *ad referendum* with the Commission in December 2004[546] or, when the

---

from all 'Community carriers' with an establishment in its territory to ensure that those interests are taken into account in negotiations. *Id.* art. 2. The Regulation also includes a 'standstill' requirement, which bars Member States (and, by implication, third countries) from *reducing* the number of Community air carriers which can be designated under existing traffic rights. *See id.* art. 3.

546. *See* European Commission, *Commission Decision 29/03/2005 on Approving the Standard Clauses for Inclusion in Bilateral Air Service Agreements Between Member States and Third Countries Jointly Laid Down by the Commission and the Member States*, pmbl., recital 2, C (2005) 943 [hereinafter European Commission, *Standard Clauses*]. The standard clauses are required to be inserted, reflecting 'Community competence and legislation.' European Commission, Air Transport Portal, A Policy Built on 3 Key Pillars: Horizontal Agreements, <http://ec.europa.eu/transport/air_portal/international/pillars/horizontal_agreements_en.htm> [hereinafter European Commission, Horizontal Agreements]. Although there is flexibility to withdraw some of these clauses in the context of specific negotiations (particularly with respect to the vexed issue of taxation of aviation fuel), the Community designation clause, which implements the Court of Justice ruling on the right of establishment and nondiscrimination is deemed non-negotiable and must be incorporated in all Member State bilaterals with third countries. *Id.* 'Such an agreement [i.e., one lacking the open designation clause for Community carriers] would continue to discriminate between companies on the ground of nationality.' *Id.* The principal standard clause implements the right of any Community carrier 'established' in a Member State, irrespective of the citizenship complexion of its ownership and control or its State of licensure or regulatory control, to be designated to serve all routes available under the bilateral agreements concluded by the State of establishment with non-Member States. European Commission, *Standard Clauses, supra*, annex 1 (offering four alternative designation and revocation clauses to regulate Member State designation of carriers; the clauses make either explicit or implicit reference to the requirement of ownership and control of Community carriers by Community citizens and to the investment rights of the non-Member States which are parties to the European Economic Area as well as of the Swiss Confederation, including their nationals). The Commission's preferred clause (Version 1), *see id.* annex 1, at 4, explicitly covers both designation and revocation. It appears that Version 1 of the clause allows a third State to accept a designation based solely on criteria of establishment in the designating State and regulatory control by that State or by another Member State. By itself, this language is a bold separation of the notions of ownership and regulatory control. *See supra* Chapter 2, Part II(D) (discussing IATA's advocacy of this separation). Nevertheless, the explanatory Annex states that Version 1 implicitly invokes the ownership/control definition of a Community carrier contained in Article 4(2) of Regulation 2407/92, *supra* note 139, on licensing of EC air carriers (now included in the consolidated regulation). *See* European Commission, *Standard Clauses, supra*, annex 1, at 4. This interpretation is not at all obvious from the actual text of Version 1, however. Interestingly, also, a supplementary standard clause makes explicit that references to 'nationals' of a Member State are understood as referring to nationals of all Member States, *inter alia* circumventing the possibility that a typical provision allowing contracting parties to refuse recognition to certificates and licenses granted to its own nationals by other States would embrace nationals of other Member States. *See id. See also infra* note 547 (setting forth the ownership and control criteria for designation under the Commission's Model Horizontal Agreement). Other standard clauses annexed to the Commission Decision relate to pricing (subjecting non-Community airlines to Community

Commission acts pursuant to its horizontal mandate, using the Commission's Model Horizontal Agreement.[547] For the foreseeable future, all amendments to these treaties, particularly but not exclusively with respect to traffic rights, will be negotiated by each Member State.[548]

By August 2008, the Member States themselves had renegotiated 118 bilateral agreements with over 60 third countries.[549] Although the Commission had been deputized to use its horizontal mandate with only 36 third countries, the 'simplicity, costs and speed' of the horizontal approach allowed the Commission to sweep nearly six times as many bilateral agreements into its purview.[550]

---

tariff law, including a prohibition on lower fares by non-Community carriers on all intra-Union routes; groundhandling (modeled on Community legislation that allows limitations on 'self-handling' but requires nondiscriminatory access to suppliers); and taxation of aviation fuel (preserving existing right of each Member State, under Community legislation, to agree with other Member States to tax aviation fuel supplied in the first State for use on intra-EU routes).

547. *See* European Commission, *[Model] Agreement Between the European Community and* [name of third country] *on Certain Aspects of Air Services*, Working Paper (Feb. 20, 2006). The Agreement is startlingly frank in its opening recital: 'Noting that bilateral air service agreements have been concluded between [several] Member States of the European Community and [name of partner country] containing provisions contrary to Community law.' *Id.* pmbl., recital 1. The final recital deflects any potential accusation that the European Union is seeking to grow the total volume of air traffic between the signatories or to affect the 'balance' between their air carriers, or indeed to advocate amendments to the provisions of existing bilaterals (other than those implicated by the Agreement itself). *Id.* pmbl., recital 8. With respect to designation, Article 2 of the Agreement requires partner countries to recognize designation by Member States of air carriers 'established' in their territories which are licensed by and under the regulatory control of another Member State and which are majority owned and effectively controlled by other Member States and/or nationals of other Member States (or by the three additional States of the European Economic Area or the Swiss Confederation as well as by their nationals). *See id.* art. 2. Thus, unlike Version 1 of the Community designation clause in Annex 1 to Commission Decision 29/03/2005, *see supra* note 546, the clause in this agreement refers explicitly to an EU ownership/control investor profile. Other standard clauses, replicating Commission Decision 29/03/05, relate to safety (including retention of 'ramp' inspection rights by partner countries for carriers with operating certificates issued by a Member State other than the designating Member State), taxation of aviation fuel, compatibility with EC competition law, and tariffs for carriage in the European Union. *See id.*

548. Again, the Commission in 1990/92 had attempted to 'sunset' all separate Member State negotiations. The continuing authority of Member States over third-country bilaterals would change only in the event that the Council awards further 'vertical' mandates to the Commission or the entire external aviation relations diplomacy of the Community becomes an exclusive Community responsibility managed by the Commission. Meanwhile, the proposed amendments do not change existing provisions of bilateral air transport agreements with respect to designation, frequency, capacity, or other traffic right restrictions. *See* European Commission, *FAQs, supra* note 541, Question 2. *See infra* Part III(G) (discussing the Commission's unsuccessful attempt to win more rights).

549. *See* European Commission, Horizontal Agreements, *supra* note 546.

550. *Id.*

The direct consequence of either the horizontal or autonomous approaches to renegotiation is that the available pool of airlines to be selected to serve international routes is enlarged for each Member State to include carriers (*i.e.*, 'Community carriers') from all other Member States. This distribution question is not problematic with respect to the open-designation provisions of open skies agreements, but creates potential discrimination in the context of bilaterals where designation is restricted. EU Member States can now *consider for designation* a much larger number of airlines, but the number of airlines which *can be designated* will remain subject to the relevant bilateral arrangements.[551]

The Commission insists, in a sanguine way, that all of this rethreading of the Member States' bilaterals will have 'no effect' on the balance of air traffic rights, which may be true as a quantitative matter but certainly is likely to have perceptible qualitative effects in terms of the identity of the carriers selected.[552] The critical issue, if the Court's opinion is to be respected, is to provide for the nondiscriminatory distribution of all of the traffic rights that might result from third-country negotiations.[553] Community legislation, surprisingly, has left it up to each Member State to distribute those rights according to national metrics that comport with the general principles of nondiscrimination and transparency.[554] Far from eliminating

---

551. *See* European Commission, *FAQs, supra* note 541, Information Note, para. 2.
552. For example, if British Airways were to become eligible to operate direct services from both London Heathrow and Frankfurt, Germany, to Tokyo, Japan, that eligibility would create a qualitatively different competitive environment for Japanese international carriers which are accustomed to direct hub-to-hub competition from BA only on its Heathrow routes. While it is true, of course, that BA cannot by itself insist upon expanding the available Germany/Japan traffic rights, at the very least the availability of unused frequencies means that BA will eventually be able to press its case for nondiscriminatory access to that bilateral market. Inevitably, therefore, the *nature* of the competitive landscape shifts even if the negotiated balance of routes and frequencies remains numerically unchanged.
553. *See* European Commission, *Relations, supra* note 545, para. 63 (observing that 'securing a non-discriminatory outcome and providing for a non-discriminatory distribution of the traffic rights that might result from a negotiation may prove to be one of the most difficult aspects of the transition from a bilateral agreements [*sic*] to a Community international air transport policy'); *see also id.* paras. 62-65 (noting that the nondiscriminatory allocation of traffic rights will be highly problematical in non-open skies agreement contexts where the applicable bilateral insists on a reciprocal division of limited traffic rights between the airlines of the parties). In this regard the Commission's function, according to Paul Gretch, in Richard Carlson's Briefing Paper for the Air Transport Association 5 (Nov. 26, 2002) (copy on file with author), is to 'decide policy, but . . . rely on the Member States to implement it.'
554. *See* Council Regulation 847/2004, *supra* note 545, arts. 5 & 6 (specifying that, whenever a bilateral agreement with a third country provides for limitations on the use of traffic rights or the number of Community air carriers eligible to be designated to take advantage of traffic rights, the Member State concerned must ensure a nondiscriminatory distribution of those rights among eligible Community carriers). The delegation of authority is surprising because the Commission had conceded the complexity of the task of distributing traffic rights between Member States but it had not resisted accepting the assignment were it to be made. The European Parliament had certainly doubted the ability of the Commission to undertake this large task. Member States, incidentally, are required by Article 6 of Regulation 847/2004 to publish their procedures in the Official Journal of the European Union. *See, e.g.*, French

'legal uncertainty' as the Commission hoped,[555] the absence of agreed common distribution criteria for existing or enhanced designation rights remains an unresolved obstacle to the operation of the post-2002 EC external aviation policy.

**2   Building the Community's External Aviation Policy II:
         More Verticality and a European Common Aviation Area**

The European Commission advocated cabining the U.S. and 'Community clause' initiatives into a full-fledged Community 'external aviation policy' which would leverage the EC as a 'heavyweight player' in a post-bilateral world.[556] Naturally, the renegotiation of all Member State bilaterals, now also a matter of Commission mandate, prompted the Commission to project an even wider intent to participate, as part of a 'new complementarity' between Member States and the Community,[557] in all Member State bilateral relations. But the essential ambiguity of the Court of Justice open skies rulings has compelled the Commission (and, indeed, its political superiors in the Council of the European Union) to adopt an oblique lexicon when describing the future shape of EC external aviation relations: the Member States 'cannot act in isolation when negotiating international air service agreements,'[558]

National Procedure for the Allocation of Limited Air Traffic Rights, 2006 O.J. (C 242) 14 [hereinafter French Procedures]; Hungarian National Procedure for the Allocation of Limited Air Traffic Rights, 2007 O.J. (C 296 11); Italian National Procedure for the Allocation of Limited Air Traffic Rights, 2008 O.J. (C 19) 14; Lithuanian National Procedure for the Allocation of Limited Air Traffic Rights, 2008 O.J. (C 31) 8. While the published procedures are supposed to conform to the 'nondiscriminatory and transparent' requirement in Article 5 of Regulation 847/2004, the Regulation offers no further guidance on how to achieve that outcome. The published procedures generally include formal application guidelines and timetables, the name of the relevant national authority making the traffic rights assessment, the evaluative criteria applied by the national authority, and the grounds for revocation of traffic rights. While all of the published procedures set forth general assessment criteria (*e.g.*, financial, technical, and those related to organizational capacity), France goes furthest in listing nine 'primary' criteria as the basis of its assessments along with six additional criteria that its authority *may* take into account. *See* French Procedures, *supra*, art. 6. Interestingly, the optional criteria include the carrier's contribution to regional planning, potential for developing the (French) tourist industry, its situation with respect to payment of national aeronautical taxes and charges, and whether the carrier operates a French language sales service. *See id.* When compared with the primary criteria, which include examining a carrier's tariff policy, quality of service, sustainability, environmental performance, and development of connecting rights for passengers, these secondary criteria appear potentially discriminatory to the extent that they favor carriers with deeper integration into the French polity. (This observation is distinct from the concerns expressed in the main text about business 'presence' and local licensing.) *See also* [Swedish] Guidelines for the Allocation of Limited Air Traffic Rights sec. 8, 2006 O.J. (L 177) 23 (stating that the Swedish Civil Aviation Administration 'may also take other factors into account if [they] are announced to the applicant before the final decision is taken').

555.   *See* European Commission, Horizontal Agreements, *supra* note 546.
556.   European Commission, *Developing the Agenda for the Community's External Aviation Policy*, at 2, COM (2005) 79 final (Mar. 11, 2005), at 2 [hereinafter European Commission, *Agenda*].
557.   *Id.* at 2.
558.   *Id.*

but the Commission concedes that the single aviation market 'does not possess an adequate external dimension.'[559] The legislative expression of this uneasy balance of responsibility is Regulation 847/2004,[560] which requires Member States, in exercising their retained power to negotiate or renegotiate bilateral air services agreements with non-Member States, to cooperate with the Commission when 'the subject-matter of an agreement falls partly within the competence of the Community and partly within that of its Member States.'[561]

Nonetheless, aside from the polemical swagger of initiatives such as EC membership of the International Civil Aviation Organization (proposed in 2002),[562] the Commission has genuinely attempted to project its experience of 15 years of progressive transnational liberalization and integration as a model for regional cooperation not just within Europe and its periphery but in (and with) other parts of the world also.[563] To that end, the Commission has sought and obtained further so-called 'vertical' mandates to negotiate a European Common Aviation Area (ECAA) with some 20 other EU aviation partners along the Union's southern and eastern borders, including Romania and Bulgaria prior to their

---

559. *Id.* at 4. Thus, while the Council has proclaimed that the Court of Justice rulings in 2002 'clarified the respective competences of Member States and the Community in external aviation relations,' the same document delivers an imprecise summons to the Commission and Member States 'to work together in a concerted manner, using all available means, to avoid interruptions in bilateral agreements between Member States and third countries.' *Id.* at 3.

560. *See supra* note 554 (explaining the operation of Regulation 847/2004, *supra* note 545).

561. Council Regulation 847/2004, *supra* note 545, pmbl., recital 4. But it must be understood that, despite this predilection for a competence-based division of labor between the Community and the Member States, there are certain relevant matters, notably the widening of designation clauses to include all Community-based carriers, which must be included on all bilateral negotiation agendas and which, therefore, implicate Community competence to act. Despite the Regulation's surface impression of light supervision, if Member States enter into *any* negotiations with third countries – and even if they do not choose to do so at all – the obligation to conform their third-country bilaterals to Community law is still paramount. Indeed, this is the burden of the sixth Recital of the Regulation, which states that all existing third-country bilateral agreements that contain provisions contrary to Community law – and all of them do, if only because their designation clauses were adopted prior to the open skies rulings of the European Court of Justice – 'should be amended or replaced by new agreements that are wholly compatible with Community law.' *Id.*, pmbl, recital 6. Further, the eighth Recital considers it 'essential' that a Member State conducting negotiations with third countries 'takes account of Community law, broader Community interests and ongoing Community negotiations.' *Id.* pmbl., recital 8. For further discussion of Regulation 847/2004, *see supra* note 545.

562. *See* European Commission, *Recommendation from the Commission to the Council in Order to Authorise the Commission to Open and Conduct Negotiations with the International Civil Aviation Organization (ICAO) on the Conditions and Arrangements for Accession by the European Community*, SEC (2002) 381 final (Apr. 9, 2002); *see also supra* Chapter 2, note 178.

563. *See* European Commission, *Agenda, supra* note 556, at 4. The Council of the European Union evidently endorses the idea of the Community experience as a demonstration model. *See* Council [of Ministers] Conclusions on Developing the Agenda for the Community's External Aviation Policy, para. 2, 2005 (C 173) 1 [hereinafter Council Conclusions] (acknowledging that the Community's internal aviation market provides 'useful references for third countries').

accession to the Community, the former Soviet satellites (including Georgia and Ukraine), the countries of the Western Balkans, and Morocco.[564] More sweeping mandates to parley with regions and countries beyond the EU's immediate neighborhood of influence in Europe – with Australia, China, India, Japan, New Zealand, the Russian Federation, Singapore, South Africa, and South Korea – have been sought and in some instances already granted by the Member States through the Council of the European Union.[565] And the Commission has latterly trained its sights on other countries in the Americas in addition to the United States, including Canada,[566] Chile, and Mexico.

In its optimal expression (from the Commission's perspective), the adhering States of a putative ECAA would accept the corpus of secondary legislation – the Community aviation *acquis*[567] – that comprises the common air transport policy (or 'single aviation market') as though they were for purposes of that policy already Member States of the EU.[568] The Community institutions (such as the Commission and the Court of Justice) would play functional roles, for example with respect to competition, and a 'Joint Committee' would filter legislation adopted after the ECAA entered into force.[569] The ambitious contours of an eventual ECAA are already discernible in some further Commission initiatives that either predated or succeeded the original ECAA mandate – the pansectoral European Economic Area (EEA), a 30-member single customs zone embracing the 27 EU Member States and the three surviving members of the European Free Trade Association (EFTA)

---

564. *See id.* para. 16. These initiatives are planned to culminate in an integrated 'European Common Aviation Area' by 2010. *See generally* European Commission, *A Community Aviation Policy Towards Its Neighbours*, para. 3, COM (2004) 74 final (Feb. 9, 2004) [hereinafter European Commission, *Community Aviation Policy*] (noting that it would not be wise, however, to impose a 'one negotiating model fits all' approach).

565. *Id.* para. 4. In this context, the Commission speaks of a series of 'targeted negotiations.' *Id.* at 11. The Council expects that each vertical mandate will require a demonstration of the 'added value' of a Community-level agreement. Council Conclusions, *supra* note 563, at 5.

566. While writing portions of this book in Canada, I have developed an improved understanding of how Canadian *amour-propre* might be jolted by the Commission's rather gratuitous reference to Canada's 'mature and not insignificant market.' European Commission, *Agenda, supra* note 556, at 10; Council Conclusions, *supra* note 563, para. 17. Following a mandate to negotiate an 'Open Aviation Area' with Canada in Oct. 2007, official negotiations opened in Brussels in 2007. *See* Press Release, Europa, EU and Canada Start Negotiations on a Broad Aviation Agreement, IP/07/1827 (Nov. 30, 2007). In keeping with its general policy of international air transport liberalization, the Commission sought a reduction of market restrictions while establishing a high degree of regulatory convergence between the two sides. *See generally* European Commission, *Developing a Community Civil Aviation Policy Towards Canada*, COM (2006) 871 final (Sept. 1, 2007). In December 2008, it was announced that the two sides had reached a comprehensive aviation agreement which envisions an eventual (although highly contingent) lifting of foreign ownership and control restrictions. *See* Press Release, Europa, Breakthrough in EU-Canada Negotiations on Far-Reaching Aviation Agreement, IP/08/1914 (Dec. 9, 2008).

567. *See* European Commission, *Community Aviation Policy, supra* note 564, para. 35.

568. *Id.*

569. *Id.*

(Iceland, Norway, and the Principality of Liechtenstein),[570] and an agreement with the Swiss Confederation which more directly captures the idea of the ECAA mandate and involved a specific *sectoral* integration of Switzerland into the entire Community air transport *acquis*.[571]

---

570. *See* Agreement on the European Economic Area, May 2, 1992, 1992 O.J. (L 1) 3, *as adopted by* Protocol Adjusting the Agreement on the European Economic Area, 1994 O.J. (L 1) 572, *as amended by* Adjusting Protocol and subsequently by the EEA Enlargement Agreement, 2004 O.J. (L 130) 3 & EEA Supp. No. 23 (Apr. 29, 2004) [hereinafter EEA Agreement]. The EEA was enlarged by a special enlargement treaty which came into force (on May 1, 2004) simultaneously with the enlargement of the European Union. Although the EEA was somewhat reduced in practical scope by the access to full membership (in 1995) of former EFTA States Austria, Finland, and Sweden, and by Switzerland's referendum decision not to participate, its structural arrangements – though cumbersome – have some value as a model for future international cooperation. In essence, the EEA Agreement attempts a homogenous application of the preexisting EC Treaty rules on free movement of the factors of production, and the competition rules, and all of the derivative jurisprudence in these fields, across the entire EEA territory. In the area of air transport, the EEA Agreement, through an Annex on Civil Aviation, applies the body of the Community air transport *acquis* with appropriate adjustments. There are important juridical limitations to the EEA project, however, that compromise its precedential value for a future plurilateral aviation treaty. Since the EFTA States were not offered direct participation in EC rulemaking or adjudicatory procedures, complex compensatory institutional mechanisms had to be devised, including a filtration tribunal, the Joint Committee, which consults with the EU institutions on *future* legislation (EEA Agreement, *supra*, art. 92), and a special EFTA Court that rules on disputes concerning (among other matters) the application of the competition rules by the EFTA Surveillance Authority (broadly equivalent to the European Commission). EEA Agreement, *supra*, art. 108. Moreover, unlike the supranational European Union, the EEA Agreement is merely an intergovernmental arrangement, and makes no transfer of sovereign authority to the institutions it establishes, relying on the EFTA States to introduce into their respective legal orders a statutory provision to the effect that EEA rules are to prevail over contrary legislative provisions. *See* Court of Justice ruling in Opinion 1/91, 1992 E.C.R. I-2821 (the constitutional nature of the EEA Agreement was the subject of Court of Justice opinions in 1991 and 1992).

571. Agreement between the European Community and the Swiss Confederation on Air Transport, 2002 O.J. (L 114) 73 [hereinafter EC/Switzerland Agreement]. Switzerland's failure to join the EEA resulted in a more limited arrangement that inserts air transport into a suite of six other sectoral agreements between the Community and Switzerland (on free movement of persons, on road and rail transport, on agriculture, on government procurement, on mutual recognition in relation to conformity assessment, and on scientific and technological cooperation) that were concluded simultaneously for an initial seven-year period. *See id.* art. 36. Article 33 of the Agreement expresses a principle that has been curiously absent (though it must certainly be implied) in the secondary air transport legislation adopted within the European Community, namely, that the terms of the Agreement would *supersede* the relevant provisions of bilateral arrangements in force between Switzerland on the one hand and EU Member States on the other. *Id.* art. 33. Structurally, the EC/Switzerland Agreement follows the EEA prototype, but it does not attempt to create special adjudicatory mechanisms, appearing on its face to consent (at least partially) to the controlling jurisdiction of the Community institutions over most of the competition rules. To the extent that anticompetitive practices only affect trade with Switzerland, or routes between Switzerland and non-EU Member States, Swiss competition jurisdiction is explicitly preserved. EC/Switzerland Agreement, *supra*, arts. 10 & 11(2). It is nonetheless unclear precisely what kind of constitutional *modus vivendi* was intended by the Agreement. The State aids provisions, for example, are to be enforced by a kind of consensus

3   **A Concluding Note on the Community's External
                    Aviation Policy**

In sum, the outcome of the Court's open skies rulings has been a delicate political
truce that allows Member States to continue to negotiate traffic rights and related
commercial matters with third countries, unless the Member States instruct
the Commission to pursue horizontal negotiations with specific third countries,
and excepting also the (rarer) ouster of all Member State authority when the
Council concedes a vertical mandate.[572] All of these negotiating channels,
however, must include the Community designation clause (irrespective of vertical
or horizontal mandates, the clause is a precept of Community law), and to that
significant extent the Community process represents a substantial shift in the
traditional understanding of the Chicago nationality rule.[573]

But the process does not attempt to break the 'internal' lock that limits foreign
ownership and control of Community airlines.[574] In fact, the Council responded to
the Commission's ambitious portrayal of a future EC external aviation policy by
reminding the Commission that 'the bilateral system of agreements between Member States and third parties will remain, for the time being at least, the principal
basis for international relations in the aviation sector.'[575]

E   A CONCEPTUAL CONFLICT: THE COMMUNITY LICENSING SYSTEM
                AND THE RIGHT OF ESTABLISHMENT

The Community's airline licensing system, however novel in the universe of the
Chicago bilateral system, remains patently incomplete from both internal and
external perspectives. Within the EC, although the system now provides even
stronger common criteria for licensing Community carriers, as we have previously

---

procedure, with Commission review ultimately displaced by the unanimity rules of a steering
body called the Joint Committee, on which the Swiss federal government and the Community
are equally represented. *Id.* art. 14. The Joint Committee is established under Article 21 of the
Agreement (and is known officially as the 'Community/Switzerland Air Transport Committee').
The Committee acts 'by mutual agreement.' *Id.* Like the EEA, the EC/Switzerland Agreement is
also intergovernmental in concept, requiring national implementation of the *acquis communautaire* and preserving the right of unilateral amendment of domestic legislation (subject to
Joint Committee procedures and the principle of nondiscrimination) on points covered by the
Agreement. *Id.* art. 23.

572. These conclusions appear from the terms of the Council's 2005 response to the Commission's
outline of a proposed Community external aviation policy. *See* European Commission, *Agenda, supra* note 556, at 4 (discussing 'general principles' regarding agreements and negotiations
between the Community and third countries).

573. As the Council has instructed, no third-country agreements can be concluded without a starting-
point acceptance of 'Community clauses.' Council Conclusions, *supra* note 563, at para. 19.

574. For the locks-and-bolts imagery used to describe the nationality rule, *see supra* Chapter 3,
Part V(B).

575. Council Conclusions, *supra* note 563, para. 5. The Council articulated this view using a
traditional Chicago narrative of stability and continuity. *See id.*

discussed the Member States retain their national licensing authorities and multiple administrative processes, subjecting the common rules to the vagaries of national implementation, and there is no comprehensive supranational register of airlines or aircraft.[576]

Moreover, following the open skies rulings of the European Court of Justice, the European Commission recognized that Community antidiscrimination law (and specifically the foundational principle of nondiscrimination in Article 12 of the EC Treaty) would require a legal methodology to reconcile the Community airline licensing regime, now premised on the existence of 'Community air carriers' owned and controlled by nationals of *any* Member State, with the exercise of the right of establishment in Article 43 of the Treaty.[577] This right (or 'freedom' – the Treaty uses both words) envisages a permanent right of economic activity in a Member State, including the right to access the legal procedures of the host State in order to conduct that activity under proper license, through subsidiary operations and otherwise.[578] For an air carrier, it means, in addition to authorization to merge with or acquire locally-established carriers, the right to establish a wholly-owned subsidiary air franchise in the territory of any Member State.[579] Thus, the chief (internal EC) purpose of the common licensing system has been and still appears to be the political one of foreclosing Member States from unilaterally imposing market access (and airport facilities) restrictions on air carriers that can lay claim to a EU 'citizenship.' While this may be its antidiscriminatory motive, however, the system (even as amended in 2008) does not per se enforce the right of establishment as the Treaty envisions it, since it offers no legal framework for establishment of subsidiary franchises by EU carriers in Member States other

---

576. Moreover, and with more than a shade of irony, the nationality rule in fact occupies a central place in this important post-Chicago experiment in multilateral deregulation: thus, if an EU carrier were to become majority-owned by a U.S. airline, for example, under current law it would presumably forfeit its right to a 'Community license' and become automatically ineligible for market access to all EU air routes. (This application of the nationality rule appears to be confirmed by the 2007 U.S./EC Air Transport Agreement, *supra* note 129, which permits the Community to impose reciprocal investment restrictions on U.S. nationals.) As between the Member States, however, as long as a carrier is owned and controlled by nationals of *any* one or more Member States, the license must be granted and must, in turn, be recognized by the other Member States.

577. For an analysis of the licensing regime, as recently amended, *see supra* in the main text.

578. EC Treaty arts. 43-44.

579. The essence of the freedom of establishment can be discerned in Article 43 of the EC Treaty: 'Freedom of establishment shall include the right . . . to set up and manage undertakings, in particular companies or firms . . . under the conditions laid down for its own nationals by the law of the country where such establishment is effected . . .' *Id.* art. 43(2). Article 43's later cross-reference to Article 48 supplies an important definitional clarification: 'companies or firms' referenced under Article 43 are those formed in accordance with the civil law of a Member State and which have their registered office, central administration or principal place of business within the European Union. Accordingly, it appears that the right of establishment can only be enjoyed and exercised by companies already established in at least one Member State (it is understood that any individual, who is a national of a Member State, can establish a company in any Member State), but the Treaty itself imposes no requirement as to the nationality of the shareholders of a company wishing to exercise such a right of establishment.

than the licensing State. That right, to the extent that it exists, falls to be considered as a matter of general supranational law.

With respect to the external dimension of the Community license, it is worth noting that the European Court of Justice in its 2002 open skies ruling also ignored the interplay between the right of establishment and the EC airline licensing laws.[580] A literal reading of Article 43 certainly suggests that Czech Airlines, for example, taking advantage of the seventh freedom traffic rights and Community designation clause incorporated in the 2007 U.S./EC Air Transport Agreement,[581] could operate turnaround air services from Paris to New York even if it has only a ticket office in France. Indeed, some U.S. officials have offered the private view that, as far as the United States is concerned, the Czech airline need only have a telephone answering machine in France. Yet the Memorandum of Consultations that accompanies the 2007 agreement makes clear that, when an EU airline seeks authorization to operate services under the agreement, the Member State where the airline's 'principal place of business' is located will be responsible for safety, security, and other regulatory oversight.[582] Bilateral treaties have traditionally included requirements about regulatory oversight, and most countries have internal laws that specify the conditions for recognition – including the identity of the State of regulatory responsibility – of airlines designated under bilateral air services agreements by third countries.[583] The International Civil Aviation Organization also has adopted rules about bilateral recognition of airlines.[584]

The elemental idea, therefore, that Czech Airlines could operate a seventh freedom service between Charles de Gaulle and New York JFK, even though the company's principal place of business is in Prague and it operates only a ticket office (or, even more reductively, a telephone answering service) in Paris, may well satisfy the letter of Article 43 of the EC Treaty. But this permissive interpretation is surely out of keeping with the probable requirements of both the French and American authorities if Czech Airlines were designated by France to serve U.S./France routes. France (if not also the U.S. authorities) would likely require something closer to full 'establishment' in the sense of being a full operating subsidiary of Czech Airlines, with a local French license and aircraft registration.

---

580. *See supra* Chapter 2, Parts III & IV.
581. *See supra* text accompanying Chapter 2, note 235.
582. 2007 U.S./EC Air Transport Agreement, *supra* note 129, Memorandum of Consultations, para. 10. While the statement in the main text is not made directly in the Memorandum, it is implied by the fact that, under EC law, only the Member State where an EU carrier has its principal place of business can issue both the air operator certificate (AOC) and the Community operating license for that carrier. Common Rules, *supra* note 120, art. 4. (Moreover, the required exercise of AOC and licensing authority by the same State was insisted upon by the Council of Ministers when it revised the Commission's draft proposal on amendments to the 1992 reform package.) *Cf. id.* art. 4 & European Commission, *Common Rules, supra* note 120, at 21, art. 4. This legal framework strongly suggests that air carriers should have established operating subsidiaries (and not merely ticket offices) in Member States where they expect to receive a designation for extra-Union air services. *See supra* in the main text.
583. *See* Brian F. Havel, International Aviation Law Institute, *Commentary on the DOT Notice of Proposed Rulemaking*, at 3, U.S. DOT Dkt. No. OST-2003-1559-28 (Dec. 2005).
584. *See id.*

In this view, France would be unlikely to designate Czech Airlines *qua* Czech Airlines to serve the France/U.S. market, but might well be prepared to designate Czech Airlines (France), a company owned and controlled by Czech Airlines but operating in France subject to the full panoply of French regulatory oversight.

The Commission itself has indicated – although not within the framework of the Community licensing regulations – that there must be 'effective and real exercise of air transport through stable arrangements,'[585] a benchmark that seems to expect more than a perfunctory presence in the designating State. While the Commission's proposed baseline *could* mean merely a ticket office (or a telephone), the safety, security, taxation, and labor implications of designation suggest that much more work needs to be done to clarify the terms of the proposed new freedom of EU carriers to operate from territories outside their home States.[586]

F   DIPPING INTO THE WELL OF PUBLIC SUBSIDY: THE BATTLE
           AGAINST 'STATE AIDS'

The Commission's early focus on market integration widened in the 1980s to include investigation and fining of some fairly prominent cartel mischief (*e.g.*, the decision in the *Woodpulp* case[587]). Later still, leveraging the enhanced prestige of competition law in the EC, the Commission reached inside the very *sanctum sanctorum* of State-sponsored commercial activity, seeking to end distortion of competition by public subsidies (State aids, in the idiom of the EC Treaty) to so-called national champion enterprises, an economic sector that courts ostentatious public recognition in the livery of the flag carriers mentioned in the introduction to this Chapter. A tolerance of some very generous capital infusions into ailing flag carriers undoubtedly tarnished the Commission's record in discouraging State-sponsored distortion of the common market,[588] but (with the important exception of Alitalia) more recent enforcement has been zealous.

---

585. Regulation 847/2004, *supra* note 545, pmbl., recital 10. *See also supra* text accompanying Chapter 2, note 144 (discussing some conceptual inadequacies of the Commission's suggested benchmark). As previously considered, this instrument relates to Commission/Member State collaboration on the negotiation of air services agreements with non-Member States. The quoted language supplies a definitional aid to a requirement in Article 2 for Member States to consult with Community carriers 'established in their respective territories' with respect to such negotiations.

586. *See infra* Chapter 6, Part III(E). (further analyzing this conceptual refinement of the 'right' of establishment within the unique juristic framework of the international airline industry).

587. Commission Decision 202/85, 1985 O.J. (L 85) 1.

588. The State aids cases in the 1990s required serial bold acts of political *lèse-majesté* by the Commission as it scrutinized (although infrequently resisted) the financial minutiae of subsidies to the flag carriers of powerful Member States like France, Spain, and Belgium. *See, e.g.*, cases discussed in HAVEL, *supra* note 229, § 4.5.4.2.1. A fear of those who planned the airline liberalization program was thus being realized: that a regime of untrammeled competition would touch off a subsidy race as the individual governments sought to underwrite the competitive performance of their national carriers, and in practical politics (as opposed to Treaty of Rome regulation) it would be impossible to get control of government aids in those circumstances. [U.K.] CAA, *Airline Competition, supra* note 279, at 41-43.

No analogue exists in U.S. law to the Community's supranational jurisdiction over State aids,[589] although arguments have been advanced that the U.S. bankruptcy laws, which can prolong airlines in service long past ordinary business viability, have a substantially equivalent effect.[590] In recent years, the rearguard defenses of their flag carriers by the Greek and Italian Governments suggest that it will be some time before an EU Member State replicates the Belgian experience with Sabena, the only example to date where EC airline deregulation matched the U.S. experience of the Federal Government watching impassively as Pan Am tumbled into liquidation.[591]

In broad principle, as we have seen, Article 87 of the EC Treaty prohibits public subsidy (State aids),[592] and the Commission has surveillance authority to review a proposed plan of aid and to approve it, or to require its withdrawal or modification (or, failing compliance by the Member State, to refer the matter under special procedures directly to the European Court of Justice).[593] The lull in battle that followed a succession of high-profile interventions in the early 1990s has ended in recent years as a further group of Member States have made efforts to brace their weakened national carriers against the competitive furies of the maturing single market. To put the issue more bluntly, survival for a number of Europe's smaller flagship airlines may come down to a matter of borrowing privileges: paying commercial market rates or enjoying cheap government-guaranteed loans.[594]

The Commission has developed a surveillance jurisprudence marked by epigrammatic catchphrases such as 'one time, last time.'[595] and the 'market economy investor principle.'[596] Despite these various assertions of broad principle, it is not a

---

589. According to David Gerber, the entire EC competition code has dramatically shifted focus from traditional concerns with private conduct toward the problem of 'government interference with the competitive process.' Gerber, *supra* note 69, at 137.

590. *See* Rod Eddington, former Chief Executive, British Airways, Address to the Aviation Club of the U.K. (Sept. 22, 2005) (criticizing 'free ride' for U.S. airlines in bankruptcy and calling for U.S. to return to 'long lost principles of real and honest competition'). Recent changes in U.S. bankruptcy laws, however, have narrowed the scope for incumbent management to propose reorganization plans.

591. The liquidation of Pan Am took place in 1991. On Pan Am's role as the *de facto* U.S. flag carrier and the fate of its storied name after its collapse, *see supra* Chapter 3, note 319.

592. *See supra* Part II(D).

593. EC Treaty art. 88.

594. The Commission has always banned pure 'operating aids,' direct support to cover operating losses on (mostly domestic) air services. It does permit certain public service exceptions for thinly-served routes in accordance with Article 73 of the EC Treaty.

595. *See* European Commission, *Report to the Council and the European Parliament on the Evaluation of Aid Schemes Established in Favor of Community Air Carriers*, SEC (92) 431 final (Mar. 19, 1992). Thus, this final tranche of aid should be given only to companies which are *in extremis*, facing exceptional circumstances which are unforeseen and external to the company. *See id. See also* Martial Tardy, *EC Clears Alitalia Rescue, Says No State Aid Involved*, AVIATION DAILY, Jun. 8, 2005, at 1.

596. Application of Articles 92 and 93 of the EC Treaty and Article 61 of the EEA Agreement to State Aids in the Aviation Sector, 1994 O.J. (C 350) 5. The principle requires that governments ought to act as commercially responsible shareholders. If a private owner (the mythical

simple matter to uncover the analytical lodestar of EC State subsidy policy. The problem for the Commission, as evidenced in past decisions, is to determine when to pass from the 'first stage' of analysis (the market economy investor principle) to the 'second stage' (when it is empowered to impose stiff conditions on an investment that is now considered to be a State aid).[597] To what extent does the Commission allow itself to be buffeted by Member State pressure – and the exigencies of industrial policy – into finding that certain government capital infusions are normal commercial transactions, even though the number of smaller, old-line European flag carriers that could attract genuine risk capital on the public exchanges (for example, in the context of a rights issue by a privatized airline) is probably minimal?[598] In considering the Commission's political predicament, a brief glance at some recent Commission decisions will be instructive.

1   Two Flag Carriers Under Scrutiny: Olympic and Alitalia

Greece's Olympic Airlines (formerly Olympic Airways) offers a specially doleful example of the Community's State aids policy. Beginning in 1994, the Commission gave its approval to the Greek Government to implement a restructuring and recapitalization plan for the 100% publicly-owned carrier.[599] The approved aid was contingent on Greece complying with 21 separate commitments,[600] including refraining from interference with the management of Olympic Airways and providing no further aid to the carrier.[601] After concerns were expressed that the government was reneging on its commitments, and following

---

'market investor') would not gamble his or her own capital in similar circumstances, then the transaction (whether in the form of a capital injection, loan financing, or guarantees) will be treated as a State aid and must satisfy certain conditions. *Id.* at 12-15. In the air transport sector, the protean language of Article 87(3) of the EC Treaty (which speaks of aid 'to facilitate the development of certain economic activities') is usually relied upon, and the requirements imposed by the Commission are supposedly designed to satisfy the Treaty proviso that such aid must not 'adversely affect trading conditions to an extent contrary to the common interest.' *Id.* at 15-17.

597. The sequence of first stage/second stage analysis is the Commission's description. *Id.* at 12.
598. Among the EU flag carriers, British Airways (fully privatized), Lufthansa (fully privatized), and Air France-KLM (partly privatized by their respective governments) have recently been successful in luring private investment capital. Old-line carriers such as Olympic Airlines (formerly Olympic Airways) and Alitalia, discussed in this Part, represent the kinds of carriers that remain unappealing to private investors.
599. Olympic's precarious financial condition, primarily the result of poor productivity and management errors, was set forth in detail in the first Commission decision on State aid to the airline. *See* Commission Decision of 7 October 1994 on the Aid Granted by Greece to Olympic Airways, 1994 O.J. (L 273) 22.
600. The Commission approved an aid package that included loan guarantees, writing-off of debt to equity, and capital injections to accompany the restructuring program. The approval was based on the exemption in what is now Article 87(3)(c) of the EC Treaty (ex-Article 92(3)(c)), which allows a derogation from the general prohibition of State aids to facilitate the development of certain economic activities or of certain economic areas. *See id.*
601. *See id.*

a Commission-sanctioned plan revision in 1998,[602] the Commission commenced an Article 88(2) proceeding to challenge the aid. The Commission's findings, contained in its Decision 2003/372, were that most of the objectives of the Olympic Airways restructuring plan had not been attained, that the Commission's conditions for the aid had not been met, and that the 1998 Commission decision had been wrongly implemented.[603] The Commission determined that in light of the violations, Olympic Airways would have to repay 41 million euro in restructuring aid back to the Greek Government along with an additional 120 million euro in new operational aid bestowed upon the airline after the 1998 decision.[604]

After all of this skirmishing, in 2003 the Commission resorted to the telescoped procedure of Article 88 to refer the Greek Government's noncompliance with the Commission's decision to the European Court of Justice.[605] Despite the special procedure, the Court took another two years to rule *inter alia* that Greece had attempted to hinder the implementation of Decision 2003/372 by transferring Olympic Airways' personnel and assets, free of all debts, to a new corporation, Olympic Airlines, and in doing so had engineered the transfer to ensure that Olympic Airways' debts were irrecoverable under Greek law.[606] The Court branded the government's behavior as having 'seriously compromised' the Commission's aim in Decision 2003/372 of 'restor[ing] undistorted competition in the civil aviation sector.'[607] Greece was found to have failed in its obligations to recover the aid it had given to Olympic Airways.[608]

---

602. *See* Commission Decision of 14 August 1998 on Aid Granted by Greece to Olympic Airways, 1999 O.J. (L 128) 1. In addition to allowing further loan guarantees and the reduction and conversion of equity debts approved in its initial 1994 decision, the Commission reduced the amount of approved capital injections into the airline from GRD 54 billion to GRD 40.8 billion. *See id.* art. 1.

603. *See* Commission Decision of 11 December 2002 on Aid Granted by Greece to Olympic Airways, paras. 41-42, 2003 O.J. (L 132) 1. Moreover, a passel of new aids, including deferment of social security and tax obligations and tolerance of defaults on airport charges, had been provided to Olympic in the intervening years. *Id.* para. 67. As the Commission noted, the concept of aid 'is wider than that of a subsidy because it embraces not only positive benefits, such as subsidies themselves, but also measures which, in various forms, mitigate the charges which are normally included in the budget of an undertaking.' *Id.* para. 211. All of these benefits contributed, in the Commission's arch phrasing, to 'artificially maintain[ing] the Hellenic carrier alive.' *Id.* para. 212.

604. *See id.* arts. 1-2.

605. Case C-415/03, Comm'n *v.* Hellenic Republic, 2003 O.J. (C 289) 14.

606. Case C-415/03, Comm'n *v.* Hellenic Republic, para. 33, 2005 E.C.R. I-3875. According to settled case law, the only defense available to a Member State in opposing a Commission application under Article 88(2) of the EC Treaty – *i.e.*, for a Court declaration of non-compliance with the Treaty – is to plead that it was absolutely impossible to implement the decision ordering recovery. *Id.* para. 35. Greece, however, could not assert this defense where it merely informed the Commission of the legal, political, or practical difficulties involved in implementing the decision and had not taken any 'real' steps to achieve recovery. *Id.* para. 43.

607. *Id.* para. 34.

608. *Id.* ruling, para. 1. As in its dealings with the Commission, Greece was in no hurry to comply with the ECJ ruling and recover the aid it had given to Olympic Airways. *See* Press Release, Europa, Greece Must Comply with Court Judgment on Illegal Subsidies Granted Before 2002

Greece's resolve to defend its flag carrier was displayed not only in its intractability with respect to recovering the already-conferred State subsidies,[609] but in its persistence in keeping Olympic aloft with further aid granted *after* the Court's 2005 ruling.[610] Despite Olympic's minor victory on the legality of aid given in the wake of 9/11,[611] however, the investigations, judicial procedures, and enormous debt load of Olympic may finally compel the Greek carrier, like Sabena before it, temporarily to close shop in order to reincarnate.[612] One thing which is not unclear

---

to Olympic, IP/06/425 (Apr. 4, 2006). Using EC Treaty procedures, the Commission returned to the Court to compel Greece through a lump sum penalty and periodic penalties to recover its aid from Olympic. *See* Press Release, Europa, Commission Requests Court of Justice to Oblige Greece to Comply with 2002 Commission Decision on Illegal Subsidies Granted Before 2002 to Olympic, IP/06/1424 (Oct. 18, 2006).

609. In an intriguing sidebar to the main proceedings, Olympic itself managed to persuade the Court of First Instance (CFI) to annul those portions of Decision 2003/372 dealing with non-notified aid alleged to have been granted by Greece to Olympic. *See* Case T-68/03, Olympiaki Aeroporia Ypiresies AE *v.* Comm'n, 2007 O.J. (C 247) 22. The non-notified aid, in the form of Greece's allowance of nonpayment or deferment of payment of a series of public levies including social security contributions, a Value Added Tax (VAT) on fuel and spare parts, airport charges and rent, and ticket taxes, was, in the opinion of the CFI, not properly justified by the Commission as constituting illegal State aid. *See* Press Release, ECFI, The Court of First Instance Partially Annuls the Commission Decision on State Aid to Olympic Airways, CJE/07/56 (Sept. 12, 2007). But the bulk of Decision 2003/372 – ordering the recovery of Olympic's restructuring aid granted between 1998 and 2002 – was left intact. *See id.*; *see also infra* note 611.

610. *See* Press Release, Europa, Commission Launches Formal Investigation into New State Aid by Greece to Olympic Airways Services and Olympic Airlines, IP/07/1963 (Dec. 19, 2007). The target of this latest challenge by the Commission is the period after 2005 when Greece allegedly provided its flag carrier with tax forbearance, government-funded aircraft leases, overpayment of arbitration awards, and credit protection. *Id.* In the Commission's opinion, this assortment of benefits would not be compatible with the common market and would violate its 'one time, last time' criterion. *Id.* The Commission takes the position, incidentally, that Olympic Airlines is the successor company to Olympic Airways for purposes of applying the 'one time, last time' principle. The Court of Justice supports this interpretation: the Commission has won another judgment against Greece for aid granted to Olympic Airlines between 2002 and 2005. *See* Case-419/06, Comm'n *v.* Hellenic Republic, 2008 O.J. (C 79) 5; Press Release, Europa, Air Transport: Commission Takes Note of Today's Court Judgment in the Olympic File, IP/08/02 (Feb. 14, 2008).

611. Here, the Court of First Instance ruled that the euro 4.8 million which the Greek Government had awarded Olympic Airways in Jul. 2002 for the cost of cancellations following 9/11 could be held compatible with the common market because of a direct causal connection with the terrorist attacks. *See* Case T-268/06, Olympiaki Aeroporia Ypiresies *v.* Comm'n, 2008 E.C.R. 00 (pending official publication). In reaching its decision, the CFI stated that the communication adopted by the European Commission after the attacks, COM (2001) 574 final (Oct. 10, 2001), recognized the legitimacy of State aid granted to airlines for extra costs incurred due to the closure of U.S. airspace, along with the additional costs of insurance, Case T-268/06, *supra*, paras. 1-5, and that the Commission had failed to adequately state reasons why the aid granted to Olympic failed to comply, *id.* para. 87.

612. *See* European Industrial Relations Observatory Online, Forced Landing for Olympic Airways, Feb. 25, 2008, <www.eurofound.europa.eu/eiro/2008/01/articles/gr0801049i.htm>. It would seem that, despite Greece's best efforts, the government may have to yield to the classic observation of fellow countryman, Xenophanes of Colophon, that 'all things are from the

is that the Olympic Airways case itself, as a recent study notes, showed the inherent tension 'of the Commission possessing executive authority in certain areas (State aids) and utilizing [this authority] across a broader agenda [for] which its competences are more limited (the form of restructuring privatization).'[613]

The study further noted that, although Brussels and Athens started from 'parallel strategies' of public divestiture of Olympic Airways and elimination of State aid, the contentious results were a product of 'differences over the clarity and consistency of the signals each gave; the time horizons each operated within; and the credibility and trust each had with the other.'[614] Based on the most recent series of rulings and the Commission's unremitting scrutiny of the Greek Government and its carrier, it appears that the case will continue to illustrate the problems of macro-level reform and State-level implementation that lies at the core of the shared governance of the EC.[615]

Meanwhile, across the Ionian Sea, Italy also serially made public capital available to its failing flag carrier, Alitalia, but until 2008 stayed largely within the Commission's interpretation of the State aid rules (or at least was able to win Commission backing for some supposedly final infusions). The Italian carrier, which has failed to turn a profit since 1998, was the beneficiary of a Commission-sanctioned capital injection from the Italian State of 1.75 billion euro in 1997.[616] With Alitalia confronting liquidation or restructuring in 2004, the Commission disapplied its 'one time, last time' maxim to approve a further 400 million euro in so-called 'rescue aid.'[617] The following year, the Commission ratified a complex 'de-merger' restructuring plan, which would have split the airline into two new autonomous companies, as also not in violation of 'one time, last time.'[618] Labor fears of job losses doomed an initial proposal by the Air France/KLM partners to expand

---

earth and to the earth all things must come in the end.' Xenophanes of Colophon, Fragments 33 (J.H. Lester ed., 1992).

613. Kevin Featherstone & Dimitris Papadimitriou, *Manipulating Rules, Contesting Solutions: Europeanization and the Politics of Restructuring Olympic Airways*, 42 Gov't & Opposition 46, 69 (2007).

614. *Id.* at 71.

615. *See id.* at 71-72.

616. *See* Europa, Press Release, Commission Confirms its Authorisation for State Aid to Alitalia in 1997, IP/01/1017 (Jul. 18, 2001) (noting the original authorization for aid in 1997 and subsequent modifications following a Court of First Instance judgment annulling minor portions of that authorization).

617. *See* Press Release, Europa, Air Transport: The Commission Authorises Rescue Aid for the Italian Airline Alitalia, IP/04/965 (Jul. 20, 2004). The Commission-approved rescue aid assertedly did not run afoul of the 'one time, last time' principle since that principle (in the Commission's interpretation) applies only to restructuring aid. The Commission cited the 'social difficulties' of terminating over 30,000 employees to justify its leniency, which had also been afforded in similar circumstances in 2001 to Belgium's Sabena. *Id.*

618. *See* Commission Decision 2006/176, 2006 O.J. (L 69) 1. Alitalia's restructuring plan involved separating the company into two parts: AZ Fly, which would cover air transport operations, and AZ Servizi, which would cover maintenance, groundhandling, information technology, and shared services. *Id.* paras. 8-9. In order to fund the restructuring, AZ Fly would receive a capital injection worth euro 1.2 billion from private investors and the Italian State while AZ

their cooperative alliance with Alitalia[619] into a full takeover of the Italian flagship.[620] That failed effort, coupled with renewed political support for an independent Alitalia following the return to power of prime minister Silvio Berlusconi in 2008,[621] prompted a new bailout in 2008, this time in the form of a 300 million euro loan intended to keep the carrier airborne long enough to secure new private investment.[622] In response, the Commission opened an investigation into whether or not the loan constituted illegal State aid and found that it had.[623]

Undoubtedly, it proved troublesome for the Italian Government to claim that the 2008 loan was the kind of transaction a private investor would make, given Alitalia's history of losses, its existential dependence on the State, and its exhaustion of the 'one time, last time' exemption. In that context, and *a fortiori* given the aeroeconomic pressures of fuel price rises, Alitalia (which declared a pre-tax loss

---

Servizi would receive euro 216 million from the State-owned holding company Fintecna. *Id.* para. 9. The Commission found that the 'dismemberment' (its unhappy choice of phrase) of Alitalia would not leave the accumulated debt in a 'public cocoon' (the attempted Olympic remedy), with the economic activity transferred to the private sector. *Id.* para. 189. So long as the involvement of both the Italian State and Fintecna remained consistent with that of private market investors, and where the participating private shareholders took part in conditions identical to the public investors, the Commission was willing to countenance the restructuring. *See id.* arts 1 & 2 (stating the decision); *see also* Alitalia, About Us, <http://corporate.alitalia.com/en/group/index.htm> (portraying the airline's post-restructuring composition).

619. *See supra* note 369.
620. Gabriel Khan, *Air France-KLM Withdraws Its Offer for Alitalia*, WALL ST. J, Apr. 22, 2008, at B3. In January 2009, however, Alitalia was relaunched as a privately owned carrier with KLM-Air France taking a 25% stake. *See supra* Chapter 3, note 304 & *infra* note 622.
621. There is no doubt that the return of a nationalist Berlusconi government provided Alitalia with a new patron. Matthew Kaminski, *Berlusconi is Back*, WALL ST. J., Apr. 15, 2008, at A18. Having made the preservation of the Italian carrier a centerpiece of his election platform, Berlusconi quickly began searching for domestic investors to bolster Alitalia. Gabriel Khan & Charles Forelle, *Berlusconi Vows to Find New Bidder for Alitalia*, WALL ST. J., Apr. 24, 2008, at B7.
622. *Alitalia to Receive Emergency Financing – State-Run Airlines Get $479 Million from Government*, WALL ST. J., Apr. 23, 2008, at B8. In January 2009, Alitalia relaunched as a smaller, privately owned carrier with Air France-KLM taking a 25% stake. In November of the previous year, the European Commission ruled that the carrier's new majority owners, the CAI consortium, would not be responsible for repaying the euro 300 million loan. *Alitalia Bidders Cleared From Repaying State Aid*, EurActiv, Nov. 13, 2008, <http://www.euractiv.com/en/transport/alitalia-bidders-cleared-repaying-state-aid/article-177110>.
623. *See* Press Release, Europa, State Aid: Commission Launches In-Depth Investigation into 300 Million Loan Granted to Alitalia by the Italian State, IP/08/919 (Jun. 11, 2008); *see also* Press Release, Alitalia: The Commission Adopts Two State Aid Decisions, IP/08/1692 (Nov. 12, 2008). As an interesting political side-story to the exchanges between the Commission and the Italian Government over the financial future of Alitalia, Antonio Tajani, longtime political ally of Prime Minister Berlusconi, assumed the role of EU Transport Commissioner from Jacques Barrot following the latter's transfer to the Freedom, Security and Justice portfolio. Despite questions about Tajani's willingness to pursue rigorously the European Commission's investigation into the Alitalia loan, he steadfastly maintained that he was 'not pocketable by any lobby' and would see to it that the Community's competition rules are enforced. *See* Press Release, European Parliament, Summary of the Hearing of Antonio Tajani (Italy), Commissioner Designate for Transport (Jun. 16, 2008); *see also* Richard Owen, *'King Silvio' Puts Old Friends and a Showgirl into His New Court*, TIMES (London), May 9, 2008, at 45.

of 215 million euro in the first quarter of 2008) showed itself as an undisciplined survivor from the long ride of the flag carriers.

2 A New State Aids Challenge: Airport Subsidies

A recent phenomenon in the praxis of State aids has been the efforts of publicly-owned regional airports to grant so-called 'start-up' aid to low-cost carriers intending to serve these airports. The most prominent case involves the relationship between Irish low-cost carrier Ryanair and the Brussels South Charleroi Airport (BSCA), a public sector company controlled by the Walloon Region in Belgium.[624] In an effort to become Ryanair's first base of operations on the European mainland, BSCA offered a substantial reduction in the carrier's landing fees, groundhandling fees at 10% of the advertised rates, and a subvention toward part of Ryanair's operating costs at the airport.[625] The deal, which included commitments from Ryanair on basing between two and four aircraft at the airport and operating at least three rotations per aircraft leaving Charleroi over a 15-year period,[626] prompted a Commission investigation following a complaint alleging that the arrangement violated Article 87 of the EC Treaty.[627]

The legality of the deal was in question once the Commission decided (reluctantly) to apply its private market investor principle, finding that the concessions granted by BSCA to Ryanair were not the kind of 'commercial hazards' a private investor would risk.[628] The Commission was unconvinced that the BSCA/Ryanair deal fell under any of the listed exceptions to Article 87,[629] although it conceded that certain forms of aid from publicly-owned airports may be compatible with the common market (and specifically its transport policy) when awarded to enhance the use of the EU's secondary airport infrastructure.[630]

---

624. Commission Decision of 12 Feb. 2004 Concerning Advantages Granted by the Walloon Region and Brussels South Charleroi Airport to the Airline Ryanair, 2004 O.J. (L 137) 1 [Ryanair Decision].
625. *Id.* paras. 10-11.
626. *Id.* para. 12.
627. *See* Press Release, Europa, The Commission's Decision on Charleroi Airport Promotes the Activities of Low-Cost Airlines and Regional Development, IP/04/157 (Feb. 3, 2004). [hereinafter Press Release, Charleroi]. According to Ryanair, no other EU airline was willing to make a similar set of commitments to Charleroi. Ryanair Decision, *supra* note 624, paras. 84-85.
628. *See id.* paras. 219 & 237. As discussed, the Commission was reluctant to apply the market investor principle to a public regulator like BSCA *ab initio*. With respect to its actual application in the decision, a red flag was raised for the Commission by the fact that BSCA's business plan was premised on contingent future revenues from hypothetical carriers which might in the future operate services at the airport, but not from Ryanair itself. Ryanair Decision, *supra* note 624, para. 192. The Commission also took a hard look at the absence of returns the airport could expect because of the concessions made to Ryanair, as well as the airport's reliance on unguaranteed subsidies, to find that it had acted imprudently and thus not in accord with Article 87 of the EC Treaty. *See* Press Release, Charleroi, *supra* note 627.
629. *See supra* note 596.
630. Press Release, Charleroi, *supra* note 627.

Having made a State aid determination, the Commission examined whether the Ryanair concessions could be declared compatible with the common market under Article 87(3) of the Treaty.[631] Since the aid was operational, the Commission declared, it 'is in principle prohibited, except in the poorest regions of Europe under exceptional circumstances and strict conditions.'[632] But Article 87(3)(c) of the EC Treaty provides that 'aid to facilitate the development of certain economic activities or of certain economic areas' may be compatible with the common market. The Commission explained that this potential exemption could not be applied on the basis of its 1994 guidelines on State aid in the aviation sector (or other existing frameworks for horizontal aid).[633] Given the economic trends generated by the deregulation of air transport in the EC, however, the application of the exemption could be considered 'in view of the role played by this aid in the development of regional airports.'[634]

In inventing a new, but limited, exemption for start-up aid to airlines departing from regional airports, the Commission's first condition is that the aid 'forms part of a coherent airport development policy characteri[z]ed by a demonstrated willingness to develop the profitability of infrastructures that are not always profitable.'[635] This policy should also result in the 'promotion of regional development, tourism, local economy, or regional image.'[636] Additional rationalizations for a regional airport exemption would include relieving the 'saturation of major airport capacities' and (relatedly) backstopping pollution and air traffic management problems.[637]

The Commission's investigation concluded that some of Ryanair's preferments were still incompatible with the new aid conditions and would have to be recovered from the carrier.[638] The 15-year reduction in landing fees, for example, was deemed impermissibly exclusive.[639] However, had the Walloon Region publicly offered limited-duration discounts on a nondiscriminatory basis to airport

---

631. Ryanair Decision, *supra* note 624, para. 254.
632. *Id.* para. 256.
633. *Id.* paras. 261-62. An updated list of the European Commission's horizontal aid frameworks, *i.e.*, categories of aid 'aimed at solving problems that may arise in any industry and country,' can be found at European Commission, State Aid Controls, Legislation: Horizontal Rules, <http://ec.europa.eu/comm/competition/state_aid/legislation/horizontal.html>.
634. Ryanair Decision, *supra* note 624, paras. 261-62. Critics suggested that impure competitive motives – and a kind of sub-State industrial policy – lay behind the BSCA/Ryanair deal: 'Despite . . . [an] attempt to portray start-up aid as part of a rational and consistent policy to promote the use of regional airports, it is readily apparent that start-up aid is designed to support a particular business model – that of low-cost carriers such as Ryanair.' Sven Völcker, *'Start-Up' Aid for Low Cost Carriers - A Policy Perspective*, COMPETITION L. INSIGHT, Apr. 12, 2005, at 6. Völcker claims that '[s]uch a move may be politically expedient given the current popularity of the low-cost business model and the low-cost carriers' skills in using regulatory proceedings to further raise their public profile. But it is bad state aid policy.' *Id.*
635. Ryanair Decision, *supra* note 624, para. 283.
636. *Id.* para 284.
637. *Id.* para. 287.
638. *See id.* paras. 338-42.
639. *Id.* para. 263-66.

users, these would have escaped censure under Article 87.[640] Ryanair's deep discounts for groundhandling fees were also impeached because they would leave BSCA unable to cover its costs for providing these services to the carrier.[641] And various 'one-shot' incentives for the opening of new routes, not directly linked to the actual costs of opening these routes (for example, pilot training) or not 'proportional or incentive in nature,' were also determined to be recoverable.[642]

The Commission would allow Ryanair to keep its 'marketing contribution' of four euro per passenger, both retroactively and prospectively,[643] provided that BSCA could demonstrate that the contribution related to the opening of a new route and was limited in time to five years.[644] The total contributions also must not exceed 50% of the 'start-up, marketing and one-shot costs' incurred and the airport must make the aid available in the future to any carrier wishing to launch service at Charleroi.[645] Finally, the contribution was disallowed for any route opened to replace a route discontinued by Ryanair during the previous five years.[646]

In its Charleroi decision, the Commission accepted the principle of start-up costs for the first time in its competitive oversight of the EU air transport industry.[647] But the explosive response of Ryanair to the investigation, including public accusations of Commission bias,[648] encouraged the Commission to build

---

640. *Id.* paras. 265-66.
641. Ryanair Decision, *supra* note 624, paras. 267-69.
642. *Id.* paras. 318-25.
643. *Id.* para. 343.
644. *Id.* paras. 311-317. A full 15-year contribution without a phased reduction, in the Commission's reasoning, was a 'simple undertaking to bear operational costs on a continuing basis.' *Id.* para. 312.
645. *See id.* paras. 326-43.
646. Ryanair Decision, *supra* note 624, para. 343. The Charleroi proceeding continues. In Mar. 2008, the Court of First Instance heard Ryanair's appeal against the Commission's 2004 Decision. Ryanair made the following arguments on appeal: (1) That the Commission had failed to apply the market economy investor principle; (2) That the Commission ignored evidence that the agreement reached with BSCA was the result of the carrier's negotiations with other low-cost airports; (3) That the Commission ignored the fact that Ryanair's cost base at Charleroi was offered to other airlines which were willing to make the same investment Ryanair did; (4) That the Commission ignored the fact that Ryanair had lower costs at other low-cost airports; (5) That the Commission ignored Charleroi's growth as a result of Ryanair's investment; and (6) That the Commission ignored that other airlines, retailers, and investors have come to Charleroi as a result of the partnership between the airport and Ryanair. *See* Press Release, Ryanair, European Court Hears Ryanair's Appeal Against Commission's Charleroi Decision (Mar. 13, 2008). In Dec. 2008, the Court of First Instance nullified the 2004 Decision, focusing its attention largely on the misapplication of the market economy investor principle by the Commission. *See* Case T-196/04, Ryanair Ltd. *v.* Comm'n, 2009 E.C.R. 00 (pending publication). The European Commission, on the other hand, is not yet done with Ryanair and its airport relationships. Separately, the Commission has launched an investigation into Ryanair's commercial relations with Frankfurt's Hahn Airport. Press Release, Europa, Commission Investigates Potential State Aid to Frankfurt Hahn Airport and to Carriers Operating From It, IP/08/956 (Jun. 17, 2008).
647. Ryanair Decision, *supra* note 624, para. 356.
648. Ryanair launched a high-profile public campaign against the European Commission, accusing the regulators of bias in the application of EC rules and of bowing to pressure from Ryanair's

a 'clear legal framework' around its BSCA decision by issuing guidelines in September 2005 to clarify its policy on start-up aid to airlines departing from regional airports.[649]

Under these guidelines, start-up aid can only be paid for routes 'linking a regional airport in category C or D [less than 5 million passengers per year] to another EU airport,'and for new routes that will lead to an increase in the net volume of passengers.[650] Moreover, the aid 'must not encourage traffic simply to be transferred from one airline or company to another.'[651] Eligible aid includes 'marketing and advertising costs' and excludes 'standard operating costs such as hire or depreciation of aircraft, fuel, crew salaries, airport charges or catering costs.'[652] Clipping the time period allowed in the BSCA decision, the Commission indicated that proposed aid must be degressive and limited to a maximum of three years,[653] and that the route receiving the aid must ultimately prove profitable.[654] Additionally, the 'amount of aid in any one year may not exceed 50% of total eligible costs for that year and total aid may not exceed an average of 30% of eligible costs,' conditions that once again sliced more narrowly the amounts approved in the BSCA/Ryanair decision.[655] To encourage transparency, the public body granting start-up aid must make the terms of the aid public and allow other interested airlines to tender their services.[656]

---

larger European competitors. *See* Press Release, Ryanair, Ryanair Responds to Further Evidence of EU Bias (Mar. 11, 2008).

649. Community Guidelines on Financing of Airports and Start-up Aid to Airlines Departing From Regional Airports, 2005 O.J. (C 312) 1 [hereinafter Airport & Airline Guidelines]. The document also includes guidelines on aid for the financing of airport infrastructure, operation of airport infrastructure, and airport services. *See id.* secs. 4.1 & 4.2.

650. *Id.* para. 79.

651. *Id.* para. 79(c).

652. *Id.* para. 79(e).

653. *Id.* para. 79(f). The period would be five years in the case of routes from 'disadvantaged regions.' Airport & Airline Guidelines, *supra* note 649, para. 79(f).

654. *Id.* para. 79(d). The airline receiving the aid must commit to operating the route for a period that is substantially greater than the period over which the start-up aid is to be received. *Id.* para. 79(f). Start-up aid must also be stopped when the airline reaches the objectives set forth in terms of passengers or when the route breaks even. *Id.*

655. *Id.*

656. *Id.* para. 69(h). The guidelines also require start-up aid to be notified to the Commission. Airport & Airline Guidelines, *supra* note 649, para. 81. The Commission requests that the Member States notify start-up aid schemes rather than individual cases. *Id.* An example of this type of notification that was approved by the Commission after publication of its guidelines is an 'air route development funds' measure put in place by regional authorities in Wales, North East and North West England. Press Release, Europa, The European Commission Approves a System for Start-Up Aid for Transport Services From Regional Airports in the UK, IP/06/627 (May 16, 2006). *See also* the notified schemes mentioned in European Commission, *Questions on State Aid for Airports and Start-Up Aid to Airlines*, Memo/07/285 (Jul. 10, 2007).

3   **Should State Aids Be a Transitional Phenomenon?**

The Ryanair case demonstrates that the provocative issue of public aids to EU airlines has not been (contrary to expectations) a transitional topic of Europe's deregulated airline industry. Certainly, the Olympic and Alitalia controversies could be described as the last reflexive gasp of a disappearing order of public dominion of the airlines themselves. Merely refloating the old flag carriers to await their next dates with economic destiny is improvident, and seriously in conflict with the economic principles of the single aviation market. Moreover, continued public assistance, as the U.K. Government argued in its European Court of Justice challenge to an earlier Air France subsidy, simply destroys the incentive for State-owned airlines to become efficient and to adopt a sound commercial approach.[657] So long as the Member States continue to support their own treaty-based credo of illegitimizing market distortion by public subsidy, the optimal course, in the end, must be to accept the absorption of the weaker carrier into a stronger EU competitor, or even its complete displacement by new entry or by the operations of a foreign carrier's subsidiary (no doubt a future wellspring of new entry).[658]

But the Ryanair/Charleroi dispute does change the equation for evaluating the legal and political wisdom of challenging State interventions in the marketplace. The Commission's reasoning is ultimately less than fully persuasive, particularly given the Treaty's conspicuous exception for economic development and the strong argument that underutilized secondary airports can make for innovative commercial arrangements with willing carriers.[659] While dogmatic positions are not helpful, as the Commission no doubt recognizes, its slide-rule approach to measuring benefits may appear overzealous when the market is capable of working out the boons and deficits of any likely arrangements. A limiting principle that permits a private airline and a public airport, in order to solve the problem of airport underutilization, to establish a joint promotion and publicity company (as Ryanair and BSCA did),[660] yet condemns the same airport for using flexible charges to incentivize the same airline, truly lacks commercial nuance. The Commission's resistance to the commercial aspirations of a 'public' regulator like an airport

---

657. *See* Case 274/94, United Kingdom *v.* Comm'n, 1994 O.J. (C 351) 4.

658. The legacy of Pan Am reminds the Europeans that airline liberalization, disciplined by the marketplace, arrives with formidable economic and political costs. While a serial analysis of the Commission's numerous State aid investigations lies outside the scope of this book, it should be noted that the procession of State-aided flag carriers has also included Aer Lingus (Ireland) and TAP (Portugal). *See* HAVEL, *supra* note 588, at 387-88 n. 857.

659. The business model of low-cost carriers feeding underutilized secondary airports has become well-practiced in Europe, especially in the United Kingdom (*cf.* Glasgow Prestwick, London Stansted, London Luton, Belfast, etc.). Airport & Airline Guidelines, *supra* note 649, para. 44. Arguably, these airports impose some competitive price and efficiency discipline on major metropolitan hubs. There is also a recognized network effect as service expansions draw in other airlines, lowering the airport's unit costs. *Id.* para. 64.

660. Press Release, Charleroi, *supra* note 627.

authority (BSCA, for example)[661] not only appears formalistic but may stifle other public/private market models that could allow municipalities, airports, and airlines to collaborate, for example, in bringing air passengers tariff-free to particular destinations.[662]

The proscription of repeated subsidies to air carriers was a necessary corollary of a multilateral deregulation project; it was also a deeply politicized process that demanded strong nerves on the part of the watchdog Commission. Special arrangements by private airports are becoming more common. Arrangements by public airports to dispense discounts in the hope of eventual regeneration are similarly localized enough and sufficiently likely to be the object of market forces that, as with global distribution technology, the argument for the smack of centralized enforcement seems less cogent. It may be best to concede the political and economic reality of the phenomenon of utilization incentives to all airlines (whether low-cost or otherwise) and all airports (public or private), and at the same time to continue to press for the enculturation among all of the Member States and their air carriers of what the Commission has called 'commercial principles' of management.[663]

G   CONCLUSION: SOME COUNTERPOINTS TO THE EC
               DEREGULATION EXPERIMENT

In broad theory, the Community's airline liberalization program constitutes a remarkable advance for international air transport law, an unprecedented consolidation of competing air sovereignties into a cohesive unitary system comparable to the U.S. federal model. And in practice, as a consumer-driven model of deregulation,[664] the three reform packages succeeded in loosening the grip of duopoly, in

---

661. The Commission was painfully reluctant to accept that the market investor principle could apply to a regulator exercising public power prerogatives (such as the imposition of airport landing charges). Ryanair argued that reductions in public levies and fees are common at non-congested (albeit private) EU airports as an incentive to launch new services or to strengthen new frequencies. Airport & Airline Guidelines, *supra* note 649, paras. 57 & 144. While Ryanair and Belgium both contended that the Commission's position discriminated against public airports in violation of the EC's Treaty principle of neutrality in public/private ownership (Article 295), the Commission responded by suggesting that private owners are just as much subject to public regulation (since an airport always serves a public function). *Id.* para. 156. While that may be true, it is certainly not dispositive of why public airports are not equally capable of acting like private owners.

662. This is one of the potential business models, after all, proposed elsewhere by Ryanair's Chief Executive Officer, Michael O'Leary, as a means to foster regional growth and development (including tourism). *See* Charlemagne, *Low-Cost Founding Fathers*, ECONOMIST, Jan. 29, 2005.

663. European Commission, *Proposal for a Decision on Community Guidelines for the Development of the Trans-European Transport Network*, at 16, COM (94) 106 final (Jul. 4, 1994).

664. The European Commission has never concealed its intention that, like the U.S. model, its deregulation of the airline industry would primarily serve consumers. *See, e.g.*, European Commission, *Third Package Consultation Paper*, *supra* note 126, para. 7 (noting that competition in the air transport industry has benefited consumers). On the other hand, the economic

opening up intra-Union cabotage, and in encouraging the rapid expansion of the low-cost airline sector[665] and the growth of direct intra-Union services from regional airports.[666] But, as the first revision of the third package takes effect,[667]

---

interests of producers (the air carriers) and of labor have visibly been compromised by the destabilization of the bilateral system, the disappearance of well-established carriers (*e.g.*, Sabena, Swissair, Air Lib), the turbulence of rapid entry and exit of new entrants, as well as (for labor) the uncertainties of differential employment laws across the Member States.

665. Low-cost carriers now have a 19.5% market share in Europe. *See* EUROCONTROL, *supra* note 456, at 3. *But see* European Commission, *Third Package Consultation Paper, supra* note 126, para. 10 (indicating that low-budget fares now represent 10% of intra-Community traffic 'with a substantial margin for growth,' while noting, however, that 'the price of fully flexible tickets has not fallen at all but even tended to rise').

666. *See id.* paras. 7-8; *see also id.* para. 9 (indicating that the 'number of links' between Member States grew to 1,290 in 2002 from 692 in 1992). *See also* Air Transport Users Council, [ATUC], *European Commission Consultation on Revision of Regulations 2407/92, 2408/ 92, and 2409/92*, para. 3, Memorandum from the ATUC (Jun. 10, 2003) [hereinafter ATUC, *Consultation*] (noting that, while these developments were partly a function of general economic growth and the improved economies of modern aircraft, 'they could not have happened in the previous regulated environment'); *see also* European Transport Workers' Federation, *ETF Contribution to the Consultation Paper with a View to Revision of Regulations 2407/92, 2408/92, and 2409/92*, at 2 (Jun. 2003) [hereinafter ETF, *Consultation*] (suggesting that it is 'sometimes hard to distinguish the direct consequences of the Third Package from actions or measures that would have come about anyway in view of current international developments (globalization, alliances, etc.)). Although the Commission stated in its paper that 'the discretionary powers of the national authorities have been curbed,' European Commission, *Third Package Consultation Paper, supra* note 126, para. 8, there remain disturbing signs of continued national protectionism in the interpretation of Community legislation. In addition to examples mentioned in these counterpoints (for example, the public service obligation process), distortions of competition through State action have been evident in earlier parts of this study which discussed slot allocation procedures and State aids.

667. *See Common Rules, supra* note 120. One quickly forms the impression, in reading the responses by stakeholders to the Commission's consultation paper on the revisions to the third package, that revision of the third package held little urgency or appeal. *See* European Commission, *Summary of the Third Package Contributions, supra* note 126, at 1; *see, e.g.*, Government of France, *Réponse Française à la Consultation Pour la Révision du Troisième Paquet*, at 1 (2003) (recommending only technical adjustments in the short term and the tackling of more ambitious reforms 'in a longer-term perspective'); *see also* U.K. Government, Department of Transport, *Response to Commission Consultation Paper on Revision of Third Package*, at 1 (2003) ('[W]e do not see the need for further regulation – indeed, in certain respects we would favour a reduction in the level of regulation'); European Regions Airline Association, *Response to the European Commission Consultation Paper with a View to Revision of Regulations 2407/92, 2408/92, and 2409/92*, at 1 (Jun. 2003) (caustically indicating that '[a]t this critical time for airlines' survival ... very few of [the members of the Association] believe that they can devote ... their senior executives' time to give a comprehensive answer to the issues raised in the consultation'). Broadly, the submissions advocated that structural adjustments to take account of the Community's evolving external relations policy, the most profound recent development in the liberalization program, should take place outside the framework of the third package. Otherwise, support for change was confined to specifics of the Community licensing system, the Community role in surveillance of safety standards, and the imposition of public service obligations on certain routes. Indeed, in May 2006 the Commission circulated a further discussion paper to Member State civil aviation authorities, indicating that revisions to the third package were less important than strict enforcement of

a number of more circumspect observations – both general and with respect to specific components of the liberalization program – can also be made.

1   Two General Counterpoints

a   *The Commission's 'Industrial Policy'*

From the perspective of a deregulation purist, there are signs that the European Commission (pressured, in this respect, by the Member States) has shown itself to be reluctant to accept the full market consequences of its own creation. The third package introduced market mechanisms into the EU's air transport industry – an acknowledgment that properly functioning markets will produce optimal outcomes – but the Commission's consultation paper on revisions to the third package[668] expressed concerns that the industry has become chronically undercapitalized, excessively fragmented, and too small by world standards.[669] As the U.K. Civil Aviation Authority indicated in responding to the Commission's paper, 'these background comments seem to suggest that the regulatory system needs to be changed if the capital and trading markets do not produce the degree of gearing and consolidation that the Commission believes is correct.'[670]

The Commission, in fact, has betrayed signs of an almost reflexive 'industrial policy' through which it interprets and evaluates the market outcome of its legislative handiwork.[671] As of 2008, this policy (as articulated in the

---

existing legislation. *See* European Commission, Directors General for Civil Aviation, *Revision of the Third Package on the Internal Aviation Market*, at 1, Discussion Paper (May 5, 2006) [hereinafter European Commission, Discussion Paper] (unpublished, copy on file with author). The Commission, in accordance with its 'better regulation' initiative, consolidated the three 1992 regulations into one. *See id.*

668. *See generally* European Commission, *Third Package Consultation Paper, supra* note 126.

669. *See id.* para. 12 (recognizing also the industry effects of the terrorist attacks of Sept. 11, 2001 and of a rapid escalation in aviation fuel costs).

670. [U.K.] Civil Aviation Authority, *Response to European Commission Consultation for Revision to Third Package*, para. 6 (Jun. 16, 2003) [hereinafter [U.K.] CAA, *Consultation*] (accepting that other factors impede market performance, including access to congested airports, foreign control impediments, the Chicago bilateral system, and State aid, and that these need to be addressed 'in their own right,' but emphasizing that financial regulation cannot lead directly to stronger balance sheets 'except by culling firms with weaker balance sheets').

671. In fairness to the Commission, the EC Treaty itself (as amended by the Maastricht Treaty) recognizes the possibility of conducting a more broadly-focused 'industrial policy.' *See* EC Treaty art. 157 (as amended), addressing measures to ensure the 'competitiveness' of EU industry. It demands much political and economic dexterity to define the frontiers of such a policy, which implicates an adaptive restructuring to meet future (most likely *foreign*) competition, and to ensure that the chosen measures do not intrude upon or impede the overriding principles of open market competition. The paradox is eloquently demonstrated by the status of the national air carriers. Competition policy expects the withdrawal of route and price monopolies and public subsidy, but the intra-EU viability and global competitiveness of the flag carriers may hinge decisively on at least some of these very factors. The value (or validity) of industrial policy has not been universally accepted by Commission mandarins. In a 1991 monograph on EC competition policy and merger control, Sir Leon Brittan, the

Commission's consultation paper) continues to reflect a concern to encourage deeper consolidation of the Union's air carriers.[672] To the extent that the current industry configuration is the product of historical and political evolution rather than economic and efficiency factors,[673] the Commission's position is at least descriptively tenable. But its normative preference for a defragmented or consolidated industry, particularly within the EU itself, has not yet been empirically supported with a detailed statistical analysis of the conjunctural events of liberalization.[674]

b   *A Partial Deregulation of the 'Aviation' Industry*

The Community's reform program was almost entirely consumed with the task of liberalizing the scheduled air passenger industry (in effect, the scheduled *airline* industry), but the *air transport* industry is a more complex value chain that also includes airport operators, air traffic control providers, global distribution systems, and groundhandling companies, all of which have inputs into determining the price of an airline's product.[675] And the chain of providers is expandable, since it also includes monopolistic practices among less direct industry participants such as caterers and fuel suppliers. All of these practices drive costs up even as ticket prices are driven down in a liberalized ticket market.

---

then-Commissioner for Competition, painted a remorselessly unflattering portrait of industrial policy, calling it an 'old-fashioned [process] where politicians and bureaucrats sat in their offices playing with industrial structures much as children do with their Lego sets.' SIR LEON BRITTAN, COMPETITION POLICY AND MERGER CONTROL IN THE SINGLE EUROPEAN MARKET 32 (1991).

672. The Commission's deregulation policy now tilts against the privileged incumbency of the remaining flag carriers, but paradoxically its industrial policy seeks to create 'Community champions' which are better placed to compete in the global marketplace. *But see* U.K. Government, Department of Transport, *supra* note 667, at 1 ('[I]n general, we do not believe that there should be a pre-determined view of the desirable shape and size of the European air transport industry, as the consultation document seems to imply').

673. *See generally* Joan Bodoff, *Competition Policies Of The US And The EEC: An Overview*, 5 E.C.L.R. 51, 56 (1984) (noting that 'Europe ... has an old mercantile tradition of public enterprises and state monopolies, and of government financial aid for troubled sectors, industries and geographic regions. These practices and habits, long ingrained, are obviously not conducive to reliance on unfettered competition or unimpeded entry and exit. . . .') *See supra* Chapter 3, Part VI (discussing the historical dominance of Europe's flag carriers).

674. *See generally* [U.K.] CAA, *Consultation, supra* note 670, para. 5 (faulting the Commission for presenting 'no evidence that the European market is too fragmented or analysis of why that is undesirable').

675. *See* British Airways, *Response to the European Commission Consultation Paper with a View to Revision of Regulations 2407/92, 2408/92, and 2409/92*, paras. 1.4 & 1.5 [hereinafter BA, *Consultation*] (observing that, '[w]hereas airlines compete in a very competitive market (subject to the rigors of the marketplace as well as the liberalized environment) our suppliers are often monopolists or oligopolists which have barely changed their working practices despite the dramatic developments ... in the airline industry'). *See also supra* note 292 (discussing the Commission's latest proposal on airport charges).

While the Commission has introduced some market access enhancement and competition scrutiny into these components of the value chain,[676] it remains true (in the United States also) that aviation as an industrial sector has not been fully liberalized and that many nonflight service providers base their economic operations on full cost recovery or even monopoly.[677] Indeed, it has been argued in recent years that private equity investors (in place of or in addition to the current activities of airline strategic investors) would be interested in an industry where all of these obstacles to creating value were removed.[678]

2   Three Specific Counterpoints

Three concluding counterpoints relate to specific aspects of the liberalization program that represent, in turn, a compromise with the free market (allowing subsidized support for certain underserved air routes); a realistic embrace of market conditions (manifested in opposition to a recent Commission suggestion of fare reregulation); or, further, a reminder of the interinstitutional challenges which still face the Community's evolving external relations policy, which is itself probably the most profound recent development in the liberalization program.

a   The Anomaly of Public Service Obligation (PSO) Routes

The existence of a Community-sanctioned procedure allowing Member States to impose PSOs on particular routes[679] – as well as the rules allowing States to

---

676. Efforts in this area, including promoting liberalizing international air transport agreements, a common aviation area with neighbors, improved access to airports, a harmonized intra-Union market, and a 'Single European Sky' are all prominently featured in the European Commission's P.R. campaign for its aviation policy. *See* EUROPEAN COMMISSION, FLYING TOGETHER: EU AIR TRANSPORT POLICY (2007); *see also* European Commission, Air Transport Portal, <http://ec.europa.eu/transport/air_portal/index_en.htm>. Groundhandling services in particular have received sustained Commission scrutiny. Council Directive 96/67/EC of 15 October 1996, 1996 O.J. (L 272) 36, opened this sector to competition by mandating at least two suppliers for certain categories of services and requiring at least one supplier to be independent of either the airport it services or the dominant carrier at that airport. While the Commission reported recently that it was pleased with the procompetitive results of the directive, a revised directive may be forthcoming which will offer further guidance on insurance requirements, quality standards, and the selection process for suppliers. *See* European Commission, *Report from the Commission on the Application of Council Directive 96/67/EC* of 15 October 1996, at 10, COM (2006) 821 final (Jan. 24, 2007).
677. *See* Association of European Airlines, *AEA Comments on the EC Consultation Paper*, para. 5.1 (Jul. 2003) [hereinafter AEA, *Consultation*]. The Commission has also been aware of the efficiency costs to its liberalization program of a lack of coordination and harmonization (both intra-Union and externally) with respect to air traffic control, safety, and security, *see* HIGH LEVEL GROUP FOR THE FUTURE EUROPEAN REGULATORY FRAMEWORK, EUROPEAN AVIATION: FRAMEWORK FOR DRIVING PERFORMANCE IMPROVEMENT (2007), as well as the social costs of the absence of a common Community labor policy.
678. Taking this argument to its next level, if private investors become interested, ownership and control provisions fall, and bilateralism falls.
679. This practice derogates from the Treaty's generally restrictive conditions for the grant of State subsidies ('aids' in the parlance of the Treaty). The U.K. Civil Aviation Authority has

restructure their airport systems[680] – have functioned (from the perspective of maintaining competition) only as well as the protective intent of the Member States applying them.[681] The existence of the PSO exception is in fundamental conflict with the EC Treaty's principle of freedom to provide services,[682] but its presence inside a deregulated system offers no more than the same philosophical contradictions reflected in the U.S. Essential Air Services Program.[683] The absence

---

suggested acknowledging this circumstance by replacing the specific PSO rules with the general rules on State aid. *See* [U.K.] CAA, *Consultation, supra* note 670, para. 49. The Authority has also criticized another competition-depleting regulatory exclusion built into the PSO – Member States can ring-fence slots for PSO services at fully slot coordinated airports. *See id.* para. 50.

680. The Commission proposed in its review of the 1992 third package that the issue of traffic distribution within an airport system (examined in the context of proceedings involving the system in Milan, Italy), would benefit from objective criteria at Community level. *See* European Commission, *Third Package Consultation Paper, supra* note 126, para. 42; *see, e.g.,* ATUC, *Consultation, supra* note 666, para. 19 (proposing capacity constraint as the principal criterion in a liberalized market, despite the strategic public policy concerns which – despite evidence of protectionist impulses – legitimately influenced the Italian Government's actions in the Milan proceedings). The 2008 amended regulation confirms that Member State traffic distribution decisions should be based on 'objective criteria,' but these criteria are not further defined in the regulation. *Common Rules, supra* note 120, art. 17(2). A different question is presented by the definition of which airports comprise a 'system' that serves a particular conurbation – an issue that has received some attention because of the consumer information questions implicated in the opening of more remote secondary airport connections by low-cost carriers such as Ryanair. *See, e.g.,* BA, *Consultation, supra* note 675, para. 3.3 (calling for redefinition to indicate which airports are actually part of a system 'rather than somewhere in the approximate vicinity of a town'). This issue is not squarely addressed in the 2008 regulation, which abandons the concept of defining an airport 'system' as a precursor to distributing traffic rights, and confines itself to defining 'conurbation' generally – and solely in relation to traffic rights distribution – as a number of cities and towns that have physically merged through population growth and expansion to form one continuous built-up area. *Common Rules, supra* note 120, art. 2(23).

681. *See, e.g.,* Ryanair, *Consultation for Revision of the Third Package,* at 5 (Jul. 11, 2003) [hereinafter Ryanair, *Consultation*] (alleging that PSO routes frequently involve disguised subsidies for national airlines, and criticizing the high number of such routes in France). Discontent with the inconsistent intra-EU operation of the PSO aroused opposition to the Commission's suggestion to widen its scope to extra-Union air routes. *See* European Commission, *Third Package Consultation Paper, supra* note 126, para. 35. *See, e.g.,* AEA, *Consultation, supra* note 677, para. 3.6; *but see* World Tourism Organization, *Response to the European Commission Consultation Paper,* at 1-2 (2003) (supporting a PSO system for extra-Union routes which provide 'essential tourism air services' for developing States). The 2008 regulation, in any event, does not address PSO services to extra-Union routes.

682. EC Treaty art. 49. The freedom to provide services furnishes a right to conduct economic activities in a Member State on a *non-permanent* basis (in contrast to the freedom of establishment, which envisages a permanent right of economic activity). *Id.* art. 50.

683. These subventions supposedly reflect a response by industrialized nations to market failure in a 'globalizing, liberalizing environment.' World Tourism Organization, *supra* note 681, at 5. On the U.S. program, *see supra* Chapter 4, Part II(D). *See generally* A.J. Reynolds-Feighan, *Subsidization Policies in the Provision of Air Services to Small Communities: European and U.S. Approaches, in* PROCEEDINGS OF THE FIRST FORUM ON AIR TRANSPORT PROVISION IN EUROPE'S REMOTE REGIONS (1999) (noting that, unlike in the Community system, U.S. carriers

of uniform application of the PSO rules, however, has allowed for great variances in how States determine the eligibility of routes. [684] In an important omission from the PSO system, the Commission publishes calls for tender in the Official Journal but lacks power to refuse State nominations of particular routes.[685]

b　　　　　*A Doomed Suggestion: Fare Reregulation*

But a deregulation mindset, in another respect, has surprised the Commission by its resilience even among those who gained most from the old protectionist system. In its 2003 consultation paper on possible revisions to the third package,[686] the Commission expressed concerns about extremes of fare levels (notably at the low-cost end of the market, where virtually 'free' pricing has become a signature marketing strategy[687]). The Commission's consultation paper on the third package

---

tendering for services themselves select the connecting airport from a subset of larger airports identified by the DOT, thereby integrating small communities into regional or intercontinental carrier networks through a carrier's hub; the Community approach, in contrast, is for Member States to impose tightly specified domestic origin/destination routes and even timetables, limiting carrier ability to integrate PSO services into larger schedules and networks); *see also* A.J. Reynolds-Feighan, *The U.S. Airport Hierarchy and Implications for Small Communities*, 37 URBAN STUDIES 557 (2000).

684. And, moreover, in how the eligibility of carriers is established. *See, e.g.,* Ryanair, *Consultation, supra* note 681 (noting Irish Government requirement that bidding airlines be members of a CRS and enter into interlining agreements, thereby excluding airlines such as Ryanair which cannot meet these *a priori* conditions).

685. As the Commission itself recognized in its consultation paper on revisions to the third package. *See* European Commission, *Third Package Consultation Paper, supra* note 126, para. 39. *See, e.g.,* AEA, *Consultation, supra* note 677, para. 3.4. As noted earlier, the Commission's *post hoc* review of designated PSO routes has been strengthened in the 2008 consolidated regulation. *See Common Rules, supra* note 120, art. 18. But, although the Commission retains its prior power ultimately to terminate PSO status, the final text of the amended regulation dropped the Commission's proposed language interposing a power to suspend PSO status pending its final decision. European Commission, *Common Rules, supra* note 120, at 41, art. 18. In fact, the transformation of national carriers into 'Community carriers,' as well as the Community's core responsibilities for regional policy, suggest that the Commission should be more centrally involved in the imposition (and even the funding) of designated routes. Moreover, PSO status should, one would think, be confined to routes connecting isolated or developing areas and that therefore have 'lifeline' status. According to British Airways, imposition of this status on intra-Union international routes – of which there is some evidence – appears inconsistent with this philosophy (even if it is not inconsistent with the language of the regulation). *See* BA, *Consultation, supra* note 675, para. 3.2; *but see* European Cockpit Association, *Consultation for Revision of the 'Third Package,' An ECA Contribution,* at 6 (May 2003) [hereinafter ECA, *Consultation*] (arguing that assistance, including State aid, for intra-Union international routes would maintain crew employment).

686. *See* European Commission, *Third Package Consultation Paper, supra* note 126.

687. Although a strategy that is under pressure through oil price rises experienced in 2008. *See supra* Chapter 1, note 2. While the existence of non-predatory but abnormally low fares (or, as sometimes advertised, 'free' fares, *i.e.,* the passenger pays the taxes) is troubling to the Commission, *see* European Commission, *Third Package Consultation Paper, supra* note 126, para. 46, it is not clear exactly why this is so. The Ryanair/easyJet model, which is

invited comments on the possibility of fare reregulation.[688] The clamor of opposition to this prospect expressed an understanding that price oscillations reveal only that market pricing is at work in a liberalized market.[689] Any principle of

---

probably the most innovative market outcome of the Community's liberalization program, claims unabashedly to derive from the Southwest 'low-cost formula' in the United States. *See* Ryanair, *Consultation, supra* note 681, at 2-3 (acknowledging the Southwest business model of minimizing costs and maximizing efficiency using uncongested secondary airports, a single aircraft-type fleet, high turnarounds and load factors, Internet sales, and strict overhead control). Moreover, Ryanair's business strategy includes sustaining profitability through non-fare channels such as ancillary revenues from onboard sales. *See id.* at 6. As early as 1994, the Comité des Sages forecast that in a competitive market, carriers with the lowest costs would set the prices: 'Consequently, Community air carriers will need to change from "cost driven pricing" to "price driven costing."' *Quoted in* IATA, *Comments on Consultation Paper on the Third Package*, at 1 (May 23, 2003) [hereinafter IATA, *Consultation*]; *see also* [U.K.] CAA, *Consultation, supra* note 670, para. 51 (calling low-cost competition 'a particularly notable success of European liberalization' that has drawn competitive responses from the full-service airlines including, for example, British Airways' abandonment of the 'Saturday night' stayover rule on fares for travel from the United Kingdom). The European Transport Workers' Federation (ETF) has alleged 'serious safety and security effects' from very low fares, as well as adverse impact on working and social conditions, but the argument (at least as presented to the Commission in response to the consultation paper on the third package) seems more rhetorical than empirical. ETF, *Consultation, supra* note 666, at 7. The European Cockpit Association has suggested that hidden or indirect subsidies for some of these fares may flow from efforts made at regional and local levels to attract carriers to secondary airports. *See supra* Part III(F) (discussing the propriety of aid to carriers by regional authorities). *See* ECA, *Consultation, supra* note 685, at 6-7 (calling for total transparency regarding cost structure).

688. A suggestion which, according to the Commission itself, 'met with a subdued reception sometimes bordering on suspicion, especially from the carriers.' European Commission, *Summary of the Third Package Contributions, supra* note 126, at 2. Although the Commission offered no prediction or explanation as to how it would propose to navigate the minefield of a fare structure infinitely more layered and complex than at the beginning of liberalization, under past Commission practice a 140% ratio between fares and costs represents the maximum permitted before fares would not be approved. This kind of analytical work on air fares, which assumes that air fares must reflect the real cost of transport, *see* European Commission, *Third Package Consultation Paper, supra* note 126, at para. 48, seems more appropriate to a marketplace with little competition.

689. Thus, pricing policies in the Community today are strongly influenced by the macroeconomic conditions of an unregulated marketplace, including the spread of low-cost competition and the greater diversification of product to include point-to-point, network, short-haul, and long-haul routes, as well as the high level of price discrimination caused by heterogeneous (flexible and non-flexible) passenger throughput. The complexity of pricing is influenced also by microeconomic variables that include route-by-route production costs, supply and demand, the pricing of direct and indirect competitors, intermodal competition, size of aircraft, and availability of feeder traffic. Very low fares will often be used for promotional purposes and to fill off-peak seats that are otherwise unused. *See* [U.K.] CAA, *Consultation, supra* note 670, para. 53. A standard calculation for fares in these circumstances seems economically inaccessible. *See* IATA, *Consultation, supra* note 687, at 2 (contending that, in a liberalized environment, 'whether tariffs reflect the real cost of provision is a commercial matter for air carriers subject to the disciplines of the market place'). For most commenters responding to the Commission's consultation paper on the third package, the general competition rules were

intervention, to use the conceptual framework of Community law, should acknowledge complete pricing freedom as long as the rates charged are not subsidized by State aid.[690] The Commission, in any event, did not further press the idea of fare re-regulation when it outlined its proposed modifications to the third package and no such provisions appear in the final instrument.[691]

c   *A Cautionary Tale of External Relations*

Stewardship of the external aviation relations of the EC remains a fascinating experiment in the shaping of international public policy. The balance of responsibilities between the Member States and the Community institutions has shifted appreciably in the latter's favor since the open skies rulings of the European Court of Justice in 2002, but an unsettled cohabitation between the Member States and the European Commission still clouds the negotiations of bilateral air services agreements with non-Member States.[692] The Commission still bridles at these restrictions, despite its success in securing vertical mandates for comprehensive negotiations with the United States and other third countries, and in using its horizontal mandate to assist the Member States in replacing the nationality rule

---

deemed sufficient to catch instances of predatory or excessive pricing. *See, e.g.*, BA, *Consultation, supra* note 675, para. 4.7; *see also* Ryanair, *Consultation, supra* note 681, at 6 ('There is already a successful measure for dealing with monopoly level fares, *i.e.*, the introduction of competition, which is what the liberalization process is all about'); [U.K.] CAA, *Consultation, supra* note 670, para. 53 (stating that 'very low fares should not be of concern unless they are offered by an airline in a dominant position in an anticompetitive fashion, in which case Article 82 already exists to deal with the problem'). The 2008 amended regulation, accordingly, maintains the general principle of pricing freedom introduced in 1992.

690. As noted earlier, the Member States' fare intervention power under Regulation 2409/92 was never invoked – and does not appear in the 2008 amended regulation. This suggests, as the U.K. Civil Aviation Authority has pointed out, that 'air markets are, for the most part, proving to be workably competitive.' [U.K.] CAA, *Consultation, supra* note 670, para. 61; *see also* ATUC, *Consultation, supra* note 666, para. 21 (noting that the market is evolving, in tandem with patterns of demand); AEA, *Consultation, supra* note 677, para. 4.3. Related questions are the extent to which air transport as a whole should cover costs associated with the provision of airport security and the environmental costs which the industry imposes on the population as a whole through noise and carbon emissions. In this regard, another 'counterpoint' to deregulation has been the Commission's efforts, culminating with a vote of the European Parliament in 2008, to incorporate air transport into its cap-and-trade emissions trading scheme. Controversially, the scheme would apply to flights departing from and arriving at all EU airports, irrespective of the points of origin or destination of the services or of the nationality of the carriers providing them. Much criticized by the global industry, this unilateral initiative – circumventing the slow-paced environmental agenda of the International Civil Aviation Organization – indicates that the deregulation agenda of the Commission's transport and competition departments is under pressure from the rising political suzerainty of the European Parliament (allied with the Commission's own Environment unit).

691. *See generally* European Commission, Discussion Paper, *supra* note 667. For the provisions on pricing in the consolidated legislation, *see* Common Rules, *supra* note 120, art. 22.

692. *See supra* Part III(D) (discussing how Community legislation has organized the shared responsibilities of the Member States and the Commission with respect to bilateral agreements).

with a new Community designation clause.[693] The Commission's displeasure at sharing external aviation relations authority with the Member States was evinced most recently by a *sotto voce* – and ultimately fruitless – attempt in its draft revision to the 1992 reform package to claim full negotiating authority for all intra-EU traffic rights with third countries.[694] The Commission even invoked its Single European Sky project for integration of EU navigational airspace to lend some plausibility to this bold jurisdictional 'land grab.'[695]

The Council of Ministers, however, 'removed' the empowering language inserted by the Commission, declaring that the proposed text was not, in its view, 'consistent with the respective competencies of Member States and the Community.'[696] In the Commission's penitent response, the Council had delivered a 'categorical' rejection of the purported realignment of Commission/Member State external authority.[697] Moreover, the Commission's audacity produced exactly the opposite result of what it evidently intended to achieve by its proposal: the Commission (no doubt under Council constraint) issued a joint statement with the Member States confirming 'to the fullest possible extent and in a co-ordinated approach, their use of the existing mechanisms and framework of Regulation 847/2004 on the negotiation and implementation of air service agreements between Member States and third countries.'[698] As we proceed to the discussion of a new U.S./EC plurilateral air services agreement in Chapter 6, therefore, this episode is a cautionary reminder that, after all that has been achieved in the past 15 years, the ultimate balance of power in the Community air transport regime still tilts toward the retained sovereignty of the Member States.

---

693. *See id.*
694. European Commission, *Common Rules, supra* note 120, at 8-9. If adopted, in the Commission's argument, this proposal would 'avoid possible inconsistencies between the internal market and individual negotiations by Member States.' *Id.* at 11. Lending support to the suggestion in the main text that the Commission's action was *sotto voce*, the draft language did not say directly that the Commission shall be accorded the requisite negotiating authority. Rather, it used a circumlocutory formula to state that non-Community air carriers shall not exercise traffic rights within the European Union 'unless they are permitted to do so by an agreement concluded by the Community with a third country.' *Id.* at 35, art. 15(6).
695. The Commission's proposal, of course, was entirely inconsistent with the division of responsibility in Regulation 847/2004, *see supra* note 545, which it purported to override by implication. European Commission, *Common Rules, supra* note 120, at 35, art. 15(6) ('notwithstanding Regulation 847/2004...'). On the Single European Sky, *see supra* Chapter 2, note 25.
696. *See Common Rules, supra* note 120, Statement of the Council's Reasons, sec. II.
697. European Commission, *Communication from the Commission to the European Parliament Concerning the Common Position Adopted by the Council in View of Adoption of the Regulation of the European Parliament and of the Council on Common Rules for the Operation of Air Transport Services in the Community (Recast)*, at 3, COM (2008) 175 final (Apr. 21, 2008).
698. European Council, *Proposal for a Regulation of the European Parliament and of the Council on Common Rules for the Operation of Air Services in the Community (First Reading)*, Joint Statement by the Member States and the Commission, 7627/08 Add 1 (Mar. 31, 2008). On the relevant provisions of Regulation 847/2008, *see supra* note 554.

Chapter 6

Conclusion: A Proposal for a Second Stage U.S./EC Air Transport Agreement

I   INTRODUCTION: THE CHANGE IMPERATIVE

In the summer of 2008, the global air transport industry had plunged into one of its periodic fits of transcendent gloom. Its chief prognosticator, the Director General of the International Air Transport Association, Giovanni Bisignani, informed his Association's annual meeting in Istanbul, Turkey, that cumulative losses caused primarily by the oil price spike and falling passenger demand could reach $6.1 billion in 2008, amidst wholesale slashing of capacity and grounding of fleets.[1] The world's airlines adopted an emergency six-point set of demands calling on governments to relieve their tax burdens, to scale back environmental taxes and charges, to invest in air traffic management modernization, and to adopt a plethora of other fixes for what ails this troubled industry.[2] Most significantly for our purpose here, one of the industry's demands also echoes the principal theme of this book. In Bisignani's words, the moment has arrived to tear up the thousands of bilateral agreements adopted under the Chicago system, to scrap all of their

---

1. *See* Giovanni Bisignani, Director General and CEO, International Air Transport Association, *State of the Air Transport Industry*, Speech to the 64th Annual General Meeting (Jun. 2, 2008); *but see* International Air Transport Association [IATA], *Financial Forecast: Lengthy Recession is Now Main Challenge*, IATA Economics (Dec. 2008) (narrowing the actual loss to $5 billion). *See also It's an ill wind . . .*, ECONOMIST, Jun. 7, 2008 (describing as 'half-right and half-wrong' the expectation that the 'no-frills' sector would suffer more from these shocks, given that Europe's dominant budget airlines, Ryanair and easyJet, have strong balance sheets, modern fleets, and strong cultures of low-cost operation; in fact, some analysts were predicting that fuel surcharges by the major airlines like British Airways could increase yields for the lower-cost providers).
2. *See* Press Release, IATA, Industry Leaders Agree to Historic Declaration, IATA Press Release No. 29 (Jun. 2, 2008).

restrictions on cross-border airline investment, and to let brands substitute for national flags. Thus, from within the maelstrom of what may be its greatest financial crisis, the airline industry is not calling for a return to regulation, but rather for the potential of deregulation to be unleashed at the global level. Whatever the structural consequences of abolishing the nationality rule (and the cabotage rule along with it) – and those consequences will be immense – that is the destiny the industry wishes now to pursue.

Whether the current crisis will indeed overturn the Chicago system remains a matter of speculation. It has long been assumed that, especially for the United States, it would take a major industry event – potential liquidation of one of the major U.S. carriers, for example, accompanied by lobbying from its hub city politicians – to push Congress toward abolition of the nationality rule. The oil price volatility, more than other exogenous events in a series of brutal assaults on industry profitability, could well trigger reform (probably within the framework of the negotiations for a second stage U.S./EC agreement).

In the analysis attempted here, oracular judgments as to the precise aeropolitical or aeroeconomic circumstances of change will not be made. Instead, in this Chapter, we will look to the end of the dialectical process that has shaped the entire book. We have already examined the decay of the traditional Chicago bilateral system, the unexpected emergence of U.S. airline deregulation, the rise of a U.S. open skies policy, EC airline deregulation and Europe's embrace of a liberalizing role in international air transport, the confluence of agendas that yielded a U.S./EC open skies agreement, as well as, inescapably, the contrast between the experiences of airlines and consumers in both jurisdictions as all stakeholders came to terms with the burdens and benefits of market freedom.

A major lesson of this book is that deregulation is an unpredictable, evolving, and challenging experiment, but it is also one that U.S. and EU airlines have yet to experience liberated from the international restrictions which have distorted the market authenticity of each of these 'model' jurisdictions. With all of that in mind, it is time now to look beyond the immediate economic turmoil of 2008, and to try to imagine the legal and policy contours of an authentically deregulated international air transport marketplace. It is time, in a phrase, to look 'beyond open skies.'

II   THE IMPERATIVES OF LIBERALIZATION AND
            GLOBALIZATION

A   THE GLOBAL REGULATORY BACKDROP TO AIRLINE DEREGULATION

Withdrawal of government intervention in transport markets, including the gradual reduction of the public ownership stake in those markets, occurred relatively recently in both the United States and Europe. Rate regulation in the railways, entry restrictions in the trucking industry, minimum levels of service in urban bus and commuter rail transport, cargo reservation for shipping, and comprehensive rate and route superintendence over the airlines, are species of regulatory control that have been long identified worldwide in both capitalist and command economic systems.[3] In our examination of the U.S. and EU air transport industries, we discussed the displacement of *a priori* governmental direction by private managerial initiative and the *ex post* discipline of a body of antitrust or competition laws.[4]

Indeed, this process of displacement is not unique either to the transport industry in general or to the airline sector in particular: competition law and principles of economic transparency, and the absence of national discrimination, have increasingly protected the public interest and marked the tempo of modern international economic affairs.[5] In seeking to extend the deregulatory franchise

---

3. See generally Paul Amos, *Public and Private Sector Roles in the Supply of Transport Infrastructure and Services: Operational Guidance for World Bank Staff*, Transport Paper TP-1, The World Bank Group (May 2004) (noting, however, that government provision of transport services to the public 'has been found disappointing in many countries,' *id.* at 2). See also the introductory comments on transport deregulation in Jose A. Gomez-Ibanez and Ivor P. Morgan's *Deregulating International Markets: The Examples of Aviation and Ocean Shipping*, 2 YALE J. ON REG. 107, 108 (1984).

4. The privatization of transport services has not been matched, however, by private ownership of transport infrastructure. Airports, for example, remain mostly publicly owned even as the airlines themselves pass into private control. This discrepancy is the result of several reasons, which apply to most basic transport infrastructure and not just to airports – the natural monopoly attributes of transport infrastructure like ports and airports, the market power vested by control of prime sites, the long-term and therefore risky financial returns, the complexities of planning, environmental, safety, and social issues, and finally a perception that transport infrastructure is 'a part of the public estate which should be provided for the common good, and not as a business for commercial gain.' Amos, *supra* note 3, at 4.

5. See generally DANIEL YERGIN, COMMANDING HEIGHTS: THE BATTLE FOR THE WORLD ECONOMY (2002) (tracing a change in intellectual climate from postwar socialism to a new paradigm of market-based competition, supported by empirical awareness of the poor performance of nationalized industries); *see also* CATO INSTITUTE, CATO HANDBOOK ON POLICY 375-84 (6th ed. 2005) (discussing strides made in U.S. transport deregulation, but noting lacunae such as Amtrak and air traffic control). World Bank expert Paul Amos has catalogued the reasons for the poor performance of nationalized industries as including contradictions in a government trying simultaneously to be policymaker, regulator, and operator; confusion in acting commercially while seeking social goals; restrictions on management freedom caused by public service norms and procedures (including cross-sectoral determination of pay scales); constraints on financial autonomy and investment due to government budgeting processes; competition for resources from core government functions of health, education, welfare, etc.; and, where the activity creates surplus, cross-subsidization of other government activities rather than reinvestment in the profitable business:

> Behind many of these issues is the reality that governments have many policy objectives in transport [including] economic, financial, social, environmental and numerous other objectives such as defense or national prestige. These objectives often conflict, some are difficult to measure, and their priority can alter day-to-day in response to political events. A government's inherent freedom to discern, pursue and reconcile multiple and changeable objectives is essential to the democratic process. But it can make it harder for governments to run businesses well.

> Amos, *supra* note 3, at 2. Conversely, private businesses in competitive markets have more focused aims and incentives, and are likely to exhibit much greater efficiency, both technical (producing outputs at the least cost) and allocative (producing outputs that most closely meet market demands). *See id.* at 3.

outside the borders of our model jurisdictions, however, we noted that the international airline industry has remained predominantly a sector of 'managed trade,' guarded by the twin legal sentries of cabotage and the nationality rule. Because of these timeworn restraints, which in turn guarantee the protected status of many State-sponsored but also many privately owned flag carriers,[6] international airline deregulation has been at best a simulacrum of the process of market deregulation we have analyzed in Europe and the United States.[7] Ironically, therefore, in a world where the 'reserved domain for national sovereignty is shrinking,'[8] global air transport in the jet age remains imprisoned within the most incongruous of legal and metaphorical borders, sovereignty over national airspace.[9]

Mindful of this paradox, IATA's 2007 briefing on global liberalization focused attention on the precedents (some positive, some considerably less so) of transnational liberalization in other service industries such as retail banking,

---

6. Commentators have noted the collaboration and mutual affinity between privately owned and controlled 'flag' airlines like British Airways and Qantas and the policy chambers of their governments. The U.K. Government's recalcitrance in the negotiations leading to the 2007 U.S./EC Air Transport Agreement, *see infra* note 12, as well as Australia's long unwillingness (until 2008) to put an open skies stamp on its U.S. bilateral air services agreement, have been attributed to the respective influences of their powerful flagship carriers. *See, e.g.*, William Echikson, *British Airways Chief Blasts Open Skies Plan – Broughton Says Treaty Favors U.S.*, WALL ST. J., Mar. 6, 2007, at A12.

7. Astonishingly, airlines have been cut off by the nationality rule from significant sources of foreign direct investment (FDI). The generally buoyant global environment for FDI has been well-captured in research produced by the Organization for Economic Cooperation and Development (OECD). *See* Hans Christiansen et al., *Trends and Recent Developments in Foreign Direct Investment, in* OECD, INTERNATIONAL INVESTMENT PERSPECTIVES: FREEDOM OF INVESTMENT IN A CHANGING WORLD 13 (2007). The authors warn, however, that hostile attitudes to foreign investment in some host countries could dissuade future FDI activity. *See id.* at 15 (commenting on a discernible 'tightening' of practices toward inward FDI on national security and other grounds); *see, e.g., supra* Chapter 3, notes 288 & 294 (discussing the Dubai Ports controversy in the United States).

8. The quoted remark of U.S. Federal Judge Diane P. Wood, formerly Assistant Attorney General for International Antitrust Policy, to the ABA Antitrust Section, *reported in* ANTITRUST & TRADE REG. REP. (BNA), Dec. 1, 1994, at 631.

9. On the 'atmospherics' of restrictions based on outmoded conceptions of sovereignty, the following remarks by a prominent former EU transport leader are especially pertinent:

   It is always perplexing to see that the air transport industry, where the most sophisticated techniques of modern science have been concentrated and where humanity has witnessed one of the most advanced examples of industrial growth, is still governed by severely antiquated regulations which do not take into account the need for close, multinational co-operation among all the players. In other words, in the world of 'globalization,' of the 'global village,' and of 'real time,' the air transport sector is still operating under economic rules that can at best be described as insufficient and antiquated, and at worst, obsolete. It is obvious that the dichotomy between the way in which air transport is regulated and the almost universal freedom of movement that exists on the ground needs to be urgently corrected and the only surprising thing is that it has not yet been done.

   Loyola de Palacio, Vice President of the European Commission and Commissioner for Transport, *Single European Sky and Passenger Protection*, Speech to the Association of European Airlines, Brussels, Speech /00/179 (May 12, 2000).

energy, telecommunications, and media.[10] Among the most striking findings of the IATA briefing is what its authors Mark Smyth and Brian Pearce label the 'Nestlé effect:' when the Swiss-based Nestlé company eliminated restrictions on foreign ownership of its registered shares in 1988, the market value of the company soared immediately by 10% as these formerly discounted shares attracted previously disqualified overseas investors. Studies of the event concluded that the opportunities provided by greater international diversification led to a decline in Nestlé's cost of capital of anywhere between 90 and 190 basis points. Because of the nationality rule, the airline industry has been substantially unable to benefit from the deregulation of capital market controls on foreign investment – a key factor behind globalization and the growth in international trade and investment flows.

B   A CONSTITUTIONAL SYMMETRY: U.S./EC AIRLINE
                DEREGULATION

Our analysis has shown that the U.S. and EC air transport experiments have evolved already to a point of constitutional symmetry: by 1997, upon full completion of the single aviation market, the 'grand cabotage' of EU airspace became juridically comparable to the federalized U.S. airspace – in the characterization of the European Commission, 'an area without internal frontiers.'[11] The relative bargaining power of the two jurisdictions was brought into parity by the legal and political process which culminated in the award of negotiating authority to the European Commission to conclude the 2007 U.S./EC Air Transport Agreement.[12] In pursuance of its widened international mandates, as we have seen, the Commission has orchestrated the creation of a European Common Aviation Area (ECAA) and set its sights on an Open Aviation Area (OAA) that contemplates an

---

10. *See* Mark Smyth & Brian Pearce, *Airline Liberalization*, ch. 4, IATA Economics Briefing No. 7 (Apr. 2007). Common to these industries (and shared, in turn, by the airline industry) are key characteristics that include political and strategic importance, cultivation of consumer brand loyalty, generation of spillover economic benefits in other sectors, network effects, and a high fixed cost and relatively low marginal cost structure. *See id.* The IATA report emphasizes that the benefits of liberalization for the airline industry will be maximized only if removal of operational restrictions (such as frequency caps) is accompanied by elimination of ownership limitations. *See id.* ch. 3.

11. *See generally* European Commission, *Completing the Internal Market: An Area Without Internal Frontiers*, COM (88) 650 final (Nov. 17, 1988). The European Commission has pronounced itself broadly satisfied with the marketplace produced by its serial liberalization packages: '[o]ld monopolies have been swept away, intra-Community cabotage has been introduced, and competition in all markets has intensified to the benefit of consumers.' *Proposal for a Regulation of the European Parliament and of the Council on Common Rules for the Operation of Air Transport Services in the Community*, at 2, COM (2006) 396 final (Jul. 18, 2006) [hereinafter European Commission, *Common Rules*]. As discussed *passim* in Chapter 5, in its 2006 proposal to amend and consolidate the leading legislative texts the Commission did not venture any major reform initiatives.

12. 2007 O.J. (L 134) 4 [hereinafter U.S./EC Air Transport Agreement].

eventual full economic merger of the ECAA and U.S. airspaces.[13] At the international level, however, the United States has so far settled for a reworking of the bilateral system 'from within' through its open skies policy. Even the vaunted 2007 U.S./EC agreement remains, at its core, a calculated stretching of the open skies template to incorporate new subjects of bilateral cooperation. But it leaves untouched the hammerlock restraints of the Chicago system – the nationality and cabotage rules.

The pivotal legal and policy challenge in international air transport regulation, then, is the conversion of support for private entrepreneurial initiative in the supply of transport services into a system of global competition unfettered by the legal archaisms of the Chicago system (including its nationality rule). International aviation is, by any definition, a global activity. 'Air transport services,' as a product, are produced and sold on a worldwide scale. Distribution channels, large investments in aircraft and facilities, and the pattern of worldwide economic integration, all compel attention toward a multilateral solution.[14] To that end, this concluding Chapter proposes that the negotiations begun in Ljubljana in May 2008 for a second stage U.S./EC air transport agreement should abandon the worn templates of the American open skies agenda[15] in favor of a merger of the juridically symmetrical U.S. and EU airspaces. Further, the new agreement should be cast as a plurilateral, the kind of cosmopolitan international law treaty that invites the full participation of likeminded third States.[16]

III   THE FOUNDATIONS OF A NEW PLURILATERAL
           AIRSPACE

A   INTRODUCTION: THE NARROWNESS OF OPEN SKIES

Without revisiting our earlier discussion in Chapter 4 on the shortcomings of the U.S. open skies policy, it is important to recognize that the animating principle of

---

13. Moreover, coupled with the formal privatization and operational commercialization of EU flag carriers, the possible emergence of a 'tiered' system of large and regional carriers, and the results of intense competition pitting major carriers against point-to-point low-cost providers, the industry profile on both sides of the Atlantic is coming to look increasingly similar.

14. *See generally* International Chamber of Commerce, *The Need for Greater Liberalization of International Air Transport*, Paper Presented to International Civil Aviation Organization [ICAO] Worldwide Air Transport Conference, ATConf/5-WP/35 (Jan. 20, 2003) (noting that bilateral air services agreements can no longer of themselves meet the rapidly changing needs of airlines, users, or of the global economy); *see also* Randall D. Lehner, *Protectionism, Prestige, and National Security: The Alliance Against Multilateral Trade in International Air Transport*, 45 DUKE L. J. 436, 458 (1995); Andras Vamos-Goldman, *The Stagnation of Economic Regulation under Public International Law: Examining its Contribution to the Woeful State of the Airline Industry*, 23 TRANSP. L. J. 425 (1996).

15. *See supra* Chapter 4, Part III(D) (discussing the legal and political tenuousness of an open skies policy that assumes the persistence of a bilateral system).

16. *See supra* Chapter 2, note 121 (discussing the nature of a plurilateral agreement).

open skies is one that can usefully be appropriated to a new multilateral enterprise: 'to rely on the marketplace and unrestricted, fair competition to determine the variety, quality, and price of air service.'[17] Certainly, the U.S. Department of Transportation's 1995 statement of international aviation policy acknowledged the limitations of the bilateral system and expressed a willingness to consider 'alternative [multilateral] forums for international aviation negotiations and agreements.'[18] Nevertheless, U.S. officials, their options constrained by political and statutory realities, have consistently sought reform of the Chicago system solely from within. Even the 2007 U.S./EC agreement, as we have discussed, continues the conceptual 'stretching' of Chicago-style bilaterals that defined the open skies project. Not coincidentally, the open skies initiative began at a time of U.S. carrier dominance[19] and the confidence of U.S. officials, not always shared by the carriers themselves, that America's airlines could successfully enhance foreign market penetration even at the cost of conceding greater access to their inbound international markets.[20] Today, with an embattled U.S. industry cut off from foreign investment capital and potential merger and acquisition partnerships,[21] continued fealty to a Chicago-style open skies model appears anachronistic when U.S. airlines have lost their almost structural dominance of the international marketplace and face intensified competition from well-positioned carriers from other economic regions, especially Asia and the Middle East.

In Chapter 1, we discussed how the open skies template applies a highly liberalized interpretation to each of the key Chicago system negotiating points.[22] But as such it is rooted in bilateralism, promoting relaxation of controls on prices,

---

17. U.S. International Air Transport Policy Statement, 60 Fed. Reg. 21,841, 21,841 (May 3, 1995) [hereinafter 1995 Policy Statement]. This statement can also be found *infra* Appendix I.

18. *Id.* at 21,843.

19. *See* Jeffrey N. Shane, Under Secretary for Policy, U.S. Department of Transportation, *Air Transport Liberalization: The U.S. Experience*, Speech at the ICAO Global Symposium on Air Transport Liberalization (Sept. 18, 2006) (recalling how the U.S. Government 'leveraged' access to the hugely attractive U.S. market in return for opportunities abroad for its strong home carriers) [hereinafter Shane, *Air Transport Liberalization*].

20. *But see id.* (noting a persistent strain of opposition by U.S. carriers to the trading away of 'hard' rights of access to the U.S. marketplace – and their success in enlisting Congressional backing for their position). Yet, as Shane emphasizes, U.S. carriers registered significant growth in their international operations as open skies unfolded. *See id.* As to the effects on foreign carriers of this American adventurism, see the following contemporaneous observation made on behalf of British Airways: 'Given the acknowledged strength of the U.S. majors, the present vision of the open skies proposition understandably creates the fear of bilateral rape and pillage, leading to calls from these quarters for further protectionism and subsidy to prevent the premature demise of the national airline industry.' British Airways, Submission to Airline Commission, Jun. 1993, *in Airline Commission Documents*, Dkt. No. 000124, at 3 [hereinafter British Airways Submission].

21. Among the shortcomings of the bilateral system – both in its classical guise and as it has evolved through the open skies policy – are capital-depleting barriers to foreign ownership and an inability to engage in routine industry consolidation. For an overview of these shortcomings, and a succinct statement of the economic argument for change, *see generally* DANIEL YERGIN ET AL., FETTERED FLIGHT: GLOBALIZATION AND THE AIRLINE INDUSTRY (2000).

22. *See supra* Chapter 1, Parts I & III.

routes, and capacity and offering to trade access to multiple U.S. international gateways, much as the EC has done internally on a multilateral basis, but without the intra-Union abolition of cabotage and abrogation of the nationality rule (through freedom of establishment and the concept of a common 'Community' airline license).[23] Indeed, given the disproportionately large size of the U.S. market, there is simply no comparable foreign market that would prompt U.S. negotiators (under the caution of domestic political opinion) to surrender cabotage and nationality restrictions within a typical bilateral setting.[24]

B   Visualizing a Multilateral Air Transport Regime

The globalization of the airline industry, even as constrained by the injunctions of Chicago orthodoxy, is now well under way. Globalization demands that the choice of which markets to enter, and how to compete efficiently in those markets, should ultimately be the province of individual carrier managements. Government intrusion should be restricted to competition law discipline and, subject to objective criteria, some limited subsidy-based public service obligation to safeguard service to peripheral destinations. Numerous models have been hypothesized for a new multilateral aviation order to supersede bilateralism. Other than in the General Agreement on Trade in Services (GATS),[25] considered in more detail in the next Part, these models assume the continuity of international air transport's trade 'exceptionalism.'[26]

It would be possible, for example, to relaunch the Chicago 'freedoms' in a new universal convention, but such an approach would risk reinstitutionalizing the basic engineering principles of the old bilateral system, where States are ultimately

---

23. British Airways, in its submission to the Airline Commission in 1993, was already arguing for the incorporation of these critical features into a revamped policy, dubbed 'Open Skies Plus,' for U.S. international aviation. British Airways Submission, *supra* note 20, at 2. This 'Open Skies Plus' agenda metamorphosed into the Association of European Airlines' blueprint for a Transatlantic Common Aviation Area in 1999, *see supra* Chapter 2, Part II(D), and remains integral to the prospects for success of the second stage of U.S./EC air transport negotiations which began in May 2008.

24. Indeed, looking toward the second stage of U.S./EC air transport negotiations, U.S. officials have signaled once again that the U.S. cabotage prohibition will not be put in play. As lead U.S. negotiator John Byerly has argued, a putative exchange of cabotage rights would be wholly incommensurate since U.S. carriers do not use intra-EU city-pair rights (other than through code-sharing with European partners). Byerly, the U.S. Deputy Assistant Secretary for Transportation Affairs, has urged that the second stage agenda should focus instead on foreign investment issues. *See* Aaron Karp, *U.S. Will Consider Relaxing Foreign Control Rules But Not Cabotage*, ATW Daily News, May 23, 2007.

25. The GATS took effect in 1995 and is incorporated as one of the Annexes to the Agreement Establishing the World Trade Organization (WTO). Any State that is a party to the WTO Agreement is also a party to the GATS. *See generally* Mary E. Footer, *The International Regulation of Trade in Services Following Completion of the Uruguay Round*, 29 Int'l Law. 453 (1995).

26. For discussion of how international air transport has historically remained (in large part) outside the conventional frameworks of the bilateral and multilateral trade negotiations that concern virtually all other economic sectors, *see supra* text accompanying Chapter 2, note 77.

responsible for a sovereign allocation of freedoms and unilateral suspension or withdrawal is an omnipresent threat.[27] Stahl proposed a more modest reform, structuring multiple 'tiers' of membership, with the junior tier offering to exchange only the first four freedoms and the highest tier granting 'all six.'[28] Stahl's theory (in its initial conception) did not contemplate conceding the seventh freedom – a limitation already surpassed in the 2007 U.S./EC Air Transport Agreement – or either type of cabotage, nor did it allow for a multinationalized system of ownership.[29] But Stahl correctly perceived the challenge: 'objective criteria, not negotiational prowess,' should determine membership in a future multinational treaty.[30]

To engineer a genuine break with bilateralism, therefore, we need to visualize how a post-Chicago multilateral regime can evolve (assuming, as this book does, that it *should* evolve). The intent of this final Chapter, therefore, is to present two (not necessarily competing) visions of a multilateralist approach to replacing the Chicago bilateral system. While the first vision, which resides in the existing policies and protocols of the World Trade Organization (WTO) and the GATS, has secured only very modest traction in recent years, it is nonetheless important to demystify the WTO/GATS as a potential forum for at least incremental change – particularly if more ambitious projects fail. Chief among a very short list of these more ambitious projects, and a recurring motif of the present book, is the potential for the negotiators of the 2007 U.S./EC Air Transport Agreement to reach 'beyond open skies' in their second stage deliberations to a comprehensive plurilateral agreement that demolishes the remaining regulatory pillars of the bilateral order. A third-generation settlement of this kind would be open to all interested States and regions, superseding the Chicago nationality rule with a 'right of establishment' model of foreign investment (as introduced in Chapter 2), and allowing the cabotage restriction to wither away within a liberal understanding of foreign ownership, while pressing forward with a broad agenda of regulatory convergence.

As we will note again in the concluding Part of this Chapter, the sustainability of either (or both) of these visions is ultimately a matter of political will: the

27. *See* discussion in Michael E. Levine, *Scope and Limits of Multilateral Approaches to International Air Transport, in* OECD, FORUM FOR THE FUTURE: NEW POLICY APPROACHES TO INTERNATIONAL AIR TRANSPORT 75 (1993). Of course, a new Chicago Convention need not necessarily be constructed on a 'Chicago' platform and could instead mirror the liberalization principles reflected in this study. That may indeed have been the sentiment behind the call by Rush O'Keefe, general counsel of FedEx Corporation, for a new Chicago Convention 'to address the remaining issues of aviation liberalization in an aviation-specific forum.' International Aviation Law Institute, DePaul University College of Law & Chicago Council on Global Affairs, *Sustainable Aviation Policies for America and the World: A Leadership Summit*, Synopsis of the Proceedings (Oct. 19, 2006) [hereinafter *Aviation Leadership Summit*]. The present study will close with a call to act upon O'Keefe's summons.
28. *See* Tycho H.E. Stahl, *Liberalizing International Trade in Services: The Case For Sidestepping the GATT*, 19 YALE J. INT'L. LAW 405, 441-43 (1994).
29. Stahl did allow for 'domestic services' and relaxation of investment rules as part of a longer process of integration, but these were not components of his initial settlement. *Id.* at 442-43.
30. *Id.* at 442.

WTO/GATS promises a more gradual path to liberalization but currently lacks the political consensus to achieve it; the plurilateral option, in contrast, links to the already notable aeropolitical success of the U.S./EC Air Transport Agreement. The plurilateral vision seeks to leverage this success to achieve a significant second-stage agreement likely to reshape global aviation by attracting adherents from across the globe.

C   GATS Gradualism: A Search for the Highest Common Denominator

1   Introduction

In one of his first speeches as WTO Director-General, New Zealander Mike Moore exhorted his member governments to consider WTO trade rules as an opportunity 'to free up the tightly controlled world of civil aviation.'[31] Air transport's 'exceptionalism' as an outlier in the international trade system is nowhere more conspicuous than within the framework of the GATS.[32] In contrast to other services sectors, which are not *a priori* blocked from coverage under the Agreement,[33] at the creation of the GATS in 1995 air transport services were explicitly excluded outside the narrow range of a brief Annex.[34] In effect, the Annex on Air Transport

---

31. Mike Moore, WTO Director General, *The Future of International Trade in Services*, Speech to the Third Debis Services Conference, Berlin (Sept. 21, 1999). Post-World War II international trade and aviation policies sharply diverged from one another. International trade policy has been rooted in and informed by the nondiscrimination philosophy of the General Agreement on Tariffs and Trade (GATT) and (since 1995) the WTO. *See* Marrakesh Agreement Establishing the World Trade Organization, Apr. 15, 1994, 1867 U.N.T.S. 31,874. Through the trade disciplines cultivated by these arrangements, national economies have been exposed to international competition. As discussed in this book, international aviation policy has avoided the disciplinary principles of international trade (including most favored nation (MFN) and national treatment (NT), discussed later in this Part) and sought protection in a system of mercantilist bilateral treaties. *See generally* William A. Dymond & Armand de Mestral, *New Destinations in International Air Policy*, 4 Policy Matters 8-10 (Oct. 2003) (discussing divergence of global trade and aviation policies and persistence of the bilateral air treaty regime). Global aviation also has a regulatory organization, ICAO, which governs air navigation and air transport safety and security, but which has sought also to superintend the progress of economic liberalization. *See supra* Chapter 2, Part II(D); *see generally* WTO, Council for Trade in Services, *Communication from the United States: Review of the GATS Annex on Air Transport Services*, at 1, Doc. No. S/C/W/198 (Oct. 3, 2001) [hereinafter WTO, *Communication from the U.S.*]
32. *See supra* note 25.
33. The GATS does not prescribe the sector scope (nor the scope of liberalization within each sector). While some Member States have limited their commitments to less than a handful of sectors, others have listed several dozen.
34. *See generally* ICAO, Economic Commission, *Regulation of International Air Transport Services*, Report by the Council on Trade in Services, at 2, A33-WP/7 (Jun. 6, 2001) [hereinafter ICAO Report 2001] (describing GATS Annex on Air Transport Services). How did air transport get into the GATS in the first place? The U.S. Government was criticized by the aviation industry for letting this happen, since aviation did not want to be 'traded' within the same framework as

Services removed so-called 'hard' traffic rights (the distribution of route access privileges between States), as well as 'services directly related to the exercise of traffic rights,'[35] from consideration under GATS procedures. The phrase 'traffic rights,' which probably captures virtually every restrictive characteristic of bilateral aviation treaties, stands as a proxy for all excluded air transport operations. The Annex included only a small subset of 'soft' rights comprising aircraft repair and maintenance, selling and marketing of air transport services,[36] and CRS.[37] The choice of these activities for coverage did not reflect deep analysis but was more

---

bananas or microprocessors or even banking or telecommunications, but inevitably it reflected a compromise offered to gain concessions in other sectors. *See* Marie-Angélique Kolivakis, *The Economic Regulation of Air Transport from the Chicago Convention to GATS* 34 (1995) (unpublished LL.M. thesis, Institute of Air and Space Law, McGill University).

35. This phrase was undefined in the Annex, and most countries have used this definitional uncertainty to interpret the exclusions so broadly that almost all air service activity is excluded. *See* Wolfgang Hubner & Pierre Sauvé, *Liberalisation Scenarios for International Air Transport*, 35 J. WORLD TRADE 973, 975 (2001). In any event, the hermeneutics of the GATS make it uncertain precisely which air transport services *not* directly related to the exercise of traffic rights might, theoretically, already be covered by the GATS (other than the listed services). *See* [U.K.] Department for Transport, *GATS 2000 and Air Transport Services*, Consultation Paper (1999) [hereinafter U.K. DOT, *GATS 2000*].

36. It is not clear how the GATS negotiators, in their zeal to obtain *some* coverage of air transport, determined that sales and marketing of air services should be treated as conceptually distinct from the provision of air services as such. As Ruwantissa Abeyratne has argued, '[a]ir traffic rights that result from the Chicago Convention's provisions are the tool with which the selling or marketing of air transport services can be carried out and the two are inextricably linked to each other.' Ruwantissa Abeyratne, *Trade in Air Transport Services: Emerging Trends*, 35 J. WORLD TRADE 1133, 1145 (2001). Resting partly on this premise, Abeyratne suggests that the explicit exclusion of air traffic rights from the GATS is necessarily 'ambivalent.' *Id.* In any event, 'selling and marketing' does not include *pricing*, which remains outside the agreement. *See Airline Commission Proceedings*, testimony of Jeffrey N. Shane, former DOT Assistant Secretary for Policy (Jun. 24, 1993), at 104-05.

37. The Annex is one of a series of similar Annexes which contain special regulations amending the scope and application of the GATS for certain services. Annexes exist for the movement of natural persons providing services under the Agreement, financial services, telecommunications, and air transportation services. Recognizing the burden and pervasiveness of existing air transport regulation, the GATS Annex on Air Transport Services carves out a massive exemption from the scope of the Agreement which covers all 'traffic rights, however granted.' Very little that takes place in the current global air transport regime merits a clear ontological separation from the concept of 'traffic rights.' Thus, the definition provided in the Annex provides a thumbnail sketch of the restrictions imposed by the bilateral system:

'Traffic rights' means the right for scheduled and nonscheduled services to operate and/or to carry passengers, cargo and mail for remuneration or hire from, to, within, or over the territory of a Member, including points to be served, routes to be operated, types of traffic to be carried, capacity to be provided, tariffs to be charged and their conditions, and criteria for designation of airlines, including such criteria as number, ownership, and control.

The words 'to operate and/or to carry' include technical stops and positioning or ferry flights without revenue traffic; 'from' and 'to' cover second, third, and fourth freedoms; 'within' covers cabotage; and 'over' includes first freedom rights. *See* WTO, *Communication from the U.S.*, *supra* note 31, at 6.

probably the outcome of 'the desire for a positive initial list.'[38] The hard/soft dichotomy, in fact, seems to be based on some intuitive sense of the economic significance (or existing degree of market openness) of the removed and included rights.

Through this 'variable geometry'[39] of hard and soft rights, the WTO member States left open a number of strategic possibilities. Hard rights could be dealt with in specialized negotiations outside the WTO framework (as in the case of the U.S./ EC Air Transport Agreement of 2007), within the WTO through a sectoral understanding or a WTO-style 'plurilateral' agreement[40] (as was done with government procurement of goods, for instance), or through the existing bilateral system. Further, additional 'soft' rights could be added to the Annex for treatment by conventional GATS disciplines, including issues related to key infrastructural services such as airport management, airline catering, or groundhandling. Contrary to a discernible trend in academic and official commentaries, however, the rule against foreign ownership and control of domestic airlines, a staple of bilateralism, should not be regarded as a 'soft' right if one assumes that economic value is indeed the premise for the hard/soft distinction drawn in the Annex.[41] That rule is used explicitly to assign traffic rights on the basis of nationality and is therefore fundamental to the discriminatory assumptions of the bilateral system.[42]

2   Applying the GATS Framework Principles to Global Air Transport

Before considering the architecture of the GATS in more detail, a piece of demystification is needed. Coverage by the GATS does not necessarily mean that a sector is being liberalized. The Agreement is set up to allow Member States to claim exemptions and exceptions with respect to its key liberalizing principles, and to

---

38.   John Gunther, *Implications of the GATS for the Air Transport Sector* (copy on file with author).

39.   The term is borrowed from EU usage, in which it means the concept of a Community or Union in which some countries may integrate more (or faster) than others. Soft rights, in this analogy, could be integrated faster than hard rights. The notion of a putative 'twin-speed' European Union, however, was debunked as politically unacceptable by EU political leaders in the wake of Ireland's referendum rejection of the Treaty of Lisbon in Jun. 2008. *See supra* Chapter 1, note 10.

40.   *See infra* text accompanying note 57.

41.   *See, e.g.*, Hubner & Sauvé, *supra* note 35, at 979 (suggesting, erroneously, that 'ownership and control' is a component of air transport that is 'not quite so jealously guarded' as hard traffic rights); *but see* UNCTAD, *Report of the Expert Meeting On Air Transport Services: Clarifying Issues To Define The Elements Of The Positive Agenda Of Developing Countries As Regards Both The GATS And Specific Sector Negotiations Of Interest To Them*, at 10, TD/B/COM.1/- EM.9./3 (Aug. 23, 1999) (explicitly linking ownership and control with route and traffic rights as 'hard rights').

42.   The nondiscrimination ethos of the GATS departs from a key premise that is still pervasive in the international airline industry, namely, that it is rational to speak of a 'United States' air carrier or a 'German' air carrier and that these descriptors are mutually exclusive. *See supra* Chapter 3, Part V (discussing the Chicago system's pervasive foreign ownership restrictions).

take unilateral commitments on specific market-opening initiatives, so that the pace of any liberalization is clearly within the sovereign remit of each participating WTO member State. While critics assert that the pace of reform is consequently set by the most resistant State,[43] that is not necessarily so because coalitions of like-minded States can create flexibility and consensus in response to particular issues.[44] The GATS is also, like its counterpart in the goods sector, a 'standstill' agreement that sets a baseline for each member State's market-restricting measures.[45]

---

43. *See, e.g.*, Peter Forsyth, *Promoting Trade in Airline Services*, 7 J. Air Transport Mgmt. 43, 49 (2001) (preferring the metaphor of 'the convoy moving at the speed of the slowest ship'). For these commentators, the bilateral system, centered in national sovereignty, is ideally suited to those States that continue to assert the wellbeing of their national carriers – whether in public or private ownership – as a priority in aviation policy. Any attempt to corral these States into a wider multilateral framework might produce agreement, but it would be pitched to the 'lowest common denominator' – *l'harmonisation à la baisse* – embracing areas of general consent that could prove even less liberal than current bilateral practice. *See also* Stahl, *supra* note 28, at 434-35 (advocating services trade liberalization among 'comparatively small groups of States united by their pursuit of common goals'); and Bruce Stockfish, *Opening Closed Skies: The Prospects for Further Liberalization of Trade in International Air Transport Services*, 57 J. Air L. & Com. 599, 640-41 (1992) (describing the failure of various ICAO-sponsored liberalization initiatives).

44. Nor does the GATS dictate a specific regulatory regime. Domestic regulations remain in force (for example, with respect to customs procedures), many of them discriminatory. But the GATS system does encourage and permit States to develop agreements on regulatory convergence and harmonization with respect to 'doing business' issues. In the arena of safety, the WTO/GATS system complements, but does not substitute for, the regulatory and standards-making functions of ICAO. *See* Hubner & Sauvé, *supra* note 35, at 978.

45. The GATS does not purport to offer a definition of 'services.' What it does do, however, is to demarcate the scope of the term 'trade in services' through various modes of supply in Article 1(2). Within this rubric, the GATS definition of the supply of a service, although not intended to cover air transport specifically, does succeed in capturing the nature of air transport services through flights originating in foreign countries and flights provided within the home country either directly through commercial presence or indirectly as extensions of inbound air services. While the GATS covers trade in services, the GATT regulates trade in goods. The theory of the GATT is that (to the extent practicable) all restrictions on imports are prohibited except as provided for in the tariff schedules. All point-of-entry restrictions, in other words, are channeled into a visible and transparent tax, the tariff, and the successive GATT negotiation rounds seek to ratchet down the level of the tariff across a wide spectrum of imported goods. Such an approach would be unworkable for services, which can either be provided without ever physically entering the country where the service is rendered, or which in many cases require that the provider is in the same physical location as the recipient. An air service from New York to New Orleans, for example, can only be provided if the foreign carrier is able to station an airplane in New York for that purpose. Prohibiting that service completely, of course, is the functional equivalent of imposing a prohibitive tariff on the foreign carrier. Moreover, the GATS recognizes that services industries have unique characteristics that cannot be treated within the understandings reached for trade in goods. Specifically, services do not necessarily enter and exit countries as discrete, quantifiable units at convenient customs ports. In addition, they are inherently more difficult to measure, nor can the value of reciprocal concessions be easily quantified or compared.

a   *The GATS Trade Principles*

Reduced to its essence, the GATS is a relatively straightforward collection of trade-enhancing principles.[46] It can be likened to a builder's toolkit from which governments may select a range of trade implements and materials depending on how high or low they wish to build their protectionist walls. In other words, the GATS is not a monolithic construct which must either be accepted in its entirety or avoided. And it is important to see the GATS process as organic and dynamic, so that initial efforts at trade discipline may (although will not inevitably) evolve into commitments to deeper liberalization.

The GATS, like the GATT, orbits around a small set of core principles – most-favored-nation (MFN), national treatment (NT), market access, and transparency[47] – which have been fundamental to the entire WTO trade regime. MFN applies universally to all services sectors unless specifically exempted by a member State in its listings. NT, in contrast, applies only to those sectors that member States specifically list. In addition, where specific sectors are rolled into the GATS, member States are allowed to make a specific commitment or series of commitments with respect to market-opening or market access. For example, if the entire international aviation sector were integrated into the GATS, then the United States could specify in its schedule of commitments that six foreign airlines could serve six listed cabotage – fully domestic – routes to be allocated on a rolling basis for the next five years.

b   *Most-Favored-Nation*

Article II (1) of the GATS sets forth the MFN principle in the following language:

> With respect to any measure covered by this Agreement, each Member State shall accord immediately and unconditionally to services and service suppliers of any other Member State treatment no less favorable than it accords to the like services and service suppliers of any other country.

---

46. Indeed, part of the demystification process being attempted here is precisely to understand that the GATS is not necessarily complex. The WTO provides an interactive tutorial on its website that presents the GATS principles in a question/answer format that requires no prior training in the esoterica of international trade law and policy. *See* World Trade Organization, GATS Training Module, <http://www.wto.org/english/tratop_e/serv_e/cbt_course_e/signin_e.htm>.

47. Transparency, a general obligation under Article III of the GATS, mandates that all laws and regulations of general application should be a matter of public record and subject to disclosure at fixed points of public inquiry. Transparency obligations are especially critical in the services area where the role of regulation – as an instrument to protect trade or as a tool of domestic policy – is likely to be more prominent than in other segments of the economy. The air transport industry, for instance, is often highly politicized and subject to secret regulatory fiat. In this setting, the notion of total transparency would in itself be a major contribution to improved market access.

'Strict' MFN is a nondiscrimination principle that universalizes the most liberal concession made to any other member State of the GATS. In the above example of market access commitments, strict MFN would technically require the United States to offer its cabotage-moderating formula to all other participating States in the GATS.[48] Strict MFN is not reciprocal – the most liberal concession will be available to all other States, even if other States (and even *all* other States but the bilateral partners) maintain more restrictive provisions on market access by foreign services providers (including U.S. providers). Every WTO member State would be required to offer to all member States the elements of its most favorable bilateral agreement, without a requirement of reciprocity. This is not the same thing as bilateralism, since it does not allow the offering State to predetermine its trading partners.[49] As a result, if bilateralism gives States the freedom to pattern different aviation relationships with different partners, MFN evidently removes that freedom. A member State will enjoy 'most favored bilateral' treatment, in other words, even if its own aviation policy requires high-protection aviation treaties. Indeed, the U.S. open skies policy would be practically inoperable under these legal conditions: the unlimited 'gateway' policy in current agreements, for example, would be available to any participant in the GATS system irrespective of its own degree of market accessibility to U.S. carrier activity.

Nonetheless, it is symptomatic of the incrementalist bias of the GATS that an exceptions clause declawed strict MFN for services from the start. Accordingly, by operation of the second clause of Article II of the GATS, the asymmetrical consequences of MFN non-reciprocity, dubbed the 'free rider' problem,[50] can be reduced or even eliminated. This clause allows member States to maintain measures inconsistent with strict MFN provided that such measures are listed in, and meet the conditions of, the GATS Annex on Article II Exemptions.[51] In the air

---

48. But Member States of the European Union, which now exist in a cabotage-free zone, could seek a special GATS dispensation for regional economic organizations to disapply MFN.

49. The process of creating bilateral relations is both quantitative and qualitative in nature. As to the latter, States will limit liberal bilaterals to partners which share a similar free market philosophy and are in rough bargaining parity. *See* Stockfish, *supra* note 43, at 635.

50. It is not difficult to perceive the trade discipline disadvantages of the free rider problem. Since the free riders have received the benefits of concessions whether or not they make reciprocal concessions, negotiating States cannot use trade concessions made during reciprocal bargaining to induce free riders to open their markets. The free rider issue disincentivizes further liberalization. For example, if State A's carriers will be forced to compete domestically with State B's carriers without access to B's home market in return, then State A will have little incentive to open its air market to B. Finally, if States avoid granting unreciprocated benefits, the multilateral exchange of trade access may be reduced to the lowest common denominator, the level set by those States unwilling to reduce their own trade barriers. *See generally* Stahl, *supra* note 28, at 417; *see also supra* note 43 (discussing the 'lowest common denominator' phenomenon of the WTO system).

51. With respect to computer reservations system, a subsector mentioned in the GATS Annex on Air Transport Services, 16 WTO members initially listed MFN exemptions on the basis of insufficient multilaterally agreed rules for the operation of CRS. *See* WTO, *Communication from the U.S., supra* note 31, at 5. By 1998, this number had risen to 28. *See* ICAO, *Regulation of*

transport sector, States reluctant to engage in liberalized market access would not be obligated to offer MFN treatment in this sector and would take an MFN exemption for their bilaterals, which many have already done even in the narrow framework of the Annex on Air Transport Services. On the one hand, a rush toward exemptions would make MFN seem superfluous. On the other hand, liberalizing member States could have an imaginative alternative to bilateralism. If enough member States were to coalesce, would this not put pressure on the member States at large to limit exemptions?

Another strategy, however, is also at least theoretically feasible. Although not technically provided for under the WTO system, a group of likeminded States could combine adherence to bilateralism with an offer of 'conditional' MFN.[52] The Annex on Exemptions could be used, contrary to its protectionist intent, to implement this conditionality. Using this method, liberal member States would unilaterally exempt themselves from MFN in order to make their most liberal bilateral agreement available to all other WTO members in return for a mirror (reciprocal) acceptance of its terms.[53] The liberal bilateral would only take effect for those member States which entered into these mutual arrangements. This would at least promote a dynamic of market-opening, although it suffers from being piecemeal and also highly contingent on the economic behavior of other States.[54] And once again, unlike the existing bilateral system, it removes from States the discretion as to which other States they will select for liberal relationships. Finally, MFN presents difficult issues with respect to the allocation of scarce resources such as takeoff and landing slots, runway capacity, and airspace.[55]

International Air Transport Services, app., at 3, Report by the Council on Trade in Services, A-32-WP/52 Addendum No. 1 (Sept. 4, 1998) [hereinafter ICAO 1998 Report Addendum]. With respect to aircraft repair and maintenance services, nearly all WTO Members took on MFN obligations because of preexisting market conditions of open access in this subsector. *See id.* Overall, it appears that exemptions outnumbered commitments and that the Annex did not have a discernible impact on liberalization in any of the listed subsectors. *See id.*; *see also* UNCTAD, *supra* note 41, at 11.

52. This is not a plurilateral agreement within Annex 4 of the GATS, however. And, unlike Annex 4 agreements, it would not require the approval of all WTO member States.

53. This would work in the following way. State A and State B have a liberal air transport agreement. State A and State C have a restrictive agreement. Under conditional or reciprocal MFN, State C would be automatically entitled to the same liberal access to State A only when State C becomes as liberal as State B. For State A, this would also mean that if State C were to sign a similar liberal agreement with State D, the elements of that agreement would be immediately available to State A and all other countries on the basis of reciprocity.

54. *See generally* Virginia Rodriguez Serrano, *Trade in Air Transport Services: Liberalizing Hard Rights*, 24 ANNALS AIR & SPACE L. 199, 213 (1999).

55. Specifically, this raises the question – how can limited resources like slots be allocated on an MFN basis? But genuine liberalization, nonetheless, requires some means to allow successful carriers to obtain more slots. The precise scope of the 'exemption' modification of strict MFN, however, is hard to evaluate in positivist terms. Under Paragraph 4(a) of the Annex, the GATS Council for Trade in Services is empowered to 'review' all exemptions which are granted for more than five years, and to determine 'whether the conditions which created the need for the exemption still prevail.' Despite these grants of authority (or at least empowerment), there is no explicit language discussing how the Council should arrive at its decision, or what will happen if the conditions no longer prevail.

Paragraph 6 of the Annex contemplates that exemptions will expire after ten years. The idea behind this implied sunsetting is that within a decade, as subsequent liberalizing rounds progress, the exemptions will inevitably be withdrawn. The GATS, like each component of the WTO global trade system, expects to be evaluated in organic terms. It can still offer a program of liberalization even if reciprocity among its members is deferred. For most sectors, the exemption loophole closed after Uruguay, but the exceptional status of aviation suggests that exemptions could still be formulated once the entire sector – or subsectors – become incorporated into the GATS disciplines. The Annex on Negotiations on Maritime Transport Services, for example, provides for the continued nonapplication of the MFN obligation in maritime transport for those member States which have not undertaken specific commitments in this sector. Therefore, exemptions are still open for maritime transport, despite the general GATS principle (in Annex II) that exemptions should apply at the date of entry into force of the Agreement (or, for newly acceding Members, the date of accession). The drafting ethos of the GATS seems to suggest that exemptions remain (at least theoretically) indefinite, which naturally grants member States an implied ability to control the pace of liberalization.[56]

The WTO system (through Article II(3) of the organization's Charter) also contemplates the creation of stand-alone specialized 'plurilateral' agreements which apply highly liberal regimes to specific arenas of trade cooperation. In this way, a transcontinental open aviation area – of the kind suggested in the next Part of this Chapter – could exist inside the WTO framework. Problematically, however, a plurilateral agreement of this kind would require the consent of the full membership of the Organization, and also could not exclude membership by any willing member State. As a result, the regional efficacy of such a proposal would inevitably be compromised. Outside the WTO framework, however, States participating in specialized economic integration agreements can be exempted as a general matter from the MFN obligation. Article V of the GATS, like Article XXIV of the GATT, permits any WTO member State to enter into agreements to further liberalize trade in services on a bilateral or plurilateral basis, provided the agreement has 'substantial sectoral coverage' and removes substantially all discrimination between participants.[57] The U.S./EC Air Transport Agreement, in both its first and second stages, would appear to be contemplated by this GATS provision.[58]

---

56. Strictly, the exemptions would lapse after ten years, but negotiations would continue during that relatively long period of time which could either forestall the sunset or make it unnecessary. In any event, the ten-year period seems to have no teeth within the GATS framework.

57. Defining 'substantially all' has proven problematical in the GATT context and is not likely to be any less problematical for services. Article V of the GATS, like its GATT cognate, makes provision to ensure that the overall level of barriers is not raised vis-à-vis nonparticipants in the sectors covered and provides a method for compensation if this happens. It is unlikely, however, that new common regimes would drift toward greater illiberality.

58. The problem with regional agreements (and even WTO-sponsored plurilaterals) is that membership of the agreement can reach a critical mass and thereafter consensus on amending the agreement can become virtually impossible to obtain. Any remaining barriers to market access may become permanently locked in place. Moreover, regional fragmentation of the global air transport market could result in inter-bloc competition but barriers could rise for competitors outside the blocs.

c   *National Treatment*

Article XVII of the GATS sets forth the NT principle as follows:

> In the sectors inscribed in its schedule, and subject to any conditions and
> qualifications set out therein, each Member shall accord to services and ser-
> vice suppliers of any other Member, in respect of all measures affecting the
> supply of services, treatment no less favorable than that it accords to its own
> like services and service suppliers.

Unlike its general applicability as part of GATT, the GATS NT principle applies
only to services with respect to which a member State has made a specific scheduled
commitment. The 'specificity' of services explains this discrepancy between the two
Agreements. Thus, universal NT for goods does not necessarily imply free trade
because imports can still be controlled by tariffs which, in turn, may be bound in a
member State's tariff schedule. By contrast, given the difficulties of applying tariff-
type measures across large segments of the services industries,[59] a general extension
of NT could be tantamount to guaranteeing free access to the domestic market.

The 'scheduling' of NT commitments (and commitments to market access) is
a more structured process than the studied vagueness that attaches to MFN exemptions. Commitments may be horizontal (multisectoral) as well as sector-specific.[60]
A horizontal commitment might necessitate that authorization is required
whenever foreigners propose to acquire land (for example, for construction of
an airport terminal or automobile factory). A sector-specific commitment, applied
solely to the air transport industry, might include a requirement that foreign equity
participation will be limited to 49%.[61]

Furthermore, the global aviation industry is governed by a variety of discriminatory rules that violate the assumptions of the NT principle (and indeed the
principle of market access). Examples include discriminatory rules which are
explicitly nationality-based, such as restrictions on foreign ownership and control
of domestic airlines,[62] reservation of domestic (cabotage) routes to nationally

---

59. *See supra* in the main text.
60. The spectrum of juristic language used in commitments ranges from full commitments without
    limitation (indicated by the term 'none'), to full discretion to apply any measure falling under
    the relevant GATS Article ('unbound').
61. This restriction is not only a violation of the NT principle, but it also serves as a limitation on
    market access. NT and market access restrictions tend to operate with the same discriminatory,
    i.e., market-closing, effect. *See generally* GATS Training Module, *supra* note 46.
62. For example, GATS Article XVI(2)(f) prohibits WTO members, when making a market access
    commitment, from placing limitations on the participation of foreign capital in terms of a
    maximum percentage limit on foreign shareholding or the total value of individual or aggregate
    foreign investment. If the United States, for example, made a commitment with respect to access
    to cabotage rights for foreign airlines, but wished to maintain its laws on foreign ownership and
    control of U.S. airlines, it could decide to specify in its schedule that the existing 25% limit on
    foreign stock ownership, and the existing substantial control test, would continue to apply.
    See generally ICAO 1998 Report Addendum, *supra* note 51, app.

owned airlines, insistence on the home nationality of crew members on internal routes, the Fly America program for United States government employees, prohibitions on inbound wet leasing from foreign carriers, discriminatory preferences favoring national airlines in the assignment of airport slot privileges,[63] and so on. The GATS, *stricto sensu*, does not proscribe any of these prevalent features of the bilateral system. Member States can simply list them in the relevant schedule as 'conditions and qualifications' that will not apply. Thus, for example, States could schedule existing foreign ownership restrictions in the form of GATS commitments, and in this way use the GATS formula as a mechanism for *freezing* existing restrictions. The United States, had it done so, would not have been able to legislate even more restrictive conditions on foreign control in 2003.[64] To this extent, of course, NT is a much weaker commitment than MFN. Ironically, NT can be discretionary under the GATS, yet compulsory under a bilateral treaty.

d   Market Access

Article XVI of the GATS, dealing with market access, provides a list of restrictions which a member State shall not maintain or adopt unless otherwise specified in its schedule (the same schedule it files with respect to limitations on NT). Among these restrictions are limitations on the number of service providers in the form of numerical quotas or the total value of service operations. If a member allows foreign airlines to operate in its domestic cabotage market, that is a market access commitment. Conversely, if it limits the number of licenses issued to foreign airlines, that is a market access limitation. Furthermore, if a foreign airline is allowed only one cabotage route while a domestic airline is allowed many, that is an exception to the NT principle.[65] Market access is conceptually part of the NT commitment. Without market access, a commitment to national treatment is meaningless.

3   A Critique of the GATS Approach to Multilateralism

As the previous Part illustrates, the GATS approach risks a scattershot approach to identifying issues that can be addressed multilaterally, even though it has the

---

63. This issue implicates the fairness of the allocation of slots among air carriers of different nationalities. Under traditional bilateral practice, a disproportionate number of slots is reserved for national carriers, antithetical to the notion that slots are best used by the most efficient and successful carriers. An objective and unbiased slot allocation system – which may be market-based – would be needed to cancel the bias of the prevailing regimes.

64. *See* Brian F. Havel, *Mixed Signals On Foreign Ownership: An Assessment*, ISSUES AVIATION L. & POL'Y ¶ 25,341, at 13,125 (2005) (discussing amendment of U.S. statute to include explicit requirement of actual control of a U.S. airline's stock by U.S. citizens).

65. Within the framework of the GATS Annex on Air Transport Services, fewer than 40 of the WTO's 140 member States committed themselves to market-opening moves. Hubner and Sauvé report that between 30 to 35 WTO Members took commitments on 'Maintenance and Repair' and 'Supporting' Services, whereas other services, including CRS services and sales and marketing of air transport services, were only committed by five WTO member States. *See* Hubner & Sauvé, *supra* note 35, at 975.

advantages of being a standstill mechanism that also encourages an organic process of liberalization to evolve. Nor is the GATS as yet a comprehensive charter for trade discipline. For example, it does not include a regime to control the grant of State aid, [66] nor does it possess a dispute settlement system that gives standing to nongovernmental actors and that therefore avoids attaching a political or diplomatic coloration to every decision to engage its forensic process.[67] Airlines prefer the kind of mediation, consultation, and informal bargaining that accompanies dispute settlement procedures (which are typically arbitral) found in bilateral aviation agreements.[68] Their access to these systems, which are still part of State-to-State diplomacy, has been nurtured by decades of bureaucratic practice.[69] To this extent, the exceptionalism of the bilateral system probably outscores the State-centeredness of the WTO/GATS procedures.[70] In any event, however, the current

---

66. In a technical sense, State aids (subsidies) are subject to MFN as an unconditional general obligation of the GATS (subject to whatever exemptions a State may claim). Similarly, the NT principle governs subject to any limitations that a State may inscribe. The WTO Agreement on Subsidies and Countervailing Measures was developed for trade in goods and is not likely to provide an ideal model for services. As things stand, Article XV of the GATS, which does deal with subsidies, is a weak compromise. While member States recognize that subsidies may in certain circumstances have a distorting effect on trade, they pledge only to enter into negotiations to develop appropriate multilateral disciplines to curb the use of subsidies. No such disciplines yet exist. At best, a member State which feels aggrieved by a foreign subsidy regime, and which believes it is suffering adverse effects, is empowered under the GATS only to request consultations with the other party. Thus, the issue of competition from State-owned or State-subsidized airlines is not squarely attacked.

67. The WTO dispute settlement system, now over a decade old, has the advantage of automaticity in that it forces recalcitrant States to endure an irreversible sequence of litigation events and timetables. But even these accelerated procedures will often prove too slow in a dynamic marketplace. Consultations, the initial step in the GATS dispute resolution process, will take a minimum of 60 days. The GATS dispute procedures are simply too cumbersome to be useful in resolving the daily skirmishes of a dynamic global industry. Richard Shell analyzes the WTO and ICAO, in contrast to the European Union, as 'contract organizations' that adopt the classic public international law contractual model of bilateral relationships between States, designed to achieve gains from cooperation without sacrificing more State autonomy than is absolutely necessary to secure those gains. *See* G. Richard Shell, *Trade Legalism and International Relations Theory: An Analysis of the World Trade Organization*, 44 Duke L.J. 829, 867 & 897 (1995). In the ICAO context, for example, States – not airlines, passenger groups, unions, or others with an interest in how States regulate air transport – have standing to participate in the ICAO governance structure or to appear before international tribunals to adjudicate disputes under the Chicago Convention. *See id.* at 867.

68. *See generally* Brian F. Havel, *International Instruments in Air, Space and Telecommunications Law: The Need for a Mandatory Supranational Dispute Mechanism*, in Permanent Court of Arbitration/Peace Palace Papers, Arbitration in Air, Space and Telecommunications Law: Enforcing Regulatory Measures 11-57 (2002) [hereinafter Havel, *International Instruments*] (reviewing the arbitration provisions of many aviation bilaterals and multilateral instruments).

69. Indeed, the bilateral system frequently allows air carriers to bring their representations directly to a foreign State, without the intermediation of their home governments. Expedited arbitration procedures are also a common feature of aviation bilaterals. *See supra* Chapter 4, note 202 and accompanying text (discussing U.S. statutory procedures).

70. *See* Shell, *supra* note 67, at 897 (noting, disapprovingly, that the WTO dispute resolution system recognizes States as the only parties with standing to bring or defend a claim).

version of the GATS Annex on Air Transport Services largely disapplies the WTO dispute resolution system in favor of existing bilateral measures.[71]

This is not to say that the GATS procedures, now that we have completed our demystification, should be discarded as being without utility. Properly applied, the GATS could deliver liberalization initiatives in any number of contested areas of global air transport regulation, including the flashpoints of nationality and cabotage.[72] The argument has also been convincingly made that a segment or subsector of the air transport industry – air cargo in general or the more specialized cargo sector of express delivery services, for example – could be decoupled for possible incorporation in an expanded GATS Annex on Air Transport Services.[73] WTO member States would then make national commitments within this area,[74] exchanging bundles of market access and traffic rights that would be inconceivable

---

71. Thus, Paragraph 4 of the Annex requires exhaustion of existing procedures in bilateral and multilateral agreements. *See* Gunther, *supra* note 38, at 4 (noting also that Paragraph 1 of the Annex in effect 'grandfathers' the terms of all existing bilateral and multilateral air transport agreements).

72. ICAO member States made suggestions in this respect during the five-year review of the GATS which took place in 2000. Among the additional 'soft' rights proposed for inclusion were a number of subsectors that could be summarized as 'groundhandling services' and which include passenger, baggage, and mail handling; ramp handling; aircraft services including cleaning, disinfecting, heating, and de-icing; and crew administration. In addition, airport services encompassing provision of air terminal services and runway operating services, as well as general aviation, are also potential targets for GATS discipline. *See generally* ICAO 1998 Report Addendum, *supra* note 51, at 4. Significantly, a few ICAO member States have also endorsed air cargo, nonscheduled, and multimodal transport as potential early candidates for inclusion in the Annex. *Id.*

73. *See generally* Brian F. Havel, *Rethinking the GATS as a Pathway to Global Aviation Liberalization*, Paper Presented to the Air Transport Research Society 2005 World Conference, Rio de Janeiro, Brazil (Jul. 3, 2005); *see also* BRIAN HINDLEY, TRADE LIBERALIZATION IN AVIATION SERVICES: CAN THE DOHA ROUND FREE FLIGHT? (2004).

74. The GATS could deliver market access and harmonization targets that are of tremendous importance to the express cargo 'integrators.' Their primary reform objective is to develop a system which permits the free and uninhibited exchanges demanded by an increasingly open economic system – a system of global manufacturing and consumption – which they have evolved to serve. American corporations FedEx and UPS have been among the most vocal supporters of the U.S./EC liberalization negotiations, calling for removal of all market or 'doing business' restrictions. They foresee liberalization as leading to the end of an unsystematic array of bilaterals, subsidiaries, partnerships and other devices which they use to guarantee door-to-door coverage on a worldwide basis. But harmonization and regulatory convergence would also be invaluable. Among the most severe of the external (non-aviation) penalties imposed on the logistics industry are inefficient and inconsistent customs procedures that afflict express delivery mail and packages even for commerce conducted in so-called developed countries. Customs account for 20% of average transport time and 25% of average transport costs. (Customs reform, however, would have to occur in tandem with the World Customs Organization. *See* U.K. DOT, *GATS 2000*, *supra* note 35. Integrators complain about arbitrary revaluation of the declared value of shipments by customs and seek harmonization (or at least regularization) of scales of charges and fees. GATS disciplines could quickly establish a single document and control procedure, as well as a fast track clearance for authorized traders.

at present for the air passenger or air cargo combination industries.[75] To this end, nothing in the GATS prevents member States, should they agree, from dividing or subdividing services sectors and making them separately subject to GATS disciplines.[76]

The aeropolitical obstacles to progress through the GATS remain substantial, however. The decoupling and fragmentation of air services liberalization negotiations, for example, is not widely favored among stakeholders within the international air transport industry. Many carriers and governments are inclined to treat their competitive position as an indivisible combination of passenger and cargo operations. Governments fear losing leverage in bilateral passenger negotiations, especially for the hybrid combination carriers.

The airline industry, meanwhile, fears the WTO system because it exposes the global airline industry to cross-sectoral trade concessions as the price for liberalization. For example, the United States Trade Representative would become engaged directly in air transport, rather than the Departments of State and Transportation which now exclusively police global air transport negotiations.[77] Jean Fleury, chair of Airports Council International, gave voice to this attitude when he discounted the WTO as 'not air-minded.' The former Director-General of IATA, Pierre Jeanniot, declared in 1999, on the eve of a scheduled review of the GATS Annex on Air Transport Services, that the airline industry did not favor a dual regulatory regime with some States applying GATS obligations and others

---

75. Interestingly, with respect to express cargo operators like FedEx and UPS, an argument can be made that their juristic assimilation to air transport (and hence to the accumulated biases of the regulatory system that governs them) has been inaccurate. Integrated multimodal transport is based on a services 'product' – express delivery – rather than a specific mode of transport. In juristic terms, a synthesis of two ontological ideas – the integrated multimodalism and time-sensitivity of logistical services – leads to the conceptual understanding that *express delivery is an activity that can be treated as juristically distinct from the provision of air transport as such.* While express logistics is conceptually multimodal, the modalities used reflect the determinant of speed rather than inherency. In other words, if the express integrators could use Olympic sprinters to deliver iPods faster than they can do with airplanes, they would do so. Express delivery services have their own 'specificity,' since aircraft are not aircraft as such but rather critical links in a global supply chain. In essentialist terms, therefore, the mode of transport is irrelevant. What is relevant is an integrated process to ensure ontime delivery. In an ontological sense, it could be argued that airlines exist only because of airplanes, but it does not appear that the speed of airplanes necessarily correlates to the driving mission of the industry. Airlines do as a matter of good business practice endeavor to move passengers speedily to their destinations, but the existence of connecting flights – indeed, of the entire hub-and-spoke system – suggests that other variables are also at play. Moreover, airlines do not (yet) offer true origin-to-destination services, including picking up the passenger at a hotel, home, or business and dropping the passenger off at a foreign hotel, residence, or business.

76. In Article XXVIII, its glossary of definitions, the Agreement defines 'sector' of a service to mean 'one or more, or all subsectors' of a service *as specified in a Member's schedule.* If a Member does not specify, the definition defaults to the whole of that service sector, including all of its subsectors. Clearly, Members could agree to subject a subsector to GATS discipline, just as they did with respect to air transport in the Annex on Air Transport Services.

77. In the air cargo sector, however, many industrial sectors intersect, including air transport, surface transport, freight forwarding, and information technology.

clinging to the existing bilateral edifice.[78] Moreover, there is a strong current of opinion among some WTO member States that ICAO should remain the primary forum for air transport liberalization efforts.[79]

On the other hand, there has been no industry consensus on which liberalizing vehicle to support. International organizations have stepped into this breach to promote their own liberalizing agendas, and one of the most persistent has been support for treating all of air cargo as a separate entry in the portfolio of services sectors under WTO discipline. Both ICAO and the International Chamber of Commerce have promoted this initiative.[80] The Association of European Airlines (AEA), representing Europe's mainline air carriers, has proposed a cautious process of GATS liberalization to cover first and second freedom rights,[81] wet leasing, groundhandling, airport and air navigation charges, and sector-specific air cargo issues including customs procedures, intermodal transport, and the harmonization of certain common rules.[82] Air cargo liberalization could be the subject of a so-called 'early harvest' deal, and ICAO has itself proposed accelerated liberalization of air cargo negotiations. These initiatives assume, however, that air cargo can be peeled away from air passenger negotiations despite the reluctance of governments and the air transport industry (dominated by the combination carriers) to do so.[83]

---

78. *See* UNCTAD, *supra* note 41, at 9.
79. *See* ICAO Report 2001, *supra* note 34, at 4. It is not clear, however, whether ICAO will eventually seek to establish a liberalized multilateral regime or prefers to see itself as the exclusive forum for any prior discussions leading in that direction. After Sept. 11, 2001, ICAO has shown itself to be increasingly assertive and less inclined to support competing (or replacement) initiatives through rival organizations such as the WTO. *See* ICAO, Economic Commission, *The Orderly Evolution of Air Transport Services: Secure and Safe Economic Regulation in an Era of Globalization*, at 4, A33-WP/227 (Sept. 28, 2001) (disparaging efforts to have civil aviation treated as 'just another international commercial service that should be dealt with by the [WTO]'). The ICAO Economic Commission does make the telling point, which resonates strongly after 9/11, that safety and security cannot be treated as entirely separate from issues of economic regulation of global air transport. *Id.* at 5.
80. *See supra* Chapter 2, Part II(D).
81. These are not insignificant privileges. The right to fly over another country without landing (first freedom) and the right to make a technical stop without picking up or letting off revenue traffic do not give access to any actual commercial market in the countries where the rights are exercised, but do enable market access in other countries and enable the provision of air transport services. While some legitimate limitations (to ensure orderly, safe, and secure air traffic/navigation management on a nondiscriminatory basis) are acceptable, these freedoms should not be seen and used as economic assets to be exploited by national governments. A large number of countries already grant first and second freedoms automatically, but some countries extract high rents for the exercise of transit privileges. Leverage to secure commitments from these high-rent States could be applied by making offers in other sectors which those countries regard as higher in priority than air transport. *But see supra* in the main text (mentioning the airline industry's dislike of cross-sectoral bargaining).
82. The AEA's support for a GATS initiative is, of course, entirely consistent with its advocacy of a U.S./EC single air transport jurisdiction and its support for the U.S./EC air transport negotiations.
83. It is often overlooked that the United States itself took a specialized view of air cargo services liberalization in 1977, deregulating air cargo in advance of the broader advance toward full

4   Conclusion: Politics and the GATS

Ultimately, the choice of forum for airline liberalization will be a political rather than legal one. As yet, no government or group of governments has articulated a coherent vision as to what kind of global air transport industry should be encouraged to emerge in a liberalized framework. There is discernible political support among certain WTO aviation powers for a GATS-driven liberalization. Australia and New Zealand,[84] as well as Norway and Sweden,[85] have expressed themselves generally in favor of increasing GATS involvement in global air transport.[86] Indeed, the EU as a whole has taken a pragmatic view that the GATS offers certain interesting options, but remains committed to the bilateral system with respect to

---

deregulation of the air passenger industry. (Indeed, from 1944 to 1977 the United States had no separate position on international air cargo regulation. The Air Cargo Deregulation Act of 1977, Pub. L. No. 95-163, became effective on Jan. 1, 1979. FedEx's colossal growth from a small commuter airline into a global integrator was powered by U.S. air cargo deregulation.) Several motivations drove that earlier flexibility with respect to air cargo. Safety concerns were less in the cargo sector, nor was air cargo a major economic sector at that time. In its first decades, it represented unused or excess capacity looking for demand, a byproduct of passenger traffic that was deployed to fill up unused passenger capacity. Accordingly, the U.S. Civil Aeronautics Board was able to promote almost a 'stealth' deregulation in 1977. That flexible policy choice later influenced U.S. actions in the international arena. Air cargo seemed much less subject to national sensitivities and more open to competition than passenger traffic. Even before its vaunted open skies initiative for air passenger services, the United States expressed interest in negotiating with the EC on air cargo issues. In 1988, U.S. aviation officials proposed a separate air cargo agreement with the Community in anticipation of an eventual much broader agreement for all segments of the air transport industry. Within the EC itself, airline deregulation in the early 1990s also began with air cargo. This sector of the air transport industry was already populated with competitive non-EU carriers, and their presence in EU airspace was regulated as much by ad hoc permissions as by effective screening by licensing authorities.

84. *See generally* WTO, *Communication from Australia: The Mandated Review of the GATS Annex on Air Transport Services*, S/C/W/167 (Sept. 18, 2000); WTO, *Communication from Australia: The GATS Review – An Opportunity For Phased Reform of Air Transport Services*, S/C/W/179 (Nov. 14, 2000); WTO, *Communication from New Zealand: The Review of the GATS Annex on Air Transport Services*, S/C/W/185 (Dec. 1, 2000).

85. *See generally* WTO, *Communication from Norway: The Negotiations on Trade in Services*, S/CSS/W/59 (Mar. 21, 2001).

86. Australia proposed that an ICAO draft Assembly resolution on trade in services should be amended to take account of the GATS as 'an effective mechanism for gradual, progressive, orderly and safeguarded change towards market access.' *See* ICAO, Economic Commission, *Relevance of the General Agreement on Trade in Services (GATS) to the Future Development of International Air Transport Regulation*, A33-WP/128 (Sept. 13, 2001) [hereinafter ICAO, *Relevance*]. Australia's chief concern, expressed in its supporting paper, was that plurilateral or regional air transport agreements are themselves discriminatory against nonfounding States and developing States which find themselves unable to influence 'the construction and composition of the core agreement.' *Id.* at 2. Moreover, once the number of adherents to such an agreement reaches a 'critical mass,' consensus on amendment becomes almost impossible and barriers to market access in the agreement may become permanent. *Id.*

traffic rights.[87] The United States, on the other hand, remains wholly opposed to any deepening of the GATS Annex on Air Transport, a position that seems to reflect carrier opposition rather than consumer interests.[88]

In this Part, I have endeavored to show that the GATS is not an arbitrary process, even though it is certainly a much misunderstood one. It exists not to trap governments, but to give them an opportunity to make rational choices based on how they perceive their national interests. The architecture of the Agreement allows member States to make sector-specific market access and NT commitments. As a 'standstill' agreement, it assures a high degree of predictability and stability in light of member States' ability to commit to freezing existing restrictive measures and not to impose additional restrictions in the sectors specified in their national schedules. But the GATS also allows the kind of flexibility to undertake additional commitments with respect to measures falling outside the market access and NT provisions of the Agreement, for example, with respect to formulation of competition and regulatory self-disciplines.

The possibility of a phased approach, rather than a 'big bang' transformation,[89] is appealing to cautious governments. As the Australian Government has argued, such an approach compares favorably with plurilateral or regional alternatives 'that are often presented as a "take it or leave it" option.'[90] In effect, the pace of the GATS tends to ensure that one of the principal advantages of bilateralism – the prerogative of individual States to maintain control over the speed and depth of liberalization – is not sacrificed to a dominant regional or plurilateral dynamic. With that said, it is precisely to the possibility of a plurilateral regime that our attention must now turn. While the GATS should not be overlooked as a creative instrument to achieve the goals of airline liberalization, and while aviation stakeholders should certainly become more familiar with its principles,[91] the 2007 U.S./EC Air Transport Agreement, and its second stage negotiations, hold the promise of a more politically viable achievement in the coming years.

---

87. *See generally* WTO, *Communication from the European Communities and their Member States: The Review of the GATS Annex on Air Transport Services*, S/C/W/186 (Dec. 4, 2000); WTO, *Communication from the European Communities and their Member States: GATS 2000 – Transport Services*, S/CSS/W/41 (Dec. 22, 2000).
88. The United States presented its case against expansion of the GATS Annex in a submission to the WTO Council for Trade in Services in Oct. 2001. The U.S. position is, succinctly, that its policy of liberal 'open skies' bilateral agreements has produced incremental liberalization not just in bilaterals involving the United States but in encouraging other countries to adopt liberal bilaterals with each other both regionally and in transcontinental relationships. *See* WTO, *Communication from the U.S.*, *supra* note 31, at 2.
89. The 'big bang' approach, considered later in this Chapter, requires a bold, decisive, and instantaneous move. *See* Hubner & Sauvé, *supra* note 35, at 977.
90. *See* ICAO, *Relevance*, *supra* note 86, at 3.
91. *See* UNCTAD, *supra* note 41, at 10 (remarks of Pierre Jeanniot, former IATA Director General).

D   A PLURILATERAL RECONCEPTUALIZATION OF THE U.S./EC
               SECOND STAGE NEGOTIATIONS

Unlike the GATS process, the bilateral U.S./EC second stage negotiations represent an unparalleled opportunity to install an expansive regime targeted at the level
of the highest common denominator of liberalization. This new political settlement
could be secured initially by the mutual leverage of these huge aviation powers,
which are similarly situated as a matter of aeropolitics and aeroeconomics.[92]
Maintaining aviation's exceptionalism,[93] and building on the political success
of their 2007 accord, they would contract in the second stage of their negotiations
for such an advanced level of integration and liberalization that *the treaty itself*,
rather than recurrent bargaining and reciprocal concession-granting, would organize *all* of their future aviation relations. Ontologically, this outcome was captured
by Professor Michael Levine in remarks delivered by way of preface to an intriguing 'mock' U.S./EC bilateral air services negotiation at the University of Leiden:

> We should focus on what it means to create a self-perpetuating process that is
> monitored to some extent by governments on both sides, but which is not
> operated by them. If you can create some process in which you have
> confidence, that produces a range of outcomes that you think are generally
> good for the publics on both sides of the ocean, then you need not be concerned
> about every micro-result that occurs in the process. . . . If you create a process
> in which you have some confidence you will create one which is self-
> expanding: it not only expands its scope among those already involved,
> but it makes much simpler the process of adding new players.[94]

---

92. The symbiotic economic and political connections between the United States and the European
    Union are too numerous and well-known to require further emphasis. Nonetheless, mention
    should be made of the curiously hybridized TransAtlantic Business Dialogue (TABD), which
    functions as an independently financed bilateral private business forum but is convened under a
    mandate from the U.S. Government and the European Commission. (Other components of the
    'dialogue' system focus on consumers, the environment, and labor.) The TABD's goal of
    'maintaining an open investment climate,' part of its proposed 'Barrier-Free Transatlantic
    Market,' remains unattainable for the air transport sector under current Chicago bilateral treaty
    practice. Nevertheless, despite having only one airline on its board in 2008 (British Airways),
    the TABD remains a potentially powerful forum for advancing the principles of air transport
    liberalization. It has become an influential voice in transatlantic economic cooperation and has
    managed to place its policy priorities directly onto the business agendas of successive U.S./EU
    summit meetings. For an overview of the TABD's structure, policies, and agenda, see Trans-
    Atlantic Business Dialogue, Homepage, <http://www.tabd.com>.
93. The airline industry has an exceptional status in global commerce as a result of, among other
    special regulatory features, the ironic persistence of the citizenship rule in the era of the global
    shareholder. While this exceptional status has clear downsides, it has also allowed the industry
    to negotiate its future as an industry apart, freed from the cross-sectoral bartering that other
    industries must confront in fora such as the WTO. Thus, the U.S./EC open skies agreement of
    2007 actually reflects the positive side of the airline industry's exceptionalism, and must be
    welcomed for its scope and for the expectation of regime change that it invites. Arguably, the
    second stage negotiations could result in changes every bit as significant as those caused by U.S.
    domestic deregulation after 1978.
94. *The Mock Negotiations Between the EEC-Bloc of Nations and the USA*, *in* EXTERNAL AVIATION
    RELATIONS OF THE EUROPEAN COMMUNITY 56, 63-64 (Henry A. Wassenbergh ed., 1992).

It can be safely assumed that unilateralism – despite some murmurings in Canada to the contrary[95] – will not force the required changes. While some analysts disparage reliance on reciprocity in international free trade negotiations,[96] the specificity of the world airline industry, coupled with the disproportionately large American internal air transport market, combine (for the moment, at any rate) to foreclose any possibility of significant unilateral concessions by the United States. Given this specificity, dismantling U.S. cabotage or abolishing inward investment laws would not be an economically (or strategically) logical predicate where other countries continue to shelter their carriers behind equivalent or stronger restrictions.

Moreover, access to the U.S. market has been the catalyst for whatever incremental liberalization we *have* witnessed in the bilateral system, and is precisely the agent of change that will also drive a multilateral effort. The United States has been, quite simply, the largest seller's market in world aviation, although recently the currency of exchange has switched to the desire for inward investment in U.S. carriers, or for code-sharing maneuvers supported by antitrust exemption, thereby stepping beyond the original open skies formula of bilateral grants of expanded gateway access for foreign carriers.[97]

If nonparticipant States choose to subscribe to the principles of a U.S./EC plurilateral, they may either seek accession upon the consent of the existing members (a 'closed' union as created by the Treaty of Rome) or adhere without specific

---

95. *See supra* Chapter 1, note 34 (mentioning Canadian Competition Bureau Commissioner Sheridan Scott's recent support for a unilateral renunciation of the Canadian cabotage embargo).

96. *See e.g.*, Brink Lindsey, *Free Trade from the Bottom Up*, 19 CATO J. 359 (2003) (arguing that the overwhelming weight of economic analysis and evidence supports the conclusion that a country benefits from opening its own markets regardless of what policies other countries choose to pursue; in this understanding, international trade negotiations serve a political or rhetorical purpose in projecting free trade as a facially reciprocal exercise – in fact, Lindsey contends, the bulk of these negotiations are more in the nature of 'coordinated unilateralism' as States reform their own national policies while adding the benefits of liberalization abroad to those of market-opening at home). Professor Wassenbergh has interpreted the multilateral effect of the Chicago Convention, which speaks in its preamble of a general 'equality of opportunity,' as excluding exchanges of commercial rights on a basis of reciprocity. *See* HENRY A. WASSENBERGH, POST-WAR INTERNATIONAL CIVIL AVIATION POLICY AND THE LAW OF THE AIR 137 (1957). 'For the reciprocity principle lies in the bilateral sphere, and is accordingly inconsistent with the multilateral character of *an equal freedom to start up air services.*' *Id.* (emphasis added). States, in other words, do not (in Wassenbergh's reading of the Convention) have an equal right to a certain protected market share, but only to an equal right to operate air services in the international sphere. Wassenbergh interprets Article 6 of the Convention, which requires the 'special permission' of each State to operate scheduled international air services over or into its territory, as a benign corollary to the right to operate air transportation, allowing States to impose rules under their national laws with respect to the admission of air services of the other contracting parties in general. *Id.* The State practice of bilateralism, of course, presents no support for Wassenbergh's reasonable textual interpretation.

97. *See supra* Chapter 3, Part VIII.

consent (an 'open' union).[98] In this regard, there is no apparent legal inconsistency between a proposed plurilateral and the Chicago Convention. The Convention, as we have seen, does not *by its terms* mandate distribution of traffic rights on a strictly bilateral basis. The logic of Article 6 of the Convention, which requires 'special permission or other authorization' of the State for operation of scheduled international air service over or into its sovereign territory, does not *per se* preclude the award of that permission through a collective mutual exchange of rights of access.[99] Indeed, our reading of Article 7 of the Convention has not disclosed any bar to the mutual repudiation of cabotage accomplished in the EC single aviation market and that would be one of the entry conditions of a new plurilateral.[100] And, with respect to a multilateral revocation of the nationality rule, we have seen that the Convention does not itself mandate the citizenship benchmarks of national ownership and control, which were transplanted into the separate Five Freedoms and Two Freedoms Agreements and have been universally incorporated as part of later *bilateral* understandings on the exchange of air services.[101]

E   Some Guiding Principles for the Negotiators

The most basic drafting principle for the new plurilateral is that it should be broad, yet simple. It would comprise a series of fundamental precepts describing a new open market in aviation – along with the substantive and procedural framework for a more effective 'Joint Committee' structure than the model created in the 2007 U.S./EC Air Transport Agreement, and a supranational appellate body dubbed the 'Air Transport Commission.'[102] Moreover, in my view the 2007 agreement obviates any need for a period of provisional 'staging' of the reciprocal concessions of the second stage. It is true that both the U.S. and EC airline deregulation experiments, as we have seen, included a systematic phased introduction of liberal principles. The case may be made that another adaptive period might be necessary, and it is easy to imagine airline support for a series of controlled exchanges of additional rights.

   Given that the proposed enterprise will be a merger of advanced competitive systems, which already operate *intra muros* on post-Chicago principles of market

---

98. Levine, *supra* note 27, at 79. Thus, regional developments outside the U.S./EC nexus hold the promise for future enlargement of a cornerstone plurilateral created between these two entities. *See* ICAO Secretariat, *Overview of Trends and Developments in International Air Transport*, at 2-3, Working Paper (Mar. 7, 2008) (periodically updated throughout the year) (cataloging regional air transport liberalization initiatives (in addition to the EC single aviation market) affecting markets in Central and South America, Africa, East Asia, and the Middle East. *See also* Tae Hoon Oum et al., *Strategic Airline Policy in the Globalizing Airline Networks*, 32 Transp. J. 14, 15 (1993); Paul V. Mifsud, *Airline Concentrations and Cross Border Arrangements*, *in* External Aviation Relations, *supra* note 94, at 11, 18-19 (detailing how a multilateral system would create possibilities for joint exploitation of new aviation markets).
99. *See supra* Chapter 3, Part IV(B).
100. *See id.*
101. *See supra* Chapter 3, Part V(B).
102. *See supra* Chapter 2, Part V(A).

competition, the justification for additional periods of adjustment is not evident. As a matter of prudence, however, certain prophylactic measures – such as a rapid-response mechanism to deter and eliminate predatory actions – could form part of the remit of the enhanced Joint Committee proposed below.[103] Indeed, prudence also counsels that we do not take the concept of 'open skies' in its most literal sense, replacing a system of State-dominated exchange by an anarchic license to compete by whatever means available throughout the stretched airspace of the new agreement. The market surveillance afforded by competition policy is critical to restrain airlines from imposing their own self-regulating oligopolies in succession to those managed and sustained (explicitly or implicitly) by the government.

Accordingly, this concluding segment offers a series of treaty-building 'principles' that would form the core elements of a truly radical second stage U.S./EC plurilateral agreement on air transport services. The principles are intended to create a uniform system, modeled to an appreciable extent on the proven integration dynamic of the EC single aviation market. Here, however, the new agreement would not form part of some larger economic union for the movement of goods and services, but would be a deliberately *sectoralized* tactic to meet the challenge of the Chicago system:[104] After all, while the plurilateral multiplies in value with each convert from traditional bilateralism, the Chicago system will still predominate outside the plurilateral framework. In addition, the specialization of the airline industry in national settings should have some correspondence in the plurilateral Joint Committee and Air Transport Commission, so that a body of supranational expertise[105] could be created to build support for the wider nullification of the *ancien régime*. This proposal would appear far less cautious were it not for the political antecedent of the 2007 U.S./EC Air Transport Agreement; because of that Agreement, the second stage negotiations can aspire to a 'big bang' deregulation that could not be contemplated in the U.S. and EC 'domestic' experiments.[106]

---

103. *See infra* in the main text. Are measures to combat predation justified, given that they will protect individual *airlines*, even though the instruments of predation – below-cost prices, for example – in the short run redound to consumer benefit? It is, after all, an article of faith in the U.S. antitrust order that competition law does not exist to protect specific competitors, but purports to protect *competition* generally. There is obviously a question of regulatory priority here: is it preferable to intervene in the short term to protect an airline under threat from rapacious competition, so that in the long run 'competition' generally is promoted, or should short-term consumer welfare predominate? *See supra* Chapter 4, Part IV(B) (discussing predation).

104. *See, e.g.*, Murray Gibbs & Mina Mashayekhi, *Services: Cooperation for Development*, 22 J. WORLD TRADE L. 81, 104 (1988) ('Given the heterogeneity of services, concrete solutions are probably most feasible in self-contained, individual service sectors').

105. The word 'supranational,' strictly speaking, has no canonical definition. *See* Laurence R. Helfer & Anne-Marie Slaughter, *Toward a Theory of Effective Supranational Adjudication*, 107 YALE L.J. 273, 287 (1997) (using the term 'supranational' to nominalize a particular type of international organization that is 'empowered to exercise some of the functions otherwise reserved to States').

106. *But see* ANDREAS LOEWENSTEIN, EUROPEAN AIR LAW: TOWARDS A NEW SYSTEM OF INTERNATIONAL AIR TRANSPORT REGULATION 167 (1991). Professor Loewenstein warns that '[t]he modifications necessary under [EC] law should ... be implemented in a very cautious manner. A long transitional period should allow European and foreign carriers, legislators and international

1   **Principle 1: The End of Managed Trade**

The foundational premise of a new U.S./EC aviation services plurilateral must be that the ultimate goal is management freedom to compete fairly, not government intervention to protect market shares. Accordingly, the participants in the plurilateral will accept that it is no longer feasible, in a market environment, for every country to have its own airline.[107] In addition, optimization of 'national' market shares can no longer be retained as an objective of the international airline system (or of national industrial policy, for that matter).[108]

Instead, true open skies requires that all air carriers, irrespective of national affiliation or quantum of public ownership, compete under uniform rules of non-discrimination and equality of competitive opportunity, with freedom to access markets, establish prices, and determine frequency of services. Under the prevailing Chicago system, carriers are presented with a bewildering array of regulatory regimes, which may be highly permissive (as in the U.S. open skies initiative) or subject to relatively rigid governmental intervention (as in the U.S./Japan relationship, for example). Corporate planning in such a fragmented and inconsistent environment is highly distorted, and even market access under relatively liberal regimes remains ever-hostage to the caprice of government policy. The subjective give-and-take of bilateral negotiations will be superseded by the objective criteria of market access and competitive behavior in the plurilateral.[109] In this way, a new universal 'freedom of the air' will be born, succinctly expressed in the old maxim *suum cuique*, 'to each [its] own.'[110] To each carrier will belong the trade that it is able to attract and build, rather than the trade which its sponsor State (whether the airline is in public or private ownership) is able to secure based on mutating aeropolitical bargains with its fellow States.

---

bodies, like ICAO and IATA, to carefully adapt their action and statutes to new requirements and desirable evolutions, maintaining the International System of Air Regulation [*sic*] based on international consensus.' *Id.* The good professor even invokes Machiavelli for his purpose. *Pace* Loewenstein, however, the EC experiment is valuable precisely because it destroys the consensus that has perpetuated the Chicago system.

107.   *But see* WASSENBERGH, *supra* note 96, at 126, n.1, who assumed (in an earlier era) that 'every *State* is entitled to at least one internationally operating airline,' while also noting that '[t]his will be the case for as long as air transport is still regarded as mainly a national affair.' (Emphasis in original.) Whether one State might be better suited than another to engage in air transport (a kind of comparative advantage in aviation) 'scarcely enter[ed] into the matter,' in Wassenbergh's view. *Id.*

108.   The Chicago Convention enshrines the traditional principle of optimization. *See id.* at 125.

109.   Fifty years ago, Professor Wassenbergh called attention to the 'closed' nature of the route systems allowed by the Chicago system, and the consequent inefficiencies for airline economic planning. WASSENBERGH, *supra* note 96, at 124-25.

110.   *See* Professor Wassenbergh's invocation of the same principle, using a more orotund Latinism, *viz.*, *trahit suum cuique tribuere*. *See* HENRY A. WASSENBERGH, PUBLIC INTERNATIONAL AIR TRANSPORTATION LAW IN A NEW ERA 153 (1976).

2   **Principle 2: The End of Cabotage and Chicago's Contrivance of 'Freedoms'**

The service of origin/destination points would be hugely magnified under a second stage plurilateral settlement. Under the first-stage U.S./EC Air Transport Agreement, a huge stride toward open route availability (and toward reducing the demand inefficiencies of the Chicago system) has already been made. Thus, designated German carrier Lufthansa operates conventional third and fourth freedom services with the United States out of Germany; but since March 2008 Lufthansa can also exercise direct traffic rights – seventh freedom rights – from Paris or Rome or London, for example, to New York.[111] (Importantly, however, this privilege is only extended so long as Lufthansa remains owned and controlled by citizens of the ECAA, as we will consider below.) Within the single aviation market, the demand inefficiencies of the required 'home' connection had already been corrected by allowing Lufthansa to exercise intra-Union seventh freedom rights, for example a Paris/Rome service (but again conditional on Lufthansa maintaining an EU ownership and control profile). Since April 1997, all Community carriers have also been able to serve all intra-Member State cabotage routes (which were traditionally embargoed under bilateral edict).

Similarly, the second stage plurilateral would release all origin/destination points in the enlarged transcontinental market, *including all cabotage routes in the United States and European Union*, into a grand network pool. Any carrier licensed within one of the plurilateral territories (or colicensed, perhaps, by a specialized subcommittee of the Joint Committee) would have the unqualified right to enter any of these origin/destination markets and to provide air transport service at price and frequency (including capacity) levels determined solely by market demand. To the extent that the right would be circumscribed in any way, it would be because of an infrastructural constraint that triggered nondiscriminatory safeguard measures notified to the Joint Committee and appealable to the plurilateral's Air Transport Commission.[112] But there would be no *a priori* determinations that a certain number of airlines provides sufficient competitive intercommunion on any given route.

A general availability of seventh freedom and ninth freedom rights would mean an implosion of the Chicago artifice of 'freedoms:' with the home connection broken, an airline would be able to begin and terminate its services using any city-pair points in the plurilateral territory. The process of home State 'designation' of airlines – whether by country or by city-pair – would terminate, just as it has (in effect) for the new generation of U.S. open skies agreements and under the 2007

---

111. *See* U.S./EC Air Transport Agreement, *supra* note 12, art. 3. Previously, Germany might have been able to negotiate *fifth* freedom (beyond) rights from Paris to New York as an extension of a service that would have to begin in Germany, but only if both the French and U.S. Governments specifically consented. Such services have typically been granted subject to negotiated caps on capacity.
112. *See infra* note 179.

U.S./EC agreement. In turn, the linear construction of Chicago system route maps could be augmented (although probably not entirely replaced) by the 'sunburst' configurations to which the U.S. public has become accustomed as a result of the hub-and-spoke phenomenon.

3   Principle 3: A New Doctrine of 'Regulatory' Nationality

It has become clear that deregulation of the global airline industry requires dismantling the citizenship purity test which appears both in bilateral air transport treaties (whereby each party requires that the other party's airlines must be majority-owned and effectively controlled by the other party's citizens), and under similarly minded domestic laws (requiring citizens to own and control the State's airlines). The EC test has been broadened to allow citizens of any of the 27 EU Member States to own and control an EU airline, but the test remains in place for relations with non-EU States. The result of this 'double lock' (international and national law operating together) is that airlines have aircraft which fly internationally, but the airline industry is not genuinely a global one. There is not even a single global competitor in the international air transport industry. As we discussed in Chapter 3, airlines have managed to construct alliances (using consumer-unfriendly devices such as code-sharing), but those alliances would probably wither rapidly if genuine transborder mergers and acquisitions could occur.

As Michael Levine has posited, the airline/State identity is 'probably the biggest single obstacle to the creation of a liberali[z]ed aviation market.'[113] If we propose a policy of 'denationalizing' the airline industry, therefore, the plurilateral must declare a broad right of establishment, enabling airlines (or private citizens of any contracting party) to establish start-up or subsidiary operations in other territories of the common airspace and to decide merger and acquisition strategy without restrictions on cross-border investment. The Chicago rules on ownership and control of licensed carriers, with their variable numerical and 'evaluative' benchmarks, would be abrogated. At a stroke, debate about the allowable degree of inward investment would be quieted, and two of the most unpredictable DOT administrative procedures – determining carrier citizenship and applying the distorting wand of antitrust immunity – would be eliminated.

Moreover, as we have noted before, the normalization of investment opportunities may well be more economically important (to carriers on both sides of the Atlantic) than the demise of cabotage. Market entry through established players, with in-place competitive networks, has been repeatedly identified as a more likely macroeconomic consequence of opening trade in international aviation.[114] Having stated these elemental precepts, and bearing in mind the surpassing importance of the investment issue to the U.S./EC second stage negotiations, it is worth refreshing some of our earlier discussion of the right of establishment – understood here as the notion of a 'regulatory' as opposed to a 'commercial' nationality.

---

113. Levine, *supra* note 27, at 81.
114. *See supra* Chapter 3, Part V(C).

Neither the U.S./EC Air Transport Agreement of 2007 nor the U.S. DOT's doomed 2005 Notice of Proposed Rulemaking (NPRM) sought to abolish the citizenship purity test, but taken together these instruments proposed significant changes to the test that drew the attention of the aviation community. First, the 2007 Agreement requires the United States to recognize the internal EC legal construct of the 'Community carrier.' Under this concession, an EU airline that is licensed in any Member State is permitted to fly to any U.S. airport from any airport in the EU regardless of the identity of the citizens who own or control it (as long as they are citizens of an ECAA State).[115] As examined in some detail in Chapter 2, the NPRM was an audacious proposal by the DOT to allow foreign investors to exercise actual control over the commercial aspects of a U.S. airline's operations, including sales, marketing, pricing, route selection, and scheduling, while ring-fencing for U.S. citizen control certain areas such as the documents of corporate organization, participation in the Department of Defense Civil Reserve Air Fleet, and issues concerning safety and security. The proposal failed, in large part because of inopportune timing, but it revealed the extent to which U.S. aviation officials have absorbed the frustrations of an industry that is captive to an obsolete ideology in an era of transnational capital and investment that the industry helped to create.

Thus, while the regime change of abolishing the citizenship purity test was not part of the 2007 Agreement or of the DOT's NPRM, these 'straws in the wind' surely point toward the eventual dissolution of tests of this nature. A broader vision of the 'right of establishment' (much broader than Article 43 of the EC Treaty) would still regard an airline's 'nationality' as important, but would de-link commercial and regulatory nationality. Commercial nationality (the right of private investors, regardless of citizenship, to own 50.1% or more of a foreign airline and to manage it without restriction) would be entirely deregulated. But an airline would still have a *regulatory* nationality, a State in which it is incorporated, where it has its principal place of business, where it pays taxes, employs local management and employees, obeys local laws, and is subject to safety, security, and fiscal supervision. The NPRM, through its creative splitting of commercial operations from operations that must be controlled by citizens, implicitly hinted at this distinction between commercial and regulatory nationality.

The 'right of establishment' is an exciting but underappreciated idea in international air transport. If implemented, it will ensure that airlines continue to have a 'national' regulatory affiliation, but without the anti-investment burdens of a narrow citizenship requirement. Congress, which has embraced the WTO, the North American Free Trade Agreement, and more recently the Central American Free Trade Agreement, surely can be informed of the advantages of the right of establishment as a trade-expanding, labor-friendly, and consumer welfare-enhancing

---

115. These so-called seventh freedom services will allow the EU Member States to claim compliance with the 2002 opinion of the European Court of Justice which struck down the ownership and control clauses in their bilateral treaties with third countries as violating the antidiscriminatory freedom of establishment rule in Article 43 of the EC Treaty. *See supra* Chapter 2, Part III(A).

approach to foreign investment in U.S. airlines. The NPRM, unfortunately, was too oblique (and too derivative of the present regime) to be able to make these arguments effectively. Instead, it was too easily depicted by its opponents as merely a collateral attempt, by appeasing the European airlines, to undermine the integrity of the citizenship purity test.[116]

4   Principle 4: An End to Pricing Controls

In both the United States and the EC, deregulation included a complicated process of pricing relaxation based on permitted adjustments to an industry or route 'standard fare.' For the second stage U.S./EC negotiations, there need be little modification of the pricing freedom article in the 2007 agreement, other than elimination of the EC's anticompetitive adherence to price leadership for Community airlines on intra-Union routes.[117] The 2007 agreement also provides for compliance by each party's airlines with requests from the other party for historical, existing, and proposed pricing information.[118] This bureaucratic imposition is a vestige of the classic Chicago system requirement of tariff filing and, at least to the extent it solicits future pricing information, should not be part of a second stage plurilateral.[119] The only form of pricing control in the post-Chicago system, therefore, would be through the *ex post* operation of the competition laws.[120]

While it is outside the scope of this study to discuss in detail the kind of pricing methodologies that might emerge from a completely unrestricted pricing environment, and especially the extent to which novel types of fares or fare restrictions might be developed, it can be assumed that many of the same criteria that currently

---

116. Indeed, it might well be the case that even generalized abstractions like 'right of establishment' are less useful than the simple statement that airline liberalization really consists of 'granting expanded rights to compete in geographically defined markets to selected countries and operators' in whose financial and operating integrity we have confidence. Michael E. Levine [formerly] Adjunct Professor, Yale Law School, Remarks to the Competitive Enterprise Institute, *in Open Aviation for a Global Industry: Removing the Last Barriers to Airline Competition*, Edited Transcript (Aug. 14, 2003).

117. *See* U.S./EC Air Transport Agreement, *supra* note 12, art. 13(2)(a) (incorporating by reference the terms of Article 1(3) of Council Regulation 2409/92 of Jul. 23, 1992). Many U.S. open skies agreements have included a prophylactic intervention mechanism that would trigger in the event of sudden pricing disequilibria that could jeopardize U.S. airlines. That provision, inconsistent with the premise of full pricing freedom, has been dropped in the 2007 Agreement and would not feature in the proposed second stage plurilateral. Note, however, that the European Community's recent consolidation of its common rules for air transport appears implicitly to have superseded the price-leadership restriction contained in the 2007 U.S./EC Air Transport Agreement. *See supra* Chapter 5, notes 128-29 and accompanying text.

118. *See* U.S./EC Air Transport Agreement, *supra* note 12, art. 13(2)(b).

119. Mandatory filing of tariffs is a remnant of regulatory intervention that has survived in U.S. oversight of foreign air transportation and even as an optional element of EC deregulation. For discussion of the U.S. tariff-filing protocols, *see supra* Chapter 4, Part III(C).

120. Even here, however, the usual admonitions about chilling competition through overzealous policing of airline pricing strategies would continue to apply. *See supra* Chapter 4, Part IV(B) (discussing the failures of price predation enforcement in the United States).

shape fare levels – the value of nonstop over direct or connecting flights, the length of time between reservation and travel, the seasonalness of demand patterns, the particular competitive structure of routes (including intermodal competition), the segmentation of business and leisure travel, and the macroeconomic profile of the national and global business climates – will all continue to drive faresetting policy in the second stage plurilateral order.[121]

<table>
<tr><td>5</td><td>**Principle 5: A 'Deep Integration' Program of Regulatory Convergence**</td></tr>
</table>

As considered in Chapter 2, Kees Veenstra's ambitious project for a Transatlantic Common Aviation Area (TCAA) foundered on its intricate proposal for supranational mechanisms to shape common regulatory standards for the contracting States. It is unlikely, given the sharp reaction of U.S. negotiators to what they saw as conceptual overreaching by their European colleagues, that the second stage negotiations will by themselves produce a raft of detailed common regulatory laws and policies. Nonetheless, the premise of the TCAA proposal remains valid: that moving 'beyond' the limitations of the open skies regime will require a truly level regulatory playing field.[122] The TCAA blueprint in fact, was seeking to move the transatlantic air transport industry closer to 'deep integration,' defined in a new glossary of international economics as 'economic integration that goes beyond the removal of formal barriers to trade and includes various ways of reducing the international burden of differing national regulations, such as, for example, mutual recognition and harmoni[z]ation.'[123] Harmonization represents the deepest quantum of integration, and is a proper objective of the second stage plurilateral.

In this concluding treaty-building exercise, therefore, it is important to recollect the lessons learned from our study of the U.S. and EC model jurisdictions and to posit a series of useful (but limited) regulatory principles that will guide the future collaborative evolution of the plurilateral agreement. Specifically, this 'balanced program' encompasses regulatory convergence in three broad spheres of commercial interest: in the competition law principles that safeguard the market freedoms of airline deregulation; in the rejection of State-funded operating aid for airlines; and in the encouragement of a regulatory 'mindset' that seeks market solutions to problems of infrastructural congestion and potential bias in distribution systems, while resisting overexuberant intervention in areas (such as passenger rights) where regulation adds costs but does

---

121. *See generally* Peter P.C. Haanappel, *Tariff Coordination, in* EXTERNAL AVIATION RELATIONS, *supra* note 94, at 33-34.
122. *See generally* Association of European Airlines [AEA], *Towards a Transatlantic Common Aviation Area*, AEA Policy Statement (Sept. 1999) [hereinafter AEA, Transatlantic Common Aviation Area].
123. *See* Deardorff's Online Glossary of International Economics, 'D,' <http://www-personal.umich.edu/~alandear/glossary/d.html#DeepIntegration>.

not necessarily deliver optimal outcomes. Finally, the new plurilateral should recognize the disparities in labor law not only between the United States and the EC, but also within the Member States of the Community, while setting forth broad principles of labor policy that will persuade airline unions on both continents that a market-based plurilateral settlement is capable of protecting and advancing their interests.

The treaty principles presented here will later introduce the possibility of a single supranational institution for dispute resolution, but it is important to recognize that U.S./EC convergence can continue in a second stage plurilateral by expanding the oversight infrastructure of the Joint Committee established under Article 18 of the first-stage agreement.[124] The Committee, which has no analogue in prior open skies bilateral agreements, holds a wide-ranging collaborative and consultative brief on areas of industry interest[125] but lacks either formal deliberative machinery or enforcement procedures to discharge its responsibilities. It should nevertheless be possible in the second stage negotiations to appoint a series of Joint Committee 'working groups' to develop specific proposals for regulatory convergence and to prepare legislative and regulatory drafts for joint adoption by the U.S. and EC political or administrative authorities. If a supranational dispute settlement mechanism becomes part of the second stage plurilateral (as proposed later in this Chapter), its institutional prestige will imbue the Joint Committee with the political clout to allow it to continue to operate by consensus but with a much greater likelihood of practical accomplishment.[126]

---

124. *See* U.S./EC Air Transport Agreement, *supra* note 12, art. 18.
125. The Joint Committee will meet 'at least once a year,' *id*. art. 18(1), and 'operate on the basis of consensus,' *id*. art. 18(6). The Committee is charged to 'develop cooperation' by measures that include 'expert-level exchanges' on new legislative and regulatory initiatives in security, safety, the environment, aviation infrastructure, and consumer protection; and, more generally, consideration of the 'social effects' (*i.e.*, labor implications) of the agreement and possible areas for amendment of the agreement, as well as maintaining an 'inventory of issues' concerning government subsidies, developing 'approaches' to reciprocal recognition of 'regulatory determinations' of airline fitness and citizenship, including a 'common understanding' of the control criteria used by the parties, and consulting on air transport issues raised in international organizations. *Id*. art. 18(4). The Committee is delegated to take a small number of decisions relating to extension of the Community designation clause to new members of the European Common Aviation Area and with respect to application of the effective control rule with respect to certain States. *Id*. annex 4, arts. 1(3) & 2(3). Interestingly, the Committee is also authorized to develop a proposal with respect to extending the Agreement to third countries. *Id*. art. 18(5).
126. *See supra* note 125 (mentioning the consensus procedures of the first-stage Joint Committee). The scrupulously nonpartisan reputation of the dispute settlement mechanism of the WTO, and in particular of its supranational Appellate Body, has undoubtedly served to raise the WTO's political standing among its members – who themselves participate in the organization through consensus rules. *See generally* JOHN H. JACKSON, SOVEREIGNTY, THE WTO AND THE CHANGING FUNDAMENTALS OF INTERNATIONAL LAW (2007); MITSUO MATSUSHITA ET AL., THE WORLD TRADE ORGANIZATION: LAW, PRACTICE, AND POLICY (2d ed. 2006).

a   *Convergence in Air Transport Competition Law and Policy*

i   Introduction: Globalizing Trends in Competition Law
           Enforcement

As our analysis of the U.S. and EC model jurisdictions has shown, liberalization of air services presents the danger of strong private actors replacing government barriers with private restraints.[127] The General Agreement on Tariffs and Trade (GATT) has never included a competition policy, although efforts in this direction are now included in both the GATS and the North American Free Trade Agreement (NAFTA) agreements and the issue has been placed formally on the so-called 'Doha agenda.'[128] Nevertheless, the 'demonstration effect' of EC competition law, a code that – notwithstanding devolution of some enforcement jurisdiction to national competition authorities[129] – is applied multilaterally by a centralized authority, has undoubtedly shaped the emergence of a body of professional and academic opinion favoring the wider transborder and even *globalized* enforcement of competition laws and policies[130] The second stage of U.S./EC air services negotiations will present a laboratory opportunity to exceed the 'sympathetic dialogue' about competition enforcement proposed 20 years ago by ICAO and which has, by and large, continued to mark the upper limits of integration.[131]

---

127. *See* John H. Jackson, *GATT and the Future of International Trade Institutions*, 18 BROOK. J. INT'L L. 11, 24 (1992).

128. *See* WTO, [Doha] *Ministerial Declaration*, paras 23-25, WT/MIN(01)/DEC/1 (Nov. 20, 2001).

129. *See supra* Chapter 5, Part II(D). *See also* ASSIMAKIS KOMNINOS, EC PRIVATE ANTITRUST ENFORCEMENT: DECENTRALISED APPLICATION OF EC COMPETITION LAW BY NATIONAL COURTS (2008).

130. Despite the macroeconomic travails of the Doha round, it is probably fair to say that the current focus on defragmenting international antitrust began with the successful conclusion of the Uruguay Round of GATT negotiations, including the GATS experiment. Specialists in other areas of economic law (securities, intellectual property, and environmental laws, for example) have also been engaged in projects on international harmonization. *See generally* REGULATORY COMPETITION AND ECONOMIC INTEGRATION: COMPARATIVE PERSPECTIVES (Geradin Damien et al. eds., 2001); CHRIS NOONAN, EMERGING PRINCIPLES OF INTERNATIONAL COMPETITION LAW (2008). For a contemporary discussion of historical efforts to multilateralize competition rules, *see* European Commission, *Competition Policy in the New Trade Order: Strengthening International Co-operation and Rules*, at 10, Report of the Group of Experts, COM (95) 359 final (Jul. 12, 1995) [hereinafter Report of the EC Group of Experts]. *See also Competition: Commission Proposes Building World Antitrust Instrument*, 1996 EUR. DOC. RESEARCH REPORT (Jun. 24, 1996), at 2 (while calling the creation of an 'International Competition Authority' premature, European Commission invited the WTO to set up a working group to promote the development of competition rules in individual countries and to promote consensus on common principles internationally).

131. In 1989, ICAO developed a model clause on competition laws to be inserted into bilateral agreements. The clause has a GATT-like focus on buffering conflicts between different systems; it does not seek a common set of substantive principles but is focused on procedural compatibility. *See* Ron Katz, *The Great GATS: General Agreement on Trade in Services and Its Impact on Aviation*, AIRLINE BUS., Sept. 1995, at 81.

Leveraging the extraordinary sectoral exceptionalism of global air transport,[132] I will propose here the feasibility of *combining* the aviation competition laws, policies, and procedural mechanisms of the two jurisdictions (and even the creation of a one-stop joint adjudication and enforcement agency).[133]

Notwithstanding the writings of influential skeptics like Paul Stephan and Judge Diane Wood,[134] fusion of the substantive and procedural competition codes of our two model jurisdictions can no longer be dismissed as the utopian fantasy of 'one-world' antitrust enthusiasts. Both jurisdictions have worked tirelessly over the last two decades to encourage a global competition culture. Among the manifestations of this leadership is the International Competition Network, a forum that connects enforcers in over 100 countries to promote parallelism in competition law theory and practice.[135] Bilaterally, the authorities in both of our model jurisdictions have become much more sensitized to the 'external' effects of their competition law enforcement. Each jurisdiction subscribes to a fairly generalized scheme of transatlantic antitrust cooperation, the result of a U.S./EC international agreement concluded in 1991.[136] This agreement speaks in the language of diplomacy rather than normative obligation, inviting each party to demonstrate 'comity' in its relations with the other, either *positive comity* (to act on the request of the other party)[137] or *negative comity* (when each party acts, to take into

---

132. *See supra* text accompanying note 93 (discussing the 'exceptionalism' of global air transport, particularly in its historical insulation from international trade talks).

133. Despite Professor Eleanor Fox's enthusiasm for internationalizing antitrust enforcement, she draws back from what she calls 'the comprehensive approach' of a world competition code. Surely she is correct in her fears of an impossible technocracy, interstate tensions and a code so generalized as to be meaningless. Eleanor M. Fox, *Competition Law and the Agenda for the WTO*, 4 Pacific Rim L. & Pol'y J. 1, 34 (1995); *see also* Michael J. Trebilcock & Robert Howse, The Regulation of International Trade 599 (2005) (stating that a world competition code would not be 'attractive even if [it] were feasible' due to the 'significant benefits to maintaining independent policies, including divergent objectives across countries and divergent means of achieving those objectives'). The plurilateral approach, in contrast, is modeled precisely on the integration accomplished by likeminded States within the original European common market.

134. *See, e.g.*, Paul B. Stephan, *Global Governance, Antitrust, and the Limits of International Cooperation*, 38 Cornell Int'l L.J. 173 (2005); Diane P. Wood, *The Impossible Dream: Real International Antitrust*, 1992 U. Chi. Legal F. 277 (1992).

135. *See generally* International Competition Network, <http://www.internationalcompetition network.org/index.php/en/home>.

136. *See* Agreement between the Government of the United States of America and the Commission of the European Community Regarding Application of Their Competition Laws, 1995 O.J. (L 95) 1 (Sept. 23, 1991), *as corrected by* 1995 O.J. (L 134) 1, *reprinted in* 4 Trade Reg. Rep. (CCH) ¶ 13,504, at 21,233-9 [hereinafter U.S./EC Antitrust Agreement]. Note, however, that on Aug. 9, 1994, the European Court of Justice, at the prompting of the French Government, invalidated this agreement on the basis that it was an international agreement that had not been duly approved by the Council of Ministers representing the Member States of the 'European Community' (as required by EC Treaty art. 300). *See* Case C-327/91, French Republic v. Comm'n, 1994 E.C.R. I-3461. The procedural irregularity was subsequently corrected in 1995 and the agreement is again current.

137. *See* U.S./EC Antitrust Agreement, *supra* note 136, art. V. Positive comity was further elaborated in the 1998 Agreement Between the European Communities and the Government of the

account important interests of the other).[138] Further, the scope of cooperation is limited to investigations and sharing of information and has no substantive law reach.[139]

Despite its self-imposed boundaries, however, the 1991 agreement should be viewed synchronically rather than diachronically as a process evolving toward more intensive case-by-case cooperation as circumstances allow (and, on occasion, toward moments of further soft normativity).[140] The dialectical thrust of the 1991 agreement and of related bilateral U.S./EC initiatives has not been so much to impress uniformity as to encourage a shared philosophical outlook that condemns the most harmful violations and seeks to reduce the expense of time and costs associated with the inevitable complexity of antitrust

---

United States on the Application of Positive Comity Principles in the Enforcement of their Competition Laws, 1998 O.J. (L 173) 28. The 1998 agreement does not, however, apply to merger control cases. *See id.* Under positive comity, States whose important interests are affected by restrictive practices in the territory of another State may call upon that other State to deal with the situation by applying its own laws. Article IV of the 1998 agreement includes a forbearance principle under which one party defers or suspends its enforcement activities in favor of the other party taking the lead against the anticompetitive activity. Some commentators regard positive comity as an empty construct, noting for example that forbearance is unlikely in respect of large-scale multinational mergers. *See* Alexandr Svetlicinii, *Cooperation Between Merger Control Authorities of the EU and U.S.*, 7 U.C. Davis Bus. L. J. 171, 178-80 (2006). In the *Boeing/McDonnell Douglas* merger, EU Competition Commissioner Karel van Miert warned that the Commission would impose prohibitive fines on Boeing, and even seize Boeing aircraft flying into EU airspace, if the merger were consummated without Commission approval. *See* Edmund L. Andrews, *Boeing Concession Averts Trade War With Europe*, N.Y. Times, Jul. 24, 1997, at A1.

138. *See* U.S./EC Antitrust Agreement, *supra* note 136, art. VI.

139. *See* Svetlicinii, *supra* note 137, at 173 (noting that the agreement is based on voluntariness and good will). The typical environment for this kind of procedural cooperation would involve harm inflicted in one jurisdiction (for example, the consequences of a horizontal boycott) by perpetrators resident or domiciled in the other. Even at this more confined level, however, the U.S. and EC authorities have cooperated not only in cartel enforcement but also concerning claims of abuse of dominance and monopolization (most notably with respect to the Microsoft Corporation). *See generally* Richard L. Gordon, Antitrust Abuse in the New Economy: The Microsoft Case (2002); William H. Page & John E. Lopatka, The Microsoft Case: Antitrust, High Technology, and Consumer Welfare (2007). Actual prosecution of the conduct, however, would remain territorial; the United States was not offering to summon U.S. companies to the federal courts for violations of EC competition law, nor will U.S. courts be accessible to the European Commission for that purpose. *See* Chapter 4, note 574 (discussing an investigation into alleged price-fixing by British Airways executives).

140. *See, e.g.*, European Commission, *Report to the Council and Parliament on the Application of the EC-US Agreement Between 1 January 1999 and 31 December 1999*, COM (2000) 618 final (Oct. 4, 2000). The arrangement is a memorandum of understanding that specifies the possibility of organizing joint hearings and meetings with the parties and both competition authorities. *See also* the U.S./EU Merger Working Group, which has prepared a 'best practices' protocol aimed at large, politically sensitive mergers and which emphasizes accepted practices such as nondisclosure waivers by the parties, joint meetings and conferences, and certain preferred timing options. *See* European Commission, US/EU Merger Working Group, *Best Practices for Cooperation in Merger Cases* (2002). *See also supra* note 137 (adverting to the 1998 U.S./EC 'positive comity' agreement).

investigations. The EC's 'cartel directorate,' for example, is an infrastructural enhancement clearly influenced by the pioneering work of the U.S. Department of Justice (DOJ).[141]

A *philosophical* convergence between the United States and the EC will ultimately prove much more significant to the future of competition law and policy than the divergent inflections of their existing substantive laws (such as the well-traversed distinction that supposedly separates the Community's notion of dominant position from the Sherman Act's precepts on monopoly).[142] Both jurisdictions now insist on open and even aggressive competition, and both accept that big companies are vital to their economies and that abuse of dominance, not dominance itself, should be the 'trigger for reproach.'[143] Of immediate pertinence, Article 20 of the 2007 U.S./EC Air Transport Agreement binds both sides to U.S. judicial precedent (and to a shared philosophy) when it confirms that the parties 'apply their respective competition regimes to protect and enhance overall competition and not individual competitors.'[144]

In its overall philosophy, however, the 2007 U.S./EC Air Transport Agreement genuflects to the current prioritization of cooperation over convergence. From a U.S. perspective, one notices immediately that the agreement governs only the limited international competition jurisdiction currently exercised by the DOT, and eschews any reference to the enforcement responsibilities or activities of the DOJ (the Department which typically acts as the U.S. Government's primary antitrust agency). Thus, in light of the impermissibility of U.S./EU transnational airline mergers and acquisitions, the sole focus of the Annex is on DOT and European

---

141. *See* Neelie Kroes, European Commissioner for Competition Policy, *Developments in Antitrust Policy in the EU and the U.S.*, Speech to the C. Peter McColough Series on International Economics, The Council on Foreign Relations, N.Y., at 2, Speech/06/494 (Sept. 15, 2006) [hereinafter Kroes Speech].

142. *See id.* at 3 (considering this distinction to be an 'overstatement'). The process of substantive convergence has accelerated in recent years and includes not just cartel and merger enforcement but also leniency policies for cooperating individuals and corporations. Of particular note is the European Commission's revised Merger Regulation in 2004 where the standard for violation changed from 'creating or strengthening a dominant position' to 'significantly imped[ing] effective competition,' which now resembles the U.S. test of 'substantial lessening of competition' in its heightened focus on effects rather than on traditional benchmarks of market dominance such as number of firms and market shares. *See* Ilene Knable Gotts et al., *Nature vs. Nurture and Reaching the Age of Reason: The U.S./EU Treatment of Transatlantic Mergers*, 61 N.Y.U. Ann. Surv. Am. L. 453, 491-92 (2005). *See supra* Chapter 5, Part II(D) (discussing the EC merger regulation). In noting these substantive alignments, however, we cannot dismiss gratuitously the real differences in competition *policy* that still separate the U.S. and EC enforcement authorities. As noted elsewhere in this study, EC competition policy has frequently blended with considerations of industrial policy and the encouragement of 'national champions,' while U.S. merger review continues to evince a bias toward consumer-friendly 'efficiencies.' For a considered treatment of some of these issues, *see* Gotts et al., *supra*.

143. *Id.*

144. U.S./EC Air Transport Agreement, *supra* note 12, art. 20 (calling also for 'differences' in the application of their respective antitrust regimes to be minimized, and for 'cooperation' to promote comparable regulatory results – especially with respect to intercarrier agreements).

Commission approval of agreements, alliances, and other cooperative arrangements among airlines involving international air transportation (including DOT-sanctioned antitrust immunity and Commission exemptions).[145]

Within that circumscribed jurisdictional framework, the Annex unfolds as a sector-specific acknowledgment and acceptance of the principles of cooperation and comity pursued by the DOJ and the European Commission under the 1991 agreement.[146] Thus, Article 2 defines the purpose of 'cooperation' between the respective agencies as including enhancement of mutual understanding, reduction of conflicts, and pursuit of compatible regulatory approaches.[147] In the matter of 'comity,' there are provisions for semiannual meetings to discuss developments in and analytical strategies to assess the international air transport industry, consultations on specific cases where requested, and pledges of timely notifications to the other party on requests for approval of cooperative agreements (including antitrust immunity or block exemption requests).[148] All of this 'comity,' however, remains subject to the confidentiality laws and practices that apply on each side, and to a nebulous (and therefore highly deployable) right to withhold information where disclosure 'would be incompatible with important interests' of the agency holding the information.[149]

---

145. *Id.* annex 2, art. 4(4).
146. *Id.* annex 2, art. 6 (expressly acknowledging that the Annex is intended to be implemented 'without prejudice' to the 1991 agreement (although that agreement is denominated with little pretense to technical accuracy)). Under the International Antitrust Enforcement Assistance Act of 1994 (IAEAA), incidentally, the United States enlarged its *general* commitment to collaborative enforcement. *See* Pub. L. No. 103-438, 108 Stat. 4597. In brief, the statute authorized the U.S. Assistant Attorney General for Antitrust and the Federal Trade Commission to enter into antitrust 'mutual assistance agreements' with competition agencies in foreign jurisdictions. The Act permits the Department of Justice and the FTC to reciprocate assistance and information provided by foreign agencies by sharing investigative information that was previously prohibited from disclosure by confidentiality provisions in the Antitrust Civil Process Act, the Federal Trade Commission Act, and the Hart-Scott-Rodino Act (grand jury secrecy rules would mostly not be affected). H.R. Rep. No. 103-772, at 8 (1994) [hereinafter IAEAA House Report] (emphasizing that only true reciprocity and strict confidentiality requirements will allow U.S. cooperation to occur). To the advantage of U.S. enforcement, the legislation enables U.S. competition agencies to obtain the aid of their foreign counterparts in gathering evidence from private firms or individuals that are beyond the jurisdictional grasp of the United States (and that have been subject in the past to so-called 'blocking statutes'). *Id.* at 11. Future-oriented business planning information filed under Hart-Scott premerger review procedures are not disclosable under the new assistance agreements, nor is information classified for national defense or foreign policy reasons. EC protection of confidential data is ensured by EC regulations, but the European Commission is entitled to conclude an international agreement that, in return for certain negotiated guarantees, derogates from the internal rules. *See* Report of the EC Group of Experts, *supra* note 130, at 14. The 1991 agreement, however, was not revised to reflect the wider collaborative authority conferred by the 1994 statute.
147. U.S./EC Air Transport Agreement, *supra* note 12, annex 2, art. 2.
148. *Id.* art. 4.
149. In brief, EC laws condition disclosure to the U.S. authorities on the express agreement of the source, *see, e.g.*, 1995 O.J. (L131) 38 (and other instruments), while the U.S. antitrust agencies

Other than sweeping a new agency into the scope of transnational antitrust cooperation, therefore, the 2007 first stage U.S./EC agreement makes little if any substantive or procedural advance on the generic undertakings of the 1991 cooperation agreement. But, once again, it is the dynamic of international comity that is interesting here, rather than the precise degree to which comity is now practiced. With a record of inconsistency in its application, and the natural effects of conflicting political and institutional interests, one can easily point to particular investigations where the cooperation mechanism performed suboptimally.[150] While we could posit numerous corrective amendments and enhancements – mandatory positive comity or preclusion of double sanctions or even an enforcement mechanism, for example[151] – the more fundamental shift towards substantive convergence, particularly with respect to the merger control process, is of immensely greater portent.[152] This slowly evolving confluence of codes may well have been inspired by the cooperation agenda, but no matter; it is a discernible trend that foreshadows the future convergence of U.S. and EC competition laws.

A final cautionary note needs to be added, however, before turning to some more specific institutional and substantive principles of enforcement. While EC and U.S. perspectives broadly coincide, any kind of commonality in enforcement – whether through domestic application of a common air transport competition code or a supranational competition authority for the international airline industry – will succeed only by accepting former European Competition Commissioner Sir Leon Brittan's longstanding premise that competition policy must be applied in its own

---

can disclose confidential information only on the basis of a reciprocity arrangement (which is obviously not the case in relations with the European Community). *See* IAEAA, *supra* note 146, sec. 12(2)(B). To avoid the destructive impact of timing differences between the U.S. and EC review processes, parties in high-profile disputes have tended to grant blanket nondisclosure waivers to the competition agencies on both sides of the Atlantic. *See* Svetlicinii, *supra* note 137, at 173-74. In the *Microsoft* investigation the company consented to the exchange, which permitted closer cooperation under which the two authorities negotiated an eventual settlement. *See* Report of the EC Group of Experts, *supra* note 130, at 7. That Report also expressed concern that an unduly restrictive interpretation of the concept of comity would make it applicable only in the (rare) cases where a firm could not comply with the requirements imposed by one jurisdiction except by infringing the law of another jurisdiction. *See id.* at 10.

150. Probably the most spectacular divergence occurred in the investigations of the GE/Honeywell merger in 2001, approved by the U.S. Department of Justice but rejected by the European Commission amidst mutual recriminations about failure to take into account the other party's critical interests. *See* Svetlicinii, *supra* note 137, at 182-87. *See also* Pinar Karacan, *Differences in Merger Analysis Between the United States and the European Union in the Context of the Boeing/McDonnell and GE/Honeywell Mergers*, 17 Transnat'l Law. 209 (2004); Kyle Robertson, *One Law to Control Them All: International Merger Analysis in the Wake of GE/Honeywell*, 31 B.C. Int'l & Comp. L. Rev. 153 (2008); Douglas K. Schnell, *All Bundled Up: Bringing the Failed GE/Honeywell Merger in From the Cold*, 37 Cornell Int'l L.J. 217 (2004).

151. Indeed, a species of mandatory comity will be proposed below as part of a framework for a common body of transnational air transport antitrust laws.

152. Thus, with respect to the IAEAA, *see supra* note 146, while the scope of that statute remains adjectival rather than substantive, the responsible House Committee explicitly encouraged 'the development of a higher degree of concordance with respect to substantive doctrine.' IAEAA House Report, *supra* note 146, at 8.

right, independently, and not merely as an adjunct to the shifting proclivities of national industrial policy (and of its handmaiden, political expediency).[153]

ii   A Proposal for Competition Surveillance of the Airlines

In examining how best to apply competition law principles to the transnational air transport industry, two distinct questions are presented. First, there is the question of which agencies – domestic or supranational – will screen intercarrier agreements, mergers, and acquisitions, as well as monitor and suppress abuse of dominance, price manipulation, and other anticompetitive practices. Relatedly, there is the second question of which tribunals – domestic or supranational – will be charged with dispute settlement when decisions of the enforcement agencies are challenged or when industry stakeholders seek autonomously to apply the competition laws against their rivals. Given the panoply of modern enforcement (in the United States, dual federal agencies, 50 state agencies, and the federal courts system; in the EC, the European Commission, the EC and national court systems, and the 27 separate national competition authorities), one may ask whether it is feasible to imagine a sectoralized common body of competition law applied within each jurisdiction or, more radically, a sectoralized supranational agency applying such a body of law. Given the recalcitrance of the U.S. air transport establishment when presented with the supranational institution-making that characterized the Association of European Airlines' (AEA) proposed TCAA, one approaches further such 'cosmopolitan' initiatives with an abiding sense of caution.

Nonetheless, while appreciating U.S. suspicions of supranational 'tribunal creep,' to encourage the second stage negotiators to boldness I propose here that the separate enforcement agencies (the U.S. DOJ and the European Commission) exercise primary jurisdiction,[154] that they apply a common body of air transport competition laws and policies, that they apply a rule of abstention whereby one agency defers to the other in accordance with established criteria, and that they accept the jurisdiction of a supranational dispute settlement and review tribunal, discussed below, which will have general jurisdiction over *all* disputes – whether or not related to competition law – arising between or among States and private parties under the second stage plurilateral. While the common code and the rule of

---

153. *See* comments in IAEAA House Report *supra* note 146, at 8-11, where the House Judiciary Committee noted an EC 'administrative' tradition (supposedly absent in the United States), of implementing competition policies, which changes 'abruptly and often with political developments,' rather than an enforcement approach that derives from antitrust being considered a 'field of law.' These statements must surely have been intended as tongue-in-cheek, given the perceptible shifts in the enforcement 'mood' that have accompanied changes in the ideological complexion of U.S. presidential administrations.

154. Given that the plurilateral will permit transnational mergers and acquisitions, it would be incongruous to maintain the DOT's inherited (and anomalous) jurisdiction in international air transportation, including its power to award antitrust immunity to would-be competitors entering alliances. *See supra* Chapter 4, Part III(C). To the extent that alliance-making remains necessary with States outside the plurilateral, the DOT should probably continue to administer these powers; for intra-plurilateral economic relations, however, the Department of Justice should henceforth act as the U.S. domestic enforcement agency (as it does for domestic U.S. airline competition).

abstention will be considered in more detail here, a full discussion of the supranational arbitral tribunal is reserved for the discussion below since the tribunal will itself constitute a general principle of the second stage plurilateral.

(a)   Shaping a Common Body of Competition Law

The existing and evolving points of symmetry between the U.S. and EC competition laws, noted above, will supply both the substantive and procedural rules to regulate *international* airline competition – or, more properly, airline competition with *international effects* – within the new unified plurilateral airspace. As Judge Diane Wood has pointed out, taking a brief hiatus from her attacks on international antitrust rules as 'utterly impractical' and 'downright dangerous,' '[t]he number of terms that require definition is surprisingly small, and the number of key principles that [a common body of laws] would need to reflect is even smaller.'[155] A coherent point of departure, for example, would harmonize the premerger notification and approval procedures that both jurisdictions have implemented through the Hart-Scott-Rodino Act and the Merger Regulation, respectively.[156] A single merger notification form and schedule could readily be adopted, as well as common data requests and common time limits for the examination of cases.[157]

Substantively, the observed linkages between the Sherman/Clayton paradigm and Articles 81 and 82 of the Treaty of Rome point unmistakably to a unified code on intercarrier agreements, merger enforcement, and abuse of market dominance, a trend that our preceding discussion has already discerned.[158] 'Hard-core' horizontal cartels relating to the fixing of prices, restriction of capacity, or the sharing of markets would also be prohibited.[159] Other types of cooperation, such as marketing alliances, would be judged (as they are today) by a standard of reasonableness, and prohibited where they are likely to have anticompetitive effects or to confer market power on the alliance partners.[160] There will no *a priori* restrictions

---

155. Diane P. Wood, *Antitrust at the Global Level (Symposium)*, 72 U. Chi. L. Rev. 309, 315 (2005). In fact, Wood lists only 16 major concepts (including merger, market power, monopoly, and cartel), not all of which would have relevance to international air transportation.
156. *See generally* Fox, *supra* note 133, at 33.
157. *See* Gotts et al., *supra* note 142, at 503 (comparing U.S. and EC approaches to 'second phase' investigations).
158. 'It is striking that, on paper, the similarities in the competition laws of major trading nations are much greater than the differences. It is only sensible therefore to build upon this developing consensus and mechanisms to ensure the proper enforcement of what exists, in the interests of more open markets and the reduction of trade friction.' Sir Leon Brittan, *Competition Law: Its Importance to the European Community and to International Trade*, Speech to the University of Chicago Law School, at 11 (Apr. 24, 1992).
159. These practices might be described, in Foxian terminology, as 'consensus principles' leading to 'consensus wrongs' by violators. Fox, *supra* note 133, at 31.
160. The detailed elaboration of a common antitrust code for international air transport lies beyond the scope of this book, but in any event an accessible model is already available in the form of the draft GATT Plurilateral Agreement on an International Antitrust Code (the 'Munich Code'), *reprinted in* 65 Antitrust & Trade Reg. Rep. (BNA) S-1, No. 1628 (Special Supp. Aug. 19, 1993)

on continued airline cooperation. To the extent that code-sharing arrangements purchase access to internal cabotage opportunities or long-haul routes subject to limited designation, they will be superfluous, but their continued employment as a cost-efficient way to build network capability cannot be discounted.

Finally, we have also noted earlier the evolving consensus that binds U.S. and EC competition *policy* – most notably, within the framework of the 2007 U.S./EC Air Transport Agreement, acceptance of the U.S. precept that competition regimes exist to enhance overall competition and not to safeguard individual competitors.[161] As Judge Wood has emphasized, the sole purpose of competition law should be to suppress business practices that harm economic welfare (practices that lead to overcharges, underpayments, or anticompetitive exclusion from markets and that in turn lead to higher prices, lower quality, and less innovation).[162] Competing objectives of industrial or business policy, such as guaranteeing employment or preserving small business operators, would be impossible to reconcile within the framework of an international antitrust code.[163]

(b)   A Rule of Abstention for Competition Enforcement Agencies

Assuming that both the U.S. and EC enforcement agencies were to apply an ever-converging code of air transport competition law and policy, problems of multiple and competing scrutiny by different jurisdictions (and hence of conflicting outcomes) would still be presented. To reduce or eliminate those contingencies, I propose to invigorate the comity principles introduced in the 1991 U.S./EC agreement using a general rule of abstention that either enforcement agency would be expected to observe in accordance with criteria assigning enforcement priority to one or the other. Under this system, only one agency would screen a particular transaction (a merger, for example) or examine a specific allegation of anticompetitive activity, but would act on behalf of both agencies.[164]

The development of criteria for enforcement priority would be a matter for the treaty negotiators,[165] but a recent article by Dutch jurist Rutger Jan toe Laer offers a sample set of criteria for prioritizing potentially conflicting agency review of

---

(with commentary, *id.* at 259-60). An alternative 'minimal' approach, comprising 15 principles, was endorsed by Professor Eleanor M. Fox and other members of the drafting group. *See id.* at S-7 to S-9.

161. *See supra* in the main text.
162. *See* Wood, *supra* note 155, at 316.
163. *See id.*
164. The conditions for the rule of abstention would have to be sufficiently adaptable to allow future plurilateral adherents to apply them in their relations with other members of the agreement.
165. To the extent that these proposed changes will require modulation of U.S. enforcement policy (though not necessarily any amendment of U.S. law), their incorporation into an Article II treaty will provide legal ballast to overcome the 'psychological' barrier of renouncing jurisdiction in favor of a foreign agency. *See* H. S. Rutger Jan toe Laer, *Kick-Starting Cross-border Alliances: Approval and Clearance; the Past, the Present and the Future*, 32 Air & Space L. 287, 314 n.95 (2007) ('being designated the exclusive agency in a one-stop approval system is something different [from mere cooperation] and will require separate (probably Treaty) language'). On the U.S. constitutional issues raised by supranational adjudication, *see infra* note 201.

transnational code-share alliances.[166] While toe Laer's analysis seems predicated on the survival of the nationality rule (the *raison d'être* of such alliances), his central thesis, which is essentially to suggest that all international airline transactions have a natural center of jurisdictional gravity, could apply with equal force to future review of transnational mergers and acquisitions in a post-Chicago order. Adapting toe Laer's 'one-stop approval system' to mergers, therefore, would allow us to designate the 'proper' enforcement agency[167] as lying in the jurisdiction identified through a range of objective and cumulative criteria including where the merger has the most important consequences for the consumer and other relevant market players, where the merger partner with the largest network is located (measuring the network by city-pairs multiplied by available revenue kilometers), and where the merger partner with the highest historical revenue base over a representative number of years is located.[168]

As a corrective to what he concedes are potential deficiencies in his analysis (large domestic networks, for example, may be 'far removed' from the main commercial hubs of the prospective merger partners),[169] toe Laer insists that the 'non-active' agency – the enforcement agency against which the priority criteria tilt – must be kept 'closely coordinated' by the selected authority.[170]

iii   Conclusion

Having sketched a competition enforcement model that relies on common substantive and procedural rules applied in the first instance by existing U.S. and EC competition agencies, I will complete the discussion in Principle 6, which examines the potential role of a new supranational agency, the Air Transport Commission, as a forum for general dispute settlement under the second stage plurilateral but also for appellate review of these agencies' determinations. Meanwhile, I turn now to revisit two further arenas of controversy – public subsidies and infrastructural manipulation and constraints – that may continue to influence the vitality of competition under the plurilateral.

b   *The End of Operating Aid for Failing Carriers*

'De-nationalization' does not necessarily implicate a wholesale privatization of flag carriers. As we discussed in Chapter 5, the EC Treaty, for example, 'adopts a neutral stance on the question of whether a State opts for public or private

---

166. *See* toe Laer, *supra* note 165, at 306.
167. U.S. civil litigation practice, for example, recognizes that the 'proper court' in which to commence suit will have at least territorial and subject matter jurisdiction. Geoffrey Hazard et al., Pleading and Procedure 145 (9th ed. 2005).
168. *See* toe Laer, *supra* note 165, at 311-312. The toe Laer analysis includes an elaborate algorithmic formula for working out the identity of the 'largest' alliance/merger partner. *See id.* at 312.
169. *See id.* at 311.
170. *Id.* at 312 (suggesting earlier U.S./EC antitrust cooperation agreements as appropriate models).

ownership' of airlines and airports.[171] Public ownership remains entirely compatible with Community law – indeed, is specifically contemplated in certain Treaty provisions – provided that States do not misapply their proprietary powers to skew the market against privately owned competitors (or rival flag carriers, for that matter).[172]

The critical issue, of course, is not whether air carriers are *per se* the property of their governments, but whether they benefit from unfair public bounty, either directly through subsidies, low-interest loans or guarantees, or indirectly through a myriad of 'targeted' preferences (such as special fuel tax exemptions, for example). In principle, direct and indirect State aids will be proscribed under the second stage plurilateral. Governments, to the extent they retain ownership stakes in airline enterprises, will be expected to act as commercially responsible shareholders and not as financial guarantors of last resort, willing to absorb operating losses or to fund the hostile takeover of troublesome competitors. Only public investment that satisfies the test developed by the European Commission – the so-called 'market economy investor' benchmark – will be sanctioned.[173]

As the Alitalia and Olympic case studies continue to demonstrate,[174] pockets of sovereign resistance will no doubt be encountered: some governments, for example, will always feel uncomfortable with the idea that a formerly 'national' airline, faced with economic extinction, could be taken over by a *State-owned* foreign carrier. Yet that contingency cannot be excluded in a transnational marketplace in which strategic industrial policy (of the kind that still permeates EC policy) will no longer be practiced.[175] Government operating aid to failing air carriers, however, should be the only explicit a prioristic restraint on public subsidies within the plurilateral. Otherwise, public grants of aid should be filtered through objective criteria modeled on prior practices of the European Commission under Article 87 of the EC Treaty and of the WTO under its subsidies agreement.[176] In particular, the WTO's brief list

---

171. Community Guidelines on Financing of Airports and Start-Up Aid to Airlines Departing from Regional Airports, para. 30, 2005 O.J. (C 312) 1. *See also* EC Treaty art. 295. The principle of public/private neutrality in Article 295 of the EC Treaty was underscored – in the context of public aids – by the EC delegation in the Memorandum of Consultations that accompanied the U.S./EC Air Transport Agreement. *See* U.S./EC Air Transport Agreement, *supra* note 12, Memorandum of Consultations, para. 34. The U.S. delegation responded, without elaboration, that government ownership of an airline 'may' adversely affect international air transport competition. Nothing is said in the Agreement or in the Memorandum about the parallel EC charge that the U.S. bankruptcy legislation sometimes functions as a statutory public safety net for U.S. carriers. *See supra* Chapter 5, note 590 and accompanying text.

172. *See supra* Chapter 5, Part III(G).

173. *See supra* text accompanying Chapter 5, note 596.

174. *See supra* Chapter 5, Part III(F).

175. As noted, one of the available prophylactic measures to screen inward investment – and to guard against potential unfair subsidization – by government-owned foreign airlines is to permit official agency review of all externally initiated air carrier mergers, acquisitions, or subsidiary set-ups. *See* text accompanying Chapter 2, note 100 (discussing the potential application of the Foreign Investment and National Security Act to foreign investments in U.S. carriers).

176. On the evolution and application of the WTO Agreement on Subsidies and Countervailing Measures, *see* SIMON LESTER & BRYAN MERCURIO, WORLD TRADE LAW 421 (2008).

of nonactionable (exempted) subsidies, including support for research and development, regional and peripheral development, and adaptive environmental compliance, was selected as minimally trade-distorting and aligns with the similar policy goals of Article 87(3) of the EC Treaty.[177]

Article 14 of the 2007 U.S./EC Air Transport Agreement recognizes the adverse effects of 'government subsidies' on international air transport competition and provides that the parties may 'submit observations' to one another (and convene the Joint Committee) if either party considers or provides a subsidy with actual or potential adverse effects. While this pusillanimous notification process is not likely by itself to have dissuasive influence, the Article also grants an unorthodox authorization to each party to 'approach' national, provincial, and even local entities of the other party with respect to suspected unlawful subsidies. While the character of the 'approach' and of any expected outcome remain undefined, the Article explicitly confers a power to make 'direct contact' with State and sub-State officials.[178]

This extraordinary license to bypass conventional aerodiplomacy – as inchoate as it seems as a matter of public international law – suggests an intent on both sides of the first-stage agreement that a challengeable subsidy should have significant transnational effects in the plurilateral territory, and that a challenge that meets these criteria should be rare. Under the second stage plurilateral, grievances concerning State subsidies would be directly actionable by affected carriers or by States using the supranational jurisdiction of the Air Transport Commission proposed earlier.

c   *Resetting the Tempo of Regulation: Abstention and Convergence*

The U.S. and EC deregulation experiences – the revocation of CRS rules in the United States[179] and the adoption of statutory passenger rights in the EC,[180] for

---

177. *See id.* at 447 (noting, however, that as a technical matter the relevant provisions of the WTO subsidies agreement are no longer in force).

178. U.S./EC Air Transport Agreement, *supra* note 12, art. 14(2)-(3).

179. The future of computer reservations systems has become a much less pressing concern for competition in a plurilateral system. Throughout this study we have been skeptical of the impulse to regulate the CRS phenomenon, and indeed the withdrawal of air carriers from 'host' ownership has caused the cessation of all CRS regulation in the United States. *See supra* Chapter 4, Part IV(B). The general principle of nondiscrimination, and the available remedies of the antitrust and competition laws (as well as appellate review by the Air Transport Commission) would seem to be a sufficient exercise of *a priori* supervision. No strong case has been made in either of our model jurisdictions for specific regulation of loyalty programs such as travel agency commissions and frequent flier programs. Although the Joint Committee might maintain a watching brief on emerging competitive trends in these programs, no regulatory intervention in either area is proposed as part of the plurilateral agreement.

180. The market-driven effects of the U.S. voluntary (and contract-based) codes of passenger rights have recently included more generous overbooking compensation for passengers as U.S. airlines maximize capacity and reduce frequency in the face of oil price spikes and economic

example – teach us that regulatory enthusiasms wax and wane, and that a general principle of abstention should guide governments in their administrative scrutiny of air transport economic regulation. To the extent that regulatory action continues to be contemplated under the auspices of the plurilateral agreement and the Joint Committee, however, it should be in the direction of convergence and harmonization (as discussed above).

It is beyond our present scope to consider safety, security, and environmental regulatory activity, although a perceptible trend toward environmental taxation and charges at Community[181] and Member State[182] levels in the EU raises

---

downturns. *See* Ed Perkins, *Bumping Compensation Shows Improvement*, CHI. TRIBUNE, Apr. 27, 2008, at C5; Laura McCandlish, *Bumped Travelers Get More Cash*, BALTIMORE SUN, Apr. 17, 2008, at 1A. The EU statutory system, as we have seen, has encountered major administrative difficulties, and is beset by noncompliance by airlines exploiting its wide 'exceptional circumstances' loophole. *See supra* Chapter 5, Part III(C).

181. The IATA/ICAO position supports a global emissions trading scheme (ETS) (although the EU Member States have filed a reservation to the ICAO proposal, *see* ICAO, *Extracts of A36-Min. EX/11 and A36-Min. EX/10*, Reservations Made to Assembly Resolutions A36-22 and A36-28 (Feb. 25, 2008)), provided that it is properly designed and in lockstep with infrastructure enhancements, technological improvements, and research and development into alternative fuels. The EC proposal, controversially, is both regional and unilateral in scope and does not prioritize technological and infrastructure improvements and research and development. Through promotion of its ETS, the Community appears to acknowledge that its antiquated air traffic management (ATM) systems cause some percentage of greenhouse gas emissions. Yet, from the U.S. perspective, the EC proposal to include aviation in the existing ETS does not give the airlines credit for emissions caused by ATM inefficiencies that are beyond the industry's control. There is also a striking difference of interpretation between U.S. and EC officials as to the compatibility of the ETS with the Chicago Convention (and in particular with Article 15 on 'airport and similar charges'). For example, in the opinion of former senior U.S. transportation official Andrew Steinberg, 'no [contracting] State [to the Chicago Convention] may condition the right of transit over or entry into or exit from its territory of any aircraft of another [contracting] State on their operator's payment of fees, dues, or other charges.' Andrew Steinberg, U.S. Assistant Secretary of Transportation, Aviation and International Affairs, Comments in the Executive Committee of the Council of the International Civil Aviation Organization on Agenda Item 17 Concerning Aviation Emissions (Sept. 22, 2007); *see also* Convention on International Civil Aviation art. 15, Apr. 4, 1947, 15 U.N.T.S. 295. In Steinberg's estimation, that is precisely the effect of the Community's ETS proposal. *See* Steinberg, *supra*. The EC perspective has been to view the ETS not as a fee, due, or charge, but rather as 'an administrative scheme which obliges air operators to monitor and report their emissions and gives them the option of whether to operate within their allocated allowances or to exceed those allowances by buying additional allowances.' *See* Letter from John Balfour, Partner, Clyde & Co., to Peter Liese, Member of the European Parliament, *The Proposed Extension of the EC Emissions Trading Scheme to Aviation and the Chicago Convention*, para. 15 (Nov. 19, 2007) (copy on file with author). *See also* CE, GIVING WINGS TO EMISSIONS TRADING 176-77 (2005) (report prepared for the European Commission) (further denying that the ETS falls under Article 15, but noting that, even if it did, 'it would just imply that foreign aircraft should be treated as national aircraft').

182. *See supra* Chapter 2, note 278 (discussing the growing incidence of 'environmental' taxes and charges among EU Member States, including the U.K.'s Air Passenger Duty, nitrogen oxide charges in Switzerland and Germany, and the introduction of a ticket tax by the Government of the Netherlands for passengers departing from Dutch airports).

significant issues of economic intervention and may introduce early conflict in the U.S./EC second stage negotiations. In this discussion, we will focus attention on two areas of pressing regulatory concern that would occupy the minds of the Joint Committee members under a plurilateral agreement – infrastructural scarcity and labor rights.

i   A Code for Airport Constraints

It is assumed, as a fundamental ordering principle, that each airline operating under the plurilateral will enjoy benefits of market access 'no less favorable' than that afforded to any other airline in the plurilateral territories, even in the latter's home State. In this expectation of equal treatment, however, lies an intractable challenge: given that the new treaty will emulate the EC Treaty and the GATT/GATS codes in incorporating a general principle of nondiscrimination, must that principle be immediately compromised in assuring fair – if not absolutely equal – treatment in slot allocation procedures, and evenhanded access to airport infrastructure and ground services (including the ability to self-handle these services)? There is obvious danger in coopting the tenets of 'safeguardism' from the EC third package, thereby condoning State intervention in the name of 'congestion,' 'environmental problems,' or other plausible excuses of statecraft.[183] But even if disguised protectionist restrictions on airport access can be exposed and proscribed, it remains true that the achievement of the comprehensive liberalization envisaged by the plurilateral is likely to be impeded for the foreseeable future by the sheer physical inadequacies of the international airport system, including slot and gate availability and air traffic control systems.

We have analyzed some of the regulatory procedures adopted by our model jurisdictions to meet these challenges, and no doubt a number of these tactics (vested grandfather rights,[184] preset quotas for new entrants,[185] perhaps a limited buy/sell protocol[186]) could be incorporated into a code of conduct for slot

---

183. As we have seen, the European Commission's 2008 consolidated legislation has attempted to narrow the scope of Member State autonomy to regulate infrastructural and environmental issues. *See supra* Chapter 5, Part III(C).

184. Given that the plurilateral territory will no longer discriminate *per se* between 'national' and 'international' flights, some reallocation of incumbent slot positions (including surrender of slots into the new entrant pool) seems likely in order to accommodate changing patterns of supply and demand. As noted, it has been suggested that, as part of the U.S./EC second stage talks, U.S. negotiators may ask for slots to be freed up for American carriers at Europe's big business hubs. Slot confiscation in a system based on the sanctity of grandfather rights presents major obstacles. *See supra* Chapter 2, note 276.

185. New entrant status should not necessarily mean 'start-up' carriers only: United would be a new entrant, for example, on a London/Rome 'seventh freedom' service, as would Air France operating a freestanding cabotage service from Boston to Los Angeles.

186. Both the U.S. and EC systems are experimenting with what is called 'secondary' slot trading (*i.e.,* sales of previously awarded slots). *See supra* text accompanying Chapter 4, note 479 & Chapter 5, Part III(C). The United States, however, has recently moved toward a more controversial market mechanism at its heavily congested New York air complexes. See *supra*

allocation to be drafted by the Joint Committee (and, again incorporating a possible right of appeal to the new Air Transport Commission). The Joint Committee, operating through a specialized subcommittee, might also be charged to work with existing slot allocation committees at airports in the plurilateral territory to assess emerging slot demand patterns and to decide on suitable reconfigurations of the code to improve market access for new competitors. To the extent that airport access must be limited because of congestion or environmental pressures, it would be consistent with abrogation of the power to impose capacity limitations to require that States will be able to act *only* with the prior authorization of the Joint Committee and upon guarantee that restraint measures will be imposed in a nondiscriminatory manner.[187]

ii   Labor Rights in a Plurilateral Setting

Liberalization has its opponents, and stakeholders like the U.S. and EU airline labor unions are a powerful and concentrated group which argues that a multilateral regulatory framework (such as the second stage plurilateral) will not take adequate account of labor protection and representation needs.[188] The unions identify a structural shortcoming at the heart of liberalization which will deprive labor of any means to negotiate with 'holding companies' (a single Lufthansa/United corporation, for example, owning airlines in both the United States and Europe) on a transnational basis. The applicable labor laws in both jurisdictions are

---

Chapter 3, note 399. Slot sales, however made, should be transparent and noted on a public register. *See generally* [U.K.] Civil Aviation Authority, *The Single European Aviation Market: Progress So Far*, at 50-51, CAP 654 (Sept. 1995). Despite the drawbacks of a buy/sell system for new or smaller carriers, it may also be true that their access to 'free' slots through the new entrant pool (and other non-market distributions) may be a cash boon that will enable them to fund new operations at less competitive times or at less densely patronized hubs.

187. *See supra* Chapter 4, Part IV(B) & Chapter 5, Part III(C) (discussing infrastructure constraints at airports).

188. In the United States, labor's position is sometimes conceptually assimilated to the quite separate issue of objections to foreign investment in critical infrastructure. James Oberstar, Chairman of the House of Representatives Committee on Transportation and Infrastructure, has been especially vocal in defense of nationally owned and controlled airlines. Chairman Oberstar proposed language amending the ownership and control statute that, in the view of some, could be interpreted by a future Administration as requiring that all middle and upper management positions in U.S. airlines be occupied by U.S. citizens. *See* Letter from Rep. John L. Mica, Ranking Republican Member, House Committee on Transportation and Infrastructure, to Rep. James L. Oberstar, Chairman, House Committee on Transportation and Infrastructure (Aug. 2, 2007). The language provided, in pertinent part, that U.S. citizens must control 'all matters pertaining to the business and structure of the air carrier, including operational matters such as marketing, branding, fleet composition, route selection, pricing, and labor relations.' FAA Reauthorization Act of 2007, H.R. 2881, 110th Cong. sec. 801 (2007) (as passed by the House Sept. 20, 2007). It has been observed that this proposed language is not in the spirit of the second stage of U.S./EC air transport negotiations, and may well conflict with the first-stage provisions for branding and franchising opportunities. Despite the failure of the 2007 bill to win support in the Senate, Rep. Oberstar has reintroduced the language into its successor. *See* FAA Reauthorization Act of 2009, H.R. 915, 111th Cong. sec. 801 (2009).

fundamentally territorial, and operate without any protective transnational effect. The unions are concerned that, as liberalization takes hold, they would be seeking an effective right to negotiate with a collective transnational entity (rather than just with a foreign investor in a U.S. airline).[189] The same is not true domestically. In the United States, when there are several airlines in one corporate 'family,' a mechanism exists to secure single representation.[190]

U.S. labor officials note that the EC, despite applying airline deregulation across 27 Member States, left territorial labor laws in place. That is one of the reasons, labor contends, why the Air France/KLM quasi-merger remains formally unconsummated.[191] The variances in EC labor laws will make it tempting for carriers to flag in countries such as Romania, where protection is weaker. This process may occur even when the original choice of flag State is commercially appropriate and legally unimpeachable. Ryanair, for example, flags in Ireland, where it is harder for unions to organize, but is now primarily a U.K. operator.[192] Labor believes that these tendencies will not be resisted and that the only way to avoid forum-shopping for weaker labor protection is to take out the variables and level the field. This would be an extraordinarily complex public policy challenge but one that would fall to the members of the Joint Committee and specialized subcommittees.

For those who favor liberalization, labor's preoccupation with protectionism seems misplaced. Some see labor as having been captured by an antimarket bias and a suspicion of foreigners, focused more on tying success to employment rather than production. Labor's agenda, in this view, protects existing jobs at the expense of future jobs and in defiance of a discernible global trend in comparable industries

---

189. *See* Captain Duane Woerth, President, Air Line Pilots Association, *Foreign Investment in U.S. Carriers*, Statement Before the Senate Committee on Commerce, Science, and Transportation (May 9, 2006).

190. *See id.*

191. Pursuant to one of the few pieces of Community labor legislation, a transnational 'Works Council' represents Air France-KLM workers. It appears to have a primarily information-giving purpose and has not displaced the country-based staff representative bodies in each company. *See* European Works Council, *Protocol for the European Works Council within the Air France KLM Group* (Feb. 13, 2006), <http://www.euro-betriebsrat.de/pdf/airfrance.pdf>; *see also* Press Release, KLM Royal Dutch Airlines, Air France KLM European Works Council Created (Feb. 14, 2006).

192. This question of the relationship between the corporate choice of establishment and the application of labor laws is topical in the European Community. Charleroi-based Ryanair pilots brought suit in Belgium claiming that social rights (including payment of irregular and supplemental working hours) must be governed by Belgian law. Ryanair asserted that Irish fiscal and labor law must govern the employment relationship. The local court found for the pilots. Article 6 of the Rome Convention on the Law Applicable to Contractual Obligations, in force in the EU Member States, provides that an employment contract is governed by the law of the State where the employee 'habitually' carries out work in performance of the contract. But the applicability of labor laws other than those of the licensing State (or even the State of principal business) can be considered unsettled in the Community. *See* Booz Allen Hamilton, The Economic Impacts of an Open Aviation Area Between the European Union and the United States: Final Report 107-08 (2007).

such as automobiles, steel, and oil. Labor responds that it is protecting existing highly paid jobs, and that it is unclear how many jobs of similar status will result from liberalization (a report prepared for the European Commission by Booz Allen Hamilton projected a five-year net gain of over 70,000 direct and indirect jobs from the 2007 U.S./EC Air Transport Agreement, not only in the airline industry itself but also through the catalytic effects of liberalization on general employment).[193] Labor's position may be an historical misjudgment, it has been argued, because U.S. labor has generally been satisfied to deal with private employers and to focus its energies on the collective bargaining process. Special interest pleading fails to recognize that a balance must be struck that will have benefits for both labor and liberalization.

The Booz Allen report[194] performed a comparative study of U.S. and EC labor laws implicated by a possible 'Open Aviation Area.'[195] Its principal focus was the status of so-called 'mobile workers' (flight and cabin crew) and the likelihood that foreign airlines would use their investment powers to favor work allocation to their own staffs even if U.S. crews were equally or more competitive.[196] In the United States, the laws are primarily federal (the Railway Labor Act of 1926),[197] whereas in the EC only a limited number of labor-related areas are harmonized at Community level. National rules, especially with respect to settlement of labor disputes, remain fundamental.[198] The report emphasizes, however, that different regulatory contexts can produce like results in an industry where technical standards and

---

193. *See id.* at 229.
194. *See id.*
195. For a quick overview of the European Commission's 'Open Aviation Area,' a 'beyond open skies' proposal toward which it hopes that second stage U.S./EC negotiations will evolve, *see infra* note 249.
196. U.S. bilateral air services agreements allow foreign airlines to bring in managerial, sales, technical, operational, and other staff provided they comply with U.S. immigration laws. In sharp contrast to EC practice, flight and cabin crews require 'alien crewman' visas. Theoretically (unless constrained by collective bargaining agreements) a U.S. airline could employ aliens on its services between the United States and other countries. The immigration laws do, however, constrain the use of foreign crews by U.S. carriers during labor disputes. Many regard the meticulous U.S. travel control rules for temporary air transport workers as inconsistent with a policy of deregulation and open skies. Also, U.S. law expressly forbids issuance of crew visas for the purpose of providing domestic transportation. *But see supra* note 188 (discussing proposed changes to U.S. airline managerial hiring laws).
197. *See* 44 Stat. 577 (1926) (codified as amended at 45 U.S.C.A. §§ 151 *et seq.* (West 2008)).
198. With respect to the right of establishment, one important working assumption is that neither the United States nor the EU Member States will provide absolute protection of employment, although arbitrary selective dismissal is generally difficult if not impossible. In individual Member States, legal restrictions on laying off staff may even be less than in the United States. But granting reciprocal rights of investment, the Booz Allen report concludes, would not remove a single existing employee legal protection. *See* Booz Allen Hamilton, *supra* note 192, at 131. The report's findings were met with skepticism by Russ Bailey, senior attorney for the Legal Department of the Air Line Pilots Association, at a panel discussion on prospects for the second stage of the 2007 U.S./EC Air Transport Agreement hosted by the German Marshall Fund of the United States in Washington, D.C. on Apr. 14, 2008. Bailey's skeptical reaction was evidently based on the fact that the report had been prepared at the behest of the European Commission.

commercial service priorities have always been strongly influenced by international standards and criteria as well as national thinking.[199]

With respect to labor fears of reallocation on lucrative transatlantic markets (including shifting of work within a networked firm to crews and aircraft working under the most flexible rules and at the most competitive wage rates), the Booz Allen study makes a number of macroeconomic findings that rely on the persistence of a dynamic marketplace and of a highly specialized labor force that can extract high rents. But, more significantly, the study seems to place more emphasis on transborder dialogue among industry professionals than on regulatory convergence. In other words, a regime of *de facto* convergence may emerge (as it has in the alliances).[200] Within the framework of a second stage plurilateral agreement, the Joint Committee will need to unscramble this juxtaposed reality of static national labor laws and dynamic transnational labor union fraternization.

6   Principle 6: A Mandatory Supranational Dispute Settlement/Appellate Mechanism

a   Introduction

In earlier writings, I did indeed adopt the cosmopolitan pose of calling for a formidable array of supranational regulatory and adjudicative institutions as

---

199. In terms of the power to terminate, national policy is dominant and there are other discernible trends toward giving employers greater flexibility to react to business cycle demand. According to the Booz Allen Report, 'any general assumption that laying off professional staff in "Europe" is much more costly or less costly and difficult than in the United States . . . is superficial if not outright wrong.' Booz Allen Hamilton, *supra* note 192, at 133. Having said that, some countries (the United Kingdom, Denmark, Spain) are manifestly more flexible to employers than others (France, Germany). According to an index established by the World Bank, measuring the difficulty under general law (*i.e.*, outside collective bargaining frameworks) of dismissing an employee, on an ease-difficulty scale of 0-100, Denmark scored 10, as did the United States, the United Kingdom, and Switzerland. Denmark leads the way, giving employers great flexibility but matching that flexibility with a commitment to social justice in the form of generous redundancy benefits and job retraining.

200. *See id.* at 111 & 122. One interesting example of this continued importance of transnational thinking springs from the labor unions themselves, which have joined forces across the existing transatlantic alliances to create the Wings Pilots Coalition, the Star Solidarity Alliance, and the oneworld Cockpit Crew Alliance. *See id.* at 79 n.90. It is conceivable that strikes of Northwest pilots, for example, could result in strikes of KLM pilots in order to maintain a balance between wages and so avoid a shift of production from KLM to Northwest (or vice versa). More significantly, the stage is being set for dialogue across national and continental borders. In January 2009, United Airlines and Aer Lingus announced an innovative partnership to begin transatlantic services between Washington Dulles and Madrid. Under the terms of the agreement, Aer Lingus would provide aircraft and new crew for the route while United would provide marketing to the U.S. customer base expected to fill the flights. *See* Press Release, United Airlines, Aer Lingus and United Airlines Announce Transatlantic Partnership (Jan. 22, 2009). The arrangement, however, was expected to draw both U.S. and EU labor union opposition.

a component of a future air transport plurilateral.[201] On reading Paul Stephan's excoriation of new global governance initiatives,[202] and reflecting on the fate of the regulatory engineering favored in the stillborn TCAA,[203] I have taken due note of the political realities and costs of further supranational agency-building. Principle 5, which advocates congruence in competition law and policy, therefore reflects a more modest proposal for first-order competition law adjudication that relies on the collaborative temperaments of existing enforcers.

Nonetheless, I remain convinced that some form of adjudicatory agency could be helpful to the management of disputes that will arise in international air transport,

---

201. For example, a 2000 article on the compatibility with U.S. constitutional law of a transfer of adjudicatory authority to supranational institutions included the following hypothetical, which was in turn based on a proposal advocated in my earlier book, IN SEARCH OF OPEN SKIES: LAW AND POLICY FOR A NEW ERA IN INTERNATIONAL AVIATION 427-33 (1997) [hereinafter HAVEL, OPEN SKIES]:

> *Chicago, December 2000: The delegates to a new global air transport conference have crafted a proposed multilateral 'open skies' agreement that would supersede the mercantilist Chicago Convention, originally signed in 1944. The new dispensation would transform commercial access to the world's airspace, eliminating the government domination of routes, prices, and market access that has limited the network expansion of the world's airlines for more than 50 years. As part of the effort, the delegates have proposed establishing two 'supranational' institutions to monitor international airline competition, an Open Skies Commission and an International Court of Air Transportation. The Commission and Court, applying a new code of international competition law, would exercise exclusive supervision over the legal relations between private citizens, between private citizens and sovereign States, and between sovereign States, in connection with the operation of international air transport routes. Accordingly, for example, a United States airline seeking to merge with a European Union airline could find the proposed deal blocked by the Open Skies Commission as anticompetitive, but would have a right of appeal to the International Court of Air Transportation. Decisions of the Commission and Court would have the status of domestic law within each contracting party's jurisdiction and no further domestic appeals or challenges would be allowed. To facilitate this regime, private citizens would be granted standing before the Commission and the Court. The United States delegation has demurred; in its view, the United States Constitution precludes the assignment of obligatory adjudicative powers over private party relationships – and possibly even over the sovereign actions of the United States itself – to supranational tribunals and judges.*

> Brian F. Havel, *The Constitution in an Era of Supranational Adjudication*, 78 N.C. L. Rev. 257, 266-68 (2000) [hereinafter Havel, *Constitution*] (concluding, *inter alia*, that supranational tribunals can be considered, along with state courts and legislative courts, to 'share' in the exercise of the Constitution's judicial power in a way that is consistent with the fundamental idea of the separation of powers).

202. *See* Stephan, *supra* note 134. To me, the saliency of Stephan's argument rests primarily on his skepticism about the burgeoning growth of international technocracy. *See id.* at 177. Given the arguments I have already marshaled about U.S./EC convergences in competition law and policy, however, I am much less persuaded by Stephan's dominating concern about continuing distinctions in competition policy between the two jurisdictions (especially Europe's 'protectionist' use of competition policy), as well as by his dislike of the 'imprecise normative judgments' supposedly made by competition policy. Stephan, *supra* note 134, at 178, 194.

203. *See supra* text accompanying note 122.

not just in the application of competition law but with respect to all the substantive issues (public aid, airport congestion controls, slot trading, and other sources of conflict) that will be addressed in the second stage plurilateral. Rutger Jan toe Laer reasonably assumes that appeals against competition agency decisions will lie only within the legal system of the jurisdiction designated under his enforcement priority criteria.[204] But, as previously noted, toe Laer's schema appears premised on the persistence of the Chicago nationality rule. Were that rule to disappear as part of a new plurilateral settlement creating a unified aviation jurisdiction, it would seem feasible to create a new, mandatory, supranational route of adjudication (or, in competition cases, of appellate review) for the entire plurilateral area. Any government regulatory decision, or any dispute between the State parties, between a State and a private party, or between two private parties, could be referred to this tribunal (which I have previously designated the 'Air Transport Commission').

b   *A Sector-Specific Supranational Tribunal*

I believe that it remains realistic, as well as jurisprudentially appropriate, to project sector-specific international dispute settlement.[205] In 1998, for example, the international community established a new international criminal court.[206] In the services sector, it makes sense to project the appearance of sectoralized tribunals to facilitate specific wealth-generating segments of the global service economy. This is particularly true within the global air, space, and telecommunications

---

204. *See* toe Laer, *supra* note 165, at 315.
205. The sectoralization paradigm should be given serious consideration. Under Article 287 of the 1982 Convention on the Law of the Sea, for example, interstate disputes may be referred not only to the International Court of Justice, but also to a new International Tribunal for the Law of the Sea and two different arbitration arrangements. *See* Karl-Heinz Böckstiegel, *Arbitration of Disputes Regarding Space Activities*, *in* PROCEEDINGS OF THE THIRTY-SIXTH COLLOQUIUM ON THE LAW OF OUTER SPACE OF THE INTERNATIONAL INSTITUTE OF SPACE LAW 137 (Graz 1994). Professor John Jackson, while praising the new General Agreement on Trade in Services, Apr. 15, 1994, 33 I.L.M. 1167, as the highwater mark of trade liberalization in services, speculated that the sheer number of service sectors (perhaps 150) presages at least 50 years of sector-by-sector negotiating. *See generally* JOHN H. JACKSON, THE WORLD TRADING SYSTEM: LAW AND POLICY OF INTERNATIONAL ECONOMIC RELATIONS 307 (2d ed. 1997). The complexity of the service sector mirrors, to some extent, the fragmentation of the discipline of public international law itself into a rich palette of new specialties including – in addition to air, space, and telecommunications law – international tort and criminal law, international resource law, international human rights law, law of the sea, communications law, unfair business practices, international antitrust and tax law, and many others. *See generally* THOMAS M. FRANCK, FAIRNESS IN INTERNATIONAL LAW AND INSTITUTIONS 5 (1995). For a recent proposal for a multilateral 'hard law' treaty asserting the existence of a right to a healthy environment, administered by a supranational adjudicatory body or court, *see* Joshua P. Eaton, *The Nigerian Tragedy, Environmental Regulation of Transnational Corporations, and the Human Right to a Healthy Environment*, 15 B.U. INT'L L.J. 261 (1997).
206. For insights into the emergence of this new court, *see* M. Cherif Bassiouni & Christopher L. Blakesley, *The Need for an International Criminal Court in the New International World Order*, 25 VAND. J. TRANSNAT'L L. 151 (1992).

sectors.[207] The glide path toward multilateralization of the international air transport industry, for example, has been fixed at least since the ratification of the Chicago Convention. In fact, Professor Bin Cheng has written that the U.K. delegation to the International Civil Aviation Conference at Chicago in 1944 already proposed the creation of a new 'International Air Authority' to serve as the world's aviation regulator.[208] A new second stage plurilateral agreement, descended from that discarded British proposal, would supersede the mercantilist Chicago Convention and its network of bilateral sovereign-to-sovereign agreements.

As part of this effort, the supranational Air Transport Commission would apply a code of substantive regulatory law to the legal relations between air carriers, between air carriers and sovereign States, and between sovereign States, in connection with the operation of international air transport routes. Accordingly, for example, a U.S. airline seeking to vitiate the imposition of high user charges at Heathrow Airport could directly challenge the U.K. Government, its competitor U.K. airlines, U.K. airport authorities, or all of these possible respondents, before the plurilaterally designated Commission. Decisions of the Commission would have the force of domestic law within each contracting party's jurisdiction, and no further domestic appeals or challenges would be permitted. To facilitate this regime, private corporations and citizens would be granted standing before the Commission.[209]

---

207. *See* JACKSON, *supra* note 205, at 307. For example, public comments on the U.S. Department of Transportation's draft predatory pricing guidelines for the domestic airline industry, *see supra* Chapter 4, Part IV(B), included an argument by the Washington Airports Task Force that the worldwide dimension of airline alliances, with the risk of anticompetitive levels of concentration, had begun to create 'a supranational situation' with respect to competition policies for the first time. In the view of the Task Force, issues created by these far-flung alliances would be increasingly difficult to resolve through the prevailing network of *bilateral* aviation agreements. *See* Washington Airports Task Force, *Response to the Request for Comment on Proposed Predatory Pricing Enforcement Policy*, U.S. DOT Dkt. No. OST-98-3713-717 (Jul. 22, 1998).

208. *See* BIN CHENG, THE LAW OF INTERNATIONAL AIR TRANSPORT 18-19, 23-24, & 422-423 (1962). Professor Cheng proposed multilateral negotiation of capacity; the New Zealand delegation suggested that the new authority own aircraft and facilities and be responsible for the actual operation of commercial air services on prescribed global trunk routes. *See also* Jeffrey N. Shane, *The Bermuda Capacity Principle: Does it still work?*, in THE USE OF AIRSPACE AND OUTER SPACE FOR ALL MANKIND IN THE 21ST CENTURY 35-37 (Chia-Jui Cheng ed., 1995) [hereinafter THE USE OF AIRSPACE].

209. Standing for individuals (and, for that matter, corporations) in international law has been historically very restrictive. John Barton and Barry Carter have explored the emergence of the private actor on the public international law plane as foreign investors and businesses sought to protect themselves from expropriation or mistreatment by a host country. John H. Barton & Barry E. Carter, *Symposium: International Law and Institutions for a New Age*, 81 GEO. L.J. 535, 538 (1993). Increased privatization of airlines and the global trend to alliances and deregulation invite consideration of why airline commercial interests should continue to be mediated through interstate dispute settlement. *See* Pablo M. J. Mendes de Leon, *Settlement of Disputes in Air and Space Law*, in THE USE OF AIRSPACE, *supra* note 208, at 325 (implying that, given the few examples that exist of dispute settlements in public international air law, airlines should be parties to international disputes that involve their commercial interests). In this context, for example, the U.S./EC hushkit dispute paradigm proved to be overly complex,

Supranationalizing dispute settlement in the plurilateral, in particular, is likely to generate a sustainable body of case law and norm-creation. Dr. Chia-Jui Cheng, Chairman of the Asian Institute of International Air and Space Law, described the content of 'international air law' as 'a vastly more complex system of law than any other system of law.'[210] As Dr. Cheng elucidated, international air law comprises a rich normative tapestry of international public law, private international law, and rules emanating from municipal law.[211] Public law norms regulate the airspace, as well as air navigation, air traffic, aviation security, the International Civil Aviation Organization, and international air transport services. Private law rules govern the liability regime of the international air carrier, product liability in aviation, surface damage and collisions, insurance, assistance, and salvage. And aspects of municipal constitutional law, administrative law, civil law, procedure, commercial law, and criminal law filter through these public and private regimes of law.[212]

Moreover, it is virtually axiomatic that a respected international tribunal, steadfast in its jurisprudence, can gain legitimacy through its processes of adjudication or appellate review. Such has been the recent experience of the European Court of Justice and of the Appellate Body of the WTO,[213] two examples of

---

unworkable, and damaging to the commercial interests most directly involved. *See generally* Havel, *International Instruments, supra* note 68, at 27-32 (discussing the consequences for various public and private stakeholders of an EC regulatory mandate imposing noise stringency standards that threatened the withholding of recognition of U.S. certificates of airworthiness for U.S. carriers which nevertheless complied with current ICAO standards). Former U.S. Under Secretary of Commerce David Aaron noted at a Brussels press briefing on Mar. 14, 2000, that an Irish hushkit manufacturer and aircraft lessor, Omega Air ('Omega'), had been attempting to retrofit and lease aircraft in the European Community but found itself potentially blocked by the new EC regulation. *See id.* at 45. Allegedly because of the regulation, Omega was unable to secure bank financing. Omega launched a triple-pronged litigation strategy that severely embarrassed EC regulators: it commenced actions challenging the EC hushkit regulation in the Irish High Court, English High Court, and before the European Court of First Instance (the junior auxiliary to the European Court of Justice). The English tribunal found that the regulation, which omitted to explain why the European Community had departed *inter alia* from ICAO noise emission guidelines, appeared to be 'wholly defective in its reasons.' *See id.* at 45-46. Omega flexed its remedial muscles within its own domestic and regional (EC) legal systems; arguably, it should also have been able to make its case directly before the ICAO tribunal. *A fortiori*, the affected U.S. hushkit manufacturers, which lacked any direct right of standing to challenge the EC regulation before any Community judicial institutions, should have been enabled to do so. (While *locus standi* before the European Court of Justice is a complex issue lying outside the scope of this discussion, it is generally the case that private litigants (even if they are citizens of the EU) will have difficulty in challenging an EC regulation *directly* before the Court.) *See generally* TREVOR C. HARTLEY, THE FOUNDATIONS OF EUROPEAN COMMUNITY LAW 343-47 (6th ed. 2007) (discussing standing of so-called 'non-privileged' applicants).

210. Chia-Jui Cheng, *New Sources of International Air Law, in* THE USE OF AIRSPACE, *supra* note 208, at 277.
211. *See id.* at 277.
212. *See id.* at 278.
213. Within the legal academy, the new WTO dispute settlement system represents what Richard Shell hails as a 'stunning victory' for international trade 'legalists' in their historic debate with

supranational radicalism that have settled into uncontested roles as powerful non-State adjudicators.[214] The WTO applies more pressure on States than past

---

      trade 'pragmatists.' Shell, *supra* note 67, at 833. The pragmatic view, Shell argues, supports formally nonbinding methods of dispute resolution; it is a power-centered approach to resolving interstate conflict. In this understanding, diplomacy 'renders trade politically sustainable in a rapidly changing world economy.' *Id.* at 833. The WTO system, in contrast, represents the triumph of a rule-based tribunal that can move world trade toward what Shell describes as a 'governance system.' *Id.* at 833-34.

214.   Professor Richard Shell's article identifies three competing normative approaches to trade legalism. Under the Regime Management Model, States are the primary actors in the international system and are motivated to achieve a set of sometimes conflicting, self-interested goals in addition to power, including wealth, political stability, and domestic distributional objectives. *See* Shell, *supra* note 67, at 860. In this context, international trade dispute mechanisms support trade regimes by allowing States to 'police violations of the "contractual" obligations that arise from trade treaties.' *Id.* at 863-64. States under this model monopolize the international judicial process, and use centralized international tribunals that limit standing to States only. *See id.* at 864. Shell cites the ICAO dispute settlement provisions as an example of classical regime management. Thus, ICAO is a contract among sovereign States designed to achieve gains from international air navigation and safety cooperation 'without sacrificing more State autonomy than is absolutely necessary to secure these gains.' *Id.* at 867. Only States – not airlines, passenger groups, unions, or other stakeholders – have standing to participate in the governance structure or to engage ICAO's dispute settlement machinery. *See id.* Disputes that cannot be negotiated are referred to a neutral international tribunal, whose decision is final and binding. *See id.* at 867-68. The Efficient Market Model, founded in pure free trade theory, assumes that States in their relationships with one another are essentially doing the bidding of strong private economic actors; this model ideally would give businesses direct access to both supranational and domestic dispute resolution machinery. *See* Shell, *supra* note 67, at 836. An indirect benefit to States within this model is its capacity to transfer accountability for adverse decisions to an extra-political body. *See id.* at 880. The model therefore views international trade laws and tribunals as devices by which governments and businesses that favor free trade may circumvent domestic protectionist groups and maximize the world's wealth. *See id.* at 884. Shell provides a few examples of this model, including the NAFTA, the Convention on the Recognition and Enforcement of Foreign Arbitral Awards (New York Convention), and the International Centre for Settlement of Investment Disputes (ICSID), to illustrate its capacity to loosen State monopoly on power and grant businesses direct standing and domestic enforceability. *See id.* at 886. The NAFTA, for example, creates a binding supranational arbitration scheme accessible directly by private business parties through which businesses can overturn final antidumping and countervailing duty decisions of domestic trade regulators. *See id.* at 887. The strongest example of an Efficient Market Model scheme is the ICSID, which permits private parties to sue States using a self-regulatory international arbitral process and incorporated appeal system. *See id.* at 889. States agree to enforcement of arbitral decisions in their own domestic courts without even the minimal 'public policy' review permitted under the New York Convention. *See* Shell, *supra* note 67, at 889. The ICSID permits private business creditors to obtain virtually automatic collection of awards against State debtors using debtor nations' own courts. *See* Shell, *supra* note 67, at 889-90. Finally, the Trade Stakeholders Model also focuses on an elevated role for private individuals and businesses, but geared less toward the advancement of pure trade interests than to accommodation of a variety of social interests including consumer, labor, and environmental protection in pursuit of 'a larger transnational society.' *Id.* at 837. Regulations enforceable under this model would include labor standards, environmental concerns, human rights, and other social issues, as well as economic rights for businesses. *See id.* at 919. Shell suggests the European Union/Community as an example of this model, having transformed itself (with jurisprudential prompting from the European Court of Justice) from a conventional trade

incarnations of supranational adjudication through appellate review and also by creating a reverse consensus rule that upholds arbitral or appellate decisions unless the membership votes by consensus (unanimity) to reject them.[215] Generally speaking, rules made 'within the . . . institutional framework of an organized community' are more likely to bind, and to contribute to rule coherency and legitimacy, than rules that are merely 'ad hoc agreements between parties' made outside that community[216] – the latter reflecting the preferred dispute settlement mechanism adopted under Chicago system bilateral air services agreements.[217]

c   *Advancing to Private Supranational Dispute Settlement*

The model of an Air Transport Commission proposed here anticipates that various party configurations would emerge, in addition to the classical international law

---

    alliance into 'a socially responsive confederation . . . that permits individuals as well as States to assert a wide array of transnational standards in legal disputes at both the regional and the domestic levels.' *Id.* at 917-18.

215. Shell calls this a 'no exit' strategy that removes the option of 'political play in the joints of the dispute resolution system.' *Id.* at 898. For Shell, this reverse consensus rule is an intrusion of the Efficient Market Model because it represents the result of private sector lobbying to prevent resort to unilateral trade sanction mechanisms (for example, under the U.S. 'Section 301' sanctions powers introduced by the Trade Act of 1974). *See* Shell, *supra* note 67, at 899. ICAO, in contrast, disqualifies only the immediate parties to the dispute from voting. *See id.* at 898.

216. Thomas M. Franck, *Legitimacy in the International System*, 82 Am. J. Int'l L. 705, 752 (1988).

217. *See* Havel, *International Instruments*, *supra* note 68, at 19-24 (examining how ad hoc arbitration is the only dispute settlement mechanism used in the U.S. directory of bilateral air services treaties). The 2007 U.S./EC Air Transport Agreement, despite its ambitious and radical provenance, offers no imaginative breakthrough on the issue of dispute settlement. It uses very conventional ad hoc arbitral mechanisms copied from U.S. bilateral practice, designating no official arbitral forum and referencing only one third party official, the President of ICAO, who appoints arbitrators if the parties do not agree on appointment of the panel. *See* U.S./EC Air Transport Agreement, *supra* note 12, art. 19 ('Arbitration'). As noted earlier, *see supra* text accompanying Chapter 2, note 242, the 2007 Agreement actually prolongs the typical ad hoc arbitral process (already notorious for delays) by adding a requirement that the Joint Committee be asked to resolve disputes in the first instance. *See* U.S./EC Air Transport Agreement, *supra* note 12, art. 19(1). Notice also that Article 20 and Annex 2 of the Agreement (both dealing with cooperation on competition matters) are excluded from the scope of the dispute settlement machinery. *See id.* The Agreement, in sum, makes no attempt to cross the Rubicon of compulsory supranational enforcement. The Agreement does borrow from recent U.S. bilateral practice by indicating that, if the parties agree, a dispute may be referred to a 'person or body' for decision prior to attempting arbitration, but again there is no attempt to identify who such a person or body might be. *See id.* art. 19(1). The vagueness of this clause, as well as its ubiquity in U.S. bilateral air services agreements, presents a clear opportunity to argue that the language opens the door to compulsory dispute settlement by a permanent institution. In other words, the phrase 'person or body' does not determine that arbitration shall be the only available mechanism, but neither does it exclude the possibility that in these agreements dispute settlement by a specific agency could be the *selected* mechanism. Ad hoc arbitration, in this setting, would remain the default option but would never be triggered because the parties would agree *a priori* on a specific dispute settlement tribunal or institution. A standard memorandum of understanding or exchange of notes could easily clarify this interpretation – and identify the selected permanent institution – if it became U.S. international aviation policy.

sovereign-to-sovereign contest, that would reject the traditional view of the individual as lacking an autonomous right of access to international tribunals.[218] Thus, while the Air Transport Commission model contemplates that the United States might press a claim against Italy because of an allegedly illegal public subsidy paid to Alitalia, that jurisdiction alone might not seem a remarkable advance on present WTO dispute settlement procedure.[219]

The authentic innovation comes in granting private parties a direct right of appearance, or standing, before the Air Transport Commission in two prototypical party configurations. First, because participation in the plurilateral treaty establishing the Commission would require an unequivocal waiver of sovereign immunity, a private party could bring suit directly against a foreign government. Accordingly, the treaty would allow a U.S. airline, for example, to bring a complaint against an EU Member State government to remove capacity restrictions unilaterally imposed by that government on air traffic routes served by the U.S. complainant. Under the proposed model, for example, Northwest Airlines could have compelled the Japanese government to arbitrate its 1993 decision to impose unilateral restrictions on Northwest's Tokyo/Sydney services.[220] Thus, unlike the dispute panel structure created under the WTO agreements in 1994, the direct access procedures proposed here would no longer compel nongovernmental complainants to lobby their national governments to raise unfair competition issues – and, failing agreement, to enter into formal dispute – with foreign governments.[221]

Second, any individual airline could demand supranational dispute settlement, or be forced to accept such dispute settlement, in managing its commercial relations with its commercial peers. For example, with respect to competition determinations, a U.S. airline could demand review by the Air Transport Commission of a U.S. or EC enforcement agency's failure to find price-fixing by two European competitors, or an alliance of U.S. and European competitors, on a major U.S./European route. It is likely, in fact, that most disputes in a fully deregulated

218. For a broad summons to expand standing in international trade tribunals, *see* Shell, *supra* note 67, at 838 (calling for 'places at the table' – including standing to litigate cases – for all trade policy stakeholders).

219. *See id.* at 898 n.325 (describing the WTO, in this specific sense, as a 'contract organization' that adopts the classic public international law contractual model of bilateral relationships between States).

220. *See* HAVEL, OPEN SKIES, *supra* note 201, at 188 (describing Northwest's complaint against Japan, pursued under the U.S. Department of Transportation's statutory administrative investigation procedures for international air transportation).

221. On the presentation of claims against foreign governments, *see generally* RESTATEMENT (THIRD) OF FOREIGN RELATIONS LAW OF THE UNITED STATES § 902, cmt. 1 (1987). For a critical evaluation of democratic weaknesses in the new WTO dispute settlement system, *see generally* Robert F. Housman, *Democratizing International Trade Decision-Making*, 27 CORNELL INT'L L.J. 699 (1994) (discussing how current international trade agreements undercut principles of democratic governance even in democratic States). Conversely, of course, ouster of domestic jurisdiction would also enable governments to invoke supranational dispute settlement against private parties directly – and mandatorily – before the proposed Commission.

international airline industry would be private in nature, especially as governments continue to withdraw from public ownership of their flag carriers.[222]

d   *Private Supranational Dispute Settlement: A Constitutional Possibility?*

Is mandatory international *private* dispute settlement a realistic prospect for the United States? Would the U.S. Government cooperate in forcing its private commercial actors to accept binding supranational dispute settlement (or in accepting such dispute settlement itself in the specific sectoral area of international air transport)? As a pragmatic matter, since the United States has already accepted binding arbitration *inter se* in the framework of the WTO dispute process, and frequently serves (as other countries do) as the surrogate for the true commercial parties in interest in a dispute,[223] it could be argued that a transition to compulsory supranational dispute resolution for private parties need not be unduly perplexing or forbidding.

As a *juristic* matter, however, the U.S. Supreme Court has never addressed the constitutional implications of moving final authority in private commercial disputes outside the domestic system, with its specific due process protections, to globalized dispute resolution panels. There is no doubt, however, that in its emphasis on the standing of private citizens, the supranational dispute settlement and review model contains an unexplored constitutional novelty for the United States. In all previous incarnations of transnational adjudication that have been accepted by the U.S. Government, American citizens either could appear before the relevant tribunals only by the sovereign consent of the United States or were represented by the United States in its sovereign capacity.[224]

While it is difficult to predict how the Court would react to a transfer of compulsory adjudication outside the traditional constitutional reach of the federal judiciary, a few positive auguries can be mentioned. First, the U.S. federal judiciary has always demonstrated a high level of pragmatic accommodation to new jurisprudential developments, as shown for example when federal judges adapted themselves to the rise of the administrative state and the creation of dozens

---

222. *See supra* Chapter 3, Part VI(A)-(B).
223. As Andreas Lowenfeld has remarked in the context of the GATT panels, for example, 'there is usually some kind of a private dispute behind these . . . cases.' Andreas F. Lowenfeld, *Transcript of Discussion Following Presentation by Kenneth W. Abbott*, 1992 COLUM. BUS. L. REV. 151, 161.
224. *See* Dames & Moore v. Regan, 453 U.S. 654 (1981) (involving an executive agreement transferring all claims of U.S. nationals against the Iranian government to international arbitration); U.S. v. Pink, 315 U.S. 203 (1942) (involving an executive agreement settling claims of American nationals against Russia and its nationals arising out of U.S. recognition of the Soviet Government); U.S. v. Belmont, 301 U.S. 324 (1937) (involving an American government action in order to complete the settlement of claims of United States nationals made by previous executive agreement with the Soviet Government).

of specialized governmental tribunals to administer statutory schemes of federal regulation (such as worker's compensation agencies).[225]

Second, the Supreme Court – and the federal judiciary generally – have historically shown great deference to the actions of the 'political' branches (the Congress and the President) in matters of foreign relations and foreign treaty arrangements, areas within which international trade and commerce are typically subsumed.[226] Third, while a right of appeal to a federal appellate court has generally been considered part of the panoply of 'due process' rights under the U.S. Constitution, within the domain of international trade, of which aviation is a highly visible but rather modest component, the individual's right to (domestic) judicial review has always been acknowledged to be contingent.[227] The United States courts have been unwilling to impose due process of law or, for that matter, a guarantee of a right to trade, as justiciable constitutional restraints on Congress's power in foreign commerce.[228]

---

225. *See generally* Havel, *Constitution, supra* note 201, 309-321 (discussing emergence of so-called 'legislative courts' created using the general powers of Congress under Article I of the U.S. Constitution). And one variant of supranational dispute resolution, international private commercial arbitration, has received the imprimatur of important U.S. courts. For example, in 1974, in *Sherk v. Alberto-Culver Co.*, 417 U.S. 506 (1974), the U.S. Supreme Court established the jurisdictional primacy of the Federal Arbitration Act of 1925 over substantive remedies found in the U.S. securities laws. The Court ruled that refusal to enforce arbitration clauses in international agreements 'would surely damage the fabric of international commerce and trade, and imperil the willingness and ability of businessmen to enter into international agreements.' *Id.* at 517. (The Federal Arbitration Act (FAA) was a response to the hostility of American courts to enforcement of arbitration agreements, a judicial disposition inherited from then longstanding English practice.)

226. Thus, one court has described foreign commerce as 'the political side of foreign affairs.' American Ass'n of Exporters *v.* U.S., 751 F.2d 1239, 1248 (Fed. Cir. 1985); *see also* South P.R. Sugar Co. Trading Corp. *v.* U.S., 334 F.2d 622, 630 (Ct. Cl. 1964) (noting that, '[i]n the intercourse of nations, changes in economic relationships have many an important political corollary').

227. Professor Andreas Lowenfeld was much less circumspect, testifying in Congressional hearings that 'I don't think there is a constitutional requirement for judicial review.' *U.S.-Canada Free Trade Agreement: Hearing Before the Senate Comm. on the Judiciary on the Constitutionality of Establishing a Binational Panel to Resolve Disputes in Antidumping and Countervailing Duty Cases*, 100th Cong. 96, 120 (1988) (statement of Professor Andreas Lowenfeld, New York University School of Law).

228. *See* Ernst-Ulrich Petersmann, *Limited Government and Unlimited Trade Policy Powers? Why Effective Judicial Review of Foreign Trade Restrictions Depends on Individual Rights, in* 8 STUDIES IN TRANSNATIONAL ECONOMIC LAW 91 (Meinhard Hilf & Ernst-Ulrich Petersmann eds., 1993). Within the framework of the European Community, the advances proposed here may appear less startling. European treaty law already allows natural and juridical persons to contest trade norms promulgated by EU institutions before the supranational Court of Justice. *See* Consolidated Version of the Treaty Establishing the European Community [EC Treaty] arts. 230 & 232, 2006 O.J. (C 321E) 37, 146-47; *see also* Helfer & Slaughter, *supra* note 105, at 276-77 (adding the tribunals established by the European Convention for the Protection of Human Rights and Fundamental Freedoms to a select category of supranational adjudication involving private parties litigating directly against State governments or against each other). The challenge within the European Community, in fact, will be to persuade the European

e   *Conclusion*

The endorsement here of a supranational Air Transport Commission does not seek
to disguise the fact that alternatives proliferate: international arbitration, regional
and specialized courts, even the transnational reach of domestic courts.[229] With
globalization as both a catchphrase and a reality, our systems of dispute settlement
must cope with the systematic and continuous flow of goods, services, capital,
ideas, and people across borders. The technical and jurisprudential absurdity of
trying to straitjacket the international aviation industry within domestic legal systems will become increasingly obvious. The premise of air travel, and of global
communications generally, inevitably requires an international approach to operations, financing, and marketing.[230] The prospect of a second stage U.S./EC plurilateral air services agreement presents an unprecedented opportunity to propose a
new kind of global dispute settlement mechanism for the air transport industry in
particular.

Even beyond the specific opportunity of the plurilateral, however, the target
for a radicalized dispute settlement system, including private party standing, is
simply expressed: the creation of a standing authority to determine finally, and on
the basis of a developed body of global air transport law, the conflicting claims of
stakeholders in the international aviation industry in potentially any area of their
relationships governed by law, and which no stakeholder can unilaterally circumvent or avoid in the particular case.[231] The question is whether the U.S./EC

Court of Justice that, as in the United States, a specialized transfer of authority, within an area
requiring distinctive treatment, can withstand constitutional scrutiny. The ECJ has indicated,
for example, that its unique jurisdiction to issue opinions on the compatibility of proposed
international agreements with the EC Treaty is a means to scrutinize 'European Community'
participation (as a party) in international arrangements that involve 'judicial control machinery' and which may impinge on the Court's own jurisdictional competence under the EC
Treaty. *See* Opinion 2/94 on the Accession of the Community to the European Human Rights
Convention, 1996 E.C.R. I-1759. The critical question, it appears, is whether the autonomy of
the 'Community legal order' is compromised. *See* Opinion 1/91 on the Draft Agreement on the
European Economic Area, 1992 E.C.R. I-2821. In this regard, it should be noted that the
proposed Air Transport Commission would not apply EC law as such, but rather a new set
of norms drawn from the synthesis of competition laws considered earlier as well as from the
interpretation and application of the plurilateral agreement.

229. *See* Graeme B. Dinwoodie, *A New Copyright Order: Why National Courts Should Create
Global Norms*, 149 U. Pa. L. Rev. 469 (2000) (arguing that national courts could and should
create global copyright norms in the context of private transborder litigation).

230. *See* Scott Kimpel, *Antitrust Considerations in International Airline Alliances*, 63 J. Air L. &
Com. 475, 476 (1997).

231. There is intentional similarity between these statements and the language adopted by the
American Society of International Law in its 1990 working party report on the jurisdiction
of the International Court of Justice (ICJ):

The [ICJ's] statutory compulsory jurisdiction . . . is the unique concrete embodiment of an
important ideal: that of a standing authority to determine finally and on the basis of general
law the conflicting claims of sovereign [S]tates in potentially any area of their relationships
governed by law, which a [S]tate cannot unilaterally circumvent or avoid in the particular
case. . . .

negotiators will stick with the loose ICAO model of generalized cooperation with benign dispute settlement provisions, as they did in their first stage agreement, or graduate to a treaty that will not only lay down substantive rules but offer a stable, fixed framework of supranational adjudication of transnational public and private disputes.

7	**Principle 7: Adopting the EC 'Community Designation Clause' for Countries outside the Second Stage Plurilateral**

The plurilateral system will need a buffering mechanism that will allow its participating States to maintain their aviation relationships with third countries while also creating a momentum that will sweep more of those countries into the network potential of the plurilateral. Two possible scenarios need to be considered. First, within the plurilateral territory, there is the issue of what we now call seventh freedom traffic rights: for example, under the traffic rights awarded to EU carriers by the 2007 U.S./EC Air Transport Agreement, the United States will allow British Airways to initiate turnaround services from Paris to New York, without a home connection to London[232] – although, as the Agreement currently is written, a formal designation by France will be required (as well as formal acceptance of the designation by the United States).[233] Within a projected plurilateral territory, there is no question that British Airways will have this authority (although, given the intended dismantling of the old edifice of Chicago freedoms, the authority is simply one of market access rather than, as at present, a privilege awarded *sub nomine* the 'seventh freedom').[234]

But a second seventh freedom issue arises, one that taxed the creativity of EC deregulators and that has been resolved, in effect, through a bold display of the EC's aeropolitical power. Air France, for example, may wish to serve a route to a destination *outside* the plurilateral, say London/Sydney, a long-haul market in which British Airways still holds a substantial market share. To compound the

---

AMERICAN SOCIETY OF INTERNATIONAL LAW, REPORT OF THE SPECIAL WORKING COMMITTEE ON THE OPTIONAL CLAUSE 8 (1990).

232. This is exactly what British Airways has done, pursuant to rights awarded under the 2007 U.S./ EC Air Transport Agreement, *supra* note 12, through its new subsidiary carrier, OpenSkies. *See* OpenSkies Website, <https://www.flyopenskies.com/os/home>.

233. *See* U.S./EC Air Transport Agreement, *supra* note 12, art. 4 (reflecting standard bilateral practice with respect to applications for authorization to provide international air services); *see also supra* Chapter 4, Part III(C) (discussing U.S. bilateral designation practice). For reasons of safety and security, but also for sheer administrative efficiency, some form of formal designation process will continue to be necessary within the plurilateral territory.

234. Curiously, under the 2007 U.S./EC Air Transport Agreement, U.S. air passenger carriers do not have reciprocal seventh freedom privileges within the European Union. *See* U.S./EC Air Transport Agreement, *supra* note 12, art. 3. This is the logical legal consequence, however, of a single sovereignty (the United States) negotiating with multiple sovereignties (the European Community/Union) to recognize the ownership/control profiles of the latter's airlines as though they operated from a single sovereignty.

puzzle, let us assume that the citizenship profile of a privatized Air France has shifted under the new plurilateral rules of transborder investment, so that the majority of Air France shareholders are of non-French citizenship (although still citizens of one or more plurilateral member States). Within the plurilateral system, the shift in ownership will be of no operational consequence, but third countries such as Australia – adhering to the Chicago nationality rule – will insist on ownership and control by citizens of the designating State (in this case, the United Kingdom). Perhaps if the majority of Air France's shareholders were now *British*, a designation would be possible if the terms of the U.K./Australia bilateral allowed for multiple carrier service, but Air France would otherwise have no legal claim to provide seventh freedom service in the London/Sydney market.

Quandaries of this kind have surfaced in the EC through the inchoate transborder mergers and acquisitions activity that began with the quasi-merger of Air France and KLM.[235] While we understandably place great reliance on the 'demonstration effect' of the new second stage plurilateral, it cannot simply be ordained that third countries will be obligated to accept or comply with the reconfigurations of the airline industry that occur within the borders of the plurilateral territory. An easy rule, therefore, would be to declare that the *status quo* will continue to regulate the designation of carriers on third country routes – only British Airways, in other words, will serve U.K./Australia routes as the designated U.K. carrier under that bilateral agreement. Where the citizenship profile changes, for example where British Airways becomes majority-owned by U.S. or other EU Member State citizens (i.e., by citizens within the plurilateral member States), it might be expected that the only workable mechanism to protect vested rights would be for the specific bilateral to be amended at the behest of the appropriate plurilateral member State to recognize the designation of a *specific named* carrier by that member State plurilateral government, provided that the named carrier is (and remains) owned and effectively controlled by a majority of natural or legal persons who are, collectively but not necessarily in direct association with each other, citizens of *any member State or member States of the plurilateral.*

The problem with these contrivances, however, is that the distribution criterion is not 'open' and that other carriers within the plurilateral territory consequently remain excluded. Until Australia subscribes to the plurilateral agreement, Air France will not – and cannot – have an independent right of market access to the London/Sydney route which it may exercise *whether or not* it does so by means of acquiring an existing service-provider on that route. These inconsistencies of external route access have been the price of the persistence of the Chicago nationality rule. The European Court of Justice decided in its open skies rulings in 2002, however, that tolerating these inconsistencies was an inequitable – and discriminatory – price for EU carriers to pay for some external destabilization of the rule.[236] As we reviewed in Chapter 5, the Court's rulings placed the EC under a legal

---

235. It is suspected, for example, that the Russian Government has raised concerns about the future nationality profile of Air France-KLM.
236. *See supra* Chapter 2, Part III(A) & Chapter 5, Part III(C).

obligation to renegotiate EU Member State bilateral agreements with third countries to remove the antidiscriminatory effects of the traditional nationality clause.

Accordingly, a combination of EU Member State negotiations and the European Commission's 'horizontal mandate' has been deployed to insert a 'Community designation clause' in each Member State's bilateral agreements with third countries to require that any EU airline which is owned and controlled by EU citizens (*i.e.*, a 'Community air carrier'[237]) can be designated by that Member State to serve all of its external routes to third countries. These actions to comply with the Court's rulings carry an ironic consequence: as in all issues of international aviation to be addressed *outside* the plurilateral system, the likelihood of success for this post-Chicago strategy depends on the practice of traditional Chicago-style aeropolitical diplomacy. Nevertheless, externalizing the plurilateral's organizing principle of nondiscrimination in market access will signal the significance of adhering to the agreement, as well as serve the practical aerodiplomatic needs of the founding States of the second stage plurilateral.[238]

IV   BEYOND OPEN SKIES: THE POLITICAL CHALLENGE
            OF AUTHENTIC LIBERALIZATION

I believe that this study has exposed a serious case for ending the Chicago system of bilateral air services agreements by moving beyond the U.S. 'open skies' policy. The inflection point for change may well be the second stage U.S./EC negotiations that commenced in May 2008, and this Chapter has submitted some ambitious ideas for the negotiators' agenda. In this closing coda, I want to pivot one more time from law to policy and to make some broad observations about the political challenges that confront the next (and potentially determinative) phase – for some, the most 'authentic' phase – of the liberalization process that has been described in this study.

The phrase 'authentic liberalization,' in fact, carries a redundancy: liberalization is neither authentic nor inauthentic, it is a continuum or a process that leads ultimately to a new paradigm of competitive behavior where a balance of benefits is replaced by a balance of opportunities. In any event, liberalization, like the

---

237. *See supra* Chapter 5, note 144 and accompanying text (discussing the term 'Community air carrier' within EC air transport jurisprudence).
238. There is, naturally, a substantial political question with respect to the propensity of certain third countries to accept the proposed plurilateral 'designation clause.' Each affected country would want to assess the changed competitive conditions that the amendment would produce in its aviation relations with the member States of the plurilateral. For example, air traffic to and from the United States is a significant economic contributor to the revenues of the major Japanese airlines, and a retaliatory suspension of even one designation of a Japanese carrier (conjoined, perhaps, with suspensions by other plurilateral member States) would likely discourage insistence on the strict terms of the Chicago nationality rule. In the international system, unfortunately, power-based leverage may sometimes be the only route to rules-based agreements.

period of restrictive bilaterals that preceded it, is essentially a political process. That process has been supported by successive U.S. Administrations but it has not been completed. The struggles faced by the DOT in its NPRM initiative on foreign ownership[239] demonstrated that the political process, for the moment, is stalled. Moreover, although we have proposed abolition of the cabotage laws and examined an expansion of traffic right allocations for U.S. and EU carriers under the 2007 Agreement, there is limited value in further initiatives that focus primarily on traffic rights. For example, it has been argued that the question – 'what are the impediments to an open skies amendment to NAFTA?' – is really the wrong way to look at the issues for future negotiation. If the liberalizing agenda of open skies, as noted earlier, has reached its culmination in the U.S./EC model, it is not clear what incremental gains can or should be achieved by pursuing that model in other directions. Arguably, U.S. carriers have already obtained most of the access rights they seek. (With over 90 open skies agreements in place, the significant holdouts remain China, Japan, Mexico, and Russia.)

If liberalization continues to be a political goal, therefore, the United States will need to be in the vanguard, persisting with the removal of limitations on foreign ownership and control and the abolition of vestiges of protectionism such as the Fly America program. In this view, liberalization will not mean more open skies bilaterals within the framework of the 'Chicago system;' it will require a much more fundamental recasting of the regulation of international air transport. By lifting restrictions on capital inflow and the right of establishment, this restructuring would deliver important benefits that are unavailable under today's open skies regime, including the ability to consolidate across national lines and, relatedly, to more efficiently allocate capacity. It would also give the industry the opportunity to move beyond the inefficient and unstable business model of the alliance.

Although U.S. airlines emerged from bankruptcy with capital raised in the U.S. marketplace (in some cases obtained at lower rates than expected), this does not mean that the capital argument for liberalization has been defeated. These investments took place at the peak of the liquidity flood, and there is no guarantee that they will be repeated. Meanwhile, private transborder equity deals are now being focused on the aviation industry (as recent investments in Iberia and Qantas have shown), and there is no good reason why U.S. airlines should be shut out of that trend. In a global finance market, it is inefficient and costly to structure this industry solely through domestic capital allocation.[240]

The supporters of liberalization claim no vatic insight into the likely performance of any airline in a transcontinental 'beyond open skies' regime, nor are they

---

239. *See supra* Chapter 3, Part V(B) (discussing an effort by the U.S. Department of Transportation to introduce a more expansive interpretive approach to the control test component of the 'nationality' rule).

240. The 'globality' of these rules, incidentally, also inhibits private U.S. equity investor Texas Pacific Group, for example, from buying an increasing stake in EU low-cost carriers such as Ryanair.

troubled by what carriers might actually do to take advantage of new marketplace opportunities. For example, until a dramatic Air France/Delta joint venture announcement that came seven months after the signing of the 2007 U.S./EC Agreement,[241] preliminary reports of the next IATA traffic season had suggested that few new routes would be introduced in the transatlantic marketplace despite the additional opportunities in the Agreement. And bmi, for example, long a proponent of transatlantic open skies, decided to concentrate its future growth plans in its Middle Eastern markets.[242] But a similar period of relative quiescence accompanied the introduction of liberalization in the EC, and eventually the low-cost industry developed across the continent without the traditional ownership restraints and some legacy carriers (like Aer Lingus, for example) even transformed themselves into low-cost operators. The same process has affected a number of U.S. legacy carriers under the discipline of bankruptcy. Airline capital cycles, in any event, are much longer than airline business cycles, and the fact that there is a tepid response to a liberalization initiative does not mean that the political reality of liberalization is thereby compromised. The quest for liberalization, in this view, always has the same purpose – to allow market forces to determine the shape of a marketplace where cost structures are so marginal that there will always be potential players who, if they have the freedom to enter the market with a perceived advantage, will exercise it.

Increasingly, also, the challenges that confront international air transport service relate less to opening markets and more to a new set of challenges that are not necessarily appropriate for bilateral arrangements. For these newer and growing challenges (*e.g.*, emissions, security, foreign ownership and control, and airport and airspace congestion), multilateral (and maybe even unilateral) approaches should be pursued. According to this approach, security and environment issues have emerged as global challenges that require ever-closer collaboration among governments in order to address the threats efficiently and effectively and to ensure that businesses and their customers are not harmed by duplicative, conflicting, or unnecessarily burdensome and costly rules and regulations. Other pressing issues, such as congested airports and oversubscribed air traffic systems, may be tackled

---

241. *See* Tim Hepher & Benoit van Overstraeten, *Air France, Delta Lead Charge on Heathrow*, Reuters News Service (Oct. 17, 2007) (describing new Air France/Delta joint venture plans with respect to Heathrow and other EU hubs); *but see supra* Chapter 5, note 367 (discussing Air France's dropping of its Los Angeles/Heathrow service after only seven months because of adverse economic conditions). The joint venture is the first use of the 'Community carrier' concept to which the United States agreed early on in U.S./EC negotiations. *See supra* Chapter 2, Part V(A). The response of Heathrow incumbents British Airways and Virgin Atlantic to this kind of incursion will be interesting, not least in terms of possible future consolidation. As noted, British Airways has already launched a subsidiary operation, OpenSkies, *see supra* note 232, to fly routes between the European mainland and New York's JFK airport. Virgin Atlantic, however, has ruled out offering similar services until at least 2010. *See* Ian Taylor, *Virgin Atlantic Rules Out Continental Europe to US Service Until 2010*, TRAVEL WKLY., Mar. 4, 2008.
242. *See* Victoria Moores, *Bmi Puts Off Transatlantic Push*, AIRLINE BUS., Oct. 2007, at 26 (noting that bmi management believes that 'everybody was caught off-guard by how quickly Open Skies came through, following many false dawns').

optimally through unilateral government intervention, but unilateralism always carries the risk of discriminatory treatment and it is clear that some international standards to protect non-national carriers will be implicated. With respect to the nationality rule – the foreign ownership and control restrictions through which this book has traced its arc of reform – the internal and external dimensions of the applicable laws (combining bilateral restrictions with domestic legislation) mean that States must focus on both multilateral and unilateral action.

The search for appropriate multilateral fora continues. Regionalism has been the preferred model (the U.S./EC and the U.S./Asian MALIAT[243] agreements, for example), but other options could include the multipolar framework of the WTO GATS and its Air Transport Annex.[244] ICAO offers a forum for global solutions on environmental issues, and NAFTA remains a potential vehicle for cooperation in air transport, a sector that the treaty has never embraced despite the 'continental thinking' that it is supposed to represent.[245]

Finally, with respect to the political challenges of the U.S./EC second stage agenda itself, a number of concluding comments should be added. Maintaining the optimal political (and policy) conditions for any aviation agreement, let alone an agreement of the magnitude proposed in this final Chapter, is always an immense challenge. The United States, through its underserved cities program[246] and then the open skies regime, changed fundamentally the way airlines across the globe look at the regulation of civil aviation (as IATA chief Giovanni Bisignani conceded with respect to open skies).[247] But the aeropolitical priorities of the United States and the EC seem to have diverged as the second stage negotiations begin.

In the first stage talks, the U.S. negotiators gave priority to the mercantilist ambition of dislodging what they perceived as London Heathrow's comfortable oligopoly. The European Commission, fronting the EC negotiations, never conceded that U.S. acquiescence in the Community designation clause as the *quid pro quo* for access to Heathrow – but without any shift in U.S. cabotage or nationality laws – was necessarily a balanced negotiation.[248] The Commission, prime architect

---

243. *See supra* Chapter 2, note 114 and accompanying text.

244. *See supra* Part III(C).

245. *See* Norman Y. Mineta, U.S. Secretary of Transportation, Remarks to the Canadian Open Skies Forum (Feb. 24, 2005). With close to 20 million passengers annually, Canada/U.S. transborder air passenger movements comprise what is almost certainly the largest bilateral air transport market in the world. *See* Bureau of Transportation Statistics, Passenger Travel Between the United States, Canada, and Mexico, <http://www.bts.gov/publications/north_american_trade_and_travel_trends/travel_us_can_mex.html>.

246. *See supra* Chapter 4, note 371 (discussing the program).

247. *See, e.g.*, Giovanni Bisignani, Director General and CEO, IATA, *Leading Change*, Remarks to the International Aviation Club, Washington, D.C. (Apr. 20, 2004).

248. And yet the Council of Ministers approved the 2007 Agreement. One senior U.K. Department of Transport official with whom I spoke reported that U.K. airline chiefs were outraged by Britain's acquiescence to the 2007 treaty without a deal on U.S. inward foreign investment. In this official's view, the U.K. Government felt that the deal unlocked certain real consumer benefits and that rejection would simply compel the European Commission to restart the tortuous and politically fraught process of enforcement proceedings against the Member States.

of EC airline liberalization, the evolving ECAA, the Single European Sky, the European Aviation Safety Agency, and a projected 'Open Aviation Area,'[249] has grasped the mantle of reform and is no longer interested in a mere balance of benefits but in a fundamental change in the dominant regulatory profile of international aviation. And, although the Commission has earned the authority to be a one-stop negotiator with the United States, it remains in an unresolved tension with the Council of Ministers and the Member States as to the ultimate assignment of responsibility for the Community's external aviation relations dossier.[250] In these circumstances, the Commission will be determined to secure a second stage agreement that unlocks the internal and external bolts of the nationality rule[251] and that has aeropolitical demonstration effects that sway not only the rest of the world but also the Commission's political masters in the Council of Ministers.[252]

The United States, in contrast, has taken the position that the second stage agenda – and especially the pivotal issue of the future of the nationality rule – is not only complicated but also legally difficult, and shows no sense of urgency in resisting the continuing opposition to full liberalization shared by the defense establishment, labor unions, and vocal factions in Congress.[253] In contrast to the Commission, the United States – as its chief negotiator John Byerly has publicly declared – does see the 2007 Agreement as a reasonable balance of interests.[254] The U.S. side, accordingly, will react strongly to any disruption of that balance if some EU Member States (as they have threatened) seek to suspend rights under the

---

249. As previously noted, the 'beyond open skies' paradigm contemplated by the European Commission is the so-called 'Open Aviation Area' (OAA) which would come into effect between the United States and the European Community. *See* Brattle Group, The Economic Impact of an EU-U.S. Open Aviation Area (2002). The OAA is derived conceptually from the 'TCAA' proposed by the Association of European Airlines in its groundbreaking 1999 policy paper. *See* AEA, Transatlantic Common Aviation Area, *supra* note 122. The OAA, regarded by some as 'the next big idea' in global aviation, would comprise full freedoms of the air (including cabotage) extended to both parties, removal of investment restrictions by both parties, unrestricted wet leasing (to include domestic routes), and a commitment to regulatory convergence and harmonization standards at a high common level in safety, security, operations, competition, State subsidies, and the environment. Thus, the OAA is intended to provide a *holistic* framework to deliver full market access. It shares with the U.S. open skies policy a consumer orientation, as well as the goal of transcending the traditional Chicago market constraints that lead to an undersupply of the 'travel commodity,' non-optimal pricing, and the discouragement of new operators and increased capacities. Given the legislative changes necessary for an OAA regime, it is thought that this capstone agreement would be adopted as a Senate treaty rather than in the form of an executive agreement, the procedure used for the 2007 first stage.
250. *See supra* Chapter 5, Part III(G).
251. *See supra* Chapter 3, Part V(C).
252. The Council, after all, has the power to award 'vertical' mandates to the Commission for comprehensive negotiations with other designated third countries in addition to the United States. *See supra* Chapter 5, Part III(D).
253. *See supra* Chapter 3, Part V(C).
254. John R. Byerly, Deputy Assistant Secretary for Transportation Affairs, U.S. Department of State, Panel Remarks at the 19th Annual European Air Law Association Conference, Dublin, Ireland (Nov. 9, 2007) (notes on file with author).

Agreement in response to a U.S. institutional unwillingness to change the foreign ownership (and possibly also the cabotage) laws as part of the second stage negotiations. As we have noted before, the missiological self-confidence of the European Commission, speaking with one voice for 27 nations, is one to which U.S. negotiators have had difficulty in adapting.[255] And the Commission, ultimately, will stand with its Member States if they seek suspension.[256]

The U.S. Government, in the past, played the role of pioneer in air transport regulation almost for its own sake: initially, the airline industry resisted domestic deregulation and resisted the open skies effort to inject a measure of liberalization into bilateral aviation relations with third countries. But the spirit of innovation has not entirely departed. In 1994, as the U.S. open skies policy was being rolled out, former American Airlines Chairman Robert L. Crandall – still today, as we have seen, a feisty contributor to the regulatory debate[257] – summoned 'theorists and observers of the air transport industry to develop a new multilateral protocol that would grant airline managements the right to exploit markets and opportunities wherever they occur.'[258] A decade later, Rush O'Keefe, general counsel of FedEx, called for a new Chicago Convention that would do precisely that.[259] Leveraged by the 2007 U.S./EC Air Transport Agreement, the idea of a plurilateral 'beyond open skies' agreement has evolved from an intellectually appealing theory to an accessible solution, anchored in the free trade principles shared by the United States and the EC, to the most challenging regulatory problem in modern international air transport. So long as governments remain the proprietors of even the most basic rights of market access, the 'aeropolitics' of the nationality rule and of piecemeal exchange will endure.[260] It is time to ask governments to reinvent their custody of this global industry. It is time, in a phrase, to move 'beyond open skies.'

---

255. The Commission has shown no reluctance to act unilaterally in international aviation matters. The most controversial recent example has been the extension of its emissions trading scheme to flights entering and departing EU airspace, defying certain assumed prerogatives of the International Civil Aviation Organization. *See supra* note 181.

256. U.S. negotiators may feel sanguine about Community or Member State suspensions given that the Community designation clause is mandated by European Court of Justice rulings and would be in jeopardy if the United States withdrew its acquiescence in the clause. Presumably, in that case, the Member States would predicate a return to pre-2007 Chicago system rules based on some type of *force majeure* argument.

257. *See supra* Chapter 4, Part IV(C) (discussing Crandall's proposals for some mild industry re-regulation to weather recent oil price volatility).

258. *See* remarks of Robert L. Crandall, Chairman and Chief Executive Officer, American Airlines, Inc., *quoted in* Frank Swoboda, *Airlines Urged to Link with Foreign Carriers: New U.S. Policy Seeks Global Market Access*, Wash. Post, Nov. 2, 1994, at F1.

259. *See Aviation Leadership Summit, supra* note 27, at 15.

260. The penetrating term 'aeropolitics,' – hitherto used only adjectivally in this book ('aeropolitical') – to describe a bilateral system of constant bartering of specific traffic rights and mutual protest of allegedly unfair competitive practices, may be a coinage of Patrick V. Murphy, DOT Acting Assistant Secretary for Policy and International Affairs, in his testimony to the Airline Commission, *Airline Commission Proceedings* (May 24, 1993), at 168.

Appendix I

Department of Transportation Statement of United States International Air Transportation Policy May 3, 1995

SUMMARY: This notice sets forth a statement of U.S. international air transportation policy.

FOR FURTHER INFORMATION CONTACT: William Boyd, Office of International Aviation, Office of the Assistant Secretary for Aviation and International Affairs, U.S. Department of Transportation, 400 7th Street SW., Room 6412, Washington, DC 20590, (202) 366-4870; or Patricia N. Snyder, Office of International Law, Office of the General Counsel, U.S. Department of Transportation, 400 7th Street SW., Room 10105, Washington, DC 20590. (202) 366-9179.

SUPPLEMENTARY INFORMATION: This statement of U.S. international air transportation policy, which was developed by the Department of Transportation in consultation with the Department of State and other executive agencies, sets forth objectives and guidelines for use by U.S. Government officials in carrying out U.S. international air transportation policy. It was first published in the Federal Register on November 7, 1994 to enable interested persons to comment.[1] On January 6, 1995, the Department asked for comments on a related report prepared for the Office of the Secretary titled 'A Study of International Airline Code Sharing.'[2] After reviewing the comments received on the policy statement and on the

---

1. An earlier statement of international air transportation policy and our request for comments on the statement was published at 59 FR 55523, Nov. 7, 1994.
2. Our request for comments on the code sharing study was published at 60 FR 2171, Jan. 6, 1995.

code sharing study, the Department of Transportation and other agencies have adopted the following final international air transportation policy statement.

Introduction

The availability of efficient international air transportation will greatly enhance the future expansion of international commerce and the development of the emerging global marketplace. Worldwide, travelers and shippers are demanding more and better quality service to more places. U.S. and foreign airlines are responding to this demand by expanding traditional forms of service and by developing new and innovative services. Increased demand and the variety of carrier responses to it challenge the existing intergovernmental system's ability to ensure the development of a competitive air transportation system that meets the needs of the rapidly evolving, expanding and increasingly integrated international aviation marketplace. In many cases, existing bilateral agreements impede the growth of the marketplace.

We must address the challenges presented by these rapid changes to meet our future civil and military air transportation needs, and to provide our aviation industry with the environment and the opportunities that will enable it to grow and compete effectively in the world market. This policy statement outlines our approach to addressing those challenges.

Our Goal

Safe, Affordable, Convenient and Efficient Air Service for Consumers

As established in our last aviation policy statement in 1978, our overall goal continues to be to foster safe, affordable, convenient and efficient air service for consumers. We continue to believe that the best way to achieve this goal is to rely on the marketplace and unrestricted, fair competition to determine the variety, quality, and price of air service. We believe that this approach will provide consumers and shippers with more and better service options at costs that reflect economically efficient operations and work best to:

- Expand the international aviation market;
- Increase airlines' opportunities to expand their operations;
- Increase productivity and high-quality job opportunities within the aviation industry;
- Address the nation's defense air transportation needs; and
- Promote aerospace exports and general economic growth.

Changing Environment

Growing economic interdependence among nations – the 'globalization' of the world economy – has expanded demand for convenient, reliable and affordable international air service. Demand for international service is growing faster than demand for U.S. domestic service, and most major U.S. airlines are now providing and planning to expand international operations. Between 1983 and 1993, the international component of U.S. airlines' route networks, measured in revenue passenger miles (RPMs), grew from around 16% to over 27%. U.S. airline revenues from international air service nearly tripled from $6.3 billion to $17.6 billion. Moreover, forecasts indicate that U.S. carrier international traffic, measured by RPMs, will increase to almost one-third of their total system traffic by the year 2000.

Just as important, the pattern of demand for international service has changed considerably. First, the regional distribution of U.S. carriers' international revenues has changed dramatically, as the primary focus of carriers' expansion moved beyond Europe to meet new demand in the emerging markets of Asia, the Pacific Rim and Latin America. In 1983, the Atlantic accounted for 48% of our carriers' international revenues, while the Pacific accounted for 32%. By 1993, the Pacific had grown to 46% while the Atlantic was only 37%. The fastest growing sectors of the international aviation market are new and relatively undeveloped markets. During this same period, revenues in the Pacific grew 286%, in Latin America 151% and in Europe 116%. Second, from 1983 to 1993, the number of international aviation city-pair markets in which U.S. airlines participate has grown by more than a third, reflecting the major expansion of air service and carrier networks throughout the world and the increased dispersion of demand. Many of these city-pair markets are relatively small, generating only a few passengers per day.

Towards a Globalized Aviation Industry

The rapid growth of demand for international air service and the wider dispersion of traffic in city-pair markets are primary factors influencing the development of the air service industry. Carriers are increasingly finding that they cannot remain profitable unless they can respond to this changed demand. To compete effectively, carriers today must have unrestricted access to as many markets and passengers as possible.

To meet demand and to improve their efficiency, many carriers are developing international hub-and-spoke systems that permit them to combine traffic flows from many routes (the 'spokes') at a central point (the 'hub') and transport them to another point either directly or through a hub in another region. Just as U.S. carriers developed hub-and-spoke systems to tap the broad traffic pool in the domestic market and to provide the most cost-efficient service for hundreds of communities that could not support direct service, international air carriers are developing world-wide hub-and-spoke systems to tap the substantial pool of international city-pairs. Internationally, an even larger portion of traffic moving over hub-and-spoke systems will require the use of at least two hubs (e.g., a hub in both the U.S. and Europe for a passenger moving from an interior U.S. point to a point beyond the European hub). This increases the complexity and interdependence of the components of the system (both the spokes and hubs) and the importance of multinational traffic rights to the success of the system.

As a result, carriers wishing to establish global networks require a higher quality and quantity of supporting route authority than they have sought in the past. Airlines will become increasingly concerned with every market that enables them to flow passengers over any part of their system network. These airlines will be looking for broad, flexible authority to operate beyond and behind hub points, in addition to the hub-to-hub market between two countries. At present, governments operating in a bilateral context naturally focus on opportunities for their respective carriers to serve the local market between their two countries. In a bilateral context, services destined for or coming from third countries receive less consideration. In the future, governments will have to adjust their focus to bargain for the bundles of rights that will permit airlines to develop global networks.

Carriers can either serve markets themselves (direct service) or provide service through commercial arrangements with other carriers (indirect service), whether on a traditional interline connecting basis or under a closer commercial agreement between the carriers, such as code sharing. Carriers will develop service products – single-plane, on-line connecting, interline connecting, joint service – that respond to the preferences of the traveling public as measured by passenger willingness to pay for differences in the quality of service and that take into account their cost structure and market strategy. To the greatest extent possible, airlines should be free to set prices and offer various service products in response to passenger preferences.

Significant challenges face carriers wishing to develop international networks using their own direct services. They need:

- Substantial access not only to key hub cities overseas, but also through and beyond them to numerous other cities, mostly in third countries. This type of access is not readily obtainable in today's bilateral system of negotiating air rights, since governments can only exchange access rights to their own countries and cannot, between themselves, deliver access to third countries, thus requiring piecemeal negotiating efforts to build the necessary package of rights;
- Access to a large number of gates and takeoff/landing slots, frequently at some of the world's most congested airports. It may become increasingly difficult for carriers to gain effective, direct access to certain airport facilities, including some in the United States;
- Considerable financial resources to establish and sustain commercially successful overseas hub systems; and
- The ability to obtain infrastructure and establish market presence in a new region quickly. Existing foreign investment laws can effectively preclude airlines from entering new markets in one of the most efficient means available: merger or acquisition.

Some carriers are taking on these challenges directly and are striving to develop their own global systems of direct service. Other carriers have chosen to side-step the obstacles, turning instead to a new network-building technique: Cross-border marketing alliances that link traffic flows between established hub-and-spoke systems in key cities of the Western Hemisphere, Europe and Asia. Some of these alliances involve cross ownership, while others do not. Under this strategy, the linking of hubs requires indirect market access through code-sharing or other cooperative marketing arrangements. Although code sharing has become a widely-used marketing device for airlines and is currently the most prevalent form of commercial arrangement, further evolution of the industry and its regulatory environment may lead to new marketing practices that could supplement or supplant code sharing.

Code sharing and other cooperative marketing arrangements can provide a cost-efficient way for carriers to enter new markets, expand their systems and obtain additional flow traffic to support their other operations by using existing facilities and scheduled operations. Because these cooperative arrangements can give the airline partners new or additional access to more markets, the partners will gain traffic, some stimulated by the new service, and some diverted from incumbents. In this way, cooperative arrangements can enhance the competitive positions of both partners in such a relationship.

Increased international code sharing and other cooperative arrangements can benefit consumers by increasing international service options and enhancing competition between carriers, particularly for traffic to or from cities behind major gateways. By stimulating traffic, the increased competition and service options should expand the overall international market and increase overall opportunities for the aviation industry. U.S. airlines should be major beneficiaries of this expansion and the concomitant increased service opportunities, given their competitive advantages.

Moreover, code sharing should also enhance domestic competition. Many international passengers traveling to or from U.S. interior cities use domestic services for some portion of their international journey. Code sharing should increase competition among domestic carriers to carry those passengers on the domestic segment of their international journey.

Although we expect the expansion of cooperative arrangements to be largely beneficial, there may be some negative effects. The greater traffic access of participants may give them considerable competitive muscle, and we may need to watch for harmful effects on competition. In addition, cooperative arrangements may affect the availability of civil aircraft to meet emergency airlift requirements. Our national defense establishment relies on U.S. civil aircraft committed to the Civil Reserve Air Fleet program to respond to worldwide crises. As set forth in our National Airlift Policy, the global mobility needs of our national defense establishment, and ensuring that the nation's defense air transportation needs are met during peace and contingency operations, are important considerations.

Global systems and the growing use of code sharing may put significant competitive pressure on carriers whose strategy does not include participation in such systems or in code-sharing alliances, or whose options to participate may be limited due to the lack of potential partners. Such carriers will have to develop other commercial responses to compete effectively. We expect these pressures and responses to lead to a restructuring of service and airlines, similar to the U.S. domestic experience in the 1980s. Overall, cities and consumers will probably enjoy improved service and access to the international transportation system, although some cities may have fewer or less convenient service options in some markets than they have today. Similarly, although some airlines will grow and prosper, others will not. Moreover, we recognize that the balance of benefits in any particular alliance will depend on the specific structure of that arrangement between the partners. Overall, this evolution should expand the level and quality of international air service for consumers.

Code-sharing arrangements are designed to address the preference of passengers and shippers for on-line service from beginning to end through coordinated scheduling, baggage- and cargo-handling, and other elements of single-carrier service. However, innovative service products, such as code sharing, can only respond to consumer preferences accurately, and thereby enable the marketplace to function efficiently, if consumers make choices based on full information. Therefore, we must ensure that airlines give consumers clear information about the characteristics of their service product, and that consumers can distinguish between code sharing and other forms of service.

In addition to the two types of global networks (sole-carrier systems and joint carrier systems), there will continue to be a role for air services outside of global networks. The U.S. experience with deregulation indicates that – absent legal barriers to entry – specialized competitors will enter the market and discipline the pricing and service behavior of the larger network operators. The introduction of technologically advanced aircraft such as the B-767, the MD-11 and the B-777 make direct service on longer or thinner routes economically viable. Moreover, airlines can viably serve heavily traveled routes with point-to-point service.

In short, as indicated by our domestic experience, a variety of service forms – global networks with carriers participating either as the sole provider or as participant in a joint network, and regional niche carriers – can exist in the international aviation market and the competition among these services will enhance consumer benefits through efficient operations and low fares. Thus, our international aviation strategy should provide opportunities for all of these forms of service so that we realize the benefits from maximum competition among them.

Our airlines are well positioned to be primary participants in all aspects of the future global marketplace. In recent years, our largest domestic carriers have become our primary international carriers, replacing specialized international operators. After operating in a deregulated domestic market for more than 15 years, our carriers have developed operating efficiencies that give them a cost advantage over their major foreign competitors. Moreover, the financial positions of our carriers are improving due to their cost-cutting measures and improving economic conditions. Coupled with their cost efficiencies, their improving financial status will further enhance their competitive capabilities. Over time, however, trends toward privatization and increased productivity of major foreign competitors may affect the current cost advantage U.S. airlines enjoy. We must try to provide our carriers with the flexible rights and economic environment that will enable them to respond to the dynamics of the marketplace.

Intergovernment Aviation Relations

International air services between two nations have traditionally been conducted pursuant to bilateral agreements. The U.S. National Commission to Ensure a Strong Competitive Airline Industry and the European Union's Comité des Sages for Air Transport have both recognized that the bilateral system is limited in its ability to encompass the broad, multinational market access required by the new global operating systems. Consequently, progress in developing global networks has been and will be extremely fragmented and may preclude or limit the development of efficient operations. We must consider alternative forums for international aviation negotiations and agreements in which we can obtain the necessary broad access rights. We should examine the feasibility of achieving multilateral air service agreements among trading partners. Although such negotiations may be more complex and difficult because of the number of parties involved, they should be undertaken when they present a reasonable prospect for further liberalization.

Moreover, some governments are taking steps to enhance their airlines' positions both by restricting the development of new, competitive services and by trying to overcome, through government fiat, their carriers' cost disadvantages that make it difficult for them to compete against U.S. airlines in a free market. These efforts underlie many of the disputes we face in international negotiations today.

Such countries are responding to the highly competitive integrated and global air transportation market, in which their airlines may not be fully prepared to compete. Most foreign airlines are only beginning to adapt to the more competitive operating environment through such mechanisms as streamlining costs and realigning their operations to achieve greater productivity and operating economies. For state-owned airlines, privatization is an important initial step as it will lead those airlines to develop cost-efficient operations and, in the longer term, to expand their markets. These governments also may be reacting to the U.S. airlines' recent operating successes in the international aviation market, which are largely attributable to the U.S. airlines' productivity and competitive gains.

Some national governments continue to give their national airlines financial aid. Some also distort the marketplace by permitting their national airlines to maintain ground-handling and other monopolies, by denying airlines access to necessary airport facilities, or by allowing user fees that equalize cost differentials between carriers. These actions distort competition and deprive the aviation system and consumers of the benefits that greater cost efficiency and lower prices would encourage. In the long run, these efforts will work against the overall best interest of the world economy. Moreover, they will be unsuccessful in providing long-term protection against the developing global aviation systems because no individual government can control all facets of its airlines' marketplace.

U.S. Objectives

We have outlined above our expectations about the future of the world air transportation industry and the role of U.S. airlines. We expect that international operations will depend more on traffic flows from multiple countries. In light of our goals, recent developments in the market and industry, and the positions and actions of our trading partners, we have designed our international aviation strategy to meet the following objectives:

- Increase the variety of price and service options available to consumers.
- Enhance the access of U.S. cities to the international air transportation system.
- Provide carriers with unrestricted opportunities to develop types of service and systems based on their assessment of marketplace demand:
  - These opportunities should include unrestricted rights for airlines to operate between international gateways by way of any point and beyond to any point, at the discretion of airline management. Carriers should be able to pursue both direct service using their own equipment and indirect service through commercial relationships with other carriers;
  - Service opportunities should not be restricted in any manner, such as restrictions on frequencies, capacity or equipment, so that carriers may provide levels of service commensurate with market demand;
  - Carriers' ability to set prices should also be unrestricted to create maximum incentives for cost efficiencies and to provide consumers with the benefits of price competition and lower fares; and
  - These opportunities should apply not only to scheduled passenger services, but also to cargo and charter opportunities, because of their growing importance to the world's economy. We have long recognized the significant differences among these types of operations. In particular, air cargo services have specific qualities and requirements that are significantly different from the passenger market. We will continue to follow our longstanding policy of seeking an open, liberal operating environment to facilitate the establishment and expansion of efficient, innovative and competitive air cargo services.
- Recognize the importance of military and civil airlift resources being able to meet defense mobilization and deployment requirements in support of U.S. defense and foreign policies.
- Ensure that competition is fair and the playing field is level by eliminating marketplace distortions, such as government subsidies, restrictions on carriers' ability to conduct their own operations and ground-handling, and unequal access to infrastructure, facilities, or marketing channels.
- Encourage the development of the most cost-effective and productive air transportation industry that will be best equipped to compete in the global aviation marketplace at all levels and with all types of service:
  - Infrastructure needs should be addressed and unnecessary regulatory barriers eliminated.

- Privately held airlines have better incentives to reduce costs and respond to public demand. Therefore, as we have in the past, we will be supportive of governments wishing to privatize their airlines so that their privatization efforts will be successful; and
- Reduce barriers to the creation of global aviation systems, such as limitations on cross-border investments wherever possible.

Plan of Action

We recognize that considerable time and effort will be required to achieve an open aviation regime worldwide. We can get there by making a concerted effort to eliminate the obstacles to that regime and by taking a more strategic and long-term approach to our overall international aviation policies. At a minimum, we must increase our focus on emerging markets and their contribution to global networks; build a coalition of like-minded trading partners committed to the principles of free trade in aviation services; work closely with our trading partners to address their concerns; develop new incentives for encouraging market reform, such as increased opportunities for cross-border investment in airlines; and devise alternatives to the bilateral aviation system for achieving our objectives. We are launching our new initiatives to create freer trade in aviation services by taking the following steps:

- Extend invitations to enter into open aviation agreements to a group of countries that share our vision of liberalization and offer important flow traffic potential for our carriers even though they may have limited Third and Fourth Freedom traffic potential. This would assist the development of global systems and increase the momentum for further worldwide liberalization.
- Give priority to building aviation relationships between the United States and potential growth areas in Asia, South America and Central Europe. This recognizes the importance of these trading partners and the need to provide air transportation to support those developing trade markets. It will also make available new markets to build global networks.
- Renew efforts to achieve liberal agreements with trading partners with which our aviation relationships lag behind those of our general trade advancements, as we have done successfully with Canada.
- Emphasize the importance of sound economic analysis based on sufficient data in developing policies and strategies for achieving our overall aviation goals. This will enable us to remain focused on the overall strategic objectives, understand developments in the industry and market, and plan for the future.
- Seek changes in U.S. airline foreign investment law, if necessary, to enable us to obtain our trading partners' agreement to liberal arrangements to the extent it is consistent with U.S. economic and security interests.
- Increase our efforts to reach out to Congress and constituent groups, such as consumers, corporations with international perspectives (aircraft manufacturers, telecommunications, travel and tourism industries), cities, airports, airlines, labor and travel agents to learn their anticipated needs over a 3-5 year

period. This will provide us with valuable information for developing our positions, as well as enlisting their support in pushing for greater liberalization.

- Establish stronger connections among U.S. government agencies whose functions are to promote U.S. business and trade interests (e.g., Departments of Commerce, State, and Transportation, Office of the United States Trade Representative, and the Export/Import Bank) as well as the Department of Defense, to ensure that we share a single vision of the future global marketplace while meeting national security requirements.

Given the diverse positions of our trading partners and their varying degrees of willingness to liberalize aviation relations, we must also have a strategy for dealing with countries that are not prepared or willing to join us in moving quickly to an unrestricted air service regime. Our approach is a practical one: It proposes to advance the liberalization of air service regimes as far as our partners are willing to go, and to withhold benefits from those countries that are not willing to move forward. Specifically, we will pursue the following strategy:

1. We will offer liberal agreements to a country or group of countries if it can be justified economically or strategically. We will view economic value more broadly than we have in the past, in terms of both direct and indirect access and in terms of potential future development. Moreover, there may be strategic value in adopting liberal agreements with smaller countries where doing so puts competitive pressure on neighboring countries to follow suit.

2. We recognize that some countries believe that they can resist the trend of economic forces and continue to control access to their markets tightly. We believe that they cannot, and that attempts to do so will ultimately fail. Nevertheless, we will work with these countries to develop alternatives that address their immediate concerns where this will advance our international aviation policy objectives. We will examine alternative approaches that may include departing from established methods of negotiation (perhaps negotiations with two or more trading partners); trying to develop service opportunities for the foreign airline to make service to the U.S. more economically advantageous for it; and continuing our efforts to help those governments and their constituencies appreciate the benefits that unrestricted air services can bring to their economies and industries.

While we work with such countries, we can consider, in the interim, transitional or sectoral agreements.

Transitional agreements – Under this approach, we would agree to a specified phased removal of restrictions and liberalization of the air service market. This approach contemplates that both sides would agree, from the beginning, to a completely liberalized air service regime that would come into effect at the end of a certain period of time.

Sectoral agreements – Traditionally, aviation agreements have covered all elements of air transportation between two countries. However, as a first step, we can consider agreements that eliminate restrictions only on services in specific aviation sectors, such as air cargo or charter services.

3. For countries that are not willing to advance liberalization of the market, we will maintain maximum leverage to achieve our procompetitive objectives. We can limit their airlines' access to the U.S. market and restrict commercial relations with U.S. airlines. When airlines request authority to serve restricted bilateral markets that is not provided for under an international agreement, we will consider their requests on a case-by-case basis in light of all our policy objectives, including, inter alia:

- Whether approval will increase the variety of pricing and service options available to consumers;
- Whether approval will improve the access of cities, shippers and travelers to the international air transportation system;
- The effect of granting code-sharing authority on the Civil Reserve Air Fleet program;
- The effect of the proposed transaction on the U.S. airline industry and its employees. In this regard, we will ascribe greater value to code-sharing arrangements where U.S. airlines provide the long-haul operations. We will also recognize the greater economic value of such arrangements where the services connect one hub to another; and
- Whether the transaction will advance our goals of eliminating operating and market restrictions and achieving liberalization.

If aviation partners fail to observe existing U.S. bilateral rights, or discriminate against U.S. airlines, we will act vigorously, through all appropriate means, to defend our rights and protect our airlines.

Conclusion

We are living through a period in which international aviation rules must change. Privatization, competition, and globalization are trends fueled by economic and political forces that will ultimately prevail. Governments and airlines that embrace these trends will far outpace those that do not. The U.S. government will be among those that embrace the future.

Dated: April 25, 1995.

Patrick V. Murphy,
Acting Assistant Secretary for Aviation and International Affairs, Department of Transportation.

Appendix II

Model U.S. Open Skies Agreement

AIR TRANSPORT AGREEMENT BETWEEN THE GOVERNMENT OF THE UNITED STATES OF AMERICA AND THE GOVERNMENT OF [country]

The Government of the United States of America and the Government of [country] (hereinafter, 'the Parties');

Desiring to promote an international aviation system based on competition among airlines in the marketplace with minimum government interference and regulation;

Desiring to make it possible for airlines to offer the traveling and shipping public a variety of service options, and wishing to encourage individual airlines to develop and implement innovative and competitive prices;

Desiring to facilitate the expansion of international air transport opportunities;

Desiring to ensure the highest degree of safety and security in international air transport and reaffirming their grave concern about acts or threats against the security of aircraft, which jeopardize the safety of persons or property, adversely affect the operation of air transportation, and undermine public confidence in the safety of civil aviation; and

Being Parties to the Convention on International Civil Aviation, done at Chicago December 7, 1944;

Have agreed as follows:

Article 1
Definitions

For the purposes of this Agreement, unless otherwise stated, the term:

1. 'Aeronautical authorities' means, in the case of the United States, the Department of Transportation and in the case of [country], the [appropriate

entity], and any person or agency authorized to perform functions exercised by the Department of Transportation or said [appropriate entity];

2. 'Agreement' means this Agreement and any amendments thereto;
3. 'Air transportation' means the public carriage by aircraft of passengers, baggage, cargo, and mail, separately or in combination, scheduled or charter, for remuneration or hire;
4. 'Airline of a Party' means an airline that is licensed by and has its principal place of business in the territory of that Party;
5. 'Convention' means the Convention on International Civil Aviation, done at Chicago December 7, 1944, and includes:
   a. any amendment that has entered into force under Article 94(a) of the Convention and has been ratified by both Parties, and
   b. any Annex or any amendment thereto adopted under Article 90 of the Convention, insofar as such Annex or amendment is at any given time effective for both Parties;
6. 'Full cost' means the cost of providing service plus a reasonable charge for administrative overhead;
7. 'International air transportation' means air transportation that passes through the airspace over the territory of more than one State;
8. 'Price' means any fare, rate, or charge for the carriage of passengers, baggage, or cargo (excluding mail) in air transportation, including surface transportation in connection with international air transportation, charged by airlines, including their agents, and the conditions governing the availability of such fare, rate, or charge;
9. 'Stop for non-traffic purposes' means a landing for any purpose other than taking on or discharging passengers, baggage, cargo, or mail in air transportation;
10. 'Territory' means the land areas, internal waters, and territorial sea under the sovereignty of a Party; and
11. 'User charge' means a charge imposed on airlines for the provision of airport, airport environmental, air navigation, or aviation security facilities or services including related services and facilities.

Article 2
Grant of Rights

1. Each Party grants to the other Party the following rights for the conduct of international air transportation by the airlines of the other Party:
   (a) the right to fly across its territory without landing;
   (b) the right to make stops in its territory for non-traffic purposes;
   (c) the right to perform international air transportation between points on the following routes:
      (i) for airlines of the United States, from points behind the United States via the United States and intermediate points to any point

or points in [country] and beyond; [and for all-cargo service, between [country] and any point or points;]

(ii) for airlines of [country], from points behind [country] via [country] and intermediate points to any point or points in the United States and beyond; [and for all-cargo service, between the United States and any point or points;] and

(d) the rights otherwise specified in this Agreement.

2. Each airline of a Party may, on any or all flights and at its option:

    a. operate flights in either or both directions;

    b. combine different flight numbers within one aircraft operation;

    c. serve behind, intermediate, and beyond points and points in the territories of the Parties in any combination and in any order;

    d. omit stops at any point or points;

    e. transfer traffic from any of its aircraft to any of its other aircraft at any point;

    f. serve points behind any point in its territory with or without change of aircraft or flight number and hold out and advertise such services to the public as through services;

    g. make stopovers at any points whether within or outside the territory of either Party;

    h. carry transit traffic through the other Party's territory; and

    i. combine traffic on the same aircraft regardless of where such traffic originates; without directional or geographic limitation and without loss of any right to carry traffic otherwise permissible under this Agreement, provided that, [with the exception of all-cargo services,] the transportation is part of a service that serves a point in the homeland of the airline.

3. On any segment or segments of the routes above, any airline of a Party may perform international air transportation without any limitation as to change, at any point on the route, in type or number of aircraft operated, provided that, [with the exception of all-cargo services,] in the outbound direction, the transportation beyond such point is a continuation of the transportation from the homeland of the airline and, in the inbound direction, the transportation to the homeland of the airline is a continuation of the transportation from beyond such point.

4. Nothing in this Article shall be deemed to confer on the airline or airlines of one Party the rights to take on board, in the territory of the other Party, passengers, baggage, cargo, or mail carried for compensation and destined for another point in the territory of that other Party.

5. Any airline of a Party performing charter international air transportation originating in the territory of either Party, whether on a one-way or round-trip basis, shall have the option of complying with the charter laws, regulations, and rules either of its homeland or of the other Party. If a Party applies different rules, regulations, terms, conditions, or limitations to one or more of its airlines, or to airlines of different countries, each airline of the other

Party shall be subject to the least restrictive of such criteria. Nothing in this paragraph shall limit the rights of a Party to require airlines of both Parties to adhere to requirements relating to the protection of passenger funds and passenger cancellation and refund rights. Except with respect to the consumer protection rules referred to in this paragraph, neither Party shall require an airline of the other Party, in respect of the carriage of traffic from the territory of that other Party or of a third country on a one-way or round-trip basis, to submit more than a notice that it is complying with the applicable laws, regulations, and rules referred to in this paragraph or of a waiver of these laws, regulations, or rules granted by the applicable aeronautical authorities.

Article 3
Authorization

Each Party, on receipt of applications from an airline of the other Party, in the form and manner prescribed for operating authorizations and technical permissions, shall grant appropriate authorizations and permissions with minimum procedural delay, provided:

    a. substantial ownership and effective control of that airline are vested in the other Party, nationals of that Party, or both;
    b. the airline is qualified to meet the conditions prescribed under the laws and regulations normally applied to the operation of international air transportation by the Party considering the application or applications; and
    c. the other Party is maintaining and administering the provisions set forth in Article 6 (Safety) and Article 7 (Aviation Security).

Article 4
Revocation of Authorization

1. Either Party may revoke, suspend, limit, or impose conditions on the operating authorizations or technical permissions of an airline where:
   a. that airline is not an airline of the other Party under Article 1(4);
   b. substantial ownership and effective control of that airline are not vested in the other Party, the other Party's nationals, or both; or
   c. that airline has failed to comply with the laws and regulations referred to in Article 5 (Application of Laws) of this Agreement.
2. Unless immediate action is essential to prevent further noncompliance with subparagraph 1c of this Article, the rights established by this Article shall be exercised only after consultation with the other Party.
3. This Article does not limit the rights of either Party to withhold, revoke, suspend, limit, or impose conditions on the operating authorization or technical permission of an airline or airlines of the other Party in accordance with the provisions of Article 6 (Safety) or Article 7 (Aviation Security).

Article 5
Application of Laws

1. The laws and regulations of a Party relating to the admission to or departure from its territory of aircraft engaged in international air navigation, or to the operation and navigation of such aircraft while within its territory, shall be complied with by such aircraft upon entering, when departing from, or while within the territory of the first Party.

2. While entering, within, or leaving the territory of one Party, its laws and regulations relating to the admission to or departure from its territory of passengers, crew or cargo on aircraft (including regulations relating to entry, clearance, aviation security, immigration, passports, customs and quarantine or, in the case of mail, postal regulations) shall be complied with by, or on behalf of, such passengers, crew or cargo of the other Party's airlines.

Article 6
Safety

1. Each Party shall recognize as valid, for the purpose of operating the air transportation provided for in this Agreement, certificates of airworthiness, certificates of competency, and licenses issued or validated by the other Party and still in force, provided that the requirements for such certificates or licenses at least equal the minimum standards that may be established pursuant to the Convention. Each Party may, however, refuse to recognize as valid for the purpose of flight above its own territory, certificates of competency and licenses granted to or validated for its own nationals by the other Party.

2. Either Party may request consultations concerning the safety standards maintained by the other Party relating to aeronautical facilities, aircrews, aircraft, and operation of airlines of that other Party. If, following such consultations, one Party finds that the other Party does not effectively maintain and administer safety standards and requirements in these areas that at least equal the minimum standards that may be established pursuant to the Convention, the other Party shall be notified of such findings and the steps considered necessary to conform with these minimum standards, and the other Party shall take appropriate corrective action. Each Party reserves the right to withhold, revoke, suspend, limit, or impose conditions on the operating authorization or technical permission of an airline or airlines of the other Party in the event the other Party does not take such appropriate corrective action within a reasonable time and to take immediate action, prior to consultations, as to such airline or airlines if the other Party is not maintaining and administering the aforementioned standards and immediate action is essential to prevent further noncompliance.

Article 7
Aviation Security

1. The Parties affirm that their obligation to each other to protect the security of civil aviation against acts of unlawful interference forms an integral part of this Agreement. Without limiting the generality of their rights and obligations under international law, the Parties shall in particular act in conformity with the provisions of the Convention on Offenses and Certain Other Acts Committed on Board Aircraft, done at Tokyo September 14, 1963, the Convention for the Suppression of Unlawful Seizure of Aircraft, done at The Hague December 16, 1970, the Convention for the Suppression of Unlawful Acts against the Safety of Civil Aviation, done at Montreal September 23, 1971, and the Protocol for the Suppression of Unlawful Acts of Violence at Airports Serving International Civil Aviation, Supplementary to the Convention for the Suppression of Unlawful Acts against the Safety of Civil Aviation, done at Montreal February 24, 1988.
2. The Parties shall provide upon request all necessary assistance to each other to prevent acts of unlawful seizure of civil aircraft and other unlawful acts against the safety of such aircraft, of their passengers and crew, and of airports and air navigation facilities, and to address any other threat to the security of civil air navigation.
3. The Parties shall, in their mutual relations, act in conformity with the aviation security standards and appropriate recommended practices established by the International Civil Aviation Organization and designated as Annexes to the Convention; they shall require that operators of aircraft of their registry, operators of aircraft that have their principal place of business or permanent residence in their territory, and the operators of airports in their territory act in conformity with such aviation security provisions.
4. Each Party agrees to observe the security provisions required by the other Party for entry into, for departure from, and while within the territory of that other Party and to take adequate measures to protect aircraft and to inspect passengers, crew, and their baggage and carry-on items, as well as cargo and aircraft stores, prior to and during boarding or loading. Each Party shall also give positive consideration to any request from the other Party for special security measures to meet a particular threat.
5. When an incident or threat of an incident of unlawful seizure of aircraft or other unlawful acts against the safety of passengers, crew, aircraft, airports or air navigation facilities occurs, the Parties shall assist each other by facilitating communications and other appropriate measures intended to terminate rapidly and safely such incident or threat.
6. When a Party has reasonable grounds to believe that the other Party has departed from the aviation security provisions of this Article, the aeronautical authorities of that Party may request immediate consultations with the aeronautical authorities of the other Party. Failure to reach a satisfactory agreement within 15 days from the date of such request shall constitute

grounds to withhold, revoke, suspend, limit, or impose conditions on the operating authorization and technical permissions of an airline or airlines of that Party. When required by an emergency, a Party may take interim action prior to the expiry of 15 days.

Article 8
Commercial Opportunities

1. The airlines of each Party shall have the right to establish offices in the territory of the other Party for the promotion and sale of air transportation.
2. The airlines of each Party shall be entitled, in accordance with the laws and regulations of the other Party relating to entry, residence, and employment, to bring in and maintain in the territory of the other Party managerial, sales, technical, operational, and other specialist staff required for the provision of air transportation.
3. Each airline shall have the right to perform its own ground-handling in the territory of the other Party ('self-handling') or, at the airline's option, select among competing agents for such services in whole or in part. The rights shall be subject only to physical constraints resulting from considerations of airport safety. Where such considerations preclude self-handling, ground services shall be available on an equal basis to all airlines; charges shall be based on the costs of services provided; and such services shall be comparable to the kind and quality of services as if self-handling were possible.
4. An airline of a Party may engage in the sale of air transportation in the territory of the other Party directly and, at the airline's discretion, through its agents, except as may be specifically provided by the charter regulations of the country in which the charter originates that relate to the protection of passenger funds, and passenger cancellation and refund rights. Each airline shall have the right to sell such transportation, and any person shall be free to purchase such transportation, in the currency of that territory or in freely convertible currencies.
5. Each airline shall have the right to convert and remit to its country and, except where inconsistent with generally applicable law or regulation, any other country or countries of its choice, on demand, local revenues in excess of sums locally disbursed. Conversion and remittance shall be permitted promptly without restrictions or taxation in respect thereof at the rate of exchange applicable to current transactions and remittance on the date the carrier makes the initial application for remittance.
6. The airlines of each Party shall be permitted to pay for local expenses, including purchases of fuel, in the territory of the other Party in local currency. At their discretion, the airlines of each Party may pay for such expenses in the territory of the other Party in freely convertible currencies according to local currency regulation.

7. In operating or holding out the authorized services under this Agreement, any airline of one Party may enter into cooperative marketing arrangements such as blocked-space, code-sharing, or leasing arrangements, with
   a) an airline or airlines of either Party;
   b) an airline or airlines of a third country; [and
   c) a surface transportation provider of any country;]
   provided that all participants in such arrangements (i) hold the appropriate authority and (ii) meet the requirements normally applied to such arrangements.
8. Airlines and indirect providers of cargo transportation of both Parties shall be permitted, without restriction, to employ in connection with international air transportation any surface transportation for cargo to or from any points in the territories of the Parties or in third countries, including to and from all airports with customs facilities and to transport cargo in bond under applicable laws and regulations. Such cargo, whether moving by surface or by air, shall have access to airport customs processing and facilities. Airlines may elect to perform their own surface transportation or to provide it through arrangements with other surface carriers, including surface transportation operated by other airlines and indirect providers of cargo air transportation. Such intermodal cargo services may be offered at a single, through price for the air and surface transportation combined, provided that shippers are not misled as to the facts concerning such transportation.

Article 9
Customs Duties and Charges

1. On arriving in the territory of one Party, aircraft operated in international air transportation by the airlines of the other Party, their regular equipment, ground equipment, fuel, lubricants, consumable technical supplies, spare parts (including engines), aircraft stores (including but not limited to such items of food, beverages and liquor, tobacco, and other products destined for sale to or use by passengers in limited quantities during flight), and other items intended for or used solely in connection with the operation or servicing of aircraft engaged in international air transportation shall be exempt, on the basis of reciprocity, from all import restrictions, property taxes and capital levies, customs duties, excise taxes, and similar fees and charges that are (a) imposed by the national authorities, and (b) not based on the cost of services provided, provided that such equipment and supplies remain on board the aircraft.
2. There shall also be exempt, on the basis of reciprocity, from the taxes, levies, duties, fees, and charges referred to in paragraph 1 of this Article, with the exception of charges based on the cost of the service provided:
   a. aircraft stores introduced into or supplied in the territory of a Party and taken on board, within reasonable limits, for use on outbound aircraft

of an airline of the other Party engaged in international air transportation, even when these stores are to be used on a part of the journey performed over the territory of the Party in which they are taken on board;

b. ground equipment and spare parts (including engines) introduced into the territory of a Party for the servicing, maintenance, or repair of aircraft of an airline of the other Party used in international air transportation;

c. fuel, lubricants, and consumable technical supplies introduced into or supplied in the territory of a Party for use in an aircraft of an airline of the other Party engaged in international air transportation, even when these supplies are to be used on a part of the journey performed over the territory of the Party in which they are taken on board; and

d. promotional and advertising materials introduced into or supplied in the territory of one Party and taken on board, within reasonable limits, for use on outbound aircraft of an airline of the other Party engaged in international air transportation, even when these materials are to be used on a part of the journey performed over the territory of the Party in which they are taken on board.

3. Equipment and supplies referred to in paragraphs 1 and 2 of this Article may be required to be kept under the supervision or control of the appropriate authorities.

4. The exemptions provided by this Article shall also be available where the airlines of one Party have contracted with another airline, which similarly enjoys such exemptions from the other Party, for the loan or transfer in the territory of the other Party of the items specified in paragraphs 1 and 2 of this Article.

Article 10
User Charges

1. User charges that may be imposed by the competent charging authorities or bodies of each Party on the airlines of the other Party shall be just, reasonable, not unjustly discriminatory, and equitably apportioned among categories of users. In any event, any such user charges shall be assessed on the airlines of the other Party on terms not less favorable than the most favorable terms available to any other airline at the time the charges are assessed.

2. User charges imposed on the airlines of the other Party may reflect, but shall not exceed, the full cost to the competent charging authorities or bodies of providing the appropriate airport, airport environmental, air navigation, and aviation security facilities and services at the airport or within the airport system. Such charges may include a reasonable return on assets, after depreciation. Facilities and services for which charges are made shall be provided on an efficient and economic basis.

3. Each Party shall encourage consultations between the competent charging authorities or bodies in its territory and the airlines using the services and facilities, and shall encourage the competent charging authorities or bodies and the airlines to exchange such information as may be necessary to permit an accurate review of the reasonableness of the charges in accordance with the principles of paragraphs 1 and 2 of this Article. Each Party shall encourage the competent charging authorities to provide users with reasonable notice of any proposal for changes in user charges to enable users to express their views before changes are made.

4. Neither Party shall be held, in dispute resolution procedures pursuant to Article 14, to be in breach of a provision of this Article, unless (a) it fails to undertake a review of the charge or practice that is the subject of complaint by the other Party within a reasonable amount of time; or (b) following such a review it fails to take all steps within its power to remedy any charge or practice that is inconsistent with this Article.

Article 11
Fair Competition

1. Each Party shall allow a fair and equal opportunity for the airlines of both Parties to compete in providing the international air transportation governed by this Agreement.

2. Each Party shall allow each airline to determine the frequency and capacity of the international air transportation it offers based upon commercial considerations in the marketplace. Consistent with this right, neither Party shall unilaterally limit the volume of traffic, frequency, or regularity of service, or the aircraft type or types operated by the airlines of the other Party, except as may be required for customs, technical, operational, or environmental reasons under uniform conditions consistent with Article 15 of the Convention.

3. Neither Party shall impose on the other Party's airlines a first-refusal requirement, uplift ratio, no-objection fee, or any other requirement with respect to capacity, frequency, or traffic that would be inconsistent with the purposes of this Agreement.

4. Neither Party shall require the filing of schedules, programs for charter flights, or operational plans by airlines of the other Party for approval, except as may be required on a non-discriminatory basis to enforce the uniform conditions foreseen by paragraph 2 of this Article or as may be specifically authorized in this Agreement. If a Party requires filings for information purposes, it shall minimize the administrative burdens of filing requirements and procedures on air transportation intermediaries and on airlines of the other Party.

Article 12
Pricing

1. Each Party shall allow prices for air transportation to be established by airlines of both Parties based upon commercial considerations in the marketplace.
2. Prices for international air transportation between the territories of the Parties shall not be required to be filed. Notwithstanding the foregoing, the airlines of the Parties shall provide immediate access, on request, to information on historical, existing, and proposed prices to the aeronautical authorities of the Parties in a manner and format acceptable to those aeronautical authorities.

Article 13
Consultations

Either Party may, at any time, request consultations relating to this Agreement. Such consultations shall begin at the earliest possible date, but not later than 60 days from the date the other Party receives the request unless otherwise agreed.

Article 14
Settlement of Disputes

1. Any dispute arising under this Agreement, except those that may arise under Article 12 (Pricing), that is not resolved within 30 days of the date established for consultations pursuant to a request for consultations under Article 13 may be referred, by agreement of the Parties, for decision to some person or body. If the Parties do not so agree, either Party may give written notice to the other Party through diplomatic channels that it is requesting that the dispute be submitted to arbitration.
2. Arbitration shall be by a tribunal of three arbitrators to be constituted as follows:
   a. Within 30 days after the receipt of a request for arbitration, each Party shall name one arbitrator. Within 60 days after these two arbitrators have been named, they shall by agreement appoint a third arbitrator, who shall act as President of the arbitral tribunal;
   b. If either Party fails to name an arbitrator, or if the third arbitrator is not appointed, in accordance with subparagraph a of this paragraph, either Party may request the President of the Council of the International Civil Aviation Organization to appoint the necessary arbitrator or arbitrators within 30 days. If the President of the Council is of the same nationality as one of the Parties, the most senior Vice President who is not disqualified on that ground shall make the appointment.

3. The arbitral tribunal shall be entitled to decide the extent of its jurisdiction under this Agreement and, except as otherwise agreed, shall establish its own procedural rules. The tribunal, once formed, may at the request of either Party recommend interim relief measures pending its final determination. If either of the Parties requests it or the tribunal deems it appropriate, a conference to determine the precise issues to be arbitrated and the specific procedures to be followed shall be held not later than 15 days after the tribunal is fully constituted.

4. Except as otherwise agreed or as directed by the tribunal, the statement of claim shall be submitted within 45 days of the time the tribunal is fully constituted, and the statement of defense shall be submitted 60 days thereafter. Any reply by the claimant shall be submitted within 30 days of the submission of the statement of defense. Any reply by the respondent shall be submitted within 30 days thereafter. If either Party requests it or the tribunal deems it appropriate, the tribunal shall hold a hearing within 45 days after the last pleading is due.

5. The tribunal shall attempt to render a written decision within 30 days after completion of the hearing or, if no hearing is held, after the last pleading is submitted. The decision of the majority of the tribunal shall prevail.

6. The Parties may submit requests for interpretation of the decision within 15 days after it is rendered and any interpretation given shall be issued within 15 days of such request.

7. Each Party shall, to the degree consistent with its national law, give full effect to any decision or award of the arbitral tribunal.

8. The expenses of the arbitral tribunal, including the fees and expenses of the arbitrators, shall be shared equally by the Parties. Any expenses incurred by the President of the Council of the International Civil Aviation Organization in connection with the procedures of paragraph 2b of this Article shall be considered to be part of the expenses of the arbitral tribunal.

Article 15
Termination

Either Party may, at any time, give notice in writing to the other Party of its decision to terminate this Agreement. Such notice shall be sent simultaneously to the International Civil Aviation Organization. This Agreement shall terminate at midnight (at the place of receipt of the notice to the other Party) at the end of the International Air Transport Association (IATA) traffic season in effect one year following the date of written notification of termination, unless the notice is withdrawn by agreement of the Parties before the end of this period.

Article 16
Registration with ICAO

This Agreement and all amendments thereto shall be registered with the International Civil Aviation Organization.

Article 17
Entry into Force

This Agreement shall enter into force on the date of signature.

Upon entry into force, this Agreement shall supersede [specify].

IN WITNESS WHEREOF the undersigned, being duly authorized by their respective Governments, have signed this Agreement.

DONE at _____, this _____ day of _____, 20_____, in two originals, in the English and _____ languages, both texts being equally authentic.

FOR THE GOVERNMENT OF THE   FOR THE GOVERNMENT OF
UNITED STATES OF AMERICA: [country]:

Appendix III

2007 U.S./EC Air Transport Agreement

AIR TRANSPORT AGREEMENT

The United States of America (hereinafter the 'United States'), of the one part; and

The Republic of Austria,
The Kingdom of Belgium,
The Republic of Bulgaria,
The Republic of Cyprus,
The Czech Republic,
The Kingdom of Denmark,
The Republic of Estonia,
The Republic of Finland,
The French Republic,
The Federal Republic of Germany,
The Hellenic Republic,
The Republic of Hungary,
Ireland,
The Italian Republic,
The Republic of Latvia,
The Republic of Lithuania,
The Grand Duchy of Luxembourg,
The Republic of Malta,
The Kingdom of the Netherlands,

The Republic of Poland,
The Portuguese Republic,
Romania,
The Slovak Republic,
The Republic of Slovenia,
The Kingdom of Spain,
The Kingdom of Sweden,
The United Kingdom of Great Britain and Northern Ireland,
being parties to the Treaty establishing the European Community and being
Member States of the European Union (hereinafter the 'Member States'),
and the European Community, of the other part;

Desiring to promote an international aviation system based on competition
among airlines in the marketplace with minimum government interference and
regulation;

Desiring to facilitate the expansion of international air transport opportunities, including through the development of air transportation networks to
meet the needs of passengers and shippers for convenient air transportation
services;

Desiring to make it possible for airlines to offer the traveling and shipping public
competitive prices and services in open markets;

Desiring to have all sectors of the air transport industry, including airline workers,
benefit in a liberalized agreement;

Desiring to ensure the highest degree of safety and security in international air
transport and reaffirming their grave concern about acts or threats against the
security of aircraft, which jeopardize the safety of persons or property, adversely
affect the operation of air transportation, and undermine public confidence in the
safety of civil aviation;

Noting the Convention on International Civil Aviation, opened for signature at
Chicago on December 7, 1944;

Recognizing that government subsidies may adversely affect airline competition
and may jeopardize the basic objectives of this Agreement;

Affirming the importance of protecting the environment in developing and implementing international aviation policy;

Noting the importance of protecting consumers, including the protections afforded
by the Convention for the Unification of Certain Rules for International Carriage
by Air, done at Montreal May 28, 1999;

Intending to build upon the framework of existing agreements with the goal of
opening access to markets and maximizing benefits for consumers, airlines, labor,
and communities on both sides of the Atlantic;

Recognizing the importance of enhancing the access of their airlines to global capital markets in order to strengthen competition and promote the objectives of this Agreement;

Intending to establish a precedent of global significance to promote the benefits of liberalization in this crucial economic sector;

Have agreed as follows:

Article 1
Definitions

For the purposes of this Agreement, unless otherwise stated, the term:

1. 'Agreement' means this Agreement, its Annexes and Appendix, and any amendments thereto;

2. 'Air transportation' means the carriage by aircraft of passengers, baggage, cargo, and mail, separately or in combination, held out to the public for remuneration or hire;

3. 'Convention' means the Convention on International Civil Aviation, opened for signature at Chicago on December 7, 1944, and includes:

   a. any amendment that has entered into force under Article 94(a) of the Convention and has been ratified by both the United States and the Member State or Member States as is relevant to the issue in question, and
   b. any Annex or any amendment thereto adopted under Article 90 of the Convention, insofar as such Annex or amendment is at any given time effective for both the United States and the Member State or Member States as is relevant to the issue in question;

4. 'Full cost' means the cost of providing service plus a reasonable charge for administrative overhead;

5. 'International air transportation' means air transportation that passes through the airspace over the territory of more than one State;

6. 'Party' means either the United States or the European Community and its Member States;

7. 'Price' means any fare, rate or charge for the carriage of passengers, baggage and/or cargo (excluding mail) in air transportation, including surface transportation in connection with international air transportation, if applicable, charged by airlines, including their agents, and the conditions governing the availability of such fare, rate or charge;

8. 'Stop for non-traffic purposes' means a landing for any purpose other than taking on or discharging passengers, baggage, cargo and/or mail in air transportation;

9. 'Territory' means, for the United States, the land areas (mainland and islands), internal waters and territorial sea under its sovereignty or jurisdiction, and, for the European Community and its Member States, the land areas (mainland and islands), internal waters and territorial sea in which the Treaty establishing the European Community is applied and under the conditions laid down in that Treaty and any successor instrument; application of this Agreement to Gibraltar airport is understood to be without prejudice to the respective legal positions of the Kingdom of Spain and the United Kingdom with regard to the dispute over sovereignty over the territory in which the airport is situated, and to the continuing suspension of Gibraltar Airport from European Community aviation measures existing as at 18 September2006 as between Member States, in accordance with the Ministerial statement on Gibraltar Airport agreed in Cordoba on September 2006; and

10. 'User charge' means a charge imposed on airlines for the provision of airport, airport environmental, air navigation, or aviation security facilities or services including related services and facilities.

Article 2
Fair and Equal Opportunity

Each Party shall allow a fair and equal opportunity for the airlines of both Parties to compete in providing the international air transportation governed by this Agreement.

Article 3
Grant of Rights

1. Each Party grants to the other Party the following rights for the conduct of international air transportation by the airlines of the other Party:

   a. the right to fly across its territory without landing;
   b. the right to make stops in its territory for non-traffic purposes;
   c. the right to perform international air transportation between points on the following routes:
      i.   for airlines of the United States (hereinafter 'U.S. airlines'), from points behind the United States via the United States and intermediate points to any point or points in any Member State or States and beyond; and for all-cargo service, between any Member State and any point or points (including in any other Member States);
      ii. for airlines of the European Community and its Member States (hereinafter 'Community airlines'), from points behind the Member States via the Member States and intermediate points to any point or points in the United States and beyond; for all-cargo service, between the United States and any point or points; and, for combination services, between any point or points in the United States and any point or points in any member of the European Common Aviation Area

(hereinafter the 'ECAA') as of the date of signature of this Agreement; and

d. the rights otherwise specified in this Agreement

2. Each airline may on any or all flights and at its option:

a. operate flights in either or both directions;
b. combine different flight numbers within one aircraft operation;
c. serve behind, intermediate, and beyond points and points in the territories of the Parties in any combination and in any order;
d. omit stops at any point or points;
e. transfer traffic from any of its aircraft to any of its other aircraft at any point;
f. serve points behind any point in its territory with or without change of aircraft or flight number and hold out and advertise such services to the public as through services;
g. make stopovers at any points whether within or outside the territory of either Party;
h. carry transit traffic through the other Party's territory; and
i. combine traffic on the same aircraft regardless of where such traffic originates;

without directional or geographic limitation and without loss of any right to carry traffic otherwise permissible under this Agreement.

3. The provisions of paragraph 1 of this Article shall apply subject to the requirements that:

a. for U.S. airlines, with the exception of all-cargo services, the transportation is part of a service that serves the United States, and
b. for Community airlines, with the exception of (i) all-cargo services and (ii) combination services between the United States and any member of the ECAA as of the date of signature of this Agreement, the transportation is part of a service that serves a Member State.

4. Each Party shall allow each airline to determine the frequency and capacity of the international air transportation it offers based upon commercial considerations in the marketplace. Consistent with this right, neither Party shall unilaterally limit the volume of traffic, frequency or regularity of service, or the aircraft type or types operated by the airlines of the other Party, nor shall it require the filing of schedules, programs for charter flights, or operational plans by airlines of the other Party, except as may be required for customs, technical, operational, or environmental (consistent with Article 15) reasons under uniform conditions consistent with Article 15 of the Convention.

5. Any airline may perform international air transportation without any limitation as to change, at any point, in type or number of aircraft operated; provided that, (a) for U.S. airlines, with the exception of all-cargo services, the transportation is part of a service that serves the United States, and (b) for Community airlines,

with the exception of (i) all-cargo services and (ii) combination services between the United States and a member of the ECAA as of the date of signature of this Agreement, the transportation is part of a service that serves a Member State.

6. Nothing in this Agreement shall be deemed to confer on:

   a. U.S. airlines the right to take on board, in the territory of any Member State, passengers, baggage, cargo, or mail carried for compensation and destined for another point in the territory of that Member State;
   b. Community airlines the right to take on board, in the territory of the United States, passengers, baggage, cargo, or mail carried for compensation and destined for another point in the territory of the United States.

7. Community airlines' access to U.S. Government procured transportation shall be governed by Annex 3.

Article 4
Authorization

On receipt of applications from an airline of one Party, in the form and manner prescribed for operating authorizations and technical permissions, the other Party shall grant appropriate authorizations and permissions with minimum procedural delay, provided.

   a. for a U.S. airline, substantial ownership and effective control of that airline are vested in the United States, U.S. nationals, or both, and the airline is licensed as a U.S. airline and has its principal place of business in U.S. territory;
   b. for a Community airline, substantial ownership and effective control of that airline are vested in a Member State or States, nationals of such a State or States, or both, and the airline is licensed as a Community airline and has its principal place of business in the territory of the European Community;
   c. the airline is qualified to meet the conditions prescribed under the laws and regulations normally applied to the operation of international air transportation by the Party considering the application or applications; and
   d. the provisions set forth in Article 8 (Safety) and Article 9 (Security) are being maintained and administered.

Article 5
Revocation of Authorization

1. Either Party may revoke, suspend or limit the operating authorizations or technical permissions or otherwise suspend or limit the operations of an airline of the other Party where:

   a. for a U.S. airline, substantial ownership and effective control of that airline are not vested in the United States, U.S. nationals, or both, or the airline is not licensed as a U.S. airline or does not have its principal place of business in U.S. territory;

b. for a Community airline, substantial ownership and effective control of that airline are not vested in a Member State or States, nationals of such a State or States, or both, or the airline is not licensed as a Community airline or does not have its principal place of business in the territory of the European Community; or

c. that airline has failed to comply with the laws and regulations referred to in Article 7 (Application of Laws) of this Agreement.

Unless immediate action is essential to prevent further noncompliance with sub-paragraph 1(c) of this Article, the rights established by this Article shall be exercised only after consultation with the other Party.

This Article does not limit the rights of either Party to withhold, revoke, limit or impose conditions on the operating authorization or technical permission of an airline or airlines of the other Party in accordance with the provisions of Article 8 (Safety) or Article 9 (Security).

Article 6
Additional Matters related to Ownership, Investment, and Control

Notwithstanding any other provision in this Agreement, the Parties shall implement the provisions of Annex 4 in their decisions under their respective laws and regulations concerning ownership, investment and control.

Article 7
Application of Laws

The laws and regulations of a Party relating to the admission to or departure from its territory of aircraft engaged in international air navigation, or to the operation and navigation of such aircraft while within its territory, shall be applied to the aircraft utilized by the airlines of the other Party, and shall be complied with by such aircraft upon entering or departing from or while within the territory of the first Party.

While entering, within, or leaving the territory of one Party, the laws and regulations applicable within that territory relating to the admission to or departure from its territory of passengers, crew or cargo on aircraft (including regulations relating to entry, clearance, immigration, passports, customs and quarantine or, in the case of mail, postal regulations) shall be complied with by, or on behalf of, such passengers, crew or cargo of the other Party's airlines.

Article 8
Safety

1. The responsible authorities of the Parties shall recognize as valid, for the purposes of operating the air transportation provided for in this Agreement,

certificates of airworthiness, certificates of competency, and licenses issued or validated by each other and still in force, provided that the requirements for such certificates or licenses at least equal the minimum standards that may be established pursuant to the Convention. The responsible authorities may, however, refuse to recognize as valid for purposes of flight above their own territory, certificates of competency and licenses granted to or validated for their own nationals by such other authorities.

2. The responsible authorities of a Party may request consultations with other responsible authorities concerning the safety standards maintained by those authorities relating to aeronautical facilities, aircrews, aircraft, and operation of the airlines overseen by those authorities. Such consultations shall take place within 45 days of the request unless otherwise agreed. If following such consultations, the requesting responsible authorities find that those authorities do not effectively maintain and administer safety standards and requirements in these areas that at least equal the minimum standards that may be established pursuant to the Convention, the requesting responsible authorities shall notify those authorities of such findings and the steps considered necessary to conform with these minimum standards, and those authorities shall take appropriate corrective action. The requesting responsible authorities reserve the right to withhold, revoke or limit the operating authorization or technical permission of an airline or airlines for which those authorities provide safety oversight in the event those authorities do not take such appropriate corrective action within a reasonable time and to take immediate action as to such airline or airlines if essential to prevent further noncompliance with the duty to maintain and administer the aforementioned standards and requirements resulting in an immediate threat to flight safety.

3. The European Commission shall simultaneously receive all requests and notifications under this Article.

4. Nothing in this Article shall prevent the responsible authorities of the Parties from conducting safety discussions, including those relating to the routine application of safety standards and requirements or to emergency situations that may arise from time to time.

Article 9
Security

1. In accordance with their rights and obligations under international law, the Parties reaffirm that their obligation to each other to protect the security of civil aviation against acts of unlawful interference forms an integral part of this Agreement. Without limiting the generality of their rights and obligations under international law, the Parties shall in particular act in conformity with the following agreements: the Convention on Offenses and Certain Other Acts Committed on Board Aircraft, done at Tokyo September 14, 1963, the Convention for the Suppression of Unlawful Seizure of Aircraft, done at The Hague December 16, 1970,

the Convention for the Suppression of Unlawful Acts against the Safety of Civil Aviation, done at Montreal September 23, 1971, and the Protocol for the Suppression of Unlawful Acts of Violence at Airports Serving International Civil Aviation, done at Montreal February 24, 1988.

2. The Parties shall provide upon request all necessary assistance to each other to address any threat to the security of civil aviation, including the prevention of acts of unlawful seizure of civil aircraft and other unlawful acts against the safety of such aircraft, of their passengers and crew, and of airports and air navigation facilities.

3. The Parties shall, in their mutual relations, act in conformity with the aviation security standards and appropriate recommended practices established by the International Civil Aviation Organization and designated as Annexes to the Convention; they shall require that operators of aircraft of their registries; operators of aircraft who have their principal place of business or permanent residence in their territory; and the operators of airports in their territory act in conformity with such aviation security provisions.

4. Each Party shall ensure that effective measures are taken within its territory to protect aircraft and to inspect passengers, crew, and their baggage and carry-on items, as well as cargo and aircraft stores, prior to and during boarding or loading; and that those measures are adjusted to meet increased threats to the security of civil aviation. Each Party agrees that the security provisions required by the other Party for departure from and while within the territory of that other Party must be observed. Each Party shall give positive consideration to any request from the other Party for special security measures to meet a particular threat.

5. With full regard and mutual respect for each other's sovereignty, a Party may adopt security measures for entry into its territory. Where possible, that Party shall take into account the security measures already applied by the other Party and any views that the other Party may offer. Each Party recognizes, however, that nothing in this Article limits the ability of a Party to refuse entry into its territory of any flight or flights that it deems to present a threat to its security.

6. A Party may take emergency measures including amendments to meet a specific security threat. Such measures shall be notified immediately to the responsible authorities of the other Party.

7. The Parties underline the importance of working towards compatible practices and standards as a means of enhancing air transport security and minimizing regulatory divergence. To this end, the Parties shall fully utilize and develop existing channels for the discussion of current and proposed security measures. The Parties expect that the discussions will address, among other issues, new security measures proposed or under consideration by the other Party, including the revision of security measures occasioned by a change in circumstances; measures proposed by one Party to meet the security requirements of the other Party; possibilities for the more expeditious adjustment of standards with respect to aviation security

measures; and compatibility of the requirements of one Party with the legislative obligations of the other Party. Such discussions should serve to foster early notice and prior discussion of new security initiatives and requirements.

8. Without prejudice to the need to take immediate action in order to protect transportation security, the Parties affirm that when considering security measures, a Party shall evaluate possible adverse effects on international air transportation and, unless constrained by law, shall take such factors into account when it determines what measures are necessary and appropriate to address those security concerns.

9. When an incident or threat of an incident of unlawful seizure of aircraft or other unlawful acts against the safety of passengers, crew, aircraft, airports or air navigation facilities occurs, the Parties shall assist each other by facilitating communications and other appropriate measures intended to terminate rapidly and safely such incident or threat.

10. When a Party has reasonable grounds to believe that the other Party has departed from the aviation security provisions of this Article, the responsible authorities of that Party may request immediate consultations with the responsible authorities of the other Party. Failure to reach a satisfactory agreement within 15 days from the date of such request shall constitute grounds to withhold, revoke, limit, or impose conditions on the operating authorization and technical permissions of an airline or airlines of that Party. When required by an emergency, a Party may take interim action prior to the expiry of 15 days. Separate from airport assessments undertaken to determine conformity with the aviation security standards and practices referred to in paragraph 3 of this Article, a Party may request the cooperation of the other Party in assessing whether particular security measures of that other Party meet the requirements of the requesting Party. The responsible authorities of the Parties shall coordinate in advance the airports to be assessed and the dates of assessment and establish a procedure to address the results of such assessments. Taking into account the results of the assessments, the requesting Party may decide that security measures of an equivalent standard are applied in the territory of the other Party in order that transfer passengers, transfer baggage, and/or transfer cargo may be exempted from re-screening in the territory of the requesting Party. Such a decision shall be communicated to the other Party.

Article 10
Commercial Opportunities

1. The airlines of each Party shall have the right to establish offices in the territory of the other Party for the promotion and sale of air transportation and related activities.

2. The airlines of each Party shall be entitled, in accordance with the laws and regulations of the other Party relating to entry, residence, and employment, to bring in and maintain in the territory of the other Party managerial, sales, technical,

operational, and other specialist staff who are required to support the provision of air transportation.

3.   a. Without prejudice to subparagraph (b) below, each airline shall have in relation to groundhandling in the territory of the other Party:
> (i)   the right to perform its own groundhandling ('self-handling') or, at its option
> (ii) the right to select among competing suppliers that provide ground-handling services in whole or in part where such suppliers are allowed market access on the basis of the laws and regulations of each Party, and where such suppliers are present in the market.

    b. The rights under (i) and (ii) in subparagraph (a) above shall be subject only to specific constraints of available space or capacity arising from the need to maintain safe operation of the airport. Where such constraints preclude self-handling and where there is no effective competition between suppliers that provide groundhandling services, all such services shall be available on both an equal and an adequate basis to all airlines; prices of such services shall not exceed their full cost including a reasonable return on assets, after depreciation.

4. Any airline of each Party may engage in the sale of air transportation in the territory of the other Party directly and/or, at the airline's discretion, through its sales agents or other intermediaries appointed by the airline. Each airline shall have the right to sell such transportation, and any person shall be free to purchase such transportation, in the currency of that territory or in freely convertible currencies.

5. Each airline shall have the right to convert and remit from the territory of the other Party to its home territory and, except where inconsistent with generally applicable law or regulation, the country or countries of its choice, on demand, local revenues in excess of sums locally disbursed. Conversion and remittance shall be permitted promptly without restrictions or taxation in respect thereof at the rate of exchange applicable to current transactions and remittance on the date the carrier makes the initial application for remittance.

6. The airlines of each Party shall be permitted to pay for local expenses, including purchases of fuel, in the territory of the other Party in local currency. At their discretion, the airlines of each Party may pay for such expenses in the territory of the other Party in freely convertible currencies according to local currency regulation.

7. In operating or holding out services under the Agreement, any airline of a Party may enter into co-operative marketing arrangements, such as blocked-space or code-sharing arrangements, with:
> a. any airline or airlines of the Parties;
> b. any airline or airlines of a third country; and
> c. a surface (land or maritime) transportation provider of any country;

provided that (i) all participants in such arrangements hold the appropriate authority and (ii) the arrangements meet the conditions prescribed under the laws and regulations normally applied by the Parties to the operation or holding out of international air transportation.

8. The airlines of each Party shall be entitled to enter into franchising or branding arrangements with companies, including airlines, of either Party or third countries, provided that the airlines hold the appropriate authority and meet the conditions prescribed under the laws and regulations normally applied by the Parties to such arrangements. Annex 5 shall apply to such arrangements.

9. The airlines of each Party may enter into arrangements for the provision of aircraft with crew for international air transportation with:

   a. any airlines or airlines of the Parties; and
   b. any airlines or airlines of a third country;

provided that all participants in such arrangements hold the appropriate authority and meet the conditions prescribed under the laws and regulations normally applied by the Parties to such arrangements. Neither Party shall require an airline of either Party providing the aircraft to hold traffic rights under this Agreement for the routes on which the aircraft will be operated.

10. Notwithstanding any other provision of this Agreement, airlines and indirect providers of cargo transportation of the Parties shall be permitted, without restriction, to employ in connection with international air transportation any surface transportation for cargo to or from any points in the territories of the Parties, or in third countries, including transport to and from all airports with customs facilities, and including, where applicable, the right to transport cargo in bond under applicable laws and regulations. Such cargo, whether moving by surface or by air, shall have access to airport customs processing and facilities. Airlines may elect to perform their own surface transportation or to provide it through arrangements with other surface carriers, including surface transportation operated by other airlines and indirect providers of cargo air transportation. Such intermodal cargo services may be offered at a single, through price for the air and surface transportation combined, provided that shippers are not misled as to the facts concerning such transportation.

Article 11
Customs Duties and Charges

1. On arriving in the territory of one Party, aircraft operated in international air transportation by the airlines of the other Party, their regular equipment, ground equipment, fuel, lubricants, consumable technical supplies, spare parts (including engines), aircraft stores (including but not limited to such items of food, beverages and liquor, tobacco and other products destined for sale to or use by passengers in

limited quantities during flight), and other items intended for or used solely in connection with the operation or servicing of aircraft engaged in international air transportation shall be exempt, on the basis of reciprocity, from all import restrictions, property taxes and capital levies, customs duties, excise taxes, and similar fees and charges that are (a) imposed by the national authorities or the European Community, and (b) not based on the cost of services provided, provided that such equipment and supplies remain on board the aircraft.

2. There shall also be exempt, on the basis of reciprocity, from the taxes, levies, duties, fees and charges referred to in paragraph 1 of this Article, with the exception of charges based on the cost of the service provided:

    a. aircraft stores introduced into or supplied in the territory of a Party and taken on board, within reasonable limits, for use on outbound aircraft of an airline of the other Party engaged in international air transportation, even when these stores are to be used on a part of the journey performed over the territory of the Party in which they are taken on board;

    b. ground equipment and spare parts (including engines) introduced into the territory of a Party for the servicing, maintenance, or repair of aircraft of an airline of the other Party used in international air transportation;

    c. fuel, lubricants and consumable technical supplies introduced into or supplied in the territory of a Party for use in an aircraft of an airline of the other Party engaged in international air transportation, even when these supplies are to be used on a part of the journey performed over the territory of the Party in which they are taken on board; and

    d. printed matter, as provided for by the customs legislation of each Party, introduced into or supplied in the territory of one Party and taken on board for use on outbound aircraft of an airline of the other Party engaged in international air transportation, even when these stores are to be used on a part of the journey performed over the territory of the Party in which they are taken on board.

3. Equipment and supplies referred to in paragraphs 1 and 2 of this Article may be required to be kept under the supervision or control of the appropriate authorities.

4. The exemptions provided by this Article shall also be available where the airlines of one Party have contracted with another airline, which similarly enjoys such exemptions from the other Party, for the loan or transfer in the territory of the other Party of the items specified in paragraphs 1 and 2 of this Article.

5. Nothing in this Agreement shall prevent either Party from imposing taxes, levies, duties, fees or charges on goods sold other than for consumption on board to passengers during a sector of an air service between two points within its territory at which embarkation or disembarkation is permitted.

6. In the event that two or more Member States envisage applying to the fuel supplied to aircraft of U.S. airlines in the territories of such Member

States for flights between such Member States any waiver of the exemption contained in Article 14 (b) of Council Directive 2003/96/EC of 27 October 2003, the Joint Committee shall consider that issue, in accordance with paragraph 4(e) of Article 18.

7. A Party may request the assistance of the other Party, on behalf of its airline or airlines, in securing an exemption from taxes, duties, charges and fees imposed by State and local governments or authorities on the goods specified in paragraphs 1 and 2 of this Article, as well as from fuel through-put charges, in the circumstances described in this Article, except to the extent that the charges are based on the cost of providing the service. In response to such a request, the other Party shall bring the views of the requesting Party to the attention of the relevant governmental unit or authority and urge that those views be given appropriate consideration.

Article 12
User Charges

1. User charges that may be imposed by the competent charging authorities or bodies of each Party on the airlines of the other Party shall be just, reasonable, not unjustly discriminatory, and equitably apportioned among categories of users. In any event, any such user charges shall be assessed on the airlines of the other Party on terms not less favorable than the most favorable terms available to any other airline at the time the charges are assessed.

2. User charges imposed on the airlines of the other Party may reflect, but shall not exceed, the full cost to the competent charging authorities or bodies of providing the appropriate airport, airport environmental, air navigation, and aviation security facilities and services at the airport or within the airport system. Such charges may include a reasonable return on assets, after depreciation. Facilities and services for which charges are made shall be provided on an efficient and economic basis,

3. Each Party shall encourage consultations between the competent charging authorities or bodies in its territory and the airlines using the services and facilities, and shall encourage the competent charging authorities or bodies and the airlines to exchange such information as may be necessary to permit an accurate review of the reasonableness of the charges in accordance with the principles of paragraphs 1 and 2 of this Article. Each Party shall encourage the competent charging authorities to provide users with reasonable notice of any proposal for changes in user charges to enable users to express their views before changes are made.

4. Neither Party shall be held, in dispute resolution procedures pursuant to Article 19, to be in breach of a provision of this Article, unless (a) it fails to undertake a review of the charge or practice that is the subject of complaint by the other Party

within a reasonable amount of time; or (b) following such a review it fails to take all steps within its power to remedy any charge or practice that is inconsistent with this Article.

Article 13
Pricing

1. Prices for air transportation services operated pursuant to this Agreement shall be established freely and shall not be subject to approval, nor may they be required to be filed.

2. Notwithstanding paragraph 1:

    a. The introduction or continuation of a price proposed to be charged or charged by a U.S. airline for international air transportation between a point in one Member State and a point in another Member State shall be consistent with Article 1(3) of Council Regulation (EEC) 2409/92 of 23 July 1992, or a not more restrictive successor regulation.

    b. Under this paragraph, the airlines of the Parties shall provide immediate access, on request, to information on historical, existing, and proposed prices to the responsible authorities of the Parties in a manner and format acceptable to those authorities.

Article 14
Government Subsidies and Support

1. The Parties recognize that government subsidies and support may adversely affect the fair and equal opportunity of airlines to compete in providing the international air transportation governed by this Agreement.

2. If one Party believes that a government subsidy or support being considered or provided by the other Party for or to the airlines of that other Party would adversely affect or is adversely affecting that fair and equal opportunity of the airlines of the first Party to compete, it may submit observations to that Party. Furthermore, it may request a meeting of the Joint Committee as provided in Article 18, to consider the issue and develop appropriate responses to concerns found to be legitimate.

3. Each Party may approach responsible governmental entities in the territory of the other Party, including entities at the State, provincial or local level, if it believes that a subsidy or support being considered or provided by such entities will have the adverse competitive effects referred to in paragraph 2. If a Party decides to make such direct contact it shall inform promptly the other Party through diplomatic channels. It may also request a meeting of the Joint Committee.

4. Issues raised under this Article could include, for example, capital injections, cross-subsidization, grants, guarantees, ownership, relief or tax exemption, by any governmental entities.

Article 15
Environment

1. The Parties recognize the importance of protecting the environment when developing and implementing international aviation policy. The Parties recognize that the costs and benefits of measures to protect the environment must be carefully weighed in developing international aviation policy.

2. When a Party is considering proposed environmental measures, it should evaluate possible adverse effects on the exercise of rights contained in this Agreement, and, if such measures are adopted, it should take appropriate steps to mitigate any such adverse effects.

3. When environmental measures are established, the aviation environmental standards adopted by International Civil Aviation Organization in Annexes to the Convention shall be followed except where differences have been filed. The Parties shall apply any environmental measures affecting air services under this Agreement in accordance with Article 2 and 3(4) of this Agreement.

4. If one Party believes that a matter involving aviation environmental protection raises concerns for the application or implementation of this Agreement, it may request a meeting of the Joint Committee, as provided in Article 18, to consider the issue and develop appropriate responses to concerns found to be legitimate.

Article 16
Consumer Protection

The Parties affirm the importance of protecting consumers, and either Party may request a meeting of the Joint Committee to discuss consumer protection issues that the requesting Party identifies as significant.

Article 17
Computer Reservation Systems

1. Computer Reservation Systems (CRS) vendors operating in the territory of one Party shall be entitled to bring in, maintain, and make freely available their CRSs to travel agencies or travel companies whose principal business is the distribution of travel-related products in the territory of the other Party provided the CRS complies with any relevant regulatory requirements of the other Party.

2. Neither Party shall, in its territory, impose or permit to be imposed on the CRS vendors of the other Party more stringent requirements with respect to CRS displays (including edit and display parameters), operations, practices, sales, or ownership than those imposed on its own CRS vendors.

3. Owners/Operators of CRSs of one Party that comply with the relevant regulatory requirements of the other Party, if any, shall have the same opportunity to own CRSs within the territory of the other Party as do owners/operators of that Party.

Article 18
The Joint Committee

1. A Joint Committee consisting of representatives of the Parties shall meet at least once a year to conduct consultations relating to this Agreement and to review its implementation.

2. A Party may also request a meeting of the Joint Committee to seek to resolve questions relating to the interpretation or application of this Agreement. However, with respect to Article 20 or Annex 2, the Joint Committee may consider questions only relating to the refusal by either Participant to implement the commitments undertaken, and the impact of competition decisions on the application of this Agreement. Such a meeting shall begin at the earliest possible date, but not later than 60 days from the date of receipt of the request, unless otherwise agreed.

3. The Joint Committee shall review, no later than at its first annual meeting and thereafter as appropriate, the overall implementation of the Agreement, including any effects of aviation infrastructure constraints on the exercise of rights provided for in Article 3, the effects of security measures taken under Article 9, the effects on the conditions of competition, including in the field of Computer Reservation Systems, and any social effects of the implementation of the Agreement.

4. The Joint Committee shall also develop cooperation by:

   a. fostering expert-level exchanges on new legislative or regulatory initiatives and developments, including in the fields of security, safety, the environment, aviation infrastructure (including slots), and consumer protection;
   b. considering the social effects of the Agreement as it is implemented and developing appropriate responses to concerns found to be legitimate;
   c. considering potential areas for the further development of the Agreement, including the recommendation of amendments to the Agreement;
   d. maintaining an inventory of issues regarding government subsidies or support raised by either Party in the Joint Committee;
   e. making decisions, on the basis of consensus, concerning any matters with respect to application of paragraph 6 of Article 11;

f. developing, within one year of provisional application, approaches to regulatory determinations with regard to airline fitness and citizenship, with the goal of achieving reciprocal recognition of such determinations;
g. developing a common understanding of the criteria used by the Parties in making their respective decisions in cases concerning airline control, to the extent consistent with confidentiality requirements;
h. fostering consultation, where appropriate, on air transport issues dealt with in international organizations and in relations with third countries, including consideration of whether to adopt a joint approach;
i. taking, on the basis of consensus, the decisions to which paragraph 3 of Article 1 of Annex 4 and paragraph 3 of Article 2 of Annex 4 refer.

5. The Parties share the goal of maximizing the benefits for consumers, airlines, labor, and communities on both sides of the Atlantic by extending this Agreement to include third countries. To this end, the Joint Committee shall work to develop a proposal regarding the conditions and procedures, including any necessary amendments to this Agreement, that would be required for third countries to accede to this Agreement.

6. The Joint Committee shall operate on the basis of consensus.

Article 19
Arbitration

1. Any dispute relating to the application or interpretation of this Agreement, other than issues arising under Article 20 or under Annex 2, that is not resolved by a meeting of the Joint Committee may be referred to a person or body for decision by agreement of the Parties. If the Parties do not so agree, the dispute shall, at the request of either Party, be submitted to arbitration in accordance with the procedures set forth below.

2. Unless the Parties otherwise agree, arbitration shall be by a tribunal of three arbitrators to be constituted as follows:

a. Within 20 days after the receipt of a request for arbitration, each Party shall name one arbitrator. Within 45 days after these two arbitrators have been named, they shall by agreement appoint a third arbitrator, who shall act as President of the tribunal,
b. If either Party fails to name an arbitrator, or if the third arbitrator is not appointed in accordance with subparagraph (a) of this paragraph, either Party may request the President of the Council of the International Civil Aviation Organization to appoint the necessary arbitrator or arbitrators within 30 days of receipt of that request. If the President of the Council of the International Civil Aviation Organization is a national of either the United States or a Member State, the most senior Vice President of that Council who is not disqualified on that ground shall make the appointment.

3. Except as otherwise agreed, the tribunal shall determine the limits of its jurisdiction in accordance with this Agreement and shall establish its own procedural rules. At the request of a Party, the tribunal, once formed, may ask the other Party to implement interim relief measures pending the tribunal's final determination. At the direction of the tribunal or at the request of either Party, a conference shall be held not later than 15 days after the tribunal is fully constituted for the tribunal to determine the precise issues to be arbitrated and the specific procedures to be followed.

4. Except as otherwise agreed or as directed by the tribunal:

    a. The statement of claim shall be submitted within 30 days of the time the tribunal is fully constituted, and the statement of defense shall be submitted 40 days thereafter. Any reply by the claimant shall be submitted within 15 days of the submission of the statement of defense. Any reply by the respondent shall be submitted within 15 days thereafter,

    b. The tribunal shall hold a hearing at the request of either Party, or may hold a hearing on its own initiative, within 15 days after the last reply is filed.

5. The tribunal shall attempt to render a written decision within 30 days after completion of the hearing or, if no hearing is held, within 30 days after the last reply is submitted. The decision of the majority of the tribunal shall prevail.

6. The Parties may submit requests for clarification of the decision within 10 days after it is rendered and any clarification given shall be issued within 15 days of such request.

7. If the tribunal determines that there has been a violation of this Agreement and the responsible Party does not cure the violation, or does not reach agreement with the other Party on a mutually satisfactory resolution within 40 days after notification of the tribunal's decision, the other Party may suspend the application of comparable benefits arising under this Agreement until such time as the Parties have reached agreement on a resolution of the dispute. Nothing in this paragraph shall be construed as limiting the right of either Party to take proportional measures in accordance with international law.

8. The expenses of the tribunal, including the fees and expenses of the arbitrators, shall be shared equally by the Parties. Any expenses incurred by the President of the Council of the International Civil Aviation Organization, or by any Vice President of that Council, in connection with the procedures of paragraph 2(b) of this Article shall be considered to be part of the expenses of the tribunal.

Article 20
Competition

1. The Parties recognize that competition among airlines in the transatlantic market is important to promote the objectives of this Agreement, and confirm that they

apply their respective competition regimes to protect and enhance overall competition and not individual competitors.

2. The Parties recognize that differences may arise concerning the application of their respective competition regimes to international aviation affecting the transatlantic market, and that competition among airlines in that market might be fostered by minimizing those differences.

3. The Parties recognize that cooperation between their respective competition authorities serves to promote competition in markets and has the potential to promote compatible regulatory results and to minimize differences in approach with respect to their respective competition reviews of inter-carrier agreements. Consequently, the Parties shall further this cooperation to the extent feasible, taking into account the different responsibilities, competencies and procedures of the authorities, in accordance with Annex 2.

4. The Joint Committee shall be briefed annually on the results of the cooperation under Annex 2.

Article 21
Second Stage Negotiations

1. The Parties share the goal of continuing to open access to markets and to maximize benefits for consumers, airlines, labor, and communities on both sides of the Atlantic, including the facilitation of investment so as to better reflect the realities of a global aviation industry, the strengthening of the transatlantic air transportation system, and the establishment of a framework that will encourage other countries to open their own air services markets. The Parties shall begin negotiations not later than 60 days after the date of provisional application of this Agreement, with the goal of developing the next stage expeditiously.

2. To that end, the agenda for the second stage negotiations shall include the following items of priority interest to one or both Parties:

    a. Further liberalization of traffic rights;
    b. Additional foreign investment opportunities;
    c. Effect of environmental measures and infrastructure constraints on the exercise of traffic rights;
    d. Further access to Government-financed air transportation; and
    e. Provision of aircraft with crew.

3. The Parties shall review their progress towards a second stage agreement no later than 18 months after the date when the negotiations are due to start in accordance with paragraph 1. If no second stage agreement has been reached by the Parties within twelve months of the start of the review, each Party reserves the right thereafter to suspend rights specified in this Agreement. Such suspension shall take effect no sooner than the start of the International Air Transport Association (IATA) traffic season that commences no less than twelve months after the date on which notice of suspension is given.

Article 22
Relationship to Other Agreements

1. During the period of provisional application pursuant to Article 25 of this Agreement, the bilateral agreements listed in section 1 of Annex 1, shall be suspended, except to the extent provided in section 2 of Annex 1.

2. Upon entry into force pursuant to Article 26 of this Agreement, this Agreement shall supersede the bilateral agreements listed in section 1 of Annex 1, except to the extent provided in section 2 of Annex 1.

3. If the Parties become parties to a multilateral agreement, or endorse a decision adopted by the International Civil Aviation Organization or another international organization, that addresses matters covered by this Agreement, they shall consult in the Joint Committee to determine whether this Agreement should be revised to take into account such developments.

Article 23
Termination

Either Party may, at any time, give notice in writing through diplomatic channels to the other Party of its decision to terminate this Agreement. Such notice shall be sent simultaneously to the International Civil Aviation Organization. This Agreement shall terminate at midnight GMT at the end of the International Air Transport Association (IATA) traffic season in effect one year following the date of written notification of termination, unless the notice is withdrawn by agreement of the Parties before the end of this period.

Article 24
Registration with ICAO

This Agreement and all amendments thereto shall be registered with the International Civil Aviation Organization.

Article 25
Provisional Application

Pending entry into force pursuant to Article 26:

1. The Parties agree to apply this Agreement from 30 March 2008.

2. Either Party may at any time give notice in writing through diplomatic channels to the other Party of a decision to no longer apply this Agreement. In that event, application shall cease at midnight GMT at the end of the International Air Transport Association (IATA) traffic season in effect one year following the date of written notification, unless the notice is withdrawn by agreement of the Parties before the end of this period.

Article 26
Entry into Force

This Agreement shall enter into force one month after the date of the later note in an exchange of diplomatic notes between the Parties confirming that all necessary procedures for entry into force of this Agreement have been completed. For purposes of this exchange, the United States shall deliver to the European Community the diplomatic note to the European Community and its Member States, and the European Community shall deliver to the United States the diplomatic note or notes from the European Community and its Member States. The diplomatic note or notes from the European Community and its Member States shall contain communications from each Member State confirming that its necessary procedures for entry into force of this Agreement have been completed.

IN WITNESS WHEREOF the undersigned, being duly authorized, have signed this Agreement.

DONE at Brussels on the twenty-fifth day of April, 2007 and at Washington on the thirtieth day of April, 2007, in duplicate.

FOR THE UNITED STATES OF AMERICA
FOR THE REPUBLIC OF AUSTRIA
FOR THE KINGDOM OF BELGIUM
FOR THE REPUBLIC OF BULGARIA
FOR THE REPUBLIC OF CYPRUS
FOR THE CZECH REPUBLIC
FOR THE KINGDOM OF DENMARK
FOR THE REPUBLIC OF ESTONIA
FOR THE REPUBLIC OF FINLAND
FOR THE FRENCH REPUBLIC
FOR THE FEDERAL REPUBLIC OF GERMANY
FOR THE HELLENIC REPUBLIC
FOR THE REPUBLIC OF HUNGARY
FOR IRELAND
FOR THE ITALIAN REPUBLIC
FOR THE REPUBLIC OF LATVIA
FOR THE REPUBLIC OF LITHUANIA
FOR THE GRAND DUCHY OF LUXEMBOURG
FOR THE REPUBLIC OF MALTA
FOR THE KINGDOM OF THE NETHERLANDS
FOR THE REPUBLIC OF POLAND
FOR THE PORTUGUESE REPUBLIC
FOR ROMANIA
FOR THE SLOVAK REPUBLIC
FOR THE REPUBLIC OF SLOVENIA

FOR THE KINGDOM OF SPAIN
FOR THE KINGDOM OF SWEDEN
FOR THE UNITED KINGDOM OF GREAT BRITAIN
    AND NORTHERN IRELAND
FOR THE EUROPEAN COMMUNITY

Annex 1

Section 1

As provided in Article 22 of this Agreement, the following bilateral agreements between the United States and Member States shall be suspended or superseded by this Agreement:

a. The Republic of Austria: Air services agreement, signed at Vienna March 16, 1989; amended June 14, 1995.
b. The Kingdom of Belgium: Air transport agreement, effected by exchange of notes at Washington October 23, 1980; amended September 22 and November 12, 1986; amended November 5, 1993 and January 12, 1994. (amendment concluded on September 5, 1995 (provisionally applied).)
c. The Republic of Bulgaria: Civil aviation security agreement, signed at Sofia April 24, 1991.
d. The Czech Republic: Air transport agreement, signed at Prague September 10, 1996; amended June 4, 2001 and February 14, 2002.
e. The Kingdom of Denmark: Agreement relating to air transport services, effected by exchange of notes at Washington December 16, 1944; amended August 6, 1954; amended June 16, 1995.
f. The Republic of Finland: Air transport agreement, signed at Helsinki March 29, 1949; related protocol signed May 12, 1980; agreement amending 1949 agreement and 1980 protocol concluded June 9, 1995.
g. The French Republic: Air transport agreement, signed at Washington June 18, 1998; amended October 10, 2000; amended January 22, 2002.
h. The Federal Republic of Germany: Air transport agreement and exchanges of notes, signed at Washington July 7, 1955; amended April 25, 1989. (related protocol concluded November 1, 1978; related agreement concluded May 24, 1994; protocol amending the 1955 agreement concluded on May 23, 1996; agreement amending the 1996 protocol concluded on October 10, 2000 (all provisionally applied).)
i. The Hellenic Republic: Air transport agreement, signed at Athens July 31, 1991; extended until July 31, 2007 by exchange of notes of June 22 and 28, 2006.
j. The Republic of Hungary: Air transport agreement and memorandum of understanding, signed at Budapest July 12, 1989; extended until July 12, 2007 by exchange of notes of July 11 and 20, 2006.

k. Ireland: Agreement relating to air transport services, effected by exchange of notes at Washington February 3, 1945; amended January 25, 1988 and September 29, 1989; amended July 25 and September 6, 1990.
(Memorandum of consultations, signed at Washington October 28, 1993 (provisionally applied).)

l. The Italian Republic: Air transport agreement, with memorandum and exchange of notes, signed at Rome June 22, 1970; amended October 25, 1988; related memorandum of understanding signed September 27, 1990; amendment of 1970 agreement and 1990 MOU concluded November 22 and December 23, 1991; amendment of 1970 agreement and 1990 MOU concluded May 30 and October 21, 1997; agreement supplementing the 1970 agreement concluded December 30, 1998 and February 2, 1999.
(Protocol amending the 1970 agreement concluded December 6, 1999 (provisionally applied).)

m. The Grand Duchy of Luxembourg: Air transport agreement, signed at Luxembourg August 19, 1986; amended June 6, 1995; amended July 13 and 21 1998.

n. The Republic of Malta: Air transport agreement, signed at Washington October 12, 2000.

o. The Kingdom of the Netherlands: Air transport agreement, signed at Washington April 3, 1957; protocol amending the 1957 agreement concluded on March 31, 1978; amendment of 1978 protocol concluded June 11, 1986; amendment of 1957 agreement concluded October 13 and December 22, 1987; amendment of 1957 agreement concluded January 29 and March 13, 1992; amendment of 1957 agreement and 1978 protocol concluded October 14, 1992.

p. The Republic of Poland: Air transport agreement, signed at Warsaw June 16, 2001.

q. The Portuguese Republic: Air transport agreement, signed at Lisbon May 30, 2000.

r. Romania: Air transport agreement, signed at Washington July 15, 1998.

s. The Slovak Republic: Air transport agreement, signed at Bratislava January 22, 2001.

t. The Kingdom of Spain: Air transport agreement signed at Madrid February 20, 1973; related agreement of February 20, March 31 and April 7, 1987; amendment of 1973 agreement concluded May 31, 1989; amendment of 1973 agreement concluded November 27, 1991.

u. The Kingdom of Sweden: Agreement relating to air transport services, effected by exchange of notes at Washington December 16, 1944; amended August 6, 1954; amended June 16, 1995.

v. The United Kingdom of Great Britain and Northern Ireland: Agreement concerning air services, and exchange of letters, signed at Bermuda July 23, 1977; agreement relating to North Atlantic air fares, concluded March 17, 1978; agreement amending the 1977 agreement, concluded April 25, 1978; agreement modifying and extending the 1978 agreement relating to North

Atlantic airfares, concluded November 2 and 9, 1978; agreement amending the 1977 agreement, concluded December 4, 1980; agreement amending the 1977 agreement, concluded February 20, 1985; agreement amending Article 7, Annex 2, and Annex 5 of the 1977 agreement, concluded May 25, 1989; agreement concerning amendments of the 1977 agreement, termination of the US/UK Arbitration Concerning Heathrow Airport User Charges and the request for arbitration made by the United Kingdom in its embassy's note no. 87 of 13 October 1993 and settlement of the matters which gave rise to those proceedings, concluded March 11, 1994; agreement amending the 1977 agreement, concluded March 27, 1997.

(Arrangements, being provisionally applied, contained in the memorandum of consultations dated September 11, 1986; arrangements contained in the exchange of letters dated July 27, 1990; arrangements contained in the memorandum of consultations of March 11, 1991; arrangements contained in the exchange of letters dated October 6, 1994; arrangements contained in the memorandum of consultations of June 5, 1995; arrangements contained in the exchange of letters dated March 31 and April 3, 2000 (all provisionally applied).)

Section 2

Notwithstanding section 1 of this Annex, for areas that are not encompassed within the definition of 'Territory' in Article 1 of this Agreement, the agreements in paragraphs (e) (Denmark-United States), (g) (France-United States), and (v) (United Kingdom-United States) of that section shall continue to apply, according to their terms.

Section 3

Notwithstanding Article 3 of this Agreement, U.S. airlines shall not have the right to provide all-cargo services, that are not part of a service that serves the United States, to or from points in the Member States, except to or from points in the Czech Republic, the French Republic, the Federal Republic of Germany, the Grand Duchy of Luxembourg, the Republic of Malta, the Republic of Poland, the Portuguese Republic, and the Slovak Republic.

Section 4

Notwithstanding any other provisions of this Agreement, this section shall apply to scheduled and charter combination air transportation between Ireland and the United States with effect from the beginning of IATA Winter season 2006/2007 until the end of the IATA Winter season 2007/2008,

    a. (i) Each U.S. and Community airline may operate 3 non-stop flights between the United States and Dublin for each non-stop flight that the airline operates between the United States and Shannon. This entitlement for non-stop Dublin flights shall be based on an average of operations over the entire three-season transitional period. A flight shall be deemed to be a non-stop Dublin, or a non-stop Shannon, flight, according to the first point of entry into, or the last point of departure from, Ireland.

(ii) The requirement to serve Shannon in subparagraph (a)(i) of this Section shall terminate if any airline inaugurates scheduled or charter combination service between Dublin and the United States, in either direction, without operating at least one non-stop flight to Shannon for every three non-stop flights to Dublin, averaged over the transition period.

b. For services between the United States and Ireland, Community airlines may serve only Boston, New York, Chicago, Los Angeles, and 3 additional points in the United States, to be notified to the United States upon selection or change. These services may operate via intermediate points in other Member States or in third countries.

c. Code-sharing shall be authorized between Ireland and the United States only via other points in the European Community. Other code-share arrangements will be considered on the basis of comity and reciprocity.

Annex 2

Concerning Cooperation With Respect to Competition Issues in the Air Transport Industry

Article 1

The cooperation as set forth in this Annex shall be implemented by the Department of Transportation of the United States of America and the Commission of the European Communities (hereinafter referred to as "the Participants"), consistent with their respective functions in addressing competition issues in the air transportation industry involving the United States and the European Community.

Article 2
Purpose

The purpose of this cooperation is:

1. To enhance mutual understanding of the application by the Participants of the laws, procedures and practices under their respective competition regimes to encourage competition in the air transportation industry;

2. To facilitate understanding between the Participants of the impact of air transportation industry developments on competition in the international aviation market;

3. To reduce the potential for conflicts in the Participants' application of their respective competition regimes to agreements and other cooperative arrangements which have an impact on the transatlantic market; and

4. To promote compatible regulatory approaches to agreements and other cooperative arrangements through a better understanding of the methodologies, analytical techniques including the definition of the relevant market(s) and analysis of competitive effects, and remedies that the Participants use in their respective independent competition reviews.

Article 3
Definitions

For the purpose of this Annex, the term 'competition regime' means the laws, procedures and practices that govern the Participants' exercise of their respective functions in reviewing agreements and other cooperative arrangements among airlines in the international market. For the European Community, this includes, but is not limited to, Articles 81, 82, and 85 of the Treaty Establishing the European Community and their implementing Regulations pursuant to the said Treaty, as well as any amendments thereto. For the Department of Transportation, this includes, but is not limited to, sections 41308, 41309, and 41720 of Title 49 of the United States Code, and its implementing Regulations and legal precedents pursuant thereto.

Article 4
Areas of Cooperation

Subject to the qualifications in subparagraphs 1(a) and 1(b) of Article 5, the types of cooperation between the Participants shall include the following:

(1) Meetings between representatives of the Participants, to include competition experts, in principle on a semi-annual basis, for the purpose of discussing developments in the air transportation industry, competition policy matters of mutual interest, and analytical approaches to the application of competition law to international aviation, particularly in the transatlantic market. The above discussions may lead to the development of a better understanding of the Participants' respective approaches to competition issues, including existing commonalities and to more compatibility in those approaches, in particular with respect to inter-carrier agreements.

(2) Consultations at any time between the Participants, by mutual agreement or at the request of either Participant, to discuss any matter related to this Annex, including specific cases.

(3) Each Participant may, at its discretion, invite representatives of other governmental authorities to participate as appropriate in any meetings or consultations held pursuant to paragraphs 1 or 2 above.

(4) Timely notifications of the following proceedings or matters, which in the judgment of the notifying Participant may have significant implications for the competition interests of the other Participant:

a. With respect to the Department of Transportation, (i) proceedings for review of applications for approval of agreements and other cooperative arrangements among airlines involving international air transportation, in particular for antitrust immunity involving airlines organized under the laws of the United States and the European Community, and (ii) receipt by the Department of Transportation of a joint venture agreement pursuant to section 41720 of Title 49 of the United States Code; and

b. With respect to the Commission of the European Communities, (i) proceedings for review of agreements and other cooperative arrangements among airlines involving international air transportation, in particular for alliance and other cooperative agreements involving airlines organized under the laws of the United States and the European Community, and (ii) consideration of individual or block exemptions from European Union competition law;

(5) Notifications of the availability, and any conditions governing that availability, of information and data filed with a Participant, in electronic form or otherwise, that, in the judgment of that Participant, may have significant implications for the competition interests of the other Participant; and

(6) Notifications of such other activities relating to air transportation competition policy as may seem appropriate to the notifying Participant.

Article 5
Use and Disclosure of Information

(1) Notwithstanding any other provision of this Annex, neither Participant is expected to provide information to the other Participant if disclosure of the information to the requesting Participant:

a. is prohibited by the laws, regulations or practices of the Participant possessing the information; or

b. would be incompatible with important interests of the Participant possessing the information.

(2) Each Participant shall to the extent possible maintain the confidentiality of any information provided to it in confidence by the other Participant under this Annex and to oppose any application for disclosure of such information to a third party that is not authorized by the supplying Participant to receive the information. Each Participant intends to notify the other Participant whenever any information proposed to be exchanged in discussions or in any other manner may be required to be disclosed in a public proceeding.

(3) Where pursuant to this Annex a Participant provides information on a confidential basis to the other Participant for the purposes specified in Article 2, that information should be used by the receiving Participant only for that purpose.

Article 6
Implementation

(1) Each Participant is designating a representative to be responsible for coordination of activities established under this Annex.

(2) This Annex, and all activities undertaken by a Participant pursuant to it, are –

   a. intended to be implemented only to the extent consistent with all laws, regulations, and practices applicable to that Participant; and
   b. intended to be implemented without prejudice to the Agreement between the European Communities and the Government of the United States of America Regarding the Application of their Competition Laws.

Annex 3

Concerning U.S. Government Procured Transportation

Community airlines shall have the right to transport passengers and cargo on scheduled and charter flights for which a U.S. Government civilian department, agency, or instrumentality (1) obtains the transportation for itself or in carrying out an arrangement under which payment is made by the Government or payment is made from amounts provided for the use of the Government, or (2) provides the transportation to or for a foreign country or international or other organization without reimbursement, and that transportation is (a) between any point in the United States and any point in a Member State, except – with respect to passengers only – between points for which there is a city-pair contract fare in effect, or (b) between any two points outside the United States. This paragraph shall not apply to transportation obtained or funded by the Secretary of Defense or the Secretary of a military department.

Annex 4

Concerning Additional Matters Related to Ownership, Investment and Control

Article 1
Ownership of Airlines of a Party

1. Ownership by nationals of a Member State or States of the equity of a U.S. airline shall be permitted, subject to two limitations. First, ownership by all foreign nationals of more than 25 percent of a corporation's voting equity is prohibited. Second, actual control of a U.S. airline by foreign nationals is also

prohibited. Subject to the overall 25 percent limitation on foreign ownership of voting equity:

   a. ownership by nationals of a Member State or States of:
      (1) as much as 25 percent of the voting equity; and/or
      (2) as much as 49.9 percent of the total equity
      of a U.S. airline shall not be deemed, of itself, to constitute control of that airline; and
   b. ownership by nationals of a Member State or States of 50 percent or more of the total equity of a U. S. airline shall not be presumed to constitute control of that airline. Such ownership shall be considered on a case-by-case basis.

2. Ownership by U. S. nationals of a Community airline shall be permitted subject to two limitations. First, the airline must be majority owned by Member States and/or by nationals of Member States. Second, the airline must be effectively controlled by such States and/or such nationals.

3. For the purposes of paragraph (b) of Article 4 and subparagraph 1(b) of Article 5 of this Agreement, a member of the ECAA as of the date of signature of this Agreement and citizens of such a member shall be treated as a Member State and its nationals, respectively. The Joint Committee may decide that this provision shall apply to new members of the ECAA and their citizens.

4. Notwithstanding paragraph 2, the European Community and its Member States reserves the right to limit investments by U.S. nationals in the voting equity of a Community airline made after the signature of this Agreement to a level equivalent to that allowed by the United States for foreign nationals in U.S. airlines, provided that the exercise of that right is consistent with international law.

Article 2
Ownership and Control of Third-Country Airlines

1. Neither Party shall exercise any available rights under air services arrangements with a third country to refuse, revoke, suspend or limit authorizations or permissions for any airlines of that third country on the grounds that substantial ownership of that airline is vested in the other Party, its nationals, or both.

2. The United States shall not exercise any available rights under air services arrangements to refuse, revoke, suspend or limit authorizations or permissions for any airline of the Principality of Liechtenstein, the Swiss Confederation, a member of the ECAA as of the date of signature of this Agreement, or any country in Africa that is implementing an Open-Skies air services agreement with the United States as of the date of signature of this Agreement, on the grounds that effective control of that airline is vested in a Member State or States, nationals of such a State or States, or both.

3. The Joint Committee may decide that neither Party shall exercise the rights referred to in paragraph 2 of this Article with respect to airlines of a specific country or countries.

Article 3
Control of Airlines

1. The rules applicable in the European Community on ownership and control of Community air carriers are currently laid down in Article 4 of Council Regulation (EEC) No. 2407/92 of 23 July 1992 on licensing of air carriers. Under this Regulation, responsibility for granting an Operating Licence to a Community air carrier lies with the Member States. Member States apply Regulation 2407/92 in accordance with their national regulations and procedures.

2. The rules applicable in the United States are currently laid down in Sections 40102(a)(2), 41102 and 41103 of Title 49 of the United States Code (U.S.C.), which require that licenses for a U.S. 'air carrier' issued by the Department of Transportation, whether a certificate, an exemption, or commuter license, to engage in 'air transportation' as a common carrier, be held only by citizens of the United States as defined in 49 U.S.C § 40102(a)(15). That section requires that the president and two-thirds of the board of directors and other managing officers of a corporation be U.S. citizens, that at least 75 percent of the voting stock be owned by U.S. citizens, and that the corporation be under the actual control of U.S. citizens. The requirement must be met initially by an applicant, and continue to be met by a U.S. airline holding a license.

3. The practice followed by each Party in applying its laws and regulations is set out in the Appendix to this Annex.

Appendix to Annex 4

1. In the United States, citizenship determinations are necessary for all U.S. air carrier applicants for a certificate, exemption, or commuter license. An initial application for a license is filed in a formal public docket, and processed 'on the record' with filings by the applicant and any other interested parties. The Department of Transportation renders a final decision by an Order based on the formal public record of the case, including documents for which confidential treatment has been granted. A 'continuing fitness' case may be handled informally by the Department, or may be set for docketed procedures similar to those used for initial applications.

2. The Department's determinations evolve through a variety of precedents, which reflect, among other things, the changing nature of financial markets and investment structures and DOT's willingness to consider new approaches to foreign investment that are consistent with U.S. law. DOT works with applicants to consider proposed forms of investment and to assist them in fashioning transactions that fully comply with U.S. citizenship law, and applicants regularly consult

with DOT staff before finalizing their applications. At any time before a formal proceeding has begun, DOT staff may discuss questions concerning citizenship issues or other aspects of the proposed transaction and offer suggestions, where appropriate, as to alternatives that would allow a proposed transaction to meet U.S. citizenship requirements.

3. In making both its initial and continuing citizenship and fitness determinations, DOT considers the totality of circumstances affecting the U. S. airline, and Department precedents have permitted consideration of the nature of the aviation relationship between the United States and the homeland(s) of any foreign investors. In the context of this Agreement, DOT would treat investments from EU nationals at least as favorably as it would treat investments from nationals of bilateral or multilateral Open-Skies partners.

4. In the European Union, paragraph 5 of Article 4 of Regulation 2407/92 provides that the European Commission, acting at the request of a Member State, shall examine compliance with the requirements of Article 4 and take a decision if necessary. In taking such decisions the Commission must ensure compliance with the procedural rights recognized as general principles of Community law by the European Court of Justice, including the right of interested parties to be heard in a timely manner.

5. When applying its laws and regulations, each Party shall ensure that any transaction involving investment in one of its airlines by nationals of the other Party is afforded fair and expeditious consideration.

Annex 5

Concerning Franchising and Branding

1. The airlines of each Party shall not be precluded from entering into franchise or branding arrangements, including conditions relating to brand protection and operational matters, provided that: they comply, in particular, with the applicable laws and regulations concerning control; the ability of the airline to exist outside of the franchise is not jeopardized; the arrangement does not result in a foreign airline engaging in cabotage operations; and applicable regulations, such as consumer protection provisions, including those regarding the disclosure of the identity of the airline operating the service, are complied with. So long as those requirements are met, close business relationships and cooperative arrangements between the airlines of each Party and foreign businesses are permissible, and each of the following individual aspects, among others, of a franchise or branding arrangement would not, other than in exceptional circumstances, of itself raise control issues:

   a) using and displaying a specific brand or trademark of a franchisor, including stipulations on the geographic area in which the brand or trademark may be used;

b) displaying on the franchisee's aircraft the colors and logo of the franchisor's brand, including the display of such a brand, trademark, logo or similar identification prominently on its aircraft and the uniforms of its personnel;

c) using and displaying the brand, trademark or logo on, or in conjunction with, the franchisee's airport facilities and equipment;

d) maintaining customer service standards designed for marketing purposes;

e) maintaining customer service standards designed to protect the integrity of the franchise brand;

f) providing for license fees on standard commercial terms;

g) providing for participation in frequent flyer programs, including the accrual of benefits; and

h) providing in the franchise or branding agreement for the right of the franchisor or franchisee to terminate the arrangement and withdraw the brand, provided that nationals of the United States or the Member States remain in control of the U.S. or Community airline, respectively.

2. Franchising and branding arrangements are independent of, but may coexist with, a code-sharing arrangement that requires that both airlines have the appropriate authority from the Parties, as provided for in paragraph 7 of Article 10 of this Agreement.

MEMORANDUM OF CONSULTATIONS

1. Delegations representing the European Community and its Member States and the United States of America met in Brussels 27 February-2 March 2007, to complete negotiations of a comprehensive air transport agreement. Delegation lists appear as Attachment A [not included].

2. The delegations reached ad referendum agreement on, and initialed the text of, an Agreement (the 'Agreement,' appended as Attachment B). The delegations intend to submit the draft Agreement to their respective authorities for approval, with the goal of its entry into force in the near future.

3. With respect to paragraph 2 of Article 1, the delegations affirmed that the definition of 'air transportation' included all forms of charter air service. Furthermore, they noted that the reference to carriage 'held out to the public' did not prejudge the outcome of ongoing discussions on the issue of fractional ownership.

4. With respect to paragraph 5 of Article 1, the EU delegation noted that flights between Member States are considered as intra-Community flights under Community law.

5. With respect to paragraph 6 of Article 1, the EU delegation noted that nothing in this Agreement affects the distribution of competencies between the European

Community and its Member States resulting from the Treaty establishing the European Community.

6. The EU delegation confirmed that the overseas territories to which the Treaty establishing the European Community applies are: the French overseas departments (Guadeloupe, Martinique, Reunion, Guyane), Azores, Madeira, and the Canary Islands.

7. In response to a question from the U.S. delegation, the EU delegation affirmed that, under European Community legislation, a Community airline must receive both its AOC and its operating license from the country in which it has its principal place of business. Further, no airline may have an AOC or operating license from more than one country.

8. With respect to paragraphs 1, 3 and 5 of Article 3, paragraph 3 of Article 1 of Annex 4 and paragraph 2 of Article 2 of Annex 4, and in response to a question from the U.S. delegation, the EU delegation explained that as of the date of signature of the Agreement the members of the European Common Aviation Area comprise, in addition to the Member States of the European Community, the Republic of Albania, Bosnia and Herzegovina, the Republic of Croatia, the Republic of Iceland, the former Yugoslav Republic of Macedonia, the Republic of Montenegro, the Kingdom of Norway, the Republic of Serbia and the United Nations Interim Administration Mission in Kosovo.

9. In response to a question from the EU delegation, the U.S. delegation explained that the following countries are implementing Open-Skies air services agreements with the United States as of the date of signature of the Agreement: Burkina Faso, the Republic of Cape Verde, the Republic of Cameroon, the Republic of Chad, the Gabonese Republic, the Republic of The Gambia, the Republic of Ghana, the Federal Democratic Republic of Ethiopia, the Republic of Liberia, the Republic of Madagascar, the Republic of Mali, the Kingdom of Morocco, the Republic of Namibia, the Federal Republic of Nigeria, the Republic of Senegal, the United Republic of Tanzania and the Republic of Uganda. The U.S. delegation also indicated that it intended to treat airlines of the Republic of Kenya in the same way as airlines of States implementing an Open-Skies air services agreement for the purposes of paragraph 2 of Article 2 of Annex 4.

10. With respect to Article 4, the U.S. delegation noted that the Department of Transportation would require any foreign air carrier seeking authority to operate services pursuant to the Agreement to indicate the responsible authority that had issued its AOC and operating license, thus making clear which authority is responsible for safety, security and other regulatory oversight of the carrier.

11. For the purposes of Article 8, 'responsible authorities' refers, on the one hand, to the U.S. Federal Aviation Administration and, on the other hand, to the authorities of the European Community and/or the Member States having responsibility for the issuance or validation of the certificates and licenses referenced in

paragraph 1 or for the maintenance and administration of the safety standards and requirements referenced in paragraph 2, as is relevant to the matter in question. Furthermore, where consultations are requested pursuant to paragraph 2, the responsible authorities should ensure the inclusion in the consultations of any territorial or regional authorities who, by law or regulation or in practice, are exercising safety oversight responsibility relevant to the matter in question.

12. With respect to Article 9, the delegations affirmed that, to the extent practicable, the Parties intend to ensure the greatest possible degree of coordination on proposed security measures to minimize the threat and mitigate the potentially adverse consequences of any new measures. The delegations further noted that the channels referred to in paragraph 7 of Article 9 are available to consider alternative measures for current and proposed security requirements, in particular the Policy Dialogue on Border and Transport Security and the EU-US Transportation Security Cooperation Group. In addition, the U.S. delegation stated that the U.S. rulemaking process for adopting regulations routinely provides the opportunity for interested parties to comment on, and propose alternatives to, proposed regulations and that such comments are considered in the rulemaking proceeding.

13. During the discussion of paragraph 6 of Article 9, the U.S. delegation explained that the Transportation Security Administration (TSA) must immediately issue a security directive when the TSA determines that emergency measures are necessary to protect transportation security. Such measures are intended to address the underlying security threat and should be limited in scope and duration. Emergency measures of a longer-term nature will be incorporated into TSA requirements using public notice and comment procedures.

14. With respect to the procedure to be established under paragraph 11 of Article 9, the delegations confirmed the need to establish a protocol for the preparation, implementation and conclusions of assessments carried out on the basis of this paragraph.

15. With respect to paragraph 2 of Article 10, the delegations affirmed their willingness to facilitate prompt consideration by the relevant authorities of requests for permits, visas, and documents for the staff referred to in that paragraph, including in circumstances where the entry or residence of staff is required on an emergency and temporary basis.

16. The delegations noted that the reference to 'generally applicable law or regulation' in paragraph 5 of Article 10 includes economic sanctions restricting transactions with specific countries and persons.

17. Both delegations recognized that, under paragraph 7 of Article 10, the airlines of each Party holding the appropriate authority may hold out code-share services, subject to terms and conditions that apply on a non-discriminatory basis to all airlines, to and from all points in the territory of the other Party, at which any

other airline holds out international air transportation on direct, indirect, online, or interline flights, provided that such code-share services:

  (i) are otherwise in compliance with the Agreement; and
  (ii) meet the requirements of traffic distribution rules at the relevant airport system.

18. The delegations discussed the importance of advising passengers which airline or surface transportation provider will actually operate each sector of services when any code-share arrangement is involved. They noted that each side had regulations requiring such disclosure.

19. With respect to paragraph 7 (c) of Article 10, the delegations expressed their understanding that surface transportation providers shall not be subject to laws and regulations governing air transportation on the sole basis that such surface transportation is held out by an airline under its own name. Moreover, surface transportation providers, just as airlines, have the discretion to decide whether to enter into cooperative arrangements. In deciding on any particular arrangement, surface transportation providers may consider, among other things, consumer interests and technical, economic, space, and capacity constraints.

20. In response to a question from the EU delegation, the U.S. delegation affirmed that, under the current interpretation of U.S. law, the carriage of U.S. Government-financed air transportation (Fly America traffic) by a U.S. carrier includes transportation sold under the code of a U.S. carrier pursuant to a code-share arrangement, but carried on an aircraft operated by a foreign air carrier.

21. The U.S. delegation explained that under Annex 3 to the Agreement, and in the absence of a city-pair contract awarded by the U.S. General Services Administration, a U.S. Government employee or other individual whose transportation is paid for by the U.S. Government (other than an employee, military member, or other individual whose transportation is paid for by the U. S. Department of Defense or military department) may book a flight, including on a Community airline, between the U.S. and the European Community, or between any two points outside the United States, that, at the lowest cost to the Government, satisfies the traveler's needs. The U.S. delegation noted further that the city-pairs for which contracts are awarded change from fiscal year to fiscal year. A U.S. Government department, agency or instrumentality, other than the Department of Defense or a military department, may ship cargo on a flight, including on a Community airline, between the U.S. and European Community, or between any two points outside the United States, that, at the lowest cost to the Government, satisfies the agency's needs.

22. The EU delegation explained that the EU does not have a similar program to Fly America.

23. Both delegations expressed their intentions to explore further possibilities for enhancing access to government procured air transportation.

24. In response to a question from the EU delegation concerning the economic operating authority that Community airlines must obtain from the U.S. Department of Transportation, the U.S. delegation began by noting that, over the years, DOT economic licensing procedures have been streamlined. When foreign airlines are seeking authority provided for in an air services agreement, their applications normally can be processed quickly. The U.S. delegation went on to explain that a Community airline has the option of submitting a single application for all route authority provided for in paragraph 1 of Article 3, which includes both scheduled and charter rights. On August 23, 2005, DOT announced further expedited procedures under which it is contemplated that foreign air carriers seeking new route authority would file concurrent exemption and permit applications. Assuming that DOT is in a position to act favorably, based on the record and on the public interest considerations germane to its licensing decisions, DOT would proceed to issue a single order (1) granting the exemption request for whatever duration would normally have been given, or until the permit authority becomes effective, whichever is shorter, and (2) tentatively deciding (i.e., show-cause) to award a corresponding permit, again for the standard duration that would normally have been given (such as indefinite for agreement regimes). Where carriers have already filed for both exemption and permit authority, and where the record regarding those applications remained current, DOT has begun to process those applications pursuant to the August 23 approach.

25. If a Community airline wishes to exercise any of the authority through code sharing pursuant to paragraph 7 of Article 10, the code-share partner airlines can file a joint application for the necessary authority. The airline marketing the service to the public needs underlying economic authority from DOT for whatever type of services (scheduled or charter) is to be sold under its code. Similarly, the airline operating the aircraft needs underlying economic authority from DOT: charter authority to provide the capacity to the other airline to market its service, and either charter or scheduled authority for the capacity it intends to market in its own right. The operating airline also needs a statement of authorization to place its partner's code on those flights. An operating airline can request an indefinite duration blanket statement of authorization for the code-share relationship, identifying the specific markets in which the code-share authority is requested. Additional markets can be added on 30 days' notice to DOT. A code-share statement of authorization is airline-specific, and each foreign code-share partnership requires its own statement of authorization, and, if applicable, a code-share safety audit by the U.S. airline under DOT's published Guidelines.

26. If, pursuant to paragraph 9 of Article 10, a Community airline wishes to provide an entire aircraft with crew to a U.S. airline for operations under the U.S. airline's code, the Community airline would similarly need to have charter authority from DOT, as well as a statement of authorization. The U.S. delegation indicated its belief that virtually all Community airlines that now provide scheduled service to the United States also hold worldwide charter authority from DOT. Therefore, from an economic licensing perspective, they

would only need a statement of authorization to provide an entire aircraft with crew to U.S. airlines. The U.S. delegation further indicated that it did not anticipate that applications from other Community airlines for charter authority would raise any difficulties.

27. The issuance of a statement of authorization, whether for code-sharing or for the provision of an entire aircraft with crew, requires a DOT finding that the proposed operations are in the public interest. This finding is strongly facilitated by a determination that the proposed services are covered by applicable air services agreements. Inclusion of the rights in an agreement also establishes that reciprocity exists.

28. With respect both to code-sharing and to the provision of an entire aircraft with crew under paragraphs 7 and 9 of Article 10, the primary focus of the public interest analysis would be on whether:

- a safety audit has been conducted by the U.S. airline of the foreign airline
- the country issuing the foreign carrier's AOC is IASA category 1
- the foreign airline's home country deals with U.S. carriers on the basis of substantial reciprocity
- approval would give rise to competition concerns.

29. With respect to the provision of aircraft with crew, the public interest analysis would additionally focus on whether:

the lease agreement provides that operational control will remain with the lessor carrier; the regulatory oversight responsibility remains with the lessor's AOC-issuing authority; approval of the lease will not give an unreasonable advantage to any party in a labor dispute where the inability to accommodate traffic in a market is a result of the dispute.

30. Statements of authorization for the provision of an entire aircraft with crew will be issued, at least initially, on a limited-term (e.g., six to nine months) or exceptional basis, which is consistent with the approach in the European Union.

31. In response to a concern expressed by the EU delegation about the discretion that DOT has under the 'public interest' standard, the U.S. delegation stated that, in the context of open-skies aviation relationships, DOT has found code-share arrangements to be in the public interest and has consistently issued statements of authorization with a minimum of procedural delay. The U.S. delegation indicated that, in relation to both code-sharing and the provision of aircraft with crew involving only airlines of the Parties, DOT, unless presented with atypical circumstances, such as those relating to national security, safety or criminality, would focus its analysis of the public interest on the elements described above. Furthermore, in the event that such atypical circumstances exist, the United States would expeditiously inform the other Party.

32. In response to a question from the U.S. delegation, the EU delegation affirmed that, under the currently applicable legislation in the EU (Council Regulation (EEC) 2407/92 of 23 July 1992), aircraft used by a Community airline are required to be registered in the Community. However, a Member State may grant a waiver to this requirement in the case of short-term lease arrangements to meet temporary needs or otherwise in exceptional circumstances. A Community airline that is party to such an arrangement must obtain prior approval from the appropriate licensing authority, and a Member State may not approve an agreement providing aircraft with crew to an airline to which it has granted an operating license unless the safety standards equivalent to those imposed under Community law or, where relevant, national law are met.

33. Both delegations recognized that the failure to authorize airlines to exercise the rights granted in the Agreement or undue delay in granting such authorization could affect an airline's fair and equal opportunity to compete. If either Party believes that its airlines are not receiving the economic operating authority to which they are entitled under the Agreement, it can refer the matter to the Joint Committee.

34. With respect to paragraph 4 of Article 14, the EU delegation recalled that, in accordance with its Article 295, the Treaty establishing the European Community does not prejudice in any way the rules in Member States governing the system of property ownership. The U.S. delegation in response noted its view that government ownership of an airline may adversely affect the fair and equal opportunity of airlines to compete in providing the international air transportation governed by this Agreement.

35. With respect to Article 15, the delegations noted the importance of international consensus in aviation environmental matters within the framework of the International Civil Aviation Organization (ICAO). In this connection, they underscored the significance of the unanimous agreement reached at the 35th ICAO Assembly, which covers both aircraft noise and emissions issues (Resolution A35-5). Both sides are committed to respecting that Resolution in full. In accordance with this Resolution, both sides are committed to applying the 'balanced approach' principle to measures taken to manage the impact of aircraft noise (including restrictions to limit the access of aircraft to airports at particular times) and to ensuring charges for aircraft engine emissions at airport level should be based on the costs of mitigating the environmental impact of those aircraft engine emissions that are properly identified and directly attributed to air transport. Both sides also noted that where relevant legal obligations existed, whether at international, regional, national or local level, they also had to be respected in full; for the United States, the relevant date was October 5, 2001, and for the European Community, the relevant date was March 28, 2002.

36. The delegations further noted the provisions on Climate Change, Energy, and Sustainable Development contained in the 2005 'Gleneagles Communiqué' of the

G8 nations as well as the framework for cooperation on air traffic management issues in the Memorandum of Understanding signed by the Federal Aviation Administration and the Commission on July 18, 2006. The delegations noted the intention of the responsible U.S. and EU authorities to enhance technical cooperation, including in areas of climate science research and technology development, that will enhance safety, improve fuel efficiency, and reduce emissions in air transport. Having regard to their respective positions on the issue of emissions trading for international aviation, the two delegations noted that the United States and the European Union intend to work within the framework of the International Civil Aviation Organization.

37. With regard to the composition of the Joint Committee, the U.S. delegation indicated that it was the U.S. intention to have multi-agency representation, chaired by the Department of State. The EU delegation indicated that the EU would be represented by the European Community and its Member States. The two delegations also indicated that stakeholder participation would be an important element of the Joint Committee process, and that stakeholder representatives would therefore be invited as observers, except where decided otherwise by one or both Parties:

38. With respect to Article 18, the delegations affirmed their intention to hold a preliminary meeting of the Joint Committee not later than 60 days after the date of signature of this Agreement.

39. The Delegations confirmed their understanding that practices such as a first-refusal requirement, uplift ratio, no-objection fee, or any other restriction with respect to capacity, frequency or traffic are inconsistent with the Agreement.

40. The EU delegation suggested that both Parties should understand as clearly as possible the extent to which representatives of the U.S. Department of Transportation (DOT) and the European Commission could exchange information on competition matters covered by Annex 2 to the Agreement under their respective laws, regulations and practices, particularly regarding data and perspectives on issues involving proceedings being actively considered by those authorities.

41. The U.S. delegation indicated that the proceedings covered by Annex 2 to the Agreement are adjudications under U.S. law and are subject to statutory, regulatory and judicial constraints to ensure that the agency decision is based only on the information that is included in the docket of the proceeding, including public information that DOT has determined is officially noticeable, on which the parties have had an opportunity to comment before final agency decision.

42. The U.S. delegation explained that these constraints do not preclude representatives advising the DOT decision-maker in an active proceeding from discussing with representatives of the Commission such matters as (1) the state of competition in any markets based upon non-confidential data; (2) the impact of existing alliances or other cooperative ventures and the results of previously imposed

conditions or other limitations to address competition issues; (3) general approaches to competition analysis or methodology; (4) past cases, including records and decisions; (5) substantive law, policies, and procedures applicable to any cases; (6) issues that might be raised by potential cases that have not been formally initiated, so long as DOT representatives do not 'prejudge' the facts or results of such cases; and (7) in active proceedings, what issues have already been raised by the parties and what non-confidential evidence has been provided for the record, again up to the point of potential prejudgment of the facts and outcome.

43. There are two basic procedural constraints on discussion of ongoing cases. The first applies largely to communications from the Commission to DOT: the latter's decision cannot be based on any substantive information or argument unavailable to all parties for comment on the record before final decision. Should such information be received, it cannot be considered in the decision unless it is made available. The second constraint involves communications from rather than to DOT: the agency cannot demonstrate or appear to demonstrate 'prejudgment' of the issues – that is, articulating a conclusion before the record in the case is ripe and a final decision has been publicly released. This constraint applies to DOT in any context, whether in discussions with the EU or with any other entity not legitimately part of the U.S. Government's internal decision-making process, interested or not. DOT intends to notify the Commission's representatives immediately whenever, in its experience, prejudgment or decisional input becomes a consideration in discussing a particular topic, so that the representatives can decide how to proceed.

44. The EU delegation requested assurance from the U.S. delegation that the statutory 'public interest' criterion is not used under the U.S. competition regime to prefer the interests of individual U.S. airlines over those of other airlines, U.S. or foreign. The U.S. delegation responded that this criterion and the competition standards that DOT must use for its decisions are designed and used to protect competition in markets as a whole, not individual airline competitors. Among other considerations, the U.S. delegation noted that the 'public interest' in international air transportation is defined by statute to include equality of opportunity among U.S. and foreign airlines, as well as maximum competition. Moreover, the public interest criterion in the statutes governing DOT approval of, and antitrust immunity for, intercarrier agreements, is not an 'exception' to the competition analysis that the agency must follow, but rather an additional requirement that must be met before DOT may grant antitrust immunity. Finally, the U.S. delegation emphasized that all DOT decisions must be consistent with domestic law and international obligations, including civil aviation agreements that uniformly contain the requirement for all Parties to provide a 'fair and equal opportunity to compete' to the airlines of the other Parties.

45. In the context of this discussion, both delegations affirmed that their respective competition regimes are applied in a manner to respect the fair and equal

opportunity to compete accorded to all airlines of the Parties, and in accordance with the general principle of protecting and enhancing competition in markets as a whole, notwithstanding possible contrary interests of individual airline competitors.

46. Regarding the European Commission's procedures, the EU delegation explained that the principal limitation on the ability of the European Commission to engage in active cooperation with foreign governmental agencies results from restrictions on the ability to communicate confidential information. Information acquired by the Commission and the authorities of the Member States in the course of an investigation, and which is of the kind covered by professional secrecy, is subject to Article 287 of the EC Treaty and Article 28 of Regulation (EC) 1/2003. Essentially, this refers to information which is not in the public domain and which may be discovered during the course of an investigation, be communicated in a reply for information or which may be voluntarily communicated to the Commission. This information also includes business or trade secrets. Such information may not be disclosed to any third country agency, save with the express agreement of the source concerned. Therefore, where it is considered appropriate and desirable for the Commission to provide confidential information to a foreign agency(ies), the consent of the source of that information must be obtained by means of a waiver.

47. Information which is related to the conduct of an investigation, or the possible conduct of an investigation, is not submitted to the above mentioned provisions. Such information includes the fact that an investigation is taking place, the general subject-matter of the investigation, the identity of the enterprise(s) being investigated (although this also may, in some circumstances, be protected information), the identity of the sector in which the investigation is being undertaken, and the steps which it is proposed to take in the course of the investigation. This information is normally kept confidential to ensure proper handling of the investigation. However, it may be communicated to DOT, as the latter is obliged to maintain the confidentiality of the information under the terms of Article 5 of Annex 2 to the Agreement.

48. In response to a question from the EU delegation, the U.S. delegation confirmed that the competent U.S. authorities will provide fair and expeditious consideration of complete applications for antitrust immunity of commercial cooperation agreements, including revised agreements. The U.S. delegation further confirmed that, for Community airlines, the U.S.-EU Air Transport Agreement, being applied pursuant to Article 25 or in force pursuant to Article 26, will satisfy the Department of Transportation requirement that, to consider such an application from foreign airlines for antitrust immunity or to continue such immunity, an Open-Skies agreement must exist between the United States and the homeland(s) of the applicant foreign airline(s). The foregoing assurance does not apply to applicants from Ireland until Section 4 of Annex 1 expires.

49. In response to a question from the EU delegation, the U.S. delegation stated that all of the DOT rules on computer reservations systems ('CRSs' or 'systems') terminated on July 31, 2004. DOT, however, retains the authority to prohibit unfair and deceptive practices and unfair methods of competition in the airline and airline distribution industries, and DOT can use that authority to address apparent anti-competitive practices by a system in its marketing of airline services. In addition, the Department of Justice and the Federal Trade Commission have jurisdiction to address complaints that a system is engaged in conduct that violates the antitrust laws.

50. With respect to Article 25, the EU delegation explained that in some Member States provisional application must be approved first by their parliaments in accordance with their constitutional requirements.

51. Both delegations confirmed that, in the event that one of the Parties decided to discontinue provisional application of the Agreement in accordance with Article 25(2), the arrangements in Section 4 of Annex 1 to the Agreement may continue to apply if the Parties so agree.

52. With respect to Article 26, the EU delegation explained that in some Member States the procedures referred to in this Article include ratification.

53. In response to a question from the U.S. delegation concerning restrictions arising from the residual elements of bilateral air services agreements between Member States, the EU delegation affirmed that any such restrictions affecting the ability of U.S. and Community airlines to exercise rights granted by this Agreement would no longer be applied.

54. The two delegations emphasized that nothing in the Agreement affects in any way their respective legal and policy positions on various aviation-related environmental issues.

55. The two delegations noted that neither side will cite the Agreement or any part of it as a basis for opposing consideration in the International Civil Aviation Organization of alternative policies on any matter covered by the Agreement.

56. Any air services agreements between the United States and a Member State the applicability of which was in question as of the signing of the Agreement have not been listed in Section 1 to Annex 1 of the Agreement. However, the delegations intend that the Agreement be provisionally applied by the United States and such Member State or States according to the provisions of Article 25 of the Agreement.

For the Delegation of the European Community and Its Member States Daniel Calleja	For the Delegation of the United States of America John Byerly

Tables of Cases and Administrative Proceedings

U.S. Administrative (CAB/DOT/FAA) Proceedings Listed Alphabetically

European Court of Justice Cases Listed Alphabetically

European Court of First Instance Cases Listed Alphabetically

Select Bibliography

Books (and Contributed Chapters to Books) Listed Alphabetically by Author

ABERLE, GERD, ED., EUROPÄISCHE VERKEHRSPOLITIK (J.C.B. Mohr, 1987)

ADKINS, BERNARDINE, AIR TRANSPORT AND EC COMPETITION LAW (Sweet & Maxwell, 1994)

ARMENTANO, DOMINICK T., ANTITRUST AND MONOPOLY: ANATOMY OF A POLICY FAILURE (Holmes & Meier, 1990)

BARLOW, PATRICIA M., AVIATION ANTITRUST: THE EXTRATERRITORIAL APPLICATION OF THE UNITED STATES ANTITRUST LAW AND INTERNATIONAL AIR TRANSPORTATION (Kluwer Law & Taxation, 1988)

Basedow, Jürgen, *Verkehrsrecht und Verkehrspolitik als Europäische Aufgabe*, in ABERLE (ED.), *supra*

BAUMOL, WILLIAM ET AL., CONTESTABLE MARKETS AND THE THEORY OF INDUSTRY STRUCTURE (Harcourt, rev. ed. 1988)

BIRNBAUM, KARL E. & HANSPETER NEUHOLD (EDS.), NEUTRALITY AND NON-ALIGNMENT IN EUROPE (Wilhelm Braumuller, 1982)

BOYFIELD, KEITH (ED.), A MARKET IN AIRPORT SLOTS (IEA, 2008)

BRAITHWAITE, JOHN & PETER DRAHOS, GLOBAL BUSINESS REGULATION (Cambridge University Press, 2000)

BRANCKER, J.W.S., IATA AND WHAT IT DOES (A.W. Sijthoff, 1977)

BREYER, STEPHEN, REGULATION AND ITS REFORM (Harvard University Press, 1982)

BUCHANAN, JAMES M. & GORDON TULLOCK, THE CALCULUS OF CONSENT: LOGICAL FOUNDATIONS OF CONSTITUTIONAL DEMOCRACY (University of Michigan Press, 1962)

Butler, Gail F., and Martin R. Keller, *Airports and Airlines: Analysis of a Symbiotic, Love-Hate Relationship*, in JENKINS (ED.), *infra*

Caratsch, Claudio, *The Permanent Neutrality of Switzerland*, in BIRNBAUM & NEUHOLD (EDS.), *supra*

CARTER, BARRY E. & PHILLIP R. TRIMBLE, INTERNATIONAL LAW (Little, Brown, 1995)

CARTER, BARRY E. & PHILLIP R. TRIMBLE, INTERNATIONAL LAW: SELECTED DOCUMENTS (Little, Brown, 1995)

CAVES, RICHARD E., AIR TRANSPORT AND ITS REGULATORS (Harvard University Press, 1962)

CECCHINI, PAOLO, THE EUROPEAN CHALLENGE, 1992: THE BENEFITS OF A SINGLE MARKET (Ashgate, 1988)

CHENG, BIN, THE LAW OF INTERNATIONAL AIR TRANSPORT (Oceana, 1962)

Crandall, Robert W., *An End to Economic Regulation?*, in ROBINSON (ED.), *infra*

DE CONINCK, FRANKY, EUROPEAN AIR LAW: NEW SKIES FOR EUROPE (Les Presses de l'Institut Aérien, 1994)

DEMPSEY, PAUL S., LAW AND FOREIGN POLICY IN INTERNATIONAL AVIATION (Transnational, 1987)

DIEDERIKS-VERSCHOOR, I.H. PHILEPINA, AN INTRODUCTION TO AIR LAW (Kluwer Law International, 8th rev. ed. 2006)

DINNAGE, JAMES & JOHN F. MURPHY, THE CONSTITUTIONAL LAW OF THE EUROPEAN UNION (LexisNexis, 2d ed. 2008)

DOGANIS, RIGAS, THE AIRLINE BUSINESS (Routledge, 2d ed. 2005)

DOGANIS, RIGAS, THE AIRLINE BUSINESS IN THE 21ST CENTURY (Routledge, 2001)

DOGANIS, RIGAS, FLYING OFF COURSE: THE ECONOMICS OF INTERNATIONAL AIRLINES (Routledge, 3d ed. 2002)

DUETSCH, LARRY L. (ED.), INDUSTRY STUDIES (Prentice-Hall, 1993)

Durham, Michael J., THE FUTURE OF SABRE, in JENKINS (ED.), *infra*

Fahy, Jr., Richard J., *The Cutting Edge of Technology and Regulation*, in JENKINS (ED.), *infra*

Forrester, Ian S., Q.C., *Competition Structures for the 21st Century*, in HAWK (ED.) (1995), *infra*

FOX, JAMES R., THE REGULATION OF INTERNATIONAL COMMERCIAL AVIATION: THE INTERNATIONAL REGULATORY STRUCTURE (Oceana, 1993)

GIDWITZ, BETSY, THE POLITICS OF INTERNATIONAL AIR TRANSPORT (Lexington Books, 1980)

Gilliland, Whitney, *Bilateral Agreements*, in MCWHINNEY & BRADLEY (EDS.), *infra*

GOYDER, DANIEL G., EEC COMPETITION LAW (Clarendon Press, 1988)

GRAHAM, EDWARD M. & DAVID M. MARCHICK, U.S. NATIONAL SECURITY AND FOREIGN DIRECT INVESTMENT (Institute for International Economics, 2006)

Haanappel, Peter P.C., *Deregulation of Air Transport In North America and Western Europe*, in STORM VAN'S GRAVENSANDE & VAN DER VEEN VONK (EDS.), *infra*

HAANAPPEL, PETER P.C., PRICING AND CAPACITY DETERMINATION IN INTERNATIONAL AIR TRANSPORT: A LEGAL ANALYSIS (Kluwer Law & Taxation, 1984)

HAANAPPEL, PETER P.C., RATEMAKING IN INTERNATIONAL AIR TRANSPORT: A LEGAL ANALYSIS OF INTERNATIONAL FARES AND RATES (Kluwer Law & Taxation, 1978)

HAANAPPEL, PETER P.C. ET AL. (EDS.), EEC AIR TRANSPORT POLICY AND REGULATION AND THEIR IMPLICATIONS FOR NORTH AMERICA (Kluwer Law & Taxation, 1990)

HANLON, PAT, GLOBAL AIRLINES: COMPETITION IN A TRANSNATIONAL INDUSTRY (Butterworth-Heinemann, 2d ed. 2002)

HARDAWAY, ROBERT M. (ED.), AIRPORT REGULATION, LAW AND PUBLIC POLICY (Quorum Books, 1991)

HARTLEY, TREVOR, THE FOUNDATIONS OF EUROPEAN COMMUNITY LAW (Oxford University Press, 6th ed. 2007)

HARVEY, DAVID, A BRIEF HISTORY OF NEOLIBERALISM (Oxford University Press, 2007)

HAVEL, BRIAN F., IN SEARCH OF OPEN SKIES: LAW AND POLICY FOR A NEW ERA IN INTERNATIONAL AVIATION (Kluwer Law International, 1997)

Havel, Brian F., *International Instruments in Air, Space and Telecommunications Law: The Need for a Mandatory Supranational Dispute Settlement Mechanism*, in THE INTERNATIONAL BUREAU OF THE PERMANENT COURT OF ARBITRATION, *infra*

HAWK, BARRY E. (ED.), ANNUAL PROCEEDINGS OF THE FORDHAM CORPORATE LAW INSTITUTE, EC AND US COMPETITION LAW & POLICY (1991) (Transnational Juris, 1992)

HAWK, BARRY E. (ED.), ANNUAL PROCEEDINGS OF THE FORDHAM CORPORATE LAW INSTITUTE, INTERNATIONAL ANTITRUST LAW & POLICY (1994) (Transnational Juris, 1995)

HAWK, BARRY E. (ED.), ANNUAL PROCEEDINGS OF THE FORDHAM CORPORATE LAW INSTITUTE, INTERNATIONAL ANTITRUST LAW & POLICY (1995) (Juris, 1996)

Hawk, Barry E., *United States Regulation of Air Transport*, in SLOT & DAGTOGLOU (EDS.), *infra*

HIGH, JACK (ED.), REGULATION: ECONOMIC THEORY AND HISTORY (University of Michigan Press, 1991)

HINDLEY, BRIAN, TRADE LIBERALIZATION IN AVIATION SERVICES: CAN THE DOHA ROUND FREE FLIGHT? (AEI, 2004)

HOVENKAMP, HERBERT, FEDERAL ANTITRUST POLICY: THE LAW OF COMPETITION AND ITS PRACTICE (West, 3d ed. 2005)

THE INTERNATIONAL BUREAU OF THE PERMANENT COURT OF ARBITRATION, 4 PEACE PALACE PAPERS: ARBITRATION IN AIR, SPACE, AND TELECOMMUNICATIONS LAW (Kluwer Law International, 2002)

JACKSON, JOHN H., SOVEREIGNTY, THE WTO AND CHANGING FUNDAMENTALS OF INTERNATIONAL LAW (Cambridge University Press, 2006)

JANIS, MARK W., INTERNATIONAL LAW (Aspen, 5th ed. 2008)

JENKINS, DARRYL (ED.), THE HANDBOOK OF AIRLINE ECONOMICS (McGraw-Hill, 1995)

JOLIET, RENÉ, MONOPOLIZATION AND ABUSE OF DOMINANT POSITION: A COMPARATIVE STUDY OF THE AMERICAN AND EUROPEAN APPROACHES TO THE CONTROL OF ECONOMIC POWER (Martinus Nijhoff, 1970)

KAHN, ALFRED E., LESSONS FROM DEREGULATION: TELECOMMUNICATIONS AND AIRLINES AFTER THE CRUNCH (Brookings Institution Press, 2003)

KASPER, DANIEL, DEREGULATION AND GLOBALIZATION: LIBERALIZING INTERNATIONAL TRADE IN AIR SERVICES (Ballinger, 1988)

KEYES, LUCILE SHEPPARD, FEDERAL CONTROL OF ENTRY INTO AIR TRANSPORTATION (Harvard University Press, 1951)

KOMNINOS, ASSIMAKIS, EC PRIVATE ANTITRUST ENFORCEMENT: DECENTRALISED APPLICATION OF EC COMPETITION LAW BY NATIONAL COURTS (Hart Publishing, 2008)

KOSKENNIEMI, MARTII (ED.), INTERNATIONAL LAW ASPECTS OF THE EUROPEAN UNION (Martinus Nijhoff Publishers, 1998).

KÖTHENBÜRGER, MARKO ET AL (EDS.), PRIVATIZATION EXPERIENCES IN THE EUROPEAN UNION (MIT Press, 2006)

KRUSEN, WILLIAM A., FLYING THE ANDES: THE STORY OF PAN AMERICAN GRACE AIRWAYS (University of Tampa Press, 1997)

LELIEUR, ISABELLE, LAW AND POLICY OF SUBSTANTIAL OWNERSHIP AND EFFECTIVE CONTROL OF AIRLINES (Ashgate, 2003)

Levine, Michael E., *Regulatory Capture*, in NEWMAN (ED.), *infra*

LOWENFELD, ANDREAS F., AVIATION LAW: CASES AND MATERIALS (Matthew Bender, 2d ed. 1981)

LOWENFELD, ANDREAS F., AVIATION LAW: DOCUMENTS SUPPLEMENT (Matthew Bender, 2d ed. 1981)

Loy, Frank E., *Bilateral Air Transport Agreements: Some Problems of Finding a Fair Route Exchange*, in MCWHINNEY & BRADLEY (EDS.)

MACAVOY, PAUL W., AND JOHN W. SNOW (EDS.), REGULATION OF PASSENGER FARES AND COMPETITION AMONG THE AIRLINES (American Enterprise Institute for Public Policy Research, 1977)

MATSUSHITA, MITSUO ET AL., THE WORLD TRADE ORGANIZATION: LAW, PRACTICE, AND POLICY (Oxford University Press, 2006)

MATTE, NICOLAS M., TRAITÉ DE DROIT AÉRONAUTIQUE (A. Pedone, 1980)

MAXEINER, JAMES, POLICY AND METHODS IN GERMAN AND AMERICAN ANTITRUST LAW (Praeger, 1986)

MCWHINNEY, EDWARD & MARTIN A. BRADLEY (EDS.), THE FREEDOM OF THE AIR (A.W. Sijthoff, 1968)

MENDES DE LEON, PABLO, CABOTAGE IN AIR TRANSPORT REGULATION (Martinus Nijhoff, 1992)

Mendes de Leon, Pablo, *Euro-Cabotage: A Lever for Liberalization of International Civil Aviation*, in HAANAPPEL ET AL. (EDS.), *supra*

MILLER, JEFFREY, THE AIRLINE DEREGULATION HANDBOOK (Merton House, 1981)

MONTI, GIORGIO, EC COMPETITION LAW (Cambridge University Press, 2007)

Morrison, Steven A., *Airline Services: The Evolution of Competition Since Deregulation*, in DUETSCH (ED.), *supra*

NAVIA, LUIS E., CLASSICAL CYNICISM: A CRITICAL STUDY (Greenwood Press, 1996)

NEWMAN, PETER (ED.), 3 NEW PALGRAVE DICTIONARY OF LAW AND ECONOMICS (Palgrave, 1998)

NOONAN, CHRIS, EMERGING PRINCIPLES OF INTERNATIONAL COMPETITION LAW (Oxford University Press, 2008)

PETERSON, BARBARA STURKEN, AND JAMES GLAB, RAPID DESCENT: DEREGULATION AND THE SHAKEOUT IN THE AIRLINES (Simon & Schuster, 1994)

PHILO OF ALEXANDRIA, PHILO VOL. I: ON THE ALLEGORICAL INTERPRETATION OF GENESIS 2 AND 3 (F.H. Colson & G.H. Whitaker trans., Loeb Classical Library, 1929)

POLANYI, KARL, THE GREAT TRANSFORMATION (Beacon Press, 2001) (1957)

PRASAD, MONICA, THE POLITICS OF FREE MARKETS: THE RISE OF NEOLIBERAL ECONOMIC POLICIES IN BRITAIN, FRANCE, GERMANY AND THE UNITED STATES (University of Chicago Press, 2006)

Rees, Ray, *Economic Aspects of Privatization*, in KÖTHENBÜRGER ET AL. (EDS.), *supra*

REICH, ROBERT B., THE WORK OF NATIONS (Vintage, 1992)

RHOADES, DAWNA L., EVOLUTION OF INTERNATIONAL AVIATION: PHOENIX RISING (Ashgate, 2003)

ROBINSON, COLIN (ED), COMPETITION AND REGULATION IN UTILITY MARKETS (Edward Elgar, 2003)

Simat, Helliesen & Eichner, Inc., *The Intrastate Air Regulation Experience in Texas and California*, in MACAVOY & SNOW (EDS.), *supra*

Slot, Pieter J., *Civil Aviation in the Community: An Overview*, in SLOT & DAGTOGLOU (EDS.), *infra*

SLOT, PIETER J. & PRODROMOS D. DAGTOGLOU (EDS.), TOWARD A COMMUNITY AIR TRANSPORT POLICY: THE LEGAL DIMENSION (Kluwer Law & Taxation, 1989)

Spode, Hasso, '*Let us Fly You Where the Sun Is:' Air Travel and Tourism in Historical Perspective*, in VITRA DESIGN MUSEUM, *infra*

STANILAND, MARTIN, A EUROPE OF THE AIR?: THE AIRLINE INDUSTRY AND EUROPEAN INTEGRATION (Rowman & Littlefield, 2008)

Starkie, David, *The Economics of Secondary Markets for Airport Slots*, in BOYFIELD (ED.), *supra*

STEPHAN, PAUL B. ET AL., THE LAW AND ECONOMICS OF THE EUROPEAN UNION (Matthew Bender, 2003)

STORM VAN'S GRAVENSANDE, J.W.E. & A. VAN DER VEEN VONK (EDS.), AIR WORTHY (Kluwer Law & Taxation, 1985)

STRUVE, GLEB, SOVIET RUSSIAN LITERATURE 1917-50 (University of Oklahoma Press, 1951)

Sundstrum, G.O. Zacharias & Bo Stahle, *Regulation of Civil Aviation in Scandinavia*, in SLOT & DAGTOGLOU, *supra*

SWANN, DENNIS, THE RETREAT OF THE STATE: DEREGULATION AND PRIVATIZATION IN THE UK AND US (University of Michigan Press, 1988)

Teubner, Gunter, *Global Bukowina: Legal Pluralism in the World Society*, in TEUBNER (ED.), *Infra*

TEUBNER, GUNTER (ED.), GLOBAL LAW WITHOUT A STATE (Dartmouth, 1996)

TRIDIMAS, TAKIS, THE GENERAL PRINCIPLES OF EU LAW (Oxford University Press, 2d ed. 2007)

VAN ANTWERPEN, NIELS, CROSS-BORDER PROVISION OF AIR NAVIGATION SERVICES WITH SPECIFIC REFERENCE TO EUROPE: SAFEGUARDING TRANSPARENT LINES OF RESPONSIBILITY AND LIABILITY (Kluwer Law International, 2008)

Van der Esch, Bastiaan, *Main Issues of Community Law Governing Access to Air Transport and Member States' Control of Fares*, in SLOT & DAGTOGLOU (eds.), *supra*

VITRA DESIGN MUSEUM, AIRWORLD (2007)

V<small>OEGELIN</small>, E<small>RIC</small>, T<small>HE</small> C<small>OLLECTED</small> W<small>ORKS OF</small> E<small>RIC</small> V<small>OEGELIN</small> V<small>OLUME</small> 17: O<small>RDER AND</small> H<small>ISTORY</small> <small>VOLUME</small> IV: T<small>HE</small> E<small>CUMENIC</small> A<small>GE</small> (Michael Franz ed., University of Missouri Press, 2000)

W<small>ENSVEEN</small>, J<small>OHN</small> G., A<small>IR</small> T<small>RANSPORTATION</small>: A M<small>ANAGEMENT</small> P<small>ERSPECTIVE</small> (Ashgate, 6th ed. 2007)

W<small>RIGHT</small>, V<small>INCENT</small> (<small>ED.</small>), P<small>RIVATIZATION IN</small> W<small>ESTERN</small> E<small>UROPE</small>: P<small>RESSURES</small>, P<small>ROBLEMS</small> <small>AND</small> P<small>ARADOXES</small> (Pinter, 1994)

Wright, Vincent, *Industrial Privatization in Western Europe: Pressures, Problems and Paradoxes*, in W<small>RIGHT</small> (<small>ED.</small>), *supra*

X<small>ENOPHANES OF</small> C<small>OLOPHON</small>, F<small>RAGMENTS</small> (University of Toronto Press, J.H. Lester ed., 1992)

Y<small>ERGIN</small>, D<small>ANIEL</small> & J<small>OSEPH</small> S<small>TANISLAW</small>, C<small>OMMANDING</small> H<small>EIGHTS</small>: T<small>HE</small> B<small>ATTLE FOR THE</small> W<small>ORLD</small> E<small>CONOMY</small> (Free Press, 2002)

Journal Articles and Scholarly Working Papers Listed Alphabetically by Author

Abeyratne, Ruwantissa I.R., *The Economic Relevance of the Chicago Convention – A Retrospective Study*, 19-2 A<small>NNALS OF</small> A<small>IR</small> & S<small>PACE</small> L<small>AW</small> 3 (1994)

Abeyratne, Ruwantissa I.R., *Trade in Air Transport Services: Emerging Trends*, 35 J<small>OURNAL OF</small> W<small>ORLD</small> T<small>RADE</small> 1133 (2001)

Alexander, Cindy R. & Yoon-Ho Alex Lee, *The Economics of Regulatory Reform: Termination of Airline Computer Reservation System Rules*, 21 Y<small>ALE</small> J<small>OURNAL</small> <small>ON</small> R<small>EGULATION</small> 369 (2004)

Argyris, Nicholas, *The EEC Rules of Competition and the Air Transport Sector*, 26 C<small>OMMON</small> M<small>ARKET</small> L<small>AW</small> R<small>EVIEW</small> 5 (1989)

Atwood, James R., Book Review, *International Aviation, How Much Competition, and How?*, 32 S<small>TANFORD</small> L<small>AW</small> R<small>EVIEW</small> 1061 (1980)

Azzie, Ralph, *Second Special Air Transport Conference and Bilateral Air Transport Agreements*, 5 A<small>NNALS OF</small> A<small>IR</small> & S<small>PACE</small> L<small>AW</small> 3 (1980)

Bailey, Elizabeth E., & John C. Panzar, *The Contestability of Airline Markets During the Transition to Deregulation*, 44 J<small>OURNAL OF</small> L<small>AW</small> & C<small>ONTEMPORARY</small> P<small>ROBLEMS</small> 125 (1981)

Baker, Jonathan B., *Predatory Pricing After Brooke Group: An Economic Perspective*, 62 A<small>NTITRUST</small> L<small>AW</small> J<small>OURNAL</small> 585 (1994)

Bamberger, Gustavo E. et al., *An Empirical Investigation of the Competitive Effects of Domestic Airline Alliances*, 47 J<small>OURNAL OF</small> L<small>AW</small> & E<small>CONOMICS</small> 195 (2004)

Barlow, Patricia M., *Aviation Antitrust – International Considerations After Sunset*, 12 A<small>IR</small> L<small>AW</small> 68 (1987)

Basedow, Jürgen, *National Authorities in European Airline Competition Law*, 9 E<small>UROPEAN</small> C<small>OMPETITION</small> L<small>AW</small> R<small>EVIEW</small> 342 (1988)

Basedow, Jürgen, *Symposium on US-EC Legal Relations: Airline Deregulation in the European Community*, 13 J<small>OURNAL OF</small> A<small>IR</small> L<small>AW AND</small> C<small>OMMERCE</small> 247 (1994)

Beane, Jerry L., *The Antitrust Implications of Airline Deregulation*, 45 J<small>OURNAL OF</small> A<small>IR</small> L<small>AW</small> & C<small>OMMERCE</small> 1001 (1980)

Bederman, David J., *Prospects for European Air Deregulation*, 21 INTERNATIONAL LAWYER 561 (1987)

Bell, Barbara A., *The Extraterritorial Application of United States Antitrust Law and International Aviation: A Comity of Errors*, 54 JOURNAL OF AIR LAW & COMMERCE 533 (1988)

Bliss, F. Allen, *Rethinking Restrictions on Cabotage: Moving to Free Trade in Passenger Aviation*, 17 SUFFOLK TRANSNATIONAL LAW REVIEW 382 (1994)

Bodoff, Joan, *Competition Policies of the US and the EEC: An Overview*, 5 EUROPEAN COMPETITION LAW REVIEW 51 (1984)

Bohmann, Kirsten, *The Ownership and Control Requirement in U.S. and European Union Air Law and U.S. Maritime Law – Policy; Consideration; Comparison*, 66 JOURNAL OF AIR LAW & COMMERCE 689 (2001)

Borenstain, Severin & Nancy L. Rose, *How Airline Markets Work, or Do They? Regulatory Reform in the Airline Industry* (NBER Working Paper Series, Working Paper No. 13452, Sept. 2007)

Boudreaux, Donald J., and Jerome Ellig, *Beneficent Bias: The Case Against Regulating Airline Computerized Reservation Systems*, 57 JOURNAL OF AIR LAW & COMMERCE 567 (1992)

Bradley, Jr., Robert L., *On the Origins of the Sherman Antitrust Act*, 9 CATO JOURNAL 737 (1990)

Brenner, Melvin A., *Airline Deregulation: A Case Study in Public Policy Failure*, 16 TRANSPORTATION LAW JOURNAL 179 (1988)

Brenner, Melvin A., *Rejoinder to Comments by Alfred Kahn*, 16 TRANSPORTATION LAW JOURNAL 253 (1988)

Brown, Jeffrey D., Comment, *Foreign Investment in US Airlines: What Limits Should be Placed on Foreign Ownership of US Carriers?*, 41 SYRACUSE LAW REVIEW 1269 (1990)

Callison, James W., *Airline Deregulation – A Hoax?*, 41 JOURNAL OF AIR LAW & COMMERCE 747 (1975)

Callison, James W., *Airline Deregulation – Only Partially a Hoax: The Current Status of the Airline Deregulation Movement*, 45 JOURNAL OF AIR LAW & COMMERCE 961 (1980)

Canetti, Craig, *Fifty Years After the Chicago Conference: A Proposal for Dispute Settlement under the Auspices of the International Civil Aviation Organization*, 26 LAW AND POLICY IN INTERNATIONAL BUSINESS 497 (1995)

Chang, Yu-Chun & George Williams, *Changing the Rules – Amending the Nationality Clauses in Air Services Agreements*, 7 JOURNAL OF AIR TRANSPORT MANAGEMENT 207 (2001)

Charney, Jonathan I., *Entry into Force of the 1982 Convention on the Law of the Sea*, 35 VIRGINIA JOURNAL OF INTERNATIONAL LAW 381 (1995)

Clarke, Virginia J., *New Frontiers in EEC Transport Competition*, 8 JOURNAL OF INTERNATIONAL LAW AND BUSINESS 455 (1987)

Cohen, Marvin S., *The Antitrust Implications of Airline Deregulation*, 28 ANTITRUST BULLETIN 131 (1983)

Cudahy, Richard D., *The Airlines: Destined to Fail?*, 71 JOURNAL OF AIR LAW & COMMERCE 3 (2006)

Cudahy, Richard D., *The Coming Demise of Deregulation*, 10 YALE JOURNAL ON REGULATION 1 (1993)

De Mestral, Armand, *Canadian-EU Bilateral Air Service Agreements* (Institute for European Studies Working Paper No. 05/05, 2005)

De Mestral, A.L.C. & H. Bashor, *International Air Transport Agreements and Regionalism: The Impact of the European Union Upon the Development of International Air Law* 18 (Jean Monnet/Robert Schuman Paper Series. Vol. 5, No. 20, July 2005)

Dempsey, Paul S., *Aerial Dogfights over Europe: The Liberalization of EEC Air Transport*, 53 JOURNAL OF AIR LAW & COMMERCE 615 (1988)

Dempsey, Paul S., *The Rise and Fall of the Civil Aeronautics Board – Opening Wide the Floodgates of Entry*, 11 TRANSPORTATION LAW JOURNAL 91 (1979)

Dempsey, Paul S., *The Role of the International Civil Aviation Organization in Deregulation, Discrimination and Dispute Resolution*, 52 JOURNAL OF AIR LAW & COMMERCE 529 (1987)

Devall, James L., *American Airlines/British Airways: An Alliance That Was Not Meant to Be?*, ISSUES IN AVIATION LAW & POLICY ¶ 10,101, at 4151 (Mar. 2002)

Dinwoodie, Graeme, *A New Copyright Order: Why National Courts Should Create Global Norms*, 149 UNIVERSITY OF PENNSYLVANIA LAW REVIEW 469 (2000)

Dolan, Stephen, *EC Aviation Scene (No. 2: 2006)*, 31 AIR & SPACE LAW 211 (2006)

Duff, John A., *The United States and the Law of the Sea Convention: Sliding Back from Accession and Ratification*, 11 OCEAN & COASTAL LAW JOURNAL 1 (2005)

Easterbrook, Frank H., *Predatory Strategies and Counterstrategies*, 48 UNIVERSITY OF CHICAGO LAW REVIEW 263 (1981)

Farmer, Susan Beth, *Chapter 9: Competitive Policy and Merger Analysis in Deregulated and Newly Competitive Industries* 39 (Dickinson School of Law Legal Studies Research Paper No. 05-2008, June 2, 2008)

Featherstone, Kevin & Dimitris Papadimitriou, *Manipulating Rules, Contesting Solutions: Europeanization and the Politics of Restructuring Olympic Airways*, 42 GOVERNMENT & OPPOSITION 46 (2007)

Fisher, Keith R., *Statutory Construction and the Kaye, Scholer Freeze Order* (MSU Legal Studies Research Paper No. 03-17, 1992)

Forrest, R.M., *Is Open Competition Preferable to Regulation?*, 6 AIR LAW 7 (1981)

Franck, Thomas M., *Legitimacy in the International System*, 82 AMERICAN JOURNAL OF INTERNATIONAL LAW 705 (1988)

Freeland, Steven, *Up, Up and . . . Back: The Emergence of Space Tourism and its Impact on the International Law of Outer Space*, 6 CHICAGO JOURNAL OF INTERNATIONAL LAW 1 (2005)

Garland, Gloria J., *The American Deregulation Experience and the Use of Article 90 to Expedite EEC Air Transport Liberalization*, EUROPEAN COMPETITION LAW REVIEW 193 (1986)

Gazdik, J.G., *Nationality of Aircraft and Nationality of Airlines as Means of Control in International Air Transportation*, 25 JOURNAL OF AIR LAW & COMMERCE 1 (1958)

Gerber, David J., *Constitutionalizing the Economy: German Neoliberalism*, 42 AMERICAN JOURNAL OF COMPARATIVE LAW 45 (1994)

Gerber, David J., *The Transformation of European Community Competition Law?*, 35 HARVARD INTERNATIONAL LAW JOURNAL 97 (1994)

Gertler, Z. Joseph, *Bilateral Air Transport Agreements*, 42 JOURNAL OF AIR LAW & COMMERCE 779 (1976)

Gertler, Z. Joseph, *Nationality of Airlines: A Hidden Force in the International Air Regulation Equation*, 48 JOURNAL OF AIR LAW & COMMERCE 51 (1982)

Gertler, Z. Joseph, *Order in the Air and the Problem of Real and False Options*, 4 ANNALS OF AIR & SPACE LAW 93 (1979)

Gibbs, Murray, and Mina Mashayekhi, *Services: Cooperation for Development*, 22 JOURNAL OF WORLD TRADE LAW 81 (1988)

Gomez-Ibanez, José, & Ivor P. Morgan, *Deregulating International Markets: The Examples of Aviation and Ocean Shipping*, 2 YALE JOURNAL ON REGULATION 107 (1984)

Griffin, Ryan, *State Aid, the Growth of Low-Cost Carriers in the European Union, and the Impact of the 2005 Guidelines on Financing Airports and Start-up Aid to Airlines Departing from Regional Airports*, 71 JOURNAL OF AIR LAW & COMMERCE 341 (2006)

Haanappel, Peter P.C., *The External Aviation Relations of the European Economic Community and of EEC Members into the Twenty-First Century, Part II*, 14 AIR LAW 122 (1989)

Hall, Frank D., *Development of the International Framework of Air Transportation*, 5 NORTHROP UNIVERSITY LAW JOURNAL OF AEROSPACE, ENERGY & THE ENVIRONMENT 1 (1984)

Hanlon, Pat, Book Review, *Kenneth Button et al., Flying into the Future: Air Transport Policy in the European Union*, 109 ECONOMIC JOURNAL F843 (1999)

Havel, Brian F., *The Constitution in an Era of Supranational Adjudication*, 78 NORTH CAROLINA LAW REVIEW 257 (2000)

Havel, Brian F., *A New Approach to Foreign Ownership of National Airlines*, ISSUES IN AVIATION LAW & POLICY ¶ 25,201, at 13,201 (2003)

Havel, Brian F., *Mixed Signals on Foreign Ownership: An Assessment*, ISSUES IN AVIATION LAW & POLICY ¶ 25,341, at 13,125 (2005)

Havel, Brian F. & Michael G. Whitaker, *The Approach of Re-Regulation: The Airline Industry After September 11, 2001*, ISSUES IN AVIATION LAW & POLICY ¶ 10,051, at 4,109 (2001)

Helfer, Laurence R. & Anne-Marie Slaughter, *Toward a Theory of Effective Supranational Adjudication*, 107 YALE LAW JOURNAL 273 (1997)

Hesse, Nicky E., *Some Questions on Aviation Cabotage*, 1 McGILL LAW JOURNAL 129 (1953)

Housman, Robert F., *Democratizing International Trade Decision-Making*, 27 CORNELL INTERNATIONAL LAW JOURNAL 699 (1994)

Hubner, Wolfgang & Pierre Suavé, *Liberalisation Scenarios for International Air Transport*, 35 JOURNAL OF WORLD TRADE LAW 973 (2001)

Jacobs, Michael S., *The New Sophistication in Antitrust*, 79 MINNESOTA LAW REVIEW 1 (1994)

Janda, Richard, *Passing the Torch: Why ICAO Should Leave Economic Regulation of International Air Transport to the WTO*, 20-1 ANNALS OF AIR & SPACE LAW 409 (1995)

Janda, Richard, *Toward Cosmopolitan Law*, 50 McGILL LAW JOURNAL 967 (2005)

Jarach, David, *Future Scenarios for the European Airline Industry: A Market-Based Perspective*, 9 JOURNAL OF AIR TRANSPORT 23 (2004)

Kaldahl, Wesley G., *Let the Process of Deregulation Continue*, 50 JOURNAL OF AIR LAW & COMMERCE 285 (1985)

Kalshoven-van Tijen, Eugenie, *The EEC Commission as the European Version of the CAB?*, 15 AIR LAW 257 (1990)

Kelleher, Herbert D., *Deregulation and the Troglodytes – How the Airlines Met Adam Smith*, 50 JOURNAL OF AIR LAW & COMMERCE 299 (1985)

Keyes, Lucile Sheppard, *A Preliminary Appraisal of Merger Control Under the Airline Deregulation Act of 1978*, 46 JOURNAL OF AIR LAW & COMMERCE 71 (1980)

Keyes, Lucile Sheppard, *The Regulation of Airline Mergers by the Department of Transportation*, 53 JOURNAL OF AIR LAW & COMMERCE 737 (1988)

Kleit, Andrew N., *Computer Reservations Systems: Competition Misunderstood*, 37 ANTITRUST BULLETIN 833 (1992)

Lehner, Randall D., *Protectionism, Prestige, and National Security: The Alliance Against Multilateral Trade in International Air Transport*, 45 DUKE LAW JOURNAL 436 (1995)

Lester, M.J., Book Review (C. CODRAI, EUROPEAN AIR FARES AND TRANSPORT SERVICES), 8 EUROPEAN LAW REVIEW 212 (1983)

Levine, Michael E., *Airline Competition in Deregulated Markets: Theory, Firm Strategy and Public Policy*, 4 YALE JOURNAL ON REGULATION 393 (1987)

Levine, Michael E., *Is Regulation Necessary? California Air Transportation and National Regulatory Policy*, 74 YALE LAW JOURNAL 1416 (1965)

Levine, Michael E., *Why Weren't the Airlines Reregulated?*, 23 YALE JOURNAL ON REGULATION 269 (2006)

Lewis, Douglas R., *Air Cabotage: Historical and Modern-Day Perspectives*, 45 JOURNAL OF AIR LAW & COMMERCE 1059 (1980)

Lissitzyn, Oliver J., *Bilateral Agreements on Air Transport*, 30 JOURNAL OF AIR LAW & COMMERCE 248 (1964)

Lissitzyn, Oliver J., *The Legal Status of Executive Agreements on Air Transport, Part I*, 17 JOURNAL OF AIR LAW & COMMERCE 436 (1950)

Lissitzyn, Oliver J., *The Legal Status of Executive Agreements on Air Transport, Part II*, 18 JOURNAL OF AIR LAW & COMMERCE 12 (1951)

Lyle, Chris, *Computer-Age Vulnerability in the International Airline Industry*, 54 JOURNAL OF AIR LAW & COMMERCE 161 (1988)

Maffeo, Dario, *Slot Trading in the Reform of the Council Regulation (EEC) No. 95/93: A Comparative Analysis with the United States*, 66 JOURNAL OF AIR LAW & COMMERCE 1569 (2001)

Mamounas, Joseph, *Controlling Foreign Ownership of U.S. Strategic Assets: The Challenge of Maintaining National Security in a Globalized and Oil Dependent World*, 13 LAW & BUSINESS REVIEW OF THE AMERICAS 381 (2007)

Mendelsohn, Allan I., *Myths of International Aviation*, 68 JOURNAL OF AIR LAW & COMMERCE 519 (2003)

Mendelsohn, Allan I., *The United States, the European Union and the Ownership and Control of Airlines*, ISSUES IN AVIATION LAW & POLICY ¶ 25,151, at 13,172 (2003)

Meunier, Sophie, *What Single Voice? European Institutions and EU-U.S. Trade Negotiations*, 51 INTERNATIONAL ORGANIZATION 103 (2000)

Mifsud, Paul V., *New Proposals for New Directions: 1992 and the GATT Approach to Trade in Air Transport Services*, 13 AIR LAW 154 (1988)

Milde, Michael, *Aeronautical Consequences of the Iraqi Invasion of Kuwait*, 16 AIR LAW 63 (1991)

Morash, Edward A., *Airline Deregulation: Another Look*, 50 JOURNAL OF AIR LAW & COMMERCE 253 (1985)

Mostaghel, Deborah M., *Dubai Ports World Under Exon-Florio: A Threat to National Security or a Tempest in a Seaport?*, 70 ALBANY LAW REVIEW 583 (2007)

Naveau, Jacques, *Arbitral Award in the Dispute between the Belgian and Irish Civil Aviation Authorities over Services between Brussels and Dublin by Sabena and Aer Lingus, given at Dublin, July 17, 1981*, 8 AIR LAW 50 (1983)

Naveau, Jacques, *Away from Bermuda? An Arbitration Verdict on Capacity Clauses in the Belgian/Ireland Air Transport Agreement*, 8 AIR LAW 44 (1983)

Naveau, Jacques, *Bilateralism Revisited in Europe*, 10 AIR LAW 85 (1985)

Oum, Tae Hoon, et al., *Strategic Airline Policy in the Globalizing Airline Networks*, 32 TRANSPORTATION JOURNAL 14 (1993)

Papatheodorou, Andreas, *Civil Aviation Regimes and Leisure Tourism in Europe*, 8 JOURNAL OF AIR TRANSPORT MANAGEMENT 381 (2002)

Pavlos, Eleftheriadis, *The European Constitution and Cosmopolitan Ideals*, 12 KING'S COLLEGE LAW JOURNAL 17 (2001)

Perrott, David L., *Regional Developments, European Communities*, 21 INTERNATIONAL LAWYER 569 (1987)

Perrott, David L., *Regional Developments, European Communities*, 21 INTERNATIONAL LAWYER 1205 (1987)

Petsikas, George, *'Open Skies' – North America*, 17 ANNALS OF AIR & SPACE LAW 281 (1992)

Pitofsky, Robert et al., *The Essential Facilities Doctrine Under U.S. Antitrust Law*, 70 ANTITRUST LAW JOURNAL 443 (2002)

Pollock, Frederick, *Cosmopolitan Custom and International Law*, 29 HARVARD LAW REVIEW 565 (1916)

Ravich, Timothy M., *Deregulation of the Airline Computer Reservation Systems (CRS)*, 69 JOURNAL OF AIR LAW & COMMERCE 387 (2004)

Ravich, Timothy M., *Re-Regulation and Airline Passengers' Rights*, 67 JOURNAL OF AIR LAW & COMMERCE 935 (2002)

Rosenthal, Daniel H., *Legal Turbulence: The Court's Misconstrual of the Airline Deregulation Act's Preemption Clause and the Effect on Passengers' Rights*, 51 DUKE LAW JOURNAL 1857 (2002)

Salzman, Alan E., *IATA, Airline Rate-Fixing and the EEC Competition Rules*, 2 EUROPEAN LAW REVIEW 409 (1977)

Saunders, Derek, *The Antitrust Implications of Computer Reservation Systems*, 51 JOURNAL OF AIR LAW & COMMERCE 157 (1985)

Schlumberger, Charles E., *Africa's Long Path to Liberalization: Status Quo of the Implementation of the Yammoussoukro Decision*, 33 ANNALS OF AIR & SPACE LAW 194 (2008)

Serrano, Virginia Rodriguez, *Trade in Air Transport Services: Liberalizing Hard Rights*, 24 ANNALS OF AIR & SPACE LAW 199 (1999)

Sheehan, W.M., *Air Cabotage and the Chicago Convention*, 63 HARVARD LAW REVIEW 1157 (1950)

Shell, G. Richard, *Trade Legalism and International Relations Theory: An Analysis of the World Trade Organization*, 44 DUKE LAW JOURNAL 829 (1995)

Shrewsbury, Stephen M., *September 11th and the Single European Sky: Developing Concepts of Airspace Sovereignty*, 68 JOURNAL OF AIR LAW & COMMERCE 115 (2003)

Silliman, Scott L., *Symposium: Responding to Rogue Regimes: From Smart Bombs to Smart Sanctions; The Iraqi Quagmire: Enforcing the No-Fly Zones*, 36 NEW ENGLAND LAW REVIEW 767 (2002)

Singh, Praveen, *Some Aspects of Australia's Bilateral Air Services Agreements*, 9 AIR LAW 160 (1984)

Sion, L. Gilles, *Multilateral Air Transport Agreements Reconsidered: The Possibility of a Regional Agreement Among North Atlantic States*, 22 VIRGINIA JOURNAL OF INTERNATIONAL LAW 155 (1981)

Smith, Barry C. et al., *E-Commerce and Operations Research in Airline Planning, Marketing, and Distribution*, 31 INTERFACES 37 (2001)

Smith, William & Robert Fine, *Kantian Cosmopolitanism Today: John Rawls and Jürgen Habermas on Immanuel Kant's* Foedus Pacificum, 15 KING'S COLLEGE LAW JOURNAL 5 (2004)

Stahl, Tycho H.E., *Liberalizing International Trade in Services: The Case for Sidestepping the GATT*, 19 YALE JOURNAL OF INTERNATIONAL LAW 405 (1994)

Staniland, Martin, Conference Report, *University of Pittsburgh Conference on 'The Future of EC-U.S. Aviation Relations*, JOURNAL OF AIR TRANSPORT MANAGEMENT 245 (2000)

Stephan, Paul B., *Global Governance, Antitrust, and the Limits of International Cooperation*, 38 CORNELL INTERNATIONAL LAW JOURNAL 173 (2005)

Stewart, Jr., John T., *United States Citizenship Requirement of the Federal Aviation Act – A Misty Moor of Legalisms or the Rampart of Protectionism?*, 55 JOURNAL OF AIR LAW & COMMERCE 685 (1990)

Stockfish, Bruce, *Opening Closed Skies: The Prospects for Further Liberalization of Trade in International Air Transport Services*, 57 JOURNAL OF AIR LAW & COMMERCE 599 (1992)

Stoffel, Albert W., *American Bilateral Air Transport Agreements on the Threshold of the Jet Transport Age*, 26 JOURNAL OF AIR LAW & COMMERCE 119 (1959)

Thaine, Colin, *The Way Ahead from Memo 2: The Need for More Competition A Better Deal for Europe*, 10 AIR LAW 90 (1985)

Thornton, Robert L., *Airlines and Agents: Conflict and the Public Welfare*, 52 JOURNAL OF AIR LAW & COMMERCE 371 (1986)

toe Laer, Rutger Jan, *Kick Starting Cross-Border Alliances*, 32 AIR & SPACE LAW 287 (2007)

Toh, Rex S., *Toward an International Open Skies Regime*, 3 JOURNAL OF AIR TRANSPORTATION WORLD WIDE 61 (1998)

Vamos-Goldman, Andras, *The Stagnation of Economic Regulation under Public International Air Law: Examining its Contribution to the Woeful State of the Airline Industry*, 23 TRANSPORTATION LAW JOURNAL 425 (1996)

Van Antwerpen, Niels A., *The Single European Sky*, ISSUES IN AVIATION LAW & POLICY ¶ 20,251, at 10,301 (2002)

Van der Esch, Bastiaan, *The Principles of Interpretation Applied by the Court of Justice of the European Communities and their Relevance for the Scope of the EEC Competition Rules*, 15 FORDHAM INTERNATIONAL LAW JOURNAL 366 (1992)

Van Gerven, Walter, *The Genesis of EEA Law and the Principles of Primacy and Direct Effect*, 16 FORDHAM INTERNATIONAL LAW JOURNAL 955 (1993)

Von Bakelen, F.A., *Aviation Wizards – Terminal Hazards: Airlines' Computerized Reservation Systems (C.R.S.): A Benefit or a Burden?*, 13 AIR LAW 77 (1988)

Wassenbergh, Henry A., *The Application of International Trade Principles to Air Transport*, 12 AIR LAW 84 (1987)

Wassenbergh, Henry A., *EEC – Cabotage After 1992?*, 13 AIR LAW 282 (1988)

Wassenbergh, Henry A., *New Aspects of National Aviation Policies and the Future of International Air Transport Regulation*, 13 AIR LAW 18 (1988)

Wassenbergh, Henry A., *Opening the Skies – The EEC and Third Countries*, 15 AIR LAW 307 (1990)

Wassenbergh, Henry A., *Regulatory Reform: A Challenge to Inter-Governmental Civil Aviation Conferences*, 11 AIR LAW 31 (1986)

Weber, Ludwig, *Air Transport in the Common Market and the Public Air Transport Enterprises*, 5 ANNALS OF AIR & SPACE LAW 283 (1980)

Weber, Ludwig, *External Aspects of EEC Air Transport Liberalization*, 15 AIR LAW 277 (1990)

Wegter, Jorn L., *The ECJ Decision of 10 January 2006 on the Validity of Regulation 261/2004: Ignoring the Exclusivity of the Montreal Convention*, 31 AIR & SPACE LAW 133 (2006)

Werden, Gregory J., et al., *The Effects of Mergers on Price and Output: Two Case Studies from the Airline Industry*, 12 MANAGERIAL & DECISION ECONOMICS 341 (1991)

Willig, Robert D., *Antitrust Lessons from the Airline Industry: The DOJ Experience*, 60 ANTITRUST LAW JOURNAL 695 (1992)

Woll, Cornelia, *The Activism of the European Commission in the Case of International Aviation* (AICGS/DAAD Working Paper Series, 2003)

Wood, Bernard, *Foreign Investment in National Airlines and the Significance of the SAS/BCAL Decision*, 13 Air Law 138 (1988)

Wood, Diane P., *The Impossible Dream: Real International Antitrust*, 1992 University of Chicago Legal Forum 277 (1992)

Speeches, Presentations, and Briefing Papers Listed Alphabetically by Speaker

Alexander, Douglas, U.K. Secretary of State for Transport, Speech to the International Aviation Club, Washington, D.C. (Oct. 4, 2006)

Bisignani, Giovanni, Director General and CEO, International Air Transport Association, *Leading Change*, Remarks to the International Aviation Club, Washington, D.C. (Apr. 20, 2004)

Bisignani, Giovanni, Director General and CEO, International Air Transport Association, *State of the Air Transport Industry*, Speech to the 64th Annual General Meeting (June 2, 2008)

Brittan, Sir Leon, Vice-President of the Commission of the European Communities, *Competition Policy in the European Community: The New Merger Regulation*, Speech to the EC Chamber of Commerce, New York, N.Y. (Mar. 26, 1990)

Brittan, Sir Leon, Vice-President of the Commission of the European Communities, *A Framework for International Competition*, Speech to the World Economic Forum, Davos (Feb. 3, 1992)

Broughton, Martin, Chairman, British Airways, Speech to the Chatham House Conference on Open Skies (Mar. 5, 2007)

Broughton, Martin, Chairman, British Airways, Speech to the Wings Club, New York, N.Y. (Jan. 19, 2006)

Byerly, John R., Deputy Assistant Secretary for Transportation Affairs, U.S. Department of State, *Liberalizing Transatlantic Aviation: The Case for Stability, Expansion, and Vision*, Speech to the USA-BIAS Conference, Washington, D.C. (Oct. 14, 2005)

Byerly, John R., Deputy Assistant Secretary for Transportation Affairs, U.S. Department of State, Remarks on the EU Open Skies Agreement (Sept. 29, 2007)

Byerly, John R., Deputy Assistant Secretary for Transportation Affairs, U.S. Department of State, *Turbulent Times: Regulation, Security, and Profitability in the Airline Industry*, Address to the Chatham House Conference, London (Mar. 5, 2007)

Byerly, John R., Deputy Assistant Secretary for Transportation Affairs, U.S. Department of State, *The U.S.-EU Air Transport Agreement: Making the Most of the Second Stage*, Remarks to the European Aviation Club, Brussels, Belgium (May 13, 2008)

Byerly, John R., Deputy Assistant Secretary for Transportation Affairs, U.S. Department of State, *U.S.-EC Aviation Relations: Success Today and Potential for the Future*, Remarks to the International Aviation Club, Washington, D.C. (Apr. 24, 2007)

Byerly, John R., Deputy Assistant Secretary for Transportation Affairs, U.S. Department of State, *U.S.-EU Aviation Relations – Charting the Course for Success*, Remarks at the International Aviation Club, Washington, D.C. (July 13, 2004)

Calleja, Daniel, Director, EC Air Transport Directorate, Speech to the International Aviation Club, Washington, D.C. (Nov. 16, 2004)

Crandall, Robert L., former Chairman and CEO, American Airlines, Remarks to the Wings Club, New York, N.Y. (June 10, 2008)

Gretch, Paul L., Director, Office of International Aviation, U.S. Department of Transportation, *The EU-U.S. Agreement: Prospects for the New Transatlantic Market*, Speech to the Future of Air Transport Conference, Institute of Economic Affairs (Dec. 2007)

Havel, Brian F., Director, International Aviation Law Institute, DePaul University College of Law, *Beyond Open Skies: Liberalization After the U.S.-EC Agreement*, Moderator's Briefing Paper for the 2007 ABA Forum on Air & Space Law (Oct. 4, 2007)

Havel, Brian F., Director, International Aviation Law Institute, DePaul University College of Law, *Rethinking the GATS As A Pathway to Global Aviation Liberalization: A 'Lead Sector' Strategy for the GATS – Express Delivery Services as a Model for Global Air Transport Reform*, Presentation to the Air Transport Research Society 2005 World Conference, Federal University of Rio de Janeiro, Brazil (July 3, 2005)

Havel, Brian F. & Dorothy Robyn, *Understanding of the Moderators*, Paper Presented to the Working Group of Aviation Experts on U.S./EU Aviation Liberalization, Washington, D.C. (May 1, 2002)

Humphreys, Barry, Director of External Affairs and Route Development, Virgin Atlantic Airways, *Liberalised Airline Ownership and Control*, Address to the Seminar Prior to the ICAO Worldwide Air Transport Conference: Challenges and Opportunities of Liberalization (Mar. 22-23, 2003)

Kroes, Neelie, European Commissioner for Competition Policy, *Competition in the Aviation Sector: The European Commission's Approach*, Address to the Conference Celebrating the 20th Anniversary of the International Institute of Air and Space Law, Leiden (Apr. 24, 2006)

Kroes, Neelie, European Commissioner for Competition Policy, *Key Developments in European Competition Policy Over the Past Two Years*, Speech to the European American Press Club, Paris (Jan. 8, 2007)

Levine, Michael E., [formerly] Adjunct Professor of Law, Yale Law School, Remarks to the Competitive Enterprise Institute (Aug. 14, 2003)

Milton, Robert, CEO and President, Air Canada, Briefing to the Air Transport Association Board of Governors, Washington, D.C. (Dec. 13, 2001)

Mineta, Norman Y., U.S. Secretary of Transportation, Remarks to the American Chamber of Commerce, Bangkok, Thailand (Apr. 18, 2005)

Mineta, Norman Y., U.S. Secretary of Transportation, Remarks to the Canadian Open Skies Forum (Feb. 24, 2005)

Moore, Mike, WTO Director General, *The Future of International Trade in Services*, Speech to the Third Debis Services Conference, Berlin (Sept. 21, 1999)

Peña, Federico, U.S. Secretary of Transportation, Remarks at the 50th Anniversary Commemoration of the Convention on International Civil Aviation (Nov. 1, 1994)

Scott, Sheridan, Commissioner of Competition, Competition Bureau Canada, *Air Liberalization and the Canadian Airports System*, Speaking Notes for Remarks to the House of Commons Standing Committee on Transport (May 4, 2005)

Shane, Jeffrey N., Associate Deputy Secretary of Transportation, *Open Skies Agreements and the European Court of Justice*, Remarks to the American Bar Association's Forum on Air and Space Law (Nov. 8, 2002)

Shane, Jeffrey N., Under Secretary for Policy, U.S. Department of Transportation, *Liberalization: More Important Than Ever*, Remarks to the 13th Annual International CEO Conference, Miami, FL, at 4 (May 9, 2005)

Shane, Jeffrey N., Under Secretary for Policy, U.S. Department of Transportation, *Air Transport Liberalization: The U.S. Experience*, Speech at the ICAO Symposium on Air Transport Liberalization (Sept. 18, 2006)

Shane, Jeffrey N., Under Secretary for Policy, U.S. Department of Transportation, *Aviation Deregulation: A Work in Progress*, Speech at the International Aviation Club, Washington, D.C. (Nov. 8, 2005)

Shane, Jeffrey N., Under Secretary for Policy, U.S. Department of Transportation, Remarks to the International Aviation Club, Washington, D.C. (Sept. 12, 2006)

Steinberg, Andrew B., Assistant Secretary for Aviation and International Affairs, U.S. Department of Transportation, Remarks before the ICAO Colloquium on Aviation Emissions, Montreal, Canada (May 16, 2007)

Tilton, Glenn, Chairman and CEO, United Airlines, *Moving the World: Global Aviation and the Global Economy*, Remarks to the Chicago Council on Foreign Relations (Apr. 21, 2005)

Van Miert, Karel, former EU Transport Commissioner, *European Air Transport Policy in the Perspective of the Achievement of the Internal Market: What Next?*, Speech at the Aviation Club of Great Britain, London (Mar. 30, 1992)

Veenstra, Kees, Deputy Secretary General, Association of European Airlines, Speaking Notes for the Future of EU-U.S. Aviation Relations Conference, Pittsburgh, PA (Apr. 7, 2000)

Whitaker, Michael G., Vice President, International and Regulatory Affairs, United Airlines, Address, *Liberalizing U.S. Foreign Ownership Restrictions: Good for Consumers, Airlines and the United States*, Address to the Seminar Prior to the ICAO Worldwide Air Transport Conference: Challenges and Opportunities of Liberalization (Mar. 22-23, 2003)

Woerth, Duane E., President, Air Line Pilots Association, Speech to the International Aviation Club, Washington, D.C. (June 28, 2001)

Institutional Reports, Papers, and Other Documents Listed Alphabetically by Entity

AIR TRANSPORT ACTION GROUP, THE ECONOMIC & SOCIAL BENEFITS OF AIR TRANSPORT (2005)

AIR TRANSPORT ASSOCIATION, AIRLINES IN CRISIS: THE PERFECT ECONOMIC STORM (2003)

AIR TRANSPORT ASSOCIATION, BALANCING THE AVIATION EQUATION: 2007 ECONOMIC REPORT (2007)

Air Transport Association, *FAA's Proposed Rule on Demand Management at LaGuardia Airport*, Issue Brief (Jan. 2007)

Allegiant Travel Company, *Investor Presentation*, Merrill Lynch Global Transportation Conference (June 18, 2008)

Association of European Airlines, *EU External Relations*, AEA Policy Statement (2003)

ASSOCIATION OF EUROPEAN AIRLINES, OPERATING ECONOMY OF AEA AIRLINES 2007 (2007)

Association of European Airlines, *Towards a Transatlantic Common Aviation Area*, AEA Policy Statement (Sept. 1999)

BOOZ ALLEN HAMILTON, THE ECONOMIC IMPACTS OF AN OPEN AVIATION AREA BETWEEN THE EUROPEAN UNION AND THE UNITED STATES: FINAL REPORT (2007)

BRATTLE GROUP, THE ECONOMIC IMPACT OF AN EU-US OPEN AVIATION AREA (2002)

CATO INSTITUTE, CATO HANDBOOK ON POLICY (6th ed. 2005)

COMITÉ DES SAGES, EXPANDING HORIZONS: CIVIL AVIATION IN EUROPE, AN ACTION PROGRAMME FOR THE FUTURE (1994)

DEUTSCHE BANK, THE FUTURE OF THE HUB STRATEGY IN THE AIR TRANSPORT INDUSTRY (2006)

EUROPEAN CIVIL AVIATION CONFERENCE, 50 YEARS OF ECAC (2005)

European Cockpit Association, *EU-U.S. Draft Air Transport Agreement*, Position Paper (Jan. 31, 2006)

European Commission, *Air Transport Agreement Between the EU and U.S.*, Information Note (Mar. 6, 2007)

EUROPEAN COMMISSION, ANALYSES OF THE EUROPEAN AIR TRANSPORT MARKET: ANNUAL REPORT 2007 (2007)

European Commission, *Annex to 'Reducing the Climate Change Impact of Aviation'*, SEC (2005) 1184 (Sept. 27, 2005)

European Commission, *Building the Single European Sky Through Functional Airspace Blocks: A Mid-Term Status Report*, COM (2007) 101 final (Mar. 15, 2007)

European Commission, *Commercial Slot Allocation Mechanisms in the Context of a Further Revision of Council Regulation (EEC) 95/93 on Common Rules for the Allocation of Slots at Community Airports*, Commission Staff Working Document (Sept. 17, 2004)

European Commission, *Communication from the Commission: A Community Aviation Policy Towards Its Neighbors*, COM (2004) 74 final (Feb. 9, 2004)

European Commission, *Communication from the Commission on the Consequences of the Court Judgments of 5 November 2002 for European Air Transport Policy*, COM (2002) 649 final (Nov. 19, 2002)

European Commission, *Communication from the Commission to the European Parliament and the Council on the Protection of Air Passengers in the European Union*, COM (2000) 365 final (June 21, 2000)

European Commission, *Communication from the Commission to the European Parliament and the Council: A Framework for Developing Relations with the Russian Federation in the Field of Air Transport*, COM (2005) 77 final (Mar. 14, 2005)

European Commission, *Communication from the Commission to the European Parliament and the Council Pursuant to Article 17 of the Regulation [EC]261/2004 on the Operation and the Results of this Regulation Establishing Common Rules on Compensation and Assistance to Passengers in the Event of Denied Boarding and of Cancellation or Long Delay of Flights*, COM (2007) 168 final (April 4, 2007)

European Commission, *Communication from the Commission to the European Parliament, the Council, the European Economic and Social Committee of the Regions on the Application of Regulation (EEC) No 95/93 on Common Rules for the Allocation of Slots at Community Airports, As Amended*, COM (2008) 227 (Apr. 30, 2008)

European Commission, *Communication from the Commission on Relations Between the Community and Third Countries in the Field of Air Transport*, COM (2003) 94 final (Feb. 26, 2003)

European Commission, *Communication on the Application of Regulation (EC) 793/2004 on Common Rules for the Allocation of Slots at Community Airports* (Nov. 15, 2007)

European Commission, *Competition Policy in the New Trade Order: Strengthening International Co-operation and Rules*, Report of the Group of Experts, COM (95) 359 final (July 12, 1995)

European Commission, *Concerning the Revision and Possible Prorogation of Commission Regulation 1617/93*, DG Competition Discussion Paper (2004)

European Commission, *Consultation Paper on the Revision of Regulation 2299/89 on a Code of Conduct for Computerised Reservation Systems*, Consultation Paper (2007)

European Commission, *Consultation Paper With a View to Revision of Regulation 2407/92, 2408/92, and 2409/92 of 23 July 1992 ('The Third Package' For Liberalization of Air Transport')* (2003)

European Commission, *Developing the Agenda for the Community's External Aviation Policy*, COM (2005) 79 final (Mar. 11, 2005)

European Commission, *Developing a Community Civil Aviation Policy Towards Canada*, COM (2006) 871 final (Sept. 1, 2007)

European Commission, *EC External Aviation Policy: Why Does the EC Want to Modify Air Service Agreements Between Its Member States and Partner Countries?*, Information Note (2006)

EUROPEAN COMMISSION, EUROPEAN COMMUNITY COMPETITION POLICY: XXVIITH REPORT ON COMPETITION POLICY (1998)

EUROPEAN COMMISSION, EUROPEAN COMMUNITY COMPETITION POLICY: XXXTH REPORT ON COMPETITION POLICY (2000)

European Commission, *[Model] Agreement Between the European Community and* [name of third country] *on Certain Aspects of Air Services*, Working Paper (Feb. 20, 2006)

EUROPEAN COMMISSION, PANORAMA OF EU INDUSTRY '94 (1994)

European Commission, *Progress Towards the Development of a Community Air Transport Policy*, Civil Aviation Memorandum No. 2, COM (84) 72 final (Mar. 15, 1984)

European Commission, *Proposal for a Council Decision on a Consultation and Authorization Procedure for Agreements Concerning Commercial Aviation Relations Between Member States and Third Countries*, COM (90) 17 final (Feb. 13, 1990)

European Commission, *Proposal for a Decision on Community Guidelines for the Development of the Trans-European Transport Network*, COM (94) 106 final (July 4, 1994)

European Commission, *Proposal for a Directive of the European Parliament and of the Council on Airport Charges*, COM (2006) 820 final (Jan. 24, 2007)

European Commission, *Proposal for a Directive of the European Parliament and of the Council Amending Directive 2003/87/EC So As to Include Aviation Activities in the Scheme for Greenhouse Gas Emission Allowance Trading Within the Community*, COM (2006) 818 final (Dec. 20, 2006)

European Commission, *Proposal for a Regulation of the European Parliament and of the Council on Common Rules for the Operation of Air Transport Services in the Community (Recast)*, COM (2006) 396 final (July 18, 2006)

European Commission, *Proposal for a Regulation of the European Parliament and of the Council Establishing Common Rules on Compensation and Assistance to Air Passengers in the Event of Denied Boarding and of Cancellation or Long Delay of Flights*, COM (2001) 784 final (Dec. 21, 2001)

European Commission, *Recommendation from the Commission to the Council in Order to Authorise the Commission to Open and Conduct Negotiations with the International Civil Aviation Organization (ICAO) on the Conditions and Arrangements for Accession by the European Community*, SEC (2002) 381 final (Apr. 9, 2002)

European Commission, *Report from the Commission on the Application of Council Directive 96/67/EC of 15 October 1996*, COM (2006) 821 final (Jan. 24, 2007)

European Commission, *Report for the Reflection Group*, Office for Official Publications of the European Communities (1995)

European Commission, *Report of the Application of Articles 4(a) and 6(3) of Council Regulation No. 2299/89 as amended by Regulation Concerning a Code of Conduct for CRS*, COM (95) 51 final (Mar. 7, 1995)

EUROPEAN COMMISSION, STUDY ON THE IMPACT OF THE INTRODUCTION OF SECONDARY TRADING AT COMMUNITY AIRPORTS, VOLUME I (2006)

EUROPEAN COMMISSION, STUDY ON THE IMPACT OF THE INTRODUCTION OF SECONDARY TRADING AT COMMUNITY AIRPORTS, VOLUME II (2006)

European Commission, *Summary of Contributions Received by the Commission Following the Consultation Paper With a View to Revision of Regulations No. 2407/92, 2408/92 and 2409/92 of 23 July 1992 ('The Third Package' For Liberalization of Air Transport')* (2003)

European Commission, *Summary of the Impact Assessment*, SEC (2006) 1685 (Dec. 20, 2006)

European Commission, *The Way Forward for Civil Aviation in Europe*, COM (94) 218 final (Jan. 6, 1994)

European Commission, *White Paper on European Transport Policy for 2010: Time to Decide*, COM (2001) 370 final (Sept. 12, 2001)

EUROPEAN COMMISSION, AVIATION WORKING GROUP, EUROPEAN CLIMATE CHANGE PROGRAMME II: FINAL REPORT (2006)

European Commission, DG Competition, *Concerning the Revision and Possible Prorogation of Commission Regulation 1617/93 on the Application of Article 81(3) to Certain Categories of Agreements and Concerted Practices Concerning Consultations on Passenger Tariffs on Scheduled Air Services and Slot Allocation at Airports*, Discussion Paper (Mar. 2, 2005)

European Council of Ministers, *Proposal for a Regulation of the European Parliament and of the Council on Common Rules for the Operation of Air Services in the Community (First Reading)*, Joint Statement by the Member States and the Commission, 7627/08 Add 1 (Mar. 31, 2008)

European Parliament, Committee on Transport and Tourism, *Draft Report for a Regulation of the European Parliament and of the Council on Common Rules for the Operation of Air Transport Services in the Community (Recast)*, Provisional 2006/0130 (COD) (Feb. 7, 2007)

European Parliament, Committee on Transport and Tourism, *Report on the [European] Commission's Report to the Council and the European Parliament on the Evaluation of Aid Schemes Established in Favor of Community Carriers*, PE 203.392 (Feb. 25, 1993)

EUROCONTROL, *Low-Cost Carrier Market Update: June 2007*, Doc 257 (Sept. 12, 2007)

EUROSTAT, PANORAMA OF TRANSPORT: EDITION 2007 (2007)

FEDERAL AVIATION ADMINISTRATION, CAPACITY NEEDS IN THE NATIONAL AIRSPACE SYSTEM 2007-2025: AN ANALYSIS OF AIRPORTS AND METROPOLITAN AREA DEMAND AND OPERATIONAL CAPACITY IN THE FUTURE (2007)

FEDERAL AVIATION ADMINISTRATION, FAA AEROSPACE FORECASTS FY 2007-2020 (2007)

FEDERAL AVIATION ADMINISTRATION & OPTIMAL SOLUTIONS AND TECHNOLOGIES, AIRPORT BUSINESS PRACTICES AND THEIR IMPACT ON AIRLINE COMPETITION: TASK FORCE STUDY (1999)

General Accounting Office, *Airline Competition: DOT's Implementation of Airline Regulatory Authority*, GAO/RCED-89-93 (June 1989)

General Accounting Office, *Airline Competition: Fare and Service Changes at St. Louis Since the TWA/Ozark Merger*, GAO/RCED-88-217BR (Sept. 1988)

General Accounting Office, *Airline Competition: Impact of Changing Foreign Investment and Control Limits on U.S. Airlines*, GAO/RCED-93-7 (Dec. 1992)

General Accounting Office, *Airline Competition: Weak Financial Structure Threatens Competition*, GAO/RCED-91-110 (Apr. 1991)

General Accounting Office, *Airline Deregulation: Changes in Airfares, Service, and Safety at Small, Medium-Sized, and Large Communities*, GAO/RCED-96-79 Report (Apr. 1996)

General Accounting Office, *Airline Ticketing: Impact of Changes in the Airline Ticket Distribution Industry*, GAO-03-749 (July 2003)

General Accounting Office, *Aviation Competition: Challenges in Enhancing Competition in Dominated Markets*, GAO-01-518T (Mar. 13, 2001)

General Accounting Office, *Aviation Competition: Effects on Consumers From Domestic Airline Alliances Vary*, GAO/RCED-99-37 (Jan. 1999)

General Accounting Office, *Aviation Competition: Issues Related to the Proposed United Airlines-US Airways Merger*, GAO-01-212 (Dec. 2000)

General Accounting Office, *Foreign Investment in U.S. Airlines*, GAO-04-34R (Oct. 2003)

General Accounting Office, *International Aviation: Airline Alliances Produce Benefits, But Effect on Competition is Uncertain*, GAO/RCED-95-99 (Apr. 1995)

General Accounting Office, *International Aviation: Measures by European Community Could Limit U.S. Airlines' Ability to Compete Abroad*, GAO/RCED-93-64 (Apr. 1993)

General Accounting Office, *Proposed Alliance Between American Airlines and British Airways Raises Competition Concerns and Public Interest Issues*, GAO-02-293R (Dec. 21, 2001)

Government Accountability Office, *Airline Deregulation: Reregulating the Airline Industry Would Likely Reverse Consumer Benefits and Not Save Airline Pensions*, GAO-06-630 (June 2006)

Government Accountability Office, *Aviation Safety: Oversight of Foreign Code-Share Safety Program Should be Strengthened*, GAO-05-930 (Aug. 2005)

Government Accountability Office, *Commercial Aviation: Legacy Airlines Must Further Reduce Costs to Restore Profitability*, GAO-04-836 (Aug. 2004)

Government Accountability Office, *Commercial Aviation: Programs and Options for the Federal Approach to Providing and Improving Air Service to Small Communities*, GAO-06-398T (Sept. 14, 2006)

Government Accountability Office, *Transatlantic Aviation: Effects of Easing Restrictions on U.S.-European Markets*, GAO-04-835 (July 2004)

Government of Venezuela, *Venezuela Recategorization Process by the Federal Aviation Administration (FAA)*, Paper Presented to the International Civil Aviation Administration Directors General of Civil Aviation Conference on a Global Strategy for Aviation Safety, DGCA/06-IP/19 (Mar. 15, 2006)

Hebdon, Robert & Hazel Dayton Gunn, *The Costs and Benefits of Privatization at the Local Level in New York State*, Community Development Report, Community and Rural Development Institute, Cornell University (1995)

HIGH LEVEL GROUP FOR THE FUTURE EUROPEAN REGULATORY FRAMEWORK, EUROPEAN AVIATION: A FRAMEWORK FOR DRIVING PERFORMANCE IMPROVEMENT (2007)

Institute of Air Transport, *Air Transport Markets in Europe and the United States: A Comparison* (June 2001)

Institute for Defense Analyses, *Sustaining the Civil Reserve Air Fleet (CRAF) Program* (May 2003)

INTERGOVERNMENTAL PANEL ON CLIMATE CHANGE, AVIATION AND THE GLOBAL ATMOSPHERE (Joyce E. Penner at al. eds., Cambridge University Press, 1999)

International Air Carrier Association, *Towards Regulatory Convergence: An IACA View*, Position Paper (June 2001)

International Air Transport Association, *Advancing the Liberalisation of Ownership and Control*, Paper Presented to the ICAO Assembly's 35th Session, A35-WP/64 (July 8, 2004)

International Air Transport Association, *Airline Views on Liberalising Ownership and Control*, IATA Working Policy Paper (2003)

International Air Transport Association, *Airline Views on Liberalizing Ownership and Control*, Paper Presented to the ICAO Worldwide Air Transport Conference, ATConf/5-WP26 (Dec. 16, 2002)

INTERNATIONAL AIR TRANSPORT ASSOCIATION, ANNUAL REPORT 2007 (2007)

INTERNATIONAL AIR TRANSPORT ASSOCIATION, IATA OPERATIONAL SAFETY AUDIT: DESIGNED FOR THE AVIATION INDUSTRY (2004)

International Air Transport Association, *Passenger and Freight Forecasts 2007 to 2011*, IATA Economic Briefing (Oct. 2007)

International Air Transport Association Secretariat, *Liberalizing Air Carrier Ownership and Control*, Paper Presented to the ICAO Worldwide Air Transport Conference, ATConf/5-WP/7 (Oct. 21, 2002)

International Aviation Law Institute, DePaul University College of Law & Chicago Council on Global Affairs, *Sustainable Aviation Policies for America and the World: A Leadership Summit*, Synopsis of the Proceedings (Oct. 19, 2006)

International Chamber of Commerce, *The Need for Greater Liberalization of International Air Transport*, Paper Presented to ICAO Worldwide Air Transport Conference, ATConf/5-WP/35 (Jan. 20, 2003)

International Civil Aviation Organization, *Analysis of the Rights Conferred by Article 5 of the Convention*, ICAO Doc. 7278-C/841 (May 10, 1952), *compiled in Policy and Guidance Material on the Economic Regulation of International Transport*, ICAO Doc. 9587 (2d ed. 1999)

International Civil Aviation Organization, *Consolidated Conclusions, Model Clauses, Recommendations and Declarations*, ATConf/5 (July 10, 2003)

International Civil Aviation Organization, *Consolidated Statement of Continuing ICAO Policies and Practices Related to Environmental Protection, compiled in Assembly Resolutions in Force*, ICAO Doc. 9848 (Oct. 4, 2004)

International Civil Aviation Organization, *Consolidated Statement of Continuing ICAO Policies and Practices Related to Environmental Protection*, Assemb. Res. A36-22 (2007), *compiled in Assembly Resolutions in Force*, at I-54, ICAO Doc. 9902 (Sept. 28, 2007)

International Civil Aviation Organization, *Convention on International Civil Aviation*, ICAO Doc. 7300/9 (9th ed. Nov. 26, 2007)

International Civil Aviation Organization, *Regulatory and Industry Overview*, Information Paper (Aug. 15, 2006)

International Civil Aviation Organization, *Report of the Conference on Air Transport*, ICAO Pub. No. 9644, ATConf/4 (1994)

International Civil Aviation Organization, *Scandinavian Airline System: Consortium Agreement and Related Agreements*, ICAO Circular 99-AT/20 (1970)

International Civil Aviation Organization, *Strategic Objectives for 2005-2010*, Consolidated Vision and Mission Statement (2005)

International Civil Aviation Organization Council, *Development and Economic Regulation of International Air Transport*, Paper Presented to the ICAO Assembly's 36th Session, A-36-WP/16 (June 26, 2007)

International Civil Aviation Organization Economic Commission, *The Orderly Evolution of Air Transport Services: Secure and Safe Economic Regulation in an Era of Globalization*, A33-WP/227 (Sept. 28, 2001)

International Civil Aviation Organization Economic Commission, *Regulation of International Air Transport Services*, Report by the Council on Trade in Services, A33-WP/7 (June 6, 2001)

International Civil Aviation Organization Economic Commission, *Relevance of the General Agreement on Trade in Services (GATS) to the Future Development of International Air Transport Regulation*, A33-WP/128 (Sept. 13, 2001)

International Civil Aviation Organization Economic Commission, *Report by the Council on Trade in Services*, A33-WP/7 (Jan. 28, 2000)

International Civil Aviation Organization Secretariat, *Case Studies on Liberalization*, ATConf/5-WP/5 (Feb. 17, 2003)

International Civil Aviation Organization Secretariat, *Industry Situation and Airline Traffic Outlook*, ATConf/5-WP/23 (Feb. 24, 2003)

International Civil Aviation Organization Secretariat, *Liberalization Developments Related to Market Access*, Paper Presented to the ICAO Worldwide Air Transport Conference, ATConf/5-WP/21 (March 3, 2003)

International Civil Aviation Organization Secretariat, *Liberalizing Air Carrier Ownership and Control*, ATConf/5-WP/7 (Feb. 11, 2003)

Larson, Alan P. & David M. Marchick, *Foreign Investment and National Security: Getting the Balance Right*, Council on Foreign Relations, CSR No. 18 (July 2006)

INTERVISTAS, THE ECONOMIC IMPACT OF AIR SERVICE LIBERALIZATION (2006)

MOTT MACDONALD, STUDY ON THE IMPACT OF THE INTRODUCTION OF SECONDARY TRADING AT COMMUNITY AIRPORTS (2006)

NATIONAL ECONOMIC RESEARCH ASSOCIATES, STUDY TO ASSESS THE EFFECTS OF DIFFERENT SLOT ALLOCATION SCHEMES (2004)

Organisation for Economic Co-operation and Development, *Background Document*, Workshop on Regulatory Reform in International Air Cargo Transportation, Paris, at 54-63 (July 5-6, 1999)

Organisation for Economic Co-operation and Development, Committee on Competition Law and Policy, *Deregulation and Airline Competition* (1988)

Organisation for Economic Co-operation and Development, Committee on Competition Law and Policy, *Regulatory Reform, Privatization, and Competition Policy* (1992)

Organisation for Economic Co-operation and Development, Directorate for Science, Technology, and Industry, *Liberalisation of Air Cargo Transport*, DSTI/DOT (2002) 1/REV1 (May 2, 2002)

Oxford Economic Forecasting, The Impact of the Express Delivery Industry on the Global Economy (2005)

Steer Davies Gleave, Review of Regulation 261/2004: Final Report (2007)

Transport Canada, *Blue Sky: Canada's New International Air Policy* (2006)

Transport Canada, *A New International Air Transportation Policy*, Consultation with Stakeholders (2006)

Transport Canada, *Straight Ahead – A Vision for Transportation in Canada*, Policy Statement (Feb. 25, 2003)

Transportation Group International, *Consumer Attitudes and Use of the Internet and Traditional Travel Agents*, A Report for the National Commission to Ensure Consumer Information and Choice in the Airline Industry (Sept. 19, 2002)

Transportation Research Board, Special Report 255: Entry and Competition in the U.S. Airline Industry—Issues and Opportunities (National Academic Press, 1999)

United Kingdom Civil Aviation Authority, *Airline Competition on European Long Haul Routes*, CAP 639 (Nov. 1994)

United Kingdom Civil Aviation Authority, *CAA Statement of Policies On Route and Air Transport Licensing*, Official Record Series 1 (Aug. 8, 2008)

United Kingdom Civil Aviation Authority, *Ownership and Control Liberalisation: A Discussion Paper*, CAP 769 (Oct. 2006)

United Kingdom Civil Aviation Authority, *The Single European Aviation Market: Progress So Far*, CAP 654 (Sept. 1995)

United Kingdom Civil Aviation Authority, *UK Regional Air Services*, CAP 754 (Feb. 24, 2005)

United Nations Conference on Trade and Development, *Report of the Expert Meeting on Air Transport Services: Clarifying Issues to Define the Elements of the Positive Agenda of Developing Countries as Regards both the GATS and Specific Sector Negotiations of Interest to Them*, TD/B/COM.1/EM.9/3 (Aug. 23, 1999)

United States Department of Justice & Federal Trade Commission, *Commentary on the Horizontal Merger Guidelines* (2006)

United States Department of Justice & Federal Trade Commission, *Horizontal Merger Guidelines* (rev. ed. 1997)

United States Department of State, Air Transport Agreement Between the Government of the United States of America and the Government of [country] (Jan. 1, 2008)

United States Department of State, Treaty Between the Government of the United States of America and the Government of [Country] Concerning the Encouragement and Reciprocal Protection of Investment, Model BIT (2004)

United States Department of Transportation, Aviation in the 21st Century: Beyond Open Skies Ministerial I (1999)

United States Department of Transportation, *Code-Share Safety Program Guidelines*, Revision 1 (Dec. 21, 2006)

United States Department of Transportation, *How to Become a Certified Air Carrier*, Information Packet (May 2005)

United States Department of Transportation, *International Aviation Developments (First Report): Global Deregulation Takes Off* (Dec. 1999)

United States Department of Transportation, *International Aviation Developments (Second Report): Transatlantic Deregulation: The Alliance Network Effect* (Oct. 2000)

United States Department of Transportation, *Secretary's Task Force on Competition in the U.S. Domestic Airline Industry: Pricing*, Executive Summary (Feb. 1990)

United States Department of Transportation, Statement of United States International Air Transportation Policy, 60 Federal Register 21,841 (May 3, 1995)

United States Department of Transportation, Office of the Assistant Secretary for Aviation and International Affairs, *Domestic Aviation Competition Series: Dominated Hub Fares* (Jan. 2001)

United States Department of Transportation, Office of Aviation Analysis, *Domestic Airline Fares Consumer Report* (Feb. 2007)

United States Department of Transportation, Office of Public Affairs, Statement of Jeffrey N. Shane, Under Secretary for Policy, Before the Aviation Subcommittee of the House Transportation and Infrastructure Committee (Feb. 8, 2006)

Van Fenema, Peter, *Ownership and Control*, Report of the Think Tank, World Aviation Regulatory Monitor, International Air Transport Association (2000)

Select Periodicals and Newspapers Listed Alphabetically

Air & Space Lawyer
Air Transport World
Airline Business
Antitrust & Trade Regulation Reporter (BNA)
Aviation Daily
Aviation Europe
Aviation Week & Space Technology
Avmark Aviation Economist
Chicago Tribune, The
Daily Telegraph, The (London)
Daily Yomiuri
Denver Post, The
EC Update (CCH)
Economist, The
European Document Research Reports
European Report
European Union News

EuroWatch (Economics, Policy & Law in the New Europe)
Financial Times, The
Frequent Flyer
Home Office Computing
IATA Weekly Bulletin
International Business & Finance Daily (BNA)
Investor's Business Daily
New Republic, The
New York Law Journal, The
New York Times, The
Journal of Commerce
Pittsburgh Post-Gazette, The
PR Newswire (LEXIS)
Reuter European Business Review
Reuter European Community Review
Reuter North European Service (LEXIS)
Times, The (London)
Transport Europe
Transportation News Digest (DOT)
Transportation Trends (DOT)
UPI News Service (LEXIS)
Wall Street Journal, The
Washington Post, The

Index

References in this index are to the first page only of a discussion that may extend through several pages. References are to topics and persons mentioned in the main text only.

AVIATION LAW AND POLICY SERIES

1. Erwin von den Steinen, *National Interest and International Aviation* (ISBN 90-411-2455-1).
2. Ludwig Weber, *International Civil Aviation Organisation: An Introduction* (ISBN 978-90-411-2622-1).
3. Niels van Antwerpen, *Cross-Border Provision of Air Navigation Services with Specific Reference to Europe: Safeguarding Transparent Lines of Responsibility and Liability* (ISBN 978-90-411-2688-7).
4. Brian F. Havel, *Beyond Open Skies: A New Regime for International Aviation* (ISBN 978-90-411-2389-3).